עם פירוש
עטרת זקנים

AVOS
Treasury

with an anthologized
commentary and anecdotes

by Rabbi Moshe Lieber
Edited, with an Overview by
Rabbi Nosson Scherman

The PIRKEI

ETHICS OF THE FATHERS

the sages' guide to living

Published by

Mesorah Publications, ltd

ARTSCROLL MESORAH SERIES®

Published by **MESORAH PUBLICATIONS, LTD.**
4401 Second Avenue / Brooklyn, N.Y 11232 / (718) 921-9000 / Fax: (718) 680-1875
e-mail: artscroll@mesorah.com

Distributed in Israel by SIFRIATI / A. GITLER
4 Bilu Street / P.O.B. 14075 / Tel Aviv 61140

Distributed in Europe by J. LEHMANN HEBREW BOOKSELLERS
20 Cambridge Terrace / Gateshead, Tyne and Wear / England NE8 1RP

Distributed in Australia and New Zealand by GOLD'S BOOK & GIFT SHOP
36 William Street / Balaclava 3183, Vic., Australia

Distributed in South Africa by KOLLEL BOOKSHOP
22 Muller Street / Yeoville 2198, Johannesburg, South Africa

Printed in the United States of America by
Noble Book Press Corp. and Edison Lithographing and Printing Corp.
Custom bound by Sefercraft, Inc. / 4401 Second Avenue / Brooklyn N.Y. 11232

ISBN: 0-89906-374-8

עטרת זקנים בני בנים ותפארת בנים אבותם

The crown of elders is grandchildren; and the glory of
children is their parents

(Proverbs 17:6)

This volume, **Ateres Zekeinim**
is dedicated to the memory of
our beloved grandparents

ר׳ חנניה יום טוב ליפא נוי ורעיתו ריזל למשפחת נוימאן הי״ד

ר׳ שמואל שמעלקא נוי ורעיתו פיגא למשפחת גרין הי״ד

ר׳ צבי אריה כהן ורעיתו חיה גיטל למשפחת טאביליצקי ע״ה

ר׳ אהרן שלמה כהן ורעיתו נעכא רוזא למשפחת גאברוביץ ע״ה

Their lives and legacy were an **Atara,** a crown for them
and a crown for us, their descendants.

They travelled different roads to the same goal: the paramount responsibility
of every Jew to cherish the past as his guide to the future.

The Noés were among the Kedoshim of Czechoslovakia.
In their home, one breathed Torah and fervent allegiance to Judaism.
When they surrendered their souls to Hashem — as victims of
Nazi hatred and murder — they left only two young survivors,
but so much of the **Ateres Zekeinim** had their children absorbed,
that they regenerated the homes that had been destroyed.

The Cohens came to England early this century and raised their families there.
They faced twin challenges — a secular spiritual wilderness and assimilation —
but they persevered in their Yiddishkeit. Their success lives in the generations
that followed — generations loyal to the legacy of their Torah-true origins.

Pirkei Avos encompasses the life-style of the fathers and mothers
of our nation. It is a guide and inspiration for our people,
as it was for our own revered grandparents.

This volume is their crown — as they were ours.

Leo and Sue Noé
Yudit, Zvi, Elisheva, Shira, and Raphael Alter

Publisher's Preface

Ⓘt is a rare privilege to present this new, anthologized commentary on Tractate *Avos* to the Jewish public. Few islands in the vast sea of the Torah are so universally frequented, so carefully studied, so revered as sources of constant guidance and information. It has aptly been called "the Torah's way of life," and, indeed, some of the major thinkers and commentators named their commentaries to reflect this concept of the tractate: *Maharal*'s work on *Avos* is named *Derech Chaim,* or "Way of Life"; and Rabbi Chaim of Volozhin's is named *Ruach Chaim,* or "Spirit of Life."

It was this feeling that prompted **Mr. and Mrs. Leo Noé** of London to dedicate this volume. They recognized it as an eternal road map and knew how it guided the lives of their grandparents ע״ה. They lived under vastly different conditions, but they persevered in passing on their devotion to the Torah — and the lessons of *Avos* — to their children and grandchildren. It is appropriate, therefore, that this commentary is named *Ateres Zekeinim,* or "Crown of the Elders." *Avos* was the crown of *their* lives, just as their memory remains the crown of their offspring.

Mr. and Mrs. Noé are gracious and distinguished friends and supporters of Torah causes, wherever they are. We are proud that they have chosen to associate themselves with our work of bringing Torah in its authentic glory to English-speaking Jews throughout the world.

We are gratified as well that we met the Noés through the good offices of our dear friends **Mr. and Mrs. Michael Gross**, of London, whose leadership in Torah causes of many varieties has made them leaders of English Jewry. Mr. Gross, as a member of the Board of Governors of the Mesorah Heritage Foundation, and a Founding Trustee of the British Friends of the Mesorah Heritage Foundation has become an integral part of our work.

It is only through the vision and generosity of people like the Noés and Grosses that Jews of all backgrounds and many lands have been able to draw upon the life-giving sustenance of the Torah in their own language and idiom. In Moses' last weeks, he inscribed the Torah in all the languages of the day. This symbolized that times would come when all those tongues would become languages of Torah (*Chiddushei HaRim*). It is happening today, as the thirst for the word of Hashem consumes Jews whose roots were thought to be severed. But the spark of the Torah is eternal within the nation and the hearts of its children.

The commentary in this volume was written by RABBI MOSHE LIEBER. His broad knowledge, skill and dedication is apparent on every page; we are grateful to him, as tens of thousands of readers will be year after year.

RABBI AVROHOM CHAIM FEUER, a familiar name to ArtScroll readers, kindly agreed to read the manuscript. He contributed many insights and valuable suggestions.

The manuscript was edited skillfully and tastefully by FAYGIE SILVERMAN.

The imaginative and beautiful page design and layout is yet another example of the unexcelled artistry of our dear friend and colleague, REB SHEAH BRANDER. He continues to outdo himself, volume after volume.

We are grateful also to the many people who contributed their skills to make this work possible. Among them are: REB AVRAHAM BIDERMAN, MRS. FAYGIE WEINBAUM, MRS. ESTHER FEIERSTEIN, CHAYA GITTI ZAIDMAN, and MRS. BASSIE GUTMAN. They were ably assisted by: MRS. DVORY BICK, MRS. MIRIAM STAVSKY, UDI HERSKOVITS, TOBY BRANDER and YEHUDA GORDON. The jacket was skillfully designed and executed by REB ELI KROEN.

We are especially grateful to the **Trustees and Governors** of the **Mesorah Heritage Foundation**. They have made many things possible in the relatively brief existence of the Foundation. They have been participants in the creation of a splendid chapter in Jewish history. With them, we look forward to many more years of productive activity in the service of Hashem, his Torah, and His people.

Rabbi Meir Zlotowitz / Rabbi Nosson Scherman

Menachem Av 5755 / August 1995

↝ An Overview /
Parents Lead the Way Back

I. Total Torah, Total Nation

We Are Their Students

All the succeeding generations are students of God, Moses, Joshua, and all the other spiritual luminaries.

*A*vos is unique among the tractates of the Talmud. Only *Avos* deals exclusively with the outlook of the Sages, with their lessons for life, with the way they lived their own lives, with the morals and ethics they wished to impart to their students, in their own study halls and in the halls of history. We, too, are their students; if we are not, then we have missed the primary lesson of the tractate, for it begins by setting forth the chain of Jewish tradition, beginning with our first Teacher, the One Who proclaimed the Ten Commandments to Moses and Israel at Mount Sinai. All the succeeding generations are students of God, Moses, Joshua, and all the other spiritual luminaries in the constellation of Jewish tradition, which is outlined in the first mishnah of this tractate.

In the simplest sense, we are their students, just as anyone who studies the Talmud is a student of all the Sages whose wisdom he absorbs, just as anyone who labors over and resolves an apparent contradiction in the *Rambam's* code is a student of the *Rambam,* and, in more modern terms, anyone who studies with the aid of a cassette series is a student of the unseen teacher who presents the Torah to him with the aid of modern technology.

Role Models

A teacher of the Torah must be a role model as a human being, as well as a scholar.

But there is another, deeper element — a particularly Jewish and an absolutely essential one — to the teacher-student relationship established by the Torah. A teacher of the Torah must be a role model as a human being, as well as a scholar. The Talmud admonishes that one should accept a teacher whom he respects as if he were an angel of God. This aspect of the learning process was never as starkly clear as in modern times, when the personal foibles and perversions of anyone who ever achieved five minutes of fame are grist for lurid gossip, exposes, and biographies. How many "great" political leaders, magnates, athletes, or entertainers of modern times have had private lives that would lead any person of middling morality to say, "That is what I want my children to be!"? And yet, general society still calls them "great," because the purveyors of culture have taught us to separate the heroics of the public arena from the antics of the private barnyard.

The teachers of Jewish eternity were always different. The Talmud teaches that one can learn as much or more from the private lives of the Sages as from their teachings in the study hall (*Berachos* 7a), and that the ordinary conversations of Torah scholars are worthy of study (*Avodah Zarah* 19b). Halachic rulings have been based — definitively so — on the private deeds of great Torah figures, even when observers have not understand the legal basis of what they did. Could the private conversations or conduct of the general run of this century's public figures be recorded as an authoritative book of law?

Clearly, the Torah's standards are different. It speaks to the total personality. It has been axiomatic since the Patriarch Abraham that sage and saint must be synonymous, that intellect, piety, ethics, and morality are part of an inseparable whole. Judaism is not a compartmentalized creed, not a religion that respects disembodied minds whose preachings are contradicted by their conduct. The Torah nation has never accepted the leadership of people who fall significantly short of that standard of aspiration. True, human beings, by definition, can almost never achieve absolute perfection, and Jews have never underestimated the difficulty of climbing that pedestal; realism and self-criticism are among Israel's most painful virtues. But the aspiration must be present. In Judaism, to speak of legal authority without moral authority is as ludicrous as accepting the Ten Commandments with the exception of the first one: "I am HASHEM, your God."

The Torah's standards are different. It speaks to the total personality.

To speak of legal authority without moral authority is ludicrous.

Thus, the Talmud would have been incomplete had it contained only discussions about ritual and law. The Torah molds total people, not just minds; it defines values, not just norms of performance.

So it was that the tractate *Avos* was compiled by the same Rabbi Yehudah *HaNasi* (the Prince) who was the redactor of the Mishnah. The tractate of ethics had to be part of the same Talmud that contains the rest of the Oral Law; there is no schizophrenia in Judaism.

Rabbeinu HaKadosh

Rabbi Yehudah was known simply as *Rabbeinu HaKadosh,* our Holy Teacher — or simply as *Rabbi*, the Teacher. He was the only Jew in over a century who had the Jewish and temporal authority to summon all the great sages to compile and redact the teachings of the Oral Law — and who was a very close friend of Emperor Marcus Aurelius Antoninus, so that the cruel and bloody Roman rulers of Israel did not interfere. He epitomized scholarship, leadership, and saintliness. The Sages exclaimed that true humility ceased to exist when he died, and that no one else in his time so combined Torah and worldly greatness.

He epitomized scholarship, leadership, and saintliness.

When Roman massacres and persecutions had so disrupted the life of the Jewish people that the oral tradition was in danger of collapse, Rabbi decided that the only way to assure the survival of the Oral Law — and with it the very existence of the nation — was to commit its essentials to writing. It is illustrative of the importance of the contents of *Avos* that he compiled it as part of the Mishnah, along with the apparently weightier tractates that perplex the intellect, and challenge courts, rabbis, and priests to plumb their meaning and apply their principles to complex and evolving situations.

The only way to assure the survival of the Oral Law — and with it the very existence of the nation — was to commit its essentials to writing.

What was it about a book of maxims about ethics, manners, and everyday conduct that earned it so much attention at a time when the nation's future hung in the balance, with the sword of Rome and the peril of dispersion poised over its neck?

II. Infusing the World with Holiness

Message of Genesis

There is a very well-known comment by *Rashi* at the beginning of the Torah. Since the Torah is essentially a book of laws, and clearly not a history book, why does it begin with the story of Creation? Why does it not begin with the very first commandment that was conveyed to the emerging Jewish people, the commandment to proclaim the New Moon and the Jewish calendar, which Moses taught the people in Egypt on the threshold of their freedom? *Rashi* explains that God wished to set forth His power as the Creator of the universe, so that no nation could question His right to give the Land of Israel to the people of Israel.

The *Sfas Emes* wonders, however, why it was necessary to devote the entire Book of Genesis to the story of the development of the Patriarchs and the emergence of their family. If God, in His wisdom, saw the need to establish His authority, the first chapter of Genesis would have been sufficient. Clearly, there is something about the first 2,255 years of history that justifies an entire book of the Torah. What is it?

Clearly, there is something about the first 2,255 years of history that justifies an entire book of the Torah. What is it?

The commandments are all part of the Written Torah and, as *Rashi*'s question indicates, the Torah's primary subject matter is the commandments; however, the material and animal worlds, too, are functions of the Torah. In the words of the *Zohar* and *Midrash*, God peered into the Torah and created the world. If the Torah is the blueprint for Creation, then it must also be the life force and ongoing plan for human activity. Indeed, the challenge of the Jewish people is to bring the sanctity of the Torah into all areas of life. As noted above, Judaism does not differentiate between "ordinary, private" affairs and the laboratory, stage, or synagogue.

Indeed, the challenge of the Jewish people is to bring the sanctity of the Torah into all areas of life.

Another Aspect of Creation

To prepare the world for the Torah was the function of the Patriarchs and Matriarchs — and even of their servants. This realm of human activity can be likened to the Oral Law, which by its nature consists not only of the immutable teachings and principles conveyed to Moses at Sinai, but also of man's potential to think, understand, broaden, interpret, and apply. The Sages teach that every innovation of an accomplished scholar to the end of time was already included in the Torah taught to Moses at Sinai — and this presupposes that such scholars will study, exert themselves, and gain Divine wisdom.

Every innovation of an accomplished scholar to the end of time was already included in the Torah taught to Moses at Sinai.

This, however, is only one aspect of man's continuous task of absorbing and teaching God's wisdom. The Torah personality's behavior in the marketplace, his interaction with kings and peasants, his personal faith and piety in situations that imperil both — all of these are mandated by a realm of the Torah that is usually not found in codes of law. But it is for man to recognize the challenge and surmount it. When Abraham as an old man recovering from his circumcision opened his tent to strangers in a brutal heat wave, when he showed the utmost courtesy and forbearance to avaricious Hittites who haggled over a burial site for Sarah, when Sarah displayed unfailing modesty and unselfishness, when Isaac endured the lust and indignities of the Philistine ruler and his people, when Jacob overcame the greed and larceny of Laban and the bloodlust of Esau, when Rebecca had to choose which of her sons could be the bearer of the world's spiritual destiny — all these and the many more stories of the developing Chosen People brought Godliness into Creation. Only people with free choice could accomplish that Divine plan. God creates, but does not impose on man's free will. So when a human being carries out God's plan and ennobles the world, he indeed becomes "God's partner in Creation," as the *Zohar* expresses it.

A realm of the Torah that is usually not found in codes of law.

When a human being carries out God's plan and ennobles the world, he indeed becomes "God's partner in Creatio."

In this sense, the entire Book of Genesis is part of the story of Creation and how God's power extends to every facet of human activity. Its first section tells very briefly how the physical universe and man came into being, but that does not affect our lives, except to prove that God, as the Creator, has the right to determine how and to whom to dispose of His universe. The rest of the story, until the commandments begin, tell how man began to carry out his own share in Creation — matching his Oral Law to God's Written Law — by shaping and breathing a soul into the universe.

Conversation of the Servant

One of the lengthy passages in Genesis can be best understood in this light. Abraham sent his servant Eliezer to Haran to find a suitable mate for Isaac. The Torah relates Eliezer's effort at great length, and then quotes his own account of the story — two lengthy accounts when it would have seemed that even a single abbreviated one would have been sufficient. In explanation, *Rashi* cites the teaching of the Sages that the ordinary conversation of the servants of the Patriarchs is more pleasing to God than the halachic verses directed at their children, for many laws are taught through implication, or through the addition or omission of a letter, while Eliezer's trip is repeated twice, in full.

The piety of Abraham and Sarah was not limited to the privacy of their souls or personal living quarters.

The piety of Abraham and Sarah was not limited to the privacy of their souls or personal living quarters. They recognized their duty to infuse their servants, neighbors, and surroundings with Godly faith and behavior. Eliezer, their servant, was typical of this, and the best way to show it is by relating how he acted in a foreign land with people who were worlds away from the atmosphere of his master's home. This, too, was part of the process of completing Creation (see *Sfas Emes, Bereishis* 5671; and *Ohr Gedalyahu* to *Toldos*).

Such conduct is the theme of *Avos*, because Creation is an ongoing process. Just as God בְּטוּבוֹ מְחַדֵּשׁ בְּכָל יוֹם תָּמִיד מַעֲשֵׂה בְרֵאשִׁית, *in His goodness renews daily, perpetually the work of Creation* (Sabbath liturgy), meaning that the universe does not exist through momentum, but through constant Divine renewal, so too, man's role in Creation — his task of bringing God's will into everyday life — must continue daily, perpetually. The Patriarchs and their servants set the pattern, the Torah provides the road map, but the behavior of great and pious Jews from the time of Abraham to today shows how it must be done.

The Patriarchs and their servants set the pattern, the Torah provides the road map.

Example of the Home

In ancient times, the "method" was to observe how it was put into practice by the "fathers and mothers" of the nation. Rabbi Yaakov Kamenetsky observed that until the time of Yehoshua ben Gamla, a Kohen Gadol of the Second Temple era, no system of public Torah education was established in Israel because, even though many of the common people were unlearned, parents were successful in conveying the traditions and values of the Torah to their children. True, this was at the cost of learning — no small price to pay — but the Sages of the nation felt that the accomplishment justified the sacrifice. Then, that situation was no longer workable, and the beginnings of what may be called the "yeshivah system" were established by Yehoshua ben Gamla approximately two thousand years ago. For nineteen centuries, there was no need for a school system for girls; Jewish mothers were more successful than Jewish fathers had been, and the home remained a powerful force for purity and devotion. Then, in the aftermath of World War I and its ravages, it became necessary to establish the Beth Jacob school system and other models of public education for Jewish girls.

For nineteen centuries, the home remained a powerful force for purity and devotion.

III. When Unity is Present

*Two Kinds
of Dispersion*

Maharal reports a blunt question put to him by a gentile, who wondered why there seemed to be less unity among Jews than would be expected of a Chosen People.

Before responding to this embarrassing condemnation, *Maharal* comments that the accusation is an old one, and that the blemish exists among the nations that are so overjoyed to find warts in the Jewish people. Nevertheless, *Maharal* agrees that it is not sufficient to point fingers back at the accusers. How, indeed, does one understand the lack of unity among Jews?

He writes, "This is our response to this matter. The very fact that our nation is not united by each one's love for his fellow is the essence of the present exile, for God has disrupted their fellowship, and divided and dispersed them. Once He divided them and dispersed them, this fact also caused people who had been of one mind and one heart to become disunited in their outlook, for if they had not become disunited in this manner, but had instead maintained their essential unity of outlook, the [exile] would not have been a true dispersion. For the fact that their hearts were still one would have united them and kept them together — but it was God's decree that they be separated. This [decree] required that there be a division and dispersion of their hearts, for if one individual had been gladdened by the greatness and desirous of the tranquility of others, could that be considered dispersion? That would not be division, but total unity!" (*Netzach Yisrael* ch. 25).

It is a fascinating concept, and one that not only sheds light on a sad phenomenon, but provides a focus for the constructive behavior that is needed to eliminate it. The purpose of exile is for the Jewish people to correct the underlying national flaws that caused the Temple to be destroyed and the nation to be dispersed. If failure to remain together is a symptom of the exile, and our love and concern for one another would recreate spiritual unity, which would inevitably lead to the ingathering of the exiles and the Final Redemption, then what more important national goal can there be?

That our nation is not united by each one's love for his fellow is the essence of the present exile.

If one individual had been gladdened by the greatness of others, that would not be division, but total unity!

*The Two
Destructions*

In a very well-known Talmudic passage, the Sages discuss the reasons for the two Destructions (*Yoma* 9b). The First Temple was destroyed because the nation collectively was guilty of the three cardinal sins of idolatry, immorality, and murder. "But the Second Temple, of which we know with certainty that [the people] were involved with Torah, commandments, and kind deeds — why was it destroyed? Because of the hatred without cause that prevailed among them."

Why was it destroyed? Because of the hatred without cause that prevailed among them.

Maharal (ibid. ch. 4) explains the difference between the two. The existence of the First Temple was based on the Divine Presence, as exemplified by the Holy Ark and the many miracles that took place there regularly. The three cardinal sins drove away God's Presence, and since God was not there, the essence of the Temple had crumbled long before the enemy's onslaught.

The Second Temple's existence was based on its status as a rallying, unifying force for the nation.

The Second Temple, on the other hand, never had the Divine Presence. The Holy Ark was never returned to it, and most of the miracles were not there, either. That Temple's existence was based on its status as a rallying, unifying force for the nation. All eyes turned to the Temple, for atonement and inspiration. It symbolized the unity of the Jewish people as the one, unique nation on earth. Sins there might be, shortcomings there might be, but unity and mutual love are very powerful forces on the Heavenly scales.

David and Ahab

The Sages contrast the reigns of David and Ahab. King David was the "Sweet Singer of Israel," one of the "Seven Historic Shepherds," the forerunner and ancestor of *Mashiach*, but he often suffered casualties in war. King Ahab was the rogue monarch who earned some of the strongest condemnations in all of Scripture, yet he was always victorious in battle and hardly suffered casualties. What was the difference between the two? Ahab's people were united in mutual affection and cooperation. David's reign was marred by recrimination and hatred (*Yerushalmi, Peah*). If bad feeling could make David's army inferior to Ahab's, surely it could disrupt a Temple founded upon national unity.

If bad feeling could make David's army inferior to Ahab's, surely it could disrupt a Temple founded upon national unity.

Living not long after the Destruction of the Temple and the Roman massacres, Rabbi Yehudah *HaNasi* saw the results of hatred and dissension, and it was to counter these disastrous effects that he compiled *Avos*. The nation fell and the Temple was destroyed because the people's moral fabric had deteriorated; it could rise again only when the fabric was mended.

Rabbi compiled the Six Orders of the Mishnah not as an orderly listing of abstract laws and principles, but as the living words of his teachers and colleagues. Historically, the vitality of the Oral Law was due to the mind and soul of teachers breathing life into new generations. That was the way he chose to formulate the teachings of ethics and morality — the charting of a דֶּרֶךְ חַיִּים, *Way of Life*. He cited the way of life of the Sages who were the great teachers and role models of the nation.

The quotes in Avos represent the way these spiritual and intellectual giants actually lived.

The quotes in *Avos* are not philosophical formulations; they represent the way these spiritual and intellectual giants *actually lived*. As will be noted in the commentary, the recurring phrase הוּא הָיָה אוֹמֵר, *he used to say*, has the sense that the normal, everyday behavior of the person declared that this was the way he lived. When Hillel urged people to love peace and pursue peace, to love people and bring them closer to the Torah (1:12), when Shammai said, "Receive everyone with a cheerful face" (1:15), they were putting into words what everyone saw them do, day in, day out. The Sages of the Mishnah never said or implied, "Do as I say, not as I do"; had they been guilty of such inconsistencies, they would not have been accepted as leaders of the people.

No One Perfect

Their teachings are not so lofty as to be unrealistic for ordinary Jews. They are goals, and goals are not disqualified because they are above the people who aspire to them. The Sages teach that every Jew's longing should be: "When will my deeds reach those of Abraham, Isaac, and Jacob?" Does this mean that every Jew is expected to become the equal of the Patriarchs and Matriarchs? Would anyone be foolhardy enough even to imagine such a possibility? Even the greatest people in our history did not attain absolute perfection, but that does not mean that perfection is not a goal.

Even the greatest people in our history did not attain absolute perfection, but that does not mean that perfection is not a goal.

In *Shemoneh Perakim*, *Rambam*'s classic, lengthy introduction to *Avos*, he writes that every human being has certain inborn character flaws that he or she must work to remedy. That is the nature of life, that people are not born perfect, yet are challenged to recognize their weaknesses and fight them. *Rambam* writes that Moses' sin at the Waters of Meribah was that he angrily chastised the nation, leading them to believe that God must be angry with them, as well — and this was not the case. Only Moses expressed anger, not God. It is perfectly true, as *Ramban* notes, that Moses had every right to be angry at people whose faith had failed them after forty years of miracles. Nevertheless, more is expected from someone of Moses' awesome greatness. The prophet Elijah, *Rambam* writes, had to be taken from this world while still alive, because his zealotry for God's honor had gone too far. Nevertheless, both Moses and Elijah were great beyond our comprehension.

Moses had every right to be angry, nevertheless, more is expected from someone of Moses' awesome greatness.

Perfect? No human being can be. Surrender? No human being has that right. And the lessons of *Avos* are that people can rise, and these are how the great leaders and teachers set examples and gave guidance.

IV. Three Areas of Life

כִּי נֵר מִצְוָה וְתוֹרָה אוֹר, וְדֶרֶךְ חַיִּים תּוֹכְחַת מוּסָר.

For a commandment is a lamp and Torah is light, and the way of life is the remonstrance of reproof (Proverbs 6:23). *

Lamp, Light, Life

This verse contains a thumbnail description of the three parts of the Torah. *Mitzvah*, the physical performance of the commandments, is like a *lamp*. It is a receptacle that contains oil and wick — or electricity and

---

* This part of the Overview is based on *Maharal*'s Introduction to his commentary to *Avos*, which, very appropriately, he entitled *Derech Chaim*, Way of Life.

filament — and provides light. So too, one uses hands to affix a *mezuzah*, feet to rush to the synagogue, wealth to contribute to charity. Like a lamp that uses physical items to provide and sustain light, the body and the appurtenances of the world combine to do God's will in a tangible way. But once the oil is consumed and the wick is spent, the lamp is still and dark. Its light is never more than temporary. Even the longest-lasting fluorescent bulb will burn out eventually. And the glow of a *mitzvah* fades away.

Once the oil is consumed and the wick is spent, the lamp is still and dark.

The Torah, however, is different in a basic way. Its light is spiritual. It unites its student with the Source of all wisdom. Just as His wisdom is timeless, so the Torah is timeless and its spiritual capital permanent.

Then there is the third component of our faith: *the way of life is the remonstrance of reproof.* The Sages derive from this phrase that man earns his share of the World to Come only through hard work and suffering (*Berachos* 5a). The way of life in this world is the highway to the World to Come. It is traversed only with difficulty, because the *remonstrance of reproof* is often unpleasant, especially for people foolish enough to resent criticism. But intelligent people welcome it, relish it, thrive on it. To aspire to the World to Come without recognizing the need for guidance and criticism is like a diamond miner who refuses to dig. Of course there is a price to pay, but man has no greater bargain.

Reproof is unpleasant, especially for people foolish enough to resent criticism. But intelligent people welcome it, relish it, thrive on it.

Way of Life

Avos is that *way of life*. It is the slow-moving conveyance to the greatest of all rewards — not an express train, because nothing is harder than polishing a flesh-and-blood creature into a spiritual gem. This slim tractate is an indispensable complement to the Torah and the commandments, and that is why it is part of the Mishnah.

The Talmud teaches that man must perform three parts of the Torah to earn the exalted title חָסִיד, *devoutly pious person*: He must be vigilant in avoiding harm to others, in carrying out the teachings of *Avos,* and in scrupulously reciting the proper blessings (*Bava Kamma* 30a).

The laws of damages symbolize the entire relationship between man and his fellow man. "Do no harm" must always be high on a person's sense of priorities; by carefully studying and conscientiously observing the laws outlining property rights, man learns never to place himself over others. It is illustrative that the tenth statement that brought the universe into being, the Divine command that brought man into existence, is paralleled by the Tenth Commandment: Do not covet anything of your fellow's. Man is a fulfillment of God's hope only if he recognizes that he may not even *covet* what God gave to another. The boundaries between one man's property and his fellow's must be as inviolate as the borders between countries.

The Divine command that brought man into existence is paralleled by the Tenth Commandment: Do not covet anything of your fellow's.

The *chassid* observe the laws of blessings, because when he thanks God for whatever he enjoys, he accepts the proper relationship between himself and God, by acknowledging that everything he has, no matter how much sweat dripped from his brow, is a gift from God.

The teachings of *Avos* express the relationship between man and himself. They urge him to strive to perfect his character, control his urges, refine his aspirations, eliminate his vices, ennoble his relations with others, learn to love his fellows, pursue what should be pursued and flee what should be fled, imitate the Sages from Sinai to our own time, who bring to us the teachings that began with Creation and extended from Abraham and all his offspring to us.

Avos does all this, if we but let it penetrate our minds and hearts.

Let us embrace its teachings and thereby bring unity and love to a dispersed nation, and thereby let us be led behind Elijah and *Mashiach* to a rebuilt Temple.

The teachings of Avos express the relationship between man and himself.

Let us embrace its teachings.

Rabbi Nosson Scherman

Menachem Av 5755 / August 1995

Introduction

❧ Why the Tractate Is Called Avos / Fathers

Parents are the ones who not only bring a child into the world, but have the responsibility to provide their child with physical and moral nurture. Teachers, too, have this role. Indeed, the Sages equate students with children, because teachers share with parents the privilege of raising them. So too, much of *Mishlei/Proverbs,* King Solomon's primer of instruction and guidance, is couched in terms of fatherly advice directed towards *my son* (e.g., *Proverbs* 1:8, 2:1, etc.).

In this sense, the Sages of the Mishnah are the fathers of the nation, for they teach the moral imperatives of the Torah and offer ethical orientation to all people. Those who live by their words are figuratively considered the sons and daughters of these teachers, and it is fitting, therefore, that the tractate containing their teachings is called *Avos,* or, as it is commonly known in English, *Ethics of the Fathers.*

Bnei Yissas'char goes a step further and says that the term *Avos* refers to our Biblical Forefathers. He notes that the beginning of the Torah until the first commandment given to the nation as a whole — the commandment of Rosh Chodesh (*Exodus* 12:2) — is the story of those incidents in the lives of the Patriarchs and Matriarchs that have shaped Jewish history through "spiritual genetics." Hence, the Sages teach that human moral and ethical development preceded the giving of the Torah by the twenty-six generations from Adam until Sinai. Those centuries were the period when the lives and example of the Patriarchs set the patterns of Jewish life and aspiration for the rest of time (see *Vayikra Rabbah* 19). Thus, all the moral and ethical instruction expressed in this tractate is gleaned from the lives of our Forefathers, *Avos,* who gave their name to the tractate.

By contrast, *Eitz Avos* and *Binah L'Itim* understand the word *Avos* to suggest that the tractate is addressed primarily *to* parents, for it is meant to be a guide for them. Every parent must master and internalize the principles elucidated in *Avos,* in order to inculcate moral values in their children.

Alternatively, the term *Avos* is used to mean "major categories," within which there are subcategories, in the same sense that there are thirty-nine primary categories of forbidden work on the Sabbath, each of which has its own subcategories. So too, the major principles of human ethical behavior are to be found here; anything else can be derived from the words of the Sages in this tractate (*Midrash Shmuel*).

Even growth in Torah knowledge must be based on the ethical training outlined in *Avos,* as the Sages teach: דֶּרֶךְ אֶרֶץ קָדְמָה לַתּוֹרָה, *Proper conduct and character development must precede the study of Torah* (*Vayikra Rabbah* 19). Since success in Torah study is a direct result of proper character

---

❧ **Three-fold perfection.** *Maharal* interprets the three opinions regarding the key to piety as complementary. Man must perfect his relationships with others (symbolized by *Nezikin*), with himself (symbolized by the moral teachings of (*Avos)*, and with God. The blessings, as expressions of our gratitude to God, express our dependence upon Him.

---

development, this tractate is the "father," the progenitor of Torah greatness. A prime example is Moses, who merited to serve as the liaison in bringing God's Torah to the nation because of his outstanding character traits. Hence, the ethical imperatives contained in this tractate are the *Avos* — the prototypical guidelines for the achievement of physical and spiritual fulfillment, and for the discharging of one's obligations to God and to his fellow man (*Tiferes Yisrael*).

◆§ Why Is Avos in Seder Nezikin?

The Mishnaic order *Nezikin* deals with the legal system: laws of damages, evidence, the processes for making restitution, and so on. Seemingly, the placement of *Avos* in this order is incongruous.

According to *Rambam*, *Avos* is the logical conclusion to the tractates dealing with the laws of judges and justice, because the courts must be permeated with a sense of ethics and morality. Judges who lack compassion and a zeal for fairness can be the source of infinite harm.

R' Yosef ibn Nachmias explains that this is based on the Talmudic teaching: "Whoever wants to be pious (חָסִיד), let him fulfill the words [and laws] of *Nezikin*. Rava, said [Let him fulfill] the words [and teachings] of *Avos*; others say, [Let him fulfill] the words [and laws] of *Berachos* [blessings recited before deriving pleasure from food, drink, or the like, and also recited prior to performing a *mitzvah*]" (*Bava Kamma* 30a).

Thus, the laws of damages in *Nezikin* and the ethical guidance of *Avos* belong together, since both are prerequisites to piety and heightened moral conduct. But what is the common denominator of laws affecting the seemingly mundane and unpleasant areas of human and property damage and contending parties in the courtroom, and the sublime topics of *Avos*?

The Mishnaic order *Nezikin* teaches man how to live with his fellow and how to protect himself and others from physical harm and monetary loss. *Avos* is a natural complement of these issues, since it teaches purity of character, which is the key to man's ability to safeguard himself and others. A moral person is never a menace to others — or himself. But unless one refines one's character and works on self-improvement in areas of interpersonal conduct, one will indeed be a danger to society, as well as himself (*Toras Avos*).

The social and personal damage resulting from a lack of ethical principles is often more severe than the damages discussed in the other tractates of *Nezikin*, which involve property. Untamed by Torah and its values and allowed to run rampant, human greed, passion, and rage can dwarf the destruction of natural disaster; *Avos*, therefore, is eminently qualified for inclusion in the order of *Nezikin* (Damages).

◆§ **A human menace.** R' Chaim Ozer Grodzenski used to say that a yeshivah without a *mashgiach* (spiritual and ethical mentor) and without the study of *mussar* (Torah ethics and morals) is analogous to an open pit in the public domain (בּוֹר בִּרְשׁוּת הָרַבִּים). Just as an uncovered pit imperils the unsuspecting person who may fall in and be injured, one who does not develop positive character traits is open to pitfalls of all kinds, and may pull other people down with him. If someone irritates him or says something which he misinterprets, he will explode, hurting himself and others. He is a danger to himself, to society, to his family and friends.

The Talmud (according to Rav; see *Bava Kamma* 3b) defines man as one of the major categories of those that do damage [מַבְעֶה]. The tractate *Avos* is meant to serve as a preventive, to keep man from becoming that damaging force (*R' A. C. Feuer*).

פרק ראשון ⊷

Chapter One

בָּל יִשְׂרָאֵל יֵשׁ לָהֶם חֵלֶק לָעוֹלָם הַבָּא, שֶׁנֶּאֱמַר:

Prologue

The following mishnah is not part of *Pirkei Avos*, but is recited as an introduction to the weekly chapter. Its origin and the reason for its insertion here are explained in the commentary.

בָּל יִשְׂרָאֵל יֵשׁ לָהֶם חֵלֶק לָעוֹלָם הַבָּא — *All Israel has a share in the World to Come.* The term *Israel* refers to any individual who has not utterly divorced himself from the Jewish nation's lofty spiritual destiny. His portion in the World to Come will vary according to his merit, but as long as he remains part of "Israel," he will never lose it entirely (*R' Hirsch*).

This maxim, from the mishnah (*Sanhedrin* 90a), is read as an introduction to each chapter of *Avos* because it increases our incentive to apply ourselves to the teachings we are about to read. Overwhelmed by the broad scope of ethical advice and moral instruction contained in *Avos*, one might despair of achieving the level of such refinement needed to assure him a place in the World to Come. Therefore, we reiterate that *all* Israel has a share in the World to Come; our ultimate reward awaits us and is within reach — we should certainly pursue it (*Midrash Shmuel, R' Moshe Almosnino*).

Knesses Yisrael adds: The lessons of *Avos* are a prescription from God to help us nurse our souls back to spiritual health. A doctor who seeks to heal his patient first reassures him that his disease is conquerable and that he need not despair; similarly, one who is beginning spiritual therapy must be bolstered emotionally against despair, which is itself a spiritually fatal malady. Even one who senses that he is in critical spiritual condition must believe that he *can* be cured. This introductory mishnah to each chapter of *Avos* provides assurance that each member of the Jewish nation can survive and flourish — because *All Israel has a share in the World to Come*.

According to *Mikveh Yisrael*, the purpose of this introduction is to explain to the Jewish people why they, more than all other nations, need the extensive ethical and moral instruction contained in *Avos*: Since all Jews have a share in the World to Come, it is imperative that they not do anything to lose such a precious gift. Everything contained in *Avos* is necessary to achieve that end.

All Israel does not mean to exclude righteous gentiles (see *Sanhedrin* 105a and *Rambam, Hilchos Teshuvah* 3:5). Rather, it teaches that even those

---

◈§ **An embarrassing guarantee.** Someone once asked the Chofetz Chaim why anyone should expend the effort to study Torah and fulfill the *mitzvos* if his share in the World to Come is already prepared for him. He replied with a story: In Kiev, Russia, there lived a wealthy magnate by the name of Yisrael Brodsky, who owned huge factories and employed hundreds of people. Skilled and unskilled workers, menial laborers, accountants, and managers, all made their living working for Brodsky. A man of extraordinary magnanimity, and a philanthropist par excellence, he supported many Torah institutions and provided full support in the famous Yeshivah of Volozhin to a group of budding geniuses known as "Brodskys." Several fellow Jews whose finances had taken a bad turn and many of his relatives were on Brodsky's payroll and received a monthly check, even though they did no productive work.

Once the magnate came to visit one of his factories. The managers showed him around and introduced him to all the workers. Mr. Brodsky inquired into the personal welfare of each worker, asking him about his role in the manufacturing process and what he received as a monthly salary. All the workers, skilled and menial alike, received this treatment from Mr. Brodsky, but from one he received an unusual response. When he asked this particular worker, "And what do you do here?," the man, one of the non-working relatives, answered, "I take a check." All the people around them broke into laughter.

"Of course," concluded the Chofetz Chaim, "all Israel has a share in the World to Come. However, some earn their keep, while others, like Brodsky's relative, do nothing more than 'take a check' and will suffer the embarrassment of doing so."

◄§ **Measuring rod.** This idea is mirrored in our Sages' explanation for the detailed laws of *kashrus*: The Jewish soul, which is linked to eternity, must be housed in a body that is carefully nourished with a spiritually refined diet; others do not have the same need.

The Midrash offers an analogy: Two patients were examined by a doctor. The examination revealed that one had a curable disease and could regain his health with proper medical care, diet, and exercise, while the second patient was incurable. The doctor told the first man: "Be careful to eat only things which are healthy and good for your condition. Follow this regimen and you will soon be a specimen of good health." Since the second man's condition was terminal, the doctor did not give any instructions that would diminish his enjoyment of the limited time he still had to live.

Likewise, the Jewish soul has a portion in the World to Come and is therefore sensitive; even its food must be closely monitored. Others, whose souls are not quite as pristine, may eat whatever they want.

In general, it is important that we appreciate the quality of our Jewish identity and set standards for ourselves in accordance with the sublimity of our mission. The Dubno *Maggid* offers a beautiful parable:

Many years ago a wealthy individual from a small town went to see the *Rosh Yeshivah* of a prestigious yeshivah. "I am looking for a *chassan* (groom) for my daughter," the gentleman began. "She is my only daughter, and I want the best for her. You can rest assured that the boy she marries will be able to continue his Torah studies unimpeded; I will guarantee that they will have no financial worries. The young man will be free to attain the heights of Torah knowledge."

Impressed with the man's obvious sincerity, the *Rosh Yeshivah* suggested an outstanding yeshivah student as a match for the young woman. His expectations were fulfilled; the two were married and went to live in the bride's small hometown. In the town's small synagogue, the young man resumed his Torah studies. His diligence and devotion were incredible. Hour after hour he would sit and learn without interruption. Many months passed in this manner, and the father-in-law was extremely proud of his daughter's husband.

About a year after the wedding, the father-in-law noticed that the young man's diligence was beginning to slacken off. At first he began his studies later in the day than usual; then he started to find excuses to leave earlier than in the past. At first, the father-in-law was hesitant to say anything, but when the young man began to skip a day or two of learning from time to time, he realized that he would have to intervene. He called the young man to his home. "My dear son," he began gently, "you know how proud I have always been of your learning and Torah accomplishments. The *Rosh Yeshivah* assured me that you would eventually be the greatest among your peers. But it grieves me to see what has become of your learning lately. I could not help but notice that there are days when you do not step into the synagogue altogether. Is this how you will continue?"

The young man looked at his father-in-law with surprise. "My dear father," he replied, "I have indeed achieved just what the *Rosh Yeshivah* said I would achieve. I am the most learned among my peers here in this town. Tell me honestly, is there anyone here who knows as much as I do? Is there anyone here who spends even half the time that I do in Torah study?"

The father-in-law looked at him and said softly, "Think for a moment. To whom are you comparing yourself? To the simpletons of our little town? They know very little and they aspire to very little. You should be comparing yourself to the companions of your yeshivah days. *They* are the true barometer of your accomplishments."

Rabbi Avraham Pam explains: If a Jew looks around him and sees a world of immorality, deceit, and fraud, if he often encounters underhandedness and an insatiable pursuit of material goals, he can easily rationalize to himself and say, "With the performance of even one *mitzvah*, I have already achieved a much greater status than those in the secular world." He might even become smug with the feeling that he has achieved a degree of holiness far beyond those who do no *mitzvos* at all. Therefore, God says, "*You shall be holy, for I,* HASHEM *your God, am holy (Leviticus 19:2).* Don't compare your holiness to the holiness of others; you are children of God and are answerable to a higher standard. Be holy, for I am holy. Use Me, not the nations of the world, as a barometer, and then you will know what is expected of you."

"וְעַמֵּךְ כֻּלָּם צַדִּיקִים, לְעוֹלָם יִירְשׁוּ אָרֶץ, נֵצֶר מַטָּעַי,
מַעֲשֵׂה יָדַי לְהִתְפָּאֵר."

Jews who are considered wicked because of their numerous sins are assured a portion in the World to Come, unless they forfeit the title "Israel" by rejecting any of the basic tenets of Judaism as enumerated in *Sanhedrin* 90a and *Rosh Hashanah* 17a (*Rambam*).

According to *Ramban* (see his *Shaar HaGemul*) and those who follow his view, the term לְעוֹלָם הַבָּא is reserved almost exclusively for the eternal world after the Resurrection of the Dead. According to *Rambam*, however, it is a much broader term that can refer to the entire period of the Afterlife or any portion thereof. (See at length, Appendix to *Sanhedrin* III, Schottenstein Edition of the Talmud.)

While all Israel has a share in the World to Come, the shares are not equal, but are dependent on the level achieved by each person through his deeds in this life (*Meiri; Sefer HaIkkarim* 4:31).

The mishnah's terminology, חֵלֶק לָעוֹלָם הַבָּא, literally means a share *"towards"* the World to Come (rather than בָּעוֹלָם הַבָּא, *"in"* the World to Come). This indicates that עוֹלָם הַבָּא is not a preexisting place in which one's share awaits him, commensurate with his good deeds. *Olam Haba* is something we create for ourselves by the way we live in this world. We gain *Olam Haba* through working *toward* it, by performing good deeds [notably, Torah study — see *Kesubos* 111] (*Ruach Chaim*).

◆§ **Parts of a great whole.** The Jewish nation's immutable connection to eternity, assured to each of its members, was revealed through Balaam, the evil, non-Jewish prophet. He prophesied: לֹא הִבִּיט אָוֶן בְּיַעֲקֹב וְלֹא רָאָה עָמָל בְּיִשְׂרָאֵל ה' אֱלֹהָיו עִמּוֹ וּתְרוּעַת מֶלֶךְ בּוֹ, *He perceived no iniquity in Jacob and saw no perversity in Israel; HASHEM, his God, is with him, and the friendship of the King is in him* (*Numbers* 23:21).

God is the רֵעַ, *friend*, of His people. [The term רֵעוּת is indicative of the strongest type of friendship. The level of יָדִיד indicates a functional friendship between two people who have joined hands (יד-יד) in a common activity; חָבֵר implies that two separate entities bond together to form a relationship. The root רֵעַ, however, can mean *to break* or *smash* (see *Psalms* 2:9: תְּרֹעֵם בְּשֵׁבֶט בַּרְזֶל, *You will smash them with a rod of iron*). Thus when this word is used to express friendship, it denotes the deep relationship of two people who sense that they share a common soul, a common longing, and that they are coming together as complementary parts of one whole. This is the relationship between God and His people; on a mystical level, they are one, and therefore all Israel has a share in the World to Come (*R' Tzadok HaKohen of Lublin*).

The Baal Shem Tov figuratively describes every Jew as a "limb" of the Divine Presence. As long as the limb is attached, there is hope that it can be healed; once severed, it withers and wastes away. A Jew, no matter how far he has drifted from God and His Torah, is still connected to eternity, unless he commits one of the sins that cause his soul to be severed from the eternity of Israel (see *Sanhedrin* 90a).

And your people are all righteous; they shall inherit the land forever; a branch of My plantings, My handiwork, in which to take pride (Isaiah 60:21).

שֶׁנֶּאֱמַר: "וְעַמֵּךְ כֻּלָּם צַדִּיקִים, לְעוֹלָם יִירְשׁוּ אָרֶץ — *as it is said: "And your people are all righteous; they shall inherit the land forever.* The mishnah applies this verse to the World to Come, since in this world not all Jews are righteous, nor is there eternal life here. Rather, in the World to Come, all Jews are deemed righteous once their souls are cleansed after death (*Tiferes Yisrael*).

The "land" that they shall forever inherit is "the land of the living" (*Psalms* 142:6), an allegory for the spiritual reward of the World to Come (*Rambam*). It may also refer to physical existence in the World of Resurrection (*Tiferes Yisrael*). This "land" is described as being *inherited* forever because it is the birthright of every Jew, just as every Jew has a portion in the Land of Israel (*Margaliyos HaYam;* see *Ramban* to *Genesis* 33:18).

נֵצֶר מַטָּעַי, מַעֲשֵׂה יָדַי לְהִתְפָּאֵר" — *a branch of My plantings, My handiwork, in which to take pride'* (*Isaiah* 60:21).

The expression *a branch of My plantings* may refer to the soul, which God planted in this world to be nurtured and developed. It has also been explained variously as a reference to the Jew planted in the World to Come (*Alshich*), to the World to Come itself (*Tiferes Yisrael*), or to the Jewish people, who are God's children [in *Shabbos* 32b, we find "the work of one's hand" used to describe one's children]. R' Yerucham Levovitz elaborates: The Jew is "planted" in this world in order to find fulfillment in the World to Come. Everything in this world gives birth to great consequences in the World to Come, and in that sense the latter is prepared even while we are still on earth.

◄§ **Work the plot.** The word חֵלֶק may be properly rendered as *a plot*. Like a plot of land which must be cultivated in order to yield produce, so every Jew is given a "plot" in the World to Come. By living a life of Torah and *mitzvos,* one spiritually cultivates this "plot" — his potential — and makes it productive. If he ignores his spiritual growth, his share in the World to Come remains the same barren plot he was given. Man's God-given potential is his key towards attaining a share in the World to Come (*Chofetz Chaim*).

◄§ **Justifiable pride.** The Beis Avraham (Slonim) homiletically interprets the second half of the verse as counterpoint to the first half: *They shall inherit the land forever* asserts that every Jew has a share in the World to Come. God imbues each and every Jew with talents and natural abilities that help him to earn that state of spiritual bliss. However, as with all God-granted gifts, man has no right to take pride in them any more than he has the right to brag about a financial inheritance. Only the branch of *his own* planting, which he cultivated and brought to fruition, is a source of true pride — *a branch of my plantings, my handiwork, in which to take pride* (interpreted here as referring to man rather than God). It is only one's spiritual handiwork, achieved by dint of his own ceaseless toil and effort, that may be deemed his own, a spiritual accomplishment in which he may justifiably take pride.

Mishnah 1

The tractate begins by tracing the links in the chain of Torah transmission through the generations, in order to emphasize the Divine origin of *Avos* and to equate its importance with that of the legal and ritual laws of the Torah. This is essential in order to differentiate *Avos* from ethical tracts composed by human beings (e.g., Aristotle's *Ethics*), for even the greatest of them are products of human intellect. *Avos*, however, was given at Sinai and transmitted through the generations, beginning with Moses; it is an integral part of the corpus of Torah that Moses received from God (*Rav*; also see *Meiri*).

This delineation of the chain of transmission indicates that even Torah study and the fulfillment of its commandments are insufficient means for man to achieve perfection, unless they are joined with refinement of character and the maintenance of proper interpersonal relationships — areas that are the subject of *Avos*. Our Sages teach (*Yoma* 86a): "Woe is to one who occupies himself with Torah yet does not conduct his business honestly and act cordially towards others" (*Tiferes Yisrael*).

מֹשֶׁה קִבֵּל תּוֹרָה — *Moses received the Torah. R'Yonah* stresses the fundamental principle of faith that the term "Torah" includes both the Written Law [תּוֹרָה שֶׁבִּכְתָב, i.e., the Five Books of Moses] and the accompanying Oral Law [תּוֹרָה שֶׁבְּעַל פֶּה], the interpretation of the text. God gave the Oral Law to Moses in its entirety and it was expounded by successive generations of sages (see *Berachos* 5a). Without the Oral Law, the Torah would be unintelligible. Thus, in the light of the Oral Law, the generic negative commandment לֹא תִגְזוֹל, *You shall not steal* (*Leviticus* 19:13), covers not only the stealing of money, but extends to liability for damages inflicted by one person or his property upon another person or *his* property. Likewise, many terms remain undefined in the written text of the Torah,

and the Oral Law identifies them [e.g., *an eye for an eye* (*Exodus* 21:24) is not literal but means monetary compensation; the ambiguous term *fruit of a beautiful tree* (*Leviticus* 23:40) refers to the commandment to take an *esrog* on Succos] (*R' Yonah*).

☐ **Like a lecturer's notes.** *R' S. R. Hirsch* compares the Written Law to the notes which a lecturer prepares for himself before making his presentation. Were an outsider, who did not hear the oral presentation, to find those notes, they would be totally unintelligible; the notes are meaningful only in conjunction with the verbal lecture. Similarly, much of the Written Torah makes sense only when accompanied by the Oral Tradition.

☐ **The Torah within us.** When He presented us with the Written Torah, God also implanted in us

⌗ **Ancient and revered.** It is commonly accepted that the more august an article's origin and the more ancient its pedigree, the more it is respected and the more it is worth. For example, an old uniform may be nothing more than a rag, but if it can be proven that it was once worn by a famous athlete or soldier, it becomes a valuable collector's item. In contrast, an article that is intrinsically precious, such as a piece of jewelry made of gold and platinum and studded with many large diamonds and pearls, is valuable even if it is of recent origin. *Avos* begins by pointing out the infinite value of the Torah. Not only is it of very ancient origin, it was given by God Himself, and treasured by the greatest people in the history of Israel.

⌗ **Intrinsically flawed.** Human definitions of ethics are unavoidably influenced by the thinking and moral climate prevalent at the time of their formulation. Rather than expressing timeless truths and objective moral certitudes, they tend to reflect circumstances. It is not surprising, therefore, that what was once unequivocally deemed murder may be considered mercy killing (euthanasia) or an expression of the right to control one's own body; and behavior once considered abominable may come to be regarded as nothing more than an "alternative life-style." Only God, through His Torah, can define truth and goodness.

1. Moses received the Torah from [God Who revealed Himself at Mount] Sinai and conveyed it to Joshua; Joshua

the intelligence and understanding to develop and penetrate the depths of its meaning — to outline its minute details and chart its pathways. As we say in our prayers, "Blessed is He, our God, Who created us for His glory, separated us from those who stray, *gave us the Torah of truth, and implanted eternal life within us.*" God "gave" us the Written Law in its entirety, but in addition He implanted within His people the national character through which God-fearing Torah scholars would have the ability and wisdom to interpret the nuances of the Written Text and apply its words to life situations as they unfold. It is in this sense that the Oral Law is described metaphorically like a tree that is *implanted . . . within us*. Just as a tree, once planted, has the capacity to grow and produce fruit and the seeds for more trees, so the Oral Law enables those who study it to elucidate the Written Law and produce ever more wisdom and applications, all emanating from the same roots.

מִסִּינַי — *from [God Who revealed Himself at Mount] Sinai.*

☐ **Not from Teacher to student.** Rather than stating directly, "Moses received the Torah from God," the Mishnah uses the word Sinai in order to emphasize that the "teacher-disciple" relationship between God and Moses was different from all others. Generally, such a relationship brings together two people who are particularly suited to each other, but in the case of God and Moses, this was not so. Any human being — even one as great as Moses — is so far removed from God that it would be irreverent and ludicrous to speak of Moses as

receiving the Torah directly from God, in the way that a student, though inferior to his teacher, can at least relate to him to some degree. Rather, as a sign of respect to God, the Mishnah speaks of Moses as receiving the Torah from Sinai (*Maharal*).

☐ **Sinai as concept.** "Sinai" refers not only merely to a location, but to the historic event that took place there, the Giving of the Law, in the sight and hearing of the entire Jewish people. In this manner, the Divine origin of the Law that came to us through Moses was established as a certainty (see *Rambam, Hilchos Yesodei HaTorah* 8:1). It is the directness of this Divine Revelation that the term *Sinai* brings to mind: the Divine origin of the Law and the authenticity of its preservation by a transmission carried on from age to age, through the leaders of each generation (*R' S. R. Hirsch*).

☐ **The mountain of humility.** The Talmud (*Megillah* 29a) teaches that the quality of humility, symbolized by Mount Sinai, is what made it the appropriate venue for the Divine Revelation. The lofty mountains are depicted as plaintiffs, complaining that they, rather than lowly, undistinguished Mount Sinai deserved to be the venue for the Revelation. God said no. "Because of your loftiness, you are all blemished compared to Sinai, and are therefore unfit to serve as the place where the Torah is given. Sinai is humble; it is upon it that the Torah will be given."

☐ **Like mountain, like Moses.** Rav Ashi said: One can learn from this that a person who is conceited is a blemished person. The mountains grew conceited on account of their loftiness and were thus

---

◆§ **God's street map.** R' Aharon Kotler likened the relationship of the two Torahs to the difference between a world map and a street map. On the huge world map New York City appears as a small black dot. Using only that map, one could never find a particular location within the city. Only with the help of a detailed map, which provides the block-by-block picture of the city, would one be able to locate his destination. Similarly, the basic map — the Written Torah — was given by God, and the Oral Torah fills out its details.

◆§ **Tone sensitive.** Similarly, one blessed with musical ability can listen to a symphony and pick up the counterpoint and the harmonies, while one who is tone deaf hears only the basic melody. The nation through its true Torah scholars, imbued with proper reverence for God and His word, has the ability to perceive the message of Torah found between the lines.

disqualified in favor of the lowly Sinai. Similarly, conceit in a human being is deemed a personal blemish. Moses, the most humble of all men (*Numbers* 12:3), was the fitting conduit through which to convey the Torah to the Jewish nation. As our Sages taught: "Why are the words of Torah compared to water? [see *Isaiah* 55:1]. Just as water leaves a higher level and goes to a lower level, so too the words of the Torah are retained only by one who is humble" (*Taanis* 7a). Our mishnah alludes to this. Moses mirrored the quality of Sinai; and it was *from Sinai* (a place symbolic of humility) that he merited to be given the Torah (*Tiferes Yisrael* et al.).

וּמְסָרָהּ לִיהוֹשֻׁעַ — *and conveyed it to Joshua.* Moses taught the Torah to the entire nation (*Deuteronomy* 31:22), but to Joshua he conveyed the reins of leadership (*Meiri*). *Midrash Shmuel* elaborates on this role. In every generation there must be Torah scholars who stand at the head of the nation and who assure that Torah regulates its daily life. Such people are called *baalei mesorah* (the masters of tradition). It was this level of Torah leadership that Moses conveyed to Joshua, along with the empowerment to enact protective legislation, according to the needs of the time and place.

Beis HaLevi defines the *baal mesorah* as the Torah scholar in each generation with the deepest appreciation of Torah and its values. Only one with a keen understanding of the priceless value of Torah can articulate and transmit its values.

Elazar, Phineas, and the seventy Elders were surely worthy to be the bearers of the tradition, but Moses chose Joshua because he had always sacrificed his personal comfort to excel in Torah knowledge and thereby earned an outstanding reputation (*Rashi*). *Yalkut* (*Pinchas* 776) elaborates that God said to Moses: "You know how much Joshua served and honored you. He arrived at your tent early and left late in order to arrange the chairs and spread out the mats [for the other disciples]. He is the one who will assume your office."

Those who fulfill this role must also be accessible to the masses of the people. The Talmud (*Bava Basra* 134a) teaches that Hillel the Elder had eighty disciples. The greatest of them was Yonasan ben Uziel. Whenever a bird flew over him, it would be consumed by exposure to the intense aura of holiness which surrounded him. The least of them was Rabban Yochanan ben Zakkai (see below 2:9), who possessed encyclopedic Torah and general knowledge. Nonetheless, *Rambam* (introduction to *Yad HaChazakah*) lists R' Yochanan ben Zakkai, not Yonasan ben Uziel, among the בַּעֲלֵי מְסוֹרָה, the links in the chain of tradition. This indicates that Yonasan ben Uziel, due to

---

◄§ **Moses learns from Sinai.** *Olelos Ephraim* notes that because of his humility, Moses showed no reluctance to accept the Torah at Sinai, as he had when God assigned him the mission to deliver the Jewish people from the Egyptian bondage. There, he had expressed misgivings about whether he was the proper agent for the task. In this case, however, taking his cue from Sinai, the lowest and symbolically most humble of all mountains, Moses was sure that he was the proper person for the job.

◄§ **Proper appreciation.** At a conference to select a committee that would defend the traditional *cheder* schools against the onslaught of the anti-religious *maskilim* ("enlightened" Jewish secularists), a motion was made to appoint a certain layman who was a confidant of the Beis HaLevi (R' Yosef Dov Soloveitchik). To the surprise of the conferees, when the rabbi was informed, he vetoed the nominee.

"Let me explain," said Rabbi Soloveitchik. "The Talmud (*Bava Kamma* 62a) relates that if someone accepted responsibility to safeguard a sack of gold coins — but the watchman was told that the sack contained silver — if it is lost, he may claim, 'I assumed responsibility only for silver. I was not willing to assume responsibility for the more precious gold.'

"We see," continued the rabbi, "that one's degree of responsibility for an item is linked to his understanding of its value. My friend is really a fine and wonderful Jew; however, his evaluation of Torah is like that of silver compared to gold. The Torah is precious to him, but he does not understand its true worth. Only a *talmid chacham* who has a real grasp of the pricelessness of Torah can serve as its guardian."

Likewise, the *baal mesorah* who serves as the guardian of the integrity of true Torah values must himself be a person with a heightened sense of its true worth.

1/1

[conveyed it] to the Elders; the Elders [conveyed it] to the Prophets; and the Prophets [conveyed it] to the Men of the Great

his exalted level, was too far above the people to serve as the conduit for the transmission of the tradition.

□ **Receive, not convey.** The Mishnah does not say that God *conveyed,* but that Moses *received.* By contrast, in Moses' transmission to Joshua, it says that Moses *conveyed.* The word "conveyed" implies that Moses, the transmitter, conveyed the entire Torah *as he knew it* to Joshua. The same term cannot be used to describe God's teaching to Moses, because God's intelligence is infinite and cannot be conveyed *in its entirety* to mortal man — not even to a Moses. Therefore, we are told that Moses *received* the Torah to the best of his ability, but not that all of God's wisdom was conveyed to him (*Tosafos Yom Tov* and *Maharal*).

וִיהוֹשֻׁעַ לַזְּקֵנִים — *Joshua [conveyed it] to the Elders.* These were the Elders who lived on after Joshua's demise [see *Judges* 2:7], and who, in turn, passed on the tradition to other groups of Elders. After the era of the Elders, responsibility for the tradition went to the Prophets, such as Eli HaKohen and Samuel (*Rav*).

The term *elders* is not indicative of age but refers to Torah scholars of any age who have acquired wisdom (see *Kiddushin* 32b).

Tiferes Yisrael, citing *Avos d'Rabbi Nosson*, identifies the זְקֵנִים as the *Shoftim* (Judges), whose exploits are recounted in the Book of Judges.

וּזְקֵנִים לִנְבִיאִים — *the Elders [conveyed it] to the Prophets.* Eli HaKohen, the last of the Judges, imparted the *mesorah-* tradition to Samuel, the first of the Prophets (*Tiferes Yisrael*). [See *Abarbanel* for a listing of the Prophets.] A prophet is a person who has had a direct communication from God, in word or vision. It is obvious from the chain of the tradition that one can be great enough to the primary leader of the nation, as were the Elders, and yet not be a prophet. Only after nearly four hundred years after the Exodus did leadership shift to the Prophets. Until then, the chain of tradition was strong enough for leaders to emerge based on their own knowledge of the Torah, without direct personal guidance from God. Later, it became necessary for prophets to replace them.

Prophets are called *Nevi'im* based on the expression נִיב שְׂפָתָיִם, *the fruit of the lips* (Isaiah 57:19; see *Rashi, Shemos* 7:1). Speech is the "fruit" of the tongue and lips, and the *Nevi'im* served in this capacity as God's spokesmen, bringing His word to His people.

Abarbanel and *Meiri* list Eli among the Elders, while *Rav* and *Rashi* consider him among the Prophets. Seemingly, at every new stage of the chain, a figure emerges who bridges two eras. Eli HaKohen was the last of the Judges and first of the Prophets; similarly, Chaggai, Zechariah, and Malachi were the last Prophets and members of the Men of the Great Assembly; Shimon the Righteous came at the end of the period of the Men of the Great Assembly and was one of the first *Tannaim* (authors of the Mishnah).

וּנְבִיאִים מְסָרוּהָ לְאַנְשֵׁי כְנֶסֶת הַגְּדוֹלָה — *and the Prophets [conveyed it] to the Men of the Great As-*

◆§ **Within reach.** R' Mordechai Pogramansky, one of the giants of the pre-World War II world of Torah and *mussar,* found this phenomenon represented by two great contemporary luminaries: "The Rogatchover Gaon (R' Yosef Rosen), a man with the mind of two Einsteins, was the storm. R' Chaim Soloveitchik of Brisk was the calm after the storm. By creating a systematic approach to Talmudic analysis and a thematic method for categorizing Torah ideas and concepts, R' Chaim served as one of the *baalei mesorah.*" [A person with a stormy temperament, like the Rogatchover, may be unapproachable; people cannot get close enough to him to benefit substantially from his knowledge.]

◆§ **Ours to pass on.** The tradition is called a מְסוֹרָה — something that is transmitted to others. Unlike a gift, which is retained by the one who receives it, a tradition is given specifically to be passed on intact to further generations (*HaChassid Yaavetz*). The Torah is not ours to dispose of as we please; it is our responsibility to pass it on intact to future generations. As Rabbi Mordechai Gifter comments, the Torah is called a heritage; it is the property of generations before *and after,* and it is incumbent upon its heirs to preserve it for the future.

הַגְּדוֹלָה. הֵם אָמְרוּ שְׁלֹשָׁה דְבָרִים: הֱווּ מְתוּנִים בַּדִּין, ‏א/א

sembly. The Men of the Great Assembly were a group of 120 Elders, including the last surviving Prophets and the greatest Torah scholars of the generation. Among them were Ezra, Zerubavel, Mordechai, Nechemiah, Chaggai, Zechariah, and Malachi. They thrived at the time of Ezra, when the Jews returned to *Eretz Yisrael* from Babylonia at the beginning of the Second Temple Era. [See ArtScroll, *History of the Jewish People: The Second Temple Era,* Chapter 4.]

Why were they called "Men of the Great Assembly?" The Talmud (*Yoma* 69b) explains that their greatness lay in their ability to perceive God's greatness even in times of exile and the apparent eclipse of His glory. Whereas others felt, with justification, that God could not be praised fully in an era when His people were subjugated and His Temple had been desecrated, these men saw and proclaimed His greatness even then — and in this lay their "greatness."

After the Babylonian Exile, the Men of the Great Assembly realized that with the end of the prophetic era there was a vacuum in Torah leadership, and they stepped into the breach. They assumed the helm and instituted many enactments to ensure compliance with the Torah (*Tiferes Yisrael*).

הֵם אָמְרוּ שְׁלֹשָׁה דְבָרִים — *They said three things.* The Men of the Great Assembly said many things; however, the three items listed are directives to assure the continued survival of the Torah (*Rav*).

Tosafos Yom Tov quotes *Rav* (from 2:10) as interpreting *they said* in the sense of *they were wont to say,* meaning that they regularly emphasized these principles.

Maharal discusses why the Mishnah reports no words of *mussar* or advice in the name of the earlier links (Joshua, Elders, Prophets). He explains that earlier generations received the necessary direction from Torah study itself; during the time of the Great Assembly, however, the generation took a spiritual downturn, requiring the leaders to provide advice on how to ensure the primacy of Torah.

Tiferes Yisrael and *Midrash Shmuel* explain *they* as referring separately to (a) Joshua, (b) the Elders, (c) the Prophets, with one of the following statements attributed to each group.

הֱווּ מְתוּנִים בַּדִּין — *Be deliberate in judgment.* This admonition is addressed to judges. Even if a similar case has come before a judge two or three times in the past, he should not be hasty to equate the cases; rather, he should deliberate before issuing a ruling.

Rambam (*Hilchos Sanhedrin* 20:7) codifies this law as follows: "One who acts irreverently in deciding the law and is quick to hand down a ruling before thoroughly investigating the issue until it is clear as day is considered a fool, a wicked person and an arrogant one. This is what the Sages commanded: 'Be deliberate in judgment.'"

☐ **A fool thinks he is wise.** *R' Yonah* elaborates:

⋙**Wherein lay their greatness?** R' Yehoshua ben Levi said: "Because they restored the crown to the Ageless One [see *Rashi* ad loc.]. Moshe [Rabbeinu] came and said [about God]: ‏'הָאֵל הַגָּדוֹל הַגִּבּוֹר וְהַנּוֹרָא, *the great, mighty, and awesome God'* (*Deuteronomy* 10:17). Jeremiah came and said: 'Foreigners revel in His Sanctuary [referring to the destruction of the Temple]; where is His awesomeness?' [Therefore,] he [Jeremiah] omitted נוֹרָא, *awesome* (see *Jeremiah* 32:18). Daniel came and said: 'Foreigners oppress His children [the Jewish people]; where is His might?' [Therefore,] he [Daniel] omitted גִּבּוֹר, *mighty* (see *Daniel* 9:4). The Men of the Great Assembly came and said: '[We arrive at the] opposite [conclusion]; this phenomenon [of God's seeming inaction in the face of His children's suffering] is itself indicative of His might. He shows His might by stifling His will and delaying the expression of His anger against the wicked. Furthermore, this shows His awesomeness as well, for if not for the fear He instills among the nations, how could one nation [the Jewish people] survive among the [other] nations?' " (*Rashi* and *Rav*). Thus, the Men of the Great Assembly recognized that Jewish survival under the trying conditions of exile and foreign domination is the greatest indication of God's might. Having restored the perception of God's greatness, they were given their name — the Men of the *Great* Assembly.

One who is quick to render a judicial decision, even though he meant to speak the truth, is not an inadvertent sinner; rather, he is considered almost as one who acts intentionally. He should have taken to heart that "the hearts of the hasty do not understand wisdom," an axiom which points out that people are prone to err. This is what our Sages meant when they said, "Be meticulous in study, for a careless misinterpretation is considered tantamount to willful transgression" (*Avos* 4:16). By taking more time for reflection, one may become aware of new aspects and approaches which his initial thoughts did not yield. Regarding this, King Solomon said (*Proverbs* 26:12): רָאִיתָ אִישׁ חָכָם בְּעֵינָיו תִּקְוָה לִכְסִיל מִמֶּנּוּ, *If you see a person who thinks he is wise, there is more hope for a fool than for him.* One who is wise in his own eyes sees no need to learn, consult with others, or reconsider;

the fool, on the other hand, may at least be aware of his deficient knowledge. For him there is yet hope.

Midrash Shmuel offers two reasons for the practice of cautious deliberation in cases of dispute: (a) Deliberation allows for compromise, but once a ruling has been issued, it is too late. (b) If a ruling is issued in haste, the credibility of the court may be undermined (זִילוּתָא דְּבֵי דִינָא). *HaChassid Yaavetz* adds that it is important that all litigants feel that the court gave them a fair hearing by carefully considering their claims and arguments.

Ritva understands מְתוּנִים as related to מַתָּנָה, *gift*, explaining the passage as a directive to appoint judges who despise money and are not liable to accept graft in payment for distorting judgment. Rather, the judges should issue rulings to the people as a "gift" — never taking or expecting anything in return.

Avos d'Rabbi Nosson (1:4) extends this maxim to all people, for each of us is a "judge" who must

---

≪§ **How to treat a "serious" inquiry.** One Erev Pesach, a woman sent her grandson to Rabbi Nisson Telushkin with a question. She had forgotten to purchase cinnamon and wanted to know if she was permitted to make *charoses* without cinnamon. Rabbi Telushkin pulled a large volume of *Shulchan Aruch* from his bookshelf and spent several minutes studying it. Finally, he closed it and told the youngster: "Tell your grandmother that this year she may use the *charoses* even without cinnamon. However, she must be careful next year and purchase kosher-for-Pesach cinnamon immediately after Purim." The Rav then went into a side room and emerged with a bottle of wine. "Give this to your grandmother and tell her the Rav wishes her a *gut Yom Tov.*"

Obviously, the question was not discussed in the *Shulchan Aruch,* nor did it require any research on the rabbi's part. But by giving the impression that he took their question seriously, he made sure that she and her grandson would not be ashamed to seek guidance on future occasions.

≪§ **Never give up.** Torah study can influence even those far removed from a Torah life-style. The people at the time of the destruction of the First Temple were involved in idolatry, bloodshed, and immorality — but even they could have been brought to repentance had they been properly involved in Torah study, "for the light [contained] in it would have returned them to [the] good [path]" (*Eichah Rabbasi* V; *Pesikta* 2).

A striking example of this principle is the story of the son of R' Elazar the son of R' Shimon. Rabbi [R' Yehudah *HaNasi*] traveled to the home town of R' Elazar after his death to inquire if he had left a son. The local residents told him, "He has a strikingly handsome son who is heavily involved in immoral behavior." Rabbi brought this son, Yose, home, ordained him as a rabbi, and asked R' Shimon ben Isi ben Lakonia, his mother's brother, to teach him Torah.

Every day the boy would complain that he wanted to go back home. Finally R' Shimon convinced him by saying, "They want to make you a sage and spread a gold garment over you and call you 'Rabbi'; yet you say, 'I want to go home to my city'?" The son dropped his request.

When he grew up, he came and sat in Rabbi's academy. Rabbi heard his voice and remarked, "This voice is similar to the voice of R' Elazar the son of R' Shimon." They told him, "This is his son." Rabbi applied this verse to him: *The fruit of a righteous man is a tree of life, and he who acquires souls is wise* (*Proverbs* 11:30). *The fruit of a righteous man is a tree of life*: This refers to R' Yose the son of R' Elazar the son of R' Shimon. *And he who acquires souls is wise*: This is R' Shimon ben Isi ben Lakonia (*Bava Metzia* 85a).

א/ב   וְהַעֲמִידוּ תַלְמִידִים הַרְבֵּה, וַעֲשׂוּ סְיָג לַתּוֹרָה.

[ב] שִׁמְעוֹן הַצַּדִּיק הָיָה מִשְּׁיָרֵי כְּנֶסֶת הַגְּדוֹלָה.

evaluate people and situations. In all matters one should act deliberately rather than in haste.

The prophets equate the practice of monetary justice with knowledge of God: *One who judges the case of the poor and destitute, that is good; for that is knowledge of Me, the word of HASHEM (Jeremiah 22:16).* Hence, the Mishnah urges careful deliberation in monetary cases even more than in questions of ritual law (*R' Yonah*). Furthermore, if one is in doubt in questions of halachah, he may adopt the more stringent view, but in monetary questions one of the two parties stands to lose if the judge decides wrongly (*Tiferes Yisrael*).

וְהַעֲמִידוּ תַלְמִידִים הַרְבֵּה — *develop many disciples.*

Avos d'Rabbi Nosson (2:9) quotes the following dispute. The Academy of Shammai said: "A Torah teacher should teach only one who is wise and humble, and who comes from a good family." The Academy of Hillel said, "Teach all, for there have been many sinners among the Jews who were brought near to Torah study and emerged as righteous, pious, and upstanding persons." Our Mishnah follows the opinion of Beis Hillel.

Alternatively, even if one developed disciples while young, he should *develop many disciples* — continuing to teach, even into old age (*Rav*). One can never know in which era or with which group of disciples he will be more successful (see *Yevamos* 62b).

This directive to *develop many students* is a charge both to Torah teachers and to men of means. The wealthy can participate in the development of Torah students by providing for their needs. One who does so merits extra Divine protection in his business ventures (*Midrash Shmuel*).

Students are catalysts to bring out their teacher's potential. R' Nachman bar Yitzchak said: Why are the words of Torah compared to a tree (see *Proverbs* 3:18)? Just as the small chips of wood are used to ignite larger pieces, so it is with Torah scholars; the younger ones sharpen the minds of the older ones with their constant questioning. This is in essence what R' Chanina said: I have learned much from my teachers, and from my colleagues more than from my teachers, but from my students more than from them all (*Taanis* 7b).

Alternatively, *Meiri* interprets this as an exhortation to judges. A judge should involve his students in the discussion, because the involvement of more people will yield a clarity unattainable even by the most brilliant individual.

Tosafos Yom Tov renders this as a charge to teachers that they should enable students to "stand on their own feet." A teacher's goal must be to enable students to be able to learn independently, by providing them with a clear and true understanding of Torah.

R' Yitzchak Kara sees this passage as a directive to parents not to be satisfied with one "token" Torah scholar in the family while the other children are involved in more worldly pursuits; instead, parents should *develop many* students.

וַעֲשׂוּ סְיָג לַתּוֹרָה — *and make a [protective] fence for the Torah.*

Preventive legislation is sometimes needed in order to keep one from violating Torah prohibi-

---

◆§ **Strictness born of love.** Rabbi Mordechai Gifter offers a parable: A young man with an insatiable appetite for non-kosher food was warned by his father never to enter the local non-kosher eatery. "If you go into that restaurant, I will punish you severely," said the father. His mother, full of maternal love and compassion, wanted at all costs to save her beloved son from his father's wrath. Aware of the boy's weakness, she assumed a strict posture and forbade the son from coming within two blocks of the restaurant. Her surface severity was in truth an expression of love for her son.

Similarly, the enactments of the Rabbis are not reflective of a cold, mechanistic protection of the system as much as an outpouring of care and compassion for the Jewish people. The rabbinic code is an effort to save people from hurting themselves spiritually by violating God's Torah.

develop many disciples; and make a [protective] fence for the Torah.

2. Shimon the Righteous was [one] of the remnants of the Great Assembly.

---

tions. This concept is familiar in many areas of activity. For example, a government will enact a margin of safety in regulating the weight limits carried by airliners, or the dosage of potentially harmful drugs. Thus the Sages prohibited certain marriages to prevent possible incest; and forbade certain activities on the Sabbath (such as מוּקְצָה, the handling of certain utensils, lest one use them to perform a labor proscribed by the Torah). The enactment of such cautionary rules is Scripturally mandated: וּשְׁמַרְתֶּם אֶת מִשְׁמַרְתִּי, *You shall safeguard My charge* (*Leviticus* 18:30), which the Sages interpret as *Make a safeguard for My charge* (*Yevamos* 21a).

Mesillas Yesharim (ch. 11) writes: Even though the main prohibition for a nazirite is the drinking of wine, the Torah forbids him to partake of anything similar to wine. The Torah uses this as an example to teach the Sages how to fulfill their mandate to safeguard the Torah's laws. Using the prohibition of

a nazirite as a prototype, the Sages forbade various acts in order to prevent one from transgressing the Torah's prohibitions. The Torah provides this model in order to show that it is the will of God that the Sages erect fences around the Torah.

Tiferes Yisrael interprets this instruction to erect barriers around *mitzvah* observance as a personal obligation. Every person, recognizing his own weaknesses, should assume stringencies beyond the letter of the law in order to protect himself against sin.

The three maxims of the *Anshei Knesses HaGedolah* provide guidance to those who try to draw people closer to Torah. The first two — *Be deliberate in judgments; develop many disciples* — illustrate the interaction between teacher and student. The third — *make a fence for the Torah* — is personal advice for the teacher. Someone who is in a non-religious environment must make a fence for *himself*, so that he should not be influenced by the surroundings (*R' Simcha Wasserman*).

Mishnah 2

שִׁמְעוֹן הַצַּדִיק — *Shimon the Righteous.* Shimon *HaTzaddik* was *Kohen Gadol* after Ezra [see *Meiri's* introduction, p. 21, footnote 40] and served in that office for forty years. During his tenure many miracles occurred in the Temple. The Talmud (*Yoma* 39a) lists them:

(1) Each Yom Kippur in his service as *Kohen Gadol,* he would put his hands into the box to draw the lots for the he-goat that would be offered on the Altar, and the lot inscribed "For God" always came up in his right hand. This was a sign of God's favor upon Israel.

(2) The scarlet ribbon that was tied to the horns of the second he-goat always turned white at the moment it was pushed over the brink of a desert cliff. This was a sign that God had forgiven His people's sins of the past year, in accordance with the verse *Even if your sins will be as scarlet, they will turn as white as snow* (*Isaiah* 1:18).

(3) The lamp of the Menorah known as the "Western Lamp" [נֵר מַעֲרָבִי] burned for twenty-four hours, even though it was filled with enough oil for only twelve hours.

(4) The fire on the Altar continued to burn strongly, even though the supply of wood placed there every morning was not replenished for the rest of the day.

(5) From each of the various grain and bread offerings — the *Omer,* the Two Loaves, and the *Lechem HaPanim* — each *Kohen* was able to satisfy his hunger with only a small portion.

Employing his influence on Alexander the Great, Shimon persuaded him to desist from conquering *Eretz Yisrael,* thus saving the Land from persecution (*Yoma* 79a). During the difficult time following the sudden death of Alexander the Great, Shimon *HaTzaddik* was the uncontested leader of Israel, both spiritually and politically. As one of the remaining sages of the Great Assembly, Shimon was the religious leader of the people; and because Alexander had decreed that the *Kohen Gadol* should be governor of the land, Shimon was also the political leader, with the power to enforce his authority. He used this power to strengthen the study and observance of the Torah throughout the land.

Shimon ben Sira, a poet who lived close to the time of Shimon *HaTzaddik*, composed a lengthy song describing Shimon in glowing terms. Among other things, the song says of Shimon: "He was the greatest of his brothers, the splendor of his people . . . How glorious he was when he left the Temple, as he departed from the Most Holy, like a star shining from among the clouds, like a full moon in the festival season . . ." (*Ben Sira* ch. 50).

הָיָה מִשְּׁיָרֵי כְּנֶסֶת הַגְּדוֹלָה — *was* [one] *of the remnants of the Great Assembly.* After the demise of its members, he remained as the *baal mesorah* (*Rav*). He was not one of the original members of the Great Assembly (see 1:1, s.v. וּנְבִיאִים מְסָרוּהָ) but joined later (*Rashi*). [See ArtScroll *History of the Jewish People: The Second Temple Era,* pp. 40-41.]

הוּא הָיָה אוֹמֵר — *He used to say.* Our Sages taught that before chastising others one must rebuke himself, making sure that his own moral house is in order (see *Bava Metzia* 107b). A leader's personal deportment must serve as an example of the type of behavior he asks of others. *R' Aharon of Kaidanov* thus homiletically explained the expression הוּא הָיָה אוֹמֵר as הוּא הָיָה אוֹמֵר, *he became,* i.e., Shimon embodied the lesson he wished to preach, internalizing it and living up to the ideals he expected of others; and only then אוֹמֵר, would he *say* it to them.

עַל שְׁלשָׁה דְבָרִים הָעוֹלָם עוֹמֵד — *The world stands on*

three things. The purpose of the creation of the world was so that human beings would find favor with God through the pursuit of these three things (*R' Yonah* and *Rav*). The world was brought into existence only in anticipation of the eventual fulfillment of these three foundation principles.

Rashi (see *Rashi,* s.v. וְעַל הָעֲבוֹדָה and s.v. וְעַל גְּמִילַת חֲסָדִים) seems to understand our mishnah as referring to justification for the continued existence of the world (see *Midrash Shmuel*). This mishnah and 1:18 seem to suggest different triads upon which the world stands. *Meiri* differentiates between this mishnah — which discusses the three things through which a person can achieve a level of perfection which justifies creation and its continued existence — and 1:18, which delineates three other attributes necessary for a functional society. [See 1:18, s.v. עַל שְׁלשָׁה דברים for additional resolutions of the seeming contradiction.]

עַל הַתּוֹרָה — *on the Torah.* If Israel had not accepted the Torah, the heavens and earth would not have been created (*Rav* — see *Shabbos* 88a). This interpretation sees *on the Torah* as referring to the historical event of the giving of the Torah.

[This idea is reflected in the words of *Rashi* (*Bereishis* 1:1): בִּשְׁבִיל הַתּוֹרָה שֶׁנִּקְרֵאת רֵאשִׁית וּבִשְׁבִיל יִשְׂרָאֵל שֶׁנִּקְרְאוּ רֵאשִׁית, *The world was created for the sake of Torah, which is called "first" or "primary," and for the sake of the nation of Israel, which is called "first" or "primary,"* meaning that God brought the world into being for the sake of the actualization of these basic values. Thus, the purpose of Creation was Israel's acceptance of the Torah.]

Tosafos Yom Tov disagrees with *Rav.* Since the next two of the three principles, *service of God* and *acts of loving-kindness,* imply directives rather than statements of history, it would be incongruent to

---

❧ **Unchanging principles.** Those who seek to dispute the primacy of Torah often do so under the guise of progress. "Times are different," they claim, "and one must move with the times; the Torah is old fashioned (God forbid), and in an ever-changing world inundated with new inventions and technology, we must not allow ourselves to atrophy by clinging to an outdated religion." Our mishnah teaches otherwise: עַל שְׁלשָׁה דְבָרִים הָעוֹלָם עוֹמֵד. While time and progress march on, there are certain timeless, unchangeable values, whose truth has stood the test of time. Many things may change, but regarding these three things, the world stands still [עוֹמֵד], for truth is immutable and eternal (*Luach Erez*).

1/2

He used to say: The world stands on three things — on the Torah, on the service [of God], and upon acts of loving-kindness.

understand *on the Torah* as a historical event rather than as another directive. Therefore, he interprets *the Torah* as the duty of studying Torah.

According to *Rashi* (see above, s.v. על שלשה דברים), who views our mishnah as a listing of those ideals which sustain the existence of the cosmos, it is *consistent* Torah study which is indicated. Torah study must never cease, even for a moment.

Were Torah study to cease, the Heavenly emanations that sustain creation would cease simultaneously, resulting in the breakdown of the world (*Ahavah B'Taanugim*).

וְעַל הָעֲבוֹדָה — *on the service* [*of God*]. This refers to the sacrificial service [generally performed in the Temple] (*Rav, R' Yonah, Rashi, Rambam*). Upon the destruction of the Temple, this service was supplanted by prayer and study of the laws regarding the Temple service (*Tosafos Yom Tov; R' Yonah*). Our Sages taught that the commandment *to serve Him with all your heart* (*Deuteronomy* 11:13) alludes to prayer, which is "service of the heart" (*Taanis* 2a).

Prayer can be even more effective than sacrifices. In seeking forgiveness for the episode of Bas-sheva, King David says (*Psalms* 51:18): *For You do not desire a sacrifice; an ascent offering You do not want* [since David's "sin" was intentional, an offering could not atone for it]. Now that I cannot bring a sacrifice, David continues, *my Lord, HASHEM, open my lips, that my mouth may declare Your praise* (ibid. 17); accept my prayers in place of a sacrifice, grant me pardon, and forgive my sin (*R' Yonah*).

וְעַל גְּמִילוּת חֲסָדִים — *and upon acts of loving-kindness.* This is based on the verse in *Psalms* (89:3): *For I said, The world will be built through kindness. Ram-*

bam (*Hilchos Aivel* 14:1) lists some of the most important acts of kindness: "It is a rabbinically ordained positive commandment to visit and inquire after the welfare of the sick, to remove the dead (for burial), to bring the bride to the wedding canopy, to accompany departing guests, and to be involved with all burial preparations including carrying the bier, eulogizing, digging the grave, and burial. Similarly, [included in this rabbinic injunction is] gladdening the hearts of bride and groom . . . Even though all these *mitzvos* are rabbinically ordained, they are included in the Biblical *mitzvah, You shall love your fellow as yourself* (*Leviticus* 19:18). [This means that] all things that you want others to do for you, you should do for [one who is considered] your brother in Torah and *mitzvos*." *Yalkut* (*Hosea* 524) quotes God: The acts of benevolence that you do for each other are dearer to Me than all the thousand sacrifices which King Solomon brought before Me.

Rambam explains the three items as a prescription for cosmic success. Through the pursuit of Torah knowledge (תּוֹרָה), exemplary character traits (גְּמִילוּת חֲסָדִים), and fulfillment of the *mitzvos* (עֲבוֹדָה), the world will achieve a balanced perfection.

"Acts of kindness are greater than charity since they can be done for both the rich and the poor, while charity can be given only to the poor. Charity can only be done with one's money, while acts of loving-kindness can be performed both personally and with one's money . . . Acts of benevolence toward the wealthy include provid-

⋅ᴪ **God's desire.** Once R' Yochanan ben Zakkai and R' Yehoshua were leaving Jerusalem. They noticed the Temple lying in ruins. R' Yehoshua said, "Woe to us that the place where we sought forgiveness for our sins is destroyed!" R' Yochanan ben Zakkai answered, "My son, don't be upset. We have a means of achieving forgiveness which is equal to the Temple service — acts of kindness, as the verse states (*Hosea* 6:6): *For loving — not sacrifice — was My desire*" (*Avos d'Rabbi Nosson* 4).

The word חֶסֶד means to go beyond established boundaries. Hence, a חָסִיד is one who goes beyond the letter of the law (לִפְנִים מִשּׁוּרַת הַדִּין). Why is the term חֶסֶד appropriate for acts of kindness? R' Shlomo Freifeld explained: A person is by nature egocentric, only concerned with his own personal needs and desires. Only when one can go beyond the boundaries of his self-centeredness is he ready to do חֶסֶד.

The term גְּמִילוּת חֲסָדִים literally means the *repaying* of a favor. Even when one does a favor for someone he never met before, he is repaying the favors that God does for him. There is really no way to pay God back; the only thing we can do is attempt to make it up to Him by helping His children or creatures (*R' A.C. Feuer*).

[ג] **אַנְטִיגְנוֹס** אִישׁ סוֹכוֹ קִבֵּל מִשִּׁמְעוֹן הַצַּדִּיק. הוּא הָיָה אוֹמֵר: אַל תִּהְיוּ כַעֲבָדִים הַמְשַׁמְּשִׁין אֶת הָרַב עַל מְנָת לְקַבֵּל פְּרָס; אֶלָּא הֱווּ כַעֲבָדִים הַמְשַׁמְּשִׁין אֶת הָרַב שֶׁלֹּא עַל מְנָת לְקַבֵּל פְּרָס; וִיהִי מוֹרָא שָׁמַיִם עֲלֵיכֶם.

---

ing them loans when needed and offering them sound advice. Included in the dictum to practice kindness is the need to be selective when offering help to give preference to God-fearing, modest persons" (*R' Yonah*).

Tiferes Yisrael and *R' Mattisyahu HaYitzhari* see the triad as describing various aspects of human relationships: *Torah* includes the intellectual pursuits that fulfill man, such as study of Torah and the cultivation of its basic beliefs. These are integral to man's relationship to himself. *Service* refers to the performance of commandments through which man serves God [מִצְוֹת בֵּין אָדָם לַמָּקוֹם]. *Kindness* encompasses all of man's interpersonal relationships [מִצְוֹת בֵּין אָדָם לַחֲבֵרוֹ].

Maharal comments that these three pillars of creation [Torah, service of God, and acts of loving-kindness] are symbolized respectively by the three Patriarchs, Abraham, Isaac, and Jacob. Since these three foundations support the world at large, they are mirrored in the persons of the three "pillars" of the Jewish nation — Abraham, Isaac, and Jacob. Abraham personified the trait of kindness as expressed by his outstanding hospitality (see *Genesis* 18:1 and *Sotah* 10a). Isaac embodied service to God. By submitting himself as a sacrifice at the *Akeidah*, he unleashed the national potential for service as expressed through offerings and prayer. Our Sages taught: On the day that Abraham placed his son Isaac on the altar, God established the continual offering [קָרְבָּן הַתָּמִיד] (*Vayikra Rabbah* 2:11). Jacob is described in the Torah as אִישׁ תָּם יֹשֵׁב אֹהָלִים, *a man of simplicity* [*and wholesomeness*], *abiding in tents* (*Genesis* 25:27); this is an allusion to constant Torah study, as evidenced by the fourteen years he spent in the Academy of Shem and Ever (see *Rashi, Genesis* 28:11).

Mishnah 3

אַנְטִיגְנוֹס אִישׁ סוֹכוֹ — *Antigonos, leader of Socho.* Antigonos was an official in Socho, a city in the section of *Eretz Yisrael* assigned to the tribe of Judah (see *Yehoshua* 15:35,48). The term אִישׁ is used in the sense of lord or leader, as in *Yoma* 1:3: אִישִׁי כֹהֵן גָּדוֹל, *my lord, Kohen Gadol* (*Tosafos Yom Tov*).

קִבֵּל מִשִּׁמְעוֹן הַצַּדִּיק — *received the tradition from Shimon the Righteous.* Due to their diminished stature, the generations after the Men of the Great Assembly [of which Shimon *HaTzaddik* was the last] were unable to integrate the entirety of the tradition that the earlier generations passed on. Hence, the mishnah speaks of what Antigonos *received*, rather than what Shimon *HaTzaddik* conveyed (*Maharal* on 1:1).

הוּא הָיָה אוֹמֵר: אַל תִּהְיוּ כַעֲבָדִים הַמְשַׁמְּשִׁין אֶת הָרַב עַל מְנָת לְקַבֵּל פְּרָס — *He used to say: Be not as servants who serve the master for the sake of receiving [even a token] reward.* Antigonos does not forbid one from serving God for reward; indeed, the Torah itself promises material reward for performance of the commandments (see *Leviticus* 26:4; however, see also *Rambam, Hilchos Teshuvah* 9:1). Certainly, then, the subsequent instruction of the

---

❧ **What can I do for You?** The Chofetz Chaim was once overheard making an accounting with God, as it were. He said, "Dear God, what have You done for me, and what have I done for You? You have given me the privilege of writing the *Mishneh Berurah, Chofetz Chaim, Shemiras HaLashon, Likkutei Halachos,* and many other *sefarim*. What have I done for You? Nothing! Please, dear God, give me an opportunity to do something for You!" To the Chofetz Chaim, whatever he did was only to be expected, and was undeserving of any reward for himself.

3. **A**ntigonos, leader of Socho, received the tradition from Shimon the Righteous. He used to say: Be not as servants who serve the master for the sake of receiving [even a token] reward, but rather, be like servants who serve the master not for the sake of receiving [a token] reward; and [nonetheless] the fear of Heaven should be upon you.

---

mishnah (2:1), *Calculate the cost of [not fulfilling] a mitzvah against its reward,* is not telling us to do the forbidden! Rather, the mishnah comes to teach that the finest way to serve God is out of pure love for Him (*Tosafos Yom Tov*). Similarly, to serve in anticipation of reward instead of for the sake of the Master is a deficient form of service (*R' Yonah*).

The term פְּרָס implies the sort of gift one gives his young child or servant as a token of appreciation for doing something on his behalf. He owes them nothing; he gives them something not in the sense of compensation, but to show his gratitude (*Rav, Rambam*).

אֶלָּא הֱווּ כַּעֲבָדִים הַמְשַׁמְּשִׁין אֶת הָרַב שֶׁלֹּא עַל מְנָת לְקַבֵּל פְּרָס — *but rather, be like servants who serve the master not for the sake of receiving [a token] reward;* but only out of love. *Abarbanel* comments that Antigonos refers to tangible reward in *this* world. The mishnah means: Do not serve God in order to receive reward in this world, since שכר

מִצְוָה בְּהַאי עַלְמָא לֵיכָּא, *there is no reward for mitzvos in this world* (*Kiddushin* 39b).

See *Rashi* here, which seems to bear out this interpretation. *Rashi* says: "Serve God out of love and let the fear of Heaven be upon you, since there is no reward in this world, as the verse teaches, *that I command you today.*" The Sages interpret this verse to imply that today, i.e., is for the *performance* of the commandments, but the reward will come *tomorrow*, i.e., in the World to Come. Certainly there *is* reward in the World to Come, and one is permitted to serve God in order to earn it. Accordingly, Antigonos means to say that if man longs for remuneration for his Divine service, he should not be disappointed if it is not forthcoming. One should never feel that all his toil was an exercise in futility. Often, God holds back even basic necessities to test the level of his commitment to God. Therefore, teaches Antigonos, *Be like servants who serve the master not for the sake of receiving [even a token] reward* — in *this* world.

וִיהִי מוֹרָא שָׁמַיִם עֲלֵיכֶם — *and [nonetheless] the fear of Heaven should be upon you.* Though we serve God out of love, we must incorporate fear of Heaven

---

◆§ **The value of a mitzvah.** The value of a *mitzvah* is so great that nothing in this world is sufficient to reward its performance. In the words of the Vilna Gaon: דְּלֵיכָּא בְּמַאי לְאִשְׁתַּלּוּמֵי, *There is nothing* [in this physical world] *with which to pay* for a *mitzvah*. Since service of God is spiritual, it is a degradation to think that something of this corporeal existence could serve as recompense for it.

One who is willing to accept a worldly reward for a *mitzvah* is like someone who boards a bus and hands the driver a hundred-dollar bill. "Mister," says the driver, "I have no change for this bill. The best I can do is let you ride for the hundred dollars." How foolish is the passenger to trade his hundred dollars for one bus ride! Likewise, how ridiculous it is to accept the currency of worldly pleasure in exchange for *mitzvos,* which are priceless. In this sense, *Haflaah* (introduction to *Kiddushin*) explains our mishnah as follows: Do not be like servants who serve the Master for partial reward (פְּרָס meaning a portion of what is really deserved). Whatever this world may offer man, it is only a small fraction of what his *mitzvos* are really worth.

As for the copious material rewards promised by the Torah (*Leviticus* 26:4ff, *Deuteronomy* 11:13ff, etc.), they are not meant in the sense of payment for performance. Instead, they are an assurance from God that all the physical conditions necessary for man to perform the commandments will be provided him, so that he will be able to serve God even more and be worthy of greater reward in the World to Come. [This is analogous to a manor lord promising his sharecroppers agricultural tools and better seed if they work his fields assiduously. Certainly, the tools are not a reward for their work; they are a means whereby the sharecroppers can do their job better.] (*Rambam, Hilchos Teshuvah* 9:1)

א/ד

[ד] יוֹסֵי בֶּן יוֹעֶזֶר אִישׁ צְרֵדָה וְיוֹסֵי בֶּן יוֹחָנָן אִישׁ יְרוּשָׁלַיִם קִבְּלוּ מֵהֶם.

into our service. Love of God is a major impetus to observe the positive commandments, while fear is the impulse that causes one to resist transgression of the negative commandments (see *Ramban* to *Exodus* 20:8). By combining both impulses, one can assure complete service of God. Our Sages said, "Serve God both from love and from fear." We must serve from love, for a lover does not forget his obligations to the beloved; and we must "serve from fear, for if you contemplate rebelliousness, know that one who is fearful is afraid to rebel" (*Rav*). [See *Rambam*.]

Tiferes Yisrael adds: Even though one does not seek reward for his actions, let him not be lulled into thinking that he can transgress without fear of retribution in this world; *the fear of Heaven should be upon you.*

The use of the expression מוֹרָא שָׁמַיִם, *fear of Heaven*, rather than יִרְאַת ה׳, *fear of God*, is meant to convey a concept that transcends mere fear of punishment (יִרְאַת הָעוֹנֶשׁ). By fear of Heaven, the mishnah means an awe that results from recognizing the gaping chasm between God's grandeur and our puny stature. This is expressed in the word *Heaven*, which connotes His all-powerful role as Creator of heaven, earth, and all that it contains (*Tosafos Yom Tov*). [See *Rambam, Yesodei HaTorah* 2:1,2.]

In the service of God there are three levels of relationship. The lowest is יִרְאַת הָעוֹנֶשׁ, *fear of retribution*, where man is basically concerned with his own self-preservation. On a higher level is אַהֲבַת הַשֵּׁם, *love of God*. Here man wants to please God and cannot do enough for Him. The most elevated form of relationship is called יִרְאַת הָרוֹמְמוּת, *fear due to God's exaltedness*. *Rambam* (ibid.) defines this as the reverence that results when one observes the physical wonders of Creation. With this awareness comes the realization of man's insignificance in the presence of the Perfect Intelligence.

This mishnah was once misunderstood, resulting in a major tragedy that roiled Jewish life for centuries. *Avos d'Rabbi Nosson* (4:2) reports that Zaddok and Boethus, students of Antigonos, were teaching their own students the dictum in this mishnah. Their students misunderstood and thought that Antigonos meant that one must serve God but will not be rewarded for doing so. They concluded that just as this statement is ludicrous, since there must be a system of reward and punishment, so all the words of the Sages are meaningless. As a result of this mistake, they came to reject all the words of the Sages [believing only in the literal written word of Torah]. The students founded deviant groups called *Zaddokim* (Sadducees) and *Boethusim*, ignominiously named after Zaddok and Boethus. [According to this version, they rejected the Oral Law as a direct result of this mishnah.]

According to *Rambam*'s version of this episode, Zaddok and Boethus *themselves* misunderstood Antigonos'

⤳ **Which plea?** When the Imrei Emes succeeded his father (the Sfas Emes) as Gerrer *Rebbe*, a group of older chassidim asked him, "Your father promised us that if we would recite the verse אָנָּא ה׳ (*Please HASHEM*) in the *Hallel* service with great devotion and intent, all our wishes would be granted from Heaven. *Rebbe*, we tried. Why didn't it work?" The new *Rebbe* replied: "Which אָנָּה ה׳ do you think my father meant: אָנָּא ה׳ הוֹשִׁיעָה נָּא, *Please, HASHEM, save now?!* No. He meant אָנָּה ה׳ כִּי אֲנִי עַבְדֶּךָ, *Please, HASHEM — for I am Your servant* (*Psalms* 116:16). Just as a mortal master must provide all the needs of his servants, so God provides for His true servants. But *first* we must commit ourselves to His service."

A Jew must consider his attitude toward life's purpose. He can be like a wagon driver, or like someone enjoying a delicious meal. If a wagon driver is hired to transport a heavy load, he is not interested in the work; he only wants the money. If somebody were to offer him the money without doing the work, he would be thrilled. If a passerby were to ask him, "Why are you carrying such a heavy load?" he will certainly answer, "In order to earn my pay."

However, if someone enjoying a delectable meal is asked, "Why are you eating that?" the answer would be obvious. He is not being paid to eat; he does it for pleasure. The enjoyment, and therefore the reward, are intrinsic.

This, taught Antigonos, should be the way we view serving God — not as a chore deserving of pay, but as an enjoyment which is an end in itself (*R' Baruch of Kossov*).

4. Yose ben Yoezer, leader of Tz'redah, and Yose ben Yochanan, leader of Jerusalem, received the tradition from them.

axiom, thinking that he was teaching that there is no Divine reward nor retribution, and no hope [or afterlife]. Consequently, they totally rejected the Torah [both Oral and Written]. However, they were unable to convince the masses of this heresy, so they modified their position and began to profess belief in the Written Torah, while still rejecting the Oral Tradition. They did this to free them-selves from all Rabbinic interpretations and enactments. In this, they succeeded into attracting many followers, and the Sadducees were able to gain ascendancy over the Sages during many periods of the Second Temple Era. [See *Tosafos Yom Tov* to 1:11. See also ArtScroll's *History of the Jewish People: The Second Temple Era*, pp. 55-56, 90.]

Mishnah 4

The Pairs. With the death of Antigonos, a change in the manner of Jewish leadership came about. No longer was a single Sage the authority over all Israel as theretofore. For the next several generations, the heads of the people were זָגוֹת, *pairs* of Sages, and both are quoted in the succeeding mishnayos. The first of each pair was the *Nasi*, president of the Sanhedrin (the High Court of the Jewish people). His civic function was to oversee the establishment of an accurate calendar and he generally acted as the political representative of the Jewish community. The second served as *Av Beis Din*, Head of the Court, and was the functional head of the Great Sanhedrin in its judicial and legislative roles.

יוֹסֵי בֶּן יוֹעֶזֶר אִישׁ צְרֵדָה — *Yose ben Yoezer, leader of Tz'redah.* Yose ben Yoezer, who served as *Nasi*, was known as the "pious one of the *Kohanim*" (*Chagigah* 20a). His city of Tz'redah was in the portion of Ephraim (*I Kings* 11:26).

וְיוֹסֵי בֶּן יוֹחָנָן אִישׁ יְרוּשָׁלַיִם — *and Yose ben Yochanan, leader of Jerusalem.* He served as *Av Beis Din*. The Talmud (*Sotah* 47a) teaches that these two were the last of the consummate Torah figures (אִישׁ הָאֶשְׁכּוֹלוֹת, lit. *man of the clusters*) who mastered all areas of knowledge and demonstrated outstanding moral deportment. A cluster of grapes symbolizes a gathering of much good in one place; similarly, these people were of such stature that they were repositories of all the virtues of greatness.

קִבְּלוּ מֵהֶם — *received the tradition from them*, i.e., from Shimon *HaTzaddik* and Antigonos (*R' Yonah*). Yose ben Yoezer and Yose ben Yochanan were students of Shimon *HaTzaddik*, and after his death, they studied under Antigonos (*R' Yosef Nechemias*). Alternatively, they were disciples of the Men of the Great Assembly (*Tiferes Yisrael*). Rashi sees them as students only of Antigonos. Since our text of the mishnah reads in the plural, *from them*, *Rashi* may mean that they were students of Antigonos and his court, or he may have the alter-nate reading: קִבְּלוּ מִמֶּנּוּ, *received the tradition from "him"* (Antigonos).

⧉ **Fear and reverence.** The lesser of the two is the primal fear of punishment or pain. The higher and more desirable fear, more aptly called reverence or awe, is overpowering respect, which in itself will prevent sin. One does not defy a gun-wielding mobster, and one does not defy a very great person whom one reveres — but the reasons are far different.

R' Asher of Stolin assumed the mantle of Chassidic leadership at a very young age. One young man, a close personal friend of R' Asher's, was thrust into an uncomfortable situation — his friend was now his leader and *Rebbe*. How should he relate to him?

R' Asher asked him, "Are you afraid of me?" The young man did not answer. R' Asher persisted: "Are you afraid of me?" Again the chassid didn't know how to react. Finally, after the new *Rebbe* repeated the question, the chassid blurted out, "I'm afraid to do something that will spoil the love between us." Angrily, R' Asher said, "Scoundrel, how dare you define our relationship in those terms? That is what true fear of Heaven is about."

יוֹסֵי בֶּן יוֹעֶזֶר אִישׁ צְרֵדָה אוֹמֵר: יְהִי בֵיתְךָ בֵּית וַעַד לַחֲכָמִים, וֶהֱוֵי מִתְאַבֵּק בַּעֲפַר רַגְלֵיהֶם, וֶהֱוֵי שׁוֹתֶה בַצָּמָא אֶת דִּבְרֵיהֶם.

[ה] **יוֹסֵי** בֶּן יוֹחָנָן אִישׁ יְרוּשָׁלַיִם אוֹמֵר: יְהִי בֵיתְךָ פָּתוּחַ לָרְוָחָה, וְיִהְיוּ עֲנִיִּים בְּנֵי בֵיתֶךָ, וְאַל תַּרְבֶּה

יוֹסֵי בֶּן יוֹעֶזֶר אִישׁ צְרֵדָה אוֹמֵר: יְהִי בֵיתְךָ בֵּית וַעַד לַחֲכָמִים — *Yose ben Yoezer, leader of Tz'redah, says: Let your house be a meeting place for Torah scholars.* Yose ben Yoezer expounds upon Shimon HaTzaddik's statement that Torah is one of the three pillars of Creation, and explains how one can achieve success at Torah study.

One's house should be constantly available as a gathering place for scholars; then the householder will benefit from their company, since it is impossible that he not assimilate wisdom from them. This is analogous to one who enters a perfumery; merely by entering, he absorbs some of the sweet scent (*Rav*). Moreover, by allowing Torah scholars access to one's home, one learns from their actions as well as from their words. The Sages taught (*Berachos* 7b): "Attending to the needs of Torah scholars is [in certain ways] greater than learning [from their Torah]" (*Tiferes Yisrael*), since their actions constitute a living lesson in how one brings the Torah into his daily life.

Since Torah scholars will not frequent the home of a person of low spiritual standards, who does not respect God-fearers, the mishnah secondarily teaches one to conduct himself in such a manner as to create an appropriate atmosphere for Torah scholars (*R' Yonah*).

וֶהֱוֵי מִתְאַבֵּק בַּעֲפַר רַגְלֵיהֶם — *you shall become dusty in the dust of their feet.* Be in close proximity to Torah scholars and follow in their footsteps. Figuratively, one who follows at the heels of another becomes soiled from the dust raised by the first person's feet. Alternatively, one should make himself a student of Torah scholars, literally sitting at their feet, in the dust. In Mishnaic times it was customarily for students to sit at their teacher's feet (*Rav*).

Rashi and *Meiri* see this clause as a continuation of the previous one, instructing us to open our homes to Torah scholars. Since familiarity breeds contempt, one may tend to become irreverent toward the Torah scholars and lax in providing for their needs. As a counterbalance, the mishnah instructs, *You shall become dusty in the dust of their feet,* i.e., perform even menial, or "dirty," chores for them.

Rambam (*Hilchos Dei'os* 6:2) interprets this figuratively, as an exhortation to cleave to God through close contact with Torah scholars and their students. One should marry the daughter of a Torah scholar, marry his own daughter to one, eat and drink with scholars, provide business opportunities for them, and generally engage in all kinds of social interaction with them.

וֶהֱוֵי שׁוֹתֶה בַצָּמָא אֶת דִּבְרֵיהֶם — *and you shall drink in their words thirstily.* One must approach words of Torah with a thirst for them (*Rashi*); not like some-

⇩§ **Spiritual dust.** Another way to think of the "dust" is as a commentary on our own spiritual state. We frequently shirk association with Torah scholars for fear that our own self-images will be deflated in comparison to their higher intellectual and spiritual standards. We would all like to think that our houses are in perfect order, with few spiritual stains, and we are uncomfortable when our shortcomings are pointed out. When the Torah scholar visits, his presence reveals that we are wallowing in "dust," in comparison with him. Nonetheless, teaches the mishnah, we should not refrain from interacting with such peoples. We should allow them to serve as the standard-bearers against which we measure the spiritual cleanliness of our homes and lives (*R' Nisson Alpert*).

Yose ben Yoezer, leader of Tz'redah, says: Let your house be a meeting place for Torah scholars; you shall become dusty in the dust of their feet; and you shall drink in their words thirstily.

5. **Y**ose ben Yochanan, leader of Jerusalem, says: Let your house be open wide; treat the poor as members of your household; and do not converse excessively with the

---

one who is so satiated that he finds that even tasty, succulent food or refreshing drink is detestable (*Rav*).

The *Vilna Gaon* cites the verse *O all who are thirsty go to water* (*Isaiah* 55:1) as the Scriptural source for this last clause of the mishnah. *Rabbi Yitzchak Hutner* explains the analogy of Torah to water. One is obligated to recite a blessing before drinking any beverage, even if he is not thirsty. An exception to this rule is water. Only if one is thirsty for water must he recite a blessing (see *Shulchan Aruch O.C.* 204:7,8; *M.B.* §40), because one derives

enjoyment and benefit from water only if one is thirsty for it. It is the same with Torah learning; in order to get the proper and maximum benefit from it, one must be thirsty for it.

Having made one's home into a meeting place for scholars, with words of Torah constantly echoing in its halls, one may tend, as we mentioned earlier, to view words of Torah with less than the proper respect. Therefore, we are taught to *drink in their words thirstily* — for a thirsty man there is nothing in the world as meaningful as a drink (*Abarbanel*).

Mishnah 5

יוֹסֵי בֶּן יוֹחָנָן אִישׁ יְרוּשָׁלַיִם אוֹמֵר — *Yose ben Yochanan, leader of Jerusalem, says.* Yose ben Yochanan expounds on Shimon *HaTzaddik*'s principle of kindness.

יְהִי בֵיתְךָ פָּתוּחַ לָרְוָחָה — *Let your house be open wide.* Your house should be as accessible as the tent of Abraham our forefather, which had entrances from all four directions in order to provide easy access (*Rav*; *R' Yonah*). *Tiferes Yisrael* renders לָרְוָחָה as *for relief*, meaning that anyone who needs help of any kind — physical comfort, money, sound advice — should be able to find it in your home.

וְיִהְיוּ עֲנִיִּים בְּנֵי בֵיתֶךָ — *treat the poor as members of your household.* It is preferable to employ a destitute Jew rather than a gentile as a servant or domestic, thus affording him or her an opportunity to earn a livelihood legitimately (*Rav, Rashi*). *Rambam*

rules: "Our Sages commanded that one's domestic help be chosen from among the poor and orphaned rather than from [non-Jewish] servants. It is preferable to employ these people, thus benefiting the children of Abraham, Isaac, and Jacob, instead of benefiting the children of Ham [i.e., non-Jews] . . . if the destitute are the members of one's household, one increases his *mitzvos* and merits at every moment" (*Hilchos Matnos Aniyim* 10:17; see *Shulchan Aruch; Yoreh Deah* 251:6).

Alternatively, *R' Yonah* and *Tiferes Yisrael* explain these words as an instruction on how to treat poor guests. One should make them feel totally at home by showing them a happy face, thus minimizing their embarrassment at being dependent. One should give them free rein of the house and chat and make small talk with them, as he would with members of his family and household. The Sages

---

◄§ Part of the mitzvah. Enjoyment of Torah study is not a contradiction to learning *lishmah* (for Torah's own sake); to the contrary, joy is an integral part of the *mitzvah* of learning. Unlike other commandments, where the blessing recited prior to their performance speaks only of the deed, the blessings for Torah study include a prayer that God make the learning sweet and pleasant. The mind best absorbs what it finds pleasurable (*Avnei Nezer*, introduction to *Eglei Tal*).

שִׂיחָה עִם הָאִשָּׁה. בְּאִשְׁתּוֹ אָמְרוּ; קַל וָחֹמֶר בְּאֵשֶׁת חֲבֵרוֹ. מִכַּאן אָמְרוּ חֲכָמִים: כָּל הַמַּרְבֶּה שִׂיחָה עִם הָאִשָּׁה — גּוֹרֵם רָעָה לְעַצְמוֹ, וּבוֹטֵל מִדִּבְרֵי תוֹרָה, וְסוֹפוֹ יוֹרֵשׁ גֵּיהִנֹּם.

taught: The impoverished one does more for his benefactor than his benefactor does for him (*Vayikra Rabbah* 34:10).

In the laws of festivals, *Rambam* writes that when one eats and drinks, he is obligated to feed the unfortunate and poor. One who eats and drinks with his family but does not give food to impoverished and bitter souls — such a person does not engage in the joy of a *mitzvah* but rather in a celebration of the stomach (*Hilchos Yom Tov* 6:18). There is no greater, more elaborate joy than to gladden the hearts of orphans, widows, and strangers. One who does so is compared to the Divine Presence, whose function the verse describes as follows (*Isaiah* 57:15): *To enliven the spirit of the lowly and the hearts of the downtrodden* (*Hilchos Megillah* 2:18).

According to *Lev Avos* the two statements of the mishnah express an order of priorities. One should be magnanimous and even incur great expense in order to open his house wide for guests; at the same time, he should treat the members of his household like the poor, allowing them to make do with necessities.

וְאַל תַּרְבֶּה שִׂיחָה עִם הָאִשָּׁה — *and do not converse excessively with the woman.* Excessive idle chatter can induce a frivolous atmosphere and may lead to

sin, but any necessary conversation, for business, domestic affairs, and the like, is permitted with any woman (*Binyan Yehoshua* to *Avos d'Rabbi Nosson* 7:3). There are situations in which limited "idle" and "light" talk with one's wife is permitted and even encouraged. (See *Rav* here and *Shulchan Aruch Orach Chaim* 240:9,10, and *Mishnah Berurah* ad loc.)

In a letter to newly married couples, the *Chazon Ish* wrote that this dictum refers only to frivolous talk meant to incite improper behavior, but one who seeks to calm, soothe, and reassure one's mate or to express affection is permitted and even encouraged to engage in small talk. This is especially true in the initial stages of marriage, when emotional bonding must occur.

Avos d'Rabbi Nosson (7:3) gives a different interpretation of these words. If one has been treated disrespectfully or has had a disagreement with a friend, he should not go home and tell his wife what words were exchanged; if he does, he embarrasses both himself and the other party. Furthermore, his wife may lose respect for him. When his antagonist hears of this, he will be doubly angry that the story was reported to the man's wife. The result is that

⋅⋖ **Members of the family.** Hospitality is a subtle art. One must show concern and interest for his guests, yet not be overbearing. There is a well-known Jew in London who maintains a separate dining room and sleeping quarters in a wing of his home for the express use of representatives of charitable institutions and people who come to England in need of medical help. He often joins his guests for meals. One evening a shabbily dressed man approached the host, unaware of his identity, and asked, "Do you know how long one may stay here?" The host answered, "Don't worry! I'm here for quite some time already and nobody has said a word to me." This man's conduct is in the true spirit of *Let your home be open wide and treat the poor as members of your household.*

In Mexico City, a prominent industrialist maintains a dining and living room in his office building for the use of travelers. Every day, his mother and wife prepare fresh-cooked lunches themselves and serve the guests personally.

The Chofetz Chaim found a relevant insight in this mishnah. Often we are reluctant to invite guests since we feel we cannot provide a sumptuous-enough meal or sufficiently comfortable lodgings. Thus the mishnah teaches that the poor should be treated literally as the members of your *own* household. Do not overburden yourself; whatever you provide for your family will be fine for your guests, so you need not hesitate to invite guests. There is another way in which one should regard his guests as family: If your son acted in an uncouth manner or was lax in performing a *mitzvah,* you might offer rebuke, but you certainly would not evict him from your house. Guests should be treated the same way.

woman. They said this even about one's own wife; surely it applies to another's wife. Consequently, the Sages said: Anyone who converses excessively with a woman causes evil to himself, neglects Torah study, and will eventually inherit Gehinnom.

---

three people will be embarrassed.

Abarbanel reads this injunction as a continuation of previous clauses dealing with hospitality. If there are women among the poor who come to your home, one should not engage in frivolous chatter with them.

בְּאִשְׁתּוֹ אָמְרוּ; קַל וָחֹמֶר בְּאֵשֶׁת חֲבֵרוֹ — *They said this even about one's own wife; surely it applies to another's wife.* The usage in the previous clause, *with "the" woman,* denotes a particular woman; hence, *one's own wife* (*Rav*).

A man who truly respects his wife will have more to offer her than idle chatter for her amusement. He will want to discuss with her the serious concerns of life and will derive enjoyment from the resulting exchange of views and counsel (*R' S. R. Hirsch*).

This statement was made regarding one's own wife during her impurity, despite the fact that she will eventually become pure and the resumption of marital relations will be permitted. Certainly, then, one should not engage in frivolous talk with another's wife, who is absolutely forbidden to him (*R' Yonah*).

מִכָּאן אָמְרוּ חֲכָמִים — *Consequently, the Sages said.* This is the statement of R' Yehudah *HaNasi,* redactor of the Mishnah (*Rav*). *Tiferes Yisrael,* however, attributes the earlier portion, *They said this even*

about one's own wife, to R' Yehudah *HaNasi,* and the present words to a group of Sages who came after him.

כָּל הַמַּרְבֶּה שִׂיחָה עִם הָאִשָּׁה – גּוֹרֵם רָעָה לְעַצְמוֹ — *Anyone who converses excessively with a woman causes evil to himself.* By telling his wife of the insult he suffered, as mentioned earlier, a man causes evil to himself, because his wife may lose respect for him (*Rav*). If she is impure, the excessive frivolity will lead to sin; hence, he *causes evil to himself* (*Midrash Shmuel*). *R' Yonah* comments that by engaging in excessive chatter with women, one incites his own evil inclination. One may legitimately claim to be overwhelmed by passion only when he himself did not provoke it [see *Berachos* 31b].

וּבוֹטֵל מִדִּבְרֵי תוֹרָה — *neglects Torah study.* Drawn into foolishness, one is sidetracked from proper involvement with spiritual matters (*Rav*). Thoughts of Torah and worldly pleasures are mutually exclusive. Idle talk with women, by its nature, causes the neglect of Torah study (*R' Yonah*).

וְסוֹפוֹ יוֹרֵשׁ גֵּיהִנֹּם — *and will eventually inherit Gehinnom.* Gehinnom is the place where the souls of the wicked are punished. The loosening of moral boundaries and bantering with other women can result in a downward spiral which eventually leads to sin and its consequences (see *Proverbs* 2:15-18).

◆§ **Husband-wife relationship.** A fascinating letter, written by R' Akiva Eiger after after his wife's death, sheds light on our mishnah. He wrote to his children in response to a proposal that he remarry. "Do you consider me so insensitive and heartless as to rush to accept a marriage proposal while still in mourning? Am I to forget the love of the beloved wife of my youth, with whom God allowed me to raise upstanding, blessed children? The little bit of Torah in me is only due to her help — she carefully kept watch over my health and bore all the financial worries of our home, so that I would not be distracted from the service of God. Now that she is gone, I am bereft and emotionally like a broken vessel. Who will pasture our young sheep (children); with whom shall I share my worries and find some respite? Who will care for me? Which human being knows better than I of her righteousness and modesty? Many times we held deep discussions on topics related to the fear of Heaven until the middle of the night" (*Igros Soferim* p. 65).

◆§ A marital relationship based on frivolity will eventually deteriorate. While such a life-style initially seems exciting, the thrill soon wears off, and all that is left is a deep disrespect for one's partner and a sense of moral shallowness. Domestic life without a solid moral foundation can become a real "purgatory on earth."

יְהוֹשֻׁעַ בֶּן פְּרַחְיָה וְנִתַּאי הָאַרְבֵּלִי קִבְּלוּ מֵהֶם. יְהוֹשֻׁעַ [ו]
בֶּן פְּרַחְיָה אוֹמֵר: עֲשֵׂה לְךָ רַב, וּקְנֵה לְךָ חָבֵר,

Mishnah 6

יְהוֹשֻׁעַ בֶּן פְּרַחְיָה — *Yehoshua ben Perachyah.* Yehoshua ben Perachyah was active during the reign of King Yannai, approximately two hundred years before the destruction of the Second Temple. When Yannai decimated most of the Sages of the Perushim camp in the wake of Yochanan the High Priest's defection to the Sadducees (see *Kiddushin* 76a), Yehoshua ben Perachyah fled to Alexandria, Egypt. When the danger passed, he was summoned back by his student Shimon ben Shatach, who enjoyed the protection of Queen Shlomis Alexandra (also known as Shlomzion), Yannai's wife, who was Shimon ben Shatach's sister.

וְנִתַּאי הָאַרְבֵּלִי — *and Nittai of Arbel.* The head of the Sanhedrin, Nittai was from Arbel in the lower Galilee, near Tiberias (see *Hosea* 10:14).

קִבְּלוּ מֵהֶם — *received the tradition from them,* i.e., from Yose ben Yoezer and Yose ben Yochanan.

יְהוֹשֻׁעַ בֶּן פְּרַחְיָה אוֹמֵר: עֲשֵׂה לְךָ רַב — *Yehoshua ben Perachyah says: Appoint a teacher for yourself.*

Even if he is equal or inferior to you intellectually, appoint him as your teacher, because studying with another person is much more efficacious than studying alone. The exchange of ideas yields greater clarity (*Rambam*). R' Yonah states additionally that one remembers that which is learned from a teacher better than what he learns by independent study. Therefore, *even* a study partner is justifiably called a teacher, since his participation in the learning process increases its success.

Rashi views the function of the teacher as insuring the intellectual honesty of the student and conveying the authentic tradition. Rabbi Chaim Soloveichik used to say, "From books, one can learn what *to* say; a rebbe teaches him what *not* to say."

Tiferes Yisrael sees in these words a charge that every city and congregation engage a rabbi who will act as a spiritual mentor.

Meiri renders עֲשֵׂה לְךָ רַב as *"make" a teacher for yourself.* If a competent teacher is unavailable, invest in an outstanding student by providing for his

---

⊷§ **A city without a rabbi.** The Beis HaLevi was offered a prestigious rabbinic position in a city whose rabbinic seat had been vacant for fourteen years. He refused the offer with the following explanation: "A woman whose husband passes away is distraught. Besides her grief over her loss, she begins to worry, 'Who will recite *Kiddush* for me on Friday night? From whom will I hear *Havdalah* at the end of Shabbos?' After a while, however, she may become self-sufficient and decide that she can do very well without a husband. Likewise, a city that has not employed a *rav* for fourteen years has adjusted to the situation. I would be afraid to accept such a position."

⊷§ **Find a medicine man.** A young man once came to visit with the Slonimer *Rebbe,* the Beis Avraham. "I learn almost all of the books of the Chassidic greats, follow their advice, and try to incorporate into my life-style *all* of the good practices they speak of. I see no need to have a *Rebbe,*" he told the Beis Avraham.

The *Rebbe* said to him: "Let me explain your situation with a parable. A man once felt ill. Rather than visiting a doctor, he decided to go to a pharmacy on his own. 'I'll buy all the medicines and take them, and that way I'll be cured of all disease. There is no need to see a doctor.'

"Of course, this is utter foolishness. One who uses drugs without proper supervision places himself in serious danger. Drugs that are beneficial in treating certain diseases may be fatal in treating others. Only a doctor, with his medical expertise and his knowledge of the patient's history, can properly diagnose the sickness and prescribe the appropriate medicine.

"Similarly, all that you learn in the books of the great Chassidic masters is like medicine. In the wrong doses or incorrectly prescribed, such 'medicines' can be fatal to your spiritual welfare. You should follow the dictum of the Sages that one should select a teacher for himself, who can serve as the doctor for your soul, diagnose your needs and prescribe the proper spiritual medicine."

6. Yehoshua ben Perachyah and Nittai of Arbel received the tradition from them. Yehoshua ben Perachyah says: Appoint a teacher for yourself; acquire a friend for yourself;

needs, thus enabling him to develop into a fitting teacher from whom you may learn.

Rashbam (quoted in *Midrash Shmuel*) views this dictum as a warning to a student against issuing rulings without consulting his teacher.

The Talmud (*Yevamos* 109b) homiletically explains the verse וְשֹׂנֵא תוֹקְעִים בּוֹטֵחַ (*Proverbs* 11:15) to mean: A student who takes a firm position [תוֹקֵעַ, as in יָתֵד תָּקוּעַ, a firmly planted peg; confidently relying on his own knowledge (בּוֹטֵחַ)] is despised (שֹׂנֵא) in the eyes of God. Hence the mishnah teaches: *Appoint a teacher for yourself.*

Every person needs a competent mentor who can correctly transmit the tradition and thereby avoid error. One should be willing to submit to his direction, for without a mentor, a person is directionless.

וּקְנֵה לְךָ חָבֵר — *acquire a friend for yourself;* even if the acquisition of this friendship entails great financial expense (*Rav*).

The expression *acquire* is inappropriate regarding a teacher, since a teacher may not receive direct remuneration for his services (see *Nedarim* 4:3). [In fact, however, a teacher of children who teaches Scripture may be compensated for the teaching of reading skills or for his service as a child-care provider. Those who teach older children may take pay as compensation for giving up other career opportunities to devote their time to teaching, but the pay is not for the teaching itself. See *Shulchan Aruch Yoreh Deah* 246:5.]

Likewise [in spite of the fact that students are a greater catalyst for Torah study than friends (see *Taanis* 7a)], the term *acquire* is incongruent with the instruction to *develop many disciples* (mishnah 1). Students seek a teacher according to their emotional make-up and temperament, and according to their perception of the benefit they might derive from him. Students cannot be "bought";

hence the mishnah never speaks of acquiring them (*Midrash Shmuel* in the name of *R' Yehudah Lirma*).

Maharal, commenting on the dictum *develop many disciples,* says that the practice of buying students is inappropriate and demeaning to the honor of Torah.

One must acquire a friend in order to correct one's actions in all areas of life. Our Sages taught the importance of friendship with the following words: "Either friendship or death" (*Taanis* 23a). One must exert great effort in cultivating a friendship, even to the extent of yielding personal preferences to the will and habits of one's friend. In this way, each of the two friends will seek to please the other, and together they will undoubtedly forge common goals and interests. How true rings the Aristotelian maxim, "One who loves, he and you are one" (*Rambam*).

A good friend serves three functions. The first is as a catalyst for increased success at Torah study (see *Taanis* 7a). The second is to insure one's *mitzvah* fulfillment, for good friends feel free to offer constructive criticism to one another. The third function is to provide good advice in all areas and to act as a discreet confidant who does not reveal secrets to others. In fact, one who breaches his friend's trust will lose him as a friend, and justifiably so (*Midrash Shmuel*). *R' Yonah* adds that a good friend also will gloss over any injustice committed by the other, thus endearing them to each other.

In a novel interpretation, *Rashi* views the instruction to secure a friend as a reference to purchasing books of Torah content; books are friends. Alternatively, it is a warning against solitary Torah study; one should find a friend with whom to learn.

◆§ **Role reversal.** Rabbi Chaim Shmulevitz explained that the instruction to acquire a friend also refers to building harmonious relationships with one's spouse on the basis of the mutual consideration of the other's needs and wants. Thus, he would counsel his students and tell them, "Our Sages teach a man to love his wife as himself and honor her even more (*Yevamos* 62b), while a wife, they teach, is deemed virtuous if she does the will of her husband (*Tanna d'Vei Eliyahu Rabbah* 9). As long as the husband abides by the former and the wife abides by the latter, their home will be blessed with marital bliss. It is when they switch quotations [the wife demanding love and respect, and the husband expecting subservience] that the troubles begin."

וֶהֱוֵי דָן אֶת כָּל הָאָדָם לְכַף זְכוּת *— and judge everyone favorably.* *Rambam* and *Rav* delineate this obligation's parameters: (a) If one sees an average person [neither confirmed as righteous (צַדִּיק) or evil (רָשָׁע)] do or say something that bears either a positive or negative interpretation, it is an act of piety (מִדַּת חֲסִידוּת) to interpret the act in a positive light. (b) If the perpetrator, confirmed as a righteous individual (צַדִּיק), does something which almost certainly is a negative act and can be interpreted positively only by means of a far-fetched explanation, nonetheless one may not suspect him of doing bad. Since it is possible to see the episode in a positive manner, he should try to do so. Regarding such an instance, our Sages taught, "One who suspects the upright will be afflicted with terrible bodily sickness" (*Shabbos* 97a). (c) If one sees a confirmed evildoer performing an act which seemingly bears only *positive* in-

⊰§ **One never knows.** The Talmud tells of an agricultural worker who spent three years working for a landowner. On the eve of Yom Kippur he went to his employer to collect the wages for the full three years in order to return home to his wife and children. The employer claimed to have no money. "Give me fruit," said the worker. "I have no fruit," the employer said. "Let me have some of your land," pleaded the worker, thinking that he could sell it and use the proceeds. Again the landowner claimed that this was impossible. Every request for equivalent payment by the worker (animals, pillows, blankets) was met with the same reply: "I have none."

Brokenhearted and penniless, the worker trudged home. After the holidays, the landowner arrived at the home of his former employee and presented him not only with his wages, but with several mules carrying foods and delicacies as a treat for the worker's family. "Tell me," asked the landowner, "when I told you I had no money, what did you think?"

"I assumed you had invested in merchandise that you were able to purchase at a good price," answered the worker.

"And when I said I had no animals?" the landowner inquired. "Oh, I assumed you had hired out your animals," was the reply.

"And what about my claim that I had no fruit?" "I assumed that you had not taken the necessary tithes," the worker replied, for it is forbidden to use fruit which has not been tithed.

"Fine; but what suspicion entered your mind when I claimed to have no pillows or covers?" "None at all. I was sure you had consecrated all your property to the Temple treasury," replied the worker.

"I swear to you," replied the landowner, "that it was exactly as you thought. I pledged all my worldly goods to the Temple in order that my son merit success at his studies. Just as you judged me favorably, so may you be judged in Heaven in a favorable manner" (*Shabbos* 127b; see other fascinating incidents there).

A more contemporary incident, recounted in ArtScroll's *Around the Maggid's Table*, also serves to bring home the lesson of this mishnah:

Mr. Usher Feingold of Ashdod was a poor man whose friends and neighbors helped raise money for his daughter's wedding. To everyone's astonishment, the wedding was catered in a large ballroom, in a very lavish manner. Many of the guests were highly offended. Was this how an ostensibly poor family had used the funds that had been raised for them? Surely the money could have been put to better use. The guests felt they had been used. After the wedding, the Feingolds could not fail to feel the resentment of the community.

Shortly thereafter, Mr. Feingold visited his rabbi and explained. He and his wife had gone to the caterer to arrange a simple and inexpensive wedding. During the course of the discussion, the caterer realized that she and her family owed their lives to Mr. Feingold's father, who had hidden them from the Nazis. She insisted on catering the wedding at her own expense, as a small expression of her gratitude — but she made the Feingolds promise that it would remain a secret.

"When we came to the hall that night, we were as shocked as everyone else, but I couldn't say anything to my guests. But when I saw the attitude of our friends, I went to her and explained. She gave me permission to tell the story, so now I beg you, please let people know the truth."

It is about such situations that we are taught *to judge everyone favorably*.

terpretation [and only a remote, improbable understanding of the episode will allow for a negative interpretation], he should [still] exercise caution in his dealings with him and may not believe that this was a good act, since it bears a negative [albeit far-fetched] reading. In reference to this evildoer, King Solomon taught: *When he intones his voice with favor, do not believe in him, for seven abominations reside in his heart (Proverbs 26:25).*

R' Yonah adds that if a completely righteous individual (צַדִּיק גָּמוּר) does something which is undeniably evil, we must assume that he already repented his transgression. Regarding this, our Sages taught, "If you have seen a Torah scholar transgress in the evening, harbor no negative thoughts about him by day, for he has surely repented" (*Berachos* 19a).

One who judges others favorably will himself be judged favorably in the Heavenly court (*Rashi*). Certainly one must judge his friends and teachers favorably, for if he does not do so, the relationships will erode and will not yield the potential benefit inherent in them (*Tiferes Yisrael*).

In order to judge a friend favorably, one must consider the totality of the person and his situation. Even if the friend is remiss in his spiritual obligations or suffers from some flaw of character, he certainly possesses other redeeming qualities which compensate for his "deficiencies." Furthermore, an understanding of the friend's circumstances may mitigate the harshness of our judgment. The mishnah implies this by saying וֶהֱוֵי דָן אֶת כָּל הָאָדָם לְכַף זְכוּת, which literally means *judge the* **entire person** *favorably* (*Sfas Emes*).

When Nathan the Prophet came to offer rebuke to King David, he began with a parable of two citizens, one wealthy and one poor. The rich man owned much cattle, while the poor man had only one small sheep; but the rich man stole the single sheep from the poor man. When David heard this story, he was appalled. "Let the man who did this die," he declared passionately. Only then did Nathan explain that this was but a parallel to David's own situation, since he had taken Bas-sheva from Uriah the Hittite. "You are the man," Nathan said to King David. In this way David indicted himself.

So, taught the *Baal Shem Tov*, does man decide his own punishment for his transgressions. He is given the opportunity to view someone else doing exactly what he did, in a slightly camouflaged form, and in a fit of righteous indignation he passes sentence. Only then is the facade lifted, and he realizes that it is he who will receive the punishment. The fashion in which man judges his friend is in reality the way in which he is judged from Heaven.

It is for this reason that we are taught *to judge everyone favorably*. One should not be in a rush to interpret his friend's actions with severity, for he may actually be passing judgment on himself. The reverse is also true; one who judges others favorably effects a favorable judgment for himself.

☙ **The whole picture.** R' Nachman of Breslov (*Likutei Maharan* 282) uses this idea to explain the verse וְעוֹד מְעַט וְאֵין רָשָׁע וְהִתְבּוֹנַנְתָּ עַל מְקוֹמוֹ וְאֵינֶנּוּ, *Just a bit more and there will be no wicked one; you will contemplate his place and he will not be there (Psalms 37:10).* Even if one seems to have no redeeming qualities, search further. Your search will certainly uncover some bit of good which justifies the person's existence. This point of goodness is what indicates that *there will be no wicked one. You will contemplate his place* — i.e., your previous negative perception of him — *and he will not be there,* for by judging the whole person favorably, you have already changed his status.

R' Nachman continues: Man must view himself in this manner as well. Rather than falling into despair over his shortcomings, he must seek out positive elements in the totality of his being and judge himself favorably on that basis. Such an attitude brings one to the joy necessary to serve God.

A young man received the following marital advice from his mentor: Whenever your wife does something that upsets you or you find yourself harboring a negative opinion of her, sit down and write up a list of everything she does for you and your family. If she lost her patience with the children today, does that mean she is impatient? What about the last ten weeks, when she exhibited the patience of a saint? If you felt she didn't show consideration for your wants and needs on a particular occasion, look at your list. Doesn't she generally anticipate your requests and fulfill them unsolicited?

Likewise, when a woman's husband cannot finance a purchase that she has requested, let her not focus on one incident; instead she should recall the countless times he has shown himself a considerate provider. The final message is to consider the entirety of the person favorably, rather than isolating particular incidents and using them as a negative barometer.

[ז] נִתַּאי הָאַרְבֵּלִי אוֹמֵר: הַרְחֵק מִשָּׁכֵן רָע, וְאַל תִּתְחַבֵּר לָרָשָׁע, וְאַל תִּתְיָאֵשׁ מִן הַפֻּרְעָנוּת.

Mishnah 7

נִתַּאי הָאַרְבֵּלִי אוֹמֵר: הַרְחֵק מִשָּׁכֵן רָע — *Nittai of Arbel says: Distance yourself from a bad neighbor.* One should keep away from a bad neighbor so as not to learn from his actions. Alternatively, one should stay away from him so as not to be caught in the path of the retribution that will befall the evildoer. The Sages taught (*Negaim* 12:6): "Woe to the evildoer; woe to his neighbor" (*Rav*).

Tiferes Yisrael views these words in a more practical sense: Distance yourself from an angry, arrogant, or jealous neighbor, for you are bound to be damaged by his company. *R' Yonah* sees this as advice to those looking for a place to live. To inquire about the neighbors is as important as investigating the living conditions themselves.

R' Yehudah Lirma takes note of the usage הַרְחֵק (literally, *remove* in the transitive form) rather than הִתְרַחֵק, which means *distance [yourself]*. One is obligated to remove others, meaning potential neighbors, from the sphere of influence of an evil resident by warning them of his presence.

וְאַל תִּתְחַבֵּר לָרָשָׁע — *do not associate with a wicked person.* Any association with the wicked is considered detrimental even if one does not learn to imitate their actions. The exposure itself causes a negative influence to rub off, much as one who enters the house of a tanner absorbs the foul odor even if he takes nothing from the house (*Rav* based on *Pirkei d'Rabbi Eliezer* 25).

Tiferes Yisrael distinguishes between a רָשָׁע and a שָׁכֵן רָע. A רָשָׁע is someone who sins but does not induce others to sin; therefore, there is no special need to distance oneself from him as long as one does not actively *associate* with him (תִּתְחַבֵּר). A bad neighbor (שָׁכֵן רָע), on the other hand, is one who is remiss in his duties toward God and bad toward people. Such a person not only sins himself but seeks to involve others in iniquity. We are thus enjoined to remain completely outside his destructive orbit (הַרְחֵק).

R' Yosef Chaim of Baghdad, the *Ben Ish Chai*, interprets this stich of the mishnah as *distance the evil from your neighbor*: rather than distancing yourself from him, help him repent, and in this way you will not fall into the trap of suffering punishment for his fellow's wickedness. One who can bring his friend to repentance, but does not, bears some of the guilt. A famous Talmudic story illustrates this approach. In R' Meir's neighborhood there were ruffians who constantly tormented him. He wanted to pray that they die, but his wise wife Beruriah said, "Rather than praying for their deaths, you should pray that they repent." He did so, and in fact they repented (*Berachos* 10a).

◆§ **Before it is too late.** The mere *threat* of retribution can often bring people to change their ways. The Sages say that the removal of Ahasuerus's ring to seal Haman's edict against the Jews brought about a greater spirit of repentance than all the admonitions of the prophets recorded in Scripture (see *Megillah* 14a). But if the threat is not sufficient, it becomes necessary to actually execute the punishments. Thus the mishnah warns us not to be apathetic to the threat of punishment lest God, so to speak, be forced to actually deliver on His threat. R' Chaim of Volozhin offered a parable:

Smugglers loaded their contraband into a casket and feigned a funeral procession, but the border guards were suspicious and searched the "mourners" and the casket. Caught in the act, the smugglers began to cry, fearful of their terrible fate.

The guards told them: "It is a shame that you are crying only now. Had you been crying when you staged the funeral procession, we would never have suspected you. But when we saw that none of the 'mourners' were crying, we became suspicious."

Likewise, if man reacts to the mere threat of retribution and puts his spiritual house in order, it is unnecessary for God to punish him, but if he does react to the threat, his spiritual situation becomes suspect.

7. Nittai of Arbel says: Distance yourself from a bad neighbor; do not associate with a wicked person; and do not despair of retribution.

וְאַל תִּתְיָאֵשׁ מִן הַפֻּרְעָנוּת — *and do not despair of retribution.* One should not look at a successful evildoer and say: "I will associate with him while fortune smiles at him, and I will abandon him when his luck passes." Instead, one should not *despair* — ignore the possibility — that retribution will suddenly befall the evil one, for eventually his time will come (*Rav* and *R' Yonah*).

Do not be deluded into thinking that Divine retribution will occur only later, in the World to Come; punishment and vengeance may be exacted even in this world. Therefore, do not give up on the certainty of retribution (*Rambam*).

Rashi offers two explanations: Do not rely on your wealth to save you, for recompense is quick to arrive. This thought should instill in man a constant fear, in line with the words of Shlomo HaMelech: *Happy is the man who is constantly afraid* (*Mishlei* 28:14). Alternatively, it is an independent clause. One should not let retribution cause him to despair; even if evil comes, one should not give up hope, for salvation can arrive quickly. In the words of *Isaiah* (59:1): *The hand of God is not too short to save.*

Midrash Shmuel quotes *R' Moshe Almosnino*: If one succumbed to his evil inclination and stumbled into iniquity, he should not fall into despair; he should not feel overwhelmed by the punishments that await him, and instead should concentrate on repentance.

⌐§ **A lost cause.** *Rejoice, young man, in your childhood; let your heart cheer you in the days of your youth; follow the path of your heart and the sight of your eyes — but be aware that for all these things God will call you to account* (*Ecclesiastes* 11:9). The opening words of the verse certainly seem to be the sweet-sounding words of the evil inclination: "Eat, drink, and be merry"; but the conclusion, *be aware that for all these things God will call you to account,* seems to be the protest of the Good Inclination.

Not so, taught the Dubno *Maggid*; the entire verse is a message from the *Evil* Inclination. He illustrated his point with a parable.

A poor, hungry man wandered through the streets wondering how he would get his next meal. Suddenly, a wealthy man approached. "My dear sir, you look hungry. Come with me to the restaurant, and I will treat you to a meal," he offered. They sat down together and proceeded to enjoy a sumptuous dinner. Toward the end of the meal, the host excused himself and disappeared. After a long wait, the owner of the restaurant came over to the table and requested payment. "I have no money," pleaded the beggar. "That unscrupulous scoundrel tricked me and left." The owner noticed a watch on the poor man's wrist. "Give me the watch as payment," he said. "If you come back and pay me, I'll return the watch." The poor man complied and left the restaurant, dejected and upset.

A few days later while walking down the street, he spotted his "host." The poor man lost no time in venting his fury upon the trickster. "How could you do such a thing to me?" he cried. The rich man attempted to appease him, offering to take him to the restaurant again and to pay both the old and the new bills. But the second time the rich man again pulled the same ruse, running away and leaving the beggar with the bill. The proprietor came to request payment, and the poor man could do nothing but repeat his tale of woe.

"You know what?" said the proprietor. "You may as well continue to eat and enjoy, since you will never succeed in redeeming your watch anyway."

"So, too," explained the *Maggid,* "we are seduced by the wiles of the *yetzer hara,* who encourages us to enjoy the good life, since we only live once. We give our souls to this great manipulator, much as the poor man gave his watch, as payment for our pleasures; but even when we contemplate repentance, his unceasing chatter continues: 'You are a lost cause,' he tells us. *'Be aware that for all these things God will call you to account* — you will never regain your soul. Punishment is certain; you have no chance to repent. You might as well continue your hedonistic ways.' It is against this ploy of the Satan that our mishnah warns us, *Do not despair.* No matter how deeply we have fallen into sin, there is still a chance for us to repent and avoid the punishment.''

[ח] **יְהוּדָה** בֶּן טַבַּאי וְשִׁמְעוֹן בֶּן שָׁטָח קִבְּלוּ מֵהֶם. יְהוּדָה בֶּן טַבַּאי אוֹמֵר: אַל תַּעַשׂ עַצְמְךָ כְּעוֹרְכֵי הַדַּיָּנִין; וּכְשֶׁיִּהְיוּ בַּעֲלֵי הַדִּין עוֹמְדִים לְפָנֶיךָ, יִהְיוּ בְעֵינֶיךָ כִּרְשָׁעִים; וּכְשֶׁנִּפְטָרִים מִלְּפָנֶיךָ, יִהְיוּ בְעֵינֶיךָ כְּזַכָּאִין, כְּשֶׁקִּבְּלוּ עֲלֵיהֶם אֶת הַדִּין.

Mishnah 8

יְהוּדָה בֶּן טַבַּאי וְשִׁמְעוֹן בֶּן שָׁטָח קִבְּלוּ מֵהֶם — *Yehudah ben Tabbai and Shimon ben Shatach received the tradition from them*, i.e., from Yehoshua ben Perachyah and Nittai of Arbel. Even though Yehudah ben Tabbai is mentioned first, there is a dispute as to whether he was the *Nasi* or the *Av Beis Din,* head of the court (see introduction to 1:4). Following the opinion that he was indeed the *Nasi,* Talmud Yerushalmi relates how he came to occupy that position: The citizens of Jerusalem sought to appoint Yehudah ben Tabbai over themselves. In his modesty he fled to Alexandria, Egypt, rather than accept such a prestigious position. The Jerusalemites sent the following message: "From the great Jerusalem to the humble Alexandria — how long will my betrothed (Yehudah ben Tabbai) reside in your midst while I sit here brokenhearted?" Yehudah ben Tabbai subsequently returned and accepted the post of *Nasi* (*Chagigah* 2:2 and *Sanhedrin* 6:6). It should be noted that the office of *Nasi* was fraught with much danger during the murderous reign of King Yannai.

Shimon ben Shatach was the brother of Yannai's queen, Shlomis Alexandra (known as Shlomzion). When Yannai purged the Torah sages, Shlomis Alexandra hid her brother, and by the time he was able to return to public life, he was the sole remaining member of the Sanhedrin still loyal to Torah Judaism; all the rest were Sadducees, who denied the validity of the Oral Law. Because of his wisdom and shrewdness, he was eventually able to oust the Sadducees from the Sanhedrin.

Among Shimon ben Shatach's many achievements were two major enactments. He instituted the *kesubah* (marriage document), expanding the protection of married women, and he established

the first Jewish elementary schools, particularly for the benefit of children orphaned from their fathers. Such children typically had no one at home to teach them Torah, so the schools were a necessity (*Yerushalmi Kesubos* 8:11; see *Korban HaEidah* ad loc.).

יְהוּדָה בֶּן טַבַּאי אוֹמֵר: עַל תַּעַשׂ עַצְמְךָ כְּעוֹרְכֵי הַדַּיָּנִין — *Yehudah ben Tabbai says: [When serving as a judge,] do not act as a lawyer.* A judge must always remain an impartial arbiter. Even if he is convinced that one of the parties is right, he should not advise that litigant on how to present his case (*Rav, Rashi* et al.). *Rambam* explains עוֹרְכֵי הַדַּיָּנִין as those who conduct a mock trial prior to the real one, thus preparing arguments and rebuttals for every eventuality. A judge may not participate in such an exercise.

In certain extraordinary instances, when particular pieces of evidence have not been properly stressed by one of the litigants due to ignorance, weakness, or awkwardness, the judges are required to intercede and "open the mouth of the speechless," presenting queries and claims on behalf of the "weak" party. For example, the court must challenge a note for collection issued against orphans, since, unaware of their late father's business dealings, they can easily be victimized by swindlers. (See *Shulchan Aruch Choshen Mishpat* 17:9, *Gittin* 37b, and *Kesubos* 36a.)

Rashi views the metaphor of "not acting as counsel" as a further instruction to judges: (a) Prior to trial, they should not offer an opinion regarding any aspect of the case, or the chances of a particular claim winning in court; and (b) they may not announce the verdict unless both parties or their representatives are present.

Some texts read כְּאוֹרְכֵי הַדַּיָּנִין, *like the great judicial figures* (*Rashi*). A student should not act like a great legal scholar by offering his opinion in the

8. Yehudah ben Tabbai and Shimon ben Shatach received the tradition from them. Yehudah ben Tabbai says: [When serving as a judge,] do not act as a lawyer; while the litigants stand before you, consider them both as guilty; but when they are dismissed from you, consider them both as innocent, provided they have accepted the judgment.

presence of his teacher; nor should a judge pressure litigants to use his court (*Rav*). [See *Shulchan Aruch Choshen Mishpat* 13-14 regarding the procedure for selecting a legal venue and a panel of judges.]

This dictum applies not only to judges. One should not offer unsolicited legal advice to a litigant that will cause loss to another party. For a Torah scholar, it is improper to do so even on behalf of a relative. It is, however, permitted to offer such advice to prevent one's own relative from incurring loss (*R' Yonah* and *Meiri*).

One way to constitute a court is for each of the litigants to choose one judge, and for those judges, in turn, to agree on the third member of the tribunal (see *Shulchan Aruch Choshen Mishpat* 13:1). This mishnah admonishes the two judges chosen by the litigants: Do not represent the position of the person who appointed you; instead you must act impartially and be open to all sides of the question.

HaChassid Yaavetz adds: Do not act as a lawyer, employing your powers of debate and persuasion to justify the litigant whose position, logically and instinctively, seems to you to be correct. Objectively weigh only the claims and counterclaims presented by the involved parties and the testimony of bona fide witnesses.

וּכְשֶׁיִּהְיוּ בַּעֲלֵי הַדִּין עוֹמְדִים לְפָנֶיךָ, יִהְיוּ בְּעֵינֶיךָ כִּרְשָׁעִים — *while the litigants stand before you, consider them both as guilty.* While the trial is in process, a judge must be skeptical of all the litigants, as if they were evildoers. This allows him to remain objective, to establish the authenticity of all statements made to the court, and to ferret out the truth (*Rav* and *Tosafos Yom Tov*). Were the judge to view all sides as righteous and honest, he would never succeed in uncovering duplicity. Furthermore, the very involvement of both litigants in a situation of strife is, in a most subtle fashion, indicative of evil (*Maharal*).

The use of the term עוֹמְדִים, *stand*, refers to the practice of judges sitting in court while the litigants stand (*Shevuos* 30a).

וּכְשֶׁנִּפְטָרִים מִלְּפָנֶיךָ, יִהְיוּ בְעֵינֶיךָ כְּזַכָּאִין, כְּשֶׁקִּבְּלוּ עֲלֵיהֶם אֶת הַדִּין — *but when they are dismissed from you, consider them both as innocent, provided they have accepted the judgment.* As long as the parties are before the judge, he must view them both as equally unreliable and evaluate the allegations

⊷§ **Two hats.** *Mei Marom* offers an insight into the dual characteristics necessary to insure true justice.

Human judges must follow the Divine model in their approach to administering justice. Just as God, the True Judge, is involved in the most intimate details of human affairs and simultaneously is totally separated from them, so the human judge must be intellectually fully aware of and empathic toward the claims of the litigants, but he may not act as counsel for them and must retain total impartiality.

Chida in *Zeroa Yemin* extends this maxim to self-judgment. We tend to employ all types of convoluted arguments and hairsplitting logic to justify our shortcomings; sometimes our creativity in arguing our innocence rivals that of the sharpest lawyer. The mishnah is showing us that when we judge ourselves, we should not act as a lawyer, who is unwilling to admit the guilt of his client. A person can never improve himself if he cannot face the reality of his shortcomings. Guilt is painful, but it is from such pain that spiritual health emerges.

⊷§ **An evildoer?** When R' Yaakov Yosef of Skwere was a young man, an old *chassid* asked him if he was considering entering the rabbinate when he grew older. The young man answered, "We are taught: *While the litigants stand before you, view them as if they were evildoers.* I am simply unable to view *any* Jew, for even a moment, as an evildoer."

[ט] **שִׁמְעוֹן** בֶּן שָׁטָח אוֹמֵר: הֱוֵי מַרְבֶּה לַחֲקוֹר אֶת הָעֵדִים; וֶהֱוֵי זָהִיר בִּדְבָרֶיךָ, שֶׁמָּא מִתּוֹכָם יִלְמְדוּ לְשַׁקֵּר.

[י] **שְׁמַעְיָה וְאַבְטַלְיוֹן** קִבְּלוּ מֵהֶם. שְׁמַעְיָה אוֹמֵר: אֱהַב אֶת הַמְּלָאכָה, וּשְׂנָא

against them objectively, dispassionately, and without regard to personalities — solely on the merit of their testimony; for there are disputes in which even the best man may be in the wrong and the worst man in the right. On the other hand, once the parties have accepted the verdict, the judge must not carry into his civilian life any adverse impressions he may have subconsciously obtained of either party. He must regard them both as equally guilt-free (*R' S.R. Hirsch*).

Lev Avos interprets the last two stiches of the mishnah as conditional. If the litigants remain standing in front of the court, arguing and protesting the verdict, then the court should view them as wicked people who are unable to yield to true justice. However, if they leave the court fully accepting its decision, then they will both be seen as

innocent people who have aligned themselves with truthfulness.

Abarbanel sees this mishnah as qualifying the axiom of Yehoshua ben Perachyah, which states that one must judge everyone favorably. That rule is not to be applied to everyone at all times. Litigants, while before the court, are to be viewed as wicked; viewing them favorably would becloud the judge's objectivity and cause him to function instead like a lawyer. Therefore, while they still stand in front of the court, they should be viewed negatively. Only after they accept the ruling of the court shall they again be viewed as innocent, and we must apply the words of Yehoshua ben Perachyah to judge them favorably.

Mishnah 9

שִׁמְעוֹן בֶּן שָׁטָח אוֹמֵר: הֱוֵי מַרְבֶּה לַחֲקוֹר אֶת הָעֵדִים — *Shimon ben Shatach says: Interrogate the witnesses extensively.* Judges must ask a set of questions to determine the basic facts of time and place. Then they should ask anything necessary to bring out all the relevant facts. Hence Shimon ben Shatach instructs judges to engage in extensive interrogation and cross-examination (*Meiri*).

Midrash Shmuel suggests further that to interrogate extensively means that the questioning should be conducted at a rapid-fire pace, never leaving the

witnesses time to tailor their answers to meet the expectations of the interrogator.

Shimon ben Shatach issued this call for extensive interrogation in response to a personal tragedy. The Sadducees who opposed zealous defense of the Torah primed false witnesses to testify against Shimon's own son. Shimon's own court accepted their testimony, and imposed the death penalty on the innocent defendant (*Rashbam;* see *Rashi, Sanhedrin* 44b, s.v. רבעיא).

וֶהֱוֵי זָהִיר בִּדְבָרֶיךָ, שֶׁמָּא מִתּוֹכָם יִלְמְדוּ לְשַׁקֵּר — *yet be cautious with your words, lest they [the witnesses]*

⊷§ **More than a judge.** To change another's actions and behavior is a formidable task, but it pales into insignificance compared to the feat of changing the person's very character. No matter how formidable, however, this must be the ultimate goal of teachers and leaders — to engender a metamorphosis in a person — and it is to them that the mishnah speaks: Do not act as a legal expert who merely delineates the scope of the halachah. Your true agenda must be to speak words of such warmth and inspiration that by the time a person leaves your presence, his life will have been totally changed. While formerly he was viewed as an evil person, your influence should make him legitimately innocent (*Kozhnitzer Maggid*).

9. Shimon ben Shatach says: Interrogate the witnesses extensively; yet be cautious with your words, lest they learn from them to lie.

10. Shemayah and Avtalyon received the tradition from them. Shemayah says: Love work; despise positions

---

learn from them [your words] to lie. Not only the witnesses but also the litigants will learn to lie (*Tosafos Yom Tov*). And what exactly does this "lying" mean? When interrogating witnesses or litigants, one must take care not to give them any indication of the direction of one's probing. Should they discern the angle of the questions, they will lie in order to accommodate the questioner (*Rashi, Rav, R' Yonah*). When issuing a verdict, do not elaborate more than necessary on the reasons for the ruling, for people may study the case in order to learn how to deceive a court in the future (*HaChassid Yaavetz*).

Ruach Chaim interprets this as referring to limitations on the judge's right to be misleading in an attempt to flush out false witnesses and trip them up on their own testimony. While the judge may do so, he must be subtle, so that the witnesses not realize and come to take license to do so themselves.

Mishnah 10

שְׁמַעְיָה וְאַבְטַלְיוֹן קִבְּלוּ מֵהֶם — *Shemayah and Avtalyon received the tradition from them*, i.e., from Yehudah ben Tabbai and Shimon ben Shatach.

Shemayah and Avtalyon were the *Nasi* and *Av Beis Din* respectively toward the end of the Hasmonean era, at the beginning of King Herod's reign. They were descendants of the Assyrian king Sennaherib (*Gittin* 57b). *Rambam* and *Rav* suggest that they themselves were converts to Judaism. *Maharal* objects, since a convert may not serve as *Nasi* or *Av Beis Din* (see *Horayos* 1:4). Rather, he says, they were descendants of converts, but were themselves born of Jewish mothers. *Magen Avos* suggests that Shemayah and Avtalyon were appointed to the Great Sanhedrin even though they were converts, since no one else of their stature was available, i.e., the rule excluding converts applies only where there is a suitable alternative. (See *Tosafos*, *Berachos* 19a ד"ה דוגמה; also see sources cited in *Chasdei Avos* here and in *Responsa Yosef Ometz* 47.)

The name Avtalyon is the Aramaic form of אַפּוֹטְרוֹפּוֹס, the Talmudic term for *guardian*. More precisely, Avtalyon is a contraction of אַב טַלְיוֹן: *father of the young.* [Similarly,

אַפּוֹטְרוֹפּוֹס is a contraction of the Latin פָּאטִיר, *father*, and פּוֹס, *minors*; thus, a surrogate caretaker.] As head of the Sanhedrin, with the responsibility to protect the interests of young orphans, Avtalyon served as their "father and legal guardian" (see *Bava Kamma* 37a and *Rashi*).

R' S. R. Hirsch explains that Shemayah's main theme here is *personal independence.* Our mishnah addresses three areas in which we must preserve our ability to follow our own principles. We are taught first of all to *love work,* for this leads one to economic independence. Secondly, we must *despise positions of power*, for leadership is enslavement. A person in power will do things to protect his own power and prestige thinking that he *must* do them. Such activities are frequently contrary to his own views and inclinations, and he would never do them were he free from political constraints. Finally, the mishnah cautions one to avoid the company of powerful friends, for they will often pressure one to conform to their own wishes and views. To avoid alienating them, one may be forced to comply. Only one who is content to live a private life, to remain in a humble position, and to support himself by dint of his own labors can be truly free (*R' S. R. Hirsch*).

שְׁמַעְיָה אוֹמֵר: אֱהַב אֶת הַמְּלָאכָה — *Shemayah says: Love work.* Even an independently wealthy person

---

◆§ **The greatest trial of all.** *Sfas Emes* views this injunction as an allegory for the great trial of life. Man must consider his actions carefully, sitting in judgment on any course of action before proceeding. The Evil and Good Inclinations are the witnesses, each testifying for the sake of its vested interest. Man must thoroughly and extensively interrogate each of these "witnesses" by examining his own motives, in order to ascertain which of the proposed paths is that of truth, and which is the pandering of falsehood.

[יא] **אַבְטַלְיוֹן** אוֹמֵר: חֲכָמִים, הִזָּהֲרוּ בְדִבְרֵיכֶם, שֶׁמָּא

should engage in some type of work; extended idleness can lead to mental atrophy [*Kesubos* 59b] (*Rav*). Thus an occupation has a benefit beyond that of producing income: It keeps one occupied and therefore productive, and prevents mental deterioration (*Tosafos Yom Tov*). However, not all occupations are equally desirable from a Torah viewpoint. The mishnah at the end of *Kiddushin* sets down guidelines:

"R' Meir says: One should always teach his son a clean and easy trade" [i.e., "clean" in that it does not lend itself to dishonesty, and "easy," in that it does not require excessive involvement, so that the person will not be prevented from studying Torah (*Maharsha* ad loc.)]. R' Meir continues: "And he should pray to Him to Whom all wealth and possessions belong, because there is no trade that does not include both want and wealth" [in every trade there are wealthy men and poor men; thus, no matter what his trade, he must rely on God].

A further guideline regarding work is that one should engage in any type of occupation, even one "below his dignity," rather than accept charity (*Rashi;* see *R' Yonah*).

וְשְׂנָא אֶת הָרַבָּנוּת — *despise positions of power.* One should try not to hold positions of command and control, for they shorten a man's life (*Rashi*). Seats of authority are a precarious perch. Jealousy abounds in any political arena, people seek to undermine one's influence, and one constantly feels forced to react in a spiritually inappropriate fashion in order to protect his power. The outcome is that power corrupts (*Rambam*).

Midrash Shmuel places this mishnah in the context of the previous ones. Just as Shemayah's teachers Shimon ben Shatach and Yehudah ben Tabbai addressed their dicta to judges, so does he. *"Love the work* of the rabbinate, i.e., cherish the rabbinic duties that require you to study day and night in order to arrive at correct decisions, and to maintain law and order by judging justly. But hate the 'rabbanus' part — despise the pomp and power that accompanies the office. Do not abuse the power inherent in the position; treat your flock instead with love and tenderness." Rabban Gamliel captured the message of this mishnah when he described the rabbinate in these words (*Horayos* 10a): "Not power do I grant you, but servitude" (*Tiferes Yisrael*).

וְאַל תִּתְוַדַּע לָרָשׁוּת — *and do not become overly familiar with the government.* Government authorities show favor to people solely for their own purposes. An intimate relationship with them is dangerous, since the moment they no longer stand to gain anything from the association, the relationship will be summarily terminated (*Rashi;* see below 2:3). In addition, maintaining this relationship demands an overwhelming degree of servitude and allegiance. One's moral and spiritual principles tend to disintegrate as the drive to maintain the favor of the authorities becomes his most overriding concern (*Rambam*).

If one actually joins the hierarchy of the government, the difficulties increase. One cannot serve two masters at once; the yoke of government places a terrible strain on one's ability to bear the yoke of Heaven. Sooner or later, officials in the upper echelons will make demands which a servant of God cannot honor, thus bringing the relationship to a sudden end (*Rambam* and *R' Yonah*).

Rambam writes in a letter to his student, R' Yosef Ibn Aknin: "Most who follow our religion lose their

---

⧉§ **Death from dignity.** R' Yisrael Salanter used to say that no one dies of hunger; anyone can find some type of occupation by which to support himself and his family. People perish instead due to prestige. They say: "This occupation is not prestigious enough for me; this one does not befit a person of my station." By contrast, the Talmud suggests: Skin carcasses in the marketplace and support yourself with the pay, and do not say, "I am a *Kohen*" or "I am a great man [and therefore I cannot do this lowly work]" (*Pesachim* 113a). Love work, teaches Shemayah — any type of work.

of power; and do not become overly familiar with the government.

11. Avtalyon says: Scholars, be cautious with your words, for

---

fear of Heaven upon attaining government office" (*Letters*, p. 32).

R' *Avraham Prizul* explains the word תִּתְוַדַּע in its

most literal sense: Do not *become known* to the great authorities. One should keep a low profile and not attempt to become involved with them.

Mishnah 11

אַבְטַלְיוֹן אוֹמֵר: חֲכָמִים, הִזָּהֲרוּ בְדִבְרֵיכֶם — *Avtalyon says: Scholars, be cautious with your words.* The mishnah speaks allegorically of the dangerous results of unclear teachings that lend themselves to misinterpretation. One should take utmost care not to express himself in a way that can be misunderstood by listeners who are unaccustomed to his mode of expression (*Rashi*). *Rambam* and *R' Yonah* view this mishnah as a reaction to the incident of Zaddok and Boethus (see comm. to mishnah 3). In that instance, the teaching that one should serve God without expectation of a reward was misinterpreted to mean that there is no reward or punishment for one's deeds, and as a result, great sections of Jewry cut themselves off from the Torah nation. Scholars, therefore, must be careful not to make statements of theological or philosophical import which are either unclear, bear dual interpretation, or may lead to a distortion in basic beliefs and principles of faith.

The words of a rabbinic scholar are potent. Disciples live by them, listeners follow them, and others

---

◆§ **A rabbi's guilt.** Among the most difficult positions in which a person can find himself is a rabbinical position. A rabbi bears responsibility for the spiritual welfare of his congregants; he must therefore rebuke them at times, difficult as that may be. Should he fail to do so, he is remiss in his duties and bears responsibility for their shortcomings.

The Chofetz Chaim told the story of a Jew who was convicted of tax evasion and was sentenced to fifteen years of hard labor in the Siberian tundra. As the police were escorting him through the town, he requested an audience with the *rav* and was given one. The rabbi asked the prisoner, "Why did you ask to see me. How can I help you?" In a broken voice the prisoner replied, "I'm going to Siberia for fifteen years, and it is your fault, *Rebbe*. You certainly knew what I was doing; why didn't you say anything? You should have made it clear to me that flouting civil law is forbidden by the Torah (see *Gittin* 10b). Why didn't you warn me what a terrible price I would have to pay for my misdeeds? As rabbi of our town, this was your job. Now I will have to toil like a slave — because of you!"

Said the Chofetz Chaim: This man knew the severity of his crimes and the harshness with which the government might treat him, yet he was sure that the *rav* bore responsibility for his fate because he had not reproved him. Certainly, when some of the *rav's* congregants are judged in the World to Come and are sentenced to fates worse than fifteen years in Siberia, the finger of liability will point to the *rav* if he was remiss in his duty to guide them on the path of virtue.

The Chazon Ish made only one stipulation with his wife before entering into marriage: that he not be pressured to assume an official position. Although he was not a rabbi, *rosh yeshivah,* or rabbinic judge, he was considered the preeminent Torah leader of his generation. In their early years, they supported themselves from the earnings of her store, and in their later years from the sale of his *sefarim*. They thus embodied the teaching of our mishnah: *Love work and despise positions of power.*

The Chofetz Chaim once advised one of his students to assume a rabbinic position. The student demurred, explaining that he feared the responsibility of ruling on questions of halachah. The Chofetz Chaim insisted: "Who should assume the position, someone who is *not* afraid of the responsibility?" Similarly, one who despises holding positions of power is by definition most suited to such positions, for it is he who will discharge his duties with the utmost caution. Thus the mishnah teaches: Despise positions of power — yet occupy them for the sake of Heaven.

תָּחוּבוּ חוֹבַת גָּלוּת וְתִגְלוּ לִמְקוֹם מַיִם הָרָעִים, וְיִשְׁתּוּ הַתַּלְמִידִים הַבָּאִים אַחֲרֵיכֶם וְיָמוּתוּ, וְנִמְצָא שֵׁם שָׁמַיִם מִתְחַלֵּל.

are influenced by them. An ambiguous statement may lead many astray if it is open to a heretical interpretation; an audience beyond the scholar's imagination may see him as the source of a doctrine he never espoused or even contemplated. Attackers of Torah tradition may claim him as one of their own, all because the scholar failed to exercise caution and did not articulate his ideas properly (*Rambam, R' Yonah, R' Moshe Almosnino*).

שֶׁמָּא תָחוּבוּ חוֹבַת גָּלוּת וְתִגְלוּ לִמְקוֹם מַיִם הָרָעִים — *for you may incur the penalty of exile and be banished to a place of evil waters [heresy].* The Torah prescribes exile as the punishment for inadvertently causing a death (see *Numbers* 35:9-34; *Deuteronomy* 19:1-10). Thus, one who kills inadvertently in a spiritual sense will also have to suffer exile.

"Evil waters" is a euphemism for heresy (*Rambam, R' Yonah*). The mishnah implies that you may be exiled to a place inhabited by heretics, who will employ the corrupted meaning of your statements as support for their own heretical ideas.

HaChassid Yaavetz views this warning as addressed to the issue of engaging in the study of philosophy and other areas of knowledge that may lead to heresy *if not studied with due caution.* Scholars are enjoined not to make statements that would give their students justification for pursuing these areas of knowledge. Such studies often are not survival tools in the exile, but rather means for the spiritual self-destruction of those who pursue them.

וְיִשְׁתּוּ הַתַּלְמִידִים הַבָּאִים אַחֲרֵיכֶם וְיָמוּתוּ — *The disciples who follow you there may drink [of them] and die.* The tragedy, the mishnah continues, is not confined to the non-believers. The evil waters may reach students of your words, both those whom you have met, and those whom you have not; either because you will already have returned from exile or because they will learn of your teachings after your death (*Meiri*). In either case, you will not have the opportunity to correct the heretics' false interpretations, and your ambiguous statement will remain unclarified. Unwary students will note how the heretical readings dovetail with your words and will conclude that such was indeed your intent; and they will transmit this erroneous reading to others. Thus, a grave error will be perpetuated, surviving the imprecise scholar and continuing to wreak ideological havoc after his death. Having imbibed the evil wa-

⌐§ **The price of silence.** Scholars are not permitted even to give the appearance of condoning heretical views. One tragic verification of this principle was the rise of the false messiah Shabtai Zvi which was accompanied by a mass movement of repentance. A few rabbis who had misgivings about Shabtai Zvi withheld them from the public so as not to rein in this welcome rededication to Torah and *mitzvos.* Their silence, however, was taken as an implicit acceptance of his messianic status. When Shabtai Zvi ultimately converted to Islam, he disillusioned thousands of Jews and sent shock waves through future generations. Rabbis who had not voiced their disapproval regretted their silence for the rest of their lives (see B. S. Hamberger, *Meshichei HaSheker*).

⌐§ **Toxic water.** Water is a metaphor for Torah and its pure and clear ideas (see *Taanis* 7a). Hence, heresy, the antithesis of Torah, is referred to as "evil waters." Although both types of "water" share a similar outward appearance, in the sense that they may be dealing with the same issues, one is the elixir of life and the other is a bitter toxin.

⌐§ **Simple faith.** Yaavetz lived in pre-expulsion Spain, where many Jews viewed expertise in secular philosophy as the key to prestige, success, and entree into the halls of government. In his analysis of the mass conversions to Christianity that took place during the Inquisition, further ravaging Spanish Jewry, he contended that the catastrophically high rate of conversions was rooted in the public adulation of philosophy. Had the faith of these "sophisticates" been simple yet genuine, the tragedy might not have been so sweeping.

you may incur the penalty of exile and be banished to a place of evil waters [heresy]. The disciples who follow you there may drink and die, and consequently the Name of Heaven may be desecrated.

ters of heresy, students will then suffer a spiritual death, and their subsequent sins may earn them a physical death as well (*Midrash Shmuel, Rav*).

וְנִמְצָא שֵׁם שָׁמַיִם מִתְחַלֵּל — *and consequently the Name of Heaven may be desecrated.* People will say, "See what happened to these people? They were true Torah students, yet they met an untimely death. Their Torah learning did not protect them, in spite of the Scriptural assurance that Torah is a tree of life" [see *Proverbs* 3:18]. When people who look up to Torah students witness their tribulations and thus lose interest in pursuing a Torah life-style, it is a desecration of God's Name (*Rashi*). The heresy, therefore, that is spawned in the long run by a lack of clarity on the part of the Torah scholar will endure, causing a desecration of the Name of God (*Rambam*).

What exactly is meant by desecration of God's Name? If someone whom other Jews look up to behaves in a way that is beneath him and causes others to lose respect for Torah and *mitzvos*, this is desecration. When people see such a person act dishonestly, speak hastily, or react intolerantly, their definition of Judaism will be drastically diminished. This is the gravest of sins. See *Yoma* 86a.

We have explained the mishnah until this point in line with the view of *Ramban* and *R' Yonah* that Avtalyon's concern was to prevent heresy. Other commentators take different approaches:

☐ Scholars, be careful with your halachic pronouncements! Perhaps they will fall into the hands of unscrupulous students, who will teach others to permit that which is prohibited. For these reasons and others, a rabbi should exercise extreme care in rendering halachic decisions (*Rashi*).

☐ Scholars, be cautions with your [choice of] words. Use precise language; phrase your teachings so that no double meanings are possible (*R' Yosef Ibn Shoshan*).

☐ Educators, beware not to say anything unless you practice what you preach. No teaching is as persuasive as personal example, and few teachings are as harmful as hypocritical ones (*Midrash Shmuel*).

⏤§ **Broad foresight.** In 1933 the Nazi-controlled Reichstag legislated that livestock could not be slaughtered without first being stunned. The ostensible aim of the law was to afford the animals a more humane death; the real aim was to prohibit *shechitah*. The Nazis knew that religious Jews would find stunning unacceptable and would forgo meat rather than comply with the law. Rabbi Yechiel Yaakov Weinberg, head of the *Beis Midrash L'Rabbanim* in Berlin, investigated the issue and wrote a detailed responsum, which concluded that, in this difficult situation, the meat of the stunned animal may be eaten if it is otherwise properly slaughtered. Rabbi Weinberg limited this leniency to children and elderly people who needed the extra nourishment that meat provides.

Before promulgating his ruling, Rabbi Weinberg sent it for approval to Rabbi Chaim Ozer Grodzensky, the leading Torah luminary of that time. R' Chaim Ozer rejected the decision, explaining that the ruling might be halachically correct, but it could have dangerous and unintended consequences. If the stunning of animals was permitted — even though it was limited to an emergency situation — other governments would feel free to enact such laws as well. As a result of this leniency, all of European Jewry might suffer!

A man of great foresight himself, Rabbi Weinberg immediately agreed and did not publish his ruling until after the war.

⏤§ **What I say and what I do.** Teachers and parents are enjoined to speak and act with full recognition that they are role models, and as such must inculcate values and morals that remain deeply rooted and unshakeable. Once children leave home, the mishnah refers to them figuratively as "in exile," where they are subject to the prevailing fads and may drink of the "evil waters" of society at large. We must provide an antidote to those insidious life-styles so that the Name of Heaven not be desecrated. But this demands behavior on the part of adults that is consistent with what they they are trying to promulgate. Students are too perceptive and skeptical to be deceived for long.

הִלֵּל [יב] וְשַׁמַּאי קִבְּלוּ מֵהֶם. הִלֵּל אוֹמֵר: הֱוֵי מִתַּלְמִידָיו שֶׁל אַהֲרֹן, אוֹהֵב שָׁלוֹם וְרוֹדֵף שָׁלוֹם, אוֹהֵב אֶת הַבְּרִיּוֹת וּמְקָרְבָן לַתּוֹרָה.

Mishnah 12

הִלֵּל וְשַׁמַּאי קִבְּלוּ מֵהֶם — *Hillel and Shammai received the tradition from them*, i.e., Shemayah and Avtalyon. Hillel and Shammai served as *Nasi* and *Av Beis Din* during the reign of King Herod, approximately one hundred years before the destruction of the Second Temple. Before Hillel, the *Bnei Beseira*, or Sons of Beseira, jointly held the position of *Nasi*, but they abdicated in his favor because of his superior knowledge (see *Pesachim* 66a). Hillel was famed for his humility (see commentary to mishnah 13) and was one of the seminal figures in the transmission of the *mesorah*-tradition (see *Succah* 20a). Before Shammai, the *Av Beis Din* was Menachem, another student of Shemayah and Avtalyon. When Menachem assumed a government position, Shammai took his place (*Chagigah* 5:2).

הִלֵּל אוֹמֵר: הֱוֵי מִתַּלְמִידָיו שֶׁל אַהֲרֹן — *Hillel says: Be*

among the disciples of Aaron. Alshich notes that the mishnah does not instruct us to be equal to Aaron; that would be impossible. Rather, we are charged to be one of his students, following in his ways to the best of our abilities.

אוֹהֵב שָׁלוֹם וְרוֹדֵף שָׁלוֹם — *loving peace and pursuing peace.* In *Malachi* 2:6, God recounts Aaron's superb qualities: *The law of truth was in his mouth, and injustice was not found on his lips; he walked with Me in peace and uprightness, and turned many away from sin.*

When Aaron saw two people at odds with each other, he would approach each one separately, without the other one's knowledge, and say, "Why are you fighting with your friend? He begged me to approach you and arrange a reconciliation." With this tactic, Aaron was able to bring about peace

⊷ **Were you really too poor?** Hillel was a descendant of King David on his mother's side. Originally from Babylonia, he went up to *Eretz Yisrael* to study under Shemayah and Avtalyon, in conditions of extreme poverty. Every day, Hillel hired himself out as a laborer for half a *dinar,* a very small sum. Half of this wage would go to the watchman of the study hall as an entrance fee, and the rest for the support of his family.

One winter Friday, he was unable to find work. Since the watchman would not admit him without the fee, Hillel climbed up on the roof and sat by the skylight in order to hear "the words of the living God." It began to snow, but he remained there. On Shabbos morning in the *beis midrash,* Shemayah commented to Avtalyon, "Every day the *beis midrash* is so bright, yet today it seems dim; could it be an overcast day?" They peered upwards and saw the form of a man over the skylight. They went up on the roof and found Hillel covered with snow. Shemayah and Avtalyon brought him down from the roof, washed him, and placed him by the fire in order to revive him. After that they ordered that he be allowed in without a fee.

The Talmud states: When a person comes before the Heavenly Court for judgment, he will be asked, "Why didn't you engage in the study of the Torah?" If the person is poor and he tries to excuse himself by saying he was busy earning a livelihood, the Heavenly Court will respond, "Were you poorer than Hillel?" (*Yoma* 35b).

⊷ **Namesakes.** Despite his Divinely anointed status and his eminence that was equal to that of Moses, Aaron did not hesitate to degrade himself in order to bring peace among Jews. In gratitude, couples whose marriages he had strengthened would often name their next son after him. At Aaron's funeral, there were eighty thousand other "Aarons" that walked behind his bier (*Kallah Rabbasi* 3).

This readiness to sacrifice personal prestige for the advancement of good was one of Aaron's greatest qualities. As Scripture relates, Aaron actually rejoiced at the preeminence granted his younger brother Moses (see *Exodus* 4:14). It was due to his ability to transcend his personal concerns that he was privileged to wear the *Choshen* (breastplate), on which were engraved the names of all the tribes of Israel. Thus the *Choshen* symbolized Jewish unity, which was maintained in great measure through Aaron's efforts.

12. Hillel and Shammai received the tradition from them. Hillel says: Be among the disciples of Aaron, loving peace and pursuing peace, loving people and bringing them closer to the Torah.

---

between the two people. Similarly, if a man and his wife were experiencing marital strife, Aaron would even allow himself to be degraded in order to restore harmony between them. If a man in a moment of anger told his wife, "I forbid you from deriving any pleasure from me until you spit in the eye of the *Kohen Gadol* (High Priest)," Aaron would approach the woman and say that he was suffering from an eye ailment. He asked her to spit in his eye, as if her saliva had some medicinal value. Thus he was able to reinvigorate the couple's faltering relationship.

In this connection, R' Shimon ben Elazar explained the verse *Turn from evil and do good; seek peace and pursue it (Psalms* 34:16). If a person keeps to himself, he is not *pursuing* peace; rather, he should go out and actively look for ways to make peace wherever he can (*Avos d'Rabbi Nosson* 12:6). Aaron not only loved peace, he incessantly and actively pursued it, and this earned him the affection of all sectors of the Jewish people. Regarding the mourning period for Moses, Scripture teaches that all the *men* mourned; Aaron, on the other hand, was mourned by all of Israel — both men and women — for his peace-making efforts (*Rashi; R' Yonah*).

Shmuel notes that the mishnah does not directly instruct one to be a "lover" of peace, because the definition of the word is so elusive; even the most contentious person will rationalize that *he* is the lover of peace and his opponents are its enemies. Therefore, the mishnah provides us with an objective standard: We should be among the disciples of Aaron and should strive to become the type of peace-lover that he was, by actively working to promote it.

Maharal comments that peace is achieved when the various segments of a society or group complement each other and form a harmonious whole, but this type of harmony is difficult to achieve since our world is inherently one of disparity. Contentiousness is so natural in this world that at the very beginning of history, strife erupted between Cain and Abel. Therefore, one must actively *pursue* peace, as one pursues a rare commodity.

אוֹהֵב אֶת הַבְּרִיּוֹת וּמְקָרְבָן לַתּוֹרָה — *loving people and bringing them closer to Torah.* Aaron brought people closer to Torah by showing them his love. If he learned of someone living sinfully, Aaron would befriend him. Overwhelmed by this display of affection, the sinner would feel ashamed and say to himself, "If the saintly Aaron were to know of my true character, he would not even look at me, and certainly not speak with me. If Aaron thinks so highly of me, let me try to make his illusion a reality." The wrongdoer would mend his ways and thus would retreat from sin (see *Malachi* 2:6). In this fashion, Aaron expressed his sincere love for all people — even sinners — and brought them closer to Torah (*Rambam, Rav,* and *R' Yonah*).

In our relationship to God, we resemble the person who was brought closer to Torah by Aaron. God constantly befriends us, showers us with His beneficence, and shows us kindness at every stage of our lives (see *Genesis* 48:15 and *Ramban* ad loc.). How

---

◁§ Aaron realized the great psychological truth that man is uncomfortable living a lie. Through his love and kindness he forced the sinner to view himself in a positive light, to be torn by feelings of internal inconsistency and therefore work to bring his actions into line with his aspirations. R' Avraham Danzig expressed this concept in *Tefillas Zakkah*, which is recited by many just before Yom Kippur: *"We are amazed at ourselves — how could this abomination have been committed?"*

In approaching sinners, Aaron followed in the ways of the Creator. Repentance in this world is achievable because God imbued man with a force for good that is impervious to the seemingly overwhelming forces of evil. God is supremely confident that man's essence is good and true, and that this essence can ultimately triumph. He therefore continually bestows kindness on us and delays the expression of His anger, waiting for us to repent and thus validate His confidence in us.

[יג] **הוּא** הָיָה אוֹמֵר: נְגִיד שְׁמָא אֲבַד שְׁמֵהּ, וּדְלָא
מוֹסִיף יָסֵף, וּדְלָא יַלִיף קְטָלָא חַיָּב,
וּדְאִשְׁתַּמֵּשׁ בְּתָגָא חֲלָף.

---

is it that we are not embarrassed to disappoint Him? How can we reject His love and friendship? By acting on this healthy sense of embarrassment and restructuring our lives, we can truly be students of Aaron (*Sfas Emes*).

The word בְּרִיּוֹת, *people*, literally means "creatures." *Midrash Shmuel* explains that we must love people simply because they were created by God. Aaron did not restrict his outpouring of love to the upper classes; his kindness shone at all levels. If someone did not know

how to pray or how to recite the *Shema*, Aaron would show him. If a person had difficulty entering the world of Torah study, Aaron would teach him (*Tanna d'Vei Eliyahu Rabbah* 13). A similar injunction is given in *Isaiah*: *When you see the naked, cover him* (*Isaiah* 58:7). This means that if you see a person bare of Torah knowledge or practice, bring him into your home and teach him. Learn with him a verse or a Torah law every day, and encourage him to perform *mitzvos* (*Tanna d'Vei Eliyah Rabbah* 27); for no one is more naked than one who lacks the royal cloak of Torah and *mitzvos* (*Chofetz Chaim*).

Mishnah 13

הוּא הָיָה אוֹמֵר: נְגִיד שְׁמָא אֲבַד שְׁמֵהּ — *He used to say: He who seeks renown loses his reputation.* One whose noble reputation is the result of self-promotion rather than the result of exemplary behavior will eventually lose that good name (*R' Yonah*). *Rashi* and *Rambam* go further, saying that even if one does not seek to promote himself, a rise to prominence may be a harbinger of disaster, for *pride precedes a fall* (*Proverbs* 16:18). The Sages cite Joseph as an example of how a position of power may "bury" one who occupies it (see *Pesachim* 87b and *Berachos* 55a), for Joseph, who ruled the Egyptian empire, died before his brothers even though he was younger than they.

Maharal explains this phenomenon as follows: God is the Source and Provider of life to all living things. One who is humble and views himself as dependent on the Source allows himself to receive life. People in powerful places, however, often perceive *themselves* to be the grand providers; thinking that others are dependent on them, while they are dependent on no one. Having emo-

tionally severed their connection to the true Source of life, they in fact tend to die early.

Midrash Shmuel and *Tiferes Yisrael* base their understanding of the mishnah on the principle *Anyone who chases after honor, the honor will flee him* (based on *Eruvin* 13a). Not only will the prestige he seeks flee him, but also any prestige he may already enjoy. He who seeks to expand the honors due him will lose even the good name he already has.

וּדְלָא מוֹסִיף יָסֵף — *he who does not increase [his Torah learning] decreases it.* This translation follows the first explanation in *Rav*. One either ascends or descends in Torah learning; if one does not continuously increase his knowledge, he will inevitably forget that which he previously learned. Included in this directive is the duty to master new areas of Torah (*Meiri*).

The Talmud teaches that when the nights grow longer after midsummer, one must utilize those

---

⌘ Oblivious to cheers and jeers. A person who cheapens himself for a bit of honor is foolish, for people will view him with scorn. By contrast, true Torah scholars are self-effacing people to whom the roar of the crowd means nothing. Rabbi Yisrael Zev Gustman was a member of the Vilna rabbinical court in his early twenties. He later survived the Nazi terror by joining partisan bands. He used to state with pride, "I no longer derive any enjoyment from honors, nor any sorrow from degradations. I saw R' Chaim Ozer Grodzensky stand up for me in Vilna, and I cannot imagine a greater honor; having suffered the humiliation of the Nazis ripping out my beard, no insult bothers me any more. I'm finished with both honors and indignities."

13. He used to say: He who seeks renown loses his reputation; he who does not increase [his Torah learning] decreases it; he who refuses to teach [Torah] deserves death; and he who exploits the crown [of Torah] shall fade away.

extra minutes and hours for learning (*Taanis 31a, Bava Basra 121b*); this is the sense of Hillel's teaching here (*Rashi*). Life is made for growth. One who feels no need to learn more is spiritually dead; the gift of life is wasted on him (*R' Yonah*).

וּדְלָא יַלִּיף קְטָלָא חַיָּב — *he who refuses to teach [Torah] deserves death.* The translation follows *Rashi*. *Tiferes Yisrael* explains that one who selfishly refuses to share his knowledge with others (either because he wishes them to remain more ignorant than he or because it is "beneath his dignity" to teach people inferior to him) is contemptible. By cutting off the supply of spiritual sustenance to others, he spiritually chokes them to death; he deserves to be paid back in kind.

Most commentators render *he who refused ever to learn deserves death.* One who had opportunities to learn and is capable of learning, yet refuses to do so, is worse than one who has learned, but does not try to increase his knowledge. Since he always refused to use his God-given faculties for even minimal spiritual pursuit and never plans to, in what way does he justify his existence as a human being? (*R' Yonah, Rav*).

Kesef Mishneh (*Hilchos Talmud Torah* 3:10) takes the opposite position: One who *has* learned, but does not want to increase his knowledge, is *worse* than one who never learned at all. The first person rejected the beauty of Torah after having tasted it; the second does not know what he is missing (see *Pesachim* 49b). This interpretation is implied by the text of the mishnah according to *Rashi*'s rendering: *he who does not add [to his Torah study] shall perish,* i.e., nothing can be done to save someone who, by refusing to add to his previously acquired knowledge, in effect rejects the Torah. But someone who never learned *deserves death,* meaning that while he may *deserve* death, other meritorious deeds may redeem him from that fate.

According to *Avos d'Rabbi Nosson* (12:13), this clause speaks of studying under Torah scholars in order to observe them and learn the practical day-to-day applications of halachah. If one's Torah knowledge remains abstract, it is deficient; only by observing the conduct of Torah scholars, whose every movement is governed by Torah, can one internalize the Torah.

וּדְאִשְׁתַּמֵּשׁ בְּתָגָא חֲלָף — *and he who exploits the crown [of Torah] shall fade away.* One who abuses his Torah knowledge by using it as a tool for personal gain shall pass away from this world (*R' Yonah, Rashi, et al.*). *HaChassid Yaavetz* renders חֲלָף in the sense of חֲלִיפִין, *barter.* He who derives personal gain from Torah study forfeits his reward in the Hereafter; by foolishly taking material reward in this world, he has bartered away the eternal for the temporal.

Alternatively, the term *crown* refers to Torah scholars, who are the crown of humanity. One may not make personal use of Torah scholars. A teacher may have his own students serve him, but not those of another teacher. Indeed, *Rambam* comments that the word תָּגָא is an acronym for תַּלְמִיד גַּבְרָא אַחֲרִינָא, *another person's student.* [See below, 4:7, for a further discussion of this clause.]

◄§ R' Aryeh Leib, son of the Chofetz Chaim, was a child genius. Once he had occasion to present a Talmudic lecture to a group of exceptional scholars, whom he dazzled by resolving a difficult problem raised in the *Shaagas Aryeh*. The listeners were impressed and expressed their admiration. The young Aryeh Leib was flattered and responded, "I hope one day to be able to resolve all of the *Shaagas Aryeh's* difficulties."

Uncharacteristically, the Chofetz Chaim stood up and publicly rebuked his son: "Such talk will never let you develop into a really great scholar." When relating this story, R' Aryeh Leib would say, "And sadly, my father's words came true."

הוּא הָיָה אוֹמֵר: אִם אֵין אֲנִי לִי, מִי לִי? וּכְשֶׁאֲנִי לְעַצְמִי, מָה אֲנִי? וְאִם לֹא עַכְשָׁו, אֵימָתַי?

Mishnah 14

הוּא הָיָה אוֹמֵר: אִם אֵין אֲנִי לִי, מִי לִי — *He used to say: If I am not for myself, who will be for me.* If I am not concerned for my own spiritual health, who will be concerned for it? No one can fulfill the commandments on my behalf (*Rav* and *Rashi*).

Rambam and *R' Yonah* interpret this as expressing the advantage of self-motivation over external inducement or coercion. If one is not motivated, no outsider can bring him to his maximum potential.

Many stimuli exist which prompt man to address his physical needs. Hunger, thirst, and desire are but a few of the ways in which the body demands attention. However, the needs of the soul may be forgotten unless one places them on his agenda and keeps them in constant focus (*Mili d'Avos*).

Tiferes Yisrael interprets: If I am not in command of myself and cannot control my delusions of self-importance, how can I expect to discipline myself or convince others to shed their own fantasies?

Man enjoys free will; his destiny is in his own hands. This cardinal principle of free will is the thought expressed here by Hillel. If one doesn't make his own life choices, no one else can make

them for him (*Meiri*). Our Sages taught: "Everything is in the hands of Heaven except the fear of Heaven" (*Berachos* 33b).

The *Chasam Sofer* taught that the mishnah refers to one's merits, relative to the merits of his ancestors. While there are great advantages to having illustrious forebears, this can sometimes work against someone. If one does not emulate his ancestors, he is deemed even more guilty than one who never had the opportunity to learn from such role models or to be genetically imbued with their positive characteristics. Thus, the mishnah reads: If I am not for myself (by conducting myself in accordance with the Torah), certainly the merits of my forebears will not protect me; if anything, they will serve as an indictment, since I do not follow in my ancestors' footsteps.

וּכְשֶׁאֲנִי לְעַצְמִי, מָה אֲנִי — *And if I am for myself, what am I.* The chasm between my accomplishments and my duties is so great that it makes my accomplishments seem insignificant (*Rav* and *Rashi*). R' Yonah understands this shortfall as a consequence of

---

◆§ **Who should know better?** The Dubno *Maggid* illustrated this with a parable. Two young men were arrested for theft, and brought before the same judge. One of them was from a family of rabbis and scholars, while the other was from a family of thieves. The judge imposed a harsher sentence on the son of rabbis and explained, "Your crime is worse, because you grew up surrounded by superb role models. For you to act as you did shows an unforgivable degree of moral corruption. The other thief did not know better. Perhaps a taste of a jail cell will teach him a lesson."

So too, a sinner cannot absolve himself because of his illustrious lineage; that very list of distinguished forebears is his condemnation.

◆§ **Facing reality.** Man often loses sight of his priorities. While we all recognize the importance of developing our relationship with God and plumbing the depths of His Torah, we feel the pressure of making a living and providing for our families, and we allow this to become our primary occupation. In truth, however, income is predetermined, and toil does not really affect our earning power (see *Niddah* 16b). Man's sustenance is decreed on Rosh Hashanah (*Beitzah* 16a), and nothing he does can change that.

On the other hand, success or failure at spiritual pursuits is completely dependent on man himself, and the degree of success is proportional to the effort expended. Hence, the mishnah instructs us to reorder our priorities. Regarding matters of the spirit, we should believe ourselves to be in full control of our efforts: *If I am not for myself, who will be for me*? However, when it comes to earning a livelihood, sustenance is completely in God's hands: *And if I am for myself* — thinking that my efforts earn my living — *what am I*? It is only the full and open Hand of God that provides for me (*Ruach Chaim*).

14. He used to say: If I am not for myself, who will be for me? And if I am for myself, what am I? And if not now, when?

man's intrinsic inclination for evil. He offers the following parable: A king told his sharecroppers that anything over thirty bushels was theirs to keep — but they were able to produce only five bushels. When the king questioned the small yield, they countered, "We worked diligently, but the field is inferior and can yield only five bushels." Similarly, man, inhibited spiritually by his *yetzer hara,* has a limited spiritual capability. Even with his free choice, his accomplishments will never attain the level his duties demand. [Nevertheless, God rewards man for his efforts in combating these built-in limitations.]

Meiri explains the clause differently: If I am concerned only with my physical needs and designs and am not involved in protecting my spiritual welfare, then of what significance is my life?

According to *Midrash Shmuel,* this is a call to outreach. While man must make his own spiritual journey, he may not ignore the spiritual welfare of his fellow Jews: If I am *only* for myself, what am I?

וְאִם לֹא עַכְשָׁו, אֵימָתַי — *And if not now, when.* The opportunity to provide for the soul is only in the present. This world is like Friday; the World to Come is like the Sabbath. Only if one prepares food on Friday will he have provisions for the Sabbath (*Avodah Zarah* 3a). Once one's time in this world is up, he can no longer do any *mitzvos. If not now,*

when? (*Rashi* and *Rav*). [See 4:21.]

One must work on the development of character while he is still young. As he grows older, he becomes set in his ways, and his negative traits become entrenched. At that stage of life it is much more difficult to redirect himself. Man is like a tree that grows crookedly. While the tree is young, one can redirect its path and make it grow straight, but once crookedness has set in, it is nearly impossible to rectify. Thus the question reads: *If not now,* i.e., if one does not repent while he is still young and flexible, *when* will he do so? (*R' Yonah* and *Rambam*).

Alternatively, *R' Yonah* explains: Do not put off your spiritual pursuits for tomorrow on the assumption that you will have time then. You may find yourself as busy tomorrow as today. Furthermore, the spiritual progress you could have experienced today is irretrievable.

Our Sages teach (*Bereishis Rabbah* 21:6) that the term וְעַתָּה, *and now* (*Deuteronomy* 10:12), is indicative of repentance. The Evil Inclination plays on a person's instinct to procrastinate, which prevents him from seizing the moment and putting his spiritual house in order. An inner voice says: "Tomorrow, when you are in the proper frame of mind, you will turn over a new leaf. Tomorrow you will be able to begin a new regimen of Torah study and *mitzvah* performance; today it is simply too much for you." In this fashion man pushes off his opportunities to

⤳ **The fleeting moment.** When visiting with the *Rebbe* of Lublin, R' Dov Ber of Radoshitz would waken those with whom he shared lodgings with the following cry: "Wake up, my brothers! A guest you've never seen has arrived. Once he leaves you will never see him again." "Who is the guest?" they asked. Said R' Dov Ber: "Today!"

Valuing time and making maximal use of it is the difference between ordinary and great people. Rabbi Reuven Zelig Bengis, *Rav* of Jerusalem, would review the Talmud regularly, completing it in its entirety every five months. Generally, he celebrated with cake and drinks. Once, however, he asked his family to prepare a more lavish meal for a *siyum.*

He explained, "This *siyum* is for a special *seder* (learning program) that I maintain during unscheduled waiting periods. People may tell me to be ready for a *bris* at eight a.m., but they don't come for me until eight-fifteen. Or they ask me to come to a wedding at six-thirty, and it does not start until seven. I have a special *seder* to review the Talmud during those waiting periods, and I've just completed *Shas.* That use of usually wasted time is worthy of a special celebration."

R' Bunam of P'shis'cha saw this same message in the verse *And from the tribe of Issachar came those who knew the wisdom of the times* (I *Chronicles* 12:33). By hearkening to the call of the mishnah and valuing the preciousness of time, the tribe of Issachar was able to achieve the wisdom of Torah.

a tomorrow that never comes.

The key to *teshuvah* (repentance) is וְעַתָּה, *and now*, the ability to seize the moment and to act immediately on one's good impulses.

This is what our mishnah comes to teach: *If not now, when?* If one listens to the soothing persuasion of his *yetzer hara*, putting off to tomorrow what should be done today, when will he finally repent? Maybe, God forbid, never (*Chofetz Chaim*).

Every person is a singular entity. In all of history and Creation there will never be two people exactly alike, with exactly the same mission. The mishnah is directed toward each of us in our unique roles: *If I am not for myself, who will be for me?* No one but I can achieve my purpose in life; no one but I can fulfill my particular part in the Divine plan.

On the other hand, man cannot be an island unto himself. A Jew's connection to his fellow Jews individually and to the nation at large is the catalyst through which he can actualize his own potential. *And if I am [only] for myself, what am I?* Alone, I will never become what I could be.

Time is not a continuum; every moment is special, every moment has a special task for which it is uniquely suited; every moment is a *now* that has never existed before and will never exist again, because tomorrow and the next day have their own opportunities and challenges. One must be sensitive to the call of the particular hour. *And if not now, when?* If I do not seize the opportunity now and imbue the moment with its particular meaning, the opportunity might not be there when I am ready (*Chiddushei HaRim*).

Mishnah 15

שַׁמַּאי אוֹמֵר: עֲשֵׂה תוֹרָתְךָ קֶבַע — *Shammai says: Make your Torah [study] a fixed practice.* Torah study must be a man's primary occupation. One's work schedule should accommodate his Torah-study periods and not vice versa (*Rav*). In addition, one should not relegate the Torah to certain hours of the day, leaving the rest of the day "Torah-free"; rather, Torah should be one's constant preoccupation, and all other business must be pursued on an ad hoc basis (*Rashi* and *Rambam*). In this respect, studying Torah is like breathing. Just as no one makes a schedule of times when he will breathe, so too no one should limit his Torah study to specific time slots: *For it is our life and the length of our days* (*Maariv* service).

However, if one is forced by circumstances to spend most of his time at work, then the opposite is true: He should set regular times for study. If he

---

◆§ **Five-step method.** *Tiferes Yisrael* offers five practical ideas to help one accord primacy to Torah study:

(1) One should not study while lying down nor in a very warm place, for this induces drowsiness and disturbs concentration. Nor should one eat or involve oneself in any other activity while studying.

(2) One should avoid intellectual distraction. By studying out loud, one can concentrate and implant the ideas firmly in one's mind.

(3) The term קֶבַע also can be taken to mean "at rest" and "relaxed." A comfortable and quiet learning atmosphere provides the proper state of mind for learning. One should study in a well-lit airy room, using books printed on fine paper [see introduction to *Responsa of R' Akiva Eiger*].

(4) The word קֶבַע also implies consistency and continuity; learning in spurts is unproductive. Likewise, too much variety of subject matter tends to leave one's mind unfocused. Even the use of different editions with varying page layouts can interfere with comprehension and retention. [According to the *Aruch HaShulchan*'s grandson, the author used to write in one draft. He could write fluidly from memory, but only when he was seated at his own table in his study. Anywhere else he suffered writer's block.] In general, through a fairly regimented schedule, one can maximize his time and energies.

(5) Another shading of the word קֶבַע connotes "firmness." One should make efforts to reach a firm and clear understanding of what he studies. Then, through careful review, he will remember what he learns. Young people especially should be encouraged to memorize their studies.

is careful to keep these set times conscientiously, and makes use of any other free time for Torah pursuits whenever he can, even his work time is considered as preparation for the *mitzvah* of Torah study. Therefore, it is of utmost importance that one be consistent in his Torah- study schedule (*Chofetz Chaim*).

Further, one's career should not be viewed as a life goal, but rather as a means to provide for his needs and thereby to free his time for Torah study and the pursuit of *mitzvos*. Torah must be one's permanent focus (*Meiri*).

By learning Torah, reviewing frequently, practicing its dictates, and teaching it to others, one's Torah will become firmly established (קֶבַע) in his mind, in his life-style, and more generally, in society (*Avos d'Rabbi Nosson*).

One of the first questions a person is asked in the Heavenly Court upon his demise is קָבַעְתָּ עִתִּים לַתּוֹרָה, "Did you make set times for Torah study?" (*Shabbos* 31a). It is difficult to stress strongly enough that one should strive to maintain a regular, non-negotiable schedule of Torah study.

The commentators find a spectrum of meanings

⋙ The Beis Ephraim (R' Ephraim Zalman Margulies) was a towering Torah scholar who also enjoyed fantastic wealth. His wife managed their widespread business dealings while her husband spent his days and nights learning. As a matter of policy, she would solicit his business advice only during his short meal breaks.

A diamond merchant once arrived in town and proposed that they invest in a business deal with the potential for huge profits. Since a large investment was needed, the Beis Ephraim's wife decided to ask her husband's opinion. She sent a messenger to the *beis midrash* to ask that her husband please come to their office immediately, since the diamond merchant had to leave town soon and could not wait.

R' Ephraim Zalman sent his apologies to his wife: "I cannot interrupt my regular learning schedule for this purpose."

Upon arriving home, he saw that his wife was crestfallen over the missed opportunity. The *Rav* told her: "Our Sages teach, 'Torah can only survive with one who is ready to kill himself for it' (*Berachos* 63b). This means that only if one is willing to view himself as 'dead' during the times set aside for Torah learning will his Torah survive and flourish. When you sent for me, I thought to myself, 'If I would be dead, Heaven forbid, would I be able to offer you my opinion about the proposed offer? Because I am living and able to study Torah, thank God, I will imagine myself dead and not interrupt my learning.' "

⋙ The answers to the questions "What do you do?" and "What do you do for a living?" should never be synonymous in one's mind. Rabbi Mordechai Gifter is fond of saying that a person does not *make* a living, he *takes* a living.

The Beis HaLevi once met a former student who had become a successful manufacturer. He asked the student, "How are you doing?" The man answered, "*Baruch Hashem, Rebbe,* I have a large factory and am doing quite well."

The Beis HaLevi asked again, "Yes, but how are *you* doing?" Again the student provided a glowing account of his commercial success. Finally, the *Rebbe* said, "Everything you've described are things that God does for you. I want to know about the areas of life that are in *your* hands. How is your spiritual agenda — your *davening,* your learning, your giving of *tzedakah*? How are *you* doing?"

⋙ **Since you knew . . .** The Talmud (*Shabbos* 31a) states that the first query posed to man by the Heavenly court is "Did you conduct your business faithfully?' and the second question is whether he had set times for study. Does this not imply that business comes first? In reality there is no contradiction. If one conducted his business with *faith in God*, realizing that He is the true Provider in Whose hands lies the success or failure of all endeavors, then one has no excuse for not maintaining a regular schedule of Torah study. However, if one lacks such faith in God, he always fears the consequences of any hour lost from the pursuit of business. Therefore, once a person answers in the affirmative about whether he conducted his business with faith, he may then be questioned about the consistency of his commitment to Torah study (*R' Shmuel Alter*).

in the word קֶבַע:

□ It means *steady* and *regular*, i.e., one should set minimum quotas for the amount of material to be covered each day (*Rashi*).

□ The instruction is addressed to halachic arbiters, who are told to be *consistent* in formulating decisions; they must not render a stringent decision for others and a lenient one for themselves, nor should they decide leniently for others and stringently for themselves. Rather, all their rulings should be consistent (*Avos d'Rabbi Nosson* 13:2, according to *Magen Avos*). [Of course, one is allowed to *act* in accordance with a stricter opinion, as long as the normative halachah is clear.]

□ Be sure that your Torah study does not remain academic; it must become a *firmly established* element of your personality. Don't simply pay lip service to what you study — act upon it (*Avodas Yisrael*).

□ The word קֶבַע also carries the connotation of theft (see *Malachi* 3:8). Hence, even if one is overwhelmed by responsibilities and commitments, he must "steal" time from his hectic schedule in order to study Torah (*Vilna Gaon* and *R' Nachman of Breslov*).

אָמַר מְעַט וַעֲשֵׂה הַרְבֵּה — *say little and do much.* When one makes a pledge to a friend or for charity, he should do more than he promises (*R' Yonah* and *Rashi*). This maxim follows the example of Abraham when he was visited by the three angels. He offered them only a morsel of bread (*Genesis* 18:5), yet *he took cream and milk and the calf which he had prepared, and placed these before [each of] them* (ibid. 7). The Sages teach that the righteous say little but do much, while the wicked make grandiose promis-

es, but don't do even a little. Ephron son of Zohar is the prototype of the wicked; he originally promised to give Abraham the Cave of Machpelah and the field around it as a gift, yet he later demanded an exorbitant payment (*Genesis* 23:10-16).

One should try not to verbalize his intentions to perform a *mitzvah* or a good deed, for once he enunciates his plans, they tend to go awry. If he says little, keeping his good plans to himself, he will succeed and do much (*Magen Avos*).

וֶהֱוֵי מְקַבֵּל אֶת כָּל הָאָדָם בְּסֵבֶר פָּנִים יָפוֹת — *and receive everyone with a cheerful face.* All one's dealings with people should be conducted in a relaxed and congenial manner; thereby one will find favor with others (*Rambam* and *R' Yonah*). The term סֵבֶר is related to סְבָרָא, which means "thought." Even if in one's heart he still bears negative feelings toward someone and is unable to truly receive him cheerfully, nonetheless he should behave in a fashion that allows his friend to think that he is happy to see him (*Meiri*).

R' Yonah adds: One who receives people cheerfully and with grace will enjoy warm camaraderie. By forgoing personal preferences for the sake of friendship, he will succeed in building enduring relationships. Conversely, one who shows others a scornful face will be hated, and other people will seek to harm him.

Midrash Shmuel applies this clause to the earlier discussions of Torah study. Even though one is preoccupied with Torah study, he should not allow himself to become anti-social or intellectually arrogant. Rather, he should receive all persons with a cheerful face.

Avos d'Rabbi Nosson (33:4) teaches: If one gives his friend all the gifts in the world with a sour face, he has given him nothing. But one who receives his

⋙ **Two-way street.** A young man once introduced himself to the Kotzker *Rebbe*, saying, "I've learned through Tractate *Kesubos* a few times." The *Rebbe* answered, "And what has *Kesubos* taught you?"

⋙ **Conservative evaluation.** When assessing your own spiritual progress, you should never feel complacent. Say to yourself that you've done little and have only scratched the surface of your obligations; push yourself to do much more (*R' Chaim of Volozhin*). Righteous people, even when they do much good, always feel that they haven't done enough. The wicked, on the other hand, are convinced — and are not even embarrassed to say — that they have done great things, when in reality they have done little. Our mishnah teaches us to follow the example of the righteous: Say you've done little, but in fact do much (*R' Yisrael of Vizhnitz*).

friend with a cheerful face, even if he has given him nothing else, has given him the greatest gift in the world.

Even though Shammai is reputed to have been impatient with people (see *Shabbos* 30-31), that was only when he sensed a breach in the honor that should be accorded to Torah and Torah scholars. His impatience was a posture assumed for the sake of Torah; the maxim *receive everyone with a cheerful face* is more representative of his intrinsic character (see *Mili d'Avos*).

Jeremiah (9:22) speaks of three types of individuals and their delusions of grandeur; our mishnah provides the antidote for each of these three delusions. *Let not the wise man laud himself for his wisdom*; rather, let him be consistent about his Torah study, always seeking to increase his knowledge. *Let not the strong man laud himself for his strength*; instead, let him exhibit strength of character by controlling his emotions and receiving all persons [even those for whom he really has no affinity] with a cheerful face. *Let not the rich man laud himself for his wealth*; rather, let him speak less about his riches and do much in the way of charity and kindness (*Rav*).

⋙**A greater debt.** Rabbi Yechiel Mordechai Gordon used to say that a sour face is comparable to a בּוֹר בִּרְשׁוּת הָרַבִּים, *an open pit in the public domain.* One's negative demeanor can be contagious, causing others to be infected with his germ of depression. The Talmud states figuratively: One who shows his friend the white of his teeth [by smiling to him] does more for him than if had offered him a drink of milk (*Kesubos* 111b). A smile is a signal to a person that he is cared for. Often, the emotional need to feel wanted is more powerful than physical hunger or thirst.

The importance of such gestures is underscored in the Talmud's account of Moses' ascent to Heaven to receive the Torah. Moses found God placing the crowns on the letters of the Torah, as it were. He did not greet God and was reprimanded, "Is it not customary in your city to offer greetings of peace?" (*Shabbos* 89a).

It is customarily that when a Jew says good morning, the response is *gut morgen, gut yohr* (a good morning and a good year); the response adds a blessing to the original greeting. Rabbi Shlomo Freifeld explained that this custom is based on *Sefer Chassidim,* which states that if one meets a poor, forlorn man in the street, takes him home, and feeds him a meal of beans, if the poor man ever finds his host in a similar predicament, he must repay the kindness with a *meat* meal. Why? Because the host not only gave him a meal; he made him feel welcome and cared about. The guest therefore owes him more than the simple return of the beans.

Likewise, a good-morning greeting sends a message in addition to the mere spoken pleasantry. It implies, "You are important to me and I am happy to see you." To repay this gift of recognition, Jews adopted the custom of responding not only good morning, but also good year, thus extending the original blessing and paying back more than was given.

In addition, by receiving people with a cheerful countenance, we emulate God's attributes. Just as He is described as giving life to all (וְאַתָּה מְחַיֶּה אֶת כֻּלָּם, *And you give them all life*; *Nehemiah* 9:6), so man must enliven all with whom he comes in contact.

⋙**Important guests.** Rabbi Eliyahu Eliezer Dessler, *mashgiach* in the Ponovezh Yeshivah, often found himself with no funds to give to people who knocked on his door for alms. Rather than turning someone away empty-handed, he would invite him in for a chat, asking about his family background and mentioning relatives of his whom he knew, or people from his town, all in an effort to make him feel comfortable. He received each person with a cheerful countenance — the greatest gift he could give.

The Rabbi of Bendin was a master host. When his brother-in-law, Rabbi Avraham Mordechai of Gur, mentioned our mishnah, *and receive everyone with a cheerful face,* he would add: "Like the Rabbi of Bendin."

A guest once entered the rabbi's study during a rabbinic conference. The rabbi excused himself, went into the kitchen, and said to his wife, "An important guest is here. Please bring him something to eat and drink, and see to his needs." After the conference adjourned, she asked her husband the identity of the guest. "I don't know — a guest," he innocently replied.

רַבָּן [טז] גַּמְלִיאֵל הָיָה אוֹמֵר: עֲשֵׂה לְךָ רַב, וְהִסְתַּלֵּק מִן הַסָּפֵק, וְאַל תַּרְבֶּה לְעַשֵּׂר אֲמָדוֹת.

Mishnah 16

רַבָּן גַּמְלִיאֵל הָיָה אוֹמֵר — *Rabban Gamliel used to say.* Known as Rabban Gamliel *HaZakken* (the Elder), in contradistinction to his grandson Rabban Gamliel of Yavneh, he was a grandson of Hillel and the first *Nasi,* after the *Zugos* (pairs), who served without an *Av Beis Din.* He functioned in the decades immediately preceding the destruction of the Second Temple and instituted many enactments, among which is the use of standard, inexpensive burial shrouds for all (see *Moed Kattan* 27b).

Noting the absence of the term *received the tradition from them,* which appears in earlier mishnayos (1:4-1:12), *Tosafos Yom Tov* quotes commentators who explain that this is due to the decrease in unanimity regarding the halachic tradition, which began after the time of Hillel and Shammai. Up until then, there had hardly ever been disputes regarding the halachah, but such disputes between the academies of Hillel and Shammai became common after the death of the two masters. Because of this lack of agreement, a uniform tradition did not exist, so it would not have been accurate to say that the tradition had been fully received by Rabban Gamliel.

עֲשֵׂה לְךָ רַב, וְהִסְתַּלֵּק מִן הַסָּפֵק — *Appoint a teacher for yourself, and remove yourself from uncertainty.* The advice to engage a teacher also appears in

mishnah 6, where it refers to a mentor for theoretical Torah study and textual acquisition; here it refers to a guide in practical matters of halachah (*Rav, Rambam*). *R' Yonah* comments that even a qualified halachic authority must be ready to consult others, even if they are less learned than he. This is because one often may have serious doubts in rendering a decision. For example, a question regarding the kosher status of a slaughtered animal cannot always be easily resolved: If one is lenient where stringency is called for, he will cause the questioner to eat non-kosher meat; and if he is stringent, he may cause the questioner to discard the meat and incur unnecessary financial loss, a serious transgression.

Midrash Shmuel, however, comments: Appoint a teacher who surpasses you intellectually and ethically, so that you will be comfortable in yielding to him.

Alternatively, *and remove yourself from uncertainty* is an independent clause unconnected to the instruction to appoint a teacher. In certain respects, situations of doubt are spiritually more dangerous than actual transgressions, because one who knows he has sinned will experience a redemptive sense of guilt that will encourage him to repent. Doubt about whether one sinned or not mitigates the pangs of conscience (see *Talmidei R' Yonah Berachos* 2b in *Rif*).

◈§ **Mentors for faith.** The Noda B'Yehudah asked R' Shmelke of Nikolsburg, a great Torah scholar and disciple of the Chassidic *Maggid* of Mezeritch, why he took precious time from his Torah studies in order to travel to visit his teacher. R' Shmelke answered with a novel interpretation of our mishnah: Appoint for yourself a teacher who will help you overcome your doubts in faith. A teacher is one who not only provides knowledge, but who strengthens one's faith in God and in his own potential.

This point is the key to understanding a comment of our Sages in regard to Jethro. After hearing of the great miracles at the splitting of the Sea of Reeds and of Amalek's attack against the Jewish nation, Jethro came to study under Moses. Why did he not come immediately after the Splitting of the Sea? From the two events he concluded that, like Amalek, one can hear about the greatest miracles and yet still remain a skeptic. One must have a teacher to dispel his doubts and to help him develop faith (*Knesses Yisrael*).

◈§ **Great enough to consult.** When Rav Ashi was presented a question concerning *treifos* (internal wounds that render an animal unkosher), he would gather all the butchers of the city for consultation "in order that we each carry only a chip from the beam" [by sharing responsibility for the decision] (*Horayos* 3b; see *Rashi Sanhedrin* 7b).

16. Rabban Gamliel used to say: Appoint a teacher for yourself, and remove yourself from uncertainty; and do not give excess tithes by estimating [instead of measuring].

וְאַל תַּרְבֶּה לְעַשֵּׂר אֲמָדוֹת — *and do not give excess tithes by estimating* [*instead of measuring*].

The commandment to tithe [*maaser*] requires that one set aside tenths of one's fruit and grain. Every year, one-tenth is for the Levite. In the first, second, fourth, and fifth years of the *Shemittah*-cycle a tenth is taken and eaten in Jerusalem; in the third and sixth years it is given to the poor. Before these tithes are separated, it forbidden to eat any part of the crop. *Yerushalmi* (*Demai* 5:2) teaches that if one gives less than ten percent for *maaser*, the remainder of the crop may not be eaten until he gives the full tenth. If he gives *more* than a tenth, his crop is permitted for consumption, but the tithe may not be eaten by the Levite, because only the exact ten percent is *maaser*; the additional amount is not considered *maaser*. Moreover, since it had been separated from the rest of the crop, it is not considered part of the remaining permitted ninety percent, and it is therefore prohibited.

The mishnah speaks of not giving *excess tithes* — even though it is also forbidden to give less than a tenth — lest one think erroneously that it is even better to give more than the required amount (*R' Yehudah ibn Shoshan*, quoted in *Midrash Shmuel*).

According to *Rav*, the mishnah speaks literally about tithing, but *Rashi* views it as a metaphor for someone who does not have a teacher. Such a person lives with doubts; he is like someone who tithes by estimate and is never really sure that he

has acted correctly. With the best of intentions, he is bound to make many mistakes.

R' Yonah interprets these words as an allegorical call to analyze carefully any proposed, logical solution to a question. Be sure that no legitimate counter-arguments to your proposal exist.

☐ **Why should it be forbidden to estimate tithes, provided one is sure to give more than a tenth?** *HaChassid Yaavetz* explains that habit is a powerful force in determining people's behavior. Once someone becomes accustomed to accommodating a *mitzvah* to his own convenience by giving more, it is a small step to go the opposite way at times and do less, when that is the more convenient course. The Torah wants people to know that God's requirements are immutable. A Jew must understand that all his actions must be regulated by the Torah and *Shulchan Aruch*.

Meiri understands the mishnah as referring simply to the disbursement of charity. One should give a tenth of one's income for charity; hence, the term *maaser*, which means literally "one tenth." In setting aside one's charity budget, one should not rely on estimates, lest there be an error and the needy people and institution not be shortchanged. On the other hand, unlike the tithes, it is permitted to contribute more than a tenth for charity.

◦§ **The right and wrong time for stringency.** Let one not think that he will be able to avoid doubt simply by adopting a more stringent course, because what may seem on the surface to be safe may result in unwitting leniency and, ultimately, transgression. One must therefore accept a teacher to be free of doubt; he should not think that he can proceed by "estimating" (*Ruach Chaim*).

◦§ **Too much leading to too little.** In the town of Kelm, home of the famous Talmud Torah, which was the seed bed of the Mussar movement, there was a small general store for the use of the yeshiva students. In order not to take anyone from his studies to tend the counter, the store operated on the honor system; customers took what they needed and left payment in a cash box. After a while, it was found that there were overpayments in the box. Hearing of this, the *Alter* (Elder), R' Simcha Zissel, ordered that the store be closed.

He explained. The reason there was too much money was probably because when the box did not have sufficient small change for customers, they would leave more money as a contribution. But by the same token, it was possible that people accustomed not to pay the exact amount might one day find themselves with too *little* money for a purchase, and they would feel entitled to *underpay*, because they had sometimes overpaid. This would be dishonest, and a situation that might encourage such a practice could not be continued.

[יז] **שִׁמְעוֹן** בְּנוֹ אוֹמֵר: כָּל יָמַי גָּדַלְתִּי בֵּין הַחֲכָמִים,
וְלֹא מָצָאתִי לַגּוּף טוֹב אֶלָּא שְׁתִיקָה. וְלֹא
הַמִּדְרָשׁ הוּא הָעִקָּר, אֶלָּא הַמַּעֲשֶׂה. וְכָל הַמַּרְבֶּה דְּבָרִים
מֵבִיא חֵטְא.

Mishnah 17

שִׁמְעוֹן בְּנוֹ אוֹמֵר — *Shimon his son says.* He was the son of Rabban Gamliel *HaZakken* (see previous mishnah), and was killed by the Romans during the period of the destruction of the Second Temple (*Tosafos Yom Tov*). Josephus writes of Shimon's great wisdom and practical sense. *Magen Avos* explains that he was not called Rabbi in this mishnah because he stated these axioms prior to assuming the post of *Nasi.*

כָּל יָמַי גָּדַלְתִּי בֵּין הַחֲכָמִים, וְלֹא מָצָאתִי לַגּוּף טוֹב אֶלָּא שְׁתִיקָה — *All my days I have been raised among the Sages, and I found nothing better for oneself than silence.* Shimon says: My life experience among wise men has taught me that one who remains silent at least *appears* to be intelligent; if he is quick to respond to people rather than silently hearing them out, he is bound to speak foolishly (*Rashi*).

Human existence consists of an ongoing debate between body and soul, with each seeking to wrest control from the other. Man is advised to try and silence the body — for its own good, as well as his spiritual benefit — allowing it minimal input in his life's decisions: *I have found nothing better for the body than silence* (*Sfas Emes*).

Although one is duty bound to provide for his and his family's physical needs, these matters should never become a major topic of conversation. There are things one must do, but he need not speak about them at length. There is nothing more offensive, for example, than the gusto with which otherwise civilized people converse about the merits of food and drink (*R' S. R. Hirsch*). Regarding matters of the soul, however, one should engage in constant discussion; it is only in regard to corporeal concerns that silence is golden (*Maharal*).

Be'er Avos adds: When in the company of scholars and sages, one is advised to keep silent and to try and absorb whatever they have to offer. Being in such company is an opportunity, and one is ill advised to waste it on listening to his own words.

Man is given a limited number of words in this world. When he uses up the quota, his life is over. Hence, nothing is as good for man's physical existence as silence (*Tiferes Tzvi*; see *Derech Pikudecha, Negative Commandments* 34).

Rav interprets these words as a call to restrain oneself from responding to insult. [*R' Avigdor Miller* adds that one who does not allow himself to be agitated by personal insults will not suffer ulcers or other such conditions that are aggravated by stress and tension.]

Rambam categorizes five types of speech:

(a) *Mitzvah* — Torah reading and study, and prayer. (b) *Forbidden* — false testimony, falsehood, tale-bearing, cursing, foul language, and *lashon hara* (gossip). (c) *Tasteless* — idle talk, general gossip and the like, or speaking disparagingly of positive ethical behavior. (d) *Worthwhile* — praising intelligent or virtuous character, degrading negative conduct or personality traits [of course, without referring to specific people]. (e) *Permissible* — business discussions, domestic issues (food, budget, etc.).

◆§ **Learn to listen.** *Mekor Baruch* tells of a conference at which one person dominated the discussion and did not allow anyone else to speak. One clever individual decided to silence this man. As soon as he quoted something he had heard from one of the greats of the past generation, the clever gentleman interrupted him, saying, "That is a lie." The speaker was shocked and demanded an explanation. The clever man replied: "It is impossible that you ever heard anything in your life; you never let anybody else talk." One must learn that there are times to be silent and listen.

17. Shimon his son says: All my days I have been raised among the Sages, and I found nothing better for oneself than silence; not study, but practice is the main thing; and one who talks excessively brings on sin.

Even in regard to the discussion of daily affairs, our mishnah teaches us to keep our speech to a minimum. [Forbidden and tasteless speech are obviously prohibited. On the other hand, it would be good if one could speak constantly of Torah worthwhile matters.]

"Reish Lakish said: Had I been at Mount Sinai, I would have requested two mouths" (one for Torah study and prayer, and one for more mundane matters). One should not waste the power of speech on insignificant matters. Man's faculties are like the vessels used in the Temple; they may not be misappropriated for any use other than the service of God (*R' Yonah*).

Tiferes Yisrael (rendering our text as *I found nothing good for the body [resulting] from silence*) interprets this as advice to a student: Do not refrain from questioning your teacher; only through inquiry will you clearly absorb his lessons (see *Bava Metzia* 84a). Specifically in the pursuit of knowledge, nothing good comes from silence. Furthermore, by enunciating aloud the words of Torah, one comes to understand them in a deeper sense (see *Vilna Gaon* to *Proverbs* 2:3) and retains them in his memory (see *Eruvin* 44a).

וְלֹא הַמִּדְרָשׁ הוּא הָעִקָּר, אֶלָּא הַמַּעֲשֶׂה — *not study, but practice is the main thing.* Even for Torah study, where verbalization is appropriate, one is not rewarded for theoretical intellectual pursuit. Torah must instead govern practical daily living — even its most minute, practical details (*Rav*).

[Torah is called תּוֹרַת חַיִּים, *a living Torah*, meaning that it must be translated into action. Since Torah is the blueprint of Creation (*Bereishis Rabbah* 1:2), it contains the key to understanding God's will, even in the most seemingly mundane arenas of our daily activity.]

One who performs *mitzvos* is greater than one who studies Torah but does not translate it into action (*Rashi*).

The wise man is not he who acquires only raw knowledge. A person becomes wise as a result of his actions. In the acquisition of wisdom, therefore, *not study, but practice is the main thing* (*Vilna Gaon*).

Preaching to others without practicing what you preach is wrong. One should make sure that his own behavior is consistent with what he expects of others (*R' Yonah*).

Midrash Shmuel explains this clause as a continuation of the previous clause, which recommends silence. Most virtues are well understood by all in their theoretical sense, but it is frequently difficult to put them into action. In the heat of the moment, for example, when one is insulted, it is difficult to bear the pain silently and not retort. The mishnah therefore teaches that it is not the theory — the mere study — but the practice that is the main thing. One must be able to draw upon his knowledge of correct conduct when the real-life situation demands a proper response, or when it demands silence.

וְכָל הַמַּרְבֶּה דְבָרִים מֵבִיא חֵטְא — *and one who talks excessively brings on sin.* This principle was demonstrated tragically on the very first day of mankind's existence. Eve extended the facts when she said that God had forbidden not only eating from the Tree of Knowledge, but even touching it. The snake then pushed her against the tree, thus proving her claim wrong. "Likewise," asserted the snake, "you

◆§ **Brilliant ignoramus.** Judaism is not a system of philosophy; it is a code of laws whose primary purpose is to regulate human conduct. The Midrash (*Bereishis Rabbah* 19:13) teaches that the main venue for God's presence is this world. God does not need angels; He seeks men whose every move is governed by Torah.

Rabbi Yisrael Salanter said: "One can possess broad Talmudic knowledge and be a fountain of deep penetrating analysis and yet he does not deserve to be considered a true *talmid chacham* (Torah scholar). If he has not allowed his Torah knowledge to refine his character and restructure his personality, he is an *am haaretz* (boorish ignoramus) who happens to know how to learn."

א/יח

[יח] **רַבָּן** שִׁמְעוֹן בֶּן גַּמְלִיאֵל אוֹמֵר: עַל שְׁלשָׁה דְבָרִים
הָעוֹלָם קַיָּם – עַל הַדִּין וְעַל הָאֱמֶת וְעַל

will not be punished for eating from it." Because of her excess words, she and her husband came to sin (*Rav*).

This principle is valid for halachic arbiters. Even though they are enjoined to make protective fences around the Torah, they should be careful to make clear to the masses what is the basic law and what is the protective measure. One may feel that once he has transgressed the protective measure, there is no need to refrain from transgressing the basic law, seeing them both as equal.

By speaking excessively and exaggerating the real severity of laws, one may come to sin.

Another interpretation is that one should not speak excessively and discuss halachic issues without adequate forethought. Decisions hastily expressed can lead to misunderstanding and ultimately to transgression (*R' Yonah*). *Meiri* explains the word חֵטְא, *mistake,* as in הֶחְטִיא אֶת הַמַּטָּרָה, *he missed the mark.* In this sense, excessive speaking leads to error.

Mishnah 18

רַבָּן שִׁמְעוֹן בֶּן גַּמְלִיאֵל אוֹמֵר — *Rabban Shimon ben Gamliel says.* Rabban Shimon ben Gamliel was the grandson of Shimon, author of mishnah 17, and the father of R' Yehudah *HaNasi,* redactor of the Mishnah. He served as *Nasi* during the Bar Kochba revolt and went into hiding at that time. The tumultuous nature of his times is reflected in his comment: "We understand the benefit of difficulties, yet were we to record them, we would not finish" (*Shabbos* 13b). His opinion is recorded more than a hundred times in the Mishnah, and he is quoted even more extensively in the *Baraisa* and *Tosefta.* His humility was exceptional — he said that Rabbi Shimon bar Yochai was like a lion, while he, Rabban Shimon, was like a jackal (*Bava Metzia* 84b-

85a) — yet in matters relating to the honor of Torah and the prestige of the position of *Nasi,* he took a very strong position, in order to defend the prestige of the office.

Meiri suggests that he is the Shimon of the previous mishnah. They view that mishnah as having been stated in his youth, while this mishnah was the product of his later years — hence, the title *Rabban. Magen Avos* questions this view, since the preface, "*All my days* I have been raised," is an inappropriate statement for a young man.

עַל שְׁלשָׁה דְבָרִים הָעוֹלָם קַיָּם — *The world endures on three things.* This mishnah seems to contradict the dictum of Shimon the Righteous in mishnah 2, who says that the world exists because of Torah, ser-

---

◆§ **Save which world?** A woman once complained to a *rosh yeshiva* who had advised her son to pursue a career in Jewish education rather than attend medical school. "How could you do this to my son?" the woman wanted to know. "Rabbi, what if he could have discovered the cure for cancer? Now you've prevented that! Do you want such a thing on your conscience?"

The *rosh yeshiva* answered with a story: Once a man from a *shtetl* sent his son to study at the University of Berlin. The people of the town were quite proud of him, since he was the first young man from their small *shtetl* to go off to the university. When the student returned home for vacation, his father was very anxious to find out about life in the big city. "Tell me about the Jewish community," he said.

"Father," the boy replied, "there are over 300,000 Jews in Berlin."

"So many Jews! What a *kehillah*! And tell me, how many non-Jews are there in Berlin?"

"Three million," answered the son.

"Three million? Why do they need so many *goyim*?"

The *rosh yeshiva* continued, "The Almighty also created non-Jews. Who says that the cure for cancer must be discovered by a Jew? Let that honor go to a gentile. Jews have problems that can be solved only by Jews. If your son has the talent to educate Jewish children, he should jump at the chance. Our people need him!"

18. Rabban Shimon ben Gamliel says: The world endures on three things — justice, truth, and peace, as it is

vice, and kindness. There is no contradiction. Mishnah 2 speaks of the virtues because of which God created the universe. He wanted a world where there would be people who are dedicated to Torah study, Divine service, and unselfish kindness to others. Indeed, even in the worst of times there have been such people even though they may have been few and unappreciated. As *Rambam* comments, all of Creation is worthwhile even if there is only one righteous person in the world. This is the teaching of Shimon *HaTzaddik* in mishnah 2, and it sets up a standard for people whose goal it is to live up to the Divine goal for Creation.

Our mishnah, on the other hand, speaks to the very practical question of how society can be maintained on an even keel, without descending into an animalistic jungle. To this Rabban Shimon ben Gamliel responds that the "social contract" cannot exist without justice, truth, and peace (*Meiri, Rav, Tos. Yom Tov*).

R' Yonah gives a slightly different view, distinguishing between a cause for Creation and what are the minimum conditions necessary for its continued existence. The world was created for the realization of the three goals enunciated by Shimon *HaTzaddik*; but it can continue to exist as long as there is a prevalence of justice, truth, and peace. *HaChassid Yaavetz* draws an analogy to a kettle of water: An intense degree of heat is necessary to bring it to boil, but a much smaller degree of heat is needed to simply maintain that boiling level.

Yalkut Yehudah views the triad of Shimon *HaTzaddik* as the positive input [עֲשֵׂה טוֹב, *do good*] that man must provide to justify Creation. Here Rabban Shimon ben Gamliel speaks of three things which, if absent (סוּר מֵרַע, *turn away from evil*], will cause the disintegration of the world and the fabric of society.

Alternatively, mishnah 2 defines the duties of Jews; the world at large is not obligated to obey the Torah, but

without justice, truth, and peace, even general society cannot endure.

Beis Avos finds the difference between the two triads implied in the different terms used by the respective Sages. In the days of Shimon *HaTzaddik,* the world *stood* (עוֹמֵד), much like a vigorous young person who stands straight and tall. So too, the Jewish people was invigorated by the presence of Torah, service, and kindness in those days. But by the time of Rabban Shimon ben Gamliel, the spiritual well-being of the nation had seriously deteriorated. Like a frail old person, the nation survived (קַיָּם) on its residue of justice, truth, and peace.

Knesses Yisrael views this triad as the underpinnings of the previous triad in mishnah 2. (1) Torah is based on truth; one must seek truth in his Torah study, since the two are synonymous. (2) Service of God is based on law and justice; it must be structured and remain within the parameters of Torah law. Innovations that are not sanctioned by halachah are illegitimate, even if they seem to enhance the honor of Heaven. (3) Peace, in its most pristine form, causes a harmonious blending of all elements of society. Hence, the pursuit of peace underlies the performance of acts of loving-kindness. (See also *Beis Yosef* to *Tur Choshen Mishpat* 10.)

עַל הַדִּין — *on justice.* Courts of law must function justly, exonerating the innocent and indicting the guilty (*Rav* and *R' Yonah*). According to *Rambam*, this is a call for countries to conduct their affairs with social justice. *Tiferes Yisrael,* on the other hand, interprets this as an interpersonal charge: One must take care not to do anything which is physically, financially, spiritually, or socially detrimental to friends.

וְעַל הָאֱמֶת — *on truth.* Truth among people is a key

◆§ **Beyond justice.** In spite of the necessity to conduct one's life with justice, one should not be a stickler regarding strict justice. The Talmud teaches that Jerusalem was destroyed because its inhabitants conducted their social interaction based on the strict letter of the law, rather than trying to help others even when the law did not require it. As an example, the Talmud says that one *should* return lost items, even in circumstances where the law would permit the finder to keep it (*Bava Metzia* 30b).

א/יח הַשָּׁלוֹם, שֶׁנֶּאֱמַר: „אֱמֶת וּמִשְׁפַּט שָׁלוֹם שִׁפְטוּ בְּשַׁעֲרֵיכֶם."

🦋 🦋 🦋

רַבִּי חֲנַנְיָא בֶּן עֲקַשְׁיָא אוֹמֵר: רָצָה הַקָּדוֹשׁ בָּרוּךְ הוּא

to survival (*Rav, Rashi*).

David, in listing the requirements for ethical conduct toward one's fellow man, speaks of a person who *speaks the truth from his heart* (וְדִבֶּר אֱמֶת בִּלְבָבוֹ; *Psalms* 15:2). The Talmud (*Makkos* 24a) points to Rav Safra as the epitome of this characteristic. *Shi'iltos d'Rav Achai Gaon* (36) explains: Rav Safra had an item for sale. While he was reciting the *Shema*, someone approached him and made an offer for the item, but R' Safra was unable to respond. The fellow understood the silence as a refusal and therefore raised his offer. When R' Safra completed his prayers, he turned to the purchaser and said, "Please take it at the first price you suggested, for in my heart, I acquiesced to your initial offer."

R' Yonah interprets "truth" as following the true path prescribed by the True God in His True Torah. Furthermore, one must emulate the attributes of God as described in the Torah.

Alternatively, one must be careful to speak the full truth, even regarding seemingly insignificant details. Lying is habit forming; once entrenched, it is almost impossible to eliminate from one's system. Almost unwittingly, one will continually slip into falsehood, even when he has nothing to gain from it.

Magen Avos notes that the very letters that spell אֱמֶת (truth) reflect its endurance, while those of שֶׁקֶר (false-

hood) reflect its instability. The letters of אֱמֶת are all flat bottomed, able to stand on their own. The word שֶׁקֶר is composed of letters which have only one leg (the *shin* has a pointy base in the script of the Torah scroll) which will inevitably topple. The Sages taught: שֶׁקֶר אֵין לוֹ רַגְלַיִם, *Falsehood has no feet* (*Tikunei Zohar* 425).

וְעַל הַשָּׁלוֹם — *and on peace*, i.e., both international and interpersonal peace (*Rav*). The attainment of peace encompasses all the good in the world; the benefit of peace is inestimable (*R' Yonah*). When one sees someone about to harm another, one must try to make peace. Alternatively, one should bestow kindness on friends by supplying monetary or physical help, or by offering good advice, thereby advancing the cause of love and peace in the world (*Tiferes Yisrael*).

The term שָׁלוֹם, *peace*, is related to שָׁלֵם, *complete*. Without peace each person is a separate, detached part of the human community, and as a result, he will suffer a lack of personal fulfillment. The need for a unified and harmonious whole exists in the macrocosmic world as well as in the microcosmic world of the human being. Man is composed of a confluence of urges, wants, needs, and ideas, many of which are at odds with each other. When peace reigns inside him, the various forces complement each other and bring him to a sense of completeness and fulfillment. Man can then achieve a peaceful

---

◆§ It is difficult to sustain any relationship which is not governed by absolute truth. Business partners, man and wife, children and parents cannot live together harmoniously and function effectively if truth is not the hallmark of their relationship. Almost every type of falsehood, whether it is a white lie, business lie, or a lie for social convenience, undermines the atmosphere of trust necessary for friendly contact between people. *Meiri* declares succinctly: The man of falsehood is as good as dead. Man's superiority over all creatures lies in his power of speech, and if he makes a mockery of his word, he is essentially dead.

◆§ **To mislead is to lie.** "One who misleads another into believing that he did him a favor or that he interceded on his behalf, when in fact he did not, is considered a deceiver of people. Our Sages taught: 'It is forbidden to delude others, even non-Jews' (*Chullin* 94a). The Sages considered this sin even more severe than robbery, for lips of deceit bear extreme guilt. We are obligated to be circumspect regarding truth, which is one of the foundations of the soul" (*Shaarei Teshuvah* 3:184).

◆§ **No peace.** Even though Hillel enjoined that we love and pursue peace (see mishnah 12), that peace will only be effective if it is accompanied by justice and truth. One who makes peace with corrupt people will tend to compromise inviolate principles. Therefore, we are taught first of justice and truth; if these can be maintained, then and only then must we seek peace (*Maharam Schick*).

said: *You shall adjudicate the verdict of truth and peace at your gates (Zechariah 8:16).*

❧ ❧ ❧

Rabbi Chanania ben Akashia says: The Holy One, Blessed is He,

relationship with God, his fellow man, and himself (*Maharal*).

שֶׁנֶּאֱמַר: ,,אֱמֶת וּמִשְׁפַּט שָׁלוֹם שִׁפְטוּ בְּשַׁעֲרֵיכֶם'' — *as it says: You shall adjudicate the verdict of truth and peace at your gates (Zechariah 8:16).* This instruction is once again directed toward judges. "At the gates of the city, where the court resides, a judge must adjudicate with complete truth. When the full truth cannot be ascertained, he should practice the art of compromise and issue a verdict which makes peace between the litigants" (*Radak* ad loc.).

Rashi interprets the verse as a promise that if the Jewish people appoints honest judges, it will be granted life and peaceful existence in its Land.

Our mishnah issues three warnings here, each addressed to a different party in the judicial process. *Justice* is demanded of the judges, who must adjudicate fairly and without bias; *truth* must be the guiding light of the witnesses, upon whom the veracity of the entire process depends; *peace* is the banner beneath which the litigants must rally. Once the verdict is issued, all animosity between them must melt under the healing warmth of peace. By joyfully accepting the decision of the court, they will restore harmony to their lives (*Beis Yosef* and *Midrash Shmuel*).

Afterword

This selection from Tractate *Makkos* is recited at the conclusion of the chapter of the week. If a quorum of ten males over *bar mitzvah* is present, the *Kaddish* of the Rabbis is recited.

רַבִּי חֲנַנְיָא בֶּן עֲקַשְׁיָא אוֹמֵר — *Rabbi Chanania ben Akashia says:* The following excerpt is from the last mishnah in Tractate *Makkos*. Rabbi Chanania ben Akashia, a fourth-generation *Tanna*, is not cited anywhere else in the entire Mishnah, and only once in *Tosefta*, regarding halachic matters (*Shekalim* 3:13).

Rashi teaches that since the Rabbis' *Kaddish* is recited only after the study of Aggadah, an Aggadic portion of the Talmud was chosen as a standard recitation after every public study session. *Mesoras HaShas* questions the need for this custom when studying *Avos*, since *Avos* itself is Aggadic material. Nonetheless, the universal custom of reciting this passage is maintained (see *Orach Chaim* 54:3, *Magen Avraham* §3 and *Mishnah Berurah* §9).

Sfas Emes considered this excerpt particularly appropriate for recitation after studying *Avos*,

---

❧ **When people are honest about truth.** At first blush, it seems strange that the mishnah should bracket truth and justice with peace; experience shows that the imposition of justice more often results in strife, and that people resort to lies in order to thwart the courts. When they lose, they may try to circumvent the verdict, and will nearly always hate the judges. This is the sad truth, but there are many people who rise above these base impulses, and when they do, justice is the prime vehicle toward peace.

Two business associates came to Rabbi Chaim Soloveichik for a *din Torah*. They had been close friends, but a bitter dispute was turning them into enemies, and they wanted the *rav* to set things right. They both produced all the necessary records; neither disputed the other's testimony, only his conclusions. R' Chaim handed down his judgment — and the losing party embraced and kissed the winner. Both thanked the *rav* profusely and handed him a bag of money in gratitude for settling the dispute.

Just then a poor man came in with a request for help. Without even opening the bag, R' Chaim, whose kindness was as legendary as his genius, handed it to the supplicant.

Such people prove how justice, truth, and peace come together to justify the continued existence of the world.

since its message is that Torah study and the performance of *mitzvos* are a Divinely conferred privilege. *Avos*, which is full of rebuke and criticism, might be perceived as an unbearable yoke; these words of R' Chanania ben Akashia remind us that the Torah's weighty demands are really for our own benefit.

רָצָה הַקָּדוֹשׁ בָּרוּךְ הוּא לְזַכּוֹת אֶת יִשְׂרָאֵל, לְפִיכָךְ הִרְבָּה לָהֶם תּוֹרָה וּמִצְוֹת — *The Holy One, Blessed is He, wished to confer merit upon Israel; therefore, He gave them Torah and mitzvos in abundance.*

An average person will be drawn after his physical instincts; only singular individuals can escape the clutches of the Evil Inclination, due to their good makeup, understanding, and their great efforts at Torah study. Most people, however, are eternally indentured to the Evil Inclination.

As a reward to our forefathers for their loyalty to Him, God gave us much Torah and many *mitzvos* so that we have the means to achieve perfection and get beyond the grasp of evil (*Meiri*).

In order to give them much reward for the performance of *mitzvos*, God gave them many opportunities to do so by issuing commandments about most life-situations; man is thus never left without a *mitzvah* opportunity (*Yarim Moshe*).

Furthermore, since each person may have a strong inclination toward a different *mitzvah*, God gave many *mitzvos*, so that every person will find his own spiritual niche and give his *mitzvah* particular care (*Derech Nichumecha*).

Many of the Torah's laws demand things which people would do anyway. For example, the Torah contains many admonitions against eating abominable creatures, crawling things, and carrion, although people abstain from them in any case. Nevertheless, God gave the commands in order to reward the people for abstaining from such foods (*Rav; Rivan*).

Likewise the prohibitions against such self-understood crimes as murder, robbery and the like would have been legislated even without the Torah, for without them society could not function. God commanded us about them so that He could reward us for keeping them (*Tiferes Yisrael*).

R' Yonah notes that many of the great moral, ethical, and spiritual principles were given as positive commandments. Man is enjoined to choose the good path with the words *and you shall choose life* (*Deuteronomy* 30:19); to study Torah (*Deuteronomy* 6:7), to follow the pathways of God (ibid. 28:9), to ponder the greatness of God (ibid. 4:39), and to remember His kindness toward us (ibid. 8:2). [See *Shaarei Teshuvah* 3:17 for more examples.] This was done in order to give man even greater opportunity for spiritual gains.

Another explanation for the abundance of commandments is that it is a fundamental principle that in order to merit life in the World to Come, a person must fulfill at least one *mitzvah* properly, with complete devotion to *God*. This *mitzvah* must be performed purely to fulfill God's will, lovingly and unselfishly. Therefore, God gave us an abun-

---

◆§ **A mitzvah suits the person.** The word מצוה is related to the word צוותא, meaning *connection*, because man connects himself to God by fulfilling His word. Since everyone's mode of connecting is different, God gave us an abundance of *mitzvos* so that each person will find his path to God.

Rambam rules that one may interrupt Torah study only in order to fulfill a *mitzvah* that no one else can do; Torah study takes precedence over any other *mitzvah*. In a letter to a student, Rabbi Shlomo Freifeld suggested that the assessment of whether someone else can do the *mitzvah* or not is subjective. There are people who by nature are so drawn to helping others that they never even think of forgoing a kindness in favor of someone else. On the other hand, those same people may not feel the same enthusiasm for other commandments.

Thus, by giving Israel a great variety of *mitzvos*, God provided all Jews with opportunities for spiritual growth.

wished to confer merit upon Israel; therefore He gave them Torah and mitzvos in abundance, as it is said: *HASHEM desired, for the sake if its [Israel's] righteousness, that the Torah be made great and glorious.*

---

dance of *mitzvos* so that every person should, in his lifetime, observe at least one *mitzvah* perfectly and thereby merit eternal life (*Rambam, Mishnah Commentary to Makkos*).

Mikveh Yisrael renders לְזַכּוֹת as *to purify*, as in שֶׁמֶן זַיִת זָךְ, *pure olive oil* (*Leviticus 27:20*). Every *mitzvah* edifies and cleanses another part of man's body and a corresponding element of his soul. The 248 positive commandments and 365 negative ones parallel man's 248 organs and 365 sinews and the corresponding parts of the soul. For this reason God gave an abundance of Torah and *mitzvos* in order to totally purify all of man's physical and spiritual parts.

— שֶׁנֶּאֱמַר: ,,ה' חָפֵץ לְמַעַן צִדְקוֹ, יַגְדִּיל תּוֹרָה וְיַאְדִּיר'' *as it is said: "HASHEM desired for the sake of its [Israel's] righteousness, that the Torah be made great and glorious"* (*Isaiah 42:21*). It was in order to make Israel righteous with abundant reward that God expanded the Torah and glorified it with many admonitions and opportunities for good deeds, thereby conferring much reward upon Israel for their observance. As Scripture states (*Psalms 31:20*): *How abundant is Your goodness which You have treasured for Your reverent ones* (*Tiferes Yisrael*).

⋙ **Scale of values.** Rambam (*Mishnah Commentary, Makkos*) sees this as the reason for R' Chanina ben Tradyon's doubt that he would merit life in the World to Come even though he risked his life to teach Torah publicly. When he was asked if he had done some good deed which would assure him a place in the World to Come, he replied he once had a wallet with money to purchase food for the Purim feast. Accidentally he distributed that money for charity, but he refused to take back the money from his charitable funds. This merit, he was assured, had earned him a place in the World to Come. (See *Avodah Zarah* 18a.)

On the surface, that good deed seems trivial in comparison with the enormous sacrifices he made to teach Torah, but it was only the gift to charity that won him a share in the World to Come. Although teaching Torah publicly is an act of spiritual greatness, R' Chanina was afraid that he might have derived honor or other forms of personal and emotional pleasure from it. Only the *selfless* distribution of personal funds for charity, a benevolent act no one would ever be aware of, earned him his place in the World of Reward.

⋙ **Cosmic function.** *Kedushas Levi* explains in a similar vein. The function of Torah and *mitzvos* is not only to protect the soul from spiritual stain (through negative commandments) and add luster to it (through positive commandments); they also help us purify and elevate the physical and mundane. For this reason we were given an array of *mitzvos* that harness and uplift physical functions in the service of God, such as the enjoyment of Shabbos and Festivals through food, drink, and relaxation. Thus, it was to *purify* even the physical functions of Jews that God gave us an abundance of Torah and *mitzvos*.

⋙ A young chassid came to R' Mendel of Kotzk to pour out his worries and woes. "I used to spend most of my time studying Torah. Recently my household expenses have grown so much that I must devote most of my day to the pursuit of a livelihood. What shall I do, *Rebbe*? My lot is unbearable. What will become of the spiritual quality of my life?"

The Kotzker replied by invoking our mishnah. "What type of merit is there in many *mitzvos*? Wouldn't we do better if we had less spiritual obligations? The answer is that the abundance of *mitzvos* gives us the ability to serve God many different ways and under all kinds of circumstances. Even a busy merchant like you can now serve God by conducting your business honestly without cheating customers or engaging in other forbidden business practices."

פרק שני ❧

Chapter Two

כָּל יִשְׂרָאֵל יֵשׁ לָהֶם חֵלֶק לָעוֹלָם הַבָּא, שֶׁנֶּאֱמַר:
„וְעַמֵּךְ כֻּלָּם צַדִּיקִים, לְעוֹלָם יִירְשׁוּ אָרֶץ, נֵצֶר
מַטָּעַי, מַעֲשֵׂה יָדַי לְהִתְפָּאֵר‟.

All Israel has a share in the World to Come, as it is said:
*And your people are all righteous; they shall inherit the land
forever; a branch of My plantings, My handiwork, in which to
take pride (Isaiah 60:21).*

[א] **רַבִּי** אוֹמֵר: אֵיזוֹ הִיא דֶרֶךְ יְשָׁרָה שֶׁיָּבֹר לוֹ הָאָדָם? כָּל שֶׁהִיא תִּפְאֶרֶת לְעֹשֶׂהָ וְתִפְאֶרֶת לוֹ מִן הָאָדָם.

Mishnah 1

רַבִּי אוֹמֵר — *Rabbi says.* "Rabbi" refers to R' Yehudah *HaNasi* (the Prince — 135-219 C.E.), son of Rabban Shimon, who is mentioned in the previous mishnah. Rabbi's primary teachers were his father and R' Yaakov ben Kurshai (see *Yerushalmi Pesachim* 6:1), but he traveled to study under many of the great men of his time.

Rabbi was the phenomenon of his generation, a man of noble character traits and superior talents, and the universally loved and acknowledged spiritual and temporal leader of Israel. His contemporaries referred to him as רַבֵּינוּ הַקָּדוֹשׁ, "our holy teacher." The Talmud states: From Moses until Rabbi, we do not find anyone with such a combination of wisdom and wealth (*Gittin* 59a). He was saintly and articulate, with an outstanding command of the Hebrew language (*Rambam,* introduction to *Mishnah Commentary*).

His service to the Jewish people was greatly enhanced by his warm and respectful relationship with the Roman emperor Marcus Aurelius, known in the Talmud as Antoninus. This rapport assured a tranquil existence for the Jews in *Eretz Yisrael* and allowed Rabbi to serve as redactor of the Mishnah, the basis of Jewish law.[1]

Despite his great prestige and power, Rabbi was so humble that the Talmud states: With the death of Rabbi, real humility and fear of sin ceased to exist (*Sotah* 49b). [See ArtScroll *History of the Jewish People: From Yavneh to Pumbedisa,* Chapters 14-15.]

אֵיזוֹ הִיא דֶרֶךְ יְשָׁרָה שֶׁיָּבֹר לוֹ הָאָדָם — *Which is the proper path that a person should choose for himself?* A cardinal principle of man's existence on earth is his ability to exercise free will. Man's life is not predestined; no one, not even God, forces him to do anything (see 3:19). He may choose goodness and

righteousness, or evil and wickedness. One can strive to be as righteous as Moses or as wicked as Jeroboam, all on the basis of his own life-choices. If man did not have free choice, God could not legitimately command us to fulfill His *mitzvos,* nor could He reward or punish us for our actions or inaction (*Rambam, Hilchos Teshuvah* 5:1-4). Rabbi advises us here about how one should choose in charting the course of life.

דֶרֶךְ יְשָׁרָה — *proper* path — rather than of a *righteous* path, which would imply the *mitzvos* between man and God (בֵּין אָדָם לַמָּקוֹם). Rabbi's stress is on the interpersonal areas that are included in the term "the proper path." *Rambam (Hilchos Dei'os* 1:6-7) defines the path of God as that which Abraham would teach his descendants (see *Genesis* 18:19), which entails imitating God's attributes of mercy, compassion, and holiness. This unselfish concern for others is יַשְׁרוּת (propriety and equity), which is the path of God. To welcome the Divine Presence is being *with* God; to receive guests is being *like* God. The Talmud (*Shabbos* 127a) teaches that hospitality is greater than receiving the Divine Presence.

The *Netziv* (introduction to *Ha'amek Davar, Genesis*) notes that the Talmud (*Avodah Zarah* 25a) refers to the Book of *Genesis* as The Book of the Upright (סֵפֶר הַיָּשָׁר) since it discusses the lives of the forefathers, who followed this path of God. In addition to their great righteousness and love of God, they were also יְשָׁרִים who lived properly and dealt in an upright, loving fashion, even with idolaters. A striking example was the length to which Abraham prayed on behalf of the incredibly sinful people of Sodom (*Genesis* 18:22-23).

כָּל שֶׁהִיא תִּפְאֶרֶת לְעֹשֶׂהָ וְתִפְאֶרֶת לוֹ מִן הָאָדָם — *Whatever [path] is a credit to himself and earns him*

---

1. The year 240 C.E., when the Mishnah was completed, is the beginning of the 2,000-year period known in the Talmud as יְמוֹת הַמָּשִׁיחַ, *the Messianic era.* It was the redaction of the Mishnah, a key stage in the revelation of the Oral Law, which began the path to ultimate redemption.

1. **R**abbi says: Which is the proper path that a person should choose for himself? Whatever [path] is a credit to himself and earns him the esteem of fellow men.

---

the esteem of fellow men. One way of earning the esteem of others is to follow the golden mean, avoiding extremism in all areas. When one follows a path of moderation, his actions are pleasant to himself and earn him the esteem of his colleagues as well. True generosity takes into consideration the needs of both the benefactor and the beneficiary. By being thrifty, yet generous to the needy, one will safeguard his assets and simultaneously earn the respect of others. By contrast, a stingy person may be proud that he has accumulated a fortune, but others will think negatively of him. On the other hand, a foolishly generous person may be popular, but he may well impoverish himself. Rabbi's golden mean must be one's guideline in all areas of his life (*Rambam* and *Rav*).

R' Moshe Alshaker interprets this mishnah as a straightforward formula for proper interpersonal dealings. Which path is the correct one when deal-

ing with others? The path that man chooses for dealing with himself. By following the golden rule alluded to by וְאָהַבְתָּ לְרֵעֲךָ כָּמוֹךָ, and doing unto others as one would do unto himself, man will please not only God, but all persons who cross his path.

Knesses Yisrael applies Rabbi's teaching to a person who serves as a role model. He must try to act in a way that others can emulate, but if he is far removed from a standard which others can replicate, i.e., he gives away most of his money to charity, people will never be able to learn from his extreme example. Rabbi teaches us to pick a moderate path in our service of God, one which befits our own level and that others feel is within their reach.

Meiri and *R' Yonah* read the word לְעֹשֶׂיהָ as לְעוֹשֶׂיהָ, *to its Maker*. According to this translation, man must choose a life path which will be pleasing to God.

⦿§ **Many Paths; One Goal.** Rabbi Simcha Bunam of P'shis'cha always emphasized that people should maintain their own individuality while defining their way of serving God; merely to imitate others is a grave error. God invests every individual with a unique set of abilities, talents, and faults, and it is with these that He wants a person to serve Him. Rabbi could have said simply "The proper path is to adhere to the Torah and all its *mitzvos.*" This is true, but would be insufficient. Rabbi means to teach that we must bring the uniqueness of our personalities to bear on our Godly service. One must choose a path that is a credit to his own blend of traits and talents.

Thus at the same time that we are achieving uniqueness in the service of God, we are reminded to respect the pathways of others. The Midrash states: Just as one person's facial features differ from those of another person, so do people's ideas differ (*Tanchuma; Pinchas* 10). The *Bais Yisrael* of *Gur* explained: Just as I cannot be upset with another person for having a nose that is different from mine, so I must respect one whose opinions are different.

This concept is reflected in the words of our Mishnah, *and earns him the esteem of fellow men.* We must be willing to confer esteem and respect upon the legitimate choices of others, never faulting them because their path is different from ours. As long as it is consistent with halachah and authentic tradition, it may, and should, reflect the individuality of its practitioner (*The Chozeh of Lublin*).

⦿§ **Aaron's question: "Is it good"?** We often assess our plans strictly on the basis of whether they are halachically permitted or forbidden, but the Mishnah suggests a second litmus test: Even if an act is permitted, we must question whether it is pleasing to God.

The *Yesod HaAvodah* discerns this principle in a question Aaron posed to Moses. Aaron's two eldest sons had just died and he felt that it would be wrong for him to eat certain offerings on the day of the tragedy. He asked: *Now that such things have befallen me [and I am in mourning], were I to eat this day's sin offering, would Hashem approve?* (*Leviticus* 10:19). Aaron did not ask whether the act was permitted or forbidden; the question was whether it would be *good* in Hashem's eyes, an even more sensitive barometer for behavior.

וֶהֱוֵי זָהִיר בְּמִצְוָה קַלָּה כְּבַחֲמוּרָה, שֶׁאֵין אַתָּה יוֹדֵעַ מַתַּן שְׂכָרָן שֶׁל מִצְוֹת. וֶהֱוֵי מְחַשֵּׁב הֶפְסֵד מִצְוָה כְּנֶגֶד שְׂכָרָהּ,

Often our actions are technically in accord with *halachah*, yet trample on the feelings of others, or they are done in ways that arouse legitimate criticism. At other times, in order to gain social acceptance, we act in ways that are not in accord with God's will. Rabbi teaches us to choose a course that is pleasing both to God and to men.

R' Yonah renders תִּפְאֶרֶת לְעֹשֵׂהָ as *a gesture of beauty toward its Maker*. This is a call to beautify the *mitzvos*. By purchasing a beautiful *esrog, tallis,* or Torah scroll, one causes people to praise and honor the *mitzvos*.

Tiferes Yisrael, however, cautions that even when seeking to beautify the *mitzvos*, one should not seek to impress people; one's excitement should be for the *mitzvah*, not for himself. In this fashion, his service of God will be a credit to himself and will earn him the respect of others.

Alternatively, *R' Yonah* sees this as a call to perform *mitzvos* in a timely fashion, King Solomon said: *"A thing in its time — how good!"* (*Proverbs* 15:23).

וֶהֱוֵי זָהִיר בְּמִצְוָה קַלָּה כְּבַחֲמוּרָה, שֶׁאֵין אַתָּה יוֹדֵעַ מַתַּן שְׂכָרָן שֶׁל מִצְוֹת — *Be as scrupulous in performing a "minor" mitzvah as in a "major" one, for you do not know the reward given for the [respective] mitzvos.*

According to *Rav* and *Rambam*, this injunction exhorts us to perform all *positive* commandments with equal zeal. The reward for fulfilling them and the punishment for not doing so is not given explicitly in the Torah, so that we remain unaware of the relative importance of the various commandments. This is an insurance that we will perform them all with the same care and enthusiasm.

The reward for keeping the negative injunctions, on the other hand, can be inferred from the punishment one receives for transgressing them. A negative commandment that carries a death penalty is certainly more stringent than one that does not.

Thus, *Rav* and *Rambam* render the mishnah as follows: Be as scrupulous in performing what you think is a "minor" *mitzvah* as you are in performing what you perceive as a "major" *mitzvah*. Since you

---

◆§ **Kosher Behavior.** R' Yosef Breuer was fond of saying that it is more important to be *glatt yosher* in one's dealings with people than to be *glatt kosher* in what one eats.

The name ישראל is a contraction of יָשָׁר, *upright,* and אֵל, *God.* The Jewish people strive not only to do God's will as expressed in the letter of the law, but also to adopt a Godly standard of uprightness and integrity (*R' A.C. Feuer*).

◆§ **A Time for Everything.** R' Chaim of Volozhin illustrates the importance of doing *mitzvos* in their proper time: The Evil Inclination begins by convincing someone that it is preferable to pray with proper intent, even if one must do so past the assigned time. The next step is, "Take your time. You have already set a precedent; pray whenever you are ready!" By indulging such laxness, a person can eventually be swayed totally from doing the *mitzvos*.

Imagine a person who spends the whole first night of Pesach in spiritual preparation for the *mitzvah* of eating matzah, only to eat it after sunrise. All his "preparations" were for naught. His friend who ate the matzah at the appropriate time, even with less than perfect intent, will have fulfilled the *mitzvah* properly.

One who fails to link his *mitzvah* performance to God's timetable is like someone who eats matzah on the night of Rosh Hashanah, fasts on the day before Yom Kippur (when it is a *mitzvah* to eat — see *Shulchan Aruch Orach Chaim* 604:1), or takes the four species on Yom Kippur.

◆§ **Variety, the spice of life.** *Rashi* offers the following analogy: A king asked his servants to tend to an orchard, telling them that he would pay more for some trees than others, but not telling them which was which. Thus, he assured himself that the servants would cultivate the entire orchard; had he given them the information they wanted, they would have cared only about those trees whose care promised greater reward and would have given less attention to the others. Similarly, had God clearly delineated the reward for each positive commandment, people would concentrate on the "major" *mitzvos*. (See *R' Yonah* for a slightly different version of this parable.)

do not know the reward for keeping the *mitzvos,* nor the punishment for not fulfilling them, you have no way to know which of them is truly minor and which is major.

Many *mitzvos* not only carry a promise of reward, but bear the additional value of conveying to man messages of supreme importance. *Ramban (Exodus* 13:16), for example, teaches that many *mitzvos* are linked to remembering the Exodus, in order to keep one's focus on the events that showed God to be the Creator Who not only controls nature, but is intimately involved in human affairs. Similarly, the Shabbos *Kiddush* implants in man's heart a deep-rooted faith in the Creator and His power to control nature. Therefore, one can never know the relative importance of *mitzvos (Meiri).*

Tiferes Yisrael adds that *mitzvos* must also be measured in terms of their intrinsic power to help man refine his soul. Each *mitzvah* contains a specific remedial aspect unique to that command. It is for this reason that there are 248 Biblically mandated positive commandments, which parallel the 248 limbs and organs of the human body. Each *mitzvah* offers perfection to a different aspect of the person, refining the spiritual counterpart of that particular organ. Therefore, one must be scrupulous in the observance of all *mitzvos* in order to gain the benefits of their refining qualities.

וֶהֱוֵי מְחַשֵּׁב הֶפְסֵד מִצְוָה כְּנֶגֶד שְׂכָרָה — *Calculate the cost of a mitzvah against its reward.* In light of the great reward one receives for a *mitzvah,* both in this world and in the World to Come, the cost in time, money, and energy expended to perform it pales into insignificance (*R' Yonah, Rashi, Rav* et al.).

⇜§ **Necessities of life.** Often, the frequency with which we must perform a *mitzvah* diminishes its importance in our eyes. We tend to view a *mitzvah* like *shofar,* which is performed only on Rosh Hashanah, as "major" and to anticipate it with enthusiasm, while constant *mitzvos* like *mezuzah* seem "minor" in comparison. But the opposite may be true, as indicated by our physical surroundings. Air, which is more fundamental to man's existence than water, exists in greater supply; water is more plentiful than bread, and bread more plentiful than meat. The more necessary something is for survival, the greater is its availability. Likewise, in a spiritual sense, the frequency with which we perform any particular *mitzvah* speaks of the important place it plays in our spiritual agenda. We must therefore be scrupulous about *all mitzvos,* even those which seem "minor" because of their frequency (*Derech Nichumecha*).

⇜§ **Allocating resources.** Rabbi seems to contradict himself. Immediately after stating that one cannot know the true reward of *mitzvos,* Rabbi asks that we calculate their relative gain and loss. How is this possible if one cannot know their true value?

In truth, it is impossible to know the reward for *mitzvos,* which is limitless. However, each person is evaluated according to his own valuation of the *mitzvah.* By calculating the temporary loss he may incur in the performance of a *mitzvah,* and demonstrating his willingness to "suffer" that loss in order to fulfill God's will, one, in effect, puts a price on the *mitzvah.* For example, a person was on his way to a business meeting to close a deal from which he stood to gain a profit of five thousand dollars. He passed a fellow Jew stranded on the road, stopped to help him, knowing full well that by coming late to his meeting, he might jeopardize the deal. By demonstrating his willingness to forego the money for the *mitzvah,* he set the minimum value of the *mitzvah,* and hence he determined his own reward (*Haflaah*).

Imrei Emes offers a similar approach. Imagine that someone were to offer you a million dollars to abstain from wearing *tefillin*; you would surely turn down the offer. If so, you should perform the *mitzvah* with as much joy as if you had received the million dollars. This is the type of creative spiritual accounting that our Sages recommended.

וּשְׂכַר עֲבֵרָה כְּנֶגֶד הֶפְסֵדָהּ. הִסְתַּכֵּל בִּשְׁלֹשָׁה דְבָרִים, וְאֵין אַתָּה בָא לִידֵי עֲבֵרָה; דַּע מַה לְמַעְלָה מִמְּךָ – עַיִן רוֹאָה, וְאֹזֶן שׁוֹמַעַת, וְכָל מַעֲשֶׂיךָ בְּסֵפֶר נִכְתָּבִים.

This need not contradict the dictum of Antigonos (1:3), who instructed that one should not seek reward for serving his Master. Certainly, one should not focus on the reward when doing a *mitzvah*; this mishnah, however, is offered as a counterargument to the claim of the evil inclination that one who performs a *mitzvah* incurs loss. Although the claim may be true, the loss is far outweighed by the reward one receives (*Abarbanel, Maharal*). *Tosafos Yom Tov* suggests alternatively that Antigonos speaks of the optimal, altruistic form of service to which one should aspire, while Rabbi, of our mishnah, teaches the proper path for most people, who are not yet able to attain the level advised by Antigonos.

HaChassid Yaavetz views this instruction to "calculate" as reflecting the *way* in which one should fulfill a *mitzvah*. Rather than ignoring the apparent "loss" entailed in fulfilling a *mitzvah,* one *should* calculate it — and then fulfill the *mitzvah* in spite of it. With this approach, you will receive an even greater reward, for you will have faced the enemy and vanquished him.

וּשְׂכַר עֲבֵרָה כְּנֶגֶד הֶפְסֵדָהּ — *and the reward of a sin against its cost.* "Gain" refers here to the temporary enjoyment one has from sin. This enjoyment pales against the backdrop of the long-term spiritual and even physical loss incurred. The enjoyment lasts for a fleeting moment and is gone, and one is left with the loss of eternity (*Rav, Rashi, R' Yonah*). *Meiri* renders: *And the reward for* [refraining from] *a sin against* [i.e., in terms of] *the loss and punishment one would incur for transgression.* If one were to gain nothing more from abstaining from sin than avoiding Divine retribution, it would vindicate his choice. One should consider the avoidance of punishment alone as ample reward for not sinning.

הִסְתַּכֵּל בִּשְׁלֹשָׁה דְבָרִים, וְאֵין אַתָּה בָא לִידֵי עֲבֵרָה — *Consider three things, and you will not come into the grip of sin:* Focus mentally and emotionally upon these three items so as not to lose sight of life's purpose. Most sin is not a result of evil intention, but rather of an unclear perspective (*Rav*).

The word לִידֵי may be rendered as *into the handles* (as in יָדוֹת נְדָרִים, *"handles"* for making vows) [see *Nedarim* 2a]. Sin is much like a pitcher with a handle, in the sense that the smaller part allows entry to the larger part. Often we are emotionally unable to transgress a sin blatantly; however, a lighter form of the sin frequently serves as a "handle" which eventually gives access to the full transgression. [For example, one would never dream of stealing his friend's money, yet he sees nothing wrong with borrowing his property without bothering to ask permission — yet Torah law deems such a person to be

⊷§ **Psychology of sin.** In the Messianic age, God will "slaughter" the Evil Inclination in the presence of both the righteous and the wicked. To the righteous, the Evil Inclination will appear as insurmountable as a tall mountain; to the wicked, it will appear as trivial and conquerable as stepping over a strand of hair. The righteous will cry, "How is it that we were able to overcome such a formidable foe?" while the wicked will weep, "How is it that we were unable to conquer such an insignificant foe?" (*Succah* 52a).

Seemingly, the reverse is true. To the victorious righteous, the forces of evil were easily conquerable; one would expect to hear them speak of evil as "a strand of hair." Only from the wicked, who fell victim to the Evil Inclination, would one expect it to be described as an insurmountable mountain!

The Talmud here enlightens us to the psychology of sin. The allure of sin lies in the promise of thrill. Before one tastes evil, it seems to be enjoyable and exciting, but once experienced, it loses its glamour, very much like a restaurant dish which may sound tantalizing on the menu but does not live up to its description.

To the righteous, who have never experienced sin, its blinding allure makes it appear insurmountable. The wicked, who have tasted the bitter fruit, cry, for they know the truth — the promise of the evil inclination is only a hollow lie. It is unfulfilling and as conquerable as a strand of hair (*Bais HaLevi*).

and the reward of a sin against its cost. Consider three things, and you will not come into the grip of sin: Know what is above you — a watchful Eye, an attentive Ear, and all your deeds are recorded in a Book.

---

guilty of thievery (see *Bava Metzia* 41a). The breakdown of the sanctity of private property can serve as the "handle" to full-fledged theft.] In this mishnah we are taught a strategy that will save us even from the "handles" of iniquity (*Midrash Shmuel*).

דַּע מַה לְמַעְלָה מִמָּךְ — *Know what is above you*. Be aware that God Who is above you — i.e., beyond human comprehension (*Tiferes Yisrael*) — is totally aware of your actions, thoughts, and speech, and that He is fully in control of your life. This is a general statement which will be subdivided into three aspects in the next part of the mishnah: that God sees all, hears all, and records all.

Meiri, however, reckons the three deterrents to sin differently, as noted below.

The mishnah can be interpreted homiletically to suggest the fact that whatever occurs in the Heavenly spheres is a result of the actions of man [see *Nefesh HaChaim* 1:4]. The *Baal Shem Tov* homiletically sees this concept conveyed in King David's words *God is your shadow* (*Psalms* 121:5). Just as one's shadow "mimics" him, so God's conduct with us depends on our own behavior. Thus, if a person is kind to his fellows, God likewise acts graciously towards him, and *vice versa*.

Thus, the mishnah can be understood to say, *Know that what occurs above* [מַה לְמַעְלָה] — the manner in which God deals with us — is מִמָּךְ, *from you* — a direct result of your own actions.

According to *Meiri*, this is the first of the three deterrents to sin: belief in a Power above Who created everything.

עַיִן רוֹאָה, וְאֹזֶן שׁוֹמַעַת — *a watchful Eye, an attentive Ear*. According to *Meiri*, these two items together form the second deterrent to sin: God is involved in human affairs, and He monitors all human activity, rewarding and punishing a person according to his actions, words, and thoughts.

וְכָל מַעֲשֶׂיךָ בְּסֵפֶר נִכְתָּבִים — *and all your deeds are recorded in a Book*. Nothing is forgotten by God. Every act is recorded and eventually is either rewarded or punished. The "Book" is the metaphorical *Book of Remembrance* mentioned in the High Holiday prayers (*R' Yonah, Tosafos Yom Tov*, et al.).

According to *HaChassid Yaavetz*, the Book is man's soul. Goodness adds luster to the soul while sin besmirches it. After death, the state of the soul

---

◁§ **Blind instinct.** The mishnah exhorts one to view life from the vantage point of eternity, and to be constantly aware of the long-term consequences of his actions. When he loses sight of the ultimate goal, he is an easy prey for the Satan.

The Chofetz Chaim offers a parable: A businessman hired a wagon driver to transport him to another city, warning him to make sure that the horse did not stray from the path. Having just eaten a full meal, the businessman settled into the wagon and promptly dozed off. The wagon driver also fell asleep.

The horse continued along the road until it spotted a grassy knoll, and it veered off to the side, overturning the wagon and waking up its passengers. The businessman berated the wagon driver for having fallen asleep and losing control over the horse. The wagon driver sought to justify himself: "My horse is highly intelligent, and I felt confident I could rely on it not to go astray."

"Fool," answered the businessman, "even if your horse is the wisest of all horses, it is still only a horse. The temptation of good feeding is too great a lure for even the smartest of horses."

Similarly, man is a synthesis of the forces of the body and soul. As long as the soul keeps an intelligent watch over the body, insuring that it will not stray from the Torah path, all is well. However, if one allows his soul to doze off, claiming that the body will stand watch, he is quite foolish, for the body, left on its own, will not be able to withstand temptation. Therefore, the Mishnah teaches, *Calculate the reward of a sin against its cost*; keep your focus trained on the long-range goal, and let these eternal needs govern temporal desires.

[כב] **רַבָּן** גַּמְלִיאֵל בְּנוֹ שֶׁל רַבִּי יְהוּדָה הַנָּשִׂיא אוֹמֵר: יָפֶה תַּלְמוּד תּוֹרָה עִם דֶּרֶךְ אֶרֶץ, שֶׁיְּגִיעַת שְׁנֵיהֶם מַשְׁכַּחַת עָוֹן. וְכָל תּוֹרָה שֶׁאֵין עִמָּהּ מְלָאכָה, סוֹפָהּ בְּטֵלָה

testifies to its owner's behavior during his life. Man builds the soul, therefore, with his deeds, either adding to or detracting from its luminescence.

Alternatively, the "Book" may refer to all of creation, which is indelibly affected by man's actions. *R' S. R. Hirsch* poetically captures the spirit of the mishnah: "Never forget that the consequences and repercussions of everything you do reach far beyond the fleeting time span in which your act occurred. God is mindful even of the least conspicuous of your actions, and all will be recalled when your life will pass in review at the end of your days; this should be sufficient reason for you to do nothing of which you might have to be ashamed in the presence of God and of your own self-respect; it should be sufficient reason to be careful, with all your deeds, to plant nothing but the seed of goodness into the soil of the future yet unborn."

R' Chaim of Volozhin interprets the words of the mishnah in a historical context. In earlier times, the nation received spiritual guidance from prophets who were blessed with a "seeing eye," able to know and articulate God's expectations. Later, when prophecy ceased, we still had people who possessed a "hearing ear," attuned to the Heavenly voice called a *Bas Kol* (see *Berachos* 52a), which gave them the spiritual guidance to lead the nation and to protect it from moral recklessness. Now even this is gone. Today one can only find his spiritual bearings in the words of Torah themselves: *And all your actions are recorded in the Book*, meaning that the guidelines for behavior can now be found only in the Torah.

Mishnah 2

יָפֶה תַּלְמוּד תּוֹרָה עִם דֶּרֶךְ אֶרֶץ — *Torah study is good together with an occupation.* The translation of דֶּרֶךְ אֶרֶץ as an occupation follows *Rav, R' Yonah, Rashi, Rambam,* et al.

Chasam Sofer comments that Torah study must be the

רַבָּן גַּמְלִיאֵל בְּנוֹ שֶׁל רַבִּי יְהוּדָה הַנָּשִׂיא אוֹמֵר — *Rabban Gamliel, the son of Rabbi Yehudah HaNasi, says.* Rabban Gamliel succeeded his father (Rabbi, of the previous mishnah) as *Nasi* and was considered the last of the *Tannaim* (authors of the Mishnah).

◆§ **Not trivial.** People tend to underestimate the significance of their actions and thoughts. The Midrash (*Vayikra Rabbah* 34:9) teaches: Had Reuben known that God would write [in the Torah, that he had wanted to rescue Joseph], Reuben would have carried Joseph on his shoulders (see *Genesis* 37:21). Had Boaz known that God would record that he had given some food to Ruth (*Ruth* 2:14), he would have given her a sumptuous meal.

The negative impact of man's deeds is cosmic as well. The Talmud tells of R' Elazar ben Durdayah, a man steeped in gross immorality. A harlot once spoke of his debased spiritual status and declared that he would never repent. Her words roused him out of his spiritual slumber, and he became fully repentant. Aware of the terrible tragedy of his life, he begged the heavens and the earth, the mountains and valleys, to implore God to show him mercy. They replied, "Before we ask mercy for you, we must ask for ourselves."

This is puzzling. What had they done that necessitated Divine mercy? R' Elya Lopian explained: When man sins, he defiles not only himself, he also taints the entire cosmos. A world after sin is a changed, impaired world. The mountains and valleys realized that they too were affected by R' Elazar ben Durdayah's immorality, and that they too needed Divine mercy.

Our mishnah therefore teaches that man's deeds are noted and recorded by God, because they are truly important. If one is constantly aware of the significance of his actions, it prevents him from stumbling into sin.

2. Rabban Gamliel, the son of Rabbi Yehudah *HaNasi*, says: Torah study is good together with an occupation, for exertion of them both makes sin forgotten. All Torah study that is not joined with work will cease in the end, and

---

scholar's primary occupation, with the pursuit of a livelihood assuming a minor role. However, those who are financially able to maintain Torah scholars and institutions should emphasize their occupations, so that they can support the study of others — but even they must not ignore their personal duty to make times for Torah study.

Alternatively, *Meiri* renders דֶּרֶךְ אֶרֶץ as *proper social conduct*, i.e., Torah study must be accompanied by ethical and moral behavior (see 3:21).

שֶׁיְּגִיעַת שְׁנֵיהֶם מַשְׁכַּחַת עָוֹן — *for exertion of them both makes sin forgotten.* The combination of Torah study and an occupation is a fine deterrent against improper conduct. Through Torah study one becomes knowledgeable of God's will and His expectations of us in daily life; financial independence assures that he will not be forced to stoop to unethical conduct in the pursuit of a livelihood (*Rashi, Rambam*). In addition, serious pursuit of Torah knowledge is a physically tiring exercise. In conjunction with a steady occupation, it leaves over little time or energy for sin (*Rav, R' Yonah*).

According to *Tiferes Yisrael*, the synthesis of Torah knowledge and proper ethical and moral conduct is the most foolproof path for preventing transgression of the Divine will. *Meiri* views the mishnah as a suggested course for the Torah scholar, whose job is to serve as the ethical and religious compass for the community. Only by striving to maintain proper ethical conduct in addition to their Torah knowledge, can they earn the confidence of the community and assure that the masses will be willing to overlook their occasional lapses.

Knesses Yisrael explains the mishnah as a directive that Torah laws and values govern the conduct of business. Through adherence to Torah-mandated business ethics, one may legitimately view the time spent earning a living as a preparation for Torah study. Thus, he causes the sin of abstaining from Torah study to be "forgotten." *Yismach Lev* elaborates on this theme: When man is called to judgment before the Heavenly Court, he will be asked: Did you conduct your business honestly? Did you engage in Torah study? (*Shabbos* 31a). The two questions are related, because one who conducts his business according to Torah principles is actually involved in Torah, in a practical and applied sense.

Binas Yissachar views this mishnah as a call for partnerships between scholars and people of means. By using one's profits to support a Torah scholar, the investor acquires a share in his merit; thus both will be saved from iniquity, since Torah study possesses the special quality of protecting one from sin (see *Sotah* 21a).

וְכָל תּוֹרָה שֶׁאֵין עִמָּהּ מְלָאכָה, סוֹפָהּ בְּטֵלָה וְגוֹרֶרֶת עָוֹן — *All Torah study that is not joined with work will cease in the end, and lead to sin.* If one is unable to

---

> ◆§ **Too busy to sin.** Dissatisfaction is a prime factor in man's vulnerability to the wiles of the Evil Inclination; unfulfilled people may fantasize that if only they had this or that pleasure, they would truly be satisfied. Thus, Rabban Gamliel teaches that if man studies Torah to satisfy his spiritual thirst, in conjunction with an occupation to provide his physical sustenance, he will achieve an overall sense of satisfaction that precludes sin.
>
> The Kotzker *Rebbe* told his followers: "I don't expect you to refrain from sin because you have no interest in it. You should be too busy to sin." *Mesillas Yesharim* (Chapter 2) writes: One of the devices of the Evil Inclination is to put unrelenting pressure on man's heart, leaving him no time or emotional space to be introspective and consider the direction his life is taking. Our mishnah, too, stresses the importance of time in the prevention of sin, by urging us to fill our hours with healthy pursuits.
>
> R' Hersh Judowitz, a grocery store proprietor in Brooklyn, always kept a volume of *Mishnah Berurah* under the counter and studied it between customers. He succeeded in finishing all six volumes.

וְגוֹרֶרֶת עָוֹן. וְכָל הָעוֹסְקִים עִם הַצִּבּוּר, יִהְיוּ עוֹסְקִים עִמָּהֶם לְשֵׁם שָׁמַיִם, שֶׁזְּכוּת אֲבוֹתָם מְסַיַּעְתָּם, וְצִדְקָתָם עוֹמֶדֶת לָעַד. וְאַתֶּם, מַעֲלֶה אֲנִי עֲלֵיכֶם שָׂכָר הַרְבֵּה, כְּאִלּוּ עֲשִׂיתֶם.

obtain basic necessities, he will become pre-occupied with the search for food — and few people can withstand the pressure of lacking basic necessities. They may either engage in dishonest practices including theft (*Rashi, Rambam*), accept gifts from others, or flatter the wicked in order to curry favor with them (*R' Yonah*).

Midrash Shmuel interprets *Torah study that is not joined with work* as any learning that remains theoretical and is not applied in practice. Such learning will not endure (see 3:12). Furthermore, if one studies Torah yet does not fulfill its precepts, he is deemed an intentional sinner, for he cannot claim to have sinned out of ignorance.

וְכָל הָעוֹסְקִים עִם הַצִּבּוּר, יִהְיוּ עוֹסְקִים עִמָּהֶם לְשֵׁם שָׁמַיִם — *All who exert themselves for the community should exert themselves for the sake of Heaven.* *Rashi's* text reads: וְכָל הָעֲמֵלִים עִם הַצִּבּוּר, *All who toil on behalf of the community.* Involvement in community affairs must never become a vehicle for self-aggrandizement, a power base, or a source

of personal benefit. Let one not say, "See what I have done for the public good." One must care for the public welfare for the sake of Heaven (*Rav, R' Yonah*).

Alternatively, one who solicits funds for charity or public concerns should do so for the sake of Heaven. He should not be afraid that he is overburdening the public; the merit of their forefathers will help them meet their fiscal commitments (*Rav*). Even though it takes time which might be spent at either Torah study or business activities, one should sacrifice himself spiritually and fiscally on behalf of his fellow Jews (*Tiferes Yisrael*).

שֶׁזְּכוּת אֲבוֹתָם מְסַיַּעְתָּם, וְצִדְקָתָם עוֹמֶדֶת לָעַד — *for then the merit of the community's forefathers aids them, and their righteousness will endure forever.*

It is not the efforts of the public functionaries that bring them success; it is the enduring merit of the community's forefathers that does so (*Rashi, R' Yonah,* and *Rav*).

৵§ **Livelihood without life.** While the mishnah stresses the danger of Torah study unaccompanied by work, it is even more dangerous to engage in work without Torah study and values; a living is nothing more than a stage on which to act out the real drama of life — to be an authentic Jew and enjoy an intimate relationship with God.

The Chofetz Chaim explained this with the parable of a woman who inherited a huge fortune from her husband, with the stipulation that she spend the money for no other purpose than to marry off their only daughter. One day the daughter became deathly ill, and it became clear that the only chance to save the young girl was to travel to a certain doctor who lived very far away. The cost of the trip and the cure would be astronomical. The woman protested: "I am not allowed to spend the money on anything except my daughter's wedding."

Her friends laughed at her. "If your daughter dies, there won't be any wedding. You must pay the doctor to heal your daughter, and then, with God's help, we will all dance at her wedding."

Thus, preparing children to earn a living becomes meaningless if we don't provide for their growth as Jews. If they are spiritually dead, of what value is anything else? The Chofetz Chaim, therefore, said that if our mishnah teaches that Torah study without work is of negligible value, certainly work without Torah study is worthless.

lead to sin. All who exert themselves for the community should exert themselves for the sake of Heaven, for then the merit of the community's forefathers aids them, and their righteousness will endure forever. Nevertheless, as for you, I [God] will bestow great reward upon you, as if you had accomplished it on your own.

Meiri renders *these words as follows: for the merit of the public officials' forefathers aids them.* Circumstances and commitment often force people involved in public service to be more lax in their standard of *mitzvah* performance than they would want to be. [For example, one involved in the distribution of food packages for the needy may lose precious time from his Torah study schedule; a health care worker may inadvertently transgress some Sabbath prohibitions; or a rabbi, charged with the responsibility to provide guidance, may speak too harshly or be overly offensive when offering reproof.] The merit of their forefathers, together with their good intentions to carry out their public duties for the sake of Heaven, will mitigate judgment against them, so that the laxity induced by community service will not be held against them.

According to *Maharal*, it is the forefathers of the nation, Abraham, Isaac, and Jacob, who actually come to the aid of the public servant. The ancestors help the public functionary in return for taking care of their descendants.

— וְאַתֶּם, מַעֲלֶה אֲנִי עֲלֵיכֶם שָׂכָר הַרְבֵּה, כְּאִלּוּ עֲשִׂיתֶם
Nevertheless, as for you, I [God] will bestow great reward upon you, as if you had accomplished it on your own. Even though it is really the merit of the community forefathers that is responsible for any good achieved by the public officials, nonetheless God rewards the officials as if they themselves had done it (*Rav, Rashi*).

God rewards those who toil for the benefit of the community, even for *mitzvos* they failed to fulfill. Even though the general rule is אוֹנֶס לָאו כְּמַאן דְּעָבִיד, one who does not perform a *mitzvah* due to circumstances beyond his control cannot be credited with its performance (*Yerushalmi Gittin* 7:5), a public servant is treated differently. God bestows great reward upon him, as if he had performed the *mitzvah* (*Rambam* and *Meiri*).

Those who attend honestly and faithfully to the affairs of the community, who know how to inspire its members to care for the institutions which they are duty bound to maintain, will be given reward as great as if they had expended all their own resources. The Sages state that he who inspires others to do good deeds and to fulfill their duties has even greater merit than he who does the same good with his own resources [*Bava Basra* 9a] (*R' S. R. Hirsch*).

◄§ **Gladdening the King.** The *Maggid* of Kozhnitz taught that one who does a favor for another Jew may give God greater pleasure than by doing a ritual *mitzvah*; the King certainly derives more pleasure from something done on his child's behalf than from something done on His own behalf. One who is involved with the community for the sake of Heaven is thereby taking care of the King's children.

◄§ **In return for service.** This is homiletically reflected in the Sabbath prayer "And all who are involved faithfully in the needs of community — may the Holy One, Blessed is He, pay their reward." Communal service earns one Divine reward even for *mitzvos* missed due to preoccupation with communal concerns.

ב/ג־ד [ג] **הֱווּ זְהִירִין** בָּרָשׁוּת, שֶׁאֵין מְקָרְבִין לוֹ לְאָדָם אֶלָּא לְצֹרֶךְ עַצְמָן; נִרְאִין כְּאוֹהֲבִין בִּשְׁעַת הֲנָאָתָן, וְאֵין עוֹמְדִין לוֹ לְאָדָם בִּשְׁעַת דָּחֳקוֹ.

[ד] **הוּא הָיָה** אוֹמֵר: עֲשֵׂה רְצוֹנוֹ כִּרְצוֹנֶךָ, כְּדֵי

Mishnah 3

הֱווּ זְהִירִין בָּרָשׁוּת, שֶׁאֵין מְקָרְבִין לוֹ לְאָדָם אֶלָּא לְצֹרֶךְ עַצְמָן — *Beware of rulers, for they befriend someone only for their own benefit.* The public servants mentioned in the previous mishnah are cautioned that in representing communal interests in the halls of government, they must be careful not to become overly friendly with the powers that be (*Rav*). One should not rely on their promises or give them excessive gifts at public expense in order to curry favor with them; respectful distrust is the safest approach when dealing with rulers. Sharing of confidences with them, on the assumption that they have the best interests of the community in mind, may be disastrous. One must be vigilant in dealing with the government, for they are interested only in what benefits them (*Tiferes Yisrael*).

One should never rely on the government, thinking that it holds the key to Jewish survival. That is to be found only with God.

According to *Machzor Vitry*, Rabban Gamliel's axiom reflects the political situation he himself faced. His father, Rabbi Yehudah *HaNasi*, had enjoyed a close relationship with Marcus Aurelius Antoninus (2:1, s.v. אומר רבי) and was of great help to the Roman government. Nonetheless, the favors Rabbi extended to the

rulers of his time were quickly forgotten. Therefore, his son Rabban Gamliel advised a policy of respectful distrust; even when rulers smile at their people, they seek their own agenda (*Mussar Avos*).

Midrash Shmuel renders רָשׁוּת as *optional matters*. Besides commandments and transgressions, there exists an entire area of unlegislated behavior in the life of a Jew. The Evil Inclination seeks to persuade man that his behavior in this area is completely optional, and that he need not concern himself with "religion" in such "secular and mundane" affairs. Man therefore may assume that in these areas he has permission (רָשׁוּת) to do what he wants. In fact, this is not true; the mishnah cautions that a Jew must scrutinize his conduct in optional areas, just as he does in the mandated ones. Rabbi Yitzchak Hutner once said, "There is no Switzerland (neutral territory) in the service of God."

Ramban teaches that the Biblical mandate that we be a holy nation (*Leviticus* 19:2) is a call to live the spirit of the law in accordance with God's will, even if there is no specific *mitzvah* or prohibition involved. One can become a degenerate within the parameters of the Torah, observing the

---

⋽§ **Facing reality.** *Ramban* (*Deuteronomy* 31:18) explains that this malady results in a vicious cycle. As a community, we believe in God yet we tend to rely on governments to bring Jewish salvation. God responds in kind to our lack of faith in Him by turning His countenance away from us. Thus, His apparent uninvolvement in Jewish history is a direct reflection of our own behavior.

At the time of the Balfour Declaration, many Jews thought that their problems would be solved by the mighty British Empire. However, they were soon disappointed when the British first limited and then virtually halted Jewish immigration to *Eretz Yisrael*. Later, Jews fantasized that the international community of nations, embodied in the United Nations, would be the source of Jewish salvation, and their hopes were dashed yet again. Again and again, Jews have relied on the nations of the world to be their saviors, only to suffer disillusionment. Thus our mishnah warns: Be wary of the ruling powers, for only God is the real Savior.

3. Beware of rulers, for they befriend someone only for their own benefit; they act friendly when it benefits them, but do not stand by someone in his time of need.

4. He used to say: Treat His will as if it were your own will, so

---

technical requirements of the commandments while surrendering to self-indulgence, gluttony, and licentiousness.

Therefore the mishnah teaches that one must take extreme care not to be deceived into thinking that the Evil Inclination is a friend who seeks to help him enjoy himself. Once a person has fallen into sin, the same Evil Inclination will show his true colors and assume the role of prosecutor. His agenda is to push the person even further into the jaws of sin (*Maharit*).

Lev Avos, in a different vein, interprets this clause as a continuation of the instructions to public servants. They are urged to solicit the permission of their constituency before pursuing any public course of action, for the community appoints leaders for their own benefit. If a public servant should do something that they view as detrimental to their welfare, even if he has done it inadvertently, they will lay the full blame on him. Hence, a public figure would do well to be sure that he has the mandate of the people.

This is true even among business partners. One should always secure a vote of confidence from his partners before embarking on a major business project. If the venture meets with success, they will

be thrilled, and if it fails, at least they will all share the blame (*R' Shmuel Alter*).

נִרְאִין כְּאוֹהֲבִין בִּשְׁעַת הֲנָאָתָן, וְאֵין עוֹמְדִין לוֹ לָאָדָם בִּשְׁעַת דָּחֲקוֹ — *they act friendly when it benefits them, but do not stand by someone in his time of need.* In difficult times, when one needs help, the rulers forget all the kindness that he performed on their behalf (*Meiri*).

R' Yonah renders: *They do not stand by someone in its* [*the government's*] *time of need.* When the government finds itself under financial pressure, it will not hesitate to bankrupt any of its subjects in order to produce the needed revenue.

The last two mishnayos of Rabban Gamliel serve as a qualifying commentary to the dicta of Shemaya enunciated in 1:10. *Love work,* said Shemaya, to which Rabban Gamliel added, "Only in conjunction with Torah study." The statement *Despise positions of power* is also not an absolute one. One may, and often must, assume a public role, and community service can be a very positive experience when it is pursued for the sake of Heaven. Even Shemaya's third injunction, *Do not become overly familiar with the government,* cannot be taken as a categorical policy; contact with the ruling power is often needed to assure Jewish survival. However, warns Rabban Gamliel, one must be wary of those who occupy seats of governance (*Midrash Shmuel*).

Mishnah 4

הוּא הָיָה אוֹמֵר: עֲשֵׂה רְצוֹנוֹ כִּרְצוֹנֶךָ, כְּדֵי שֶׁיַּעֲשֶׂה רְצוֹנְךָ כִּרְצוֹנוֹ — *He used to say: Treat His will as if it were your own will, so that He will treat your will as if it were His will.*

We are advised here to expend as much money, time, and effort on *mitzvos* as we expend on our personal pleasures. In return, God will treat our will — to enjoy His beneficence and to bask in His

---

◄§ **No longer needed.** A striking example of this took place in the royal house of Spain. Don Yitzchak Abarbanel served as royal treasurer to Ferdinand and Isabella, and enabled Spain to finance the reconquest of the country from Moslem domination. Once this was accomplished, however, Spain no longer needed its Jews and issued the infamous decree of expulsion. In 1492, Abarbanel pleaded for a stay of the expulsion and even offered a huge bribe, but to no avail. All of Abarbanel's service to the national cause became worthless in a moment. His efforts on the royals' behalf were quickly forgotten, and his ungrateful employers turned their backs on him and his people.

goodness — as His own, and reward our efforts handsomely (Rav).

When building or furnishing a home, one will spend extra money and effort in order to obtain an item of superior quality that will provide good service for a long time. The extra expenditure is justified, one does not want to be "penny-wise and pound-foolish." The mishnah enjoins us to maintain the same standard regarding God's will as we maintain for our own needs, settling for nothing less than the best (Ruach Chaim). Tiferes Yisrael adds: One should approach his spiritual pursuits with the same excitement, alacrity, and single-mindedness with which he approaches his business dealings. In reward, God will provide sustenance without any undue stress. The Talmud teaches that when Jews do God's will, the burden of earning a living will be assumed by others (Berachos 35b).

According to Rashi and R' Yonah, this mishnah is a call to live only for the sake of Heaven by making one's own will synonymous with God's. Since real purity of heart is to will only one thing — the will of Heaven — one should never want anything different for himself than what God gives him.

Chovos HaLevavos records the motto of one who places true trust in God: "I never awoke in the morning in a particular situation wanting to find myself in different circumstances."

The key to achieving this perspective is to realize that everything a person has — money, talent, even life itself — is entrusted to him by God, to be invested in ventures that can be expected to yield spiritual profits. To use one's life for anything else is a gross misappropriation and a breach of trust. For example, one might feel some slight remorse over giving away one's *own* money for charity, but if he were to realize fully that he is disbursing *God's* funds, that he is actually in God's employ, he would feel no compunction whatsoever.

If we make His will and ours inseparable, He will respond by making our will and our physical needs His intimate concern and will provide for us amply.

Midrash Shmuel cites an alternative text: עֲשֵׂה רְצוֹנוֹ בִּרְצוֹנֶךָ, *Do His will with your own desire.* Often, a person performs commandments, but with a heavy heart, as though under duress. When that happens, God may, in response, do man's will "with a heavy heart." Rabban Gamliel teaches us here to serve Him willingly, so that He in turn will do *our* will willingly.

בַּטֵּל רְצוֹנְךָ מִפְּנֵי רְצוֹנוֹ, כְּדֵי שֶׁיְּבַטֵּל רְצוֹן אֲחֵרִים מִפְּנֵי רְצוֹנֶךָ — *Nullify your will in the face of His will, so that He will nullify the will of others in the face of your will.* The previous clause referred to the active fulfillment of positive commandments; this clause

⌘ **The business of Torah life.** The blessing recited prior to Torah study is לַעֲסוֹק בְּדִבְרֵי תוֹרָה, *to engross ourselves in the words of Torah.* The word עֵסֶק generally refers to a business or occupation. Just as a businessman constantly seeks to increase his profits, one who engages in spiritual "commerce" must always devise strategies to increase his "bottom line" (Chofetz Chaim).

⌘ **Not shared.** One should dedicate even his emotions to God. A touching example of such sensitivity was related by the Chofetz Chaim in his eulogy for his young and extremely gifted son. He related that in 1648-1649, during the Chmielnicki pogroms, there lived a widow with her only son in a small town in Poland. The woman prized nothing in the world as much as her dear young boy; he was the apple of her eye. One day the Cossack marauders broke into her home and violently murdered the boy in front of his mother.

The woman, her wellspring of tears already dried up, stood in front of her son's lifeless body, her hands raised up toward Heaven. "Master of the Universe!" she said. "In the chest of every person beats a heart capable of loving You. I, Your sinful maidservant, was never able to give You all my heart in love; half of it was always filled with love for my son. Now that You have taken him from me, I will fill my heart entirely with love for You!"

"So," said the Chofetz Chaim, "I always wanted to love God will all my heart; yet I'm only a human being, and some part of my capacity to love is expended on my children. Now that my son is gone, that bit of heart can be focused on loving You."

that He will treat your will as if it were His will. Nullify your will in the face of His will, so that He will nullify the will of others in the face of your will.

---

is addressed to one's efforts to avoid transgressing negative commandments (*Tosafos Yom Tov*). When one's will stands in conflict with God's directive, he must nullify his desire. In reward, God will nullify the designs of those whose will conflicts with his will (*Meiri, Rav*).

Another interpretation of this clause revolves around the concept of free will. While man is blessed with free choice, he would be wise at times to forgo the privilege and pray that God take it away from him. When sorely tempted by the Evil inclination, man should pray: "I totally yield to Your will, dear Father. Take my free will from me;

I want neither free will nor the reward for proper choice that it can bring me." Man may then be assured that since he willfully nullified his power of free choice to the Will of God, God will in turn nullify the will of *others* — in this case, the Evil Persuader — in the face of his will (*Kozhnitzer Maggid*).

When man follows the word of God because he "agrees" with Him, his commitment is weak, since he may later change his mind and decide to "disagree."

Therefore, our Sages teach that one should refrain from forbidden foods not because he dislikes

---

•§ **A father's satisfaction.** God, as we have mentioned before, always "mirrors" our behavior. If we do what He asks begrudgingly, He will provide for us "begrudgingly," in a less-than-optimal way. However, if we do His will full-heartedly, then He, in kind, "will want" to do good for us. Therefore, we are taught: Do His will with as much joy as you act upon your own desires. Just as nothing in the world will stop you from exercising your own will, so let nothing impede your fulfillment of God's wishes. God will then respond in kind and allow nothing to stand in the way of providing for our needs and desires (*HaChassid Yaavetz*).

It is the nature of a father to support his son under almost any circumstances, even if the son is undeserving. However, it is a joy to do so when the son not only does what the father expects of him, but does so wholeheartedly. The mishnah therefore tells us: *Treat His will as if it were your own will, so that He will treat your will as if it were His will*; act so that God will bestow His goodness upon you willingly and out of love, not merely as a father begrudgingly discharging a parental duty (*Kozhnitzer Maggid*). Further, a father wants nothing more than the special pleasure he feels when his child gives him satisfaction. Likewise, as God's children, we should perform *mitzvos* and fulfill His will with joy and excitement, thereby seeking to awaken His fatherly love for us (*Ohr HaMeir*).

•§ **Setting desire aside.** *Sfas Emes* explains the directive בַּטֵּל, *nullify*, in terms of the halachic principle of בִּיטוּל אִיסוּר בְּהֶיתֵּר, the nullification of forbidden substances in larger amounts of permitted items. For example, if a drop of milk falls into a pot of meat whose contents are at least sixty times the volume of the milk, the meat does not become unkosher. The rule of nullification states that the milk in such a small proportion loses its identity and assumes the identity of the kosher meat. Likewise, one must nullify his personal will, not by disregarding it but by subordinating it to such an extent that it takes on the character of God's will and loses its own identity.

R' Chaim of Volozhin was involved in protracted negotiations regarding a marriage proposal for one of his grandchildren. At every turn difficulties arose, and it seemed as if the match would not materialize. One day R' Chaim suddenly told his family that the time had come to seal the match. That day, the family of the other party came to Volozhin, and the match was indeed finalized. The family asked R' Chaim, "Was it prophecy or holy prescience that made you so sure about the outcome?"

"No," he answered. "Today was the first time I was able to free myself of personal emotions and follow the advice of our Sages to nullify your will to the will of God. Having done so, I was sure God would nullify the will of others (i.e., resolve the other party's doubts) and convince them to come to an amicable agreement with our family."

[ה] **הִלֵּל אוֹמֵר:** אַל תִּפְרוֹשׁ מִן הַצִּבּוּר, וְאַל תַּאֲמִין בְּעַצְמְךָ עַד יוֹם מוֹתְךָ,

them, but rather because God disapproves (*Toras Kohanim, Kedoshim*). [Similarly, if one accepts 612 of the 613 *mitzvos,* he has broken the yoke of his Master and in truth is really following only himself (see *Shaarei Teshuvah* 1:6).] Hence, the mishnah instructs us to nullify our own will in the face of His.

Alternatively, the term *the will of others* is a respectful reference to God. By nullifying their personal agendas, the righteous can even cause God to rescind a Heavenly decree (*Rav* and *Tiferes Yisrael*).

Mishnah 5

הִלֵּל אוֹמֵר — *Hillel says.* Hillel (see 1:12) was the grandfather of Rabban Gamliel of the last three mishnayos. In the following passage he amplifies Rabban Gamliel's dictum (2:2) regarding people involved in community service and teaches the general relationship of individuals to the community [or, according to *Tiferes Yisrael,* as instructions to public servants]. Furthermore, this mishnah and the three that follow, which are all attributed to Hillel, are an introduction to mishnah 9, which links Rabban Yochanan ben Zakkai to Hillel and Shammai in the chain of tradition (*Tosafos Yom Tov*).

אַל תִּפְרוֹשׁ מִן הַצִּבּוּר — *Do not separate yourself from the community.* One must participate emotionally [and physically] in the concerns of the community, bearing its pains and difficulties. One who does so will merit to share in the eventual consolation of the Messianic era (*Rav* based on *Taanis* 11a).

One who separates himself from community activities has no share in the World to Come. Even if he does not transgress any particular sin, he views himself as a separate entity, neither participating in the communal performance of *mitzvos* nor sharing the pains and travails of his co-religionists; and therefore he is deemed outside the Jewish pale (*Rambam, Hil. Teshuvah* 3:11).

When the community is actively involved in the pursuit of Torah and *mitzvos,* the honor of the King of kings is enhanced by every additional participant, each of one whom is one more jewel in the crown of God. One should not separate himself from the community and thereby diminish the glory of His Kingdom. It is praiseworthy, however, to shun completely a community which is willfully set on an improper course (*R' Yonah*), and if there is no alternative, even to live in solitude, rather than be forced to mingle with a corrupt society (*Rambam, Hilchos Dei'os* 6:1).

Even if one can save himself from a catastrophe threatening the community, he should not separate himself from them. Rather, he must seek ways to achieve general salvation for the entire community. If he looks only to save himself, he will not succeed, but the community will be saved through another of God's myriad messengers. *Meiri* cites the story of Mordechai and Esther as a classic example of this concept: When Esther said that it would be dangerous for her to approach Ahasuerus, Mordechai warned her that the Jewish people would somehow be saved without her, but she would be doomed (*Esther* 4:13-14).

According to the *Zohar,* we are instructed in this

⋑ Different ways to serve. During the Nazi Holocaust, great Jewish leaders interpreted this mishnah in diametrically different ways. Some felt that their duty was to remain with the community even if they themselves would perish along with it, while others ruled that they were obligated to escape in order to be able to rebuild vibrant Torah communities in other places. Both felt that the communal need came first, it was only the form that this took that was in doubt. The self-doubt which tormented these sensitive souls is aptly expressed in a letter written by Rabbi Shlomo Weinberg of Slonim, explaining why he did not leave the bloodbath of Europe when he could have: "Maybe I should have taken up your offer to flee when I still was able. But what shall I do? The children [i.e., the community] are dependent on me."

5. Hillel says: Do not separate yourself from the community; do not believe in yourself until the day you die;

mishnah to pray with the community. The prayers of the community at large are far more effective than that of any single individual. Also, the prayers are written in the plural form, because Jews should include the community's needs in their personal prayers. When R' Yitzchak Hutner was deathly ill, he explicitly told his students not to pray for him unless they asked God to allow him a speedy recovery among the other sick people of Israel.

[The word צִבּוּר is an acronym for צַדִּיקִים, *righteous*; בֵּינוֹנִים, *average people*; and רְשָׁעִים, *wicked people*. The community is comprised of disparate types who blend together to create a harmonious service to God. The Sages in fact teach that any public fast in which there are no participants from among the wicked is not truly a public fast (*Kerisos* 6b).]

וְאַל תַּאֲמִין בְּעַצְמְךָ עַד יוֹם מוֹתְךָ — *do not believe in yourself until the day you die.* Never rely on the fact that a good character trait is ingrained in your personality. Until death one must be afraid of ethical backsliding (*Rambam*). Even in terms of belief, one is susceptible to lapses. Yochanan served as *Kohen Gadol* for eighty years, and yet he became a Sadducee toward the end of

his life (*Rav, Rashi,* based on *Berachos* 29a).

According to *Tiferes Yisrael,* these words speak of the temporary nature of success. One should never become complacent about his financial or professional achievement. King Solomon, the epitome of royalty and success, was dethroned temporarily in his later years (see *Gittin* 68a).

The Evil Inclination is a tireless foe. One should therefore not delude himself into thinking that because he has won the battle, he has also won the war. Even to listen to the spurious arguments of heresy is a dangerous practice. A person should not be overconfident in his ability to interact with heretics and sift through their rhetoric for nuggets of truth. While Rabbi Meir succeeded in doing this with Elisha ben Abuyah, his former mentor turned heretic (see *Chagigah* 15b), in most cases it is an exercise in spiritual fatality (*R' Yonah*). King Solomon, the wisest of all men, was convinced that he was above such temptation when he disregarded the prohibition for a king to marry many wives (see *Deuteronomy* 17:17). He learned the bitter lesson contained here in our mishnah when his foreign wives persuaded him to ignore the

⊷§ **Communal prayer.** Upon meeting the Shunamite woman, the prophet Elisha asked her what she wished to request from the king (*II Kings* 4:13). The *Zohar* interprets "the king" as a reference to God. Her answer was, "I reside among my people." Rather than entering a personal plea, she linked her destiny to that of her people. R' Bunam of P'shis'cha compares this to a coin which is worn out and of diminished value. If a dishonest person tried to pass it off on a banker, it would certainly be rejected. However, if it were among many good-quality coins, no one would notice its defects. Likewise, in the company of the community God does not focus on personal faults. It is for this reason that He never totally rejects the entreaties of the community (*Berachos* 8a).

⊷§ **When the chips are down.** Rabbi Aharon Luria elaborates: One can be sure of the permanence of a good character trait only when it is put to the test. For example, one may exhibit a calm demeanor under normal circumstances and yet lose his temper when he is under extreme pressure. This is analogous to a person who holds something in his hand. We can never be sure how tightly he is holding it until someone tries to remove it. Similarly, we can only assess how entrenched a character trait is when it is under attack.

This dictum seems to contradict the words of the Talmud: "Once man has spent the majority of his life sinlessly, he will no longer sin" (*Yoma* 38a). Why, then, does the mishnah suggest that one beware of a spiritual lapse until his dying day? Rabbi Yisrael of Vizhnitz views the mishnah not in terms of sin but in terms of spiritual accomplishment. One should never become complacent, feeling that he has achieved his life's goals. There is no "early retirement" from the service of God; one must constantly nurture his spiritual growth. Thus Hillel says, *Do not believe in yourself;* you still have a long way to go to achieve your potential. Therefore, strive onward and upward, always seeking greater spiritual accomplishments, and continue to do so *until the day you die.*

idolatry and sin in his kingdom [see *Sanhedrin* 21b] (*Meiri*).

וְאַל תָּדִין אֶת חֲבֵרְךָ עַד שֶׁתַּגִּיעַ לִמְקוֹמוֹ — *do not judge your fellow until you have reached his place.* According to *R' Yonah,* this is a continuation of the previous clause: One should not believe that he is better able to withstand temptation than others who succumbed, for one never knows how he would react in the same predicament (*Rav, Rashi*). The Talmud (*Sanhedrin* 102b) relates that King Menashe, one of Israel's most notorious rulers, appeared to R' Ashi in a dream. R' Ashi asked him why a man as wise as he would stoop to idolatry. Menashe answered: "Had you been there, you would have lifted your cloak and run speedily after the idols. [It is only because the desire for idolatry was eradicated before your time that you have the moral fortitude to withstand temptation." See *Rashi* ad loc.]

[Until one finds himself in the same place, time, and circumstances, it is realistically impossible to judge a friend; one would be like a magistrate who lacks critical evidence.]

When King Solomon finished building the Temple, he placed the keys under his pillow. One of his wives, the daughter of Pharaoh, tricked him into oversleeping, causing him to miss bringing the morning offering. When Jeroboam, an infamous idolater, gathered the tribe of Ephraim to rebuke King Solomon, a Heavenly voice was heard to say, "Evil one [i.e., Jeroboam], he is only an inadvertent sinner, while you are a rebellious idolater." This is a striking illustration of judging someone without having arrived at his place (*Machzor Vitry*).

Meiri offers a novel interpretation: Do not judge someone when he is away from their familiar surroundings, because people tend to behave better when they are away from home and trying to make a good impression. Therefore, *do not judge your fellow until you have reached his place* of residence; there, his guard is down and he will behave naturally, showing his true character.

וְאַל תֹּאמַר דָּבָר שֶׁאִי אֶפְשָׁר לִשְׁמוֹעַ, שֶׁסּוֹפוֹ לְהִשָּׁמַע — *do not make a statement that cannot be easily understood, on the ground that it will be understood eventually.* One should speak clearly, leaving no doubts as to his intent. *Rambam* adds that teachers must not speak or write so cryptically that their ideas yield meaning only upon careful investigation. Similarly, *Tiferes Yisrael* decries the excessive use of abbreviations in books.

Alternatively, *Rav* comments that one should be discreet regarding secrets. One should not make a statement which is not intended to be heard by others, for eventually it will be heard. The walls have ears when it comes to secrets; *the bird of the skies may carry the sound, and some winged creature may betray the matter* (*Ecclesiastes* 10:20).

Meiri comments: Do not speak cryptically in public on the assumption that those who are not intended to know your message will not understand it. Eventually, even the uninformed will figure out what you mean, and your secret will now become public knowledge.

וְאַל תֹּאמַר לִכְשֶׁאֶפָּנֶה אֶשְׁנֶה, שֶׁמָּא לֹא תִפָּנֶה — *and do not say, "When I am free I will study," for perhaps you will not become free.* One should never postpone Torah study to a more opportune moment. It may never come. He must seize the moment now and increase his intellectual and spiritual wealth; he must not assume that tomorrow it will be easier for him to work Torah study into his schedule.

◆§ **Keep it sealed.** A secret is very much like a balloon. If tightly knotted, it will contain all the air blown into it. However, the slightest pinhole will allow everything to escape. A secret revealed to one person is as good as revealed to the whole world. A wise man once said: "If someone tells you a secret with the warning not to tell anybody, you should never entrust him with anything *you* want to remain a secret."

do not judge your fellow until you have reached his place; do not make a statement that cannot be easily understood, on the ground that it will be understood eventually; and do not say, "When I am free I will study," for perhaps you will not become free.

Every day has its preoccupations and distractions. This mishnah echoes 1:15, *Make your Torah study a fixed practice* (*Rav, R' Yonah*).

According to *Tiferes Yisrael*, אֶשְׁנֶה should be rendered *I will review* [my studies]. The key to success in Torah study is constant review, even though it is a tedious task that one prefers to push off, and therefore the injunction is a necessary reminder.

⋙ **In your own arena.** One who feels hunger pangs must eat immediately; if he ignores the need for food, his health may suffer. Likewise, one who ignores his soul's hunger risks spiritual harm (*Vilna Gaon*).

Even if one eventually finds the time to learn, he can never make up the time lost. Every breath of life granted man is an opportunity to pursue Torah and *mitzvos*. One can never use his free time to compensate for time lost in the past (*R' Yonah*). Based on this, the *Bach* would write any new insights he developed while studying during the Intermediate Days of Succos and Pesach, when it is forbidden to write unless the matter cannot be postponed until after Yom Tov. His rationale for permitting this was that it would be impossible to come back to these thoughts later on, when he would have to attend to *other* learning. Furthermore, he would have to review the material after the holiday to refresh his memory before committing his ideas to paper, a further loss of time (see *Mishnah Berurah* 545 §47).

A disciple of the Chozeh of Lublin once spent Rosh Hashanah with his *Rebbe*. During the visit, he offered the following prayer: "Please, God, allow me to earn enough for my weekly needs early in the week, even though it means I may earn less money overall. This way, I will have the peace of mind to devote the rest of the week to my Torah studies."

The following day when he went to take leave of his teacher, the *Chozeh* told him: "Yesterday your prayer elicited amusement in Heaven. Do you really think the few rubles a week you are willing to forgo play a significant role in Heaven? Do you think God lacks money to give, or that He is — Heaven forfend — stingy? And as far as the peace of mind you seek — who tells you that God wants you to conduct your Torah study and prayer under idyllic conditions? Maybe He wants you to perform *mitzvos* while you are harried. Maybe what pleases Him is the special holiness and purity that you achieve despite difficulty. Maybe God has more satisfaction in how you overcome your burdens and create light in the midst of darkness."

R' Mendel of Kotzk explained this mishnah in a similar vein: Don't wait until you are free to learn, for your special task in life may be to learn while under stress and pressure. If you wait until the pressures subside, you may wait forever.

According to the Chofetz Chaim, this principle is reflected in God's words to Moses: *The place on which you stand is hallowed ground* (*Exodus* 3:5). Despite all its difficulties, your present situation is an opportunity for holiness and growth. There is no rule that greatness can bloom only under optimal conditions.

⋙ Rabbi Aharon of Belz said that review is a *segulah* for remembering one's learning. This is rather enigmatic, since generally the term *segulah* indicates a supernatural rather than a natural way of insuring the desired result. R' Shlomo Freifeld explained that man's ability to understand the infinite wisdom of God is indeed incomprehensible and unnatural. It is only because of God's mercy that He allows us access to His wisdom — and this only in response to our demonstrated desire to understand. The process of review, therefore, is not merely to facilitate retention; it is a way to express how badly we yearn for His word, our silent prayer for enlightenment.

[It is interesting to note that the word for "review" and for "different" is the same — שׁוֹנֶה. Both meanings are connected. The purpose of reviewing is not merely to repeat the old; it is done in order to reach new levels of understanding. Material which is reviewed assumes new and different meanings and therefore, each time one reviews, he again expresses his thirst for the word of God. In response, God allows him to penetrate new levels of understanding.]

[ו] **הוּא** הָיָה אוֹמֵר: אֵין בּוּר יְרֵא חֵטְא, וְלֹא עַם הָאָרֶץ חָסִיד, וְלֹא הַבַּיְשָׁן לָמֵד, וְלֹא הַקַּפְּדָן מְלַמֵּד,

Alternatively, this clause is directed toward communal leaders, who are constantly preoccupied with public issues. They should not wait until all the tumult dies down before taking time to study, for it is unlikely that there will ever be a time when they will be free. Instead, they should seize any breaks in their schedule for Torah study.

Mishnah 6

הוּא הָיָה אוֹמֵר: אֵין בּוּר יְרֵא חֵטְא — *He used to say. A boor cannot be fearful of sin.* A boor is a person of no substance, without even the minimal intelligence necessary to conduct basic business (*Rashi, Rav*). In the context of our mishnah, a boor is one who is completely lacking in Torah knowledge, good deeds, and character refinement. Unaware of right and wrong, he is unable to maintain fidelity to Torah law or ethics (*R' Yonah; Rambam*).

Like an unplowed field (שָׂדֶה בּוּר), no spiritual growth is possible for the boor (*Meiri*).

Tiferes Yisrael differentiates between one who is fearful of sin (יְרֵא חֵטְא) and a God-fearing person (יְרֵא אֱלֹהִים). While a boor may act properly out of fear of Divine retribution, he has not developed a true sensitivity to the abhorrent nature of sin.

וְלֹא עַם הָאָרֶץ חָסִיד — *an unlearned person cannot be scrupulously pious.* [The term *chassid* refers to someone who is aware of the law and chooses to do more than it requires.] An unlearned person can be fearful of sin, but he can never be scrupulously pious (*Rashi, Rav*) as long as he lacks knowledge of the extent of the law and what is considered desirable behavior.

According to *Meiri*, our mishnah uses the term עַם

⊸§ **Every minute counts.** Rabbi Aharon Kotler always carried a *Mishnah Berurah* with him and learned it whenever there were brief intervals in his hectic and demanding communal activities. The lesson is equally applicable to the average person, who may be disheartened at the thought that his limited Torah study is of negligible value. Not so, every moment is precious.

The Chofetz Chaim illustrated this idea with a parable: A man was warned by his doctors not to enter the bathhouse since the excessive heat and steam were dangerous to his health. One day he passed the bathhouse and could not resist the temptation to enter. The heat indeed weakened him, and he felt that he might faint. Mustering his last bit of strength, he headed toward a cold pool in order to resuscitate himself, but to his chagrin, the door to the pool was locked. He called for help, and a bystander tried to sprinkle cold water from a bucket on him. "I need a cold pool," the sick man protested. "These few drops will not help!" Replied his rescuer, "You are right — but until we can open the pool, be refreshed from this little bit of cool water. It is still better than fainting!"

One would certainly prefer to immerse himself totally in the refreshing waters of Torah; but even if this is not possible, it is foolish to refuse a partial rescue by denying the benefit of a limited exposure to the waters of Torah. This is the wisdom imparted us in the mishnah: In the meantime, we can revive our soul even with droplets of God's refreshing Torah.

⊸§ **No greater waste.** The Kotzker *Rebbe* explained this clause in his typically sharp style: *A boor cannot be fearful of sin,* for if he were to be truly fearful of sin, he would never allow himself to remain a boor. There is no sin greater than leaving human potential undeveloped.

⊸§ **Transcending law.** A scrupulously pious individual (חָסִיד) is one who goes beyond the letter of the law and follows its spirit as well. While no specific legislation exists for many areas of behavior, the חָסִיד is able to ascertain the Heavenly will in these areas with his own insight and sensitivity. One can only achieve this level if he has been sufficiently exposed to the Godly intelligence, which is revealed in the full spectrum of Torah. Hence, the unlearned cannot be scrupulously pious.

6. He used to say: A boor cannot be fearful of sin; an unlearned person cannot be scrupulously pious; a bashful person cannot learn, and a quick, impatient person cannot teach;

הָאָרֶץ to refer to someone preoccupied with business matters. Such a person is by habit accustomed to thinking in terms of exact measures and weights, and he therefore finds it difficult to aspire to being a *chassid*, which demands dealing with others *beyond* the strict letter of the law.

The Talmud teaches that even if one studied much Torah, he is considered unlearned if he has not served and observed Torah scholars in their daily lives. While one can fulfill the basic legal and ethical requirements of Torah through textual learning alone, it takes a personal involvement with the righteous to develop a sense of right and wrong, especially regarding life situations which are not explicitly addressed in the Scriptures. Hence, one unlearned in the ways of scholars can never

achieve scrupulous piety (*Doresh LePerakim*).

וְלֹא הַבַּיְשָׁן לָמֵד — *a bashful person cannot learn.* While bashfulness generally is a positive trait (see 5:24), it is counterproductive to success in Torah study (*R' Yonah*). One must unembarrassedly seek to grow spiritually, for if one is afraid of being ridiculed for his questions, he will never be able to clarify his doubts (*Rav*). It is better to risk being thought a fool than to remain silent and relinquish intelligence (*Tiferes Yisrael*).

וְלֹא הַקַּפְּדָן מְלַמֵּד — *and a quick, impatient person cannot teach.* A teacher who is impatient with his students and intolerant of their questions will never succeed at teaching. His students will fear his

⤳ **The seeker excels.** R' Chaim Shmulevitz related that he once visited with his uncle, R' Avraham Joffen, *Rosh Yeshivah* of the Novarodoker Yeshivah in Bialystok. He asked his uncle to point out the most astute scholar (*lamdan*) in the yeshivah, and R' Avraham indicated one particular student. "Who is the greatest *baki*, with the broadest knowledge?" asked R' Chaim. R' Avraham pointed to a second student. When R' Chaim asked to see the young man who was most proficient in the theory and practice of *mussar*, the ethical system for which Novarodok was famous, his uncle pointed out yet a third student. Finally, R' Chaim asked, "Uncle, tell me who is the best *bachur* in the yeshivah?" To his surprise, R' Avraham pointed out a fourth person and said, "He is the best." "But if the other three excel in *lamdanus, mussar,* and *b'kius,* how can this young man be the best?" questioned his nephew. R' Avraham replied, "He is the greatest מבקש — the greatest *seeker.* He, more than all the others, is tireless in his efforts to achieve growth. He shows no signs of bashfulness and forges ahead in his search for greatness in Torah knowledge and character." That student was Rabbi Yisrael Yaakov Kanievsky, who became world famous as the Steipler Gaon.

Just as one is not embarrassed to ask directions of a passerby in order to reach his destination, so he must not be ashamed to enlist aid in understanding Torah, the road map which guides man from this world to the next.

⤳ **Patience is perfect.** The classic instance of a teacher's patience is recorded in the Talmud (*Eruvin* 54b):
R' Preida had a student who had to have each lesson repeated four hundred times before he understood it. One day R' Preida was asked to attend to a certain matter involving a *mitzvah.* Before leaving, he taught the student the lesson the usual four hundred times, but the student still did not grasp it. R' Preida asked him, "Why is today different?" The student answered, "From the very moment they told the *rebbe* that there is a *mitzvah* matter for him to attend to, my attention was diverted because I thought that at any moment the *rebbe* would get up and leave." R' Preida said to him, "Pay attention, and I will teach you," and he taught him another four hundred times. A Heavenly voice emanated and asked R' Preida, "Do you prefer that four hundred years be added to your life, or that you and your generation merit the life of the World to Come?" R' Preida replied, "That I and my generation merit the life of the World to Come." The Holy One, Blessed is He, said, "Give him both."

R' Mordechai Gifter describes Rav Preida's student not necessarily having meager intellect, but rather as one whose inquisitive mind constantly sought new angles of interpretation and new levels of understanding which caused him to incessantly question his teacher. Rav Preida never tired of answering his perpetual questioner.

sharp retorts and will be afraid to seek clarification. Instead, a teacher must exhibit a cheerful disposition toward his students so that they will feel free to make any inquiries (*Rav* and *Rashi*). *Rambam* renders קַפְּדָן as a perfectionist. Such a person is unsuited for teaching; every mistake on the part of his students will elicit his anger, undermining their self-confidence and impeding their growth. *R' Yonah* adds that one must be ready to repeat the lesson to his or her students time and time again until it penetrates.

According to *Tiferes Yisrael*, the axiom לֹא הַקַּפְּדָן מְלַמֵּד is based on the teaching of King Solomon, *The gentle words of the wise are heard* (*Ecclesiastes* 9:17). Students should never feel that their relationship with their teacher is an adversarial one. Only when the teacher senses that his students are inattentive may he instill fear in them (see *Kesubos* 103b); and even this rebuke should be given in a way that allows his love for his child-student to shine through.

וְלֹא כָל הַמַּרְבֶּה בִּסְחוֹרָה מַחְכִּים — *anyone excessively occupied in business cannot become a scholar.*

Our Sages (based on *Deuteronomy* 30:13) taught: Torah knowledge is not to be found among international business travelers. Since their business dealings dominate their schedule, with Torah study occupying a secondary role, they will never taste real success in learning (*Rav, R' Yonah*).

Rashi and *Tosafos Yom Tov* note that the mishnah speaks of *excessive* involvement in commerce. Of course, the ordinary pursuit of a living is not only permitted but is important [see mishnah 2, and 3:21: *If there is no flour* (sustenance), *there is no Torah*]. It is

overinvolvement, an excessive emphasis on the means rather than on the end, that the Sages viewed as detrimental to success in learning.

Alternatively, *Rashi* explains: To be truly wise, one must possess knowledge spanning the full spectrum of the disciplines. Limiting oneself to business knowledge may be a fatal flaw in the acquisition of wisdom. Therefore, one who is excessively involved in business, to the exclusion of other areas, will not acquire wisdom.

Unlike the previous statements of the mishnah, which are absolute and unequivocal, Rabban Gamliel states here that not *all* who are excessively involved in business can become wise, indicating that some exceptional individuals may be able to achieve both. Indeed, there were persons who succeeded at the acquisition of both wisdom and wealth. The Talmud cites R' Eliezer ben Charsom as an example [see *Kiddushin* 49b] (*Midrash Shmuel*).

Tiferes Zvi renders מַחְכִּים as "succeed." Success in business is ultimately in God's hands. Greater effort does not necessarily result in greater success. Only in spiritual pursuits is success linked to exertion. Hence we are taught: *Anyone excessively occupied in business cannot succeed*, for his efforts are no guarantee.

וּבְמְקוֹם שֶׁאֵין אֲנָשִׁים, הִשְׁתַּדֵּל לִהְיוֹת אִישׁ — *and in a place where there are no leaders, strive to be a leader.* When there is a dearth of leaders who can issue decisions, one must make every effort to fill that role, even though it entails great responsibility (*Rav*).

R' Yonah and *Meiri* warn that someone should not practice excessive humility. If the times or location suffer from spiritual decline and no one more qualified is available, he should step into the leadership role.

Alternatively, they comment that if one cannot

◆§ **The best investment.** Raphael Goetz, an alumnus of the Telshe Yeshivah in Lithuania, married the only child of Kalman Wissotsky, who controlled the monopoly on tea in Czarist Russia. Goetz took over the business upon his father-in-law's passing. He employed Rabbi Yehudah Leib Graubart on full retainer and ensconced him in a book-filled room next to his own office. Rabbi Graubart's company duties were twofold: He was to rule on any pertinent halachic questions involving the business and he was to learn with Goetz whenever his employer had a free moment. The rest of the time, he was free to pursue his own studies.

◆§ **Warped outlook.** One who is involved excessively in business indicates that he views success as a product of human effort. Such a person will use any and all means at his disposal in order to be successful; ethical behavior will fall to the wayside. One who is blessed with the insight that his business efforts will not necessarily translate into fiscal success will make a normal effort to earn a living but will be wary of excessive involvement. [See 3:21.]

find a friend or mentor to teach him and offer him constructive criticism, he should strive to be his own leader and to offer himself corrective advice, striving to grow until he becomes a man of distinction.

Furthermore, a person should never be satisfied with his spiritual attainments, no matter where he is. Even in a place where there are no people who occupy a greater spiritual plane than he, he should not rest on his laurels. Under such circumstances, the mishnah instructs him that he must still *strive to be a man*, seeking to emulate the great people of earlier times and working toward greater achievements.

A different interpretation is that the mishnah is referring to private behavior. One is often tempted to relax his religious, moral, or ethical standards when he is not under the scrutiny of the public eye. He should never say to himself, "No one is looking; I can let my guard down." Even *in a place where there are no people* observing one's conduct, one must still *strive to be a man* and retain his moral standards (*Midrash Shmuel*).

◆§ **Everyone's job.** This situation is comparable to a soldier's status in the army. In peacetime one may take the liberty of proceeding leisurely through the ranks, eventually rising to high status. On the battlefield, however, when no officers are there to lead, everyone must be ready to step into the breach and be a commander no matter what his official rank is. It is the same in the eternal war of spiritual growth.

The Chofetz Chaim offered the following parable: An innkeeper once offered a cup of tea to the *poritz*, the lord of the manor. The *poritz* took one sip and spit it out, smashing the cup. "Don't you know that one must use filtered water to make a cup of tea? This water is full of impurities. Make sure the next time to use only distilled water!"

A while later, a fire broke out in the inn. The flames raged, and yet the innkeeper did nothing to put them out, and before long, the inn and the surrounding buildings burned to the ground — including the mansion of the *poritz*. The angry landowner confronted his tenant: "Why didn't you fetch water and put out the fire? There is plenty of water in the well; why did you let the fire spread?" The innkeeper answered, "I couldn't do that. You told me to use only distilled water. I couldn't use water from the well."

Answered the *poritz*, "Fool! For a glass of tea, you must use only pure water. But when a fire is burning, even unrefined water can put it out!"

Similarly, taught the Chofetz Chaim: In days gone by, when the spiritual climate in the Jewish community was as it should be, and the Torah was supreme, Torah teachers had to be only the best and most refined people of the nation. Like a glass of tea, only "distilled" water could be used. Today, however, a spiritual conflagration threatens to consume the entire nation. In such circumstances, even people of a lesser caliber must take positions as teachers, rabbis, and *roshei yeshivah*. Today, even water which is not 100-percent pure is needed to extinguish the engulfing flames.

◆§ **Not good enough.** The Sages taught: "A person should say, "When will my actions reach [the spiritual level of] those of my forefathers?'" (*Tanna d'Vei Eliyahu* 25). R' Bunam of P'shis'cha questioned this premise. Can one actually reach such an exalted level? Rather, he explained, one must attempt to at least *touch* the level his forefathers attained [the word יַגִּיעַ, *reach*, is rendered in this case as יַגַע, meaning to touch]. One will grow by attempting to barely touch the level of those who came before him, for by doing so he will emotionally stretch himself to his limits.

This tendency to settle for mediocrity in spiritual matters is, according to the Ponovezher Rav (Rabbi Yosef Kahaneman), the key to understanding a rather puzzling prophecy: *Behold, days are coming, says God, and I will send famine in the land. Not famine for bread nor thirst for water, but rather [hunger] to hear the word of God* (Amos 8:11). This does not seem to be a terrible tragedy at all; if anything, it seems to portend a spiritual awakening.

Explained the Ponovezher Rav: A hungry person is so desperate for food that he will eat anything, even unappetizing food, and if he is thirsty, even filthy water will seem refreshing. The prophet teaches that the unbearable lack of food for the soul will be so oppressive at that time that people will settle for diluted versions of Torah and synthetic religious experiences. Rather than experiencing the full vibrancy of Torah, they will settle for poor imitations of the real thing. Our mishnah teaches us not to be satisfied with any spiritual status that is less than the best we can possibly achieve.

[ז] **אַף** הוּא רָאָה גֻּלְגֹּלֶת אַחַת שֶׁצָּפָה עַל פְּנֵי הַמָּיִם.
אָמַר לָהּ: ,,עַל דַּאֲטֵפְתְּ אַטְפוּךְ, וְסוֹף מְטַיְּפָיִךְ
יְטוּפוּן.''

[ח] **הוּא** הָיָה אוֹמֵר: מַרְבֶּה בָשָׂר, מַרְבֶּה רִמָּה;

Mishnah 7

אַף הוּא רָאָה גֻּלְגֹּלֶת אַחַת שֶׁצָּפָה עַל פְּנֵי הַמָּיִם. אָמַר
לָהּ — *He* ,,עַל דַּאֲטֵפְתְּ אַטְפוּךְ, וְסוֹף מְטַיְּפָיִךְ יְטוּפוּן''
*also saw a skull floating on the water. He said to it:
"Because you drowned others, they drowned you;
and eventually those who drowned you will be
drowned."* (This is the second incident related in
Avos d'Rabbi Nosson regarding Hillel, indicated by
the word *also*.)

Hillel spoke to the skull (see *Rashi, Succah* 53a,
who opines that Hillel recognized the skull as that
of a known murderer) as if it were alive in order to
explain the system of Divine justice. "Since you
were wicked and murdered others, you were
yourself murdered. However, even the one who
murdered *you* is subject to punishment, for God
picks as an instrument of retribution someone who
previously transgressed and is liable. Even though
your murderer was an agent of Divine retribution,
he too will be punished" (*Rav*).

Ramban clarifies the concept alluded to here in
his commentary (*Genesis* 15:14): "Know and understand that if a person has been inscribed and sealed
for a violent death on Rosh Hashanah, the bandits
who kill him will not be guiltless [simply] because
they fulfilled that which had been decreed against
him. *That wicked man shall die in his iniquity* (*Ezekiel*
3:18), but his blood will be sought from the
murderer(s). However, when a decree is issued from
the mouth of a prophet, there are different laws
concerning the one who fulfills it. If he heard it and
he wishes to fulfill the Will of his Creator as
decreed, he incurs no sin for doing so. On the

contrary, it is accounted to him as a merit, just as it
is said concerning King Jehu: *Because thou hast
done well in executing that which is right in Mine
eyes, and hast done unto the house of Ahab
according to all that was in My heart, thy sons of the
fourth generation shall sit on the throne of Israel* (*II
Kings* 10:30). However, if he heard the command
and killed the guilty person out of personal hatred
or in order to take his wealth, he is subject to
punishment, for his intention was to sin, and it is
accounted to him as a transgression." [See *Ramban*
ad loc. for a historical analysis of this matter.]
Furthermore, overzealousness and excessive cruelty are factors which indict one who assumes the
role of executing God's retributive plans.

*He said to it: "Because you drowned others, they
drowned you."* Moved by this sight of a floating
skull that had been deprived of proper burial
(*Tiferes Yisrael*), Hillel remarked aloud about the
justice of Divine retribution: "God punishes man
'measure for measure.' Nothing man experiences
in life is without reason." The commentators agree
that Hillel made his statement only in *general* terms
and did not mean that every corpse was that of a
murderer. Certainly such a victim had not necessarily committed murder, but Hillel's point was that
there is always justice in God's scheme.

According to *Rambam*, this teaches us that one's
bad deeds come back to haunt him. Man himself
suffers from the suffering he inflicts on others.
Conversely, and to an even greater extent, man is
always the beneficiary of his own good deeds.

◆§ Man is treated by God in the same fashion that he treats his fellow man. This is certainly true for
good treatment as well as bad. Homiletically, this clause is the message of the famous verse
(*Leviticus* 19:18): וְאָהַבְתָּ לְרֵעֲךָ כָּמוֹךָ אֲנִי ה', *You shall love your fellow like yourself; I will be God*: In proportion
to your love for your fellow man, I will be God [i.e., I will shower you with My beneficence] (*R' Avraham
Yaakov of Sadigur*).

7. He also saw a skull floating on the water. He said to it: "Because you drowned others, they drowned you; and eventually those who drowned you will be drowned."

8. He used to say: The more flesh, the more worms;

Mishnah 8

Of the mishnah's ten clauses, the first five speak of stages of life, the excesses one might indulge in during those stages, and the unfortunate result of these excesses. The last five clauses present the antidote to such indulgence (*Tiferes Yisrael*).

הוּא הָיָה אוֹמֵר: מַרְבֶּה בָשָׂר, מַרְבֶּה רִמָּה — *He used to say: The more flesh, the more worms.* In a denunciation of gluttony, the mishnah teaches that overeating and drinking fatten one's body only in order to sustain the maggots in his grave. The Talmud (*Shabbos* 152a) teaches that in addition, maggots are as painful to the dead as sharp needles are to the living.

That pain is not felt by the body; after death, the body feels nothing. The soul, which lives on after death, senses the pain inflicted by the worms and realizes that this is punishment for not having properly tended in life to spiritual needs (*Tosafos Yom Tov*).

This is just one example of the basic life principle that all excess is detrimental to man — except for great indulgence in Torah study, charity, and the pursuit of wisdom (*Rav*). Pleasure and the good life, symbolized by the words *the more flesh*, are no assurance of long life; on the contrary, they are a source of embarrassment and an attraction for the maggots on the day of death (*R' Yonah*).

◆§ The Baal Shem Tov captures the essence of the seventh mishnah with a haunting parable: An impoverished woman who lived in a shanty on the outskirts of town spent her days collecting alms from door to door. Whenever people offered her charity, she would take it and respond, "Everything man does he does not for others, but for himself." People became accustomed to her strange response.

On her rounds she once approached the royal palace and received a contribution from the queen. As usual, she offered her customary maxim, "Everything man does he does not for others, but for himself." Soon the destitute woman became a regular visitor at the palace, each time receiving a tidy sum from the queen and offering the enigmatic rejoinder. Initially, the queen bore the seemingly ungracious remark of the woman with patience, but eventually the poor woman's lack of appreciation became so annoying that she could no longer take it. She decided to teach her a fatal lesson and ordered the royal bakery to prepare a loaf of bread laced with deadly poison. The poor woman was delighted to receive the bonus loaf on her next visit, and as always, she offered her predictable response, "Everything man does he does not for others, but for himself." The woman took the loaf home but decided not to eat it right away, planning to merely gaze at it and smell it for awhile.

At that time the prince went out to the forest on a hunting expedition, accompanied by his servants. The hunt was tiring, and the prince was therefore happy to come upon a shanty at the edge of the woods where he hoped to rest a bit before returning home. The shack belonged to none other than the queen's regular charity case. The woman immediately recognized the prince and was honored to be able to host the son of her benefactress. She immediately offered him the delectable loaf of bread, and the prince, ravenously hungry, took a slice. He had eaten but a bite or two when he collapsed, dead — a victim of the powerful poison with which the royal bakers had laced the loaf. The members of the prince's entourage were so aghast that they could not react.

The poor woman ran quickly to the palace to tell the queen of the terrible tragedy. The queen fainted as a result of her great shock. When she revived, she turned to the poor woman and said, "I now understand the bitter truth of your aphorism, 'Everything man does he does not for others, but for himself . . .'"

Certainly this is true of our good deeds which return to help us.

מַרְבֶּה נְכָסִים, מַרְבֶּה דְאָגָה; מַרְבֶּה נָשִׁים, מַרְבֶּה
כְשָׁפִים; מַרְבֶּה שְׁפָחוֹת, מַרְבֶּה זִמָּה; מַרְבֶּה עֲבָדִים,
מַרְבֶּה גָזֵל. מַרְבֶּה תוֹרָה, מַרְבֶּה חַיִּים; מַרְבֶּה יְשִׁיבָה,

According to *Tiferes Yisrael*, the mishnah defines different stages of life. From one's earliest years, his first desire is to eat, drink, and increase the flesh. He is cautioned here not to indulge this desire, since it only results in parasites and ill health caused by obesity.

מַרְבֶּה נְכָסִים, מַרְבֶּה דְאָגָה — *The more possessions the more worry.* As one grows a little older, he progresses from a desire for food to a desire for money (*Tiferes Yisrael*). Worldly possessions do not assure a good life. Property can be stolen, damaged, seized by the government, or lose its value based on the fickleness of the market. Hence, possessions can often be a source of incessant worry (*Rashi, R' Yonah, Rav*).

One who possesses one hundred dollars wants two hundred, while he who has two desires four (see *Koheles Rabbah* 1:34). Similarly, the more one possesses, the greater the amount he needs to compensate for a loss. The wealthy have more to lose and therefore more to worry about than those of more modest means.

Chovos HaLevavos (quoted by *Rav*) cites the prayer of a righteous man who made the following request of God: המקום יצילני מפזור הנפש, *May the Omnipresent rescue me from a scattering of the soul.* His intent was that God should prevent him from owning properties and posses-sions in too many locations, causing the preoccupation of his heart and mind to be dispersed over the seven seas.

Financial success is ordained in Heaven. One cannot earn a penny more than what was inscribed for him on Rosh Hashanah. Hence, by increasing his possessions, one does not increase his income; he only increases the things he has to be worried about (*Ruach Chaim*).

מַרְבֶּה נָשִׁים, מַרְבֶּה כְשָׁפִים — *the more wives the more witchcraft.* During the time when polygamy was permitted, the jealousy between rival wives would often cause them to resort to all kinds of ploys — even witchcraft — to capture their husband's affection (*R' Yonah, Meiri*).

Although it is Biblically permitted, Ashkenazic Jews adopted the ban on polygamy enacted by Rabbeinu Gershom (known as the Light of the Exile) [c. 960-1040]. [See *Shulchan Aruch Even HaEzer* 1:10.]

מַרְבֶּה שְׁפָחוֹת, מַרְבֶּה זִמָּה — *the more maidservants the more lewdness.* As one matures, the need for possessions assumes an external role: the desire for prestige. By surrounding himself with the accouterments of wealth, such as maidservants and other domestic help, one seeks to enhance his

◆§ **Welcome stranger.** A well-to-do man came to visit the Chozeh of Lublin for Shabbos. On Friday night after the prayers, everybody passed by the *Rebbe* to exchange Shabbos greetings. When the wealthy merchant passed by, the *Rebbe* stretched out his hand. "*Shalom Aleichem*, welcome," he said. The guest was surprised. "*Rebbe*, you welcomed me today upon my arrival in Lublin; why again?"

"Yes, my friend, you are right," the *Rebbe* replied. "However, I noticed during the prayers that you seemed preoccupied. Since much of your business is based at the market in the port city of Danzig, your mind wandered off to Danzig to check up on your dealings even while your body was here in the synagogue in Lublin. Now that you have returned, it is only right that I welcome you back."

◆§ **Useless responsibility.** The *Mussar* disciples of Novarodok considered private property as similar to *chametz* on Passover. From a legal standpoint, *chametz* on Passover is valueless and hence can be declared ownerless. Nonetheless, if *chametz* is found in one's possession during Pesach, he is deemed the owner and is considered culpable for it. Similarly, one's possessions are really not his own, only on loan, so to speak, from God — and yet he is deemed the owner and suffers the constant worry that comes with them.

the more possessions the more worry; the more wives the more witchcraft; the more maidservants the more lewdness; the more manservants the more thievery. [However,] the more Torah the more life; the more study the

prestige in the eyes of the public. However, maidservants often maintain a low moral standard and may introduce him to immoral behavior. His behavior will become public knowledge, thus bringing him infamy rather than the prestige he sought (*Tiferes Yisrael*).

Even if it is not he but only those around him who are ensnared by the lewd behavior of these women, he bears much of the responsibility and shame, since such abominable behavior took place in his home under his nose (*R' Yonah*).

The Talmud suggests that even the wife of a wealthy man, who can afford extensive domestic help, should not completely remove herself from some type of involvement in the running of the household; "Total inactivity can lead to lewd behavior" (*Kesubos* 59b). Too many maidservants often provide the mistress of the house with too much free time, which may lead to immorality (*Doresh LePerakim*).

מַרְבֶּה עֲבָדִים, מַרְבֶּה גָזֵל — *the more manservants the more thievery.* The fifth step on the ladder of excess comes in old age, when man is weak and tired, and seeks assistance in maintaining and expanding his financial holdings. He hires servants and staff, but they only deplete his fortune, by defrauding him (*Tiferes Yisrael*). According to *Rashi* and *R' Yonah,* manservants are a terrible liability to their masters. Sooner or later they will rob from others, and the blame will be attributed to the master.

Like the servants of Lot (see *Genesis* 13:7, *Rashi* ad loc.), they will rob and steal *on behalf* of their masters, thus bringing them disrespect and leading them to sin. *Sfas Emes* interprets this clause as a warning similar to 1:5, which teaches one to *let the poor be members of your household* by employing only Jewish domestic help. One who hires non-Jewish manservants "increases thievery" by robbing potential Jewish employees of the means to earn a living.

According to *R' Yosef ibn Nachmias,* our mishnah decries the practice of maintaining a standard of living above one's means. By hiring too many servants, one may be forced to stoop to "thievery" in the sense of questionable business practices in order to maintain his opulent life-style.

Unlike *Tiferes Yisrael,* who views this mishnah as a series of chronological progressions in the stages of indulgence, *Rav* sees each step as a *result* of the preceding step. He organizes them as follows: One begins with a life-style of conspicuous consumption and then seeks to expand his finances in order to support his indulgences. With the achievement of fiscal success, he feels comfortable and is sure he can afford to support more than one wife; however, in order to make each wife feel like a queen, he must provide maidservants. Having thus expanded the size of his family and household, he needs to maintain a larger agricultural operation in order to feed all the extra mouths; and to do this, he will need to hire extra manservants. Each increase produces a need for the next.

⊷§ **Introduction:** The previous overindulgences appear on the surface to assure man happiness, but are in fact roads to spiritual oblivion. The mishnah now outlines five items which can act as antidotes to such excesses. These items all seem to involve difficulty for man, but in truth they are pathways to happiness. Regarding these virtues, no amount of indulgence is considered excessive.

מַרְבֶּה תוֹרָה, מַרְבֶּה חַיִּים — [However,] *the more Torah the more life.* Unlike overindulgence in bodily pleasures, which appears to give life but actually diminishes it, Torah study actively enriches life. Although it demands a rigorous commitment of time and effort, Torah study produces increased health and a longer and more enriched life.

Torah scholars live on beyond their physical demise in the words and values of the Torah way that they taught to others in their lifetimes. The Talmud teaches (*Yevamos* 97a) that when one repeats a Torah thought of a great teacher, the teacher's lips move in the grave, as if for the moment he is alive again. Hence, one who involves

חרבה חָכְמָה; מַרְבֶּה עֵצָה, מַרְבֶּה תְבוּנָה; מַרְבֶּה צְדָקָה, מַרְבֶּה שָׁלוֹם. קָנָה שֵׁם טוֹב, קָנָה לְעַצְמוֹ; קָנָה לוֹ דִבְרֵי תוֹרָה, קָנָה לוֹ חַיֵּי הָעוֹלָם הַבָּא.

himself extensively in Torah study and in teaching extends his life beyond his death (*Magen Avos*).

Meiri interprets חַיִּים as *eternal* life. Through Torah study, one is able to achieve life in the World to Come, whose glowing reward is the ability to perceive the glory of God.

מַרְבֶּה יְשִׁיבָה, מַרְבֶּה חָכְמָה — *the more study the more wisdom.* Through establishing yeshivos (houses of study) and teaching students, one's own knowledge and wisdom is increased. Just as small wood chips ignite large logs, so students ignite and fan the flame of wisdom in their teacher. By questioning and challenging him, they force him to clarify and expand his ideas. The Talmud (*Taanis* 7a) teaches: "I have learned much from my teachers, even more from my friends, and the most from my students" (*Rashi, Rav* et al.).

Through financial investment in the establishment and continued support of yeshivos and Torah scholarship, one can make a significant contribution to increased knowledge. Unlike speculation in worldly ventures, which are often fraught with worry and the danger of sudden loss, investment in Torah is eternal and always produces profits (*Midrash Shmuel*).

According to *Tiferes Yisrael*, increasing study refers to developing the analytical skills necessary for extrapolating rulings not found explicitly in the text. Furthermore, by plumbing the depths of

Torah and learning to "read between the lines," Torah scholars will develop worldly wisdom that will serve them well in social, vocational, and practical situations. Through the wisdom acquired from in-depth Torah study, man may develop a business acumen that will release him from much of the worry associated with making a living.

R' Yonah and *Rav* invert the text to read מַרְבֶּה חָכְמָה מַרְבֶּה יְשִׁיבָה, *the more wisdom the greater the yeshivah,* i.e., by developing the depth and breadth of his knowledge, the Torah scholar will attract students seeking knowledge. This statement serves as a counterpoint to the earlier clause which taught that more maidservants result in increased lewdness. Just as the householder is held responsible for the increase in immorality brought about by the extra maidservants he brought to the scene, so, in a positive sense, the teacher who develops an attractive and exciting methodology will reap the reward of the increased Torah study generated by the students he attracts.

מַרְבֶּה עֵצָה, מַרְבֶּה תְבוּנָה — *the more counsel the more understanding.* Through constantly seeking advice, one expands his ability to understand situations and to apply his knowledge to everyday life (*Rav*). The folk saying has it that people seek advice and then do what they want anyway; if so, why do they seek counsel? Answered *R' Chaim of Volozhin*: One who offers advice can never fully understand the questioner's problem. Only the one who has lived through the experience can understand the

⊷ **Source of life.** We are taught, *But you who cling to HASHEM, your God — you are all alive today* (*Deuteronomy* 4:4). Cleaving to God is the means by which man can tap into the Source of Life. Since the most effective access to God is through the study of His Torah (see *Nefesh HaChaim*, *Shaar* 4), the greater the attachment to Torah study, the greater the connection to life.

Anyone who has experienced the surge of joy and vitality that comes from a penetrating Talmudic insight of Rabbi Akiva Eiger or the like has existentially experienced the words of this mishnah, which equates more Torah study with a more enriched life.

In the *Maariv* prayer we say, "We will rejoice with the words of Your Torah and with Your commandments for all eternity; for they are our life and the length of our days." Of course one is happy to be alive, but does he really rejoice from the mere fact that he is living? Rabbi Yitzchak Hutner explained: If one was saved from drowning at the moment he was about to go under, he is certainly excited to have his life back. A Jew without Torah is on the brink of spiritual death; it is Torah that brings him back from the dead. Can one minimize the joy of one saved from spiritual oblivion?

more wisdom; the more counsel the more understanding; the more charity the more peace. One who has gained a good reputation has gained it for his own benefit; one who has gained himself Torah knowledge has gained himself the life of the World to Come.

---

subtle nuances and conflicting issues involved.

On the other hand, the person with the problem bears a narrow perspective which is shaded by his subjectivity. He needs to seek the *counsel* of others, who are impartial, and then decide on his own what to do. Thus the mishnah tells us that one who consults others will gain a better understanding of the problem demanding a solution.

Tiferes Yisrael views this as advice to leaders to solicit the counsel of teachers and colleagues. A spectrum of opinion produces a clarity of understanding that cannot be achieved in solitude, even by the most brilliant mind. Furthermore, one feels more secure about his decisions after hearing the ideas of others. King Solomon taught: *Salvation comes from the counsel of many (Proverbs* 11:14). This clause is the antidote to the confusion and weakness of mind caused by indulgence in licentiousness, which was mentioned earlier.

By serving as counsel for others and exerting oneself intellectually and emotionally to fully comprehend another's situation, one in reality expands his own powers of understanding (*Talmid HaRitva*).

מַרְבֶּה צְדָקָה, מַרְבֶּה שָׁלוֹם — *the more charity the more peace.* One who distributes charity is beloved and thus promotes peace among people; even one who advises *others* to give charity is looked upon favorably. In this way, the clause is the positive counterpart to the earlier mention of excessive manservants, which was considered a doorway to thievery. Just as people are antagonistic towards the owner for his servants' theft of their property, by contrast people are grateful to the one who advised

them to contribute to charity (*R' Yonah*).

Midrash Shmuel views charity as a peacemaker between God and the destitute. If the poor lack essential needs, they will cry out to God with a tinge of anger. When we provide for their needs, we act as a broker between man and God. *Rambam* (see 3:19) writes that it is preferable for one to distribute smaller amounts of charity to more people rather than giving larger amounts to fewer people. In this way, he will cultivate the trait of giving and develop into a charitable person. Increased charity is the key to increased ethical perfection and to being at peace with oneself [the word שָׁלוֹם, *peace,* shares the same root as שָׁלֵם, *complete*]. In addition, one who gives smaller amounts to more people assures that at least each poor person will receive something, thus promoting peace among the poor (*Pri Chaim*).

קָנָה שֵׁם טוֹב, קָנָה לְעַצְמוֹ — *One who has gained a good reputation has gained it for his own benefit.* A sterling reputation lasts forever. Unlike material wealth, which one must leave behind when he passes on, a good name belongs to a person for eternity. Hence, while a man who increases his fortune must always worry that he may lose it, a good reputation is forever (*R' Yonah*). *Tosafos Yom Tov* amplifies this concept by teaching that a name is indicative of the essential quality of the item (see *Genesis* 2:19-20). One who enjoys a good reputation has apparently actualized his potential in life, an accomplishment of note.

קָנָה לוֹ דִבְרֵי תוֹרָה, קָנָה לוֹ חַיֵּי הָעוֹלָם הַבָּא — *one who has gained himself Torah knowledge has gained*

◁§ The Chazon Ish cites the power of Torah scholars to assess real-life situations as the reason that the halachic decision-making process was given exclusively to them. The slightest change in the details of the case under discussion can drastically affect the ruling. Only Torah scholars, blessed with the insight and intuition granted to those who drink deeply of Torah's wells, can be trusted to interpret these subtle nuances (see *Collected Letters* 1:31). [The daily prayer וְהָאֵר עֵינֵינוּ בְּתוֹרָתֶךָ, *Enlighten our eyes in Your Torah,* may also be understood as "enlighten our eyes *through* Your Torah" [to understand the world around us]. Since Torah is the blueprint of Creation (see *Bereishis Rabbah* 1:2), the more one understands the blueprint the greater his understanding of the world.

[ט] רַבָּן יוֹחָנָן בֶּן זַכַּאי קִבֵּל מֵהִלֵּל וּמִשַּׁמַּאי. הוּא הָיָה אוֹמֵר: אִם לָמַדְתָּ תּוֹרָה הַרְבֵּה, אַל תַּחֲזִיק טוֹבָה לְעַצְמְךָ, כִּי לְכָךְ נוֹצָרְתָּ.

himself the life of the World to Come. Torah knowledge is the catalyst for human growth. Since it is Divine intelligence, it serves as a guidebook to enable man to actualize the image of God which lies within his soul. By acquiring Torah knowledge and making it an integral part of his personality and thought processes, one can transform himself into a person deserving of a place in the World to Come.

Yalkut Yehudah adds: One who experiences the beauty of Torah gets a taste of the World to Come in the present.

Mishnah 9

רַבָּן יוֹחָנָן בֶּן זַכַּאי קִבֵּל מֵהִלֵּל וּמִשַּׁמַּאי – *Rabban Yochanan ben Zakkai received the tradition from Hillel and Shammai.* One of the greatest of his generation of *Tannaim,* Rabban Yochanan ben Zakkai lived through the destruction of the Second Temple and was instrumental in the national recovery from that cataclysmic event. His huge investment of talent and ability expressed itself in his establishment of the academy at Yavneh (see *Gittin* 56b for the fascinating story). He was also responsible for the many enactments which fanned the flames of hope for a national rebirth and helped the nation come to grips with the reality of life without the Temple (see *Rosh Hashanah* 4:1-4). Rabban Yochanan was among the younger disciples of Hillel, who predicted a bright future for him because of his purity of speech (see *Pesachim* 3b). He lived 120 years; forty years were spent in business pursuits, forty years in study, and forty in teaching (see *Rosh Hashanah* 31b). Even though he was not a member of the family of Hillel, which occupied the position of *Nasi,* he still received the title "Rabban." During his years in commerce he lived in the lower Galilee, where he issued halachic rulings (see *Shabbos* 16:7). Unappreciated by the residents of Arav, most of whom were ignorant, he

◆§ **Acquisition beyond compare.** Interestingly, the mishnah speaks of *gaining* or *acquiring* Torah knowledge instead of *learning.* Even one who is unable to learn because of constraints may still acquire the special merit of Torah study by supporting those who make it their full-time occupation. Women, who are not obligated to study Torah, nonetheless also have an opportunity to avail themselves of this special reward. By being supportive of their husbands' efforts to grow in Torah, even at the expense of financial comfort or social pleasures, women will be blessed with the unique reward given for Torah study. Furthermore, by encouraging her children to advance in their Torah learning, the mother herself will have a full share in the reward for that learning. Such support includes taking the children to school, motivating them to succeed at Torah study, and sending a clear message that growth in Torah learning and good character are the most important things to acquire, all of which guarantee a mother a special place in the "exclusive neighborhood" in the World to Come reserved for those who study Torah.

One day, a student at Beth Medrash Govoha passed by the office of R' Aharon Kotler and saw the *Rosh Yeshivah* dancing — all alone! The student watched in amazement until R' Aharon noticed him and requested that he ask one of the yeshivah's outstanding students to come to the office.

R' Aharon spoke privately with the second young man for some time. When their discussion ended, the first student approached the second, related what he had seen, and asked why R' Aharon had summoned him. The second *talmid* replied, "For more than twenty years the *Rosh Yeshivah* has been struggling to understand a comment of the *Vilna Gaon* in *Choshen Mishpat,* chapter 28. Today, he finally arrived at what he is certain is the correct understanding. This is why the *Rosh Yeshivah* danced. He summoned me to share the explanation and his joy."

Some people have the good fortune to experience the joy of the next world in this world.

9. Rabban Yochanan ben Zakkai received the tradition from Hillel and Shammai. He used to say: If you have studied much Torah, do not take credit for yourself, because that is what you were created to do.

---

moved to Jerusalem, where he taught at large public gatherings (see *Pesachim* 26a, *Rashi* ad loc.).

A strong opponent of the Sadducees, he successfully debated them on many issues and thus protected the authentic tradition. (See *Megillas Taanis*, Chapters 1, 5, and 8; see also *Menachos* 65a-b, *Bava Basra* 115b, and *Yadaim* 4:6.) Nonetheless, he was a man of peace. The Talmud relates that no one (not even gentiles) ever succeeded in greeting him first (*Berachos* 17a). His regard for human dignity is expressed clearly in his explanation for why a man who steals and slaughters or sells a sheep must pay a smaller fine (four times its value) than one who steals an ox (five times its value) [see *Exodus* 22:17]: that one who steals a sheep must carry it on his shoulder, so the Torah decreases the fine (*Bava Kamma* 79b). Few of his halachic rulings are quoted in the Mishnah; many are likely related as the opinion of Beis Hillel, which he headed. In the waning days of the Second Temple, he saw the hotheadedness of the zealots as a destructive force, and opposed their futile desire for armed revolt against the Romans (see *Gittin* 56a).

In Rabban Yochanan's parting words to his students, he blessed them that they should fear God as much as they fear man. "Rebbi, not more?" they asked. "May you *at least* be worried, when contemplating sin, that no one should see you," was his reply. The radiance of wisdom disappeared when he died (*Sotah* 9:15).

הוא הָיָה אוֹמֵר — *He used to say.* Having covered the entire corpus of Torah learning (see *Succah*

28a and *Bava Basra* 134a), Rabban Yochanan ben Zakkai was able and entitled to state the following (*Rashi, Rav*).

אִם לָמַדְתָּ תוֹרָה הַרְבֵּה, אַל תַּחֲזִיק טוֹבָה לְעַצְמְךָ, כִּי לְכָךְ נוֹצָרְתָּ — *If you have studied much Torah, do not take credit for yourself, because that is what you were created to do.* One should not take pride in his accomplishments in the study of Torah; its study and the fulfillment of its directives is his *raison d'etre*. In fact, all of Creation hung tentatively in the balance until Jews accepted the Torah at Sinai (see *Shabbos* 88a). At that point Creation assumed a degree of permanence, but it could only be sustained by man's constant delving into the depths of Torah. Hence, man is commanded to study Torah so that the world can continue to exist (*Rashi*). *R' Yonah* amplifies the point: Just as one understands that he deserves no thanks from his creditor for paying back a debt, so he deserves no special credit for discharging his obligation to study Torah. It is for this purpose that he was brought into the world.

Sfas Emes notes the usage *If you have studied "much" Torah.* Torah study has a humbling effect on man. Therefore, only one who has learned *much* Torah realizes that his pride is misplaced; if he has learned only a little, he is often captivated by delusions of greatness.

This is true not only of Torah study but of fulfilling *mitzvos*. Man was set on this earth to fulfill God's will. Since we owe him everything, we deserve no thanks for anything we do at His behest.

Furthermore, one can take no credit for having learned much, since no matter how much one

---

◄§ **Self-preservation.** Man was created with 248 limbs corresponding to the 248 positive commands, and 365 veins and sinews corresponding to the 365 Biblical prohibitions. Through the fulfillment of all the 613 *mitzvos*, man is able to lend spiritual splendor to the entirety of his being. Hence, no matter how much of the Torah one learns or fulfills, he is only doing his duty — to perfect all parts of the person created by God.

[It is for this reason, teaches *R' Chaim Vital,* that Moses yearned to enter the Holy Land, for some of the *mitzvos* which are of an agricultural nature can only be performed there (see *Sotah* 14a). Even though he was not obligated to fulfill these *mitzvos* outside the Land, he yearned for the opportunity to keep *all* of the *mitzvos* so as to attain perfection for the entirety of his person.]

[יז] חֲמִשָׁה תַלְמִידִים הָיוּ לוֹ לְרַבָּן יוֹחָנָן בֶּן זַכַּאי, וְאֵלּוּ הֵן: רַבִּי אֱלִיעֶזֶר בֶּן הֻרְקְנוֹס, רַבִּי יְהוֹשֻׁעַ

learns, it is but a drop in the bucket compared to the vast sea of knowledge contained in the endless Torah (*R' Yonah*).

Tiferes Yisrael renders כִּי לְכָךְ נוֹצָרְתָּ, *for [with abilities] to do this you were created.* Let one not assume airs of superiority for having learned much; the intelligence, memory, and sharpness are God-given abilities for which he deserves no special recompense. Others may deserve greater reward for lesser accomplishments, since their attainments are the result of greater efforts. Intelligence was given to a person only for the purpose of acquiring knowledge, and he has no more right to become arrogant for utilizing this knowledge than a bird has for using his wings to fly (*Mesillas Yesharim*).

Lev Avos offers the following rendering: If you have learned much Torah, אַל תַּחֲזִיק טוֹבָה לְעַצְמְךָ, *do not hoard the good [Torah] for yourself.* One who has knowledge must share it with others, for that is the purpose for which he was created — both to learn *and* to teach Torah.

Mishnah 10

חֲמִשָׁה תַלְמִידִים הָיוּ לוֹ לְרַבָּן יוֹחָנָן בֶּן זַכַּאי, וְאֵלּוּ הֵן — *Rabban Yochanan ben Zakkai had five [primary] disciples. They were.* Rabban Yochanan ben Zakkai had so many students that he had to deliver his lectures outdoors, in front of the Temple, since no study hall could contain the enormous crowds in attendance (see *Pesachim* 26a and *Rashi* ad loc., s.v. ורבא). The mishnah speaks of his primary students, to whom he conveyed the tradition (*Magen Avos*).

Midrash Shmuel views these five as the disciples who enabled Rabban Yochanan ben Zakkai to grow in Torah stature, in the spirit of the words וּמִתַּלְמִידַי יוֹתֵר מִכֻּלָּם, *and from my students more than from all the rest* (*Taanis* 7a).

רַבִּי אֱלִיעֶזֶר בֶּן הֻרְקְנוֹס — *Rabbi Eliezer ben Hyrkanos.* A second-generation *Tanna*, R' Eliezer ben Hyrkanos entered adulthood unlettered and ignorant (see, however, *Yerushalmi Megillah* 1:9). In his twenties he decided, against his father's wishes,

⌐§ One is not considered deficient for lacking an attribute deemed out of the ordinary. For example, musical ability is a special gift from God, but one who is tone deaf certainly is not considered lacking. On the other hand, the lack of a basic attribute, such as a limb, would certainly be considered a tragic handicap; having it, however, is no cause for boasting.

Similarly, if man views his Torah accomplishments as a source of pride, it follows that he views Torah study as a luxury, not a necessity. In reality, however, Torah is the most basic necessity in the life of a Jew. Therefore, we are taught: *If you have studied much Torah, do not take credit for yourself.* It is not a superfluous luxury — it is the basic purpose of life for which man was created (*Knesses Yisrael*).

⌐§ **Greatness of humility.** Tiferes Shlomo of Radomsk offers the following insight: While he had many students, Rabban Yochanan ben Zakkai only enumerated the praises of these five. All the others were well aware of their own praises; these five, however, were so humble that their teacher needed to cite their praises. They themselves were unaware of their own stature. It was because of their humility that they were considered Rabban Yochanan ben Zakkai's primary disciples, appropriate channels for the transmission of the *mesorah*.

Another great disciple whose humility won him the right to become the bearer of the *mesorah* was Joshua, who was the disciple and successor of Moses. When Joshua was about to go to *Eretz Yisrael*, as one of the spies whose mission ended in a disastrous loss of faith, Moses gave him a special blessing that he should not succumb to the fears of his colleagues. The reason for the blessing, *Targum Yonasan* explains, was because Joshua was humble and might not have stood firm against the ten spies who opposed him. This same humility was also part of his personal greatness as a person and eventual leader.

to begin studying Torah and fled to the academy of Rabban Yochanan ben Zakkai in Jerusalem. He was successful at his studies and became an accomplished scholar. Hyrkanos, who went to Jerusalem to disinherit Eliezer at the behest of his other sons, was pleasantly surprised to find his son lecturing at a gathering of the wise men of Jerusalem and instead decided to give Eliezer all his money. R' Eliezer, however, refused to take a share larger than that of any of his brothers (*Avos d'Rabbi Nosson* 6).

Even before the destruction of the Temple, he was considered one of the greats of the generation. He was among the "pallbearers" who carried Rabban Yochanan ben Zakkai to his meeting with Vespasian (see *Gittin* 56a). After the fall of Jerusalem, he moved along with the Sanhedrin to Yavneh and played a major role in its activities, and was a member of a delegation to Rome to negotiate on Jewish issues (*Yerushalmi Sanhedrin* 17b).

רַבִּי יְהוֹשֻׁעַ בֶּן חֲנַנְיָא — *Rabbi Yehoshua ben Chanania.* A Levite, R' Yehoshua served as one of the choir members in the Temple [Levites served either as gatekeepers or choir members in the Temple]. Rabban Yochanan ben Zakkai, who or-

dained him (*Yerushalmi, Sanhedrin* 1:2), also taught him the kabbalistic areas of Torah (*Chagigah* 14b).

After the death of Rabban Yochanan ben Zakkai, when the office of *Nasi* reverted to the family of Hillel, Rabban Gamliel assumed that position, with R' Yehoshua serving as *Av Beis Din* (*Bava Kamma* 74b). An accomplished linguist (*Sanhedrin* 17b) and mathematician (*Horayos* 10a), he acted as a spokesman for the Jewish people in the halls of government. On his way to Rome to lobby against anti-Jewish edicts, he visited Alexandria and Athens (see *Niddah* 69b and *Bechoros* 8b).

Aware of the political realities of his time, he sought to promote peaceful coexistence with the Roman government. When Hadrian effectively reneged on the promise he had made to allow the Jews to rebuild the Temple (he told them to build it at a different, totally unacceptable location), R' Yehoshua counseled *against* civilian revolt, offering the following parable: A bone once became stuck in the throat of a lion. The lion announced that he would handsomely reward anyone who succeeded in removing the bone. An ostrich came and extended his long neck into the mouth of the lion, thus extracting the bone, and then demanded the

---

◄§ **Rabbi Eliezer the Great.** R' Eliezer married Aima Shalom, the sister of Rabban Gamliel of Yavneh, and resided in Lod, where he presided over the local *beis din* (see *Sanhedrin* 32b). He was very firm in defending his rulings, even if it meant refusing to accept the majority opinion (*Taanis* 25b), a trait that sometimes had painful consequences. At a time when the strengthening of the Sanhedrin's authority was a national priority, R' Eliezer disputed the majority opinion in a particular halachic dispute regarding the ritual purity of a type of oven known as the "the oven of Achnai." Convinced that he possessed the authentic tradition in the matter, he refused to yield. Unable to tolerate such dissent, his colleagues, including his brother-in-law Rabban Gamliel, had no other choice but to excommunicate him (see *Bava Metzia* 59b for the amazing story of the dispute).

He remained at home in Lod under the ban for the rest of his life. (The ban was lifted only at the end of his life.) Nonetheless, when he became ill, his colleagues and students came to visit him. He predicted the terrible times to come in the wake of the Bar Kochba revolt. In an attempt to calm him, his visitors spoke of his greatness, comparing him to the rain and the sun, and asserting that he was of more benefit to the nation than a parent to a child.

Among his famous dicta are the following: One who rules on a point of law in the presence of his teacher is liable to the death penalty (*Eruvin* 63a); one who has bread for today and asks, "What will I eat tomorrow," is a person of limited faith (*Sotah* 48b); one who refuses to have children is considered a murderer (*Yevamos* 63b).

The Midrash known as *Pirkei d'Rabbi Eliezer* is attributed to him. R' Akiva and R' Elayi are among his more famous disciples.

בֶּן חֲנַנְיָא, רַבִּי יוֹסֵי הַכֹּהֵן, רַבִּי שִׁמְעוֹן בֶּן נְתַנְאֵל, וְרַבִּי אֱלִיעֶזֶר בֶּן עֲרָךְ. ב/יא

[יא] **הוּא** הָיָה מוֹנֶה שִׁבְחָן: (רַבִּי) אֱלִיעֶזֶר בֶּן הֻרְקָנוֹס,

promised reward. Replied the lion, "Here is your reward: go and brag that you entered and emerged alive from the jaws of the lion." Said R' Eliezer, "We too should be happy that we have survived this nation [the Romans — and we should not do anything else to antagonize them]" (*Bereishis Rabbah* 64:10).

Although R' Yehoshua was physically unimpressive (*Taanis* 7a) and in constant poverty (*Berachos* 28a), his opinion on theological and practical matters was solicited even by non-Jewish royalty (see *Shabbos* 119a, *Chullin* 59b, *Bereishis Rabbah* 28:3, et al.). He used these political connections to benefit his fellow Jews (see *Shabbos* 127b). The Talmud records his debates with heretics and non-Jewish scholars, including his triumphant debate at Bei Avidan in the presence of the Roman Caesar (see *Shabbos* 152a; see also *Sanhedrin* 90b). *Yerushalmi* (*Sotah* 9) notes the comment of the Sages upon his death: "When R' Yehoshua died, good counsel and planning disappeared from Israel."

R' Yehoshua was so beloved by the people that Rabban Gamliel lost his post as *Nasi* because of his high-handed behavior towards him. When Rabban Gamliel came to appease R' Yehoshua and took note of his extreme poverty, the latter rebuked the deposed *Nasi* sharply. "Woe to the generation whose leader you are; you are unaware of the difficulties its scholars face in supporting themselves." Only upon eliciting R' Yehoshua's forgiveness was Rabban Gamliel reinstated (see *Berachos* 28a).

During the famous debate with R' Eliezer over the impure status of the oven of Achnai (see *Bava Metzia* 59b), he made his famous response to the miracles that R' Eliezer marshalled to prove that the majority opinion was wrong: "It [the Torah] is not in Heaven." He thus asserted the scope of the intellectual sovereignty and great decision-making power of the Sages.

A man of moderation, he was opposed to undue stringency in matters of halachah out of fear that one who was unable to uphold them would also reject the basic laws (see *Shabbos* 153b). He similarly rejected excessive mourning over the Temple (*Bava Basra* 60b). The famous dictum כַּבְּדֵהוּ וְחָשְׁדֵהוּ, *Honor him, yet be wary of him*, seems to be based on his statement "One should always view people as bandits, yet honor them as if they were Rabban Gamliel" (*Derech Eretz Rabbah* 5).

רַבִּי יוֹסֵי הַכֹּהֵן — *Rabbi Yose the Kohen*. Together with R' Yehoshua, R' Yose studied the esoteric portions of the Torah known as *Maaseh HaMerkavah* (literally, The Workings of the Divine Chariot), an achievement which greatly pleased their teacher, Rabban Yochanan ben Zakkai (see *Chagigah* 14b). His halachic opinion is recorded only once in the Mishnah (*Eduyos* 8:2) [see *Rosh Hashanah* 17b].

רַבִּי שִׁמְעוֹן בֶּן נְתַנְאֵל — *Rabbi Shimon ben Nesanel*. Little is known about this second-generation *Tanna*. A *Kohen*, he was the son-in-law of Rabban Gamliel *HaZakken* (*Tosefta, Avodah Zarah* 4:10).

וְרַבִּי אֱלְעָזָר בֶּן עֲרָךְ — *and Rabbi Elazar ben Arach*. An intellectual giant in both the revealed and hidden areas of Torah, Rabbi Elazar was a favorite of Rabban Yochanan ben Zakkai. Of all the disciples, he was the one able to comfort his teacher upon the death of Rabban Yochanan's son (*Avos d'Rabbi Nosson* 14:6).

Interestingly, little of his Torah has come down to us. *Tosefta* (*Nedarim* 6:5) indicates that he died prematurely. It is more probable that upon the death of his teacher, he, unlike his colleagues, did not remain with the academy at Yavneh. Upon the urging of his wife, he moved instead to Amaos, a vacation resort famous for its fine cuisine and refreshing baths, thinking that his colleagues would follow him. They did not come and he found himself alone and without the intellectual ferment necessary for growth. The Talmud (*Shabbos* 147b) reports that he completely forgot his learning, to the extent that he was unable to read from a Torah

ben Chanania, Rabbi Yose the Kohen, Rabbi Shimon ben Nesanel, and Rabbi Elazar ben Arach.

11. He used to enumerate their praises: (Rabbi) Eliezer ben

---

scroll. Instead of reading, *"This month shall be for you [the beginning of the months]"* (הַחֹדֶשׁ הַזֶּה לָכֶם [רֹאשׁ חֲדָשִׁים], *Exodus* 12:2), he read, *"Their hearts became deaf"* (הַחֵרֵשׁ הָיָה לִבָּם). *Yalkut Koheles* (973) reports that eventually Elijah the Prophet restored his knowledge. This tragic story serves as a living validation of R' Nehorai's statement (*Avos* 4:18):

Exile yourself to a place of Torah, and do not assume it will come after you, for it is your colleagues who will cause it to remain with you. A similar sentiment is expressed in *Proverbs* (3:5): *Do not rely on your own understanding.* It is noteworthy that some are of the opinion that R' Nehorai is a pseudonym for R' Elazar ben Arach (see *Shabbos* ibid.).

Mishnah 11

הוא הָיָה מוֹנֶה שִׁבְחָן — *He used to enumerate their praises.* Only Rabban Yochanan ben Zakkai would speak of his students' praises; they themselves would never do so (*Midrash Shmuel*). Generally one should not speak excessively about another person, even to praise him, since it may arouse his own jealousy or bring him to speak disparagingly of the other. However, parents and teachers are not

jealous of their children or students (see *Sanhedrin* 105b), and therefore, Rabban Yochanan ben Zakkai was permitted to praise his students (*Magen Avos*). He enumerated their virtues in order to inspire his other students to emulate them. None of these praises is a God-given gift; even R' Eliezer's flawless memory was the product of incessant review (*Maharam Schick*).

❧ **A deafness of the spirit.** Rabbi Shlomo Freifeld explained the significance of R' Elazar ben Arach's inability to read this particular verse, which underscores man's power to infuse time with sanctity. (The verse describes the power of the court to declare a new month based on evidence of a "new" moon, thus establishing the dates of holy days, and transforming them into times of a sacred rendezvous in time between God and Israel.) Caught up in the pursuit of the "good life," he lost the perspective expressed in the words of the Sages that "A Torah scholar is like the Sabbath" (*Zohar* 3:29). Every moment of a Torah scholar's time is an opportunity for growth and sanctity. By involving himself with an environment that was excessively immersed in mundane matters, he lost this spiritual sensitivity and his heart became deaf to the message of Torah. Thus, instead of *This month shall be for you,* he read, *Their hearts became deaf.*

❧ **Too important to forget.** The Chofetz Chaim related the following anecdote to provide a different understanding of the praiseworthiness of R' Eliezer's memory: "One only remembers things which made a deep impression on him when he experienced them. I remember an old man in our town of Radin who was able to describe in vivid detail the visit of Czar Nikolai, which had occurred over seventy years ago. The old man described precisely the royal carriage, the majestic horses, the decorative trim around the edges of the wagon driver's uniform, and he even portrayed the hand movements of the driver as he held the reins. Yet, that same elderly gentleman could not describe many things he had seen or heard maybe a day or two earlier. Only those things that have great significance and impact at the time leave an indelible impression upon us."

R' Eliezer ben Hyrkanos was so excited and captivated by words of Torah, and their impact was of such intensity, that he never forgot them.

The *Chasam Sofer* expressed the same concept in a semi-humorous manner. He said that he did not really have a good memory, but it would have been a shame for him to forget something that he had learned with great effort.

[On a deeper level, one never forgets to perform bodily functions, such as breathing, which are of a life and death nature. The more a function is linked to the essence of the person's life the more likely that he will remember it. To R' Eliezer ben Hyrkanos, Torah was life itself — something impossible to forget.]

בּוֹר סוּד שֶׁאֵינוֹ מְאַבֵּד טִפָּה; (רַבִּי) יְהוֹשֻׁעַ בֶּן חֲנַנְיָא, אַשְׁרֵי יוֹלַדְתּוֹ; (רַבִּי) יוֹסֵי הַכֹּהֵן, חָסִיד; (רַבִּי) שִׁמְעוֹן בֶּן נְתַנְאֵל, יְרֵא חֵטְא;

According to *Tiferes Tzvi*, Rabban Yochanan ben Zakkai intended to pass the mantle of leadership to these five disciples. It was in order to enhance their prestige in the eyes of the public that he praised them; he sought to insure that they would command the respect of the people and thus be effective leaders. [Our mishnah mentions this in order to teach the proper procedure for passing the torch of leadership from teacher to student.]

(רַבִּי) אֱלִיעֶזֶר בֶּן הֻרְקָנוֹס, בּוֹר סוּד שֶׁאֵינוֹ מְאַבֵּד טִפָּה — *(Rabbi) Eliezer ben Hyrkanos is [like] a cemented cistern that loses not a drop.* In many early texts of the mishnah, Rabban Yochanan did not append the title "*Rabbi*" to the names of his disciples. As their teacher, he did not use the title (*Rashi, Midrash Shmuel*).

In mishnaic times, water was stored in cisterns dug into the earth, which served as family reservoirs. In order to keep the water clean and prevent it from being absorbed into the ground, the cisterns were cemented. R' Eliezer ben Hyrkanos is compared to a cemented cistern because of his flawless capacity to remember all he had learned. He never forgot anything — not even a "drop" (*Rashi, R' Yonah, Rav*).

Although a cemented cistern retains all its contents, it also has certain drawbacks: (a) Its water generally is stale and not very refreshing; and (b) unlike a spring, it does not release any new waters. In these aspects, R' Eliezer

ben Hyrkanos did *not* resemble a cemented cistern. His Torah thoughts were always refreshing, and his emphasis on constant review and mastery of large amounts of material did not preclude an ability to generate new ideas (*Midrash Shmuel*).

Sfas Emes interprets this as indicative of R' Eliezer's self-control in repeating only what he had heard from his teachers (see *Succah* 28a); all his own ideas he kept to himself. In this way he was like a cemented cistern which loses not a drop.

(רַבִּי) יְהוֹשֻׁעַ בֶּן חֲנַנְיָא, אַשְׁרֵי יוֹלַדְתּוֹ — *(Rabbi) Yehoshua ben Chanania, praiseworthy is she who bore him.* Rabbi Yehoshua ben Chanania was of such sterling character that people envied his mother for having borne such a child. His combination of encyclopedic knowledge, practical intelligence, and influence in the halls of government (see *Taanis* 7a) made him respected and beloved by his contemporaries and a source of pride to his mother (*Rashi, Rambam, Rav*).

Yerushalmi (*Yevamos* 1:6) reports that when his mother was pregnant with him, she would go every day to all the study halls of the city and ask the Torah scholars to pray that her child would grow up to be a scholar. After he was born, his mother would take his crib to the study hall so that his ears would be filled exclusively with words of Torah. Because his mother was largely responsible for the great

⏤§ **Acute hearing.** Rabbi Chaim Shmulevitz notes the Sages' teaching that R' Eliezer taught words of Torah שֶׁלֹּא שְׁמָעָתַן אֹזֶן מֵעוֹלָם, *that no ear had ever heard before* (*Pirkei d'Rabbi Eliezer*), which seems to contradict the statement that he taught only that which he heard from his teachers. In fact, however, there is no contradiction. A real disciple does not merely parrot his mentors; he repeats what he knows his teacher *would* say about any given subject. Having mastered the teacher's thought patterns, he can independently replicate his conclusions.

An example of this type of student was Rabbi Nisson Alpert, a disciple of Rabbi Moshe Feinstein. Once, Rabbi Aharon Kotler called Mesivta Tifereth Jerusalem, to solicit his halachic opinion regarding a tragic episode in which the parents of a groom were killed in a car accident on the way to their son's wedding. The young man who answered the phone informed R' Aharon that the *Rosh Yeshivah* was not in the building at the moment. R' Aharon replied, "Please call Nisson Alpert to the phone. He will know what his *rebbi* would say about the matter."

Rabbi Mordechai Gifter resolved the contradiction by defining R' Eliezer's greatness. While all of the students heard the teacher's words, only R' Eliezer fully penetrated the depth of their meaning. He later taught things which no ear [except his] had ever heard, but which *he* had heard and understood from his mentor.

Hyrkanos is [like] a cemented cistern that loses not a drop; (Rabbi) Yehoshua ben Chanania, praiseworthy is she who bore him; (Rabbi) Yose the Kohen is a scrupulously pious person; (Rabbi) Shimon ben Nesanel fears sin;

person that he grew to be, Rabban Yochanan stressed, *praiseworthy is she who bore him* (*Rashi, Rav*).

The Talmud sees in the Biblical dictum *You shall love God, your Lord* (*Deuteronomy* 6:5) a call for man to serve as an open representative of Godliness. By studying Torah and conducting his affairs honestly, he causes people to declare: "Praiseworthy are his parents, who taught him Torah and its values; how pleasant are his actions" (*Yoma* 86a). R' Yehoshua ben Chanania was such a person.

רַבִּי) יוֹסֵי הַכֹּהֵן, חָסִיד) — (Rabbi) Yose the Kohen is a scrupulously pious person. One who goes beyond the letter of the law is deemed scrupulously righteous. Yose the *Kohen* did not seek to observe only the minimum; he was scrupulously pious (*Rav, R' Yonah*). According to *Rambam* and *Meiri*, the term חָסִיד indicates one who is a model of ethical and moral perfection. *Tosafos Yom Tov* (end of *Sotah*)

cites two definitions of חָסִיד: (a) one who performs all his activities, even mundane ones, for the sake of Heaven, channeling all his actions into his service of God; and (b) one who, in a spirit of compromise, forgoes money and entitlements in business.

רַבִּי) שִׁמְעוֹן בֶּן נְתַנְאֵל, יְרֵא חֵטְא) — (Rabbi) Shimon ben Nesanel fears sin. Rabbi Shimon would adopt stringencies in his personal behavior, avoiding even things that were permitted, out of fear of transgression (*Rav*).

Since simple fear of sin can be achieved by ignorant people (see 2:6), it would seem to be rather a faint praise to say that Shimon ben Nesanel was one who fears sin (*Rav*, see *Meiri*). According to *Rambam*, the term יְרֵא חֵטְא indicates alacrity — the active and energetic pursuit of the proper path and refraining from any type of negative behavior. *Magen Avos* interprets these words in past tense, explaining that R' Shimon was always fearful that perhaps he had sinned in the past.

⇒ **Indelible memory.** Many people would attend the lectures of R' Aharon Kotler even if they understood little. The experience of witnessing his excitement and fire was moving and exhilarating, and it left an impact even if one could not follow the *shiur*.

The Torah commands us to bring small children to the Temple in fulfillment of the *mitzvah* of *hakhel* (*Deuteronomy* 31:12); for even they, who do not who understand a word, will be deeply affected by what they see and hear (*M'lo HaOmer*)

⇒ **The stamp of honesty.** A famous incident involving Reb Yaakov Kamenetsky — and one which he felt was a *mitzvah* to publicize — may serve as a classic instance of this type of responsibility for the public image of Jews and Judaism. Shortly after Reb Yaakov assumed the position as *rav* of Tzitevian, Lithuania, a Jew came to him and reported that the postmaster had mistakenly given him change for a hundred-*lit* note instead of for the ten-*lit* note with which he had paid. Reb Yaakov advised the man to return the money.

Several weeks later, Reb Yaakov was in the post office, and this same postmaster gave him more stamps than he had paid for, and Reb Yaakov returned the excess stamps. The sly smile on the postmaster's face convinced Reb Yaakov that the postmaster was deliberately testing him to see whether the new rabbi was honest. Reb Yaakov was delighted that he had been presented with such an opportunity for *kiddush Hashem*.

Years later, he learned from survivors of Tzitevian that the postmaster had been one of the few locals who had been willing to hide Jews from the Nazis. Reb Yaakov was convinced that such displays of honesty had been a major factor in that decision.

⇒ **Oblivious.** *Chasdei Avos* quotes a letter purportedly written by the *Rambam* to a person who did not want to recite the *Viduy* (confessional prayer) on Yom Kippur since he was sure he had not sinned. The *Rambam* replied: "If you were to understand truly what the service of God is about, you might realize that not only have you sinned, but that your sins are much greater than anything described in the *Viduy*. The greater one's level of understanding, the more intensely he is judged. Just for your comment about not having sinned, a person like you will have to justify yourself in front of the Heavenly Tribunal."

[יב] הוּא הָיָה אוֹמֵר: אִם יִהְיוּ כָל חַכְמֵי יִשְׂרָאֵל בְּכַף מֹאזְנַיִם, וֶאֱלִיעֶזֶר בֶּן הֻרְקָנוֹס בְּכַף שְׁנִיָּה, מַכְרִיעַ אֶת כֻּלָּם. אַבָּא שָׁאוּל אוֹמֵר מִשְּׁמוֹ: אִם יִהְיוּ כָל חַכְמֵי יִשְׂרָאֵל בְּכַף מֹאזְנַיִם, וְ(רַבִּי) אֱלִיעֶזֶר בֶּן הֻרְקָנוֹס אַף עִמָּהֶם, וְ(רַבִּי) אֶלְעָזָר בֶּן עֲרָךְ בְּכַף שְׁנִיָּה, מַכְרִיעַ אֶת כֻּלָּם.

[יג] אָמַר לָהֶם: צְאוּ וּרְאוּ אֵיזוֹ הִיא דֶּרֶךְ טוֹבָה

The *Kozhnitzer Maggid* states that it was not the *punishment* for the sin that made R' Shimon fearful; it was the sin itself. He suffered extreme consternation at the thought that he might have upset his Father in Heaven and beclouded the purity of his soul. Such thoughts caused him to recoil from sin, as one recoils from a snake.

R' Shmuel Alter renders חֵטְא as *deficiency*. R' Shimon always feared that even his good actions were incomplete, both in quality and in quantity.

וְ(רַבִּי) אֶלְעָזָר בֶּן עֲרָךְ, כְּמַעְיָן הַמִּתְגַּבֵּר — *(and Rabbi) Elazar ben Arach is like a spring flowing stronger and stronger.* With his penetrating mind and broad understanding, R' Elazar ben Arach was able to formulate new ideas and interpretations in Torah. Unlike R' Eliezer ben Hyrkanos, who repeated only what he had been taught (*Doresh LePerakim*), R' Elazar applied creative thinking to his learning (*Rav, R' Yonah*).

The intensity of a spring diminishes as its waters move outward. Therefore, a spring which grows constantly stronger is a supernatural phenomenon. R' Elazar ben Arach possessed such rare intellectual ability (*Midrash Shmuel*).

Rambam sees an additional meaning in the metaphor of the spring. In order to partake of well water, one must drop a bucket deep into the well, while spring water is more easily accessible. Similarly, R' Elazar ben Arach was easily able to comprehend deep issues. *Meiri* adds that words of Torah wisdom poured out of him in torrents, like a rushing stream.

Mishnah 12

הוּא הָיָה אוֹמֵר: אִם יִהְיוּ כָל חַכְמֵי יִשְׂרָאֵל בְּכַף מֹאזְנַיִם, וֶאֱלִיעֶזֶר בֶּן הֻרְקָנוֹס בְּכַף שְׁנִיָּה, מַכְרִיעַ אֶת כֻּלָּם — *He used to say: If all of the sages of Israel were on one pan of a balance scale, and Eliezer ben Hyrkanos were on the other, he would outweigh them all.* In assessing the respective intellectual abilities of his students, Rabban Yochanan ben Zakkai found the scope of R' Eliezer ben Hyrkanos's knowledge to be of such magnitude and breadth as to outweigh all the sages of Israel together. None among them possessed his encyclopedic knowledge (*R' Yonah*). Knowledge of such magnitude is indispensable to the community as the Talmud teaches: "Everyone needs the one who possesses the wheat" — i.e., the one who has mastered all areas of Torah knowledge (*Berachos* 64a). If the wheat for flour is unavailable, even the greatest baker cannot produce bread. Likewise, the brightest and sharpest minds are limited in their Torah creativity if they lack a broad base in Torah knowledge.

(and Rabbi) Elazar ben Arach is like a spring flowing stronger and stronger.

12. He [Rabban Yochanan ben Zakkai] used to say: If all of the sages of Israel were on one pan of a balance scale, and Eliezer ben Hyrkanos were on the other, he would outweigh them all. Abba Shaul said in [Rabban Yochanan's] name: If all the sages of Israel with even (Rabbi) Eliezer ben Hyrkanos among them, were on one pan of the balance scale, and (Rabbi) Elazar ben Arach were on the other, he would outweigh them all.

13. He [Rabban Yochanan ben Zakkai] said to them [the five disciples]: Go out and discern which is the proper path

---

אַבָּא שָׁאוּל אוֹמֵר מִשְּׁמוֹ: אִם יִהְיוּ כָל חַכְמֵי יִשְׂרָאֵל בְּכַף מֹאזְנַיִם, וְ(רַבִּי) אֱלִיעֶזֶר בֶּן הִרְקָנוֹס אַף עִמָּהֶם, וְ(רַבִּי) אֶלְעָזָר בֶּן עֲרָךְ בְּכַף שְׁנִיָּה מַכְרִיעַ אֶת כֻּלָּם — *Abba Shaul said in [Rabban Yochanan's] name: If all the sages of Israel with even (Rabbi) Eliezer ben Hyrkanos among them were on one pan of the balance scale, and (Rabbi) Elazar ben Arach were on the other, he would outweigh them all.* The Talmud (*Horayos* 14a) records that Rabban Shimon ben Gamliel and the Sages disagree regarding which kind of sage is superior: a *"Sinai"* (who

has mastered all the subject matter of the Torah) or an *"Oker Harim"* (an *uprooter of mountains*, i.e., one whose sharp mind can perform great intellectual feats of creative reasoning in the halachic process). This seemingly is the point of contention in our mishnah. The first anonymous report gives primacy to R' Eliezer ben Hyrkanos, the *Sinai* figure, with total knowledge and recall. Abba Shaul's version prefers R' Elazar ben Arach, the sharp-minded *Oker Harim* (*Ruach Chaim, Tiferes Yisrael*).

Mishnah 13

אָמַר לָהֶם: צְאוּ וּרְאוּ — *He [Rabban Yochanan ben Zakkai] said to them [the five disciples]: Go out and discern.* The expression *Go out and discern* is based on *Song of Songs* 3:11: *Go forth and gaze, O daughters of Zion.*

Rav explains that the phrase is a behest to explore this question intellectually. To which question does it refer? According to *Midrash Shmuel* and *Tiferes Yisrael*, *Go out* is a call to these five

great students of Rabban Yochanan ben Zakkai to transcend the confines of their own exalted existence in order to prescribe a purposeful life course for the common man.

Rabban Yochanan asked his five great disciples to *go out* figuratively from the study hall where they were surrounded by peers of exceptional piety and intellectual capacity. He wanted them to put themselves in the place of ordinary people

---

◆§ Majority does not always rule. Rabbi Yechezkel Abramsky wondered why it was necessary for the mishnah to weigh which of the disciples was superior; what does this teach us? And if there is no teaching of permanent value, it would seem to be improper to praise one at the expense of all the others. Rabbi Abramsky explained that the mishnah teaches that when major decisions must be made for the benefit of the nation, one cannot decide merely by polling the various sages. A key factor in the determination must be the relative caliber of the discussants. Thus our mishnah makes a point of discussing which of the five great disciples was the superior one.

שֶׁיִּדְבַּק בָּהּ הָאָדָם. רַבִּי אֱלִיעֶזֶר אוֹמֵר: עַיִן טוֹבָה.
רַבִּי יְהוֹשֻׁעַ אוֹמֵר: חָבֵר טוֹב. רַבִּי יוֹסֵי אוֹמֵר: שָׁכֵן טוֹב.

---

and choose the best life-path for everyone (*Mikveh Yisrael*).

Not every personality attribute which is good for the study hall is appropriate in the marketplace. For example, being satisfied with little is, generally, a positive trait, but not in Torah study, where one must always seek to know and understand more (*Yalkut Yehudah*). The same is true of envy, which is a pernicious and degenerative trait, but is desirable among Torah scholars, if they use it as a spur to excel and accomplish more in their studies (see *Bava Basra* 21a).

אֵיזוֹ הִיא דֶּרֶךְ טוֹבָה שֶׁיִּדְבַּק בָּהּ הָאָדָם — *which is the proper path to which a man should cling.* While all of the character traits that follow are important elements of a complete Torah personality, no one can expect to master every desirable trait; perfection in one area is preferable to partial success in multiple areas, for one unblemished good trait can serve as the catalyst for the refinement of the total personality. One must pick a solitary trait and cleave to it until he masters it. In addition, one good attribute can serve as the

trailblazer for the overall pursuit of a proper path (*R' Yonah; Meiri*).

Chessed L'Avraham gives an interesting interpretation for the use of the word יִדְבַּק, *to cling* or *cleave*. The physical and spiritual aspects of man must achieve a *modus vivendi* which is mutually beneficial. A healthy body is needed to carry the spirit, and a vibrant spirituality is the lifeblood of an otherwise animalistic body. Rabban Yochanan ben Zakkai was asking his students which character trait could serve as the "glue" to bond body and soul together and enable them to serve each other's needs: אֵיזוֹ הִיא דֶּרֶךְ טוֹבָה, *which is the proper path* through which the physical and spiritual aspects of man will be pulled together.

If one cleaves to this particular trait under all circumstances, it will be a deterrent against sin; and even if, God forbid, one lapses, it will help him recover spiritually. This trait should serve as his spiritual compass, charting a course as he advances toward his destination (*Nesivos Shalom* of *Slonim*).

רַבִּי אֱלִיעֶזֶר אוֹמֵר: עַיִן טוֹבָה — *Rabbi Eliezer says A good eye*, i.e., a charitable and benevolent attitude toward others (*R' Yonah*).

◆§ **A realistic assessment.** Many Jews have the custom on Yom Kippur of adopting resolutions to improve specific areas of their lives. The Chofetz Chaim counseled his students to choose one area to concentrate on, and to move on to another area only after mastering the first. "A train," he said, "must be pulled by the powerful engine in its first car. Likewise, one improvement fully accomplished can draw man along the proper path."

◆§ **Let someone else succeed.** The ability to view life with a positive eye is based on deep-rooted faith. A man can actually delight in the success of his friend, without the slightest misgiving about his own lesser status, since it is clear to him that God, for perfectly good reasons which he may not fully comprehend, granted each one of them exactly what he should have (*Avodas Yisrael*).

On the commandment to love one's fellow as one loves himself, *Ramban* comments that it is impossible to say that the Torah literally expects every Jew to feel the same love for someone else that one feels for himself and his immediate family. Rather, the sense of the commandment is that one should be happy at another's successes and not begrudge his good fortune.

A person with a positive eye sees only the good in people and things and mentally blocks out the negative. The charge to adopt such a perspective is homiletically reflected in the words of King David, *And see the good of Jerusalem* (*Psalms* 128:5); even in the Holy City there are negative aspects, but one should have an eye only for the *good*.

In a more specific way, this refers to one who feels satisfied with himself and his lot in life, and is therefore not envious of others (*Rambam, Rav*); he even enjoys witnessing their success. Such a person is beloved by all (*Meiri*). [The untranslatable Yiddish term פַארגִינֶער, *farginner*, captures the spirit of עַיִן טוֹבָה.]

רַבִּי יְהוֹשֻׁעַ אוֹמֵר: חָבֵר טוֹב — *Rabbi Yehoshua says: A good friend.* One must have a good friend who is willing to offer constructive criticism and corrective advice (*Rav, Meiri*).

The strength of a friendship may be measured by its ability to withstand the strain of constructive criticism. Furthermore, one must have a close friend with whom he can share unashamedly his innermost thoughts and dreams — as well as his shortcomings (*R' Bunam of P'shis'cha*).

According to *Midrash Shmuel*, the "good friend" refers to a compatible spouse, who can be of the greatest help in one's spiritual quests. Living in such close quarters with another person allows endless opportunities for positive motivation. The prophet Malachi refers to one's wife as *your friend and your covenantal mate* (see *Gittin* 90a).

One must *be* a good friend. By acting as a good friend, even to one other person, one can train himself to find favor in the eyes of people in general. This is crucial to the maintenance of good relationships (*R' Yonah*). A good friend is often of greater help than a positive outlook. One can be overwhelmed by bitterness or a vested interest, lose his positive outlook, view life negatively, and

therefore fall into sin. However, while a friend may not be ready to engage in *self*-criticism he will always remind you of *your* obligations (*Magen Avos*).

רַבִּי יוֹסֵי אוֹמֵר: שָׁכֵן טוֹב — *Rabbi Yose says: A good neighbor.* A good neighbor is even more influential than a good friend. Because of his proximity, one enjoys constant contact with him and has greater opportunity to learn from his good behavior (*Rav*). One's good neighbor constantly observes his behavior, and he will be more conscious of behaving in an upright fashion in order not to disappoint his neighbor (*Meiri*, see *Rashi*).

According to *R' Yonah*, the key to developing a proper path is to *be* a good neighbor rather than simply to *have* one. By helping those who live nearby and cultivating strong relationships with them, one learns to relate to people. [Having good neighbors is not always in one's hands, but *being* a good neighbor certainly is.] Good neighbors provide opportunities to help others even at one's own personal expense. By practicing acts of kindness, one can evolve into a kind and good person (*Tiferes Yisrael*).

The Hebrew word אַהֲבָה, *love*, comes from the root הב, *to give*. Giving is not a result of love as much as love is a result of giving. Much of mother love is the product of the constant nurture that a mother gives her child (*Michtav MeEliyahu*).

⋖§ **She knows best.** When the Sages were contemplating the appointment of R' Elazar ben Azariah as *Nasi*, the suggestion was made that they discuss the idea with his wife to see if he was fit for the position (see *Berachos* 28a). Explained Rabbi Shlomo Freifeld, "The first one to know if a man is truly of elevated spiritual stature is his wife, for she lives with him every day."

⋖§ **True love.** "It was from two drunken Ukrainian peasants that I learned the true meaning of friendship," taught R' Mendel of Rimanov. "I heard one say to the other, 'Ivan do you really love me?' 'Yes,' answered his friend.' 'But do you *really* love me?' Again came the positive response. Said the first one, 'If you really love me, Ivan, why is it that you don't know what bothers me?'" From then on, R' Mendel insisted that he was obligated to try and find out what troubled another Jew, even if he insisted, as most people do, that "everything is fine."

רַבִּי שִׁמְעוֹן אוֹמֵר: הָרוֹאֶה אֶת הַנּוֹלָד. רַבִּי אֶלְעָזָר אוֹמֵר: לֵב טוֹב. אָמַר לָהֶם: רוֹאֶה אֲנִי אֶת דִּבְרֵי אֶלְעָזָר בֶּן עֲרָךְ מִדִּבְרֵיכֶם, שֶׁבִּכְלַל דְּבָרָיו דִּבְרֵיכֶם.

[יד] **אָמַר** לָהֶם: צְאוּ וּרְאוּ אֵיזוֹ הִיא דֶרֶךְ רָעָה שֶׁיִּתְרַחֵק מִמֶּנָּה הָאָדָם. רַבִּי אֱלִיעֶזֶר אוֹמֵר: עַיִן רָעָה.

רַבִּי שִׁמְעוֹן אוֹמֵר: הָרוֹאֶה אֶת הַנּוֹלָד — *Rabbi Shimon says: One who considers the outcome* [of a deed]. While no one today is a prophet, one can and should consider the probable consequences of any planned course of action. He can do this by predicting the future based on what had happened in the past in similar circumstances (*Rambam*). A little forethought will enable him to assess whether the immediate gains from a proposed activity are outweighed by any possible loss (*R' Yonah* and *Rav*). Forethought is the greatest form of preventive medicine. One who plans ahead will be saved from physical, spiritual, and emotional maladies (*Meiri*).

Minchas Shabbos renders הָרוֹאֶה אֶת הַנּוֹלָד as one who *envisions* the outcome of a deed, literally trying to imagine what will result and trying to imagine that he actually sees it. He gives an example of two students who were warned by their teacher that they would be severely punished if they didn't behave. One child was able to conjure up in his mind the expected punishment, and on the basis of that mental image alone, he was able to control himself. For the second child, nothing short of the punishment itself had an effect. Visualization of the consequences of one's actions can deter him from iniquity, and by the same token, vision of reward can give him the impetus to follow the good path.

רַבִּי אֶלְעָזָר אוֹמֵר: לֵב טוֹב — *R' Elazar says: A good heart.* One's heart is his emotional control center. From a good heart flow all good actions and character (*Rav*). R' Yonah defines a good heart as

the ability to be patient with people and to contain anger. A good-hearted person always responds to people softly and considerately, and is always ready to do them favors (*Tiferes Yisrael*). One can deal with the difficulties of life if he possesses a good heart. King Solomon teaches: *A good heart is always at a banquet* (Proverbs 15:15). [In fact, this verse is quoted as the very last words in *Shulchan Aruch Orach Chaim*, signifying that it should be one's goal to achieve a happy frame of mind throughout life.] This means that one who is happy with his lot in life is always in a festive frame of mind, never fazed by life's vicissitudes (*Beis Avos*).

אָמַר לָהֶם: רוֹאֶה אֲנִי אֶת דִּבְרֵי אֶלְעָזָר בֶּן עֲרָךְ מִדִּבְרֵיכֶם, שֶׁבִּכְלַל דְּבָרָיו דִּבְרֵיכֶם — *He said to them: I prefer the words of Elazar ben Arach to your words, for your words are included in his words.* Everything in life is dependent on the feelings of the heart (*Rashi*). Rabban Yochanan ben Zakkai views a good heart as a trait that includes all the virtues mentioned by his other disciples. A good-hearted person is not consumed by jealousy and is happy when other people enjoy success; hence, a good heart includes Rabbi Eliezer's *good eye.* Likewise, a good heart enables one to be a *good friend* and a *good neighbor.* Even the ability to *consider the outcome of one's actions* is related to emotional sensitivity. All the other virtues are therefore included under the all-encompassing category of the *good heart* (*R' Yonah* and *Rambam*).

◆§ **Dominos.** The mishnah (4:2) teaches that one *mitzvah* leads to another, and that one sin leads to another. Hence, the consequence of a good deed is to get one on the track toward another good deed. Likewise, one transgression sets off a "domino-like" progression of sin. Therefore, one should consider carefully the nature of any proposed course of action, bearing in mind that it will trigger either a positive or negative chain reaction (*R' Shmuel Alter*).

Rabbi Shimon says: One who considers the outcome [of a deed]. R' Elazar says: A good heart. He said to them: I prefer the words of Elazar ben Arach to your words, for your words are included in his words.

14. He said to them: Go out and discern which is the evil path from which a man should distance himself. Rabbi Eliezer says: An

---

R' Yonah notes further that a good and sensitive heart is a fundamental tool in the service of God. While the physical performance of *mitzvos* is possible even by rote, only one who is endowed with a feeling heart can focus on serving his Master out of love [which is considered the optimal level].

A serene and happy person has a sanguine view of life; people will enjoy his friendship and seek to be his neighbors. Furthermore, his calm and equanimity will enable him to assess the future clearly (*Tiferes Yisrael*). A good-hearted person empathizes with others and is flexible enough to accommodate their needs. This is a key to all the other character traits spelled out in our mishnah (*Sfas Emes*).

Mishnah 14

אָמַר לָהֶם: צְאוּ וּרְאוּ אֵיזוֹ הִיא דֶרֶךְ רָעָה שֶׁיִּתְרַחֵק מִמֶּנָּה הָאָדָם — *He said to them: Go out and discern which is the evil path from which a man should distance himself.* Even though it might have seemed obvious that the *evil path* is the exact opposite of the desirable paths the five disciples listed in the previous mishnah, this is not necessarily the case. For example, while satisfaction with one's lot or magnanimity towards others are certainly desirable, one may not automatically assume that a desire for luxuries or excessive thriftiness are negative, since they generally do no harm to others. [Similarly, while scrupulously righteous behavior is admirable, one would be hard-pressed to condemn those who do not maintain such a rigid standard.] Therefore, even after hearing their definitions of the good path, Rabban Yochanan ben Zakkai inquired of his students which path they considered evil; he intended to make it clear that the negative counterparts of the five virtues are *specifically* evil (*R' Yonah, Rav*).

According to *Chida*, Rabban Yochanan ben Zakkai solicited his disciples' opinions regarding the evil path in order to ascertain whether they had accepted his assessment that a good heart is the epitome of the good path. Each answered from his own perspective.

רַבִּי אֱלִיעֶזֶר אוֹמֵר עַיִן רָעָה — *Rabbi Eliezer says: An evil eye.* An evil eye refers to parsimony (*Rav*). Alternatively, it refers to the pursuit of luxuries (*Rambam*), implying that the term connotes a corrupt sense of values. According to *R' Yonah*, it refers to selfishness: While a generous spirit prompts all types of virtuous behavior, monetary and emotional stinginess are the root of most unethical and evil activities.

The term עַיִן רָעָה also indicates a jealous outlook. Such jealousy can bring harm to the person viewed.

A person with an evil eye, who has a negative view of life, lives in constant dissatisfaction and

---

◆§ **Harmful eye.** It is for this reason that one should always try to maintain a low profile and not arouse the jealousy of others. It is explained that such jealousy can cause harm to its victim because the victim may have been responsible for arousing such baseness in others. [See *Perakim BeEmunah VeHashgachah* (printed in *Amudei Olam*, p. 254) by R' Chaim Friedlander for an incisive understanding of the damaging effect of עַיִן רָעָה.] Interestingly, the Sages always refer to the evil *eye* (in singular) rather than to the *eyes*. It is only by shutting one eye to the Godliness inherent in every man — and instead looking only at his human, flawed side — that one is able to look upon others negatively (*Chasdei Avos*).

רַבִּי יְהוֹשֻׁעַ אוֹמֵר: חָבֵר רָע. רַבִּי יוֹסֵי אוֹמֵר: שָׁכֵן רָע. רַבִּי שִׁמְעוֹן אוֹמֵר: הַלֹּוֶה וְאֵינוֹ מְשַׁלֵּם. אֶחָד הַלֹּוֶה מִן הָאָדָם כְּלֹוֶה מִן הַמָּקוֹם, שֶׁנֶּאֱמַר: ,,לֹוֶה רָשָׁע וְלֹא יְשַׁלֵּם, וְצַדִּיק חוֹנֵן וְנוֹתֵן"

jealousy. Furthermore, he imputes bad motives to his friends and teachers, and doubts their sincerity. Because of his cynicism, he may even question his own values and beliefs (*Tiferes Yisrael*).

רַבִּי יְהוֹשֻׁעַ אוֹמֵר: חָבֵר רָע — *Rabbi Yehoshua says: A wicked friend.* This refers to oneself. One must be careful not to *be* a bad friend by acting unkindly toward others (*R' Yonah*). According to *Tiferes Yisrael,* it is *having* a wicked friend that invites spiritual disaster. The negative influence of a bad friend draws one off the proper path.

רַבִּי יוֹסֵי אוֹמֵר: שָׁכֵן רָע — *Rabbi Yose says: A wicked neighbor.* A wicked neighbor is a bad role model and must be avoided at all costs.

Rambam (*Hilchos Dei'os* 6:1) writes: By nature, people adapt their behavior to their surroundings, and to think and act like their friends. Hence, it is imperative that one befriend righteous people and live among them in order to emulate them. Likewise, one must keep a distance from evil people. If he lives in a place inhabited by wicked persons, he should move to one that is inhabited by upright individuals; and if such a place is not to be found, he should dwell in solitude. If the evil people of his place will not allow him to live in solitude, he must run away even to an uninhabited desert in order to escape their decadent influence.

רַבִּי שִׁמְעוֹן אוֹמֵר: הַלֹּוֶה וְאֵינוֹ מְשַׁלֵּם — *Rabbi Shimon says: One who borrows and does not repay.* This

mishnah is the counterpart of Rabbi Shimon's previous statement (הָרוֹאֶה אֶת הַנּוֹלָד) in the sense that borrowing without sufficient forethought as to how one will repay the debt is the equivalent of not foreseeing the future. When one cannot repay, he damages his credit standing and will not be able to secure any loans in the future (*Rav*).

According to *R' Yonah,* this is a case where not acting with an eye to future consequences is actually evil since it may incur the transgression of defaulting on a loan. One must make an objective assessment of his ability to repay before accepting a loan; and if he is in doubt, he should not succumb to the pressure of his circumstances and accept it. Instead, he should suffer the temporary discomfort of forgoing necessities. He may not seek to be excused for non-payment on the basis that he could not resist the pressure of his needs.

Rather than misleading the lender, let the potential borrower swallow his pride and ask for a gift. It certainly is better to be shamed in this world than to be shamed in the World to Come (*Ri ben Shlomo*).

אֶחָד הַלֹּוֶה מִן הָאָדָם כְּלֹוֶה מִן הַמָּקוֹם — *One who borrows from man is like one who borrows from the Omnipresent.* God repays the lender whose debtor is unable to make good on the loan. Hence, the borrower is really indebted to the Omnipresent (*Rav*).

◆§ **Where are the deserts today?** The Chazon Ish would often tell people that escape to academies of Torah study is the only way to save oneself from the immorality prevalent in society. "The yeshivos are the deserts," he would say. [Even if one must operate in a decadent world, he should at least prepare himself by spending years studying in Torah institutions. In this way he will build up an immunity to the spiritual contamination that dominates the culture.]

◆§ **Repaying God.** *Midrash Shmuel* interprets this label as an allegorical expression for a sinner. One who disregards God's word is indebted to Him, and *teshuvah* is the means by which he can repay the debt. One who does not repent fails to foresee the future, for without repentance he will sooner or later have to pay the price of his misdeeds. *Chiddushei HaRim* notes that *teshuvah* literally means "return." All sin is actually a form of theft, for man misappropriates the abilities endowed by God, and uses them against Him. Repentance entails making restitution for the theft by rededicating one's talents, abilities, and very life to his Creator.

evil eye. Rabbi Yehoshua says: A wicked friend. Rabbi Yose says: A wicked neighbor. Rabbi Shimon says: One who borrows and does not repay; one who borrows from man is like one who borrows from the Omnipresent, as it says: *The wicked one borrows and does not pay, while the Righteous One is gracious and gives (Psalms 37:21).*

God is called Omnipresent since He is not located in the world; He is more all-encompassing than it and envelops the entire cosmos.

According to *Yalkut HaGershuni*, the mishnah equates the importance of loans taken for personal use with those taken in order to meet philanthropic commitments. Whether borrowing for human or Godly purposes, one must take extreme care to make full and timely restitution; God is not interested in charity which is given at the expense of others.

R' Yonah adds that even if the court absolves an indigent man of his debt, he still has the moral obligation to pay back; for it is as if he borrowed from God, and a Heavenly duty is still incumbent upon him. *Meiri* views this as a reiteration of the severity of retaining loans. One tends to justify delays in paying back since he came into the money legally and is only temporarily retaining the money, which in his eyes is a far cry from stealing. Nonetheless, this is considered a sin in God's eyes, as if one had borrowed from God Himself.

R' S. R. Hirsch explains these words in the more global sense of one's attitude toward property. The person *who borrows and does not pay back* is irresponsible and thoughtless, for he never stops to consider the effects of his neglect in a communal context. He must always consider the fact that he does not exist solely for himself, and that whatever he receives in this world has been given him to advance the welfare of the world in accordance with God's will. The greater the "loan" he has been granted in terms of material possessions, the greater his obligation to use his assets for public benefit, and the greater the achievement that may be expected of him in return. Therefore, one who lives only for *himself* and is content to build his happiness at the expense of his fellow men, without thinking of the return which he is expected to make and for which God has created him, borrows from the world without repaying his debt. With every breath he takes, he becomes more deeply indebted to the world; and the greater the wealth and pleasures he has borrowed, the greater and the more crushing will be the spiritual bankruptcy of his life.

שֶׁנֶּאֱמַר: לֹוֶה רָשָׁע וְלֹא יְשַׁלֵּם, וְצַדִּיק חוֹנֵן וְנוֹתֵן — *as it says: "The wicked one borrows and does not pay, while the Righteous One is gracious and gives"* (*Psalms* 37:21). When a wicked person does not repay his loan, God, whose essence is righteousness, graciously serves as a guarantor and repays the lender (*Rav*).

According to *R' Yonah*, the verse contrasts two types of debtors. One who does not repay a loan is

---

⮜ **No excuse.** Under the strain of their debts, people often justify delaying repayment, saying, "The other man is comfortable enough to carry me. The few dollars won't really make a difference to him." Therefore, the mishnah teaches that one must view loans from a person as if they came from God. Just as God does not need the money back, so too, one must meet his lender's payment schedule, even if the lender has no pressing need for his money (*Avos al Banim*).

⮜ **Giving till it does not hurt.** A Jew who had lost his fortune came to Rebbe Mordechai Dov of Hornesteipel to cry his heart out and request help. The *Rebbe* groaned under the impact of the man's tragic tale and took out a very respectable sum of money to help alleviate his plight. He then reread the man's petitional note and offered him even more money. The man, however, felt uncomfortable. "*Rebbe*, please, it was hard enough to accept the first sum." The *Rebbe* answered, "We are taught, *Give and give again and let your heart not be pained when you give him* (Deuteronomy 15:10). A Jew must keep giving until the pain he feels for the plight of his fellow Jew disappears. What else should I do, since my heart still hurts for you?"

This is the way of the righteous; they are merciful and give.

רַבִּי אֶלְעָזָר אוֹמֵר: לֵב רָע. אָמַר לָהֶם: רוֹאֶה אֲנִי אֶת דִּבְרֵי
אֶלְעָזָר בֶּן עֲרָךְ מִדִּבְרֵיכֶם, שֶׁבִּכְלַל דְּבָרָיו דִּבְרֵיכֶם.

[טו] **הֵם** אָמְרוּ שְׁלֹשָׁה דְבָרִים. רַבִּי אֱלִיעֶזֶר אוֹמֵר: יְהִי
כְבוֹד חֲבֵרְךָ חָבִיב עָלֶיךָ כְּשֶׁלָּךְ, וְאַל תְּהִי

not deemed evil if he is really destitute and unable to pay. The evil exists if he borrowed without having objectively evaluated his ability to make restitution. The righteous person, on the other hand, assumes only as much of an obligation as he feels he can reasonably handle. While one who pays his debts is only fulfilling an obligation for which he deserves no gratitude or honor, an honorable borrower returns the money graciously and earns the gratitude and love of his creditors. Hence, he is referred to as a righteous person.

רַבִּי אֶלְעָזָר אוֹמֵר: לֵב רָע — *Rabbi Elazar says: A wicked heart.* Avos d'Rabbi Nosson (14:5) defines לֵב רָע in reference to three areas: (a) a wicked heart toward Heaven is ready to transgress Torah prohibitions; (b) a wicked heart is reluctant to make the effort to fulfill the 248 positive commands; (c) a wicked heart toward fellow men.

Rambam (*Hilchos Dei'os* 7:7-8) comments that the Biblical prohibitions of taking revenge and bearing a

grudge (לֹא תִקּוֹם וְלֹא תִטּוֹר) are rooted in the framework of a good heart. For example, a man asked his friend to lend him an item and the friend refused; a few days later their roles were reversed. The second man is cautioned not to refuse on the basis of his friend's refusal; rather, he should give his friend the item wholeheartedly, and not seek to pay back the friend with a similar action. One must not even bear a grudge, but must seek to *totally erase his friend's indiscretion from his heart.* It is this refined attitude that fosters civilized life and promotes proper commercial and social interaction among men.

אָמַר לָהֶם: רוֹאֶה אֲנִי אֶת דִּבְרֵי אֶלְעָזָר בֶּן עֲרָךְ מִדִּבְרֵיכֶם, שֶׁבִּכְלַל דְּבָרָיו דִּבְרֵיכֶם — *He* [Rabban Yochanan ben Zakkai] *said to them: I prefer the words of Elazar ben Arach to your words, for your words are included in his words.* The heart is the root of all man's emotions, thoughts, and actions. Just as decay in the roots of a tree will spread to the tree itself, destroying all its vigor and beauty, so a wicked heart will spread its moral decay throughout man's entire being (*Tiferes Yisrael*).

Mishnah 15

הֵם אָמְרוּ שְׁלֹשָׁה דְבָרִים — *They each said three things.* Each of the five disciples of Rabban Yochanan ben Zakkai made three statements on the subject of ethics, values, and proper conduct.

But regarding ritual law, we find many statements of these great men (*Rashi* and *Rav*).

Alternatively, although they made many statements regarding ethical issues, the mishnah refers to the statements on these issues that they constantly reiterated in public (*Rav* and *R' Yonah*).

רַבִּי אֱלִיעֶזֶר אוֹמֵר: יְהִי כְבוֹד חֲבֵרְךָ חָבִיב עָלֶיךָ כְּשֶׁלָּךְ, וְאַל תְּהִי נוֹחַ לִכְעוֹס — *Rabbi Eliezer says: Let your fellow's honor be as dear to you as your own, and do not anger easily.* According to *Rav*, these two stiches together form the first of R' Eliezer ben

Hyrkanos's statements. By controlling one's anger one may be sure not to diminish his fellow's honor. A person lost in a fit of anger is bound to demean his fellow; hence, the second part is a means for achieving the first.

Tiferes Yisrael views these instructions in exactly the opposite fashion: Anger is the result of a belittlement of the other person's honor. Indeed, arguments usually begin with one party slighting the other; angry words ensue, and the tone and heat of the quarrel escalate. R' Eliezer therefore advised extreme sensitivity to the honor of others. Just as one does not want to be demeaned, even by innuendo, so he should be careful not to degrade his friend even the

Rabbi Elazar says: A wicked heart. He [Rabban Yochanan ben Zakkai] said to them: I prefer the words of Elazar ben Arach to your words, for your words are included in his words.

15. They each said three things. Rabbi Eliezer says: Let your fellow's honor be as dear to you as your own, and do not

---

slightest bit. [The Talmud compares discord to an overflowing river which swells the streams in the land adjacent to it. If these streams are not immediately dammed, they will continue to expand and eventually flood the area. Similarly, if a dispute is not quelled in its early stages, it will escalate out of control (see *Sanhedrin* 7a and *Rashi* ad loc.).]

According to *Rambam* and *R' Yonah*, however, these are two separate instructions. One must not only treat his fellow with respect, but must make all efforts to see that *others* treat his friend in a prestigious fashion. The honor of a fellow Jew must be as primary a concern as one's personal prestige — even to the extent of assuring others' attitudes toward the person. Secondly, one should not be quick to anger.

Midrash Shmuel offers a few alternative insights into a proper perspective on human honor and dignity. (a) The mishnah (4:1) says that the honor one is accorded parallels the extent to which he honors others (*Who is honored? He who honors others*). His friend's honor should therefore be as dear to him as his own, for it is by honoring others that he earns honor for himself. (b) People have a tendency to feel that they honor others above and

---

◆§ **Perspectives on honor.** The mishnah (4:28) teaches that honor is one of the three things which remove a man from the world. Why, therefore, are we enjoined here to honor others? Do we really want to give someone else something that is spiritually detrimental?

The answer lies in a keen insight illustrated by the following story. The Kotzker *Rebbe* was famous for his very exacting standard of honesty. Once a certain well-known *Rebbe* came to spend a Shabbos with the Kotzker. The Kotzker's followers were surprised to see their teacher accord the guest great honor, since they knew he did not have a very high opinion of the gentleman. When they questioned their teacher, he explained his actions by quoting the Talmudic teaching regarding charity: One must provide for a poor man whatever he was accustomed to in the past, even a horse to ride on and a servant to lead the horse (see *Kesubos* 67b). Said the Kotzker: "I can understand that one who finds it difficult to walk should be provided with a horse for transportation, but why a servant to lead the horse? That seems foolish! The answer is that part of charity is even to provide a fool with his foolishness."

Subjective needs are real! Even if it is objectively foolish to require honor and prestige (see comm. to 4:28), one who is accustomed to them needs them. Honoring others, therefore, is an exercise in charitable behavior. Hence, even someone who avoids honor for himself, because he understands its shallowness, should honor others, rather than considering it a foolish need. Let him imagine that he personally *does* need honor; than he will sympathize with others.

A story told of R' Shmelke of Nikolsburg offers an entirely different perspective on the requirement to equate others' honor with one's own. When R' Shmelke assumed his rabbinical position, the community held a welcoming reception. Before entering the hall, he requested the use of a side room. Much to their disbelief, his congregants overheard him talking to himself in his room, saying, "Welcome, honored rabbi; it is our pleasure to have such a genius grace our city," and similar expressions of welcome and praise. When the *Rebbe* emerged, the notables of the community, somewhat nonplused, asked him to explain his strange behavior. He said: "I am aware that I will soon hear accolades similar to those I just repeated to myself. I wanted to get the feeling of how meaningless such honor really is. I therefore followed the words of the Sages: 'Let the honor given you by your friends and colleagues have the same value and be as [meaningless and ludicrous to you as] the honor you accord yourself.'"

beyond the call of duty, yet others honor them in a less-than-appropriate manner. It is to address this slanted perspective that we are taught: "Let the honor one *receives* from others *seem as special* as the honor one *gives* others." (c) When one sees his fellow receiving greater honor than he himself receives, he should not be upset. Rather, the honor others receive should give him as much pleasure as the honor he himself receives. [It is possible that his friend has some positive character trait that he himself lacks. Possibly it is that good trait which evokes the prestige his fellow enjoys.]

The next words of R' Eliezer, וְאַל תְּהִי נוֹחַ לִכְעוֹס, instruct us not to anger easily. It is really impossible never to get angry, so the mishnah instructs us not to anger *easily*. We must be level headed enough to assess whether the incident that sparked our anger is sufficient cause for an outburst. We should actively attempt to find reasons not to be angry. The difference between the intelligent and the foolish can be measured by their propensity toward anger; the wise exercise some self-control, while the foolish are controlled by their stormy emotions.

The Sages teach that one's character can be discerned by the way he acts when he is under financial pressure, intoxicated, or angry (*Eruvin* 65b). [In these three instances, the restraining power of the mind becomes largely inoperative, and man's inherent instincts surface (*R' Yonah*).] *Rambam* views the prohibition against anger as rooted in the Talmudic equation of anger with idolatry (see *Shabbos* 105b).

וְשׁוּב יוֹם אֶחָד לִפְנֵי מִיתָתְךָ — *repent one day before your death.* Does one ever know when he will die? Rather, he must always assume that today is the last day of his life and not push off his repentance. Hence, he will spend all his life in perpetual self-improvement (*Rashi, R' Yonah, Rambam*).

King Solomon teaches in *Ecclesiastes* (9:8): *Let your garments always be white.* One's soul — his inner garment — must always be kept clean of spiritual stains through repentance. The Talmud offers the following analogy: A king invited all his subjects to a royal feast without specifying when the banquet would begin. The intelligent among his subjects donned their finest attire in preparation. "Since the king lacks nothing to prepare a feast, we must be ready at a moment's notice," they said. The foolish among them rationalized instead, "A

⇥ **Planned outbursts.** *Yismach Yisrael* emphasizes that *any* spontaneous anger is misplaced, for anger is sinful. Even when it may be a *mitzvah* to show anger (i.e., over a public breach of halachah), it certainly should be done like all other *mitzvos* — calmly and with much forethought. A well-known yeshivah principal used to urge his teachers to show anger only on rare, but well-thought-out occasions, and to do so only several minutes before recess, so that learning time should not be lost, and they would have time after recess to show affection to the class.

HaChassid Yaavetz views this dictum as reflective of R' Eliezer ben Hyrkanos's general emphasis on having a "good eye," which is the cornerstone of ethical development. One who has a positive outlook on life and on others will not anger easily.

⇥ **False premises.** This seemingly exaggerated comparison must be understood in light of a dazzling insight of the *Sefer HaChinuch* §241 regarding the prohibition against revenge.

Everything that happens to man is part of a Divine plan; there is no such thing as coincidence or accident (see *Ramban* to *Exodus* 13:16). Even when a man is harmed by his fellow, it is an expression of God's will, with the perpetrator acting merely as a Heavenly messenger. When one becomes angry with another person or takes revenge on him for a wrong, he is assuming that his fellow had the independent ability to harm him in the first place and does not take God's will into account. Otherwise, he would look to God as the source of his trouble and would have no reason to be angry with the person who hurt him. Such anger is a form of idolatry, for he assigns independent power to another human being when there is really no such thing. Therefore, we are taught not to become angry easily; it is a form of denial of the Source of all events in the world.

feast takes time to prepare. What is our rush?" Suddenly, the king summoned his subjects. The intelligent ones appeared in proper attire, while the foolish came in front of the king in their filthy clothes. Those who were properly dressed were allowed to partake of the feast, and the others could only sit by in envy.

Similarly, man is invited to partake of the feast of reward that awaits him after his sojourn in this world. Those who think ahead are sure to be cleanly and properly cloaked with *mitzvos*; even if God summons them suddenly, they will be prepared to join the feast and partake of their reward. The foolish fantasize that they will repent later, and in the interim they besmirch their souls. When their day comes suddenly, it is too late; they will not be allowed to appear at the royal feast since they are not properly attired. They can only sit on the sidelines and gaze jealously.

וֶהֱוֵי מִתְחַמֵּם כְּנֶגֶד אוּרָן שֶׁל חֲכָמִים — *warm yourself by the fire of the sages.* Merely learning from books or even listening to the words of the wise is

insufficient. One must cultivate a more intimate relationship with sages and bask in the warmth of their personalities. One may enjoy the light of Torah even from afar, but its greatest warmth and excitement comes only from close contact with Torah personalities. The fire of their commitment can melt even the coldest hearts. We are enjoined here not to be satisfied with a distant relationship with Torah scholars, but instead to warm ourselves directly opposite their fire (*Tiferes Yisrael*).

According to *Rav*, this is the third of R' Eliezer ben Hyrkanos's ethical statements (the first two are interpersonal respect as an antidote to anger, and repentance before death); *Rambam* and *R' Yonah* view this as an additional statement which R' Eliezer did not emphasize quite as frequently as the others.

וֶהֱוֵי זָהִיר בְּגַחַלְתָּן שֶׁלֹּא תִכָּוֶה — *but beware of their glowing coal lest you be scorched.* Although we are advised to maintain close contact with the sages,

---

◄§ **The time may be now.** *Koheles Rabbah* (9:8) paints a poignant picture of a sailor's wife who dressed every day in her finest clothes. When questioned about her practice, she replied: "My husband is a sailor. A strong wind can bring his ship into port in any moment, and I will be very ashamed if he finds me ungroomed and unattractive."

Lev Avos reminds us that man can rectify his entire life in one moment through *teshuvah*. By repenting even on his dying day, he can redefine his entire life and turn it into a prelude for that one moment of greatness. Let one not feel imprisoned by the detours and lapses of his past; he can recreate himself at any time. *Repent* even *one day before your death.*

◄§ **Fire versus pot.** Parents are sometimes deluded into thinking that minimal Jewish education is sufficient to insure that their children will grow up to be good Jews. They are sure that the positive influence of the home will provide the backbone missing in the education process.

The Chofetz Chaim explained otherwise: There are two items which give off heat, the flame itself and a pot warmed over the fire. The fire itself is always hot, no matter where one moves it; not so the pot, which cools down if it is not directly on the fire. Furthermore, the fire itself can ignite other fires; the pot cannot. The contents of a pot get progressively cooler when poured into other pots, but a fire remains as hot as ever, no matter how many other flames are lit from it.

In a similar vein, Torah study can maintain the fire of one's commitment to Judaism even if one is removed from the influence of parents and home. However, if one hopes that a sketchy or incomplete Jewish education will suffice, and relies only on parental influence, he takes great risk. Once out of the parental orbit, his commitment tends to cool down, much like the hot pot; and even if his commitment remains vibrant, it loses warmth with each generational transfer. It is highly doubtful whether his children or grandchildren will remain strongly linked to their heritage.

With regard to people who feel that their faith can remain firm even without a strong Torah education, Dr. Leo Deutchlander, a pioneer of the Beth Jacob movement in Poland, once said, "If you show me someone who swam across the rapids of the Danube River, I will admire him greatly, but if you show me someone who is planning to undertake that hazardous stunt, I will consider him a suicidal fool."

שֶׁנְּשִׁיכָתָן נְשִׁיכַת שׁוּעָל, וַעֲקִיצָתָן עֲקִיצַת עַקְרָב,
וּלְחִישָׁתָן לְחִישַׁת שָׂרָף, וְכָל דִּבְרֵיהֶם כְּגַחֲלֵי אֵשׁ.

[טז] רַבִּי יְהוֹשֻׁעַ אוֹמֵר: עַיִן הָרָע, וְיֵצֶר הָרָע,

we are warned here not to be overly friendly, which may bring us to act disrespectfully toward them. We should allow them to initiate the points of contact and to monitor the extent of the relationship. This is similar to one who sits near a fire: If he sits too far away, he will not derive any benefit from the warmth of the fire, yet if he gets too close he will be hurt rather than helped. Overfamiliarity breeds contempt, and contempt or even irreverence toward Torah scholars is a grave sin with major consequences (*Rav, Ramban, R' Yonah*).

Rashi views these words instead as referring to the consequences of not following the dictates of Torah scholars, which is as dangerous as "playing with fire."

שֶׁנְּשִׁיכָתָן נְשִׁיכַת שׁוּעָל — *for their bite is the bite of a fox.* A fox bite is particularly painful and difficult to heal. The results of acting casually with Torah scholars are similarly enduring and painful (*Rav*).

Rambam interprets the fox bite as referring to the stinging admonition one may receive from a sage if he oversteps his bounds.

Meiri sees the significance of the fox metaphor as follows: A fox has thin and slanted teeth. At the moment of the bite, the pain is not felt; however, when the fox removes its teeth the pain is unbearable. Likewise, one who tampers with the honor of Torah scholars may not initially feel the repercussions, but afterward they will be felt severely.

⊷ **Deceptive surface.** Many times, Torah sages are easygoing people who enjoy amicable relationships with their followers. This should not lead one to abuse the exalted position of the Torah scholar, who is compared to a glowing coal covered by gray ash; on the surface, no fire is apparent, but inside there is a flame that harbors danger for those who tamper with it (*Baal Shem Tov*). Thus, one must maintain a delicate balance in his dealings with Torah scholars. *R' Yedayah HaPenini* (*Mivchar HaPenenim* 34:5) captures this process in the following analogy: A wise man once instructed his son in the art of surviving royal service. "When you serve royalty, imagine that you are standing in front of a raging fire. Do not be too far removed from it, lest you suffer from the excess cold; yet do not get too close, for you may be fatally burned."

⊷ **Mirror of the soul.** Irreverent behavior toward Torah scholars not only elicits punishment, it is symptomatic of an underlying weakness in one's character, one which may spread and poison his general value system.

R' Yonah (*Shaarei Teshuvah* 3:148) offers a penetrating analysis of the fashion in which men assign values: *The refining pot is for silver, and the furnace for gold, and a man according to his praise* (*Proverbs* 27:21). That is, a man's qualities can be assessed by what he praises. If he praises good deeds and righteous men, we know that he is a good man who appreciates and loves righteousness. Even though he may transgress from time to time, he does not approve of sin; he still reveres the lovers of righteousness, and he is among those who honor God. On the other hand, one who praises repulsive deeds and extols the wicked is a confirmed evildoer, who desecrates the service of God.

Sometimes a person is somewhere between these two levels. When he sees that he is not on the elevated level of true Torah scholars, he is often psychologically tempted to drag them down by imputing that their decisions are based on personal interests and considerations of private gain. [The *Chazon Ish* (*Emunah U'Bitachon* 3:30) asserts vehemently that authentic Torah scholars are not subject to this type of pettiness. If that were so, God forbid, the bedrock of Judaism — belief in the Sages — would be irreparably smashed. A person who thus debases a Torah scholar gives evidence of the wayward inclination of his soul.]

you be scorched — for their bite is the bite of a fox, their sting is the sting of a scorpion, their hiss is the hiss of a serpent, and all their words are like fiery coals.

16. Rabbi Yehoshua says: An evil eye, the evil inclination,

וַעֲקִיצָתָן עֲקִיצַת עַקְרָב — *their sting is the sting of a scorpion.* A scorpion releases deadly poison along with its sting (*Rashi, Tiferes Yisrael*).

וּלְחִישָׁתָן לְחִישַׁת שָׂרָף — *their hiss is the hiss of a serpent.* Unlike other dangerous reptiles, the serpent, once incited, cannot be charmed or restrained from attacking. Likewise, one should not fool himself into thinking that after slighting a Torah scholar it will be possible to appease him (*Rav* and *R' Yonah*).

Even if scholars take no action against their detractors, merely praying to God to intervene on their behalf, the "hiss" of prayer will be answered (*Tiferes Yisrael*).

Rambam cites as historical evidence the story of Gechazi, who impudently sought to interpret the prophet Elisha's reason for refusing to accept gifts from Naaman (see *II Kings* 5:20-27). As a result, Gechazi was struck with incurable leprosy.

וְכָל דִּבְרֵיהֶם כְּגַחֲלֵי אֵשׁ — *and all their words are like fiery coals.* The word "all" warns us not to ignore rabbinic enactments that may seem minor to us. Such a light attitude will cause us to be spiritually scorched (*Rashi*).

Even words uttered inadvertently and unintentionally by great men have a powerful effect (*Torah Temimah*).

According to *Tiferes Yisrael*, R' Eliezer ben Hyrkanos addresses three areas in this mishnah: good character development, practical fulfillment of the *mitzvos*, and Torah study. Regarding one's character we are taught to avoid anger; in order to keep our priorities straight and act correctly rather than indulging in our own comfort, the mishnah enjoins us to repent. Finally, regarding Torah study, we are told how to maximize the benefit we may derive from Torah mentors and role models.

Mishnah 16

רַבִּי יְהוֹשֻׁעַ אוֹמֵר: עַיִן הָרָע — *Rabbi Yehoshua says: An evil eye.* This mishnah describes three negative qualities that destroy a person's life in this world. The first is the "evil eye," which may refer to a number of things. One is a "roving eye" that incessantly seeks luxuries. Alternatively, the evil eye may refer to the attitude of one who seeks to harm the property or family of others (*Rav*).

⯈ The metaphor of the serpent is intended to refer to the manner in which a Torah scholar takes "revenge": "Any Torah sage who does not take revenge like a serpent is not considered a true scholar" (*Yoma* 22b). As a result of God's curse (see *Genesis* 3:14), the serpent tastes everything as dust and derives no pleasure from eating. A true Torah scholar, similarly, reacts sharply only to one who scorns the honor of Torah, and not out of the pleasurable sense of a personal vendetta. Like a serpent, his "hiss" is deadly — but he derives no pleasure from his bite (*Baal Shem Tov*).

⯈ As a young man, the Malbim visited Pressburg and was asked to present a public Torah discourse. After a three-hour lecture, he was extremely tired, and he inadvertently sat down and dozed off on the chair of the *Rav* of Pressburg, the Chasam Sofer. When the Chasam Sofer entered the synagogue, everybody arose in a show of respect. The *Malbim,* stirred by the noise, began to rise, but the Chasam Sofer said to him: "Young man, remain in your place."

While the Chasam Sofer meant nothing more than to calm the Malbim, the latter complained bitterly in later years: "From the moment the great Chasam Sofer told me to remain in my place, my growth in areas of halachah has been seriously impeded." [Before this incident, the Malbim had published *Artzos HaChaim*, a very well-received work on the laws of *tzitzis* and *tefillin*. Later, he published his famed commentary on *Tanach* but never produced another halachic work.]

[יז] רַבִּי יוֹסֵי אוֹמֵר: יְהִי מָמוֹן חֲבֵרְךָ חָבִיב עָלֶיךָ

R' Yonah speaks of the evil eye as a cancerous jealousy. One who is unhappy with his lot in life constantly views others with envy and has an insatiable desire to usurp their wealth and position. The object of his envy is likely to suffer loss as a result of the evil eye, and the perpetrator also will be emotionally scarred and suffer endless heartache as a result of his unquenchable thirst for that which is not destined to be his. A person's inner world is completely destroyed by such consuming jealousy.

In *Rambam's* view, the evil eye which our mishnah warns against is stinginess. [One who is stingy never enjoys life. He is always afraid that he is on the doorstep of poverty.]

Avos d'Rabbi Nosson extends the concept of an evil eye to one who feels upset by his friend's success in Torah study. While jealousy in regard to spiritual pursuits is generally positive [see *Bava Basra* 21a], this is only true if it motivates the one who is "jealous" to study in order to surpass the object of his jealousy. The possessor of an evil eye, however, does not want his friend to be successful.

וְיֵצֶר הָרָע — *the evil inclination.* According to *Rambam,* this is a generic term for all man's lusts and negative desires. The Talmud (*Shabbos* 105b) describes the Evil Inclination as a "strange god ingrained in the body of man"; it begins its conquest by inducing one to commit a minor infraction and constantly increases its influence until the person is so imprisoned that he is ready to transgress the most sordid of sins.

Meiri renders יֵצֶר הָרָע as the drive toward immorality and notes the fact that the Evil Impulse in man predates the force of good in him by thirteen years (or twelve for women) [see *Koheles Rabbah* 4:15]. While the Good Inclination only becomes fully activated at *bar* (age thirteen) or *bas mitzvah* (age twelve), man is born with an aggressive drive toward evil which he must temper and tame. *Meiri* adds that this force for evil seeks to destroy man's life utterly (*Meiri*). Our Sages (*Berachos* 61a) compare the Evil Inclination to a mosquito. Even if one chases it away, it keeps coming back again and again, seeking a way to suck a person's blood.

Avos d'Rabbi Nosson adds an encouraging note by comparing the evil inclination to brass. When placed in fire, brass becomes malleable and can be shaped. Similarly, the fire of Torah can transform the evil impulse into a force for good.

וְשִׂנְאַת הַבְּרִיּוֹת — *and hatred of other people.* This refers to causeless hatred (שִׂנְאַת חִנָּם) (*Rashi*). *Rambam* renders שִׂנְאַת הַבְּרִיּוֹת as *misanthropy,* referring to one who detests human company and prefers to be alone. Such a person will eventually suffer from melancholy. [The disinclination toward human company discussed in our mishnah is not rooted in a desire to be free of others' negative influence (see *Rambam, Hilchos Dei'os* 6:1) but is simply antisocial behavior.]

According to *Magen Avos,* *Rambam's* rendering is inappropriate, since this mishnah discusses social and moral failings, rather than physical or, in this case, psychological sicknesses.

❧ **A mystery.** The Chazon Ish (*Choshen Mishpat, Likkutim*) writes that one of the mysteries of Creation is the ability of man, by means of his intellect, to unleash hidden forces in everyday existence. Man's thought processes alone can cause physical things to be destroyed. In the instance of the mishnah, when a person experiences excessive agitation over successful people and coveted items, he places them in extreme danger.

❧ **With cause.** Meiri notes a distinction between causeless hatred and that which has a basis. We are told specifically that those who blatantly transgress the word of God are not to be loved (see *Psalms* 139:21, *For indeed those who hate You,* HASHEM, *I hate them*). Just as one could never prevent himself from hating a person who slapped his father in the face, so our natural reaction should be abhorrence for anybody who defames or rebels against our Father in heaven.

17. Rabbi Yose says: Let your fellow's money be as dear to you

Rav (based on *Magen Avos*) sees this person as one who, by his difficult and antipathetic behavior, brings upon himself the hatred of others. *Midrash Shmuel* adds that people who hate him will curse him. The Talmud (*Megillah* 15a) teaches that even the curse of a simple person can be efficacious and should be treated seriously.

מוֹצִיאִין אֶת הָאָדָם מִן הָעוֹלָם — *remove a person from the world.* Someone characterized by these three distinctive qualities is in danger of a premature death. The drive for money and possessions can become so obsessive as to cause him unbearable anxiety; lust induces all kinds of physical sicknesses; and extreme hatred of others is life-threatening (*Meiri*). These three things also undermine a man's spirituality.

Tiferes Yisrael sees R' Yehoshua's triad as the forces that might undermine the three foundations of the world given in 1:2: *Torah, the service [of God]* and *kind deeds.* He thus renders עַיִן רָעָה as *evil views.* One loses his foothold both in this world and in the next when his views on these three foundations are corrupt: Such a person has failed to adopt the Torah viewpoint regarding fundamental areas of faith; he allows his evil inclination to impede his service of God and fulfillment of *mitzvos*; and he lets a senseless hatred of people paralyze the ingrained Jewish trait of loving-kindness. Such a person loses both worlds.

Mishnah 17

רַבִּי יוֹסֵי אוֹמֵר: יְהִי מָמוֹן חֲבֵרְךָ חָבִיב עָלֶיךָ כְּשֶׁלָּךְ — *Rabbi Yose says: Let your fellow's money be as dear to you as your own.* One should be as concerned for someone else's property and money as for his own.

This is an extension of Hillel's statement (*Shabbos* 31a) "Whatever you find hateful to yourself do not do to your friend" (*Meiri*). *Avos d'Rabbi Nosson* (17) offers an example. One should never publicly

Unwelcome occupier. A man was once possessed by an insatiable desire to acquire his friend's house.

He begged, pleaded, and cajoled his friend to sell it, but to no avail. Finally, in a desperate attempt to rid himself of the other man's incessant pleas, the owner agreed to sell him a tiny space in the house — large enough for a hook to hang his hat. The owner was paid handsomely, yet he soon realized his mistake, for the buyer began to show up every day and request passage into his "area." The owner had no choice but to allow him in. He eventually became such a nuisance that the owner was ready to give away the house altogether and move out.

Such is the craft of the Evil Persuader. He pesters us incessantly until we allow him a foothold in our lives. But that is the beginning of the end. He soon drives us out of house and home, assuming total control of our bodies and souls. Hence, he *removes a person from the world* (*Baal Shem Tov*).

Ohr HaChaim elaborates: Once man allows any evil to penetrate his defenses, he is no longer able to see the truth or accept the rebuke. He becomes spiritually deaf and blind. Like a sentry, the evil inclination stands guard at the entrance to his heart, preventing any talk of change or growth. This is similar to a king who appoints thieves as his palace guards. They would certainly never allow people who want to complain about them to enter the palace.

Based on this idea, Rabbi Shlomo Freifeld explained an anomaly in the Torah's report of the sale of Joseph by his brothers. When Joseph, as the Egyptian ruler, demanded the presentation of their younger brother Benjamin, they began to feel pangs of guilt. *Then they said to one another, "Indeed we are guilty concerning our brother, inasmuch as we saw his heartfelt anguish when he pleaded with us and we paid no heed"* (*Genesis* 42:21). *Ramban* (ad loc.) wonders why this report of Joseph's pleadings is not to be found in the initial account of the episode. R' Freifeld explained: In the heat of sin, man is so captivated by the force of evil that he really hears and sees no legitimate counter argument. Only when they were overcome by therapeutic guilt and spiritually began to disengage themselves from the hold of the evil inclination did the brothers realize that Joseph had begged for mercy all during their sale of him. At the time, they had been spiritually so deaf that they heard nothing.

criticize the quality of any goods being offered for sale, since this may dissuade potential buyers. If the merchandise is of good quality, he should praise it; if it is inferior, he should say, "I don't know."

Meiri supplements: One should be concerned with his friend's potential monetary loss just as he would be with his own. If he sees his friend's ship about to capsize or his house about to burn down, he is obligated to make all efforts to save the friend's property, acting no differently than if the imminent loss were his own.

This can also be seen as a call for man to rejoice over his fellow's success. Rather than feeling jealousy, one should help his friend and view his success as if it were his own (*Tiferes Yisrael*).

Additionally, if one has undertaken to manage his fellow's investments, he should make all reasonable efforts to invest it profitably and prudently. Just as he uses his own capital to increase his wealth, he must do the same with his friend's property. A classic example of this approach is recorded in the Talmud: A person inadvertently left some chickens on R' Chanina ben

Dosa's doorstep. R' Chanina warned his family not to eat the chickens' eggs since they belonged to the original owner. Unaware of the owner's identity, he was unable to return them and instead tended to them. Eventually the chickens produced so many eggs and chicks that they became a nuisance. R' Chanina sold the chickens and eggs and purchased goats. When the original owner finally passed by R' Chanina's house, he remembered his chickens and inquired as to their whereabouts. R' Chanina was finally able to return a fortune in goats (*Taanis* 25a).

A more emotional interpretation asks that we consider money given to charity as though it were spent on a personal need or desire. Such money actually remains our own, safely invested in our Heavenly bank account, since we have not really parted with it (*R' Yehoshua Heschel* of *Monostrich*).

וְהַתְקֵן עַצְמְךָ לִלְמוֹד תּוֹרָה, שֶׁאֵינָהּ יְרֻשָּׁה לָךְ — *apply yourself to study the Torah, for it is not yours by inheritance.* One must not delude himself into thinking that by virtue of the fact that his father and forefathers were scholars, he too will become a scholar, even without sweat and toil. Success at

---

◆§ **Honest equivalence.** If one is ready to part with his own money on behalf of a charitable cause, then and only then may he ask the same of his friends; he should not be a philanthropist with someone else's money. This is the mishnah's instruction: *Let your fellow's money be as dear to you as your own.* Only if you are ready to commit your own money to a cause are you allowed to expect the same of others (*Tiferes Tzvi*).

It is a universal malady to see the belongings of others as special and beautiful rather than to appreciate one's own blessings. *Maharam Schiff* understands this piece of psychological insight as the key to the words of the Sages: "Man does not die with even half of his desires in hand" (*Koheles Rabbah* 1:34). This statement seems to contradict the one that follows: "He who possesses one hundred desires two hundred" (ibid.), which would seem to indicate that one *does* attain half of his desire. The answer is that the second hundred — the unachieved half — always seems bigger and better than the first. It is to this end that we are taught, *Let your fellow's money be* [*at most as*] *dear to you as your own* — but not dearer than your own, for one should be satisfied with his own possessions and not assume that others are more precious (*Beis Shmuel*).

◆§ **Conveying love.** The Talmud (*Pesachim* 49b) states regarding the verse מוֹרָשָׁה קְהִלַּת יַעֲקֹב, *It is the heritage of the Congregation of Jacob* (*Deuteronomy* 33:4): Do not read it as מוֹרָשָׁה, *heritage,* but instead as מְאוֹרָשָׂה, *betrothed.* Unlike a financial inheritance, which the children receive without lifting a finger, Torah cannot be given to one's children unless they themselves expend the necessary effort. Hence, the term מוֹרָשָׁה is not quite an appropriate term to use for the acquisition of Torah.

However, one's love and passion for Torah, unlike Torah knowledge, can indeed be inculcated in one's children. This is symbolized by the word מְאוֹרָשָׂה, *betrothed.* The groom's joy in his fiancée is something that can be conveyed to others. Likewise, when children see the love of parents for Torah, it becomes infectious and inspires the children to love, learn, and live Torah (*R' Chanoch Ehrentrau*).

Torah study is achieved only through the investment of personal effort. Unlike a monetary inheritance, which is acquired effortlessly, Torah knowledge can be achieved only by those who actively seek it (*Rashi, Rav*).

One may be blessed with towering intellect, yet without toil he will not succeed in his Torah study. *Meiri* poetically captures this message: "How many rivers have dried up? How many rocks have yielded water?" [Many people imbued with great natural talent did not utilize their Godly gifts and spiritually dried up, while others, ostensibly with limited abilities, have by dint of great effort made themselves into prolific scholars.]

Rambam interprets this clause as a general rule of human development: *No man is born with predestined superior qualities nor with built-in deficiencies.* Every person is endowed with potential of a specific nature, but he must expend the effort to actualize it (*Shemoneh Perakim* Chapter 8). It is this that our mishnah teaches: Prepare yourself through study and effort to achieve success, for it is not a God-given inheritance achieved without exertion.

According to *R' Yonah*, the mishnah prescribes preparatory stages that are necessary to make oneself a fitting receptacle for the Divine intelligence. Only one who has developed a refined and elevated character is a fitting vessel for Torah.

The quality of the receptacle must always befit the contents. Hence, a human being must make himself Godly in order to be a fitting receptacle for Torah.

Furthermore, the lustful pursuit of luxuries and creature comforts is incompatible with growth in Torah. One must prepare himself for Torah study by creating in himself a fitting abode for it. In the words of *Tanna d'Vei Eliyahu Rabbah* 26, "Before man prays that words of Torah enter him, let him pray that excessive delicacies not enter his body."

When one sits down to learn Torah, he must set his emotional and intellectual agenda aside and concentrate fully on whatever he is studying. Concerns of health, work, inadequate intelligence to understand the words of Torah or other important and legitimate worries can sidetrack one from the single-mindedness that Torah study demands. *Apply yourself to study the Torah* by making every effort to lay aside other concerns (*Tiferes Yisrael*).

The *Sfas Emes* explains that preparation for Torah study means that one must be ready to submit to the Torah's way of thinking even if he understands things differently. He should seek only God's will in Torah, not

---

 ⛉ **Reluctant acceptance.** Torah scholars who are hesitant to accept the support by others for their study must remember that Torah scholarship is the *raison d'etre* of the Jewish community. Furthermore, they will eventually serve as both the official and unofficial leadership of the nation. We are taught here that such hesitation is misplaced. *Let your fellow's money*, which he invests in the future of the nation, *be dear in your eyes as if it were your own* — earned by you legitimately.

The words *and apply yourself to study the Torah* refer to innovation and creativity in learning, which may also require outside support. The development of novel approaches to Torah *is not yours by inheritance*; such understanding is achieved only by one who makes Torah study his major occupation. One who is preoccupied with the concerns of making a living cannot apply himself adequately to the complexities of in-depth study. Therefore, one should accept the help of others so that he may seek greatness in Torah — but he must be sure that his motive for doing so is pure: *Let all your deeds be for the sake of Heaven* (*R' Shimon Sofer*).

[While King Solomon taught *one who hates gifts shall live* (*Proverbs* 15:27), this does not preclude the acceptance of support by Torah scholars. A careful reading notes that the maxim does not say that one must *not* accept gifts; instead it implies that although one must accept them, one should hate the need to do so. A Torah scholar who accepts public support in spite of the discomfort of doing so is the true hater of gifts. Only out of a sense of Heavenly duty, to assure the existence of true Torah personalities and teachers, does he accept the public's investment in his — and their — future.]

[יח] **רַבִּי שִׁמְעוֹן** אוֹמֵר: הֱוֵי זָהִיר בִּקְרִיאַת שְׁמַע

the validation of his own preconceived notions. Only thus will Torah leave its mark on him.

The words שֶׁאֵינָהּ יְרֻשָּׁה לָךְ, *for it is not yours by inheritance,* seem to contradict the Biblical verse which teaches that Torah is *the inheritance of the Congregation of Jacob (Deuteronomy 33:4).* The explanation is that the inheritance of Torah is the property of the nation as a whole. However, every individual must be prepared to persevere in Torah study in order to receive his personal share in the national heritage (*Tiferes Yisrael, Ruach Chaim, Sfas Emes*).

Beis Yisrael offers a different explanation. Torah knowledge itself is the heritage of the Jewish nation. However, one must *apply himself to study the Torah, for it* [the necessary preparation one needs to acquire that precious heritage] *is not yours by inheritance* — one must exert himself in the preparation (see *R' Yonah* above). [This is analogous to a group of orphans who were to receive a large inheritance from their father, consisting of money and precious gems. The executor of the estate instructed them to bring luggage to carry away their shares. "What!" they exclaimed. "Such a magnificent

estate and we must bring suitcases? Aren't there any among the items left to us by our father?" "No," answered the executor. "Your father bequeathed you a fantastic fortune, but he didn't leave you even one basket or piece of luggage. That you must provide yourself."

Our Father granted us the most precious legacy — His Torah. However, we must provide the proper receptacle for that inheritance. By refining our characters and freeing ourselves from the shackles of decadence and narcissism, we shape ourselves into fitting vehicles to bear our Godly heritage.

וְכָל מַעֲשֶׂיךָ יִהְיוּ לְשֵׁם שָׁמָיִם — *and let all your deeds be for the sake of Heaven.* All areas of life are a venue for increasing the honor of Heaven. Even the most seemingly mundane functions of life are elevated when they are performed in the service of God. In this clause we are charged to let *all* our deeds be done for the sake of Heaven — even the common, everyday practices of eating and drinking, which should be elevated from a biological need to an exercise in preparing a healthy body to fulfill the will of God (*R' Yonah* and *Rav*).

⇜§ **The honor of Torah.** Rabbi Yonason Steif, *Rav* of Pesht, would often consult with Rabbi Moshe Feinstein on halachic matters. Rabbi Steif's widow related that even when her husband spoke to Rav Feinstein on the phone, he would first don his hat and jacket, and he would stand during the conversation. In this way he fulfilled the principle of our mishnah: *Apply yourself to study the Torah.*

A person is often unaware of the extent to which the values of the surrounding culture, which are sometimes totally antithetical to Torah, have colored his thinking. A classical example concerns the laws of damages. Western man is inclined to think that he should have to make restitution if his child (a minor) damages someone's property, but that he is certainly not obliged to pay for his pet's indiscretions. ("It was my dog who did it. What do you want from me?") In fact, Torah law is exactly the opposite. One whose property has been damaged by a minor cannot demand payment either from him or from his parents. [See *Choshen Mishpat* 424:8. According to some authorities, the child has a moral obligation, upon achieving majority, to make restitution; see *Rashi* to *Bava Kamma* 98b, s.v., וְאַכְפֵּיהּ; *Taz, Orach Chaim* 343⇜§2 and *Mishnah Berurah* ad loc. §9. See also *Taz, Choshen Mishpat* 349:3.] On the other hand, he can demand full payment from the owner when his property is damaged by an animal.

R' Yitzchak Isaac of Ziditchov proposed an insight into the juxtaposition of these two maxims (to consider another person's money dear, and to apply oneself to study the Torah):

People often say: Let my friend learn on my behalf. Yet when it comes to earning money, no one is ready to allow another to possess money on his behalf! Our mishnah teaches us to adopt the opposite perspective. When dealing with issues of finances, we should consider another's money as dear to us as our own; it should be sufficient for us that someone else came into money, and we should have satisfaction from it. However, in regard to Torah, apply *yourself* mightily to study — don't allow someone else to act as your proxy.

18. Rabbi Shimon says: Be meticulous in reading the Shema

Rambam (*Shemoneh Perakim* ch. 5) extends this dictum to all areas of life. Even activities that generally are viewed negatively may be harnessed for a greater goal. For example, levity, while generally frowned upon, can be used to put people at ease and in a relaxed frame of mind, thus allowing them to concentrate on their Torah study and *mitzvah* performance. In this fashion, what might in some cases be a transgression is transformed into service of Heaven (see *Berachos* 63a). The Talmud relates that Elijah the Prophet once introduced R' Beroka to two people who were destined for the World to Come. When R' Beroka asked their professions, they replied that they were comedians who cheered up the depressed and used their humor to patch up quarrels (*Taanis* 22a). It was this positive use of humor that earned them a place in the World to Come. The Talmud also indicates that it was sometimes customary among Torah teachers to relate a humorous matter before beginning the lecture in order to lessen the pressure felt by the students (see *Shabbos* 30a).

Mishnah 18

רַבִּי שִׁמְעוֹן אוֹמֵר: הֱוֵי זָהִיר בִּקְרִיאַת שְׁמַע וּבִתְפִלָּה — *Rabbi Shimon says: Be meticulous in reading the Shema and in prayer.* This is Rabbi Shimon ben Nesanel (see 2:10). He warns us here to be punctual in reading the *Shema* and in praying at the proper time (*Rav, Rashi*).

There are set times for the reading of the morning and evening *Shema* and for the *Shemoneh Esrei* prayer, and here R' Shimon urges that Jews be meticulous in adhering to those schedules. The morning *Shema* must be recited during the first quarter of the daylight hours, and the morning *Shemoneh Esrei* prayer must be recited during the first third of the daylight hours. The evening *Shema* must be recited after nightfall.

The afternoon *Minchah* prayer should be recited sometime between a half hour after midday and sunset, and the evening *Maariv* must be recited after nightfall.

‑§ **Even piety must be sincere.** Often one justifies extreme cruelty or other undignified behavior on the basis that the motive is for the sake of Heaven. One should check his motives carefully and be sure that even what he ostensibly does for the sake of Heaven is *truly* for Heaven's sake and in tandem with God's standards (*R' Bunam of P'shis'cha*).

This thought is reflected in the words of King Solomon (*Proverbs* 13:25): *The righteous one eats and his soul is satisfied, while the stomach of the wicked constantly lacks.* He who eats for his own pleasure is never satisfied, since the eating is an end in itself. The righteous, however, use food as a vehicle to serve God, and they achieve true satisfaction (*R' Yonah*).

‑§ **Everything for a purpose.** Dr. Henry Rhein, a prominent pediatrician and a true *tzaddik,* was eulogized by R' Shlomo Freifeld specifically in reference to his sense of humor. He spoke of the doctor's uncanny ability to use humor to calm the nervous mothers of sick children who visited his office. This is a prime example of the use of *all* one's deeds for the sake of Heaven.

‑§ **Three times, three symbols.** *Maharal* explains the significance of the appointed times for prayer: The time slot for each of the three daily prayers allows man to exhibit a willingness to forgo his own interests and comfort, and to express his dependency on God. In the morning, he would much prefer to pamper himself by remaining comfortably asleep. Instead, he arises for the morning prayers in recognition that he must seek his needs from God.

In the heat of the business day, when he is engaged in the pursuit of a livelihood, he stops to turn to God in the *Minchah* prayer, thus reminding himself that it is God Who is the true Provider of a livelihood.

At the end of a tiring day, when he seeks only rest and peace of mind, he delays his sleep in order to turn once more to God in thanks for the success of the day and to pray for continued Divine help.

Midrash Shmuel views this dictum as addressed especially to a late sleeper, admonishing such a person to arise on time to pray with a *minyan* and to recite *Shema* at its proper time.

According to *Meiri* and *Tiferes Yisrael*, the mishnah is not concerned at all with the obligation to *recite* the prayers, nor with the duty to pray at the prescribed time. Rather, the mishnah speaks of the benefit derived from these *mitzvos*, for the consistent and conscious recitation of *Shema* and prayer help man to develop a strong sense of God's Presence and a great desire to relate to Him.

Shema contains many of the main articles of Jewish faith, including belief in the unity of God, the duty both to love and to fear Him, the obligation to study His Torah and fulfill its commandments, and the doctrine of Divine reward and punishment. In the third portion of the *Shema,* we are taught to be cautious of the forces of desire and heresy, which seek to detour man from the righteous path. Prayer, by its very nature, is an act of faith, wherein man recognizes God as the Source of all blessings.

R' Yonah's reading of the mishnah is: *Be more meticulous in reading the Shema than in prayer.* He explains that while the morning prayers may be recited at any point during the first third of the day, the most meritorious time for reciting the morning *Shema* is exactly at sunrise. [This is the practice of those who were meticulous about *mitzvah* performance, known as *vasikin* (see *Berachos* 9a).] Hence, we are enjoined to be especially meticulous about reading the *Shema* during that narrow time frame (see *Tosafos Yom Tov*).

וּכְשֶׁאַתָּה מִתְפַּלֵּל, אַל תַּעַשׂ תְּפִלָּתְךָ קֶבַע, אֶלָּא רַחֲמִים וְתַחֲנוּנִים לִפְנֵי הַמָּקוֹם — *when you pray, do not make your prayer a set routine, rather [an entreaty for] mercy and a supplication before the Omnipresent.* The word קֶבַע connotes a steady obligation one seeks to be rid of (*Rambam* and *R' Yonah*), but prayer should never be performed perfunctorily, as a burdensome duty that one seeks to be done with.

Alternatively, קֶבַע is used to mean an established amount. Thus, one must never view prayer merely as nothing more than a recitation of a certain number of prescribed verses; he should seek to add his own personal prayer (in any language, at the proper point in the service) to the standard text. Just as one always seeks the right words to elicit a favor from a friend, so he should go beyond the words of the *siddur* and express the feelings of his heart to God (*Tiferes Yisrael*).

⊷§ **Bringing faith to life.** Doctrines of faith often remain abstract ideas rather than live realities in a person's life. Constant verbal expression of these principles coupled with concentration on what they mean gives them life and makes them a vibrant part of one's existence. Rabbi Avraham of Slonim homiletically renders the verse הֶאֱמַנְתִּי כִּי אֲדַבֵּר (*Psalms* 116:10) as *I believed* [the cardinal principles of Judaism] *when I spoke* [of them, constantly reiterating them to myself]. The constant daily repetition of the *Shema* and the prayers inculcate the basic tenets of the Torah.

⊷§ **Ask of yourself.** The Kozhnitzer *Maggid* offers a novel understanding of R' Yonah's version. It is not difficult to be meticulous about a prayer in which man makes personal requests of God. However, the recitation of *Shema*, which enjoins him to make commitments to love and fear God and which teaches him to be ready for the ultimate sacrifice on God's behalf [since life without God is not worth living], is more difficult. Therefore, we are taught to be more meticulous in the recitation of *Shema*, which asks for self-sacrifice, than in our general prayers for personal necessities.

and in prayer; when you pray, do not make your prayer a set routine, rather [an entreaty for] mercy and a supplication before the Omnipresent, as it is said: *For He is gracious*

The Sages refer to prayer as the service of the heart. One should beg for God's mercy as if he were a beggar at the door, who senses that this is the only place where his needs can be met (*Rav*); and he must concentrate on the meaning of the words he says (*Rashi*). [While there is dispute among the Sages regarding whether lack of intent impedes the fulfillment of other *mitzvos* (*Berachos* 13a), all agree that prayer without intent is lifeless and in certain instances halachically invalid (see *R' Chaim Brisker* on *Rambam, Hilchos Tefillah* 4:1). Prayer is not just saying the words; it is talking to God and sharing one's heartfelt problems, wants, dreams, and aspirations.]

R' Moshe Alshakar explains the mishnah as teaching the correct approach to prayer.

The Midrash teaches that God showed Moses many Heavenly storehouses of Divine reward; one for those who study Torah, one for those who do good deeds, yet another for those who perform acts of kindness, and so on. Finally God showed him the largest storehouse of all. "Who is this for?" inquired Moses. God answered, "The others are for those who have merits; this storehouse is מַתְּנַת חִנָּם, *free*, for those who lack merit." The *Avnei Nezer* explained: Those who base their claim to reward on their personal merits are limited in their entitlement. However, those who realize that all the good they may have done is insignificant in comparison to the endless favors God bestows upon them come to Him with תַּחֲנוּנִים, *entreaties*, for מַתְּנַת חִנָּם, an undeserved gift, which is not related to their merits. That storehouse is the largest, for it is not limited by what man deserves; its treasures are bestowed in accordance with God's beneficent will.

This is the message of the mishnah: Do not make your prayers an established routine, in which you expend a limited effort to elicit a prescribed reaction from God. Rather, it should be an entreaty for mercy and a supplication that God shower you from the infinite treasures of His free storehouse.

❦ **In conversation with Father.** Prayer is likened to a woman who is speaking with her husband when their young child starts tugging on her sleeve. The mother turns to the child and says, "One moment, let me finish talking to Daddy. It is impolite to interrupt while I'm speaking to someone else, and certainly when I'm talking to your father."

When one prays, he is talking to his Father. Even if he has finished his prayers, it is impolite for him to speak or make noise while his neighbor is still in the midst of speaking to God.

This is also the idea behind the law which forbids walking in front of someone who is in the midst of the *Shemoneh Esrei* prayer (see *Shulchan Aruch Orach Chaim* 102); just as it is rude to walk between two people who are engrossed in conversation, it is improper to cross between man and God, so to speak, while they are conversing.

The Chofetz Chaim used to point out the wonder of the opportunity provided to man through prayer; he can actually address God directly in the second person, and say, "Blessed are *You*."

❦ **On God's mercy.** When Moses prayed to be allowed to enter the Land of Israel, he employed the term וָאֶתְחַנַּן, *I implored* (*Deuteronomy* 3:23). According to *Rashi* (ad loc.) this is to indicate that even though he could have made his request on the basis of his merits, he nonetheless asked for it as a free, undeserved gift. The Midrash (ad loc.), however, sharpens the point. Moses asked to be allowed admission to the Land as a totally undeserved gift. This teaches that no person has any right to make even the slightest demand on the Creator. In prayer one throws oneself totally on the mercy of God.

שֶׁנֶּאֱמַר: ,,כִּי חַנּוּן וְרַחוּם הוּא אֶרֶךְ אַפַּיִם וְרַב חֶסֶד וְנִחָם ,,עַל הָרָעָה״ — *as it is said: "For He is gracious and compassionate, slow to anger, abounding in kindness, and relentful of punishment"* (*Joel* 2:13). God is gracious and responds mercifully to pleas for grace, even when the supplicant cannot justify them. Hence one should pray for His mercy (*Rashi and Rav*).

By describing God this way, the verse alludes to three kinds of prayer:

(a) *Slow to anger* — entreaties for Divine mercy, asking God to await man's eventual repentance, and save him from the punishments he deserves for his sins.

(b) *Abounding in kindness* — requests for Divine beneficence, even though man does not deserve it.

(c) *Relentful of punishment* — entreaties for atonement of previously committed sins and of the punishment man should receive for them.

Even if man has been granted a stay of immediate punishment, he must pray for God's mercy through prayer, for God's extended mercy and slowness to anger can be suspended at any moment (*R' Yonah*).

According to *Meiri*, the verse teaches that God responds to man with the attributes through which man addressed Him. If man turns to Him in supplication as a gracious and merciful God, He responds with graciousness and kindness.

וְאַל תְּהִי רָשָׁע בִּפְנֵי עַצְמֶךָ — *and do not judge yourself to be a wicked person.* This follows *Rambam's*

⮜ **God knows how.** R' Levi Yitzchak of Berditchev renders קֶבַע as *set,* i.e., one's prayer should not be as if etched in stone. Instead of asking for specific ways in which he wants God to help him, rather one should ask God for general mercy — and rely on Him to define what is really good, since He certainly knows better than we what will benefit us.

A fascinating story about R' Bunam of P'shis'cha sheds light on this. Rabbi Ephraim Fishel of Strikov was famed for his miraculous powers. People from many lands came to his doorstep to be blessed with health, wealth, and prosperity. One day he suddenly closed his door and refused to receive any more supplicants. Removing his rabbinic hat, he declared, "I am no longer a miracle-working rabbi."

His close disciples were shocked, and after much entreaty they elicited the reason for his sudden decision. R' Fishel had instructed an upstanding, impoverished person to purchase a lottery ticket, promising him that God would bless the purchase. The destitute man followed the rabbi's instruction and purchased the ticket. Two days before the drawing, on a Friday, the man found himself without money to purchase his Shabbos necessities, and seeing no other choice, he sold the ticket. Two days later that ticket was drawn, and its holder won 75,000 rubles.

When R' Fishel heard what had happened, he became convinced that in Heaven he was no longer acceptable as an agent to help Jews. He therefore decided to refuse any more supplicants.

R' Bunam of P'shis'cha heard of R' Fishel's abdication, and went to Strikov. He presented R' Fishel with the following question: "We know that a righteous man may issue a decree, which God will honor (see *Shabbos* 59b); yet Scripture teaches, *And who can tell You what to do?* (*Job* 9:12). How are we to resolve this seeming contradiction? The answer is that while the righteous may decree whom Heaven must help, it is not for man to dictate what *form* that help should take. Let the righteous pray for one's health, but let God decide which medicine or doctor will help; let man pray for financial prosperity, but let Heaven decree what business or occupation will be the agent of his success. A father wants his son to seek his help, but he does not want the son to tell him how exactly to provide it. What made you so sure that the poor man's salvation was to come through a lottery ticket?

"A man once came to me on the verge of mental and fiscal collapse," R' Bunam continued. " 'I am at wit's end,' he said. 'There is no way for me to survive.' I answered him, 'May God help you as only He knows how — but woe is to Bunam if he serves a God who needs his guidance in helping a Jew in need.' "

R' Fishel learned the lesson of our mishnah and resumed the task of helping his brothers in need.

and compassionate, slow to anger, abounding in kindness, and relentful of punishment (Joel 2:13); and do not judge yourself to be a wicked person.

rendering. A person's standard of behavior is to a large extent influenced by his self-image. One who perceives himself as an evil person has no psychological safety net to prevent him from committing the worst of sins. "I am a wicked person anyway," he tells himself. "Why should I not indulge my baser instincts?"

R' Yonah elaborates: One may become a prisoner of his self-image, unable to free himself of the burdens of his past and repent. He rationalizes: "Compared to the terrible sins I have committed in the past, the sin I now contemplate is insignificant." One should not view himself as a wicked person hopelessly entrapped in the web of iniquity.

R' S. R. Hirsch explains the flow of ideas in the mishnah: "Do not allow yourself to be taken in by the erroneous idea advanced by alien philosophies that man must be crushed by the weight of his guilt and that only through the gracious intercession of another can he be delivered from the burden of his

sin. In reality the one person able to free you from the chains of sin and raise you to the level of pure and free service of God is none other than you yourself. Prayer uttered in the proper spirit will be that source from which you will derive the strength and Divine aid that you need in all your efforts at self-liberation from evil."

The Talmud instructs us to consider ourselves as being among the wicked, even if all our contemporaries claim we are righteous (*Niddah* 30a). This does not contradict our mishnah, since both edicts must be followed. One must view his life as a perfectly balanced combination of good and evil. One good deed will overweigh the balance in favor of the virtue, while one misstep can tip the scales against us.

Rashi renders: *Do not act in a fashion that will cause you to view yourself as wicked.* Be careful how you act today so that you will not come to question later how you came to do such evil.

Rav renders: *Do not become evil by isolating yourself.* Separating oneself from the community

---

⤎§ **God cherishes your frailty.** A young man came to R' Boruch of Mezhibozh and asked him for advice.
 "Rebbi, please teach me how one can thwart his evil inclination."

R' Baruch answered: "Believe me when I tell you that my evil inclination is no less persuasive than yours. How do I stave off his attacks? I tell him, 'Listen here. How will I appear in *your* eyes if I listen to you?' "

Thus, the mishnah says, *Do not be a wicked person in front of yourself.*

A negative self-image not only can lead a person to sin, but can prevent him from doing good. In a moment of weakness, a man may think to himself: "Who am I, a creature of flesh and blood, to stand in prayer in front of God? Even a being as exalted as the angels cannot fathom His greatness." This thought has the power to induce total spiritual paralysis; we should recognize that this is nothing but the insidious whisper of the evil inclination in man. Since no creature can fully praise God, He accepts praise from *all* His creatures. In fact, He particularly cherishes the praise of man, who suffers from human frailties and yet still finds it within himself to rise above them and pray anyway (*Kedushas Levi*). [This essential principle is poignantly expressed in the prayers for Yom Kippur: *While the force of Your praise is rendered by heavenly angels that glow like lightning, yet You desire praise from those who pray with passion and await graciousness, whose accomplishment is meager, whose livelihood is bitter as gall, who hunger for forgiveness — for this is Your (true) honor.*]

R' Michel of Zlotchov reported: "When I am about to start praying, I am overcome by a terrible sense of embarrassment. How can I approach God in prayer when my life is so riddled with sin? On second thought, however, I realize that this must be my evil inclination talking, trying to dissuade me from praying. How do I know it's him? Because this never happens when I'm ready to eat."

Hence, our mishnah teaches, *When you pray, do not view yourself as an evil person.* It is *your* praise and *your* prayer that God awaits.

רַבִּי אֶלְעָזָר אוֹמֵר: הֱוֵי שָׁקוּד לִלְמוֹד תּוֹרָה, וְדַע מַה שֶׁתָּשִׁיב לְאֶפִּיקוֹרוֹס; וְדַע לִפְנֵי מִי אַתָּה [יט]

and not caring for others is in itself a form of wickedness. [See *Rambam, Hilchos Teshuvah* (3:11).]

Lev Avos adds a further dimension to the words בִּפְנֵי עַצְמֶךָ. One should not maintain a double standard of behavior. He should not lower his standards in private, a form of wickedness (*Lev Avos*). Some texts of the morning prayer [לְעוֹלָם יְהֵא אָדָם יְרֵא שָׁמַיִם] read: *One shall*

always be God-fearing בְּסֵתֶר כְּבַגָּלוּי, *in private* **just as** *in public.*]

According to *Midrash Shmuel*, the words בִּפְנֵי עַצְמֶךָ teach the far-reaching consequences of our actions. *Do not be wicked by yourself*, for your actions have a ripple effect. They do not affect only you; all Jews are responsible for each other, and the balance of the world's judgment may hang on a single one of our actions.

⇜§ **A balanced approach.** Yismach Yisrael of Alexander offers another resolution of this apparent contradiction. When you are among people who tell you that you are righteous, do not let the praise go to your head; instead, view yourself as wicked. However, when you make a self-assessment, do not allow yourself to fall into depression and self-negation, which leads to sin. וְאַל תְּהִי רָשָׁע בִּפְנֵי עַצְמֶךָ, *Do not be wicked in your own eyes "when you are by yourself."* [See also *Likutei Amarim, Tanya* chapter 1.]

This approach is reminiscent of the credo of R' Bunam of P'shis'cha, who enjoined every Jew to have two "pockets." In one pocket he should carry around the verse *For I am dust and ashes* (*Genesis* 18:27), and in the second pocket should be found the words, "Man is obligated to say, 'The world was created for my sake' " (*Sanhedrin* 37a), reflective of the great heights to which man can aspire. The trick in life, said R' Bunam, is to know when to pull out the contents of each pocket.

The Chofetz Chaim offered another example of the need to judge one's deeds on more than one level. Since our mishnah cautions against judging *oneself* to be wicked, the implication is that the opinions of others do not matter, as long as one knows he is doing the right thing — but the Moses said, *you shall be vindicated before God and before Israel* (*Numbers* 32:22), implying that one must seek public approval, as well. The Chofetz Chaim explained that there is a greater responsibility on leaders and people who are in the public spotlight. They must keep themselves above suspicion, for if their behavior is not impeccable, they may cause God's Name to be desecrated.

⇜§ **Ritual is personal.** Rabbi Elchonon Wasserman offered a startling insight into the nature of *mitzvos*. We generally categorize *mitzvos* as either ritual (בֵּין אָדָם לַמָּקוֹם) or interpersonal (בֵּין אָדָם לַחֲבֵרוֹ). In truth, these labels are misnomers. All interpersonal *mitzvos* are actually ritual in nature, since only God can establish ethical standards and legislate proper behavior. What we may consider to be immoral is truly so only if God decreed that it is wrong. Stealing, therefore, is immoral only because God in His infinite wisdom has deemed it so. On the other hand, it is permissible to eat the flesh and use the hide of animals because the Torah permitted it, even though there may be people who proclaim that animals have the same rights as humans.

Furthermore, every omission of a ritual duty affects the quality of life of the entire world. One good act of a ritual nature (which ostensibly does not affect others) can shift the spiritual balance of the world to the positive side, thus sustaining the lives of all its inhabitants. In that sense, a ritual act can constitute an interpersonal kindness. Thus, one can never be wicked [or virtuous] purely on his own account, for what he does affects everybody around him. *Ecclesiastes* (9:18) captures this principle succinctly: וְחוֹטֶא אֶחָד יְאַבֵּד טוֹבָה הַרְבֵּה, *for a single sinner can ruin a great deal of good.*

The Kozhnitzer *Maggid* adds that if one's personal conduct is not up to par, he should not remain alone. *Do not be wicked by yourself*; instead, associate with righteous people. Often, one has difficulty freeing himself from an evil past, but by associating with righteous people, he will be swayed toward the good.

Mishnah 19

רַבִּי אֶלְעָזָר אוֹמֵר: הֱוֵי שָׁקוּד לִלְמוֹד תּוֹרָה, וְדַע מַה שֶׁתָּשִׁיב לְאֶפִּיקוֹרוֹס — *Rabbi Elazar says: Be diligent in the study of Torah, and know what to answer a heretic.* According to *R' Yonah, Rambam* and *Meiri,* these two clauses together form the first of R' Elazar ben Arach's three dicta. One must study Torah diligently in order to achieve sufficient mastery of it to refute the theories of disbelievers. One who is unable to refute their heretical falsehoods allows the masses to become vulnerable to these distortions. Any ideological victory of the heretics causes a profanation of God's Name and honor.

Rambam posits that this instruction applies only to answering non-Jewish heretics. The Talmud teaches (*Sanhedrin* 38b) that debate with a Jewish heretic is futile, and even counterproductive. Since he has turned his back on his former beliefs, it will be virtually impossible to convince him that his abandonment of Torah was a mistake. *R' Yonah* defines a heretic as one who denies the Divine origin of the Oral Law, or who interprets Torah law in an inauthentic fashion.

The term אֶפִּיקוֹרוֹס, *heretic,* is based on the word הֶפְקֵר, meaning *ownerless.* A heretic disparages the ideas of Torah, as if they had no originator. Alternatively, a heretic figuratively deems himself ownerless, open prey to the Divine retribution which is the lot of one who treats Torah or its scholars disdainfully (*Rav*).

Magen Avos sees the term אֶפִּיקוֹרוֹס as related to Epicurus, the Greek philosopher who lived 400 years before the destruction of the Second Temple. Epicurus preached disbelief in God and advocated the narcissistic pursuit of pleasure as life's goal. He maintained heretical beliefs regarding the afterlife of the soul and other basic Jewish tenets. The term אֶפִּיקוֹרוֹס was extended to include those who deny God, those who express contempt for Torah or its scholars, and other non-believers (see *Rambam, Hilchos Teshuvah* 3:7-8).

Historically, many of the earliest movements away from traditional Judaism were led by people who distorted basic beliefs and the meaning of the Scriptures in order to promote their own deviant ideologies. Not only did they try to lead Jews astray through example and persuasion, they used their political power to oppress observant Jews and slander them to the anti-Semitic Roman government. It was against these people that the Sages instituted a new blessing in the *Shemoneh Esrei* prayer (thus increasing the number of its blessings to nineteen) known as the "Blessing Regarding the Heretics" (ברכת המינים). (See *Berachos* 28b and *Megillah* 17b; *Rambam, Hilchos Tefillah* 2:1.)

According to *Rashi,* these are the first *two* of R' Elazar ben Arach's statements, rather than a simple composite statement. [One must study Torah diligently for it does not easily yield its secrets, and, in addition, one must be able to respond to the heretics.] The mishnah places these two clauses together to teach us that it is unnecessary to study *anything else but Torah* in order to have the relevant information to answer a heretic. The mishnah teaches (5:26): *Delve into it [the Torah] and continue to delve into it [the Torah] for everything is in it.* Torah is the repository of all knowledge, including the refutation of heresy (*Zeroa Yemin*).

Midrash Shmuel interprets this as a prescription for the priorities of Torah study. First, one must study the Torah diligently and master its halachic

⇜§ **Constructive "heresy."** If heresy is so insidious, why does God allow it to flourish? R' Bunam of P'shis'cha, in his ironic style, explained it thus: If not for heresy, wealthy men would refuse to help support the poor. "There is a God in Heaven," they would declare. "He will take care of His unfortunate children." Therefore, God allows the wealthy to entertain the "heretical" thought that if they don't provide for the poor, nobody else will.

עָמֵל; וְנֶאֱמָן הוּא בַּעַל מְלַאכְתֶּךָ, שֶׁיְּשַׁלֶּם לְךָ שְׂכַר פְּעֻלָּתֶךָ.

[כ] **רַבִּי** טַרְפוֹן אוֹמֵר: הַיּוֹם קָצֵר, וְהַמְּלָאכָה מְרֻבָּה,

portions. Only then may one move on to in-depth study of the *Aggadah* portions of the Torah, which address philosophical and ideological issues.

Alternatively, the order of study may be seen as Torah first and secular knowledge second. Only after studying and *totally* absorbing the entire corpus of Torah knowledge may one study areas of general knowledge which are needed to refute the heretics.

It is noteworthy that the mishnah emphasizes that we must know what to *answer* a heretic, i.e., how to respond to his questions and challenges. One who engages in disputes with disbelievers must understand their positions clearly; parroting formulae out of books is sure to lead to defeat. Furthermore, the mishnah teaches us that we must *answer* the heretic, but we should never initiate the debate (*Midrash Shmuel*).

וְדַע לִפְנֵי מִי אַתָּה עָמֵל — *know before Whom you toil.* Rambam, Rav, and *R' Yonah* count this as the second statement of R' Elazar. He warns that debate with heretics can often infect a believer with their poisonous ideas. Therefore, R' Elazar tells us to

remember before Whom we stand, and not to allow the residue of non-belief to adhere to us.

According to *R' Yonah,* this is also a continuation of the charge to study Torah diligently. One must be aware that Torah is God's most precious possession, from which He has always, so to speak, derived enjoyment. Man likewise should view Torah study as a pursuit which yields endless pleasure and as an exercise in enjoyment. Hence, he must commit all his energies to Torah study.

Another explanation is that one should not be deterred by the effort needed to master the complexities of Torah study because of the great effort involved. Upon considering *before Whom one toils* at Torah, the effort becomes justified (*Meiri*).

In a historical interpretation reflective of the bitter episodes of his times, *Abarbanel* renders this clause as referring to debates on matters of faith and heresy: *Know before whom it is that one toils* — know who will serve as judge of the debate, for it is only worthwhile to debate in front of intelligent judges, who can be objective; to respond to heresy in front of judges with predetermined conclusions is futile. The famous debate at Tortossa

---

≈§ **Marriage to the Torah.** Torah is compared to a woman in terms of the requirement to engage in it with diligence. [*It is the heritage* (מוֹרָשָׁה) *of the Congregation of Jacob* (*Deuteronomy* 33:4) is homiletically interpreted as מְאוֹרָשָׂה, *betrothed* (see *Pesachim* 49b); the Torah is the betrothed of God's nation. Similarly, *Rashi* explains the אֵשֶׁת חַיִל in *Proverbs* (31:10-31) as an allegory for Torah.] Just as one must court a woman with persistence if he hopes to marry her, so he must pursue Torah study diligently if he hopes to achieve true understanding of it.

The Chazon Ish, in a letter to a budding young scholar, portrays the meaning of diligence. Diligence is not defined strictly by the amount of time one spends in study or by the rigidity of his learning schedule. Instead, it refers to the wholehearted commitment of one's entire personality, the total surrender of one's emotions and will, to the in-depth study of Torah. Achieving such diligence entails making non-negotiable decisions about the purpose of life and subordinating one's baser instincts to his better judgment. It is a path which may initially seem bitter but is eternally sweet.

≈§ **Go to the experts.** R' Isaac of Komarna tells us that the mishnah may be addressed to the greatest heretic of all — the one that resides in man's heart, always seeking to undermine his faith: *And know* [you should know that the best answer to the inner heretic is to say] מה, *what* [*am I* ?]. The mishnah tells us to quell our doubts by telling the heretical alter ego, "I'm neither a philosopher nor a student of the esoteric *Kabbalah,* and I am not even involved in the study of metaphysics. I'm nothing more than a simple Jew who wants to believe. Please take your doubts someplace else."

toil; and [know] that your Employer can be relied upon to pay you the wage of your labor.

20. Rabbi Tarfon says: The day is short, the task is abundant,

---

(1413-1414) was a classic example of a case where the subjective views of the clergy and royalty decided the contest before it began.

A slightly different reading is that intense Torah study will not only yield answers to heretical questions, it will also teach one to recognize the Creator before whom one toils (*Knesses Yisrael*).

וְנֶאֱמָן הוּא בַּעַל מְלַאכְתֶּךָ, שֶׁיְּשַׁלֶּם לְךָ שְׂכַר פְּעֻלָּתֶךָ — *and [know] that your Employer can be relied upon to pay you the wage of your labor.* The efforts expended at Torah study will not be for naught (*R' Yonah* and *Meiri*).

Rambam's text reads: *and [know] Who your employer is.* God, Who knows the innermost recesses of our hearts and minds, can ascertain whether any of the noxious fumes of heresy have penetrated our consciousness. Therefore, one must constantly reinforce his faith in God and in the cardinal principles of Judaism, especially after encounters with skeptics.

Tiferes Yisrael views the entirety of the mishnah as a three-part formula for success in Torah study: (a) *Be diligent in the study of Torah.* One must study with diligence and constantly review in order to retain his knowledge. (b) *Know what to answer a heretic.* One must never accept any Torah concept without attempting to penetrate its meaning intellectually. He should not be satisfied with a surface understanding based on faith and tradition. One must approach his Torah studies with incisive questions, not unlike a heretic who must have every point proven to him. This will guarantee full comprehension of every concept. (c) *Know before Whom you toil.* Since it is the word of God one studies, he must not allow any other preoccupations to intrude on his search for Torah knowledge. Furthermore, concern over physical sustenance should not sidetrack one from his Torah learning. Man's livelihood comes totally from God's hand. Hence, *know that your Employer can be relied upon to pay you the wage of your labor;* He will not abandon you, but will provide you with physical sustenance if you make Torah study your primary occupation.

Mishnah 20

רַבִּי טַרְפוֹן אוֹמֵר — *Rabbi Tarfon says.* A student of Rabban Yochanan ben Zakkai and a *Kohen* (see *Kiddushin* 71a), Rabbi Tarfon was one of the most prominent members of the Academy at Yavneh. His opinion was always the first solicited (see *Yadaim* 4:3 and *Sanhedrin* 101a). Rabbi Akiva was his student (see *Bechoros* 4:4) and his colleague (see *Kesubos* 84b). His encyclopedic Torah knowledge was legendary; all who came to discuss Torah topics with him left greatly enriched (see *Avos d'Rabbi Nosson* 18). A resident of Lod, **he** spent his vast wealth supporting less fortunate Jews. Talmud Yerushalmi (*Yoma* 1:1) refers to him as "the father of all Israel."

He and R' Akiva promulgated the famous statement, "Had we been members of the Sanhedrin, we would never have administered capital punishment" (*Makkos* 1:10). [They would have sought

---

◆§ **Not piecework.** The Chofetz Chaim notes: Ordinarily, pieceworkers are paid only for the amount they produce. If they must expend greater amounts of time than projected to meet the quota, it is their problem; they may not request greater compensation once the price for each item is fixed. However, God repays man for his *effort* as well as his actual production. A person who is not blessed with great intelligence is not penalized for the extra time and effort he exerts in order to learn the necessary laws or the proper procedure to perform a *mitzvah* — on the contrary, he is rewarded *according to his efforts* (see 5:26). This thought is conveyed in the words of the mishnah, *your Employer can be relied upon to pay you the wage of your* **labor** — your effort, not just the outcome.

וְהַפּוֹעֲלִים עֲצֵלִים, וְהַשָּׂכָר הַרְבֵּה, וּבַעַל הַבַּיִת דּוֹחֵק.

[כא] **הוּא הָיָה** אוֹמֵר: לֹא עָלֶיךָ הַמְּלָאכָה לִגְמוֹר, וְלֹא אַתָּה בֶן חוֹרִין לְהִבָּטֵל מִמֶּנָּה. אִם לָמַדְתָּ תוֹרָה הַרְבֵּה, נוֹתְנִים לְךָ שָׂכָר הַרְבֵּה;

technical grounds on which to avoid killing the murderer and instead would have administered a sentence of life imprisonment.]

הַיּוֹם קָצֵר, וְהַמְּלָאכָה מְרֻבָּה — *The day is short, the task is abundant.* Life is short, and the Torah is seemingly endless (*Rav, Rashi* et al.). One should not waste a moment of the precious few years he is granted in this world. Life is a fleeting opportunity to gather treasure; once the time is up, he can no longer earn anything.

The Midrash (*Shemos Rabbah* 47:7) draws the following analogy: A king gave his servant twenty-four hours to count the gold coins in the treasury. Whatever the servant counted was his to keep. The servant said to himself, "How can I sleep during these twenty-four hours? Every minute slept is treasure irretrievably lost." It was for this reason, teaches the Midrash, that Moses did not sleep during the forty days and nights he spent in Heaven; he did not want to miss a moment of the glorious opportunity to partake of God's mission.

Tosefta (*Terumos* 1:1) defines a fool as one who loses what is given to him. If one is considered a fool simply for losing an object, certainly wasting time — the most precious commodity — earns one this ignominious title (*Midrash Shmuel*).

Chiddushei HaRim used this concept to explain the custom of presenting a groom with a gold watch. When a young man assumes the responsibility of a family, it is imperative that he realize that time is more precious than gold.

וְהַפּוֹעֲלִים עֲצֵלִים — *the laborers are lazy.* The over-whelming spiritual work incumbent upon man can bring on laziness, since one may feel he cannot finish his allotted tasks no matter what he does (*Meiri*).

וְהַשָּׂכָר הַרְבֵּה, וּבַעַל הַבַּיִת דּוֹחֵק — *the reward is great, and the Master of the house is insistent.* Unlike a human employer, who doesn't care if the contractor doesn't do the job (he simply will not pay him), God wants each of us to complete His spiritual work. If we are lax, it will be our loss, for God wants to give us reward and can only do so when we perform our duties (*R' Yonah*).

According to *Rambam,* the phrase *the wage is great* underscores the laziness of the laborers. In spite of the tremendous payment one can earn for serving God, man is too lazy to undertake the effort. *Tiferes Yisrael* views *the laborers* as man's limbs, which become paralyzed because of his laziness. Our mishnah warns that we must take steps that man emotionally and psychologically overcome this natural lassitude (*R' Yonah*).

Beis LeAvos sees the phrase *the task is abundant* as the reason for *the laborers are lazy.* Over-whelmed by the enormity of one's spiritual duties, one can easily despair of accomplishing them. We are therefore taught that *the wage is great.* Even if one cannot do all that is incumbent upon him, he will still be amply rewarded for whatever he is able to do.

∽§ **The sale will soon be over.** The Vilna Gaon lived with this sense of the fleeting opportunities this world presents us. Shortly before he died, he was seen holding his *tzitzis* and crying. He explained to his followers, "Soon I will be leaving this world. Here, for just a few pennies, I can buy *tzitzis* and fulfill the *mitzvah* every minute of the day, and day after day. Before long, I will be in a world where I will not be able to purchase that opportunity even for millions.

21. He [R' Tarfon] used to say: You are not required to complete the task, yet you are not free to withdraw from it. If you have studied much Torah, they give you great reward;

Mishnah 21

הוּא הָיָה אוֹמֵר: לֹא עָלֶיךָ הַמְּלָאכָה לִגְמוֹר, וְלֹא אַתָּה בֶּן חֹרִין לְהִבָּטֵל מִמֶּנָּה — *He [R' Tarfon] used to say: You are not required to complete the task, yet you are not free to withdraw from it.* R' Tarfon comments on his own statement in the previous mishnah regarding man's overwhelming spiritual tasks in this world. One may feel, "Why should I begin when I will never be able to complete all my duties? Since the day is short and the task abundant, it is useless to try." Therefore, R' Tarfon tells us that we are not absolved of our tasks, even though they seem too heavy for us (*Midrash Shmuel*).

God does not engage man in His service with the expectation that he can complete the task, and He does not penalize him for being unable to finish. On the other hand, man is obligated to commit his best efforts to the service of the Creator. He should not think that if he is willing to forgo the reward, he may be absolved of the duty. The work is not optional — it is a burden that must be borne (*Rav* and *R' Yonah*).

Were man enjoined with the impossible duty to complete the task, he could expect no reward. However, it is the full effort that God seeks; not success. The more effort expended, the greater the reward (*Rashi* and *HaChassid Yaavetz*).

The Midrash speaks of an ignoramus who enters the study hall, requesting instruction on how to succeed in Torah study. "Begin with Scripture," he is told, "go on to mishnah and Talmud, follow this with Midrash and Aggadah, etc." Discouraged, he declares, "How will I ever learn all of this?" and leaves the hall. He doesn't realize that Torah is compared to water. Drop by drop it accumulates until it becomes a powerful stream. Likewise, day-by-day effort will yield prodigious results (see *Devarim Rabbah* 8 and *Shir HaShirim Rabbah* 1).

Chiddushei HaRim views the two clauses as a connected thought: Man is given an endless task, and for this reason alone he can never absolve himself of it.

אִם לָמַדְתָּ תוֹרָה הַרְבֵּה נוֹתְנִים לְךָ שָׂכָר הַרְבֵּה — *If you have studied much Torah, they give you great reward.* It is not knowledge for which one is rewarded — it is the effort exerted in its pursuit that elicits God's magnanimity. One is rewarded in accordance with his efforts. Unlike other tasks, where incomplete work is worthless, spiritual challenges which are even partially met are deserving of reward (*HaChassid Yaavetz*).

Man is commanded to serve his Master constantly and totally. Yet while the servant of an earthly lord can expect no special reward for greater service, man will indeed receive reward that is commensurate with the level of his Godly service (*Machzor Vitry*).

◆§ **Adrenalin in learning.** The city of Dvinsk was blessed with two world-renowned geniuses who served its two congregations during the same period. The Rogatchover Gaon (R' Yosef Rosen) outlived the Ohr Some'ach (R' Meir Simcha *HaKohen*) and eulogized him with the following observation: "One trapped under a fallen beam in a burning building can find the strength to move the beam and escape the flames, even though under ordinary circumstances he would never be able to push the beam even an inch. R' Meir Simcha always tapped into that strength when he learned." Such strength is the result of pure willpower, the only effective weapon against the "natural" limitations of laziness.

וְנֶאֱמָן הוּא בַּעַל מְלַאכְתֶּךָ, שֶׁיְּשַׁלֵּם לְךָ שְׂכַר פְּעֻלָּתֶךָ. וְדַע שֶׁמַּתַּן שְׂכָרָן שֶׁל צַדִּיקִים לֶעָתִיד לָבֹא.

❧ ❧ ❧

רַבִּי חֲנַנְיָא בֶּן עֲקַשְׁיָא אוֹמֵר: רָצָה הַקָּדוֹשׁ בָּרוּךְ הוּא לְזַכּוֹת אֶת יִשְׂרָאֵל, לְפִיכָךְ הִרְבָּה לָהֶם תּוֹרָה וּמִצְוֹת, שֶׁנֶּאֱמַר: ,,יהוה חָפֵץ לְמַעַן צִדְקוֹ, יַגְדִּיל תּוֹרָה וְיַאְדִּיר.''

— **וְנֶאֱמָן הוּא בַּעַל מְלַאכְתֶּךָ, שֶׁיְּשַׁלֵּם לְךָ שְׂכַר פְּעֻלָּתֶךָ** — *and your Employer can be relied upon to pay you the wage of your labor.*

Unlike a human employer who can go bankrupt, God will always have the means at His disposal to reward man amply for his efforts (*R' Yonah*).

In truth, all man's spiritual accomplishments benefit none other than himself; God receives "nothing" from them, even though they give Him, so to speak, immeasurable pleasure. None-theless, God rewards man as if he has done something that benefits his Master: *Your Employer can be relied upon to pay you the wage of your labor.*

Even though man could never succeed at any pursuit, even a spiritual one, without God's help, he is nonetheless rewarded for his successes as if he himself brought them about. *Your employer* can be trusted to pay you the wage of "your" labor.

2/21 and your Employer can be relied upon to pay you the wage of your labor, but be aware that the reward of the righteous will be given in the World to Come.

❧ ❧ ❧

Rabbi Chanania ben Akashia says: The Holy One, Blessed is He, wished to confer merit upon Israel; therefore He gave them Torah and *mitzvos* in abundance, as it is said: *"HASHEM desired, for the sake if its [Israel's] righteousness, that the Torah be made great and glorious."*

וְדַע שֶׁמַּתַּן שְׂכָרָן שֶׁל צַדִּיקִים לֶעָתִיד לָבֹא — *but be aware that the reward of the righteous will be given in the World to Come.* According to *R' Yonah,* this is an incentive for one to strengthen his commitment to follow the Divine path. Contemplation of the great reward in store for those who loyally follow God's word induces in man a fervent love of his Creator and an insatiable desire to please Him.

Tiferes Yisrael et al. view this clause as a source of encouragement. Even if one notices that those who follow the Divine dictates are seemingly not rewarded, and that they even seem to suffer in this world, he should not be disheartened. The reward of the truly righteous takes place mainly in the World to Come. [The wicked are rewarded completely in this world, while those of mediocre spiritual stature receive partial payment in this world and the rest in the World of Truth (*Sfas Emes*).]

פרק שלישי &
Chapter Three

כָּל יִשְׂרָאֵל יֵשׁ לָהֶם חֵלֶק לָעוֹלָם הַבָּא, שֶׁנֶּאֱמַר: ,,וְעַמֵּךְ כֻּלָּם צַדִּיקִים, לְעוֹלָם יִירְשׁוּ אָרֶץ, נֵצֶר מַטָּעַי, מַעֲשֵׂה יָדַי לְהִתְפָּאֵר''.

All Israel has a share in the World to Come, as it is said:
And your people are all righteous; they shall inherit the land forever; a branch of My plantings, My handiwork, in which to take pride (Isaiah 60:21).

[א] **עֲקַבְיָא** בֶּן מַהֲלַלְאֵל אוֹמֵר: הִסְתַּכֵּל בִּשְׁלֹשָׁה דְבָרִים וְאֵין אַתָּה בָא לִידֵי עֲבֵרָה: דַּע מֵאַיִן בָּאתָ, וּלְאָן אַתָּה הוֹלֵךְ, וְלִפְנֵי מִי אַתָּה עָתִיד לִתֵּן דִּין

Mishnah 1

עֲקַבְיָא בֶּן מַהֲלַלְאֵל אוֹמֵר — *Akavia ben Mahalalel says.* A contemporary of Hillel, Akavia ben Mahalalel lived during the Second Temple era. The Mishnah (*Eduyos* 5:6) describes his greatness in glowing terms: "No person found in the Temple Courtyard for the slaughtering of the Pesach offering [when most Jews were present] was his equal in Torah knowledge, fear of sin, or humility." His stature was of such magnitude as to preclude the use of any honorific titles, such as Rabbi or Rabban. [This is in the spirit of גָּדוֹל מֵרַבָּן שְׁמָן, *his name is [a] greater [compliment] than [the title] Rabbi (Tosefta, Eduyos* 3:4).]

He rejected a motion that he be appointed *Av Beis Din* (head of the court), since the appointment was made conditional on the retraction of four halachic decisions he had made. "I prefer to be considered a fool my entire life rather than to be deemed wicked in God's eyes for even a moment. Let people not say that the lure of power made me renege on my decision." [He was certain that his opinion concurred with that of the majority of Sages in a previous generation, and he was not willing to compromise his integrity in order to assume a prestigious position.]

Akavia refused his son's request that he ask his colleagues to treat him (the son) preferentially. "Your actions will bring you close or keep you afar," i.e., the type of relationship you enjoy with my contemporaries will be determined by your own actions, he replied to his son (*Eduyos* 5:7).

Chronologically, a statement from Akavia should follow immediately after that of Hillel; however, the mishnah preferred to finish the line of people who served as *Nasi* from Hillel through Rabban Gamliel, son of R' Judah the Prince (2:2-4). The mishnah then returned to Hillel (2:5-8) and continued with Rabban Yochanan ben Zakkai who received the tradition from Hillel (2:9) and his

students (2:10-20). The second chapter ends with quotations of R' Tarfon, which are essentially a commentary on R' Elazar's statements in 2:19. Only then does the third chapter begin with Akavia ben Mahalalel (*Tosafos Yom Tov*).

הִסְתַּכֵּל בִּשְׁלֹשָׁה דְבָרִים וְאֵין אַתָּה בָא לִידֵי עֲבֵרָה — *Consider three things and you will not come into the grip of sin.* Sin is the result of a distorted perspective. Focusing on these three injunctions will enable one to develop a healthy attitude and to remove many of the major root causes of sin from his life. *Tiferes Yisrael* renders לִידֵי as *to the stems* of sin (as in יַד לִפְּרִי, *the stem of a fruit*; see *Uktzin* 1:1). Iniquity stems from arrogance, lust, and blindness regarding an ultimate reckoning. The mishnah teaches us how to counteract these sources of negativity.

Akavia pronounced these three principles at a time when the Temple still stood and Jews enjoyed financial security. In an era of plenty, desire becomes the mortal enemy of spirituality. It is against such desire that Akavia offered his prescription. Rabbi (2:1), on the other hand, lived after the destruction of the Temple, when Jews were in a state of depression and were vulnerable in areas of faith. He therefore offered ways to bolster it, by focusing on God's Omnipresence and full involvement in human affairs, concepts which boost one's faith in God (*Derech Avos*).

דַּע מֵאַיִן בָּאתָ, וּלְאָן אַתָּה הוֹלֵךְ, וְלִפְנֵי מִי אַתָּה עָתִיד לִתֵּן דִּין וְחֶשְׁבּוֹן — *Know whence you came, whither you go, and before Whom you will give justification and reckoning.* The mishnah first posits the questions and later repeats them with answers. According to *Tiferes Yisrael,* this follows a general Mishnaic pattern of first listing categories and explaining them afterward. [See *Bava Basra* 108a for an example of this.]

R' Moshe Almosnino views this first part of the mishnah as addressed to man's soul. *Know, O soul,*

1. Akavia ben Mahalalel says: Consider three things and you will not come into the grip of sin: Know whence you came, whither you go, and before Whom you will give justification and

---

whence you come. The human soul, a spark of the Eternal God, emanates from beneath the Heavenly Throne. Imbued with such Divinity, man is enjoined to retain the purity of his soul and not besmirch it with sin. Additionally, realize *whither you go;* you must return your soul to your Maker as spotless and pristine (if not more pristine, enhanced by your good deeds) as you received it.

[Furthermore, by living your life correctly, you can go on to a world of eternal reward, where you will bask in the goodness of the Almighty.] Thirdly, focus on the One *before Whom you will give justification* [*for yourself*] *and reckoning* [*for your misdeeds*]. A person's life is so significant that every move must be reported to the Creator; he must never consider himself an unimportant being

---

◆§ **Dual approach.** The mishnah initially suggests a positive approach toward protection from sin. It encourages a positive self-image in man, who runs the risk of falling into despair when he loses his confidence. Only when this approach does not succeed in awakening him from his spiritual slumber is the shock treatment of the latter part of the mishnah suggested.

The Talmud gives similar advice to one who finds himself the victim of seemingly causeless pain and aggravation. Since this is most likely the result of one's sins, it initially suggests Torah study as an antidote for the sway of the Satan. If that is unsuccessful, the Talmud suggests that the person read the *Shema,* which teaches love and fear of God. If all else fails, then and only then should he be reminded of the harsh reality of the day of death (*Berachos* 5a).

Mili d'Avos suggests that the two approaches, one softer and one harsher, are addressed to the soul and body respectively. He illustrates the idea with an enchanting parable: A wealthy rabbi sent his son to a famous yeshivah located in another city. The head of that yeshivah was a world-renowned scholar at whose feet, the father was certain, his son would develop into an accomplished scholar.

On the way, the son stopped overnight at an inn owned by his wealthy father. There he was befriended by a young man of inferior character, whose life was devoid of any meaningful activity. The rabbi's son decided to stay for a while. He very quickly became infected with his new-found friend's spirit and began spending late nights involved in fun and games. One of his father's employees, who worked at the inn, was pained to see the level to which the son had fallen, and he began to speak to the young man. "Remember, young man, *where you come from.* Your father is a great and fine man, and a scholar of note. Do not forget your roots! Furthermore, never lose sight of *whither you go:* to the great yeshivah, home of highly intelligent and learned young men. There, you will have to meet the dean, who will test your knowledge and abilities. Think of the great shame you will experience if you do not make a good impression or if you are unable to answer his questions. How will you explain it to your father? Don't waste your life away in the company of that empty-headed rascal."

He then turned angrily to the other boy. "You low life, remember *where you come from.* How dare you corrupt someone of such distinguished lineage? Do not forget *whither you go.* If your new associate's father gets word of your negative influence on his son, he will have you driven from the inn and you will be forced to return to the hovel of your lowly parents. Moreover, aren't you afraid of having to account to this boy's father for ruining him?"

The parable incorporates all parts of the mishnah. To the soul, represented by the rabbi's son, Akavia suggests focusing on its eminent origins, the great potential it has to achieve lofty levels of sanctity and reward, and the terrible shame it will suffer if it disappoints its Maker.

It is to the body — the miscreant friend — that Akavia's words assume a different tone. "Realize you are from a putrid drop," Akavia tells the body. "What gives you the audacity to entice your soul toward sin? Even more, realize that if you allow your evil inclination control over your soul, you will never achieve any sense of meaning in life. You come from the earth and will return there (see *Genesis* 3:19). Finally, are you not afraid of having to account to God for having ruined the life of His most precious child?"

וְחֶשְׁבּוֹן. מֵאַיִן בָּאתָ? מִטִּפָּה סְרוּחָה. וּלְאָן אַתָּה הוֹלֵךְ?
לִמְקוֹם עָפָר, רִמָּה וְתוֹלֵעָה. וְלִפְנֵי מִי אַתָּה עָתִיד לִתֵּן דִּין
וְחֶשְׁבּוֹן? לִפְנֵי מֶלֶךְ מַלְכֵי הַמְּלָכִים, הַקָּדוֹשׁ בָּרוּךְ הוּא.

whose actions or misdeeds are ignored in the grand scheme of the world. Thus aware of his nobility, man can save himself from spiritual oblivion.

Toras Avos interprets the first part of the mishnah as follows: *Know from whence you come.* When the heat of desire overcomes one, he should be aware of its source. It is the darker side of him that is lustful, yet he often fools himself into believing that his motives are above reproach. He must realize that it is not a friend but a foe who seeks to incite him.

Furthermore, focus on *whither you go.* One tends to deny that even one sinful deed has a far-reaching effect on him, but the spiritual blemish imprinted on man's soul by iniquity is deep and difficult to remove.

Finally, one must realize that his actions can have a negative influence upon others who witness them. In this context, *before whom you will give reckoning* refers not to God, but to people with whom we come in contact. When others learn from our actions, we bear responsibility for *their* misdeeds as well.

The term הוֹלֵךְ is in present tense. Man is constantly "going"; he is either merely on the way to the cemetery or the path to Paradise, depending on how he lives.

The *Chofetz Chaim* explains that man is always on the go, moving not only physically, but, more importantly, spiritually. He never stands still. The crucial question, therefore, is for man to know *whither you go*; are you going spiritually up or down? Do you sense growth or recession? Stating that there is no such thing in human life as stasis, King Solomon describes the resolution of this dilemma: *The path of life goes upward for the intelligent and successful person, in order to avoid descending into the abyss (Proverbs 15:24); one must go up in order to avoid falling down.*

The next clause speaks of man giving a reckoning for his deeds in the next world. The words לִתֵּן דִּין mean literally *to give judgment* — but, *R' Shlomo of Lutzk* notes: One does not *give* judgment, he is *subject* to it. Why does our mishnah speak of *giving* judgment? In the world of truth, man will realize the extent of the damage he has inflicted on himself due to his sins. He will beg to be judged so that God may prescribe some type of therapeutic punishment to purify his soul. Thus, man will willingly surrender himself to judgment.

⧫ **Pay for the consequences.** This concept of דִּין וְחֶשְׁבּוֹן may be likened to a merchant who sold defective seeds to farmers. When the seeds yielded no produce, the farmers demanded to be reimbursed not only for the price of the seed, but also for the profit they would have earned from the field had the seeds been of proper quality. Likewise, the time employed by man for sin is not only defective in the sinful action itself, but it is also responsible for the damage of potential spiritual produce that it *could have* yielded.

⧫ **Ripples of sin.** On a deeper level, every episode of sin pollutes the spiritual atmosphere of the world, permeating it with a negative aura. The Talmud relates that Elazar ben Durdayah, a notoriously immoral person, realized the extent of his depravity and sought Divine mercy. He implored the mountains and valleys to intercede with God on his behalf. They replied, "Before we seek mercy for you, we must seek Divine mercy for ourselves" (*Avodah Zarah* 10b). Even though they had not sinned, the hills and valleys, and indeed all of the physical world, had been polluted by his sins. [For this reason, teaches *Beis HaLevi*, the entire world had to be laid waste during the Flood, not only the people who sinned. In a climate of hedonism, the air we *all* breathe is spiritually contaminated. Conversely, one who performs good deeds purifies the spiritual climate of the world and induces in all people a greater proclivity toward good.] Thus, דִּין refers to judgment of our own actions, while חֶשְׁבּוֹן refers to the reckoning we will have to make for disturbing the world's quality of existence through our sins.

reckoning. "Whence you came?" — from a putrid drop; "whither you go?" — to a place of dust, worms and maggots; "and before Whom will you give justification and reckoning?" — before the King Who reigns over kings, the Holy One, Blessed is He.

Alshich suggests that indeed, man will judge himself. Act by act, his entire life will be portrayed in front of him; regarding each misdeed, he will be questioned: "Do you now remember that the Torah mandates retribution for this act?" Of course, he will answer in the affirmative and thereby seal his own fate. Hence, man himself *gives* judgment.

The difference between דִין, *justification,* and חֶשְׁבּוֹן, *reckoning :* The *Vilna Gaon* explains that דִין, *justification,* is the futile attempt to justify one's misdeeds and sins. חֶשְׁבּוֹן, *reckoning,* refers to an assessment of the misuse of the time which one spent sinning. Because he could have been busy doing *mitzvos,* he will be called upon to account for the his failure to use the time properly.

Mussar Avos adds further that one must offer justification for the sin itself and provide a reckoning of the resulting damage. For example, one who murders the father of children is not only culpable for the murder, but he must also calculate the damage inflicted by robbing the children of their source of support, their role model, and their educator (*Mussar Avos*).

מֵאַיִן בָּאתָ? מִטִּפָּה סְרוּחָה — *"Whence you came?"* — *from a putrid drop.* Man's physical existence begins ignominiously in the form of a putrid seminal drop (see *Rav*). He should not become arrogant, therefore, and think he is above God's law. By focusing on his ignoble origin, man will be saved from haughtiness, which God finds abominable (*R' Yonah, Rambam,* et al.).

Although man begins from a putrid drop, he has the ability to grow far beyond that. By compounding his accomplishments and building upon them, the man of today can be born of the man of yesterday (*Yalkut Yehudah*).

וּלְאָן אַתָּה הוֹלֵךְ? לִמְקוֹם עָפָר, רִמָּה וְתוֹלֵעָה — *"whither you go?"* — *to a place of dust, worms and maggots.* The ultimate destination of the human corpse is the grave; physical pleasure is but a fleeting experience. Man should be aware of the futility of concentrating on physical fulfillment, for he toils only for the benefit of the maggots. Money and worldly goods become insignificant when one realizes that after his temporary sojourn on earth, he cannot take them along (see *R' Yonah*). King David expresses this succinctly: *For upon his death he will not take anything; his splendor will not descend after him (Psalms* 49:18).

Burial shrouds are made without pockets because only good deeds and acts of kindness belong to someone after death; everything else remains behind.

וְלִפְנֵי מִי אַתָּה עָתִיד לִתֵּן דִּין וְחֶשְׁבּוֹן? לִפְנֵי מֶלֶךְ מַלְכֵי הַמְּלָכִים, הַקָּדוֹשׁ בָּרוּךְ הוּא — *"and before Whom will you give justification and reckoning?"* — *before the King Who reigns over kings, the Holy One, Blessed is He.* Contemplation of the exalted status of the Master of the Universe will encourage man to follow all of His dictates scrupulously (*Rambam*). Man could not possibly rebel against God's

---

ᴖᴥ **Haughty clod.** R' Avraham, son of the great *Maggid* of Mezritch, known as the *Malach,* or "Angel," came to visit his father-in-law. All the dignitaries of the community came to greet R' Avraham. Overcome by the excessive honor and fearful of its detrimental effect, he walked over to a window and stared out at a large mountain in the distance, ignoring his guests.

A young, wealthy, and rather haughty scholar who was present took affront at being ignored and sought to put the *Malach* in his place. "Haven't you ever seen a tall peak before?" he asked cynically. "Why do you gaze so intently out the window?"

The *Malach* quietly replied, "I am amazed how a simple clod of earth can become so infatuated with itself that it grows into so mighty and tall a mountain."

One must never lose sight of his beginnings; *know whence you came.*

---

expectations if he is truly aware that he will have to account in front of the Ultimate Judge for every act and thought. Furthermore, contemplation of the

retribution he can expect for his iniquities and the embarrassment he will suffer should be a sufficient deterrent against sin (*R' Yonah*).

Mishnah 2

רַבִּי חֲנִינָא סְגַן הַכֹּהֲנִים אוֹמֵר — *Rabbi Chanina, the deputy Kohen Gadol, says.* R' Chanina served as *s'gan*, or deputy, to the *Kohen Gadol* (High Priest). *Rambam* (*Hilchos Klei HaMikdash* 4:16) describes the *s'gan's* functions as follows: The administrator [or deputy] to the *Kohen Gadol* was appointed to serve the *Kohen Gadol* in his dealings with the other *Kohanim*. He stood to the right of the *Kohen Gadol* constantly, and any directions transmitted by the *Kohen Gadol* to the other *Kohanim* were conveyed by the *s'gan*. He also assisted the *Kohen Gadol* in his ritual duties. "His relationship to the *Kohen Gadol* was that of a prime minister to a king." [See *Yad Avraham* to *Yoma* 1:1, s.v וּמַתְקִינִין.] He would also replace the *Kohen Gadol* on Yom Kippur when necessary (see Yoma 39a).

R' Chanina attested to many of the practices in the Temple (see *Eduyos* 2:1-3), as well as laws related to *Kohanim* and the Temple service (see *Menachos* 10:1 and *Zevachim* 12:4). His emphasis on peace in our mishnah is reflected in his statement "Great is peace. It is as valuable as all of Creation" (*Sifri, Bamidbar* 42).

The rather strange plural usage סְגַן הַכֹּהֲנִים, *deputy of [many] priests,* is specific to R' Chanina. He lived during the Hasmonean dynasty, toward the end of the Second Temple era. The Talmud (*Yoma* 18a) teaches that the Romans auctioned off the office of *Kohen Gadol* during this period; many grossly unqualified people bought the august position and died prematurely during their terms. R' Chanina should have been appointed *Kohen Gadol*,

but the corrupt authorities would not do so, and R' Chanina was not willing to pay for the privilege. Hence, he served as deputy to many High Priests (*R' Meir Shapiro* and *Mussar Avos*).

הֱוֵי מִתְפַּלֵּל בִּשְׁלוֹמָהּ שֶׁל מַלְכוּת — *Pray for the welfare of the government,* even for a non-Jewish government (*Rav*). This is based on the verse (*Jeremiah* 29:7): *You shall seek the welfare of the city to which I have exiled you and entreat God on its behalf.*

The seventy bullocks offered in the Temple during the Succos holiday were an example of Jewish service on behalf of the nations (*Rashi*).

This mishnah is the source for the custom of offering a prayer on behalf of the government during the Sabbath morning services (*Tiferes Yisrael*). According to *R' Yonah*, it is a call for Jews to take an interest in public issues. We must be concerned with and pray for the general welfare, and any human suffering should pain us. King David was a paradigm of such sensitivity, praying even for his enemies: *But as for me, when they were ill, my clothing was sackcloth and I afflicted myself with fasting* (*Psalms* 35:13). One must not confine his prayers to his own personal concerns; instead he should pray on behalf of all men, including the government, which assures peace and tranquility.

Mili d'Avos interprets this clause as a continuation of the previous mishnah, which offers Akavia's formula on ways to keep from sinning against God. R' Chanina, however, suggests that while contemplation of man's lowly beginnings and his ultimate

⧫§ **The shame of recognition.** R' Tzadok *HaKohen* of Lublin explains that the purgatory one experiences for his sins in the afterworld is the scalding embarrassment of having to face the truth of his mistakes in life. Much like being forced to watch a film of everything he has done wrong, he will have no choice but to hang his head in shame. For this reason, the Talmud teaches: "He who commits a sin and is embarrassed by it is forgiven" (*Berachos* 12b). The profound sense of shame is in itself a form of the "pains of *Gehinnom*" that an unrepentant person will eventually suffer for his misdeeds.

2. Rabbi Chanina, the deputy Kohen Gadol, says: Pray for the welfare of the government, because if people did not fear it, a person would swallow his fellow alive.

destination will weaken his urge to sin against God, it is less effective against transgressions against one's fellows. Man rationalizes: "Although I originated from a putrid drop, I still have achieved more in life than my friend, and that entitles me to take advantage of him and act abusively toward him." To counter this attitude, R' Chanina says that it is only fear of governmental intervention that can stop one from devouring his fellow man, as described in the next passage.

שֶׁאַלְמָלֵא מוֹרָאָה, אִישׁ אֶת רֵעֵהוּ חַיִּים בְּלָעוֹ — *because if people did not fear it, a person would swallow his fellow alive. Rav* quotes the Talmudic elucidation of this verse, *And You have made men like the fish of the sea (Habakuk* 1:14): Just as the larger fish in the sea swallow the smaller ones, so would stronger people devour the weak if not for fear of the ruling powers *(Avodah Zarah* 4b). The government maintains social order and peace, and by instilling fear of the law, it prevents anarchy and wanton crime.

Meiri gives an added dimension to the importance of prayer for the welfare of the government. Human affairs are influenced largely by scholars and politicians. While legislators can function without intellectuals, those in the intellectual realm cannot flourish unless there is political stability. We are therefore directed to pray for the welfare of the government, to assure the peaceful conduct of day-to-day living, so that intellectuals will be able to set the tone for society *(Meiri)*.

Ritva interprets this as a directive to pray for the welfare of the Heavenly Kingdom and the realization of God's will in the world. If not for the fear which God induces in the hearts of mortal rulers, they might unleash destructive forces that would totally consume Israel.

Ruach Chaim sees this as a call to pray for the welfare of the Kingdom, placing the attainment of a world run according to God's will ahead of our own personal agendas.

In truth, our personal and collective welfare is dependent on the attainment of God's agenda; when the Kingdom is on sound footing, all the King's subjects stand to benefit. Furthermore, if not for the fear of Heaven, men would devour each other, thus destroying personal welfare. Abraham's words of rebuke to Abimelech over the kidnaping of Sarah focused on this axiom: *Because I said [to myself], "There is no fear of God in this place, and they will slay me because of my wife" (Genesis* 20:11).

When a government is preoccupied with wartime concerns or other foreign crises, it often cannot protect its citizens against violence and crime. Domestic policy concerns are frequently shunted aside at times of national emergency. Therefore, we must pray for peace among governments in general, for only when our own government is active on its home territory, without foreign distractions, can it prevent chaos among men *(Tiferes Tzvi)*.

◁§ **Ever-present peril.** Even those who give the appearance of relating to Jews as אִישׁ אֶת רֵעֵהוּ, *a man to his fellow*, and who seemingly harbor no ill will toward Jews, are often tempted to swallow us alive. The deafening silence of the community of nations in the face of the Nazi savagery clearly underscored the stark reality that we can rely only on our Father in Heaven.

Based on this, Rabbi Eizel Charif gave a caustic explanation of the revenge strategy used by Shimon and Levi when their sister Dinah was kidnapped by Shechem. The brothers suggested that all the males of Shechem undergo circumcision, and then took advantage of their infirmity to kill them. "Had they killed them uncircumcised, they would have enraged world opinion. Once the Shechemites were circumcised [and therefore considered to be members of the covenant of Abraham], Shimon and Levi felt confident that killing them would elicit nary a whimper from the community of nations." Hence, we must pray for the welfare of the Heavenly Kingdom, our only Patron and Protector. If the forces of evil are allowed free reign and are not kept under check by God, civilization can self-destruct.

The Kotzker *Rebbe* interpreted these words differently: *Pray when the kingdom is at peace.* When governments are preoccupied with external enemies, they have no time to involve themselves in anti-Semitic schemes. When the rulers are at peace, however, the Jews have cause to fear intrigues against them, and that is when they must pray for Jewish survival.

[ג] **רַבִּי חֲנִינָא** בֶּן תְּרַדְיוֹן אוֹמֵר: שְׁנַיִם שֶׁיּוֹשְׁבִין וְאֵין בֵּינֵיהֶם דִּבְרֵי תוֹרָה, הֲרֵי זֶה מוֹשַׁב

Mishnah 3

Much of the rest of this chapter discusses the primacy of Torah study and the serious consequences of minimizing one's involvement in it.

רַבִּי חֲנִינָא בֶּן תְּרַדְיוֹן אוֹמֵר — *Rabbi Chanina ben Tradyon says:* A third-generation *Tanna*, he lived in Sichnin (present-day Suchnin), in the lower Galilee, where he headed a yeshivah and presided over a court (*Sanhedrin* 32b). The Sages invoked him as a role model for charity collectors and distributors: "One should deposit charity only to funds overseen by a scholar the likes of R' Chanina ben Tradyon" (*Bava Basra* 10b, *Avodah Zarah* 17b).

R' Chanina was one of the עֲשָׂרָה הֲרוּגֵי מַלְכוּת, the ten sages executed by the Roman government for teaching Torah publicly in defiance of the ban that the Roman conquerors imposed in order to extinguish the sparks of faith in God. The Talmud relates that when he went to visit the ailing R' Yosi ben Kisma, the latter challenged him about this dangerous course of action. "Don't you know that this nation [Rome] was enthroned by God? They have destroyed the Temple, decimated the righteous people among us, and are still in ascendance. I am told that you teach Torah at large public gatherings, holding the Torah scroll as you speak." R' Chanina answered, "Heaven will show mercy." R' Yosi rejected this approach, saying, "I speak reasonable words and you tell me 'Heaven will show mercy'! I would not be surprised to hear that they burn you alive along with the Torah scroll."

The Romans did in fact arrest R' Chanina, wrap him in his Torah scroll, and burn him alive. In their cruelty, they placed wet sponges on his heart in order to cause him a slow and torturous death. His daughter cried out, "Father, must I witness this?" He answered, "God, Who will certainly redress the degradation of His Holy Torah scroll, will also avenge my debasement." To his students he said, "I see the parchment burning, but the letters ascend," conveying his deep faith that while Israel may suffer physical pain and death, its spirit is everlasting. The eternal and indestructible Torah will carry the nation forever (see *Avodah Zarah* 18b). Beruriah, the famous intellectual and wife of the *Tanna* R' Meir, was R' Chanina ben Tradyon's daughter.

שְׁנַיִם שֶׁיּוֹשְׁבִין וְאֵין בֵּינֵיהֶם דִּבְרֵי תוֹרָה, הֲרֵי זֶה מוֹשַׁב לֵצִים — *If two sit together and there are no words of Torah between them, it is a session of scorners.* "Scorn" here is not meant in the active sense of one who speaks disparagingly of other people or of spiritual goals. The mishnah speaks of people who meet for the sole purpose of engaging in frivolities, which constitutes scorn of the Torah. If there are no pressing business or other serious matters that need to be discussed, there is no excuse for them not to engage in Torah study or discussions of a spiritual nature; to do otherwise implies contempt for Torah (*R' Yonah*).

The term לֵיצָנוּת refers to the mindset of one who cannot bear to accord honor to anybody or anything. The Midrash characterizes Amalek, the nation that attacked the Jews in the desert after the Exodus, as a *scorner* (*Proverbs* 19:25 and *Rashi* ad loc.). In spite of the supernatural events of the Exodus, which paralyzed all the nations and prevented them from taking any action against Israel, Amalek remained unmoved. They refused to recognize the superiority of Israel and brazenly

---

◆§ **Making every minute count.** A businessman who does not use every available means to maximize his profits can be viewed, to some extent, as neglecting his business. Similarly, since one can learn and sharpen his understanding through discussion with colleagues (see *Taanis* 7a), to sit with another person and not avail oneself of the knowledge that their combined efforts may yield is a rebuff of the Torah.

Panim Yafos interprets the word לֵץ, *scorner*, as an acronym of the words לַמְדָּן צַדִּיק, *scholar, saint*. Apparently he considers himself such a paragon of brilliance and virtue that he is superior to others and is entitled to ignore or ridicule them.

3/3

3. Rabbi Chanina ben Tradyon says: If two sit together and there are no words of Torah between them, it is a session

attacked (*R' Yitzchak Hutner*).

Scorn for the Torah is compared to one who is given the opportunity to count money for an hour, with the added incentive that he may keep whatever he counts — and yet he refuses. This is the worse kind of scorn, for such a person shows contempt both for the money and for the one who made the offer. Similarly, one who is aware of the great value of and reward for Torah study, and has the audacity to pass up such an exalted opportunity, is contemptuous of both Torah and its Giver. The Baraisa teaches: *Every single day a Heavenly voice emanates from Mt. Horeb: "Woe to them, the people, because of [their] insult to the Torah"* (*Avos* 6:2) (*HaChassid Yaavetz*).

Midrash Shmuel notes that the mishnah does not speak of two separate people who do not learn Torah; rather, it speaks of two people who do not have words of Torah *between them,* implying that each of them may be studying, but there is no exchange of ideas between them. Even though the two individuals engage in independent Torah study, they are still deemed scorners, for each one may privately lack respect for his fellow's intellectual abilities and therefore refuse to join his friend in study. Such scorn earns one the title לֵץ.

HaChassid Yaavetz applies the mishnah in a broader sense, commenting that it does not speak of people who do not study Torah at all, but rather of those who do not bring the Torah into all areas of their lives. Two people engaged in commerce who do not use Torah as a guideline in their affairs are scorners of the Torah. [To confine Torah to patently "religious" matters rather than allowing it to govern all areas of one's life is a degradation of Torah. Furthermore, we must ensure that all of our activities yield some spiritual profit. If two people engage in any type of social interaction or commercial venture which produces no spiritual benefit or does not increase the honor of God and His Torah (וְאֵין בֵּינֵיהֶם דִּבְרֵי תוֹרָה), their meeting is one of scorners. How can two Jews eliminate God from their everyday activities?]

The mishnah seems to speak in extreme terms. Are two people who do not exchange words of Torah really the equivalent of a session of scorners? *Rashi* offers clarification: The Torah teaches, "Beware lest your heart be seduced and you turn astray [from Torah study] and serve others" (*Deuteronomy* 11:16, *Rashi* ad loc.). The Torah seems to equate neglect of study of Torah with idolatry, another seemingly extreme comparison. However, they are really not so far apart; for just as nature, in a physical sense, abhors a vacuum, so too a spiritual vacuum is quickly filled up — sometimes with the worst of sins. Thus the mishnah means to teach that the absence of words of Torah and spiritual content creates a vacuum in a person which will be filled up with the worst forms of scorn and nonsense (*R' Yitzchak Hutner*).

⋙ **No compartmentalization.** The Chazon Ish makes a strong statement about those who neglect to bring all their daily activities under the umbrella of Torah jurisdiction. "The practice of dividing Torah into two separate domains by yielding subserviently to the decisions of the scholars of the generation in ritual matters while seeking to retain freedom of choice in the 'marketplace of life' is a reincarnation of the attitude of the disbelievers who caused the degeneration of German Jewry and its almost survivorless assimilation into the general culture. The demarcation between [the license of Torah scholars to rule on] ritual questions and their power to legislate [rabbinic] enactments and preventative measures is [indicative of] abuse of Torah and its scholars. Those who practice such compartmentalization are counted among those who have no share in the World to Come, who are invalid as witnesses, etc." (*Collected Letters* 3:92).

⋙ **Effect of a vacuum.** A puzzling incident recorded in the Talmud may be understood in light of this axiom of "spiritual physics." When R' Akiva was imprisoned by the Romans, R' Shimon bar Yochai asked that he teach him Torah, but R' Akiva refused. R' Shimon said to him, "If you don't teach me, I will have my father turn you over to the authorities [for even greater punishment than imprisonment]" (*Pesachim* 112a). The story is astounding! Even an ordinary person would never steep so low as to turn a fellow over to such cruel authorities as the Romans — and certainly not a *Tanna* as great as R' Shimon bar Yochai! Rather, R' Shimon meant to give expression to the tragedy of a life without Torah; one deprived of Torah can fall into a moral abyss, even stooping to מְסִירָה (informing).

לֵצִים, שֶׁנֶּאֱמַר: ,,וּבְמוֹשַׁב לֵצִים לֹא יָשָׁב". אֲבָל שְׁנַיִם
שֶׁיּוֹשְׁבִין וְיֵשׁ בֵּינֵיהֶם דִּבְרֵי תוֹרָה, שְׁכִינָה שְׁרוּיָה בֵּינֵיהֶם,
שֶׁנֶּאֱמַר: ,,אָז נִדְבְּרוּ יִרְאֵי יהוה אִישׁ אֶל רֵעֵהוּ, וַיַּקְשֵׁב
יהוה וַיִּשְׁמָע, וַיִּכָּתֵב סֵפֶר זִכָּרוֹן לְפָנָיו, לְיִרְאֵי יהוה
וּלְחֹשְׁבֵי שְׁמוֹ." אֵין לִי אֶלָּא שְׁנַיִם; מִנַּיִן שֶׁאֲפִילוּ אֶחָד
שֶׁיּוֹשֵׁב וְעוֹסֵק בַּתּוֹרָה, שֶׁהַקָּדוֹשׁ בָּרוּךְ הוּא קוֹבֵעַ לוֹ שָׂכָר?
שֶׁנֶּאֱמַר: ,,יֵשֵׁב בָּדָד וְיִדֹּם, כִּי נָטַל עָלָיו."

שֶׁנֶּאֱמַר: ,,וּבְמוֹשַׁב לֵצִים לֹא יָשָׁב" — *as it is said: "In the session of scorners he does not sit"* (Psalms 1:1). The next verse in *Psalms* continues, *Rather, his desire is in the Torah of God* (ibid. 1:2). Thus, King David equates lack of desire for the word of God with scorn (*Rambam, R' Yonah*).

Even if the people at the session do not engage in levity and scorn, their blatant lack of interest in spiritual matters stamps it as a session of scorners (*Meiri*). In addition, our Sages taught (*Sanhedrin* 99a): Any person who can devote himself to Torah and refrains from doing so is counted among those of whom it is stated, *For they have degraded the word of God* (*Numbers* 15:31).

אֲבָל שְׁנַיִם שֶׁיּוֹשְׁבִין וְיֵשׁ בֵּינֵיהֶם דִּבְרֵי תוֹרָה, שְׁכִינָה שְׁרוּיָה בֵּינֵיהֶם — *But if two sit together and words of Torah are between them, the Divine Presence rests between them.* By studying Torah, which is the repository of Godly intelligence, the learners are able to perceive a degree of God's glory (*Meiri*).

According to *Tiferes Yisrael*, two who study God's word together are blessed with enlightenment in their studies and enjoy God's personal concern.

Unlike scorners, who never merit the Divine Presence (see *Sotah* 42b), those involved in Torah study sense the immanence of God (*Tosafos Yom Tov*).

שֶׁנֶּאֱמַר: ,,אָז נִדְבְּרוּ יִרְאֵי ה' אִישׁ אֶל רֵעֵהוּ, וַיַּקְשֵׁב ה' וַיִּשְׁמָע, וַיִּכָּתֵב סֵפֶר זִכָּרוֹן לְפָנָיו, לְיִרְאֵי ה' וּלְחֹשְׁבֵי שְׁמוֹ" — *as it is said: "Then those who fear Hashem spoke to one another, and Hashem listened and heard, and a book of remembrance was written before Him for those who fear Hashem and give thought to His name"* (Malachi 3:16). The phrase *one another* indicates that the verse refers to two people (*Rashi, Rav*). Those who fear God spoke

⅏ **It's up to us.** The term שְׁכִינָה denotes God's presence in this world, for although God is transcendent, He projects His Presence into the physical sphere. Following *HaChassid Yaavetz*, when people allow the Torah to dictate the way they conduct the mundane details of their lives, they allow Divinity to permeate their daily existence. This is שְׁכִינָה, the *Divine Presence*. More profoundly, the greatest access we have to God is through the Godly intelligence He reveals to us in the Torah. The deeper one drinks of that well, the more Godliness enters his life.

The Kotzker *Rebbe* once asked a young follower: "Where is God to be found?" Answered the newcomer: "The world is full of His glory." "No, no," said the Kotzker. "God is found wherever man allows Him to enter."

⅏ **Reward for joy.** Rabbi Avraham Pam compares people conversing in Torah to the newly engaged young woman who shows off her engagement ring to others. The girl is so excited that she wants to share the tangible evidence of her joy with everybody. Likewise, one who appreciates the sparkling beauty of the Torah's wisdom wants everybody else to share in his joy. God remembers these moments of passion and repays man for them.

of scorners, as it is said: *In the session of scorners he does not sit* (*Psalms* 1:1). But if two sit together and words of Torah are between them, the Divine Presence rests between them, as it is said: *Then those who fear HASHEM spoke to one another, and HASHEM listened and heard, and a book of remembrance was written before Him for those who fear HASHEM and give thought to His Name* (*Malachi* 3:16). From this verse we would know this only about two people; how do we know that if even one person sits and occupies himself with Torah, the Holy One, Blessed is He, determines a reward for him? For it is said: *Let one sit in solitude and be still, for he will have received [a reward] for it* (*Lamentations* 3:28).

---

words reflective of that awe (i.e., words of Torah) to one another, and God listened [intently, as if in close proximity to them] and heard. This implies that God is present when two persons converse on Torah topics (*Meiri*). R' Yonah adds that the mishnah refers to the reward that the righteous will receive in the future: "It is because they exchange words of Torah with one another that God recorded this in a book of remembrance and is now rewarding them for it."

The verb נִדְבְּרוּ is in the causative form. In studying Torah one should not only speak, but also seek to elicit his study partner's opinion (*R' Avraham Azulai*).

אֵין לִי אֶלָּא שְׁנַיִם; מִנַּיִן שֶׁאֲפִילוּ אֶחָד שֶׁיּוֹשֵׁב וְעוֹסֵק בַּתּוֹרָה, שֶׁהַקָּדוֹשׁ בָּרוּךְ הוּא קוֹבֵעַ לוֹ שָׂכָר — *From this verse we would know this only about two people; how do we know that if even one person sits and occupies himself with Torah, the Holy One, Blessed is He, determines a reward for him?* Since the merit of many people who fulfill the Torah's dictates is disproportionately greater than that of an individual who does so (see *Rashi, Leviticus* 26:8), one might suspect that the solitary learner does not merit a Godly Presence (*Tiferes Yisrael*).

Rambam cites the Talmud (*Berachos* 6a), which differentiates between the two cases: Of course, a person who studies alone merits the Divine Presence, but the Torah of two people is recorded in God's book of remembrance, while the Torah of one person is not. *Maharsha* (ibid.) explains: When two people investigate a Torah topic together, the intellectual give-and-take will generally result in a correct halachic application. Hence, their efforts are recorded in a book of remembrance for posterity.

While it is proper to study the words of Torah aloud (see *Eruvin* 54a), individual learners often do not do so. Hence, unlike the earlier stich of the mishnah, which discusses two who sit with audible *words* of Torah between them, one person is characterized merely as being occupied with Torah (*Tosafos Yom Tov*). Nonetheless, God determines and establishes a proper reward for him.

שֶׁנֶּאֱמַר: ,,יֵשֵׁב בָּדָד וְיִדֹּם, כִּי נָטַל עָלָיו'' — *For it is said: "Let one sit in solitude and be still, for he will have received [a reward] for it"* (*Lamentations* 3:28). His mental occupation with Torah is deemed in God's eyes as if he engaged in verbal study (*R' Yonah*).

> ◆§ **Guaranteed dividend.** The mishnah uses the word קוֹבֵעַ, *establish*, which implies not only that there is a reward for Torah study, but that the reward is guaranteed. While a transgression can cancel out the merit and reward for another *mitzvah*, Torah study is an immutable source of recompense. Furthermore, the merit of Torah study constantly shields man from troubles, both during study and after (see *Sotah* 21a).

[ד] **רַבִּי** שִׁמְעוֹן אוֹמֵר: שְׁלֹשָׁה שֶׁאָכְלוּ עַל שֻׁלְחָן אֶחָד וְלֹא אָמְרוּ עָלָיו דִּבְרֵי תוֹרָה, כְּאִלּוּ אָכְלוּ מִזִּבְחֵי מֵתִים,

Mishnah 4

רַבִּי שִׁמְעוֹן אוֹמֵר — *Rabbi Shimon says.* The legendary Rabbi Shimon bar Yochai (see *Meilah* 17b) was a student of Rabbi Akiva and a fourth-generation *Tanna*. He was one of the youngest students at the Academy of Yavneh and the one who proposed the question regarding the obligation to recite *Maariv* that precipitated the impeachment of Rabban Gamliel from the office of *Nasi* (see *Berachos* 27b-28a). Together with R' Chanina ben Chachinai (see next mishnah), he studied at the yeshivah of R' Akiva in Bnei Brak for thirteen years. When R' Akiva was imprisoned by the Romans for teaching Torah publicly, R' Shimon bar Yochai followed him in order to continue learning from him (*Pesachim* 112a). R' Akiva said of him: "It is sufficient that I and your Creator are aware of your ability" (*Yerushalmi Sanhedrin* 1:2). In recognition of the greatness of his teacher, R' Shimon instructed his own students to model themselves after him, "for my attributes are but tithes of the tithe of R' Akiva's." After R' Akiva's death, R' Shimon was given *semichah* (ordination) by R' Yehudah ben Bava (see *Sanhedrin* 14a).

Some of R' Shimon's more famous statements evidence his deep love for Torah, the Jewish people, and the Land of Israel: "God gave Israel three gifts, all of which can only be acquired through suffering: Torah, the Land of Israel, and the World to Come" (*Berachos* 5a); "God took moral and ethical measure of all the nations of the world and found none as fitting as the Jewish people to receive His Torah. God assessed all the lands of the world and found none as fitting as the Land of Israel to be given to the children of Israel" (*Vayikra Rabbah* 13:2). R' Shimon viewed all Jews as royalty (see *Shabbos* 14:4) and taught: "Whoever helps a Jew is considered to have helped the Divine Presence" (*Tanchuma, Vayechi* 5).

In his view, the Land of Israel lacked nothing (*Sifre, Devarim* 37). One of his students once left the

---

◆§ **The Cave and the Zohar.** R' Shimon's undisguised animosity toward the Roman occupiers of the Land earned him their deep enmity and a death sentence, which forced him to go into hiding (see *Shabbos* 33b). He and his son, R' Elazar, hid in a cave for thirteen years, sustained by a brook that flowed nearby and carobs that grew at the entrance of the cave. As a result of their seclusion and total immersion in Torah study, they developed a disdainful attitude toward non-spiritual matters. When they emerged, they had great difficulty adjusting to the mundane world. The Talmud relates that when they set eyes on agricultural workers — whom they criticized for neglecting Torah study — the intense flame of their other-worldliness consumed the people. A Heavenly voice rebuked them: "Have you left the cave to destroy My world? Return!" When they emerged again a year later, they observed Jews fulfilling the *mitzvos* with joy, and were better able to adjust.

In spite of this experience, R' Shimon advocated a life-style of total immersion in Torah study and viewed his own experience in the cave as proof that "when Jews follow the will of God, their physical needs will be tended to by others [as agents of God]." Nonetheless, he respected and valued work. "Great is work, for it honors those who occupy themselves with it," he said (*Nedarim* 49b).

Of himself and his son he stated: "I have seen few who live with an elevated standard. If there are only two in the world, I and my son Elazar are the two" (*Succah* 45b).

Famous as a miracle worker, R' Shimon was often sent as an emissary of the Jewish community to Rome, where he miraculously saved the Jews from terrible decrees (*Megillah* 17a).

His literary legacy includes all the anonymous statements in the *Sifri* (a halachic Midrash on *Numbers* and *Deuteronomy*) and the *Mechilta of Rashbi* (on *Exodus*), only part of which is extant. His magnum opus is the *Zohar* (Book of Splendor), the basic text of the esoteric *Kabbalah*. In addition to mystical Biblical commentary, it records much biographical information about R' Shimon and his students.

4. Rabbi Shimon says: If three have eaten at the same table and have not spoken words of Torah there, it is as if they have eaten of offerings to the dead idols, as it is said:

Land and subsequently made a large fortune. Other students who were jealous wanted to follow his example and seek their fortunes in the Diaspora. R' Shimon took them to a valley near Meron and prayed that the valley be filled with gold coins, which miraculously occurred. R' Shimon told his students: "If it is gold you seek, take as much as you want — but know that whoever takes now does so at the expense of his share in the World to Come" (*Shemos Rabbah* 52:3).

שְׁלֹשָׁה שֶׁאָכְלוּ עַל שֻׁלְחָן אֶחָד וְלֹא אָמְרוּ עָלָיו דִּבְרֵי תוֹרָה, כְּאִלּוּ אָכְלוּ מִזִּבְחֵי מֵתִים — *If three have eaten at the same table and have not spoken words of Torah there, it is as if they have eaten of offerings to the dead idols.* The absence of words of Torah at a gathering of three is a greater travesty than at a meeting of two. Three people are needed to recite the introductory invitation (*zimun*) before *Bircas Hamazon* (Grace After Meals), since three constitute a group. When an entire group shows disrespect for the Torah by not discussing it at all, the scorn is compounded (*HaChassid Yaavetz*).

Three who eat together are obligated to wait for each other in order to recite the *Bircas Hamazon* together (see *Shulchan Aruch Orach Chaim* 193:1). Hence, three who have eaten together are apparently not in a rush to finish and leave, so they have no legitimate excuse for not speaking words of Torah at their meal (*R' Yonah*; *Tiferes Yisrael*).

According to *Rav* and *Rashi*, one can fulfill the obligation to recite words of Torah at the table by reciting *Bircas Hamazon*, which contains many Scriptural verses.

Tosafos Yom Tov elaborates: The first blessing of *Bircas Hamazon* was composed by Moses and represents the Pentateuch. The second blessing was established by Joshua, first of the Prophets, and is symbolic of the Books of the Prophets, while the third blessing, authored by King David, represents the Writings. Hence, all three sections of Scripture are represented.

Nonetheless, it is laudatory not to rely on the recitation of *Bircas Hamazon* and to engage instead in Torah study or conversation (see *Tosafos Yom Tov* and *Magen Avraham O.C.* 170). *Sfas Emes* suggests that while recitation of *Bircas Hamazon* elevates the meal above the level of זִבְחֵי מֵתִים, only actual discussion of Torah will raise it to the level where it is considered God's table.

The rendering of זִבְחֵי מֵתִים as *offerings to dead idols* is based on *Psalms* (106:28): *Then they attached themselves to Baal Peor* (a form of idolatry) *and ate the sacrifices of the dead* (*Rashi*, *Rambam*). When three people join in a culinary feast, indulging their bodies but allowing no accommodation for their souls, it is considered an abominable rejection of Torah (*R' Yonah*). Only the soul of man is eternal and lives forever; the body dies when man's time in this world is up. Serving the needs of the body and not those of the soul is comparable to serving dead and useless idols rather than the Eternal, Living God (*Tiferes Yisrael*, *R' Moshe Alshaker*).

⤳§ **Choose life.** Just as food fortifies and sustains the body, so words of Torah are the food of the soul. This is true both for individuals and for the nation as a whole (*Raya Mehemna, Pinchas 227a*).

Offerings for idol worship are called offerings to the dead, since idols are as powerless as the dead. When man eats and pays no homage to God, he indicates that he considers his sustenance a result of his own abilities and efforts. In truth, no mortal human can provide sustenance; only the Living God can do so. One who refrains from words of Torah at the table is in effect worshiping himself as provider, when in fact he is powerless. His meal is therefore an offering to a dead god (*Minchas Shabbos*).

Man may legitimately kill animals or destroy vegetation for his own consumption only if he has risen spiritually above the level of animal or vegetation. To do so, he must employ the power of speech — an endowment which is his exclusively — for good. By speaking words of Torah, man elevates the food he eats by giving it a new life and meaning. Otherwise, he has done nothing more than kill the animal or vegetable (*Mili d'Avos*).

שֶׁנֶּאֱמַר: ,,כִּי כָּל שֻׁלְחָנוֹת מָלְאוּ קִיא צוֹאָה, בְּלִי מָקוֹם";
אֲבָל שְׁלֹשָׁה שֶׁאָכְלוּ עַל שֻׁלְחָן אֶחָד וְאָמְרוּ עָלָיו דִּבְרֵי
תוֹרָה, כְּאִלּוּ אָכְלוּ מִשֻּׁלְחָנוֹ שֶׁל מָקוֹם, שֶׁנֶּאֱמַר: ,,וַיְדַבֵּר
אֵלַי, זֶה הַשֻּׁלְחָן אֲשֶׁר לִפְנֵי יהוה."

[ה] **רַבִּי חֲנִינָא** בֶּן חֲכִינַאי אוֹמֵר: הַנֵּעוֹר בַּלַּיְלָה,

---

שֶׁנֶּאֱמַר: ,,כִּי כָּל שֻׁלְחָנוֹת מָלְאוּ קִיא צוֹאָה, בְּלִי מָקוֹם" — *as it is said: "For all tables are full of vomit and filth, without the Omnipresent" (Isaiah 28:8). The verses immediately preceding this one speak of people who neglect Torah study due to excessive preoccupation with food and drink (Rambam).*

The mishnah deduces that the verse in *Isaiah* speaks of three people sharing a meal, because the prophet had previously been discussing the activities of three people: a scholar, a prophet, and a Kohen. Had there been only two people, perhaps they would not have been judged so harshly, but in a group of three, at least one of them should have reminded his colleagues to stop their idle chatter (*Tosafos Yom Tov*).

Their obsessions block their intelligence and good sense, causing them to spurn the corrective words of Torah and prophecy (*Rashi* to *Isaiah* 28:7). Their table is reprehensible since God occupies no place at it (*Rashi and Meiri*); they have excluded Torah from their table as though it were a place of filth where Torah study is forbidden (*Tiferes Yisrael*).

אֲבָל שְׁלֹשָׁה שֶׁאָכְלוּ עַל שֻׁלְחָן אֶחָד וְאָמְרוּ עָלָיו דִּבְרֵי תוֹרָה, כְּאִלּוּ אָכְלוּ מִשֻּׁלְחָנוֹ שֶׁל מָקוֹם — *But if three have eaten at the same table and have spoken words of Torah there, it is as if they have eaten from the table of the Omnipresent.* By taking in spiritual nourishment along with his physical sustenance, a person

consecrates his table (*Rashi*). Just as Kohanim eat from offerings brought on the Altar, so those who give Torah a place at their table transform the food into offerings and their table into an altar (*Tosafos Yom Tov*).

Our Sages taught: "As long as the Temple stood, it was the Altar that brought about forgiveness for Jews; now it is man's table that does so" (*Berachos* 55a).

— שֶׁנֶּאֱמַר: ,,וַיְדַבֵּר אֵלַי, זֶה הַשֻּׁלְחָן אֲשֶׁר לִפְנֵי ה' " — *as it is said: "And he said to me, 'This is the table that is before God'" (Ezekiel 41:22).* Although the table in the verse refers to the Temple Altar, which an angel showed to the prophet Ezekiel, the Sages understand it in addition to be an allusion to the table of human beings. Thus, it teaches that we can invest our dining tables with a sanctity that makes them like sacred vessels *before HASHEM* (*R' Meir Zlotowitz*).

According to most religious philosophies, there is a dichotomy between the physical and the spiritual. They consider man to be basically a sensual being, who achieves a degree of spirituality only when he is involved in "religious" activities such as prayer and ritual, but his body and spirit never really coexist. For this reason the Talmud teaches that if an idolater brings a peace offering to the Temple, all of it is offered on the Altar, unlike

---

◆§ **Home and Temple.** *Rashi* quotes a midrash (*Vayikra Rabbah* 21) stating that whenever R' Yochanan entered his house, he would make noise on his way in, following the rule of R' Akiva that one should never enter even his own house to the surprise of others. This is derived, teaches the Midrash, from the verse *Its sound* [of the gold bells suspended from the hem of the Kohen Gadol's robe] *shall be heard when he enters the Sanctuary before God* (Exodus 28:35). The Alter of Slabodka inferred from this midrash that every man's home can be as special as the Holy of Holies in the Temple, and that every man can strive to attain the spiritual heights of the Kohen Gadol. Just as the Holy of Holies was sanctified by the Ark, which contained the Torah, so man's home and table can be elevated by the presence of Torah study and scholars.

For all tables are full of vomit and filth, without the Omnipresent (Isaiah 28:8). But if three have eaten at the same table and have spoken words of Torah there, it is as if they have eaten from the table of the Omnipresent, as it is said: *And he said to me, "This is the table that is before* HASHEM*"* (Ezekiel 41:22).

5. Rabbi Chanina ben Chachinai says: One who stays awake at

a peace offering brought by a Jew, which is eaten. Even a Kohen may not eat of the idolater's offering. The Talmud states the reason for this: "An idolater intends [his offering] only for Heaven" (*Menachos* 73b). An idolater cannot fathom conceptually that a mortal human being can engage in the physical act of eating and thereby elicit forgiveness for the owner of the offering.

Judaism views the matter in exactly the opposite way. Not only is physical existence impossible without the satisfaction of spiritual needs, but spirituality must be realized through physical vehicles. The enactment of spiritual principles must assume concrete forms. Man is a physical being elevated by the soul God blew into him (see *Genesis* 2:7); for this reason, offerings brought in the Temple must be eaten by the Kohanim and the owners of the offering. Man achieves spiritual fulfillment by sanctifying the mundane.

Our mishnah emphasizes this difference of approach. One who engages in the physical act of eating without introducing a spiritual element into his meals establishes a demarcation between the physical and spiritual domains; in effect, he is declaring that they share no interaction. His meal is therefore the equivalent of an offering brought to an idol.

People who follow the Torah by giving physical garb to spiritual concepts, and by elevating the physical with an infusion of spirituality, eat from God's table. Their meals reflect the Jewish view as expressed in the laws of offerings (*Emes LeYaakov*).

Mishnah 5

רַבִּי חֲנִינָא בֶּן חֲכִינַאי אוֹמֵר — *Rabbi Chanina ben Chachinai says.* Of the fourth generation of *Tannaim*, R' Chanina was a student of R' Akiva and studied both the revealed Torah and esoteric portions of *Maaseh Bereishis* and *Maaseh HaMerkavah* (see *Chagigah* 14b). His devotion to Torah study was legendary. He left his home for twelve years in order to pursue his studies undisturbed. Finally his wife sent him a message: "Your daughter is of marriageable age. Return home and arrange for her marriage." When he returned, he did not recognize the streets of the town, which had expanded in his absence, and he could not find his way home. He sat down to rest and suddenly heard someone calling out, "Daughter of Chachinai, fill up your pitcher." Realizing it was his daughter, he followed her home. His wife, shocked to see him, passed away; he prayed for her resurrection, and his prayer was miraculously granted (see *Kesubos* 62b and *Vayikra Rabbah* 21:8). R' Chanina's wife, who was committed loyally to her husband and his spiritual growth, was admired as the quintessential woman who loved the Torah (*Bereishis Rabbah* 17:3). Her husband was one of the ten martyrs killed by the Romans (*Midrash Eleh Ezkerah*).

הַנֵּעוֹר בַּלַּיְלָה — *One who stays awake at night.* The commentators offer various explanations for R' Chanina's harsh condemnation of being awake at night and traveling alone:

☐ *R' Yonah* says that the quiet of night and the solitude of travel are particularly suited for spiritual pursuits, for a person who is uninterrupted by the hubbub of daytime activity can devote himself to Torah study and personal growth. Thus, someone who purposely refrains from doing so is extremely derelict.

☐ *Rambam* writes: Even though one is commanded to study Torah both during the day and at night, most of man's intellectual achievements

וְהַמְהַלֵּךְ בַּדֶּרֶךְ יְחִידִי, וּמְפַנֶּה לִבּוֹ לְבַטָּלָה – הֲרֵי זֶה מִתְחַיֵּב בְּנַפְשׁוֹ.

[ו] **רַבִּי** נְחוּנְיָא בֶּן הַקָּנָה אוֹמֵר: כָּל הַמְקַבֵּל עָלָיו עֹל תּוֹרָה, מַעֲבִירִין מִמֶּנּוּ עֹל מַלְכוּת וְעֹל דֶּרֶךְ אֶרֶץ;

occur at night. Therefore, one who wishes to merit the crown of Torah should act appropriately at night, being careful not to waste even one night on excessive sleeping, eating, drinking, idle talk, or any other such distractions. He should occupy himself solely with Torah study and words of wisdom (*Hilchos Talmud Torah* 3:13). *Rambam* (cited in *Magen Avos*) calls the nighttime "the blessed hours."

☐ *Meiri* views these words as a simple directive to get sufficient rest. One should sleep eight hours out of every twenty-four (*Rambam, Meiri*).

☐ *Rav* comments that Torah study is a protection against dangers that are prevalent at night and during lone travel.

The Talmud debates whether night was created for sleep or study (see *Eruvin* 65a). One who is awake at night and yet ignores the opportunity to study Torah follows neither opinion; he abuses the creation called night (*Sfas Emes*).

While it is an axiom of our faith that everything that happens to man is an act of Divine Providence, consti-

tuting either reward or punishment, there are times and places that are inherently dangerous, and there are "natural" occurrences that are detrimental to man's health. Lack of sleep is one cause of ill health, which man is encouraged to avoid.

וְהַמְהַלֵּךְ בַּדֶּרֶךְ יְחִידִי — *or who travels alone on the road.* A lone traveler is not distracted. as noted above (*R' Yonah*). Alternatively, it is dangerous to travel alone, which leaves one especially vulnerable to attack by thieves and bandits (*Rav, Meiri*).

וּמְפַנֶּה לִבּוֹ לְבַטָּלָה — *but turns his heart to idleness.* According to *R' Yonah* and *Rav,* this is the critique of someone who squanders the quiet, uninterrupted opportunity for spiritual growth, and turns his heart to idleness, instead of drinking of the well of wisdom with a clear head (*R' Yonah*). According to *Rav,* the protective power of Torah would shield him from the dangers of the night or of solitary travel. He ignores the opportunity and instead abandons himself to emptiness.

Meiri's text reads וְהַמְפַנֶּה לִבּוֹ, **and** *one who turns his heart.* Thus he views this as the *third* dangerous

◆§ **An unblemished crown.** R' Aharon Kotler explained the metaphor of a crown. A royal crown from which one diamond is missing is fatally flawed. It is not merely a diamond that is missing; the entire crown is imperfect. Likewise, the totality of commitment required for Torah study does not allow for even one wasted night. The beauty of the crown lies in its completeness.

◆§ **Blocking out the night.** Night is often used as a metaphor for troubled times (*R' Shmuel Alter*). Alternatively, one who travels only on the road of proper living, never worrying about the spiritual welfare of his fellow man, is culpable for his own soul. His spiritual egocentricity will prevent even his own soul from achieving its potential (*Knesses Yisrael*).

Much of life is spent in deep spiritual slumber while opportunities for growth slip away. Occasionally, however, a person can be found who is awake during the night of exile (הַעֵר בַּלַּיְלָה) and who is sensitive to the call of the eternal and the duties it entails. Such a person rises above the herd mentality that induces most people to shape their lives based on what others decide to be good or nice. Occasionally there arises a person who drums his own beat, making his own decisions based on the Torah's teachings, even if he must make his way through life alone (וְהַמְהַלֵּךְ בַּדֶּרֶךְ יְחִידִי). If such a person abuses his heightened sensitivity and focuses his heart on the mundane and foolish (מְפַנֶּה לִבּוֹ לְבַטָּלָה), he has sold his soul cheaply (מִתְחַיֵּב בְּנַפְשׁוֹ).

night or who travels alone on the road, but turns his heart to idleness — indeed, he bears guilt for his soul.

6. Rabbi Nechunia ben Hakanah says: If someone takes upon himself the yoke of Torah — the yoke of government and the yoke of worldly responsibilities are removed from him.

---

situation against which man must take precaution, and whose consequences are a result of man's lack of concern rather than of God's hand. The Talmud (*Kesubos* 59a) teaches that idleness eventually leads to intellectual dullness and ultimately to forms of mental illness.

הֲרֵי זֶה מִתְחַיֵּב בְּנַפְשׁוֹ — *indeed, he bears guilt for his soul.* He is morally guilty for the squandered spiritual opportunity since no legitimate justification exists for the waste of precious time (*R' Yonah*).

In quiet moments, man's mind is naturally preoccupied by the thought of things that are deeply rooted in his subconscious and to which he is emotionally attached. Since the Torah defines

our national essence, it must be so embedded in our consciousness that at such moments our minds and hearts are naturally captivated by its ideas and thoughts. One whose mind moves instead toward idleness has forfeited his spirit and soul (*HaChassid Yaavetz*). By turning his heart to idleness and not utilizing the situations described in the mishnah to engage in study, he exposes himself to danger — and has only himself to blame (*Rav*).

One may not "blame" God for the consequences of these three behavior patterns (remaining awake at night, traveling alone on the road, and engaging in idleness). The negative results are self-induced and man has no one to blame but himself (*Meiri*).

Mishnah 6

רַבִּי נְחוּנְיָא בֶּן הַקָּנָה אוֹמֵר — *Rabbi Nechunia ben Hakanah says.* A contemporary of R' Yochanan ben Zakkai and teacher of R' Yishmael (see *Shevuos* 26a), R' Nechunia was an amiable person who avoided interpersonal conflict at all costs. When asked for the secret of his longevity, he replied, "I never derived honor at the expense of my colleagues; I never lay down to sleep if I was cursed by a friend (without eliciting his forgiveness); and I was always liberal with my money" (*Megillah* 28a).

His entrance to and exit from the study hall were always accompanied by a prayer. When asked about its content, he said: "When I enter, I ask that no error in the law occur because of me. When I leave, I thank God for the privilege of being among those who study His Torah" (*Berachos* 28b). Many mystical works, among them the *Sefer HaBahir,* are attributed to him, as is the prayer *Ana Becho'ach,* which is recited every morning and before *L'chah Dodi,* on Friday evenings.

כָּל הַמְקַבֵּל עָלָיו עֹל תּוֹרָה — *If someone takes upon himself the yoke of Torah.* Accepting the yoke of Torah means accepting the obligation to study Torah under all conditions, just as a yoke is borne by a plowing animal under all circumstances (*Rambam*). According to *R' Yonah,* this mishnah refers to one who considers Torah study and spiritual pursuits his primary goal and relegates all other areas of life to a secondary role. All else is optional, but Torah is a yoke that must be carried.

Tiferes Yisrael notes the phrase *takes upon himself* which connotes a voluntary assumption of obligation. He interprets it as a reference to one who is legitimately exempt from the yoke of Torah due to preoccupation with a livelihood or a government position, and nonetheless assumes it, devoting himself to Torah study beyond his apparent limitations, is rewarded in kind.

מַעֲבִירִין מִמֶּנּוּ עֹל מַלְכוּת וְעֹל דֶּרֶךְ אֶרֶץ — *the yoke of government and the yoke of worldly responsibilities are removed from him.* The yoke of government may assume the form of taxes and levies, or the support of military forces and expeditions (*Rambam*). The clause can also mean that one who assumes the burden of Torah will be freed from military or governmental conscription (*R' Yonah*).

The pressures of daily living are lifted from the shoulders of one who bears the yoke of Torah. The Talmud (*Eruvin* 54a; see *Avos* 6:2) homiletically reads חָרוּת עַל הַלֻּחוֹת, *engraved upon the Tablets* (*Exodus* 32:16) as חֵרוּת עַל הַלֻּחוֹת, *freedom is upon the Tablets.* One who accepts upon himself that which is engraved on the Tablets (the Ten Commandments, which encapsulate the entire Torah) will gain freedom from the burdens of life and from government service (*Rambam*).

R' Nechunia ben Hakanah lived at the time when Torah study was outlawed by the Roman government. He taught this mishnah in order to strengthen Jewish resolve to withstand the government's pressure. Torah carries within it a literal power to transcend the yoke of government and throw it off the neck of the nation (*Mussar Avos*).

According to *Tiferes Yisrael*, the removal of the yokes of government and worldly responsibility is a supernatural reward given for the *voluntary* assumption of the yoke of Torah. *Rav*, however, interprets the mishnah to mean that one's business

⋙ **A welcome burden.** In spite of Israel's willingness to accept the Torah, God found it necessary to place Mount Sinai above their heads and threaten them with instantaneous death if they refused it (see *Shabbos* 88a and *Tosafos* ad loc., s.v. כפה). *Maharal* explains that the Torah is not an optional luxury; it is a necessity, without which man (and the world) cannot survive. Thus, even though Israel was anxious to accept the Torah, God wanted them to understand that without it they would be doomed.

It is for this reason that King David was punished for saying of the Torah *Your statutes were "music" to me* (*Psalms* 119:54) [see *Sotah* 35a]. Torah has a dual character; it provides the greatest of all pleasures, and it is simultaneously a necessity of life without which survival is impossible. One must always retain both these perspectives. King David emphasized the luxury of Torah at the expense of its necessity, and he was therefore punished. Even while experiencing the sheer joy — the *music* — of the Torah, one may never forget that it is a yoke to be carried consciously throughout life (*R' Yitzchak Hutner*).When a student of the Chofetz Chaim took leave of him during World War I, the venerable sage offered this advice, as a guide through life: "Always remember the words of the mishnah, that someone who assumes upon himself the yoke of Torah will be freed from the yoke of government. You may wonder: How is it that many yeshivah students are forced into an anti-Semitic army, while others are not, or are able to be discharged without long or harsh service? The key is that Torah, even though it is the greatest pleasure and joy in the world, begins as a burden that must be borne. In proportion to how sincerely and intensely one accepts the burden, that is how much he is freed from the yoke of government. Whoever earnestly carries the Torah *with all his strength* merits immediate and total freedom from the other yoke; those who bear the Torah half-heartedly receive only partial freedom from the yoke of government."

The Chofetz Chaim would give practical counsel based on the wisdom of this mishnah: Since everyone must have cares and worries in life, it makes more sense to carry the burden of *spiritual* struggles, which ultimately lead to blessing and happiness, rather than to waste our efforts on mundane cares, which drain a person emotionally and offer little in return.

⋙ **To whom will you pay?** According to *Mikveh Yisrael,* this mishnah speaks of those who bear the financial burden of supporting Torah scholars and institutions. As reward for assuming this yoke, they will merit Divine help in their business affairs, thus earning the necessary money to pay their government taxes and their household expenses. However, if they are not working for God by endowing Torah causes, they will have to bear the full brunt of the yoke of government (taxes) and the yoke of worldly responsibilities (domestic expenditures).

God needs loyal soldiers. If one does not serve in His army, he will have to serve in somebody else's army.

affairs will be blessed, alleviating the burden of earning a living.

The Talmud teaches that when Jews act in accordance with God's will, their toil is assumed by others [thus freeing their time and energy for spiritual activities]. However, when they do not follow His will, their work will be burdensome and physically difficult (*Berachos* 35b).

The righteous person who accepts the yoke of Torah will find disproportionately great success in the small effort he expends to earn a living. Furthermore, since he is satisfied with his lot, he needs little and does not suffer the anxiety of worldly concerns (*R' Yonah*).

This mishnah has halachic ramifications. See *Shabbos* 114a, which obligates the citizens of a city to assist Torah scholars and free them from the yoke of worldly responsibilities from him. Likewise, municipal taxes for protective items (walls, doors, bridges, guards, etc.) are not to be collected from Torah scholars (see *Rambam, Hilchos Sh'cheinim* 6:6). [Of course, this is only relevant when a Jewish Torah-oriented government is in power.] The Talmud (*Bava Basra* 8a) relates that Darius absolved the Men of the Great Assembly (see 1:1) from paying royal taxes since they were involved in God's work (see *Ezra* 7:24).

Rabbi Gifter qualifies this exemption: Only a Torah scholar who deeply believes in the protective power of Torah and views his learning as a shield against harm is entitled to the exemption accorded those who provide the nation with its lifeblood.

וְכָל הַפּוֹרֵק מִמֶּנּוּ עֹל תּוֹרָה — *But if someone throws off the yoke of Torah from himself.* This refers to

⋖⋗ **Applying the experience.** *Bnai Yissaschar* gives an interesting interpretation on the stich in the *Hoshana* prayers, כְּבוּשָׁה בַּגּוֹלָה לוֹמֶדֶת יִרְאָתֶךְ, *Oppressed in exile, they learn to fear you.* He cites this as an example of Israel's ability to transform all of life's experiences into lessons on the service of God, rendering, "Oppressed in exile, they [use the experience] to learn to fear You." The same thought is reflected in this mishnah. The governments and kingdoms of the world exist in order for us to take the fear we have for them as an example for how we should fear God. One who assumes the yoke of Torah and has internalized the lesson need not be subject to the yoke of government.

⋖⋗ **Like deer, like man.** This sentiment is expressed in the words of R' Shimon ben Elazar: "I have yet to see a deer spreading figs to dry, or a lion serving as a porter, or a fox engaged as a shopkeeper; yet they are sustained without trouble, even though they were created only to serve me. Certainly I should be supported without having to endure any trouble. However, since I have engaged in bad behavior, I have brought about restrictions on my livelihood" (*Kiddushin* 82b). One who accepts the yoke of Torah is in fact sustained without trouble.

In light of this principle, a rather puzzling incident in the Talmud (*Eruvin* 22a) becomes readily understandable. As Rav Adda bar Masna was leaving home to travel to a Torah academy, his wife asked how she should feed their young children in his absence. He said to her, "Are there no more reeds and wild vegetables in the marsh?" On the surface, this seems to be a cruel remark; did he not care for his family? The *Maggid* of Mezritch explains: Of course Rav Adda did not mean that his wife should feed the children grass. He intended to open her eyes to an important reality: Just as God provides wild grass for the animals without any effort on their part, so He will, in the merit of our spiritual efforts, provide us our necessities with limited or even no toil on our part.

⋖⋗ **A taste of freedom.** Even while in exile, under the dominion of foreign powers, a Jew can experience a taste of freedom and redemption by accepting the yoke of Torah. Likewise, even one who must work hard to earn his bread may break the shackles of this drudgery by embracing one of the Torah's fundamental *mitzvos* — Shabbos. God granted us Shabbos as a day of rest, a time to reorder our priorities. By devoting the day to Torah study, we can free ourselves of a psychological enslavement to our weekday work routine. Thus, one who accepts upon himself the yoke of Torah will be mentally absolved of the yoke of government and the yoke of worldly responsibilities — even though he is physically oppressed by his mortality and his struggle for survival (*Sfas Emes*).

[ז] רַבִּי חֲלַפְתָּא בֶּן דּוֹסָא אִישׁ כְּפַר חֲנַנְיָא אוֹמֵר: עֲשָׂרָה שֶׁיּוֹשְׁבִין וְעוֹסְקִין בַּתּוֹרָה, שְׁכִינָה שְׁרוּיָה בֵינֵיהֶם, שֶׁנֶּאֱמַר: „אֱלֹהִים נִצָּב בַּעֲדַת אֵל.״ וּמִנַּיִן אֲפִילוּ חֲמִשָּׁה? שֶׁנֶּאֱמַר: „וַאֲגֻדָּתוֹ עַל אֶרֶץ יְסָדָהּ.״

one who claims that the yoke of Torah is too difficult and restrictive for him to carry. "I am unready and unable to place my neck in its yoke," he claims (*Rav, Rambam*).

Another explanation is that this is one who [without legitimate excuse (*Tiferes Yisrael*)] fritters away his time in trivial pursuits rather than concentrating his efforts on Torah and *mitzvos* (*Meiri*).

**נוֹתְנִין עָלָיו עֹל מַלְכוּת וְעֹל דֶּרֶךְ אֶרֶץ — *the yoke of government and the yoke of worldly responsibilities are placed upon him.* Man must toil at something — *For man was born to toil* (*Job* 5:7); if not at Torah, he will be forced to toil for the government or to provide for his worldly needs (*Magen Avos*). One who cuts back on the time he allots for Torah pursuits in order to amass wealth will not achieve his aim, for God will create political circumstances that will leave him with no more money and much more heartache. Likewise, one who shuns the sweet shackles of Torah will search far and wide for his daily bread but will experience great difficulty in

finding it; and even when he succeeds, he will not derive satisfaction from his lot in life, for *a lover of money will never be satisfied with money* (*Ecclesiastes* 5:9). He will spend his life in the never-ending pursuit of money, a heavy yoke of worldly responsibility from which one never has rest (*R' Yonah*).

The Jew bears a dual burden: The government of the country in which he resides imposes upon him a burden because it treats him as a stranger; secondly, he bears the burden entailed by day-to-day secular living. He who harnesses all of his thoughts and actions in the service of the Torah will not feel oppressed by these burdens. In fact, he will accept and bear them cheerfully as part of the purpose ordained for him by God Himself. He who shirks the Torah service which he owes God may indeed imagine that he has freed himself; however, once he has cast off the yoke of the Law, he will lack the staying power which can be derived from serving the Torah; he will lack that serene contentment and vitality which can be gained only through service of the Torah (*R' S. R. Hirsch*).

Mishnah 7

**רַבִּי חֲלַפְתָּא בֶּן דּוֹסָא אִישׁ כְּפַר חֲנַנְיָא אוֹמֵר — *Rabbi Chalafta ben Dosa of Kfar Chanania says.* A fifth-generation *Tanna* and a student of R' Meir, R' Chalafta resided in Kfar Chanania (present-day Kfar Aina), a town on the border between the upper and lower Galilee (*Bava Metzia* 94a).

**עֲשָׂרָה שֶׁיּוֹשְׁבִין וְעוֹסְקִין בַּתּוֹרָה — *If ten people sit together and engage in Torah study.* The number ten signifies completeness. [All numbers up to ten can be added to, but ten is a complete set. The number eleven, for example, consists of one which is added to ten, and so on.] God's Presence similarly creates

> **◆§ No time for sin.** The term נוֹתְנִין עָלָיו, literally *it is given to him,* is used here because these yokes are, in their own way, a gift from Heaven. If man were to be without any sense of burden, his life would veer recklessly out of control. God therefore gives him worries and difficulties, leaving him no time or energy for sin or foolishness (*R' Moshe of Kobrin*). R' Mendel of Kotzk used to tell his followers: "I don't want you to refrain from sin because you have no desire; I want you simply to have no time for such nonsense."
>
> Many of the great *Tannaim* held menial jobs as a source of support. Are we to assume that they, God forbid, threw off the yoke of Torah?! R' Mendel of Kotzk explained that one who bears the yoke of Torah will not sense that earning a living is a burden. If he throws off the yoke of Torah, however, he will find providing for himself and his family an insufferable load.

7. Rabbi Chalafta ben Dosa of Kfar Chanania says: If ten people sit together and engage in Torah study, the Divine Presence is present among them, as it is said: *God stands in the assembly of God* (*Psalms* 82:1). How do we know this [is true] even of five? For it is said: *He has established His bundle upon earth* (*Amos* 9:6).

---

completeness in an incomplete and flawed world. Hence, ten persons involved in Torah merit the Presence of God (*Maharal*).

Rav quotes an alternative text: The ten people are those who sit as a court. The continuation of the text cited in proof (see below), *in the midst of judges He shall judge* (*Psalms* 82:1), which refers directly to judges, would seem to bear this out.

שְׁכִינָה שְׁרוּיָה בֵּינֵיהֶם — *the Divine Presence is present among them.* They are afforded the opportunity to sense the presence of God's honor according to their spiritual level (*Meiri*). They will merit Divine assistance and enlightenment in understanding God's wisdom (*Tiferes Yisrael*).

Magen Avos notes that the Talmud (*Berachos* 6a), in teaching of the power of ten in prayer, employs the term עִמָּהֶם, the Divine Presence is *with them,* while here the mishnah speaks of the *Shechinah* resting *among* them. Prayer is a *mitzvah* whose merit protects man only while he is involved in it. The Divine Presence is therefore *with them* while they pray; when the group disbands, the Divine Presence, so to speak, departs. Not so when ten people are engaged in words of Torah. Its protective aura and merit remain even after they are no longer involved in study. Therefore, the Divine Presence remains *among* them, i.e., in the place where they studied, awaiting their return.

שֶׁנֶּאֱמַר: ,,אֱלֹהִים נִצָּב בַּעֲדַת אֵל" — *as it is said: "God stands in the assembly of God"* (*Psalms* 82:1). Any group of at least ten men involved in prayer or Torah study is deemed a Divine assembly.

That the term עֵדָה refers to a group of ten people is derived from the incident of the spies in the Wilderness, who returned from their mission to Israel and spoke critically of the Land. God asked: *How long for this evil "assembly" that provokes complaints against Me?* (*Numbers* 14:27). Of the twelve spies, only Caleb and Joshua spoke favorably of the land; the other ten slandered it. Thus, when God expressed His anger at the *assembly*, he was referring to the ten, indicating that the word עֵדָה, *assembly,* means a group of ten (*Rashi, R' Yonah, Rambam;* based on *Berachos* 21b).

וּמִנַּיִן אֲפִלּוּ חֲמִשָּׁה? שֶׁנֶּאֱמַר: ,,וַאֲגֻדָּתוֹ עַל אֶרֶץ יְסָדָה" — *How do we know this [is true] even of five? For it is said: "He has established His bundle upon earth"* (*Amos* 9:6). A bundle is something that can be grasped by the five fingers of one hand. Hence, a group of five involved in Torah study is deemed God's "bundle." The proof-verse from *Amos* begins *He Who builds His attics in Heaven.* Thus, the entire verse implies that God descends from His abode in Heaven to join His "bundle" on earth (*Rav, Rambam*).

Often the hand itself is called אֲגוּדָּה because of its five fingers (*R' Yonah*).

Meiri cites a text in which the proof-verse is *In the midst of judges He shall judge* (*Psalms* 82:1). The minimum number of people in a court case is five: three judges and two litigants. The verse from *Psalms* therefore proves that five involved in judgment (and certainly in Torah study) enjoy the company of the Divine Presence, for God comes to assist them in their deliberation.

See *Succah* 13a and *Tosafos* ad loc., s.v. אגד, which discusses the relative merits of the two versions.

◄§ **Two degrees of Divine Presence.** R' Shneur Zalman of Liadi writes (*Iggeres HaKodesh* 23): "I was taught by my teachers that were an angel to be found in the presence of ten Jews, even if they were not speaking words of Torah, the angel would be overcome by such unbearable fright from the Divine Presence which rests upon them that it would cease to exist. This Divine Presence which is present in collective prayer is something man can sense — but the Divine Presence that rests upon ten men involved in Torah study is too exalted for human beings to sense."

וּמִנַּיִן אֲפִילוּ שְׁלֹשָׁה? שֶׁנֶּאֱמַר: ,,בְּקֶרֶב אֱלֹהִים יִשְׁפֹּט.'' וּמִנַּיִן אֲפִילוּ שְׁנַיִם? שֶׁנֶּאֱמַר: ,,אָז נִדְבְּרוּ יִרְאֵי יהוה אִישׁ אֶל רֵעֵהוּ וַיַּקְשֵׁב יהוה וַיִּשְׁמָע.'' וּמִנַּיִן אֲפִילוּ אֶחָד? שֶׁנֶּאֱמַר: ,,בְּכָל הַמָּקוֹם אֲשֶׁר אַזְכִּיר אֶת שְׁמִי, אָבוֹא אֵלֶיךָ וּבֵרַכְתִּיךָ.''

[ח] **רַבִּי** אֶלְעָזָר אִישׁ בַּרְתּוֹתָא אוֹמֵר: תֶּן לוֹ מִשֶּׁלּוֹ, שָׁאַתָּה וְשֶׁלְּךָ שֶׁלּוֹ; וְכֵן בְּדָוִד הוּא אוֹמֵר:

וּמִנַּיִן אֲפִילוּ שְׁלֹשָׁה? שֶׁנֶּאֱמַר: ,,בְּקֶרֶב אֱלֹהִים יִשְׁפֹּט'' — *How do we know this [is true] even of three? For it is said: "In the midst of judges He shall judge"* (*Psalms* 82:1). I.e., God Himself is present when judges are taking up a case.

The minimum number of judges for a court is three (*Rambam, R' Yonah*). Again citing an alternative text, *Rashi, Rav,* and *Meiri* bring the verse in *Amos* (9:6), *He has established His bundle on earth,* as proof of a Divine Presence even among three. The term אֲגוּדָה (or אֲגֻד) indicates a bundle of three elements. One example is the *lulav* (palm branch), which is bound together with willow and myrtle branches on Succos. Another is the hyssop (אֲגוּדַת אֵזוֹב) used to spread the blood of the pesach offering on the doorposts, which was also comprised of three stalks (see *Exodus* 12:22 and *Rashi* ad loc.).

וּמִנַּיִן אֲפִילוּ שְׁנַיִם? שֶׁנֶּאֱמַר: ,,אָז נִדְבְּרוּ יִרְאֵי ה' אִישׁ אֶל רֵעֵהוּ וַיַּקְשֵׁב ה' וַיִּשְׁמָע'' — *How do we know this [is true] even of two? For it is said: "Then those who fear HASHEM spoke to one another, and HASHEM listened and heard"* (*Malachi* 3:16). The word וַיַּקְשֵׁב indicates intent listening. When two people join in

a spiritual partnership, God, so to speak, "eavesdrops" on them, listening intently to their words of holiness and allowing His Divine Presence to join them (*Magen Avos*).

וּמִנַּיִן אֲפִילוּ אֶחָד? שֶׁנֶּאֱמַר: ,,בְּכָל הַמָּקוֹם אֲשֶׁר אַזְכִּיר אֶת שְׁמִי, אָבוֹא אֵלֶיךָ וּבֵרַכְתִּיךָ'' — *How do we know this [is true] even of one? For it is said: "In every place where I cause My Name to be mentioned, I will come to you and bless you"* (*Exodus* 20:21). Even a solitary student of God's word enjoys His Presence. God's Presence is with any person in whose heart resides the intelligence and sensitivity to mention His Name. The singular usage *will come to "you"* in the verse of proof indicates that even one person is intended (*Rashi*).

Since even a single individual merits the Divine Presence when he is engaged in matters of the soul, why does the mishnah enumerate groups of two, three, five, and ten? *R' Yonah* explains: The more people who join in the performance of a good deed, the greater is its cumulative value; a multitude studying Torah together is better than an unassembled group of individuals (see *Berachos* 6a for an alternative explanation).

---

 musical⁀§ **Exponential growth.** King Solomon describes Torah as being dearer than pearls and diamonds (*Proverbs* 3:15). The Chofetz Chaim comments: The monetary value of diamonds goes up exponentially, depending on the number of carats. If a one-carat stone is worth a thousand dollars, a two-carat stone is valued at much more than two thousand dollars, and a five- carat diamond is worth at least thirty times that amount; the increase in value is disproportionate to the increase in size. Good deeds performed by a large group of people are similar. Their value is increased many times over as the number of participants increases.

3/8

How do we know this [is true] even of three? For it is said: *In the midst of judges He shall judge* (Psalms 82:1). How do we know this [is true] even of two? For it is said: *Then those who fear HASHEM spoke to one another, and HASHEM listened and heard* (Malachi 3:16). How do we know this [is true] even of one? For it is said: *In every place where I cause My Name to be mentioned, I will come to you and bless you* (Exodus 20:21).

8. Rabbi Elazar of Bartosa says: Give Him from His Own, for you and your possessions are His. And so has David said:

Mishnah 8

רַבִּי אֶלְעָזָר אִישׁ בַּרְתּוֹתָא אוֹמֵר — *Rabbi Elazar of Bartosa says.* R' Elazar ben Yehudah of Bartosa, a Tanna of the third generation, was a colleague of R' Akiva and a student of R' Yehoshua (*Tevul Yom 3:4-5*). He was so famed for his magnanimity that charity collectors actually hid from him out of fear that he would donate his last penny. The Talmud reports that he once met a charity collector while on the way to purchase a trousseau for his daughter. The collector tried to run away, but R' Elazar accosted him and forced him to reveal the cause for which he was collecting. When told that it was for the weddings of orphans, he declared, "They come first" and proceeded to hand over almost all of his money (*Taanis 24a*; see *Maharsha* ad loc.).

תֵּן לוֹ מִשֶּׁלוֹ, שֶׁאַתָּה וְשֶׁלְּךָ שֶׁלּוֹ — *Give Him from His Own, for you and your possessions are His.* Man should withhold neither himself nor his wealth from being used to fulfill the wishes of Heaven. All that he has and is belongs to God; hence, he gives not his own, but is merely returning to God what is His (*Rav*). This is a call against stinginess in matters of charity or expenditures for *mitzvos*. Realizing he is spending God's money and not his own, man should give happily and magnanimously (*Meiri*).

All man's wealth is given to him by God for safekeeping. Unlike human depositors, God allows man to use part of the deposit for his personal needs, but the rest must certainly be used only according to the Depositor's instructions (*R' Yonah*).

God only asks man to give back *part* of what He bestows upon him: *from His,* מִשֶּׁלוֹ, i.e., part of His. All one's strength comes from God, yet He demands only part of it back. "Spend *part* of your time at the task of Torah study," God asks of man. "All your wealth comes from My coffers, yet I ask that only part of it be returned to the destitute who collect on *My* behalf" (*Ruach Chaim*).

The Midrash teaches: [God says to man:] "Were you able to affix a *mezuzah* before I gave you a house? Did you have a place for *tzitzis* fringes before I gave you a garment?" (*Vayikra Rabbah 27:2*).

Even talents should not be perceived as one's own. If one is blessed from Heaven with any talent or ability — be it wealth, strength, a good memory, artistic or musical ability, or intelligence — he

⊷§ Jews throughout the generations were able to find the strength of character to offer themselves to God in martyrdom because they viewed life through the lens of this inspiring principle. When God calls on man to make the ultimate sacrifice, man must understand that he is being asked to return to God what is really His (*Midrash Shmuel*). [It is for this reason that Jewish law prohibits suicide. Man does not "own" his own life. Life itself is a safekeeping entrusted to him to be employed and invested according to the will of the Depositor. Man has no right to squander, misappropriate, or willingly relinquish the deposit of life.]

[ט] **רַבִּי** יַעֲקֹב אוֹמֵר: הַמְהַלֵּךְ בַּדֶּרֶךְ וְשׁוֹנֶה, וּמַפְסִיק

---

should employ it only for Heavenly goals. Ulti- mately, it is not really his, merely a grant in trust from the Source of all abilities and talents (*Tiferes Yisrael*).

As a practical matter, the mishnah advises us to separate funds immediately from our income and earmark them for charity. Thus, when the destitute or representatives of institutions come to solicit, one will

⋖§ **Escrow agent.** *Lev Avos* renders our mishnah as *Give him* [the poor man] *what is his, for you and your possessions are* [really] *his.* All the money one dispenses for charity actually belongs to the poor man. The benefactor is only God's agent, and he must provide the poor man with the sustenance that really is his; hence, even the benefactor himself is in some sense the property of the destitute.

Toldos Yaakov Yosef elaborates: The Talmud (*Bava Basra* 131b) teaches that if a person bequeaths all his property to only one of his sons, we assume that he meant to appoint that son as a legal guardian to distri- bute the inheritance to all the children. We make the assumption that no one would act so inequitably with his own children. Nonetheless, God differentiated between *His* children, bestowing wealth on some and depriving others. Can it be that God does not follow His own Torah? The answer is that the wealthy are really legal guardians appointed by God to distribute a fair share to *all* of His children, just as the single heir must distribute his father's property among his siblings. When the wealthy provide for the poor, they really are giving them what is rightfully theirs: *For you and* [what you think are] *your possessions are* [really] *his.*

⋖§ **Realistic humility.** This mishnah sheds light on the true definition of humility. Moses certainly believed in the thirteen *Ani Maamin* principles of faith, including the credo that Moses was the greatest of all prophets — and yet the Torah teaches that he was the most humble of all men (*Numbers* 12:3). How is this possible?

The Steipler Gaon explained: If a destitute woman were to borrow an elegant gown to attend a wedding, she certainly would not spend the evening bragging about "her" dress. She knows it is not hers and that tomorrow morning she must return it to its owner. Similarly, a portfolio manager may handle millions of dollars, yet he knows he is merely playing with someone else's fortune; at the end of the day he must return the money with every penny accounted for.

God endows man with a living soul and invests him with many abilities and talents — but it is all on loan, to be wisely invested on God's behalf and eventually returned to Him.

Humility does not mean being oblivious to one's unique capabilities; it is the recognition that one's uniqueness is on loan, and that such a loan cannot be a source of personal pride. Moses had no doubt that he was the greatest of all prophets; but he knew also that his prophecy was a gift from God.

A puzzling comment in the Talmud assumes new meaning in this light. The Talmud (*Sotah* 49b) states that humility ended when R' Yehudah *HaNasi* died. R' Yosef objected: "Do not speak of the death of true humility, for I am still alive."

R' Yosef's comment, however, reflects the paradoxical understanding that one can be conscious of his talents and yet be humbly aware that they are no cause for pride. Such a person knows that all his abilities are on loan, to be used properly during his lifetime. R' Yosef was actually speaking of his own unimportance, and his statement can be read thus: "Humility is not dead, for I know that everything I am *comes from Him.*"

Even **time** is a loan from God. Often, one's business and social obligations leave him no time for any spiritual activity during the workweek; but on Shabbos, a day which he may spend productively in Torah study, he may be reluctant to give up his "free time" for spiritual pursuits, feeling that he must relax. It is in response to this attitude that our mishnah teaches: *Give Him from His own* — use the leisure time He provides you for His purposes, *for you and your possessions*; the Shabbos day of rest *are His* — God gave us the Day of Rest for relaxation from our mundane concerns, not from spiritual affairs (*R' Yosef Chaim of Baghdad*).

For everything is from You, and from Your Own Hand we have given You (I Chronicles 29:14).

9. Rabbi Yaakov says: One who walks on the road while reviewing [a Torah lesson] and interrupts his review,

---

feel no remorse in parting with the funds since he already considers them the property of the poor (*Pri Chaim*). For this reason, many people follow the commendable practice of keeping a separate *maaser* (charity tithe) account, and to deposit a tenth of their earnings in it as soon as they are paid. Then, when they write out their charity checks, they are truly not taking it from their own funds.

— וְכֵן בְּדָוִד הוּא אוֹמֵר: ,,כִּי מִמְּךָ הַכֹּל, וּמִיָּדְךָ נָתַנּוּ לָךְ'' — *And so has David said: "For everything is from You, and from Your Own Hand we have given You" (I Chronicles 29:14).* King David said this about the gold and silver he collected for the building of the Temple (*Rashi*).

The verse cited is an allusion — not an absolute proof — to the concept expressed in the mishnah. One might argue that one's income and possessions must be returned to God only for such causes as the building of the Temple, because the entire Jewish public was responsible to erect it (*Derech Chaim*).

The verse from *I Chronicles* cited in the mishnah begins with King David's statement: *For who am I and who are my people that we gathered enough strength* [i.e., wealth] *to donate so magnanimously?* Only due to the grace of God were we blessed with such a fortune. Nonetheless, we do not perceive this fortune as our own; it is from Your hand that we take, to give back to You (*Malbim, I Chronicles ad loc.*).

Mishnah 9

רַבִּי יַעֲקֹב אוֹמֵר — *Rabbi Yaakov says.* *Tosafos Yom Tov* identifies him as R' Yaakov Kurshai, the father of R' Eliezer ben Yaakov and a teacher of R' Yehudah *HaNasi* (see *Yerushalmi Shabbos* 10:5). He displayed his loyalty to his colleague Rabban Shimon ben Gamliel by thwarting the plans of R' Meir and R' Nosson to embarrass him. Having overheard their plan to question his friend on the difficult tractate *Uktzin*, he purposely studied the subject aloud, within hearing distance of Rabban Shimon. Noting R' Yaakov's strange behavior, Rabban Shimon also began to study *Uktzin*. The following day, when R' Meir and R' Shimon arrived, Rabban Shimon was well prepared (see *Horayos* 13b).

R' Yaakov taught that reward for the performance of commandments is given only in the World to Come — the world which is completely good and endlessly long (see *Chullin* 142a and *Kiddushin* 39b). One of his most famous statements is: "He who is without a wife lacks goodness, assistance, joy, and atonement" (*Bereishis Rabbah* 17).

Some texts attribute this mishnah to R' Shimon, but *R' Yonah* and *Tosafos Yom Tov* reject this (see *Tosafos Yom Tov*).

הַמְהַלֵּךְ בַּדֶּרֶךְ וְשׁוֹנֶה, וּמַפְסִיק מִמִּשְׁנָתוֹ — *One who walks on the road while reviewing [a Torah lesson] and interrupts his review.* Since danger lurks on the road, the interruption of Torah study under such circumstances is a particularly grave error. By forfeiting the protective power of Torah, one leaves oneself vulnerable to the dangers. Alternatively, this dictum is equally applicable at home, but the

---

⋦§ At the end of his prayer King David adds the following request: *May You preserve this forever as the realization of the thoughts in the heart of Your people, and may You direct their heart toward You (I Chronicles 29:18).* Even man's will to serve God and to grow spiritually is God given. King David prays: "Since You, God, are Eternal, we ask that You always give us the inspiration to serve You wholeheartedly, and to give You reason to be happy with us. Prepare and direct our hearts so that we always seek Your love and closeness" (*R' Tzadok HaKohen*).

מִמִּשְׁנָתוֹ, וְאוֹמֵר: ,,מַה נָּאֶה אִילָן זֶה! וּמַה נָּאֶה נִיר זֶה!" —
מַעֲלֶה עָלָיו הַכָּתוּב כְּאִלּוּ מִתְחַיֵּב בְּנַפְשׁוֹ.

[יז] רַבִּי דּוֹסְתַּאי בַּר יַנַּאי מִשּׁוּם רַבִּי מֵאִיר אוֹמֵר:

mishnah uses a situation where interruption is most likely to occur — on the road, where one is easily distracted (*Tosafos Yom Tov*, see *Magen Avos*).

The obligation to study God's Word is constant and all-encompassing: *You shall speak of them while you sit in your home, while you walk on the way, when you retire, and when you arise* (*Deuteronomy* 6:7). In response to this constant focus, the Torah spreads its protection over man. As long as he does not allow himself to be distracted, his Torah knowledge shields him from danger. This is the import of the words of the Wise Man (*Proverbs* 6:22): *When you walk it shall lead you, when you lie down it shall watch over you* (*Machzor Vitry*).

וְאוֹמֵר: ,,מַה נָּאֶה אִילָן זֶה! וּמַה נָּאֶה נִיר זֶה!" — *and exclaims: "How beautiful is this tree! How beautiful is this plowed furrow!"* This is a common form of interruption. When he is on the road, man tends to be distracted by the attractions of the scenery. Alternatively, the mishnah teaches that even the recognition of God as Creator, which results from taking note of the wonders of nature (see *Berachos* 58b), is an unjustified distraction from Torah study (*Rav*).

The great Chassidic masters explained the mishnah in a novel but penetrating fashion: One who becomes enraptured by his own growth during study (he interrupts his study to note "how beautiful is this tree") has forfeited his soul.

מַעֲלֶה עָלָיו הַכָּתוּב — *Scripture considers it.* *Rashi* and *R' Yonah* delete the phrase *Scripture considers it,* since the mishnah cites no verse as proof of the point. Their text reads: *it is considered.* *Maharal* suggests that the verse cited in the next mishnah, *But beware for yourself and guard your soul exceedingly, lest you forget the things your eyes have seen* (*Deuteronomy* 4:9), is in fact the Scriptural source referred to here. *Midrash Shmuel* cites as the proof text הַקֹּטְפִים מַלּוּחַ עֲלֵי שִׂיחַ, *those who scrape moss from the trees* (*Job* 30:4). This verse is interpreted in the Talmud (*Avodah Zarah* 3b) as a reference to those who interrupt their Torah studies with casual talk and idle chatter (see *Rashi* ad loc.).

Since *Targum* (*Job*, ibid.) interprets the verse in this sense, its meaning is obvious. Hence, the mishnah saw no need to quote the verse, relying on the reader's basic knowledge of Scripture (*Tosafos Yom Tov*).

⊷§ **Mind your focus.** The Talmud teaches: When a teacher is involved in the study of one Talmudic tractate or area of research, one should not make inquiries of him regarding a different tractate or area (*Shabbos* 3b). True Torah study allows for no distraction; all of one's faculties must be entirely committed to this pursuit, with no room for any other involvements — even the study of another area of Torah.

This exclusivity of focus is alluded to in the Talmud (*Shabbos* 88b), which teaches that upon utterance of each of the Ten Commandments, the entire cosmos became filled with sweet incense. Only a wind specially released by God cleared out space for the next utterance, a clear indication of the all-encompassing concentration needed to understand Torah concepts. [According to many commentators, the dictum "one may not do *mitzvos* in bundles" (see *Sotah* 8a) is based on this concept (see *Moed Kattan* 8b and Tosafos ad loc., s.v. לפי).] When one is involved in the performance of a *mitzvah* or particular area of Torah study, it stakes a claim of exclusive rights to all his energies, time, and concentration. At that moment there can be no room in his life for anything else — even a second *mitzvah*, unless, of course, the halachah requires that the other *mitzvah* should be performed without delay.

Upon the death of R' Moshe of Kobrin, his students were asked: "What was the main focus of your teacher?" They replied: "Whatever good deed he was busy with at the moment was the focus of his total being."

and exclaims: "How beautiful is this tree! How beautiful is this plowed furrow!" — Scripture considers it as if he bears guilt for his soul.

10. Rabbi Dostai bar Yannai says in the name of Rabbi Meir:

כְּאִלּוּ מִתְחַיֵּב בְּנַפְשׁוֹ — *as if he bears guilt for his soul.* Having relinquished the protection provided one who is immersed in Torah study, he bears responsibility for whatever adversity he suffers on the danger-laden road. [Traveling in olden days was a dangerous exercise] (*Rashi*). Since Torah is God's crown, one must afford it the proper respect. By interrupting his studies with mundane talk, he indicates his lack of awe, thus indicting himself (*R' Yonah*).

The reason for such strong condemnation is that man, by nature, is drawn to the mundane and meaningless, and one seemingly minor interruption could be the first step in a series of distractions, leading ultimately to the rejection of the yoke of Torah (*Meiri*). The Talmud explains the Scriptural analogy of men to fish (see *Habakuk* 1:14): Just as fish die when they come onto dry land, so men die spiritually when they withdraw from Torah (*Avodah Zarah* 3b). One who cuts his link to Torah has severed his spiritual life support (*Magen Avos*).

Mishnah 10

רַבִּי דוֹסְתַּאי בַּר יַנַּאי מִשּׁוּם רַבִּי מֵאִיר אוֹמֵר — *Rabbi Dostai bar Yannai says in the name of Rabbi Meir.* R' Dostai was a fifth-generation *Tanna*. This and his only quoted halachic statement (*Eruvin* 5:4) are both reported in the name of R' Meir, which would seem to indicate that R' Meir was his primary teacher.

Nonetheless, he is quoted in *Tosefta* as reporting in the name of R' Yose (*Taharos* 5:5) and R' Eliezer (*Shabbos* 15:14).

Many of his aggadic statements are cited, among them "One who gives even a penny to a poor person merits to experience the Divine Presence" (*Bava Basra* 10a), which he based on the words of King David: *And I — because of righteousness* [i.e., charity] *I shall behold Your face* (*Psalms* 17:15).

◆§ **Take the high road.** This dictum seems to contradict the principle that observation of natural wonders is a legitimate path to the love and fear of God. *Rambam* writes: "What is the way to attain love and fear of Him? When man contemplates God's great and wondrous creatures and perceives from them His inestimable and endless wisdom, he immediately loves and praises Him and is overcome by an intense desire to know His Great Name. As King David said: *My soul thirsts for the Lord, for the living God* (*Psalms* 42:3). When one ponders these things, he is immediately overtaken by fear, realizing that he is an insignificant, lowly creature who stands with limited intelligence in the face of the One of Perfect Knowledge" (*Hilchos Yesodei HaTorah* 2:2). The answer is that this path to God is nonetheless secondary to the one provided by studying His Torah. [See *Rambam, Sefer HaMitzvos,* Positive Commandments §3.] Therefore, the mishnah warns against abandoning the primary highway to God in order to travel on the back road.

R' Dov Ber of Mezritch offered the following analogy: A royal officer was awarded a diamond-studded crown by the king. The crown was sent to the officer in a package enhanced with an impressive floral bouquet. The officer foolishly began praising the flowers, ignoring the gift of the crown.

◆§ **Wrong pleasure.** One may certainly interrupt his Torah activities in order to earn a living. It is only when the enjoyment of the good life becomes his major focus that he begins to forfeit his soul. The words of the mishnah may be interpreted to reflect this: *One who interrupts his* [Torah] *review and exclaims, "How beautiful is this tree!"* — how beautiful it is to pursue life's pleasures — throws away the entire meaning of his life.

כָּל הַשּׁוֹכֵחַ דָּבָר אֶחָד מִמִּשְׁנָתוֹ, מַעֲלֶה עָלָיו הַכָּתוּב כְּאִלּוּ מִתְחַיֵּב בְּנַפְשׁוֹ, שֶׁנֶּאֱמַר: ,,רַק הִשָּׁמֶר לְךָ, וּשְׁמֹר נַפְשְׁךָ מְאֹד, פֶּן תִּשְׁכַּח אֶת הַדְּבָרִים אֲשֶׁר רָאוּ עֵינֶיךָ.'' יָכוֹל אֲפִילוּ תָקְפָה עָלָיו מִשְׁנָתוֹ? תַּלְמוּד לוֹמַר: ,,וּפֶן יָסוּרוּ מִלְּבָבְךָ כֹּל יְמֵי חַיֶּיךָ'', הָא אֵינוֹ מִתְחַיֵּב בְּנַפְשׁוֹ עַד שֶׁיֵּשֵׁב וִיסִירֵם מִלִּבּוֹ.

R' Dostai offered an analogy to explain why, in the halachic procedures of marriage, man is the active partner while the woman offers passive consent: "One who has lost an item searches for it; the item does not seek its owner." [Eve was created from a part of Adam. Hence, man's spouse is, figuratively, a lost part of himself; in marriage, they are reunited to form an integrated whole] (see *Niddah* 31b).

כָּל הַשּׁוֹכֵחַ דָּבָר אֶחָד מִמִּשְׁנָתוֹ — *Whoever forgets anything of his Torah learning.* Constant review is the key to retaining one's knowledge. The mishnah issues such a harsh indictment on one who forgets due to lack of review (*Rav, R' Yonah*). One is obligated to review his studies regularly in order to minimize the natural process of forgetting. Negligence, indifference, or laziness are not acceptable reasons for forgetfulness, because they are the fault of the student, not out of his control (*Tiferes Yisrael, Midrash Shmuel*). [One must not only study Torah, one must master Torah knowledge and retain it.]

Shulchan Aruch HaGraz (*Yoreh Deah, Talmud Torah* 2:8) rules that one with a memory span of no more than thirty days must review his studies every thirty days rather than proceeding to new material.

Since all areas of Torah knowledge are interconnected, forgetting even one bit of Torah knowledge is a tragedy of colossal proportions (*Midrash Shmuel*). [See *Tosafos Yom Tov* for a possible source for this.]

מַעֲלֶה עָלָיו הַכָּתוּב כְּאִלּוּ מִתְחַיֵּב בְּנַפְשׁוֹ — *Scripture considers it as if he bears guilt for his soul.* Due to lack of review, one may inadvertently issue an incorrect ruling which will cause others to sin. Even though this is unintentional, he bears guilt for his soul since he could have prevented it by reviewing (*R' Yonah, Rav*). Alternatively, the protective power generated by Torah study is only operative if one retains his knowledge. Having forgotten his learning, he is vulnerable to all destructive forces (*Rav*).

שֶׁנֶּאֱמַר: ,,רַק הִשָּׁמֶר לְךָ, וּשְׁמֹר נַפְשְׁךָ מְאֹד, פֶּן תִּשְׁכַּח אֶת הַדְּבָרִים אֲשֶׁר רָאוּ עֵינֶיךָ'' — *as it says: "But beware and guard your soul exceedingly, lest you forget the things your eyes have seen"* (*Deuteronomy* 4:9). According to *Tiferes Yisrael, the things your eyes have seen* cannot be referring to the great miracles that were witnessed by the Israelites in the desert. If so, the injunction would be addressed only to that generation, but not to the later ones

⤖ **Review and prayer.** R' Yosef ibn Nachmias notes: One's initial study of a Torah subject may be rooted in a general thirst for knowledge, or the challenge of the subject matter. *Review,* however, is indicative of studying Torah for its own sake. *Rashi* (*Avodah Zarah* 8a) teaches that one who feels he is forgetting his learning should pray for Divine help in the fourth blessing of the *Shemoneh Esrei* prayer: אַתָּה חוֹנֵן, "You graciously endow man with knowledge and teach insight to a frail mortal. Endow us graciously from Yourself with wisdom, insight, and knowledge."

⤖ **Forgetting the One.** *Avodas Yisrael* offers a novel but powerful idea. One who forgets the *One* — i.e., God — while studying Torah has taken the greatest gift in life without giving proper recognition to its Giver. The words *I am HASHEM, your God* (*Exodus* 20:2) were taught to the Jewish people by God Himself, and one who forgets this fundamental fact is spiritually ruined.

3/10 Whoever forgets anything of his Torah learning, Scripture considers it as if he bears guilt for his soul, as it says: *But beware and guard your soul exceedingly, lest you forget the things your eyes have seen* (Deuteronomy 4:9). Does this apply even if [he forgot because] his studies were too difficult for him? [This is not so, for] Scripture says: *And lest they be removed from your heart all the days of your life* (ibid.); thus, one bears no guilt for his soul unless he sits [idly] and [through lack of concentration and review] removes them from his consciousness.

who did not witness those events. It must therefore refer to concepts perceived by the "eye of the mind," namely, one's Torah knowledge.

See, however, *Ramban* to *Deuteronomy* 4:9, as well as his addendum to *Rambam Sefer HaMitzvos,* negative commandments §2, where he indeed interprets the verse as a reference to the *events* surrounding the Sinaitic revelation.

Tikkun Moshe suggests that the proof text is cited merely to prove that one may legitimately be commanded not to forget, even though memory is seemingly an involuntary function.

יָכוֹל אֲפִילוּ תָּקְפָה עָלָיו מִשְׁנָתוֹ — *Does this apply even if [he forgot because] his studies were too difficult for him?* I might think that he is held responsible even if the subject matter was complicated and difficult to remember (*Rav, Rashi*), or was forgotten due to illness (*R' Moshe Alshakar*).

Tiferes Yisrael explains תָּקְפָה מִשְׁנָתוֹ as referring to subject matter so complex that it was not fully understood the first time, and thus with the passage of time was forgotten. One might think that even in such an instance the prohibition of forgetting applies and therefore one must spend even inordinate amounts of time at mastering the subject in order to never forget it.

תַּלְמוּד לוֹמַר: "וּפֶן יָסוּרוּ מִלְּבָבְךָ כֹּל יְמֵי חַיֶּיךָ"; הָא אֵינוֹ מִתְחַיֵּב בְּנַפְשׁוֹ עַד שֶׁיֵּשֵׁב וִיסִירֵם מִלִּבּוֹ — [*This is not so, for*] *Scripture says: "And lest they be removed from your heart all the days of your life"* (ibid.); thus, one bears no guilt for his soul unless he sits [idly] and [through lack of concentration and review] removes them from his consciousness. A person transgresses only if he refrains from review; but if he forgets his learning as a result of sickness or old age, he is absolved of any responsibility, much as he would be for any other unwilling omission [see *Bava Kamma* 28b] (*R' Yonah*).

One should not study matters initially in their full depth and profundity; instead one should clarify in his mind the basic intellectual structure and only afterward seek to master all the minute details and underlying reasons for the law by reviewing [see *Shabbos* 63a]. Only through incessant review does Torah reveal itself to those who seek its secrets [its intimacy] (*Tiferes Yisrael*).

Yerushalmi (*Berachos* 9:5) teaches: "If one forsakes Torah for a day, the Torah forsakes him for two."

⇜ **Forget to live?** A disciple once asked the Chiddushei HaRim for advice on how to remember his Torah studies. The *Rebbe* asked him in return: "Did you ever forget how to eat? Did you ever put a spoonful of food into your ear instead of into your mouth? No! Why not? Because your life depends on eating, and no one can forget an essential life process. Similarly, when a person comes to the realization that Torah is actually keeping him alive, he never forgets a word of his life-giving studies. Thus David said, *I will never forget Your orders, for with them You keep me alive* (Psalms 119:93)."

In a mystical sense, one's Torah insights are an expression of how the word of God filters through his soul. One who develops a new idea in Torah gives expression and life to his own soul; hence, if he forgets anything of *his* own Torah learning, he is deemed guilty for his own soul, for he has extinguished one of its sparks (*Chasdei Avos*).

[יא] **רַבִּי** חֲנִינָא בֶּן דּוֹסָא אוֹמֵר: כָּל שֶׁיִּרְאַת חֶטְאוֹ
קוֹדֶמֶת לְחָכְמָתוֹ, חָכְמָתוֹ מִתְקַיֶּמֶת; וְכֹל
שֶׁחָכְמָתוֹ קוֹדֶמֶת לְיִרְאַת חֶטְאוֹ, אֵין חָכְמָתוֹ מִתְקַיֶּמֶת.

Mishnah 11

רַבִּי חֲנִינָא בֶּן דּוֹסָא אוֹמֵר — *Rabbi Chanina ben Dosa says.* A first-generation Tanna and a student-colleague of Rabban Yochanan ben Zakkai, R' Chanina lived during the end of the Second Temple era. His power of prayer was renowned, and many asked him to intercede on their behalf. When R' Yochanan ben Zakkai's son took ill, he asked R' Chanina ben Dosa to pray on his behalf. Placing his head on his lap (a show of submission), R' Chanina prayed, and the son was saved. When R' Yochanan ben Zakkai's wife asked him why his own supplications were not effective, he replied: "I am like an officer who visits with the King infrequently, while R' Chanina ben Dosa is like a servant who is constantly in the presence of the King and can therefore make requests and be answered" (*Berachos* 34b).

Rabban Gamliel also sent messengers to R' Chanina to pray on behalf of his son. R' Chanina ascended to his attic to pray and afterward told the messengers that they could return, for the son's fever had passed. The messengers noted the time and verified upon their return that in fact the fever had passed at that particular moment, and the sick boy had requested a drink of water (ibid.). [See *Yoma* 53b, *Berachos* 5:5, and *Yevamos* 121b for other examples of the power of his entreaties.]

With his great faith in God, R' Chanina was able to perform many miraculous feats. His daughter once accidentally lit Shabbos candles with vinegar instead of oil. Said R' Chanina: "He [God] Who instructed the oil to burn will instruct the vinegar to burn" — whereupon it promptly did so (*Taanis* 25a). Once a poisonous reptile attacked and killed several people, R' Chanina went to its habitat and placed his foot at the entrance of the reptile's lair. The creature bit his heel and promptly died. R' Chanina brought the dead reptile to the study hall and held it up as evidence that "it is not the reptile that kills; it is sin that kills" [the reptile is only the messenger to mete out God's retribution] (*Berachos* 33a).

A poor man all his life, he bore his poverty with grace and refused to benefit from others. The Talmud (*Taanis* 25a) relates that his wife once found abandoned chickens on their doorstep. In spite of their own bare cupboard, they would not eat the chickens or the eggs they laid. The chickens laid so many eggs that the mess became unbearable. They sold the chickens and bought goats with the money (see *Bava Metzia* 28b), which they eventually returned when they learned the identity of the long-lost owner of the chickens.

They would often have nothing to eat for the Sabbath, yet they went to great lengths to hide this from others. They would light their oven on Friday and let it emit smoke so as to give the impression that they were baking something. R' Chanina's wife fully supported his wish to maintain this lifestyle. Once, they miraculously received a golden table leg in response to her heartrending pleas for Heavenly mercy, but upon dreaming that this gift would diminish their share in the World to Come, she asked her husband to pray that the golden table leg be taken back by Heaven. [See the introduction to *Koheles Rabbah* and *Taanis* 24-25 for more fascinating incidents about this couple.]

The Sages viewed R' Chanina as the person in whose merit the entire generation found favor in God's eyes (*Chagigah* 14a) and about whom a Heavenly voice stated: "The entire world is sustained in the merit of Chanina, My son — while Chanina, My son, subsists on a mere *kab* of carobs from one Friday to the next Friday" (*Taanis* 24b). Upon his passing, the Sages said that men of action and extreme righteousness were no longer to be found (*Sotah* 49b).

11. Rabbi Chanina ben Dosa says: Anyone whose fear of sin takes precedence over his wisdom, his wisdom will endure; but anyone whose wisdom takes precedence over his fear of sin, his wisdom will not endure.

כֹּל שֶׁיִּרְאַת חֶטְאוֹ קוֹדֶמֶת לְחָכְמָתוֹ, חָכְמָתוֹ מִתְקַיֶּמֶת — *Anyone whose fear of sin takes precedence over his wisdom, his wisdom will endure.* This concept is alluded to in the words of the Psalmist: *The beginning of wisdom is the fear of God (Psalms 111:10).*

A goal must always be viewed as having primary importance, while the means to achieve it are relegated to secondary status. One who accords fear of sin priority in his scale of values, and views Torah knowledge as a means to achieve that fear, will reach his goal. His wisdom will endure and be translated into action through a reverent fulfillment of the *mitzvos* (*R' Yonah* and *Rav*).

An apparent contradiction exists between this mishnah and 2:6, where Hillel states, *A boor cannot be fearful of sin,* indicating that wisdom is a *prerequisite* of fear of sin. Based on the interpretation of *R' Yonah*, *Tosafos Yom Tov* and *Magen Avos* resolve the incongruency as follows: One who is a boor, with no potential to achieve wisdom, will indeed never become fearful of sin. However, one who has the potential to become wise in Torah must predicate his intellectual pursuit on a deep emotional commitment to a higher goal: achieving the fear of offending God through sin.

Alternatively, *R' Yonah* suggests that fear of sin must precede one's wisdom and serve as his moral and spiritual compass. His newly acquired wisdom will thus deepen his will to follow the good path to which he is accustomed. *Rashi* renders חָכְמָתוֹ as *his actions.* One who is conscious of a fear of sin and precedes any action by assessing its legitimacy is sure to act properly, thus giving his activities value and permanence.

It is a philosophical truth that a person enjoys the pursuit of knowledge only when it validates his life-style. Hence, he who develops good habits prior to studying will find that his wisdom endures since he will find pleasure in study. However, if he has become habituated to negative behavior, he will shirk the burden of any knowledge which contradicts his way of life (*Rambam*).

Meiri adds that refinement of character is the most effective means to prevent sin, as well as to achieve perfection of the spirit. Wisdom without the fear of sin is like a building without a foundation.

Avos d'Rabbi Nosson (22) draws the following analogy: One who is both wise and fearful of sin is compared to a craftsman who has not only the skill but the tools to create a work of art. The wise person who lacks fear of sin is a craftsman without tools; one who is fearful of sin but lacks wisdom possesses the tools but lacks the skills to use them.

Tiferes Yisrael interprets חָכְמָתוֹ as worldly knowledge. One who approaches secular knowledge with a heightened sense of fear of sin will be able to avoid the subtle pitfalls in issues of faith that sometimes complicate secular disciplines. The knowledge he gains will endure without undermining his faith.

וְכֹל שֶׁחָכְמָתוֹ קוֹדֶמֶת לְיִרְאַת חֶטְאוֹ, אֵין חָכְמָתוֹ מִתְקַיֶּמֶת — *but anyone whose wisdom takes precedence over his fear of sin, his wisdom will not endure.* Knowledge may never serve as an end unto itself if is not accompanied by a level of piety that will make the person appreciate what his wisdom teaches him. But without fear of sin, a person will come to despise the wisdom that tells him not to do what he wishes, or commands him to do what he does not enjoy (*Rav, Rambam, R' Yonah*). One will only succeed in Torah study if he views it as an applied science, which is meant to

---

◆§ **Actualizing abstractions.** *Ramban* (*Emunah U'Bitachon* Chapter 19) homiletically interprets a verse from *Shir HaShirim* (2:7) as emphasizing that Torah knowledge must be realized in practice in the everyday world: אִם תָּעִירוּ וְאִם תְּעוֹרְרוּ אֶת הָאַהֲבָה עַד שֶׁתֶּחְפָּץ, *That you not awaken or stir up the love* [of God] *unless you concretize it,* translating it into action by making it into an *object* (חֵפֶץ).

---

be carried into practice, not as a theoretical discipline (*R' Yonah*).

Wisdom needs to be housed in a proper environment in order to endure. *The fear of Heaven is its storehouse* (Isaiah 33:6); knowledge without fear of sin is meaningless (*Rashi*). Proper ethical development and a sense of awe toward God and His word is the bedrock upon which true knowledge is built. Lacking a solid foundation, the building is certain to crumble (*Meiri*).

The opposite path has serious consequences. If one makes knowledge and human understanding a prerequisite to his fear of sin and is unwilling to refrain from a course of action unless he understands it to be negative, he will never possess enough knowledge to do the right thing. He must develop a fear of sin before acquiring knowledge, and he must follow the path of Torah even if parts of it are temporarily unfathomable due to his limited understanding of right and wrong (*Sefer HaMussar*).

Mishnah 12

הוּא הָיָה אוֹמֵר: כֹּל שֶׁמַּעֲשָׂיו מְרֻבִּין מֵחָכְמָתוֹ, חָכְמָתוֹ מִתְקַיֶּמֶת — *He [R' Chanina ben Dosa] used to say: Anyone whose good deeds exceed his wisdom, his wisdom will endure.* The previous mishnah mandated a strong commitment to refraining from transgression as a precondition to acquiring enduring wisdom; this mishnah refers to a commitment to fulfill *positive* commandments as a prerequisite (*Rav*).

The term מְרֻבִּין, *exceed*, implies greater quantity or importance (*Tosafos Yom Tov*). Thus, one should perform good deeds in greater quantity and frequency and with greater care than is called for by his intelligence. Even if, in a narrow halachic sense, he has no obligation, he should go beyond the demands of the law and his own perceptions and seek to perform deeds that please God,

whether toward God or towards his fellow man (*Meiri*).

In areas of doubt, where one cannot ascertain with his own judgment whether he is obligated to fulfill a certain *mitzvah* or not, he should nevertheless fulfill it (*Midrash Shmuel*). Another explanation is that even when one does not understand the rationale for a *mitzvah*, he must still perform it. One's actions must exceed his limited understanding (*Tiferes Yisrael*).

Rashi renders מִתְקַיֶּמֶת *is of everlasting value.* Only if one's learning results in increased good deeds and charity is the wisdom he acquires of eternal value.

The *mitzvah* of *tefillin* is symbolic of this precept. One places the *tefillin* on the hand first and then on the head; and when he removes them, the *tefillin* of the hand remain on until those of the head are taken off. Thus, the head *tefillin*, representing wisdom, are never worn

⊷§ **No foundation, no house.** R' Chaim Vital suggests that the reason why there is no special *mitzvah* to have good character traits is because these ethical, moral, and social values are the foundation upon which the entire edifice of Torah and *mitzvos* is built. R' Elya Lopian offered the analogy of someone who hired a contractor to build a house for him. They settled on a price and the contractor began work. When he finally finished the house, he presented a bill to the customer, who was surprised to see an additional ten-thousand-dollar fee on it. "Oh," said the builder, "that is for the foundation." "You must be joking," replied the customer. "The initial price we discussed *included* the foundation. It is understood that when one buys a house, he gets the foundation with it; without a foundation the house cannot stand." The Torah need not spell out that one must develop good character, which is the very foundation of Torah. It is self-understood that one must build his life on a solid foundation.

⊷§ **Action before words.** A public figure can have the greatest impact if his words are consistent with his own life-style. Constructive criticism offered by such a person is respected and accepted. Homiletically, therefore, the mishnah teaches that if one's acts are plentiful מֵחָכְמָתוֹ, *as a result of* his wisdom, i.e., he practices what he knows to be true, his wisdom will endure and take root in the hearts of his charges (*Lev Avos*). Since a person's actions speak louder than his words, his actions must exceed his words in their power of persuasion (*Minchas Shabbos*).

without the hand *tefillin,* representing action. Ideas and wisdom are only valuable if they are translated into action.

The question arises, however, that it seems impossible for one's good deeds to exceed his wisdom. Since he cannot act without foreknowledge of what he plans to do, his wisdom perforce must always exceed his deeds. *R' Yonah* explains: On the first day of Nissan, Moses commanded the Children of Israel to bring the Pesach offering on the fourteenth, yet as soon as he finished giving them the commandment, the Torah states, *And the Children of Israel went and did so* (*Exodus* 12:28). The Sages explained that since they took it upon themselves to do so, the Torah credits them as if they had done so immediately (*Mechilta, Bo* 12:2).

[God deems a sincere commitment as a completed act.] A general commitment to fulfill God's *mitzvos*, even those that one may not yet have learned, makes one's actions greater than his knowledge.

Avos d'R' Nosson (22:11) writes: "One whose deeds exceed his wisdom, his wisdom endures, as it is said, *We will do and we will hear*" (*Exodus* 24:7), for the Jews committed themselves to carry out all the commands of the Torah even before they knew what would be demanded of them. The verse from *Exodus* is cited as a perfect example of the principle in our mishnah; for if one commits himself wholeheartedly to the ways of the Torah, he receives merit for what is revealed to him as well as for that which is still unknown, as did Israel

---

⥀ **Intended incident.** As one's understanding of the true meaning of life matures and he better appreciates God's expectations of him, he constantly refines his character and behavior and his increasing wisdom is linked to eternity. However, if his experiences do not change his approach to God, then his wisdom, never fully realized, exceeds his actions. Such wisdom is of negligible value; it is certainly not enduring.

According to R' Menachem Mendel of Vitebsk, this idea sheds light on an enigmatic statement of the Sages (see *Rashi, Numbers* 6:2): "Why is the section regarding a *nazir* placed immediately after that of a *sotah*? To teach that one who sees a *sotah* [an unfaithful wife] degraded [by the terrible punishment visited upon her (see *Numbers* 5:27)] should become a nazirite and abstain from wine, since wine can lead to immoral behavior." If wine leads to immorality, then shouldn't everybody abstain from it? Why is a nazirite vow particularly appropriate for one who witnessed a *sotah's* downfall?

Our mishnah provides the answer. Every human experience, understood properly, is really a lesson from God on how to serve Him better. There are no accidents, only messages. That someone witnessed a *sotah's* downfall was not coincidental; he must analyze the experience and use it to better himself spiritually. Thus he is advised to take on the vow of a *nazir*. If his wisdom exceeds his actions because he does not bring into deed the lessons taught him through his life experiences, the lessons accrue no eternal value.

There is a story of Rabbi Saadiah Gaon which finely illustrates the importance of learning from experience. Rabbi Saadiah was asked by his disciples why he engaged in constant repentance. What sins had he committed? He replied that once, as a traveler, he had spent a day at an inn, where the innkeeper treated him as he would any other guest. The next morning, the leading citizens of the town converged on the inn to greet R' Saadiah and benefit from his wisdom. After they departed, the innkeeper approached him and said tearfully, "Please, Master, forgive me for not serving you properly."

"But you treated me very well. Why do you apologize?"

"I treated you as I treat all my guests. Had I only known yesterday who you were, I would have served you as befits a person of your stature!"

R' Saadiah told his students that the innkeeper's reaction illustrates the feelings that a Jew should have. The innkeeper was not remiss in his behavior, but if he had known the truth a day earlier, he would have acted differently. In our service to God, we should take the same approach. Surely we realize when we are middle aged that our youthful service of God was immature and unsophisticated; if only we knew then what we know now, we would have acted differently. The same holds true when we examine our deeds of yesterday. Every life experience must teach us how to better fulfill our spiritual mission. Should we not repent, therefore, for failing to serve God yesterday as we do today?

חָכְמָתוֹ מִתְקַיֶּמֶת; וְכֹל שֶׁחָכְמָתוֹ מְרֻבָּה מִמַּעֲשָׂיו, אֵין חָכְמָתוֹ מִתְקַיֶּמֶת.

‏[יג] **הוּא הָיָה** אוֹמֵר: כֹּל שֶׁרוּחַ הַבְּרִיּוֹת נוֹחָה הֵימֶנּוּ, רוּחַ הַמָּקוֹם נוֹחָה הֵימֶנּוּ;

at Sinai when they declared, "We will do and we will hear," placing their acceptance of the deed before their hearing of it. Otherwise, it is impossible that a man's deeds can be more than what he knows (*Shaarei Teshuvah* 2:10).

וְכֹל שֶׁחָכְמָתוֹ מְרֻבָּה מִמַּעֲשָׂיו, אֵין חָכְמָתוֹ מִתְקַיֶּמֶת — *but anyone whose wisdom exceeds his good deeds, his wisdom will not endure.* One who does not allow his studies to shape his conduct would do better not to study, for his learning has no real significance. [Furthermore, his knowledge serves as an indictment, since he can no longer claim ignorance as an excuse for his behavior.] He is like someone who sows but does not reap or a woman who gives birth to children only to bury them. So too, one who studies Torah but does not fulfill it brings life to the world — and subsequently buries alive the eternal word of God (*Rashi*).

One who will fulfill only the commandments that he thinks he understands uses his wisdom to limit his commitment to God. Such wisdom is counterproductive and can never flourish. When such a person is tempted to sin, his intellectual understanding of the spiritual danger involved will not keep him on the right path (*Tiferes Yisrael*).

Similarly, wisdom must be employed to create protective fences around the laws of Torah, increasing the pattern of action beyond one's understanding of what is minimally expected of him. If he allows his wisdom to remain static and does not use it to build safeguards against sin, his knowledge is severed from any connection to the Eternal (*Tikkun Moshe*).

Only wisdom attained through toil and activity endures; that which is the result of inborn talent can be easily lost. Hence, the wisdom of one whose actions exceed it will endure; not so for one whose wisdom [i.e., native intelligence] exceeds his good deeds [and efforts in Torah study]. Furthermore, when a person's actions exceed his wisdom because he has achieved beyond his innate abilities, both his wisdom and his abilities are endowed with enduring meaning. However, if one's potential remains greater than his achievements, he allows his wisdom to wither; eventually, it is buried altogether (*Mabit*).

[It is a common tragedy that very bright youngsters excel in younger grades without exerting themselves, because everything comes easy to them, but when they reach higher grade levels they are surpassed by classmates with less innate ability who were forced to concentrate and develop good study habits.]

Mishnah 13

הוּא הָיָה אוֹמֵר: כֹּל שֶׁרוּחַ הַבְּרִיּוֹת נוֹחָה הֵימֶנּוּ, רוּחַ הַמָּקוֹם נוֹחָה הֵימֶנּוּ — *He used to say: If the spirit of one's fellows is pleased with him, the spirit of the Omnipresent is pleased with him.* A person beloved on earth is certainly beloved in Heaven (*Rashi*;

Meiri). A person who is pleasant and honest in his dealings with others becomes a model of the Torah's way of life. Thus he sanctifies God's Name, and the spirit of the Omnipresent is pleased with him (*R' Yonah*).

◆§ **Easy come, easy go.** The Sages taught (see *Nedarim* 81a) that the children of the poor are the most likely to succeed in their Torah studies. The Vilna Gaon explains that this is because they must rely on their own efforts. The children of the wealthy, who can afford tutors and other supports, often rely on them and do not exert the difficult effort needed for success.

wisdom, his wisdom will endure; but anyone whose wisdom exceeds his good deeds, his wisdom will not endure.

13. He used to say: If the spirit of one's fellows is pleased with him, the spirit of the Omnipresent is pleased with him;

The Talmud (*Yoma* 86a) interprets *You shall love HASHEM, your God* (*Deuteronomy* 6:5) as an implied commandment call to make the Name of God beloved among men. Hence, one who causes God to be loved among people by living an exemplary life in all areas earns for himself the reciprocal love of God (*Tiferes Yisrael*).

R' Yosef ibn Nachmias notes that the mishnah does not speak of one who pleases *all* others; such a person certainly cannot be true to himself or to God. There are times when one must stand up and fight those who tear down the authority of the Torah or who weaken Israel's allegiance to the commandments. Our Sages teach that even the great Mordechai of the *Megillah* was only beloved and acceptable to *most* of his brothers (see *Esther* 10:3 and *Rashi* ad loc.).

The use of the word בְּרִיּוֹת, *creatures*, instead of a word that refers specifically to human beings, implies a relationship to the concept of בְּרִיָּה, a *significant* creature which can never be nullified and lose its identity (see *Tosafos, Chullin* 100a, s.v. בריה). *Knesses Yisrael* thus understands the mishnah to mean that one should seek to please people who are worthy of respect, not those who lack the qualities of piety and integrity. Thus, he renders: If *men of spirit* are pleased with someone, the spirit of the Omnipresent is pleased with him. But to be pleasing to sinners is not significant or desirable.

◄§ **Choose your description.** The wife of a rabbi, whose unreciprocated kindness towards his congregants was legendary, once complained to the Chofetz Chaim about the grief she suffered because of her husband's goodness. The Chofetz Chaim replied: "One who is kind by nature suffers from others, while someone with a bad disposition causes *others* to suffer. Is it not preferable that in the next world they say about you, 'This is Rabbi X, who suffered from everyone,' rather than 'This is Rabbi X, who caused everyone to suffer'?"

It is difficult for a spiritual leader to satisfy everyone if he is truly doing his job properly. R' Yisrael Salanter is reputed to have told a student contemplating assuming a rabbinic post: "A rabbi whose congregants don't want to fire him is not a real rabbi; but a rabbi whom they actually fire is not a *mensch*!" The Talmud teaches that when a rabbi is universally loved by his congregants, it is not because of his goodness but because he does not offer them guidance and rebuke in spiritual matters (*Kesubos* 105b).

◄§ **The Divine gift of favor.** *Tosafos Yom Tov* cites as the source of this mishnah the verse: וּמְצָא חֵן וְשֵׂכֶל טוֹב בְּעֵינֵי אֱלֹהִים וְאָדָם, *So you shall find grace and good understanding in the sight of God and man* (*Proverbs* 3:4). *Sfas Emes* questions this verse as the Scriptural source of our mishnah, since its priorities are reversed, listing pleasantness in the eyes of God as a prerequisite to finding favor in the eyes of people. The mishnah, however, seems to give priority to finding favor in the eyes of one's fellows. He explains that it is no small feat to please people and find favor in their eyes. Only one who first finds favor in God's eyes will be blessed with חֵן, the inner charm that makes him pleasant to people.

When Rabbi Chaim Heller resigned his rabbinic post in Lomza after only a few short months, he expressed the difficulty of earning people's favor. "One must first find favor in God's eyes," he said, "and then, and only then, in the eyes of man. In the rabbinate these two tasks are often incompatible."

R' Boruch of Kossov expounded on the idea of God's favor. When God wants Reuben to earn a profit, He puts it into his mind to go to the market and purchase some goods to sell. There he meets Shimon, who has fox skins to sell. God causes the skins to seem substandard in both men's eyes so that Reuben will make a low offer and Shimon will sell it cheaply. The deal is done, and Reuben takes his fox skins home. Along the way, God infuses those same skins with great charm and beauty, in the eyes of both Reuben and his potential customers, so that he is able to fetch a good price for them and earn his living. When man finds favor in God's eyes, God endows him with an unexplainable חֵן, *favor*, in the eyes of others. [The Vilna Gaon explains that חֵן is related to the word חִנָּם, *free*. One becomes beloved in the eyes of another for no identifiable reason — for free.]

וְכֹל שֶׁאֵין רוּחַ הַבְּרִיּוֹת נוֹחָה הֵימֶנּוּ, אֵין רוּחַ הַמָּקוֹם נוֹחָה הֵימֶנּוּ.

[יד] רַבִּי דּוֹסָא בֶּן הָרְכִּינַס אוֹמֵר: שֵׁנָה שֶׁל שַׁחֲרִית, וְיַיִן שֶׁל צָהֳרָיִם, וְשִׂיחַת הַיְלָדִים, וִישִׁיבַת

One who finds favor in the eyes of people is actually pleasing God by making His children happy. A father is most pleased when someone causes his children to rejoice. Certainly God is pleased when man brings joy to the life of another, for every interpersonal *mitzvah* is really a charge from God to take care of His children (*R' Klonymos Kalman of Piaseczna*).

וְכֹל שֶׁאֵין רוּחַ הַבְּרִיּוֹת נוֹחָה הֵימֶנּוּ, אֵין רוּחַ הַמָּקוֹם נוֹחָה הֵימֶנּוּ — *but if the spirit of one's fellows is not pleased with him, the spirit of the Omnipresent is not pleased with him.* One who is lax in his interpersonal duties is by definition deficient in his obligations to God as well (*R' Yonah, Tiferes Yisrael*). In a sense it is even more serious than sins against God, because one cannot atone on Yom Kippur for sins against God unless he seeks forgiveness for his interpersonal transgressions. If his fellow man does not view him favorably, neither does God (*Chavos Yair*).

Proper conduct in interpersonal relationships is Divinely mandated. Thus, pleasing man is a form of pleasing God.

Mishnah 14

רַבִּי דּוֹסָא בֶּן הָרְכִּינַס אוֹמֵר — *Rabbi Dosa ben Harkinas used to say.* A colleague of R' Yochanan ben Zakkai, R' Dosa was blessed with great wealth and longevity, in addition to his great Torah knowledge.

In the introduction to his Mishnah Commentary, Chapter 4, *Rambam* writes that R' Dosa lived from the time of Shimon the Just until the time of R' Akiva (who lived until after the destruction of the Second Temple). *Yuchasin* (see entry *Dosa*) bases this time frame on R' Dosa ben Harkinas's testimony regarding a halachic quandary pondered by Chaggai, Zechariah, and Malachi, who were members of the Great Assembly. [See *A. Heiman, Toldos Tannaim V' Amoraim* (entry *R' Dosa ben Harkinas*) for a full discussion.]

The Talmud records that the Sages received a report that R' Dosa had ruled according to the Academy of Shammai, contrary to the normative *halachah,* which follows the Academy of Hillel, regarding an aspect of levirate marriage [*yibum*]. Because he was elderly and blind, the Sages visited him at home to inquire about the matter. He seated them on golden couches, an indication of his personal fortune. As the matter turned out, the report of his ruling was erroneous; it was his

---

◆§ **How to rebuke.** One should be pleasant toward others even when he offers rebuke. Criticism which attacks the person himself rather than his negative behavior is bound to backfire, while that offered in a palatable way may be very productive. *Shelah* and *Alshich* interpret the verse in *Proverbs* (9:8) in this light: *Do not offer rebuke to a scoffer lest he hate you; chastise a wise man and he will love you.* When offering chastisement, one must take care not to be insulting to the target of his criticism, treating him as if he is a scoffer. Instead one should appeal to the other person's dignity, saying, "You are an intelligent and upstanding individual. Such behavior as you have exhibited in the past is below your dignity and does not befit somebody as wise and special as you." The person will then love you and accept your constructive criticism. When one's words of corrective advice do not find favor in his fellow's eyes, God Himself views with disfavor the fruitless insult hurled upon him (*Baal Shem Tov*).

but if the spirit of one's fellows is not pleased with him, the spirit of the Omnipresent is not pleased with him.

14. Rabbi Dosa ben Harkinas used to say: Late morning sleep, midday wine, children's chatter, and sitting at

younger brother Yonasan, a member of the Academy of Shammai, who had permitted the marriage in question (see *Yevamos* 16a).

R' Chanina ben Dosa is seemingly not his son (see *Heiman* ibid.).

In this mishnah, R' Dosa ben Harkinas lists several pleasurable activities that squander time and distract one from his real mission on earth.

שֵׁנָה שֶׁל שַׁחֲרִית — *Late morning sleep.* I.e., oversleeping the prescribed time for reading the *Shema* or reciting the morning prayers [see *Shulchan Aruch, Orach Chaim* 580 and 89] (*Rav, R' Yonah*). Drawn by the enjoyable relaxation of sleeping late, one may stay in bed during the hours most conducive to spiritual growth (*Rashi*).

The Midrash (*Bereishis Rabbah*) teaches: "Sleep is the beginning of human downfall." Sinking into sleep rather than awakening early to pursue spiritual and practical agendas weakens one's resolve and induces laziness (*Magen Avos*). Other commentaries say that sleep here is a metaphor for excessive relaxation. In moderation, respite is necessary to preserve one's health, and in fact one should be careful to relax after any strenuous activity, be it physical or mental. The mishnah criticizes someone who had a good night's sleep, and has no legitimate excuse for staying in bed late (*Meiri, Tiferes Yisrael*).

וְיַיִן שֶׁל צָהֳרַיִם — *midday wine.* One should refrain from intoxicating drink during the day (*Rashi*). Wine as a stimulant in the morning or as a relaxant in the evening can serve as an aid to man's physical and spiritual welfare. It is midday, when he is fully functioning, that it serves to dull his senses and induce sluggishness (*Tiferes Yisrael*). His mind beclouded by drink, a man can neither study Torah nor exercise proper moral or spiritual judgment. In such a state he is bound to sin (*R' Yonah*). Psychologically, the frequenting of taverns and other places of pleasure induces in one the attitude that life is nothing more than a party, intended purely for physical enjoyment (*Magen Avos*). Enjoyed in moderation, the pleasures of life enable a person to maintain his emotional stability, as well as a healthy sense of *joie de vivre*. These qualities are essential for spiritual activity and growth. It is when "the good life" becomes one's sole reason for existence that he has lost direction (*Meiri, Tiferes Yisrael*).

וְשִׂיחַת הַיְלָדִים — *children's chatter.* This refers to involvement with the foolish pastimes of youth to which men are attracted (*Rashi*). Young people view their elders as role models. If adults engage in childish frivolities, the young will adopt similar behavior and will always remain children. Having misdirected their offspring by example, the adults

⋖§ **Unbridled youthfulness.** The mishnah is an excellent metaphor for constructive activity in the "morning" of one's life — the youthful years. The beauty of youth lies in its impulsive confidence in achieving the impossible. It is a time when one may set the tone for the rest of his life, a time when one makes his greatest push to ascend to the peaks of the spirit. Spiritual slumber is particularly deadly in the morning of one's life.

Some people have the special ability to remain eternally young, always optimistic and hopeful. The Ponevezher Rav (R' Yosef Kahaneman) escaped from the impending Nazi inferno and later went to Israel, where he immediately began planning to rebuild the Torah glory of his town. Standing on a hill in Bnei Brak (present-day sight of the Ponevezher Yeshivah), he declared his intention to build a yeshivah. German Field Marshall Erwin Rommel's army was knocking on the gates of Palestine at that time, and the prospect of building a new yeshivah seemed impossible, even insane. Skeptical bystanders said to him, "Rebbe, you are dreaming." He replied, "You are right, I am dreaming — but I am not asleep."

ג/טו בָּתֵּי כְנֵסִיּוֹת שֶׁל עַמֵּי הָאָרֶץ – מוֹצִיאִין אֶת הָאָדָם מִן הָעוֹלָם.

[טו] רַבִּי אֶלְעָזָר הַמּוֹדָעִי אוֹמֵר: הַמְחַלֵּל אֶת הַקֳדָשִׁים,

leave no legacy of spiritual worth in the world (*Midrash Shmuel*).

Another interpretation is that one's spiritual growth may be retarded if he is overly involved in his children's lives and activities (*Rav, R' Yonah*).

Tiferes Yisrael interprets "children's chatter" as humor which has fallen to a foolish level. Humor and light talk are generally positive tools in the ongoing battle against negativism. [As *R' Aharon of Karlin* said: "Nowhere does the Torah forbid morbidity, yet it is at the root of all transgression; nowhere does the Torah say that to be happy is a *mitzvah*, yet from a joyous heart emanates the motivation to fulfill all the *mitzvos*.] However, when the tone becomes immature, foolish, and — God forbid — base, humor and casual conversation lose their redeeming value (*Tiferes Yisrael*).

Parents frequently express concern about their children's future. Too often their worries are focused on the social and financial security of their offspring, and not on spiritual planning. It is precisely such lack of

forethought that makes this world a missed opportunity for one's children (*Knesses Yisrael*).

וִישִׁיבַת בָּתֵּי כְנֵסִיּוֹת שֶׁל עַמֵּי הָאָרֶץ — *and sitting at gatherings of the ignorant.* Spending time in casual conversation and idle chatter is the pastime of the ignorant. When one frequents places where this is the major occupation, he develops a cavalier attitude toward his spiritual duties (*Rav, R' Yonah*). The light conversation of Torah scholars, on the other hand, is of value, since they speak in a dignified manner even about mundane matters. Furthermore, such talk provides them with a refreshing respite from their rigorous studies. Among the unlearned, however, casual talk usually contains elements of slander, gossip, profanity, off-color humor, and other forms of forbidden speech (*Tiferes Yisrael*).

מוֹצִיאִין אֶת הָאָדָם מִן הָעוֹלָם — *remove a man from the world.* One forfeits the World of Eternity if he becomes enmeshed in the claws of these desensitizing practices (*Tiferes Yisrael*). *Avos d'Rabbi Nosson* teaches: "He who

---

⇜ **Grow up!** Parents must maintain a balance in rearing children, attempting to understand the child from his mindset, while at the same time being careful not to act childishly themselves. We are instructed: חֲנֹךְ לַנַּעַר עַל פִּי דַרְכּוֹ, *Educate the lad according to his way [of thinking]* (Proverbs 22:6), meaning that we investigate our children's thought processes in order to understand how to instruct them. On the other hand, we must guard against the unsophisticated *chatter of children,* which can lead us to develop an immature system of values and priorities.

Youth is a time of playfulness; however, as one matures he should not remain in a childish frame of mind. One who gets caught up in *children's chatter,* considering the most recent ball-game scores as the most important news of the day, has divested his life of meaning.

In addition, adults must always remember: We are the parents and mentors of our children, and not the other way around. As someone once said, "I don't want to be my child's pal; I want to be his parent." While we shower children with love and protection, we should never feel the emotional need to befriend them out of our own sense of insecurity. One who spurns his obligation to educate his children, and instead overindulges them to serve a personal need, harms both them — and himself.

⇜ **Where is that child?** On the other hand, planning for one's children can become so obsessive that one totally ignores his own spiritual needs.

A man of means once came to visit with R' Bunam of P'shis'cha. A workaholic, he spent all his energies in expanding his business. When the *Rebbe* questioned his spiritual shortsightedness, he replied, "Rebbe, I work hard so that my child will be able to study Torah without worries."

"Yes, my friend" replied R' Bunam. "And your child will tell me that he toils for *his* child, who in turn will say that he does so for *his* child. This has gone on for eternity. I am still looking to find that one child who was worthy of the sacrifices of so many generations."

15. Rabbi Elazar the Moda'ite used to say: One who desecrates

refrains from these four pitfalls is second only to the angels."

All these vices undermine one's spiritual orientation and destroy his potential for real virtue. He never attains the spiritual peaks for which he was destined and leaves the world as an unfulfilled person (*Rambam*). According to *R' Yonah*, involvement in these negative habits actually *shortens* one's life. Torah study and practice is the key to longevity: *For He* [God] *is your life and the length of your days* (*Deuteronomy* 30:20). Life is an investment opportunity. Like capital, it is provided by God for the purpose of wise investment. One who misappropriates the funds is not given more capital; likewise, he who abuses the gift of life is deprived of it.

R' Moshe Alshakar tells us that the vices described in the mishnah are really allegories for different stages of life. In the morning of his existence, one is lulled into spiritual slumber and neglects to prepare spiritually for the journey through life. As he matures and enters the noon of his life, when he is at the height of his powers, he often becomes intoxicated by his social and financial success, and he does not pause to consider whether he is addressing the real issues of life. It is in old age that the tendency to engage in trivial pursuits and pleasures overcomes him. As his life wanes, he yearns only for the comforting company of the ignorant, who waste their days in banal conversation and gossip.

It is the abuse of these stages of life that distances man from the wonderful world of reward that awaits only those who make use of every precious moment of life (*R' Moshe Alshakar*).

Mishnah 15

רַבִּי אֶלְעָזָר הַמּוֹדָעִי אוֹמֵר — *Rabbi Elazar the Moda'ite says.* A third-generation *Tanna*, R' Elazar was from the city of Modiin, famous as the birthplace of the Hasmoneans. His special strength lay in his aggadic expositions, particularly in Scriptural exegesis, rather than in halachic rulings. Rabban Gamliel viewed him as expert in matters of Aggadah and often concluded discussions of such matters with the statement, "We still need [to rely on the opinion of] the Moda'ite" (see *Shabbos* 55b, *Megillah* 15b and *Bava Basra* 10b). Once, at a conclave of sages at Yavneh, he spoke in seemingly exaggerated terms of the miracles surrounding the Biblical episode of the manna. R' Tarfon, ever the seeker of the simple meaning of the Biblical text, questioned the veracity of his words. R' Elazar replied that all his explanations were rooted in a careful reading of the text (*Yoma* 76a).

According to Rabbinic tradition, he supported his nephew Shimon bar Kochba in his revolt against the occupying Roman government. Eventually, however, Bar Kochba accepted a slanderous accusation of treachery and treason against his uncle and in a fit of rage killed him. The Jerusalem Talmud relates that "A voice emanated from Heaven and proclaimed, 'You have killed R' Elazar the Moda'ite, the strong arm and right eye of Israel. Therefore your own arm will wither, and your right eye shall grow dim.' Soon after, Beitar fell to the Romans and Bar Kosiba [Bar Kochba] was slain" (see *Yerushalmi Taanis* 4:5 and *Eichah Rabbah* 2:2).

הַמְחַלֵּל אֶת הַקֳּדָשִׁים — *One who desecrates sacred things.* This refers to the Temple offerings, which must be kept in a strict state of sanctity and are subject to specific restrictions as to their consumption.

> ◄§ **The secret of longevity.** The Talmud frequently seeks the secret of the longevity of one or the other of the Sages (see *Megillah* 28a, *Taanis* 20a), but the answers never involve diet or other physical aspects of one's life-style; it is axiomatic to the Sages that physical existence is dependent on spiritual health. Hence, R' Dosa ben Harkinos, who lived to a ripe old age (see *Yevamos* 16a), is the fitting spokesman for this truth. It is not the pampering of the body which assures long life, but rather the development of the soul (*Derech Avos*).

One who does not take the necessary precautions when preparing or consuming sacred items desecrates their holy status. Included is one who profanes an offering by intending to consume it after its prescribed time (פִּגּוּל) or who renders it impure (טָמֵא) and hence unfit. Other members of this category are one who leaves over parts of the offerings that should be eaten beyond the prescribed time (נוֹתָר), and one who misappropriates offerings or sacred property of the Temple treasury for personal benefit (מְעִילָה) (*Rav, R' Yonah, Rashi*).

Sefer HaMussar offers an alternative explanation. A *Kohen* who attempts to coerce people into giving the priestly portion of the offering to him is considered as having desecrated sacred objects. The sons of Eli *HaKohen* were a prime example of such behavior. Scripture states that they forced the people to give them such portions, and the Torah is unforgiving in its criticism of their behavior (*I Samuel* 2:17).

One who does not show proper respect for a Torah scholar is included in this category. Such disrespect may take the form of a flippant attitude toward the scholar's rulings: "Just yesterday it was an ordinary animal. How did it suddenly become sacred?" Similarly, people may say of the scholar himself, "When I knew him, he was merely another person on the street. What drastic change came about that he is now a man of distinction?" (*Ri ibn Sasson*).

Chida extends this to one's attitude toward himself: One who does not believe in his own innate potential to achieve a life of sanctity has forfeited his share in eternity. *Alshich* views this opinion as the reason the Biblical call to sanctity (see *Leviticus* 19:2 and *Rashi* ad loc.) was taught at once to the entire assemblage of the Jewish people. One should not be deluded into thinking that sanctity is something to which only a select few may aspire. Every person, on his or her own level, can and must strive to realize the potential for holiness with which God has endowed him. Seeking anything less is considered a desecration of the sacred.

The Talmud (*Sanhedrin* 99a) cites as the Scriptural source of all the profanations in the mishnah the verse *That person shall be cut off from among his people, for he scorned the word of HASHEM* (*Numbers* 15:30-31). The words *and nullified His commandment* (ibid. v. 31) alludes to one who nullifies the covenant of circumcision (see *Rashi* here and *Sanhedrin* ad loc.).

וְהַמְבַזֶּה אֶת הַמּוֹעֲדוֹת — *who disgraces the festivals.* The mishnah does not speak of one who profanes festivals themselves by doing forbidden labor

⪧ **Permanent image.** The Ponovezher Rav offered a striking example of this phenomenon from personal experience: When he began his career as a rabbi, he left his hometown of Kula to search for a *shteleh* (rabbinical position). Years later, after having served successfully as a rabbi in a few Polish cities, a position opened up in his hometown. Rabbi Kahaneman eagerly wrote the selection committee to apply for the post, only to receive a very polite letter of rejection. The committee would not even give him a hearing. He wrote again, asking for clarification; since he knew all the people in the committee, he was sure they had mistaken his application for someone else's. He waited for a reply, but after a few weeks it became clear that they were not going to answer him and, for some reason, did not want him as their rabbi.

Many years later, at the height of his career as *Rav* of Ponovezh, he noticed one of the leading congregants of Kula in his synagogue, one Shabbos. Not only that, this man had been a member of the search committee that had rejected his rabbinical application years earlier. After Shabbos, Rabbi Kahaneman asked his old townsman why the community had turned him down.

The man was frank with the now-famous rabbi. "Rebbe, now you are renowned and respected. You preside over a very large community. But you must understand that at the time you wanted the post in Kula, all we knew about you was what we remembered from the time you were growing up in our town. We remembered you as a child playing marbles in our streets. It may sound unfair, but to us you were still that child. Nobody would have thought of you as the rabbi, the leader, the one from whom we had to learn. Who in Kula would accept reproof from a player of marbles?"

The rabbi thanked him for his honesty. When he good-humoredly told the story after many successful years in Ponovezh and Israel, he would remark that it was a good thing he had not grown up in Ponovezh, for he might have been remembered there too as "the child who played marbles in the streets!"

on the *Yom Tov* days (מְחַלֵּל), but instead of one who disgraces (מְבַזֶּה) the *Yom Tov* quality of the Intermediate Days of Pesach and Succos (*Chol HaMoed*) by performing labors which are forbidden then, or by treating them with less honor than the major days of the festival (*Rashi; R' Yonah*).

Regarding whether work on *Chol HaMoed* is prohibited Biblically or Rabbinically, see *Introduction to Moed Kattan 1:1* in *Yad Avraham*.

It is also deemed a disgrace of the festivals if one refrains from the added expense of purchasing delicacies or fine clothing for his children or wife [according to his financial ability] (see *Rambam, Hilchos Yom Tov 6:18*) (*Sefer HaMussar*).

According to *Meiri*, this *disgrace of the festivals* refers not to labor, and it applies not only to *Chol HaMoed* but even refers to the major days of the festivals. Since most of the festivals relate to the Egyptian Exodus, one who profanes them essentially denies the principle of God as the All-Powerful Creator and Force of Providence, conveyed through the great miracles which accompanied the Exodus (see *Ramban, Exodus 13:15*). The Talmud considers disgrace of the festivals the moral

equivalent of idolatry (*Pesachim 118a*). Denial of the themes of faith embodied in the festivals is an expression of denial of God.

וְהַמַּלְבִּין פְּנֵי חֲבֵרוֹ בָּרַבִּים — *who humiliates his fellow in public.* The phrase הַמַּלְבִּין פְּנֵי חֲבֵרוֹ literally means *one who causes his fellow's face to turn white.* One's face becomes red and then pale white when he is embarrassed (*Rav;* see *Bava Metzia 58b*). Public embarrassment is an ancillary of murder. Just as murder is one of the three cardinal sins for which one must be ready to surrender his life in this world (see *Sanhedrin 74a*), so one who publicly humiliates his fellow surrenders his eternal life in the World to Come.

See *Tosafos, Sotah 10b,* s.v. נוח. *Pnei Yehoshua* points out a halachic implication of the severity of shaming someone in public. One who commits suicide forfeits his portion in the World to Come (see *Chidushei MaHarit, Kesubos p. 152* and *Shevet Mussar 20*); yet suicide is permitted in order not to bring humiliation upon a fellow, even justifiably. [Once the Sages instituted this ruling, such sacrifice of one's life is no longer considered suicide.]

◄§ **Justifiable suicide.** The Talmud relates the story of a couple that preferred possible death to causing a fellow Jew to be embarrassed. Very early every morning, Mar Ukva used to put money inside a poor man's door hinge. One day, the man decided that he would try to learn the identity of his secret benefactor, so he waited in hiding. Mar Ukva and his wife were late that day, and when the poor man saw them coming, he emerged from his hiding place to get a good look at them. Before he could recognize them, Mar Ukva and his wife fled, with the poor man in pursuit. As they ran, they saw a furnace that had been recently cleaned of its coals, but was still piping hot. They jumped into the furnace and Mar Ukva's legs were singed.

◄§ **A matter of choice.** This ruling is derived from Tamar, who was ready to be put to death by fire rather than embarrassing Judah by revealing that she was carrying his child [actually twins] (see *Genesis 38:24-25*). Had Judah not owned up to his misdeed, he would have allowed an innocent woman and her two fetuses to go to a fiery death. Thus, even someone capable of such injustice must also be saved from public humiliation (*R' Yitzchak of Bohosh*).

It is noteworthy that the Sages expressed the gravity of inflicting shame publicly in relative terms; they said it is *preferable* to fling oneself into a furnace rather than publicly humiliate one's fellow. R' Leib Chasman offered the following illustration: Imagine being trapped in a burning building. Only two escape routes are available to flee the flaming inferno and both entail a passage through the flames. Some pain from the heat must be endured, but of course one will pick the route where the fire is smaller. This is the import of our Sages' observation: the ''heat'' one must suffer for inflicting public humiliation is of such intensity that a fiery furnace seems cool by comparison.

The Brisker Rav explained, regarding the case of Mar Zutra and his wife in the previous footnote: '' The Sages did not say that someone is *obligated* to enter a fiery furnace rather than humiliate another person. They taught that a fiery furnace is *easier* on a person than the punishment for public embarrassment. Mar Ukva and his wife therefore chose the more comfortable course for themselves.''

וְהַמֵּפֵר בְּרִיתוֹ שֶׁל אַבְרָהָם אָבִינוּ, וְהַמְּגַלֶּה פָנִים בַּתּוֹרָה שֶׁלֹּא כַהֲלָכָה, אַף עַל פִּי שֶׁיֵּשׁ בְּיָדוֹ תּוֹרָה וּמַעֲשִׂים טוֹבִים — אֵין לוֹ חֵלֶק לָעוֹלָם הַבָּא.

The draining of blood from the victim's face is tantamount to actually spilling his blood. The Sages taught: One should sooner fling himself into a fiery furnace than cause his fellow public humiliation (*Sotah* 10b).

The Talmud (*Sanhedrin* 99b) includes under this rubric one who refers to another person with a demeaning nickname or who gains honor at another's expense. Although not a severe infraction in ritual terms, inflicting public embarrassment is an ethical flaw, indicative of a grievous lack of basic human decency. God has little tolerance for such people and finds no place for them in His world of reward (*Meiri*).

According to *Torah Temimah*, public humiliation of a fellow is also an instance of scorning the word of HASHEM (see *Sanhedrin* 99b and *Maharsha* ad loc.). Man is created in the image of God and imbued with a spark of the Divine — the soul. One who humiliates another human being exhibits blatant disregard for the Godliness present in his fellow. [See *Rambam, Hilchos Dei'os* 6:8 for the halachic guidelines regarding the obligation to provide rebuke vis-a-vis the issue of public humiliation.]

וְהַמֵּפֵר בְּרִיתוֹ שֶׁל אַבְרָהָם אָבִינוּ — *who nullifies the covenant of our forefather Abraham.* By refusing to circumcise himself (if he was not circumcised as a child) or his children, or by surgically concealing his circumcision, he nullifies the covenant God made with Abraham and his children (*Rav*). One who does so demeans God's commandments (*R' Yonah*).

The Midrash (*Bereishis Rabbah* 48:7) relates that Abraham sits at the entrance to *Gehinnom* and refuses admission to any uncircumcised Jew.

Tikkun Moshe elaborates: Circumcision is a physical expression of the exclusive covenant between God and His people. One who nullifies this covenant turns his back on his national identity and thus expresses a deep-seated self-hatred.

וְהַמְּגַלֶּה פָנִים בַּתּוֹרָה שֶׁלֹּא כַהֲלָכָה — *or who perverts the meaning of the Torah contrary to halachah.* This refers to one who interprets verses of the Torah in ways contrary to the Rabbinic and halachic tradition (*Rav, Rashi*).

Under this category, *Rashi* includes one who, like King Menashe, an evil ruler of Judah in the First Temple era, heretically questions why Moses included certain seemingly inconsequential details in the Torah (see *Sanhedrin* ibid.).

The term מְגַלֶּה פָנִים, literally *reveals a face*, is used as in the Talmudic principle "There are ע' פָּנִים (seventy faces, meaning interpretive approaches) to Torah" (see *Osiyos d'Rabbi Akiva* and *Bamidbar Rabbah* 13:15).

Meiri includes one who rejects the manifest meaning of the Torah's dictates, claiming that particular commandments are not meant in a literal sense, but instead are metaphorical and symbolic. To interpret the prohibition against eating swine as an allegorical condemnation of "swinish, unethical behavior" is an example of the illegitimate explication of the commandments. Furthermore, one who is contemptuous of Torah

⊰§ **Respect even for the least worthy.** The respect due a human being as a reflection of his Godliness underlies the law regarding those who are executed by the court for idolatry or blasphemy. The body is hanged on display to remind the people of the gravity of the crime and as a deterrent; nonetheless, it must be buried before nightfall. *You shall not leave his body overnight on the gallows, rather you shall surely bury him on that day, for a hanging person is a curse of God* (*Deuteronomy* 21:23). Since a human being is created in the image of God, and God calls the Jews His children, the hanging body is disgraceful to God Himself, as it were. It can be likened to a king's twin brother, who is a bandit and is hanged for his crimes. People who see the body think it is the king (*Rashi*).

The practice of the courts was that the body would be hanged just before sunset, and then taken down immediately.

in public, who nullifies the covenant of our forefather Abraham, or who perverts the meaning of the Torah contrary to halachah — though he may have Torah and good deeds, he has no share in the World to Come.

scholars, the true bearers of God's wisdom, is likewise denied a place in the World to Come.

Alternatively, *Rambam* and *R' Yonah* render מְגַלֶּה פָנִים as *one who acts brazenly* toward Torah and its dictates.

One who has a sense of shame tends to hide his face rather than to "reveal" it. A head held high and a face looking straight ahead may often be symptomatic of arrogance and brazenness.

Other opinions say this goes further than misinterpretation of Torah laws and refers to one who publicly and shamelessly desecrates them, the ultimate heresy. *Yerushalmi* (*Pe'ah* 1:1) cites Yehoyakim ben Yoshiyahu as a prototype (see *II Kings* 24:5 and *Vayikra Rabbah* 19:6 for various opinions about his heinous crimes).

אַף עַל פִּי שֶׁיֵּשׁ בְּיָדוֹ תּוֹרָה וּמַעֲשִׂים טוֹבִים — *though he may have Torah and good deeds.* The misdeeds enumerated in the mishnah are not sins of passion, such as theft, eating forbidden foods, or engaging in illicit liaisons; and so one cannot absolve himself of full responsibility for them with the claim that he is generally a Torah observant person whom the evil inclination seduced to commit them. The misdeeds are the result of heretical leanings [for which no excuse is sufficient] (*Meiri*). The good deeds once performed and the Torah once studied cannot save a person from losing his eternity if he has succumbed to heresy. He must thoroughly reorientate his beliefs and approach to life. Only full and complete repentance can snatch him from the fatal effects of heresy; even the curse of pain [which can atone for sins] is insufficient to undo the spiritual damage inflicted by heresy (*Rambam, Rav, R' Yonah*).

אֵין לוֹ חֵלֶק לָעוֹלָם הַבָּא — *he has no share in the World to Come.* The verse teaches, *That person shall surely be cut off; his sin is upon him* (*Numbers* 15:31). The Talmud explains the double term הַכָּרֵת תִּכָּרֵת to mean that such a person will be spiritually cut off in both this world and the World to Come (see *Sanhedrin* ibid.). Another opinion is that any reward that he earned for his past Torah study or good deeds will be paid him in this world, but his heretical beliefs will cause him to lose *any* reward in the World to Come (*Chasdei Avos*).

See Appendix to the Schottenstein Edition of the Talmud, *Sanhedrin III,* for a definition of the term "the World to Come."

The Talmud (*Sanhedrin* 90a) lists many categories of people whose belief is so seriously flawed that they have no share in the World to Come. *Tiferes Yisrael* views the five transgressions listed in this mishnah as qualifications of those categories:

(1) Deniers of God inherently reject the concept of sanctity and profaneness. One who desecrates sacred property essentially does not believe in a Holy One who can sanctify the mundane. Furthermore, he considers offerings meaningless altogether, since in his warped sense there is no God to serve.

(2) The festivals, given to commemorate the Creator's active intervention in human affairs and His ability to override the laws of nature, serve to testify that He created everything and everybody. One who profanes the festivals denies these basic articles of faith.

(3) Those who admit to the existence of the Creator yet deny that man is created in His image can easily come to humiliate a person publicly. They lack the respect that should be accorded man as the bearer of a Divine soul.

ᴥ **A Jew remains beautiful.** The Talmud views circumcision as a mark of national identity. One who takes a vow not to derive any benefit from circumcised people is only obligated to distance himself socially from Jews — even uncircumcised ones. He may derive benefit from any non-Jew, even one who is surgically circumcised (see *Nedarim* 31b). Circumcision is therefore a symbol of Jewish identity.

(4) One who nullifies the covenant of circumcision indicates a basic lack of understanding regarding the qualitative difference between God's people and others. This, in a subtle fashion, indicates a denial of Torah as a Divine gift, since the giving of the Torah at Sinai invested Israel with its exclusive national character.

(5) One who espouses interpretations of Torah which contradict the tradition denies the veracity of the Oral Law.

According to *Yalkut Gershuni*, the mishnah here describes a spiritually degenerative chain reaction.

One who loses his perspective and is unable — or unwilling — to differentiate between the holy and profane will eventually lose this faculty regarding many of the major themes of Torah and Judaism. Desecration of the sacred is rooted in not recognizing the marked difference between the hallowed and the unsanctified. One who does not see a difference between the elevated spirit of the Sabbath and festivals and the mundane quality of the weekdays may come to disgrace the festivals. This, in turn, may lead to a perverted sense of the value of a human being; for if he sees no distinctions between

⧁§ **You are beautiful.** On Friday afternoons Reb Aryeh Levin would always go early to the synagogue and chant the *Song of Songs*. Once Rabbi Chaim Berlin, the *Rav* of Jerusalem, was sitting next to him, also chanting the *Song of Songs*. Suddenly R' Chaim began to cry. "Why are you weeping?" Reb Aryeh asked him.

Rabbi Chaim Berlin answered with a story:

"When I was the rabbi of Moscow, a distinguished man approached and asked to speak with me in private. The man told me, "I have become the father of a son, and I should like you, dear rabbi, to perform the circumcision."

"Why, of course," I replied. "That will be fine. But why the need for secrecy about this?"

"I am a man of considerable means, dealing in crosses to the Christian market," he explained. "No one in my neighborhood knows that I am Jewish. I therefore wish to have the circumcision take place in secrecy; it must be kept hidden from my neighbors."

R' Chaim continued, "I advised him to let the Christian servant-girls in his home have the day off, and he did so. This man himself served as *sandak* and held the child on his knees, and I performed the circumcision; only the two of us were in attendance. When it was over I asked the infant's father to let me know three days later how the child was faring.

"Three days later, he came to see me, and he put down a sum of money on the table, for my trouble. 'I do not take money for performing circumcisions,' I told him. Being a businessman, he thought that I meant that he given me too little, so he put down a larger sum and then an even larger sum — but I remained firm in my refusal. Finally, I asked him, 'Tell me something: Your home is totally bereft of any trace of our Jewish heritage. In addition, you yourself make every effort to be sure that no one even suspects you are a Jew. Why did you want your son circumcised? What made you go to all that trouble, with such sacrifice, for this *mitzvah*?' "

"Rabbi," he replied, "I know how completely estranged I am from Judaism. Frankly, I doubt if I will ever be able to return to my faith. Even this newborn child will most likely know nothing about Judaism. I at least grew up among Jews and had whom to learn from; he will have nobody and nothing. Nevertheless, should the boy find out when he grows up that he is Jewish, and should he wish to be a complete Jew, I want nothing to stand in his way . . ."

R' Chaim Berlin concluded: "Whenever I read the verse — *Behold you are beautiful, my love; behold, you are beautiful, your eyes are doves* (Song of Songs 1:15) — I am reminded of that incident, and I understand why Scripture states the same phrase twice *Behold, you are beautiful* refers to the Jewish people before they sin; the repetition means *behold, you are* [still] *beautiful* even after you sin. Why are the Jewish people *beautiful* (still held in the Almighty's affection) even after sinning? — because *your eyes are doves*: As the Talmud (*Bava Basra* 23a) indicates, even when a dove flies off from the dovecote, it never goes too far away, and always remains within the range of sight of the dovecote. Even when a Jew drifts very far from his roots, the covenant of Abraham still focuses him on the warm, cozy nest of his heritage."

people and does not consider the specialness of his friend, he may come to humiliate him publicly.

Finally, he may lose sight of the chosenness of God's people and adopt a perverted, universalist philosophy that expresses itself in the nullification of the covenant of circumcision of our forefather Abraham. Ultimately, he will take liberties with the interpretation of the Torah, for he will forget that the Torah, unlike books of human authorship, is the word of God. Such blasphemy is the final expression of a lack of discrimination in matters of sanctity.

Mishnah 16

רַבִּי יִשְׁמָעֵאל אוֹמֵר — *Rabbi Yishmael says.* Rabbi Yishmael was one of the greatest of the third generation of Tannaim. There is disagreement whether he was R' Yishmael the Kohen Gadol who was martyred by the Romans, or his grandson. A colleague of R' Akiva, he was a student of R' Yehoshua ben Chanania, who ransomed him when he was a young boy from a Roman prison, paying an exorbitant sum. R' Yehoshua predicted a great future for him because he exhibited insight far beyond his years. His teacher's predictions were quickly realized (see *Gittin* 58a).

R' Yishmael was the first to codify the thirteen hermeneutic principles for Biblical interpretation, and much of the halachic Midrash (*Mechilta* to *Exodus, Sifrei* to *Numbers,* and part of *Sifri* to *Deuteronomy*) is a legacy of his Academy. R' Tarfon attested to the fact that his expertise was not limited to halachic areas, saying: "He is a great scholar, with broad knowledge of Aggadah" (*Moed Kattan* 28b).

R' Yishmael's great belief in the corrective power of Torah was expressed in his statement: "If one sees a Torah scholar sin by night, let him harbor no suspicions regarding the scholar by day — for he certainly has repented" (*Berachos* 19a).

His ability to admit mistakes is highlighted in an incident recorded in *Tosefta* (*Shabbos* 1:13). Reading by candlelight on the Sabbath was prohibited by the Sages, who feared that one might inadvertently tamper with a flickering wick. R' Yishmael, confident that he would exercise sufficient caution, ignored their ruling and once read by candlelight on the Sabbath and, indeed, he adjusted the wick. He wrote in his personal journal: "I, Yishmael ben Elisha, read by candlelight and tampered with the wick. When the Temple is rebuilt, I will bring a robust sin offering."

R' Yishmael lived during the time of the destruction of the Temple and felt deeply the pain of that tragedy and said that the grief was so great that it would be proper to forbid the consumption of meat and wine, but this could not be done because the majority of people would find it too difficult (see *Bava Basra* 60b).

His concern for poverty-stricken young Jewish women was legendary. A young man once vowed not to marry a certain young lady because of her unattractiveness. R' Yishmael brought her to his home and invested his own money to feed her well and to hire cosmeticians to improve her appearance. The change convinced the young man that he had erred, and R' Yishmael found halachic grounds to nullify the vow. "Jewish daughters are [really] beautiful," he said; "it is only abject poverty that makes them repulsive." [Jewish women bewailed his death with the elegy "Jewish daughters! Cry for R' Yishmael" (see *Nedarim* 9:10).]

הֱוֵי קַל לְרֹאשׁ — *Be yielding to a superior.* One should exhibit subservience when in the presence of men of stature, rather than seeking to inflate his own image (*Rambam*). One should view himself as a lightweight — insignificant — in comparison to those of great spiritual eminence.

Alternatively, the word קַל may be interpreted as *light* (lightweight). One should be light and swift footed in tending to the needs of great men who are older than he and who occupy leadership positions (*Rav*). *Rav* and *Rashi* also interpret this mishnah as a reference to one's approach to God, Who stands at the head of everything and everybody. One should be contrite and emotionally

ג/יז   לְתִשְׁחֹרֶת, וֶהֱוֵי מְקַבֵּל אֶת כָּל הָאָדָם בְּשִׂמְחָה.

[יז] רַבִּי עֲקִיבָא אוֹמֵר: שְׂחוֹק וְקַלּוּת רֹאשׁ מַרְגִּילִין אֶת

submissive in his relationship with God, always yielding his own will to that of his Creator.

According to *Rashi* and *R' Yonah*, the mishnah calls for submissiveness towards those at the head of government. King Solomon encapsulated this lesson: *Do not glorify yourself in the King's presence* (*Proverbs* 25:6). Furthermore, arrogance in the presence of great men is dangerous (*Meiri*).

Accordingly, the word לְרֹאשׁ may be rendered as an acronym for לַעֲשׂוֹת רְצוֹן אָבִיךְ שֶׁבַּשָּׁמַיִם, "Be light and emotionally pliant *to do the will of your Father in Heaven*" (*R' Moshe Alshakar*).

וְנוֹחַ לְתִשְׁחֹרֶת — *pleasant to the young.* While subservience is not called for in dealing with younger people, one is well advised to act pleasantly toward his juniors. Even if they are sometimes rash and disrespectful, their youthful indiscretions should sometimes be indulged (*Midrash Shmuel*).

תִּשְׁחֹרֶת is rendered as *the young*, i.e., those whose hair is still black (שָׁחוֹר) (*Rav*), or those who are still in the morning (שַׁחַר) of life.

R' Yonah renders תִּשְׁחֹרֶת as a government official [or functionary]. Even minor government officials exercise power over ordinary citizens. In the absence of the king or head of government, the appointee is empowered to exact retribution from anyone who crosses him.

Rashi gives an entirely different explanation, claiming that תִּשְׁחֹרֶת refers not to youth but to old age; the root שָׁחוֹר, *black,* indicates one whose face has been "blackened" by life's experiences. Thus, this clause is a continuation of the previous one. One should seek to please God even into his old age.

By bending one's will to God's when he is still young, one develops a proper orientation, which will stand him in good stead and render him pleasant and affable in God's eyes even when he is old (*Knesses Yisrael*).

Midrash Shmuel interprets תִּשְׁחֹרֶת homiletically as related to שָׁחוֹר, *black.* Even when one endures a life that seems dark and gloomy, he should try to remain pleasant in his attitude toward God and not harbor any resentment.

וֶהֱוֵי מְקַבֵּל אֶת כָּל הָאָדָם בְּשִׂמְחָה — *and receive every person cheerfully.* One should speak pleasantly with all people, young and old alike (*Rashi*). Although older people should maintain their dignity in dealing with youth, this should not be misconstrued as a call for an intimidating or sullen demeanor. One should receive all people with joy, no matter their age or social class. This is a greater spiritual plateau than the instruction of Shammai (see 1:15; *Rambam*).

Shammai only instructed that one receive all people with a cheerful countenance, something that may not truly reflect one's inner feelings (see *Meiri* ad loc.). R' Yishmael goes further and speaks of receiving people בְּשִׂמְחָה — with happiness. [See, however, *Meiri* here, who surprisingly equates the two statements.]

Alternatively, *Meiri* interprets the mishnah as an instruction in how to react to personal requests. One should respond easily and quickly to requests from one's elders, or superiors, but not necessarily to one's juniors. But if one acquiesces to the request of a younger person, he should do so affably. One the other hand, if one must refuse a request, he should do so amicably, making sure to convey that he would like to comply, but is unable to do so.

 ◆§ **Discard excess baggage.** *Toldos Yaakov Yosef* offers an allegorical rendering. In order to ascend a mountain, one must free himself of excess baggage and bulky clothing so that he may travel as lightly as possible. This is doubly true in the attempt to scale spiritual heights. One who is unencumbered by the weight of possessions and social commitments can *be light* [in order to rise] *to the top.*

 ◆§ **Youth not an obstacle.** R' Yishmael lived through the deposing of Rabban Gamliel as *Nasi* and the appointment of the young R' Elazar ben Azariah in his place. He therefore warned his colleagues and students to treat the young *Nasi* pleasantly (*Mussar Avos*).

17. Rabbi Akiva says: Mockery and levity accustom a man

Knesses Yisrael renders the mishnah in an entirely different way, seeing it as a primer for those who are able to lobby on behalf of the weak and unfortunate. One should be light and easy going in approaching leaders of society on behalf of others. In addition, he should be agreeable in the first place (לְשַׁחֵר פָּנָיו) when asked to intervene on behalf of those in need. He should receive joyously all who need his help, and make them feel instead as if *they* are helping *him*.

Mishnah 17

רַבִּי עֲקִיבָא אוֹמֵר — *Rabbi Akiva says*. Rabbi Akiva was a third-generation Tanna, one of the most famous of all Tannaim. During his lifetime, the Temple was destroyed. Of modest and humble beginnings (see *Berachos* 27b) [his father Yosef is identified by *Rambam* (*introduction to Mishneh Torah*) as a convert], he grew to epitomize multi-faceted greatness.

Although he was ignorant in Torah until a late age, he was able to become a great scholar thanks to his outstanding mind, great willpower, and the selfless encouragement of his wife.

The Talmud relates that as a young man he had been a shepherd in the employ of one Kalba Savua, a wealthy Jerusalemite, whose daughter Rachel was attracted to him because of his refinement and humility. She asked him, "If I marry you, will you dedicate yourself to Torah study?" He agreed, and they were secretly married. When word of the marriage reached her father, he was incensed and forbade her any access to his considerable wealth. Forced into a life of abject poverty, R' Akiva and his wife were homeless and took shelter in a hay stall, but she remained loyal and supportive, insisting that she was ready for any sacrifice in order for him to become a scholar. Once he said to her, "If only I could, I would have an artisan create for you a יְרוּשָׁלַיִם שֶׁל זָהָב, a gold tiara in the form of the skyline of Jerusalem."

According to *Avos d'Rabbi Nosson*, R' Akiva was inspired to begin his Torah studies at the age of forty, when he observed how water could wear grooves into solid stone after years of constant dripping. He said to himself, "If soft water can penetrate hard stone, certainly the iron-strong Torah can leave its imprint on my heart." He began learning the *alef-beis* and continued his studies until he mastered the entire Torah.

R' Akiva studied under R' Eliezer ben Hyrkanos and R' Yehoshua ben Chanania, and returned home after twelve years. As he approached his home, he overheard an old man chiding his wife: "How long will you be the widow of a live man?" She replied selflessly: "If he were to listen to me,

⊷§ **Happy "reunion"** R' Moshe Rosenstein, *mashgiach* of Lomza, recounted his first day, as a young boy, at the famed Talmud Torah of Kelm. Knowing not a soul among the students, he stood uncomfortably in the corridor outside the study hall, afraid and embarrassed to enter. Suddenly the door swung open, and one of the married students approached him with a smile, shook his hand in welcome, and offered a hearty *"Shalom Aleichem."* "How are you doing, my friend? We are so happy that you came! Please come and have a bite; you certainly are hungry."

R' Moshe was overjoyed. In fact, it seemed clear that the young man knew him from someplace. "Maybe our paths have crossed in the past," he thought.

Suddenly another young man came out of the study hall and greeted R' Moshe with the same effusive warmth, inviting him a second time to eat and rest. R' Moshe was pleasantly surprised at the coincidence of meeting two people who seemed to have known him from before.

It was only much later that he realized that in Kelm, the charge to *receive every person cheerfully*, like all Torah dictates, was not merely an idea — it was a way of life.

he would remain even longer in his studies." R' Akiva immediately turned back and devoted himself to Torah study for another twelve years.

Upon his triumphant return home, R' Akiva was escorted by his 24,000 students. His wife went out to greet him dressed in simple clothes that indicated her poverty. Unaware that she was his wife, his students sought to deny her access to their great teacher. Said R' Akiva, "Allow her through, for my [Torah] and yours is really hers" (Kesubos

---

⊰§ **Two times twelve.** In spite of R' Akiva's enormous gratitude to his wife, he turned back without even taking a moment to enter his home and gladden her heart with his presence. R' Chaim Shmulevitz derives from this incident the destructive power of interruption. R' Akiva realized that life is like a kettle on the stove. One can heat and reheat the water countless times, but if the kettle is removed before the water boils, then all the heating is useless. Likewise, man's spiritual progress needs to be compounded without interruption in order to reach its culmination. R' Akiva understood his heroic wife and knew that she would also appreciate the fact that two times twelve is *not* the equivalent of twenty-four uninterrupted years of Torah study.

⊰§ **Teacher in life and death.** A master at explicating the Written Torah in order to reveal the basis for much of the Oral Law, R' Akiva felt that every word of the written text carried an exact meaning, and he derived countless laws even from the "crowns" of the letters of the Torah (*Menachos* 29b). Much of the Tannaitic literature can indeed be traced to him. R' Yochanan attributes anonymous mishnayos to R' Meir, anonymous *Toseftas* to R' Nechemiah, anonymous *Sifra* to R' Yehudah, anonymous *Sifri* to R' Shimon — and all of them in accordance with the opinion of R' Akiva (*Sanhedrin* 86a).

R' Akiva enjoyed the admiration of young and old. R' Dosa ben Harkinas, a first-generation *Tanna,* exclaimed upon meeting him, "Are you the world- renowned Akiva ben Yosef? May there be many like you in Israel" (*Yevamos* 16a). *Mitzpeh Eisan* (ad loc.) notes that the words of R' Dosa ben Harkinas — "That your name reaches מִסּוֹף עוֹלָם וְעַד סוֹפוֹ" [*from one end of the world to the other*] — are the equivalent in *gematria* of 564, exactly the number of times R' Akiva's name is mentioned in the Talmud.

R' Akiva's life was riddled with tragedy. As a punishment for not showing each other proper respect, his 24,000 students were decimated in a plague (see *Yevamos* 62b). He also suffered the political disappointment of the times. As an active supporter of Bar Kochba and his revolution, he viewed Bar Kochba as a possible Messiah, only to see those hopes dashed; he also suffered the anguish of the Roman persecution that followed Bar Kochba's break with the Sages and his eventual defeat.

Refusing to succumb to the iron fist of the Romans, R' Akiva continued to teach Torah publicly. When he was challenged about this dangerous practice, he replied by comparing the Jewish people to fish: Just as fish cannot survive out of water, so the Jewish people will perish without Torah (see *Berachos* 61b). Eventually he was arrested and imprisoned for this "crime." Even while in prison, he maintained high spirits and continued to teach Torah clandestinely to his students. He refused to allow himself halachic leniencies even under the severe conditions of imprisonment. Once, when he only had enough water either for drinking or for washing his hands, he decided in favor of washing, saying, "I prefer to die of thirst rather than transgress the words of my colleagues" (*Eruvin* 21b).

His martyr's death is described in the Talmud in heart-rending terms. Arrested for the crime of teaching Torah publicly, he was taken to be killed in the early morning, at the time when the *Shema* is usually recited. The Romans began flaying his skin with iron rakes, but all the while he recited the *Shema.* His students gazed in awe and asked, "Our teacher, must one go so far?" He answered, "All my life I was distressed because I never had the opportunity to fulfill the Biblical directive to 'love God with all one's soul' (see *Deuteronomy* 6:5). Now that the opportunity presents itself, should I not fulfill it?" His soul departed as he reached the word *echad* (*God is one*) in the *Shema* (*Berachos* 61b).

R' Akiva was beloved in life and revered in death. The Sages applied to him and his colleague-martyrs the words of King David: "*Gather unto Me My devout ones, sealers of My covenant through sacrifice* (*Psalms* 50:5); these are R' Akiva and his friends, who made the ultimate sacrifice" (*Yalkut* ad loc.).

62b-63a and *Nedarim* 50a).

When he became a famous rabbinic figure, his father-in-law, Kalba Savua, annulled his vow of disinheritance and gave R' Akiva half of his fortune. R' Akiva remembered his promise to his wife and commissioned an artisan to make a "Jerusalem of Gold" brooch for Rachel. Rabban Gamliel's wife asked her husband for a similar gift, and he answered, "Would you, like Rachel, be ready to sell your braids so that your husband could study Torah?" (*Yerushalmi, Shabbos* 6:1). R' Akiva's love and appreciation for his wife's dedication to him is given vivid expression in his aphorism: "Who is wealthy? One who has a wife whose deeds are beautiful" (*Shabbos* 25b).

His clarity of thinking and expression gave rise to R' Tarfon's declaration: "Akiva, one who separates himself from you separates himself from life itself" (*Kiddushin* 66b).

שְׂחוֹק וְקַלּוּת רֹאשׁ מַרְגִּילִין אֶת הָאָדָם לְעֶרְוָה — *Mockery and levity accustom a man to immorality.* Uninhibited merriment and light, foolish conversation lead to immoral behavior. A refined seriousness and fear of God are the best deterrents to such behavior (*R' Yonah*)

Midrash Shmuel notes that the mishnah gives the negative consequences for undesired behavior, unlike the subsequent clauses, which offer protections for virtues. This is done in order to stress that mockery and levity are generally unacceptable modes of behavior. The mishnah speaks of the moral consequences of such behavior to teach that fear of God is not merely a tactic to achieve extra spiritual greatness; it is a strategy for survival.

Tiferes Yisrael discusses the psychological dynamics of immoral behavior as the key to understanding R' Akiva's advice. One's ultimate protection against sin and lust is self-respect. Immoral behavior, unlike many other sins, involves two participants; jesting and uninhibited merriment break down the barriers of inhibition between the two parties and lead to vulgarity. However, if one has a healthy sense of self-respect, he will feel a sense of embarrassment — whether before the other participant, before the public or before God — and this will deter him from such base behavior.

מָסוֹרֶת סְיָג לַתּוֹרָה — *The transmitted Oral Torah is a [protective] fence around the Torah.* The traditional Masoretic text of the Torah protects its integrity, allowing us to interpret its words properly and to derive the halachah from them. In addition to the correct interpretation of the Written Torah, this tradition includes such basic elements as which words are written with their full spelling and which are abridged, items which sometimes affects the derivation of laws. [For example, the requirement that a *succah* must have a minimum of two walls plus a partial third wall is derived from such variations in spelling (see *Succah* 6b).] Our Scriptural text has been handed down intact from Sinai, allowing for an exact tradition of interpretation and leaving little room for distortion by impostors or misbelievers who might alter the text according to their own notions. Just as one erects a fence around his vineyard so that outsiders do not trespass and trample it, so the tradition serves to safeguard the Torah from mishandling by

---

◆§ **Self-respect, the antidote to sin.** Rambam (*Hilchos Eidus* 11:5) teaches that one who eats openly in the market place, who does menial work while partially undressed (e.g., digging ditches while stripped to the waist) or who exhibits any other type of behavior indicative of a lack of shame is Rabbinically unfit to be a witness. Rabbi Aharon Kotler explained: The ultimate safety net against sin is self-respect. Unlike all other preventive measures, which are external, self-respect is an internal sensor which warns one of impending spiritual danger. Once self-respect is gone, there are no shields against sin, and one may even give false testimony.

Judaic linguists saw an allusion to this concept in the verse מִדְּבַר שֶׁקֶר תִּרְחָק, *Distance yourself from a false word* (*Exodus* 23:7). The letters of שֶׁקֶר are the initials of שְׂחוֹק (laughter, playfulness) and קַלּוּת רֹאשׁ (lightheadedness) proscribed by our mishnah.

irresponsible "experts" (*Magen Avos, Rav, Machzor Vitry, R' Yonah*).

Meiri interprets *mesorah* as the mnemonic devices which one develops in order to remember what he learned. *Sefer HaMussar* explains it as the way in which one classifies and categorizes his learning, explaining *mesorah* as related to the verb אסר, *to bind* (see *Psalms* 149:8). By properly organizing one's knowledge and classifying it logically, one can retain great amounts of material.

מַעַשְׂרוֹת סְיָג לָעשֶׁר — *tithes are a [protective] fence for wealth*. Gifts and tithes to a Kohen, Levite, or the poor do not diminish one's wealth; on the contrary, they increase it. Hence, they serve as a fence protecting one's wealth from erosion (*Midrash Shmuel*). The discipline of contributing tithes to charity makes one cognizant of the true Owner of all wealth, and thereby makes him worthy of an even greater fortune. On the words עַשֵּׂר תְּעַשֵּׂר, literally *you are to give tithes* (*Deuteronomy* 14:22), the Sages homiletically expound: עַשֵּׂר בִּשְׁבִיל שֶׁתִּתְעַשֵּׁר, *give tithes so that you will become wealthy* [see *Taanis* 9a].

Although in general the Torah teaches, *You shall not test HASHEM your God* (*Deuteronomy* 6:16), which by extension also forbids serving God to test whether He will give rewards (see *Ramban* ad loc.), charity is an exception. As the prophet Malachi exhorted: *Bring the entire tithe to the storehouse, let there be food in My House — and test Me now thereby . . . if I will not open for you the windows of heaven and pour down for you incessant blessing beyond your capacity* (*Malachi* 3:10). Thus, regarding tithes (and charity as well) one may, so to speak, test God by giving in order to be rewarded.

Wealth often leads to arrogance, for man becomes convinced that it is his own efforts and acumen that lead to his success. The "self-made" may proclaim, *It is my strength and the might of my hand that has brought me all this success* (*Deuteronomy* 8:17), and if so, his very success can become a spiritual stumbling block. Therefore we are taught to give tithes, in recognition of the fact that all belongs to God and that we are merely sharecroppers in His vineyard, whom He allows to share some of the yield (*Tiferes Yisrael*).

In a more general sense, God responds in kind to the way man uses his wealth. Reflecting on his openhandedness toward his fellow man, God also opens His Hand and showers the charitable with wealth (*Midrash Shmuel*).

נְדָרִים סְיָג לַפְּרִישׁוּת — *vows are a [protective] fence for abstinence*. One who is in control of himself and who is capable of self-denial without making vows is best advised not to make them. But someone who is unable to subdue his darker side by the willful exercise of self-control may invoke a vow to strengthen his resolve. However, he should do so for a prescribed amount of time; an open-ended vow may be too difficult to keep indefinitely (*R' Yonah*).

When someone makes vows of abstinence and keeps them, he develops self-restraint. As this ability grows stronger, he finds it easier to refrain from indulging in forbidden pleasures (*Rambam*). *Rashi* and *Rav* recommend the use of vows only when one embarks on a path of abstinence from sensual matters. Fearful of weakness, one may battle his evil inclination with the weapon of the solemn word.

Abstinence even from permitted pleasures is considered a trait which enhances the service of God.

The ambiguous role of abstinence in the Torah *weltanschauung* is highlighted in the Torah's dual descriptions of a *nazir*. He is deemed both a holy person

---

⊷ **The man who fooled God.** The Midrash illustrates this reality with a striking story. A person owned a field that yielded one thousand bushels annually, from which he gave one hundred as a tithe. On his deathbed he commanded his children to follow this practice. Eventually, his son began ignoring his instructions, giving less than the one-tenth requirement. As a result, the field began yielding less and less, until it finally produced only one hundred bushels — a tenth of its original yield. The man's relatives reproached him by pointing out the irony of his situation: "Until now you were the landowner and God was the Kohen, receiving one tenth of the produce; now He is the landowner, taking ninety percent, while you are the 'priest,' getting only the tithe" (see *Magen Avos*).

and a sinner (*Numbers* 6:8,11). R' Elazar HaKappar calls him a sinner for his abstinence from wine, inferring from this that the Torah generally frowns upon abstinence (see *Taanis* 11a). Nonetheless, the Torah calls the abstainer a holy person. How can he be both?

Rema provides the perspective. Extremes of behavior are not desirable; the ideal is the golden mean. Thus, neither indulgence nor asceticism is optimal, but rather a course between the two. When one's behavior inclines too far in one direction, however, it becomes necessary to incline towards the other extreme for a time, in order to regain one's balance (*Rambam, Shemonah Perakim, introduction to Avos*). Now, it is evident from numerous laws in the Talmud that thirty days represent the minimum time necessary for a particular action to become a habit that is ingrained in one's nature. Since a primary function of the *nezirus* vow is to establish a mechanism by which a self-indulgent person can curb his excessive appetites [as evidenced from the story of Shimon *HaTzaddik* (see *Nedarim* 9b and *Nazir* 4b)], it follows that at least a thirty-day period of abstinence is necessary to effect a lasting modification of his behavior. Thus, the minimum term of *nezirus* is a minimum of thirty days.

It is interesting that the Scriptural source for the thirty-day minimum is the verse קָדֹשׁ יִהְיֶה, *it shall be holy* (*Numbers* 6:5). The numerical value of יִהְיֶה is thirty (*Nazir* 5a). The use of this word in the future tense — literally, *he will be* holy — indicates that he is not yet holy during his abstinence; he *will be* holy at the conclusion of this period, when the temporary excursion into abstinence restores him to the practice of moderation, and he is again able to drink wine without fear of over-indulgence (*Rema*, in *Toras HaOlah* 3:71).

סְיָג לַחָכְמָה שְׁתִיקָה — *a [protective fence] for wisdom is silence.* Silence from slander, tale-bearing, gossip, or foul language is a Biblically mandated duty and need not be spelled out. Conversely, one should not remain silent when engaged in Torah study. Rather, the mishnah speaks of the virtue of silence in ordinary, mundane, "harmless" areas; even here one should keep his conversation to a minimum. King Solomon taught: *Even a silent fool is considered wise (Proverbs* 17:28). The Talmud elaborates: "Silence is good for the wise; certainly it is so for the foolish" [*Pesachim* 99a] (*Rav, Rashi, Machzor Vitry*). According to *Tiferes Yisrael*, silence is the most foolproof method for avoiding all types of improper speech.

R' Yonah renders שְׁתִיקָה very literally as an instruction to students in the presence of their mentors, as well as to all who seek wisdom. By remaining silent and listening carefully in the presence of one greater than oneself, or by admitting that he is deficient in certain areas [and waiting silently to be enlightened], one can increase his knowledge [but one who is smug about his knowledge cannot learn from others]. Likewise, a student who refrains from offering his own opinion while his mentor is speaking is able to follow his teacher's argument without being distracted by his own words. Rather than assuming that he understands the teacher's point and is now able to disagree, he should wait silently for the end of the discourse, think the master's words through carefully, and only then offer his own view. King

---

◆§ **Need for moderation.** Man is a delicate balance of the sensual and the spiritual, with his body and soul competing for control. When physical pleasures are pursued with moderation, and as a means of providing the soul with an arena for its agenda, they assume a very positive meaning. Food, drink, the needs of the flesh, honor, and power may all be legitimate tools in fulfilling God's will. However, when these items become the primary focus of life, they serve the body at the expense of the soul. Vows are man's way of warding off his lust for pleasure. Much like a surgeon who must use radical surgery to remove a life-threatening cancer, man should make vows in order to control the spiritually ravaging effects of a life mired in desires.

◆§ **Speech of quality.** Silence is the protective fence for wisdom. However, wisdom itself is the ability not necessarily to remain completely silent but to control one's speech so that he can engage *appropriately* in discussion. The Chofetz Chaim, famous for his caution regarding all areas of speech, was far from a recluse. He could talk with people for hours and yet take care to do so in a halachically proper way.

[יח] **הוּא הָיָה** אוֹמֵר: חָבִיב אָדָם שֶׁנִּבְרָא בְּצֶלֶם; חִבָּה יְתֵרָה נוֹדַעַת לוֹ שֶׁנִּבְרָא בְּצֶלֶם,

Solomon depicted the futility of one who is enamored of his own voice: *A fool does not seek enlightenment; [he] only [wishes] to reveal his own thinking* (Proverbs 18:2).

The mishnah changes its syntactical form here. Instead of following the style of the previous three stiches and saying, "Silence is a [protective] fence for wisdom," it states "A [protective] fence for wisdom is silence." *Chassid Yaavetz* explains: Among the qualities that characterize a wise man (see 5:9) are that he refrains from speaking in the presence of those wiser or older than him; he does not interrupt others; he does not offer an opinion about things with which he is unfamiliar; and he is not quick to answer. These may all be classified under the generic term "silence." Hence, silence is not merely one of many paths to wisdom (as in the previous recommendations, which offer one protection of many for the valued item); silence may be the *primary* approach — the [protective] fence which leads to wisdom. *Orach LeChaim* offers a slightly different approach: Silence does not necessarily *lead* to wisdom.

However, wisdom, or at least the appearance thereof, is protected by limiting one's speech.

Mikveh Yisrael offers a humbling perspective on the mishnah. Since Torah is given only to those who humble themselves before its grandeur, one does well not to speak too much of his achievements. The way to protect one's wisdom and guarantee its endurance is not to talk about it.

R' Yosef Nachmias tells of one who observed someone talking more than he listened. The observer told him: "God created man with two ears and one mouth. Apparently, one should listen twice as much as one speaks." This is the truth expressed in the adage, "A word is worth a *sela* coin; silence is worth two" (*Megillah* 18a).

In a similar vein, *R' Dov Ber of Mezritch* noted that while God created two eyes to see and two ears to hear, He made only one mouth both to eat and to talk. Apparently talk alone, without action, is not worthwhile enough to merit an exclusive organ, and the mouth therefore performs more than one function.

Mishnah 18

הוּא הָיָה אוֹמֵר — *He [R' Akiva] used to say.* As a counterpoint to 3:1, where Akavia ben Mahalalel spoke of the ignoble, putrid drop that is the genesis of man, R' Akiva portrays the nobility of man, who is created in the image of God. Whereas Akavia

described man's grave as a place of dust and maggots, R' Akiva teaches here that physical death is only the end of the temporal body of man; a Jew's soul is eternal. For the children of the living God, death is merely their return to their Father, no

⧫§ **Silence and wisdom.** The mishnah says that silence is a protector of wisdom; but what is wisdom itself? R' Mordechai of Husyatin taught his followers the secret: One who remains silent in the face of argumentative and insulting individuals has acquired the protective fence of wisdom. Wisdom is the ability to maintain equanimity under such circumstances and not allow the insult to penetrate or cause distress.

After his return to Poland from his first visit to *Eretz Yisrael,* the Imrei Emes of Gur was asked if he had experienced the Sages' promise that the air of the Land gives wisdom. (see *Bava Basra* 158b). Smiling, he replied, "Yes, the Sages did make that promise, but they also said that the protective fence for wisdom is silence." Intelligent people know of what they speak; fools speak of what they know (*Minchas Shabbos*).

⧫§ **Grooming the image.** The Midrash relates that Hillel the Elder once took leave of his students, telling them that he had to tend to a *mitzvah*. In the spirit of תּוֹרָה הִיא וְלִלְמֹד אֲנִי צָרִיךְ, [everything a true Torah sage does] *is Torah and I [the disciple] must learn [see Berachos 62a]),* his students asked where he was going. He replied, "To use the bathhouse." "What type of *mitzvah* is that?" his disciples asked. Hillel replied, "If the caretakers in theaters and stadiums wash and shine the statues there and are paid to do so, certainly I, who was created in the image of God, have need to wash and groom myself" (*Vayikra Rabbah* 34).

18. He [R' Akiva] used to say: Beloved is man, for he was created in [God's] image; it is indicative of a greater love that it was made known to him that he was created in [God's] image,

---

cause for undue sadness. It is in preparation for the spiritual reckoning of which Akavia ben Mahalalel speaks that God gave the Jewish people His most precious vessel, the Torah. Properly followed, it serves to temper the sway of the evil inclination and to guide man on a path of righteousness, which leads to exoneration on the eventual day of judgment beyond the grave (*Ruach Chaim*).

חָבִיב אָדָם שֶׁנִּבְרָא בְצֶלֶם — *Beloved is man, for he was created in [God's] image.* "More beloved than whom? More beloved than animals? Isn't that obvious? More beloved even than the angels" (*Maharal*). Man is the pinnacle and focal point of Creation. More precious to God than any other creature, he was created in the image of his Maker. This is true of all men, Jew and non-Jew alike (*Tosafos Yom Tov;* see *Sfas Emes*).

Since God has no physical form, the term *image* is employed in a borrowed sense and indicates that man is endowed with some Godly element which sets him apart from all other creatures. *Rambam* (*Guide* 1:1) defines this "image" as man's ability to perceive ideas intellectually and to recognize the Creator. *Maharal* objects to this definition, since angels share this quality with man. Instead, he, followed by *Tiferes Yisrael*, views man's *freedom of choice* as the Godly element in man, a quality which even angels do not enjoy. Just as God's actions are

not controlled by any other force in the heavenly spheres, so man's activities are not controlled by any earthly creature. Since man is endowed with this quality of Divinity, it is incumbent upon him to do God's will (*Rashi*).

Maharal offers insight into the term "image." A picture drawn with ink is not a true replication of the flesh-and-blood person it seeks to portray. Rather, it is a representation *in a totally different medium* of the original. Man is a physical representation of God, Who is other-worldly and non-physical.

חִבָּה יְתֵרָה נוֹדַעַת לוֹ שֶׁנִּבְרָא בְצֶלֶם — *it is indicative of a greater love that it was made known to him that he was created in [God's] image.* The translation follows *Rav, Rambam* and *R' Yonah*. Often one does favors for others out of pity and does not even bother to let his beneficiary know what he has done for him. This is because he considers the beneficiary beneath him. God, however, acts differently; by letting man know of the great favor He has done for him by creating him in His own image, God exhibits His extraordinary love of man. Thus, man's creation entails a double gift: (a) being created in the image of God; (b) being given an awareness of this fact.

Rashi renders: God showed a greater love to man by creating him in God's image. [The creation in His image itself is the expression of greater love.]

⏃⏃ **Jew and gentile alike.** All men must therefore be accorded proper respect, and one must deal with them honestly and forthrightly. In his *Be'er HaGolah* notes to *Choshen Mishpat*, R' Moshe Rivkash writes with uncharacteristic elaboration of the proper attitude to adopt in business dealings with non-Jews. Just as one should return a lost object to a non-Jew in order to sanctify God's Name and to portray Jews as honest and loyal people (see *Choshen Mishpat* 266:1), so one should not exploit a monetary mistake made by a non-Jew (ibid. 348:2, *Rema,* and *Be'er HaGolah* §4). He writes: "I write this for posterity, for I saw many who became great and wealthy through dishonest dealings with non-Jews, only to see their fortunes disappear, allowing them to leave nothing for their children. Those who sanctified the Name of God by returning even sizable sums of money which were earned through the oversight of non-Jews were blessed with great fortune and success."

Tanna d'Vei Eliyahu (quoted in *Be'er HaGolah* to *Choshen Mishpat* 231:1) tells of one who sold dates to a non-Jew and cheated him on the weight. With the profit he earned from his larcenous sale, he bought a pitcher of oil, which cracked in transport and spilled out completely. Eliyahu *HaNavi* commented: "Blessed is the Omnipresent, Who shows no favoritism. We are taught that one may not steal — even from a non-Jew."

שֶׁנֶּאֱמַר: ,,כִּי בְּצֶלֶם אֱלֹהִים עָשָׂה אֶת הָאָדָם." חֲבִיבִין יִשְׂרָאֵל, שֶׁנִּקְרְאוּ בָנִים לַמָּקוֹם; חִבָּה יְתֵרָה נוֹדַעַת לָהֶם שֶׁנִּקְרְאוּ בָנִים לַמָּקוֹם, שֶׁנֶּאֱמַר: ,,בָּנִים אַתֶּם לַיהוה

Man's ability to experience a closeness to God is the greatest gift in life, and it is possible only because he possesses inherently Godly qualities. It is thus in a great outpouring of His love that He creates human beings in His image (*Maharal*).

שֶׁנֶּאֱמַר: ,,כִּי בְּצֶלֶם אֱלֹהִים עָשָׂה אֶת הָאָדָם" — *as it says: "For in the image of God He made man"* (*Genesis* 9:6). The quoted verse is the instance where God told Noah of his Divine aspect, whereas the earlier verses in *Genesis* (1:25,26 etc.) that speak of man as a physical *representation* of Godliness are statements of fact (*Tiferes Yisrael*).

The verse cited by R' Akiva is the Torah's explanation of why murder is treated as such a heinous crime that a murderer is liable to the death penalty. The complete verse reads: *Whoever sheds the blood of man, by man shall his blood be shed, for in the image of God He made man.* Human life is so valuable to God that one who takes it deserves to

die. The severity of the punishment reflects the severity of the crime (*Maharal*). This verse was stated to Noah after the deluge, and emphasizes that even after man's stature was diminished in the wake of his sin, he still remains in the image of God (*Magen Avos*).

חֲבִיבִין יִשְׂרָאֵל, שֶׁנִּקְרְאוּ בָנִים לַמָּקוֹם — *Beloved are the people of Israel, for they are described as children of the Omnipresent.* Although all people are created in the image of God, they can, through misdeed, cause the Divine image to leave them. Jews, however, are deemed spiritual children of God; just as a child can never lose his status as a child no matter how much he sins against his father, so the people of Israel can never lose their special status as children of their Father in Heaven (*Tiferes Yisrael*).

The Talmud (*Kiddushin* 36a) cites a dispute between R' Meir and R' Yehudah. R' Yehudah says that Jews are considered children of God only when they comply with

---

⋘§ **Don't waste the opportunity.** The Chofetz Chaim offers an interesting parable to illustrate the connection between man's Divine image and his duty to fulfill God's will: A wealthy person once chanced upon a less fortunate acquaintance. The poor man was thrilled to see him. "Would you perchance be able to lend me a thousand rubles?"

"A thousand rubles is a hefty sum," replied the rich man. The pauper begged, "You know that until recently I was doing well. My business took a drastic turn for the worse, and I need to get back on my feet. A great opportunity has presented itself, and I need a thousand rubles to complete the deal."

Impressed by his friend's earnest plea, the wealthy man finally agreed to grant the loan. After arranging the terms of repayment, they parted company. The poor man took the money home, but instead of investing it in some worthwhile venture, he carefully placed it in his drawer and left it there untouched. On the day of repayment, he took the stack of bills out of his drawer and returned them to his benefactor.

The wealthy person looked carefully at the pile of currency and realized that the bills were the exact ones he had originally given the poor man — and that they were even stacked the same way. He could not control his annoyance. "How do you have the nerve to return this money? You begged me for the loan in order to survive, and it was not easy for me to give it to you. After all that, you simply let the money sit and made no attempt to use it profitably?"

Similarly, we are the paupers and God is our Benefactor. He creates us in His Image, lending us a precious soul and giving us the opportunity to use the loan in order to produce spiritual profit in the form of Torah and *mitzvos*. We, however, like the foolish pauper, let the power of our souls lie dormant and never bother to use our loan for any worthwhile investment. We must not return the soul in the original state it was given to us; it is our duty instead to add luster to it by perfecting our existence. When the time finally comes to return our souls to God, how annoyed He will be to see that they are in their original condition! Man is especially beloved to God, and the gift that He gives us is meant to be used, not ignored.

as it is said: *For in the image of God He made man* (*Genesis* 9:6). Beloved are the people of Israel, for they are described as children of the Omnipresent; it is indicative of a greater love that it was made known to them that they are described as children of the Omnipresent, as it is said: *You are children of HASHEM,*

His wishes. R' Meir disagrees: even when they behave towards Him without proper filial respect and devotion, they still enjoy the special favored status of being "God's children." *Rashba* (*Responsa* I:194 and 242) notes that although the law generally follows R' Yehudah in his disputes with R' Meir (see *Eruvin* 46b), here the ruling follows the opinion of R' Meir. Accordingly, Jews are irrevocably considered children of the Omnipresent.

The Prophets refer to Israel as "God's children" even while chastising them for their worst sins. Jeremiah (4:22) calls them foolish children, blind to the ramifications of sin; Moses deems them disloyal sons (*Deuteronomy* 32:20). Isaiah accuses them of the corruption of idolatry, yet still calls them children (*Isaiah* 1:4).

חִבָּה יְתֵרָה נוֹדַעַת לָהֶם שֶׁנִּקְרְאוּ בָנִים לַמָּקוֹם — *it is indicative of a greater love that it was made known to them that they are described as children of the Omnipresent.* Since God seeks the love of the Jewish people, He explicitly expresses His love of them and waits for them to reciprocate (*Maharal*).

The Talmud (*Eruvin* 18b) instructs that one must never utter more than partial praise of a person in his presence. If God calls the people of Israel His children, it certainly follows that the Godly love they enjoy is even greater than that of a father for a son (*Ohr HaChaim*). By informing the people of Israel of their privileged status, the Almighty not only gave them cause for pride, but also let them know their potential and what their spiritual goals should be (*R' Meir Zlotowitz*).

שֶׁנֶּאֱמַר: ,,בָּנִים אַתֶּם לַה׳ אֱלֹהֵיכֶם׳׳ — *as it is said, "You are children of HASHEM, your God"* (*Deuteronomy* 14:1). The Jewish people are *children of God* and must conduct their lives in accordance with this exalted station. This is why God forbade them to engage in the mutilating, self-destructive mourning practices of the Amorites. As *children of God,* Jews should be beautiful, and they therefore must not cut themselves or make a bald spot between their eyes (*Rashi, Deuteronomy* ibid.).

In addition, as *children of God,* a Jew must understand that even though the body eventually

---

⚜ **Irreplaceable.** Even when he sins, a Jew remains a Jew (see *Sanhedrin* 44a); his elevated status as a member of God's chosen people is immutable. This is the key to understanding a very perplexing incident recorded in the Talmud. God told the prophet Hosea, "Your children [the nation of Israel] have sinned." The prophet answered, "Master of the World, the whole world is yours; take another nation in their place" (*Pesachim* 87a). Why would the prophet make the condemnatory proposition that God (Heaven forbid) exchange His holy nation for another? Explains R' Elimelech of Lizhensk: Hosea meant to say to God, "Search through Your whole world and *see if You can find a nation as good as they are.* No matter how much they sin, they are still better than anyone else Your world has to offer, and no one can be substituted for them."

The awareness of one's specialness in his father's eyes gives him the strength to bear the father's occasional harshness and punishment. When times are hard, the Jewish people, aware that they are "God's children," are able to rise above the difficulties, supremely confident that whatever their merciful Father in Heaven sends upon them is ultimately for their benefit (*Toldos Yaakov Yosef*).

⚜ **Full capacity.** R' Mattisyahu Friedman offers an example. A father bought his child a very sophisticated computer, complete with state-of-the-art software. One day he observed the child doing simple computations on the machine. As he entered the room, the boy said to him, "Father, thank you for the present. Now I can easily do my addition and subtraction homework." The father responded in surprise, "The capabilities of this computer go far beyond simple arithmetic! Let me show you what it can do."

God showed us extraordinary love by informing us of our potential for spiritual greatness. Had He not done so, we might never realize what we really can become.

perishes, the soul remains intact and is gathered in by God. Thus, despite the natural grief that one feels at the loss of a loved one, a Jew should never be so terrified by death that he would mutilate his body. Such behavior is fit only for those to whom death is chillingly final (*Ramban; Sforno*).

HaChassid Yaavetz explains why the verse of proof is the one from *Deuteronomy*, rather than the verse from *Exodus*, where God says to Moses, *You shall say to Pharaoh, "So said HASHEM: My firstborn son is Israel"* (*Exodus* 4:22). Even though these words indeed convey the thought that Israel is God's most worthy and beloved nation, just as a firstborn has a special place in his parents' affections, nonetheless it was never stated directly to the people. The verse cited in our mishnah was stated to the nation, thus *conveying explicitly to them* a sense of God's overwhelming love for them.

Maharal explains alternatively that the knowledge of God's extraordinary love for His people does not come from a verse, but from the prohibition to engage in excessive mourning practices, a *mitzvah* which gives concrete expression to that love. According to *Toras Avos*, this verse, stated after the cataclysmic episode of the Golden Calf, proves that even after experiencing the throes of sin, a Jew retains his elevated status as a "child of God." The verse in *Exodus* 4:22 was taught before the incident of the Golden Calf occurred and would not prove the point quite as forcefully. [See also *Tosafos Yom Tov.*]

חֲבִיבִין יִשְׂרָאֵל, שֶׁנִּתַּן לָהֶם כְּלִי חֶמְדָּה — *Beloved are the people of Israel, for a cherished utensil was given to them.* The Torah is the tool that God used to create the world. King Solomon speaks in the name of the Torah when he says, *Then I was by Him as the*

implement of His craft (*Proverbs* 8:30), as the Torah states figuratively, "I was the instrument used by the Holy One at the very beginning — for He looked carefully at the Torah and then created the universe accordingly." It was this precious implement which God gave exclusively to His beloved nation, the children of Israel (*Rashi, Machzor Vitry*).

R' Yonah (based on a text that reads כְּלִי חֶמְדָּה שֶׁבּוֹ נִבְרָא הָעוֹלָם, *a precious implement with which the world was created*) explains: Like an artisan who expresses his affection for someone by presenting them with the tools of his trade — tools which the artisan created with his own hands — so God gave us His Torah. Alternatively, this text may be rendered, "*for which* the world was created." All of creation came into existence in order that man learn and fulfill the Torah. God made everything in order to provide for the needs of one who studies Torah and practices its dictates. *Rambam* states that a man who plants a lavish orchard may have done so by Divine plan, for the sole purpose that a pious individual who passes by on one occasion will be able to find shade there.

King David speaks of the inestimable preciousness of Torah: *They* [the words of Torah] *are more desirable than gold — than even much fine gold; and sweeter than honey, than drippings from the combs* (*Psalms* 19:11). In this sense Torah is called כְּלִי חֶמְדָּה, *a precious utensil*. The other commentators offer various shades of meanings to explain the phrase: According to *Midrash Shmuel,* כְּלִי חֶמְדָּה means *a coveted instrument* [as in לֹא תַחְמֹד, *thou*

⋖§ **Remember who you are.** The greatest sin a Jew can commit is to forget that he is a member of a royal family, a child of the King (*R' Shlomo of Karlin*). According to R' Avraham of Slonim, this is the homiletic meaning of the words of King Solomon, מוּסַר ה׳ בְּנִי אַל תִּמְאָס, *The rebuke of God, my son, do not detest* (*Proverbs* 3:11). God chastises us in order to help us direct our lives. What does He say to us? "בְּנִי, you are My son, a prince of Royalty. אַל תִּמְאָס, do not make yourself detestable, staining yourself with the soil of sin. Conduct yourself as one of royal descent and thus protect the honor of the King."

⋖§ **Tool of autonomy.** R' Meir Dan Plotzki notes the mode of expression in the mishnah: "A precious implement *was given to them.*" This means that the power to make proper interpretations and halachic decisions was given completely to man. The Talmud (*Bava Metzia* 59b) relates that in response to Godly intervention in a halachic dispute, R' Yehoshua said, "It [the Torah] is not in Heaven." Men, by means of the office of the Sanhedrin, have full autonomy to establish halachic practice. Thus, we are blessed that God gave us the Torah, His creative tool, that we may also enjoy full creative autonomy. [See *HaChassid Yaavetz.*]

shalt not covet (Exodus 20:14)]. When Moses went up to Heaven to receive the Torah from God, the Heavenly angels coveted it. "Place Your splendor on the Heavens," they asked of God, questioning why something so precious was to be given to mere mortals. Nonetheless, God gave the Torah to man (see *Shabbos* 88b).

Alternatively, the term חֶמְדָּה implies constant desire. The more one tastes of Torah, the greater is his appetite for it. One who studies the word of God develops an insatiable need for more. The

Zohar teaches that God created the emotions of pleasure so that man would develop a passion for Torah.

R' Mendel of Kotzk renders חֶמְדָּה in the sense of a [proper] receptacle for one's desire. Every man is born with innate passion and desire. The fool, under the sway of his evil inclination, channels his desires into the vanity of worldly pleasures, while the informed soul pours all its passion into the exhilarating experience of participating in God's infinite wisdom.

◂§ The Talmud (*Shabbos* 88b) reports that God asked Moses to refute the argument of the angels. Moses did so by describing man's vulnerability. "The Torah teaches, *You shall have no other gods (Exodus* 20:3). Do you [angels] live among idolaters [that you need to be taught to avoid their influence]? Do you angels need a Sabbath as a day of rest? Is there jealousy and hatred among you that you need to be commanded not to murder? Are you susceptible to the human stirrings of passion that necessitate the prohibition of adultery?" Torah addresses the human condition, seeking to elevate man and make him into a human angel. Celestial angels have no need for a Torah.

R' Shneur Zalman of Liadi (in another context) offered an enchanting tale which captures this message: A king sent his only son to a faraway land to study at several prestigious universities. In this way, the king hoped, the prince would acquire proficiency in many areas of knowledge and become an accomplished scholar and an enlightened human being.

One day, the king received terrible news; his son had fallen victim to a terrible disease and was rapidly approaching death. All the great doctors of that land had given up hope of finding a cure for the young prince. Overcome by the gravity of the situation, the king issued a royal proclamation, promising untold wealth to anybody who could find a way to save his dear son. Many people came forward to offer ideas, medicines, or therapies, but nothing succeeded. Finally, one person offered the following solution: "The only hope for the boy is if we can find a certain rare and expensive jewel, grind it into powder, and add the powder to wine. If the prince drinks that potion, he will be cured."

Hoping against hope, the king sent emissaries across the length and breadth of his kingdom in search of the precious stone, but to no avail. Finally, one of his attendants whispered to him, "There is one place where this stone can be found."

"Where, where?" cried the king. "I'm ready to send messengers anywhere in the world to save my precious son, the apple of my eye."

The attendant replied quietly, "There is no need to send anyone anyplace. The stone is right here — in the center of the king's crown; but how can we remove it and ruin the symbol of royal authority?"

"Don't delay," the king interrupted. "Of what worth is my entire kingdom if my only son dies? And if he is saved, it is the greatest glory for my kingdom. Remove the stone."

Without the Torah, man is spiritually dead. It is the nation of Israel, God's children, who carry the banner of His kingdom in this world. If they are dead, the King has no one to bring His message to the world. Therefore, God is ready to give away His most precious stone, the Torah, to save His son, Israel, from the debilitating spiritual ravages of our world.

◂§ **Growing appetite.** Torah is the food of the soul. Like food, which expands the stomach and thereby the appetite, the learning of Torah stretches one's capacity and appetite for the word of God. The Jewish nation is royalty and cannot subsist on standard fare; as the children of God, they must have Torah for their spiritual sustenance.

יְתֵרָה נוֹדַעַת לָהֶם, שֶׁנִּתַּן לָהֶם כְּלִי חֶמְדָּה, שֶׁנֶּאֱמַר: „כִּי לֶקַח טוֹב נָתַתִּי לָכֶם, תּוֹרָתִי אַל תַּעֲזֹבוּ.‟

[יט] **הַכֹּל** צָפוּי, וְהָרְשׁוּת נְתוּנָה. וּבְטוֹב הָעוֹלָם נָדוֹן,

---

These two clauses of the mishnah are connected as cause and effect. Since Israel are the children of God, He therefore gave them His most precious possession — His Torah.

חִבָּה יְתֵרָה נוֹדַעַת לָהֶם, שֶׁנִּתַּן לָהֶם כְּלִי חֶמְדָּה — *it is indicative of a greater love that it was made known to them that they were given a cherished utensil.* The centrality of Torah to the existence of the world was revealed only to Israel. Torah is the blueprint of Creation and also the key to its continued existence. In a gesture of love toward His people, God revealed this to them (*Shaar Asher*).

Maharal comments that God placed Mount Sinai above the heads of the Jewish people and threatened to bury them alive if they would not accept the Torah (see *Shabbos* 88a) in order to impress upon them that all of Creation is meaningless and unjustified without the Torah.

According to *Tiferes Yisrael*, this part of the mishnah refers to Torah scholars. It is upon them that God showers His extraordinary love by allowing them to understand His Torah. [Therefore, one who does not accord a Torah scholar proper respect is especially vulnerable to God's wrath.]

שֶׁנֶּאֱמַר: „כִּי לֶקַח טוֹב נָתַתִּי לָכֶם, תּוֹרָתִי אַל תַּעֲזֹבוּ‟ — *as it is said: "For I have given you a good teaching; do not forsake My Torah"* (*Proverbs* 4:2). [See *Rashi*

ibid. and *R' Yonah.*] God describes Creation as something good: *And God saw all that He created, and it was very good* (*Genesis* 1:31). All of Creation was brought into being for the express purpose of the fulfillment of the Torah. Torah is therefore called a "good" teaching (*Rav*). Success in life is dependent upon one's loyalty to Torah.

People pay attention to the words of others for one of three reasons: (a) The words are intrinsically true and interesting; (b) they offer practical advice; (c) the speaker is worthy of respect. The verse from *Proverbs* included all three conditions: (a) The Torah is intrinsically good (לֶקַח טוֹב); (b) it teaches a Jew how to conduct his life (לָכֶם — it was given to *you*); (c) it is the word of God (תּוֹרָתִי), which in and of itself makes it so precious (*Mili D'Avos*).

The Midrash invokes this verse to teach that God, so to speak, gave Himself to His nation along with His Torah and offers a parable: A king married off his only daughter to a prince. When the young couple were ready to move back to the prince's country, the king was faced with a dilemma. He could not demand that they stay with him, yet he could not bear to part with his daughter. He finally asked that they build him a small chamber wherever they lived. Similarly, God wanted to give the Jews the Torah, yet He could not part with it. He asked them to build Him a Tabernacle so that He could come and dwell among them and thereby remain with His Torah (see *Shemos Rabbah* 33:1).

Mishnah 19

הַכֹּל צָפוּי — *Everything is foreseen. Rambam* and *R' Yonah* explain that all of man's actions, past and future, are known to God. He is aware of how man will act long before man even thinks of acting. King Da-

vid stated this cardinal truth: *O* HASHEM, *You have scrutinized me and You Know. You know my sitting down and my rising up, You understand my thought from afar [even before I conceive it]* (*Psalms* 139:1-2).

⋙ **King and Father.** The Vilna Gaon explained the fifth blessing in the *Shemoneh Esrei* prayer, "Bring us back, our **Father**, to Your Torah, and bring us near, our **King**, to Your service." Why does the word Father apply to the Torah and the word King to His service? All people, Jews and non-Jews alike, are enjoined to *serve* God; this explains the second part of the blessing, which asks the King to draw all His servants near to His service. However, the King will allow only His children into the deep recesses of His treasury, to enjoy His most prized possession: Torah study is only given to Israel, God's spiritual progeny, and therefore it is our *Father* whom we beseech to bring us back to His Torah.

greater love that it was made known to them that they were given a cherished utensil, as it is said: *For I have given you a good teaching; do not forsake My Torah (Proverbs 4:2).*

19. Everything is foreseen, yet the freedom of choice is given. The world is judged with goodness, and everything

---

All of man's actions, even those done in private and in the utmost secrecy, are revealed to God; nothing can be hidden from Him (*Rav* and *Rashi*).

וְהָרְשׁוּת נְתוּנָה — *yet the freedom of choice is given.* No preordained force in the universe, not even God, forces man to act the way he does (*Rashi* and *Rav*). *Rambam* and *R' Yonah* render: *and yet man is granted free choice.* Even though God knows what man will do, this advance knowledge in no way affects man's choice. Man's path is not predestined; he enjoys total freedom of choice. The Torah teaches this axiom of faith: *I have placed life and death before you, blessing and curse; and you shall choose life (Deuteronomy 30:19).*

Machzor Vitry emphasizes that this is a fundamental concept of Divine Providence. Although God foresees the course man will adopt, this in no way restricts his complete autonomy to do as he pleases. Nothing is imposed upon him, and God's foreknowledge in no way impedes his free will. Even if God sees someone prepared to sin, He does not intervene.

In spite of man's absolute freedom of choice, however, God always knows what he will do. How these two inviolable yet seemingly irreconcilable truths can coexist is, according to *Rambam*, beyond human understanding. He cites the verse *For My thoughts are unlike your thoughts (Isaiah 55:8)* as referring to this contradiction: Man's limited intelligence is incapable of fathoming how God's knowledge is acquired or how it functions (see *Rambam, Hilchos Teshuvah 5:5* and *Raavad ad loc.*).

Tosafos Yom Tov suggests that this contradiction is only problematic if one views God as bound by time.

Since God is *not* bound by the strictures of time, His knowledge of events is unrelated to the human understanding of past and present; He sees all events as if they were happening simultaneously. Hence, the mishnah can be rendered to say that everything is *seen* [indicative of the present], rather than saying that everything is *known,* which indicates foreknowledge and therefore a context of time. Perhaps, states *R' Moshe Almosnino,* this is the thrust of *Rambam's* citation of the verse *For My thoughts [and knowledge] are unlike your thoughts;* meaning that all God's thoughts take place in the "present," and that all events are therefore known, while human beings cannot perceive the future. Thus, God can know what we *will* do in the future without affecting our actions or choices.

Be'er Avos offers an enlightening interpretation: Even though a person has genetic or socially habituated inclinations, whether positive or negative, he is not a prisoner of these tendencies. God allows us the free choice to rise above our so-called "natural" limitations. Man can recreate himself through the spiritual metamorphosis of *teshuvah.* Even though *everything is seen* by God and a man's future can seemingly be predicted based on pre-existing conditions and circumstances, nonetheless he is granted full permission to supersede these "natural" obstacles.

וּבְטוֹב הָעוֹלָם נָדוֹן — *The world is judged with goodness.* God does not judge the world in general or any of its inhabitants [even the wicked (*R' Yonah*)] with strict justice; Divine mercy is always a factor in His judgment (*Rav, Rashi*). *Rambam* explains: God goes beyond the strictures of pure justice and is *slow to anger and abundant in kindness (Exodus 34:6),* both to the righteous and to the evil (see *Eruvin 22a*).

⋖§ **Free to change.** Sometimes we are spiritually paralyzed by others' perception of us. We tend to adopt a desired self-image, which does not allow us to pursue a true spiritual identity. This mishnah inspires in us the courage to become different people. Even God's foreknowledge of our actions, which is exact and irrefutable, need not be an insurmountable obstacle to our will to change. Certainly, we should not allow our fellow man's narrow view of us to confine or limit what we can become.

[כ] **הוּא הָיָה** אוֹמֵר: הַכֹּל נָתוּן בָּעֵרָבוֹן, וּמְצוּדָה

Tiferes Yisrael gives a different rendering: *Justice is meted out to the world for good.* Although God does administer justice, He never does so in a narrow, punitive sense. His judgment is intended to cleanse the soul of the spiritual impurities of sin and to break down the emotional barriers that sin erects between man and God. [Furthermore, it arouses one from his spiritual lethargy.]

According to *Meiri*, the goodness referred to here is the opportunity to repent. God created both the good and evil impulses in man, and He gave us the ability to repent to counteract the successes of the evil inclination. The words *the world is judged with goodness* mean specifically that God accepts repentance.

Mesillas Yesharim (Chapter 4) defines the mercy involved in God's acceptance of repentance. Since the evil deed has already been committed, how does repentance "undo" it? God in His mercy deems the change of the will [that precipitated the evil act] as if the act itself was transformed from evil to good.

[This is indicative of His goodness. King David taught: *Good and upright is HASHEM, therefore He guides sinners on the way* (of repentance) (*Psalms* 25:8).]

Rav offers an alternate reading of *Rambam* in which this clause is explained as a result of the previous one: Since man has free choice, he and the world he lives in are judged according to the choices they make, whether good or, God forbid, bad. Free choice means responsibility, and therefore culpability or merit.

In a homiletic vein, *Midrash Shmuel* explains: One form of Divine justice is that God gives a sinner reward in this world for his few good deeds. Hence, *the world is judged with goodness*, which is dispensed in the here and now, thus effectively excluding the evildoer from the truly meaningful eternal reward.

וְהַכֹּל לְפִי רוֹב הַמַּעֲשֶׂה — *and everything depends on the abundance of good deeds.* Man is condemned or acquitted on the basis of the quality of the majority of his actions, good or bad (*Rashi*). *Rav* and *R' Yonah* alternatively offer: *Everything* — meaning the scope of God's mercy — is commensurate with man's deeds. The more good deeds he does, indicating his desire for good, the greater degree of Divine mercy he is shown. Even the wicked are beneficiaries of Divine goodness, although not to the degree that the righteous enjoy it.

Rashi further suggests that this entire clause refers to the process by which God is able to judge the world benevolently. By *temporarily* looking aside from man's continuous pattern of transgression, God can allow the continued existence of the world. However, everything must ultimately be accounted for; hence even though He *judges the world with goodness* [וּבְטוֹב הָעוֹלָם נָדוֹן], eventually *everything is dependent on the abundance* [i.e., majority] *of deeds* [וְהַכֹּל לְפִי רוֹב הַמַּעֲשֶׂה], be they good or evil.

◆§ **Enduring love.** Rebbetzin Rischel Kotler (widow of the late Rabbi Shneur Kotler, *Rosh Yeshivah* of Lakewood) is a woman of formidable emotional and spiritual strength, who overcame the double tragedy of losing her husband and a gifted son to cancer. A woman she knew, who was only marginally committed to traditional Judaism, had also had many strains placed on her faith. She asked the Rebbetzin, "Isn't it enough already?" the Rebbetzin replied compassionately, "God still loves you. If He had given up on you, He would have stopped the *petch* (blows) long ago."

◆§ **A call from Above.** *Rambam* (*Hilchos Teshuvah* 6:5) explains that God shows man the way back to Him by sending prophets to teach His ways and to awaken people to repentance. On a more subtle level, this may mean that God implanted in man an ability to learn and grow: "For as long as man is drawn to wisdom and righteousness, he passionately chases them. This is what the Sages taught: 'One who attempts to purify himself is given Divine assistance [in his search for purity and truth].'"

20. He used to say: Everything is given on collateral, and a net

---

Rambam, however, separates the two expressions, viewing the second one as an independent idea. He renders רוֹב הַמַּעֲשֶׂה as the frequency with which one performs a deed. Man's virtue is determined by the frequency with which he repeats good deeds. For example, it is preferable to dispense many small gifts of charity to many individuals, rather than to give one large gift to one person. A single great act may be the product of a temporary stirring of kind feelings that quickly dissipates and does not allow one to internalize the trait of magnanimity. It is only through habituation to virtuous behavior that one firmly acquires good character. The mishnah therefore teaches that

everything is dependent on the *number* of times that one performs a good deed, rather than on the magnitude of a particular act.

A good deed is also defined by its context. One who goes against his nature to act virtuously (e.g., when one who is naturally stingy gives charity) deserves and receives a greater reward. Likewise, a poor man who gives beyond his means receives a commensurate reward. Motivation also plays a role; charity dispensed with fanfare for the honor it brings is not as deserving of reward as that which is given quietly and with dignity. Hence, the term רוֹב הַמַּעֲשֶׂה should be translated as *the greatness inherent in the act* (*Tiferes Yisrael*).

Mishnah 20

This mishnah is an expansion of mishnah 19, and explains the manner in which Divine justice is dispensed (*Tosafos Yom Tov*). It likens God's conduct of the world to that of a business enterprise. Man is granted the goodness of the world and the freedom to partake of all its opportunities. He may borrow — meaning that he may enjoy the world's pleasures and riches — on the pledge "that he will use it all for good and Godly purposes." However, no debt that he has left unpaid — long outstanding as it may be — is ever canceled; no one can evade his responsibilities.

הוּא הָיָה אוֹמֵר — *He used to say.* R' Akiva would offer the analogy in this mishnah to describe the terms of man's life in this world and the guidelines he must follow. God conducts His world much like a business, defining credit terms for His people, taking collateral, eventually collecting all debts, and returning great profits for those who work hard to make the business a success. The mishnah outlines each portion of this process.

הַכֹּל נָתוּן בָּעֵרָבוֹן — *Everything is given on collateral.* Man's life and death are totally in the hands of

God, much like collateral for a loan, which may be collected at any time; no one can keep God from calling in the debt (*Rav* and *Meiri*).

Man's soul is his "co-signer" before God, taking responsibility for all his actions. If he uses his body to live properly, he earns merit for his soul; if not, the soul must come in judgment before God. Alternatively, every Jew is a guarantor that his fellow Jew produce spiritual profit for God, as the Talmud states: "All Jews are responsible for each other"(*Sotah* 37a). Thus, God's investment in the well-being of an individual Jew is assured by his fellow Jews (*Rashi*).

◂§ **Your need is mine.** This concept of joint responsibility has halachic ramifications, in that one may perform certain *mitzvos* on behalf of a fellow Jew and thus fulfill his obligation for him. For example, one who has already recited *Kiddush* may recite it again on behalf of others who have not yet done so. Since all Jews are responsible for each other, to enable a fellow Jew to fulfill his obligation is deemed a *mitzvah* act in itself, even though the first person has already fulfilled his personal obligation (see *Orach Chaim* 273:4; *Chazon Ish, Orach Chaim* 29:1).

According to *R' Yonah, everything* refers to all of life's pleasures and enjoyments, which are given on collateral. Whatever one takes from this world, even the inheritance he receives from his parents, does not really belong to him; it is given to him by God as a loan, and he must repay it by "spending" it eventually on God's behalf. In this world man is like one who enters an apparently deserted house and finds a fully set table laid out with a gourmet meal. He immediately eats the food, never realizing that the owner of the house is watching him all the while from a hidden location, calculating every bite. So too, the Master of the Universe reckons every bit of worldly pleasure we indulge in. The bill will eventually be presented, and we will have to pay up. [But as long as we fulfill our obligations to the Master of the house, He graciously provides us with all our needs, just as a benevolent human master gives his loyal servants whatever they need to enjoy life (*R' A.C. Feuer*).]

Tiferes Yisrael explains further that one cannot rely on his abilities, intelligence, money, or success, all of which are a loan from God which He may call in at any time. God waits for a person to use his abilities for a higher purpose, and if he should be remiss in this task, God might revoke the loan. Further, it is easier to fall into failure than to achieve success; it is easier to lose wealth than to accumulate it; and to lose one's health is easier than to recuperate fully from sickness. Likewise, it is much easier to remain ignorant than to acquire knowledge. Hence, one must make all efforts to retain his God-given assets by using them in God's service, thus guarding God's safekeeping (*Tiferes Yisrael*).

וּמְצוֹדָה פְרוּסָה עַל כָּל הַחַיִּים — *and a net is spread over all the living.* The net of the Angel of Death is always spread out, searching for victims on whom to inflict suffering and death (*Machzor Vitry, Rav*). Like the fate of fish ensnared in the net of the fisherman, eventual judgment and death are unavoidable (*Rashi, R' Yonah*). The Evil Inclination acts as a hunter who spreads out his bait-filled net. A foolish bird believes that the hunter has put the food out for its benefit, but it is intended only to lure the bird into the inescapable trap [see *Proverbs* 1:17-18] (*R' Yosef Karo* and *Tiferes Yisrael*).

⇜§ **Member of a wedding.** Whatever one has enjoyed in this world will eventually have to be paid for. Often, the price is a diminished share in the world of *true* reward.

The Talmud likens life to a wedding (see *Eruvin* 54a). Rabbi Mendel Kaplan explained this to mean that the immediate gratification one enjoys at a wedding is in inverse proportion to his enduring pleasure. The guests, for example, generally have a great time. Good food, fine wine, music, dancing, and socializing all add up to a pleasure-filled evening. Once they go home, however, they are left with nothing but a memory of an enjoyable few hours.

The parents of the bride and groom are often preoccupied with the managerial details of the celebration, such as the seating and arrangements with the caterer, and are unable to enjoy the wedding in a relaxed way. Once it is over, however, they go home satisfied and grateful that they have seen their children united in marriage.

The people who are the most harried during the evening are the bride and groom themselves. Directed by photographers, forced to smile at all the guests (half of whom they do not even know), tired from the pre-wedding fast combined with the long hours of dancing, they hardly remember anything that took place, until they see the pictures. But, of course, they are the greatest beneficiaries. Their whole lives now lie ahead of them, and they can look forward to long years spent in a fruitful, loving relationship. Thus, the greater enjoyment one has now, the less he tastes later, and vice versa.

The world is very similar. Every bit of pleasure enjoyed here is at the expense of true reward in the next world; conversely, every thrill one forgoes here will earn him a great increase in the quality and quantity of his eternal reward.

is spread over all the living. The shop is open; the Merchant extends credit; the ledger is open; the hand writes; and whoever wishes to borrow, let him come and borrow.

הֶחָנוּת פְּתוּחָה — *The shop is open.* Like a department store, life offers all types of opportunities: A "shopper" may purchase whatever type of merchandise he seeks, bitter or sweet, hot or cold, hard or soft. Likewise, he has freedom to do as much good or evil as he chooses (*Meiri, Rav*).

Rashi emphasizes the lure of negative temptations. Just as one who visits an inn may drink as much wine as he pleases, so one who seeks impurity in his life is granted the opportunity to find it. R' Yonah adds that man is often so dazzled by the array of things to be had that he takes more of this world than he can afford. He must take care to exercise both financial and spiritual restraint, not "buying" more on credit than he can eventually pay for [by using them as a tool for the service of God].

וְהַחֶנְוָנִי מַקִּיף — *the Merchant extends credit.* God does not exact immediate retribution for man's misdeeds (*Rav, Rashi, Meiri*).

Midrash Shmuel understands the *merchant* to be one's evil impulse, which induces him to buy beyond his means in the shop of sin, thus burdening him with eternal debt. As long as man continues to sin, the evil inclination does not report man's outstanding moral debts for fear that he may stop his overindulgence. Only when he has seemingly satisfied his desires is the statement of charges issued and the collection begun. *Tiferes Yisrael* extends this idea by rendering the word מַקִּיף as "solicit": The *merchant* goes around soliciting "business," offering his sinful wares to potential customers. [Just as modern advertising first creates "needs" in man and then supplies the goods to satisfy them, so the hidden persuader subliminally convinces a person that the sinful wares being offered are just what the customer is lacking.]

Midrash Shmuel offers a positive alternative interpretation: God has such confidence that man will live correctly that He is willing to offer him an "advance" by providing him with his physical needs even before he legitimately earns them through his Torah study and *mitzvah* performance.

וְהַפִּנְקָס פָּתוּחַ, וְהַיָּד כּוֹתֶבֶת — *the ledger is open; the hand writes.* Let man not be fooled. The Heavenly Ledger is always open; no deed is unrecorded or forgotten; the Shopkeeper is never too busy to enter man's deeds in His ledger (*Rav*). Like the innkeeper who records every drop of wine consumed by his patrons, God notes every misdeed of man in His Book of Remembrance (*Rashi*).

Meiri cites the Talmud: "Anyone who claims that God forgoes [exacting retribution for sin], may he lose his innards. Rather, God is patient — but eventually collects that to which He is entitled" (*Bava Kamma* 50a).

וְכָל הָרוֹצֶה לִלְווֹת יָבֹא וְיִלְוֶה — *and whoever wishes to borrow, let him come and borrow.* With his free choice, man can control the extent of his involvement in the pleasures of this world, and he can therefore control his debt to Heaven. The wicked foolishly overindulge themselves and are quickly overburdened when payment comes due. The righteous borrow only the capital (worldly pleasures) that they need to conduct the *real* business of life (Torah study, *mitzvah* fulfillment, and acts of

---

≈§ **Giving another chance.** God accepts man's heartfelt repentance even if He knows that the person may sin again; as long as someone earnestly wants to come back to God and settle his account, God will receive him with grace. This is but one of the myriad ways in which God is unlike mortal man, who would never forgive his fellow if he knew that the misdeed would be repeated. God is therefore likened to a sympathetic shopkeeper who is kind enough to offer credit, even though he suspects that the customer is not a very good risk. This is homiletically implied in God's response (*Exodus* 33:19) to Moses' when he entreated that Israel be forgiven for the sin of the Golden Calf: *I shall show favor* [i.e., accept no repentance] *to one who I will* [have to] *show favor* [after he sins again in the future], *and I will show mercy* [and forgive] *to one who I will show mercy* [again, after he backslides again] (*Doresh LePerakim*).

וְהַגַּבָּאִים מַחֲזִירִין תָּדִיר בְּכָל יוֹם וְנִפְרָעִין מִן הָאָדָם,
מִדַּעְתּוֹ וְשֶׁלֹּא מִדַּעְתּוֹ, וְיֵשׁ לָהֶם עַל מַה שֶׁיִּסְמְכוּ. וְהַדִּין
דִּין אֱמֶת, וְהַכֹּל מְתֻקָּן לִסְעוּדָה.

---

kindness toward the needy), never allowing themselves to become mired in the staggering debt of iniquity (Rav, R' Yonah, Rambam).

Free choice can have a further harmful consequence; for man not only has the freedom to sin, but the Evil Inclination also sees to it that he has whatever monies he needs to support his sinful habits (Midrash Shmuel).

וְהַגַּבָּאִים מַחֲזִירִין תָּדִיר בְּכָל יוֹם וְנִפְרָעִין מִן הָאָדָם — The collectors make their rounds constantly, every day, and collect payment from the person. "The collectors" is a figure of speech for death and other forms of punishment that are visited on man (Rambam, Meiri). All life's pains and difficulties are God's messengers to collect payment for one's moral debts (Rashi, Rav).

The Talmud (Arachin 16a) teaches that even the slightest inconvenience one may suffer, such as putting his hand in the wrong pocket when looking for change, is considered יִסּוּרִין, suffering. This is God's merciful way of allowing us to pay off our debts in this world.

מִדַּעְתּוֹ וְשֶׁלֹּא מִדַּעְתּוֹ — whether he realizes it or not. Sometimes man remembers his debts — i.e., the cause of his pain and difficulty — and understands the justice of God's punishment; other times he forgets his debts and sees God's judgment as unreasonable (Rav).

When a person recognizes the personal flaws that precipitated his travails, he will repent, correcting the shortcomings that took him into debt. However, a self-righteous person is astounded by suffering. "Why is this happening to me?" he asks incredulously. Such a person may die without ever understanding the need to repent. His wasted life is analogous to one who is indebted to the king. The king sends his sheriff to seize collateral against his debt, but the debtor, unable to admit to himself that he owes anything, cannot fathom why the item is being taken (R' Yonah).

All the difficulties one undergoes in life, whether self-inflicted (one goes into deep water and drowns at the beach, or one lends money to his fellow and is not repaid) or seemingly of an arbitrary nature

---

◆§ **The pain of inconsistency.** While we often find it hard to pay for important things in life — tuition, charity, support of Torah scholarship, the extra few dollars to enhance and beautify our fulfillment of mitzvos — we somehow always manage to find room in our budgets for non-essential and even negative items that do nothing for our spiritual growth.

Beis HaLevi explains that this concept explains the Midrashic expression "Woe to us on the day of judgment; woe to us on the day of rebuke," which was uttered by Joseph's brothers when he revealed himself to them (see Genesis 45:3 and Bereishis Rabbah 93:11). What is the difference between judgment and rebuke? The "day of judgment" is the time when a person will be shown the glaring inconsistencies in his behavior. He may have claimed that he could not wake up early enough to pray at the synagogue, yet he was in his car at 5:30 a.m. on his way to a vacation. Approached for a charitable contribution, he may have excused himself by saying that times were hard, yet somehow he found the wherewithal to host the extravagant wedding or bar mitzvah that all his friends were talking about, or the extra suit or dress that was not really needed.

Joseph used this same idea in rebuking his brothers. He said to them, "I am Joseph; is my father living?" His message was a caustic one: "You, my dear brothers, have lived with internal inconsistency. You constantly appealed to me not to force you to bring Benjamin down to Egypt, since it might fatally affect our father's health. Where was your concern for his health when you sold me?! I am Joseph, whom you sold down to Egypt; is my father still living after you broke his heart by selling me?"

Acknowledging the stinging truth of his words, the brothers understood that not only is one eventually judged for his actions, but he will also have to account for his hypocrisy and face the morally atonal music.

The collectors make their rounds constantly, every day, and collect payment from the person, whether he realizes it or not. They have proof to rely upon; the judgment is a truthful judgment; and everything is prepared for the [final festive] banquet.

(a natural disaster or theft), are from God. His collectors are doing their job (*Tiferes Yisrael*).

וְיֵשׁ לָהֶם עַל מַה שֶׁיִּסְמֹכוּ — *They have proof to rely upon.* Even though man sometimes forgets the actions for which he is now punished, God's "ledger" does not forget. The "collectors," i.e., God and His agents, thus have proof of their right to collect (*Rav*).

Meiri says that "they" refers to the sinners themselves: *and they have something* [i.e., repentance] *to rely upon.* No matter how deeply one becomes mired in sin, it is always possible for him to straighten out his affairs through true heartfelt repentance; and even if he cannot totally eradicate his iniquities, he can certainly lighten the punishment.

Even suffering and sorrow visited upon the righteous are justified. Sometimes it is the result of the righteous person having placed himself in a dangerous situation, from which he could be saved only by miraculous intervention, and he may not have sufficient merit for such a rescue. Or the pain may be a test of his commitment (see 5:4 for the purpose of trials and tests). Or it may be that God was being particularly exacting in his expectations of the righteous, because their very righteousness imposes greater responsibilities upon them to maintain a higher standard of conduct. What may be considered a minor infraction for lesser people may be deemed a significant sin for the righteous. More is expected of them, and they are judged accordingly [see *Bava Kamma* 50a] (*Tiferes Yisrael*).

וְהַדִּין דִּין אֱמֶת — *the judgment is a truthful judgment.* God does not make unreasonable or unrealistic demands of man (*Rav* from *Avodah Zarah* 3a). He is just in expecting men to meet their obligations, and is fair in exacting payment for their spiritual debts.

Meiri continues: First, God tries to arouse a person to repent by inflicting partial punishment on him. If he does not respond, the Eternal Judge is completely justified to impose full punishment.

וְהַכֹּל מְתֻקָּן לִסְעוּדָה — *and everything is prepared for the [final festive] banquet.* The "banquet" is a figurative term for the world of reward, the World to Come. According to *Rav*, the mishnah teaches that once the wicked have received appropriate punishment for their misdeeds, they also have a share in the World to Come. Hence he renders: *And all persons* [rather than "everything"] *are ready for the banquet.*

An earlier mishnah (3:15) and *Sanhedrin* 11:1 list the exceptions, those who do *not* have a share in the World to Come under any conditions (*Tosafos Yom Tov*).

Sefer HaMussar gives a different rendering: *Everyone's share in the banquet is prepared* — whether it is large, small or non-existent. The righteous, who used their lives properly to prepare for the afterlife, will enjoy the fruits of their labors, while the wicked will be denied admission to the banquet and will have to stand aside, enviously observing the rewarding of the righteous (see *Isaiah* 65:13). Further, just as the quality of one's meal depends on the ingredients he purchased, so

---

◆§ **The hidden sheriff.** The Talmud relates that the prophet Samuel saw a frog carry a scorpion across a river, where the scorpion bit a person and caused him to die. Samuel invoked the words of King David: *To fulfill Your decree they stand until this day, for all are Your servants* (Psalms 119:91). Once a man's time has come, all creatures are poised to execute His judgment (*Nedarim* 41; *Rashi* ad loc.).

◆§ **A fool's waste.** *Koheles Rabbah* (6:32) compares one who does not avail himself of the opportunity to repent to a prisoner who ignores a subterranean tunnel that offers him an escape to freedom. The jail warden who observes the scene slaps the prisoner and says to him contemptuously, "Fool, the tunnel is already dug! Why did you not save yourself?" (see *Shaarei Teshuvah* 1:2).

the taste and quality of man's ultimate "banquet" is directly linked to the manner in which he prepared for it in this world. [The Sages taught: "He who makes the effort on Friday (i.e., this world) will eat on the Sabbath (i.e., the World of Reward)" [*Avodah Zarah* 3a] (*Meiri*).

Rambam and *R' Yonah* view this clause as a statement of Divine purpose. All of the processes described in the allegory of this mishnah were put into place by Divine plan so as to provide reward in the World to Come for the good choices a person has made in his lifetime.

Abarbanel, in a novel explanation, renders מְתֻקָּן as *rectified*. All the perceived injustices of this world, wherein the wicked prosper and the righteous suffer, are only temporary. God is just and will redress these imbalances at the final festive banquet, in the world of true reward.

Mishnah 21

רַבִּי אֶלְעָזָר בֶּן עֲזַרְיָה אוֹמֵר — *Rabbi Elazar ben Azariah says.* R' Elazar ben Azariah was a tenth-generation descendant of Ezra the Scribe and a third-generation Tanna. R' Yehudah *HaNasi*, in enumerating the special qualities of each of the Sages, compared him to an itinerant peddler who offers a full array of wares, for his knowledge was so vast that one could learn from him all the myriad areas of Torah (*Avos d'Rabbi Nosson* 18). He was also blessed with great material wealth (*Shabbos* 44b): in fact, the Talmud teaches that one to whom he appears in a dream may expect to acquire wealth (*Berachos* 57b). Due to his combination of wealth and family lineage, he was

---

◄§ **Understanding the inconceivable.** The Holocaust is perhaps the greatest example of this phenomenon, a tragedy which cannot be fully understood by human intellect, but this mishnah assures us that all accounts will eventually be settled. A student of Reb Elchonon Wasserman, who had been in hiding with him in the Kovno ghetto until he was murdered by Lithuanian anti-Semites, related the following: A few days before he was killed, Reb Elchonon told four of his students that he never went to sleep at night until he had an answer for whatever *kashya* (difficulty) a student had asked him during the day. Sometimes he would have to stay up all night working on the problem, but by the next morning he always had a solution for the *bachur*.

Only one question he had been unable to answer: Why? "Why my *zeide*?" "Why my *bubbe*?" "Why my mother and father?" "Why my wife and children?"

"I still don't know the answer to that question," Reb Elchonon told his students, "but at least I understand *why* the question cannot be answered." He then proceeded to relate the following parable.

A man who knew nothing at all about agriculture came to a farmer and asked to be taught about farming. The farmer took him out to the field and asked him what he saw. "I see a beautiful piece of land, lush with grass and pleasing to the eye," the visitor replied. He then watched aghast as the farmer plowed the grass under and turned the beautiful green field into a mass of shallow brown ditches.

"Why did you ruin the field?" he demanded.

"Be patient. You will see," said the farmer.

Then the farmer showed his guest a sackful of plump kernels of wheat and said again, "Tell me what you see." The visitor described the good qualities of the grain, and then once more watched in shock as the farmer walked up and down the furrows he had just plowed, dropping kernels into the open ground and covering them with clods of soil.

"Are you insane?" the man demanded. "First you destroyed the field, and then you ruined the grain!"

"Be patient. You will see."

Time went by, and once more the farmer took his guest out to the field. Now they saw endless straight rows of green stalks sprouting up from all the furrows.

appointed to the post of *Nasi* when Rabban Gamliel was deposed (see *Berachos* 28b), even though he was only eighteen years old (see *Berachos* 1:5; but see *Rambam Commentary* ad loc. and *Yerushalmi Berachos* 1:6). Even when Rabban Gamliel was reinstated, R' Elazar ben Azariah shared the office with him.

Among R' Elazar's more famous statements: "There is no forgiveness on Yom Kippur for sins against another human being unless one appeases his [injured] friend" (*Yoma* 8:9); "A Sanhedrin that executes [a criminal] more frequently than once in seventy years is deemed a murderous court" (*Makkos* 1:10). In spite of his wealth, another of his statements shows his empathy with the common man's struggle to earn his daily bread: "Man's sustenance is as difficult [a feat] as the splitting of the Sea of Reeds" (*Pesachim* 118a). The public's love of him is captured in the touching statement

quoted in *Avos d'Rabbi Nosson* (18): "Happy are you, Abraham our forefather, to have a descendant like R' Elazar ben Azariah."

אִם אֵין תּוֹרָה, אֵין דֶּרֶךְ אֶרֶץ — *If there is no Torah, there is no worldly occupation.* The laws of Torah regulate commerce and business ethics; therefore, Torah knowledge and fidelity to its laws are imperative in order to conduct one's business properly (*Rav*).

This is reflected in the Talmudic statement: He who seeks to be exceedingly righteous should be involved with the laws of damages (*Bava Kamma* 30a).

R' Yisrael Salanter would advise any student about to enter the world of commerce to prepare himself by studying the pertinent laws in the halachic codes of *Choshen Mishpat* and *Yoreh Deah*.

Machzor Vitry and *R' Yonah* render דֶּרֶךְ אֶרֶץ as *proper conduct.* One who is ignorant of Torah is

---

The visitor smiled broadly. "I apologize. Now I understand what you were doing. You made the field more beautiful than ever. The art of farming is truly marvelous."

"No," said the farmer, "we are not done. You must still be patient."

More time went by, and the stalks were fully grown. Then the farmer came with a sickle and chopped them all down. His visitor watched open mouthed as the orderly field became an ugly scene of destruction. The farmer bound the fallen stalks into bundles and decorated the field with them. Later, he took the bundles to another area, where he crushed them until they became a mass of straw and loose kernels. Finally, he separated the kernels from the chaff and piled them up in a huge hill. Always he told his protesting visitor, "We are not done; you must have more patience."

The farmer brought his wagon and piled it high with grain. He took it to a mill, where it was ground into formless, choking dust. The visitor complained again: "You have taken grain and transformed it into dirt!" Again, he was told to be patient.

The farmer put the dust into sacks and took it back home. He took some of the dust, mixed it with water, and fashioned the "mud" into the shape of a loaf. The visitor saw the perfectly formed loaf and smiled broadly, but his happiness did not last. The farmer kindled a fire in the oven and put the loaf into it.

"Now I know you are insane. After all that work, you burn what you have made!"

The farmer only laughed. "Have I not told you to be patient?"

At last, the farmer opened the oven and took out a freshly baked bread — crisp and brown, with an aroma that made the visitor's mouth water.

"Come," the farmer said. He placed the loaf on the kitchen table, cut it, and offered his now-pleased visitor a liberally buttered slice. "Now," he said, "you understand."

God is the Farmer, and we are the fools who cannot begin to understand His ways or to predict the outcome of His plan. Only at the great festive banquet, when the process is complete, will the Jewish people know why everything has happened. Then, when *Mashiach* has finally come, we will know why even those events that seem destructive and painful are part of a process that will produce goodness and beauty. Everything will be rectified on that great day when we will recognize that all of human history was a preparation for the great banquet.

דֶּרֶךְ אֶרֶץ; אִם אֵין דֶּרֶךְ אֶרֶץ, אֵין תּוֹרָה. אִם אֵין חָכְמָה,
אֵין יִרְאָה; אִם אֵין יִרְאָה, אֵין חָכְמָה. אִם אֵין דַּעַת,

bound to fail morally and ethically in many areas of conduct, for the Torah contains explicit guidelines for the vast majority of worldly dealings, and only the Torah can truly imbue one's behavior with fairness, as defined by God. Laws about proper weights and measures, usury, the payment of timely wages, the disbursement of tithes and charities are all delineated in the Torah; so too are guidelines for social interaction. Without its guiding hand, no one, even someone temperamentally predisposed to moral and ethical standards, can achieve perfect behavior in his daily life. Only through attachment to Torah can one truly ascend to the peak of human potential (*Meiri*).

HaChassid Yaavetz views this clause as descriptive of the interdependent relationship between the Torah and a functional world. If there is no Torah — in both study and practice — the world will cease to exist. There is no reason for God to bother to sustain a world if His Will is not the foremost concern of man. [On the other hand, without the world there can be no Torah, for the actualization of Torah ideals demands a real world as its arena. Without worldly activity, Torah would remain theoretical, prevented from elevating the mundane and infusing it with holiness.]

אִם אֵין דֶּרֶךְ אֶרֶץ, אֵין תּוֹרָה — *if there is no worldly occupation, there is no Torah.* A livelihood enables people to devote themselves properly to study; without it, people will eventually forget their Torah learning (*Rav*).

Many other commentaries interpret דֶּרֶךְ אֶרֶץ not as a livelihood but as a person's moral conduct. Only one who has cultivated his personality in accordance with Torah standards is a fitting receptacle for Godly wisdom. Man must therefore perfect himself morally as a prerequisite to successful pursuit of Torah knowledge (*R' Yonah*).

──────────

◆§ **Relative morality.** *Tiferes Yisrael* questions this premise on the basis that there are people devoid of Torah knowledge (Jewish or gentile) who are nevertheless paragons of ethical and moral virtue. Accordingly, he interprets this mishnah to mean that a code of conduct based purely on human understanding is inherently flawed and fragile, because human standards are constantly changing, based on new political, economic, and philosophical conditions. Only allegiance to a code that is above human control can be trusted to remain strong and constant. Thus, he interprets *Torah* in this mishnah to refer to a triad of basic truths: one who has not internalized belief in (1) the Divine origin of the Torah, (2) Divine reward and punishment, and (3) the eternal existence of the human soul.

Without these foundations, one is unable to appreciate that man is endowed with a spark of Divinity; an ethical code based on anything other than this view of man is fragile.

Although many people who are ignorant of the Torah uphold impeccable moral standards, it is only Torah study and practice which can guarantee that morals stand the tests of time and the corrosive influence of society. Aristotle, whose classic *Ethics* is at the core of much enlightened Western thought, succumbed to his baser instincts in his personal life.

◆§ **Torah and "mensch."** Much like a princess who is appalled at the mere thought that a commoner might embrace her, the Torah cannot reside in a human being whose character and behavior are anything less than royal. Moses was instructed to inform the children of Israel of this principle. Before offering them the Torah, he relayed God's message to them: *You shall be to Me a kingdom of ministers and a holy nation* [*Exodus* 19:6] (*Nesivos Shalom*).

When R' Chaim Ozer Grodzenski became engaged to the granddaughter of R' Yisrael Salanter, founder of the Mussar movement, the bride's proud father sent R' Yisrael a brilliant scholarly exposition written by the young man. R' Yisrael Salanter responded, "Scripture quotes a man who has betrothed his daughter: אֶת בִּתִּי נָתַתִּי לָאִישׁ הַזֶּה, *I gave my daughter to this man* (*Deuteronomy* 22:16). The word אִישׁ in the verse indicates a *mensch*, a man of ethics and refined character. First and foremost, I need to know if this young genius is also a mensch."

worldly occupation; if there is no worldly occupation, there is no Torah. If there is no wisdom, there is no fear of God; if there is no fear of God, there is no wisdom. If there is no knowledge,

Torah study is meaningful only if it causes one to conduct his relationships with his fellow men in an upright and dignified manner. Torah must never become a purely intellectual exercise. If proper conduct does not result from it, then there really is no Torah (*Sefer HaMussar*).

While Torah study and the performance of *mitzvos* will generally give one a proper direction, character development is also necessary, and not all of its guidelines are explicitly spelled out in the Torah. From the stated truths of Torah, one must extrapolate solutions to ethical quandaries and learn to adopt good character traits. For example, by studying the Torah's dietary prohibitions, one may design a personal program to regulate his appetite and eliminate gluttony from his makeup. In addition to what is explicitly stated in the Torah, one must internalize a sense of Divine morality and ethics (*Meiri*).

אִם אֵין חָכְמָה, אֵין יִרְאָה — *If there is no wisdom, there is no fear of God.* **Wisdom** refers to Torah wisdom. Fear of God is strengthened, deepened, and clarified by knowledge of the Torah (*R' Yonah*). King Solomon teaches: *Let your ear listen attentively to wisdom . . . then you will truly perceive fear of God* (*Proverbs* 2:2-5). While one can achieve a primitive fear of Divine retribution, just as the horse fears the whip, our mishnah refers to a deeper fear of God, an intelligent awe that strikes one who perceives the gaping chasm between man and his Creator. This refined form of fear is attained only through a conscious understanding of the awesomeness of the Master of the Universe. *Rambam* (*Hilchos Yesodei HaTorah* 2:2) contends that in-depth observation of God's creations is the key to developing this heightened awareness and fear of God.

A servant who rebels against his powerful master is a fool. Similarly, one who has not acquired, to the best of his ability, an adequate picture of God's greatness will never develop proper reverence for Him, and thus there is nothing to prevent him from insubordinate behavior toward God. If one lacks the wisdom and knowledge of right and wrong, he cannot fear God (*Sefer HaMussar*).

אִם אֵין יִרְאָה, אֵין חָכְמָה — *if there is no fear of God, there is no wisdom.* R' Yonah explains: Fear of God must precede the acquisition of His wisdom. If one does not first imbue his conduct with a fear of God, he will find the Divine wisdom despicable and

---

◄§ **Unwritten laws.** *Ramban* writes that two Biblical commandments that are not specific are essential guidelines for developing this sense of morality:

(1) *You shall be holy* (*Leviticus* 19:2) teaches us to avoid self-indulgence and gluttony even when there are no halachic prohibitions involved. A person must examine areas of behavior that are not explicitly commanded or forbidden — and it is there that he can sanctify himself. One who refuses to budge from the letter of the law can easily become a contemptible person.

(2) *You shall do what is fair and good in the eyes of HASHEM* (*Deuteronomy* 6:18) is a spiritual yardstick by which all unlegislated actions should be measured. After exhorting Israel to observe the commandments scrupulously, Moses told them that the rest of their actions, specifically their dealings with people, should be guided by a sense of what is *fair and good* in God's eyes. How to do so in any given situation depends on the sensitivity of the individual, for it is impossible for the Torah to spell out all potential situations. Specific guidelines must be interpolated from the Torah's general requirements to show compassion and forbearance to others, to show respect for the learned and the aged, to be sensitive to the danger or financial loss which threatens others, and similar-type *mitzvos*. For example, one *should* pay incompetent workers because they need money to support their families, even though they have not carried out their responsibilities, and one *should* return lost items, even in cases where he is not halachically required to do so. The expression "the fifth *Shulchan Aruch*" refers to the development of this extra moral sense, which dictates that there are duties not spelled out in the four printed sections of the codes.

reject it. [One cannot live a lie while constantly exposed to truth; so he will deny the validity of the truth. See *Rambam* to 3:11.] The wisest of all men captured this sentiment with these pithy words: *Of what use is the price of wisdom* [i.e., the funds to pay for a teacher] *in the hand of the fool, if there is no heart [to fear God]?* (*Proverbs* 17:16).

Reverence of God is the beginning of wisdom (*Psalms* 111:10). God imparts His Wisdom only to those who treasure it and realize that it is a Divine gift. One who fears God and seeks to live by His word indicates thereby that he realizes the sacredness of Torah wisdom. Even the practical sense one acquires from Torah study is only granted to those who value the word of God and assume the obligations it imposes (*Tiferes Yisrael*).

אִם אֵין דַּעַת, אֵין בִּינָה — *If there is no knowledge, there is no understanding. Knowledge* [דַּעַת] is the ability to perceive the underlying logic behind a fact. *Understanding* [בִּינָה] is the ability to deduce one fact from another. Sometimes such deductions are not based on logic, but on intuition, but if someone lacks an understanding of the logic of the phenomena he is studying, his deductions will not be accurate or even correct (*Rav*). Knowing a fact without understanding the reason is not real knowledge (*Rashi*).

There are three categories of intellect: חָכְמָה, *wisdom;* בִּינָה, *understanding;* and דַּעַת, *knowledge.* "Wisdom" includes facts and ideas acquired from others. "Understanding" is deduced knowledge. "Knowledge" consists of the conclusions one reaches independently, on the basis of observation and inquiry. The mishnah is speaking of the complementary relationship of knowledge and understanding. One can infer new ideas only from facts he fully understands. But if he lacks this basic background of clearly comprehended facts [i.e., knowledge], he is bound to err in his deductive reasoning (*R' Yonah*).

Meiri sees דַּעַת and בִּינָה as the elements of productive thinking. *Knowledge* is innate intellectual ability; *understanding* denotes the perceptions one achieves as a result of his efforts in study and research. One must combine natural ability and effort to succeed in intellectual endeavors.

Machzor Vitry offers another interpretation of these two terms: The knowledge [דַּעַת] one acquires from mentors serves as a framework of tradition which assures intellectual honesty in Torah study. However, one must also apply his own intellect [בִּינָה] to Torah concepts, making the knowledge dynamic rather than static.

אִם אֵין בִּינָה, אֵין דַּעַת — *if there is no understanding, there is no knowledge.* This clause complements the previous one; one's inability to extract new ideas from his base knowledge indicates that he really does not fully understand what he learned. [Knowledge should serve as building blocks for new concepts] (*R' Yonah*).

אִם אֵין קֶמַח, אֵין תּוֹרָה — *If there is no flour, there is no Torah.* Man is comprised of body and soul. One cannot survive without the other, and both must receive sustenance. The body must be nourished properly in order to function effectively; without nourishment one cannot study properly (*Rav, Rashi*).

When earning a living proves to be too difficult a task, it leaves little time or energy for serious Torah study. [As it is often said, we are often so

⊰§ **To explain is to know.** Real knowledge includes the ability to explain concepts verbally. R' Chaim Soloveitchik, the famous originator of the Brisker system of Talmudic discourse, is reputed to have said, "The extent to which one is unable to explain a concept indicates the extent to which he does not understand it himself. Let one never fool himself into thinking that he understands a concept and merely has difficulty explaining it." Only if one sufficiently understands something to be able to explain it can we say that he knows it.

there is no understanding; if there is no understanding, there is no knowledge. If there is no flour, there is no Torah; if there is no Torah, there is no flour.

---

preoccupied with earning a living that we are left with little time to *live*, in the true sense — to tend to the needs and aspirations of the soul.] The insecurity and worries engendered by poverty do not allow for the concentration and unburdened state of mind necessary for Torah study (*Machzor Vitry*).

Poverty can cause one to lose his moral anchor. In the battle to sustain himself, one's survival instinct often overwhelms all other values. A lack of "flour" can therefore cause him to lose the sense of honesty which is so basic to a Torah way of life (*Lev Avos*).

אִם אֵין תּוֹרָה, אֵין קֶמַח — *if there is no Torah, there is no flour.* Man's material wealth is a means to an end, a tool to provide him with enough time for spiritual pursuits. If he does not dedicate his life to follow the path of Torah, there is no reason for God to provide him with the means to *sustain* life (*Rav, R' Yonah*).

Alshich offers a homiletical interpretation. People generally excuse their limited involvement in Torah on the basis that all their energies are consumed in making a living. They claim that since there is "no flour" — they must work for their bread — there is no time for Torah. Our mishnah teaches that such an argument confuses the cause with the effect. Lack of involvement in Torah *causes* a lack of "flour," not vice versa.

R' Yosef ibn Nachmias gives these last two stiches a global meaning. If everyone were completely involved in Torah study, without attending to the maintenance of the physical world — plowing, sowing, harvesting, and all the other tasks necessary to produce sustenance — the world would perish, and along with it any hope to realize the Torah's potential in this life. Therefore, *if there is no flour, there is no Torah.* However, if everyone were occupied exclusively with ensuring the world's physical sustenance and Torah was, God forbid, completely ignored, the world could not survive; *if there is no Torah, there is no flour.*

⊷§ The same trough. *Meiri* finds this idea reflected in the Talmud's statement (*Pesachim* 118a) regarding the consequences of Adam's sin. God initially spoke to Adam and told him, *"You shall eat the grass of the field"* (*Genesis* 3:18). Adam cried out: "Am I and my donkey to eat from the same trough?" God responded by allowing him to eat more refined foods, since man must have sustenance in order to study and practice the Torah. If not for Torah, there is no reason why man cannot eat with his donkey from the same trough. Hence, if there is no Torah, there is no [reason for God to provide] flour.

The Torah lends dignity to man. Without its humanizing quality, the beast in him is likely to become dominant. If there is no Torah, therefore, man truly deserves to share his meals with his donkey. It is only his refinement of character which legitimates his need for a finer quality of food.

⊷§ There are two types of people, physical providers and spiritual providers. Ideally they should create alliances for the furtherance of God's goals. The classic Yissachar-Zevulun partnership, in which the businessman provides the Torah scholar with the means to pursue his studies free of worry in exchange for an equal share in the special reward for the scholar's learning, is a wonderful means of combining "Torah" and "flour" to everyone's advantage.

The Talmud (*Berachos* 35b) debates the merits of a life-style exclusively committed to Torah study, as personified by R' Shimon bar Yochai, and concludes: "Many have attempted to be like R' Shimon bar Yochai, but did not succeed." The commentators take note of the expression "many," which implies that some imitated R' Shimon and *did* succeed. A select few may choose such a framework, but only if they possess a passion for God and His Torah, and are firmly committed to the idea that they were created for this holy task. Those who have not yet achieved such an elevated determination may follow the approach of R' Yishmael (see ibid.), studying when they can and sharing their piece of this world with Torah students, and, in turn, earning a share of the scholars' reward in the World to Come.

[כב] **הוּא** הָיָה אוֹמֵר: כֹּל שֶׁחָכְמָתוֹ מְרֻבָּה מִמַּעֲשָׂיו,
לְמָה הוּא דוֹמֶה? לְאִילָן שֶׁעֲנָפָיו מְרֻבִּין
וְשָׁרָשָׁיו מוּעָטִין, וְהָרוּחַ בָּאָה וְעוֹקַרְתּוֹ וְהוֹפַכְתּוֹ עַל פָּנָיו,
שֶׁנֶּאֱמַר: "וְהָיָה כְּעַרְעָר בָּעֲרָבָה, וְלֹא יִרְאֶה כִּי יָבוֹא טוֹב,
וְשָׁכַן חֲרֵרִים בַּמִּדְבָּר, אֶרֶץ מְלֵחָה וְלֹא תֵשֵׁב." אֲבָל כֹּל
שֶׁמַּעֲשָׂיו מְרֻבִּין מֵחָכְמָתוֹ, לְמָה הוּא דוֹמֶה? לְאִילָן
שֶׁעֲנָפָיו מוּעָטִין וְשָׁרָשָׁיו מְרֻבִּין, שֶׁאֲפִילוּ כָּל הָרוּחוֹת
שֶׁבָּעוֹלָם בָּאוֹת וְנוֹשְׁבוֹת בּוֹ, אֵין מְזִיזִין אוֹתוֹ מִמְּקוֹמוֹ,

---

Mishnah 22

הוּא הָיָה אוֹמֵר: כֹּל שֶׁחָכְמָתוֹ מְרֻבָּה מִמַּעֲשָׂיו, לְמָה הוּא דוֹמֶה — *He [R' Elazar ben Azariah] used to say: Anyone whose wisdom exceeds his good deeds, to what is he likened.* R' Chanina ben Dosa taught this maxim in an earlier mishnah (see 3:12), and R' Elazar ben Azariah adds emphasis to it. He offers an analogy here that clearly makes the point that Torah knowledge is a *result* of proper behavior rather than its source. As the Sages taught: "Not study but practice is the main thing" (1:17). One's actions are roots from which his wisdom sprouts forth, as symbolized by the branches [in the next clause] (*Magen Avos*).

לְאִילָן שֶׁעֲנָפָיו מְרֻבִּין וְשָׁרָשָׁיו מוּעָטִין, וְהָרוּחַ בָּאָה וְעוֹקַרְתּוֹ וְהוֹפַכְתּוֹ עַל פָּנָיו — *to a tree whose branches are numerous but whose roots are few; then the wind comes and uproots it and turns it upside down.* The commentaries explain this "root-edness" in various ways:

□ *Rashi* says that one who studies much but does not live according to what he studies [or preaches (*Maharam Alshakar*)] is like a tree with few roots. His commitment to the word of God is shaky and easily.

□ *HaChassid Yaavetz* comments that a person whose intelligence is not borne out in action can easily fall prey to heretical ideas, for good deeds and *mitzvah* performance are the guardrails that keep him on the straight path. Those who fulfill His *mitzvos* receive God's assistance in resisting the sway of heresy.

□ *Chelek Yaakov* gives a very practical interpretation. He states that this mishnah is an exhortation to public speakers to use their pulpit not as a means to show off their intellectual prowess, but rather to offer their listeners guidance in real-life, everyday issues. One who uses his role as a public speaker to showcase his brilliance will find that the prevailing winds of society to which his listeners are exposed will very quickly overturn the message he sought to impart.

Avos d'Rabbi Nosson (24) offers an analogy for the person whose wisdom exceeds his actions: One who mounts a horse that wears no bridle will be

---

◆§ **Mute is beautiful.** R' Avraham of Slonim once met an itinerant *maggid* (preacher) who was always on the search for new material. "Please tell me a nice Torah thought," the *maggid* requested. R' Avraham replied with a homiletic interpretation of a phrase from the Sabbath hymn *D'ror Yikra*: דְּרוֹשׁ נָוִי וְאוּלָמִי, *Seek My Temple and My Hall.* He rendered instead: "If one's purpose in teaching Torah is merely to give a beautiful (נָוִי) discourse (דְּרוֹשׁ), he might do better to remain silent (וְאוּלָמִי) — from אִלֵּם, which means *mute*)."

22. He [R' Elazar ben Azariah] used to say: Anyone whose wisdom exceeds his good deeds, to what is he likened? — to a tree whose branches are numerous but whose roots are few; then the wind comes and uproots it and turns it upside down, as it is said: *And he shall be like an isolated tree in an arid land and shall not see when good comes; he shall dwell on parched soil in the wilderness, on a salted and uninhabited land (Jeremiah 17:6).* But one whose good deeds exceed his wisdom, to what is he likened? — to a tree whose branches are few but whose roots are numerous; even if all the winds in the world were to come and blow against it, they could not budge it from its place,

---

quickly thrown off. Similarly, one who studies but does not put what he learns into practice will quickly lose control of himself.

Maharal analyzes the metaphor of the tree. Man is a combination of intelligence (שֵׂכֶל) and earth (אֲדָמָה), from which his body is formed (see *Genesis* 2:7). Nonetheless, he is called Adam from the word אֲדָמָה, *earth*, indicating that his basic substance of man is his physical being, for it is the flesh-and-blood human being who must perform God's commandments and thereby rise to spiritual heights, through overcoming the pull of his physical desires and the pull of nature. True, with his intelligence he can strive for great heights like a tree's branches reaching toward heaven, but, also like a tree, he will topple unless he is firmly rooted in his earthly existence. These roots are the *mitzvos*, performed with the physical body, and are thus analogous to the roots buried in the earth. These roots support the intellectual growth, symbolized by the branches of the tree. The greater one's understanding of Torah, the greater is his obligation to fulfill it. One whose wisdom expands must develop a concurrent commitment to a higher standard of observance. If he does not do so, he will find himself spiritually toppled.

שֶׁנֶּאֱמַר: ,,וְהָיָה כְּעַרְעָר בָּעֲרָבָה, וְלֹא יִרְאֶה כִּי יָבוֹא טוֹב, וְשָׁכַן חֲרֵרִים בַּמִּדְבָּר, אֶרֶץ מְלֵחָה וְלֹא תֵשֵׁב'' — *as it is said: "And he shall be like an isolated tree in an arid land and shall not see when good comes; he shall dwell on parched soil in the wilderness, on a salted and uninhabited land" (Jeremiah 17:6).* The

prophet speaks of one who places his trust exclusively in human efforts (be it his own or others) rather than relying on God, whether he earns his living through legal or illegal means. He is compared to an isolated tree which will never receive sustenance from God or yield fruit (*Rashi*).

Tiferes Yisrael explains how the verse from *Jeremiah* cited in the mishnah helps to explain this point: One who is strong in Torah wisdom, yet relies on his own intellect and at the same time follows the strong pull of his physical desires, is cursed. Increased wisdom (חָכְמָתוֹ) without concurrent physical restraint (מְרֻבָּה מִמַּעֲשָׂיו) will cause a person's heart to turn from God. He will become like a tree on parched earth, which cannot develop strong roots; and without such roots, he will fall.

אֲבָל כֹּל שֶׁמַּעֲשָׂיו מְרֻבִּין מֵחָכְמָתוֹ, לְמָה הוּא דוֹמֶה? לְאִילָן שֶׁעֲנָפָיו מוּעָטִין וְשָׁרָשָׁיו מְרֻבִּין, שֶׁאֲפִילוּ כָּל הָרוּחוֹת שֶׁבָּעוֹלָם בָּאוֹת וְנוֹשְׁבוֹת בּוֹ, אֵין מְזִיזִין אוֹתוֹ מִמְּקוֹמוֹ — *But one whose good deeds exceed his wisdom, to what is he likened? — to a tree whose branches are few but whose roots are numerous; even if all the winds in the world were to come and blow against it, they could not budge it from its place.* Intellectual arrogance, lust, and the passion for wealth are forces that seek to uproot man from his spiritual destiny. However, one who is firmly rooted by his fear of God and his active fulfillment of all that he learns cannot be budged from his spiritual commitments (*Tiferes Yisrael*).

A person who fears God will not succumb to any strategy used against him. Even if he cannot refute

שֶׁנֶּאֱמַר: "וְהָיָה כְּעֵץ שָׁתוּל עַל מַיִם, וְעַל יוּבַל יְשַׁלַּח
שָׁרָשָׁיו, וְלֹא יִרְאֶה כִּי יָבֹא חֹם, וְהָיָה עָלֵהוּ רַעֲנָן, וּבִשְׁנַת
בַּצֹּרֶת לֹא יִדְאָג, וְלֹא יָמִישׁ מֵעֲשׂוֹת פֶּרִי."

[כג] **רַבִּי** אֶלְעָזָר בֶּן חִסְמָא אוֹמֵר: קִנִּין וּפִתְחֵי נִדָּה

---

the arguments presented against him, he will still stand firm in his commitment to the word of God (*Meiri*). One who understands that practice is the main thing and that unapplied wisdom is of negligible value possesses the attitude that will enable him to prevail against any spiritually distorting winds.

שֶׁנֶּאֱמַר: "וְהָיָה כְּעֵץ שָׁתוּל עַל מַיִם, וְעַל יוּבַל יְשַׁלַּח שָׁרָשָׁיו, וְלֹא יִרְאֶה כִּי יָבֹא חֹם, וְהָיָה עָלֵהוּ רַעֲנָן, וּבִשְׁנַת בַּצֹּרֶת לֹא יִדְאָג, וְלֹא יָמִישׁ מֵעֲשׂוֹת פֶּרִי." — *as it says: "And he shall be like a tree planted by waters, spreading its roots toward the stream, and it shall not notice the heat's arrival, and its foliage shall be fresh; in the year of drought it shall not worry, nor shall it cease from yielding fruit"* (*Jeremiah* 17:8). The verse proves that when man acts properly he may also be compared to the tree (*Maharal*). The subject of the verse from *Jeremiah* is one who

places his trust in God. That trust will be rewarded, and man, like a tree planted by nourishing waters, will enjoy God-given success (*Rashi*).

Tiferes Yisrael interprets the verse from *Jeremiah* homiletically as an expression of the mishnah's theme: Blessed is the one with the strength of character to withstand temptation (see 4:1), who fulfills all the *mitzvos* even when he doesn't understand them, trusting that God's wishes are for our benefit. This person thus acquires the merit of more deeds than he can understand intellectually. Firmly planted on the waters of Torah, his roots are everlasting; the heat of passion will never overtake him, and he will always enjoy spiritual freshness. Even during the figurative times of famine, when life is full of difficulties, he will not experience any lapses of faith, but will continue to follow God's word and produce abundant fruit of the spirit.

Mishnah 23

רַבִּי אֶלְעָזָר בֶּן חִסְמָא אוֹמֵר — *Rabbi Elazar ben Chisma says*. R' Elazar ben Chisma was a third-generation Tanna. He studied primarily under Rabban Gamliel and R' Yehoshua (see *Horayos* 10a and *Chagigah* 3a), but also under R' Akiva (*Vayikra Rabbah* 23:4).

Once, as they traveled together on a ship, Rabban Gamliel expressed surprise at R' Yehoshua's vast knowledge of geometry and physics.

R' Yehoshua replied, "Rather than being impressed with *my* knowledge, be astonished at the knowledge of two of your students, R' Elazar Chisma and R' Yochanan ben Goodgoda, who can compute exactly how many drops of water are contained in the sea; and yet, in spite of their knowledge, they suffer extreme poverty and have neither food nor clothes." [This passage indicates that the name was R' Elazar Chisma, not ben Chisma.]

❧ **Resist the wind.** People who had the privilege to meet the Chazon Ish were overwhelmed by his originality in all areas of Torah interpretation and of life. His opinion on any subject was totally the result of his own thinking, based on the way Torah filtered through his soul. There was no influence in the world that affected his decisions. A sensitive visitor recalled that as he left the house he was struck by this profound quality and its stark contrast so vividly portrayed by King David: *Not so the wicked, rather they are like chaff that is carried by the wind* (*Psalms* 1:4). The wicked do not think for themselves — their opinions are formed by the wind of the times.

as it says: *And he shall be like a tree planted by waters, spreading its roots toward the stream, and it shall not notice the heat's arrival, and its foliage shall be fresh; in the year of drought it shall not worry, nor shall it cease from yielding fruit* (Jeremiah 17:8).

23. Rabbi Elazar ben Chisma says: The laws of bird offerings, and the laws regarding the beginning of menstrual periods

Taking R' Yehoshua's words to heart, Rabban Gamliel decided to appoint R' Elazar and R' Yochanan to positions in the Academy at Yavneh, thus providing them with a way to earn a living. Initially they refused the offer, but Rabban Gamliel convinced them to accept it with the following argument: "Do you think that I am giving you power, and is that why you seek to flee the honor? In truth, I am offering you servitude" (*Horayos* 10a) [public positions are a burden one must bear rather than a source of glory and power (*Rashi* ad loc.)].

The appellation "Chisma" was given to R' Elazar as a result of the following incident. He once visited a city where the local inhabitants asked him to lead the service. He did not have expertise in this area and had to refuse. They replied, "It is for naught that you are called Rabbi." Terribly hurt, he went to visit his teacher, R' Akiva, who gave him instruction in leading services; and upon his return to that city, he was able to do so. The local inhabitants then said, נִתְחַסֵּם ר' אֶלְעָזָר, *R' Elazar has become stronger*. The name חִסְמָא, *Chisma,* meaning *stronger,* stuck (see *Vayikra Rabbah* ibid.).

Midrash Shmuel derives the name from the root חסם, meaning to close, as in the Biblical prohibition of לֹא תַחְסֹם, *you shall not muzzle* (Deuteronomy 25:4), which forbids the "closing" of a plow animal's mouth, i.e., muzzling. Thus the name is indicative of his brilliance, which was so overwhelming that it caused others to close their mouths in his presence and smack their lips in sheer wonderment.

According to *Rashi* and *Rav*, the mishnah offers a perspective on the relative value and complexity of different areas of Torah study. *Meiri*, along the same lines, sees it as a proposal for the proper program of study, naming those areas that should be given priority.

קִנִּין — *The laws of bird offerings.* The word קִנִּין, literally *Nests*, is the title of a tractate at the end of the order of *Kodashim*. It consists only of Mishnah, with no Gemara, and deals with the laws of bird offerings. There are many complexities in these laws; they address, for example, what must be done if a bird designated for a voluntary offering and one designated for an obligatory offering were exchanged, or if a bird brought as a sin offering (*chatas*) and one brought as a burnt offering (*olah*) were inadvertently switched. Since each offering has its own specific laws and rituals, any exchange creates many halachic problems (*Rashi, Rav* et al.).

וּפִתְחֵי נִדָּה — *and the laws regarding the beginning of menstrual periods.* These laws are important because there are extensive halachic ramifications when a woman loses track of her personal calendar. When her next period begins, there is doubt whether she has become a *niddah* or a *zavah*, which have different laws of varying degrees of severity [see *Yad Avraham* to *Arachin* 2:1, p. 29, for the Biblical definition of these terms].

Alternatively, this is a reference to a woman who is unsure of her *vesses* (וֶסֶת), the day on which it is probable, based on past history, that she will begin menstruation again (*Rashi*). [See *Yoreh Deah* 184 for the halachic ramifications of this and the complex laws involved.]

⌇ **Priorities.** R' Elazar ben Chisma is a fitting spokesman for the primacy of Torah study, which eclipses all other disciplines. He himself displayed great proficiency in many areas of knowledge (see *Horayos* 10a), yet he insisted that they are all peripheral in comparison to Torah (*Derech Avos*).

הֵן הֵן גּוּפֵי הֲלָכוֹת; תְּקוּפוֹת וְגִמַטְרִיָּאוֹת — פַּרְפְּרָאוֹת לַחָכְמָה.

❧ ❧ ❧

רַבִּי חֲנַנְיָא בֶּן עֲקַשְׁיָא אוֹמֵר: רָצָה הַקָּדוֹשׁ בָּרוּךְ הוּא לְזַכּוֹת אֶת יִשְׂרָאֵל, לְפִיכָךְ הִרְבָּה לָהֶם תּוֹרָה וּמִצְוֹת, שֶׁנֶּאֱמַר: "יהוה חָפֵץ לְמַעַן צִדְקוֹ, יַגְדִּיל תּוֹרָה וְיַאְדִּיר".

הֵן הֵן גּוּפֵי הֲלָכוֹת — *these are essential laws.* These two types of laws are examples of mathematical computations that must be made in order to resolve a halachically doubtful situation. The mishnah teaches that they are essential laws and that their study is a true example of optimal Torah study, even though they address only situations of uncertainty (*Tosafos Yom Tov*). In researching these areas, one will discover great depth and profundity (*Rashi*); they are also prime examples of the study of the Oral Law, for which one is richly rewarded (*Rav*).

A subject such as קִנִּין may appear unworthy of a scholar's attention, and a subject such as פִּתְחֵי נִדָּה may be an unappealing topic; but the mishnah emphasizes that *no* Torah topic should be taken lightly. All the laws are essential (*Kessef Mishnah* to *Rambam, Hilchos Yesodei HaTorah* 4:13). *Ruach Chaim* adds that these important areas must be studied even if one will never be asked to rule on them.

Vilna Gaon suggests that these topics are presented by the mishnah as examples of applied mathematical formulas. Once one masters the basic formula, all the laws flow from simple application of it. One might be led to believe that only the general formula and not the applications were given at Sinai; therefore, the mishnah teaches that even *these* are essential laws, part and parcel of the Sinaitic tradition.

Meiri notes that these two areas of halachah are found in the last tractates of the last two Mishnaic orders (*Kodashim* and *Taharos*). He deduces from this that one should complete the Talmud and its related studies in their entirety before embarking on other courses of study.

תְּקוּפוֹת — *astronomy.* I.e., study of the orbits of heavenly bodies and constellations. [The word תְּקוּפָה is from the root הַקֵּף, which means to go around.] Alternatively, it refers to the ability to chart the quarterly equinoxes and solstices (*Rashi; Rav*).

Although the mishnah describes astronomy as a "seasoning," relegating it to secondary status, this refers only to a *theoretical* knowledge of astronomy, without regard to its halachic aspects. During R Elazar's time,

---

⋖§ **Number messages.** Many of the Torah's messages are alluded to by means of *gematria. Tosafos* (*Gittin* 2a) suggests that the numerical value of the word גט, used particularly for a bill of divorce, is twelve, to allude to the customary twelve lines used in its writing. On a homiletic level, *Notzer Chessed* notes that וְאָהַבְתָּ אֶת ה׳ אֱלֹהֶיךָ, *You shall love* HASHEM, *your God* (*Deuteronomy* 6:5), and וְאָהַבְתָּ לְרֵעֲךָ כָּמוֹךָ אֲנִי ה׳, *You shall love your fellow as yourself — I am* HASHEM (*Leviticus* 19:18), share the same numerical value (493), underscoring that the *mitzvah* to love Jews (אַהֲבַת יִשְׂרָאֵל) is equated with the love of God (אַהֲבַת ה׳). Similarly, the maxim that "nature is a pseudonym for God" — meaning that God's greatness is revealed in nature and that He controls nature — is conveyed by the *gematria* for הַטֶּבַע (the [laws of *nature*), which is the numerical equivalent of אֱלֹהִים, *God* (86).

— these are essential laws; astronomy and mathematics are like seasonings to wisdom.

❧ ❧ ❧

Rabbi Chanania ben Akashia says: The Holy One, Blessed is He, wished to confer merit upon Israel; therefore He gave them Torah and mitzvos in abundance, as it is said: *Hashem desired, for the sake if its [Israel's] righteousness, that the Torah be made great and glorious.*

---

however, astronomy and its related areas of study were needed as practical tools in determining the new moon (see *Rambam, Hilchos Kiddush HaChodesh* 5:3) and the intercalated month, i.e., the thirteenth month that is added to the Hebrew calendar, when necessary. As such, they were not secondary at all, but were essential building blocks in the halachic process (*Tosafos Yom Tov*).

וְגִמַטְרִיָאוֹת — *and mathematics.* According to most commentators, this refers to the study of the numerical values of Hebrew letters and acronyms [נוֹטְרִיקוֹן] (see *Rashi, Rav*).

Meiri and *Tosafos Yom Tov,* et al., interpret it as geometry.

פַּרְפְּרָאוֹת לַחָכְמָה — *are like seasonings to wisdom.* This rendering follows *R' Yonah:* Just as seasonings add sharpness to food and bring out its taste, so the study of these disciplines sharpens the mind and enriches one's understanding of Torah.

Tiferes Yisrael and *Sefer HaMussar* render פַּרְפְּרָאוֹת as *condiments* (see *Berachos* 42a); these areas of study are analogous to butter and other such condiments. Spread on bread, they enhance the flavor and enjoyment of the bread; but they are of little nutritional value and do not offer much pleasure when eaten alone. Likewise, astronomy and mathematics are valuable when studied to enhance one's understanding and enjoyment of Torah; but pursued as an end in themselves, they have limited redeeming value.

Rashi renders פַּרְפְּרָאוֹת as the non-essential dishes served before or after a meal, such as an appetizer or dessert. These foods are likened to areas of study that are interesting and enjoyable but not central. [*R' Wolf Heidenheim* (based on *Aruch*) suggests in a similar vein that the word can be read פְּרַפְּרָיוֹת, meaning the peripheries. The center and focal point of study must be the essential laws; anything else is considered peripheral and does not merit great attention.]

Following *Meiri,* this mishnah teaches that only after completing the entire Torah may one devote time and effort to other areas of study. One should begin with math and related subjects, followed by the applied sciences, and then finally the metaphysical areas of inquiry.

❧ The verse *For it is your wisdom and discernment in the eyes of the peoples* (Deuteronomy 4:6) is understood by the Talmud (*Shabbos* 75a) as referring to the study of astronomy and mathematics. While knowledge of these disciplines certainly enhances Jewish prestige in the eyes of the nations, our Mishnah teaches that inquiry into these areas is non-essential in comparison to true Torah study (*Ruach Chaim*).

Nonetheless, *gematria* is a valuable tool for conveying many Torah lessons. The words of the verse כִּי לֹא דָבָר רֵק הוּא מִכֶּם, *For it is not an empty thing for you* (Deuteronomy 32:47), add up numerically to 679, the same value as the word גִימַטְרִיָאוֹת (*gematrias*) itself. This teaches that *gematria* is a substantial adjunct of Torah study.

פרק רביעי ‎‏
Chapter Four

כָּל יִשְׂרָאֵל יֵשׁ לָהֶם חֵלֶק לָעוֹלָם הַבָּא, שֶׁנֶּאֱמַר: „וְעַמֵּךְ כֻּלָּם צַדִּיקִים, לְעוֹלָם יִירְשׁוּ אָרֶץ, נֵצֶר מַטָּעַי, מַעֲשֵׂה יָדַי לְהִתְפָּאֵר‟.

All Israel has a share in the World to Come, as it is said:
And your people are all righteous; they shall inherit the land forever; a branch of My plantings, My handiwork, in which to take pride (Isaiah 60:21).

Mishnah 1

In the following mishnah, Ben Zoma offers the most meaningful definitions of wisdom, strength, and wealth. In doing so, he elaborates on a prophecy of Jeremiah that denigrates wisdom, strength, and wealth, as they are narrowly and selfishly defined and lauded by most people. Ben Zoma offers the counterpoint: Of course Jeremiah is right, but these qualities have a loftier role, and it is to that one that people should aspire. Jeremiah prophesied as follows:

> So says HASHEM: "Let not the wise man laud himself with his wisdom, and let not the strong man laud himself with his strength, and let not the rich man laud himself with his wealth. Only with this may one laud himself — discernment in knowing Me, for I am HASHEM Who does kindness, justice, and righteousness in the land; for in these is My desire," the words of HASHEM (Jeremiah 9:22-23).

Ben Zoma comes to teach that wisdom, wealth, and strength may indeed engender legitimate pride and lead to *discernment in knowing Me*, which Jeremiah states is the only desirable form of pride. This occurs with the understanding that all virtues should ultimately be used in the service of God. One who is "wise" — who learns from all people — will develop a proper fear of Heaven. One who is "strong" possesses the strength of his conviction and is able to rebuff his evil inclination and to quell his anger against his fellow man. One who is wealthy understands that his assets are merely tools for the service of God (*R' Yonah*).

בֶּן זוֹמָא אוֹמֵר — *Ben Zoma says.* Shimon ben Zoma, a third-generation *Tanna* and student of R' Yehoshua ben Chanania, was one of a quartet of scholars named Shimon. In order to avoid confusion, they were referred to as sons of their fathers (ben Zoma, ben Azzai, ben Nanas) or in conjunction with their place of residence (*HaTaimani*). [See *Machzor Vitry.*]

Ben Zoma was a scholar almost without equal (see *Kiddushin* 49b and *Rashi* ad loc.), whom the Talmud considered a symbol of wisdom (see *Berachos* 57b). He was qualified to receive the *semichah* ordination (*Horayos* 2b), but because he never did he is not referred to as "Rabbi" (*Rav*, *Rashi*). Alternatively, he never received the title because he died prematurely. His strength in Torah lay in his ability to establish connections between the text of the Written Law and the Oral Tradition, and to show clearly the Scriptural sources for many laws. As testimony, the Passover Haggadah states: "R' Elazar ben Azariah said: 'I am like one seventy years old, yet I never merited to have my opinion accepted [regarding the obligation to remember the Egyptian Exodus every night] until ben Zoma provided a Biblical source'" (See *Berachos* 1:5). The Sages eulogized him as the last of the experts in Biblical exegesis (*Sotah* 49a).

Ben Zoma's respect for the uniqueness of each person is expressed in his dictum כְּשֵׁם שֶׁאֵין פַּרְצוּפֵיהֶן שָׁוִין זֶה לָזֶה, כָּךְ אֵין דֵּעוֹתֵיהֶן שָׁווֹת, *Just as their facial features are not alike, so their opinions are not alike.* [People must respect each other's opinions even if they are different than their own.]

אֵיזֶהוּ חָכָם — *Who is wise?* Ben Zoma is looking for the true definition of the virtues listed in the mishnah. The common denominator is that any of them must be internalized and integrated into one's personality, or he is not entitled to be called by the name of the virtue. For example, one can possess much wisdom and yet not deserve the title "wise person," if his wisdom did not change him intrinsically (*Maharal*). *Nesivos Shalom* of *Slonim* adds: God-given virtues and talents are gifts and do not entitle their recipients to any recognition. Ben Zoma seeks to define the *effort* one must expend in order to deserve the appellations in this mishnah.

Rabbi Chaim Shmulevitz was fond of saying: "A poor man who wins the lottery does not always become a wealthy person. Sometimes he remains a *schnorrer* — with money."

Ben Zoma does not mean to say that people cannot be wise, strong, rich, happy, or honored unless they comply with his definitions. Rather, he is telling us that people are entitled to take pride in their achievements only when their efforts have been in accordance with the Torah's moral teachings — in the spirit of "let all your deeds be for the sake of Heaven" [see 2:17] (*Tosafos Yom Tov*).

הַלּוֹמֵד מִכָּל אָדָם — *He who learns from every person.* One who truly values wisdom will seek it wherever it can be found. He will not refuse to learn from someone because he dislikes him or considers him of lower status; such an attitude indicates that he values his own ego more than the pursuit of knowledge. Willingness to learn from every person demonstrates a pursuit of wisdom that is spiritual in nature and not a means of self-aggrandizement (*Rav, Rashi*).

The title of "wise person" is not related to the quantity of one's knowledge as much as to his thirst

---

◆§ **Constant search.** A Torah scholar is not called a *chacham* (wise man); rather, he is referred to as a *talmid chacham* (a *wise student* or the *student of a wise man*). A *talmid chacham* should always think of himself as a student, constantly seeking to learn from others.

Rabbi Shlomo Wolbe, one of the great *mussar* masters of our time, was a student of Rabbi Yerucham Levovitz, the *mashgiach* of the Mirrer Yeshivah in Poland. He later went on to study with the *Rebbe* of Ozerov, R' Moshe Yechiel. When the Ozerover passed away, Rabbi Wolbe was a mature, respected teacher who had raised generations of students, but he sought out Rabbi Yitzchak Hutner as a mentor — he was a *talmid chacham* who valued knowledge too much to be content with his own considerable attainments.

◆§ Even someone not endowed with great intelligence can, with hard work, achieve a degree of success in Torah study. A verse in *Daniel* teaches us this truth: *He gives wisdom to the wise* (2:21). The verse at first is puzzling; if God gives wisdom only to the wise, what designates them as wise in the first place? Ben Zoma's dictum provides the answer. A thirst for knowledge and an appreciation of its importance are prerequisites for the acquisition of knowledge. One who is ready to learn from all persons indicates that he possesses the initial *wisdom* — the desire for understanding — that makes him a fitting receptacle for enlightenment. An essential ingredient in this desire is humility; it is a key to true wisdom, because it enables someone to admit to ignorance and to be ready to seek answers without regard to the status of the person who can enlighten him.

The author of the *Toldos Yaakov Yosef* (R' Yaakov Yosef of Polnoye) was originally a vehement opponent of the Baal Shem Tov and the Chassidic movement. Once the Baal Shem Tov told him that one can derive instruction on how to serve God from *everything* one hears or sees.

As they were speaking, a gentile handyman knocked on the door. "Do you have any broken utensils to be fixed?" he asked, to which the Baal Shem Tov replied, "Thank God, everything in my home is in excellent shape. Nothing needs fixing."

The man was persistent. "Check carefully. Maybe after looking through everything, you will notice something that needs to be fixed."

The Baal Shem Tov turned to R' Yaakov Yosef. "Of course, he is talking about pots, pans, and the like. But from my standpoint he is really a messenger of God, sent to reprove me and to remind me that much in my life is not the way it should be. This repairman has made me realize that I must carefully search my actions and life-style, and make a reckoning of my spiritual condition."

The *Toldos* scoffed at what seemed to him to be an outlandish understanding of a rather innocuous statement. Could a simple handyman really be a messenger from Heaven?

After the *Toldos* took leave of the master, a gentile approached and asked him for help. "Jew, help me pick up my overturned wagon," he demanded brusquely of the *Toldos*. The rabbi replied, "I'm too weak for this. I can't help you."

The ruffian began to shout. "You *can* help me, Jew. You don't *want* to."

The *Toldos'* heart was pierced by this rebuke, for he understood it in a spiritual fashion: Righting the wagon of one's life is something that one *can* do — if he only wants to.

He returned to the Baal Shem Tov to admit the truth of the master's words. "You are right. One *can* learn from all persons."

---

for wisdom. Furthermore, one who loves and has a passion for wisdom can be considered a wise man *even if* while he is still acquiring knowledge, since his desire guarantees that he will ultimately attain wisdom and the knowledge of God. Thus, true wisdom is the *appreciation* of wisdom. Ben Zoma taught that only one who so passionately loves knowledge that he is ready to seek it anywhere (even from individuals of lesser prestige than he) is considered wise; for is it not true that one who has lost a precious object, however small it is, will search for it everywhere? (*R' Yonah*).

Calling a house a "man" is a misnomer; a house *shelters* man, but it is not man himself. Likewise, a person may contain much knowledge, yet not embody or personify that knowledge. One who passionately seeks wisdom, sensing that it is essential to his existence, and is ready to learn from any person is the true wise man (*Maharal*).

Zeroa Yemin elaborates: One may learn some lesson applicable to his own spiritual endeavors from almost anyone. Take a laborer or craftsman who rises early and works assiduously in order to sustain himself and his family. Certainly one can learn from him to invest maximum time and effort in matters that affect his and his family's spiritual welfare.

שֶׁנֶּאֱמַר: ,,מִכָּל מְלַמְּדַי הִשְׂכַּלְתִּי״ — *as it is said:* *"From all my teachers I grew wise"* (*Psalms* 119:99). The above verse ends: *for Your testimonies are my conversation.* King David is saying: "Since I wanted to be perpetually involved with the study of God's Torah, I sought enlightenment from anybody and turned all whom I met into my teachers (*Rav*). I was not embarrassed to learn

from any of them" (*Rashi*). Even if someone of inferior knowledge presented King David with an idea or thought, he would not treat his words with contempt, but would instead listen carefully in order to glean a new bit of wisdom (*Machzor Vitry*). According to *Ibn Yachna*, King David said, "*I loved Your Torah so much* (*Psalms* 119:97) that I sought to gain *wisdom from **all** my teachers* (ibid. 99); I was even willing to lower myself by seeking instruction from my enemy if he had something worthwhile to teach and if I could learn from him."

King Solomon teaches that one will find knowledge of God if he searches for it as he would for silver and hidden treasure (see *Proverbs* 2:4-5). No one demeans the value of silver just because it comes from the ground; likewise, one should seek knowledge and enlightenment even from people who seem lowly (*Yemin Moshe*).

אֵיזֶהוּ גִבּוֹר? הַכּוֹבֵשׁ אֶת יִצְרוֹ — *Who is strong? He who subdues his personal inclination.* True strength is exhibited when one is in control of himself and can refuse the advances of his evil inclination (*Rashi*). This is a spiritual strength in which man may take pride (*Rav*).

The battle between the positive and negative forces in man is a more precarious one than a physical war in three ways: (a) While a physical enemy can be vanquished permanently, the Evil Inclination can at most be subdued, but he will return again and again; the war is life long. (b) At stake in a physical war is physical security; the war against one's personal impulses is one of spiritual life or death. (c) One is well aware of physical enemies and knows that they seek

---

◆§ **Worthwhile competition.** The *Yid HaKadosh* (Holy Jew) of P'shis'cha spent the first years of his marriage in the home of his in-laws. It was from the blacksmith who lived next door that he learned to study assiduously. "Every morning when I would arise for prayer and Torah study, I would hear his hammer hitting the anvil. I thought to myself, 'If he is ready to get up early to work simply for money, I, who stand to gain eternity, certainly should be up bright and early.' I therefore began to arise earlier.

"When the smith noticed that I was up before him, he began to get up even earlier. I later discovered his reasoning. He said, 'If that young man, who earns not a penny for studying, is up before dawn, then I, who must provide for my family, certainly cannot waste the time lying in bed.'

Eventually," concluded the Holy Jew, "I became a committed student by competing with my neighbor, the blacksmith."

as it is said: *From all my teachers I grew wise* (*Psalms* 119: 99). Who is strong? He who subdues his personal inclination,

---

nothing less than his death; his spiritual enemies, however, attempt to pass themselves off as his best friend. Thus, they have greater power and are more deadly (*Midrash Shmuel*).

Ethical philosophers stated: There are three types of dominion: Rulership over one's country, one's household, and oneself. All three must rule with justice, punish evildoers, and strengthen and support those who do good. Man must subdue anything that arouses his negative impulses, elicits his anger, or incites any inclination toward excess. Conversely, he must strengthen all his

---

⊷§ **Unlikely teachers.** Ben Zoma's principle that one should learn from everyone has been a guiding light to great people throughout the centuries. Here are only a few examples:

Rabbi Zussia of Anipoli said that in his service of God, he learned three things from babies, and seven from burglars.

From babies: (a) A baby is always busy and is not unoccupied even for a minute. (b) When he lacks something, he isn't embarrassed to cry for what he needs. (c) Whenever his basic needs are satisfied, he is happily content.

From burglars: (a) A thief does his work only under cover of night, away from the eyes of people. [People should do good deeds quietly and secretly.] (b) Even if today's attempt fails, he tries again tomorrow. He never gives up hope that eventually he will succeed. (c) He is loyal to his comrades and will never steal from them or turn them in. (d) Even a seemingly insignificant item or sum of money is important in his eyes and justifies the risk of stealing it. [One should make every effort to do the same even for seemingly insignificant *mitzvos*.] (e) He is ready to sell for a minimal price even that which he expended great effort to steal, not considering his catch of great importance. The main thing he is interested in is to cover his tracks. [Whatever good deeds we do should not cause us to think arrogantly that we have produced something for which God should reward us handsomely. Our main concern should be whether we have covered our debts to Him.] (f) He tells no one of his successes, nor does he divulge his plans for the future. (g) He loves his profession and would not exchange it for anything in the world.

The famed R' Elimelech of Lizhensk used to relate something that he learned from a neighbor, a furrier, also coincidentally named Elimelech. The furrier worked long hours to eke out a living. Once after midnight, he fell asleep at his workbench. Suddenly he was startled out of his stupor by his wife, calling out to him in Yiddish, „אלימלך פארריכעט דאס פעלצעל כל זמן עס ברענט נאך דער ליכט‟ — *"Elimelech, fix the skin while the candle still burns."* R' Elimelech would often relate this story, adding, "Her words still ring in my ears and give me no rest — day or night. As long as the light of the soul is still burning, we must make repairs. Later it will be too late."

One who receives a letter from the king is proud, even if the messenger is dressed in ragged, dirty clothes. Likewise, one should be ready to learn Torah and grow spiritually from his contact with *all* people (*Knesses Yisrael*). From a sinner who transgresses with excitement and joy, and is often willing to place himself in danger in order to achieve his goal, one can derive some very important lessons on how to serve God with passion and dedication. King David captured this idea with the words מֵאֹיְבַי תְּחַכְּמֵנִי מִצְוֹתֶךָ, *From my enemies I became wise regarding Your commandments* (*Psalms* 119:98).

This offers some insight into a puzzling comment of *Rashi*. Our forefather Jacob says, "עִם לָבָן גַּרְתִּי, *I sojourned with Laban"* (*Genesis* 32:5). *Rashi* (ad loc.) paraphrases, rearranging the letters of the word גַּרְתִּי to form תרי"ג: "I sojourned with Laban, fulfilling the תרי"ג (613) *mitzvos*, and I did not learn from his evil ways." This is an apparently arrogant claim, however, from someone as humble as Jacob. R' Meir Shapiro explained that Jacob actually did speak with great humility: "Although I kept all 613 *mitzvos*, I did not learn from Laban's evil ways as I should have. Had I followed the advice of the Sages, I would have adopted Laban's passion for evil and channeled it into serving God."

יִצְרוֹ, שֶׁנֶּאֱמַר: "טוֹב אֶרֶךְ אַפַּיִם מִגִּבּוֹר, וּמֹשֵׁל בְּרוּחוֹ מִלֹּכֵד עִיר." אֵיזֶהוּ עָשִׁיר? הַשָּׂמֵחַ בְּחֶלְקוֹ,

positive attributes, bringing them to expression (*Meiri*).

שֶׁנֶּאֱמַר: "טוֹב אֶרֶךְ אַפַּיִם מִגִּבּוֹר, וּמֹשֵׁל בְּרוּחוֹ מִלֹּכֵד עִיר" — *as it is said: "He who is slow to anger is better than a strong man, and a master of his passions is better than a conqueror of a city"* (*Proverbs* 16:32). The verse from *Proverbs* does not speak of physical strength, which animals, too, possess. Ben Zoma instead weighs two other types of strength, which are the exclusive province of human beings: the *strategic* strength used in waging war, and the strength of character and heart necessary to master one's passions. He cites the words of King Solomon to show that the defeat of overpowering passion is a greater feat than victory in a physical battle (*R' Yonah*).

According to *R' Yonah*, the verse cites two comparisons: one who is slow to anger versus a strong man, and one who is a master of his passions versus the conqueror of a city.

One who defeats an external enemy in battle may not be truly strong; his enemy may simply be weak. Not so when man overcomes the evil inclination which is so integral a part of his personality — he is then both the victor and the vanquished, for he has overpowered a very powerful side of *himself* (*Maharal*).

Magen Avos emphasizes the fact that the mishnah speaks of internal strength. The donkey possesses a greater ability than man to carry burdens, and the lion is a greater warrior. Only in strength of character can man take pride.

Rav explains: It is better that one is slow to anger out of strength and self-control rather than out of natural docility. Likewise, a conqueror of a city

---

ะ§ **Stay at your post.** Many wise men have emphasized the importance of gaining control over oneself, and have sought to define its guidelines. For example, one must be careful to conquer his *own* Evil Inclination — the one that is troubling to him, personally — not somebody else's. People often are busy correcting others' failures and never stop to see their own (*R' Naftali of Ropshitz*). Every person's Evil Inclination is unique, seeking to entrap him in a particular area of weakness, and trying to capitalize on his own particular passions. It was specifically in order to withstand that particular temptation that this person was sent into the world. Hence, one must conquer *his own* Evil Inclination. R' Yisrael Salanter once said that people should worry about their own spiritual needs and their friend's physical ones, not the other way around.

Often, the Evil Inclination seeks to subvert people by pushing them to assume spiritual roles of others rather than allowing them to do their own jobs. For example, a *rav*'s main task is to spend the majority of his time on Torah study in order to provide his congregation with halachic guidance and leadership; a wealthy congregant's task is to assume responsibility for the charitable affairs of the city. The evil inclination may come to the *rav* and whisper in his ear, "As leader of your flock, you must tend to the charities of the city." While charity is important, it would be a mistake for the *rav* to invest most of his energies in raising and distributing funds, when they are better spent elsewhere.

Likewise, the householder must spend an appropriate amount of time at Torah study, but he should not be swayed by the pandering of the Evil Inclination, which reminds him that "the study of Torah is equal to all other *mitzvos*," and therefore he should not be overly concerned with the plight of the city's poor. Let each person subdue his *own* Evil Inclination — not someone else's.

As the Chofetz Chaim once told a wealthy and charitable person who decided to scale down his business so that he could dedicate himself to Torah study: "In wartime, if an officer decides that he can do more for the common good by leaving his post and fighting at the front, he will be court-martialed. A soldier must obey orders and man the position assigned to him. Your responsibility is to *support* Torah study and the poor. By ending your business success, you are jeopardizing the cause you were assigned to support. You are a deserter."

as it is said: *He who is slow to anger is better than a strong man, and a master of his passions is better than a conqueror of a city (Proverbs 16:32). Who is rich? He who is happy with his lot,*

who controls his passions and forgoes the opportunity to exact revenge from those who rebelled against him is stronger than one who gives vent to this desire (see *Tosafos Yom Tov*).

One should subdue and conquer his Evil Inclination, but not break it totally. The Midrash (*Bereishis Rabbah* 9:12) explains that when the Torah ends the account of physical creation with the words *and it was very good (Genesis* 1:31), it is referring to the Evil Inclination. All life forces, even those which seem irredeemably evil, can and should be harnessed for the greater glory of God. Our Sages taught, "*And you shall love God with all your heart* — with both your Good and Evil Inclinations" (see *Berachos* 54a). Men would not marry and start families if not for their procreative drive, which can potentially be misdirected as well (see *Sanhedrin* 64a). Hence, the Evil Inclination has a legitimate role in life and should only be conquered, but not destroyed (*Ri ben Shlomo*).

The *Vilna Gaon* interprets the proof text in this fashion. He explains that the one exception to the rule is anger, which must be totally eradicated, as it has almost no redeeming value; hence, "one who is slow to anger is better than a strong man." Passion, however, must be saved and redirected. Therefore "a master of his passions is better than a conqueror of a city," for a conquered city is seldom razed or emptied of its inhabitants; a deserted city is of no value. Similarly, Torah and *mitzvos* performed without passion are also deficient, and therefore the mishnah says that passion should be mastered, not destroyed.

אֵיזֶהוּ עָשִׁיר? הַשָּׂמֵחַ בְּחֶלְקוֹ — *Who is [truly] rich? He who is happy with his lot.* One who graciously accepts whatever God gives him is constantly happy. Such a person does not allow himself to be caught up in the senseless pursuit of pleasures and possessions. The truly wealthy person is the contented one, for what good is wealth if it does not provide happiness? (*Rashi, Magen Avos*).

Hafla'ah elaborates on this point by analyzing the human tendency to rejoice over a new possession. As time passes, however, one gets used to the new item and begins to take it for granted. The truly wealthy person, on the other hand, *always* rejoices in his portion. Not only does he appreciate it when he gets it, but even long afterward, when it has become his own [חֶלְקוֹ], he is still happy and thankful to God.

He who constantly desires material wealth will never achieve emotional satisfaction. Like a pauper, he is always in search of what he thinks he lacks (*Tiferes Yisrael*), but if one can support himself and his family, and engage in the development of his spiritual life as well, he has everything he needs. What is the purpose of material wealth if not to allow one the opportunity to address his spiritual agenda? However, one who is unhappy with his lot in life, dissatisfied with what God provides him, is truly impoverished.

King Solomon captured this contrast in the following verse: *All the days of the pauper are bad, but the good hearted constantly celebrate (Proverbs* 15:15). One who suffers pangs of hunger for material wealth is like a pauper who never has enough. Those who have emotional satisfaction,

> ⇜ **Turn the tables.** The Baal Shem Tov offered the following parable: To test the loyalty of his subjects, a king hired men to incite them to revolt. Many people were swayed by the "revolutionaries," while others remained unswervingly loyal. Among the loyalists was a bright fellow who saw through the "fifth column" and countered their arguments, saying, "Fools, you yourselves show loyalty to the king by executing his mission. Why do you expect us to be less loyal to the king than you are?"
>
> Man should use the same argumant against the Evil Inclination. "When you incite me against the Great King, you are following His instructions! Why do you expect less of me? You do your job — but let me do mine!" Thus, one can even transform the evil inclination itself into a force for good.

however, enjoy life and find it a constant celebration (*R' Yonah*). *Abarbanel* quotes the famous saying, "One who has one hundred wants two hundred" (see *Koheles Rabbah* 1:34). Someone who covets money can never have enough, so he can never be truly rich. Only one who has an inner sense of contentment is really wealthy.

Ruach Chaim notes the usage חֶלְקוֹ, literally, *his portion*. Most men never achieve more than a *portion* of their desires, but for the true magnate, this portion is sufficient.

שֶׁנֶּאֱמַר: ,,יְגִיעַ כַּפֶּיךָ כִּי תֹאכֵל אַשְׁרֶיךָ וְטוֹב לָךְ'' — *as it is said: "When you eat the labor of your hands, you are praiseworthy and all is well with you"* (*Psalms* 128:2). One can achieve happiness even from the little bit of wealth yielded by the labor of his hands. The Talmud teaches that a person has more enjoyment from something he made himself than from something he acquired from others. [A multimillionaire who derives no joy from the fruits of his toil suffers from true poverty, for true wealth is in the heart and mind.] (*Rashi, R' Yonah*).

The *Rebbe* of Kotzk offers a beautiful interpretation of the verse cited here. King David is teaching us: "Eat of the labor of your *hands*, but not of your heart and soul. Of course you must toil with your hands in order to earn a livelihood, but never allow your entire being to be totally consumed by your occupation. Even as you toil with your hands, concentrate your thoughts upon lofty spiritual goals."

The truth of this definition of wealth is actually self-evident. Ben Zoma cites the verse from *Psalms* 128 (which begins, "Praiseworthy is the person who fears God") as an additional proof that satisfaction with one's lot in life engenders true fear of Heaven, and thereby guarantees a good life both here and in the Hereafter (*Magen Avos*).

Metzudas David (*Psalms* ad loc.) gives a different explanation of the proof verse: One who is self-supporting need not share the rewards of his Torah study with others in exchange for their financial help. Thus, all the rewards and benefits are solely his.

,,אַשְׁרֶיךָ'' – בָּעוֹלָם הַזֶּה, ,,וְטוֹב לָךְ'' – לָעוֹלָם הַבָּא — *"You are praiseworthy" — in this world; "and all is*

⋖§ **Be content with the good.** The Chofetz Chaim had many pithy comments and observations on the mishnah's advice that people must learn to be content with their lot:

☐ Once he overheard someone say about his financial condition. "Thank God, but it wouldn't hurt if business was a little better."

"Who says it wouldn't hurt?" interjected the Chofetz Chaim. "Everything God does is for the good (*Berachos* 60b). If this is the lot God granted you in life, it is good for you. Be happy with *your* lot."

☐ The Chofetz Chaim once encouraged a wealthy acquaintance to spend more time in spiritual pursuits such as prayer or Torah study. The gentleman demurred, claiming, "I have no time." Answered the sage of Radin, "If you have no free time, you aren't truly wealthy. You are nothing but a pitiful pauper. There is no greater poverty than yours."

☐ A carpenter needs a large saw. If we were to take it from him and replace it with a very fine diamond saw, he would effectively be out of business, even thought the diamond saw is much more expensive than a carpentry saw; for his job, the carpenter needs the right tools. One's lot in life constitutes the tools God gives him for his own role in life. Some need financial wealth in order to function as distributors of God's money; others need poverty in order to achieve the personal growth that is born of adversity. Only God knows who needs which tool. A truly wealthy person is one who is happy with the portion God has designed uniquely for him (*Chofetz Chaim*).

The Steipler Gaon poetically captured the sentiment of the mishnah, when he wrote: בְּטָחוֹנִי בְּצוּרִי הִיא אוֹצְרֵי, *My faith in my Creator — that is my treasure.* A person's faith in God is the treasure that allows him to be satisfied with his lot.

as it is said: *When you eat of the labor of your hands, you are praiseworthy and all is well with you (Psalms 128:2). You are praiseworthy* — in this world; *and all is well with you* — in the World to Come.

---

well with you" — in the World to Come. One who is satisfied with the share that God grants him needs nothing from anyone. Such independence is a primary condition for happiness in this world. Furthermore, one who is content with his lot has no reason to stoop to thievery, trickery, or any other Torah prohibition in an effort to acquire wealth; perfectly content with what is his, he will not ever covet his neighbor's property. His independence is his wealth; he earns his own and is not indebted to anybody.

Additionally, the avoidance of these grave sins is a guaranteed way to enjoy the goodness of the World to Come (*Rashi, Machzor Vitry, Tiferes Yisrael*).

Alternatively, *Machzor Vitry* views the mishnah's interpretation of the words from *Psalms* as referring to one who endures poverty gracefully, never doubting God's judgment. He is happy in this world since he is not overwhelmed by depression, and he gains the next, for his loving acceptance of God's plan is an atonement for him.

According to *Meiri*, the two parts of this statement are contingent upon each other. A person who has enough for his daily needs and does not seek luxuries will be able to devote the rest of his time to the service of God, and he will thus merit both this world and the World to Come.

R' Moshe Alshakar offers an insightful piece of advice. A person can hoard money his entire life, never spending it either on himself or on *mitzvos* and charity. The truly wealthy person is content and happy with *his* portion; he uses it both for his own legitimate enjoyment in this world, and as a tool to produce merits that will provide him a share in the World to Come. This is the lesson of the words of King David: "If you eat the fruits of your labors instead of leaving your wealth for others,

---

◆§ **Heads up.** The *Rebbe* of Sochatchov (the author of *Shem MiShmuel*), the grandson of the *Kotzker* Rebbe, cited a Talmudic dictum which vividly illustrates his grandfather's lesson. The Talmud (*Kiddushin* 29a) teaches that a father has numerous obligations toward his son to prepare him for life: "A father must . . . teach his son Torah . . . and teach him a trade or profession. Others say that a father must teach his son how to swim in the water." Why is swimming singled out as the one physical fitness pursuit which a father must teach his son? If it is for safety, then the Sages could have found many other examples; i.e. self-defense, first aid, or survival techniques.

Rather, the Sages were alluding to a very special lesson by juxtaposing swimming with the importance of teaching a trade, for the techniques of swimming should be applied to earning a livelihood. A swimmer places his entire body in the water and then churns vigorously with his arms and legs to propel himself. However, he must constantly lift his head out of the water so as not to drown. Similarly, someone working at his livelihood must strain every fiber of his body to succeed — but he must never forget to limit the scope of his labor, and never to let his heart and soul "drown" in his mundane pursuits. Like a swimmer, he must keep his head above water, concentrating his mental powers mainly on Torah study and character improvement. One of the fundamental and perilous errors of life is to think that what we *do* is what we *are*.

King David alludes to this when he says, *"Eat the labor of your hands,"* meaning that one should labor with *his hands* not *his head*. He should not sink his whole mind into his work, but save the best of his intellectual powers for spiritual pursuits.

◆§ **Beyond your reach.** The commentators question how man can be commanded not to covet another's property, which is a natural emotional reaction. *Ibn Ezra* offers an enlightening response by way of a parable: Even a coarse village bumpkin with minimal sophistication would not fantasize that he could marry the royal princess; it is simply beyond the realm of possibility for him. Similarly, we must understand that all acquisitions in life are gifts from Heaven. If God has given something to someone else, it is no more our right to request it than to request wings to fly. Both are delusionary.

אֵיזֶהוּ מְכֻבָּד? הַמְכַבֵּד אֶת הַבְּרִיּוֹת, שֶׁנֶּאֱמַר: ,,כִּי מְכַבְּדַי אֲכַבֵּד, וּבֹזַי יֵקָלּוּ.''

[ג] בֶּן עַזַּאי אוֹמֵר: הֱוֵי רָץ לְמִצְוָה קַלָּה, וּבוֹרֵחַ

---

you will attain happiness in this world; and by making wise spiritual investments, you will benefit in the World to Come.

אֵיזֶהוּ מְכֻבָּד? הַמְכַבֵּד אֶת הַבְּרִיּוֹת — *Who is honored? He who honors others.* The three previously mentioned virtues ennoble man in the eyes of God and make him worthy of honor, whether or not his neighbors acknowledge it. Ben Zoma offers practical advice on how to *gain* the respect of others as well: Show respect and honor to others, and they will honor you (*Rav*).

Another explanation is that one who honors others really honors only himself. He adds nothing to the honoree by his show of respect, for if the other person is truly worthy, the expression of esteem adds nothing, and if the other person is *not* worthy, hollow accolades will not alter his status [and in fact will only embarrass the flatterer]. The only thing honor does is to enhance the stature of those who *give* it in the eyes of their beholders. Thus, whenever a person honors others, he is really honoring himself (*R' Yonah*).

Rashi and *Meiri* render: *Who is honored [by Heaven]? He who honors others.* Not only does man

naturally receive reciprocal honor from those whom he honors, but God too honors such a person, for one who respects others recognizes man as created in the image of his Maker. Therefore, sensitivity to human dignity is in essence showing honor to God. In return, *Tiferes Yisrael* adds, his own Godliness will shine, causing others to honor him.

Abarbanel comments: Man can give only what he possesses; only an honorable person can accord honor to others.

שֶׁנֶּאֱמַר: ,,כִּי מְכַבְּדַי אֲכַבֵּד, וּבֹזַי יֵקָלּוּ'' — *as it is said: "For those who honor Me I will honor, and those who scorn Me shall be degraded" (I Samuel 2:30).* Though this verse refers to God, one may infer a guideline for proper human behavior from it by means of a *kal vachomer* (a fortiori) argument. If God Himself [Who created the universe for His Own Glory — see 6:11] repays honor with honor, surely people should do the same (*Rav, R' Yonah*).

Rashi offers alternative interpretations: (a) One who follows God's dictates by honoring elders and scholars will himself be honored. (b) One should honor those who honor him so that they

---

ᐸᕼ **Invest now.** The Talmud (*Eruvin* 54a) teaches that Rav told Rav Hamnuna: "My son, if you have the means, treat yourself well now; for in the grave there is no enjoyment, and death comes soon. Do not say, 'I will leave my wealth for my children' — they will find support for themselves even without your money." The commentators explain Rav's meaning: A person should spend his fortune on *mitzvos* and charitable acts as soon as he possibly can, "treating himself well" in a spiritual sense, because he may die suddenly, and then it will be too late.

ᐸᕼ **A glutton for someone else's honor.** R' Avigdor Halberstam (brother of the *Divrei Chaim*) was once a guest for Shabbos in the home of a wealthy *chassid*. The custom in that house was to give a distinguished guest the honor of tasting the *cholent* and then serving portions to everyone else. When the *cholent* was brought to R' Avigdor, he took a taste and then another taste and yet another, finally finishing the contents of the large serving bowl down to the last bean. "Is there more?" he asked. He finished every morsel of the *cholent*, leaving nothing for any of the shocked people at the table.

Later it was discovered that the cook had accidentally poured kerosene instead of oil into the *cholent*. R' Avigdor preferred to appear as a glutton and suffer personal embarrassment rather than allow the hapless woman to be humiliated in front of the others. He thus honored others at the expense of his own prestige. Is there anything more honorable than that?

Who is honored? He who honors others, as it is said: *For those who honor Me I will honor, and those who scorn Me shall be degraded* (I Samuel 2:30).

2. **B**en Azzai says: Run to [perform even] a "minor" *mitzvah,*

---

will continue to honor him, thus perpetuating the cycle.

Tiferes Yisrael views this citation from *I Samuel* as proof of the Heavenly honor which one receives as a result of honoring others. God is pleased when we respect His creatures and He responds by granting us prestige and honor.

The verse does not mean that God actively degrades those who scorn Him. According to *Rashi*, the degradation is a direct result of, rather than a punishment for, scorning God. Such a person has lost his nobility and is intrinsically degraded. *Rav* and *Magen Avos* view this verse as an expression of God's humility, for it suggests that God will, so to speak, not actively intervene to defend His own honor. Instead, the scorners will, so to speak, passively become scorned. Regarding those who debase the righteous, however, God actively takes up the cause, as He told Abraham: *"And he who curses you, I will curse"* (Genesis 12:3).

Mishnah 2

בֶּן עַזַּאי אוֹמֵר — *Ben Azzai says.* Shimon ben Azzai, a third-generation *Tanna,* was a student-colleague of R' Akiva (see *Bava Basra* 155b), but his main teacher was R' Yehoshua, whose halachic opinion he followed even against that of R' Akiva (see *Taanis* 26a and *Yevamos* 49a). Like his colleague Ben Zoma, he did not receive the *semichah* ordination and thus is usually not referred to as "Rabbi" [see, however, *Yevamos* 49a and commentary to 4:1].

A model of diligence in Torah study, he remained a lifelong bachelor. Interestingly, he himself is quoted as saying, "One who does not marry and have children is considered to have spilled blood" (*Yevamos* 63b). When confronted with his own words, he responded, "What shall I do? I have an unquenchable passion for Torah [and cannot be burdened with the responsibility of a wife and family]. Let others worry about the existence of the world" (ibid.). [See *Kesubos* 63a, which reports that he was betrothed to R' Akiva's daughter who — like her mother — agreed to the marriage on the condition that her husband immerse himself completely in Torah study. Nonetheless, the marriage did not last (see *Sotah* 4a). *Tosafos* ad loc., s.v. ברתיה דרבי עקיבא, reports that the *eirusin* (betrothal) was completed, but not the *nisuin* (marriage). See *Rambam, Hilchos Ishus* 15:3, regarding the halachic permissibility of Ben Azzai's course of inaction.]

A resident of Tiberias, Ben Azzai became known for his incisiveness and strong logic in Talmudic issues. "I am like Ben Azzai in the marketplace of Tiberias" became the slogan of those who claimed Talmudic prowess.

His abiding faith in God's fairness is expressed in his opinion regarding the fear of losing the source of one's livelihood to another: "בְּשִׁמְךָ יִקְרָאוּךְ וּבִמְקוֹמְךָ יוֹשִׁיבוּךְ וּמִשֶׁלְּךָ יִתְּנוּ לָךְ, *You will be summoned by your **name** and assigned **your** proper place.* Sustenance will be provided for you by Heaven, not from what has been prepared [by Providence] for another. No person can touch what God has designated for you nor may one kingdom stand in the way of another kingdom's rise to power" (*Yoma* 38a).

His love for Torah study emanated from a burning love for God Himself. His understanding of the Biblical dictum *to love God with all your soul* (Deuteronomy 6:5) was that one's love of the Almighty must penetrate to the core of his soul (see *Sifri* ad loc.). These two passions did not diminish his high regard for his fellow human beings. In response to R' Akiva's claim that the dictum *Love your fellow as yourself* (Leviticus 19:18) is *the* cardinal principle of the Torah, Ben

Azzai claimed that citing the verse *This is the Book of the generations of man; He made him in the image of God* (Genesis 5:1) is more fundamental. He argued that according to R' Akiva, one who is degraded by his fellow would be legitimately entitled to retaliate since the Torah only demands *equal* treatment for one's fellow — not better treatment. However, morality and ethical fellowship based on a respect for the Godliness in man is absolute and not conditional on anyone's behavior (see *Bereishis Rabbah* ad loc.).

Along with a brilliant mind, Ben Azzai possessed a sensitive heart, which he considered an integral element of Godly service. "Both he who does much and he who does little [are deemed worthy], as long as his heart is directed toward [fulfilling the will of] Heaven" (*Berachos* 5a), i.e., God looks into man's heart, for He desires action that is sincere rather than mechanistic.

Ben Azzai's rare combination of love for Torah, man, and God defines an individual of whom the Sages taught: "One to whom Ben Azzai appears in a dream may expect to achieve exceptional righteousness" (*Berachos* 57a).

The Midrash (*Eichah Rabbasi* 2:4), however, lists him among the martyred victims of Roman emperor Hadrian's reign of terror. His death signaled to the Sages the end of true diligence in Torah study (*Sotah* 49a).

הֱוֵי רָץ לְמִצְוָה קַלָּה — *Run to [perform even] a "minor" mitzvah.* In addition to the rationale for performing even "minor" *mitzvos* offered in 2:1, Ben Azzai adds that when someone performs a *mitzvah* — any *mitzvah* — he becomes conditioned

to obey God's will (*R' Yonah*). Alternatively, the performance of "light" *mitzvos* will lead to performance of more difficult ones, those for which the penalty is more severe (*Rashi*).

According to *Rambam*, the mishnah teaches alacrity in the performance of *mitzvos*. One should not procrastinate when a *mitzvah* opportunity presents itself; he should seize the moment and act.

Sfas Emes elaborates: This does not mean that one should ignore a *mitzvah* of seemingly greater consequence in deference to a light one. Ben Azzai simply means that "light" *mitzvos* should be pursued *as* passionately as difficult ones.

Moses exemplified this lesson in his approach to the *mitzvah* of establishing cities of refuge for those who commit unintentional murders. He was commanded to establish three such cities on the east bank of the Jordan and three on the west bank, which is in *Eretz Yisrael* proper (*Deuteronomy* 4:41). Those on the east bank were to become functional only upon the establishment of the three in the Land. Nevertheless, Moses established those in Transjordan without delay, even though their status would not take effect until Joshua established the other three cities much later. Moses said, "I will seize the *mitzvah* opportunity that came to me and fulfill it" (see *Makkos* 10a). If someone of the stature of Moses, who understood the significance and great reward of a *mitzvah*, yearned to perform even a partial *mitzvah*, then certainly we, who suffer from the advanced stages of spiritual malaise, would do well to practice alacrity in the performance of *mitzvos* in order to cure our own souls and hearts of the spiritual diseases from which they suffer.

◆§ **Temporary vs. eternal.** The dictum of our mishnah may be homiletically interpreted in light of the Talmud (*Avodah Zarah* 3a) which refers to the *mitzvah* of dwelling in the *succah* as a מִצְוָה קַלָּה, a "light" *mitzvah*. The lesson of *succah* is that this world is very temporary, while the world of reward is eternal. Thus, our mishnah teaches that one should run to perform the "light" *mitzvah* of *succah* and to learn its lesson; by internalizing its message, one will be saved from sin (*Toras Avos*).

◆§ **Stay fresh.** One should never be spiritually satisfied; the key to spiritual growth is thirst for increasing closeness to God. We are therefore taught to run after the opportunity to perform a *mitzvah* with as much enthusiasm as if it were the very first time we had been able to perform it. The Baal Shem Tov explains that it is this freshness of approach that we implore God to grant us when we recite the words of King David: *Do not cast us away in old age; when our strength gives out, do not forsake us* (Psalms 71:9). We plead with God not to let us become old and tired in our service of Him.

and flee from sin; for one *mitzvah* leads to another *mitzvah*, and one sin leads to another sin; for the consequence of a

Tiferes Yisrael explains the term קַלָּה as *easy.* Even a *mitzvah* which is easy to perform and which one assumes he will always have opportunity to perform should nonetheless be performed joyfully and without delay.

In the verse וּשְׁמַרְתֶּם אֶת הַמַּצּוֹת, *You shall oversee the matzos* (Exodus 12:17), the Sages read the word המצות as הַמִּצְוֹת, *the commandments,* i.e., the verse alludes to a similarity between the attitude needed toward matzos and that needed toward the proper observance of commandments. Unless one kneads and bakes the dough with utmost haste and efficiency, it will become *chametz,* unfit for consumption on Pesach. Likewise, if opportunities to perform *mitzvos* are left unexploited, they may well sour and no longer be available (see *Mechilta* ad loc.). Thus, when there is an opportunity to perform a commandment, one should do so with alacrity and without delay.

Alternatively, the *mitzvos* spoken of here are "minor" in the sense that they are easy and enjoyable to perform for one of the following reasons: (a) The act itself entails little physical exertion; (b) one is habituated to it, such as the daily prayers; (c) it is a "logical" *mitzvah,* such as honoring one's parents; or (d) it is an enjoyable *mitzvah,* such as the Shabbos meals, or one which lends us prestige, such as wearing a beautiful *tallis* or purchasing a nice *esrog.* One should run to perform a *mitzvah* even of this type, for the sake of Heaven rather than for personal enjoyment, just as one would perform a *mitzvah* which is less personally satisfying or beneficial (*Tiferes Yisrael*).

וּבוֹרֵחַ מִן הָעֲבֵרָה — *and flee from sin.* Each wrongful act dulls the conscience and makes the next sin all the more easy to do. In addition to the basic spiritual havoc it wreaks, misdeed therefore has the long-lasting effect of conditioning one to a sinful life-style (*R' Yonah, Rashi*).

Ruach Chaim offers the following: The Mishnah employs terms such as *run after,* or *chase a mitzvah,* and *flee* from sin in order to stress the seriousness of the war between good and evil. The force of evil in man seeks perpetually to keep *mitzvah* opportunities out of his grasp, and he must therefore chase after these golden opportunities. In addition, it seeks to victimize him by actively thrusting sin in his path. Man, therefore, must operate on two tracks: He must flee sin, always staying a step ahead, and he must also create the circumstances for doing *mitzvos.* Hence, Ben Azzai directed us to run after even a "minor" *mitzvah,* and to *flee* from sin, as from fire.

The Mishnah does not use the term *light* regarding sin, as it does regarding *mitzvos.* Every sin is, at least initially, highly enjoyable to the sinner and quite easy to transgress (*Maharal*).

שֶׁמִּצְוָה גוֹרֶרֶת מִצְוָה, וַעֲבֵרָה גוֹרֶרֶת עֲבֵרָה — *for one mitzvah leads to another mitzvah, and one sin leads to another sin.* The performance of one *mitzvah,* even a "minor" one, unleashes a spiritual chain reaction, opening up opportunities for another *mitzvah* and yet another. Hence, even a "minor"

⋅§ **Chain reaction.** Spiritual abilities are similar to muscles: Lifting heavy burdens strengthens one's muscles, and the accomplishment of spiritual tasks expands one's spiritual capacity. R' Yehudah Leib Ashlag told his students: "I once heard a glutton say that one knows if food is good and tasty only when he hears people ask for more. It is the same in the service of God; if the performance of the first *mitzvah* creates an appetite for more, one can rest assured that the first one was performed with great sincerity."

We are taught that there is no reward for *mitzvos* in this world because nothing in this world is of sufficient quality to serve as reward for a *mitzvah.* Only the opportunity to do another *mitzvah* can adequately compensate one for the invaluable act of following God's will.

Thousands of people attended the ground breaking ceremonies for the Yeshivas Chachmei Lublin in Poland. The site of the yeshivah, a piece of prime real estate in downtown Lublin, was donated by Shmuel Eichenbaum, a childhood friend of the *Rosh Yeshivah,* Rabbi Meir Shapiro. The Chortkover *Rebbe,* R' Yisrael, spoke at the occasion. During his remarks, he turned to R' Shmuel Eichenbaum and said: "I don't especially envy you for the *mitzvah* of donating the building site, since it is a *mitzvah* done publicly, for which you get much honor. It is the *mitzvah* that you must have once done privately, that was the catalyst for this *mitzvah,* which makes me envious."

mitzvah should be sought out vigilantly. Conversely, a sin must be avoided at all costs, for in its wake many more will follow (*Rashi*).

This domino effect, both in its positive and negative manifestations, is a natural phenomenon since it creates a spiritual groove and habituates us to a particular pattern of action. The reward one receives for fulfilling a *mitzvah* is the Heavenly gift of being able to do another *mitzvah*. Having thus developed good habits, goodness becomes almost second nature; having fallen under the sway of the seemingly Eternal Enemy, however, one quite naturally begins to follow his call increasingly, until one is ready to engage even in the most abominable behavior (*R' Yonah*).

Rambam (*Hilchos Teshuvah* 7:4) reckons the entrapping nature of sin as the reason the repentant are considered of a more elevated stature than those who have always been righteous (see *Berachos* 34b). Having tasted sin, they are more deeply bound by its influence and must call upon greater spiritual resources to free themselves of its viselike grip. *Midrash Tanchuma, Vayikra* 6 explains this phenomenon as the tragedy of inadvertent sin. While man is not culpable for a sin he committed accidentally, his act nonetheless opens the door for premeditated iniquity.

The Evil Inclination slowly but surely wears down man's resistance. Beginning with the lure of mild transgressions, he keeps raising the stakes in his campaign for one's soul (see *Shabbos* 108b). Thus one light sin leads to another more severe transgression.

שֶׁשְּׂכַר מִצְוָה מִצְוָה, וּשְׂכַר עֲבֵרָה עֲבֵרָה — *for the consequence of a mitzvah is a mitzvah, and the consequence of a sin is a sin.* Besides the natural process of habituation, in which one becomes accustomed to perform *mitzvos,* God rewards the performance of a *mitzvah* by providing the opportunity for an additional *mitzvah.* Thus, the performance of a *mitzvah* earns dividends, since it sets in motion a chain of events that permit one to perform other *mitzvos.* Conversely, one who sins is afforded more opportunities to follow the path he has chosen (*Rav, Rashi*).

Tosafos Yom Tov, seeking to resolve this mishnah with the basic Torah principle of free choice, cites the words of the Sages: "One who seeks purity will be aided from Above [in his quest]; one who seeks impurity will be allowed [to find opportunities to do so]" (*Yoma* 38b, *Shabbos* 104a). God provides active help to those in search of a righteous life. To those who unfortunately seek the opposite path, He opens the gate and allows them to follow their hearts' perverted desires.

R' Yonah elaborates: Man is given free choice to chart his own life course. Once he chooses repeatedly to follow a certain path, God responds to his choice by turning his wish into a reality. The first *mitzvah,* so to speak, "sends a signal" to God, indicating the will and choice of man; the second *mitzvah* is God's response to that choice.

⇜§ **Creating conditions.** *Avnei Nezer* questions why one should be punished for his later sins. Since they are the result of the chain reaction triggered by the initial sin, it would seem that he almost had no choice regarding his later misdeeds. The answer is that the punishment is indeed for the initial sin, which contained the seeds of destruction that came in its wake. Man must take precaution not to unleash a spiritual avalanche for he will bear the guilt for all the ensuing damage.

Rambam (*Hilchos Teshuvah* 6:3) teaches that man may, as a result of having committed many sins or severe ones, be punished by losing the opportunity to repent. Notwithstanding that he no longer has free choice, he is still culpable for *all* his actions since he is responsible for placing himself in such a situation.

Tosafos (*Bava Basra* 17a s.v. שלשה לא שלט) explains in this light the statement of the Talmud that there were four people over whom the Evil Inclination had no sway. If they were never subject to the sway of iniquity, would it not seem that they never had free choice to begin with and therefore did not deserve reward for either their active or passive deeds? *Tosafos* concludes that initially they had so fervently fought their innate force of evil that God rewarded them by silencing it altogether. Nevertheless, they were rewarded for the good they did even afterward, since they themselves were responsible for their status.

[Of course, the actual *reward* for the *mitzvah* is to be paid out in the World to Come.]

Negative choices also elicit a Heavenly reaction. Once man indicates his preference for iniquity, God allows that choice to play itself out, to man's own detriment. Thus, one sin results in another, until man is almost inextricably caught in the traffic of sin. Once he chooses this track, he may lose his moral bearings and will encounter extreme difficulty in finding them again.

Rav offers an alternative interpretation, rendering the clause as follows: *Since the enjoyment one had from [performance of] a mitzvah is [itself] a mitzvah.* One receives reward not only for the act of performing the *mitzvah* itself, but also for whatever enjoyment he derives from its performance. Likewise, man is punished not only for a sinful act, but also for whatever pleasure and benefit it brought him. [שָׂכָר thus means *benefit derived* rather than *reward*. See 2:1 *Meiri* et al.]

Tiferes Yisrael and *Orach LeChaim* offer a variation on *Rav*. God created man in order that He would have people upon whom to bestow His goodness: *God wished to confer merit on Israel; therefore, He gave them Torah and mitzvos in abundance* (*Makkos* 23b). When man fulfills *mitzvos*, he provides God with the opportunity, so to speak, to concretize His will to bestow goodness upon us. Hence, the enjoyment and reward one receives for a *mitzvah* is in itself a *mitzvah*, since man's receiving reward is itself something that, so to speak, pleases God.

HaChassid Yaavetz offers the following understanding: The greatest reward for a *mitzvah* is the *mitzvah itself*. The opportunity to come closer to God by doing His will is the greatest reward one could ever dream of. The tragedy of sin lies not in the punishment one will receive for it, but rather in the obstacles it interposes in his relationship with God.

R' Moshe Alshakar explains שְׂכַר מִצְוָה as the expense one goes to in order to perform a *mitzvah*. Not only does God pay for the *mitzvah* itself, He also rewards one for any additional outlay of money, energy, or emotion in the execution of his spiritual duties. Similarly, when one chases after a *mitzvah* or flees from sin, he is duly rewarded for the extra effort.

◆§ **The finest dowry of all.** A wealthy and learned Jew decided to tour all the yeshivos in order to find a scholar to marry his daughter. He prepared an elaborate Talmudic discourse, leaving a few difficult questions out of his presentation so that he could pose them to the students he met. When he arrived in each yeshivah, he made it known that whoever could resolve his difficulties would be granted his daughter's hand in marriage, along with a dowry lavish enough to provide them lifetime financial security. Of course, many of the best and brightest students vied for the prize, yet none were able to answer the questions to the man's satisfaction.

On the third morning of his stay at a particular yeshivah, the wealthy Jew was visited by yet one more young man who carried a *Gemara*. The student entered the house, wished the wealthy Jew a good morning, and said to him, "I have worked on this topic for days, yet I have no answers. Please be so kind as to tell me the answer to these questions. I *must* know."

The man reacted with great surprise. "Apparently, you don't understand. I have spent a small fortune traveling to all the yeshivos in search of a major scholar, to whom I wish to give my daughter and my fortune. I need somebody who is able to *answer* the questions. If I tell you the answers, my trip was for naught."

The young man quietly responded, "Sir, it is you who misunderstand. I don't want your daughter or your money. Please tell me the resolution of the questions; that is what really interests me."

Duly impressed by the young scholar's love for Torah itself, the wealthy man took him as a son-in-law.

King David implored God: *Guide me on the path of Your commandments for I desire it* (*Psalms* 119:35). Lest one claim that he deserved no reward since God helped him to spiritual success, David was careful to add that he greatly desired it; it is the Torah and the *mitzvos* themselves that he wanted, for to him, the opportunity to fulfill a *mitzvah* was itself a greater reward than anything else he could have received. *The reward of a mitzvah is the mitzvah* (*Mili d'Avos*).

[ג] **הוּא** הָיָה אוֹמֵר: אַל תְּהִי בָז לְכָל אָדָם, וְאַל תְּהִי מַפְלִיג לְכָל דָּבָר, שֶׁאֵין לְךָ אָדָם שֶׁאֵין לוֹ

Mishnah 3

הוּא הָיָה אוֹמֵר — *He used to say.* In the previous mishnah Ben Azzai spoke of the hidden dividends of *mitzvos*, stating that even seemingly "minor" *mitzvos* carry great reward. Here he teaches of the hidden potential of persons and things (*Abarbanel*). *Toras Avos* views Ben Azzai's words as commentary on Ben Zoma's aphorisms in mishnah 1 (see below).

אַל תְּהִי בָז לְכָל אָדָם — *Do not be scornful of any person.* One must not insult people, verbally or otherwise. Even the most inferior person must be treated respectfully (*Rashi, R' Yonah, Machzor Vitry*). Meiri adds: Harbor contempt for no man, thinking to yourself, "What can he do to me?" Even if now he has no power to harm you, he may eventually be in a position to do so.

Yerushalmi (*Terumos* 8:4) relates an incident in which the Jews narrowly escaped severe retribution for such folly. A group of Jews once physically and verbally abused a gentile pig-keeper by the name of Diocletian, calling him "Diocletian the Pig." Eventually, he became emperor of the Roman Empire, and, remembering his mistreatment at the hands of the Jews, he planned revenge in the form of anti-Jewish decrees and pogroms. The Sages sought to appease him: "We insulted Diocletian the Pig, and now we honor Diocletian the Caesar," they claimed. "Nonetheless, you have insulted me," he said. "Be careful from now on." Diocletian pardoned them and rescinded his decrees.

Rambam and *R' Yonah* offer another very practical interpretation: One should not be scornful of any person, since there does not exist a person in the world from whom one cannot, at one time or another, enjoy some slight benefit or harm.

HaChassid Yaavetz advises us that we must treat people properly because all people play a role in God's plans; nobody was created for naught, be it a fool, an ignoramus, or even an evil person. They are all part of the Divine scheme. We may not understand how this can be, but God created everything and everyone so that something good and beneficial will come from each of them. *Tiferes Yisrael* adds that we must not insult any person,

Mature perspective. Rabbi Shmuel Blech relates that Rabbi Aharon Kotler would often repeat the following explanation offered by Avraham ben Avraham, the famous *ger tzedek* [righteous convert] of Vilna, while being taken to be burned at the stake, for the "crime" of becoming a Jew. The executioner told the victim that he was fearful he would be punished for executing such a holy person.

Replied the saintly proselyte: "King David said, *Praise HASHEM all nations; praise Him all states. For His kindness has overwhelmed us* (*Psalms* 117:1-2). Why should the nations praise God for His overwhelming kindness to *us*?" Avraham ben Avraham explained with a story:

"A young crown prince used to play with the children of his father's subjects. One day he got into a scuffle with one of the children, who beat him up. The young heir to the throne promised to avenge his hurt when he grew up. The commoner was frightened and dreaded the day that his royal "victim" would become king. Years later, the king passed away and his only son became his successor. The new king's old childhood assailant, fearful of retribution, came to plead his case and begged for mercy. 'Please don't take revenge. I really meant nothing when I beat you up years ago,' he said.

"Answered the newly crowned monarch. 'Don't worry. I won't do anything to you. At the time I was angry and really wanted revenge, but now, when I look around at my new greatness, that ancient incident falls into perspective. Now I realize that it was mere child's play.'

"So," concluded the soon-to-be-martyred Jew, "when *Mashiach* comes and the Jewish nation will assume the mantle of greatness, we will view all the torment we received at the hands of the nations of the world as inconsequential childishness. Now we want revenge, but then it will all pale into insignificance. Thus the nations of the world will praise God for His overwhelming kindness *to us*."

4/3

3. He used to say: Do not be scornful of any person, and do not be disdainful of anything, for you have no person without

because it is an insult to the Creator to imply that His creature is superfluous.

R' Shlomo Kluger renders the mishnah differently: *Do not let* **yourself** *be the subject of abuse for every man*. While one must avoid haughtiness, one must not allow himself to become vulnerable to the cheapening insults of inferior people. [Torah scholars in particular must be careful to assure that they and their colleagues are treated with respect and reverence — not for their own sake, but for the honor of the Torah they carry within them. In the pursuit of knowledge and spiritual growth, however, one should indeed allow himself to be "demeaned" by seeking knowledge from all — even those of lesser standing or intelligence. In this sense, the mishnah is a qualification of Ben Zoma's earlier exhortation to learn from all people.

Mussar Avos offers an additional rendering: Do not debase *the entire person* [לְכָל אָדָם] on the basis of a particular character flaw (see 1:6, s.v. וֶהֱוֵי דָן אֶת כָּל הָאָדָם). There is no person who does not

have redeeming value, and one should never dismiss him based on one fault.

וְאַל תְּהִי מַפְלִיג לְכָל דָּבָר — *and do not be disdainful of anything*. The translation follows *Rav, Rashi, and Meiri*.

According to *Tiferes Yisrael*, the mishnah warns against denying meaningfulness to any part of God's Creation. Even such seemingly insignificant and repulsive creatures as insects and poisonous snakes play a role in the world, and therefore take part in God's glory. Insects, for example, purify the air of microbes, thus enhancing the quality of life for all living creatures.

Magen Avos explains: One should not be disdainful of any *possibility*, including the chance of danger, and therefore one should not entirely dismiss his fears as ridiculous. Far-fetched though they may seem, legitimate fears must not be discounted as paranoia. People often say that one should go about his business, and that there is nothing to fear, since whatever will happen will

---

&§ **Respect for oneself.** One must avoid being scornful even about himself. The most powerful weapon in the arsenal of the Evil Inclination is the ability to convince someone that he is spiritually worthless, because if that is so then there is no reason for the person to try and better himself. The mishnah enjoins us never to fall prey to this debilitating strategy. Every person can grow in spirit. *Rashi* defines the humility of Moses as שָׁפָל וְסַבְלָן, *lowly and patient* (see *Numbers* 12:3). Explained *R' Bunam of P'shis'cha*: One must be patient with *himself* and bear his lowliness with grace.

&§ **Sensitivity.** In sensitive and respectful Jewish communities, it is considered abhorrent for guests at a celebration or other public gathering to talk or eat while a rabbi or Torah scholar is speaking. This is a sign of respect for the Torah, to indicate that it is the word of God and not an "after-dinner" entertainment. Similarly, when offering a gratuity to a rabbi or teacher, one should be careful about how it is given. To hand cash directly to a Torah scholar rather than placing it in an envelope is crass and demeaning, and may lead one eventually to view the scholar disdainfully. Even the tipping of teachers in a camp should be done through an intermediary in order to set an example for children in the proper respect for Torah teachers. (See *Sanhedrin* 52b.)

&§ **Everything has its day.** King Solomon teaches: *One who despises something will suffer from it* (*Proverbs* 13:13). His father, King David, experienced this truth personally on three occasions. The Midrash relates that King David questioned the need for insanity, flies, and spiders. When he was captured by Achish, King of Gath, he escaped harm by feigning insanity (see *I Samuel* 21). When David wanted to take the spear of the sleeping King Saul, a flea bit Saul and caused him to lift his leg, thus allowing David access to the spear (see *I Samuel* 26). Lastly, when David was hiding from Saul in a cave, the Holy One sent a spider to spin a web across the entrance. Saul came, saw the web, and thought, "Surely no man has entered here," thus sparing David once again from harm (*Aleph Beis d'Ben Sira, Otzar HaMidrashim* 47).

happen, and whatever will not will not. Ben Azzai says no; "Consider nothing impossible" (*Magen Avos*).

שֶׁאֵין לְךָ אָדָם שֶׁאֵין לוֹ שָׁעָה — *for you have no person without his hour.* There comes a time when every person can either help or harm his fellow. Hence, everyone should be treated respectfully, no matter what his present station in life (*R' Yonah, Rambam*). [Yiftach of Gilad, the Biblical judge, is a classic example. Of lower-class background, he was stripped of his paternal inheritance and exiled from his city, whereupon he became the leader of a band of ruffians. But when his fellow Giladites needed military aid, they turned to Yiftach — who became their leader and savior (see *Judges* 11).]

In addition, the mishnah reminds us that every human being has a significant role to play in life, and it is not for us to judge how minor or major that role may be. There comes a special moment in life when that particular person, whatever his faults and shortcomings, has a contribution to make which is uniquely his (*Tiferes Yisrael*).

Avodas Yisrael explains a person's "hour" as his remarkable ability to recreate himself in an instant through repentance. This august potential is not merely to correct flaws; it is the possibility of a complete metamorphosis which occurs in a mo-

ment of spiritual clarity. *There is no person without his hour*, i.e., without a moment when his whole life can assume new meaning and direction. As the Talmud (*Avodah Zarah* 10b) says of the notorious Elazar ben Durdayah, whose life-style was the epitome of moral depravity but who repented with extraordinary sincerity, a Heavenly voice called out, "*Rabbi* Elazar ben Durdayah, you are fit for the World to Come." R' Yehudah *HaNasi* commented, "There are those who acquire their world [the World to Come] in one hour [i.e., in an instant]."

It is to that "hour" that our mishnah refers. We are taught not to be scornful of any person, dismissing him as one of little or no spiritual substance, for every person has his "hour," the capability to restructure his life completely (*Orach LeChaim*). [The "hour" referred to here is described also in 4:22. "Better one hour of repentance and good deeds in this world than the entire life of the World to Come" (*R' Yechiel of Mush*).]

וְאֵין לְךָ דָּבָר שֶׁאֵין לוֹ מָקוֹם — *and you have no thing without its place.* According to *R' Yonah* and *Magen Avos*, the mishnah continues its earlier thought: At some place or time, danger may be present, even from a source that one had dismissed as implausible (*R' Yonah*).

Rashi and *Sefer HaMussar* explain the *thing* as

≈§ **Be vigilant.** *Ruach Chaim* interprets the first two parts of the mishnah as complementary statements: One should never jump to conclusions when informed of another's intent to harm him. *Do not be scornful of any person,* assuming that he has evil designs against you. On the other hand, one should not naively dismiss such reports altogether; perhaps they are not as unfounded and implausible as they may seem.

The Talmud (*Niddah* 61a) gives guidelines regarding such instances of *lashon hara* (slanderous gossip): While one may not believe reports accusing someone else of evil designs, he should *suspect* that they are true and take appropriate precautions. A case in point was Gedaliah ben Achikam, the governor of Palestine under the Babylonians, after the destruction of the First Temple, who was informed that a Jewish rival was conspiring to assassinate him. Gedaliah discounted the whole matter. He did not exercise proper precautions, and was indeed assassinated (see *Jeremiah* 40:13-16).

≈§ **Never write someone off.** *Avodas Yisrael* renders שָׁעָה as *turning* [as in וְאֶל מִנְחָתוֹ לֹא שָׁעָה, *But to Cain and his offering He did not turn* (*Genesis* 4:5)]. In a moment one can turn his life around, averting his head and heart from the treacherous path down which he was headed and asking God for help. Hence, one must never be scornful of any person, for the object of his scorn may turn toward the path of goodness at any moment and thus save himself.

4. Rabbi Levitas of Yavneh says: Be exceedingly humble in spirit,

referring to knowledge. All bits of knowledge are precious; never deem any tidbit of knowledge irrelevant, for it may sooner or later prove itself useful. The mishnah's general philosophy is that everything, in its proper place and time, be it an idea or a thing, adds its hue and tone to the Royal tapestry: "*All that the Holy One, Blessed is He, created in His world, He created solely for His glory*" (6:11). Let man not think even for a moment that something in this world is superfluous; *everything* has its place in enhancing God's glory and advancing His goals.

Mishnah 4

רַבִּי לְוִיטַס אִישׁ יַבְנֶה אוֹמֵר — *Rabbi Levitas of Yavneh says*. Rabbi Levitas was a third-generation *Tanna* and one of the most prominent members of the Academy of Yavneh (*Midrash Shmuel*), but little is known about him; this teaching is the only one attributed to him in the entire six Orders of the Mishnah.

מְאֹד מְאֹד הֱוֵי שְׁפַל רוּחַ — *Be exceedingly humble in spirit*. In almost all areas of life, one should try to follow a moderate approach. Excessive stinginess or generosity, for example, are both inappropriate.

Likewise, although mercy is generally a positive attribute, one must be careful not to show excessive mercy to those who abuse God and His Torah. Such people often should be treated with tempered aloofness, and sometimes tempered harshness.

R' Levitas tells us in this mishnah, however, that arrogance is an exception to this rule of moderation. Due to its repugnant character and the ease with which people fall into its grip, one must go the extreme and become *exceedingly humble* of spirit [מְאֹד מְאֹד] (*Rav, R' Yonah, Rambam*).

⏤§ **He is everywhere.** One of God's Names is מָקוֹם, *The Omnipresent*. *Notzer Chesed* comments in a homiletic vein: God is everywhere in the sense there is no thing that does not contain a reflection of the Omnipresent. Nature is not an independent force; it is the living reflection of God, and every molecule is imprinted with His signature. [The word הַטֶּבַע (nature) is the numerical equivalent of אֱלֹהִים, *God*. Both equal 86.]

Sfas Emes interprets the call of our Sages, שֶׁתִּהְיוּ עֲמֵלִים בַּתּוֹרָה, *that you shall toil at the study of Torah* (see *Rashi* to *Leviticus* 26:3), as an injunction to seek the meaning of everything in life through the prism of Torah. This is the message of our mishnah: אַל תְּהִי מַפְלִיג לְכָל דָּבָר, *Do not view anything as removed* [*from its roots in Torah*], because אֵין לְךָ דָּבָר שֶׁאֵין לוֹ מָקוֹם, *you have no thing that does not have its place*, i.e., everything has an intrinsic place in a world, as defined by the word of God.

⏤§ **Arrogant humility.** *Chasdei Avos* tells us that arrogance is analogous to *chametz*. Since people are accustomed to partake of it all year, the Torah found it necessary to be stringent in forbidding the consumption of *chametz* on Passover, even in the smallest amounts. According to R' Levitas, arrogance shares this quality; people are inclined toward arrogance more than toward other negative character traits. Therefore, we are taught to be *exceedingly* humble of spirit.

Machneh Levi offers an alternative explanation for the double expression מְאֹד מְאֹד. People often act in an ostensibly humble fashion when in fact they suffer from exaggerated delusions of superiority. Their humble protestations are only for the purpose of having people note their "humility."

R' Eliyahu Kitov paints a portrait of just such a character, the fictional R' Yerucham the Ascetic, a humble person who was reputed to fast all week long. A Kotzker *chassid* named Eliezer Bialystoker was convinced that R' Yerucham's humility was a fraud and tried to devise a plan to prove it. "What shall I say when I see him in the company of others?" he thought to himself. "If I say, 'Do you know that R' Yerucham fasts all week?' he will deny it, and people will think, 'He fasts all week long but is too humble to admit it.'"

When the Kotzker *chassid* finally met R' Yerucham, he told those who accompanied him, "He fasts every Monday and Thursday." R' Yerucham protested vehemently, "It's not true; I fast every day!" Thus he exploded the myth of his humility. The mishnah therefore teaches מְאֹד מְאֹד הֱוֵי שְׁפַל רוּחַ, *be* **extremely** *and* **authentically** *humble*.

Tiferes Yisrael explains that there are three characteristics in this category. At one extreme is arrogance, which God despises and which must be avoided. A desirable quality is modesty, which was best characterized by Moses. The Torah testifies that he was the most modest man who ever lived, but he was certainly aware that he surpassed all his contemporaries in prophecy, that the mantle of leadership lay only on his shoulders, and that only he spoke with God face to face, and that "the *Shechinah* spoke through his throat." Nevertheless, Moses did not let his greatness affect his modesty. R' Levitas urges even more. His model is King David, who was so humble that he always focused on his shortcomings, even those of which only he was aware, and saw himself as inferior to all others. This is the preferred path.

Rambam quotes a pious individual who was questioned as to the happiest day of his life. He replied, "I was once traveling on a ship. Because of my poverty, I was assigned the worst quarters imaginable — in the lowest hold, together with the cargo. A group of rich, arrogant, and uncouth merchants were also on board. Once, as I lay in the hold, one of the merchants actually urinated on me. I must have appeared so despicable in his eyes that he felt I was unworthy of elementary respect as a human being, but I was not offended in the least, nor did I react in any way. When I realized how indifferent I was to my own prestige, I was overcome with joy, because I had achieved a level of genuine humility and self-effacement and was able to ignore the disparagement of that person." This is the true sense of שְׁפַל רוּחַ.

The Talmud (*Sotah* 5a) records two opinions regarding the proper degree of humility. One opinion holds that both excessive arrogance and excessive humility are to be avoided; one must follow the middle path. The other school of thought sees any degree of arrogance as dangerous. *R' Yonah* views R' Levitas's words as an expression of the second view. *Rambam* (*Hilchos Dei'os* 2:3) concurs. (See, however, *Meiri, Chibbur HaTeshuvah*, First lecture, Part I:5.)

R' Yonah continues: The havoc wreaked by arrogance is spotlighted by the Talmud: "Arro-

---

◈§ One should not make judgments about a person who is less accomplished than he. If someone is less learned, one should consider how much of his own knowledge he has translated into action; his friend may actually be superior to him in that regard. Similarly, if one is wealthy, let him stop for a moment and reflect on whether he uses his God-given gifts for the betterment of others. He may find that his less fortunate brother gets more "spiritual mileage" out of his lot in life. Life is replete with so many such examples that one with open eyes will easily find the path to extreme humility (*R' Nachum of Chernobyl*).

R' Shlomo Wolbe makes the following observation: One who craves attention from others lacks self-esteem; unaware of his true worth, such a person almost never finds happiness within himself. He depends on the opinion of others, hungers for their praise and feels worthless without it. When people fail to applaud him, he feels helpless, and therefore hostile and angry (*Alei Shur I*, p.42).

◈§ **The joy of self-negation.** R' A. C. Feuer notes that the word שִׂמְחָה, *joy*, contains the word מָחָה, *to erase*.

If one truly wishes to rejoice, he must first abandon the conscious desire to place his own needs first. In a sense, he must "erase" himself.

R' Raphael of Bershad spoke of the pitfalls of arrogance: "When I am judged after 120 years, I will be able to defend myself against all charges — *except* the charge of arrogance. When I am questioned about whether I did business honestly (see *Shabbos* 31a), I will answer simply that I was never involved in business. When I'm asked about my commitment to Torah study, I will plead that I was too ignorant to succeed at Torah study. Even regarding the disbursement of charity, I will be able to claim that I myself was impoverished and couldn't help others.

"But what do I answer when they say, 'If you were poor, ignorant, and never a successful businessman, why did you act as if you were so special?' I will have no answer!"

On another occasion he spoke of how much we must thank God for not commanding us to be haughty. "Imagine if there were such a *mitzvah*. How would someone like me be able to fulfill it? What could I be arrogant about?"

gance is comparable to idolatry" (*Sotah* 4b). Most sin is rooted in arrogance, since man feels that he is above Heavenly scrutiny and not accountable to God. The Torah warns of this: *And your heart will become haughty and you will forget HASHEM, your God* (*Deuteronomy* 8:14).

The comparison is based on the false claim that God is too exalted to be bothered with human affairs, and that He must have some intermediary to handle His affairs with men. An arrogant person is convinced that since he himself disdains his inferiors, certainly God would not want to have anything to do with *His* inferiors, and that He must allow for other deities to come between Himself and man (*Kli Chemdah*).

שֶׁתִּקְוַת אֱנוֹשׁ רִמָּה — *for the anticipated end of mortal man is worms.* By what right can man become haughty when he, with all his hopes and aspirations, is doomed to serve as food for worms? (*Rashi, Machzor Vitry*). The ignominious end that

awaits man's body serves as a most humbling deterrent against delusions of grandeur (*Rambam*).

Magen Avos writes: God cloaks Himself in גֵּאוּת, grandeur (see *Psalms* 93:1). A commoner who wears the cloak of a mortal king deserves to be beheaded; one who appropriates God's cloak certainly deserves such a punishment. It is told that Aristotle instructed his disciple Alexander the Great that it is unbecoming even for a king to exalt himself over his people, saying, "I saw the following in a book: A king once summoned one of his distinguished subjects. When the man arrived, the king said to him, 'What were you doing?' The subject replied, 'I was considering that in comparison with the highest sphere, the planet earth is no more than a swampy pool in the great sea; and even on the earth, only about one quarter is inhabited, and even in the inhabited part there are mountains and hills and seas and rivers and deserts and fields

---

⊷§ **The last hope.** The concept of גֵּאוּת, *grandeur*, represents God's revelation as mightier than any force in nature. In man, grandeur — or arrogance — is a contemptible trait, because man's power is limited at best. But to God, *grandeur* is becoming because all forces owe their existence to Him while He is dependent on nothing (*Midrash Shocher Tov*).

God "dons" grandeur (*Psalms* 93:1). It is similar to a person donning a garment; our comprehension of him is guided by the contours and quality of the garment, but the garment is hardly his essence. So too, the greatest measure of God's grandeur cannot reveal any degree of His essence; no matter how much of God's greatness we think we understand, our puny intellect grasps but the minutest fraction of His infinite greatness. He does us the favor of allowing mankind this degree of perception only so that we can aspire to the privilege of praising Him.

Literally, שֶׁתִּקְוַת אֱנוֹשׁ רִמָּה should be rendered "for the *hope* of mortal man is worms"; the word סוֹף, *end*, would seem a more appropriate expression. *Chelek Yaakov* explains: The Talmud offers a few tactics that can save one from the magnetic pull of iniquity. Optimally, one should become engrossed in Torah study, the greatest protection against sin. If this does not work, let him read the *Shema*, thereby subjugating his will to that of God. If neither of these tactics works, one should consider the day of death as a reminder of the futility of sin (see *Berachos* 5a). The remembrance of man's ignominious end is thus his last hope for quashing his inner forces of negativity. The mishnah instructs us to be exceedingly humble and to avoid indulging ourselves in the arrogance that leads to sin, for the last *hope* for man's spiritual survival lies in remembering the worms.

According to *Chasan Sofer*, it is because of man's limitations and inherent weaknesses that God has compassion and is willing to forgive a penitent his sins. This is reflected in the *Ne'ilah* prayer of Yom Kippur: "You know that our end is worms and rot; therefore You have granted us [access to] forgiveness." Our mishnah suggests that one be exceedingly humble, for the hope of man to have his misdeeds forgiven is rooted in the realization that he is powerless, a mortal who will one day feed the appetite of the worms.

[One who was sentenced to death but was granted clemency on the basis of a claim that he was terminally ill would be foolish to deny his illness, since it is the key to his survival. Similarly, one who suffers from delusions of grandeur blinds himself to the reality of his own mortality and thus forfeits his pass to salvation.]

and vineyards; comparatively small is the inhabited part of cities; and I am in one of these innumerable cities. And in that very city there are shops and yards and marketplaces, and I am in one spot and am no more than a fragment of the place in which I dwell. If so small is my portion in this world, and this whole world in the sight of the Creator is of so little value, how shall I carry myself with pride in His presence!' " (*Magen Avos*).

A powerful king once gave one of his servants a piece of paper and said to him: "If you ever see me enraged, give this to me." Written on it was the following: "Stop your anger. You are not God, merely a flesh-and-blood body who will soon return to earth and be consumed by its worms."

HaChassid Yaavetz interprets this description of man's end as a reason why man should be exceedingly humble spirited and suffer insult gracefully. Just as one does not feel "insulted" by a dog who barks at him, so he should never feel too hurt by the disparaging remarks of his fellow man, a temporary creature who eventually will be food for the maggots. The mishnah does not say, "*Your end is worms*," but rather that the eventual "*end of man* [i.e., the one who offered the insult] *is worms*."

In a novel interpretation *Tosafos Yom Tov*

renders שְׁתִקֹּנַת אֱנוֹשׁ רִמָּה as *for a person's measuring stick should be the worm* [as in תִּקְוַת חוּט הַשָּׁנִי, *a length of scarlet cord* (*Joshua* 2:18)], i.e., a person should measure his own standing against the performance of the lowly maggot. Worms play an important role in the ecology, softening the earth so that roots can spread out and allow the rain water to reach them, and turning fallen leaves into rich earth which fertilizes the growing plants. Nonetheless, the worm, unlike many other animals, remains silent, never bragging of its importance. Man should measure himself against the worm in trying to assess whether he too goes about his business, without fanfare and arrogance.

According to *Knesses Yisrael*, the mishnah emphasizes the futility of relying on human endeavor. He renders רִמָּה as *deception* [as in Jacob's words to Laban upon discovering that he had been given Leah in marriage instead of Rachel: "לָמָּה רִמִּיתָנִי, *Why have you deceived me?*" (*Genesis* 29:25)]. Thus, the mishnah reads, "*The hopes of man are a deception*"; his dreams and his reliance on himself are illusory. We are told this clearly by King Solomon: רַבּוֹת מַחֲשָׁבוֹת בְּלֶב אִישׁ וַעֲצַת ה' הִיא תָקוּם, *Many designs are in man's heart, but the counsel of* HASHEM — *only it will prevail* (*Proverbs* 19:21). One should be exceedingly humble, for human hopes are deceptive and disappointing. Without God's help, one can achieve nothing.

Mishnah 5

רַבִּי יוֹחָנָן בֶּן בְּרוֹקָא אוֹמֵר — *Rabbi Yochanan ben Beroka says.* Quoted many times in the Mishnah and more extensively in the *Tosefta* and *Baraisos*, this student of R' Yehoshua ben Chanania was a third-generation *Tanna*. When he and his colleague, R' Elazar Chisma, once visited with R' Yehoshua at Peki'in, their teacher asked them if they could report any new ideas or Torah thoughts advanced in the study hall that day. They replied, "We are your students and we drink of *your* waters (i.e., what can

we teach you?)." Nonetheless, under his insistence, they repeated the lecture of R' Elazar ben Azariah. R' Yehoshua was impressed and praised it: "You had a precious jewel in your hands and [almost] did not allow me to enjoy its brilliance" (see *Chagigah* 3a, see also *Avos d'Rabbi Nosson* 18).

R' Yochanan was apparently a bridge figure between the third and fourth generations of *Tannaim*, since his disputants are occasionally those of the later generation (see *Eruvin* 8:2, 10:15).

⌾ **From infancy.** R' Yochanan and R' Elazar Chisma reported the explanation for why the Torah commands us to bring even infants to the *Hak'hel* reading of the *Book of Deuteronomy* (see 31:12). "In order to give reward to the adults who bring them" (*Chagigah* 3a). R' Yehoshua was particularly overjoyed with this interpretation, since his mother had always brought him, as an infant, into the study hall to be exposed to the beautiful and inspiring sound of Torah study [see 2:11] (*Meshech Chochmah* to *Deuteronomy* ibid.).

Many of his statements indicate his concern with the rights and honor of women. He said: "One is obligated to support his daughters"; the Talmud explains that this includes the father's obligation to make sure that his estate will provide for his daughters posthumously, so that they will not be forced into the embarrassing predicament of collecting alms — (see *Tosefta Kesubos* 4:8 and glosses of *Vilna Gaon* ad loc.). Regarding the ordeal of a *sotah* (a woman whose behavior created a suspicion of adultery, see *Numbers* ch. 5), he said: "One should not debase the daughters of Israel to a greater degree than is mandated by the Torah" (*Sifre, Naso* §11).

כָּל הַמְחַלֵּל שֵׁם שָׁמַיִם בְּסֵתֶר — *Whoever desecrates the Name of Heaven in secret.* Desecration of the Name involves the sort of conduct that leads onlookers to think or say that observant Jews act in an unworthy manner. The sort of conduct that causes this varies from person to person: for some of the great Talmudic sages, even to take a few paces without studying Torah constituted such a desecration; for ordinary people, rudeness, dishonesty, and the like would be considered a desecration.

According to this understanding, a private desecration of God's Name would seem to be a contradiction in terms, since it does not affect outsiders' opinions of the Jewish people. *Rashi* explains that a sin done in private can cause a desecration of God's Name, because those who witness the punishment of the perpetrator, but are unaware of his sins, may view this as a flaw in Divine justice. Thus, the Name of God will be desecrated.

Meiri interprets the mishnah as referring to one who sins privately because he believes that God is not involved in the lowly affairs of human beings and that He does not oversee their actions. Attempting to hide from God, as one can from man, he sins privately. This is deemed a desecration of God's Name and honor.

According to *R' Yonah*, certain sins such as idolatry or swearing falsely — which is a use of God's Name to conceal dishonesty — are intrinsically a desecration of His Name and prestige, no matter in what venue in which they are conducted. Hence, it is possible to desecrate God's Name privately, since only He Who sees the heart knows of the falsehood.

According to *Ritva* this mishnah offers an exception to R' Levitas's previous exhortation to extreme humility. Misplaced humility is counterproductive and wrong. Let one not be humble and quiet when a Torah scholar is degraded or moral principles are

---

◄§ **Denying God's presence.** The term חִלּוּל הַשֵּׁם is commonly viewed as rooted in the term חוּלִין, *profane* or *mundane.* One who treats the honor of God without the proper reverence profanes His Name. *Avodas Yisrael* and *Ruach Chaim* interpret חִלּוּל as related to the word חָלָל, *empty* or *vacuum* (see *Psalms* 109:22). God is everywhere: מְלֹא כָל הָאָרֶץ כְּבוֹדוֹ, *the entire universe is full of His honor* (see *Isaiah* 6:3); every molecule is evidence of His existence. One who philosophically or emotionally entertains the notion that there can be an area of life that is "empty" of His involvement has desecrated His Name. Thus, חִלּוּל הַשֵּׁם can be a private sin, because the desecration takes place within the sinner's own perception of God.

Mili d'Avos compares one who sins in private to a person who asks a friend to leave the room so that he can talk privately with another friend. A sin done in private implies that man thinks he can ask God not to be present to witness his folly, as it were.

◄§ **Relative reputations.** The Chofetz Chaim always cautioned his son to avoid any behavior that could cause a *chillul Hashem.* Once the young man protested that he was not a rabbi or outstanding scholar, and no one could consider his errors as grounds for denigrating God and His servants. The Chofetz Chaim replied, "You are wrong. If you were to chastise others, they would probably say that you are not qualified to offer criticism. But if you once make a mistake, people will say, 'Look at the terrible thing that *gaon* and *tzaddik* did!'"

The point is that everyone is viewed in various ways, and that people will usually describe him in terms that suit their own selfish interests at any particular moment.

[ו] **רַבִּי** יִשְׁמָעֵאל בַּר רַבִּי יוֹסֵי אוֹמֵר: הַלּוֹמֵד עַל מְנָת לְלַמֵּד, מַסְפִּיקִין בְּיָדוֹ לִלְמוֹד וּלְלַמֵּד;

---

trampled upon. One who does so causes a private and silent desecration of God's Name. Rather, one must speak up and not be a silent accomplice to the desecration of God's honor.

נִפְרָעִין מִמֶּנּוּ בְּגָלוּי — *they will exact punishment from him in public.* Since the perpetrator's sin was committed privately and his punishment was exacted publicly, it is necessary that his sin become public knowledge so that people will not question God's sense of justice (*Rashi*). Man will not succeed in hiding from God or from his fellow man behind a facade of righteousness. Even though he sinned privately, he will be publicly punished (*Meiri*).

When one sins because he lacks fear of God rather than out of weakness of character, he will often do so privately to protect his own reputation. Such a person deserves to be publicly punished in order to besmirch the reputation he so fervently sought to protect. However, one who cannot resist temptation, but sins privately in order not to desecrate God's Name publicly, is repaid in kind; because he was concerned with God's honor, the True Judge will preserve the sinner's prestige and punish him privately, not publicly (*Tiferes Yisrael*).

אֶחָד שׁוֹגֵג וְאֶחָד מֵזִיד בְּחִלּוּל הַשֵּׁם — *unintentional and intentional, both are alike regarding desecration of the Name.* By definition, the unintentional sin described by the word שׁוֹגֵג involves carelessness, so that even though the person did not mean to sin, the transgression would not have taken place if the sinner had had a proper sense of the seriousness of what might occur. Similarly, a driver who killed a pedestrian through careless driving would not be

charged with murder, but is nonetheless responsible to a degree. One who does things that bring God's Name into disrepute ח״ו shows contempt for Him, and this is the most serious of all sins, especially because of the effect it has on others. Even an unintentional desecration is serious if it is the result of insufficient care or concern. Just as people would not be careless when the health and life of a loved one is involved, so too, one who is truly concerned with the honor of God will not permit an unintentional desecration to take place. Because it is so serious a sin, one who could have avoided or prevented it cannot excuse himself by saying it was unintended.

Rashi and *Rambam* comment that intentional and inadvertent sins are equated with regard to the *public nature* of the punishment, because even an inadvertent sin is still considered a sin (see *Numbers* 15:27). [Certainly, the fact that it was unintentional mitigates the severity of its *punishment*, but the negative consequences of any sin (especially חִלּוּל הַשֵּׁם) exist even in cases of private sin and call for some punishment.] An intentional transgression, of course, is of greater severity than one committed without any forethought, and will undoubtably receive a more severe punishment.

Meiri, however, holds that inadvertent and purposeful transgressions are equated even for the severity of the punishment itself, so that one who does not correct his unintentional misdeed when he becomes aware of it shows a contemptuous attitude toward the yoke of Heaven and its demands. Such a person clearly denies God's providence and all-knowingness.

Mishnah 6

רַבִּי יִשְׁמָעֵאל בַּר רַבִּי יוֹסֵי אוֹמֵר — *Rabbi Yishmael bar Rabbi Yose said.* Although this is the version found in most *siddurim,* the text of the Mishnah reads *Rabbi Yishmael his son* [i.e., of Rabbi Yochanan ben Beroka, of the previous mishnah]

said. A fourth-generation *Tanna,* R' Yishmael studied under his father, R' Yochanan ben Beroka (see *Bava Basra* 130a), and also attended the academy at Yavneh (*Tosefta Yevamos* 6:7 and 10:3). He was a colleague of R' Yehoshua ben Karcha and Rabban

him in public; unintentional and intentional, both are alike regarding desecration of the Name.

6. Rabbi Yishmael bar Rabbi Yose said: One who studies [Torah] in order to teach is given the means to study and to teach;

Shimon ben Gamliel the *Nasi* (see *Tosefta Yevamos* 13:4). His opinions are rarely cited in the Mishnah (*Bava Kamma* 10:2, *Sanhedrin* 11:1 and here), but are frequently quoted in *Tosefta* and the *Baraisos*.

הַלּוֹמֵד עַל מְנָת לְלַמֵּד, מַסְפִּיקִין בְּיָדוֹ לִלְמוֹד וּלְלַמֵּד — *One who studies [Torah] in order to teach is given the means to study and to teach.* This does not mean that he studies only to teach, but not to fulfill the Torah's precepts, for such Torah study cannot lead to anything positive (*R' Yonah*). Rather,

according to *Rav*, the mishnah speaks of one who wants to study and teach without involving himself in the performance of kind deeds on behalf of others. Even though he ignores an integral facet of Torah life, his wish to study and teach will be granted. On the verse וְתוֹרַת חֶסֶד עַל לְשׁוֹנָהּ, *And a lesson of kindness is on her* [the Torah's] *tongue* (*Proverbs* 31:26), the Talmud asks, "Is there a Torah of kindness and a Torah not of kindness?" The Torah life-style in its very essence calls for acts of kindness.

◆§ **Unselfishness and its reward.** One should teach certain disciplines to his students even if he personally stands to gain nothing from them. This is what the mishnah refers to as "learning in order to teach." Our teacher Moses was of this mold; even though he knew that he would not enter the Land, he told the Children of Israel, *"See I have taught you decrees and ordinances, as HASHEM my God has commanded me, to do so in the midst of the Land to which you come, to possess it"* (*Deuteronomy* 4:5). Since Moses would not enter the Land, he had no practical use for the knowledge of laws pertaining only to Land, but he learned them in order to teach the Jewish people (*Chasam Sofer*). One who thus places the spiritual needs of others ahead of his own will be rewarded with unparalleled success in his own Torah study (*K'sav Sofer*).

Even one's children, who apparently suffer from their parents' involvement with students, will succeed in the merit of that dedication. The Chasam Sofer devoted virtually every waking moment to his hundreds of students and to his large and well-organized *kehillah* (community) of Pressburg, and to the endless stream of halachic inquiries addressed to him from all over the world. A student of his, Rabbi Chaim Avrohom Orenstein, the *Rav* of Bardiov, once visited him and found him sorely distressed. The Chasam Sofer sighed, "I am so overwhelmed with responsibility that I do not have enough time to devote to my own children. Look at my young son, Shimon; it's been quite a while since I gave him a thorough examination on everything he recently learned, but what can I do? My time is not my own!"

The Bardiover *Rav* consoled his beloved teacher, saying: "Do not be overly concerned. King David has already offered you a blessing in the verse, כָּל הַיּוֹם חוֹנֵן וּמַלְוֶה וְזַרְעוֹ לִבְרָכָה, *All the days he graciously lends, and his children are a blessing* (*Psalms* 37:26). King David is not referring to a man who lends money, because then he would have described him as תָּמִיד מַלְוֶה, *one who constantly lends*. Rather, he is referring to a Torah teacher who literally gives away his days (כָּל הַיּוֹם, *all the days*), meaning that he devotes all his time to others and has little left for himself or his family. What is his reward? וְזַרְעוֹ לִבְרָכָה, *his children are a blessing*; God will see to it that his children receive special סִיַּעְתָּא דִשְׁמַיָּא, *Divine assistance*, and that they will see extraordinary blessings in their studies!"

This blessing was amply fulfilled in all of the Chasam Sofer's children, particularly in Shimon, who grew up to be the renowned Rabbi of Cracow. [The Chasam Sofer would often point to his hat, an oversized style typically worn by Hungarian rabbis. "I succeeded with my children by praying to God; with the tears of my prayers I filled up this hat."]

The Chofetz Chaim once told R' Moshe Schneider, founder of the famous Schneider's yeshivah in London: "Success with children is based totally on Divine help. All the efforts we expend are only so that when we come before the Heavenly tribunal we can claim that we tried. But ultimately success is in God's hands. Therefore, remember — one must really pray for his children."

וְהַלּוֹמֵד עַל מְנָת לַעֲשׂוֹת, מַסְפִּיקִין בְּיָדוֹ לִלְמוֹד וּלְלַמֵּד, לִשְׁמוֹר וְלַעֲשׂוֹת.

[ז] **רַבִּי** צָדוֹק אוֹמֵר: אַל תִּפְרוֹשׁ מִן הַצִּבּוּר; וְאַל תַּעַשׂ עַצְמְךָ כְּעוֹרְכֵי הַדַּיָּנִין; וְאַל תַּעֲשֶׂהָ עֲטָרָה לְהִתְגַּדֵּל

R' Yonah interprets *in order to teach* as learning with the goal of superficial understanding — enough to teach, but not enough to understand the subject with clarity and depth. Such a person fears a thorough understanding of the subject because it may lead him to discover that something which he formerly thought was permitted is really forbidden. Study of this type will yield only its intended goal — to study and teach — but not to observe and practice.

While Torah should be studied for its own sake, it must be a goal-oriented activity. It should encourage one to grow in self-awareness, to perfect his practice, and, finally, to share his knowledge with others (*Meiri*).

The words *in order to teach* indicate one who concentrates on the theoretical aspects of Torah (including theological issues, laws such as those of divorce or *chalitzah* which occur infrequently, and laws of sacrifices or ritual purity, which are not applicable in the absence of the Temple); however, he contents himself with a surface knowledge of the practical laws necessary for daily fulfillment of the *mitzvos*. God will help him to master his subject matter and send him students so that he can fulfill his goal (*Tiferes Yisrael*).

Rashi and *Magen Avos*, based on *Avos d'Rabbi Nosson*, have a text which reads: הַלּוֹמֵד עַל מְנָת לְלַמֵּד — אֵין מַסְפִּיקִין בְּיָדוֹ לִלְמוֹד וּלְלַמֵּד — *One who studies in order to teach* [and receive the title and honor accorded to rabbis and scholars] *will*

not *be provided with the opportunity to study and teach.*

This version is supported by the juxtaposition of this mishnah with the next one, which portrays the fate of those who exploit the crown of Torah. *Rav* nonetheless prefers the text מַסְפִּיקִין בְּיָדוֹ.

וְהַלּוֹמֵד עַל מְנָת לַעֲשׂוֹת, מַסְפִּיקִין בְּיָדוֹ לִלְמוֹד וּלְלַמֵּד, לִשְׁמוֹר וְלַעֲשׂוֹת — *and one who studies [Torah] in order to practice is given the means to study and to teach, to observe and to practice.* One who studies Torah with an eye toward practical application will succeed not only in achieving his goal of action but will taste success in studying and teaching as well (*Mili d'Avos*). *Rav* interprets "practice" as acts of kindness. The combination of Torah study with acts of interpersonal kindness is the true path to Godliness. One who aspires to such a course will be blessed with spiritual success according to his wishes.

R' Yonah views the expression *in order to practice* as reflective of a penetrating level of study, where one searches for subtle details in order to arrive at a true determination of halachic practice. Alternatively, *practice* means the active fulfillment of positive and negative commandments. לִשְׁמוֹר, a separate concept, is rendered as retaining in memory: One who learns in order to act properly will be blessed with the ability to remember whatever information he needs in order to address the practical questions that arise (*Tiferes Yisrael*).

≈§ **Kindness and longevity.** The descendants of Eli HaKohen were destined to die prematurely. The Talmud (*Rosh Hashanah* 18a, see *Rashi* ad loc.) relates of Rava and Abaye [some texts read Rabbah], who were from that family, that Rava, who was involved exclusively in Torah study, lived only until forty, while Abaye, who not only studied but performed many acts of kindness, lived until sixty.

and one who studies [Torah] in order to practice is given the means to study and to teach, to observe and to practice.

7. Rabbi Tzadok says: Do not separate yourself from the community; [when serving as a judge] do not act as a lawyer; do not make the Torah a crown for self-glorification,

---

Mishnah 7

רַבִּי צָדוֹק אוֹמֵר — *Rabbi Tzadok says.* A first-generation *Tanna,* Rabbi Tzadok was already an old man at the time the Second Temple was destroyed. He had fasted and prayed for forty years to avert that catastrophe. When Rabban Yochanan ben Zakkai left Jerusalem clandestinely to meet with the Roman general Vespasian, the newly appointed emperor granted him three wishes. One of R' Yochanan's requests was that the emperor provide a doctor for R' Tzadok, whose esophagus had shriveled from excessive fasting, and whose digestive system was seriously weakened. He survived on the juice he sucked out of figs (see *Gittin* 56a-b).

Originally a follower of Beis Shammai, R' Tzadok later began to follow the rulings of Beis Hillel (*Yevamos* 15b). R' Yochanan ben Zakkai held him in high esteem, remarking, "If there had been just one more person of his caliber, Jerusalem could never have been conquered" (*Eichah Rabbah* 1:5).

After the destruction of the Temple, R' Tzadok moved from Jerusalem to a small town near Haifa. From there he sent halachic queries to the academy at Yavneh (*Tosefta, Niddah* 4:3-4). When he visited Yavneh, he was accorded great respect by Rabban Gamliel II. *Yerushalmi* (*Sanhedrin* 1:4) reports in the name of R' Elazar, his son, that R' Tzadok would sit to Rabban Gamliel II's right — a sign of prestige.

At the feast that Rabban Gamliel tendered in honor of his son's wedding, he personally served the sages in attendance. When R' Eliezer protested, R' Tzadok replied: "Just as God Himself provides winds and rain clouds and makes the earth sprout in order to provide all men — good and evil alike — with their needs, so it is proper that Rabban Gamliel serve the scholars and sons of the Torah" (see *Sifre, Devarim* 11:10 and *Kiddushin* 32b).

Revered by the masses as a holy man, R' Tzadok's words left a deep imprint on all who heard them. Once, two Kohanim were racing up the ramp to the Temple Altar to seize the opportunity to present an offering. The one who lost the race pulled out a knife and killed the other Kohen. R' Tzadok proclaimed in the Temple Courtyard that the people must examine themselves. Did the tragedy indicate vileness on the part of the Kohanim, or was it due to a general breakdown of morality and ethics? Everyone in the Courtyard began to cry profusely (*Tosefta, Yoma* 1:12).

A *Kohen* himself, R' Tzadok asked whether a *Kohen* has a right to declare a firstborn animal as blemished. This question spawned one of the confrontations between R' Yehoshua and Rabban Gamliel the *Nasi* in which Rabban Gamliel felt forced to assert the authority of the office against R' Yehoshua (see *Bechoros* 36a).

אַל תִּפְרוֹשׁ מִן הַצִּבּוּר — *Do not separate yourself from the community.* [See 2:5.]

וְאַל תַּעַשׂ עַצְמְךָ כְּעוֹרְכֵי הַדַּיָּנִין — *[when serving as a judge] do not act as a lawyer.* [See 1:8.] These two dicta of Hillel and Yehudah ben Tabbai were apparently adopted by R' Tzadok as his credo. In most editions they do not appear in this mishnah, which begins with the next phrase.

וְעַל תַּעֲשֶׂה עֲטָרָה לְהִתְגַּדֵּל בָּהּ — *do not make the Torah a crown for self-glorification,* Do not say, "I will study in order that others will call me 'Rabbi' and accord me honors." Learn out of love [for God and His Torah] and honor will eventually come

בָּהּ, וְלֹא קַרְדֹּם לַחְפָּר בָּהּ. וְכָךְ הָיָה הִלֵּל אוֹמֵר: וְדְאִשְׁתַּמֵּשׁ בְּתָגָא חֲלָף. הָא לָמַדְתָּ: כָּל הַנֶּהֱנֶה מִדִּבְרֵי תוֹרָה, נוֹטֵל חַיָּיו מִן הָעוֹלָם.

(*Rav, Rashi* based on *Nedarim* 62a). Although assuming the crown of Torah for personal glorification is forbidden, a Torah scholar may expect that others honor him as a way of honoring the Torah he possesses. If he does so with pure motives and intends no self-aggrandizement, it is fully permitted (*R' Yonah*).

Torah knowledge should not be used to achieve power over others or to assume an air of superiority. Truth should be sought for truth's sake (*Meiri*).

וְלֹא קַרְדֹּם לַחְפָּר בָּהּ — *nor a spade with which to dig.* This "spade" is the spade of livelihood. One should teach Torah to others without taking compensation for the work. He should not regard himself as the equivalent of a hired man using his axe as a source of income (*Machzor Vitry*).

Moses establishes the basis for this principle in the verse *See, I have taught you decrees and ordinances, as HASHEM my God has commanded me* (*Deuteronomy* 4:5). The Talmud explains these words as forbidding the charging of a fee for teaching Torah, which is not a commodity to be marketed. "Just as I [Moses] was taught [by God] gratis, so I teach you [the people of Israel] without a fee. And when you teach others, you should also teach them without remuneration" (*Nedarim* 37a; see *Rambam, Hilchos Talmud Torah* 1:7).

Teachers of youngsters may be paid for watching over their charges or for teaching the *trop* (cantillation). Even teachers of older students, or judges who rule on cases, may take money for their time, which could have been used to earn income. A judge must take equal payment from both litigants, lest he show favoritism to the one paying more.

One who uses the Torah as a vehicle to generate income has misappropriated the sanctified. He deserves death by the hands of Heaven, much as one who misappropriates hallowed property (*Rav*).

In a lengthy presentation, *Rambam* strictly forbids Torah scholars to request or accept either pay or gifts for their services. He views such a practice as a profanation of God's Name and a cause of making Torah and its practitioners contemptible in the eyes of the masses. Only three financial favors are permitted by *Rambam*: (a) A Torah scholar may invest money with a business person who will manage it free of charge. One who provides this service for a Torah scholar deserves great reward. [The Talmud (*Berachos* 34b; *Kesubos* 111b) states that one of the ways one can cleave to the Divine Presence is by managing the business affairs of a Torah scholar so that he may be free to pursue his studies.] (b) If a Torah scholar is a merchant, local authorities may forbid anyone to compete with his merchandise until he sells out his inventory (see *Bava Basra* 22a). (c) Torah scholars are exempted from paying many different types of taxes. *R' Yonah* concurs with *Rambam* on these rulings.

Many other commentators, however, disagree with *Rambam's* position, taking a broader view of the monies that a Torah figure is permitted to accept. [See *Kessef Mishneh* (R' Yosef Karo) to *Rambam, Hilchos Talmud Torah* 3:10, and *R' Yaakov Emden*, glosses to *Avos.*]

Magen Avos and *Rav* summarize the latter position as follows: A distinguished person who is needed by a community may receive compensation, just as he is permitted to be honored when the Torah is thereby honored. These are not examples of exploiting the Torah for personal advantage; rather they are for the honor of the Torah and the benefit of the community. Such a person may

---

◆§ **Torah does not bury.** Rendering לַחְפָּר as *to embarrass* (see *Isaiah* 24:23), *Notzar Chessed* explains the mishnah as a call to refrain from using the Torah as a means of indulging one's ego. Torah knowledge should never be used as a means of degrading others by pointing out their ignorance. One should not turn his Torah into a spade, building up his ego by "burying" others.

nor a spade with which to dig. So too, Hillel used to say: He who exploits the crown [of Torah for personal benefit] shall fade away. From this you derive that whoever seeks personal benefit from the words of Torah removes his life from the world.

even be paid a handsome sum beyond his needs in order to increase his prestige in the eyes of his congregation so that he will be able to enforce the Torah way of life among them. We find that the Kohen Gadol had to be wealthy; if he was not, the community had to provide him with financial wealth (see *Yoma* 18a), because honoring a scholar constitutes an honor to the Torah itself. The scholar is not putting the Torah to his own service; rather, he is serving it! To be sure, there were many sages who were woodchoppers, water drawers, and humble laborers, but they adopted these occupations out of a desire for the ways of saintliness; or perhaps they did so before they were appointed heads of academies, or out of a wish not to be a burden to the community. But there is no legal prohibition against accepting such compensation.

וְכָךְ הָיָה הִלֵּל אוֹמֵר: וּדְאִשְׁתַּמֵּשׁ בְּתָגָא חֲלָף — *So too, Hillel used to say: He who exploits the crown [of*

Torah for personal benefit] shall fade away. Hillel's teaching is recorded in 1:13. The Talmud teaches that one who makes use of the crown of Torah will be uprooted from the world (*Nedarim* 62a) — both from this world and the World to Come. Thus חֲלָף refers to the person who exploits Torah. According to *Rashi* and *Rambam*, the expression חֲלָף, "to fade away" is related to חֲלִיפִין, a barter agreement. One who exploits the crown of Torah for personal benefit has bartered away his eternal reward for temporal benefit. According to *Tiferes Yisrael*, חֲלָף should be rendered as *changes it.* Exploited for personal purposes, the crown of Torah is stripped of its sanctity and is changed into something mundane.

הָא לָמַדְתָּ: כָּל הַנֶּהֱנֶה מִדִּבְרֵי תוֹרָה, נוֹטֵל חַיָּיו מִן הָעוֹלָם — *From this you derive that whoever seeks personal benefit from the words of Torah removes his life from the world.* One loses his reward in the next world if

> ◄§ **Necessity to support scholars.** *Sefer HaMussar* elaborates: "Needless to say, when a scholar can support himself, he is especially praiseworthy . . . But if it is impossible for him to make a living from his own labors without neglecting the study of Torah at the same time, what shall he do? If he spends all his time at study, he will die of hunger; if he spends all his time trying to make a living, he will neglect the study of Torah! . . . When the *Geonim,* of blessed memory, saw that unless some arrangement for the scholar's support was made, he would worry about his livelihood, be unable to study Torah, and the Torah would be forgotten . . . they established rules for the support of scholars, so that scholars would be free to study.
>
> "Now, even though some of these scholars might be suspected of engaging in study only for the sake of the stipend and not for the sake of study itself, nevertheless we have been taught (*Sanhedrin* 105b): 'Let a man devote himself to the study of Torah and to the commandments even for an ulterior purpose, because from an ulterior purpose he will eventually arrive at the real purpose.' By means of the stipend set aside for them, men will be drawn to study, will finally understand the Torah properly and go on studying it for the right reasons . . . Wherever it is not possible for a scholar to survive without deriving profit from his study of Torah, let him derive profit; he is not guilty of any transgression."
>
> In recent generations, especially, Torah authorities have held that the *Rambam*'s strictures do not apply, because unless the nation supports those with the potential to become its scholars, leaders, and teachers, Torah knowledge and observance will decline to dangerous levels. In the aftermath of the Holocaust, had there been no financial incentives for people to become Torah scholars, a spiritual Holocaust would have come in the wake of the physical one.
>
> See *Shulchan Aruch, Yoreh Deah* 246:21 and *Responsa Tashbetz* 1:142-148 for an extensive analysis of this issue; see also *Responsa Avkas Rochel* 2 and *Igros Moshe Y.D.* II.

he uses the words of Torah as a tool for achieving personal benefit (*Rambam, Rashi*).

Meiri and *Rambam* cite the story of R' Tarfon as an example of one who unnecessarily used his standing as a Torah scholar for personal benefit. A gardener who suspected R' Tarfon of stealing from his garden grabbed the sage, whom he did not recognize, and began dragging him toward the river, intending to drown him. R' Tarfon screamed, "Woe is to Tarfon, whom they want to kill." Upon hearing this, the gardener freed him. The wealthy R' Tarfon regretted all his life having used his status rather than his money to free himself (see *Nedarim* 62a-b).

The Talmud teaches that those who learn Torah for its own sake merit life, wealth, and honor. Those who study for self-serving reasons lose the gift of long life. Thus the mishnah teaches that one who exploits the crown of Torah for personal benefit actually forfeits part of his life in the world (*Tiferes Yisrael*).

According to *Midrash Shmuel*, this mishnah is addressed to public speakers, who should not become enamored of themselves when they speak and derive personal pleasure from their profundity and oratorical skills.

Mishnah 8

רַבִּי יוֹסֵי אוֹמֵר — *Rabbi Yose says.* R' Yose bar Chalafta, a fourth-generation *Tanna*, was a student of R' Akiva (see *Pesachim* 18a, *Yevamos* 62b). In the wake of the aborted Bar Kochba revolt, R' Akiva was martyred by the Roman emperor Hadrian, before he was able to ordain R' Yose and other distinguished disciples who were needed to fill the vacuum in leadership. Therefore, one of the senior sages of the time, R' Yehudah ben Bava, ordained R' Yose and his four colleagues, R' Meir,

---

✒ **Forsaking the world.** Rabbi Nachman of Breslov interpreted the mishnah in a very positive manner. No pleasure can equal the ecstasy of plumbing the depths of a Talmudic issue. One who has savored the intoxicating taste of Torah can no longer find any real enjoyment in this world. This is the homiletic message of our mishnah: The deeply satisfying experience of Torah study takes one away from his life in this world; the world loses its allure and has nothing to offer him.

✒ *Sefer HaChassidim* (cited in *Mishnah Berurah, Orach Chaim* 53:35) reports that when Rabban Shimon ben Gamliel was being led to his death at the hands of the Romans, he turned to his fellow martyr, R' Yishmael the *Kohen Gadol*, and asked him, "Brother, why am I being taken to be killed (i.e., what sins have I done to deserve such punishment)?" R' Yishmael replied: "Is it perhaps because you once derived personal enjoyment from Torah while speaking in public?" R' Shimon ben Gamliel responded, "You have comforted me," indicating that something of this nature had, in fact, once happened; he now understood that his life was being taken as a consequence of having sought personal benefit from the words of Torah.

A fascinating incident occurred in Safed in the times of the Holy Arizal. R' Moshe Alshich, who held the position of town *maggid* (preacher), would deliver a homiletic discourse every Shabbos afternoon. The Arizal and many of his students were in attendance, and all those present were enraptured by the deep content of the Alshich's words and his soaring oratory. Suddenly, for no apparent reason, the Arizal and his entourage picked up and left.

After Shabbos the Alshich asked the Holy Arizal why he had left.

"When you speak," the Arizal said, "all the angels in heaven descend to listen to your presentation. Not only the angels but even the *Tannaim* and *Amoraim* in the Heavenly academy are all in attendance. While you were speaking today, you suggested an absolutely brilliant idea — but for a moment, a twinge of arrogance overcame you. You thought to yourself: 'My idea is as good as any that might be offered by the *Tannaim* and *Amoraim* who are in attendance.' At that moment you snapped your fingers. The celestial angels flew away in droves, and the *Tannaim* and *Amoraim* also returned to their Heavenly abode. Seeing this, I too left, and my students followed." Thus, even the greatest of the great had to take caution not to seek the slightest personal benefit from the words of Torah.

R' Yehudah bar Elai, R' Shimon bar Yochai, and R' Elazar ben Shamua. The Talmud relates that these ordinations were conferred under harrowing conditions.

The Romans had issued an edict which forbade, under threat of death, anyone conferring or receiving *semichah* [ordination], and which threatened cruel reprisals even against the towns where such ordinations took place. The elder sage R' Yehudah ben Bava took the five disciples outside city limits in order to forge the next link in the chain of tradition, but government authorities discovered them. R' Yehudah ben Bava warned his disciples of the imminent danger and urged them, "Run, my children, run," while he himself, too infirm to escape, was pierced by countless spears, which "caused his blood to run as through a sieve" (see *Sanhedrin* 13b-14a and *Avodah Zarah* 8b).

R' Yose bar Chalafta resided in Usha, where he supported himself by processing hides (*Shabbos* 49a). He was later exiled to Tzipori as a punishment for not protesting R' Shimon bar Yochai's criticism of Rome. He founded a court in Tzipori that was considered a model of judicial propriety (see *Sanhedrin* 32b). Upon the death of his childless brother, he married his sister-in-law [in compliance with the Biblical *mitzvah* of *yibum,* levirate marriage], who bore him R' Yishmael, R' Elazar, R' Chalafta, R' Avtilas, and R' Menachem. He referred to them as the "five cedar trees" since they grew tall and strong in Torah (*Shabbos* 118b). R' Yochanan (*Yevamos* 82:) ascribes to him the authorship of *Seder Olam*, an authoritative historical work that dates Scriptural incidents.

One of his more famous sayings is: "God is the Place of the world; it is not His place" (*Yalkut, Habakuk*). He is also known for his reply to the question about what God has been doing since He finished Creation: "He is making matches — X's daughter to Y's son. Others say God sits erecting ladders — elevating some, humbling others" (*Tanchuma, Ki Sisa*).

Beloved by his neighbors, his death elicited an outpouring of grief and mourning. The Talmud poetically captures their sentiment: "When R' Yose passed away, the drains of Tzipori [figuratively] overflowed with blood" (*Moed Kattan* 25b).

— כָּל הַמְכַבֵּד אֶת הַתּוֹרָה, גּוּפוֹ מְכֻבָּד עַל הַבְּרִיּוֹת *Whoever honors the Torah is himself honored by people.* Honor to the Torah assumes many forms. A learned person pays tribute by explicating its textual nuances and showing how every word, letter, and phrase is significant, incorporating multiple layers of meaning. Others do it by showing respect to a Torah scroll and scholars and students (*Rav*).

Rashi and *Machzor Vitry* list others who display appropriate honor for Torah. They include one who is careful not to place the Torah scroll on a bench where people sit or to place one scroll on top of another, one who teaches Torah only to suitable students, and one who listens carefully to the public Torah reading and does not carry on conversation while it is being read.

According to *Rambam*, a person who "honors the Torah" is one who exhibits an eagerness to live by its teachings, as well as to honor its bearers — the scholars — and the books they have written.

Tiferes Yisrael adds the proper care of Torah books, binding them properly and returning them to the shelf after use.

R' Yonah explains the significance of honoring the Torah as reflective of man's innermost essence. King Solomon taught how one can determine the quality of precious metals and of people: *A refinery for silver and a furnace for gold, and a man according to his praise* (*Proverbs* 27:21). Just as the refinery purges silver of its impurities and the furnace produces unadulterated gold, so we may discover

---

◈ **Misplaced tribute.** Those people who stand up in deference to a Torah scroll yet do not do so in honor of a Torah scholar are foolish (see *Makkos* 22b, *Kiddushin* 33b and *Ran* ad loc.). The Torah was given to us so that its words and messages will produce a great man; thus a Torah scholar is the living embodiment of the Torah itself, and is equally worthy of honor (*R' Tzadok HaKohen of Lublin*).

[ט] רַבִּי יִשְׁמָעֵאל בְּנוֹ אוֹמֵר: הַחוֹשֵׂךְ עַצְמוֹ מִן
הַדִּין, פּוֹרֵק מִמֶּנּוּ אֵיבָה וְגָזֵל

a person's essence by seeing what he praises. Not the accolades that he receives, but the praise that he offers to others is what mirrors his values. Someone who speaks positively about the righteous and praises students of the Torah reveals himself to be a righteous person, or, at least, someone who reveres such people and wishes he could be like them. [See *Shaarei Teshuvah* 3:248, which explains this concept in a powerful and poetic way.] On the other hand, one who speaks positively of the wicked and justifies their behavior, or who views the righteous negatively, indicates his own inner wicked orientation. Thus, one who honors the Torah reveals to all the kind of person he really is — one who himself deserves honor (*HaChassid Yaavetz*).

Noting the usage גוּפוֹ, literally: *his body*, *Tiferes Yisrael* comments that this word implies that his external appearance, rather than his inner qualities, will be honored. He explains that this mishnah is an amplification of the previous one, in which R' Tzadok called for Torah scholars to seek financial independence even at the expense of performing menial tasks. Such a scholar may fear that his grimy exterior will cause the Torah to be degraded in the eyes of simple people, who, unlike other scholars, cannot appreciate his knowledge and inner worth. To this, R' Yose responds that if a scholar performs menial chores because he wishes to honor the Torah, in accordance with R' Tzadok's

dictum, then God assures him that he will be respected by all, even very common folk.

Meiri explains that one who "honors the Torah" becomes its "goodwill ambassador." When he comports himself in an upright, ethical fashion, those who note his exemplary behavior will regard him as a true Torah personality, and gain heightened respect for the Torah that molded him. This is what our Sages meant when they interpreted the Biblical command to love God as an instruction that one should behave in such a way that he will cause God to be beloved among people (see *Yoma* 86a).

וְכָל הַמְחַלֵּל אֶת הַתּוֹרָה, גּוּפוֹ מְחֻלָּל עַל הַבְּרִיּוֹת — *and whoever disgraces the Torah is himself disgraced by people.* Disgracing the Torah implies the opposite of all the actions and attitudes enumerated above (*Rambam*). R' Yonah includes under this generic heading one who questions the need for the Torah to record seemingly insignificant details [such as the phrase *And Timna was a concubine of Eliphaz* (*Genesis* 36:12)]. This disgraces the Torah since it casts aspersions on the sacredness of its every word.

Meiri (based on *Yoma* 86a) explains that unethical or antisocial conduct on the part of a Torah scholar is a blatant disgrace of the Torah. People will say, "Look at that person who learns Torah. Woe to his parents and teachers; see how ugly his behavior is,

---

◆§ **Imprint on the body.** One must honor even an aged Torah scholar who has forgotten his learning (see *Berachos* 8b). This is derived from the fact that the shards of the First Tablets, which Moses smashed, were placed in the Holy Ark along with the complete, Second Tablets.

Maharal explains: The words of the First Tablets were erased with the smashing, yet the stones upon which they were engraved retained their holiness. Likewise, the body of a scholar is the surface upon which his Torah learning is engraved. Even if the words are now gone from his mind, the initial etching leaves an imprint on his body; he is no longer the person he was before Torah elevated him. Hence, one must honor a former scholar, not for what his mind once knew but for what his body became. The Torah leaves its effect even on the physical being of the one who honors it (see *Minchas Shabbos*).

9. Rabbi Yishmael [R' Yose bar Chalafta's] son says: One who withdraws from judgment removes from himself hatred,

---

how debased his conduct!" Alternatively, *Tiferes Yisrael* equates disgracing the Torah with using one's Torah knowledge for personal gain.

In a broad application, *Chelek Yaakov* interprets this mishnah as a survival tactic in exile. People often think that by hiding their Judaism they will find favor in the eyes of their gentile neighbors. The mishnah teaches that *one who honors Torah by*

wearing his Judaism with pride will be honored by all people, even his gentile neighbors. People respect those who respect themselves and their heritage; one who disgraces the Torah, however, and is ashamed of his religious heritage will be viewed with disdain by others. If we suffer from self-hatred, there is no reason for our host culture to respect us.

Mishnah 9

רַבִּי יִשְׁמָעֵאל בְּנוֹ אוֹמֵר — *Rabbi Yishmael [R' Yose bar Chalafta's] son says.* He was oldest of R' Yose bar Chalafta's sons (see 4:8, s.v. *Rabbi Yose says*), and R' Yose was his primary teacher; almost all of R' Yishmael's halachic quotations are cited in his father's name (see *Yevamos* 67a and 105b). His admiration for his father can be seen in his comparison of the differences between his own generation and that of his father to "the difference between sand and gold" (*Yerushalmi, Gittin* 6:7). His life parallels his father's in many respects: Both resided in Tzipori, served as halachic adjudicators, and were confidants of the royal house of the *Nasi*. The *Nasi* in R' Yishmael's time was R' Yehudah *HaNasi,* who spoke glowingly of him: "Happy is the generation that enjoys the presence of you and R' Chiya" (*Yerushalmi, Megillah* 4:1).

The Talmud relates that R' Yishmael, a corpulent and slow-moving individual, once arrived late at a lecture of Rabbi Yehudah *HaNasi* and slowly made his way through the rows of students towards his place. A man named Avdan, who was in charge of seating, chided R' Yishmael for his lateness, saying, "Are you fit to study Torah from Rabbi?" Rabbi Yishmael countered, "Was Moses fit to study under God?" Avdan retorted, "Do you think you are Moses?" Answered R' Yishmael, "Do you think your teacher is God?" The Talmud reports that Avdan suffered severe Divine punishment for having insulted R' Yishmael (*Yevamos* 105b).

Famed as a Biblical expert, R' Yishmael's recall of Scripture was so precise that it was claimed that one could write a Torah scroll based on his dictation (*Yerushalmi, Megillah* 4:1). A famous saying of his: "As scholars age, their intelligence increases; as ignoramuses age, their foolishness increases" (*Shabbos* 152a).

הַחוֹשֵׂךְ עַצְמוֹ מִן הַדִּין — *One who withdraws from judgment.* If more competent judges are available to settle a legal dispute, one should withdraw in their favor; otherwise, the most qualified judge has a responsibility to accept the case (*R' Yonah*).

Rashi interprets that a judge should attempt to bring about compromises rather than render definitive judgments.

Alternatively, *Rashi* explains that this is addressed to the litigants. The disputants should find a way to compromise and engineer an out-of-court settlement rather than allow their case to go to trial.

Baal HaTurim notes on the verse וְאֵלֶּה הַמִּשְׁפָּטִים, *These are the statutes* (*Exodus* 21:1), that הַמִּשְׁפָּטִים is an acronym for הַדַּיָּין מְצֻוֶּה שֶׁיַּעֲשֶׂה פְּשָׁרָה טֶרֶם יַעֲשֶׂה מִשְׁפָּט, *The judge is commanded to seek a compromise before imposing exact justice.*

פּוֹרֵק מִמֶּנּוּ אֵיבָה — *removes from himself hatred,* The losing litigant often resents the judge, convinced that he did not sufficiently weigh the merits of his arguments. One who withdraws from serving as a judge or who convinces the litigants to compromise avoids being subjected to this hatred (*Rav, R' Yonah* et al.). Likewise, this is directed to the litigants. By arranging an amicable compromise, both of the parties will conclude the case without harboring animosity toward each other (*Rashi*).

וְגֵזֶל — *robbery.* A judge is always at risk of issuing an erroneous decision, effectively depriving one of the parties of what is legally his. By refraining from accepting this role or by suggesting a compromise. one avoids this pitfall (*Rav* et al.). A litigant may be tempted to bend the facts, thus robbing his adversary of his rightful property. Compromise

enables one to avoid this type of larceny (*Rashi*).

Rav said of himself when entering the court to preside over a trial: "Of his own volition, this man (meaning himself) is going to his death" (*Sanhedrin* 7b). He prayed that he would not be punished for an erroneous judgment (*Rashi* ad loc.).

וּשְׁבוּעַת שָׁוְא — *and [the responsibility for] an unnecessary oath.* A judge may incorrectly and unnecessarily obligate a disputant to swear (*Rav, Tiferes Yisrael, R' Yonah*). Alternatively, this may refer to one of the litigants; convinced of the correctness of his position, he may be tempted to

---

◦§ **Seeing through self-interest.** R' Mordechai of Neshchiz gives us a sharp insight into these words: A judge must withdraw עַצְמוֹ, *himself*, i.e., his personal prejudices, from the judicial process. Only then will he arrive at true justice, for even the brightest person may find his perspective colored by his own personal agenda.

A fascinating incident from the life of Rabbi Chaim of Volozhin highlights this principle. R' Chaim had two former students who were famed rabbis in their own right — R' Dovid Tevel of Minsk and R' Dovid of Novarodok, author of the Talmudic work *Galia Masechta*. They had a dispute and appeared before R' Chaim for a *din Torah* (halachic litigation). R' Chaim ruled for R' Dovid Tevel, but though the *Galia Masechta* complied with the ruling, he felt that R' Chaim had erred.

Almost a year later, the leading rabbis of Russia, Lithuania, and Poland were invited to an important rabbinic conference. R' Dovid of Novarodok was a poor man and could ill afford the cost of traveling to the conference, but a good friend lent him the money, to be paid back whenever it was convenient. As soon as he arrived, he went to visit R' Chaim of Volozhin. R' Chaim greeted him and asked him for a favor. "Two businessmen have asked me to preside over a *din Torah* between them. My responsibilities at the conference do not permit me to comply with their request — could you take the case?" R' Dovid agreed. "I will send them to your lodgings tomorrow afternoon," said R' Chaim.

The next day two young men appeared at R' Dovid's door and told him that R' Chaim had sent them to present their case. After both sides had presented their arguments, R' Dovid said that he would render his decision the next day. Late into the night he pondered the issues and came to a conclusion. The next morning the two litigants returned, he issued his ruling, and the men paid him for his time and left.

That afternoon, R' Chaim asked him about the case. After R' Dovid reviewed the dispute and explained his decision, R' Chaim said, "It seems to me that the underlying principles of these two arguments are similar, if not exactly the same, as those of last year's *din Torah* between you and R' Dovid Tevel."

"Yes, *Rebbe,* you are right," replied R' Dovid.

"And I think that you ruled in this instance exactly as I did in your case," said R' Chaim.

Shamefacedly, R' Dovid conceded that R' Chaim was right, and that he had been blinded to the truth of the ruling only because of his own vested interest.

Many years later R' Dovid met one of the two merchants who had appeared before him at that *din Torah.* "Tell me," he asked, "did the two of you settle your accounts?"

The man laughed. "R' Dovid, there never was a case between my friend and me. We are both former students of R' Chaim of Volozhin. He asked us to stage the *din Torah* and coached us on the exact arguments and counterarguments to present. Not only that, he gave us the money to pay you."

Through his rare combination of intelligence and sensitivity, R' Chaim had demonstrated to his student the power of a vested interest to blind the wise, and he had simultaneously helped him with his financial difficulties!

robbery, and [the responsibility for] an unnecessary oath, but one who is too self-confident in issuing legal decisions is a fool, wicked, and arrogant of spirit.

swear falsely, thus violating one of the Ten Commandments (*Rashi, Rav*). An out-of-court settlement allows one to avoid all of these ethical and halachic pitfalls.

וְהַגַּס לִבּוֹ בְּהוֹרָאָה — *but one who is too self-confident in issuing legal decisions.* This refers to one who has no fear of ruling incorrectly and who does not take the time or patience to investigate the matter thoroughly, weighing all the arguments again and again (*Rashi, Rav*). Two types of people fall under this category: (a) one who is too sure of his knowledge and who renders decisions presumptuously, without providing sources or proof, confident that if he is challenged, he possesses sufficient legal prowess to defend his ruling; (b) one who contentiously seeks to justify his mistaken rulings. *Machzor Vitry* interprets this as a reference to self-appointed legal experts who arrogantly seek opportunities to display their skill.

שׁוֹטֶה — *is a fool.* Only a fool is conceited enough to assume a judicial role recklessly and to issue decisions in haste (*Magen Avos*). Such a misguided person foolishly and arrogantly takes credit for Torah knowledge which is not his. Furthermore, he never realizes his mistakes (*Rashi*). *R' Yonah* emphasizes that one who is wise in his own eyes is the ultimate fool, for he will never repent.

Furthermore, only a fool will voluntarily earn himself enemies. One who renders judicial decisions presumptuously does just this. In addition, he brings Divine punishment on himself if he is in any way responsible for a miscarriage of justice. The Talmud teaches: A judge should always view himself as if a sword rests on his neck and *Gehinnom* is open beneath him (*Tiferes Yisrael*; see *Sanhedrin* 7a).

רָשָׁע — *wicked.* He is wicked since his behavior indicates that he learned Torah with the ulterior motive of self-aggrandizement (*Rashi*). One who fears God would never rush headlong into a situation where mistakes are so prevalent (*R' Yonah*). Someone unafraid to issue erroneous rulings and unconcerned that he may cause others to lose their money or swear falsely is a wicked person (*Tiferes Yisrael*).

וְגַס רוּחַ — *and arrogant of spirit.* One who is incompetent or unfit for judicial office, but seeks it anyway, displays unmitigated arrogance. His pursuit of power and authority is haughtiness personified, for he is mainly interested in impressing people with his ability to adjudicate quickly yet wisely (*Rashi, R' Yonah*).

Mikveh Yisrael homiletically interprets the mishnah as a note of caution to those who try to rule for themselves on personal halachic questions rather than seeking competent counsel. Their attempts to extrapolate the proper ruling from something they heard in the past may be misguided. Furthermore, this is an exercise in wickedness, for only one who is lacking a basic fear of God would attempt to rule in areas where he is ignorant. Thirdly, it is an exaggerated sense of self-importance and vanity that *keeps* him from consulting a competent authority in the first place.

Doresh LePerakim views the three appellations of the mishnah as follows: A litigant will view an incompetent judge sometimes as a fool who did not understand the issues of the case, sometimes as a wicked person who probably accepted graft, and always as one who is too stubbornly proud to exercise intellectual humility and suggest a compromise.

◆§ **Know the facts.** Every halachic decision is really comprised of two distinct areas of knowledge: (a) One must know the pertinent citations from the corpus of halachic literature; and (b) one must have a thorough and accurate understanding of the details of the case, so that he can correctly choose the applicable rulings. The slightest difference in even a minute detail could affect the propriety of the adjudicator's approach. He may walk a very fine line between permitting and forbidding the act in question, and may easily and inadvertently step over the line if he does not correctly understand the relevant facts of that particular situation. It is because of the *second* condition, the absolute necessity of ascertaining the facts, that the power to rule on halachic questions — even those regarding which the law is clear and well known — was given to Torah scholars, rather than to the masses (see *Chazon Ish, Collected Letters* I:31).

[י] **הוּא** הָיָה אוֹמֵר: אַל תְּהִי דָן יְחִידִי, שֶׁאֵין דָּן יְחִידִי אֶלָּא אֶחָד. וְאַל תֹּאמַר: "קַבְּלוּ דַעְתִּי!" שֶׁהֵן רַשָּׁאִין וְלֹא אָתָּה.

[יא] **רַבִּי** יוֹנָתָן אוֹמֵר: כָּל הַמְקַיֵּם אֶת הַתּוֹרָה מֵעֹנִי,

Mishnah 10

הוּא הָיָה אוֹמֵר: אַל תְּהִי דָן יְחִידִי — *He used to say: Do not act as a judge alone.* This mishnah expands on the theme of the previous one, which speaks of the benefits of avoiding judicial service. While a recognized judicial expert (מֻמְחֶה) is legally permitted to adjudicate cases alone (see *Sanhedrin* 5a and *Rambam, Hilchos Sanhedrin* 5:8), it is morally correct to avoid doing so (*Rav, Rashi, R' Yonah*).

Rav suggests that if the litigants agree to present their case to a solitary judge he may, without any moral compunction, accept. *Tosefos Yom Tov* questions this premise and concludes that this moral obligation not to serve as a solitary judge always applies, even when the litigants are willing to accept his judgment.

Always endeavor to be part of a tribunal (at least of three), so you will be able to discuss the relative merits of the arguments and the different aspects of the case. In this way you will be sure to render proper judgment (*Machzor Vitry* and *HaChassid Yaavetz*). Furthermore, all the responsibility [and enmity of the litigant who views himself as judi-

cially aggrieved (*Tosefos Yom Tov*)] will not fall on one person (*R' Yonah*).

The Talmud reports that R' Huna would always bring in ten scholars as consultants when judging a case, in order that "each of us carry only a splinter of the beam," i.e., that in case we were mistaken in our conclusions we at least share the responsibility (*Sanhedrin* 7b).

According to *Lev Avos*, this mishnah forbids a judge to listen to the arguments of only one of the litigants. Only God may legitimately do so since He knows the truth. Thus the Torah teaches that God heeds the cry of the oppressed, *And it shall be when he cries out to Me, I will listen, for I am merciful* (*Exodus* 22:26).

Any judge who issues true rulings becomes a partner of God in sustaining the world. Hence, a judge who rules fairly and honestly is not alone — he shares the "bench" with God. Rule truthfully and you will *not act as a judge alone* (*Zechus Avos*).

שֶׁאֵין דָּן יְחִידִי אֶלָּא אֶחָד — *for none judges alone except One.* I.e., only God with His infallible wisdom

⯌ **Fairness and equality.** The word תָּשִׂים in the verse, וְאֵלֶּה הַמִּשְׁפָּטִים אֲשֶׁר תָּשִׂים לִפְנֵיהֶם, *These are the statutes which you shall place before them* (*Exodus* 21:1), alludes to this exhortation: The first letters of the phrase תִּשְׁמַע שְׁנֵיהֶם יַחַד מְדַבְּרִים, *Listen to both of them speaking together,* form the word תשים.

⯌ **The Whole Picture.** *Matnas Avos* renders homiletically, "Do not judge the Unique One [יְחִידִי]." Do not stand in judgment on God and the way He runs His world. Lovingly accept His judgment.

The Chofetz Chaim compared the narrow vision of man regarding Divine Providence to the attitude of a guest at a synagogue. After watching the *gabbai* assign different people with *aliyos* (being called to the Torah), he approached the *gabbai* and asked, "Why do you pick certain people and skip others? Would it not be fairer to go in order, skipping no one?"

The *gabbai* answered, "Had you been here the last few weeks you would understand everything. The ones I skipped today had received an *aliyah* in the last few weeks. Some had a family *simchah* or the like, and were given the proper privileges. On the other hand, many of the people I honored today have not had an *aliyah* in weeks. You cannot judge because all you know is what you saw this morning."

Man in this world is like a guest. In his seventy or eighty years here, one never gets to see the whole picture. Hence it is foolish to think that one can fully understand how God runs His world. Therefore let one not try to "second-guess" God.

10. He used to say: Do not act as a judge alone, for none judges alone except One; and do not say, "Accept my view," for they are permitted to, but not you.

11. Rabbi Yonasan said: Whoever fulfills the Torah despite

---

may judge alone. The verse *But He is alone and who can reverse Him* (*Job* 23:13) teaches us that only God can judge alone (*Machzor Vitry, R' Yonah* et al.).

This is seemingly contradicted by the words of the Sages that "the Holy One, Blessed is He, does not do anything without first consulting the Heavenly Court" (*Sanhedrin* 38b). *Magen Avos* explains: Although God consults with His court [in order to teach man humility, that they should consult with peers], He alone renders the verdict. *Zeroa Yemin* comments that God rules alone when His decision is beneficial to people, but when the ruling is harmful to people, He consults with His Heavenly entourage.

According to *Rambam*, this does not only include judges. One should never force his opinions on others.

— וְאַל תֹּאמַר: ,,קַבְּלוּ דַעְתִּי!'' שֶׁהֵן רַשָּׁאִין וְלֹא אָתָּה — *and do not say, "Accept my view," for they are permitted to, but not you.* According to *Rav* this clause, too, is addressed to the expert jurist. Do not force your colleagues to accept your opinion, claiming that since you are an expert you could rule without them. Once you have made them part of the tribunal, they constitute the majority opinion.

Even about things that seem obvious to you, do not expect your colleagues to yield to your position; bolster your own argument with logical proofs and offer refutation of their view. If you are unable to do so or they counter your arguments, do not stand on your own intellectual superiority, saying, "Accept my view since I am greater than you" (*Sefer HaMussar*).

Mishnah 11

רַבִּי יוֹנָתָן אוֹמֵר — *Rabbi Yonasan says.* A *Tanna* of the fourth generation, Rabbi Yonasan studied under R' Yishmael and was greatly influenced by his method. One area where he clearly adopted his teacher's perspective concerned the question of textual redundancies. R' Akiva was of the opinion that the Scriptural text contains no words that serve as mere stylistic accouterment; he elucidated every word and letter, and even the crowns over the letters (see *Bava Kamma* 65a, et al.). R' Yishmael, however, often explained such redundancies by saying that "the Torah speaks in the language of people." R' Yonasan followed his opinion and interpreted the Scripture accordingly (see *Sifre* to *Numbers* 5:29).

After the Bar Kochba revolt was quashed and the Roman government forbade public Torah study,

Rabbi Yonasan left *Eretz Yisrael*, along with R' Yehudah ben Beseira, R' Masya ben Charash, and others. Unable to bear the separation from their homeland, they returned (*Sifre, Re'eh*) but were eventually forced to leave again.

Rabbi Yonasan's keen understanding of the true quality of Jewish leadership is highlighted in this comment: "Jonah was ready to allow himself to be drowned at sea [in order to save his fellow travelers]. Moses did the same during the Golden Calf incident; [he said,] 'And now, if You would but forgive their sin! — but if not, erase me now from this book that You have written' " (*Exodus* 32:32) (*Mechilta, Masechta d'Pischa Introduction*). This is the only place Rabbi Yonasan is cited in the Mishnah; he is frequently mentioned in *Mechilta*

◄§ **Not only the defendant.** A mortal judge tries not only the defendant; his decision affects many others.

In a capital case, the lives of all the defendant's potential descendants are at stake. Even in a monetary case, a wrong decision could strip potential heirs of their inheritance. Hence, one is never really judging only the solitary defendant. Only God Who can truly make restitution of life or money can judge the person without His judgment adversely affecting others (*R' Yaakov Dovid of Amshinov*).

---

and *Sifre* on *Bamidbar*, which were products of the academy of his mentor, R' Yishmael.

כָּל הַמְקַיֵּם אֶת הַתּוֹרָה מֵעֹנִי, סוֹפוֹ לְקַיְּמָהּ מֵעֹשֶׁר — *Whoever fulfills the Torah despite poverty will ultimately fulfill it in wealth.* Rav and R' Yonah explain that one who suffers poverty, yet takes off time from his work to study Torah or perform *mitzvos*, will eventually find his financial situation relaxed, and will have the time and peace of mind to concentrate joyfully on his spiritual agenda. Torah knowledge and its pursuit are the guarantors of prosperity and serenity. When given a choice between wealth or wisdom, King Solomon chose the latter (see *Proverbs* 30:8).

Tiferes Uziel explains the words of King David in this manner: *"From the straits* [of poverty] *did I call upon God. God answered me with expansiveness* [providing me with wealth]*" (Psalms* 118:5)..

R' Yonah quotes the following analogy from the Midrash: A king offered to give his servant whatever he requested. The servant thought to himself, "If I ask for gold and silver, he will give it to me. If I merely request properties, they will be mine. However, if I request the hand of the princess in marriage, the king will fulfill *all* my needs and desires." Similarly, King Solomon asked for Torah knowledge, thus "marrying the daughter of the King" (see *Berachos* 57a, אַל תִּקְרֵי מוֹרָשָׁה אֶלָּא מְאוֹרָסָה) and acquiring everything he might need. As God responded, because he did not ask for wealth, victory over enemies, or the other things that a young king would wish, he would be granted not only wisdom, but everything else, as well. *For to sit in the shelter of wisdom is to sit in the shelter of money (Ecclesiastes* 7:12).

Rambam adds emphasis: One who is able to overcome the debilitating effects of poverty to leave his woes at the door of the study hall and force himself to concentrate on his studies will eventually be granted the wealth and serenity to learn unperturbed.

Tiferes Yisrael offers a different perspective: Poverty can be a terribly difficult test of one's spiritual and emotional mettle; yet it pales when compared to the threat posed by wealth. King Solomon makes the point clearly: *Lest I become sated and deny, saying "Who is God?" or lest I become impoverished and* [stoop to] *steal (Proverbs* 30:9). One who fulfills the Torah despite poverty, which is the easier test, will be granted Heavenly aid to pass the greater trial of wealth, if he finds himself in that position.

Midrash Shmuel interprets the mishnah as speaking of one's degree of success at Torah study and intellectual understanding. One who suffers from *intellectual* poverty, attempting to study and fulfill the word of God in spite of limited understanding, will eventually be blessed by God with a deeper intelligence.

Midrash Shmuel offers several interpretations. One who holds steadfast to the Torah in spite of poverty will merit the eternal wealth of the World to Come.

Another idea is that one who fulfills the word of God even though he does not yet derive pleasure from it will eventually sense the richness that serving God adds to his life.

In yet another interpretation, *Midrash Shmuel* renders מְקַיֵּם as *supports.* One who supports Torah scholarship, reducing his personal budget in order to help meet the needs of scholars and students, will merit increased wealth, which will allow him even greater opportunities to give.

Chasdei Avos views this mishnah as a source of comfort to teachers. Teachers are often frustrated by a poor enrollment or by the inferior intellectual abilities of the students they attract. The mishnah homiletically teaches that teachers who expend all their energies to succeed with even a few weak students will eventually be blessed with many bright and talented disciples.

◆§ **Intrinsic Wealth.** Only one who is involved in Torah study is truly free, since Torah has the ability to teach man how to minimize his needs. Thus, a person who studies Torah enjoys the emotional wealth of one satisfied with his lot (see 4:1) (*Sfas Emes*).

poverty will ultimately fulfill it in wealth; but whoever neglects the Torah because of wealth will ultimately neglect it in poverty.

— וְכָל הַמְבַטֵּל אֶת הַתּוֹרָה מֵעֹשֶׁר, סוֹפוֹ לְבַטְּלָהּ מֵעֹנִי — *but whoever neglects the Torah because of wealth will ultimately neglect it in poverty.* One who is so involved in the management of his wealth that he has no time for a life of the spirit will eventually be reduced to poverty, and he will continue to ignore his Torah activities because of the pressures of his new circumstances (*Rav, Magen Avos*).

According to *Rambam*, it is the "good life" associated with wealth that distracts man from his true goals in life. One who becomes a prisoner of this pleasure syndrome and neglects Torah because of it will ultimately neglect Torah due to the unremitting battle for his day-to-day existence.

More than one type of wealth can cause neglect of Torah. Financial wealth may engender an arrogant contempt toward the Torah lifestyle. Intellectual prosperity, for example, can sometimes cause one to rely on his innate abilities instead of expending energy and toil in his Torah study.

R' Yonah renders מֵעֹשֶׁר as *in spite of wealth*, reading the mishnah as follows: *One who neglects the Torah in spite of wealth will ultimately neglect it in poverty.* He explains that wealth provides leisure, giving one ample opportunities to pursue a full spiritual agenda. If he spurns these options and neglects the Torah, he will be stripped of his luxuries and will be forced into the neglect of Torah that is a consequence of poverty.

Chida sees this mishnah as addressed to supporters of Torah. One who is unwilling to share his wealth and who holds back financial support of Torah students and projects will eventually, God forbid, be reduced to poverty and will be unable to purchase a share in Torah through a partnership with the scholars.

◦§ **Different kind of poverty.** Rabbi Yitzchak Hutner once told the following story to Rabbi Aharon Kotler:

In Europe, many years ago, a man was looking for a *shidduch* (partner in marriage) for his daughter. A certain young man was suggested as a suitable match, but after making some inquiries, the prospective father-in-law had serious doubts about him. The young man in question had a reputation as being very pious and sincere, and was known for his exceptional *hasmadah* (diligence in Torah study). However, he did not possess a very sharp mind and his comprehension of the Talmud was not as outstanding as the prospective father-in-law had been led to believe. The gentleman was in a quandary, for he wanted only the very best *bachur* for his daughter, and this fellow seemed to be lacking in superior abilities. He decided to seek the counsel of Rabbi Yehoshua Leib Diskin, the rabbi of Brisk.

He explained the situation to the *rav*, who cited our mishnah that *Whoever fulfills the Torah despite poverty will ultimately fulfill it in wealth.* "It is my understanding that this refers not only to money but to talent and ability as well. Just as we are guaranteed that those who uphold Torah and *mitzvos*, even though they are poor, will eventually uphold the Torah in wealth, in the very same way those who are diligent in their studies and persevere even though they suffer intellectual 'poverty' are also assured of 'wealth,' meaning that they will attain great heights in Torah. [Torah has the power to expand one's intellectual capabilities. *The testimony of HASHEM* [*Torah*] *is trustworthy, making the simple one wise* (Psalms 19:8).] Thus, if the young man in question is indeed diligent in his learning and sincere in his performance of *mitzvos*, even though he may presently be 'poor' in comprehension, in time he will surely attain 'wealth' — superior comprehension — and achieve prominence in Torah. I therefore suggest," concluded the *rav*, "that you agree to the *shidduch*, because this young man will someday achieve the eminence in Torah that is so important to you."

The gentleman gave his approval to the marriage, and the *chassan* eventually became the renowned rabbi of Aishishok, R' Yosef Zundel, and the author of many works on *Shulchan Aruch*, including the noted *Chadrei Deah.*

Rav Hutner related that R' Aharon cried when he heard the story. "R' Aharon was a born genius who never suffered from that type of intellectual poverty," he said. "Therefore, the special *siyata dishmaya* (Divine assistance) given to those who struggle intensely to overcome that poverty was something he never merited." For R' Aharon not to be the recipient of any aspect of *siyata dishmaya* in Torah, regardless of the reason, was in his mind a personal tragedy.

[יב] **רַבִּי מֵאִיר** אוֹמֵר: הֲוֵי מְמַעֵט בְּעֵסֶק, וַעֲסֹק
בַּתּוֹרָה; וֶהֱוֵי שְׁפַל רוּחַ בִּפְנֵי כָל אָדָם;

Mishnah 12

רַבִּי מֵאִיר אוֹמֵר — *Rabbi Meir said.* R' Meir was perhaps the central figure of the fourth generation of *Tannaim*. According to the Talmud, he was a descendant of the Roman Caesar Nero. His wife, Beruriah, daughter of R' Chanina ben Tradyon, was famous in her own right; she was a very learned woman, who is frequently mentioned in the Talmud. Rabbi Meir's colleagues and students were in awe of him. The great R' Yehudah *HaNasi* attributed his own success in Torah study to having viewed R' Meir "from the back." "Had I viewed him from the front, I would have achieved much more," he said (see *Eruvin* 13b).

His brilliance was of such magnitude that most of his colleagues were unable to understand him fully. In spite of a Heavenly proclamation that he had no equal in the generation, the halachah does not follow his opinion (ibid.). He was ordained both by R' Akiva (see *Sanhedrin* 14a) and by R' Yehudah ben Bava, and was among the five disciples of R' Akiva who rebuilt the tradition after the tragic decimation of R' Akiva's 24,000 students (see *Yevamos* 62b).

An accomplished halachist and homileticist, he devised a successful formula for public speaking (one-third halachic content, one-third homiletics, and one-third illustrative stories and parables), which kept his audiences spellbound (*Yerushalmi, Sotah* 1:4). His opinions play a major role in the compilation of the Mishnah. The Talmud attributes *mishnayos* of anonymous authorship to R' Meir in the name of R' Akiva; the attribution "others say" is, in fact, his opinion. This relative anonymity was the price he paid for his role in the controversy regarding the respective roles of *Nasi* and *Av Beis Din*, in which he sided with R' Nosson against R' Shimon ben Gamliel (see *Horayos* 13b).

The primacy of Torah study in his world view is mirrored in many of his maxims: "One who engages in Torah study for its own sake merits many things" (*Avos* 6:1); "Anyone who lives in a city with a study hall but does not attend it has no share in the World to Come" (*Avos d'Rabbi Nosson* 36). According to him, Torah accomplishment is of greater significance than the most exalted lineage: A *mamzer* who is a Torah scholar takes precedence over an ignorant Kohen Gadol [High Priest] (*Horayos* 13a). Emphasizing the teaching of Torah as an enhancement of God's honor, he condemned those with the ability to teach who refused to do so, saying that they "degraded the word of God" (see *Sanhedrin* 99a). Nonetheless, he advocated that one should teach his child a clean trade and pray for a livelihood — for no trade guarantees wealth, without God's blessing.

Out of deep humility, Rabbi Meir would often follow the halachic opinion of his colleagues, even though he disagreed with them (see *Shabbos*

◆§ **From the back.** According to *Rashi* (ad loc.), R' Yehudah *HaNasi* (Rabbi) studied under R' Meir, but his seat at the lectures was positioned so that he did not have a frontal view, and he therefore lost out on the extra clarity one gets from seeing the teacher's facial expressions [see *Maharsha* ad loc.].

According to *Yerushalmi* (*Beitzah* 4:2), the expression "viewing from the back" is the result of an incident: R' Meir once passed by Rabbi's house on Shabbos and heard the sound of one hand clapping on the back of the other. Of the opinion that this is forbidden on the Sabbath — and not knowing whose house it was — R' Meir called out, "Who permitted the desecration of Shabbos?" Rabbi, who held that this type of clapping is permitted, responded, "Who came to annoy us in our own home?" R' Meir fled, and Rabbi, looking out of the window, saw his back. It was to this incident that the Talmud refers.

[Homileticists explain that Rabbi meant to say that even though he never enjoyed a close relationship with R' Meir and in fact only saw him once from the back, the mere experience of seeing such a great man left an impact on him and inspired him to greatness. "Imagine," he said, "had I 'seen him from the front' (i.e., had I actually developed a close relationship with him), how much more I could have grown in Torah!"

4/12

12. Rabbi Meir said: Limit your business activities and engage in Torah study. Be of humble spirit before every person.

134a). He would rise in the presence of elders, even those who were unlettered (*Yerushalmi, Bikkurim* 3:3).

His love for the Land of Israel was extraordinary. He saw sanctity even in the stones of Jerusalem (*Kiddushin* 54a) and considered living in the Land a key to the World to Come (*Yerushalmi, Shabbos* 1:3): "Anyone who steadily lives in *Eretz Yisrael*, the Land itself will cause God to grant him atonement" (*Sifre, Haazinu*).

Unhappily, he was forced to leave the Holy Land and eventually settled in Asia Minor, where he supported himself as a scribe (see *Bava Metzia* 67a and *Sotah* 20a). Longing eternally for Zion, he commanded that his remains be returned to *Eretz Yisrael*, and asked that until that was possible, his casket should be placed on the Mediterranean sea-shore opposite the Land, so that he would remain connected to his homeland by means of the waves that lick the shore (*Yerushalmi, Kilayim* 9:3).

הֱוֵי מְמַעֵט בְּעֵסֶק וַעֲסֹק בַּתּוֹרָה — *Limit your business activities, and engage in Torah* study. One should keep his commercial affairs to a minimum in order to have sufficient time and energy to make Torah study his major occupation (*Rav, R' Yonah*).

Maharal notes: One should limit his business activities only in order to free his time for Torah study. There is no merit in curtailing business affairs out of laziness or fear of the difficulties of commerce.

One should engage in business only as is necessary to earn a living. [Any involvement beyond that is at the great expense of Torah study] (*Sefer HaMussar*).

The Talmud explains that the phrase *nor is it* [the Torah] *across the sea* (*Deuteronomy* 30:13) teaches that Torah is not to be found among international business travelers (see *Eiruvin* 55a). A business life-style with its constant demands keeps one so preoccupied that it allows little room for real growth. Our mishnah calls for diminished involvement in business and a primary focus on matters of the spirit (*Meiri*).

Ruach Chaim suggests rendering הֱוֵי מְמַעֵט בְּעֵסֶק as *gradually reduce your business involvement*. One can wean himself of addiction to the pursuit of wealth only by disengaging slowly. Rapid changes of direction are most often counterproductive.

וֶהֱוֵי שְׁפַל רוּחַ בִּפְנֵי כָל אָדָם — *Be of humble spirit before every person. Rav* and *Magen Avos* interpret this as referring to Torah study: One must be ready

---

◆§ **Bad investment.** R' Yehudah Leib Ashlag spoke of the foolishness of those who sacrifice their spiritual growth in order to earn more money: "Imagine someone hoarding currency which the government has announced will shortly be taken out of circulation. How futile an enterprise! Man does not live forever; in a few short years *he* is taken out of circulation, and then all his money is worthless."

◆§ **Time and money.** The Chofetz Chaim said: "The world says that time is money, but I say that money is time. In order to earn enough money to satisfy his desires, one must sacrifice inordinate amounts of time. For me, that sacrifice is too great." He owned few *sefarim* (Torah books) and advised people that the time spent earning money to buy books would be better spent studying the books one already owned.

◆§ **Carrying your own weight.** The Dubno *Maggid* gives a wonderful parable to discourage any excessive involvement in business: A poor fellow was walking on the road, his pack on his back, when a wagon passed by. The wagon driver offered him a ride, which he gratefully accepted. When the poor man climbed in, he continued to hold his pack rather than putting it down. The wagon driver asked him to explain his puzzling behavior. "My dear friend," the poor man replied, "it is kind enough of you to allow me to ride on your wagon. Why should you also have to carry my package?" Replied the wagon driver, "Fool! Don't you realize that just as I carry you on my wagon, I also carry your pack?" Just as God grants us life and carries us through it, so does He bear all our burdens, including our sustenance.

The mishnah teaches us to minimize our business involvements and allow God to carry us financially to some extent; He is better equipped to provide for us than we are ourselves. Our job is to earn our own *spiritual* sustenance.

to learn humbly from any person, even one of lesser caliber. *Rambam* notes the phrase *before "every" person*. One should act humbly in general in the presence of all people, even those of lesser spiritual stature. When speaking to others, he should behave as though they are his spiritual superiors. *R' Yonah* combines these two ideas by connecting this stich to the previous one: Not only should one be exceedingly humble in everyday affairs (see 4:4), but he must stifle any arrogance concerning his spiritual achievements as well.

Abarbanel interprets the command to be humble as advice on how to successfully diminish one's business involvements. The obsessive pursuit of money is not an issue of consumption, for one can only spend so much. Instead, it is rooted in a desire for honor and prestige. The mishnah teaches that if one wants to limit his business involvement, he should be of humble spirit, forsaking the glory that money can buy him.

Haflaah notes that humility is also the key to success in Torah study [see 1:1, s.v. מסיני]. One who forfeits the world of commerce for the world of Torah need not fear; his humility will bring him success in his Torah endeavors. *Maaseh Avos* reverses the cause and effect, rendering: *Limit your*

business involvement and engage in Torah study, and [you will] thus be humble of spirit. Deep immersion in the study of Torah *results* in true humility, for one who is exposed to God's overwhelming intelligence is forced to realize his own insignificance.

וְאִם בָּטַלְתָּ מִן הַתּוֹרָה, יֶשׁ לְךָ בְּטֵלִים הַרְבֵּה כְּנֶגְדֶּךָ — *If you should neglect the [study of] Torah, you will have many excuses to neglect it.* There are always compelling reasons why it is "impossible" for someone to study Torah. If his resolve weakens and he gives in to "necessity," he will find it harder and harder to study with diligence. Thus, Heaven will prevent him from receiving the reward for Torah study (*Rashi*). Man is destined to toil in some form. If he neglects to make Torah his labor of love, his precious time and talents will be frittered away on the trivial and meaningless issues that clutter life. When he fully involves himself in Torah, however, his everyday concerns will be tended to by others [see *Berachos* 35a] (*Rambam*).

Rav and *R' Yonah* render: *If you neglect the study of Torah, there are many [things that are] unoccupied [which can be employed as agents of punishment] against you.* Wicked men and wild animals,

---

◦§ **Greatness equals humility.** A cardinal principle of Jewish law demonstrates that one must be humble even towards the simplest Jew. If one is presented with an ultimatum either to be killed or kill another Jew, he must forfeit his own life, because "Who says your blood is redder [i.e., your life is more valuable to God]; perhaps your friend's blood is redder" (*Pesachim* 25b). Since this law is applicable to any Jew, no matter what his spiritual station, it proves that we must be humble in the presence of all people (*R' Bunam of P'shis'cha*).

Ruach Chaim explains the usage *before every person* as follows: Many people realize their shortcomings when they are alone, but exhibit selective memory and carry themselves arrogantly when among people. The mishnah therefore advises, *Be of humble spirit before* **every** *person,* not only when you are alone.

The greatest Torah scholars were also the humblest of men, following the model of Moses. A telling instance of this characteristic occurred during the nineteenth century, when the Jews of Warsaw greeted two of the greatest of their generation. Many thousands of men, women, and children lined the streets to pay honor to Rabbi Akiva Eiger of Posen and Rabbi Yaakov Lorberbaum of Lisa (author of *Nesivos HaMishpat* and other classics). The men of the city unhitched the horses, grabbed hold of the wooden shafts, and began pulling the coach themselves, in a dramatic display of honor to the two great visitors.

Inside the coach, the two giants of Israel sat in opposite corners, engrossed in their thoughts. Each was thinking that this magnificent welcome must be for the other. Yearning to take part in this *mitzvah* of honoring the Torah, they each slipped quietly out of the doors on either side of the wagon and joined those pulling the vehicle. And so the multitudes continued their joyous reception of the rabbis, unaware that they were pulling a coach empty of its humble passengers.

uninvolved in anything positive, stand ready to inflict Divine retribution for the neglect of Torah study.

In a novel interpretation, *Meiri* explains the mishnah as a comparison between the relative values of a life of Torah and the pursuit of worldly goals. If one neglects Torah study in order to pursue a career in business, what unique gain will come of it? Even if one becomes a successful merchant, there are many others who are similarly successful; likewise, success in the trades or arts have been attained by many. Torah study is the only field where only a few truly succeed. As the moralists said: "Truth is heavy; therefore, few are ready to bear the burden." The true Torah scholar is a rare and irreplaceable commodity. The mishnah warns that the many people who have involved themselves in relatively meaningless careers at the expense of their spiritual growth have wasted their lives — and if one neglects Torah to follow their path, he too is destined for spiritual oblivion.

Yalkut Gershuni offers an eye-opening thought. Eating, drinking, making a living, even leisure and recreation may assume meaning if harnessed to the service of Torah. The peace of mind provided by these activities allows for vibrant Torah study and spiritual growth. However, if one neglects Torah study, then all these activities are transformed into meaningless wastes of time. Thus he renders: *If you neglect Torah, then you will have many other areas of your life that are for naught.*

◆§ **Into every life ...** Abraham Pinchas Landau of London was a businessman and one of the most community-minded Orthodox Jews of London. He was *gabbai* of the *Machzikei Hadas* synagogue and head of a Talmud Torah, as well as other institutions. His business, however, had suffered of late because of his involvements, and his family was beginning to pressure him not to neglect their own needs in deference to others. Mr. Landau attended the *Knessiah Gedolah* (World Convention) of Agudath Israel held in Vienna, hoping to consult with the Chofetz Chaim. He went to the Schreiber home, where the sage of Radin was staying, but gave up any hope of a private audience when he saw that the house was mobbed. Still, it was a rare privilege to spend some time in the same room as the Chofetz Chaim, in close enough proximity to hear him talk; it was an opportunity afforded few spectators at the *Knessiah Gedolah* in those days before the microphone, when the elderly sage's remarks could never be heard beyond the first few rows. So Landau stood and waited.

As was his custom, the Chofetz Chaim concluded his meal with a Torah thought before reciting the *Bircas HaMazon*: He quoted the verse אַךְ טוֹב וָחֶסֶד יִרְדְּפוּנִי כָּל יְמֵי חַיָּי, *Only goodness and kindness shall pursue me all the days of my life (Psalms 23:6)*. "A remarkable thing!" he began. "People sometimes suffer for performing deeds of goodness and kindness. The truth is that every human being suffers some sort of tribulations in life; and if he must suffer, it is far better to suffer for good deeds than for evil ones. That is what King David meant. If I *must* be 'pursued' in my lifetime, then please, God, let it be for deeds of goodness and kindness!"

Abraham Pinchas Landau trembled. "How could he know what I wanted to ask him? He was talking to me!" The Chofetz Chaim had taught him the lesson of our mishnah, and resolved his personal dilemma.

◆§ **The paramount function.** Bar Kappara eulogized Rabbi with the following words: נָצְחוּ אֶרְאֵלִים אֶת הַמְּצוּקִים וְנִשְׁבָּה אֲרוֹן הַקּוֹדֶשׁ, *The angels overpowered the righteous mortals, and the Holy Ark was taken captured (Kesubos 104a)*. Of all the different vessels found in the Temple, Bar Kappara chose to compare Rabbi to the Holy Ark. Why? Rabbi Yitzchok Hutner explained: Unlike all the other vessels of the Temple, the Holy Ark did not play a specific *functional* role in the Temple service. Even the Yom Kippur service of sprinkling sacrificial blood between the poles of the Ark did not require the physical presence of the Ark; during the Second Temple Era, when the Ark was not there, the blood was sprinkled anyway.

Similarly, Bar Kappara meant to say that the main loss Jewry suffered with the death of Rabbi was not the loss of his brilliant Torah, not his great deeds and piety, nor even his function as the leader of the nation. The main loss was that Rabbi no longer walked the face of the earth — and the world had been diminished by his absence. The greatest significance of a true *talmid chacham* lies not in what he *does*, but in what he *is*. His value is not functional, but rather existential.

[יג] **רַבִּי אֱלִיעֶזֶר** בֶּן יַעֲקֹב אוֹמֵר: הָעוֹשֶׂה מִצְוָה אַחַת קוֹנֶה לוֹ פְּרַקְלִיט אֶחָד;

Pri Chaim interprets the mishnah as a warning. Just as one who must cut his expenses will generally abridge his charitable activities rather than his personal pleasures, so people who hope to expand their business activities often take the time they need from their Torah study rather than from their leisure time. Our mishnah advises the opposite: If you must neglect something for the sake of your business, let it not be Torah study; there are many other options to choose from.

וְאִם עָמַלְתָּ בַּתּוֹרָה, יֵשׁ לוֹ שָׂכָר הַרְבֵּה לִתֵּן לָךְ — *but if you labor in the Torah, He has ample reward to give you.* Unlike the punishment for neglecting Torah study, which is meted out through intermediaries, the reward for making Torah one's labor of love is given by God Himself. This is analogous to a king who commissioned an artisan to create beautiful vessels for him. When the artisan had completed the task, the king instructed his servants to withdraw funds from the royal treasury and reward him handsomely. They promptly complied, but since the money was not theirs, they skimped a bit. Had the king paid the artisan himself, he would certainly have been much more

magnanimous. Likewise, when God Himself rewards man's good deeds, He showers him unstintingly with His beneficence (*R' Yonah, Rav*).

Meiri views *ample reward* as a reference to the provision of man's worldly needs. He should not fear that his involvement in Torah will adversely affect his ability to support his family; God lacks nothing and will provide man with everything he needs.

R' Meir taught this mishnah as a rebuttal to *Acher* (Elisha ben Abuyah), who had become an apostate (see 4:25, s.v. אֱלִישָׁע) and sought to dissuade young Torah students from pursuing their special calling. "Become a carpenter, become a tailor," he would cry. "Learn a trade that provides a living" (see *Yerushalmi, Chagigah* 2:1). R' Meir refuted him by emphasizing that one who labors at Torah will indeed earn ample reward from God.

R' Yehudah Lirma notes that the mishnah speaks of *laboring* at Torah, not *learning* much Torah. The ample Godly reward is for the toil and labor one expends at Torah study.

⇜§ **Earning God's provenance.** *Rambam* captures this sentiment in *Hilchos Shemittah V'Yovel* (13:13), where he writes: "Not only the tribe of Levi is considered the special portion of God; but any human being in the world who is emotionally inspired and intellectually committed to separating himself in order to stand before God in His service — to know God and to walk upright as He has created him, and who is ready to unburden himself of the yoke of mundane considerations, which are the concern of the masses — such a person is sanctified with extreme holiness, and God will be his portion and inheritance forever and ever. God will provide him in this world with his basic necessities, just as He did [in ancient times] for the Kohanim and Levites. King David says: '*HASHEM is my allotted portion and my share; You guide my destiny*' (*Psalms* 16:5)."

One who earnestly engages in Torah study will be able to earn a living with little effort. This message is reflected in the fact that a cask of manna was placed alongside the Holy Ark and the Tablets of the Law in the Temple (see *Yoma* 52b).

Sustenance, symbolized by the manna, is intricately connected to Torah activities, symbolized by the Ark and the Tablets. One who makes Torah his major endeavor will find his sustenance, like manna, provided from Heaven.

The Chazon Ish writes: "For us, physical sustenance is something we receive through constant miracles" (*Collected Letters* 1:161).

excuses to neglect it; but if you labor in the Torah, He has ample reward to give you.

13. Rabbi Eliezer ben Yaakov said: He who fulfills even a single *mitzvah* gains himself a single advocate,

Mishnah 13

רַבִּי אֱלִיעֶזֶר בֶּן יַעֲקֹב אוֹמֵר — *Rabbi Eliezer ben Yaakov said.* A fourth-generation *Tanna* and one of R' Akiva's last students (*Yerushalmi, Chagigah* 3:1), Rabbi Eliezer ben Yaakov was among those in attendance at the conclave held at Usha after the Bar Kochba revolt. He spoke warmly of the local residents, who joyfully and graciously accommodated the participants, and he compared them to the generation that stood at Mount Sinai and jubilantly accepted the Torah (*Shir HaShirim Rabbah* 2:5). *Magen Avos* assumes that this R' Eliezer is actually the second-generation *Tanna* of the same name [see *Hyman: Toldos Tannaim V'Amoraim*, Vol. I, p. 181].

Yerushalmi (*Peah* 8:8) gives an example of R' Eliezer's great humanity. He once befriended a blind man who visited his city, and in response to his example, the local residents saw to the blind man's needs. In gratitude, the man offered a prayer on behalf of his benefactor: "Since you showed kindness to one who is seen but cannot see, may the One Who sees but cannot be seen accept your entreaties and show you kindness."

R' Eliezer affirmed his belief in the eternal survival of the Jewish people by explaining the Scriptural metaphor that compares the Jewish masses to the sand of the seashore (see *Hosea* 2:1): "Just as a hole dug at night is refilled by morning, so too, Jewish masses decimated in one era [the days of King David] are replenished in another era [Solomonic times]" (*Pesikta d'Rav Kahana*).

הָעוֹשֶׂה מִצְוָה אַחַת קוֹנֶה לוֹ פְּרַקְלִיט אֶחָד — *He who fulfills even a single mitzvah gains himself a single advocate.* Man's actions are the "character witnesses" that testify before the Heavenly Court (*Rashi, R' Yonah* et al.). A person should not belittle the significance of performing even the smallest *mitzvah*, for every good deed creates an argument in his defense, an agent who pleads his case at the Divine tribunal (*Meiri*).

◆§ **A friend indeed.** A man had three friends. One loved him deeply and spent as much time as possible with him; the second one was not quite as intimate, but nonetheless maintained a close relationship with him; a third friend was merely an acquaintance.

One day the man was summoned to the royal palace to be tried for heinous crimes against the king. Terrified, he asked his very dear friend to accompany him to the trial. To his surprise, the friend refused. Afraid to appear alone in front of the king, the man asked his second friend to strengthen his spirits by accompanying him on his trek. "I will accompany you to the palace, but I can't go in," replied the second friend.

Fearful for his life and with no other options, he asked his casual acquaintance to keep him company on his way to the trial. "I understand your predicament and am ready to help you out. Don't worry! Let us go together, and when we get there I will plead your case," answered the third friend.

The three friends are analogous to man's three "friends" in life: his money, his family, and his good deeds. Money is often such a priority in his life that the pursuit of it seems to be his constant preoccupation — his "best friend." Yet when he will have to give a final reckoning, his riches will be of no help to him. His family, unfortunately, is often shunted to a secondary role in his concerns. Nonetheless, they love him and would want to help him in any way they can. However, they can only accompany him as far as the cemetery; once in front of the Heavenly court, he is on his own. Only man's third friend, his charity and good deeds — with which he often maintains only a distant relationship — will accompany him to the Great Trial and testify on his behalf.

וְהָעוֹבֵר עֲבֵרָה אַחַת, קוֹנֶה לּוֹ קַטֵּיגוֹר אֶחָד. תְּשׁוּבָה וּמַעֲשִׂים טוֹבִים כִּתְרִיס בִּפְנֵי הַפֻּרְעָנוּת.

Our Sages taught that one should always view himself as having equal amounts of good and bad deeds. One good deed can tip the scales of Divine justice toward acquittal (see *Kiddushin* 40b). The performance of even one *mitzvah*, therefore, is of paramount significance, since the single Heavenly advocate it spawns may be the one that saves him (*Avos al Banim*).

וְהָעוֹבֵר עֲבֵרָה אַחַת קוֹנֶה לוֹ קַטֵּיגוֹר אֶחָד — *and he who commits even a single transgression gains himself a single accuser.* Man's sins are his greatest indictment; they argue the case against him before God. The Talmud teaches that just as one's good deeds precede him, paving his way into the World of Reward, so too his spiritual flaws herald his arrival before the Heavenly Court (*Sotah* 3a).

Rashi and *Magen Avos* suggest that the word קַטֵּיגוֹר is a contraction of קוֹרֵא תַּגָּר, one who issues a challenge. A prosecutor challenges the presumption of the accused's innocence, while *Tiferes Yisrael* suggests that its etymology is from the Greek *categoris*, meaning prosecutor or complainant.

Rambam and *R' Yonah* define a קַטֵּיגוֹר as one who bears tales of indiscretion to the king, seeking to have the disloyal subject killed. This reflects the words of the Talmud: "Reish Lakish said: He is Satan, he is the Evil Inclination, he is the selfsame Angel of Death. He first descends to incite man to sin, then ascends to the Heavenly Court to prose-cute; and having won his case, he returns to this world in order to carry out the sentence and take man's life" (see *Bava Basra* 16a).

Maharal explains that God, in His infinite wisdom, gives almost free reign in this world to the forces of negativity. They assume three roles: the Satan, the Evil Inclination, and the Angel of Death, all of which have but one goal — the ruination of man. When man succumbs to the Evil Inclination, he creates Satan, the prosecutor, who eventually becomes the hangman; they are three guises of the evil force that seek to destroy him.

It is this phenomenon to which the Sages refer when they speak of the good angels created by *mitzvos* and the bad ones created by sin (see *Shabbos* 32a).

Meiri and *Midrash Shmuel* infer from the mishnah the basic doctrine that God cannot be bribed. Every *mitzvah* is rewarded, every transgression punished; nothing is canceled out.

תְּשׁוּבָה וּמַעֲשִׂים טוֹבִים כִּתְרִיס בִּפְנֵי הַפֻּרְעָנוּת — *Repentance and good deeds are like a shield against retribution.*

Repentance offered to rectify transgressions already committed or good deeds one undertakes may serve to ward off calamity (*Rambam, R' Yonah*). *Meiri* views this clause as a chronological continuation of the previous one: Even if man has created accusers by means of his sins, he should not despair. Repentance and good deeds (i.e., the

---

⇨ **By one point.** It is noteworthy that the numerical value of סַנֵּיגוֹר, *defense attorney* (329), is one more than קַטֵּיגוֹר, *prosecutor* (328). A person needs only one more merit to outweigh the demerits and gain him acquittal. It is that one additional *mitzvah* to which our mishnah refers.

⇨ **Unscrupulous angels.** That sin is a person's undoing is illustrated by the following story: An opponent of the Baal Shem Tov once sat in his *succah* among friends and spoke disparagingly of the great sage. The next day the Baal Shem Tov upbraided him: "How does a person of your caliber speak *lashon hara* (slanderous gossip) in the *succah*?"

Shocked, the man asked, "Who told you?"

"An angel," answered the Baal Shem Tov.

His detractor laughed. "Since when do angels speak *lashon hara*?"

"Some do," answered the holy man. "Every time a person does a good deed, he gives birth to a good angel; and every time he sins, he creates an evil angel. The angel you created by speaking slanderously against me is the one who told me. Evil angels, like their creators, are not afraid of sinning."

and he who commits even a single transgression gains himself a single accuser. Repentance and good deeds are like a shield against retribution.

improvement of his actions) can serve as a shield and armor against Divine punishment which takes the form of life's tribulations.

Life is full of difficult times, but if someone constantly seeks to improve himself, God grants him protection from such natural occurrences (*R' Meir Zlotowitz*).

R' Yosef ibn Nachmias takes note of the order of the words: Repentance is mentioned before good deeds because the repentant are deemed of greater spiritual standing than those who are occupied with good deeds (see *Berachos* 34b). *Baal HaTanya* offers a different perspective on the role of repentance. Following God's *mitzvos* is a means of connecting to God; sin creates a chasm between man and his Maker which is difficult to bridge. King David gives expression to this idea: כִּי עִמְּךָ הַסְּלִיחָה לְמַעַן תִּוָּרֵא, *For with You is forgiveness, [in order] that You may be feared* (*Psalms* 130:4). Hence, repentance must precede good deeds in order that they close the gap and create the conditions for a true Godly connection.

⋘ **Body and soul.** The Talmud teaches, "The Jewish people are holy. Some want to [give charity] but don't have the means; others have the means, but don't want to give" (*Chullin* 7b). *Tosafos* write that even those who give unwillingly and out of embarrassment are considered holy. The premise seems incredible; how can one who gives only out of shame be deemed holy?

R' Zusia of Anipoli explained, based on our mishnah, that every *mitzvah* creates an angel. The performance of the good deed creates the "body" of the angel, while the person's good intent imbues the angel with a "soul." When a person earnestly intends to do a *mitzvah* but lacks the wherewithal, he creates a "soul" for an angel, but it lacks a body. Conversely, when one performs a *mitzvah* without proper intent, he creates a "body" without a soul. Since all Jews are part of the same organism — *Klal Yisrael* — the "soul" created by the well-intentioned person and the "body" created by his unwilling fellow join forces, and together they form a complete angel. Hence, when Jews pool their spiritual resources, they are collectively deemed holy.

Just as one searches for the most competent lawyer to plead his case, so we are well advised to perform *mitzvos* with alacrity and excitement, thus creating for ourselves an advocate who is sound of body and soul.

The quality of the angel-advocate created by a good deed is directly related to the completeness of the *mitzvah*. A *mitzvah* done by rote, without understanding or feeling, will create an incomplete angel. One who does a *mitzvah* with every fiber of his being, however, creates an articulate and convincing advocate for himself.

In this light, *Peh Kadosh* homiletically explains the angel's call to Abraham at the *Akeidah*, when Abraham was commanded not to slaughter Isaac: "Now I know that you are a God-fearing man, since you have not withheld your son, your only one, [מִמֶּנִּי] from Me" (*Genesis* 22:12).

The simple meaning is that the angel is speaking in God's Name, but in this interpretation, the angel is speaking for himself. How so? Having been created by Abraham's absolute determination to obey God by sacrificing Isaac, the angel tells him that his dedication and sense of commitment were so complete that he — the angel himself — was perfect. "You did not withhold your son מִמֶּנִּי, *from me*; my completeness is reflective of the way in which you followed God's will.

The Chofetz Chaim used to say sadly that people will be shocked when they come to face the Heavenly Tribunal after they die. They will see robust, overpowering angels, and they will see angels who are limping, crippled, and famished. The robust angels will be the ones produced by *mitzvos* and sins that were done with alacrity; the sick angels will be the ones created by the *mitzvos* and sins done half-heartedly and under compulsion. To be vindicated in that most harrowing of all trials, a Jew must be sure that his angelic advocates are strong enough to protect him.

[יד] **רַבִּי** יוֹחָנָן הַסַּנְדְּלָר אוֹמֵר: כָּל כְּנֵסִיָּה שֶׁהִיא לְשֵׁם שָׁמַיִם, סוֹפָהּ לְהִתְקַיֵּם; וְשֶׁאֵינָהּ לְשֵׁם שָׁמַיִם, אֵין סוֹפָהּ לְהִתְקַיֵּם.

Mishnah 14

רַבִּי יוֹחָנָן הַסַּנְדְּלָר אוֹמֵר — *Rabbi Yochanan the Sandler said.* Rabbi Yochanan, a student of R' Akiva (*Berachos* 22a), earned his livelihood as a shoemaker. *Yerushalmi* (*Chagigah* 3:1) suggests instead that he was called *HaSandlar* after the name of his native city, Alexandria, Egypt.

During the period of intense Roman persecution, when R' Akiva was in prison, R' Yochanan was sent surreptitiously to solicit his opinion regarding the permissibility of performing the *chalitzah* rite without the presence of a panel of three. Disguised as an itinerant peddler, he passed by the prison where R' Akiva was held and cried out, "Who needs needles and other knitting tools? *Chalitzah* just between him and her (i.e., without the panel of three) — what is the law?" R' Akiva replied, "Do you have a thimble? It is permitted" (*Yerushalmi, Yevamos* 12:5).

Seeking to escape the jaws of the Roman lion, R' Yochanan traveled to Netzivin, Babylonia together with R' Elazar ben Shamua (see 4:15), to study under R' Yehudah ben Beseira. When they arrived in Netzivin, however, they were so overwhelmed by longing for *Eretz Yisrael* that they began to cry and tear their clothes. Unable to quell their anguish, they returned to the Land and proclaimed, "Dwelling in *Eretz Yisrael* is equal to all the *mitzvos* of the Torah" (*Sifre, Re'eh*).

During a reprieve from the Hadrianic reign of terror, a conclave of R' Akiva's most prominent students was convened at Bikas Rimon, at which R' Yochanan *HaSandlar* was among the prestigious group of fourth-generation *Tannaim*, who discussed plans to resuscitate the fallen Land physically, financially, emotionally, and spiritually.

The Midrash (*Bereishis Rabbah* 61:3) describes this group of Sages as having refilled the Holy Land with Torah. Their assemblies at Bikas Rimon and Usha were a living representation of R' Yochanan's statement that an assembly convened for the sake of Heaven will be successful.

כָּל כְּנֵסִיָּה שֶׁהִיא לְשֵׁם שָׁמַיִם — *Every assembly that is dedicated to the sake of Heaven.* Any gathering convened in order to advance the cause of Torah study and the performance of *mitzvos* is considered an assembly for the sake of Heaven (*R' Yonah*). *Avos d'Rabbi Nosson* (40) considers the assemblage of the Jewish people at Mount Sinai an example of such a gathering.

According to *Tiferes Yisrael*, the mishnah is not limited to religious gatherings. Even assemblies whose agenda is mundane in nature can be deemed "for the sake of Heaven" if their motive is to advance the realization of God's will in the world.

◆§ **United for Heaven.** The Sages teach that at Sinai the entire Jewish nation was כְּאִישׁ אֶחָד בְּלֵב אֶחָד, *with a single desire, like a single person* (see *Exodus* 19:2 and *Rashi* ad loc.). Only when it was united in its desire to hear the word of God could Israel receive the Torah. It was this unity of purpose that enabled the Torah to endure and its message to reverberate throughout the generations.

On a deeper level, it was this single-minded focus that preserved the *integrity* of the Torah. *Ramban* (*Deuteronomy* 4:9) explains that the basis of our belief in the truth of the Torah is the axiom that "a person does not give his children a false inheritance." A nation of millions of men, women, and children witnessed the Sinaitic Revelation, and there was no doubt in anyone's mind as to the truth of that event. Passed down from generation to generation, it is the account of that Revelation that has provided the underpinning for our explicit belief in the Torah's authenticity.

14. Rabbi Yochanan the Sandler said: Every assembly that is dedicated to the sake of Heaven will have an enduring effect; but one that is not for the sake of Heaven will not have an enduring effect.

A business gathering conducted in a spirit of honesty and forthrightness will produce enduring results, but when an atmosphere of distrust hovers over it, nothing good will come of the meeting (*Meshivas Nefesh*).

Midrash Shmuel notes that the word כְּנֵסִיָּה is a contraction of כֶּנֶס and יָהּ, a Godly gathering. Even those who gather for a meeting which is spiritual in nature must remember to conduct their affairs for the sake of Heaven rather than for self-aggrandizement. Since group gatherings tend to become contentious, it is important that all participants focus on one goal — to strengthen the love and fear of God. This spiritual tone will serve as a unifying factor (*Abarbanel*).

סוֹפָהּ לְהִתְקַיֵּם — *will have an enduring effect.* The resolutions and decisions of such a Godly assembly will come to fruition (*Rashi*). According to *Midrash Shmuel*, it is the assembly itself that will endure. Since the goal of the gathering is to discover truth and to adopt a course of goodness and upright living, it will never be broken up. When everyone in the group has only one wish — to seek truth — the group as a unit will endure (*Sefer HaMussar, Meiri*). If the participants in groups sincerely mean to serve God, even though they began on a pessimistic, inauspicious note, they will eventually succeed in their undertakings (*R' Meir Zlotowitz*).

וְשֶׁאֵינָהּ לְשֵׁם שָׁמַיִם, אֵין סוֹפָהּ לְהִתְקַיֵּם — *but one that is not for the sake of Heaven will not have an enduring effect.* This refers to a gathering of people whose purpose is to exercise their power and derive honor from each other (*R' Yonah*). By nature, people are contentious and unite only with great difficulty. Only the presence of God in a group can serve as a binding force; any assembly that lacks Godliness is bound to disintegrate eventually (*Maharal*). Self-interest nearly always becomes the dominant factor sooner or later, but when people are loyal to the Torah and God-fearing, their self-interest becomes His service and they are afraid to do anything that will desecrate His Name; thus they will strive to stay united in the common purpose of advancing the Divine agenda.

Even when people are ostensibly involved in good deeds, it is important that they be carried out in a peaceful fashion, without any political maneuvering (*Tiferes Yisrael*). *Avos d'Rabbi Nosson* cites the *Dor Haflagah* — the generation that built the Tower of Babel (see *Genesis* 11:1-9) — as the personification of unity which was *not* for the sake of Heaven.

Meiri underscores one of the most prevalent human failings as the basis for this mishnah. Interpersonal relationships must never be based on a desire to triumph over the other person. If someone has a need to control others, he is bound to stoop to falsehoods in order to maintain his superior status. The divisiveness caused by such falsehood can irreparably damage the fabric of society. Any gathering where victory rather than veracity is the main goal will be short lived.

⳹ **Survival in Egypt.** *Midrash Rabbah* (*Shemos* 1:32) teaches that Moses asked the Egyptians to allow the Jews to choose the Sabbath as their day of rest. On that day the Jews would gather together and strengthen each other's faith in God. It was this weekly assembly, convened for a Godly purpose, which reinforced the Jews' resolve and enabled them to survive the torturous Egyptian ordeal.

⳹ **Dangerous unity.** Since it was the unity of this generation which made their blasphemous project nearly successful, God declared that He would destroy that unity. He divided them by causing them to speak many different languages, resulting in a breakdown of communication and a general dispersion (*Akeidas Yitzchak*).

[טו] **רַבִּי** אֶלְעָזָר בֶּן שַׁמוּעַ אוֹמֵר: יְהִי כְבוֹד תַּלְמִידְךָ
חָבִיב עָלֶיךָ כְּשֶׁלָּךְ; וּכְבוֹד חֲבֵרְךָ כְּמוֹרָא רַבָּךְ;

Mishnah 15

רַבִּי אֶלְעָזָר בֶּן שַׁמוּעַ אוֹמֵר — *R' Elazar ben Shamua said.* R' Elazar ben Shamua was a fourth-generation *Tanna* and one of the five students of R' Akiva who was ordained by R' Yehudah ben Bava after their mentor was tortured to death.

R' Yehudah *HaNasi* was among his most prominent disciples and often reports events that occurred while he studied under R' Elazar (see *Yevamos* 84a; *Yoma* 79b). A popular teacher who loved his students deeply, R' Elazar was always surrounded by many disciples who filled the study hall (see *Eruvin* 53a).

Later generations spoke of R' Elazar in glowing terms. Rav called him the "happiest of scholars" (*Kesubos* 40a), while R' Yochanan described the breadth of his knowledge and understanding in vivid terms (*Eruvin* 53a). His fundamental concern with human honor and dignity is reflected in his reaction to the famous Kamtza-Bar Kamtza incident, when a man named Bar Kamtza was publicly humiliated in the presence of sages who remained silent and did not protest. To get revenge, the angry Bar Kamtza devised a scheme to convince the Roman powers that the Jews were rebellious (see *Gittin* 57a). Successful, it precipitated the destruction of the Second Temple. R' Elazar ben Shamua said: "See the power of embarrassment [and how God takes up the cause of the victim]. God helped Bar Kamtza bring about the destruction of His house and the burning of His palace."

When asked why he thought he had merited such a long life, R' Elazar replied that he had always been careful to show regard for others. He never entered the study hall after the other students had already sat down, so as not to give the appearance of arrogantly stepping above their heads (see *Sotah* 39a, *Rashi* ad loc.).

The Midrash tells a fascinating story of his humanity and the huge dividend it brought the Jewish people. R' Elazar was once walking along the seashore when he spotted a sunken ship. All was lost except for one Roman, who was washed ashore without his clothes. The survivor's request for clothing was ignored by all except R' Elazar, who took off one of his own garments and gave it to the naked man. R' Elazar then took him home, fed him, gave him some money, and accompanied him to the door as he left. Years later this Roman achieved prominence in the government and promulgated many anti-Jewish laws. R' Elazar traveled to Rome to visit him. The ruler instantly recognized him; he canceled the decrees and presented R' Elazar with a sizable financial gift (*Koheles Rabbah* 11:1). When asked how one might save himself from the travails which will accompany the coming of the Messiah, R' Elazar replied, "Let him be involved in Torah study and acts of kindness" (*Sanhedrin* 98b).

יְהִי כְבוֹד תַּלְמִידְךָ חָבִיב עָלֶיךָ כְּשֶׁלָּךְ — *Let the honor of your student be as dear to you as your own.* Since you, as a teacher, have a share in your student's accomplishments, his honor is actually yours. You

---

◆§ **Grooming for the future.** *Rambam* (*Hilchos Talmud Torah* 5:8) teaches that while generally one may not show honor to a student in the presence of his teacher, it is permitted if the teacher is accustomed to demonstrate honor for the student. This practice often takes the form of the teacher assigning some of his duties or roles to the student. With shrewd judgment, the teacher can assess when the student is ready for the responsibility and honor him with an assignment at which he can succeed.

Rabbi Yisroel Belsky relates that one day after *davening*, someone approached R' Yaakov Kamenetzky with a halachic question (*she'eilah*). R' Yaakov nodded in the direction of R' Belsky and said, "He'll answer your *she'eilah.*" Rabbi Belsky had trained rigorously in R' Yaakov's method, but until that moment it had never occurred to him that he was ready to rule on such a matter. With this show of honor, R' Yaakov, always the consummate educator, gave his student the confidence to succeed.

15. R' Elazar ben Shamua said: Let the honor of your student be as dear to you as your own; the honor of your colleague as the reverence for your teacher;

should therefore cherish your student's prestige as if it were your own (*Rashi*).

R' Yonah's version of the mishnah reads: יְהִי כְבוֹד תַּלְמִידְךָ חָבִיב עָלֶיךָ כִּכְבוֹד חֲבֵרָךְ, *Let the honor of your student be as dear to you as the honor of your colleague.* Clearly, the mishnah does not call upon a teacher to grant his students as much honor as he does his colleagues; rather, one should not diminish in any way from the honor his students deserve, just as he honors his colleagues according to what they deserve.

Rav (citing *Avos d'Rabbi Nosson*) teaches that the obligation to honor students is derived from the way Moses addressed his disciple Joshua concerning the battle strategy against Amalek: "Let *us* choose men" (see *Exodus* 17:9). Moses did not say, "Choose men for me"; rather, he spoke to Joshua as an equal even though Joshua was his student.

"Just as students must honor their teachers, so teachers should honor their students and develop a close relationship with them. One must take extreme care with his disciples and love them, for they are his children who give him pleasure in this world and in the World to Come" (*Rambam, Hilchos Talmud Torah* 5:12).

Tiferes Yisrael says that one must honor his students because they make great contribution to his own achievements in Torah study. A teacher should listen carefully to the words of his students; often they are like a diamond in the rough, which merely needs some polishing in order to shine brilliantly. This is but one aspect of the growth a teacher can experience as a result of his relationship with his students. The Sages taught (*Taanis* 7a) that one can often learn more from students than from mentors or colleagues.

R' Shlomo Kluger renders כְּבוֹד תַּלְמִידְךָ as "the honor you *receive* from your student." One may never discourage his students from honoring him since it is beneficial for them (see *Rambam, Hilchos Talmud Torah* 5:8). Through honoring their mentor, they come to view themselves as subservient to him and will therefore allow themselves to be molded spiritually. However, a teacher should never take the honor so seriously that he allows it to inflate his ego. The honor one receives from his students should be as insignificant in his eyes as if he had accorded the honor to himself.

וּכְבוֹד חֲבֵרָךְ כְּמוֹרָא רַבָּךְ — *the honor of your colleague as the reverence for your teacher.* This principle is derived from Aaron, who called his

---

Honoring students. Rabbi Shlomo Heiman, *Rosh Yeshivah* of Torah Vodaath, treated his students with a rare and deep warmth. Whenever a student would advance a possible explanation, R' Shlomo would begin to repeat the student's words, no matter how ridiculous they initially seemed: "So you probably mean to say . . . yes, yes, that is a deep insight. Perhaps we might want to answer the question we had in the *Gemara* based on your thought as follows . . ." By the time R' Shlomo was done refining the student's garbled thought, a multifaceted piece of insight had emerged. The *Gemara* was now clear, the student felt confident of his ability, and R' Shlomo had ably fulfilled the dictum of our mishnah.

R' Akiva Eiger's sons write in the introduction to their father's responsa that he had instructed them to delete the title "my student" from any responsa they planned to print. He told them: "I never called anyone my student, even those who came to study in my yeshivah; for who knows which one of us learned more from the other?"

Sense of proportion. A great rabbi who was about to be installed as *rav* of an important Jewish community went into his room and closed the door behind him. To their surprise and chagrin, the people in the house overheard him speaking eloquently and enthusiastically about his *own* greatness. When they inquired later, he explained. "When the ceremonies begin, the speakers will make exaggerated statements about my prowess in learning and piety. I want to be sure not to let these compliments go to my head, so I spent some time praising myself. Just as my own compliments are meaningless, so I will remember that I should not take their compliments seriously."

[טז] **רַבִּי** יְהוּדָה אוֹמֵר: הֱוֵי זָהִיר בְּתַלְמוּד, שֶׁשִּׁגְגַת

younger brother Moses "my master" (*Numbers* 12:11).

The Talmud (*Bava Metzia* 33a) relates that the scholars of Babylonia would stand up for each other and would tear their clothes in mourning when a colleague died. Since they studied together and benefited from each other's wisdom, each viewed his colleagues as his teachers (*Midrash Shmuel*).

According to *Tiferes Yisrael*, the mishnah teaches the attitude one must maintain toward an adversary in an argument over a Torah topic. While one has an obligation only to honor a student but need not yield to his opinion, he should be more flexible and accepting regarding the opinion of a colleague. Unless it is clear that his opinion is mistaken, one should never flippantly reject the position of his colleague, just as he certainly would never reject that of his teacher.

Maharal sees this mishnah as a commentary on the previous one, which offered advice on how an assembly of people can gain permanence. Respect and honor — be it of students, colleagues, or teachers — is the key to ongoing, fruitful relationships.

R' Aharon Luria (author of *Avodas P'nim*) elaborates. Equating collegial respect to reverence for a mentor teaches that just as one fears his teacher but never expects reciprocal reverence, so one should honor his friend but expect no honor in return.

וּמוֹרָא רַבָּךְ כְּמוֹרָא שָׁמָיִם — *and the reverence for your teacher as the reverence for Heaven.* The Torah teaches: אֶת ה' אֱלֹהֶיךָ תִּירָא, *HASHEM, your God, you shall fear* (*Deuteronomy* 6:13). R' Akiva interprets the extra word אֶת as indicating that Torah scholars are to be feared along with God (see *Bava Kamma* 41b). God has placed the reverence of scholars on the same plane as reverence for Himself because one achieves life in the World to Come through the teachings of the scholars (*Sefer HaMussar*).

This principle is derived from the Biblical episode in which Joshua suspected Eldad and Meidad of disrespect and insubordination towards Moses (*Numbers* 11:28). He said that they deserved to die, since revolt against the teacher of Israel is tantamount to revolt against God (*Rav*).

The Talmud details the specific forms this reverence must take. Some of them are: One may not sit or stand in the place that the scholar generally occupies, nor may he contradict his words (see *Kiddushin* 31b).

The relationship between fear of God and reverence for a teacher is reciprocal. One who possesses strong feelings of יִרְאַת שָׁמַיִם is enjoined to fear his teachers; one who reveres his mentors should transfer that feeling to his relationship with God (*B'nayos B'Ramah*).

Ruach Chaim connects all the phases of the mishnah through a reality of human nature. Since

---

⏴ A higher law. However, one must never fear any man more than he fears God. R' Moshe of Kobrin described the awe and trepidation that the great *Maggid* of Mezeritch felt for his teacher, the Baal Shem Tov. It was of such magnitude that when he discovered a handkerchief with a pinch of snuff on it that had belonged to his late master, he fainted! Nevertheless, he never allowed his great reverence for the Baal Shem Tov to interfere with his fear of God.

Once, the *Maggid* served as a judge at a *din Torah* in which one of the litigants was a relative of the Baal Shem Tov. He looked out at the assembled crowd and saw the master pass by. Afraid that the sight of his mentor would bias his judgment, he called out, "We decree as a court that anybody who has no business with the court leave immediately." He would not allow his reverence for the Baal Shem Tov to compete with his fear of the master's Master.

[For a profound elucidation of R' Akiva's statement see *Maharal, Nesiv HaTorah* (9:1).]

R' Yitzchak of Ziditchov explained homiletically that one's fear for his teacher is directly related to the degree of the teacher's fear of God. Students have a sixth sense in determining how authentically their teachers or parents practice what they preach.

16. Rabbi Yehudah said: Be meticulous in study, for a careless

man's instinct is to degrade those who are on a higher spiritual plane, it is necessary for him to compensate by "over-honoring" others. Thus, a student who is actually of a lower standing than you should be treated like a colleague, while a colleague who is equal to you should be treated as a superior. A teacher, who is truly superior, should be revered along with God (*Ruach Chaim*).

Mishnah 16

רַבִּי יְהוּדָה אוֹמֵר — *Rabbi Yehudah said*. The Rabbi cited in Mishnah is usually R' Yehudah bar Ila'i, a fourth-generation *Tanna,* who was one of R' Akiva's students who rebuilt Torah study and Jewish life after the terrible persecution that followed the defeat of Bar Kochba's revolt. The Romans respected R' Yehudah because of his conciliatory attitude toward them, and this enabled him to win several concessions for his people (see *Shabbos* 33b).

While still a youngster in Lod, R' Yehudah studied under R' Tarfon (*Megillah* 20a), and the Talmud lists many laws that he learned from him (see *Yevamos* 101b and *Shabbos* 28b). His primary mentor, however, was R' Akiva, and he authored the *Toras Kohanim (Sifre)*, the halachic Midrash on *Leviticus,* based on R' Akiva's teachings.

More than six hundred *halachos* are quoted in the Mishnah in his name; only in Tractate *Kinnin* does he not appear. The *Tosefta* is replete with his quotations, and he was prolific as well in matters of *Aggadah*, with hundreds of citations in the Midrash. Due to his vast knowledge of customs, traditions, and historical precedents, he was "the major speaker in all places" (רֹאשׁ הַמְדַבְּרִים בְּכָל מָקוֹם), speaking first at communal and rabbinic conferences (*Shabbos* 33b).

Among his famous statements: "Man is recognized through his cup, his pocket, and his anger" [meaning that a person's true character can be ascertained by how he behaves when he drinks too much, how generous he is with his money, and how quick he is to anger]. He also said: "The Jewish people are compared to sand and stars. When they fall [spiritually], they descend to the sand, and when they rise, they rise to the stars" (*Megillah* 16a).

Famous for his piety, he is the one meant when the Talmud speaks of "a happening with a pious man" (*Bava Kamma* 103b). (Some say the man referred to is R' Yehudah ben Bava.) He suffered poverty with grace; for a period of time he and his wife shared one coat. When Rabban Shimon ben Gamliel became aware of his circumstances, he sent him a coat, which R' Yehudah refused to accept (*Nedarim* 49b).

The Sages cited the phrase *a God-fearing woman, she is praiseworthy* (*Proverbs* 31:30) as referring to the generation of R' Yehudah bar Ila'i, when six impoverished Torah scholars would cover themselves with only one cloak and study Torah, an unprecedented level of dedication (*Sanhedrin* 20a).

His disciples included R' Elazar son of R' Shimon (*Sotah* 34a), R' Yishmael son of R' Yose (*Succah* 18a), and R' Yehudah *HaNasi* (*Shevuos* 13a). His son, R' Yose bar Yehudah, was a prominent personality in the Academy of R' Yehudah *HaNasi.*

הֱוֵי זָהִיר בְּתַלְמוּד — *Be meticulous in study.* Addressing himself to Torah students, R' Yehudah teaches that one must carefully analyze what he learns to be sure that he fully understands the ideas and their halachic ramifications (*Rashi, Rav*). According to *R' Yonah,* this is a call for constant review. Since forgetfulness tends to make issues unclear, one should not rely on his initial understanding. Instead, he should review his studies until they are perfectly clear to him.

Meiri views this mishnah as directed particularly toward those whose intellectual bent leads them to *horaah,* the practical application of halachah. One who assumes responsibility for ruling on questions of halachah must understand the law with pristine clarity, and should have almost instant recall of the relevant sources. Only if his knowledge is carefully

[יז] רַבִּי שִׁמְעוֹן אוֹמֵר: שְׁלשָׁה כְתָרִים הֵם: כֶּתֶר תּוֹרָה,

organized in his memory will the appropriate section of the law be accessible to him, so that he will be able to rule correctly.

Midrash Shmuel and *Tiferes Yisrael* have a version which reads, הֱוֵי זָהִיר בְּתַלְמִיד, *Be meticulous with a student.* A teacher must be careful to convey his lessons in a fashion that allows no room for his students to misunderstand him.

שֶׁשִּׁגְגַת תַּלְמוּד עוֹלָה זָדוֹן — *for a careless misinterpretation is considered tantamount to willful transgression.* If one errs in his understanding and application of Torah laws because of carelessness, his offense is not pardonable as an unwitting error. One who studies superficially is bound to make mistakes for which he has only himself to blame. He will be punished as if he deliberately transgressed, since he should have studied carefully but did not (*Rashi, Rav, Machzor Vitry*). [A misinterpretation of Torah principles is judged so harshly only if it was due to the student's failure to apply himself according to his ability. An

earnest mistake is regarded as an unintentional error.]

Since error is common among human beings, one must take this to heart and take precaution by reviewing what he has learned. Anyone who does not do so and sins because of incomplete study is regarded as "negligent bordering on willful" (פּוֹשֵׁעַ קָרוֹב לְמֵזִיד), since he could have avoided the sin (*R' Yonah*). One who issues halachic decisions has a great responsibility not to be a stumbling block for his fellow man. If he wants to rule for others, he must toil at his studies until they are carefully organized in his mind. Anything less is considered willful sin (*Meiri*).

According to *Tiferes Yisrael* and *Midrash Shmuel*, the inadvertent sin of a student is considered a willful transgression on the part of the teacher if it resulted from a lack of clarity in the teacher's lessons. Alternatively, one must be careful in his understanding even when he is engaged only in theoretical study, for ideas once entertained often become engraved in one's thought processes and

⊷§ **Exemplary unselfishness.** *Margaliyos HaYam* (ibid.) suggests that the students of R' Yehudah bar Ila'i achieved such a level of dedication to Torah study because they had role models like their teacher and his wife. Having seen R' Yehudah and his wife sharing one coat (see *Nedarim* 49b), they took the example to heart and shared one coat among six people. The generation was compared to a God-fearing woman, for it was indeed from the God-fearing wife of R' Yehudah that its scholars learned true dedication to God and His Torah.

R' Chaim Shmulevitz sees in the Talmud's exceptional praise of R' Yehudah's generation an indication that self-sacrifice and concern for others is the key to success in Torah. The Jewish people's level of internalization of the Torah is in direct proportion to the harmony among them — the extent to which they are בְּלֵב אֶחָד כְּאִישׁ אֶחָד, *with one heart, like one* man (see *Rashi* to *Exodus* 19:3). "Let us ask ourselves: If six people cover themselves with one blanket, can any one of them stay warm? The answer is that if each one pulls the blanket to himself, no one will be covered. But if each one pushes the blanket to his fellow, to ensure that his friend is sufficiently covered, then all six of them will be warm.

"The Sages sought to emphasize that it is this single-minded devotion to the welfare of one's fellow, the true בְּלֵב אֶחָד, that resulted in a generation singular in its scholarly attainments. The generation of Moshe stood at Sinai and witnessed Divine Revelation; yet this was false charm relative to the later generation. Chizkiyahu imbued Israel with a spirit of scholarship so powerful that every man and child knew the most difficult laws of ritual purity; this, too, comparatively speaking, was but empty beauty. It was R' Yehudah's disciples, who lived with such deep-seated unity and cared so much for each other, who were singled out as the God-fearing generation which alone is praiseworthy.

"It was their בְּלֵב אֶחָד that enabled them to receive Torah at its highest level."

may be applied later. One cannot justify imprecision in study by claiming that it has no consequences, since in the realm of the practical it will indeed cause sin.

Taam Zekeinim elaborates: One should never fantasize

that ignorance is bliss, and that not studying serves as a legitimate excuse for his shortcomings. The mishnah teaches that "inadvertent" sin due to ignorance actually places one in double jeopardy, for he is liable not only for his lack of study, but for the sin itself.

Mishnah 17

רַבִּי שִׁמְעוֹן אוֹמֵר — *Rabbi Shimon said.* See 3:4 for biographical details about R' Shimon bar Yochai.

שְׁלשָׁה כְתָרִים הֵם — *There are three crowns.* One must honor the three crowns of Torah, priesthood, and kingship by showing respect to those who wear them (*Rav*). According to *R' Yonah* et al., this refers to the three types of elevated status which Jews may achieve. *Rambam* adds that these three crowns were given to the Jewish people at Mount Sinai.

Rashi notes that the three crowns do not indicate the same degree of greatness. One who is not a descendent of Aaron cannot aspire to *Kehunah*

(priesthood), nor can anyone but a member of the Davidic house legitimately seek to be a king. However, the crown of Torah is the greatest, since it is open to anyone who is ready to toil for it.

Even though one could count the items enumerated in the mishnah, the number three is spelled out so that one not make the mistake that a good name is a fourth crown in the same category as the others. That crown is in a class by itself (*R' Moshe Alshakar*).

כֶּתֶר תּוֹרָה — *The crown of Torah. Rav* cites the verse *you shall honor the presence of a sage* (*Leviticus* 19:32) as indicating that one must honor scholars, who bear the crown of Torah.

◆§ **Extra care.** *Mattisyahu HaYitzhari* interprets mishnah 16 as a warning to Torah scholars to recognize that people scrutinize their actions and learn from them. Torah scholars must therefore take extra precaution to do nothing, even inadvertently, from which the masses can learn wrongly. While a scholar's personal transgression may be accidental, he bears full blame for the transgressions which others have learned from him.

Bris Avraham sees this thought homiletically mirrored in the verse *If the anointed Kohen will sin, bringing guilt upon the people* (*Leviticus* 4:3): *When the anointed Kohen,* who is a representative of the learned class, *will sin* even inadvertently, the masses will learn from his way and transgress willfully. Thus the misdeeds of the scholars may bring guilt upon the people.

◆§ **Priorities.** *Abarbanel* explains the order in which the mishnah lists the three crowns. The crowns of Torah and priesthood were both given at Sinai, but the crown of Torah takes precedence because it includes the two categories of observance: the commandments between God and man [בֵּין אָדָם לַמָּקוֹם] and those between man and man [בֵּין אָדָם לַחֲבֵרוֹ]. The crown of priesthood is listed next, since the Kohanim, through the Temple service, are intermediaries between man and God. The crown of kingship is mentioned last because the monarchy was to be established only after the Jewish people entered the Land (see *Deuteronomy* 17:15).

Chelek Yaakov suggests that the mishnah speaks of these three crowns in order to comfort Jews during the long night of exile. The crown of Torah is symbolic of the promise that Torah knowledge will always be present in the Jewish nation, as God said: *My spirit that is upon you, and My words that I have placed in your mouth shall not be withdrawn from your mouth, nor from the mouths of your offspring, nor from the mouths of your offspring's offspring* (*Isaiah* 59:21). This truth is clearly evident in the post-Holocaust renaissance of Torah study and practice. The crown of *Kehunah* reminds us that the priesthood will return to the rebuilt Temple in times to come; and the crown of kingship alludes to the reestablishment of the Davidic dynasty with the arrival of the Messiah.

Rambam defines the all-encompassing and exclusive commitment to Torah study necessary for one to merit the "crown of Torah": "One whose heart has elevated him to fulfill properly the command to study Torah and to want to be crowned with the crown of Torah, let him not shift his focus to any other pursuits. Let him not entertain the thought that he can acquire Torah along with wealth and honor" (*Hilchos Talmud Torah* 3:6). He also states: "One who wants to merit the crown of Torah should not lose even one of his nights to sleep, food, drink, idle talk, or the like; [he should] be involved only in Torah study and wisdom" (ibid. 3:13).

Tiferes Yisrael defines the crown of Torah as the assumption of a position as a rabbinic judge, communal rabbi, or Torah teacher.

וְכֶתֶר כְּהֻנָה — *the crown of priesthood.* Priesthood carries certain privileges. These include the right to be the first to address an assemblage, the right to recite the blessing first at a meal [be it the blessing on the bread in the absence of the master of the house (see *Rema, Orach Chaim* 167:14) or the right to lead the Grace After Meals (see *Orach Chaim* 201:2)], and the right to read first from the Torah scroll in the synagogue. These privileges are derived from the Biblical verse *You shall sanctify [the Kohen], for he offers the food of your God; he shall be holy to you* (*Leviticus* 21:8). This last phrase teaches that the Kohen's sanctity places him first in every respect, not only in matters of ritual [see *Gittin* 59b] (*Rav*).

וְכֶתֶר מַלְכוּת — *and the crown of kingship.* The Torah teaches, *You shall surely set over yourself a king, whom HASHEM your God shall choose* (*Deuteronomy* 17:15). The Sages (*Kesubos* 17a) interpret this to mean that the nation must fear and revere its king. In speaking of two of the most tragic incidents that occurred after Israel arrived in the Holy Land — the graven image of Micah (*Judges* ch. 17-18) and the

atrocity of the concubine at Gibeah (ibid. ch. 19-21) — Scripture states that they were possible only because there was no king in Israel (ibid. 18:1, 19:1); a righteous king who provided leadership and discipline would never have permitted such outrages to take place.

Rambam (2:1-6) delineates the prohibitions associated with reverence for a king: "One may not ride on his horse, sit on his throne, or make use of his royal scepter, crown, or any of his clothes. Upon his death they are all burned in the presence of his corpse" [see *Rambam*, ibid., for more details].

The Midrash (*Shemos Rabbah* 34) relates in the name of R' Shimon bar Yochai (the R' Shimon of our mishnah) that these three crowns are representative of the three golden tiaras found in the Tabernacle and later in the Temple. The crown of kingdom is embodied in the tiara on the *Shulchan* (Table), for the Jewish people's wealth and power emanated from there [see *Exodus* 25:24, *Rashi* and *Ramban* ad loc.]; just as it is the king's responsibility to insure the safety and prosperity of his country, so the Jewish people enjoyed prosperity because of the merit of the Table.

The crown of the Altar was symbolic of the crown of priesthood, for on the Altar the priests brought offerings to God from His children.

Rashi, however, sees the Altar as representing the crown of kingship since all Jews must depend on the Altar for forgiveness of their sins just as a king's subjects depend on him for all their needs. The crown of priesthood is instead symbolized by the Table, on which rests the showbread (לֶחֶם הַפָּנִים) that may only be eaten by *Kohanim*. [See, however, *Yoma* 72b.]

The third tiara was found around the Holy Ark, repository of the Torah and Tablets of Law, and it corresponds to the crown of Torah. *Rambam* adds that the crown of Torah is the greatest of the three since the

---

◆§ **Conduit of prosperity.** *Ramban* explains the process of this miracle of prosperity. He writes that from the time God brought the universe into existence from a vacuum, He has not created anything from absolute nothingness. Instead, when He wishes to bring about a miraculous increase, He causes it to flow from something that is already in existence. We find this in the case of the prophet Elisha, who caused a single jug of oil to produce an unceasing flow for as long as there were empty jugs to be filled (*I Kings* 17:16). So it was with the Table; by virtue of the bread that was placed on it weekly, prosperity flowed to the entire nation. In another more immediate manifestation of this miracle, the Talmud teaches that a Kohen who ate even a tiny piece of the previous week's showbread from the Table would be fully satisfied. In the expression of the Sages, it "became blessed in his innards" (*Yoma* 39a).

other two are dependent on it. *R' Yonah* sees an allusion to this primacy of Torah in the fact that while the Altar and Table were placed outside the Holy of Holies (קֹדֶשׁ הַקֳּדָשִׁים), the Ark was placed inside.

The Talmud captures this idea with the observation that while a king or a Kohen Gadol who dies is replaceable, a Torah scholar is an irreplaceable loss (*Horayos* 13a).

The Talmud (*Horayos* 13a) teaches that the honor of a Torah scholar of impure lineage takes precedence to that of an ignorant Kohen Gadol, an example of the Torah's fundamental importance in Jewish life. All high posts, including the priesthood and kingship, are effective only when governed by the objective standards of rightness and fairness promulgated in the laws and spirit of the Torah.

These three crowns correspond to the three things on which the world stands: Torah, the Temple service, and acts of kindness (see 1:2). The Torah corresponds to the crown of Torah; the Temple service corresponds to the crown of priesthood; acts of kindness correspond to the crown of royalty, because wealth (here symbolized by royalty) enables one to be generous to others. It also refers to the kings of Israel themselves, who were characterized by kindness (*Magen Avos*).

וְכֶתֶר שֵׁם טוֹב עוֹלֶה עַל גַּבֵּיהֶן — *but the crown of a good name surpasses all of them.* This crown adorns someone whose deeds earn him the respect and affection of his fellows. Even scholars, priests, and kings are lacking if they fail to earn this crown (*Rav*).

The crown of a good name is superior even to the crown of Torah, for if a scholar behaves in an uncouth manner, he causes people to despise him, as the Talmud (*Moed Katan* 17a) teaches: "If a teacher is like an angel of the Lord of Hosts, then seek Torah from his mouth; but if his relationship with human beings is bad, he is guilty of profaning the Name of God, and if he is guilty of misconduct, he is worse than an ignorant boor.

The crown of a good name is also superior to the crown of kingship. The Sages of the Talmud (*Bava Basra* 4a) taught: It is written, *You shall not curse a leader among your people* (*Exodus* 22:27); it is forbidden to curse him only if he is *among your people*, i.e., when he acts as a proper Jew . . . The righteous kings of Israel were praised only for doing God's will; the wicked ones were disgraced only for doing what He considers evil.

Finally, the crown of a good name is also superior to the crown of priesthood. We are told in the Talmud (*Yoma* 71b) that a certain Kohen Gadol had insulted the sages Shemayah and Avtalyon because they were descendants of proselytes. They retorted: "Let welcome be extended to descendants of heathens who act the way Aaron acted, and let there be no welcome to descendants of Aaron who do not act as Aaron acted" (*Magen Avos, Rav*).

All the crowns require the crown of a good name along with them, and a good name is dependent upon the crown of Torah. For what gives man a good name if not the study of the Torah and the practice of its commandments? (*R' Yonah, Rambam*). If one does not acquire a good name, everybody despises him; thus, whatever crown he may have had is useless (*Machzor Vitry*).

Bigdei Meshi offers an enlightening insight. The first three crowns are gifts. Wisdom and intelligence are God given; priesthood is a familial inheritance. Even the wealth associated with kingship is the result of a Heavenly decree. It is only a good name which man earns for himself, through his good deeds and pleasant personality, that is truly his. For this reason it is greater than all other crowns.

◆§ **Power of a good name.** R' Shimon bar Yochai himself stated in the Midrash: "A good name is more precious than the Holy Ark. While the Holy Ark went only three days' distance before the Israelites in the Wilderness, a man's good name precedes him all over the world" (*Koheles Rabbah* 7:3).

◆§ **Legitimately yours.** *Alshich* homiletically explains the words of *Jeremiah* (9:22-23) in this vein: "Let not the wise man laud himself with his wisdom and let not the strong man laud himself with his strength and let not the rich man laud himself with his wealth. Only with this may one laud himself — discernment in knowing Me, for I am God Who does kindness, justice and righteousness in the land, for in these is My desire." Man may not laud himself for his wisdom, strength or wealth for these are gifts with which God imbues him: *for in these I desired* to grant to man. Only for his fear of God and his following in the Godly path, areas where man is granted free choice so that he acquired them through his own efforts, does one have a right to be proud.

[יח] **רַבִּי** נְהוֹרַאי אוֹמֵר: הֱוֵי גוֹלֶה לִמְקוֹם תּוֹרָה, וְאַל
תֹּאמַר שֶׁהִיא תָבוֹא אַחֲרֶיךָ, שֶׁחֲבֵרֶיךָ יְקַיְּמוּהָ
בְיָדֶךָ. וְאֶל בִּינָתְךָ אַל תִּשָּׁעֵן.

Mishnah 18

רַבִּי נְהוֹרַאי אוֹמֵר — *Rabbi Nehorai said.* Rabbi
Nehorai was a student of R' Yehoshua and R'
Tarfon, as evidenced by his quotations in their
names (see *Nazir* 5a, *Bereishis Rabbah* 91:9, etc.).
His exact identity is shrouded in mystery. Some
are of the opinion that R' Nehorai is R' Meir, others
say that he is really R' Nechemiah, and yet others
identify him as R' Elazar ben Arach (see *Rashi* here
and *Seder HaDoros,* s.v. רַבִּי נְהוֹרַאי). He was given
the name Nehorai, meaning *enlightened*, since he
enlightened the eyes of the Sages in their approach to halachic matters (*Eruvin* 13b; see *Maharsha* ad loc.). [It is noteworthy that the mishnah in
Nazir 9:5 mentions an argument that he had with
R' Yose bar Chalafta who lived many years after R'
Elazar ben Arach.]

הֱוֵי גוֹלֶה לִמְקוֹם תּוֹרָה — *Exile yourself to a place of
Torah.* If there are no Torah scholars, or none of
sufficient stature, in one's place, he should uproot
himself and move to a place where he will find

Torah mentors to teach and stimulate him (*Rav,
Rashi*). *Rambam* views this as a call to seek out a
place where many study so that one can find study
partners.

According to *Tiferes Yisrael,* even if ample
opportunity to study exists in a young person's
own place, he should still move away from home in
order to succeed. *Chasam Sofer* (*Responsa,
Choshen Mishpat* 9) mentions the son of R' Yehudah *HaNasi* as one who fulfilled this dictum. Even
though his father headed a great yeshivah, he was
sent to study under Rav and stayed with him for
twelve years.

In spite of the difficulty of parting from the
comforts of family, friends, and home, this is the
best way to insure success in one's studies, and in
life in general. Like a plant that flourishes only
after the gardener uproots and replants it, so a
person achieves success in character development
and Torah study only when he is removed from his
home town. Even if a move entails lowering one's

⸹ **Exiled elite.** The Chofetz Chaim took particular pleasure in the young men who came from America
to study in his yeshivah in the small hamlet of Radin. He would often declare passionately, "Master
of the Universe, look at Your children. A young man is ready to leave family, home, and the comforts
of America and suffer privation in order to learn Torah. He has yeshivos in his homeland, yet he feels
that he will grow more here. For whom does he do that? For You and Your holy Torah. For that reason
alone You should have mercy on Your people. In merit of the exile that these young scholars endure,
You should gather all Jews from their own bitter exile." With these words the Sage of Radin would burst
into tears.

⸹ **Reasons for change.** There are three reasons why such exile may be desirable: (a) One must abandon
the fun and games of his early years in order to ascend the ladder of achievement, and this is difficult
to do at home, where one is accustomed to the life-style of his youth. (b) In his parent's home, one always
remains a child. Parents often spoil children, albeit with good intentions, and do not allow them to grow
up. Leaving home opens the door to increased maturity and responsibility. [Furthermore, one is often a
prisoner of the image people have of him as a youth. Even when he is ready to shed the foolishness of
immaturity, it is often emotionally difficult to move beyond this impression. In new surroundings, where
one is unknown, one can more easily start afresh and build a new self.] (c) Mature people learn to act of
their own free will rather than waiting for the instruction of others. Away from the projection of the
parental home, one can develop the self-discipline and sense of internal direction from which greatness
is born (*Tiferes Yisrael*).

18. Rabbi Nehorai said: Exile yourself to a place of Torah — and do not assume that it will come after you — for it is your colleagues who will cause it to remain with you; *and do not rely on your own understanding (Proverbs 3:5).*

standard of living, it is worthwhile to trade temporary comforts for eternal reward (*Midrash Shmuel*).

וְאַל תֹּאמַר שֶׁהִיא תָבוֹא אַחֲרֶיךָ — *and do not assume that it will come after you.* One should never move to a place devoid of adequate Torah study or personalities on the assumption that a competent scholar will eventually move there (*Rav, Rashi*). This may never happen, and even if it does, every day spent outside a proper spiritual climate is time irretrievably lost (*Meiri*).

שֶׁחֲבֵרֶיךָ יְקַיְּמוּהָ בְּיָדֶךָ — *for it is your colleagues who will cause it to remain with you.* This rendering follows *Rav, Rashi*, and *Rambam* (second interpretation) and explains the beginning of the mishnah: One must leave home to live in a Torah environment, for it is only in the company of scholars that one can study Torah properly and succeed in resolving questions of halachah.

In addition, the Torah that a man studies with his companions is more firmly mastered than that which he studies on his own; colleagues challenge one another and try to find answers, and through such give-and-take a subject is thoroughly clarified (*Sefer HaMussar*).

R' Yonah, Rav, and *Rashi* translate this stich slightly differently, seeing it as another false assumption made by one who may not want to leave his home to study: One must not depend on his friends to report the teachings they learned from their teacher; he must chase after Torah and go to learn from the master himself. Hearing something secondhand from a student does not compare to learning directly from a teacher.

וְאֶל בִּינָתְךָ אַל תִּשָּׁעֵן — *"and do not rely on your own understanding"* (*Proverbs* 3:5). One must not think that he can succeed on his own without the help of a mentor, for no one can plumb the depths of Torah with his own intelligence exclusively. In addition, he must keep questioning his teacher until he fully understands. He should not assume that he will eventually comprehend the words of his mentor with his own understanding (*Rashi*).

A person must not say to himself, "It is enough for me to read books." From books one derives only what is written; but the men of learning will also tell him what they learned from their teachers, what they added to the tradition as a result of their own thinking, what they derived from books, and how they trained themselves in good conduct and correct thinking (*Midrash Shmuel*).

R' Yisrael Salanter is reputed to have commented: "Both the *chassidim* and their opponents erred. The *chassid* thinks since he has a *rebbe*, he does not need books. The *misnaged* is sure that since he has his books, he does not need a mentor."

According to *R' Yonah*, this advice follows the advice of the earlier part of the mishnah. One who goes off to study and becomes an accomplished

---

◄§ Source of life. Teaching is not merely the transmission of information; it entails a deep and personal connection between the teacher and student, by which the life force of the teacher is conveyed to his students through words and example. We are therefore taught to exile ourselves to a place of Torah to experience a soul-to-soul encounter with the words of the Living God, which only a teacher can provide (*Kozhnitzer Maggid*).

The obligation to teach Torah to students is derived from the verse *You shall teach them thoroughly to your children* (*Deuteronomy* 6:7), which indicates that students are called children in order to capture the essence of the teacher-student relationship. Strangers can provide children with many things in life, such as food and shelter, but only parents can provide *life itself*. Similarly, a true Torah teacher gives his students the most precious thing — spiritual life (*R' Yitzchak Hutner*).

scholar must be careful not to become intellectually arrogant. He should consult with wiser people about everything he plans to do, to be sure that it is in consonance with Torah values.

R' Moshe Alshakar connects the pieces of the mishnah in an interesting way. The Talmud (*Shabbos* 147b) relates that Rabbi Elazar ben Arach (see above, s.v. רַבִּי נְהוֹרַאי) visited the city of Diomsith in the Upper Galilee and was attracted to it despite the fact that it was not a place of learning. Subsequently, he forgot his learning and became an ignorant person. His former colleagues prayed for him, and his learning was restored. As a result of

this experience he said, "Move to a place where Torah is studied." He also advised, "Do not rely on the prayers of your colleagues to have your knowledge restored to you, as happened to me."

B'nayos B'Ramah offers a novel interpretation of our mishnah. Even though one who supports Torah scholars is promised a share in their reward, he still does not savor the incomparably enriching experience of learning Torah himself. He should therefore not be satisfied with the *reward* for Torah; instead, he should go into exile in *search* of Torah knowledge. He must not say, "The scholars whom I support will cause Torah to remain with me," for God gave him the intelligence to study on his own.

Mishnah 19

רַבִּי יַנַּאי אוֹמֵר — *Rabbi Yannai said.* Rabbi Yannai was the father of R' Dostai ben Yannai (see 3:10) and R' Elazar ben Yannai. Except for this citation, he is never quoted in the six Orders of Mishnah. *Tosefta* (*Sanhedrin* 2:5) quotes him as relating a law in the name of Rabban Shimon ben Gamliel, thus indicating that he was a fourth- or fifth-generation *Tanna*. R' Yannai lived in the terrible times of severe Roman persecution, which may explain the sense of despair that permeates this mishnah.

אֵין בְּיָדֵינוּ לֹא מִשַּׁלְוַת הָרְשָׁעִים וְאַף לֹא מִיִּסּוּרֵי הַצַּדִּיקִים — *It is not in our power to explain either the tranquility of the wicked or the suffering of the righteous.* The age-old question of why the wicked prosper while the righteous suffer is beyond the scope of human understanding. While we know that God has good reasons for allowing both, we, with our limited intelligence and view of only

minute parts of the total flow of life, cannot fathom them (*Rav, R' Yonah*).

Sometimes God pays the wicked for their few good deeds in this world and reserves their punishment for the World to Come. Similarly, the righteous are purged of their few sins here on earth so that they will receive only reward in the World of Eternity (*Rashi*).

The righteous, who uphold truth in this world, are rewarded in the eternal World of Truth, for it is only there that they can gain reward commensurate with their achievement. The wicked, however, who glorify temporal pleasures and whose good deeds ring hollow, do not aspire to the truth of the world to come, so they are recompensed in our fleeting world of falsehood (*Maharal, Yalkut Gershuni*).

Alternatively, *Rav* and *R' Yonah* explain that R' Yannai comes to assess the situation of Jews in the dark exile. Apparently, God does not consider

---

⏴§ **Keep buying.** The Chiddushei HaRim continued to travel to R' Mendel of Kotzk long after he had become famous in his own right as a towering scholar and saint. People asked him, "Why do you still feel a need for a mentor when you yourself could be a mentor to others?" He answered, "King Solomon teaches us in *Proverbs* (23:23): *Buy truth, do not sell.* As long as one still has someone from whom he can 'purchase' truth, he does well not to get involved in 'selling' (i.e., teaching) truth to others."

19. Rabbi Yannai said: It is not in our power to explain either the tranquility of the wicked or the suffering of the righteous.

us either totally wicked or fully righteous. We do not enjoy the tranquility He generally grants the wicked in this world in order to lock them out of the next; nor do we suffer the tribulations of the righteous (i.e., the type of travail that does not cause any suspension of Torah study). [Instead, such troubles seem to be meted out as punishment (*Machzor Vitry*).] *Midrash Shmuel* adds that R' Yannai means to help us strike a balance. On the one hand, we should realize that we are not irredeemably wicked; on the other hand, we should not be fooled into thinking that we have done all we must to advance ourselves spiritually.

Alternatively, the mishnah notes the combination of wisdom and compassion with which God maintains us in exile. Too much tranquility and comfort would lull us into spiritual apathy, or even worse, into the insubordination born of wealth. On the other hand, excessive trials and travails might be too much to bear. God therefore strikes a balance, giving us neither the tranquility of the wicked nor the suffering that only the extremely pious can bear (*Midrash Shmuel*).

If all the righteous were afflicted with suffering and all the wicked blessed with tranquility, we would be able to understand that it is a temporary condition that exists only in this world. The problem, however, is that we see exceptions; there are many righteous people who are blessed with material success and wicked people who live in misery and poverty. Hence, both success and suffering are beyond our understanding (*HaChassid Yaavetz*).

To determine the relationship between the visible fate of a man and his moral worthiness is utterly beyond our power. We do not have sufficient insight to determine a person's moral worth or to understand his motivations, and therefore we cannot know with certainty if what befalls him is a blessing or a calamity. The mishnah warns us that we should abstain from passing judgment in either case, and not permit our own short-sighted view of the events to influence our decisions (*R' S. R. Hirsch*).

◦§ **Sublimating prayer.** The Talmud (*Berachos* 7a) teaches that this question troubled even Moses, who asked God: "הוֹדִעֵנִי נָא אֶת דְּרָכֶךְ, *Make Your way known to me*" (*Exodus* 33:13). The Sages explain that he meant, "Please tell me the answer to the ancient question of צַדִּיק וְרַע לוֹ, רָשָׁע וְטוֹב לוֹ; why the righteous suffer and the wicked prosper in this world."

In the early 1900s, Rabbi Yisrael of Modzhitz underwent the amputation of a leg in a Berlin hospital. Instead of being anesthetized, which was then a new and unpolished technique, he asked the surgeon for a few extra minutes before the procedure. He began singing, becoming so enraptured that he felt little pain. During the operation, he composed the famous lengthy and beautiful musical composition known as *Ezkerah*, *I shall remember*.

Afterward, the surgeon said to R' Yisrael, "I told the government minister in the next room to learn from you. He screams uncontrollably from pain, while you are tranquil and are able to sing."

R' Yisrael replied, "Sir, you are mistaken. I also am in pain; but I take my pain and translate it into prayer, and then my suffering is turned into tranquility." The true *tzaddik* takes pain and transforms it into prayer.

◦§ **Accepting judgment.** The Chiddushei HaRim lost all thirteen of his children during his lifetime. When one of his daughters was near death, he was overheard saying, "When Heaven slaps a person in the face, he should pause for a moment to contemplate what lesson God is trying to teach him."

When the last of the thirteen died, the *rebbetzin* broke down. Her husband said, "God in his mercy has allowed us to be a source of comfort for others. Whenever a parent suffers the heartbreak of the loss of a child, people will say, 'Look at Yitzchok Meir and his wife. They lost thirteen good and beautiful children. Have you suffered nearly as much?' "

[כ] **רַבִּי** מַתְיָא בֶּן חָרָשׁ אוֹמֵר: הֱוֵי מַקְדִּים בִּשְׁלוֹם כָּל אָדָם, וֶהֱוֵי זָנָב לָאֲרָיוֹת, וְאַל תְּהִי רֹאשׁ לַשׁוּעָלִים.

[כא] **רַבִּי** יַעֲקֹב אוֹמֵר: הָעוֹלָם הַזֶּה דּוֹמֶה לִפְרוֹזְדוֹר

Mishnah 20

רַבִּי מַתְיָא בֶּן חָרָשׁ אוֹמֵר — *Rabbi Masya ben Charash said.* R' Masya lived during the third and fourth generation of *Tannaim.* He was a student of R' Eliezer ben Hyrkanus (see *Yoma* 12a) and R' Elazar ben Azariah (*Yerushalmi, Yoma* 8:7), and was a model of piety and fear of sin (see *Yalkut* 1:161).

Together with R' Yehudah ben Beseira and R' Chananiah, the nephew of R' Yehoshua, he founded a yeshivah in the Diaspora. Upon taking a tearful leave of the Land of Israel, he expressed his great love for it by saying, "Dwelling in the Land of Israel is equal to all of the *mitzvos*" (*Sifrei, Re'eh*). R' Masya's new home town was Rome, where he led a yeshivah and operated a court that was praised by the scholars of Israel (*Sanhedrin* 32b). When R' Shimon bar Yochai and R' Elazar ben R' Yose visited Rome, they answered many questions he posed to them, in halachic and Aggadic matters.

R' Masya was knowledgeable in medical science and emphasized the halachic principle that the Sabbath must be violated to save a life, even if it is doubtful that the potential victim's life is in danger (see *Yoma* 84a and *Yerushalmi, Yoma* 8:5). His delineation of the four categories of sinners and the steps they must take to receive Divine pardon (see *Yoma* 86a) are the basis for many of the laws of *teshuvah* (repentance).

הֱוֵי מַקְדִּים בִּשְׁלוֹם כָּל אָדָם — *Initiate a greeting to every person.* Every person, even non-Jews whom one meets on the street and people of lower social standing, should be greeted cordially (*Rav, Tiferes Yisrael*). The Talmud praises Rabban Yochanan ben Zakkai as one who never allowed anyone, even a non-Jew, to greet him first (*Berachos* 17a). One must not only love his fellow man, he must also make himself beloved to them. By initiating greetings, one elicits such love (*Meiri*).

Human dignity must be respected and honored in both word and deed. R' Akiva's 24,000 students died in a calamitous plague because they did not show each other the proper respect (see *Yevamos* 62b). Even enemies should be greeted (*Midrash Shmuel*). [Often their enmity is softened by the disarming expression of concern and respect that is conveyed by a greeting. Conversely, the snub of a failure to say hello or, much worse, to respond to a greeting, can cause animosity.] Thus, הֱוֵי מַקְדִּים might be rendered: *Take the initiative* בִּשְׁלוֹם in pursuing *peace* with all men. Don't wait for your antagonist to approach you; extend the branch of peace to him first. He will eventually respond in kind (*Pri Chaim*). *Toldos Yaakov Yosef* renders מַקְדִּים as *give precedence.* The peace and welfare of others should come before one's own comfort and well-being.

⋖§ **Greeting everyone.** A Monsey resident was surprised to be stopped one day by the mother superior of a convent down the block from Rabbi Yaakov Kamenetsky's home. She asked why the convent's Jewish neighbors averted their eyes or crossed to the other side of the street whenever one of the nuns passed by — except for the elderly rabbi, who always made a point of giving them a friendly greeting and a warm smile.

One should greet even a wicked person. Since he does not consider himself wicked, he will never understand why he is ignored, and will feel that he has been unfairly insulted (*Maharab*).

20. Rabbi Masya ben Charash said: Initiate a greeting to every person; and be a tail to lions, rather than a head to foxes.

21. Rabbi Yaakov said: This world is like a lobby before

וֶהֱוֵי זָנָב לַאֲרָיוֹת, וְאַל תְּהִי רֹאשׁ לְשׁוּעָלִים — *and be a tail to lions, rather than a head to foxes.* It is better to be a follower of the righteous [from whom one can learn] than to be a leader of common people (*Rashi, Machzor Vitry*). One should prefer to be the disciple of wiser people rather than the mentor of inferiors. The former will only benefit him, while the latter will be to his spiritual detriment (*Rambam*).

The organization of the Sanhedrin mirrored this idea. Its seating protocol reflected the intellectual hierarchy; the greater the sage, the closer he sat to the center. When a member died, everyone moved up a seat. The last seat, then empty, was filled by the highest-ranking member of a lower court. Thus, the new member, who was formerly a "head of foxes," now became a "tail of lions" (see *Sanhedrin* 37a). It is preferable to be the least distinguished member of an elite group than to be the most distinguished member of a lesser group.

Even though one who leads his inferiors stands to gain in prestige by comparison to them, it is still preferable for him to dwell among more illustrious people (*R' Shlomo Kluger*). The mishnah employs the metaphor of lions and foxes to allude to a lesson: One should be subservient to those who show strength in following God's word — symbolized by the king of beasts — even when he doesn't fully understand their actions. This is preferable to leading people who consider themselves to be sophisticated and shrewd — symbolized by foxes — who may be lacking in the qualities that are truly meaningful to a servant of God (*Mili d'Avos*).

Mishnah 21

רַבִּי יַעֲקֹב אוֹמֵר — *Rabbi Yaakov said.* See 3:9 for biographical details on Rabbi Yaakov.

הָעוֹלָם הַזֶּה דּוֹמֶה לִפְרוֹזְדוֹר בִּפְנֵי הָעוֹלָם הַבָּא — *This world is like a lobby before the World to Come.* The word פְּרוֹזְדוֹר is of Greek origin and refers to the vestibule immediately outside a king's chamber. *Rashi* renders it *portico. Bayis LeAvos* explains the analogy: One who stands in the king's waiting room is not concerned with mundane matters. Food and drink are meaningless to him; his only concern is whether he will be granted a royal audience and whether the king will be receptive to his requests. While waiting in the foyer, he repeats in his mind again and again the pleas he hopes will elicit the king's favor. Likewise, the only real agenda that should preoccupy man in this world is his eventual audience with the King.

The Talmud offers variations on the theme of this world as a preparatory stage for the next. "This world is like Friday, the next [world] like the Sabbath. Only he who prepares on Friday will eat on the Sabbath" (*Avodah Zarah* 3a). Only one who does good in this world will be able to enjoy the great reward of the World of Eternity.

The mishnah, furthermore, teaches a sense of perspective. Investing time and energy to beautify the portico while leaving the main chamber unadorned is senseless. Likewise, one who wastes his resources on the pleasures of this world and does not utilize them in order to purchase a respectable portion in the World to Come has a false perception of the meaning of life (*Likutei Basar Likutei*).

This world is like a vestibule. If one prepares properly here, then the World to Come is like a banquet hall. If not, the World to Come may be a very painful experience (*Hadar HaCarmel*). This is analogous to one who travels to a resort town. If he is headed there to enjoy a pleasure-filled vacation, then the destination is one of joy. However, if he is being sent there to be executed, then his trip is full

בִּפְנֵי הָעוֹלָם הַבָּא, הַתְקֵן עַצְמְךָ בַּפְרוֹזְדוֹר, כְּדֵי שֶׁתִּכָּנֵס
לַטְּרַקְלִין.

[כב] **הוּא** הָיָה אוֹמֵר: יָפָה שָׁעָה אַחַת בִּתְשׁוּבָה וּמַעֲשִׂים
טוֹבִים בָּעוֹלָם הַזֶּה מִכֹּל חַיֵּי הָעוֹלָם הַבָּא;

---

of pain and sorrow. This world is a vestibule; the final destination depends on man.

— **הַתְקֵן עַצְמְךָ בַּפְרוֹזְדוֹר, כְּדֵי שֶׁתִּכָּנֵס לַטְּרַקְלִין**, *prepare yourself in the lobby so that you may enter the banquet hall.* Before someone enters the inner chamber of an important person, he prepares

himself; so too, a man first prepare himself through repentance and good works, so that he may merit entrance into the World to Come (*Machzor Vitry*). One who waits in the antechamber must always be ready to enter the king's presence. He has no time to waste, and he must not delay getting dressed properly or grooming himself, for

---

◆§ **Seductive banquet.** Rabbi Pesach Pruskin illustrates this concept with a parable: Three people who saved the king's life were rewarded with permission to enter the royal treasury for one day and take whatever they wanted. The king's inner circle was jealous of the three rescuers and decided to stop them from enjoying their good fortune. On the appointed day, the courtiers gave a lavish party in honor of the three "heroes." With tables full of delicacies and wine, they were sure they could divert the attention of the three, if not induce them to drink themselves into a stupor.

On the day of the feast, the conspirators provided food, drink, and endless compliments about the heroism of the rescuers. The most intelligent of the three was not impressed. "Who needs their food and their accolades? It won't make me wealthy." Not wasting a minute, he left the banquet hall and hurried to the treasury, where he filled his sacks with gold, silver, and other precious items. By nightfall he had enough wealth to last a few lifetimes.

The second rescuer, not as perceptive as the first, was seduced by the great praise of his heroism and the succulent aroma of the feast. Surrounded by the king's officers and advisors, he enjoyed the royal banquet and forgot why he was in the palace. Suddenly, he remembered the king's offer! "The day is almost over, and I haven't taken any of the king's riches!" Excusing himself from the revelry, he rushed to the treasury. Working frantically, he was able to amass a respectable fortune before nightfall.

The third hero was totally blinded by the overtures of the royal circle. After a long day of eating, drinking, and merriment, he collapsed into a drunken slumber, exactly as the royal advisors had hoped. When he finally awoke, night had fallen and the opportunity had been squandered. He was forced to return home empty-handed.

Similarly, this is a world of opportunity. God gives us carte blanche to collect the most precious items in His treasury — Torah study and *mitzvos*. At the same time, the King's servant — man's Evil Inclination — stages a lavish party for him, full of food, drink, and all the other pleasures of this world, in order to make him forget why he is here, and to prevent him from partaking of the royal wealth.

An intelligent person is not blinded by the pleasures of this world; he remembers his purpose, and goes immediately to enrich himself spiritually. He knows the real honor will come in the next world. Others wake up only during mid-life; then, they repent the sins of their youth and make up for lost time, so that by the end of their lives they are able to amass a respectable fortune of spiritual accomplishments.

The unfortunate people in the last category, however, intoxicated by the heady wine of the good life, squander away their years. Excited by a false sense of self-importance, they place their hopes in the wisdom of those who honor them, and believe that the prestige they enjoy is authentic. They indulge mindlessly in the worldly banquet, and do not come to their senses until it is too late. They return to their Maker empty-handed.

the World to Come; prepare yourself in the lobby so that you may enter the banquet hall.

22. He used to say: Better one hour of repentance and good deeds in this world than the entire life of the World to Come;

the king may summon him at any moment. Likewise, man in this world must continually groom himself spiritually by the way he lives; he must be ready with *mitzvos* to enter the palace of the King (*Doresh LePerakim*).

Tiferes Yisrael renders כְּדֵי as *sufficiently*. Just as one needs sufficient fuel to reach his destination, so he must utilize his time and talents to earn enough merit to carry him to his spiritual destination.

Mishnah 22

הוּא הָיָה אוֹמֵר: יָפָה שָׁעָה אַחַת בִּתְשׁוּבָה וּמַעֲשִׂים טוֹבִים בָּעוֹלָם הַזֶּה מִכָּל חַיֵּי הָעוֹלָם הַבָּא — *He used to say: Better one hour of repentance and good deeds in this world than the entire life of the World to Come.* Only in this world can one perform *mitzvos* and earn Divine reward. In the next world, it is too late; there he cannot add to his spiritual fortune but only collect what he earned in life. "Today [i.e., this world] was made to perform the command-

ments, not tomorrow [i.e., the World to Come]" (see *Eruvin* 22a). In the World to Come, a person has only as much as he has prepared for himself during his earthly sojourn. Thus, one hour spent in repentance and good deeds is time that will yield spiritual profits. This is a much better opportunity than the entirety of the World to Come, where one can enjoy the profits of his previous labors but can earn nothing new (*Rav; Rashi*).

◆§ **The tourist.** Mrs. Necha Golding, whom Rabbi Aharon Kotler called the last real *tzaddekes*, was the host and supporter of many causes and great Torah leaders, among them the Chofetz Chaim. She wanted to meet him, so she decided to visit him in Radin. It was at that meeting that a famous exchange took place — an exchange which truly reflected our mishnah's description of this world as nothing more than a corridor.

After noting the sparse wooden benches in his home, Mrs. Golding offered to buy the Chofetz Chaim more comfortable furniture. He asked, "Where is your furniture?"

Answered Mrs. Golding, "At home. I'm only traveling through!"

"So am I," answered the Chofetz Chaim. "This is not my true home."

◆§ **Don't return empty-handed.** R' Moshe Leib of Sassov once returned from a long journey. His children met him at the door, and one of the youngest immediately asked him, "Tatte, what did you bring for me?" R' Moshe Leib had brought nothing. The disappointed child continued to implore him, "Tatte, what did you bring for us? When you return from a long trip, you must bring something back with you. You can't return empty-handed."

R' Moshe Leib fainted. When he regained consciousness, his wife said to him, "Just because you can't satisfy the children, it is no reason to be so distressed."

The *tzaddik* of Sassov replied, "I didn't faint because of that. When I heard what the children said, I began to think. When I return home to the next world after my long sojourn here, what will I answer when I'm asked what I brought back with me? The mere thought of 'coming home empty-handed' overcame me, and I fainted."

◆§ **According to the hardship.** Ben Hei Hei teaches (5:26) that man is rewarded for his good deeds in proportion to the effort he exerts and the difficulties he overcomes. R' Yechezkel of Kuzmir interpreted our mishnah in this spirit: Even one hour of repentance and good deeds performed in this world — when man is inundated with problems and temptations — is of greater value than an entire lifetime of serving God in the next world, which is done in a worriless atmosphere of Heavenly bliss.

[כג] **רַבִּי** שִׁמְעוֹן בֶּן אֶלְעָזָר אוֹמֵר: אַל תְּרַצֶּה אֶת חֲבֵרְךָ

King Solomon alluded to this truth in *Ecclesiastes* (9:10): *Whatever you are able to do with your might, do it. For there is neither doing nor reckoning nor knowledge nor wisdom in the grave where you are going.* Once a person leaves this world, he remains at the level of development he attained during his lifetime; he can proceed no further after death. Therefore, he must use his temporary stay in this world to accrue merits that will later stand him in good stead. Intelligent people understand this and devote most of their efforts to the search for spiritual enhancement, careful not to squander on material concerns any more time or talent than is absolutely necessary. Others waste their lives in the senseless pursuit of vanities, remaining as empty when they leave this world as they were when they entered it. Woe to those who mistake darkness for light, and in the process exchange light for darkness. The entire Book of *Ecclesiastes*, carefully read, comes to clarify this reality (*Rambam*).

People of depth and understanding appreciate the gift of life precisely because it is their only opportunity to plant seeds that will yield spiritual fruit (*R' Yosef ibn Nachmias*).

The mishnah may also refer to the opportunity to repent, which is available only in this world. Repentance comes to repair the spiritual damage inflicted on the soul of one who sins; good deeds lend new luster to the soul. Only in this world is such work possible (*Tiferes Yisrael*). Through great effort and a powerful commitment, one can attain great spiritual heights in a very short time. Elazar ben Durdayah was the prime example of such commitment, for after a lifetime of immorality, he repented in a moment of greatness. About him Rabbi said: "יֵשׁ קוֹנֶה עוֹלָמוֹ בְּשָׁעָה אַחַת, *There are those who acquire [their share in] the World to Come in one hour (i.e., in a moment)*" (see *Avodah Zarah* 10b). It is to this hour that our mishnah refers (*R' Yonah*).

וְיָפָה שָׁעָה אַחַת שֶׁל קוֹרַת רוּחַ בָּעוֹלָם הַבָּא מִכֹּל חַיֵּי הָעוֹלָם הַזֶּה — *and better is one hour of spiritual bliss in the World to Come than the entire life of this world.*

⋅⋅§ **Not for chicken.** Those who do not share the Torah's belief in a world of reward are hard pressed to justify the prolonging of life under terminal and debilitating conditions. This has brought about support for euthanasia. To a Jew, however, life is the opportunity to wear *tefillin* one more time or to do one more *mitzvah* for family or a friend; this attitude has given many a sick Jew the courage to fight for his life. Aharon Stern told his grandson shortly before his death: "If I can't pray anymore or do another *mitzvah*, what is it all worth? Do you think I want to live just to eat chicken?"

⋅⋅§ **A new person.** *Teshuvah* (repentance) is not merely a repair, as one would patch a worn fabric. *Teshuvah* means to be reborn, a totally new person. *Rambam* captures the essence of repentance when he teaches that one who repents should change his name, as an indication of his new identity: "I am someone else, not the one who did those (terrible) acts" (see *Rambam, Hilchos Teshuvah* 2:4). As the *Alter* of Slobodka put it, "תשובה איז נישט בעסער ווערין; ס"יז אנדערש ווערן, *Teshuvah* is not becoming better; *teshuvah* is becoming different."

A man once came to pour his heart out to R' Asher of Stolin. "I have committed the worst transgressions and long ago lost my portion in the World to Come. Even repentance won't help me. What should I do? I'm desperate."

The *Rebbe* replied: "Repent anyway. You will be a new and different person. This is what the mishnah in *Avos* means: *An hour of repentance and good deeds is more valuable than all of the World to Come.* Even if one will not regain his share in the World to Come, it is still worthwhile to repent."

and better is one hour of spiritual bliss in the World to Come than the entire life of this world.

23. R' Shimon ben Elazar said: Do not appease your fellow

True peace of mind is a rare commodity in this world, with its hardships and woes, but the World to Come offers serenity. One hour of spiritual bliss in the next world is worth more than anything this world can provide (*Rashi*).

The prophets left descriptions of the Messianic Age, but they found the World to Come beyond human comprehension. There is nothing comparable to it in this world; a moment of the tranquility of the World to Come is far superior to anything this world can offer, and it is beyond human powers of description. All the enjoyments of earthly existence pale into insignificance against the bliss in the Great Hereafter (*R' Yonah*).

R' Eliyahu Dessler (quoting *Rabbi Zvi Hirsch Broide* and *Rabbi Nochum Zev Ziv*) elaborates: "Imagine if one were able to compact all the hours of joy he experienced in his own lifetime, along with all the happiness of his friends and neighbors, into one moment. Can you fathom the utter ecstasy of that moment? Compound that moment with the total bliss of the lifetimes of all his contemporaries found any place on the globe, and imagine that someone will experience that intense joy. Is the sensation describable? Yet *all* the delight of *all* the generations of human history in the entire world, concentrated in *one solitary intoxicating moment*, still falls short of the spiritual bliss of the World to Come.

"What is spiritual bliss? It is a whiff. A destitute, ravenously hungry beggar passes the royal palace on the eve of a gala ball. Uninvited, he cannot partake of the sumptuous cuisine; he must make do with the delectable and teasing aroma that wafts out into the street. One who does not deserve a real and full taste of the bliss of the World to Come may be given a diminutive form of that joy — a fleeting whiff of its aroma. And yet that whiff is greater, more enjoyable, enduring, and meaningful than all the happiness of this world."

Mishnah 23

רַבִּי שִׁמְעוֹן בֶּן אֶלְעָזָר אוֹמֵר — *R' Shimon ben Elazar said.* This fifth-generation *Tanna* was a student of Rabbi Meir, and attributed his Torah knowledge to the fact that he faithfully tended to R' Meir's needs: "It was R' Meir's walking stick in my hand that enlightened me" (*Yerushalmi, Moed Kattan* 3:1). In addition to his many quotations of R' Meir in halachic matters (see *Shabbos* 154b and *Eruvin* 29a), he was famous as a prolific expositor of homiletics and *Aggadah.* He was also a contemporary and frequent halachic adversary of R' Yehudah HaNasi (see *Megillah* 30a, *Yevamos* 85a).

From the incident of Rechavam, son of King Solomon (see *I Kings* 12), R' Shimon inferred that one should seek advice from mature and experienced people who view things from a long-term perspective. "If the young advise you to build and the old suggest that you demolish, follow the counsel of the aged, not that of the young. The construction of the young is [in reality] destructive,

---

◆§ **Welcome reprieve.** A warrior loves war, for nowhere else can he taste the intoxicating wine of victory.

On the other hand, he pines for peace, because fear of defeat is never far from his mind. These dual emotions are no less true in the war of all wars — the lifelong battle of good and evil. One hour of repentance and good deeds provides the exhilarating taste of spiritual victory, which one can no longer taste once he is in the World to Come, yet a total reprieve for the battle weary comes only in the next world. *Better is one* [peaceful] *hour of spiritual bliss in the World to Come than the entire life* [of victory on the battlefield] *of this world (Maharam Schick).*

בִּשְׁעַת כַּעְסוֹ; וְאַל תְּנַחֲמֵהוּ בְּשָׁעָה שֶׁמֵּתוֹ מֻטָּל לְפָנָיו; וְאַל תִּשְׁאַל לוֹ בִּשְׁעַת נִדְרוֹ; וְאַל תִּשְׁתַּדֵּל לִרְאוֹתוֹ בִּשְׁעַת קַלְקָלָתוֹ.

---

while the destruction of the old is [in truth] constructive" (*Nedarim* 40a). Had Rechavam heeded the advice of the elders and followed a course of self-depreciation, he would have earned the loyalty of his subjects. Instead, he accepted the counsel of the young, who suggested that he make ever greater demands on his subjects. The approach backfired, resulting in rebellion.

An astute observer of human nature, R' Shimon suggested that one exercise a mixture of softness and severity in his dealings. "[Three things] one's sexual drive, children, and women should be kept at a distance [i.e., discouraged] with the left [weaker hand] and be brought close [i.e., encouraged] with the right [stronger hand]" (*Sotah* 47a). [This means that while one's passions must be controlled, it is counterproductive to crush them completely. Procreation would not be possible if passion were not given some reign (see *Yoma* 69b). Similarly, one must make demands of children; however, excessive pressure can cause terrible calamities. Likewise, women, who are sensitive by nature, will react adversely to inordinate tyrannical pressure (see *Rashi*, ad loc.).]

R' Shimon learned of the need to treat people sensitively from experience. He once met a very ugly person, and exclaimed, "Are all the people of your city so coarse?" The man answered, "I don't know; go ask the Craftsman Who made me." Chastened, R' Shimon begged the man's forgiveness. At first the man refused, but finally he relented, warning R' Shimon never to repeat such unkind behavior. After he was forgiven, the *Tanna* entered the study hall and taught, "A person should always be as soft [in interpersonal matters] as a reed and not hard as a cedar. It was for this

reason that the reed merited to be the writing tool for Torah scrolls, *tefillin*, and *mezuzos*" (see *Avos d'Rabbi Nosson* 41 and *Taanis* 20b-21a).

R' Shimon offers advice in this mishnah about speaking only at the proper moment and holding one's peace when appropriate. Timing is a key to improving interpersonal affairs (*Rambam*).

אַל תְּרַצֶּה אֶת חֲבֵרְךָ בִּשְׁעַת כַּעְסוֹ — *Do not appease your fellow at the time of his anger.* When approaching an angry person who is under strain, one should exercise utmost tact in order not to add fuel to the fire. It is useless to attempt to appease a person when he is in the heat of his anger, almost like seeking to extinguish a fire with kerosene. He is emotionally unable to accept pacifying words; at that moment, he is convinced that no one empathizes with him. Instead, he should be left alone to calm down (*Rashi, Machzor Vitry*).

R' Yonah emphasizes that an attempt at rapprochement at such a moment can be counterproductive, inflaming the victim's anger and causing him, out of pain, to respond inappropriately. This is derived from God's instruction to Moses when he came to plead on behalf of the Children of Israel after the catastrophic incident of the Golden Calf. *[God] said to him, "My Presence will go and provide you rest"* (Exodus 33:14). God told Moses: "Allow My stern countenance to pass, and then you may beseech on their behalf" (see *Berachos* 7a). This was an indication that in human relationships as well, one must allow the other person's anger to pass before approaching him. As the Talmud teaches, "Just as one is commanded to speak up when his words will be listened to, so it is

---

⌁§ **Punishment may backfire.** R' Yaakov Kamenetsky often cautioned parents and teachers to be careful when threatening children with punishment for infractions. "Remember that the fear of punishment may compel a child to lie. One may have to forgo punishing the child as a reward for being honest; otherwise, the child will feel pressured and will have no choice but to lie. A child who feels total disapproval from his parent or teacher can even be dangerous to himself."

at the time of his anger; do not console him while his dead lies before him; do not question him about his vow at the time he makes it; nor attempt to see him at the time of his degradation.

---

a *mitzvah* to remain silent when he will not be listened to" (*Yevamos* 65b).

According to *Beis Avos*, the mishnah is concerned with the reaction of the one who seeks to appease, not with that of the angry person, for one who is unsuccessful in appeasing his friend will become disgruntled, and not want to try again at a more opportune moment. Scorned once, he fears a second rejection.

וְאַל תְּנַחֲמֵהוּ בְּשָׁעָה שֶׁמֵּתוֹ מֻטָּל לְפָנָיו — *do not console him while his dead lies before him.* A mourner is inconsolable while his dead one lies before him; his loss is too immediate. Only later, when the deceased is no longer before him, can he be comforted (*Rashi, Machzor Vitry*). The mourner feels that the comforter does not really understand or fully empathize with his loss. This may evoke his anger and cause him to react inappropriately both toward the comforter and toward the True Judge (*R' Yonah, Midrash Shmuel*).

We are also taught that mourning and grief are beneficial and should not be interrupted or disturbed prematurely. In addition to their cathartic function, they also temper a person's arrogance. It is unwise to try to remove him from the mourning

state of mind before he is ready (*Lev Avos*). This is derived from God's response to the angel's attempt to "comfort" Him after the destruction of the Temple. He told them, "Don't rush to console Me" (*Rav*).

וְאַל תִּשְׁאַל לוֹ בִּשְׁעַת נִדְרוֹ — *do not question him about his vow at the time he makes it.* Rashi offers three explanations: (a) One should not question the circumstances under which another made a vow, in an attempt to find a disclaimer as a basis for nullification. Do not raise questions like, "Are these or those the terms of the vow?" In anger he may blurt out that the vow was made unconditionally, thus effectively ruining any possibility for annulment (see *Machzor Vitry, Rav, R' Yonah*). (b) When one vows to do a good deed, one must never demand that he fulfill it immediately. Such pressure may cause him to regret having vowed to do a good deed in the first place. (c) If one seeks to have a vow nullified, he should not request that another person who has also made a vow serve on the panel. The second person will be reminded of his own vow, and it will cause him pain to assist in the annulment.

According to *Rabbeinu Ephraim*, the mishnah's

◆§ **Ask, don't announce.** Rabbi Shlomo Freifeld remarked: "The same *mitzvah* to offer constructive criticism to others also demands silence when one's words will fall on deaf ears. Why? Because every rejection of criticism throws up a psychological barrier that makes it more difficult to help the person next time. The very *mitzvah* of reproof, which demands speaking out, sometimes demands silence; one must wait for the moment when his friend is emotionally able to hear him."

A student of Rabbi Freifeld once came to him excitedly to request permission to join the *Daf Yomi* study cycle. Rabbi Freifeld agreed. About half a year later, the young man found the program too demanding and decided to quit. When he informed his *rebbe* of his decision, he received a verbal tongue-lashing. "*Daf Yomi* is not for a yeshivah student your age. It will not allow you to maintain your other learning programs properly. I always felt it was a mistake for you." The student was hurt and said, "But I asked the *rebbe* before I started!"

Replied R' Freifeld, "Asked? You were so excited about your plan that it was impossible even to attempt to dissuade you. You didn't ask me, you *told* me. Only now that you have come to your senses are you ready to hear the truth."

◆§ **One at a time.** *Midrash Shmuel* extends this idea: One who solicits charity funds should avoid asking a donor to support a second cause after he has just pledged money to the first. The donor may feel inundated by requests and change his mind about his original commitment. *Do not ask him* [to support another cause] *at the time of his* [initial] *vow.*

[כד] **שְׁמוּאֵל** הַקָּטָן אוֹמֵר: "בִּנְפֹל אוֹיִבְךָ אַל תִּשְׂמָח,
וּבִכָּשְׁלוֹ אַל יָגֵל לִבֶּךָ. פֶּן יִרְאֶה יהוה וְרַע
בְּעֵינָיו, וְהֵשִׁיב מֵעָלָיו אַפּוֹ".

---

teaching is somewhat different: If one has severed ties with a friend by means of a vow, the friend should not request resumption of the relationship immediately. It is best to wait a while until the one who took the vow calms down before seeking a reconciliation.

וְאַל תִּשְׁתַּדֵּל לִרְאוֹתוֹ בִּשְׁעַת קַלְקָלָתוֹ — *nor attempt to see him at the time of his degradation.* People should be accorded the privilege of maintaining a positive public persona. In a moment of weakness, when one has sinned or harmed someone, he is overcome with shame. The company of his friends is no solace at such a time; on the contrary, it only increases his embarrassment (*Rashi, Rav, Tiferes Yisrael, R' Yonah*). The principle is derived from the way in which God confronted Adam and Eve after they sinned. He first provided them with clothes to minimize their shame, and only then did He address their misdeed (*Rav*).

Maharam Schick views this clause as guidance in the art of constructive criticism. At the time when one sins, the heat of his passion creates a psychological barrier to any corrective criticism. Of such a time, the Talmud suggests, "It is a *mitzvah* not to utter words of rebuke that will not be heard" (*Yevamos* 65b). One should therefore not attempt to see a person in his hour of iniquity.

The expression *do not attempt* teaches that when one encounters difficulty in approaching a friend who has sinned, he should realize that his friend might prefer not to see him and is avoiding him purposely (*Avos al Banim*).

Sefer HaMussar extends the scope of this dictum. There are times of personal distress when friends should leave a victim alone. At the moment of calamity, one's pain is compounded when others witness his suffering, and his situation is only aggravated by shame.

Mishnah 24

שְׁמוּאֵל הַקָּטָן אוֹמֵר — *Shmuel HaKattan said:* A second-generation *Tanna*, Shmuel was called *HaKattan* (the Small) either because of his humility or as an indication that he was not of the same spiritual stature as the great prophet Samuel (*Yerushalmi, Sotah* 9:13). Infrequently quoted in Aggadic matters and never cited in halachah, he nevertheless captured the hearts and minds of the Jewish people because of his upstanding behavior and warm demeanor.

An incident that demonstrated his sensitivity occurred when Rabban Gamliel summoned seven great scholars and members of the Sanhedrin to a secret location in order to proclaim an official leap year. Eight people, however, arrived at the scene. When Rabban Gamliel requested that the uninvited individual leave, Shmuel *HaKattan* arose and said, "I am the one who came uninvited. I did not come to participate, but rather to observe the process firsthand." R' Gamliel asked him to remain, stating,

---

✒ **Without undue delay.** On the other hand, to allow grievances to fester is also very dangerous. Strife has a way of multiplying far beyond the proportions of its origin. Rabbi Nisson Alpert explained that the term שִׂנְאַת חִנָּם, does not necessarily mean *causeless hatred*, as it is usually translated, since animosity is often precipitated by very real and justifiable factors. Instead, שִׂנְאַת חִנָּם is the *extra* hatred caused by allowing the animosity to rankle. When the parties discuss the point of contention soon, the problem can often be resolved; if instead they keep their feelings pent up inside, the anger only grows and becomes more intense. This extra enmity exists for no good reason — it is חִנָּם, *without cause.*

24. Shmuel *HaKattan* said: *When your enemy falls do not be glad, and when he stumbles let your heart not be joyous, lest HASHEM see and it displease Him, and He turn His wrath from him [to you] (Proverbs 24:17-18).*

"You are fit to be involved in the process; however, the Sages have stated that only those who are designated may take part." The Talmud says that in truth, it was someone else who came uninvited; Shmuel *HaKattan* made his "admission" only to save the intruder from embarrassment.

At the request of Rabban Gamliel, Shmuel *HaKattan* composed the text for the twelfth blessing of the weekday *Amidah*. This blessing, known as *Bircas HaMinim* (וְלַמַּלְשִׁינִים), was directed at the early Christians who had begun to flourish at the time and who campaigned to enlist Roman persecution of traditional Judaism. Shmuel *HaKattan* was chosen because he was free of any *personal* animosity toward these heretics, and was therefore best qualified for the task of creating a prayer for the destruction of heretics and slanderers (*Berachos* 28b).

A Heavenly voice testified to his greatness, saying, "There is a person among you who deserves to have the Divine Presence rest upon him, but the generation is not worthy of it." All the Sages turned to Shmuel *HaKattan*, certain that he was the one. Before his death, he predicted the brutal death of many of the *Tannaim*. This "prophecy" came true, justifying the Heavenly proclamation that he was indeed deserving of the *Shechinah*. [In this way he was similar to Samuel the Prophet, his namesake (see *Tosafos Yom Tov*).]

Beloved in his lifetime, he was eulogized by the nation upon his death as a saint and a model of true humility (see *Sanhedrin* 11a). To his bier, they attached his keys and notebook, symbolizing the closing of an era and the loss of someone irreplaceable. He died childless, and R' Gamliel and R' Elazar ben Azariah expressed the national sentiment by saying: "Over this one it is fitting to cry and mourn. When kings die, they leave their crowns to their children; the wealthy leave their money to their heirs. Shmuel *HaKattan* took all the desirable things of this world along with him" (*Maseches Semachos* 8).

בִּנְפֹל אוֹיִבְךָ אַל תִּשְׂמָח, וּבְכָּשְׁלוֹ אַל יָגֵל לִבֶּךָ. פֶּן יִרְאֶה ה׳ וְרַע בְּעֵינָיו, וְהֵשִׁיב מֵעָלָיו אַפּוֹ — "When your enemy falls do not be glad, and when he stumbles let your heart not be joyous, lest HASHEM see and it displease Him, and He turn His wrath from him [to you]" (Proverbs 24:17-18). The entire dictum is a quotation from the *Book of Proverbs*. Shmuel *HaKattan* adopted it as his motto (*Rashi*) and apparently was in the habit of quoting it when he admonished people against taking delight in the misfortune of others (*Rav, Meiri* et al.).

He apparently felt it necessary to emphasize this lesson of King Solomon since the masses do indeed rejoice at the failures of their foes. Even if one's enemy is wicked, it is improper to rejoice

§ **Self-respect.** This is true in all humiliating circumstances, not only in moments of moral weakness.

When the Boyaner *Rebbe*, R' Mordechai Shlomo Friedman, was hospitalized, he was visited by the Satmar *Rebbe*, who was accompanied by a large entourage. The *gabbai* (personal attendant) of the Boyaner *Rebbe* asked the Satmar *Rebbe* to wait in the hall until the patient was ready to receive him. They waited ten minutes, twenty minutes. . . and still were not allowed into the room. The Satmar *Rebbe's* followers were distressed at what they took to be disrespect.

Finally, after half an hour, the *Rebbe* was allowed to enter. The Boyaner *Rebbe* was sitting in a chair, fully dressed in his rabbinical garb, hat, and tie. "Satmar *Rebbe*," the Boyaner addressed him, "excuse me for keeping you waiting. As you know, we are descendants of the royal *Rebbes* of Rizhin. Out of respect to them, I could not allow you to see me in my pajamas."

Royalty is a state of mind. A person must be allowed to maintain his royalty even under the most demeaning conditions.

[כה] **אֱלִישָׁע** בֶּן אֲבוּיָה אוֹמֵר: הַלּוֹמֵד יֶלֶד, לְמָה הוּא דוֹמֶה? לִדְיוֹ כְתוּבָה עַל נְיָר חָדָשׁ. וְהַלּוֹמֵד

---

over his downfall; only if one's joy is *totally* rooted in the vindication of God's honor may he indulge in a sense of elation. Furthermore, such a feeling is permitted only for the righteous, whose personal behavior upholds God's honor. One who does not maintain a higher spiritual standard than his adversary, however, is not permitted to rejoice over the other's difficulties (*R' Yonah, Tiferes Yisrael*).

HaChassid Yaavetz offers a different and fascinating perspective. Since God rebukes and punishes only those whom He loves, one must conclude that God, in a certain sense, loves his enemy. Therefore, if one rejoices over his enemy's "misfortune," God will take up the enemy's cause by taking revenge for the extra pain he suffers, redirecting it toward the one who rejoiced.

Mishnah 25

אֱלִישָׁע בֶּן אֲבוּיָה אוֹמֵר — *Elisha ben Avuyah said.* This third-generation *Tanna* became a heretic, and from that time on, he was known in the Talmud as *Acher* (the Other One).

By his own account, his father decided at his circumcision to consecrate him to a life of Torah study. "My father was a wealthy man, and he invited all the sages of Jerusalem, including R' Eliezer and R' Yehoshua, to my circumcision. After the meal, the singing and dancing began. R' Eliezer and R' Yehoshua sat on the side and discussed Torah topics. They went from the Bible to the Prophets to the Writings. Their words and

demeanor evoked the same sort of joy as there was at Mount Sinai when the Torah was given. A flaming fire surrounded R' Eliezer and R' Yehoshua. When my father saw this, he said, 'If this is the great power of Torah, I will have this son dedicate his life to it.' Since his intent in doing so was not purely for the sake of Heaven, but only because of his jealousy of R' Eliezer and R' Yehoshua's honor, my Torah was not sustained [and I became a heretic]" (*Yerushalmi, Chagigah* 2:1).

The incident that precipitated his apostasy is described in *Yerushalmi* (ibid.): "Once he was

---

◆§ **The only candidate.** Sometimes it is necessary to perform an unpleasant task directed against another individual. In such a case, one is not permitted to derive any pleasure from the act, or to delight in the other person's discomfort. The Mishnah (*Yoma* 18b) relates, for example, that due to the prevalence of heretics occupying the office of Kohen Gadol in the Second Temple, it became necessary for the Sanhedrin to administer an oath to the occupant that he not conduct the Yom Kippur ritual according to the heretical Saducean version, but rather according to the Torah tradition. After the administration of the oath, both the Kohen Gadol and the Sanhedrin would retire to their chambers and weep. The Kohen Gadol would weep in shame that he had been suspected of such a heinous crime; the members of the Sanhedrin, who had no choice but to administer the oath, would weep out of remorse for having suspected an upstanding person of heresy.

Similarly, it was Shmuel *HaKattan*, free of any sense of personal vendetta, who was the proper person to establish a text for the blessing against heretics. Motivated only by the desire to establish God's will in the world, his intentions would give the greatest authority and public acceptability to such a blessing.

This attitude toward the wicked is also reflected in the rebuke Beruriah offered her husband, R' Meir, who sought to pray for the death of wicked neighbors, who made his life unbearable. "King David calls for the end of *sin* from the earth," she said, "not for the destruction of the *sinners* (see *Psalms* 104:35). Pray that they repent" (see *Berachos* 10a).

25. Elisha ben Avuyah said: One who studies [Torah] while [he is still] a child, to what can he be likened? — to ink written on fresh [clean] paper. And one who studies [Torah]

---

studying in the valley of Ginosar when he saw someone climb up a tree and take baby birds while sending away the mother, in fulfillment of the Biblical precept (*Deuteronomy* 22:6-7). When the person came back down, he was bitten by a snake and died. He [Elisha] said: 'The Torah promises a long and good life for fulfilling the *mitzvah*; where is the goodness he deserves; where is the long life?' " Another version says that he saw the tongue of R' Yehudah *HaNachtom* — one of those martyred by the Romans — in the mouth of a dog and oozing blood. He said: "זו תוֹרָה וְזוּ שְׂכָרָה, This is Torah and this is its reward?" He concluded that there is neither reward and punishment, nor an afterlife and resurrection.

According to the Talmud (*Chagigah* 14b), he was one of the four people who engaged in the study of Kabbalah. This area of philosophical inquiry, reserved for a select few, affected him adversely, and he became a heretic. He was a vehement and vocal opponent of Torah study, and sought to dissuade young men from pursuing their studies. Nonetheless, his student R' Meir continued to learn from him. The Talmud says: "R' Meir found a fruit. He ate the inside and discarded its peel," meaning that R' Meir was great enough to absorb his former mentor's Torah without being influenced to follow his path (*Chagigah* 15b).

R' Meir's deep love for Elisha ben Avuyah and hope that he might be convinced to repent kept their relationship alive. One Shabbos in Tiberias, R' Meir was interrupted in the middle of his public discourse and was told that Elisha was outside — on a horse. He immediately went outside and began accompanying his former teacher, all the while repeating the discourse and discussing Torah topics. Suddenly, Elisha stopped and said to R' Meir, "Meir, return; you are at the *techum* (boundary) beyond which you may not go on Shabbos." "How do you know?" asked R' Meir. Acher replied, "I measured the steps of my horse."

R' Meir said, "You, too, should return [to traditional Judaism]." Elisha answered, "I heard from behind the Heavenly partition a voice that said, *'Return, O you wayward sons* (*Jeremiah* 3:14) — except for *Acher'* " (*Chagigah* 15b), meaning that he had been so sinful that he did not deserve a chance to repent.

When he was near death, Elisha was visited by his ever-loyal student R' Meir, who again asked him to repent. "Will Heaven accept me?" he asked. R' Meir answered, "*You reduce man to pulp and You say, 'Repent, O sons of man'* (*Psalms* 90:3). Even when man approaches death (i.e., he is reduced to pulp), God still calls out to him to return." Elisha wept as he took leave of this world. With joy in his heart, R' Meir said, "I believe that my teacher left the world a penitent" (*Yerushalmi* ibid.).

הַלּוֹמֵד יֶלֶד, לְמָה הוּא דוֹמֶה — *One who studies [Torah] while [he is still] a child, to what can he be likened.* This rendering follows *Rashi* and *Rambam*, who view the mishnah as referring to students, i.e., one should learn while he is young, when his mind is fresh and receptive.

The metaphor of paper which indicates the recipient rather than the teacher — the writer — would seem to bear this out (see below).

R' Yonah, Midrash Shmuel, and *Maharal* understand it, however, as discussing the teacher and the relative benefits of students of different ages. They translate הַלּוֹמֵד יֶלֶד not as *the one who* **learns** *as a child*, but as *the one who* **teaches** *a child*.

See *Tosafos Yom Tov* for an explanation, in this case, of the use of the passive paper metaphor rather than the active writing one.

לְדִיוֹ כְּתוּבָה עַל נְיָר חָדָש — *to ink written on fresh [clean] paper.* When one writes on a clean, white piece of paper, every line is perfectly legible. Likewise, things learned in one's youth, when his mind is fresh and receptive, are absorbed with clarity. Furthermore, things written on an unmarked piece of paper do not seep into the paper and become invisible after the ink dries. Similarly,

זָקֵן, לְמָה הוּא דוֹמֶה? לִדְיוֹ כְתוּבָה עַל נְיָר מָחוּק.

[כו] **רַבִּי** יוֹסֵי בַּר יְהוּדָה אִישׁ כְּפַר הַבַּבְלִי אוֹמֵר:
הַלּוֹמֵד מִן הַקְּטַנִּים, לְמָה הוּא דוֹמֶה? לְאוֹכֵל
עֲנָבִים קֵהוֹת, וְשׁוֹתֶה יַיִן מִגִּתּוֹ. וְהַלּוֹמֵד מִן הַזְּקֵנִים, לְמָה

---

ideas taught to young people leave an indelible impression on their hearts and minds. The Sages taught: "That which one learns when he is young is not easily forgotten" [*Shabbos* 21b and *Rashi* ad loc.] (*Rav, Rashi, Tiferes Yisrael, R' Yonah*).

וְהַלּוֹמֵד זָקֵן, לְמָה הוּא דוֹמֶה? לִדְיוֹ כְתוּבָה עַל נְיָר מָחוּק — *And one who studies [Torah] as an old man, to what can he be likened?* — *to ink written on smudged paper.* People who begin to learn late in life have difficulty absorbing new material. Even that which they learn is not understood accurately, since their minds are already crowded with a lifetime of information. Furthermore, this overabundance of old information causes them to forget the new. In

all these ways an older person is like a piece of paper which is smudged due to frequent erasures (*Rashi, Rambam, Tiferes Yisrael*). *Avos d'Rabbi Nosson* (24) teaches: "One who studies while young absorbs the words of Torah in his blood. They emanate from his mouth with pristine clarity. Not so one who studies in old age." *Meiri* and *R' Yonah* (quoting *Mivchar Peninim*) offer the following comparison: "Teaching Torah to the young is like engraving in stone, while teaching to the old is like engraving in sand."

Nonetheless, an older person who encounters difficulty in retaining what he learns should not feel discouraged. God will repay him handsomely for his efforts in Torah study, even if he retains little of

---

◆§ **Youth and maturity.** The Chiddushei HaRim interprets the phrase *while [he is still] a child* figuratively.

The excitement one experiences while studying clearly has an effect on his ability to retain what he learns. If he is exhilarated when he studies, as though he were just born and is experiencing Torah for the first time in his life, he will remember what he learns. The mishnah is speaking of this childlike wonderment at the sheer beauty of Torah. [For this reason, man's Good Inclination is referred to as a child (see *Ecclesiastes* 4:13). This force for good constantly renews him and rejuvenates his service of God.] One who comes to Torah old, tired, and without youthful exuberance stands little chance of achieving much spiritual growth.

The *Alter* of Kelm noted, however, that while child-like enthusiasm is desirable, it is also important as one matures to outgrow the childish thinking that characterized his early learning. Many people go through their lives with an infantile understanding of the Patriarchs because they are still carrying around the oversimplified images their teachers used when first introducing them to the narratives of the *Chumash*. Thus many go through life thinking of Jacob and Esau as the personification of "good guys and bad guys," because they were given such versions in kindergarten. But as people become more mature, they must look for the subtle lessons inherent in the Scriptural narratives.

◆§ The Kozhnitzer *Maggid* suggests a homiletical approach. One who prepares himself to study Torah by repenting his misdeeds is like a child — for he is reborn again. The metamorphosis of *teshuvah* creates a new person, with a fresh and uncluttered mind and heart.

The *Chozeh* of Lublin exemplified this kind of *teshuvah*. He would begin his Torah studies each day with a tearful prayer: "How can I open my mouth to study the words of Your Torah, dear God? King David taught us, *But to the wicked, God said, 'To what purpose do you recount My decrees?'* (*Psalms* 50:16)." He would pause for a moment and then continue, "But I promise You, Master of the Universe, that from now on I will change my ways"; and then, "But I promised God yesterday and the day before that I would improve, and I didn't keep my promise." Finally, he would conclude his discussion with himself by saying, "Yes," but now, God, I *really* mean what I say." Then and only then would he open his *Gemara* and begin to study.

as an old man, to what can he be likened? — to ink written on smudged paper.

26. Rabbi Yose bar Yehudah of Kfar HaBavli says: One who learns [Torah] from the young, to what can he be likened? — to one who eats unripe grapes or drinks unfermented wine from his vat. But one who learns [Torah] from the old, to what

---

what he learns. Like a worker hired to fill up punctured barrels with water, the old man who learns is rewarded for his efforts, not for his results (*R' Yonah*).

Tikkun Moshe explains instead that the lesson of the mishnah is a proper attitude toward Torah mentors. The Talmud teaches that "If the earlier sages were like angels, we are like humans. If the earlier sages were like humans, we are like donkeys" (*Shabbos* 112b). *Chasam*

Sofer explains: "If we understand the greatness of those who preceded us, then we are human. But if we think they were mere mortals, then we are no more enlightened than the donkey."

If one comes to Torah like a child, with reverence for his elders and mentors, he will absorb the lessons of Torah. However, if he approaches Torah with the attitude of a wizened and cynical old man, he will never succeed.

Mishnah 26

רַבִּי יוֹסֵי בַּר יְהוּדָה אִישׁ כְּפַר הַבַּבְלִי אוֹמֵר — *Rabbi Yose bar Yehudah of Kfar HaBavli says.* It is unclear in which generation Rabbi Yose bar Yehudah lived. This is the only statement of his reported in all of Mishnah.

הַלוֹמֵד מִן הַקְטַנִּים, לְמָה הוּא דוֹמֶה — *One who learns [Torah] from the young, to what can he be likened.* The previous mishnah discusses students of different ages; this mishnah compares *teachers* of different ages.

לְאוֹכֵל עֲנָבִים קֵהוֹת, וְשׁוֹתֶה יַיִן מִגִּתּוֹ — *to one who eats unripe grapes or drinks unfermented wine from his vat.* Like unripe grapes that have a bitter taste and are unappetizing, so the wisdom of the young is intellectually unattractive. Furthermore, unfermented wine still contains sediment in it; similarly, a young scholar has yet to sift out the unclarified issues that cloud his wisdom. One who imbibes

such unripened wine will reach a state of intellectual stagnation (*Rav, Rashi, Meiri*).

Tiferes Yisrael explains the double metaphor: One who eats unripe grapes tastes their bitterness immediately. Unfermented wine, however, may initially taste good but eventually causes a stomach ache. Similar are the teachings of young people. Much of what they say is patently incorrect, obviously the product of unripened thought, like the bitter grapes. But even ideas that sound convincing are, when carefully scrutinized, found to be flawed — like the unfermented wine, which tastes sweet at first, but is indigestible. Young people may have ideas that seem original and scintillating, but they may not have the knowledge and skill to provide them with a solid foundation, nor the intellectual breadth to guarantee that their concepts do not conflict with other areas of Torah.

◆§ **Reverence for a teacher.** To a great extent, one's perception of his teacher affects the fruitfulness of their relationship. A student who looks up to his teacher and respects him as a wise elder will savor his intoxicating words, experiencing the type of joy that comes from a good, aged wine. Not so the student who looks at his teacher as a peer; he will not derive benefit or pleasure from his teacher (*Kozhnitzer Maggid*).

Rabbi Zusia of Anipoli sees this idea mirrored in the statement of the Sages: "If the teacher is comparable to an angel of God, seek Torah from his mouth, but if not — do not seek" (*Moed Kattan* 17a). If one reveres his teacher as an angel, elevated far above him, one may seek Torah from him. However, if he considers the teacher no better than himself — he should not seek to learn from him.

הוּא דוֹמֶה? לְאוֹכֵל עֲנָבִים בְּשׁוּלוֹת, וְשׁוֹתֶה יַיִן יָשָׁן.

[כז] רַבִּי מֵאִיר אוֹמֵר: אַל תִּסְתַּכֵּל בַּקַּנְקַן, אֶלָּא בְּמַה שֶׁיֵּשׁ בּוֹ; יֵשׁ קַנְקַן חָדָשׁ מָלֵא יָשָׁן, וְיָשָׁן שֶׁאֲפִילוּ חָדָשׁ אֵין בּוֹ.

[כח] רַבִּי אֶלְעָזָר הַקַּפָּר אוֹמֵר: הַקִּנְאָה וְהַתַּאֲוָה וְהַכָּבוֹד

וְהַלּוֹמֵד מִן הַזְּקֵנִים, לְמָה הוּא דוֹמֶה? לְאוֹכֵל עֲנָבִים **בְּשׁוּלוֹת, וְשׁוֹתֶה יַיִן יָשָׁן** — *But one who learns [Torah] from the old, to what can he be likened? — to one who eats ripe grapes or drinks aged wine.* Like old wine, which is a joy to the palate, the wisdom of the elderly is satisfying to the mind and the heart (*Rashi*).

As wine ages, it becomes better and more aromatic; so is it with wisdom. As time passes, one's knowledge increases and deepens, constantly becoming clearer. *Job* (12:12) captures this thought:

Wisdom resides with the elderly; with the length of days — understanding (*R' Yonah*).

Tiferes Yisrael addresses the second part of the double metaphor. Like ripe grapes which are sweet, one can savor the wise words of the elderly. Even those thoughts which the listener finds difficult to understand will, with the passage of time, prove themselves correct and satisfying. Thus, the wisdom of elders is like a wine served in the proper time.

Mishnah 27

רַבִּי אוֹמֵר — *Rabbi said.* See 2:1 for biographical details about Rabbi. This text follows *Rambam*, *Rashi*, and *R' Yonah*. Some versions have instead *Rabbi Meir said* (see *Meleches Shlomo*).

אַל תִּסְתַּכֵּל בַּקַּנְקַן, אֶלָּא בְּמַה שֶׁיֵּשׁ בּוֹ — *Do not look at the jug, but at what is in it.* In the previous mishnah, R' Yose bar Yehudah made an unqualified statement of preference for older teachers over younger ones. In contrast, Rabbi suggests looking at every individual separately, rather than drawing conclusions based merely on age (*Rav, R' Yonah* et al.).

Alternatively, this is a general statement not referring to all people. One must take care not to be deceived by appearances; people of regal bearing who have a commanding physical appearance may, in fact, be devoid of Torah or good deeds, and deserve no special respect. Conversely, a rough exterior often hides a good heart and soul. One must look past the exterior trappings and seek out the essential person.

Bayis LeAvos notes how appropriate it is that R' Meir (see above, s.v. רַבִּי אוֹמֵר) makes this statement. It was this ability to penetrate beyond surface impressions that induced him to continue studying with *Acher* (see 4:25,

---

⊷§ **Improving with age.** The Talmud teaches that Joseph sent his father Jacob aged wine, which pleases the elderly (*Megillah* 16b). What do the elderly find so pleasing about aged wine? Rabbi Yitzchak Hutner explained: Almost everything in the world gets worse and deteriorates with age. Wine is an exception to the rule; it improves with age. Similarly, as Torah scholars get older, they become more intellectually mature (*Kinnim* 3:6). Old wine reminds the elderly of their special quality of improving with age.

⊷§ **Focus on contents.** *Midrash Shmuel* cites an interesting variation on this theme. Man is a synthesis of body and soul. Without a body, the soul could not function, but nonetheless, the soul is certainly the focal point of the partnership. This is comparable to the relationship between wine and its vessel. The wine is the main thing; the vessel is only there to contain it. Thus we are taught to focus on the contents, not on the earthen jug.

can he be likened? — to one who eats ripe grapes or drinks aged wine.

27. Rabbi said: Do not look at the jug, but at what is in it; there is a new jug filled with old wine, and an old jug that does not even contain new wine.

28. Rabbi Elazar HaKappar said: Jealousy, lust and glory

אֱלִישָׁע בֶּן אֲבוּיָה אוֹמֵר .s.v.

Tiferes Yisrael applies the same concept to other aspects of character, citing Talmudic sources for instances where people appeared to be learned when, in fact, they were ignorant, and vice versa (see *Pesachim* 111b and *Bava Kamma* 117a), or for people who appear wicked and are really righteous (see *Taanis* 22a).

יֵשׁ קַנְקַן חָדָשׁ מָלֵא יָשָׁן, וְיָשָׁן שֶׁאֲפִילוּ חָדָשׁ אֵין בּוֹ — *there is a new jug filled with old wine, and an old jug that does not even contain new wine.* There are young men whose level of learning and insight has outstripped that of their seniors. In spite of their youth, they may be full of the old, ripe wine of Torah. Conversely, one may have come to old age empty of Torah content, and be of lesser stature than some who are many years his junior (*Rashi, Rav*). Just as old wine is not ruined by being in a new jug, so an incisive body of Torah knowledge may reside in the young (*R' Yonah*).

R' Moshe Almosnino notes that Rabbi invokes only the wine image of the previous mishnah, but not that of the grapes. He explains: Grapes allude to the corpus of Torah knowledge and the basic laws. Regarding these, both Rabbi and R' Yose agree to the superiority of the older and more experienced teacher. It is only in regard to analytic skills that Rabbi disagrees, stating that sometimes a young person may be sharper and more incisive than an older one.

According to *R' Yonah,* the opinions of R' Yose and Rabbi are alluded to in the opening words of Elihu's first speech in *Job* (32:6-9). *I am young in days, and you are old. Because of this I trembled and was afraid of expressing my opinion to you. I had thought, "Let days have their say; let years dispense wisdom."* These statements support R' Yose's position that wisdom is a function of age. However, Elihu then recanted: *But truly, it is a kind of prophecy in man; the breath of the Almighty inspires them with understanding. Therefore, there are not many who are truly wise; oldsters do not necessarily understand justice.* These latter thoughts reflect the view of Rabbi.

Elihu had waited for the elders to end their debate over the issues of God's stewardship of human affairs and the age-old questions of why the righteous suffer and the evil prosper. He assumed that they were the repository of true wisdom by virtue of their years. Now that he saw that they failed, he realized that wisdom is not a property of years, but comes as a gift from God. He may grant it to whomever He wishes — even a youngster (*R' Yosef Kara*).

Mishnah 28

רַבִּי אֶלְעָזָר הַקַּפָּר אוֹמֵר — *Rabbi Elazar HaKappar said.* R' Elazar HaKappar is mentioned only once in the Mishnah, but is cited many times in *Tosefta* and *Baraisos*. His son was Bar Kappara, and among his most prominent students was R' Yehoshua ben Levi (*Chullin* 56b). Apparently he was a resident of Lod, as indicated by the *Tosefta* (*Oholos* 18:8), which records a discussion among him, R' Yehudah *HaNasi*, R' Yishmael ben R' Yose,

and R' Pinchas ben Yair at the shop of Ben Pazi in Lod.

He considered peace the key to all blessing and explained that this is why the *Amidah* prayer concludes with the blessing for peace (*Sifre, Naso*). His son amplified this idea to the extent of stating that even idolaters who coexist peacefully with each other are protected against evil (ibid.). Another famous statement of his conveys the intrinsic link of all holy places to the Holy Land: "The synagogues and study halls in Babylonia will be relocated in the future to the Land of Israel" (*Megillah* 29a).

R' Elazar had a keen understanding of the vanity of the vices discussed in this mishnah, and he emphasized the enduring quality of offering oneself in service to others, even at the cost of being abused. His advice is recorded in *Avos d'Rabbi Nosson* (26): "One should never be like the lintel [of a door], out of reach for most people; instead be like the doorstep, which, though trod upon by all, lasts forever, long after the rest of the building has been destroyed."

הַקִּנְאָה — *Jealousy.* One who is jealous of his friend's possessions, position, or power seeks to outdo him in these areas (*Rashi, Tiferes Yisrael*).

Jealousy can be a positive life force, however, if one is envious of the righteous and strives to emulate them. This is an example of transforming a poor motive into a positive one. Our Sages taught: "קִנְאַת סוֹפְרִים תַּרְבֶּה חָכְמָה, *Rivalry between scholars increases wisdom*" (*Bava Basra* 21a).

Regarding wealth and possessions, there are also various levels of envy. The most extreme form is that of one who begrudges others' wealth, since he lacks it himself. Such a person is truly inferior, since he has no interest in human welfare. One who has a lesser degree of envy cannot tolerate the fact that others are wealthier than he is. [In his eyes, wealth is honor, and he wants to be more important than others.] The most tolerable level of envy is one who is envious of his friend's riches and simply wishes to possess such wealth himself.

Nonetheless, all types of jealousy are emotionally debilitating. King Solomon teaches: וּרְקַב עֲצָמוֹת קִנְאָה, *But envy is the decay of bones* (*Proverbs* 14:30), i.e., jealousy penetrates to and corrodes the inner being of a person.

Rashi offers two historical examples of the detrimental effects of envy: (a) The angels envied the great honor and pleasure that Adam experienced in the Garden of Eden, and as a result they caused the Evil Inclination, in the form of the snake, to entice him. (b) Korach's jealousy was the reason that he foolishly contested the power and position of Moses and Aaron. The end of this shameful episode was that he and his followers were swallowed alive by the earth.

וְהַתַּאֲוָה — *lust.* The lust for money or physical pleasures can be a debilitating force; even permitted pleasures can become obsessive if one overindulges in them (*Rashi, R' Yonah, Rav*).

The *Vilna Gaon* (*Iggeres HaGra*) quotes *Mivchar HaPeninim*, who compares indulging one's lust to drinking salty water; the more you drink, the thirstier you get. The Talmud teaches about lust: "מַרְעִיבוֹ שָׂבֵעַ מַשְׂבִּיעוֹ רָעֵב, *Starve it and it is satisfied; satisfy it and it is starved*" (*Succah* 52b).

R' Yonah reminds us that wealth and comfort need not necessarily impede the service of God if one's intentions are properly channeled. R' Yehudah *HaNasi* was a man of fantastic wealth who had all the comforts of this world. Before he died, he lifted his ten fingers and testified that he had not derived the slightest bit of *personal* pleasure from this world (see *Kesubos* 104a). All his wealth and comfort were harnessed for a higher purpose.

King David makes an impassioned plea to achieve this level: "*My Lord, before You is all my yearning* (*Psalms* 38:10), i.e., the sum total of all my yearnings and the goal to which I wish to dedicate all my desires is to stand before You and faithfully fulfill Your will" (see *Meiri* ad loc.).

Just as *Rashi* noted some of the historical effects of jealousy, he also mentions those that exhibit the cancerous effect of lust: (a) Adam and Eve's lust for the forbidden fruit in the Garden of Eden had fatal consequences (see *Genesis* 3). (b) Gechazi, a

---

◆§ **Wiser than a horse.** "Somebody opened a store right next door to mine, and I am surely going to lose my livelihood. He will take all my business away!" complained a storekeeper to R' Meir of Premishlan. The sage replied, "Have you ever seen a horse drink water from a river? He walks into the water and stamps his hooves. Do you know why he does that? He looks down at the water and sees another horse also drinking. Envious and afraid that the 'other' horse will drink up all the water, he kicks his mirror-image. That is the attitude of the horse," continued R' Meir'l, "but you know better. You realize that there is enough water in the river for all the horses, and that no one can touch what God has prepared for his friend. Place your trust in God, and you will have nothing to fear and no reason to be jealous of."

student of the prophet Elisha, was so overcome with a lust for wealth that he could not bear to see Elisha refusing to accept a gift from Naaman. Under false pretenses, he himself took a sizable gift from Naaman, an act that angered Elisha (see *II Kings* 5:20-27).

וְהַכָּבוֹד — *and glory.* The love of honor and glory is a despicable trait, and forcing others to honor oneself is a base form of this spiritual malady. Worse still is allowing oneself to be honored for qualities one does not possess. Even scholars or righteous people who deserve honor should not seek it; and even the king of Israel, whom we are commanded to revere, is enjoined to be careful that *his heart does not become haughty over his brethren* (see *Deuteronomy* 17:20). Honor is legitimate only when one accepts it in order to enhance respect for Torah and its Giver (*R' Yonah*).

R' Moshe Chaim Luzzatto (*Mesillas Yesharim* ch. 22) graphically portrays the pitfalls of glory: "Honor is nothing but pure vanity, which causes a man to deny his own mind and the will of his Master. One who recognizes it for what it is will certainly find it despicable and will hate it. The praise of men will be a burden to him, for when he sees men heaping praises upon him for qualities he does not possess, he will be ashamed. He will detest honor, realizing not only that he does not possess the virtues for which he is being praised, but that men are adding to his shame by praising him falsely."

In Chapter 11 he writes: "The desire for honor is even greater than the desire for wealth, for it is possible for a person to overcome his inclination for wealth and the other pleasures and still be entrapped by the desire for honor, unable to tolerate being, and seeing himself, beneath his friends."

"Many were caught and destroyed by the desire for honor. Jeroboam ben Nebat was barred from the World to Come because of his desire for honor. The Sages taught (*Sanhedrin* 102a): "The Holy One, Blessed is He, seized his garment and said to him, 'Repent, and you and I and [King David] the son of Jesse will walk together in the Garden of Eden.' Jeroboam asked, 'Who will go first?' God answered, 'The son of Jesse'; and Jeroboam said, 'If so, I refuse' " (*Sanhedrin* 102a).

"The desire for honor tugs at a person's heart more than any of the other longings and desires in the world. If not for concern over his honor, a person would be content to eat whatever is at hand, to clothe himself with whatever will cover him, and to dwell in a house which will protect him from the elements. He would obtain his livelihood with little effort and would feel no need to exert himself to become rich. But in order not to see himself as lower or lesser than his friends, he places a yoke upon his neck, and there is no end to his labors.

"In summation, the desire for honor is one of man's greatest stumbling blocks. One cannot be a faithful servant to his Master as long as he is concerned with his own honor; for in all circumstances, his foolishness will lead him to detract from the honor of Heaven."

Rashi cites two examples of the detrimental effect of pursuing glory: (a) The honor which the angels accorded Adam contributed to his undoing. (b) Jeroboam, fearful of the loss of prestige that would result from his having to stand in the

⤷ **He means me!** The need for glory is addictive and makes one totally dependent on others, constantly seeking their approval. Such a person is truly a prisoner of a "herd" mentality. What makes his situation all the more tragic is that those who honor him publicly often scorn him privately.

A *chazzan* (cantor) once asked R' Yisrael Salanter for advice on how to overcome the conceit he felt about his talent and the pride he took in his congregants' compliments. R' Yisrael quietly replied: "Simply take the *tallis* off your head and see how they are laughing at you."

To illustrate the psychological truth that glory is really a fantasy, Rabbi Chaim Shmulevitz once related an incident that took place when he was a student in the Mirrer Yeshivah in Poland. Rabbi Yerucham Levovitz, the *Mashgiach*, received a letter from a former student of the yeshivah who had moved to America. R' Yerucham read the letter to his students, and when he came to the sentence, "I repeated a Talmudic insight of R' Chaim to a group of young men here. They enjoyed it immensely," he stared directly at R' Chaim Shmulevitz. Years later, R' Chaim commented: "I knew the letter was referring to R' Chaim Brisker, but nonetheless I felt flattered." Honor is but a fantasy.

⤷ **Say it again.** Jeroboam's question is rather puzzling. Why did he ask who would go first? God had told him the order: "You and I and the son of Jesse." R' Chaim Shmulevitz, in a humorous but pointed remark, explained that Jeroboam wanted to hear the statement again. The pursuit of honor is so addictive that one can never get enough of it.

[כט] **הוּא** הָיָה אוֹמֵר: הַיִּלּוֹדִים לָמוּת, וְהַמֵּתִים לִחְיוֹת,

Temple Courtyard [which was under the monarchy of his rival Rechavam], erected golden calves in order to not permit anyone to make the pilgrimage to Jerusalem for the festivals (see *I Kings* 12:25-33).

R' Chaim Volozhiner suggests that the three vices are in chronological order. Almost from birth, one suffers from jealousy. Lust fully develops only as one approaches maturity. A powerful desire for honor comes later in life; only as one gets older and becomes more emotionally and spiritually sophisticated do his desires become more refined, and glory becomes more important to him than physical pleasures. Therefore, honor is mentioned last in the mishnah.

Tosafos Yom Tov and *Midrash Shmuel* see a parallel between this mishnah and 2:16, which lists three other failings that remove a person from the world: the evil eye, the Evil Inclination, and hatred of other people. An *evil eye* results in jealousy since one begrudges others their accomplishments and

successes; the *Evil Inclination* is the source of lust; and the desire for glory spawns *hatred of people* in two ways: (a) It draws the hatred of others upon the one who seeks honor. No one is more despised than such a person; even though others may outwardly honor him, in their hearts they scorn him and talk about him behind his back. (b) Conversely, it causes the one who seeks honor to hate others. One who needs to have his ego constantly stroked will always feel that are others are begrudging him the respect he deserves.

מוֹצִיאִין אֶת הָאָדָם מִן הָעוֹלָם — *remove a man from the world.* A man with such reprehensible qualities will inevitably lose his faith in the Torah and will attain neither intellectual nor ethical excellence (*Rambam*).

According to other commentators, the "world" mentioned here refers to the World to Come. In addition to the great calamities which befall a person in this world as a result of these vices, he

◆§ **Last hurrah!** Another explanation of why a person desires honor more strongly as he gets older is that he begins to face the imminence of death, which challenges his sense of personal worth. On one hand, he is obligated to say "The world was created for me" (*Sanhedrin* 37a). On the other hand, the existence of death stands in sharp contradiction to the notion of individual importance, for one can hardly claim that his existence justifies a world that will continue to exist after he is gone. [It is only faith in the ultimate resurrection of the dead which enables him to continue to assert his eternity in the face of death (see *Pachad Yitzchak, Shavuos* 21).] As man begins to sense his mortality, he feels an increasing need to make his mark in the world, and this desire awakens an inordinate appetite for glory.

◆§ **Fantasy world.** R' Nochum Mordechai of Novominsk translates הָעוֹלָם as *reality*. One who is a prisoner of the three spiritual maladies of jealousy, lust, and glory loses touch with reality and enters a psychological world of fantasy. [Jealousy can induce paranoia, which paints demons in every corner of one's existence; lust can induce someone to destroy his life and career for a cheap thrill; and glory, when taken too seriously, can foster delusions of grandeur.]

R' Simcha Zisel of Kelm compares these three moral flaws to a leech. While the leech initially derives great enjoyment from sucking blood, eventually it gets so full that it simply explodes. The blood is nothing short of a deadly poison. Likewise, the obsessions of jealousy, lust, and glory are pleasurable at first, but ultimately result in spiritual suicide.

Yaina Shel Torah homiletically renders the words מוֹצִיאִין אֶת הָאָדָם מִן הָעוֹלָם as [jealousy, lust, and glory] *remove man from the rest of the world.* One who suffers the triple curse of these crippling spiritual diseases becomes so egocentric that everyone around him ceases to exist.

29. He [Rabbi Elazar HaKappar] used to say: The newborn will die; the dead will live again; the living will

---

may lose his share in the World to Come, for jealousy, lust, and glory are the roots of most sins.

Mivchar HaPeninim offers a clever parable to illustrate the futility of envy and excessive desire. Two people, an envious person and a glutton, once stood before the king, who made them the following offer: "If either one of you will ask for something, you will receive it, but your comrade will get a double portion." The envious one did not want to ask first, because he begrudged his companion a double portion. The glutton wanted two portions, so he pressed his companion to ask first. The envious fellow finally asked to have one of his own eyes gouged out, so that the glutton should lose both of his. Such is the nature of gluttony and envy; they are so overpowering that they cause senseless loss, and even self-destruction.

Ben Ish Chai extends this analogy: One who suffers from all three of these maladies finds himself entangled in such contradictions that his life becomes unbearable. If he is offered a choice like that which was presented to the envious man and the glutton, he faces terrible dilemmas. He will not want to request something painful because of his lust for comfort, nor will he ask for something demeaning because of his need for prestige. The only avenue left is to ask for something comfortable and prestigious — but he simply cannot bring himself to allow his friend the double pleasure. Such a person is a victim in every sense of the word.

Yamin Moshe explains the potent mix of these three human weaknesses. Jealousy is a prolific source of interpersonal strife (בֵּין אָדָם לַחֲבֵרוֹ); gossip, talebearing, and revenge all are stirred up by envy. Lust is the root cause of many sins against God (בֵּין אָדָם לַמָּקוֹם) which take the form of obsession with forbidden pleasures. Both of these areas are rectifiable if one is ready to repent. Repentance in interpersonal areas demands that one ask the aggrieved party for forgiveness, just as one must ask God to forgive transgressions against Him. The person who is enslaved by his own self-importance can never find the humility of heart to come before either God or his friend to ask for a new start. Jealousy and lust, compounded by glory, thus truly prevent one from finding a place in the World to Come.

Mishnah 29

הוּא הָיָה אוֹמֵר: הַיְּלוֹדִים לָמוּת — *He* [*Rabbi Elazar HaKappar*] *used to say: The newborn will die.* This is a call for repentance. Since man is alive today and in the grave tomorrow, he would do well to stop and take stock of his spiritual life (*R' Yonah*).

[לָמוּת is in the passive form, since man is actually approaching death from the day he is born.]

וְהַמֵּתִים לִחְיוֹת — *the dead will live again.* The resurrection of the dead is a cardinal principle of Jewish belief. (See Appendix to *Sanhedrin III*, the Schottenstein Edition of the Talmud, for a discussion of this phenomenon.) Usually the active form לְהַחֲיוֹת, *to enliven*, rather than the passive לִחְיוֹת, *to live*, is used to describe this, since awakening the dead is a supernatural phenomenon which demands God's active intervention (*Tiferes Yisrael, Midrash Shmuel*).

At the time of the resurrection all souls will be judged. Some will achieve eternal life while others will suffer everlasting abhorrence in the eyes of God (see ibid.).

⧉§ **Constructive use.** These same vices of jealousy, lust, and glory, when directed constructively, can also lead a person *into* the World to Come. Envy of those who do good deeds may bring a person to a closer relationship with God. Similarly, passion in the service of God will help him scale the heights of greatness. Honor given to others is one of the most effective passkeys to a place in the World to Come (*Kozhnitzer Maggid*).

וְהַחַיִּים לָדוּן – לֵידַע לְהוֹדִיעַ וּלְהִוָּדַע שֶׁהוּא אֵל, הוּא
הַיּוֹצֵר, הוּא הַבּוֹרֵא, הוּא הַמֵּבִין, הוּא הַדַּיָּן, הוּא הָעֵד, הוּא
בַּעַל דִּין, הוּא עָתִיד לָדוּן. בָּרוּךְ הוּא, שֶׁאֵין לְפָנָיו לֹא עַוְלָה,

Man should seek to be among those who achieve eternal life (*R' Yonah*).

R' Saadia Gaon has a different view. The Torah promises that at the time of redemption "many of those who sleep in the dusty earth shall awaken" (*Daniel* 12:2). The intent is not that among those who are resurrected, some will be rewarded and some punished, for those who deserve punishment will not be resurrected at all at the time of the redemption. Rather, these words mean that those who will awaken will have everlasting life, and those who will not awaken will be shamed and suffer everlasting abhorrence. For all the righteous, including those who repented, will live; only the unbelieving and those who died without repentance will not be resurrected (*Emunos V'Dei'os* ch. 7) [see ArtScroll *Daniel*, pp. 320-321, for divergent views].

וְהַחַיִּים לָדוּן — *the living will be judged.* Those who are resurrected will be judged. Alternatively, this may refer to those who are still alive when the great day of judgment comes. They will all be brought before the Heavenly tribunal (*Rashi, Rav, Machzor Vitry*). Even though the ultimate function of death is to free the soul from the body so that it may enjoy eternal life, this freedom is granted only in accordance with one's merits. Therefore, the soul, too, will experience judgment (*Tiferes Yisrael*). According to *Meiri*, the mishnah

teaches that even in this world, we — the living — may experience partial punishment for our misdeeds.

לֵידַע לְהוֹדִיעַ וּלְהִוָּדַע שֶׁהוּא אֵל — *in order that they know, teach, and become aware that He is God.* This rendering follows *Rav, Rashi, Machzor Vitry* et al., who understand this phrase to mean that at the time of resurrection, man will realize the truth of these ideas on his own, without instruction or prodding. He will come to know the strength and omnipotence of God, and will teach this doctrine to others. *Tiferes Yisrael* adds that man is told about death, resurrection, and the process of judgment, in order that he will learn, teach others, and know that He is [a strong] God.

God punishes us as a Father — not to hurt us, but to help us help ourselves, to awaken us to the gravity of our spiritual condition. All of the fears to which God subjects us in our lifetimes (animals, thieves, calamities, the oppression of the nations) are for the purpose of teaching us to fear Him. One who is truly God fearing need fear nothing else (*Ruach Chaim*).

הוּא הַיּוֹצֵר, הוּא הַבּוֹרֵא — *He is the Fashioner, He is the Creator.* All of the cosmos is in God's hands,

⤷§ **Goodness is life.** Rabbi Yitzchak Hutner explained why death is passive while resurrection is active, and he explained the Talmud's comparison of good with life and evil with death. The process of going from life to death is natural, but the path from death back to life is supernatural. It is the same in spiritual matters. If one does not provide himself with spiritual sustenance, he automatically dies; therefore, if he regrets having done a good deed, he strips it of its value and thereby deprives it of its spiritual sustenance. The good deed automatically "dies" for lack of sustenance. The process of resurrection, on the other hand, is a supernatural phenomenon; merely providing a corpse with food will not bring it back to life. In the spiritual realm as well, a mere change of heart is normally not enough to "revive" the victim of sin. A miracle is needed to resuscitate him spiritually. Therefore, only God, Who "resuscitates the dead with abundant mercy," can provide us the means of repentance.

The novelty of the concept of *teshuvah* (repentance) lies in the fact that God deems one's change of heart as though he actually undid his sinful act. Such a reversal is beyond rational expectation and could only occur through God's mercy.

be judged — in order that they know, teach, and become aware that He is God, He is the Fashioner, He is the Creator, He is the Discerner, He is the Judge, He is the Witness, He is the Plaintiff, He will judge. Blessed is He before Whom there is no iniquity,

---

like clay in the hands of the sculptor. Having created everything *ex nihilo*, He does with it as He pleases (*Rav*).

Meiri interprets בּוֹרֵא as the One Who originally created and יוֹצֵר as the One Who continues to sustain Creation. *Tiferes Yisrael* explains בּוֹרֵא as the Creator of man's physical being and יוֹצֵר as the One Who fashioned the human soul.

הוּא הַמֵּבִין — *He is the Discerner*. God oversees human activity; He understands the exact circumstances surrounding each of a person's acts [see *Psalms* 33:15] (*Rashi, Tiferes Yisrael*). *Machzor Vitry* elaborates: Since God created man, He is fully aware of his innermost secrets. He discerns everything; nothing can be hidden from Him.

According to *Rav*, this phrase is connected to the next: Since God knows all of our actions and thoughts, He is able to bring us to judgment.

הוּא הַדַּיָּין, הוּא הָעֵד, הוּא בַּעַל דִּין — *He is the Judge, He is the Witness, He is the Plaintiff*. God plays all these roles when He judges man. Not only does He judge him for his sins, but He also testifies against him since He is fully aware of his actions. Furthermore, God is the Plaintiff since it is against Him that man sins. Even interpersonal misdeeds (בֵּין

אָדָם לַחֲבֵרוֹ) are in truth sins against God (*R' Yonah, Rav, Tiferes Yisrael*).

God's roles in judgment are not listed according to the order in which they take place, but in the order of their increasing novelty to us. Not only is He the Judge, He is also the Witness and even the Plaintiff [roles which we may not have been aware of] (*Tosafos Yom Tov*). *Vilna Gaon* quotes a verse from *Malachi* (3:5) as proof that God is both Witness and Plaintiff: "*I shall approach you for judgment, and I will be an urgent witness.*" The Talmud relates that R' Yochanan would cry when he reached this verse and say, "What shall a servant say if his master testifies against him?" (*Chagigah* 5a).

הוּא עָתִיד לָדוּן — *He will judge*. God will judge us in the World to Come (*Rashi, Rav, R' Yonah*). *Rambam* distinguishes between this phrase and the earlier one *He is the Judge*, which refers to God's judgment of man in *this* world. Earthly judgments include such things as those given in the liturgy of the New Year: "Who will live and who will die, who will be impoverished and who will be enriched, who will be degraded and who will be exalted."

בָּרוּךְ הוּא, שֶׁאֵין לְפָנָיו לֹא עַוְלָה — *Blessed is He before Whom there is no iniquity*. God does not bend His judgment to favor anybody; He rules according to the law and metes out punishment with exact justice (*Rashi, R' Yonah*).

⋖§ **Equal partners.** Since the body plays an indispensable role in earning a person's reward or punishment, God insists that the body be resurrected, so that it may receive its just reward. A Talmudic parable illustrates the vital interconnection of the body and the soul: A blind man and a lame man both desired to raid a certain orchard, but because their physical limitations hindered them, they formed a partnership. The blind man took the lame man on his shoulders, and the lame man directed him to the orchard. They then shared the fruits of their "labors."

When the two were caught by the owner of the orchard, each one claimed that he was innocent because he could not have plundered the orchard by himself. The owner then took the lame man, set him back on the blind man's shoulders, and punished them as a unit (*Sanhedrin* 91b).

Man, too, is also composed of two "partners," body and soul, which collaborate for good or for ill. The righteous will arise at the time of resurrection to collect the material good due them for having utilized their bodies for good. The evil will stand up *for shame* and *for everlasting abhorrence* for having turned their souls to the service of evil (*R' Hersh Goldwurm*).

וְלֹא שִׁכְחָה, וְלֹא מַשּׂוֹא פָנִים, וְלֹא מִקַּח שֹׁחַד; שֶׁהַכֹּל שֶׁלּוֹ. וְדַע, שֶׁהַכֹּל לְפִי הַחֶשְׁבּוֹן. וְאַל יַבְטִיחֲךָ יִצְרֵךָ

וְלֹא שִׁכְחָה — *no forgetfulness*. One should not be deluded into thinking that God will overlook a portion of his spiritual debt. Everything is recorded; He forgets nothing (*Rashi*).

We highlight this point in our prayers on *Rosh Hashanah*, the Day of Judgment: "For it is You Who eternally remembers all forgotten things, and there is no forgetfulness before Your Throne of Glory."

וְלֹא מַשּׂוֹא פָנִים — *no favoritism*. God shows no favoritism. Even a perfectly righteous person will be held accountable for a minor transgression (*Rav*). One is not absolved of responsibility because of his great wisdom or piety (*R' Yonah*). Additionally, God, unlike human rulers, does not show favor to the rich and eminent. Instead, *He carries out the judgment of orphan and widow* (*Deuteronomy* 10:18) (*Ramban*). Neither does He favor the evil son of a righteous father (*Sforno*).

וְלֹא מִקַּח שֹׁחַד — *and no acceptance of bribery*. This is difficult to understand, for it is ludicrous even to entertain the thought that God can be bribed; what type of bribe could one offer Him? Instead, "bribery" here means that God does not accept the performance of commandments as atonement for transgressions; there is no such thing as trading one for the other. Rather, He gives reward for the performance of *mitzvos* and punishment for transgressions (*Rambam, R' Yonah*).

Rambam continues: Even Moses, in spite of his towering spiritual stature, was punished for the anger he displayed at *Mei Merivah* when he excoriated the people for their complaints, and called them rebels (see *Numbers* 20:10). This sin of anger was compounded because the Jews assumed that whatever Moses said was a reflection of God's will, and if Moses was angry with them, then God must be angry. [To portray God as anything less than a Merciful Father is a desecration of His Name and honor.]

Similarly, despite his deep-rooted wickedness, Esau was rewarded for the meticulous way in which he honored his parents. The Midrash quotes Rabban Shimon ben Gamliel: "All my life I served my father, yet it was not even one hundredth of the service that Esau provided his father Jacob. When I served my father, I did so dressed in dirty clothes; only when I went outside did I change into clean clothes. Esau, however, would always wear royal garb when he attended his father. He said, 'It is only fitting for the honor of my father that I wear clothes of royalty' " (*Bereishis Rabbah* 65:16). As reward for honoring his parents, Esau's descendants were sought as marriage partners for the royalty of the world (see *Bereishis Rabbah* 82; see also *Devarim Rabbah* 1:16).

The Talmud gives another example of God's exact recompense for individual deeds: Nebuchadnezzar, the wicked Babylonian king, was allowed

⊰§ **What to remember.** The first part of the text of the prayer asserts that God remembers the *forgotten* things, yet the second phrase indicates that He forgets nothing. R' Yisrael of Rizhin explained: וואס מ'פארגעסט דא געדענקט מין אויבען. וואס מיר גדענקט מין אויבען, "Whatever is forgotten [by man] here [on earth] is remembered in Heaven. Whatever man on earth remembers is forgotten in Heaven." This principle includes both good deeds and sins. If a person "forgets" about his good deeds in the sense that he does not carry around the feeling that he deserves credit for them, then God remembers them and rewards him. However, if he remembers his good deeds and arrogantly expects to be recognized for them, then God, so to speak, forgets what he has done.

Rabbi Gedaliah Schorr would never discuss his efforts to save Jews during the Holocaust. When he was pressed, he would quote the above comment of the Rizhiner.

The same principle applies to sins. King David said, *"My sin is always before me"* (*Psalms* 51:5). If a person adopts this attitude, then God is ready to forgive and forget his sin. If, however, he forgets about his *sins*, thinking he has repented sufficiently, then God will remember those sins.

to destroy the Temple as a reward for once having gone out of his way to show respect for God. A messenger from King Merodach Baladan once was carrying a letter to King Hezekiah. Nebuchadnezzar felt that the text of the letter showed a lack of respect for God, and he ran four paces after the messenger in order to retrieve the letter and change it.

The Talmud concludes that the angel Gabriel stopped Nebuchadnezzar after four paces. Otherwise, his merit would have been so great that it would have enabled him to exterminate the Jewish people entirely (*Sanhedrin 96a, Rashi ad loc.*).

Maharal understands וְלֹא מִקַּח שֹׁחַד to mean that an unrepentant sinner cannot bribe God by bringing an offering or contributing to charity; God is angered by those who steal or otherwise obtain money dishonestly and then use their ill-gotten profits to bless or serve Him (see *Psalms* 10:3).

Midrash Shmuel comments that these virtues (lack of iniquity, forgetfulness, favoritism, and bribery) correspond to the above-mentioned three roles that God assumes in judgment. A litigant may lie to win his case; God, however, commits no such iniquity. As a witness, there is no concern that a poor memory will cause Him to give inaccurate testimony, for He forgets nothing. Lastly, as a judge, God shows no favoritism, nor does He accept any type of bribe.

שֶׁהַכֹּל שֶׁלּוֹ — *for everything is His.* Since everything belongs to Him, He cannot be bribed (*Rashi*). According to *Rambam*, the mishnah says this to explain why man's good deeds cannot compensate for his transgressions: even his ability to do *mitzvos* is God given. If God would not assist a person, he could never do even the simplest *mitzvah*. King David prays, *"May God complete on my behalf"* (*Psalms* 138:8), indicating that man takes the initial step, but it is God Who brings the

good deed to completion. Those who come forward seeking purity merit His Divine assistance [see *Yoma* 38a] (*Midrash Shmuel*).

וְדַע, שֶׁהַכֹּל לְפִי הַחֶשְׁבּוֹן — *Know that everything is according to the reckoning.* God makes an exact reckoning of a person's good and bad deeds. Like many small coins adding up to a large sum, many minor transgressions add up to a large debt (*Rashi, Rav*).

The greater a person's status, talents, and opportunities to do good, the more God demands of him. One who possesses greater intelligence, good character, and abilities may receive greater punishment for a minor transgression than a person of lesser intellect and abilities may receive for a major transgression (*Rambam*). [God judges the righteous with hairline precision (*Yevamos* 121b). What for a less righteous person is considered an inconsequential act is deemed a sin for someone on a higher spiritual plane.]

Meshivas Nefesh elaborates: One who is by nature compassionate but who does not perform acts of kindness is more culpable than one who tends toward cruelty. Conversely, one who overcomes his natural inclination to cruelty and helps another person will receive greater reward than one who is naturally kind.

According to *Tiferes Yisrael*, God considers all the circumstances surrounding a person's actions when He assesses reward and punishment. His passion or distaste for a sin as well as his joy or reluctance in doing a *mitzvah* are all taken into account.

Knesses Yisrael suggests yet another factor which is taken into account in the Heavenly Court: the intensity of a person's rebelliousness. One who has transgressed ten ordinary sins is more rebellious than a person who transgressed one severe sin; having repeatedly disregarded God's will, he is more condemnable.

◆§ **Changed person.** Repentance would hardly be accomplished in any case by a "trade-off" of good deeds for bad; it misses the point entirely. True repentance is a process of internal metamorphosis, where the penitent emerges as a totally new and different person. If he has not erased his sins by changing himself, a person has hardly repented.

שֶׁהַשְּׁאוֹל בֵּית מָנוֹס לָךְ – שֶׁעַל כָּרְחֲךָ אַתָּה נוֹצָר; וְעַל כָּרְחֲךָ אַתָּה נוֹלָד; וְעַל כָּרְחֲךָ אַתָּה חַי; וְעַל כָּרְחֲךָ אַתָּה מֵת;

וְאַל יַבְטִיחֲךָ יִצְרְךָ שֶׁהַשְּׁאוֹל בֵּית מָנוֹס לָךְ — *And let your Evil Inclination not promise you that the grave will be an escape for you.* One should not delude himself into thinking, as heretics do, that in the World to Come there is (God forbid) no judgment and no Judge (*R' Yonah*). The grave offers no refuge from the obligation to pay the price of sin. One should not dismiss everything he has been told earlier in the mishnah about the Day of Judgment, thinking that after he leaves this world, he will no longer have to account for his actions (*Rashi*).

Meiri renders בֵּית מָנוֹס as *a way to escape*. Once in the grave, a person's fate is sealed. No effort in the world can save him from the Divine retribution he has brought upon himself.

שֶׁעַל כָּרְחֲךָ אַתָּה נוֹצָר — *for against your will you were created.* A soul is reluctant to descend from Heaven to earth, but an angel forces it to enter the womb (*Rashi, Rav*).

Tiferes Yisrael renders עַל כָּרְחֲךָ as *beyond human comprehension*, for it impossible to understand how flesh-and-blood human beings can create new life. How could one entertain the notion that the soul belonging to such a supernatural being is anything less than eternal, and is surely destined to live beyond the grave?

⧢ **No escape.** *Rambam* writes in *Iggeres HaShmad:* "It is a fundamental principle of our religion that even people as wicked as Yeraboam ben Nebat and his like are punished for all their minor sins, just as they are punished for sins as severe as the erection of the idolatrous calves. God punishes man for all iniquities, no matter what their level of severity."

R' Shmuel of Slonim, in a letter to someone who had abandoned his connection to Torah and *mitzvos*, wrote: "Even an apostate should not delude himself into thinking that he will receive one great punishment for abandoning his heritage and then be free to live as he pleases. Cutting one's ties to his spiritual home in no way absolves him of even his most minor duty."

While traveling, the *Gaon* of Vilna once met a Jewish apostate. The apostate asked the *Gaon's* host for a glass of whiskey, and the *Gaon* told the host to be sure that the apostate recited the appropriate blessing before drinking.

"Why should I recite a blessing?" asked the apostate. "I'm no different from a gentile."

The *Gaon* replied, "Don't speak such foolishness. You are a full-fledged Jew, with all the duties it entails. You will be punished for even the slightest infraction." Shocked by these powerful words, the apostate eventually became a complete penitent.

The Chasan Sofer anticipates yet another of Satan's ruses: One must not think that the grave is a refuge since he will no longer sin there. This is not so; the effects of one's sins outlive him and continue to have an influence on others, obligating him to account for ongoing effect of his deeds.

Likewise, a person's good deeds are eternal. The Talmud teaches that upon his death, a Torah scholar must be accompanied to his final resting place by at least 600,000 people. Just as the Torah was given at Mount Sinai in the presence of 600,000 men, so the Torah is figuratively returned to God with this number of people in attendance. "This is true for one who studied Torah. For a scholar who studied *and taught* Torah, no number of people is sufficient" (*Megillah* 29a). R' Moshe Feinstein explained: One who teaches Torah to others implants seeds which produce fruit — which in turn produce other fruits, for students will, with God's help, become teachers one day. The process is ongoing and endless. A Torah teacher can never know upon how many people he has left an imprint; therefore, it is impossible to calculate the number of people who must pay him the final honor.

⧢ **Only through a Creator.** Merely by studying the complexities of something as small as the human eye, one's faith in the Creator can be immeasurably enhanced. *Chazon Ish* (*Emunah u'Bitachon* 1) expresses poetically how endless wellsprings of faith can flow from contemplation of the human body.

that the grave will be an escape for you — for against your will you were created; against your will you were born; against your will you live; against your will you die; and against your

וְעַל בָּרְחֲךָ אַתָּה נוֹלָד — *against your will you were born*. The human fetus enjoys a perfect existence, sustained by means of the umbilical cord. In addition, the unborn child, in the words of the Sages, sees "from one end of the earth to the other" and is taught the entire Torah by an angel. When the time comes to be born, the child does not want to leave the warm and protective womb; an angel must force it to come into this world [see *Niddah* 30b] (*Rashi, Rav*).

וְעַל בָּרְחֲךָ אַתָּה חַי — *against your will you live*. Man is often so debilitated by pain and woe that his greatest hope is to die. When he lies down to sleep at night, his soul, aware of the terrible troubles he suffers, does not want God to return it to him in the morning, but God returns man's soul even against man's will (*Rashi, Rav*).

וְעַל בָּרְחֲךָ אַתָּה מֵת — *against your will you die*.

Man is powerless over the spirit — to restrain the spirit; nor is there authority over the day of death (*Ecclesiastes* 8:8). When death approaches, man does whatever he can to prevent it — but to no avail. Grasping at straws, he searches for any means to save himself from the Angel of Death, but he has no choice. When his time comes, he is forced to leave this world; he can neither escape nor elude death (*Machzor Vitry*).

Rambam notes that the mishnah lists only those realities that are not in the scope of man's free choice. About these we are taught: "Everything is in the hands of Heaven except the fear of Heaven" (*Berachos* 33b). Other areas such as sinning, doing good deeds, and all physical activities are subject to human choice and discretion.

The *Vilna Gaon* questions the structure of the mishnah. The fact that man is born and forced to live against his will would seem to absolve him of

⊷§ **Your own choice.** The Vilna *Gaon* offers a halachic analogy to his commentary on the mishnah. The Talmud (*Bava Basra* 4a) rules that if Reuben fences in three of his fields, which surround an inner field owned by Shimon, Shimon need not share the expense. Even though he gains some protection from the fences, he may claim that since the fourth side is still open, he has no real benefit from them. However, if he himself fences in the fourth side, he becomes obligated to reimburse Reuben for a fair share of the first three fences, for by erecting the fourth fence, he showed that he wanted his property enclosed.

Similarly, the first three statements of the mishnah (that man is created, is born and lives against his will) are good reasons why man should not have to pay for his misdeeds; he was coerced to live! However, the fact that he *dies* against his will refutes such an argument. A person who fights tenaciously for life cannot honestly claim that he would prefer to be absolved of life and its responsibilities — so he must ultimately account for his deeds.

The Dubno *Maggid* illustrates this idea with a parable. Two women, one ugly and one a shrew, could not find anybody to marry them. Finally, someone proposed a blind man for the ugly woman and a deaf man for her vociferous friend. The marriages took place, and the couples enjoyed happy lives; the deaf man heard none of his shrewish wife's diatribes, and the blind man could not see his unattractive wife.

One day a miracle-working doctor promised the two men that for a hefty sum he could cure their maladies; and so he did. No sooner were they cured than their domestic bliss was ruined. The once-blind man was taken aback by his wife's appearance, and the once-deaf man could not bear his wife's curses. They refused to pay the doctor, whereupon he sued them. After hearing the arguments, the judge ordered the doctor to reverse his cures and return the men to their former conditions.

But they both protested: "No, we don't want to go back to the way it was. This way is still better." The judge replied, "If so, then you must pay the doctor, for you have proved that you are satisfied with his cures."

Thus our mishnah states that even though we are born against our will, we do not want to die — which proves that we want to live. If so, then we must account to God for what we do with our lives.

וְעַל כָּרְחֲךָ אַתָּה עָתִיד לִתֵּן דִּין וְחֶשְׁבּוֹן לִפְנֵי מֶלֶךְ מַלְכֵי הַמְּלָכִים, הַקָּדוֹשׁ בָּרוּךְ הוּא.

❧ ❧ ❧

רַבִּי חֲנַנְיָא בֶּן עֲקַשְׁיָא אוֹמֵר: רָצָה הַקָּדוֹשׁ בָּרוּךְ הוּא לְזַכּוֹת אֶת יִשְׂרָאֵל, לְפִיכָךְ הִרְבָּה לָהֶם תּוֹרָה וּמִצְוֹת, שֶׁנֶּאֱמַר: ,,יהוה חָפֵץ לְמַעַן צִדְקוֹ, יַגְדִּיל תּוֹרָה וְיַאְדִּיר.''

---

facing judgment for his actions. "I didn't ask to be born; why should I be held responsible for my sins?" he might claim. "Since I am coerced me to live, why should I be responsible for my failures? I would prefer to die." This seems to be a very logical argument. However, when a person is terminally ill, he fights for life with every fiber of his being; suddenly

he wants life at all costs. Thus, he provides the answer to his own question. He may have been born against his will, but his life is desirable and precious. The Gaon renders: *Even though* you were created and were born against your will, and *in spite* of the fact that you claim to live against your will, nonetheless, since you die against your will — proving will you are destined to give an account before the King Who rules over kings, the Holy One, Blessed is He.

❧   ❧   ❧

Rabbi Chanania ben Akashia says: The Holy One, Blessed is He, wished to confer merit upon Israel; therefore He gave them Torah and *mitzvos* in abundance, as it is said: HASHEM *desired, for the sake if its [Israel's] righteousness, that the Torah be made great and glorious.*

---

that you want desperately to live — you will be forced to give an accounting of your life before God.

וְעַל כָּרְחֲךָ אַתָּה עָתִיד לִתֵּן דִּין וְחֶשְׁבּוֹן לִפְנֵי מֶלֶךְ מַלְכֵי הַמְּלָכִים, הַקָּדוֹשׁ בָּרוּךְ הוּא — *and against your will you are destined to give an accounting before the King Who rules over kings, the Holy One, Blessed is He.*

There is no escaping God's judgment, even in the grave. As King David taught: *Where can I go from Your spirit? And where can I flee from Your Presence? If I ascend to heaven, You are there; if I make my bed in the lowest depths, behold, You are there (Psalms 139:7-8).* [See 3:1 for the difference between דִּין and חֶשְׁבּוֹן.]

פרק חמישי ❧ Chapter Five

> **כָּל** יִשְׂרָאֵל יֵשׁ לָהֶם חֵלֶק לָעוֹלָם הַבָּא, שֶׁנֶּאֱמַר: ,,וְעַמֵּךְ כֻּלָּם צַדִּיקִים, לְעוֹלָם יִירְשׁוּ אָרֶץ, נֵצֶר מַטָּעַי, מַעֲשֵׂה יָדַי לְהִתְפָּאֵר".

> All Israel has a share in the World to Come, as it is said:
> *And your people are all righteous; they shall inherit the land forever; a branch of My plantings, My handiwork, in which to take pride (Isaiah 60:21).*

[א] **בַּעֲשָׂרָה** מַאֲמָרוֹת נִבְרָא הָעוֹלָם. וּמַה תַּלְמוּד לוֹמַר? וַהֲלֹא בְמַאֲמָר אֶחָד יָכוֹל לְהִבָּרְאוֹת? אֶלָּא לְהִפָּרַע מִן הָרְשָׁעִים, שֶׁמְּאַבְּדִין אֶת הָעוֹלָם שֶׁנִּבְרָא בַּעֲשָׂרָה מַאֲמָרוֹת, וְלִתֵּן שָׂכָר טוֹב

Mishnah 1

T his chapter, in addition to ethical and moral teachings, includes historical information and several of the foundation principles of Creation. It begins with numerical sets, the first of which is the ten utterances of Creation, a fundamental Torah doctrine (*Meiri*).

בַּעֲשָׂרָה מַאֲמָרוֹת נִבְרָא הָעוֹלָם — *With ten utterances the world was created.* The entire cosmos and all that it contains was created when God called it into existence. This act of creation was comprised of a series of ten utterances that appear in the account of Creation in the first chapter of *Genesis.* The Talmud (*Rosh Hashanah* 32a) notes that the term וַיֹּאמֶר, *And God said,* appears only nine times, and the tenth "utterance" is the word בְּרֵאשִׁית, *In the beginning,* with which the Torah begins. That term refers to the creation of heaven and earth, as mentioned in *Genesis* 1:1.

The *Vilna Gaon* lists the ten utterances as follows:

1) *In the beginning of God's creating the heavens and earth* (*Genesis* 1:1).

2) *God said, "Let there be light"* (1:3).

3) *God said, "Let there be a firmament"* (1:6).

4) *God said, "Let the waters beneath the heaven be gathered into one area, and let the dry land appear"* (1:9).

5) *God said, "Let the earth sprout vegetation"* (1:11).

6) *God said, "Let there be luminaries in the firmament of the heaven"* (1:14).

7) *God said, "Let the waters teem with teeming living creatures"* (1:20).

8) *God said, "Let the earth bring forth living creatures"* (1:24).

9) *God said, "Let us make man in Our image after Our likeness"* (1:26).

10) *God said, "Behold, I have given to you all herbage yielding seed that is on the surface of the entire earth, and every tree that has seed-yielding fruit; it shall be yours for food"* (1:29).

See *Bereishis Rabbah* 17:1 and *Pirkei d'Rabbi Eliezer* (3) for alternative reckonings of the ten utterances. See also *Meleches Shlomo.*

וּמַה תַּלְמוּד לוֹמַר? וַהֲלֹא בְמַאֲמָר אֶחָד יָכוֹל לְהִבָּרְאוֹת — *What does this come to teach us? Indeed, could it have not been created with one utterance.* R' Yonah views the mishnah's main question as the second one, i.e., why did God not bring the entire universe into existence with one utterance? According to *Maharal,* however, the real question is the first one: "What are we to learn from the fact that God created the world with ten utterances?"

Midrash Shmuel tells us that the mishnah incorporates both questions. Why did the Creation necessitate ten separate utterances? And for what purpose did the Torah inform us of this?

Rav understands the question in yet a third way: "Why did God spread the different elements of Creation over a period of six days rather than creating everything on one day?"

אֶלָּא לְהִפָּרַע מִן הָרְשָׁעִים, שֶׁמְּאַבְּדִין אֶת הָעוֹלָם שֶׁנִּבְרָא בַּעֲשָׂרָה מַאֲמָרוֹת — *This was to exact punishment from the wicked, who destroy the world that was created with ten utterances.* Each element of creation was brought into existence with a separate utterance to teach man that every part of creation is important, part of an ordered system. One who ruins the world through his wicked conduct has destroyed something of great value, for the human soul has the capacity to maintain and perfect the universe, and by sinning, a person harms his soul, which is the focal point of this ordered system (*Rambam*). *Rav,* based on *Avos*

1. **W**ith ten utterances the world was created. What does this come to teach us? Indeed, could it have not been created with one utterance? This was to exact punishment from the wicked, who destroy the world that was created with ten utterances, and to bestow goodly reward upon the

---

d'Rabbi Nosson (31), interprets the mishnah as expressing the maxim כָּל הַמְאַבֵּד נֶפֶשׁ אַחַת מִיִּשְׂרָאֵל כְּאִילוּ אִיבֵּד עוֹלָם מָלֵא, *Whoever destroys even one Jewish soul is considered to have destroyed an entire world* (*Sanhedrin* 37a). The "world" referred to in this statement is man's own inner world — his soul.

According to *Rashi*, the reason that God "bothered" to use ten utterances was so that He would be able to exact greater retribution from the wicked for destroying the world in which He, so to speak, invested such great effort. *Maharal*, among others, questions this explanation, for it would seem incongruent with God's mercy that He would create the world in a fashion designed to increase the punishment of the wicked.

Maharal explains that the Mishnah means as follows: The number ten denotes a thing that has multiplicity and diversity, but which forms an integrated whole. This characteristic is peculiar to ten; for the numbers from one to nine are discrete entities, but ten is an inclusive number, a single integrated entity.

For this reason the letter י, *yud*, is used to signify ten. The *yud* is small — so small that it cannot be split into two halves; it is a single point, to teach us that the ten parts form a single entity.

Maharal continues, "Now, when a thing is integrated into a single entity, a disruption of its order by interfering with an individual component is a

disruption of the entire order. Similarly, each instance of maintaining the order upholds the entire order. This explains why our Sages said, 'The world was created with ten utterances.'

"The world was created with ten utterances and not with one, for if it had been created with one, we would have had no indication of its integrated unity. Because the world was created with ten utterances, the righteous, who maintain the order established by God, thereby sustain the entire universe; while evildoers, who forsake the Torah and violate the order of the Creation, thereby devastate the entire universe, because all the world is a single unified whole, and a departure from the order established by God is a disruption of the whole. The righteous enjoy great rewards, therefore, for they sustain the entire world, while evildoers suffer dire penalties, for they destroy the whole."

In contrast to *Maharal*'s view that the ten utterances are an expression of integrated unity, *Ruach Chaim* comments that they reflect a disparity, which God built into Creation to protect evildoers from devastating punishment. The world was created in separate units so that the wicked would not be able to ravage it completely, for if they were to have the ability to do so, they would remain eternally indebted to God for wreaking such havoc. Thus, it was an act of mercy that God

---

◆⧽ **Prerequisite for honor.** R' Yitzchok Hutner notes that diversity is required in God's scheme because it enables us to keep the world in existence. How so? By performing the commandments of the Torah, man asserts that the purpose of Creation is to honor God. By definition, "honor" implies the recognition that not all things or people are of equal value, because if all things are of equal worth, it is impossible to say that one should be honored more than another. The existence of multiple levels of value, however, is possible only in a world of diversity, not in a world of uniformity. Thus, the ten utterances, which established the principle of diversity in the world, were a prerequisite to the concept of honor, thus enabling man to honor God, by fulfilling the Torah, in the merit of which the world continues to exist. Diversity, therefore, is one of the practical underpinnings of the functional world (see *Pachad Yitzchak*, *Shavuos* 8).

לַצַּדִּיקִים, שֶׁמְּקַיְּמִין אֶת הָעוֹלָם שֶׁנִּבְרָא בַּעֲשָׂרָה מַאֲמָרוֹת.

[ב] עֲשָׂרָה דוֹרוֹת מֵאָדָם וְעַד נֹחַ, לְהוֹדִיעַ כַּמָּה אֶרֶךְ אַפַּיִם לְפָנָיו; שֶׁכָּל הַדּוֹרוֹת הָיוּ מַכְעִיסִין וּבָאִין, עַד שֶׁהֵבִיא עֲלֵיהֶם אֶת מֵי הַמַּבּוּל.

---

created a world of independent units, as a way of curtailing the scope of the damage they could inflict. [This construction of the world is analogous to a ship which is built with many separate, watertight compartments; even if one of the compartments gets flooded, the ship will still stay afloat.]

וְלִתֵּן שָׂכָר טוֹב לַצַּדִּיקִים, שֶׁמְּקַיְּמִין אֶת הָעוֹלָם שֶׁנִּבְרָא בַּעֲשָׂרָה מַאֲמָרוֹת — *and to bestow goodly reward upon the righteous, who sustain the world that was created with ten utterances.* The world was created to give man a place in which to serve God. Those who do so sustain the world (*R' Yonah*) and are entitled to great reward (*Rashi*). The world was created with ten utterances in order to grant greater reward to the righteous for sustaining such a complex and supremely important system (*Meiri*).

Sfas Emes renders מְקַיְּמִין as *validate* (as in קִיּוּם שְׁטָרוֹת, *validation of* [signatures] *on a document*). Through following the Godly path, the righteous attest to the fact

that God created and sustains the world; they "legitimate" His Creation.

According to *HaChassid Yaavetz*, the world was created in steps rather than all at once to teach that man is the *raison d'etre* of Creation. Each utterance brought the world closer to its purpose — the existence of righteous human beings who are deserving of God's beneficence.

Another reason for the ten utterances may be that diversity camouflages the Oneness of the God Who created all. Only man can pierce this veil of diversity and recognize the world as a unified entity under God. The world was created with ten utterances to support the principle of man's free choice, giving him the opportunity (God forbid) to perceive existence as comprised of disparate elements that come from different sources. But righteous people who see beyond this facade are amply rewarded for their recognition of Creation as a unified whole, the work of One God.

Mishnah 2

עֲשָׂרָה דוֹרוֹת מֵאָדָם וְעַד נֹחַ — *There were ten generations from Adam to Noah.* *Meiri* lists these ten generations:

1) אָדָם — *Adam:* died in the year 930 from Creation

2) שֵׁת — *Seth:* born in the year 130 from Creation; died in 1042.

After his time, people begin to do evil.

3) אֱנוֹשׁ — *Enosh:* 254-1140

4) קֵינָן — *Kenan:* 325-1235

5) מַהֲלַלְאֵל — *Mahalalel:* 395-1290

6) יֶרֶד — *Jared:* 460-1422

7) חֲנוֹךְ — *Enoch:* 622-987

❧ **Sustenance through charity.** Rabbi Yosef Adler renders this portion of the mishnah as follows: *and to bestow reward upon the righteous by allowing them to sustain the world that was created with ten utterances.* He explains that the greatest joy for truly righteous people is to be able to do things for the benefit of others. Thus they can have no greater reward than the privilege of providing the merits that maintain the world's existence.

As the Talmud states: "Every day a voice emanates from Mount Sinai and proclaims, 'The whole world is sustained in the merit of My son, Chanina [ben Dosa], and My son Chanina himself subsists on a mere *kav* of carobs from Friday to Friday'" (*Berachos* 17b).

righteous, who sustain the world that was created with ten utterances.

2. **T**here were ten generations from Adam to Noah — to show the degree of His patience; for all those generations angered Him increasingly, until He brought upon them the waters of the Flood.

---

8) מְתוּשֶׁלַח — *Methuselah*: 687-1656

9: לֶמֶךְ — *Lamech*: 874-1651

10) נֹחַ — *Noah*: 1056-2006

Many details of human history do not appear in the Bible; even the lives of the spiritual giants are not portrayed in full. For example, the years in Moses' life, from when he initially left Egypt until he arrived at the home of Jethro, receives not a word in the Scriptures. This is because the Torah is not meant to be a history book; it instructs man on how to live. If the Torah lists the names and lifespans of the ten generations from Adam to Noah, it can only be that there is a lesson to be learned, and this is what the mishnah teaches (*Tiferes Yisrael*).

According to *Maharal*, however, the mishnah does not seek to explain the Torah's reason for reporting these ten generations, but rather to explain their existence. Why did God find it necessary to bring ten generations into the world before the Flood?

לְהוֹדִיעַ כַּמָּה אֶרֶךְ אַפַּיִם לְפָנָיו — *to show the degree of His patience.* In spite of the wickedness of these ten

generations, God did not destroy them immediately in order to allow them the opportunity to repent (*Rashi, Meiri*). Further, His patience is not a result of forgetting, or overlooking, man's sins. Rather, He often awaits the birth of a descendant who will be more righteous than his ancestors. If God, for example, had killed Terach for his sins, Abraham might have never been born. His trailblazing role in introducing knowledge of God to the world could not have existed had God not been patient and delayed retribution. God, Who knows the future, exercises patience with the wicked so that their righteous descendants may be born (*HaChassid Yaavetz*).

שֶׁכָּל הַדּוֹרוֹת הָיוּ מַכְעִיסִין וּבָאִין, עַד שֶׁהֵבִיא עֲלֵיהֶם אֶת מֵי הַמַּבּוּל — *for all those generations angered Him increasingly, until He brought upon them the waters of the Flood.* God waited patiently for them to repent. His patience, however, does not last forever, as the Talmud teaches: Anyone who claims that God waives the punishment of sin will have to waive his life (*Bava Kamma* 50a). If man does not repent,

---

◄§ **The missing years.** The fascinating details of Moses' life are reported in *Yalkut Shimoni* (*Shemos* 168):

"When Moses fled from Egypt he came to the camp of [King] Kokanus [of the land of Cush]. He was eighteen years old at the time, and was as tall as a cedar, as radiant as the noontime sun, and as strong as a lion. He became the king's adviser. Nine years later, the king fell sick and died. [After] he was buried, [the people] seated Moses on a platform and cried, 'Long live the king!' Then [using a clever strategy devised by Moses] they fought against the city of their enemies and captured it. On that day, a thousand of the city's population died, and Balaam the sorcerer and his two sons fled to Egypt. Moses was seated on the throne, a crown was placed on his head, and the Cushite queen was given to him as a wife. But Moses feared the God of his fathers and did not approach her; neither did he stray from the path which Abraham, Isaac, and Jacob had trod.

"[Forty years later,] the queen said to the ministers, 'For forty years now, this person has been ruling over Cush and he has not come near me; neither has he worshiped the gods of the Cushites. It is better for you to serve the son of your master than to serve a stranger.' They then crowned Muncham, son of Kokanus, king, and to Moses they gave costly gifts and sent him off with great honor.

"Moses was sixty-seven years old when he left Cush. [From there he] went to Midian, for he was afraid to return to Egypt because Pharaoh might avenge the Egyptian whom Moses had killed many years earlier.

[ג] **עֲשָׂרָה** דוֹרוֹת מִנֹּחַ וְעַד אַבְרָהָם, לְהוֹדִיעַ כַּמָּה אֶרֶךְ אַפַּיִם לְפָנָיו; שֶׁכָּל הַדּוֹרוֹת הָיוּ מַכְעִיסִין וּבָאִין, עַד שֶׁבָּא אַבְרָהָם אָבִינוּ וְקִבֵּל שְׂכַר כֻּלָּם.

[ד] **עֲשָׂרָה** נִסְיוֹנוֹת נִתְנַסָּה אַבְרָהָם אָבִינוּ וְעָמַד

the natural consequence is that he *must* be punished, so after all these generations, God brought the Flood upon the world (*Machzor Vitry*).

R' Yonah see this mishnah as a source of comfort to us in our long exile. Even though God extended His patience for ten generations, He eventually exacted retribution and brought the Flood. Let no one wonder why God allows our enemies to oppress us and keeps us in exile for so many long years. Just as His patience eventually gave way to the Flood, so His seemingly endless patience with our oppressors will end, and God will repay them for their terrible deeds. God is forbearing even with the enemies of Himself and His people, but in the end He will redeem us and punish them for their iniquities.

Mishnah 3

עֲשָׂרָה דוֹרוֹת מִנֹּחַ וְעַד אַבְרָהָם — *There were ten generations from Noah to Abraham.* These generations, beginning with Noah's son Shem, are listed in *Genesis* (11):

1) שֵׁם — *Shem*: 1558-2158
2) אַרְפַּכְשַׁד — *Arpachshad*: 1658-2096
3) שֶׁלַח — *Shelah*: 1693-2126
4) עֵבֶר — *Eber*: 1723-2187
5) פֶּלֶג — *Peleg*: 1757-1996
6) רְעוּ — *R'eu*: 1787-2026
7) שְׂרוּג — *Serug*: 1819-2049
8) נָחוֹר — *Nahor*: 1849-1997
9) תֶּרַח — *Terach*: 1878-2083
10) אַבְרָהָם — *Abraham*: 1948-2123

Meiri, however, includes Noah and excludes Shem.

לְהוֹדִיעַ כַּמָּה אֶרֶךְ אַפַּיִם לְפָנָיו; שֶׁכָּל הַדּוֹרוֹת הָיוּ מַכְעִיסִין וּבָאִין — *to show the degree of His patience; for all those generations angered Him increasingly.* God gives man freedom of choice to live according to His expectations and thus implement His will in the world. After the Flood, God built a new world through Noah and his family, and patiently waited another ten generations for renewed mankind to exercise its freedom of will properly. Instead, many incidents occurred during this waiting period that ignited His wrath, most prominently the building of the Tower of Babel and the resultant dispersion (see *Genesis* 11:1-9). Nonetheless, God did not decimate the people of that era.

Pri Chaim notes that God's patience during these ten generations was even greater than during the first ten generations. The knowledge of the cataclysmic Flood should have shocked its survivors and their descendants out of their spiritual lethargy. Even though they continued to sin, God patiently awaited the appearance of Abraham.

עַד שֶׁבָּא אַבְרָהָם אָבִינוּ וְקִבֵּל שְׂכַר כֻּלָּם — *until our forefather Abraham came and received the reward of them all.* Abraham's good deeds equaled what could have been expected from the ten previous generations, hence, they were all saved in his merit. On the other hand, since he assumed their responsibilities in this world, he also received the reward earmarked for them in the World to Come (*Rav*). [According to *Rav*, the mishnah might be rendered "until our forefather Abraham came and received the reward *that would have been theirs.*"]

Only Abraham was great enough to earn all the reward of the earlier generations. Noah was not sufficiently righteous to deserve the reward of his predecessors (*Rashi*).

Machzor Vitry and *Meiri* say that Abraham received the reward of all ten generations because he was the one who brought humanity back to God by teaching them the proper path. When the Torah speaks of "the souls that they [Abraham and Sarah] made in Haran" (*Genesis* 12:5), it refers to the people they had converted to faith in God. Hence, he

3. There were ten generations from Noah to Abraham — to show the degree of His patience; for all those generations angered Him increasingly, until our forefather Abraham came and received the reward of them all.

4. Our forefather Abraham was tested with ten trials and he

was responsible for the good deeds of all those people and was rewarded in kind.

According to *Tiferes Yisrael*, Abraham's reward was the privilege of being the one who would implement God's will in the world. Initially, God had created Adam and *all* his descendants to fulfill this charge of living a sanctified life. When man's stature was diminished by twenty generations of failure and sin, the universal scope of the Godly mission was narrowed and assigned specifically to Abraham and his descendants. All the great spiritual opportunities, including Godly revelation, the giving of the Torah, prophecy, Divine miracles, and

a covenantal relationship with God, might have been the privilege of all men. Now, however, all of these gifts were reserved for Abraham and his descendants.

Sefer HaMussar explains somewhat differently that God lavishly rewards the righteous person who comes after generations of wicked people. Since he rejects their negative influence and does not adopt the life-style of his environment, turning instead to truth and the ways of God, he deserves all the reward the previous generations might have received, because their sinful lives and the culture they created constituted his challenge.

Mishnah 4

עֲשָׂרָה נִסְיוֹנוֹת נִתְנַסָּה אַבְרָהָם אָבִינוּ — *Our forefather Abraham was tested with ten trials.* Abraham's faith in God was put under stress ten times. The commentators differ on the precise identity of the ten trials, for more than ten incidents in Abraham's life could be so designated.

According to *Avos d'Rabbi Nosson* (33), he was tested as follows:

☐ *Twice* when he had to move — when God commanded him to leave his ancestral home; and when, after God's glowing promise to him of a good life in Canaan, he was forced to go to Egypt in the face of a famine.

☐ *Twice* in connection with his two sons — the difficult decision to heed Sarah's insistence that

he drive away Ishmael (21:10), and the supreme test of binding his beloved son Isaac to the altar as a sacrifice (ibid. 22:1-2).

☐ *Twice* in regard to his two wives — when Sarah was taken from him to Pharaoh's palace, and when he was required to drive Hagar from his home (21:10). [Other commentators include the banishment of Hagar with that of Ishmael as a single test. In place of the deleted item, they include among the list of the trials Sarah's abduction to the palace of Abimelech (20:2).]

☐ *Once* on the occasion of his war with the kings (14:14).

☐ *Once* at the Covenant Between the Parts (15:7-21), when he was told that his descendants

---

◆§ **Frustrated desire.** What reward would they have deserved in any case if, as the mishnah says, they *angered Him increasingly*? *Sfas Emes* explains the origin of the reward that Abraham was given. God, the epitome of goodness, always seeks to bestow benefits upon people, but His wisdom decreed that man must earn and deserve that beneficence. If he sins, he "frustrates" God's will to shower His goodness upon mankind, and the people of the ten generations angered God by denying Him that opportunity. This is similar to the frustration of a host who prepares a magnificent banquet — for a guest who never arrives. Only when Abraham came and assumed the spiritual responsibilities of his predecessors and contemporaries did God find someone worthy to receive the beneficence He longed to bestow.

would be enslaved and exiled for four hundred years.

☐ *Once*, in Ur Kasdim, when he was thrown into a fiery furnace by Nimrod (see *Rashi* to 11:28).

☐ *Once* at the covenant of circumcision (17:9-11), which was an unprecedented act, as well as a dangerous undertaking at his advanced age.

☐ Other trials are cited by various commentaries.

According to *Rashi*, one of them is the fact that Abraham had to hide underground for thirteen years from Nimrod. *Rambam* includes Abraham's decision to marry Hagar after concluding that Sarah would not bear his children. *R' Yonah* lists among the ten the difficult negotiations to purchase a burial site for Sarah.

These ten trials were not only significant in terms of Abraham's reward or his designation as the progenitor of the Jewish people; they had vast, monumental consequences for our national character. Abraham is called our forefather because his descendants reap much benefit from his firm faith (*Tosafos Yom Tov*). How is this so? It is an established principle of Jewish spiritual history that the actions of our forefathers portend the future of their descendants. Many of the attributes the forefathers displayed were transmitted to their children as part of a spiritual genetic code. For example, the Jewish willingness throughout the generations to sacrifice their lives for the sake of God is rooted in Abraham's willingness to allow himself to be thrown into the fiery furnace, and later in his readiness to slaughter Isaac, if that was God's will. Likewise, the Jewish people's passionate love for their ancestral home became part of our spiritual make-up through Abraham's bravery in uprooting himself from his home to go to the Holy Land. By bringing famine to the Land and forcing Abraham to emigrate temporarily to Egypt, God conditioned us historically to exhibit unques-

tioning loyalty to Him and to believe that everything He brings upon us is for the good (*Ruach Chaim*).

Machzor Vitry and *Rashi* note the parallelism of the number ten, in God's ten utterances and Abraham's ten trials. The trials corresponded to the Divine utterances which brought the world into existence (see 5:1), for the loyalty that Abraham displayed ten times is the kind which sustains and justifies Creation.

וְעָמַד בְּכֻלָּם — *and he withstood all of them.* Since God knows what a person will and will not do, and He knows a person's capabilities, what is the purpose of a trial? Further, the Sages teach that a person is never tested beyond his capabilities, which implies that a Divine test is inflicted only upon people whose greatness is already proven. Clearly, therefore, God inflicts trials for a purpose that goes far beyond one's apparent abilities.

In introducing Abraham's climactic trial, the *Akeidah* of Isaac (see *Genesis* 22:1), *Ramban* explains that the trial is not for God's benefit, in the sense that a teacher may administer a test to evaluate the performance of a student. That sort of test benefits the teacher by providing information; but God's test is for the benefit of the person. God already knows what he can and will do; but He cannot reward a person for potential and fine intentions alone. God's reward and punishment are reserved primarily for voluntary *performance* of deeds. Thus when God puts a great man to the test, it permits him to translate potential into reality, so that the person is not only afforded the opportunity to achieve a higher spiritual level by overcoming obstacles in his service of God, but he can be rewarded for the performance itself.

Ramban (22:1) emphasizes: "Know that HASHEM tests [only] the righteous; when he knows that the righteous *tzaddik* will do His will and He wishes to

---

⏴ **Committed exile.** *Mili d'Avos* adds: The courage exhibited by parents who allow and encourage their children to commit their best years to intensive Torah study is also a spiritual heritage from our forefather Abraham. Such parents and their children emulate Abraham by following God to an unknown destination, where their livelihood would seem to be questionable. Such people are true descendants of the one whom God called "Abraham, My beloved" (*Isaiah* 41:8).

5/4

withstood all of them — to show the degree of our forefather Abraham's love for God.

benefit him, He will command him [to undergo] the trial. But He will not test the wicked, who will not obey. Behold, therefore, that all trials [mentioned] in the Torah were [administered] for the benefit of the one being tested."

Sforno adds that God wants the righteous to demonstrate in deed their love for and fear of God; by translating their feelings into action, they emulate God Himself, Whose merciful deeds are continuing and endless. In actualizing their great potential, the righteous fulfill the purpose of Creation — that man emulate God to the greatest extent possible, thus allowing Him to shower His goodness upon humanity.

Many commentators note that the word נִסָּיוֹן, *trial*, is related to נֵס, *banner*, an item that is raised up high. In this sense, the purpose of a trial is not to test a person in the usual sense of the word, to see if he can pass it; and most assuredly it is not intended as a trap for the wicked, for if it were, they would be tested. Rather, a trial is meant to "raise up" the righteous by lifting them to new spiritual heights. It is a well-known human phenomenon that those who successfully survive the crucible of difficult experiences emerge as better people. No matter what his circumstances, someone who turns theory into practice in difficult situations gains wisdom and strength of character. Abraham was already a great man, but he became greater with each triumphant navigation of a new trial. This, indeed, is the purpose of a trial — not to prove to God what He already knows, but to raise the subject to new heights, just as a banner is lifted higher and higher on its pole. Furthermore, just as a banner acts as a signal to the viewer for that which lies out of sight below it, so man's hidden qualities remain out of sight until they are brought to light by means of a trial.

Sfas Emes relates the word נִסָּיוֹן to נֵס, *miracle*. Just as a miracle is God's way of helping man by going beyond the limitations of nature, a trial of faith calls on man to supersede his own natural limitations for the sake of God.

The mishnah speaks of Abraham *withstanding* (literally, *standing*) the ten trials. Rather than withdrawing in the face of adversity, he "stood" firm; thus he grew from the experience and achieved an even more elevated status (*Midrash Shmuel*).

לְהוֹדִיעַ כַּמָּה חִבָּתוֹ שֶׁל אַבְרָהָם אָבִינוּ — *to show the degree of our forefather Abraham's love for God.* This rendering follows *Rashi* and *R' Yonah*. Through his trial, people became aware of the depth of Abraham's loyalty and commitment to God, and could gain inspiration from it. According to *Meiri*, and as amplified by *R' Shlomo Kluger*, however, the converse is indicated: Abraham's success in overcoming the ten trials indicate *God's love for Abraham*. Incessant trials are a sign of the innate potential which God invests in a person, and which the trial is intended to actualize. By withstanding his trials, Abraham revealed the depth of his personality, indicating the great potential with which God had endowed him.

⏴⏴ **Parallel people.** The Midrash explains the angel's repetition of Abraham's name at the *Akeidah* with the phrase: אַבְרָהָם דִּלְעֵילָא אַבְרָהָם דִּלְתַתָּא, *Abraham above*, *Abraham below*. *Abraham above* is the Abraham that God imbued with almost superhuman potential; *Abraham below* is the fully developed person he became when he actualized all that potential by overcoming the ten trials. At the tenth and final trial, the last bit of potential imbued in the *Abraham of above* was realized and became synonymous with the flesh-and-blood *Abraham below*. Thus, the ten trials manifested the greatness of God's love for Abraham, for through them it became clear to what extent God had endowed him (*R' Gedaliah Schorr*).

Abarbanel suggests that sometimes the righteous are tested in order to benefit those who witness their trial and their ultimate triumph. Through being exposed to the deep commitment of those who are willing to follow God's word even under trying circumstances, they will come to realize the value of a life molded by subservience to His will.

[ה] **עֲשָׂרָה** נִסִּים נַעֲשׂוּ לַאֲבוֹתֵינוּ בְּמִצְרַיִם וַעֲשָׂרָה עַל הַיָּם. עֶשֶׂר מַכּוֹת הֵבִיא הַקָּדוֹשׁ בָּרוּךְ הוּא עַל הַמִּצְרִים בְּמִצְרַיִם וְעֶשֶׂר עַל הַיָּם.

[ו] **עֲשָׂרָה** נִסְיוֹנוֹת נִסּוּ אֲבוֹתֵינוּ אֶת הַקָּדוֹשׁ בָּרוּךְ

Mishnah 5

עֲשָׂרָה נִסִּים נַעֲשׂוּ לַאֲבוֹתֵינוּ בְּמִצְרַיִם — *Ten miracles were performed for our ancestors in Egypt.* Only through Divine intervention were our ancestors saved from the ten plagues that God brought upon the Egyptians. The Torah states about each of the plagues [except lice — see *R' Yonah*] that God differentiated between the Jews and the Egyptians. Since Divine retribution operates on the principle that "once the forces of destruction are unleashed, they do not differentiate between good people [who deserve to be spared] and evil people [who deserve to be punished]" (see *Bava Kamma* 60a), it is due only to the miraculous intervention of God that the Jews were spared from the suffering of the plagues (*Rambam, R' Yonah, Tosafos Yom Tov*; see also *Magen Avos*).

Derech Avos notes that even though Pharaoh increased the Jews' backbreaking workload after Moses and Aaron's initial visit, he did not do this after the other plagues. These reprieves, he suggests, are the miracles referred to here — but they number only nine. The tenth miracle occurred in conjunction with the plague of the firstborn, when the Jews used a sheep, the Egyptian deity, for the Pesach offering and yet suffered no retribution from the Egyptians.

Ramban notes the difference in usage between the first and second parts of the mishnah. In the following statement, the mishnah says that God inflicted the plagues on the Egyptians, using the active form of the verb. The present clause states passively that miracles *were performed* [literally, *were done*] for our ancestors. The reason for this is that the ten plagues were targeted *directly* at the Egyptians, and the Jews were miraculously saved as a result.

HaChassid Yaavetz reverses this emphasis by pointing out that the mishnah mentions the miracles performed for the Jews *before* the punishment of the Egyptians. This is because the primary purpose of the ten plagues was *not* the punishment of the Egyptians, but rather the clear expression of Israel's chosenness, as demonstrated through the fact that they were totally spared the suffering of the plagues.

וַעֲשָׂרָה עַל הַיָּם — *and ten at the Sea.*

The commentators (*Rav, R' Yonah,* and *Rambam*), based on *Avos d'Rabbi Nosson* (33), list the ten miracles as follows: (1) The Sea split; (2) tunnels were formed in the Sea; (3) the seabed was dry, allowing the Jews to pass through comfortably and unimpeded; (4) the seabed turned into a muddy morass, stopping the Egyptians in their pursuit of the Jews; (5) the waters solidified into a rock like substance that caused injury to the Egyptians; (6) the seawaters formed into perfectly shaped bricks; (7) the walls formed by the waters created twelve separate corridors, thus allowing each of the twelve tribes an independent passage; (8) the walls were transparent, allowing each tribe to see the others passing through the Sea; (9) the sweet water in the Sea remained in liquid form to quench the thirst of the Jews; (10) the remaining sweet water froze in place, ready for when the Jews would need to drink again.

Magen Avos notes that God's Ineffable Name is mentioned ten times in the Song by the Sea, a clear allusion to these ten miraculous events.

עֶשֶׂר מַכּוֹת הֵבִיא הַקָּדוֹשׁ בָּרוּךְ הוּא עַל הַמִּצְרִים בְּמִצְרַיִם — *Ten plagues did the Holy One, Blessed is He, bring upon the Egyptians in Egypt.* The ten plagues are given in the Torah as follows: (1) All the water in Egypt turned into *blood.* (2) *Frogs* overran

5. Ten miracles were performed for our ancestors in Egypt and ten at the Sea. Ten plagues did the Holy One, Blessed is He, bring upon the Egyptians in Egypt and ten at the Sea.

6. [With] ten trials did our ancestors test the Holy One, Blessed

---

the land of Egypt. (3) *Lice* infested man and beast. (4) *Swarms of wild animals* filled the land. (5) An epidemic of *pestilence* struck the Egyptian livestock. (6) *Boils* broke out on the Egyptian people and their animals. (7) *Fire-filled hailstones* rained on the country, destroying foliage, plants, and trees. (8) Foliage spared by the hail was eaten by unprecedentedly large droves of *locusts*. (9) The country was enveloped by palpable *darkness*. (10) Every *firstborn* in Egypt, both human and animal, died at midnight of the fifteenth of Nissan.

וְעֶשֶׂר עַל הַיָּם — *and ten at the Sea.* *Rashi* and *Rav* enumerate the Biblical references to these ten plagues found in the Song by the Sea (*Exodus* 15:1-19): (1) רָמָה בַיָּם, *He hurled* [*horse and rider*] *into the Sea.* (2) יָרָה בַיָּם, [*Pharaoh's chariots and army*] *He threw into the Sea.* (3) טֻבְּעוּ בְיַם סוּף, *They* [*the Egyptians*] *were mired in the Sea of Reeds.* (4) תְּהֹמֹת יְכַסְיֻמוּ, *Deep waters covered them.* (5) יָרְדוּ בִמְצוֹלֹת, *They descended in the depths.* (6) תִּרְעַץ אוֹיֵב, [*Your right hand,* HASHEM,] *smashes the enemy.* (7) תַּהֲרֹס קָמֶיךָ, *You shatter Your opponents.* (8) יֹאכְלֵמוֹ כַּקַּשׁ, [*You send forth Your wrath, and*] *it consumes them like straw.* (9) כִּסָּמוֹ יָם, *The Sea enshrouded them.* (10) צָלֲלוּ כַּעוֹפֶרֶת, [*The mighty*] *sank like lead* [*in water*].

R' Yonah gives a different listing of the ten plagues inflicted on the Egyptians at the Sea of Reeds: (1) Darkness descended on the Egyptians, while for the Jews the night was lit up. (2) The pillar of cloud that led the Jewish camp descended to the seabed, turning it into soft clay. (3) The pillar of fire that led the Jewish camp at night heated the ground, dislocating the hooves of the Egyptian horses. (4) God removed the wheels of the Egyptians' chariots. (5) God caused them great difficulty in driving. (6) They were prevented from escaping from the Sea. (7) God stirred the Egyptians' bodies in the Sea, as one stirs up the contents of a pot. (8) They were swallowed up at the bottom of the Sea. (9) They sank like lead (*Exodus* 15:10). (10) The bodies of the Egyptians were washed up on the banks of the Sea, displaying them in front of the Jews. [See *Vilna Gaon* based on *Avos d'Rabbi Nosson* for a variant listing.]

This mishnah seems to contradict the passage from the *Mechilta* (incorporated in the Passover *Haggadah*), in which one opinion holds there were fifty miracles at the Sea, another that there were two hundred miracles, and yet a third posits that two hundred and fifty miracles occurred at the splitting of the Sea. This clearly indicates that many more — at least five times as many — plagues occurred at the Sea than in Egypt. *Magen Avos* views this as a point of contention between the two Tannaitic sources. *Rambam* writes that while there were more plagues at the Sea, they were all of the same ten categories as those that occurred in Egypt.

Maharal explains the redemption of Jews as a two-stage process. Man is susceptible to harm both from other human beings and from the forces of nature; God redeemed Israel from both sources. Pharaoh and the mighty Egyptian empire were defeated during the Exodus, thus exhibiting that no human power can stand up against God; and the splitting of the sea proved beyond a shadow of a doubt that the Creator has full control of His world and can change the "immutable" laws of nature on behalf of His people. Our mishnah tells of the miracles of these two equally important stages of redemption.

Mishnah 6

עֲשָׂרָה נִסְיוֹנוֹת נִסּוּ אֲבוֹתֵינוּ אֶת הַקָּדוֹשׁ בָּרוּךְ הוּא בַּמִּדְבָּר — [*With*] *ten trials did our ancestors test the Holy One, Blessed is He, in the Wilderness.* The Sages identify these ten trials as follows: (1) When the Egyptians pursued the Israelites to the Sea, the Jews told Moses they would have preferred to remain slaves in Egypt than to die in the Wilderness (*Exodus* 14:11). (2) They complained when they had nothing to drink but the bitter waters of Marah (ibid. 15:24). (3) They complained again when they

ה/ז הוּא בַּמִּדְבָּר, שֶׁנֶּאֱמַר: ,,וַיְנַסּוּ אֹתִי זֶה עֶשֶׂר פְּעָמִים, וְלֹא שָׁמְעוּ בְּקוֹלִי".

[יז] עֲשָׂרָה נִסִּים נַעֲשׂוּ לַאֲבוֹתֵינוּ בְּבֵית הַמִּקְדָּשׁ:

ran out of food (ibid. 16:3). (4) They left manna over, even though they had been told not to (ibid. 16:20). (5) They left the camp to gather manna on the Sabbath, even though they had been told there would not be any (ibid. 16:27). (6) They complained against Moses when their water ran out at Rephidim (ibid. 17:2). (7) They worshiped the Golden Calf (ibid. 32:4). (8) They rebelled against God's commandments (*Numbers* 11:1). (9) They complained that the manna was not good (ibid. 11:4). (10) They believed the spies' evil report about *Eretz Yisrael* (*Arachin* 15a).

Rambam includes the time at Rephidim when the nation questioned whether God was present among them (*Exodus* 17:7).

Since many of these incidents were blatant sins, the term "trials" is rather puzzling. *Tiferes Yisrael* and *Tosafos Yom Tov* differentiate between sins, which are the result of misguided desire, and those that result from man's doubts of God's power or of the veracity of particular prophecies. Sins in the second category are considered a challenge to and trial of God.

The ten sins listed were of such magnitude that they "tempted" God to destroy His people. Hence the Nation tested God by not listening to Him (*R' Shmuel Alter*).

Even though these ten trials cast the Jewish people in a negative light, they are listed to teach us the extent of God's patience with us. He always awaits our

repentance; in spite of our disloyalty, He will never disown us or exchange us for another nation (*Avos al Banim*).

Maharam Shick also sees a positive side to the Jewish nation's incessant testing of God. The Talmud teaches that God chose the Jewish people as His nation since they are the most obstinate of all peoples (*Beitzah* 25b). *Ramban* (*Deuteronomy* 7:7) explains: "A lover desires someone with the stubborn perseverance to maintain the relationship under the duress of life's difficulties. The Jewish people are particularly suited for this role since they are the most obstinate of the nations. They will withstand all stresses placed on their relationship with God, and overcome all trials and tribulations." This quality of being "stiff necked" serves as the bedrock of the Jews' chosenness. Had they not originally manifested this "hardheadedness" in a negative way, later generations might have claimed that their forefathers' belief in God and acceptance of His Torah was the product of a pliable and easygoing character. Thus, our mishnah teaches that these obstinate people, who experienced ten serious crises in their faith, ultimately accepted the word of God and became His Chosen People.

The juxtaposition of the miracles performed for the Jews at the Exodus and at the Splitting of the Sea with their ten trials of God comes to teach us that experiencing miracles does not guarantee fidelity in matters of faith. We often decry our own times, so far removed from the spiritual exposure of our ancestors, claiming that an open manifestation of God's Presence would remove our doubts of faith and elevate us to greater spiritual heights. The mishnah teaches us not to delude ourselves that

⋅≈§ **A wall.** The words of the *Hoshana* prayer אוֹם אֲנִי חוֹמָה, *Nation [that declares], "I am like a wall,"* reflect this idea. Israel's nationhood (אוֹם) is based on its eternal protestation: "אֲנִי חוֹמָה — I am like an immovable wall." Nothing can move Israel from its dedication to God.

⋅≈§ **Miracles not enough.** Rabbi Eliyahu Lopian explained in this vein the famous comment of *Rashi* regarding Jethro's conversion (see *Exodus* 18:1 and *Rashi* ad loc.): "What did he hear that induced him to come [to the Jewish people]? The Splitting of the Sea and the battle with Amalek." But Amalek had also heard of the supernatural events at the Sea, yet remained unmoved by them — and was even audacious enough to attack God's nation. Jethro realized that miracles do not always bolster faith or transform the beliefs of the Amaleks of the world; those who refuse to recognize the hand of God will always interpret events to suit their own purposes.

7. Ten miracles were performed for our ancestors in the Holy Tem-

---

living in an age of miracles would necessarily ensure our spiritual stature. The people who experienced the miraculous events in Egypt and at the Sea were nonetheless capable of gaping lapses of faith and of rebellion against God (*Darkei Yosher*).

שֶׁנֶּאֱמַר: ,,וַיְנַסּוּ אֹתִי זֶה עֶשֶׂר פְּעָמִים, וְלֹא שָׁמְעוּ בְּקוֹלִי'' — *as it said: "They have tested me these ten times and did not heed My voice" (Numbers 14:22).* This was God's reaction to the report of the spies,

who doubted God's ability to conquer the inhabitants of the Holy Land; it was the tenth time the people tested Him (*Rav*). The mishnah quotes this verse to teach that the number ten is not used in a figurative sense to mean "many" trials (see *Rashbam* and *Ibn Ezra* ad loc.); it is an exact number and refers to ten specific incidents as enumerated in the Talmud [*Arachin* 15a] (*Magen Avos*).

Mishnah 7

עֲשָׂרָה נִסִּים נַעֲשׂוּ לַאֲבוֹתֵינוּ בְּבֵית הַמִּקְדָּשׁ — *Ten miracles were performed for our ancestors in the Holy Temple.* Many miracles occurred in the Holy Temple, some of which were to indicate that the Divine Presence resides among Jews. [See *Yoma* 21b, which relates, among others, the miracle of the western lamp of the Menorah, which was the first lamp to be lit, yet the last to be extinguished (see 1:2, s.v. שִׁמְעוֹן הַצַּדִּיק).] These miracles occurred *for* [the benefit of] *our ancestors.*

The previous mishnayos need not list the miracles or trials, because they are specified or alluded to in the Bible, but the miracles that took place in the Temple are not found in Scripture, so they must be listed in the mishnah (*Tosafos Yom Tov*).

In the Holy Temple, the abode of the Divine Presence, many of the laws of Nature were transcended. *HaChassid Yaavetz* explains: Spoilage

and destruction are a result of Adam's sin. In the world which God originally created according to His will, everything was to be perfect and eternal. Many things that seem miraculous to us are in fact nothing more than a manifestation of conditions that existed before Adam's sin. For example, the prophecy וְגָר זְאֵב עִם כֶּבֶשׂ, *The wolf and the sheep shall live [peacefully] together (Isaiah 11:6)*, expresses the idea that in Messianic times, as in God's original design of nature, animals will not be carnivorous. [See *Ramban* to *Leviticus* 26:6 who takes such prophecies literally; but *Rambam, Hilchos Melachim* 12:1, views these prophecies as allegorical.] The Holy Temple, a microcosm of Creation (see *Ramban* to *Exodus* 25:24), was not subject to the familiar laws of nature, but instead functioned according to the conditions that defined the world before the sin — conditions that now seem miraculous.

◆ᶊ **Back to the origins.** *Ramban* explains that after the six days of Creation, while God does not create anything *ex nihilo*, He may cause blessing to flow from a minimal source that He causes to grow, as He wishes. The golden crown on the *Shulchan* (Table) in the Tabernacle, and later in the Temple, was a source of prosperity for all Israel, for God lifted the limitations that were placed on the natural world after the sin. God punished Adam with the curse of "By the sweat of your brow you shall eat bread" (*Genesis* 3:19). Prior to this curse, his food came to him effortlessly, and in the Holy Temple, where the restrictive laws of nature after the sin were suspended, man was able to return to a world of sustenance without toil. [See *Daas Chochmah U'Mussar* 1:22 for a beautiful presentation of this concept.]

לֹא הִפִּילָה אִשָּׁה מֵרֵיחַ בְּשַׂר הַקֹּדֶשׁ; וְלֹא הִסְרִיחַ בְּשַׂר הַקֹּדֶשׁ מֵעוֹלָם; וְלֹא נִרְאָה זְבוּב בְּבֵית הַמִּטְבְּחַיִם; וְלֹא אֵרַע קֶרִי לְכֹהֵן גָּדוֹל בְּיוֹם הַכִּפּוּרִים; וְלֹא כִבּוּ הַגְּשָׁמִים אֵשׁ שֶׁל עֲצֵי הַמַּעֲרָכָה; וְלֹא נִצְּחָה הָרוּחַ אֶת עַמּוּד הֶעָשָׁן;

לֹא הִפִּילָה אִשָּׁה מֵרֵיחַ בְּשַׂר הַקֹּדֶשׁ — *No woman miscarried because of the aroma of the sacrificial meat.* The tantalizing aroma of the meat of the Temple offerings could arouse in a pregnant woman such a desire to eat it that she might miscarry. Miraculously, this never occurred (*Rashi, R' Yonah*), even though it would have been permitted to feed it to her in order to save her life. Alternatively, even though a woman under such circumstances would have been allowed to eat sacrificial meat (or any other forbidden substance), pregnant women might have refrained from entering the Courtyard, lest they be forced to rely on this leniency. Thus, our mishnah teaches that no such fear ever existed, because of the miracle that no woman was ever overcome with such an uncontrollable craving (*Tiferes Yisrael*; see *Rishon LeTzion*, who emends a text of *Rashi* to read וּבָאַת לְטַעוֹם מֵהֶן שׁוֹמְעִין לָה, deleting the word אֵין; see also *Tosafos HaChadashim*).

Mili d'Avos (Warsaw) adds that a desire for food is related to a person's physical desires. The sacrificial meat was of such sanctity that it did not arouse these desires in man.

וְלֹא הִסְרִיחַ בְּשַׂר הַקֹּדֶשׁ מֵעוֹלָם — *the sacrificial meat never became putrid.* Most minor offerings

(קָדָשִׁים קַלִּים) may be eaten for two days and one night after they are offered (see *Zevachim* 55a), but even though they were not refrigerated and were exposed to a hot climate, they never spoiled. Alternatively, this refers to instances when one was unable to burn the limbs of a burnt offering immediately. In such cases, he was permitted to place them on the Altar and burn them later, and they did not become unfit even if they were not burned for a few days. Nevertheless, they did not spoil (*Rashi, Tosafos Yom Tov*).

Midrash Shmuel notes the expression מֵעוֹלָם, *never.* This miracle persisted during the years that Jews brought offerings in the Tabernacle at Nob, Gibeon, and Shiloh, and even during the eras when it was permissible to sacrifice on the private altars known as *bamos.*

וְלֹא נִרְאָה זְבוּב בְּבֵית הַמִּטְבְּחַיִם — *no fly was seen in the place where the [sanctified] meat was butchered.* The meat of offerings was slaughtered, butchered, and washed on marble tables erected in the Temple Courtyard, just to the north of the Altar (*Shekalim* 6:4). Even though blood and internal tissue and organs normally attract flies, they were miraculously never seen on the meat (*Meiri*), nor in the Temple slaughterhouse, a phenomenon that was

---

◆§ **Back to the source.** *Ruach Chaim* suggests that this mishnah teaches metaphorically that sanctity, by definition, rejects the filth of spiritual impurity. *Bnei Yisaschar (Adar)* notes that man's sense of smell is the only one of the senses that played no part in Adam's sin; it is the only remnant of man's original, elevated nature. Man's task on earth is to regain the exalted spiritual dimensions with which God initially endowed man. Thus, a pleasant odor is reminiscent of a heightened degree of sanctity. [It may be for this reason that before Yocheved and Miriam placed the baby Moses in the wicker basket, they smeared it with clay on the inside and with pitch only on the outside, "so that the righteous person [Moses] not smell the foul odor of pitch" (see *Exodus* 2:3; *Rashi* ad loc.).] The mishnah teaches that the sacrificial meat gave off no putrid odor, indicative of its high degree of sanctity.

◆§ **Immune.** In a homiletical vein, the *Maggid* of Mezritch renders מֵעוֹלָם as *from the world.* Truly righteous people who have elevated the physical aspects of their lives — who have "sanctified the meat," so to speak — can have contact even with people who are obsessed with worldly pleasures, and not be influenced by them. The holy "meat" never becomes spiritually putrid מֵעוֹלָם — from the world.

---

ple: (1) No woman miscarried because of the aroma of the sacrificial meat; (2) the sacrificial meat never became putrid; (3) no fly was seen in the place where the [sanctified] meat was butchered; (4) no seminal emission occurred to the High Priest on Yom Kippur; (5) the rains did not extinguish the fire on the Altar pyre; (6) the wind did not disperse the vertical column of smoke from

---

indicative of the Divine Presence resting in the Temple (*Rashi*). According to *Tiferes Yisrael*, God performed this miracle in order to spare the Kohanim who served there the discomfort of such a repulsive sight.

וְלֹא אֵירַע קֶרִי לְכֹהֵן גָּדוֹל בְּיוֹם הַכִּפּוּרִים — *no seminal emission occurred to the High Priest on Yom Kippur.* The Temple service of Yom Kippur could be performed only by a Kohen Gadol (High Priest). A seminal emission, among other causes of *tumah* (ritual impurity), renders any Kohen spiritually impure and unfit to officiate in the Temple. Such an impurity, because it emanates from the body, would be humiliating for the Kohen Gadol; miraculously it never occurred in the Temple, in order to save him from embarrassment (*Rav, Rashi*).

According to *Rashi*, the mishnah in *Yoma* (1:1), which requires that an alternate Kohen Gadol be prepared before Yom Kippur, is concerned only with other types of *tumah* (impurity). Tumah due to a seminal emission,

however, was miraculously non-existent in the Temple. (See *Yerushalmi, Yoma* 1:1, and *Korban HaEdah* ad loc. s.v. שֶׁאֵירַע קֶרִי). According to *R' Yonah*, the prescription of the mishnah in *Yoma* to prepare an alternate Kohen Gadol was established despite the miracle described here, in accord with the dictum אֵין סוֹמְכִין עַל הַנֵּס, *We may not rely on a miracle* (see *Pesachim* 64b). Meiri quotes *Tosafos Yeshanim* (*Yoma* 21a, s.v. וְלֹא אֵירַע), which suggests, based on *Yerushalmi Yoma* 1:4, that this miracle occurred only during the First Temple era; if so, it was indeed necessary to prepare an alternate Kohen Gadol.

וְלֹא כָּבוּ הַגְּשָׁמִים אֵשׁ שֶׁל עֲצֵי הַמַּעֲרָכָה — *the rains did not extinguish the fire on the Altar pyre.* The Altar was situated in the Temple Courtyard, which had no roof. Nonetheless, the rains never extinguished the fire, which was fueled by wood stacked on the Altar (*Rambam, Rav*).

וְלֹא נָצְחָה הָרוּחַ אֶת עַמּוּד הֶעָשָׁן — *the wind did not disperse the vertical column of smoke from the Altar.* The smoke from the offerings on the Altar rose in

---

◆§ **The fire never goes out.** God could just as well have made a miracle that it never rain over the site of the Temple and the Altar. Why was it necessary that it rain and yet not extinguish the flame? R' Chaim of Volozhin offers a homiletical answer based on an interpretation of the word גֶּשֶׁם, *rain,* as a reference to גַּשְׁמִיּוּת, *physicality.* No matter what worries and concerns inundate one's life, he must always be sure that the torch of his commitment to the Torah burns strongly. People often claim that making a living stands in the way of their serious involvement in Torah study and the performance of commandments. The lesson of this miracle in the Temple was that one's physical needs and desires [גֶּשֶׁם] must never, God forbid, dampen his spiritual pursuits. One must never let the גַּשְׁמִים — the physical concerns — extinguish the fire of his innate burning passion for the spiritual.

Sefer HaChareidim quotes the moving prayer of a sincere servant of God: בְּלִבָּבִי מִשְׁכָּן אֶבְנֶה לַהֲדַר כְּבוֹדוֹ, וּלְמִשְׁכָּן מִזְבֵּחַ אָשִׂים לְקַרְנֵי הוֹדוֹ וּלְנֵר תָּמִיד אֶקַּח לִי אֶת אֵשׁ הָעֲקֵדָה וּלְקָרְבָּן אַקְרִיב לוֹ אֶת נַפְשִׁי הַיְחִידָה, *In my heart I will build a Tabernacle dedicated to His glory. In that Tabernacle I will place an altar for the elevation of His splendor. As a continuous flame I will take the fire of the Akeidah, and as an offering I will offer Him my one and only soul.* Man must figuratively fulfill the Scriptural dictate, *A permanent fire shall remain aflame on the Altar; it shall not be extinguished* (*Leviticus* 6:6).

The mishnah allegorically informs man that his heart should be fired by a burning love of God, so intense and passionate that *many waters [physical pleasures] cannot extinguish the fire of this love, nor can rivers [of royal seduction or torture] wash it away. If anyone will offer all the treasures of his house for the love, he will be scorned to the extreme* (*Shir HaShirim* 8:7).

וְלֹא נִמְצָא פְסוּל בָּעְמֶר, וּבִשְׁתֵּי הַלֶּחֶם, וּבְלֶחֶם הַפָּנִים;
עוֹמְדִים צְפוּפִים, וּמִשְׁתַּחֲוִים רְוָחִים; וְלֹא הִזִּיק נָחָשׁ
וְעַקְרָב בִּירוּשָׁלַיִם מֵעוֹלָם; וְלֹא אָמַר אָדָם לַחֲבֵרוֹ:

---

a vertical column in order not to discomfit the Kohanim by going into their eyes.

Even on windy days, the smoke, miraculously, did not float downwards toward the Kohanim (*Rav, Meiri*; see *Yoma* 21b). According to *Rambam*, the miracle was slightly different. While the offerings were being burned, the wind would blow softly rather than stormily, allowing the smoke to ascend.

Rashi (based on *Yoma* ibid.) deletes these two last items (the rain and the column of smoke) from the list of the ten miracles of the Temple and compensates by viewing the next three items (the Omer, Two Loaves, and Showbread) as separate miracles. *R' Yonah* seems to concur.

וְלֹא נִמְצָא פְסוּל בָּעְמֶר — *no disqualification was found in the Omer.* A meal offering of barley was offered in the Temple on the morning of the sixteenth of Nissan, the second day of Pesach, after which the people were allowed to eat grain from the new crop (see *Leviticus* 23:19). A limited amount of barley was cut the night before and offered in the morning. Had a ritual defect been found in the barley or occurred in any other part of the service, the offering could not be brought that year, since the cutting and gathering of the barley is permitted only on the night of the sixteenth [see *Menachos* 68b and *Tiferes Yisrael* here]. Miraculously, no such problem ever occurred.

Rashi and *R' Yonah* list some of the possible problems that might disqualify the Omer: a) if it became *tamei*; b) if the frankincense was not placed on the handful (קְמִיצָה) of the offering that the Kohen scooped out for placement on the Altar; c) if one took the Omer out of the Temple Courtyard; or d) if he did not offer it before sundown.

וּבִשְׁתֵּי הַלֶּחֶם — *the Two Loaves.* Grain of the new crop was only permitted to be used for Temple offerings only after the two loaves were offered.

These had to be baked before the onset of Shavuos and offered on the festival itself. If they became disqualified by a defect, replacements could not be baked, and no offerings could be made from the new crop for the next year (*Rav, Rashi* et al.). No such defects were ever found.

וּבְלֶחֶם הַפָּנִים — *or the Show Bread.* Twelve loaves were baked each Friday and placed on the Table in the Temple on the Sabbath, where they remained until new loaves replaced them on the following Sabbath (see *Exodus* 25:30 and *Leviticus* 24:5). If a defect were found, the *mitzvah* could not be performed because new loaves could not be baked on the Sabbath; but no defect was ever found (*Rav, R' Yonah* et al.). *R' Yonah* notes that the loaves of the Show Bread miraculously remained as fresh during the entire week as when they were placed there (see *Menachos* 96b).

As mentioned earlier, *Rashi* and *R' Yonah* delete the miracles of the Altar pyre and the pillar of smoke from our mishnah, considering the last three items (Omer, Two Loaves, and Show Bread) instead as completing the count of ten miracles. *Rav, Meiri*, and others view all three instances as a collective single miracle among the ten. *Tiferes Yisrael* suggests that the reason the three cases are reckoned as one is that they are variations of the same theme, i.e., that God made a miracle since a defect would leave irreparable damage.

עוֹמְדִים צְפוּפִים, וּמִשְׁתַּחֲוִים רְוָחִים — *the people stood crowded together, yet there was ample space when they prostrated themselves.* Throngs of pilgrims gathered in the Temple Courtyard on the festivals and Yom Kippur, filling it to capacity. Yet miraculously, though there was not even enough room to stand comfortably, each person had ample room to prostrate himself and confess his sins on Yom Kippur, or

---

◆§ **Standing out in the crowd.** R' Yehoshua Heschel of Monostrisht views the mishnah as testimony to the abiding faith of the Jewish people and their ability to thank God for their lot in life, whatever it may be. Even though Jews sometimes stand ''crowded,'' oppressed by the vicissitudes of life, they still thank God for providing amply for their needs.

the Altar; (7) no disqualification was found in the Omer, the Two Loaves, or the Show Bread; (8) the people stood crowded together, yet there was ample space when they prostrated themselves; (9) neither serpent nor scorpion ever caused injury in Jerusalem; (10) nor did any man say to his fellow, "The

---

to recite personal prayers on the festivals, without being overheard by his neighbors (*Rashi, Rav*). *Meiri* renders צְפוּפִים as *suspended*, as in צָף עַל פְּנֵי הַמַּיִם, *floating on the surface of the water*. The Temple Courtyard was so crowded that many people were literally suspended in midair, supported by those surrounding them, with their feet off the ground. Nonetheless, they were able to bow down comfortably.

Shelah, Ruach Chaim, and *R' Aharon of Karlin* all offer the following homiletical explanation: When people are "standing" tall with their own pride and selfishness, they feel "crowded"; everyone seems to be in their way. However, when they prostate themselves by acting humbly and bending their own wishes to the needs of others, they find that there is ample room for everyone.

וְלֹא הִזִּיק נָחָשׁ וְעַקְרָב בִּירוּשָׁלַיִם מֵעוֹלָם — *neither serpent nor scorpion ever caused injury in Jerusalem.*

No serpent or scorpion ever bit a person fatally in Jerusalem (*Rashi*). The sanctity of the city protected its inhabitants (*Machzor Vitry*) so that the many snakes and scorpions found in Jerusalem miraculously did no harm (*Meiri* and *Tiferes Yisrael*).

Homiletically, *Ruach Chaim* explains our mishnah based on the Talmudic axiom אֵין הַנָּחָשׁ מֵמִית אֶלָּא הַחֵטְא מֵמִית, *It is not the snake, but rather the sin that kills* (*Shemos Rabbah* 3:16; see also *Berachos* 33a). Sin is deadly; the venomous snake is nothing more than God's agent of punishment. The Midrash (*Bamidbar Rabbah* 21:19) teaches that the continual-offering [*tamid*] of the evening atoned for sins committed by day, and the one in the morning for those committed at night. Hence, the city of Jerusalem was always free of sin, and the serpents and scorpions were not used as Divine agents of inflicting retribution.

◆§ **When the heart bows.** True humility and subservience toward God — and even toward man — are not measured as much by actions as by one's innermost emotions and thoughts. When one ponders the greatness of God, he senses his own insignificance and his dependence on Him. Such emotions constitute true prostration before God. Likewise, a truly humble person is one who understands that he must provide for the emotional needs of others, even at his own expense.

The following passage from the Sabbath prayers refers homiletically to such serene humility: וְכָל קוֹמָה לְפָנֶיךָ תִשְׁתַּחֲוֶה, *Every erect spine shall prostrate itself before You*, meaning, "Even while erect, [one should] prostrate himself before You." One must "bow" to God even when physically erect. Bowing is not merely a physical action; it is a state of mind and heart (*R' Yechiel* [son-in-law of the *Baal Shem Tov*).

Egotistical people often suffer from emotional claustrophobia, feeling that people are not allowing them the space they need. This idea is expressed succinctly in the pithy folk expression מִי שֶׁאֵינוֹ תּוֹפֵס מָקוֹם בְּשׁוּם מָקוֹם יֵשׁ לוֹ מָקוֹם בְּכָל מָקוֹם, *Anyone who does not seize a place any place* [i.e., view himself with an exaggerated sense of importance] *has a place* [i.e., feels welcome] *every place*.

◆§ **Good will and prosperity.** The two last stiches of the mishnah — about the snakes and scorpions, and the spaciousness of Jerusalem — are related. Serpents and scorpions allude allegorically to gossipers and rumor mongers, who inject the insidious poison of *lashon hara* into society. When people are preoccupied with such deadly pastimes, everyone feels threatened by his fellow, and bad will escalates. Jerusalem, however, was free of this viper of slander, so that people could find ways to make a living. Peace thus leads to prosperity. This is the homiletic lesson of King David's words: *He [God] Who makes your borders peaceful, and with the cream of the wheat He sates you* (Psalms 147:14), implying that peacefulness and good will are associated with satiety. Our mishnah teaches as well that the absence of the viperous practice of gossip among the citizens of Jerusalem put them at peace with one another, and no one ever felt that his livelihood was threatened (*R' Chanoch Zvi of Bendin*).

[ח] **עֲשָׂרָה** דְּבָרִים נִבְרְאוּ בְּעֶרֶב שַׁבָּת בֵּין הַשְּׁמָשׁוֹת,
וְאֵלּוּ הֵן; פִּי הָאָרֶץ, וּפִי הַבְּאֵר, פִּי

וְלֹא אָמַר אָדָם לַחֲבֵרוֹ: "צַר לִי הַמָּקוֹם שֶׁאָלִין בִּירוּשָׁלָיִם" — *nor did any man say to his fellow, "The space is insufficient for me to stay overnight in Jerusalem."* Because of the holiness of the city, God provided for the needs of all its residents, so that no one ever had to move to another city to seek a livelihood. Thus, no one ever complained, "The place is too confining for me — I don't find enough economic opportunity here" (*Rashi, Rav, Machzor Vitry*). Alternatively, this refers to those who came to Jerusalem for the pilgrimage festivals. No one complained that there was no room for him — that he lacked space or that things were too expensive. Though throngs of people came to the city, it was miraculously able to accommodate all of them sufficiently (*Rav*)

R' Yonah homiletically interprets the following words of King David as a reference to the expansive properties of Jerusalem. יְרוּשָׁלַיִם הַבְּנוּיָה כְּעִיר שֶׁחֻבְּרָה לָהּ יַחְדָּו, *The built-up Jerusalem is like a city that is united together* (*Psalms* 122:3). When God built Jerusalem, He provided it with the ability to contain all of Israel and to host all its visitors in a flourishing atmosphere.

Mishnah 8

עֲשָׂרָה דְּבָרִים נִבְרְאוּ בְּעֶרֶב שַׁבָּת בֵּין הַשְּׁמָשׁוֹת, וְאֵלּוּ הֵן — *Ten things were created on Sabbath eve, at twilight. They are.* When God created the world, He provided even for future miracles and exceptions to the natural order. These ten items were set into place just before the first Sabbath.

According to *Rambam*, the miraculous items themselves were not created then; rather, the working potential for them was woven into the tapestry of nature at that time. From the beginning of Creation, God instilled in the nature of every creature the potential to fulfill the Divine Will in any circumstance. In most cases, creations would behave uniformly in accord with the Divine laws of nature, but there would be instances when they would perform on a supernatural level, which is commonly called a miracle. The mishnah teaches that the occurrence of these ten phenomena was ordained on the sixth day.

Sefer HaMussar clarifies this concept: All the miracles and wonders performed by the prophets, as well as anything destined for the future, were planned and created in potential during the first six days of Creation. When a prophet was to announce or perform them, God simply informed him of the time and the occasion when He would perform them. Why does the mishnah mention only these ten phenomena, and why were they created immediately prior to the onset of Shabbos, after everything else? These ten have a different property from the rest of Creation. Everything God created during the first six days was designed as a prototype, which could be replicated constantly. This is implied by the words אֲשֶׁר בָּרָא אֱלֹהִים לַעֲשׂוֹת, *which God created to make* (*Genesis* 2:3). This means that all of Creation was invested with the ability to *continue* to "make" — to reproduce itself. The ten items mentioned in our mishnah were created separately because they would not be reproduced. Since their creation was for a specific time and

⋖§ **In the mind and in the place.** The mishnah does not say that the space was actually sufficient; perhaps it was not, but no one complained. Their love for the Holy City and the Temple was so great that they did not feel crowded (*Chasam Sofer*).

R' Tzemach Duran (author of *Magen Avos*) wrote in a letter: "I have been told that when the local residents come to the synagogue of Jerusalem it is filled to capacity. Nonetheless, during the festivals when thousands of pilgrims arrive in the city from the surrounding areas, all of them fit without crowding. The holiness of the place still clings to it!" (*Magen Avos*).

8. Ten things were created on Sabbath eve, at twilight. They are: The mouth of the earth, the mouth of the well, the mouth of

---

purpose, they were also created at a different time from everything else.

The lesson of our mishnah is encapsulated in the famous dictum of the Maharal: יֵשׁ סֵדֶר לְנִסִּים, *There is an order to supernatural occurrences* (Introduction to *Gevuros Hashem*). Miracles are not accidental aberrations of the rules of nature that occur, God forbid, without the guiding Hand of Heaven. All miracles are woven into the tapestry of nature, planned and waiting for the circumstances under which they are to occur (see *Meiri*).

Ramban (*Exodus* 13:15) notes that great miracles are indicative of the controlling hand of God over all of nature; from such great supernatural events one comes to realize that *everything* in nature is miraculous. What we call "nature" or the "regular order of things" is what God has ordained should take place daily or regularly; we do not think of them as miracles because we are accustomed to them, not because they are more readily comprehensible. In the *Modim* blessing of *Shemoneh Esrei*, we thank God for נִסֶּיךָ, *Your miracles*, that occur *every day*, for, indeed, the daily wonders of Creation are no less of Divine origin than the Splitting of the Sea. Based on this concept, *Tiferes Yisrael* explains the significance of the fact that these items were created immediately before the Sabbath. Everything that was created earlier seems to follow rules of nature, and we might easily make the mistaken assumption that they are not necessarily the result of a Divine guiding force. The Sabbath, however, proclaims specifically that God is the Creator Who brought the universe into being in six days and Who rested on the seventh. Israel's observance of the Sabbath laws constitutes devoted testimony to the fact that God is King and that He controls all of nature. For this reason these supernatural items were created just before the advent of the Sabbath.

פִּי הָאָרֶץ — *The mouth of the earth.*

When Korach and his fellow conspirators challenged the Divine nature of Moses' mission and the veracity of his prophecy as emanating directly from God [see *Rambam*, introduction to *Sanhedrin*, Chapter 11], Moses asked God to cause something unprecedented to happen, something so unusual that it would convince everyone of his truthfulness. This plea was not for an ordinary earthquake; such an event, though unusual, is not totally unnatural. In this case, the earth opened up, swallowed the rebels, and simply closed again, without a trace that anything had happened. *Rashi* notes that the opening itself was created and covered until the proper time (see *Numbers* 16:28-32 and *Ramban* ad loc.). According to *Rambam*, it was not the opening itself, but the potential for this phenomenon that was created on Friday at twilight.

⏎ **Unprecedented challenge, unprecedented response.** Moses' authority had been defied before, but he had never made a request from God for such a supernatural response. It was the nature of Korach's challenge that impelled Moses to seek such a stark punishment. He stated that if God did not grant his plea, it would prove to the people that *"it is not HASHEM Who has sent me."* This implies that Korach and his followers denied the Divine nature of Moses' mission; and if they were permitted to prevail, anyone could claim that even the Exodus was carried out at Moses' initiative and was not a Divine plan. Such a heresy could not be permitted to stand, lest the entirety of Moses' prophecy be denied (*Ramban*).

Moses took the very great risk of calling publicly for this unprecedented miracle, even though he knew that if it did not occur, he and his entire prophecy would be called into doubt. He felt, however, that he had no choice. If a large group of distinguished leaders — who had experienced the miracles of the Exodus, the Revelation at Sinai, and all the other wonders in the Wilderness — could doubt him, then all his teachings were worthless, for there would always be those who would attempt to cast doubt on the truth of his prophecy. In order to establish the validity of the Torah, therefore, he felt compelled to call for a demonstration of Divine intervention that would silence all possible skeptics. And if it did not occur, the danger of rebellion would be no greater than it had been before Korach's emergence (*R' Yaakov Kamenetsky*).

וּפִי הַבְּאֵר — *the mouth of the well.* During the forty years that the Jewish people spent in the Wilderness, they were provided with water from a spring that miraculously traveled along with them. The well was provided to the Jews in the merit of Miriam the Prophetess, sister of Moses and Aaron, and existed as long as she lived. Alternatively, the mishnah refers literally to the *mouth* of the well, for one of the miracles was that expressions of praise gushed forth from the well, recounting God's great miracles on behalf of His people [see *Numbers* 21:17 and *Rashi* ad loc.] (*Rashi, Rav*).

פִּי הָאָתוֹן — *the mouth of [Balaam's] donkey.* That Balaam's donkey would have the power of speech with which it reproached him (*Numbers* 22:28-30) was decreed at twilight on the eve of the first Sabbath (*Rashi, R' Yonah* et al).

The purpose of that miracle was to show Balaam that even man's normal functions are under God's control. If a beast could speak intelligently, then surely Balaam could be forced to say what God wanted him to say, and he could be silenced if he wished to oppose God's will. This proved to him that his sorcery could not prevail against God (*Ramban*), and that man is ultimately only a pawn in God's hands (*R' Elie Munk*).

וְהַקֶּשֶׁת — *the rainbow.* In the wake of the Flood, God established a covenant with Noah, his descendants, and all living beings until the end of time. This covenant would be signified by the rainbow. After a rainstorm, which could have been the harbinger of another deluge like that in Noah's time, the appearance of the rainbow would be a reminder of God's pledge never again to wash away all of mankind in a flood. *Rashi* and *R' Yonah* maintain that the rainbow, which had existed since Creation, was first seen after the Flood and was designated as a covenantal sign from that time on (see *Genesis* 9:9-17).

R' S. R. Hirsch teaches that the rainbow is the eternal sign that, no matter how bleak the future may seem, God will lead mankind to its ultimate goal.

וְהַמָּן — *the manna.* The manna that God provided for forty years as food for the Children of Israel in the Wilderness was prepared at twilight of the first Sabbath [see *Exodus* 16:4-21] (*Rashi, Rav* et al.).

R' Akiva and *R' Yishmael* disagree regarding the miraculous nature of the manna. According to *R' Akiva*, it was the food that sustains the angels — זִיו הַשְּׁכִינָה, *the glow of God's Presence*. This spark of the Divine had merely been given a material form so that human beings could eat it. According to *R' Yishmael*, it was not the food of the angels, but it was still so sublime that all of it was absorbed into the body without producing any waste [see *Tiferes Yisrael*] (*Yoma* 75b).

וְהַמַּטֶּה — *the staff.* This refers to the sapphire rod with which Moses performed the miracles in Egypt (see *Exodus* 4:17). [This indicates that the Exodus and the birth of the Jewish nation were part of God's plan from the beginning of Creation.] According to rabbinic tradition, it belonged to Adam and was transmitted through the generations to Moses. The ineffable four-letter Name of God was engraved on it (*Rashi, Rav, R' Yonah*; see *Pirkei d'Rabbi Eliezer* ch. 40). According to the Midrash (*Shemos Rabbah* 5:6), the initials of the Ten Plagues, דְּצַ״ךְ עַדַ״שׁ

◆§ **The gift of speech.** Baalam's power lay in his mouth. God taught him that it is He Who grants the power of speech; just as He gives man the ability to speak, so He may give it to a donkey (*Kozhnitzer Maggid*).

God's greatest gift to humanity is the power of intelligent speech. When God blew the breath of life into Adam, He gave him רוּחַ מְמַלְלָא, *a spirit of speech* (*Onkelos* to *Genesis* 2:7). God may bestow this gift on dumb animals as well, for regarding Balaam's donkey the Torah says: *And God opened the mouth of the donkey* (*Numbers* 22:28). *Sforno* (ibid.) observes: The gift of intelligent speech to a donkey reminds us of the words of the Psalmist (51:17): *My Lord, open my lips, so that my mouth may declare Your praise.*

Rabbi Yaakov Yitzchok Ruderman explained that *Sforno* is teaching us to appreciate human speech as no less a miracle than the speech of a donkey. Man should never take this gift for granted; he should regard his every utterance as a renewal of the Almighty's blessing of verbal communication.

באח"ב, were also inscribed on it.

וְהַשָּׁמִיר — *the shamir worm.* This was a small worm that could cut and split large stones. Since no swords or iron — symbols of violence — could be used to hew the stones for the Temple (*Deuteronomy* 27:5), the *shamir* took the place of conventional chisels when King Solomon built the Temple (*Rambam, Rashi* et al.).

See *Gittin* (68a-b) for the fascinating story of how Benayahu ben Yehoyada acquired the *shamir* for King Solomon.

The Talmud teaches that the *shamir* was used to engrave the names of the Twelve Tribes on the precious stones of the *ephod* and breastplate worn by the Kohen Gadol (High Priest). Each name was outlined on the stones, and the *shamir* was coaxed to crawl along the outlines. As it passed over the outlines, the letters were etched out (*Sotah* 48b).

הַכְּתָב — *the script.* This refers to the Torah, which, though given later, was written in black fire on a surface of white fire from the time of Creation (*R' Yonah*). According to *Rashi* and *Rav*, the script refers to the forms of the Hebrew alphabet, which were engraved on the Tablets.

Although the Torah existed two thousand years before Creation, it assumed written form only at the end of the sixth day of Creation.

וְהַמִּכְתָּב — *the inscription.* I.e., the instrument used by God, as it were, to engrave the Tablets, with the Ten Commandments, which were miraculously "written on both their sides." This instrument was created just before the onset of the first Sabbath (*Rashi, R' Yonah*). According to the Talmud, the inscription itself was miraculous. Since the engraving pierced the stone completely, the letters ךְ סמ, *samech,* and final מם, *mem,* had no place to attach themselves to the Tablets. The middle of these letters remained suspended in midair supernaturally (*Megillah* 2b).

וְהַלוּחוֹת — *and the Tablets.* The first Tablets, which were later broken by Moses, were created at that time, and God kept them with Him until he gave them to Moses (*Rashi*). The second Tablets were carved by Moses. Both sets of Tablets were kept in the Holy Ark (*Berachos* 8a).

וְיֵשׁ אוֹמְרִים: אַף הַמַּזִּיקִין — *Some say also the destructive spirits.* God created Adam and Eve on Friday, the sixth day of Creation (see *Genesis* 1:26). Afterward He created many other spirits, but the Sabbath began before He gave them bodies. God rested from creative work on the Sabbath, leaving these beings as spirits without physical form (*Rav*). *Meiri* explains that these spirits are the many forms of the Evil Inclination.

Magen Avos identifies these spirits as שֵׁדִים, demons. [See ArtScroll *Tehillim* 91:6, fn. 1.] According to *Tiferes Yisrael,* they are the evil angels who serve as God's messengers to exact retribution from man for his sins.

וּקְבוּרָתוֹ שֶׁל מֹשֶׁה — *Moses' grave.* The location of Moses burial site is unknown. It was created at the

---

◆§ **Moses' grave.** The Torah relates that Moses was unsure whether the "mouth of the earth" which would swallow Korach had already been created or not (*Numbers* 16:30; *Rashi* ad loc.). Was he not aware of the mishnah which teaches that it was created at the end of Creation? *Chasam Sofer* explains that God did not reveal this mishnah to Moses since it also alludes to his death. God did not want Moses' spirits to be dampened by the awareness that he, too, would one day occupy a grave. Thus, he knew nothing of the existence of this mouth of the earth.

Tradition has it that those who die outside the Land of Israel will have to undergo suffering at the time of the Messianic resurrection of the dead in order to come to the Holy Land (see *Rashi* to *Genesis* 47:29), but this applies only to those who did not have a deep love of the Land. Those who treasured it, however, during their lifetime will remain connected to it forever, and will thus painlessly ascend to the Land. Moses, who yearned to enter the Land, but was buried outside of it, will be brought back to Israel painlessly, and with him will come all those who shared his passion for the Land of their forefathers (*Sefer HaChamim*).

וְאֵילוֹ שֶׁל אַבְרָהָם אָבִינוּ. וְיֵשׁ אוֹמְרִים: אַף צְבָת בִּצְבַת עֲשׂוּיָה.

[ט] שִׁבְעָה דְבָרִים בְּגֹלֶם, וְשִׁבְעָה בְּחָכָם. חָכָם אֵינוֹ מְדַבֵּר לִפְנֵי מִי שֶׁגָּדוֹל מִמֶּנּוּ בְּחָכְמָה וּבְמִנְיָן;

---

end of the six days of Creation, and after Moses was buried, the site simply disappeared. The Torah states that *no one knows his burial place to this day* [Deuteronomy 34:6] (*Rashi, R' Yonah*).

Even Moses did not know where he would be buried; and it remained concealed after his death, so that his tomb would not become a shrine of pilgrimage for those who deify national heroes. It has been noted that the hiddenness of the tomb is a symbolic affirmation of Moses' humble self-effacement [see *Sotah* 13a].

וְאֵילוֹ שֶׁל אַבְרָהָם אָבִינוּ — *and the ram of our forefather Abraham*. At the moment that Abraham was ready to offer his son Isaac as the ultimate sacrifice, God told him to stop. *And Abraham raised his eyes and saw — behold, a ram! — afterwards, caught in the thicket by its horns; so Abraham went and took the ram and offered it up as an offering instead of his son* (Genesis 22:13). It was ordained from the time of Creation that the ram would be caught in the thicket so that Abraham could offer it to God in place of Isaac (*Rav, Rashi, Magen Avos*).

Pirkei d'Rabbi Eliezer (31) relates that the ram was

running toward Abraham to offer itself as a replacement for Isaac when Satan stood in its way and forced it into the thicket. Abraham saw the ram, freed it, and offered it instead of his son. The *Akeidah* took place on Mount Moriah, the site of the future Temples. The sweet savor of this offering remains forever, reminding God of the merit of our forefathers.

No part of that ram was wasted. Its ashes became the base of the Altar; its sinews became the strings on King David's ten-string lyre; its skin became the cloak of Elijah the Prophet (see *II Kings* 1:8). The smaller of its two horns became the *shofar* blown at Mount Sinai when the Torah was given, and the larger of the two awaits the great day when it will be used to herald the ingathering of the exiled Jewish nation, in fulfillment of the prophecy וְהָיָה בַיּוֹם הַהוּא יִתָּקַע בְּשׁוֹפָר גָּדוֹל וּבָאוּ הָאֹבְדִים בְּאֶרֶץ אַשּׁוּר וְהַנִּדָּחִים בְּאֶרֶץ מִצְרָיִם וְהִשְׁתַּחֲווּ לַה' בְּהַר הַקֹּדֶשׁ בִּירוּשָׁלָיִם, *And it will be on that day that a great shofar will be blown, and then will come those lost in the land of Assyria and those cast away in the land of Egypt, and they shall prostrate themselves to HASHEM on the holy mountain in Jerusalem* (Isaiah 27:13).

וְיֵשׁ אוֹמְרִים: אַף צְבָת בִּצְבַת עֲשׂוּיָה — *And some say*

◄§ **Cannot be buried.** The Talmud (*Sotah* 14a) teaches that the nations of the world searched at *Beis Peor* for Moses' grave. Those who searched at the top of the mountain came to think it was below; those who sought it below thought it was on top.

R' Meir Dan Plotzki views this as an allegorical comparison to the situation of the Jews in exile. Many of the nations would like to "bury" Moses and all he stands for. The Jewish nation, which carries a message of morality, truth, and Divinity, is a thorn in their side, and they would like to "bury" it. Some suggest that the burial site is located at the "top of the mountain" — that by granting Jews full rights and access to societal opportunities, they will succeed in severing the Jewish people from their historical mission, and will thus "bury Moses." Others seek the burial site of the Jews at the "bottom of the mountain" — through physical persecution, pogroms, and oppression. Neither strategy will work; the nations will never discover the key to the spiritual annihilation of God's people. The "burial site of Moses" will never be discovered.

◄§ **Mother of invention.** *Be'er Avos* views the first tongs as a metaphor for the human ability to invent. In truth, no invention is really new, for all the raw material and creative thinking needed to develop new technology was given to man by God. Man has to apply the ideas to the physical world in order to discover "new" inventions; but everything which he discovers can ultimately be traced back to the original "tongs" and their Inventor.

ram of our forefather Abraham. And some say also tongs, which are made with tongs.

9. Seven traits characterize an uncultivated person and seven a learned one. A learned person does not begin speaking before one who is greater than he in wisdom or in years; he

---

also tongs, which are made with tongs. Tongs are made with another pair of tongs, which holds the red-hot metal for the smith. According to this view, God provided man with the original pair of tongs with which to make others (*Rashi, R' Yonah*).

The Talmud (*Pesachim* 54a) challenges this idea, since the first tongs could have been made with a man-made mold. *Tiferes Yisrael* suggests that, nonetheless, the original pair was created by God prior to the first Sabbath in order that later sets of tongs, which would be used to create the vessels for the Temple, would have some connection to the original set made by God.

Mishnah 9

Having completed the sets of ten, the mishnah now commences to discuss groups of seven.

שִׁבְעָה דְּבָרִים בְּגֹלֶם, וְשִׁבְעָה בְחָכָם — *Seven traits characterize an uncultivated person and seven a learned one.* The term גֹּלֶם, meaning an *uncultivated person*, indicates one who has never developed his God-given raw intelligence and potential. Like an unformed vessel (see *Keilim* 12:6), he has not put forth the effort to perfect himself intellectually, morally, or socially. Even if he has learned a lot and possesses moral and intellectual virtues, they are in an incomplete state; constantly confused and disorganized, he functions improperly, like an unfinished implement in the hands of a craftsman. The mishnah teaches that this rawness manifests itself in a failure to develop the seven virtues listed here (*Rashi, R' Yonah*). [See *Psalms* 139:16: גָּלְמִי רָאוּ עֵינֶיךָ, *Your eyes saw my unshaped form.*]

A חָכָם, *learned person*, is one in whom these virtues are fully developed and internalized. The seven virtues enumerated here are fundamental to the improvement of one's character and social behavior, and to the ability to study, teach, and practice Torah. One who aspires to be a truly learned person should cultivate these virtues (*Rambam, Meiri*).

חָכָם אֵינוֹ מְדַבֵּר לִפְנֵי מִי שֶׁגָּדוֹל מִמֶּנּוּ בְּחָכְמָה וּבְמִנְיָן — *A learned person does not begin speaking before one who is greater than he in wisdom or in years.* A learned person remains silent and allows the one with greater wisdom to speak first. This is crucial to his success in study (*R' Yonah*). As an example *Rav* cites Elazar and Ithamar, the sons of Aaron. When Moses rebuked them for what he thought was a failure to carry out their responsibility as Kohanim, they did not respond, for it would have been disrespectful for them to speak in their father's presence or to take issue with their teacher Moses (see *Leviticus* 10:16-19).

Tiferes Yisrael elaborates: Even an accomplished scholar should allow one with greater knowledge to speak first. An incisive mind is no competition for one who has received the authentic tradition.

An example of this is found in *Eduyos* (1:3), where all the Sages of Israel yielded to the opinion of Shemaya and Avtalyon based on a report by two lowly weavers from the Dung Gate in Jerusalem.

Likewise, one should never speak before someone who is greater in *years*, since older people must be honored for their superior theoretical knowledge, as well as for the knowledge they have gained through life experience (see *Kiddushin* 33a).

Avos d'Rabbi Nosson (37) cites Moses as an example. Even though Moses heard instruction directly from God and Aaron heard only from Moses, nevertheless Moses asked Aaron to relate the message of redemption to the Children of Israel (see *Exodus* 4:30).

Rashi and *Meiri* explain וּבְמִנְיָן, *in number*, as a reference to a greater number of students. [Since one's greatest understanding of Torah comes from his students (see *Taanis* 7b), a teacher who has more students gains superior wisdom and *should* be given preference.]

Rambam's text does not have the word וּבְמִנְיָן. The terms בְּחָכְמָה וּבְמִנְיָן, (literally: in knowledge and in number), appear together in *Eduyos* 1:5, where the mishnah rules that a court may overrule another only if it is greater בְּחָכְמָה וּבְמִנְיָן, *in knowledge and in the number of its members*. The word וּבְמִנְיָן might inadvertently have slipped into our mishnah.

וְאֵינוֹ נִכְנָס לְתוֹךְ דִּבְרֵי חֲבֵרוֹ — *he does not interrupt the words of his fellow.* He listens without interrupting, waiting courteously until the speaker finishes his point, before refuting or commenting (*Rambam, R' Yonah*) so as not to confuse the other person's thought processes (*Rav*).

B'nayos B'Ramah suggest that the mishnah offers the intelligent response to criticism or talk. When confronted by someone who is upset, a learned person lets the other one vent his feelings before responding. An uncultivated lout, however, jumps into the fray and only aggravates the situation.

In intellectual debate, whether with a colleague or student, it is unfair and arrogant to interject one's comments before the other person has finished presenting his argument. The learned person, who seeks only truth, allows his intellectual adversary the opportunity to state his case clearly. Furthermore, it is a sign of disdain to interrupt another's flow of ideas, for this sends the message: "I'm not interested in what you have to say" (*Tiferes Yisrael*). As an example of this practice, *Rav* cites God's request to Moses, "Hear now my words"

(*Numbers* 12:6), which means: "Wait until I finish speaking."

Avos d'Rabbi Nosson cites God's patience in allowing Abraham to request that Sodom be saved. When Abraham asked that God save the city if fifty righteous people were to be found, God could have responded immediately that even a few righteous people would have prevented the Sodomites from sinking to such an abysmal level of moral depravity. Instead, God waited for Abraham to finish his plea.

וְאֵינוֹ נִבְהָל לְהָשִׁיב — *he does not answer impetuously.* A learned person is in no rush to answer. He listens carefully, allowing the other person to present all of his arguments, and only after thoroughly weighing the merits of his case is he ready to offer his opinion. This lack of impetuousness is a sign of wisdom, since it assures that one will answer intelligently (*R' Yonah*).

Rambam questions this interpretation, for it seems to indicate that this phrase is synonymous with the previous one, [*a learned person*] *does not interrupt the words of his fellow.* He therefore translates נִבְהָל as *hesitate* rather than *impetuous*, rendering the phrase as *he does not hesitate to answer.* The wise man quickly assesses the value of his colleague's argument and does not hesitate to point out its inconsistencies.

According to *R' Moshe Almosnino*, the word נִבְהָל can be translated as *excited* or *agitated*. He explains

---

⨳ **Better questions than answers.** Rabbi Elchanan Wasserman offered his son an important piece of advice on achieving success in his Torah studies: "Seeking answers to the questions of *Tosafos* should be left for one's later years, when one's mind is less innovative. When one is young and fresh, all his energies should go into 'listening' to *Tosafos*, trying to fully understand the question. Discovering an answer to a question is no cause for celebration; if anything, it may be a loss, for it usually indicates that one has not fully understood what bothered the *Tosafos* in the first place."

A young man once approached Rabbi Boruch Ber Leibowitz. He repeated a question posed by R' Akiva Eiger and began to suggest an answer.

"One moment," interrupted R' Boruch Ber. "First allow me some time to enjoy and savor the sweet taste of R' Akiva Eiger's words. Then I will be ready to hear what you think may be the answer."

[In general, writes the Chazon Ish, one who truly loves Torah prefers a good question to a proof for an idea already stated. R' Yochanan complained about the colleague who had replaced the deceased Reish Lakish: "Reish Lakish asked me twenty-four questions on every statement I made, but he brings me twenty-four proofs!" [*Bava Metzia* 84a].

the mishnah as describing the sensitive fashion in which a learned man points out the intellectual mistakes of others. In order to insure that a student or colleague will not hesitate to ask a question again, the truly wise man answers in a non-critical fashion. He does not get excited or carried away when he replies. Not so the uncultivated man, who answers impetuously and with rancor.

Atzei Ya'ar renders נִבְהָל as *afraid*. The fool is afraid to respond, fearful that he may answer incorrectly and cast himself as stupid. Not so the learned person, who answers to the best of his ability and is not afraid to make a mistake."

שׁוֹאֵל כְּעִנְיָן, וּמֵשִׁיב כַּהֲלָכָה — *he asks relevant questions, and replies appropriately.*

This rendering follows *Rav*. A wise student asks questions of his teacher only regarding the issue at hand. The teacher, who is totally involved in that subject, can then provide correct and appropriate answers. When a student asks a tangential question, the teacher will often be unable to orient himself sufficiently to be able to reply intelligently and to the point. It was for this reason that R' Chiya told Rav, "When Rabbi is engaged in the study of one tractate, do not question him concerning another tractate" (*Shabbos* 3b).

Meiri renders כְּעִנְיָן as *timely*; the learned person's questions come at the right time. For example, he inquires about the laws of Pesach before the onset of the festival.

According to *Tiferes Yisrael*, the mishnah speaks of the learned person's intellectual honesty and search for truth. Such a person asks only relevant questions and does not use halachic discussion as a forum to display his intellectual prowess. Like-

wise, when he answers questions, he seeks the most simple and straightforward response, rather than engaging in an exegetic display which may disintegrate under the scrutiny of straight thinking. His major concern in both cases is to discover the truth.

Miuchar HaPeninim quotes the famous aphorism שְׁאֵלַת חָכָם חֲצִי תְשׁוּבָה, *A learned man's question is half the answer*. By posing his questions carefully and presenting the underlying doubts in a clear fashion, the wise person provides a basis for developing an answer. Half the work of answering the question is already done.

The mishnah praises the learned man as one who does not mix domains of knowledge, either in questioning or in answering. He does not ask for logical proofs in areas of faith, nor does he offer theoretical answers to practical questions. His answers are always relevant to the type of question asked and are within the parameters of the discipline under discussion (*Rambam, R' Yonah*).

וְאוֹמֵר עַל רִאשׁוֹן רִאשׁוֹן, וְעַל אַחֲרוֹן אַחֲרוֹן — *he discusses first things first and last things last.* A learned person answers questions in the order in which they were asked. One who answers sequentially shows that he has an orderly and organized mind. The principle is learned from God, Who answered Moses' two questions in the order they were asked. Moses asked: a) "Who am I that I should go to Pharoah?" b) "[Who am I] that I should take the Children of Israel out of Egypt?" (*Exodus* 3:11). [By this he meant to ask what merit would justify the Jews being redeemed.] First God told Moses that he need not fear Pharaoh, because He would be with him. As to the merit of the Jewish people, God informed Moses that they were destined to receive

---

◆§ **Unflustered.** *Avodas Yisrael* suggests a homiletic interpretation: The mishnah informs man how to react to adversity. He should follow the example of the learned man, who does not become flustered by anything Heaven sends his way. He understands that everything God brings upon him, although it is often beyond his understanding, is for his own good. He is not impetuous in his reactions to God's plans.

◆§ **Potential.** This teaches that people can be judged and even rewarded on the basis of their potential. The very fact that the nation had the capacity for growth that would enable them to listen to God's word and accept His Torah was sufficient merit to justify the Exodus (*R' Nosson Scherman*).

אַחֲרוֹן; וְעַל מַה שֶׁלֹא שָׁמַע אוֹמֵר: „לֹא שָׁמַעְתִּי"; וּמוֹדֶה
עַל הָאֱמֶת. וְחִלּוּפֵיהֶן בְּגֹלֶם.

[יז] **שִׁבְעָה** מִינֵי פֻּרְעָנִיּוֹת בָּאִין לָעוֹלָם עַל שִׁבְעָה גּוּפֵי

the Torah on Mount Sinai within three months after leaving Egypt [see ibid 3:12 and *Rashi* ad loc] (*Rashi, Rav, Tiferes Yisrael*).

Rashi on *Genesis* 24:23 cites the Matriarch Rebecca as an example of one who exhibited this characteristic. When Eliezer came to Aram Naharaim seeking a wife for Isaac, he met Rebecca at the well and asked her who her father was and whether there was lodging space in his house. She replied to his questions in order.

R' Yonah notes however, that it is not always appropriate to answer in strictly sequential order. Rather, the learned man answers questions in *logical* order, providing background with his first answer in order to lead up to the next. Therefore, it is sometimes preferable to answer the second question first since its resolution may provide the background for the answer to the first question.

Rambam comments that the mishnah exhorts those who seek wisdom to study in a systematic fashion, attacking preliminary concepts first and only then moving on to the more complex areas.

וְעַל מַה שֶׁלֹּא שָׁמַע אוֹמֵר: „לֹא שָׁמַעְתִּי" — *about something he has not heard he says, "I have not heard."* A learned man will not offer a ruling of his own and give the impression that it is based on something he heard from his teachers. [Instead he states clearly: "This is my own idea. I did not hear it from my teachers." The questioner may then decide whether to accept the ruling or not (*Meiri*).] On the other hand, one who says something he did *not* hear from his teacher, giving the impression that he did, causes the Divine Presence to leave the Jewish people (see *Berachos* 27b) (*Rashi*). This sensitivity is something an uncultivated person does not possess (*R' Yonah*).

Rambam renders this phrase in a most straightforward fashion, explaining that one should not talk of something which he knows nothing about, and he should not be ashamed to admit his ignorance in that area.

Rav adds that the principle of admitting that one does not know something is derived from an incident involving Jacob. When Jacob came to Haran, he inquired of the local inhabitants regarding Laban. They told him: "It is well [with him]; and see — his daughter Rachel is coming with the flock!" (*Genesis* 29:6). Realizing that Jacob wanted to know more about Laban's personal life than they could tell him, they pointed out his daughter, as if to say: "*Look, his daughter is coming* — perhaps you should ask her your questions directly."

Midrash Shmuel renders לֹא שָׁמַעְתִּי as *I did not understand.* One who is truly wise is never ashamed to ask for further clarification on a matter which he does not understand.

Mishberei Yam interprets this as a directive to express appreciation when one is taught something new. If one remains silent after learning a thought or idea, his intellectual benefactor may get the impression that he already heard it. A truly learned person expresses his appreciation by saying, "I never heard this before. Thank you for introducing me to a new idea."

וּמוֹדֶה עַל הָאֱמֶת — *and he acknowledges the truth.* The learned person is not embarrassed to admit a mistake (*Rashi, Tiferes Yisrael*). A wise person is not dominated by the need to control, and therefore he will not use his intellectual persuasiveness to triumph over his fellow, even though he knows his own position is incorrect. The wise person's guid-

---

◆§ **A boor's discourtesy.** An uncultivated person exhibits the opposite trait. It is the height of discourtesy and a cause of great disappointment when one interrupts a friend who is relating a thought or a story with the words "I heard this already." A wise man thanks his benefactor for the new thought, even if he really did hear it before, but a boorish person dashes his friend's enthusiasm with his display of insensitivity.

10. Seven types of punishment come to the world for seven

---

ing principle is truth, even if its pursuit is at the expense of his ego (*Rabbeinu Yonah, Rav, Rambam*).

This principle also applies to constructive criticism. A person whose yearning for truth is stronger than his ego is happy and grateful when someone points out his shortcomings, for then he can begin to correct them. Such a person is called one who is מוֹדֶה עַל הָאֱמֶת, thankful for being told the unadulterated truth (*Atzei Ya'ar*).

Moses was the paragon of this scholarly trait. When he confronted Elazar and Ithamar about their burning of the he-goat of Rosh Chodesh instead of eating it, Aaron replied that only the specific offerings of that day should have been eaten, but not those that are always brought (see *Leviticus* 10:12-20). Moses immediately conceded that Aaron's reasoning was correct. In a demonstration of the humility that was the essence of his greatness, Moses did not attempt to defend his position. Instead, he admitted without embarrassment that God had instructed him only with regard to the specific offerings of the day, just as Aaron and his sons had assumed — but that he had forgotten (*Rav* based on *Zevachim* 101a).

The seven characteristics of a learned person are listed chronologically:

1. One should be careful not to speak before another who is wiser than he.
2. Once the other person has begun to speak, he should not interrupt.
3. When the person has finished, he should not be in a rush to reply.
4. When he does begin to speak, he should ask relevant questions and provide pertinent answers (*Tiferes Yisrael*).
5. He should reply in a sequential fashion.

6. When he is in doubt, he should say, "I didn't hear this."
7. After replying, he should be ready to recant and admit to the truth.

וְחִלּוּפֵיהֶן בְּגֹלֶם — *And the reverse of these [traits] characterizes an uncultivated person.* The uncultivated person, who does nothing to develop his innate abilities, will never attain the virtues of the learned (*R' Yonah*).

This mishnah only highlights the virtues of the learned, but does not specify the flaws of the boorish person. This is consistent with the Talmudic teaching (*Pesachim* 3a) that the Torah refers to an impure animal as אֲשֶׁר אֵינֶנָּה טְהֹרָה, *which is not pure* (*Genesis* 7:8), instead of directly calling it טְמֵאָה, *impure*. The Torah goes out of its way to use a longer expression rather than the single word in order to teach a moral lesson: One should never utter a gross expression. The Torah, which is supremely succinct, added several extra letters to the Hebrew text of this verse to avoid using the unseemly expression *unclean*. Likewise, the mishnah prefers to speak the praises of the learned rather than to elaborate on the failings of the uncultivated.

Alternatively, the characteristics of the uncultivated are not listed since generally such people have no intrinsic character. Their entire being is a reaction to the learned man. The defining characteristic of such a person is that he passively hopes to be everything the learned person is not (*Chelek LeOlam Haba*).

Mishnah 10

Of the seven categories mentioned by the mishnah, three are listed in this mishnah,
and the other four in mishnah 11.

שִׁבְעָה מִינֵי פֻרְעָנִיּוֹת בָּאִין לָעוֹלָם עַל שִׁבְעָה גוּפֵי עֲבֵרָה — *Seven types of punishment come to the world for seven kinds of transgressions.* Divine retribution is meted out מִדָּה כְּנֶגֶד מִדָּה, *measure for measure,*

with the punishment reflecting the crime. By carefully analyzing the form of punishment he has received, a spiritually sensitive person will understand which failings need to be corrected. This

עֲבֵרָה: מִקְצָתָן מְעַשְּׂרִין וּמִקְצָתָן אֵינָן מְעַשְּׂרִין, רָעָב שֶׁל
בַּצֹרֶת בָּא, מִקְצָתָן רְעֵבִים וּמִקְצָתָן שְׂבֵעִים; גָּמְרוּ שֶׁלֹּא
לְעַשֵּׂר, רָעָב שֶׁל מְהוּמָה וְשֶׁל בַּצֹרֶת בָּא; וְשֶׁלֹּא לִטֹּל אֶת
הַחַלָּה, רָעָב שֶׁל כְּלָיָה בָּא;

---

mishnah discusses seven instances of punishment that come to the world in ways that might seem "natural," such as drought, but which calamities are really punishments and are meant to arouse people to self-scrutiny and repentance for very specific transgressions (*Meiri*).

The term גּוּפֵי עֲבֵרוֹת means *primary*, or severe, transgressions (see 3:23, s.v. הֵן הַן). Furthermore, the word גּוּף, literally *body*, is used because it is through sin that the "bodies" of evil angels come into being (see 5:8, s.v. וְיֵשׁ אוֹמְרִים אַף הַמַּזִּיקִין). Every time a person ignores God's will, he creates an evil angel that prosecutes him (*Midrash Shmuel, Ruach Chaim*).

Be'er Avos renders גּוּפֵי עֲבֵרוֹת as *established* or *entrenched transgressions*. Unlike a private sin, which may be judged as a fleeting aberration, public sins such as those enumerated in this mishnah assume a sense of permanence and are thus more severe.

R' Shlomo Kluger suggests that the punishments mentioned here are meted out for the sinful act itself (for example, the sin of eating untithed food) — the גּוּף, meaning the *body*, or *essential act*, of the sin. In addition, however, such transgressions have an additional, ripple-like effect, which the mishnah does not address. One who eats untithed food, for instance, deprived the Levite of his rightful due.

מִקְצָתָן מְעַשְּׂרִין וּמִקְצָתָן אֵינָן מְעַשְּׂרִין, רָעָב שֶׁל בַּצֹרֶת בָּא, מִקְצָתָן רְעֵבִים וּמִקְצָתָן שְׂבֵעִים — a) *If some people tithe and others do not, a famine caused by lack of rain ensues; some go hungry and some are satisfied.* When some people are lax about giving *maaser* (one tenth of the crop, which is given to a Levite) or *terumah* (one fortieth, fiftieth, or sixtieth of the yield, which is given to a Kohen), the punishment is inflation. When the economy is inflationary, those who can afford to buy food will be satisfied, while those who cannot will go hungry (*Rashi, Rav*).

Rambam, R' Yonah et al. do not render *lack of rain*, but rather *uneven rainfall*. As a result of such selective giving, God will respond with sporadic rainfall; some rain will fall in certain places, and none will fall in others. Thus, only some people's needs will be met. The Talmud teaches that as a result of not giving *terumah* and *maaser*, "the heavens withhold rain and dew, the economy is plagued with constant inflation, one's paycheck disappears quickly, and people chase futilely after a living" (*Shabbos* 32b).

This punishment is measure for measure, for when tithing becomes inconsistent and people become tightfisted, God responds in kind, by closing His hand and giving His blessings selectively (*Sefas Emes*).

גָּמְרוּ שֶׁלֹּא לְעַשֵּׂר, רָעָב שֶׁל מְהוּמָה וְשֶׁל בַּצֹרֶת בָּא — b) *if all decided not to tithe, [general] famine caused by armed bands and drought ensues.* When large segments of the population do not tithe, as in the first case of the mishnah, only the miserly people are forced to suffer the hunger induced by inflation. But if such callousness to the needs of others becomes institutionalized as a public policy, everybody suffers the consequences (*Mussar Avos*). In

---

◆§ **Everything is a message.** Rabbi Yosef Kahaneman. the *Rav* of Ponevezh, used to visit the Chofetz Chaim often, especially when he returned from a fund-raising tour overseas, for the benefit of his yeshivah. Once, upon his return from a visit to South Africa, the Chofetz Chaim inquired about the plight of the blacks in that country, saying that he had heard they were persecuted. Rabbi Kahaneman expressed surprise at his interest, to which the Chofetz Chaim explained, whatever calamity happens in the world, it is a message to Jews to examine themselves and repent. Whether it is an earthquake in Japan, a famine in India, or suffering in South Africa, Jews must take it as a warning to improve themselves.

kinds of transgressions. a) If some people tithe and others do not, a famine caused by lack of rain ensues; some go hungry and some are satisfied; b) if all decided not to tithe, [general] famine caused by armed bands and drought ensues; c) if [they also decided] not to separate *challah,* a famine caused by fatal drought ensues.

such a case, the heavens completely hold back rain and dew, so that men toil but cannot provide for themselves (*Avos D'Rabbi Nosson*).

An all-consuming famine of this kind may also be caused by calamities such as war, and exposure to roaming bands of ruffians, all of which prevent people from planting and harvesting (*Rambam, R' Yonah, Rav*). Furthermore, the frightful, chaotic conditions make it impossible to escape to a more financially secure place (*Tiferes Yisrael*). According to *Rashi*, רָעָב שֶׁל מְהוּמָה does not indicate a literal famine, but rather a condition where one never feels satisfied. This is one of the travails of the *Tochachah*, the Divine Admonition, which Israel will undergo as a result of its sins (see *Leviticus* 26:26).

וְשֶׁלֹא לִטֹל אֶת הַחַלָּה, רָעָב שֶׁל כְּלָיָה בָּא — c) *if [they also decided] not to separate challah, a famine caused by fatal drought ensues.* The Torah commands that from every batch of dough kneaded for baking, a portion — known as *challah* — must be given to a Kohen, just as they must receive a part of the produce of the field. Until *challah* is separated, the dough (or bread) may not be eaten (see *Numbers* 15:17-21).

Our rendering follows *Tosafos Yom Tov, Rashi,* and *R' Yonah,* who see the withholding of *challah* as a separate sin from the curtailing of *terumos* and *maaseros.* According to *Midrash Shmuel,* a resolu-

tion to refrain from setting aside *challah* can, by itself, evoke the calamitous consequences mentioned above.

By obligating the nation at large to provide gifts for the Kohanim and Levites, making them dependent upon their brethren, God links even those not involved in spiritual matters with those who devote themselves to Torah study, the Temple service, and matters of the spirit (see *Numbers* 15:17-21).

When it becomes a public policy not to give *challah,* the world will suffer devastating hunger. No rain will fall and rivers will dry up. This terrible punishment is described in the Divine admonition: *Your heavens over your head will be [like] copper, and the land beneath you will be [like] iron (Deuteronomy 28:23)* (*Rav, Rambam, R' Yonah*).

One who begrudges the Kohen his share could circumvent the need to separate *challah* altogether, simply by kneading less than the minimum amount from which *challah* must be taken (see *Eduyos* 1:2). If, on the other hand, he kneads the required amount and then refuses to separate *challah,* he displays both insubordination toward God and callousness toward the Kohen. This constitutes a compound sin, which can bring both fatal drought and famine on the nation.

This amount was established based on the portion of manna that fell daily for each Jew in the Wilderness, which was an *omer,* or the volume of 43.2 eggs.

◆§ **Unacceptable policy.** People who are callous toward others but who act without forethought might find some slight justification for their behavior by saying that in a moment of moral weakness, they succumbed to the panderings of their Evil Inclination. However, premeditated cruelty is unpardonable. Once a considered policy decision is made to stop tithing, a full-fledged famine is in order (*Avos al Banim*).

◆§ **The first portion.** Adam was created from the combination of a soul with a body made of mud, which God kneaded and formed as a baker makes bread (see *Genesis* 2:6-7 and *Rashi* ad loc.). Thus, he was the figurative *challah*, the most pristine "first portion," of the world. When he ate of the Tree of Knowledge, his sin diminished his spiritual stature. Among the curses he endured were the fact that he would now have to toil for food, and that eventually he would die. When one gives *challah*, he recognizes that all his creative powers to produce life and to earn a livelihood really belong to God. A decision not to give *challah* brings in its wake the curse that was placed on Adam: "Accursed is the ground because of you" (*Genesis* 3:17).

[יא] **דֶּבֶר** בָּא לָעוֹלָם – עַל מִיתוֹת הָאֲמוּרוֹת בַּתּוֹרָה
שֶׁלֹּא נִמְסְרוּ לְבֵית דִּין, וְעַל פֵּרוֹת שְׁבִיעִית;
חֶרֶב בָּאָה לָעוֹלָם – עַל עִנּוּי הַדִּין, וְעַל עִוּוּת הַדִּין, וְעַל

Mishnah 11

The seven types of punishment begun in the previous mishnah are concluded here:

דֶּבֶר בָּא לָעוֹלָם – עַל מִיתוֹת הָאֲמוּרוֹת בַּתּוֹרָה שֶׁלֹּא נִמְסְרוּ לְבֵית דִּין — d) *pestilence comes to the world for death penalties prescribed by the Torah that were not carried out by the court.* When the court did not comply with their Divine mandate to impose the death sentence in appropriate instances, God addresses the miscarriage of justice by sending pestilence to kill those who deserve death (*Rashi, Rav*). Pestilence is an epidemic which kills many people suddenly (*Tiferes Yisrael*).

The Talmud (*Sanhedrin* 37b) teaches that even after the Sanhedrin ceased to function, transgressors liable to the four types of death sentences could still die by the hand of God, through forms of death that resembled those that should have been executed by the court.

For example, a person sentenced by a court to stoning (סְקִילָה) would be pushed from a height to the ground below. If this did not kill him, he was crushed by a heavy stone (see *Sanhedrin* 45a). Since the disbandment of the Sanhedrin, Divine Providence brings this type of punishment upon one who deserves it by causing him either to fall from a roof and be killed, or to be thrown to the ground and trampled by a wild animal (*Rashi on Kesubos* 30b). [The same would apply to someone killed by an automobile.]

The second type of death carried out by the Sanhedrin was burning (שְׂרֵיפָה), in which case hot lead was poured down the guilty person's throat. Such persons might die in an actual fire or through a snakebite, which sends a burning venom through the body.

One who deserved decapitation (הֶרֶג) might receive the equivalent at the hands of bandits or civil authorities who execute by beheading.

A person who deserved death by strangulation (חֶנֶק) might die of suffocation by drowning, or from a disease (אַסְכָּרָא) often associated with diphtheria, where the throat becomes so constricted that the person cannot breath (see *Rashi on Kesubos* 30b).

R' Yonah gives a different rendering: *pestilence comes to the world for crimes punishable by death that are not in the court's jurisdiction to execute.* The Sanhedrin could not punish those who committed crimes that deserved either כָּרֵת, *excision of the soul*, meaning Divinely imposed premature death, or מִיתָה בִּידֵי שָׁמַיִם, early *death by the Hand of Heaven.* God often uses pestilence as a way to slay the perpetrators of such crimes. *R' Yosef ibn Nachmias* also includes those whom the court could not execute for lack of witnesses or proper warning. Another person in this category is one who escaped before execution; he, too, will find justice at God's hand.

וְעַל פֵּרוֹת שְׁבִיעִית — *and for [illegal use of] fruits of the seventh [Sabbatical] year.* During *Shemittah*, the last year of each seven-year cycle, one must renounce ownership of whatever grows during that year; anyone is permitted to enter his field and

---

◆§ **Lesson of Shemittah.** The *Shemittah* year awakens our awareness that everything in God's universe has a role; from the huge African elephant to the microscopic ant, God made everything for a reason. During the *Shemittah* year, when man is forced to realize that the earth and all that it contains belongs to God, we must leave the fruit of our labor for *all* of God's creatures — even the animals (*Darchei Yosher*).

The produce of *Shemittah* is endowed with a special sanctity (*Avodah Zarah* 54b), and its uses are regulated. As long as *Shemittah* produce has not been picked, it must be made accessible to all (*Exodus* 23:11; *Rambam, Sefer HaMitzvos*, positive precepts 134). Once a person has picked it, it is no longer ownerless, but it remains sacred and its uses are governed by special laws [see introduction to *Yad Avraham*, *Sheviis* pp. 9-15]. There are two other general restrictions affecting *Shemittah* produce: a) It may not be wasted (*Pesachim* 52b); and b) it may not be used for commercial purposes (*Avodah Zarah* 62a).

11. d) Pestilence comes to the world for death penalties prescribed by the Torah that were not carried out by the court, and for [illegal use of] fruits of the seventh [Sabbatical] year; e) the sword [of war] comes to the world for the delay of justice, for the perversion of justice, and for rendering

---

take produce for himself. But everything that grows must be used as food; it may not be used for commerce (see *Bechoros* 12b).

Also, the produce of *Shemittah* must be treated with appropriate sanctity and may not be discarded indiscriminately. Furthermore, one may keep food at home for his own animals only as long as there is food available in the field for ownerless beasts. Once there is no food left in the fields, one must make his own food available to people and animals alike.

During the *Shemittah* year, when no one harvests, there are no tithes available for the Levite or the poor; their only possible source of food is the fields to which they are given access. The owner of a field who cuts off this supply is literally responsible for allowing them to die of hunger, and he deserves to die measure for measure. *Tiferes Yisrael* explains that in retribution for not making his field free for the poor to take at will, God gives the Angel of Death free reign to take his life.

Maharam Shick sees the withholding of the fruits of *Shemittah* from the poor as a flaw in faith. Were man to understand that מַאן דְּיָהִיב חַיֵּי יָהִיב מְזוֹנָא, *He Who gives life gives sustenance* (see *Taanis* 8b), he would not fear a personal loss from allowing the poor to take from his field. Instead, God takes him from the world and leaves his harvest for others, to show that both life and a livelihood are in God's hands.

חֶרֶב בָּאָה לָעוֹלָם – עַל עִנּוּי הַדִּין — e) *the sword [of war] comes to the world for the delay of justice.* I.e., delay in the execution of a sentence. Once someone is convicted of a capital crime, his sentence must be carried out that very day, so as not to keep him waiting in mental agony for his punishment (*Rashi, R' Yonah, Rambam* et al.) (see *Rambam, Hilchos Sanhedrin* 12:4).

To impose such agony upon the convicted man violates the Scriptural injunction (*Leviticus* 19:15) against committing a perversion of justice (*Rambam, Hilchos Sanhedrin* 20:6) [true justice entails fair treatment even for the criminal]; it also violates the Scriptural command (*Leviticus* 19:18) to "love your neighbor as yourself" (*Yad Ramah*).

According to *Machzor Vitry*, this sin includes a court's delay in trying the case. When the judge turns instead to other cases, the defendant is filled with suffering and worry, as he awaits the impending trial. For this crime, the sword of war comes to the world (*Tiferes Yisrael*).

B'nayos B'Ramah extends this crime to a judge who refuses to sit on a case for fear that one of the litigants will

---

⧉ **Sharing with animals.** This obligation, known as the law of *biur*, concerns *Shemittah* produce which a person has picked from the fields and taken home. A verse in *Leviticus* (25:7) pertains to this law: *For your animal, and the beast which is in your land, shall all its produce be to eat.* *Toras Kohanim* comments that the juxtaposition of "your animal" and "beast" teaches that a domestic animal may be fed *Shemittah* produce only so long as such produce is also available in the fields for wild animals. Once a type of produce is no longer available in the fields, however, it must be removed from the house as well.

The nature of this removal, known as *biur*, is the subject of a dispute. According to *Rambam* (*Hilchos Shemittah* 7:3), when any particular type of *Shemittah* produce is no longer available in the fields, it becomes forbidden for consumption and must be destroyed. On the other hand, *Ramban* (*Commentary to Lev.* 25:7) and *Rashi* understand *biur* as the process of removing the produce from one's home and declaring it ownerless. Once this is done, the produce is permitted for consumption, and even the person who just declared it ownerless can repossess it. This view, which is followed in practice (*Chazon Ish, Sheviis* 11:7), essentially reduces *biur* to a formality. Nevertheless, if someone negligently allowed the deadline to pass without performing *biur*, the produce thereafter becomes forbidden for consumption (*Maharil* Vol. 2 #43; *Chazon Ish Sheviis* 26, *Seder HaSheviis* #15).

take revenge if he rules against him. The Torah warns: "You shall not tremble before any man" (*Deuteronomy* 1:17). *Zeroa Yemin* cites other examples of the delaying of judgment: תַּלְמִיד שֶׁהִגִּיעַ לְהוֹרָאָה וְאֵינוֹ מוֹרֶה, *a student who is competent to rule but who refuses to do so, and* תַּלְמִיד שֶׁלֹּא הִגִּיעַ לְהוֹרָאָה וּמוֹרֶה, *an unqualified student who nonetheless rules.*

וְעַל עִוּוּת הַדִּין — *for the perversion of justice.* I.e., accepting bribes (*Rashi*). *Rambam* and *Meiri*, among others, include one who vindicates the guilty and indicts the innocent. *Machzor Vitry* adds: One who wrongly takes the wealth of one person and gives it to another perverts justice. The Talmud teaches: One who robs his fellow is considered to have taken his soul (*Bava Kamma* 119a).

וְעַל הַמּוֹרִים בַּתּוֹרָה שֶׁלֹּא כַהֲלָכָה — *and for rendering decisions contrary to the halachah.* This refers to one who permits the forbidden and forbids the permitted in regard to ritual matters (*Rashi, Rav, R' Yonah* et al.). *Midrash Shmuel* and *Machzor Vitry* also include one who renders decisions in the presence of his teacher, and one who rules on questions of law in spite of his incompetence [in the latter case, the phrase is rendered as *those who illegitimately render decisions in Torah*].

Meiri explains that the reason these specific sins "bring the sword" to the world is because the one who has been victimized by the perversion of justice may seek to avenge the wrong by killing the person responsible. Thus, a perversion of justice in any form engenders conflict in the world. *Yalkut Yehudah* elaborates, explaining that justice and physical force operate inversely; where justice prevails, brute strength can gain no foothold, but when justice is a sham, the sword of destruction swings freely. One who perverts justice unleashes this sword on the world.

Doresh LePerakim offers a novel perspective: When approaching a case, a judge must literally envision a sword held over him, which will instill in him the fear of tampering with the truth. A judge who perverts justice has apparently overlooked that imaginary sword and must therefore fall victim to a real one.

Mili d'Avos renders חֶרֶב as destruction (as in the root of the word חוּרְבָּן). The three instances of judicial misconduct mentioned in the mishnah, respectively, undermine the three foundations of the world — justice, truth, and peace (see 1:18) — the breakdown of which constitutes the most ruinous destruction. *Perversion of justice* contradicts the *justice* that R' Shimon ben Gamliel defines as fundamental to the world's existence. Those who *render decisions contrary to the halachah* trample on the *truth* that is so vital to the functioning of the human community and finally, the *delay of justice* is an attack on the *peace* that should exist between people.

According to the Talmud, if one sees that the generation suffers many troubles, he should investigate the conduct of its judges, for punishment comes to the world as a result of judicial misconduct. God does not let His Presence rest among Jews until the nation is rid of evil judges and officials. In reference to such a time, Isaiah prophesied: *Then I will return your judges as in earliest times and your counselors as at first; after that you shall be called City of Righteousness, Faithful City* (*Isaiah* 1:26).

חַיָּה רָעָה בָּאָה לָעוֹלָם – עַל שְׁבוּעַת שָׁוְא — f) *wild beasts come upon the world for vain oaths.* The third of the Ten Commandments (see *Exodus* 20:7) is the prohibition against vain oaths. The Sages (*Shevuos* 29a) explain that the commandment forbids the

---

⋘ **Higher calling.** Not only are judges warned not to allow fear to sway their judgment in favor of an influential party, but they may not even excuse themselves from such a case (*Gur Aryeh; Taz*). They must recognize that they are agents of God in administering justice, and nothing but fear of God may enter their deliberations. A judge should rule even if a litigant threatens him with bodily or financial harm. This matter is treated with great seriousness because if a judge allows anyone to entertain the notion that the Torah's law can be bent or ignored for personal considerations, it borders on the desecration of God's Name (*R' Yaakov Kamenetsky*).

use of God's Name to validate either of two varieties of vain oaths: (a) to swear that a marble object is marble, which is vain because it is so obvious that there is no reason for such an oath (see *Yerushalmi, Shevuos* 3:8); and (b) to swear that an obviously wooden object is gold, which is vain because the oath is patently false and serves no purpose [see *Rashi* on *Shabbos* 33a]. *Tiferes Yisrael* sees this as a general category, referring to those who swear falsely by making any misleading statement.

R' Yonah explains that the gravity of oaths uttered in vain is a necessary condition of the uniqueness of man's power of speech. This ability not only differentiates him from the beasts, but gives him dominion over them. One who abuses the power of speech by uttering oaths in vain has sunk to the level of animals and becomes vulnerable to them.

וְעַל חִלּוּל הַשֵּׁם — *and for Desecration of God's Name.* This includes sinning publicly in brazen defiance of God and His Torah, or acting in a manner that will cause others, who emulate him, to sin (*Rav, Tiferes Yisrael*). Man is given dominion over the animals only if he lives on a more elevated plane than they; if not, he can become their victim. One who desecrates God's Name and honor may become prey to wild animals; not having taken sufficient precaution regarding God's honor, such a person deserves to be trampled by them (*R' Yonah, Meiri*).

⋘ **Sinking to the animals.** *Ramban* (*Leviticus* 26:6) teaches that the animals became carnivorous only after Adam sinned, in order to serve as messengers to exact Divine retribution. If man were on a sufficiently high spiritual level, the animals would again revert to their original nature as described in *Genesis* (1:30). *And to every beast of the earth . . . every green herb is for food.* This will happen in the Land of Israel when Jews live there according to the Torah. According to *Ramban*, this is the thrust of the Messianic vision of Isaiah (11:6-8): *A wolf will dwell with a sheep, and a leopard will lie down with a kid . . . and a lion will eat hay like cattle. A suckling will play by the hole of a viper.* This will not be a supernatural phenomenon; rather, nature will return to the pristine beauty and peace it enjoyed before Adam's sin, and will consequently will be freed of the aberrations of flesh-eating animals. [See, however, *Rambam, Hilchos Melachim* 12:1.]

Hence, one who loses his spiritual dimension by uttering an oath, one of the most flagrant abuses of the power of speech, abandons his uniqueness and sinks to a non-human level, and he thereby allows the animals dominion over him.

⋘ **Image of God.** The *Zohar* explains that in man's ideal state, the image of God in which he was created would be sufficient to frighten the animals. But when the generation of the Flood degraded itself and sank to the level of the animals, it forfeited this Divine quality. After the Flood, Noah was afraid that the few surviving people would be in constant danger from wild animals. God assured him that He had implanted in animals an instinctive fear of human beings (*Abarbanel*): *The fear of you and dread of you shall be upon every beast of the earth* (*Genesis* 9:2). This concept means that as long as man is true to his Godly image, he need not fear beasts; but if he falls from his calling, as did the generation of the Flood, he must indeed fear the beasts of the wild.

Everything that God created in His world He created solely for His glory (see 6:11). The culmination of His work was the creation of man, a being blessed with the intelligence to understand the scope of God's beneficence, and imbued with the power of speech to verbalize the fact that we are His creatures (see *Ramban* to *Exodus* 13:17). These two gifts are exclusive to man. When he loses his focus on the purpose of Creation — the sin called חִלּוּל הַשֵּׁם — and debases the gifts that God bestowed upon him — the sin called שְׁבוּעַת שָׁוְא — he is no better than his predator.

Conversely, Rabbi Nosson Adler and his student, the Chasam Sofer, were once traveling in a coach through a forest, when a wild bear menaced the driver. Hearing his terrified screams, Rabbi Adler looked throught the window. The bear saw him and fled. In response to the surprised reactions of his fellow passengers, he said simply, ''Perhaps the image of God has not left me.''

Abarbanel elaborates: One who desecrates God's Name indicates that he does not realize God's supremacy over man. God punishes him in kind by allowing the animals not to recognize human domination.

גָּלוּת בָּאָה לָעוֹלָם – עַל עוֹבְדֵי עֲבוֹדָה זָרָה, וְעַל גִּלּוּי עֲרָיוֹת, וּשְׁפִיכוּת דָּמִים — g) *exile comes to the world for idolatry, for immorality, for bloodshed.* These three crimes are the most severe commandments in the Torah; they are the exceptions to the principle that the preservation of human life supersedes the observance of the commandments. As a general rule, the preservation of life supersedes all other commandments, so that, for example, a Jew is required to desecrate the Sabbath if another Jew's life is in danger. The Sages (*Yoma* 85b) derive this from the expression that God gave the commandments *by which he shall live* (*Leviticus* 18:5), which implies that the *mitzvos* were given for the sake of life, not death (see *Rambam*, *Hilchos Yesodei HaTorah* 5:1-3).

Homiletically, *Chiddushei HaRim* interpreted these words from *Leviticus*, *by which he shall live*, to teach that a person should not perform the *mitzvos* apathetically. Rather, he should find in them his primary source of joy, enthusiasm, and life — he should *live* through them.

Only in times when there is general persecution that is intended to force Jews to give up the Torah, or when the intent is to force even an individual Jew into apostasy, is one obligated to forfeit his life to avoid the transgression of even minor *mitzvos* or Jewish customs. Otherwise, if the performance of a commandment may endanger life, the preservation of life is supreme. For the three cardinal sins, however — idolatry, forbidden relationships, and murder [and cases where violation of commandments would cause public desecration of God's Name (*Sanhedrin* 74a)] — one must be prepared to sacrifice his life even under all circumstances.

The most severe punishment for the nation as a whole is to be banished from the Land, and to be placed under the domination of others, and to witness the destruction of the Temple. This extraordinary punishment fits the crime of having transgressed the most severe, cardinal prohibitions (*Tiferes Yisrael, Sefer HaMussar*).

R' Yonah (quoting *Shabbos* 33a) cites the Scriptural sources teaching that exile is a result of these cardinal sins. Regarding idolatry it is written: וַהֲשִׁמּוֹתִי אֶת מִקְדְּשֵׁיכֶם, וְגוֹ' וְאֶתְכֶם אֱזָרֶה בַגּוֹיִם, *And I will make your sanctuaries desolate . . . ; And I will scatter you among the nations* (*Leviticus* 26:31,33) [see *Shabbos* 33a]. Regarding immorality it is written: וַתִּטְמָא הָאָרֶץ וָאֶפְקֹד עֲוֹנָהּ עָלֶיהָ וַתָּקִא הָאָרֶץ אֶת יֹשְׁבֶיהָ, *And the Land became contaminated, and I recalled its iniquity upon it* (*Leviticus* 18:25); and וְלֹא תָקִיא הָאָרֶץ אֶתְכֶם בְּטַמַּאֲכֶם אֹתָהּ, *Let not the Land disgorge you for having contaminated it* (ibid. 28).

The Torah teaches that while murder is an unpardonable crime in all places, it is especially so in the Land of Israel. Hence, *You shall not bring guilt upon the Land in which you are, for the blood will bring guilt upon the Land . . . You shall not contaminate the Land in which you dwell, in whose midst I rest* (*Numbers* 35:33,34).

Bloodshed includes unintentional or accidental killing, as indicated by the law of the עָרֵי מִקְלָט, cities which were set aside to provide sanctuary for those who kill through carelessness. Such people were required to live in the cities of refuge as atonement for having caused a death.

◆§ **Critical sins.** *Nesivos Shalom* of Slonim elaborates: These three sins undermine the three dimensions of the human being. Idolatry is an intellectual sin which contaminates a person's mind, his ideas and opinions; immorality is a crime of passion rooted in the desires of the heart; and murder transforms man's physical power into a force for destruction. When people are involved in these three evils, they leave no place for the Divine Presence, and the nation suffers exile as a result. On a personal level as well, these three sins remove a person from his spiritual moorings: Idolatry affects man's faith, immorality devastates his inherent sanctity, and murder is symptomatic of an egomania that does not allow productive contact with others.

וְעַל שְׁמִטַּת הָאָרֶץ — *and for working the earth during the Sabbatical year*. One may not plow or sow the Land during the *Shemittah* year (see *Leviticus* 25:4-5). Regarding failure to observe the year of rest, the Torah teaches אָז תִּרְצֶה הָאָרֶץ אֶת שַׁבְּתֹתֶיהָ כֹּל יְמֵי הָשַּׁמָּה וְאַתֶּם בְּאֶרֶץ אֹיְבֵיכֶם, *Then the Land will be appeased for its Sabbaticals during all the years of its desolation, when you are in the land of your foes* (*Leviticus* 26:34). From this verse the Sages derive that exile results from Israel's failure to observe the commandments of the Sabbatical year. If the people do not let the Land rest in their presence, it will rest in their absence (*Shabbos* 33a).

Because of the seventy Sabbaticals that Israel had violated prior to and during the period of the First Temple, the Babylonian exile lasted for seventy years. During that time, the Land made up for the rest of which it had been deprived (*Rashi* on *Leviticus* ibid.).

Exile is the fitting punishment for ignoring the Sabbatical of the Land. The earth and everything it contains belong to God; man is merely a temporary tenant. *Shemittah* is given to us to teach us the truth of God's words: כִּי לִי כָּל הָאָרֶץ, *For Mine is the whole world* (*Exodus* 19:5). Man must relinquish his control over his holdings — his land and loans — in order to internalize this lesson. One who continues his regular activities during *Shemittah* declares instead, כֹּחִי וְעֹצֶם יָדִי עָשָׂה לִי אֶת הַחַיִל הַזֶּה, *My strength and the might of my hand has made me all this wealth* (*Deuteronomy* 8:17). Since his possessions are a spiritual stumbling block, God takes them away by sentencing him to exile (*R' Moshe Alshakar*).

Ri bar Shlomo offers another approach: Part of the *Yovel* observance is the freeing of slaves and the return of lands to their original owners (see *Leviticus* 25:9-10). Those who do not do so are punished by being exiled and sold as slaves.

◆§ **The nature of the land.** This mishnah provides an important insight into the nature of *Eretz Yisrael*. Its holiness is such that it cannot tolerate the sort of sins described here, and it vomits out those who commit them. In *Rashi's* parable, the Land is like a prince with a delicate constitution. If he is given spoiled food, he cannot digest it and regurgitates it. Similarly, the Holy Land cannot abide sinners in its midst, so that when the Jews began to indulge in such behavior, they were exiled.

It is illuminating that the Egyptians, despite their rampant corruption and immorality, were not spewed out of their land. Though the sins of immorality set forth in the Torah apply everywhere in the world, their perpetrators are not expelled from Egypt or any other land; only *Eretz Yisrael* expels those who contaminate it. This is because the Holy Land, unlike other lands, is not assigned to intermediate heavenly forces. *Eretz Yisrael* is under God's personal supervision, and as such it demands a higher standard of behavior.

It is this heightened sanctity of the Land that caused the Patriarchs to recognize instinctively that they should observe all the commandments in *Eretz Yisrael*, even before the Torah was given. Thus, although Jacob married two sisters in Charan, he could not be married to both of them in the Land. As soon as he and his family arrived in the Holy Land, Rachel died. Because of her righteousness, she was privileged to die in the Land; because of Jacob's righteousness, he did not live with sisters once he had arrived in *Eretz Yisrael* (*Ramban*).

◆§ **Personal redemption.** Exile is not only geographical; it is a personal condition suffered by one whose heart and will are pulled in disparate directions. The Talmud teaches: גְּדוֹלָה תְּשׁוּבָה שֶׁמְּבִיאָה הַגְּאוּלָּה, *Great is repentance, which brings redemption* (*Yoma* 86b). This refers to the power of repentance to bring about a *personal* redemption, when a person regains the spiritual station to which he truly aspires. *Maharal* teaches that for this reason the *shofar*, which signals the onset of *Yovel* and the freeing of slaves, is blown on Yom Kippur, the climax of the days of repentance. In its truest sense, repentance is a declaration of independence from enslavement to one's desires, and a return to one's ancestral heritage.

Those who remain impervious to the message of *Shemittah* and *Yovel*, who never realize that man has the capacity to come home spiritually, suffer the worst type of exile — that of the eternally wandering Jew.

[יב] **בְּאַרְבָּעָה** פְּרָקִים הַדֶּבֶר מִתְרַבֶּה: בָּרְבִיעִית, וּבַשְּׁבִיעִית, וּבְמוֹצָאֵי שְׁבִיעִית, וּבְמוֹצָאֵי הֶחָג שֶׁבְּכָל שָׁנָה וְשָׁנָה. בָּרְבִיעִית, מִפְּנֵי מַעְשַׂר עָנִי שֶׁבַּשְּׁלִישִׁית; בַּשְּׁבִיעִית, מִפְּנֵי מַעְשַׂר עָנִי שֶׁבַּשִּׁשִּׁית; בְּמוֹצָאֵי שְׁבִיעִית, מִפְּנֵי פֵּרוֹת שְׁבִיעִית; בְּמוֹצָאֵי הֶחָג שֶׁבְּכָל שָׁנָה וְשָׁנָה, מִפְּנֵי גֶּזֶל מַתְּנוֹת עֲנִיִּים.

Mishnah 12

Having finished listing sets of seven, the mishnah begins listing sets of four (*Magen Avos*).

בְּאַרְבָּעָה פְּרָקִים הַדֶּבֶר מִתְרַבֶּה — *At four periods* [*of the seven-year Sabbatical cycle*] *pestilence increases.* This mishnah elaborates on one of the themes of the preceding one, the appearance of דֶּבֶר, *pestilence*, upon the earth. As noted above, pestilence strikes for a variety of sins, among them denying the poor access to the yield of *Shemittah*. Even during a time of general affliction, however, the nation must feel a special responsibility to help the poor, for they suffer more than anybody else in a crisis. If they are ignored, the pestilence will intensify (*Tosafos Yom Tov*).

בָּרְבִיעִית, וּבַשְּׁבִיעִית, וּבְמוֹצָאֵי שְׁבִיעִית, וּבְמוֹצָאֵי הֶחָג שֶׁבְּכָל שָׁנָה וְשָׁנָה — *in the fourth year, in the seventh year, in the year following the Sabbatical year, and annually at the conclusion of the* [*Succos*] *festival.* During these four periods, special caution must be taken to provide for the needs of the poor.

Because of this obligation, the poor look forward to receiving support during these four particular periods. The loss of revenue which they experience when people are not forthcoming is aggravated when their hopes are dashed. Similarly, the Talmud teaches that מַתְּנוֹת לָאֶבְיוֹנִים, the *gifts to the poor* that are a major commandment of the Purim festival, must always be given on the day the Megillah is read, since "the poor people anxiously await the Megillah reading in anticipation of receiving gifts" (*Megillah* 4b).

בָּרְבִיעִית, מִפְּנֵי מַעְשַׂר עָנִי שֶׁבַּשְּׁלִישִׁית; בַּשְּׁבִיעִית, מִפְּנֵי מַעְשַׂר עָנִי שֶׁבַּשִּׁשִּׁית — *In the fourth year* [*of the Shemittah cycle*] *for* [*neglecting*] *the tithe of the poor in the third; in the seventh year for* [*neglecting*] *the tithe of the poor in the sixth.* Tithes are given during the first six years of every seven-year *Shemittah* cycle. *Maaser Rishon*, the first tithe, is given to the Levite every year. *Maaser Sheini*, the second tithe, is set aside to be eaten in Jerusalem in all years except the third and sixth, when it is replaced by *Maaser Ani*, the tithe of the poor; the latter is given to the destitute (*Machzor Vitry*). The harvests of the third and sixth years are therefore times of special responsibility to the poor. When one curtails their sustenance by withholding the gifts due them, one causes God to cease sustaining man's life, thus

---

∙⧉ Getting your way. Very often we justify limiting our aid to the poor with the claim that we must provide for our old age. The mishnah teaches us that in truth, it works the other way around; one merits old age by providing for others.

Knesses Yisrael portrays the metaphoric scene of a double trial. A family that had been deprived by its miserly husband and father summoned him to court. At the same time, the judge was trying the case of a woman who accused her husband of giving away too much to the poor. Each defendant presented his defense. The miser claimed that he had to hoard his money for his old age, while the spendthrift expressed fear that he might die young and not have time to distribute enough charity. The judge ruled that God should save each one from the thing he most feared: The miser's life should be shortened, and the open-handed philanthropist should live to a ripe old age. When one neglects to give tithes to the poor, he may have more money — but pestilence or the like will not allow him the peace of mind to enjoy it.

12. At four periods [of the seven-year Sabbatical cycle] pestilence increases: in the fourth year, in the seventh year, in the year following the Sabbatical year, and annually at the conclusion of the [Succos] festival. In the fourth year [of the Shemittah cycle] for [neglecting] the tithe of the poor in the third; in the seventh year for [neglecting] the tithe of the poor in the sixth; [immediately] following the Sabbatical year for [violating the laws of] the Sabbatical produce; annually, at the conclusion of the festival [of Succos], for robbing the poor of their gifts.

---

making him vulnerable to the deadly pestilence (*R' Moshe Almsonino*).

בְּמוֹצָאֵי שְׁבִיעִית, מִפְּנֵי פֵּרוֹת שְׁבִיעִית — [*immediately*] *following the Sabbatical year for* [*violating the laws of*] *the Sabbatical produce.* During the Sabbatical year, when everyone — including the poor — is entitled to take whatever grew in the fields that year, one who attempts to retain ownership or control over his yield invites the devastating effects of pestilence. By denying the poor access to his field, he opens the door to death (*Rashi*).

Midrash Shmuel notes that, unlike the earlier stich of the mishnah, which speaks of punishment in the *following* year for neglecting the tithe of the poor, the punishment for not allowing the poor to benefit from the Sabbatical produce comes quickly, immediately at the end of the *Shemittah*

year. He explains that neglecting tithes is a passive sin and can always be rectified; hence, God delays punishment while awaiting man's repentance. Denying access to the fields or taking the harvest for oneself, however, is an active sin which elicits immediate retribution.

בְּמוֹצָאֵי הֶחָג שֶׁבְּכָל שָׁנָה וְשָׁנָה, מִפְּנֵי גֶּזֶל מַתְּנוֹת עֲנִיִּים — *annually, at the conclusion of the festival* [*of Succos*], *for robbing the poor of their gifts.* Succos is the time of the harvest when those who own fields are commanded by the Torah to leave לֶקֶט, שִׁכְחָה — the harvest gleanings, the forgotten and dropped sheaves, and a corner of the field — for the poor (see *Leviticus* 19:9-11).

Likewise, one who harvests grapes must leave עוֹלְלוֹת, single grapes which have not formed clusters, or פֶּרֶט, those which have fallen to the

---

◆§ **Too careful.** In the days before he became famous, R' Zusia of Anipoli had a secret benefactor who would give him one gold coin every week. The benefactor became fantastically wealthy, and his friends constantly begged him to reveal the secret of his success. Finally, he told them of his support of the holy R' Zusia. His friends replied: "If that is the key to wealth, you would do even better to support the famed Holy *Maggid* of Mezritch, instead. You will become even wealthier." The man listened to their advice, and stopped his stipend to R' Zusia, and gave it instead to the great R' Dov Ber of Mezritch. No sooner had he done so than his fortune plummeted, leaving him with almost nothing.

Realizing that he had done something wrong, he went to appease R' Zusia. The holy *tzaddik* of Anipoli told him, "Listen, my dear friend. As long as you gave me without investigating whether I was the most worthy recipient, the Heavenly agents also did not check too carefully to see if you were the one most deserving of wealth. However, now that you are careful to give charity only to a great *tzaddik* like the *Maggid*, they are also more careful in Heaven about whom they bless with prosperity."

[We are sometimes tempted to reevaluate where we will spend our charity dollar. We might be wise, however, not to remove persons or institutions from our list of causes too hastily, even if we feel we have found worthier recipients. Our regular beneficiaries rely on our contributions and experience great disappointment when we are not forthcoming. Furthermore, we never know which charitable cause is the one for which God rewards us. If we become selective about whom we support, God may also reevaluate whether or not we deserve His support.]

[יג] **אַרְבַּע** מִדּוֹת בָּאָדָם. הָאוֹמֵר: „שֶׁלִּי שֶׁלִּי וְשֶׁלְּךָ שֶׁלָּךְ,‟ זוֹ מִדָּה בֵּינוֹנִית, וְיֵשׁ אוֹמְרִים: זוֹ מִדַּת סְדוֹם; „שֶׁלִּי שֶׁלָּךְ וְשֶׁלְּךָ שֶׁלִּי,‟ עַם הָאָרֶץ;

---

ground (see *Rambam*). King Solomon advises: *Do not rob the impoverished . . . for God will take up their cause and despoil the life of those who despoil them* (Proverbs 22:22-23). Once the Succos festival is over and all agricultural work is done, either one has met his obligations, or he has robbed the poor of what is rightfully theirs and will be punished immediately (*Machzor Vitry, Rambam, Rashi*).

The phrase גֶּזֶל מַתְּנוֹת עֲנִיִּים, *robbing the poor of their gifts*, seems to be a contradiction in terms. How can one who does not give a *gift* be accused of *theft*? *Midrash Shmuel* sees in this an expression of God's mercy. Even though one is obligated to support the poor and deserves

no special recognition for meeting this obligation, God still rewards charity as if it were done willingly rather than dutifully. Nonetheless, if one refrains from contributing, it is as if he had stolen God's property. Thus, the poor recipient has received a gift, magnanimously given by the giver; but the one who refuses to give is regarded as a thief, for he has stolen from God, by keeping something that was given him only to pass along to the poor.

Mikveh Yisrael views this as an allusion to a donor who formerly spread his contributions among many poor people, but now contributes the same sum to only a few, to the deep disappointment of the former recipients, who always relied on his contributions. This, too, is tantamount to stealing the gifts of the poor.

Mishnah 13

אַרְבַּע מִדּוֹת בָּאָדָם — *There are four character types among people.* This mishnah continues the sets of four, but unlike 5:16, which speaks of attitudes toward philanthropy and those dependent on it, this mishnah defines attitudes of equals toward each other (*Midrash Shmuel, Magen Avos*). The topic includes all areas of exchange among people, including material or financial assistance to people we do not know well. Because people frequently rationalize to excuse themselves from helping others, the approach one takes in interpersonal dealings is a mark of one's character (*Meiri*).

a) הָאוֹמֵר: „שֶׁלִּי שֶׁלִּי וְשֶׁלְּךָ שֶׁלָּךְ‟ זוֹ מִדָּה בֵּינוֹנִית — *One who says, "My [property] is mine, and yours is yours," is an average character type.* This person's attitude is "I don't want others to derive any pleasure from me, nor do I want to derive any pleasure from them" (*Rashi, Rav*). He is an average character type, falling somewhere between the wicked, who want only to take, and the pious, who seek only to benefit others. While not exemplary, he is certainly an acceptable type of person (*Tiferes Yisrael*).

Meiri renders בֵּינוֹנִית as *consistent*. This person's attitude toward his own property is consistent with his attitude toward others'; he feels everyone is

entitled to his own. On the one hand, this attitude is strangely antisocial, but it is not worthy of censure. *R' Yonah* adds that such a person would seem to be the subject of King Solomon's observation וְשׂוֹנֵא מַתָּנֹת יִחְיֶה, *One who despises gifts shall live* (Proverbs 15:27); he is neither a giver nor a taker.

וְיֵשׁ אוֹמְרִים: זוֹ מִדַּת סְדוֹם — *but some say this is characteristic of Sodom.* The residents of Sodom epitomized selfishness: *She did not strengthen the hand of the needy* (Ezekiel 16:49) is how the prophet described Sodom; they prevented outsiders from coming into their city even though they lacked nothing and had plenty to spare. In spite of their awareness that people of other cities would retaliate by not receiving them, the Sodomites were not deterred from their institutionalization of cruelty (see *Sanhedrin* 109a).

The Talmud (*Eruvin* 49a, *Bava Basra* 12b) teaches that the attitude of refusing to allow others to benefit from one's property even when no loss will be incurred [זֶה נֶהֱנֶה וְזֶה לֹא חָסַר], is characteristic of Sodom. According to this view, the notion of "each man for himself" is not merely average but unethical, since it negates the entire concept of benevolence and will eventually lead to stinginess

13. There are four character types among people: a) One who says, "My [property] is mine, and yours is yours," is an average character type, but some say this is characteristic of Sodom; b) "Mine is yours, and yours is mine," is an unlearned

and even cruelty (*Rav, Tiferes Yisrael*).

R' Yonah explains the divergence of opinion in the mishnah on whether this trait is innocuous or actually evil. The first opinion, which claims that שֶׁלִּי שֶׁלִּי וְשֶׁלְּךָ שֶׁלָּךְ is an average characteristic, refers to one who disburses charity out of a sense of religious obligation in spite of an inner selfishness.

He means to say, "Whatever I'm entitled to keep, I will keep; whatever I am halachically obligated to give to others, I will give." Even though his attitude is not exemplary, he is considered "average" because, although he would prefer not to give anything away, his behavior is acceptable, since he does the right thing. The second opinion, claiming

⊷ **Sodom — an economic decision.** The seed of Sodom's wickedness lay in its failure to abide by the principles of kindness and caring that Abraham would inculcate in his offspring. The cruelties of Sodom have become synonymous with selfishness, callousness, and depravity, but the real root of their evil was greed. Sodom was a rich and fertile region, and as such, it was a magnet for people seeking to make their fortunes, as it was for Abraham's nephew Lot. The wealthy and well-connected Lots of the world were welcome in Sodom, because they would give more to the economy than they would take. The Sodomites, however, wanted to insulate their prosperity and guard it against a possible flood of poor immigrants. To discourage such undesirable newcomers, they institutionalized state cruelty, so that it became a crime to feed a starving person or offer alms to a beggar. Even the perversion for which Sodom is notorious was employed to keep visitors away. According to the opinion of the Sages expressed here, this cruelty stemmed from the attitude "What is mine is mine, and what is yours is yours," or, in the popular idiom, "Neither a lender nor a borrower be." Such selfishness degenerates into cruelty and perversion — and a metropolis that elevates such behavior to a legitimate way of life forfeits its right to exist (*R' Nosson Scherman*).

⊷ **What's new.** When Rabbi Levi Yitzchak assumed his rabbinical post in Berditchev, he stipulated that he not be called to any communal meetings unless some new general enactment was on the agenda. At one such meeting, a proposal was made to forbid beggars from collecting house to house. Instead, they would only be allowed to congregate outside the local synagogue, where anyone so disposed could offer a contribution.

R' Levi Yitzchak was upset. "Why did you ask me to attend this meeting?" he wanted to know.

The elders were surprised. "But the proposal under discussion is new," they said. "We need the Rav's approval."

R' Levi Yitzchak replied: "This is not a new idea. The idea of limiting opportunities for the poor and not wanting to help others originated in Sodom!"

⊷ **Attitude is everything.** Charity must be given joyously, for the Talmud teaches: "Charity is rewarded according to the kindness involved" (*Succah* 49b). *Rashi* (ad loc.) explains that the effort one makes to anticipate and provide for the needs of the poor is the barometer of his kindness. The benefactor may show his concern in many ways, not merely in the amount of money he gives. By providing food that is ready to eat or clothes that are ready to wear, and by delivering them personally, one shows that he wishes to ease the lot of the needy, not merely to satisfy his own conscience. And, of course, the manner in which one renders assistance is all important. Assistance given with a cheerful, friendly smile encourages the recipient; a lavish gift tossed off with a frown demeans the recipient.

The Chazon Ish once replied to someone who had written to him in regard to providing for his less fortunate brother: "If you decide to help him through this difficult time, do so joyfully, as you would if you were building a *succah* or listening to the *shofar*. The main thing in the performance of a *mitzvah* is the elation we experience from having merited the opportunity" (*Collected Letters II*, 93).

that this is a Sodomistic trait, holds that one's action should be a direct expression of his attitude. It is not enough simply to give charity; one must actively develop a sense of magnanimity. Anything short of this borders on Sodomism.

Lachmei Todah homiletically offers the following: Individuals who adopt the attitude of the בֵּינוֹנִי, *the average person*, may be pardoned for their lack of sensitivity, since a streak of self-centeredness is a common human trait. Others with more generous hearts will bear the burden of the more unfortunate members of society. It is for this reason that the first opinion uses the singular term הָאוֹמֵר, the *individual* who says, "Mine is mine, and yours is yours"; the second opinion, however, uses the plural וְיֵשׁ אוֹמְרִים, to indicate that when such an attitude becomes prevalent among *many* members of society,

the poor are in great danger of being neglected. A society in which generosity and caring is not public policy will eventually evolve into another Sodom.

שֶׁלִּי שֶׁלָּךְ וְשֶׁלְּךָ שֶׁלִּי," עַם הָאָרֶץ — b) *"Mine is yours, and yours is mine," is an unlearned person.* The translation of עַם הָאָרֶץ as *an unlearned person* follows *Rashi*. Such a person lacks a sense of moral sophistication, and therefore has no appreciation for the sanctity of private property. Alternatively, this expression personifies a glutton who will shamelessly take from others.

R' Yonah and *Rav* explain the term עַם הָאָרֶץ in a non-derogatory fashion. He is literally *a man of the people*, an ordinary, viable member of society who is interested in promoting good will, harmony, and

---

⊷ **Be involved.** *Knesses Yisrael* elaborates: When one adopts this attitude of detachment — that he does only what is required — as a *personal* policy, it places him somewhere between wicked and pious. However, when he advocates this approach as the norm for everyone, he removes kindheartedness from the public domain and emulates the Sodomites, who would neither entertain guests nor allow others to do so.

Rabbi Yitzchak of Vorki offered a charming homiletical interpretation of our mishnah: It is within the boundaries of decency to decline to support causes outside of one's immediate locale with the justification that *"Mine is mine* — the indigent and the institutions of *my* city are *my* responsibility," and *"Yours is yours* — the problems of *your* town are the responsibility of *your* fellow citizens." It is true that the Sages teach עֲנִיֵּי עִירְךָ קוֹדְמִין, *the poor of your own city take precedence (Bava Metzia* 71a), but this applies only if one actually helps the local poor. If he merely offers this principle as an excuse in order not to help outsiders, then it is מִדַּת סְדוֹם, and his behavior borders on cruelty.

⊷ **Ignorance is lawlessness.** One who does not know halachah may be tempted to rule on monetary matters on the basis of his instincts, which may be contrary to Torah law. Out of ignorance, he may give away what is rightfully his, and he may even claim monies that belong to his fellow (*Ruach Chaim*).

As a classic example of this type of ignorance and the havoc it can wreak, the Chazon Ish (*Emunah U'Vitachon* 3:14) cites a responsum of Rabbi Yosef Saul Nathanson (*Yad Shaul (Yoreh Deah* §145). New teachers moved into his town and began recruiting students. The local teachers, fearing that the intruders were violating their territory, sought to enlist the help of the regional government in order to have the new teachers evicted from town. R' Yosef Shaul responded: "The prohibition against infringing on another person's livelihood does not apply to the teaching of Torah. The Talmudic dictum that competition and rivalry among scholars serves to increase wisdom (see *Bava Basra* 21a) applies equally to those who teach youngsters and to those who teach mishnah and Talmud. God forbid to suggest that any responsible and competent halachic authority ruled otherwise."

The Chazon Ish adds that if the halachah indeed forbade the new teachers to establish a new school, not only would it be permitted to enlist the government's aid in preventing them from doing so, it would be a *mitzvah*. However, since the Torah permits them to come, it is those who want to see them leave who are at fault; they are considered in the category of מוֹסֵר, one who indiscriminately hands over Jews to the non-Jewish powers. Thus, our eyes must always be raised to the *Shulchan Aruch* and to the great scholars of the generation to teach us the halachah, for ignorance can result in erroneous decisions about ownership — in this case, about territory and rights. R' Yosef Shaul, whose heart was permeated with a love for truth and justice, was able to exhibit "cruelty" toward the old teachers in order to uphold the truth of Torah.

commerce among men, and would like people to share with each other; however, he is ignorant of the Torah's principle that considers one who detests taking from others an alive and vibrant person (see *Proverbs* 15:27); the ideal behavioral framework is to give and not to take. According to *Tiferes Yisrael*, one who displays such an approach to interpersonal relationships is a normal member of society, who wants to benefit his neighbors and benefit from them.

Meiri renders עַם הָאָרֶץ as *a social creature*, who needs the social benefits of reciprocity. This is an acceptable mode of behavior for most people.

Sefer HaMussar points out cautiously, however, that the desire to derive benefit from others is an inherent character deficiency. It may lead one to covet the wealth of other people and to an obsessive preoccupation with other people's belongings. It is almost impossible to find even two brothers or two partners who share without jealousy.

,,שֶׁלִּי שֶׁלָּךְ וְשֶׁלָּךְ שֶׁלָּךְ,'' חָסִיד — c) *"Mine is yours, and yours is yours," is scrupulously pious.* The term חָסִיד denotes someone who does more than what is required by the letter of the law. One is entitled to derive benefit from others (with their permission), and is likewise not obligated to allow others to benefit from him; but the scrupulously pious person allows others to derive enjoyment freely from whatever he owns, and yet he does not permit himself to benefit from the property of others (*Rashi, Rav*).

Samuel the Prophet exhibited this type of piety. He would bring along whatever household items he needed when traveling so that he would not have to derive benefit from others (see *I Samuel* 7:17 and *Berachos* 11a).

Midrash Shmuel comments that a pious person speaks of others' property before speaking of his own, in order to reassure those who benefit from him that he expects nothing in return: "שֶׁלִּי שֶׁלָּךְ, take from me whatever you would like — but וְשֶׁלָּךְ שֶׁלָּךְ, *what is yours is yours,* so do not think about repaying." Alternatively, a pious person seeks to calm those who are embarrassed about taking. "What is mine is yours to the same extent that your own belongings are yours. You should feel no more embarrassed about taking from me than you would about using your own possessions."

However, it is forbidden to carry out this principle to an extreme, giving away so much that he has nothing left for himself. Acting with piety does not allow him to become a ward of the community (*Maharal*). The Talmud (*Kesubos* 67b) teaches, in fact, that even for charity one should not spend more than one fifth of his assets.

,,שֶׁלָּךְ שֶׁלִּי וְשֶׁלִּי שֶׁלִּי,'' רָשָׁע — d) *"Yours is mine, and mine is mine," is wicked.* Such a self-centered person is concerned only with what he can take from life. He wants only to benefit from others, even at their expense or to their detriment, but he cannot

---

◆§ **Skewed perspective.** Rabbi Bunam of P'shis'cha explains the ignorance of the unlearned person in terms of the balance between reliance on God and human effort. The unsophisticated person thinks that his spiritual growth is dependent on God, when in fact, his spiritual successes and failures are in his own hands: "הַכֹּל בִּידֵי שָׁמַיִם חוּץ מִיִּרְאַת שָׁמַיִם", *Everything is in the hands of Heaven except for the fear of Heaven* (*Berachos* 33b), i.e., whether or not a person is pious is up to him exclusively. On the other hand, man's livelihood is completely dependent on God's beneficence. Yet an unsophisticated person foolishly thinks that he himself makes a living. He says, "My spiritual station (שֶׁלִּי) — which is really up tp the man himself — is in *Your*, i.e., God's hands (שֶׁלָּךְ); and my livelihood (וְשֶׁלָּךְ) — which is really from God — depends on *my* efforts (שֶׁלִּי)."

◆§ **Fooling God.** According to the Kozhnitzer *Maggid*, the contrast alludes to one's approach to the service of God. A pious person tells God: "שֶׁלִּי שֶׁלָּךְ — I recognize that my things are really Yours, and I will perform even my personal activities, such as eating, sleeping, and leisure activities as a means to serve You. Not only that, but שֶׁלָּךְ שֶׁלָּךְ — what is Yours is Yours. I will try to do the *mitzvos* for Your sake, not for the purpose of self-aggrandizement, prestige, or reward." The wicked see life from a different vantage point: "שֶׁלִּי שֶׁלִּי — my good times, God, are my business; and even שֶׁלָּךְ שֶׁלִּי — when I do an occasional *mitzvah*, it is only for a self-serving purpose." The most mundane activities of the righteous are for the sake of God; but even the good deeds of the wicked are for no one's sake but their own.

[יד] **אַרְבַּע** מִדּוֹת בְּדֵעוֹת: נוֹחַ לִכְעוֹס וְנוֹחַ לִרְצוֹת, יָצָא שְׂכָרוֹ בְּהֶפְסֵדוֹ; קָשֶׁה לִכְעוֹס וְקָשֶׁה לִרְצוֹת, יָצָא הֶפְסֵדוֹ בִשְׂכָרוֹ; קָשֶׁה לִכְעוֹס וְנוֹחַ לִרְצוֹת, חָסִיד;

---

fathom doing something for someone else, even if it costs him nothing (Rashi, Rav) This potential for wickedness exists in one who is obsessed with money; he will eventually come to thievery (Magen Avos).

The obvious contrast between the pious and the wicked lies in their *basic* attitudes toward other people's money as opposed to their own. The pious person says, "I prefer to forgo something I'm entitled to in order to be sure that you get whatever is coming to *you*." The wicked, however, say, "Certainly what is mine is mine — and I am even willing to take from others in order to be sure that I am not shortchanged" (R' Shaul Brach).

Mishnah 14

אַרְבַּע מִדּוֹת בְּדֵעוֹת — *There are four types of temperament.* Having discussed the various attitudes that people have toward money and personal property, the chapter now delineates four basic temperaments, based on how one handles anger and the wide-ranging effects that each may have.

The Sages taught: אָדָם נִכָּר בְּכִיסוֹ בְּכוֹסוֹ וּבְכַעְסוֹ, *A person's character can be determined through his wallet [his attitude toward money], his cup [his behavior when he is intoxicated], and his anger"* (Tanchuma, Korach Ch. 12). Since the issue of money is frequently the subject of arguments and the cause of anger, the Sages' first suggestion was to verify a person's approach to money. The mishnah follows the same pattern.

The mishnah makes clear judgments about the relative value of each of the four temperaments, but such value judgments would be unfair and misplaced if man could not change the temperament with which he was born. Rather it is implicit in the mishnah that self-transformation is inextricably bound up with the principle of free will. The mish-

nah thus teaches us indirectly that it is possible for a person to restructure and modify his most basic characteristics (Sefer HaMussar, Maharam Shick).

a) **נוֹחַ לִכְעוֹס וְנוֹחַ לִרְצוֹת, יָצָא שְׂכָרוֹ בְּהֶפְסֵדוֹ** — *One who is angered easily and pacified easily, his gain is offset by his loss.* One who becomes angry over trivial matters is bound to be provoked often. Even if he is pacified easily, another outburst is certain to be imminent. Thus, the positive aspect of his character is offset by his general vulnerability to even minor frustration. Furthermore, a moment of anger may cause damage that cannot be easily erased by appeasement (R' Yonah, Rashi, Rav).

According to *Meiri*, *Rambam*, and *Magen Avos*, the correct text reads: נוֹחַ לִכְעוֹס וְנוֹחַ לִרְצוֹת, יָצָא הֶפְסֵדוֹ בִשְׂכָרוֹ, *One who is angered easily and pacified easily, his loss is offset by his gain.* According to this reading, any loss caused by one's anger will be mitigated, if not eliminated, by the ease with which he is pacified. *Meiri* explains that this has less to do

---

⁀⁆ **Restore the relationship.** Rabbi Gershon Henoch of Radzin observed that some people get out of bed in the morning already angry; all they need is an object for their wrath. About such people the Sages taught: "One who gets angry, all forms of *Gehinnom* rule over him" (Nedarim 22a), for the inability to control one's emotions traps him in a living purgatory.

The greatest loss suffered by a habitually angry person is that he becomes a slave to his mood. Rabbi Yitzchak Waldshein, one of the great *mussar* masters of Novarodok, points to the words of the Sages, "One who gets angry loses his wisdom." This is an unqualified fact of life. Even a bit of anger can cause a person to lose his perspective totally and forfeit control over his emotional world.

Words uttered in anger can often destroy relationships; even if the parties become reconciled, the outburst may have irreversibly damaged the quality of the relationship, and the fact that a person is easily appeased may not be enough to counteract the effects of a quick temper.

14. There are four types of temperament: a) One who is angered easily and pacified easily, his gain is offset by his loss; b) one who is hard to anger and hard to pacify, his loss is offset by his gain; c) one who is hard to anger and pacified easily is pious;

with the external results of anger as much as with the spiritual damage that an angry person can potentially inflict on himself. If he is able to free himself easily from his wrathful state, he reduces to a great extent the negative impact on his soul.

R' Mattisyahu HaYitzhari explains: People typically react to an adversary's anger with frustration, which in turn increases the agitated person's distress. This spiraling effect can turn a mere difference of opinion into a serious conflict. But when a person's friends and family are aware of his temperament, and know that he is easily appeased, they can temporarily ignore his outbursts and wait until he is pacified. Thus, the potential for damage that his negative disposition can cause is to some extent tempered by his propensity to be appeased easily.

קָשֶׁה לִכְעוֹס וְקָשֶׁה לִרְצוֹת, יָצָא הֶפְסֵדוֹ בִשְׂכָרוֹ — (b *one who is hard to anger and hard to pacify, his loss is offset by his gain.* Even though this person is hard to appease, his flaw is not very damaging since he is slow to anger in the first place. His occasional outburst is more than offset by his generally calm demeanor (*R' Yonah, Rashi, Rav*). Such a person will be saved from the physical and spiritual damage caused by anger (*Tiferes Yisrael*).

Sfas Emes comments that one who is easily angered and easily appeased (the first case of the mishnah) is worse off than one who is hard to anger, even though he is hard to appease. This is because it is easier to find ways to prevent such a person's anger from exploding in the first place. Furthermore, one who falls into a pattern of easy anger and easy appeasement can lose perspec-

tive and begin to accept his anger as natural. "It doesn't matter if I'm angry, it will soon pass," he says to himself; and once it passes, he quickly forgets the bitterness he experienced when he was enraged. This is not so with one who is hard both to anger and to appease. When he *does* become angry, he suffers the consequences of his temper for so long and with such intensity that he might well attempt to cure himself of his fault. In the long run, therefore, he is better off.

Meiri, however, again inverts the text to read יָצָא שְׂכָרוֹ בְּהֶפְסֵדוֹ, *his gain is offset by his loss.* The emphasis here rests on the negative result of his occasional outbursts because when he does lose his temper, the effect is lasting.

קָשֶׁה לִכְעוֹס וְנוֹחַ לִרְצוֹת, חָסִיד — (c *one who is hard to anger and pacified easily is pious.* One who has great patience and is forbearing to such an extent that he is almost never aroused to anger is truly pious. He silently bears whatever Divine Providence allots him in life and does not allow himself to be provoked by insults (*Rambam*). Saintly people can defuse their anger in midstream before it is fully spent, unlike the wicked who must vent their rage completely before they can be pacified (*R' Yonah*). [A classic exemplar of this trait was King David. When Shimi ben Gera cursed him, he would not allow his servants to retaliate. *"God told him to curse me,"* he said to them humbly (see *II Samuel* 16:11).]

The mishnah does not speak of one who *never* gets angry; this is virtually impossible. Even Moses,

---

King David was motivated by this dynamic when he begged God to forgive him for his sin in the incident of Uriah and Bathsheba (see *II Samuel* 12-13 and ArtScroll *Tehillim*, Overview, Part IV). He wanted not only forgiveness, he longed for the close relationship he had had with God before the sin. According to R' Yonah (*Shaarei Teshuvah* 1:23), this plea, which is contained in Psalm 51, is the "Chapter of Repentance," because it was David's plea for forgiveness for that sin and in it can be found the primary principles of repentance. In commenting on verse 10 and 14, R' Yonah (ibid. 1:42) writes: It is possible that a person can be forgiven for his transgressions and yet not regain the degree of closeness that had existed previously in his relationship with God. It is the return of this love that the true penitent passionately seeks, and this is what David meant when he asked God to sustain him with a "generous spirit," and "Restore me to the joy of Your salvation; let me be as beloved to You as in days gone by." It is this restoration of the old relationship that often becomes impossible due to outbursts of anger.

נוֹחַ לִכְעוֹס וְקָשֶׁה לִרְצוֹת, רָשָׁע.

[טו] **אַרְבַּע** מִדּוֹת בְּתַלְמִידִים: מָהִיר לִשְׁמוֹעַ וּמָהִיר
לְאַבֵּד, יָצָא שְׂכָרוֹ בְּהֶפְסֵדוֹ; קָשֶׁה
לִשְׁמוֹעַ וְקָשֶׁה לְאַבֵּד, יָצָא הֶפְסֵדוֹ בִּשְׂכָרוֹ; מָהִיר
לִשְׁמוֹעַ וְקָשֶׁה לְאַבֵּד, זֶה חֵלֶק טוֹב; קָשֶׁה לִשְׁמוֹעַ

---

the humblest of all men, exhibited anger [see *Numbers* 31:14] (*Midrash Shmuel*). *Tosafos Yom Tov* cites Moses' rebuke of the Israelites, *Listen now, O rebels* (*Numbers* 20:10), as another instance of his anger. [See 4:29, s.v. וְלֹא מִקַּח שֹׁחַד.]

Noting that the mishnah does not say that the pious person never becomes angry, *R' Yonah* comments that there are times when anger is appropriate. Phineas displayed "anger" on God's behalf when he took zealous action against the rampant immorality to which the Israelites were incited by the Moabite and Midianite women (see *Numbers* 25:1-15). [See *Yoma* 22b and *I Kings* 2:6 for other examples.] Similarly, King Saul was rebuked for not showing anger when the honor of his kingdom was defamed by ruffians who refused to recognize him as king after Samuel anointed him.

Sfas Emes adds that one who is slow to anger and easily pacified is the truly pious person. Since he becomes angry in spite of his gentle nature, one can assume that he had a good reason; his piety is manifested in his ability to control his emotions and to allow himself to be appeased in spite of the good reason for his anger.

נוֹחַ לִכְעוֹס וְקָשֶׁה לִרְצוֹת, רָשָׁע — (d) *one who is angered easily and hard to pacify is wicked*. According to *Rashi*, one who is always angry is considered wicked since his temper will eventually cause him to transgress the word of God. The Talmud shows this progression when it teaches, "Don't become angry and do not sin" (*Berachos* 29b).

Tiferes Yisrael elaborates: One who is quick to anger is clearly not in control of himself; one who is slow to be pacified suffers from paralyzing obstinacy. The combination of these two character flaws opens the doorway to sins against God and against one's fellow man.

According to *Rambam* and *Maharal*, someone with this combination of a quick and enduring temper is already considered evil. The Talmud (*Nedarim* 22b) derives from the words of King Solomon *An angry person incites strife and one possessed by rage brings much sin* (*Proverbs* 29:22) that habitual anger is an indication that one has transgressed many sins.

Maharal explains: Sin is a loss of spiritual equilibrium. One who angers easily and has difficulty being appeased suffers from a lack of stability. Emotionally, this instability is expressed as anger; spiritually, it takes the form of sin.

Mishnah 15

אַרְבַּע מִדּוֹת בְּתַלְמִידִים: מָהִיר לִשְׁמוֹעַ וּמָהִיר לְאַבֵּד, יָצָא שְׂכָרוֹ בְּהֶפְסֵדוֹ — *There are four types of students:* (a) *One who grasps quickly and forgets quickly, his gain is offset by his loss.* One who has a quick intellectual grasp but a poor memory will never acquire a large fund of knowledge; the advantage of

his good mind is offset by his forgetfulness (*Rashi, Rav,* et al.). However, such a person can overcome his weakness through constant review and thus capitalize on his quick grasp (*Tiferes Yisrael*).

Even if one forgets his learning due to a weak memory, he should not become dissuaded or dis-

---

⏀ **The right time.** One would never think twice before standing up to someone who insulted his parents or his teacher. Therefore, pious people who are generally calm and placid are nonetheless ready to stand up against someone who seeks to demean their Father, since it is a time when anger is certainly in order.

d) one who is angered easily and hard to pacify is wicked.

15. There are four types of students: (a) One who grasps quickly and forgets quickly, his gain is offset by his loss; (b) one who grasps slowly and forgets slowly, his loss is offset by his gain; (c) one who grasps quickly and forgets slowly, this is a good portion; (d) one who grasps slowly

---

couraged, for the act of studying Torah is in itself of great significance, even if he retains little. Much like a person hired to draw water with a sieve, man is rewarded by God for his efforts in Torah study, not only for the results (*R' Yonah*).

Maharal and *Midrash Shmuel* render *One who grasps quickly and **therefore** forgets quickly*. They explain that if he had listened carefully to the teacher's words instead of trying to digest them too rapidly, the lesson would have made a lasting impression on him. He forgets quickly because his initial grasp of the material was rapid, but shallow. [This explains why youngsters with superior intellect often fall behind their less gifted classmates as the years go by. Since they grasped their lessons so easily when they were young, they never had to develop the knack of concentration and good study habits that are required when the material becomes more complex.]

According to this rendering, the expression יָצָא שְׂכָרוֹ בְּהֶפְסֵדוֹ means that the loss is a result of the gain. It is precisely because this person has a quick mind that he does not retain his knowledge.

(b) — קָשֶׁה לִשְׁמוֹעַ וְקָשֶׁה לְאַבֵּד, יָצָא הֶפְסֵדוֹ בִּשְׂכָרוֹ *one who grasps slowly and forgets slowly, his loss is offset by his gain.* This person's difficulty in grasping material is offset by his retentive ability. Ultimately, he will acquire permanent knowledge; if he is patient with himself and continues to review until he fully understands, he will succeed in Torah study (*Rashi, Rav*).

When limited funds are available for the support of Torah students, priority should be given to one

who has poor grasp but a strong memory over a quick-minded individual who does not retain well. The student with the good memory has a better chance to succeed in his own learning as well as in teaching (*R' Yonah, Rav*). Such a person should not be disheartened by the slow pace at which he acquires wisdom. God amply rewards every ounce of effort and every bit of progress. Furthermore, his incessant efforts will eventually be rewarded with a fundamental understanding of what he has learned (*R' Yonah*).

On the other hand, Rabbi Chaim of Volozhin wrote that his teacher, the *Vilna Gaon*, counseled him to give extra attention to the children of poor families because their parents' lack of funds prevented them from getting the best tutors and study arrangements; consequently, their true potential was probably untapped.

According to *Maharal*, cited above, such a student's strong retention may well be a direct result of his slow apprehension. By absorbing his lessons slowly and systematically, he achieved a clarity of understanding that enables him to remember it.

(c) — מָהִיר לִשְׁמוֹעַ וְקָשֶׁה לְאַבֵּד, זֶה חֵלֶק טוֹב *one who grasps quickly and forgets slowly, this is a good portion.* One who is blessed with the ability to grasp concepts quickly and to retain what he learns has truly been granted a good lot from the Source of All Knowledge. Even though he possesses great natural talent, however, he is cautioned to review constantly, rather than rely on his strong memory. To learn and then to allow forgetfulness to cause a natural erosion of the material is equivalent to sow-

---

⤷ **Antidote.** Memory has been compared to a kerchief. If it is folded over and over again, it eventually develops creases and can be folded neatly and easily along them. Similarly, even someone who was born with a weak memory can, by means of incessant review and self-discipline organize and strengthen his memory, so that everything he learns falls into place in his mind (*Peirush Man*).

[טז] **אַרְבַּע** מִדּוֹת בְּנוֹתְנֵי צְדָקָה: הָרוֹצֶה שֶׁיִּתֵּן וְלֹא

ing and not reaping (*R' Yonah*).

Some texts read חָכָם, *this person is wise*. The mishnah does not speak in terms of "righteous" and "wicked" in this case, since natural intellectual capacities are God-given gifts which are not in man's control (*Rambam, Rav* et al.). While moral strength is acquired with toil, intelligence is Divinely endowed (*R' Yonah*).

קָשֶׁה לִשְׁמוֹעַ וּמָהִיר לְאַבֵּד, זֶה חֵלֶק רָע — (d) *one who grasps slowly and forgets quickly, this is a bad portion.* Lack of intellectual capacity is a major handicap in life in general, and especially in Torah study. One who is not endowed with natural abilities has a difficult lot and must expend strenuous efforts to succeed. Nonetheless, the effort is worthwhile. God rewards a person's efforts commensurate with the difficulty he encounters. Furthermore, the very involvement with the words of the Torah has a sub-

liminal effect on one's character, immaterial of his level of intellectual understanding (*R' Yonah*).

King David tells us in *Psalms* (19:8) that the Torah is *the testimony of HASHEM . . . making the simple one wise*. This is a literal guarantee that one of deficient intellect can merit expanded abilities through exposure to Torah.

One should never become dismayed by the fact that his peers are smarter and quicker than he, or that they have better memories; he can still experience success on his own level. Effort, hard work, and prayer are always rewarded, and often result in expanded ability and intelligence (*Bigdei Sheish*).

Ultimately, success is not dependent on intrinsic abilities. Our Sages taught: "What should a person do in order to become wise? Let him study diligently and limit his business activities. But [isn't it true that] many have done so without success?

⇘ **Respect engenders knowledge.** *Lev Avos* suggests that one's attitude toward his teachers and toward knowledge in general affects the functioning of his innate abilities. A student with the proper respect for his teacher may grasp concepts quickly, yet since he lacks a burning love of wisdom, he is quick to forget. Conversely, one who lacks proper reverence for his teachers but who loves wisdom does not fully concentrate on the lesson and is slow to grasp, but he will retain whatever knowledge penetrates his mind. A healthy respect for one's mentors, coupled with a keen understanding of the value of knowledge, is the ideal combination. One who has neither will not grasp the lesson quickly, and he will not retain what he does learn.

The Chasam Sofer once deflected praise of his prodigious memory by saying that his memory was not exceptional, but that Torah knowledge was so important to him and was acquired with so much effort that it would have been a shame to forget it. His personal humility aside, he expressed a fundamental principle of successful study.

⇘ In his younger years, Rabbi Pesach Pruskin was considered a rather mediocre scholar. One day, while he was serving as *mashgiach* (spiritual mentor) in the Yeshivah of Slutsk, the turning point of his life took place. Several students were involved in a Talmudic discussion, and R' Pesach joined in, offering his opinion. His comment was not penetrating, and even revealed a lack of thought on his part. A heavy silence blanketed the group, with a mocking smirk flickering here and there. Brokenhearted, R' Pesach retreated to his corner, and, feeling very foolish, wept over his *Gemara* until he fell asleep. As he related many years later, he dreamt that he was told to renew his efforts with an in-depth study of the tractate *Bava Kamma*, and he was promised *siyata diShmaya* (help from Above).

R' Pesach began to study with new vigor and confidence, and in only a short time he changed recognizably, expounding on the Talmud with a depth and clarity that amazed everyone. As time went on, he amassed a great store of knowledge and comprehension and later became the *rosh yeshivah* in Shklov. Among his students there was a young man known as "Moshe Starobiner," who later became famous as Rabbi Moshe Feinstein.

16. **T**here are four types of donors to charity: (a) One who wishes

Rather, let him beseech mercy from the Source of All Wisdom, as it says (*Proverbs* 2:6): *For God grants wisdom; from His mouth comes knowledge and understanding.* Just as a king, at the royal feast, sends portions from his own plate to his most loyal subjects, so God grants wisdom directly from His mouth, so to speak, to those whom He loves" (see *Niddah* 70b).

Notzar Chesed offers a Mussarist interpretation of the mishnah, explaining it as four approaches to the process of *teshuvah*, penitence: If one is quick to hear the call of Heaven to repent [*Return, O you wayward children (Jeremiah* 3:14)] and yet forgets quickly, meaning that his spiritual arousal dissipates as fast as it came, his gain is offset by his loss. On the other hand, if one is not easily aroused to *teshuvah*, but acts upon those impulses when they do come, his loss is offset by his gain; eventually, he is fully prepared to find his way back to God.

The last two categories address the extremes. One who is quick to hear the call of return and slow to lose its message enjoys a good lot in life. Not so the unfortunate one who rarely hears God calling him to spiritually come home, and even when he does, never allows the message to penetrate fully. His lot in life is nothing short of tragic.

Mishnah 16

אַרְבַּע מִדּוֹת בְּנוֹתְנֵי צְדָקָה — *There are four types of donors to charity.* This mishnah is strategically placed between two others that discuss various types of students (5:15) and their relationship to the house of study (5:17). This teaches the value of supporting Torah scholars; people of means who engage in this kind of charity merit the same special reward that God prepares for those who study His word (*Midrash Shmuel*).

In his final blessings of the Jewish people, Moses said: *Rejoice, O Zebulun, in your excursions, and Issachar in your tents (Deuteronomy* 33:18). Issachar and Zebulun had a unique and inspiring partnership. Zebulun engaged successfully in maritime commerce and supported Issachar, who devoted his time to Torah pursuits, acting as teacher, judge, and cultivator of the spiritual treasure of the Jewish people (see *I Chronicles* 12:33-34). Although Issachar was older, Zebulun is mentioned first because it was he who made Issachar's Torah study possible (*Tanchuma* and *Rashi* ad loc.; see *Rashi* to *Genesis* 49:13).

The tradition of this partnership has been perpetuated by many over the years. Wealthy people have even drawn up formal contracts stipulating that the merit of the Torah scholar's study would be shared by both. By doing so, a businessman may thus find joy and meaning in his commercial activities, since he takes an equal portion of the reward for his partner's Torah studies. *Sifre* expounds that in the merit of Zebulun's support of Torah study, he will rejoice when he leaves this world and embarks on man's final excursion — to the World to Come. The *Vilna Gaon* maintained that the ultimate human joy comes from attaining a higher level of understanding. Thus, when the supporters of Torah depart this

---

⁌§ **The honest "donor."** Rabbi Meir Shapiro, founder and builder of the famed Yeshivas Chachmei Lublin, traveled the world in search of funds. Based on his experience, he gave a more benevolent interpretation of why our mishnah refers to all four types as *donors*.

Often one approaches a person who is very quick to make a pledge to charity. Furthermore, he promises, "Rebbe, I will give, and I will even get my friends involved." Unfortunately, however, this person may not keep his word, and the fundraiser must start again in his search for support. If the person had at least been forthright and said plainly that he did not intend to give and that he would not solicit others, one would know where he stood and what he had to do. With God's help he would find the funding elsewhere.

Thus, one who says that he will not give nor will he involve others in support of the cause is also among the "donors," because his straightforward refusal, in its own way, is helpful.

world, they will rejoice, for they will not only be rewarded for their charity, but they will gain the privilege of knowing and understanding all the Torah learning that they made possible (*Rabbi Aharon Kotler*).

Although the mishnah speaks of *donors*, this would seem to be a misnomer, for the second and fourth types mentioned here do not want to donate at all. *Rav* explains the mishnah as referring to four *attitudes* towards giving, rather than to the donors themselves. *R' Moshe Alshakar* explains alternatively that these are four types of people who are *obligated* to donate to charity, whether they do or not.

R' Moshe Almosnino notes that the community, through the offices of the rabbinical courts, is entitled to coerce individuals into contributing to charity (*Bava Basra* 8b); thus, even those who do not want to give will eventually be among the donors. Nonetheless, one who must be forced to contribute is deemed wicked (see below).

הָרוֹצֶה שֶׁיִּתֵּן וְלֹא יִתְּנוּ אֲחֵרִים, עֵינוּ רָעָה בְּשֶׁל אֲחֵרִים — (a) *One who wishes to give himself but wants others not to give, he begrudges* [lit., *his eye is evil with regard to*] *others.* One who seeks to monopolize the giving of charity often does so in order to

prevent others from sharing the blessings of increased wealth and good reputation that are the result of charitable acts (*Rashi, R' Yonah, Rav*). Sometimes such a person is motivated by the need to inflate his own image. He wants others to appear stingy so that he can portray himself as the "magnanimous benefactor." Thus, the "others" referred to here are other potential contributors (*Meiri*).

According to *Tiferes Yisrael*, it is the needy whom he begrudges any "extra" funds.

HaChassid Yaavetz explains that this person is actually stingy at heart. Even though he considers the amount he gave sufficient for the needs of the poor, it bothers him that they should receive more from others. This miserliness is expressed by the term עַיִן רָעָה.

B'nayos B'Ramah sees here a reference to wealthy people who seek to benefit only those who have no other source of aid. Regarding an impoverished person who has wealthy relatives or friends, their attitude is "Let his family worry about him," even if those relatives or friends actually do nothing to help. Such a person actually begrudges the others their money; he wants them to spend it on their less fortunate relative so that it will be

---

Everyone's privilege. Rabbi Yechezkel Landau, the famed rabbi of Prague and author of *Noda B'Yehudah*, was once asked to contribute to a fund to ransom Jewish captives, which was a common problem in Eastern Europe. The delegation explained that 300 *rendlich* were needed to free a Jew from captivity. The *Noda B'Yehudah* went into a side room and returned with 290 *rendlich*. "This is my contribution. Please solicit the rest of the money from others," he said.

The rabbi sensed that the collectors, although thrilled with the donation, wondered why he had chosen not to complete the *mitzvah*, when it was in his power to give another ten *rendlich*. He explained, "You have forgotten the mishnah: *One who wishes to give himself but wants others not to give begrudges others.* I want others, as well, to share in the *mitzvah*."

According to the Chofetz Chaim, it is this principle that underlies the interesting contrast between the support systems of secular and Torah institutions. A secular institution, such as a university, is often funded by one wealthy benefactor who is ready to endow fully the building of its structures. Yeshivos, on the other hand, must solicit hundreds, if not thousands, of small contributions in order to fund even a modest building. The reason is that all Jews must have a share in the support of Torah. God, in accordance with the dictate of the mishnah, does not allow one person a monopoly on philanthropy. He added that the merit of supporting Torah study is so great that it can only be shared by the masses of Jews; no individual is worthy of the entire merit.

to give himself but wants others not to give, he begrudges others; (b) that others should give but that he should not give, he begrudges himself; (c) that he should give and that others should give

---

diminished. Were he of better character, he himself would grab the opportunity to do the *mitzvah*. Thus, the mishnah describes one who wants to give only where others do not give as a person who begrudges others their wealth.

Chasam Sofer offers a deep psychological insight into the emotional needs of the poor. Merely providing them with their physical necessities is insufficient; the poor must be provided with the feeling that they are "normal," productive, functioning members of society. One must therefore give them enough so that they in turn can give charity to others. The mishnah can be rendered: יִתֵּן, *one who gives*, וְלֹא יִתְּנוּ אֲחֵרִים, *but does not give enough to allow the poor to give to others*, begrudges them that vital feeling of vibrancy and self-esteem.

יִתְּנוּ אֲחֵרִים וְהוּא לֹא יִתֵּן, עֵינוֹ רָעָה בְּשֶׁלּוֹ — (b) *that others should give but that he [himself] should not give, he begrudges himself.* This person constrains himself unnecessarily; unable to part with his

money, he begrudges himself the freedom of spending it as he sees fit (*R' Yonah*).

Tightfistedness is often the result of a person's fears for his financial security. One who believes in charity, but is afraid to contribute personally because he does not know what the future holds, suffers from a narrow perspective on life, a condition labeled here as עַיִן רָעָה (*Meiri*).

Rashi renders the expression עֵינוֹ רָעָה as *he is cheap*, meaning that he cannot motivate himself to help others at his own expense. Alternatively, according to *Rashi*, this person is skeptical of the Divine guarantee that charity increases, rather than decreases, one's wealth (see 3:17). Afraid of depleting his assets, he is not prepared to involve himself in philanthropic activities.

Midrash Shmuel notes that this type, unlike the first one, is not deemed wicked since he at least wants others to help. According to *Sfas Emes*, however, יִתְּנוּ אֲחֵרִים does not merely indicate a passive willingness to allow others to give; instead

---

◆§ **The best investment.** Since the giving of charity increases one's wealth, a person who refrains from giving only hurts himself. Thus, עֵינוֹ רָעָה בְּשֶׁלּוֹ, *his evil eye affects only himself*. The Sages taught: מֶלַח מָמוֹן חֶסֶר, *One who seeks to preserve* ("salt away") *his money, let him be charitable and do acts of kindness* (*Kesubos* 66b). Otherwise, like meat left unsalted, his wealth may eventually *rot* and disappear.

According to his daughter, Nakdimon ben Gurion, a fantastically wealthy Jerusalemite who lived during the waning days of the Second Temple, lost his entire fortune because of insufficient concern and involvement with the plight of the poor.

A more contemporary episode involved Kalman Wissotzky, who owned the tea concession for the Russian Czar's entire military operation. Since the Czar's armies numbered in the millions and drinking tea was a daily Russian custom, this concession made Wissotzky very rich. One day he was approached by members of a group interested in the development of the tea business in *Eretz Yisrael*, but Wissotzky laughed at this "preposterous" idea. The Turks governed Palestine and they were notoriously difficult to deal with; besides, he pointed out, Palestine could not produce its own tea, and tea leaves from India were too costly to import.

He was assured that all these problems could be surmounted; furthermore, he was reminded, the venture would enable him to provide employment for many Jews. Although not convinced, he sent enough money to Israel to start a small tea business.

In 1917, the Czar and his army were swept from power. The Communists seized all the businesses the Czar had franchised, including Mr. Wissotzky's tea business. After the revolution, the only asset remaining to the family was the small company he had set up in Palestine, and they fled there and built up the business. To this day, the Israeli company sells tea under the Wissotzky label. The family feels it merited this protection only because of the Jewish families who benefited from their employment in the company.

חָסִיד; לֹא יִתֵּן וְלֹא יִתְּנוּ אֲחֵרִים, רָשָׁע.

[יז] אַרְבַּע מִדּוֹת בְּהוֹלְכֵי בֵית הַמִּדְרָשׁ: הוֹלֵךְ וְאֵינוֹ עוֹשֶׂה, שְׂכַר הֲלִיכָה בְּיָדוֹ; עוֹשֶׂה וְאֵינוֹ

---

it refers to one who actively seeks to involve others in the *mitzvah.* This activism entitles him to a place in the category of donors. Furthermore, it is for this reason that one who does not personally contribute is nonetheless not considered wicked, for getting others to do their share is also a charitable act.

Mikveh Yisrael takes a novel approach, explaining that the person in this category is actually not a favorable type. He is the one who remains on the sidelines during an appeal, waiting to see what others will donate. He is willing to give if need be, but he is in no rush to initiate. He is given a place among the charitable, since he will respond when necessary; nonetheless, he is considered to *begrudge himself* since he is not quick to give.

יִתֵּן וְיִתְּנוּ אֲחֵרִים, חָסִיד — (c) *that he should give and that others should give is saintly.* While a righteous person is concerned with his own spiritual endeavors, one who is truly pious (חָסִיד) seeks the spiritual welfare of all people. Such a person wants others to benefit from the *mitzvah* of giving charity and offers them a share in it (*R' Moshe Almosnino*). Similarly, *Alshich* defines the saintly person as one

---

⋙ **Charity does not end at home.** The Sages view one who enlists the aid of others in acts of charity as greater than one who participates personally (*Bava Basra* 9a). [In this light, one may understand the first stich of the mishnah, which criticizes one who is satisfied when he himself gives but others do not. We may find ourselves easily in this category, in the sense that we find it easier to make charitable donations ourselves than to enlist the aid of others. Asking others to give is uncomfortable for a variety of reasons; we may not want to put pressure on our friends, or perhaps we feel that by soliciting from them, we will become morally indebted to them when they solicit for their own cause. Whatever the reason, many people find it compelling. Our mishnah teaches that one must even make himself uncomfortable on behalf of a brother in need. If he is unwilling to ask favors, he begrudges the poor what they might receive from others. One who gives and gets others involved, however, is righteous.]

⋙ **Honor by sharing.** The Talmud teaches: רְבִּי הָיָה מְכַבֵּד אֶת הָעֲשִׁירִים, *Rabbi would honor the wealthy (Eruvin* 86a). In a homiletic rendering, Rabbi Shmuel Alter commented that R' Yehudah *HaNasi,* who was fantastically wealthy, was able to support any given philanthropic endeavor singlehandedly. Nonetheless, he shared the merit with other wealthy men, giving them a chance to participate in the *mitzvah*, according to the mishnah's dictate. In this sense, Rabbi honored the wealthy, by sharing with them the privilege of contributing to worthy causes.

⋙ **Be a model.** *Avos Al Banim* offers a variation on this theme of giving through an intermediary. Even though giving charity secretly is the most elevated form of philanthropy, it suffers one drawback: One who provides for others is not a role model, since others do not know what he does. It is admirable, therefore, for one to forgo the opportunity to perform the *mitzvah* in its highest form, and give visibly so that others will also give.

According to *Atzei Ya'ar*, the mishnah teaches us to seize the opportunity to help others without fear that we may someday need the money ourselves. A truly saintly person gives freely (הוּא יִתֵּן) and never worries that he may deplete his resources one day, so that others may have to give to him (וְיִתְּנוּ אֲחֵרִים). God will certainly repay him and see to it that he is provided for.

[The mishnah might even be rendered as reflective of the greatest form of charity described by the *Rambam* (*Hilchos Matnos Aniyim* 10:7) — giving an indigent Jew a loan, a job, or the opportunity to enter into a partnership, any of which preserves the recipient's sense of self-sufficiency. Thus, the most pious person gives a poor one the means to be self-supporting so that others — his employer or customers — will give him, not as a handout but in terms of an ordinary business relationship.]

is saintly; (d) that he should not give and that others should not give is wicked.

17. There are four types among those who go to the house of study: (a) One who goes but does not study has the reward for going; (b) one who studies [at home] but does not

---

who gives in order that others follow his example.

Chelek Yaakov offers a novel interpretation based on the eight levels of charity enumerated by the *Rambam* (*Hilchos Matnos Aniyim* 10:7-14). The lowest form of *tzedakah* is to hand charity directly to a needy person, because this will embarrass the recipient. The highest form is to offer a job or a loan to start a business, so that the recipient can not only retain his self-respect, but pull himself out of poverty. The penultimate form of charity is where an intermediary is used, so that neither the giver nor the recipient is aware of the other's identity. Hence, a saintly person is one who gives to *others* — to intermediaries — who will then give to the poor person. He thereby protects the indigent from the indignity of receiving.

לֹא יִתֵּן וְלֹא יִתְּנוּ אֲחֵרִים, רָשָׁע — (d) *that he should not give and that others should not give is wicked.* One who has no desire to help those in need but also begrudges them the help of others is truly cruel and wicked (*Tiferes Yisrael*). His refusal to give is itself a sign of wickedness. This is compounded by the fact that he sees others doing nothing, and yet he remains unmoved to help (*B'nayos B'Ramah*). *Mikveh Yisrael* offers: One who refuses to contribute to charity is guilty of a double wickedness, a) for not giving himself; b) for not inspiring others to give.

Mishnah 17

אַרְבַּע מִדּוֹת בְּהוֹלְכֵי בֵית הַמִּדְרָשׁ — *There are four types among those who go to the house of study.* This mishnah discusses the four attitudes people display in regard to attending a *beis hamidrash*, a house of study. It does not refer to four types of people who attend, since two of the four never go (*Rambam, Magen Avos*). According to *Lechem Shamayim*, it refers to people who at one point did frequent a *beis hamidrash*; some of them continue to do so, while others have stopped. The mishnah evaluates the conduct of each type.

הוֹלֵךְ וְאֵינוֹ עוֹשֶׂה, שְׂכַר הֲלִיכָה בְּיָדוֹ — (a) *One who goes but does not study has the reward for going.* This follows *Rashi* and *Rav*, who render עוֹשֶׂה as *study*. These people go to the study hall and listen, but they do not sit down to study themselves. Nonetheless, God rewards them for going.

◆§ **Importance of atmosphere.** Why are people rewarded for going to the study hall if they do not study?

Rabbi Mendel of Kotzk explained: One who stays home, surrounded by his creature comforts and distracted by domestic concerns, stands little chance of achieving any spiritual improvement. If he goes to the study hall, he may at least be able to focus on spiritual activity. The very act of pulling himself away from home is worthy of reward.

A great *rosh yeshivah* advised all of his students to begin married life enrolled in a *kollel* (Talmudic study program for married scholars). Certain laymen questioned his counsel. "Not everybody has the potential to be a scholar," they countered. "Furthermore, aren't we overtaxing the resources of the Jewish community by having *everyone* join the *kollel* and receiving stipends?"

The *rosh yeshivah* responded: "Of course, not everyone will become a great scholar. But it should be clear that besides the inestimable value of the Torah the young man will learn, his *kollel* stay is justified for other reasons. The standard of Judaism and the philosophical foundation of the home are established in the first years of marriage. One who spends those years in a *beis midrash* is bound to be affected positively. The *kollel* is an investment in the future of the entire community."

הוֹלֵךְ, שְׂכַר מַעֲשֶׂה בְּיָדוֹ; הוֹלֵךְ וְעוֹשֶׂה, חָסִיד; לֹא הוֹלֵךְ
וְלֹא עוֹשֶׂה, רָשָׁע.

According to *Midrash Shmuel*, this refers to one who indeed goes to study on his own, but does not encourage others to do so, i.e., he is not עוֹשֶׂה, does not *make* others follow his example. He receives the reward for his own actions, but forfeits the merit he could have earned for inspiring others to learn.

Meiri interprets the *one who goes* as one who leaves his home to study from a better teacher or in a better environment, following the instruction of R' Nehorai: "Exile yourself to a place of Torah" (4:18). Even if he does not achieve exceptional success in his studies, he still receive great reward for his effort and self-sacrifice in abandoning the comforts of home in search of God.

R' Yonah renders עוֹשֶׂה as *carried out in practice*: one who studies but does not practice what he learns, meaning that he performs the commandments if the opportunity presents itself, but he will not go out of his way to look for ways to fulfill them.

Tiferes Yisrael renders similarly. One who attends the ethical and moral lectures given in the study hall in the hope of improving the spiritual quality of his life is rewarded for attending. Even if his Evil Inclination subverts his efforts to act upon what he hears, it may be hoped that the Torah he heard will eventually be internalized and translated into action.

עוֹשֶׂה וְאֵינוֹ הוֹלֵךְ, שְׂכַר מַעֲשֶׂה בְּיָדוֹ — *(b) one who studies [at home] but does not attend [the house of study] has the reward for accomplishment.* The translation follows *Rashi* and *Rav.* One who learns at home is rewarded for the study itself; however, he misses out on the special reward for attending the study hall. *Maharal* explains why there is a specific reward for the act of going to a house of study [or a synagogue]. Study, unlike all other *mitzvos*, is purely intellectual. By going physically to a place of study, one involves not only his mind but his body in the pursuit of the Torah.

Along the same guardedly optimistic lines, one who encourages others to study or supports their efforts financially, although he does nothing to foster his own spiritual growth, will still be rewarded for the role he played in others' development (*Midrash Shmuel, HaChassid Yaavetz*).

According to *Meiri*, the Mishnah speaks of one who learns in his hometown rather than seeking a more profound learning experience in another locale. In spite of the opportunity he has squandered, he is still rewarded for his limited efforts.

Following their interpretation of עוֹשֶׂה as *carried out in practice*, *R' Yonah* and *Tiferes Yisrael* explain this stich to refer to someone who does fulfill the commandments, yet is uninterested in deepening his religious commitment any further. He does not consult Torah scholars or seek to expand his

⇥§ **Going for what?** Unlike the first two clauses, this one does not speak of reward; it says only that such a person is pious. The martyred Slonimer *Rebbe*, R' Shlomo, explained that a truly pious person has no interest in reward for his actions. He expects nothing and is elevated simply by the opportunity to serve God. The greatest reward for a pious person is the privilege of being pious, so no mention of reward is necessary.

The Chofetz Chaim notes the attitude one takes to the study hall is of serious consequence. Sometimes one's journey and presence there can be a grave sin. How often do we go to hear the rabbi speak, only to react cynically and comment on how ignorant or naive he is? Or we sometimes accuse him of hypocrisy or of doing what he does only for the money? We are especially quick to fault him when he points out our failings or asks that we subscribe to higher moral and ethical standards. If we carefully scrutinize our motives, we may realize that our disenchantment is the result of something he said that he preferred not to hear. Thus, the visit to a *beis midrash* can often be a spiritual calamity. Our mishnah teaches us the perspective with which we should enter it — that one should go to study.

attend [the house of study] has the reward for accomplishment; (c) one who goes and studies is pious; (c) one who does not go and does not study is wicked.

---

knowledge by attending the house of study. Since he is willing to carry out God's wishes only in accordance with his limited understanding of them, his reward is also limited.

הוֹלֵךְ וְעוֹשֶׂה, חָסִיד — *(c) one who goes and studies is pious.* One who does not rely on his own understanding of God's will but who goes to the study hall seeking to improve the quality of his service is truly pious (*R' Yonah*).

Meiri comments that one who makes an extra effort to seek out the finest environment and teachers, and who exerts his full energies in his studies, is pious. *HaChassid Yaavetz* explains that he not only promotes others' learning, whether through moral or financial support, but he learns and lives a Torah life-style himself.

לֹא הוֹלֵךְ וְלֹא עוֹשֶׂה, רָשָׁע — *(d) one who does not go and does not study is wicked.* He neither seeks opportunities to do *mitzvos* (הוֹלֵךְ, *goes after*), nor is he willing to fulfill God's word when circumstances present him with the chance. Such a person sustains deep spiritual scars (*R' Yonah*).

The wicked person does not seek the strengthening quality of communal study — and he does not even try to advance himself spiritually in the solitude of his own home (*Tiferes Yisrael*).

According to *Mikveh Yisrael*, עוֹשֶׂה means *to support* and refers to the upkeep of the house of study. The entire mishnah can be explained thus: One who goes to the study hall and learns but gives nothing towards its upkeep is rewarded only for his learning. On the other hand, if he helps finance the operating costs of the *beis midrash*, yet is unable to come and learn himself, he is at least rewarded for his support. One who both studies and contributes to the maintenance of centers of learning is truly righteous; and one who ignores both his own spiritual needs and those of the community is thoroughly wicked.

Two other commentaries also give a global interpretation of the mishnah. According to *Meshivas Nefesh*, all of the people listed here actually go to the study hall but maintain different levels of focus. One person wants to go to study, but upon arriving there is distracted. Nonetheless, his good intention in going is rewarded. A second type goes to the study hall to socialize or simply to idle the time away; however, once there, he puts in a few moments of study. Although he has come for the wrong reason, he still deserves credit for the studying he did as an afterthought. The third type goes for the right reason and does the right thing; he is pious. The wicked go for the wrong reasons and they augment their misdeed by not studying at all once they are there.

Mussar Avos explains that our mishnah outlines the relationship of talent to effort. If one moves upward (הוֹלֵךְ) and achieves excellence (וְעוֹשֶׂה) due to his great talent rather than his hard work, he is still rewarded for his achievements. One who expends great energy (עוֹשֶׂה) despite his limitations yet does not taste success (הוֹלֵךְ) is nonetheless rewarded for his effort. One who overcomes all obstacles in his path to greatness and enjoys success in his spiritual pursuits (הוֹלֵךְ וְעוֹשֶׂה) is truly righteous; one who never succeeded because he never made the effort is wicked; he is a victim of self-neglect.

‎◆§ **To go and to do.** The father of a young student who attended his hometown yeshivah in Lakewood insisted on paying a sizable portion of the tuition. Since the boy lived at home, he questioned why his father should do so. The father replied, "Doesn't electricity cost money? Doesn't water in the building cost money? The upkeep of the library, stipends for the *kollel* people with whom you study, the salaries of the *roshei hayeshivah* and administrators — are any of these items free? Besides that, we must also participate in the cost of running the yeshivah." He was a living example of the understanding that one must go to the house of study and also offer it concrete support.

[יח] **אַרְבַּע** מִדּוֹת בְּיוֹשְׁבִים לִפְנֵי חֲכָמִים: סְפוֹג, וּמַשְׁפֵּךְ, מְשַׁמֶּרֶת, וְנָפָה. סְפוֹג, שֶׁהוּא סוֹפֵג אֶת הַכֹּל; וּמַשְׁפֵּךְ, שֶׁמַּכְנִיס בְּזוֹ וּמוֹצִיא בְּזוֹ; מְשַׁמֶּרֶת, שֶׁמּוֹצִיאָה אֶת הַיַּיִן וְקוֹלֶטֶת אֶת הַשְּׁמָרִים; וְנָפָה, שֶׁמּוֹצִיאָה אֶת הַקֶּמַח וְקוֹלֶטֶת אֶת הַסֹּלֶת.

Mishnah 18

אַרְבַּע מִדּוֹת בְּיוֹשְׁבִים לִפְנֵי חֲכָמִים — *There are four types among those who sit before the sages.* An earlier mishnah which spoke of four types of students (5:15) addressed variations in comprehension and retention. This mishnah continues with two other aspects of intellectual ability: the power of logic and the ability to discern one item or idea from another (*Rav, Tiferes Yisrael*).

Rather than referring to them as students, the mishnah calls these four types "those who sit before the sages," to teach that the key to success is to remain constantly in the presence of one's teachers (*Midrash Shmuel*). A student learns not only from his teacher's words but also from his actions. The Talmud teaches: גְּדוֹלָה שִׁמּוּשָׁה שֶׁל תוֹרָה יוֹתֵר מִלִּמּוּדָהּ, *[One can learn] more [from a] Torah [scholar] by tending to his needs than from his formal instruction* (see *Berachos* 7b and *Tanna d'Vei Eliyahu Rabbah* 5).

Mili d'Avos explains that learning from a teacher in person improves one's understanding of his studies. An example of this idea was expressed by Rabbi, the redactor of the Mishnah, who attributed his incisive understanding of Torah to having viewed his teacher, R' Meir, from the back; and he bemoaned not having merited to view him from the front: "Had I viewed him from the front, I would have been even sharper." (See *Eruvin* 13b, *Rashi* and *Maharsha* ad loc., who explains that a teacher's facial expressions convey meanings that do not come across in the words alone. See also *Yerushalmi Beitzah* 5:2.)

סְפוֹג, וּמַשְׁפֵּךְ, מְשַׁמֶּרֶת, וְנָפָה — *a sponge, a funnel, a strainer, and a sieve.* These items are symbolic of the four types of people who sit before the sages. The "sponge" retains everything indiscriminately; the "funnel" retains nothing; the "strainer" retains the wrong things; and the "sieve" has the power of discernment to retain only the good (*Avos d'Rabbi Nosson*).

סְפוֹג, שֶׁהוּא סוֹפֵג אֶת הַכֹּל — *(a) a sponge, which absorbs everything.* Though this person remembers everything, he lacks the power to exercise selectivity, to distinguish between the true and the false, the meaningful and the trivial. He is like a sponge that absorbs all the water, whether it is clear or dirty (*Rashi, R' Yonah, Rav*, et al.). *Midrash Shmuel* explains another negative quality of one who quickly absorbs a great deal of knowledge: Just as one must squeeze a sponge in order to release its contents, a scholar who has learned much may have to be pressured into teaching others and releasing his vast knowledge.

Tiferes Yisrael comments: The clear and dirtied waters become mixed inside the sponge, so that when they are released, they are all contaminated. So it is with the student who does not exercise discrimination in his learning and who does not classify his knowledge; his ideas will be randomly blended, and he will certainly be unable to express himself clearly to others (see *Ruach Chaim*).

וּמַשְׁפֵּךְ, שֶׁמַּכְנִיס בְּזוֹ וּמוֹצִיא בְּזוֹ — *(b) a funnel, which lets in from one and lets out from the other.* Like a funnel quickly channeling all its contents out the

18. There are four types among those who sit before the sages: a sponge, a funnel, a strainer, and a sieve — (a) a sponge, which absorbs everything; (b) a funnel, which lets in from one and lets out from the other; (c) a strainer, which lets the wine flow through and retains the sediment; (d) and a sieve, which allows the flour dust to pass through and retains the fine flour.

---

other end, this student almost immediately forgets everything he learns.

מְשַׁמֶּרֶת, שֶׁמּוֹצִיאָה אֶת הַיַּיִן וְקוֹלֶטֶת אֶת הַשְּׁמָרִים — *(c) a strainer, which lets the wine flow through and retains the sediment.* The third type of student retains only the minor, trivial points [or falsehoods (*Rambam*)] of his learning and allows the important truths — the wine — to slip out of his memory (*R' Yonah, Rav*).

Ruach Chaim and *Tiferes Yisrael* object. They interpret the strainer as symbolic of a student who is able to isolate the flaws in an idea and to perceive the truth with clarity. He allows only refined and truthful ideas to pass through the strainer of his mind to others by repeating them, and he retains, i.e., he does not repeat, anything that is not fully logical or sound.

(d) — וְנָפָה, שֶׁמּוֹצִיאָה אֶת הַקֶּמַח וְקוֹלֶטֶת אֶת הַסֹּלֶת *and a sieve, which allows the flour dust to pass through and retains the fine flour.* A sieve symbolizes the best student, who retains the essential and truthful points of a matter and rejects any superfluous or false "chaff" (*Rashi, R' Yonah, Rambam, Rav*). *Ruach Chaim* and *Tiferes Yisrael,* however,

view the sieve as the worst type of student, the one who retains the coarsest elements, the unproven initial hypotheses suggested by his teachers, and allows the truthful ideas to slip by him.

Minchas Shabbos gives a global view of the mishnah as referring to four attitudes that one may have toward his familial heritage. Some people, like sponges, absorb and follow every practice they saw in their parents' home — both the good and the bad, the sophisticated conduct and the customs that may have had no basis. Others, who consider themselves wiser than their parents, reject everything, throwing out that which is spiritually valuable in the process. They are analogous to the funnel, which allows everything to pass through and retains nothing. The third type is symbolized by the strainer. These people let the fine wine of Torah and *mitzvos* pass through and retain only a vestige of Jewish identity in the form of symbolic, non-halachic observances and customs. The best type of all is the sieve; those individuals who are able to perceive clearly the authentic spiritual legacy of their ancestors and to discard anything which is without basis or, even worse, contrary to halachah.

⋘ Nature of sediment. There is disagreement among the commentaries about whether or not it is better to retain flawed or superficial knowledge. *Rashi* considers it better to retain at least the minor points; *Rambam,* however, seems to feel that it is better to lose knowledge than to retain it in an imperfect form. The difference lies in their understanding of what the mishnah means by "sediment." *Rashi* compares the sediment to the secondary, minor aspects of an issue, which do have some redeeming value. *Rambam,* however, regards the sediment as falsehoods, in which case it is better to remain ignorant.

Magen Avos differentiates between the types of material involved. In halachic matters, he suggests, flawed knowledge might be better than nothing; in matters of belief, however, it is better to remain ignorant than to subscribe to a flawed system of beliefs and values.

כָּל אַהֲבָה שֶׁהִיא תְלוּיָה בְדָבָר, בָּטֵל דָּבָר, בְּטֵלָה אַהֲבָה; וְשֶׁאֵינָה תְלוּיָה בְדָבָר, אֵינָה בְּטֵלָה לְעוֹלָם. אֵיזוֹ הִיא אַהֲבָה שֶׁהִיא תְלוּיָה בְדָבָר? זוֹ אַהֲבַת אַמְנוֹן וְתָמָר. וְשֶׁאֵינָה תְלוּיָה בְדָבָר? זוֹ אַהֲבַת דָּוִד וִיהוֹנָתָן.

Mishnah 19

כָּל אַהֲבָה שֶׁהִיא תְלוּיָה בְדָבָר, בָּטֵל דָּבָר, בְּטֵלָה אַהֲבָה — *Any love that depends on a specific cause, when that cause is gone, the love is gone.* This mishnah explores new territory by giving instruction for the heart. It establishes the profound principle that love which is based on anything besides emotional closeness and true friendship will not endure (*Rashi*). Superficial motivations create only temporary results. The desire for food, for example, disappears as soon as one is satiated. Likewise, the emotion of love, if based only on a temporary need, will dissolve. Only that which is based on eternal and deep-rooted foundations can endure (*Rav* and *Rambam*).

A person may "love" another because of the favors he receives from him, but his love is for the favors, not the person. Such love is self-love, which has no future (*Tiferes Yisrael*). For example, if one loves a woman only for her beauty, and she falls sick and loses her beauty, he will lose his love for her; likewise, if he loves a friend for his wealth and the generosity comes to a halt, so too will his love for him end. The same is true for any attachment which is based on physical and material needs alone; when the motivation is gone, the love ceases to exist (*Sefer HaMussar*).

Rambam and *Rav* have a text which translates the word בָּטֵל as *temporary*. It reads: כָּל אַהֲבָה שֶׁהִיא תְלוּיָה בְדָבָר, בָּטֵל, בְּטֵלָה אַהֲבָה, *Any love that depends on a temporary factor, the love will cease to exist.*

Chelek LeOlam Haba notes the inclusive form כָּל אַהֲבָה, *any love*. No matter what type of relationship it is, no matter how intense or passionate, it will not endure if it is based on temporal considerations. According to *R' Yonah*, this refers to those who enter relationships in order to be admired and loved, rather than to love others.

וְשֶׁאֵינָה תְלוּיָה בְדָבָר, אֵינָה בְּטֵלָה לְעוֹלָם — *but if it does not depend on a specific cause, it will never cease.* A relationship that does not depend on material benefits, such as wealth or beauty, but instead is an unselfish attachment based on mutual respect and concern, will endure (*Rambam*, *Rav*). For example, the love of a disciple for his master, or the love of scholars who assemble to study, never vanishes. Since they are motivated by their search for truth and wisdom, which is a lasting value, their love for each other will also last forever (*Sefer HaMussar*).

According to *Tiferes Yisrael*, the expression שֶׁאֵינָה תְלוּיָה בְדָבָר indicates a natural, intrinsic love that cannot necessarily be articulated. If one were asked why he loves his children, for example, or why he loves righteous and wise people, he could not identify the reason. There is no identifiable cause for this love, it is unconditional and therefore it will endure. *Tanna d'Vei Eliyahu Rabbah* (28) gives as an example the love of Abraham, Isaac, and Jacob for God, and of God's love for them, their children, and grandchildren throughout all generations.

According to the *Kozhnitzer Maggid*, the mishnah

◅§ **Tenses of love.** The Torah describes Isaac's love for Esau in the past tense. Isaac **loved** *Esau, for game was in his mouth* (*Genesis* 25:28). Since it was based on material considerations — that Esau caught game to prepare delicacies for his father — the love was temporary, and therefore was described in the past tense since it could easily dissipate. On the other hand, Rebecca's love for Jacob is described in the present tense: *And Rebecca* **loves** *Jacob"* (ibid.). Her love for Jacob was based on his intrinsic good character and his involvement in the spiritual — values which endured for her continually and permanently (*Shelah*).

19. Any love that depends on a specific cause, when that cause is gone, the love is gone; but if it does not depend on a specific cause, it will never cease. What sort of love depended on a specific cause? — The love of Amnon for Tamar. And what did not depend upon a specific cause? — The love of David and Jonathan.

homiletically defines a proper relationship with God. When man loves God as a result of everything good that He has done for him, the bond is tenuous and may even, God forbid, collapse. However, if one's love of God is for its own sake, even if he undergoes the travails of Job, he will emerge with pristine faith and an enduring love of his Maker.

Based on a homiletical reading of the mishnah, *Atzei Yaar* offers a deep insight into the strength of friendship. True friends are able to offer and accept constructive criticism from each other; a friendship that cannot bear the strain of honest and loving criticism is not solid. Thus, any love that increases or diminishes depending on the power of דָּבָר, *words,* is false. This includes not only spoken words that are wrongly received, but those left unspoken out of fear of their consequences; the mishnah may be read בְּטֵלָה דָּבָר, *if a word of constructive rebuke is* **not** *offered,* בְּטֵלָה אַהֲבָה, *the love is meaningless.* Love that knows how to administer and receive criticism lovingly, however, will endure.

אֵיזוֹ הִיא אַהֲבָה שֶׁהִיא תְלוּיָה בְדָבָר? זוֹ אַהֲבַת אַמְנוֹן וְתָמָר — *What sort of love depended on a specific cause? — The love of Amnon for Tamar.* Amnon and Tamar were half brother and half sister, children of King David. Amnon lusted for her, and one day, under the guise of illness, he requested that she tend to his needs. When they were left alone, he forcefully satisfied his lust. Afterwards, his love turned to a hate that was far more intense than his original love (see *II Samuel* 13). His love did not endure because it was motivated only by lust for her beauty. Once he had satisfied his desire, the love was gone (*Rashi, Rav*); his passion left him and was replaced by hate (*Meiri*).

Amnon's love was not for Tamar, but for himself. She was nothing more than a means for him to satisfy his lust (*Tiferes Yisrael*).

וְשֶׁאֵינָהּ תְּלוּיָה בְדָבָר? זוֹ אַהֲבַת דָּוִד וִיהוֹנָתָן — *And what did not depend upon a specific cause? — The love of David and Jonathan.* No two people were in a position more conducive to rivalry than David and Jonathan. Jonathan was the crown prince, the natural successor to his father Saul as king of Israel. He was also a man of great stature, righteous and beloved by the people; he would have been a source of pride to the nation. David was the rival, the interloper who had been anointed by Samuel to take away the throne that should have been Jonathan's.

⊷ **Mutual love.** When man loves God unconditionally, God responds by loving man unconditionally (*Nesivos Shalom*). *Chovos HaLevavos* (*Shaar Ahavas Hashem* 1) tells the metaphorical tale of a man who suffered abject poverty; he had nothing to eat or wear, nor even a candle. In the middle of a dark night he offered the following heartrending profession of faith: "Dear God, You have starved me and left me naked, and placed me in the pitch darkness of night. However, You have taught me Your strength and greatness. If You were to burn me in fire, I would only continue to love You and rejoice in You."

Job, too, said: "Were He to kill me, I would still yearn for Him" (*Job* 13:15). [The Talmud (*Sotah* 27b and 31a) states that Job's love for God was total and unconditional. Even though God had sent the worst imaginable afflictions upon him, he still adored Him undyingly and continued to yearn for His closeness.]

The Jewish nation as a whole enjoys this type of relationship with God. *Rashi* (*Songs of Songs* 1:1) teaches that *Song of Songs* is the holiest of all books because it is the song of praise and adoration that Israel, metaphorically presented as a young woman, offers to God even in her most troubled times of exile and spiritual widowhood. No affliction diminishes Israel's unceasing yearning for the love for her Beloved.

⊷ **True love.** R' Yisrael Salanter once overheard someone say that he loved chicken. R' Yisrael responded: "If you loved the chicken, you would never slaughter it. It is *yourself* that you love; you love to *eat* chicken."

בָּל [כ] מַחֲלֹקֶת שֶׁהִיא לְשֵׁם שָׁמַיִם, סוֹפָהּ לְהִתְקַיֵּם;
וְשֶׁאֵינָהּ לְשֵׁם שָׁמַיִם, אֵין סוֹפָהּ לְהִתְקַיֵּם. אֵיזוֹ
הִיא מַחֲלֹקֶת שֶׁהִיא לְשֵׁם שָׁמַיִם? זוֹ מַחֲלֹקֶת הִלֵּל וְשַׁמַּאי.

The potential explosiveness of the situation was compounded by King Saul's hatred of David, an enmity so intense that it prompted the king to attempt to kill him more than once. In spite of all this, David's and Jonathan's souls were bound together. Even though each knew that the other stood in the way of his succession to the throne, their love for each other was not affected (see *I Samuel* 18).

I Samuel 20 best demonstrates the nature of this quintessential friendship. Jonathan ignored his selfish interests — even his father's fury — and devised a plan to warn David of danger and save his life.

One may learn from David and Jonathan's story that it is wise to place a friend's interests over one's own, even if one suspects that he will suffer financial damage or embarrassment by doing so (*R' Yonah, R' Moshe Alshakar*).

Tiferes Yisrael defines their love as the sympathetic understanding two people sometimes enjoy instantaneously upon meeting; a certain chemistry occurs between them which seals their love permanently.

Mishnah 20

בָּל מַחֲלֹקֶת שֶׁהִיא לְשֵׁם שָׁמַיִם, סוֹפָהּ לְהִתְקַיֵּם — *Any dispute that is for the sake of Heaven will have a constructive outcome.* *Rambam* explains that the "constructive outcome" of a dispute for the sake of Heaven refers to the fact that even the view of those whose opinion is not adopted will be remembered and discussed.

Machzor Vitry explains the term סוֹפָהּ לְהִתְקַיֵּם literally, the dispute *will endure*, i.e., when people argue in search of truth rather than out of contentiousness (see *Shabbos* 55a), their words will be lasting and productive. In the category of an argument for the sake of Heaven, *Machzor Vitry* includes one that results from constructive criticism. When one gives such advice out of concern for the other, with no hint of self-glorification, it will achieve its goal by finding its place in the other person's heart.

According to *R' Yonah*, the mishnah refers specifically to debate on Torah topics. Those engaged in such debate will literally *endure*; their sincere involvement in Torah will add years to their lives. In addition, their involvement will be sustained. Since their disputes result in a clearer understanding of the Torah, they will continue to have such disputes, and the exchange between them will continue all their lives.

Rav says that the words סוֹפָהּ לְהִתְקַיֵּם refer to the disputants rather than to the dispute itself. Unlike

⧉ **Test for the sake of Heaven.** The *Zohar* explains that even the Evil Inclination's continual dispute with the force of spirituality in the world is for the sake of Heaven, and this is why the contestants endure. In order for man to receive true reward in the World to Come, he must choose to do good in spite of the blandishments of the Satan; and so the latter is ultimately in the service of Heaven. Like a king who hires a woman to seduce his son and then instructs the son not to fall prey to her wiles, God created an Evil Inclination and then gave man the Torah to instruct him how to avoid the pitfalls of evil (*Mikveh Yisrael*).

⧉ **Enduring dispute?** R' Zorach Eideltz offers a homiletic approach: The litmus test which determines if a dispute is for the sake of Heaven is whether or not it flares up again after it has been settled. If it is indeed for the sake of Heaven, סוֹפָהּ, *its resolution,* לְהִתְקַיֵּם, *will endure.* An argument which people engage in for its own sake will be reignited in time.

Furthermore, if the dispute was sincere, the disputants themselves will become good friends. The Talmud teaches that even if a father and son, or a teacher and student, become "enemies" through debate in Torah topics, they will ultimately become "friends" again by reaching agreement (see *Kiddushin* 30b and *Meiri* to 4:14).

20. **A**ny dispute that is for the sake of Heaven will have a constructive outcome; but one that is not for the sake of Heaven will not have a constructive outcome. What sort of dispute was for the sake of Heaven? — The dispute between Hillel and Shammai.

Korach and his cohorts, the disputants in a controversy for the sake of Heaven will survive. Alternatively, the phrase may be rendered as *Rav, its intended goal will be realized.* When they are motivated purely by a need to find the truth, the disputants will succeed.

וְשֶׁאֵינָהּ לְשֵׁם שָׁמַיִם, אֵין סוֹפָהּ לְהִתְקַיֵּם — *but one that is not for the sake of Heaven will not have a constructive outcome.* When people argue in order to exert control or to triumph over each other, the argument will not have any constructive outcome (*Machzor Vitry*). According to *Rav* and *R' Yonah*, אֵין סוֹפָהּ לְהִתְקַיֵּם refers again to the disputants. In a controversy which is not for the sake of Heaven, the disputants will not survive; on the contrary, they will perish in the very first round, as did Korach.

Even if only one party in the dispute has selfish motives, nothing substantial will result. Only when there is a common goal shared by all can a controversy produce enduring positive effects (*Tiferes Yisrael*).

אֵיזוֹ הִיא מַחֲלֹקֶת שֶׁהִיא לְשֵׁם שָׁמַיִם? זוֹ מַחֲלֹקֶת הִלֵּל וְשַׁמַּאי — *What sort of dispute was for the sake of Heaven? — The dispute between Hillel and Shammai.* Hillel and Shammai are the prototypes of disputants engaged in debate for the sake of Heaven. In their halachic disputes, they were concerned not with triumph but with a sincere search for the true understanding of Torah. In spite of their disputes, they enjoyed amicable relations and lived in harmony and true brotherhood (see *Yevamos* 14b) (*Rav, Yaaros Devash*).

The Talmud (*Sanhedrin* 88b) teaches that in the tumultuous times after Hillel and Shammai, students could not spend sufficient time studying with their teachers. This lack of internship resulted in increased controversy over the authentic halachic tradition. It is for this reason that Hillel and Shammai rather than their respective disciples are considered the exemplars of proper conduct in dispute (*Tosafos Yom Tov*). The mishnah does not invoke the academies of Hillel and Shammai as examples of a dispute for the sake of Heaven; apparently some of the students may have had other motives in their debates (*Tiferes Yisrael*).

Hillel and Shammai's debates are ongoing. Wherever students of Torah gather to learn together, their words are still studied (*R' Yehudah Lirma*). *Ruach Chaim* suggests that only people

---

◆§ **What will God gain?** R' Yerucham Levovitz notes in the name of R' Yisrael Salanter the interesting paradox that simple farmers can fight among themselves about straw, grass, and other fairly inconsequential things, and yet come to an amicable solution without much delay. However, when honorable, more sophisticated people fight presumably "for the sake of Heaven," the destructive fire of controversy cannot be extinguished. When pompously self-righteous people convince themselves that their stubbornness is an expression of their concern for God's honor, dangerous consequences can ensue. A person can commit the worst sins under the false conviction that he acts for the sake of God.

Rabbi Tzadok HaKohen of Lublin was considered one of the greatest Torah scholars in Poland while he was still a youngster. He once met a famed senior sage who had heard of the young genius's reputation. "Let us converse in learning," the older rabbi offered. "Tell me a novel interpretation of a *gemara* or a *Rambam.*" Replied R' Tzadok, "You are a famous scholar; I, too, am capable. So I will tell you my brilliant ideas to prove to you that I am a genius, and you will tell me your dazzling thoughts. But what will God have from all of this?"

◆§ **More lofty disputes.** R' Yitzchak Hutner suggested that this mishnah may refer to various pathways in the service of God. The *Chassidim* and *Misnagdim*, the separatist German Orthodoxy of Rabbi Samson Raphael Hirsch and the opposing school of the *Rav* of Wuerzberg, the deep piety of the proponents of the *Mussar* Movement and their opposition all sought the will of Heaven. Their contributions to the full spectrum of the Torah *Weltanschauung* therefore live on.

וְשֶׁאֵינָהּ לְשֵׁם שָׁמַיִם? זוֹ מַחֲלֹקֶת קֹרַח וְכָל עֲדָתוֹ.

[כא] **כָּל** הַמְזַכֶּה אֶת הָרַבִּים, אֵין חֵטְא בָּא עַל יָדוֹ; וְכָל

with motives as pure as those of Hillel and Shammai are entitled to engage in heated debate. Lesser people should refrain from the all-consuming fire of מַחֲלֹקֶת.

Chida quotes *Ritva*, who reports in the name of the Kabbalists that while the normative halachah presently follows the academy of Hillel, the law will follow the academy of Shammai in the Messianic era. They explain the phrase סוֹפָהּ לְהִתְקַיֵּם to mean that both views will endure, since eventually Shammai's view will prevail.

וְשֶׁאֵינָהּ לְשֵׁם שָׁמַיִם? זוֹ מַחֲלֹקֶת קֹרַח וְכָל עֲדָתוֹ — *And which was not for the sake of Heaven? — The dispute of Korach and his entire company.* Korach incited the Jewish people to rebel openly against Moses and Aaron and overthrow them as the leaders of the nation, in spite of the fact that he was their cousin and fellow Levite. As is typical of would-be usurpers who must attract a popular following, Korach posed as a champion of the people and tried to discredit Moses and Aaron. He accused

them of selfishly taking power and prestige for themselves at the expense of the rest of the nation, which was full of people as qualified as they. Then he continued to curry favor with the masses by saying that since all Jews were equally holy, Moses and Aaron had no right to take for themselves the two highest positions in the nation.

Korach's own resentment began when Aaron was made Kohen Gadol, or when their cousin Elizaphan son of Amihud was placed in charge of the Kohathite family (*Numbers* 3:30), thus making him Korach's superior and giving him a position that Korach felt should have been his. At that time, however, Korach did not dare criticize Moses, who was so beloved by the people that they would not have tolerated any resistance to him. But after the fiasco of the Spies and the decree that an entire generation would die in the Wilderness without ever seeing the Holy Land, Korach took advantage of the national unrest to foment rebellion.

This was a clear example of a controversy not for the sake of Heaven. Korach and his clan came to undermine Moses and his position only out of envy,

⊷§ **A short and tragic step.** R' Hersh Goldwurm suggests that once Korach found an excuse to challenge Moses' legitimacy, it was a short step for him to deny the Divine origin of the commandments and hold them up to ridicule; for if Moses could be suspected of appointing his brother Kohen Gadol, an act of apparently gross nepotism, why could he not be accused of fabricating the commandments? This explains why Korach, as the Midrash relates, had his followers dress in garments of *techeiles,* turquoise wool, and confront Moses publicly with the derisive question "Does a garment made entirely of *techeiles* require a single *techeiles* thread in its *tzitzis*?" Moses said, "Yes" (see *Numbers* 15:38) — whereupon Korach scoffed, "If a single strand is enough for an entire garment made of a different color of wool, does it not stand to reason that an all-*techeiles* garment should not require the required strand?" By means of such challenges, Korach sought to convince the people that such "illogical" laws must have been the product of Moses' own imagination.

⊷§ **Look beyond the dispute.** People who find reasons to challenge the authority of Torah leaders and to cast aspersion on their level of observance generally claim that they do so for the sake of Heaven. How is one to determine if this is true? What is the mark of a dispute for the sake of Heaven? *Noam Elimelech* explains: If the different groups are at peace among themselves and enjoy a good relationship, one may assume that the dispute is for the sake of Heaven. If, however, contention and strife run rampant among them in all other areas besides their campaign against the righteous, one may be sure that the dispute is for anything *but* the sake of Heaven.

Thus, the mishnah tells us that Korach and his entire assemblage were really antagonists. Only against Moses could they find common ground; regarding all else, they exhibited only enmity — a sure sign that their dispute was ignoble.

21. **W**hoever influences the masses to become meritorious shall not be the cause of sin; but one who influences the

---

contentiousness, and a desire for victory (*Meiri* and *Rav*). Therefore, they perished, and the rebellion against Moses died an eternal death with them. They had sought honor and power for themselves, but instead they died an ignominious death (*Rav*).

Midrash Shmuel notes that the mishnah does not refer to both parties in the dispute (Korach and

Moses) as it does with Hillel and Shammai. *R' Yehudah Lirma* suggests that while both Hillel and Shammai argued for the sake of Heaven, only Moses had such pure intentions. Moses and Aaron lived altruistically, dedicated completely to God. They answered Korach only in order to sanctify God's Name, but they were not truly parties to the dispute he had instigated.

Mishnah 21

כָּל הַמְזַכֶּה אֶת הָרַבִּים, אֵין חֵטְא בָּא עַל יָדוֹ — *Whoever influences the masses to become meritorious shall not be the cause of sin.* One who seeks to direct others onto the path of righteousness (*Rambam*), by teaching them Torah, inculcating them with a fear of God, or influencing them to perform the commandments (*Tiferes Yisrael*), will be kept from sinning himself.

Rashi, Meiri, and *Rav* quote the Talmud (*Yoma* 87a) that such a person merits Divine protection from sin, because it is inconceivable that his disciples should be in the World to Come, while he, who elevated them, should languish in *Gehinnom*.

This is derived from the verse *For You will not abandon my soul to the lower world, nor allow Your devout ones to witness destruction* (*Psalms* 16:10). If someone inspires others, God will not him allow to suffer the punishments

of *Gehinnom*, not only for his own sake, but in order to prevent his disciples from witnessing the spiritual destruction of their mentor (*Tosafos Yom Tov*).

According to *R' Yonah* (ms.), this is an application of the principle of מִצְוָה גוֹרֶרֶת מִצְוָה, *the reward of a mitzvah is another mitzvah* (see 4:2). One who acts as a catalyst for the increased fulfillment of God's will in the world is rewarded with the continual opportunity to fulfill the *mitzvah* of fearing God. If he leads people to righteousness, he himself will be blessed to stay on the right path.

Midrash Shmuel suggests that the mishnah actually describes a feature of human nature. Since a person of conscience suffers inner conflict when his words and his deeds are divergent, one who inspires the public to virtue will be especially careful not to sin himself; he will not want to appear hypocritical or cause others to be cynical.

◆§ **No one lacking.** *Yismach Moshe* renders the word חֵטְא in this mishnah as *failing* or *loss* (see *I Kings* 1:21). Thus the mishnah states that one who expends his time and effort to minister to the spiritual needs of the public will not suffer any loss in his own spiritual growth or physical welfare because of it. Rabbi Moshe Adler adds: One should not worry that the Evil Inclination will focus especially on him and his family to "avenge" his involvement with the spiritual welfare of others. To the contrary, both he and his children will be bolstered by the merit of all those whom he has affected positively, and they will suffer no spiritual harm.

A contemporary example of this principle is the experience of Rabbi Mordechai Yoffe, the first student of Rabbi Aharon Kotler to found a new yeshivah far from the established centers of Torah life. When he went to Kansas City, Missouri to plant the seeds of Torah, R' Aharon blessed him that his children not be adversely affected by the non-observant atmosphere where they would grow up. Although R' Mordechai and his new yeshivah suffered great privation for the cause of Torah, every one of his children and their families are the fulfillment of R' Aharon's blessing.

הַמַּחֲטִיא אֶת הָרַבִּים, אֵין מַסְפִּיקִין בְּיָדוֹ לַעֲשׂוֹת תְּשׁוּבָה. מֹשֶׁה זָכָה וְזִכָּה אֶת הָרַבִּים, זְכוּת הָרַבִּים תָּלוּי בּוֹ, שֶׁנֶּאֱמַר: ,,צִדְקַת יהוה עָשָׂה, וּמִשְׁפָּטָיו עִם יִשְׂרָאֵל". יָרָבְעָם בֶּן נְבָט חָטָא וְהֶחֱטִיא אֶת הָרַבִּים, חֵטְא הָרַבִּים תָּלוּי בּוֹ, שֶׁנֶּאֱמַר:

Rabbi Moshe Adler suggests a novel reading of the mishnah. One who judges people sympathetically, even when they act improperly, runs the risk of becoming desensitized and may eventually be tempted to lower his own spiritual standards. It is against this pitfall that the mishnah offers reassurance: One who views the public favorably will not lose any personal sensitivity; no sin will occur as a result of his positive approach to others.

וְכָל הַמַּחֲטִיא אֶת הָרַבִּים, אֵין מַסְפִּיקִין בְּיָדוֹ לַעֲשׂוֹת תְּשׁוּבָה — *but one who influences the masses to sin will not be given the means to repent.* One who leads others astray by inciting them to sin or creating opportunities for them to transgress the will of God (*Tiferes Yisrael*) will not merit Divine assistance in his attempts to repent.

As the Talmud (*Yoma* ibid.) teaches: "So that he not be in *Gan Eden* while his students are in *Gehinnom.*" While God generally helps those who seek to repent, in the case of someone who is responsible for the spiritual downfall of others, it would be unfair to help him escape punishment while his victims must suffer for their sins. Even so egregious a sinner can certainly repent, but he will have to do so on his own; he will not receive Divine assistance (*Rashi, Meiri, Rav*).

This is derived from the words of King Solomon: *A man*

⊷§ **Guaranteed investment.** The Chofetz Chaim once traveled to a rabbinic conference by train, accompanied by R' Meir Dan Plotzki. At one of the stops, a large group of people gathered, all hoping to get a glimpse of the sage of Radin. A delegation of rabbis and community elders was sent to the train to ask the Chofetz Chaim to step out to greet the crowd, but he graciously refused.

R' Meir Dan asked the Chofetz Chaim why he refused to go out when so many Jews were waiting to see him.

"Honor is poisonous," the Chofetz Chaim replied. Rabbeinu Yehudah *HaChassid* says that while other pleasures of this world do not detract from one's share in the World to Come, honor, which is a spiritual pleasure, takes away from one's eternal reward. How can you ask an old Jew to seek honor?"

R' Meir Dan responded: "I have two things to say. First of all, it is worthwhile to lose some of one's share in the World to Come in order to make so many Jews happy. Secondly . . ."

The Chofetz Chaim interjected: "Enough! The first reason is sufficient." And the elderly sage stepped onto the platform to meet the crowd.

It may be assumed that the sage had in mind the message of the mishnah. Although it would have been a personal sacrifice for the Chofetz Chaim to accept the plaudits of the crowd, by giving them the spiritual satisfaction of meeting him, he would surely have been rewarded, not deprived.

⊷§ **Double vision.** A loving mother who knows her child has done wrong will chastise him in private, but will defend him before his principal or a judge. Moses, who carried his people as a *nurse carries a suckling* (*Numbers* 11:12), followed the same pattern, as is expressed in the latter part of the Mishnah, which can be interpreted homiletically as follows: Moses זָכָה, he sought to *purify* the nation by offering it private rebuke. Simultaneously, however, וְזִכָּה אֶת הָרַבִּים, he *found justification for the multitude* when he pleaded with God to be merciful. צִדְקַת ה' עָשָׂה, *[Moses] performed the righteousness of* HASHEM, *seeking* the good in man, just as God only seeks our good, and וּמִשְׁפָּטָיו עִם יִשְׂרָאֵל, *His ordinances together with Israel,* by demanding privately that they follow God's Torah (*Knesses Yisrael*).

A perceptive student of human behavior once expressed the proper perspective one should adopt: "One should view others with the eyes of R' Levi Yitzchak of Berditchev [famed for his ability to see only the good in others] and himself with the eyes of the Kotzker *Rebbe* [known for his uncompromising search for truth]." It is always important to look upon others with a benevolent eye, but to engage in self-criticism.

masses to sin will not be given the means to repent. Moses was meritorious and influenced the masses to be meritorious, so the merit of the masses was to his credit, as it is said: *Carrying out God's justice and His ordinances with Israel (Deuteronomy 33:21).* Jeroboam ben Nebat sinned and caused the masses to sin, so the sin of the masses is charged against him, as it is said:

---

involved with the [spiritual] blood of a person will hasten his own steps to the pit with no support (Proverbs 28:17). One who murders a friend spiritually by inciting him to sin (see Bamidbar Rabbah 21:5) will receive no support from Heaven to thwart his own fall into Gehinnom.

R' Yonah (ms.) and Rambam consider this an application of the rule that the consequence of sin is sin. They render אֵין מַסְפִּיקִין בְּיָדוֹ לַעֲשׂוֹת תְּשׁוּבָה as: *They* [God] *do not allow him to repent.* The punishment for inciting others to sin is that one is *unable* to get rid of his own sins.

Rambam (Hilchos Teshuvah 6:3) elaborates: There are cases where one's sins are so numerous or of such gravity that he is punished by being denied the opportunity to repent; God decrees that he perish in his wickedness. In addition, he is punished even for those sins that he commits after he loses his free will, since his inability to repent is self-inflicted. [See Rambam's example of Pharaoh.]

R' Moshe Alshakar adds that one who causes others to sin cannot fully repent for the simple reason that he cannot correct *their* errors, for which he was responsible. His personal repentance alone is insufficient; he is comparable to one who is טוֹבֵל וְשֶׁרֶץ בְּיָדוֹ, a person who seeks purification by *immersing* in a *mikveh* while holding an *impure creature in his hand.*

The mishnah now cites examples:

מֹשֶׁה זָכָה וְזִכָּה אֶת הָרַבִּים, זְכוּת הָרַבִּים תָּלוּי בּוֹ — *Moses was meritorious and influenced the masses to be meritorious; so the merit of the masses was to his credit.* Moses not only achieved the highest degree of spiritual, moral, and ethical perfection to which

a human being can aspire; he also taught Torah to the Jewish nation, developing their latent spiritual abilities — and thus their potential to fulfill their role as God's chosen nation. Since he brought them to fulfill the *mitzvos* and accrue spiritual merit, he deserves the credit (Rashi, Rav). This follows the Talmudic dictum: גָּדוֹל הַמַּעֲשֶׂה יוֹתֵר מִן הָעוֹשֶׂה, *One who causes others to do* [mitzvos] *is greater than one who does* [mitzvos] *himself (Bava Basra 9a).*

שֶׁנֶּאֱמַר: ,,צִדְקַת יהוה עָשָׂה, וּמִשְׁפָּטָיו עִם יִשְׂרָאֵל" — *as it is said: "Carrying out God's justice and His ordinances with Israel" (Deuteronomy 33:21).* This verse teaches that Moses figuratively carried out all the laws of the Torah along with the people of Israel. Their actions are deemed his, since he inspired them to live the Torah way (Rashi, Meiri).

R' Moshe Alshakar renders צִדְקַת ה׳ as the "charity" given to God. God considers the Jews' fulfillment of the *mitzvos* as "charity" given to Him by Moses. Since Moses brought the people to this spiritual plateau by guiding them and offering them rebuke when needed, he is considered to have "given" God something of his own.

Moses even received credit for the nation's performance of the *mitzvos* which can only be kept in the Land of Israel, even though he never kept them himself, because they were fulfilled only as a result of his instruction and inspiration (Tiferes Yisrael).

יָרָבְעָם בֶּן נְבָט חָטָא וְהֶחֱטִיא אֶת הָרַבִּים, חֵטְא הָרַבִּים תָּלוּי בּוֹ — *Jeroboam ben Nebat sinned and caused the masses to sin, so therefore the sin of the masses*

◆§ **Without delay.** According to *Avos al Banim,* one who brings others to iniquity is not granted the delay of punishment, which God generally extends through His attribute of אֶרֶךְ אַפַּיִם, *enduring patience.* On the other hand, someone who sins because he could not withstand temptation is granted additional time in the hope that he will come to his senses and repent when the heat of passion passes. However, one who persuades others to sin does so only out of a cynical attitude toward God and toward life. Such a person does not deserve the opportunity to repent. *Chelek LeOlam Haba* adds that he is punished immediately so that he will no longer have a ruinous influence on the lives of others.

עַל חַטֹּאות יָרָבְעָם אֲשֶׁר חָטָא, וַאֲשֶׁר הֶחֱטִיא אֶת יִשְׂרָאֵל.״

[כב] **כָּל** מִי שֶׁיֵּשׁ בְּיָדוֹ שְׁלֹשָׁה דְבָרִים הַלָּלוּ, הוּא מִתַּלְמִידָיו שֶׁל אַבְרָהָם אָבִינוּ; וּשְׁלֹשָׁה דְבָרִים אֲחֵרִים, הוּא מִתַּלְמִידָיו שֶׁל בִּלְעָם הָרָשָׁע. עַיִן טוֹבָה, וְרוּחַ נְמוּכָה, וְנֶפֶשׁ שְׁפָלָה, תַּלְמִידָיו שֶׁל אַבְרָהָם אָבִינוּ.

is charged against him. Jeroboam ben Nebat was a servant of King Solomon, and after Solomon's death he led the secession of the ten northern tribes and became their king. Jeroboam was afraid that if he made pilgrimages to the Temple in Jerusalem, his authority would be undermined when people saw him standing in the Temple courtyard while his rival, King Rehavam of Judah, sat, a privilege that was reserved only for the legitimate heirs to the Davidic dynasty. He was also apprehensive that his own subjects would be weaned away from him when they went to the Temple. To safeguard his claim to the throne, he made two golden calves, claiming that they were repositories of the Divine Presence and that one could worship God through them just as in the Temple. In this way, he sinned by preventing the people from going to Jerusalem for the pilgrimage festivals. Furthermore, he caused them to sin by inducing them to serve idols (see *I Kings* 12). Thus,

Jeroboam was responsible for their sins as well as his own (*Magen Avos*).

Tiferes Yisrael notes that the mishnah cites the case of Jeroboam only to prove that one is responsible for the sins one causes others to commit, not as an example of one who found repentance either difficult or impossible. It is obvious that one cannot repent for the sins of others that are a result of his influence.

שֶׁנֶּאֱמַר: ,,עַל חַטֹּאות יָרָבְעָם אֲשֶׁר חָטָא, וַאֲשֶׁר הֶחֱטִיא אֶת יִשְׂרָאֵל״ — *as it is said: "For the sins of Jeroboam that he committed and that he caused Israel to commit"* (*I Kings* 15:30). The entire household of Jeroboam was decimated, in punishment for both his own sins and those he caused others to commit. We may infer from this that the converse is also true: The good deeds one inspires others to do are considered his as well (*Magen Avos*). The sins which he incited others to do are, in fact, called his own, rather than being referred to as the sins of the Jewish nation (*Rav*).

Mishnah 22

כָּל מִי שֶׁיֵּשׁ בְּיָדוֹ שְׁלֹשָׁה דְבָרִים הַלָּלוּ, הוּא מִתַּלְמִידָיו שֶׁל אַבְרָהָם אָבִינוּ — *Whoever has the following three traits is among the disciples of our forefather Abraham.* Whoever emulates our forefather Abraham by living according to the three positive character traits listed below is considered his student and protege (*Meiri, Rav*). The mishnah makes this introduction before enumerating the character traits, rather than merely stating that the disciples of Abraham possess these three virtues, in order to teach that the possession of these three *alone* is deemed a sufficient degree of perfection to qualify one as a student of Abraham. These three are the bedrock of the type of ethical development that makes one a follower of Abraham; all other charac-

teristics are subdivisions of these three. Hence, if one possesses other attributes yet lacks these three, he cannot be numbered among the disciples of Abraham (*R' Yonah*)

The mishnah does not speak of the students of Moses, since one would have to fulfill the Torah in its entirety to achieve that title.

Even non-Jews can aspire to be considered followers of Abraham whom Scripture describes as "father of a multitude of nations" (*Genesis* 17:4) and who taught monotheism and proper ethical development to the human family. By subscribing to the moral code expressed in this mishnah, even a non-Jew can become a disciple of Abraham (*Tiferes Yisrael*).

For the sins of Jeroboam that he committed and that he caused Israel to commit (I Kings 15:30).

22. **W**hoever has the following three traits is among the disciples of our forefather Abraham; and [whoever has] three different traits is among the disciples of the wicked Balaam. Those who have a good eye, a humble spirit, and an undemanding soul are the disciples of our forefather Abraham.

וּשְׁלֹשָׁה דְבָרִים אֲחֵרִים, הוּא מִתַּלְמִידָיו שֶׁל בִּלְעָם הָרָשָׁע — *and [whoever has] three different traits is among the disciples of the wicked Balaam.* God, in His wisdom, ordained that the gentile nations should have a prophet comparable to Moses — though much inferior to him — so that they could not contend that if only they had had someone who could communicate to them the will of God, they would have been as righteous as Israel (see *Ramban* to *Deuteronomy* 34:10). Balaam was that prophet and a man of great wisdom; nevertheless, the three corruptions of character described below led him to great immorality. Anyone who possesses these three negative traits holds the key to moral failure and may be considered a follower and disciple of the wicked Balaam (*Tiferes Yisrael*), despite any other fine attributes he may have; he is a soul mate of Balaam.

עַיִן טוֹבָה — *Those who have a good eye.* I.e., who does not suffer from jealousy and to whom a friend's honor is as dear as his own (*Rashi*).

According to *Rambam* and *Rav*, עַיִן טוֹבָה, *a good eye,* is the knack of being satisfied with one's own lot in life and being happy over the success of others. He does not begrudge others anything, nor does he desire that which belongs to them. According to *R' Yonah*, he is magnanimous, both financially and emotionally. *Sfas Emes* interprets the term as referring to having a positive outlook.

One who finds evidence of God's goodness and kindness in everything he sees is a disciple of Abraham. One who is firm in his faith in God, even when he cannot fathom His ways, exhibits a good eye towards God (*Tiferes Yisrael*).

וְרוּחַ נְמוּכָה — *a humble spirit.* I.e., exceptional humility and modesty of spirit (*Rashi, Rav* et al.), toward both God and man (*R' Yonah*) [See 4:4].

וְנֶפֶשׁ שְׁפָלָה — *and an undemanding soul.* One who can exercise restraint and self-control over forbidden physical desires (*Meiri, Rav*) or even over excessive luxuries (*Meiri*) enjoys a spiritually healthy soul without desire for lust or sin (*R' Yonah*). According to *Tiferes Yisrael*, this also connotes a sense of satisfaction with one's lot.

◄§ **Purity of desire.** Rabbi Shalom of Belz was once sent by his mentor, the *Chozeh* of Lublin, to go to the back of the study hall and to sit near the oven, where the unlearned people generally congregated. There R' Shalom heard two simple Jews pouring out their bitter hearts to each other. They felt that they had traveled to the *Rebbe* for nothing, since they felt no spiritual uplift from being near him.

R' Sholom understood that it was to encourage these sincere but depressed people that the *Chozeh* had sent him. He said, "Once the angels brought all of the merits of Jews in front of the Heavenly Court. Charity, hospitality, kindness, the merit of helping poor brides — all were presented as evidence of the Jewish people's righteousness. Satan countered by presenting evidence that the nations of the world perform the same meritorious deeds. Triumphantly, Satan cried, 'This is no reason to favor the Jews!' Finally the angel Michael came forward with 'some broken Jewish hearts,' those saddened that they had not accomplished more spiritually. These won the day; Satan could not find anything to match them.

"King David says, *a broken and depressed heart, God will not scorn* (*Psalms* 51:19). There is nothing as dear to God as a broken Jewish heart. Even if one deserves to be scorned, his broken heart will save him."

The Kotzker said, "Nothing is as whole as a broken heart."

Midrash Shmuel renders נֶפֶשׁ שְׁפָלָה as a *diminished soul*. Man's animalistic element seeks to be the most prominent part of his life and decisions. When man *diminishes* its prominence in his decisions, he possesses an undemanding soul.

Chida views these three positive traits as counterpoint to the three fatal faults listed in 4:28: jealousy, lust, and glory. One blessed with *a good eye* is happy with his own lot and does not suffer the cancer of *jealousy.*. The *humble spirited* are free from the spiritually suicidal search for *honor* and prestige. Furthermore the key to freedom from *lust* is an *undemanding soul;* one who is not tempted by the beckoning call of the flesh does not constantly seek new thrills.

According to *HaChassid Yaavetz*, these traits parallel the ethical and moral plateaus highlighted in the last three mishnayos. One who loves God unconditionally (see 5:19) enjoys a *good eye,* always happy with the quality of life God grants him. *A humble spirit* is the root cause for one to conduct disputes without rancor or out of a desire for victory in debate. A dispute for the sake of Heaven (see 5:20) is the approach of one who argues his point only in search of truth and uses his intelligence as a tool to enhance and broaden his fear of Heaven. The *undemanding soul* needs little for himself and is able to devote himself to the spiritual welfare of others, always seeking to influence them toward a meritorious existence.

תַּלְמִידָיו שֶׁל אַבְרָהָם אָבִינוּ — *are the disciples of our forefather Abraham.* Abraham enjoyed all these qualities: When the king of Sodom offered him the spoils of war, Abraham refused, even though, according to the accepted pratice of the time, he was entitled to it (see *Bava Kamma* 114a). Abraham, who was not plagued by the insatiable thirst for money, was able to forgo the windfall of war, and say, "*I lift up my hand to God [and swear] . . . . if so much as a thread to a shoelace; or if I take from anything of yours!*" (Genesis 14:22-23). Thus, a *good eye* is an identifying characteristic of Abraham and those who follow in his footsteps (*Rambam*, *Rav*). *R' Yonah* establishes this trait of Abraham from his hospitality to three bedraggled visitors. *Then Abraham ran to the cattle, took a calf tender and good, and gave it to the youth who hurried to prepare it* (Genesis 18:7). Even though Abraham thought his visitors were lowly, idol-worshiping nomads, he nonetheless exhibited magnanimity by bringing each one a separate calf so that they might enjoy the delicacy of tongue served with mustard (see *Rashi* ibid. 7 ad loc.).

Tiferes Yisrael, who views a good eye as indicative of deep seated faith, cites Abraham's unquestioning belief in the promise that he would be blessed with descendants as innumerable as the stars: *And he trusted in God and He reckoned it to him as righteousness* (Genesis 15:6), despite his advanced age and lack of children until then.

According to *Rambam*, *Rav*, et al., Abraham's trait of *humility* is given its fullest expression in his petition to God on behalf of Sodom: "*I am but dust and ash*" (Genesis 18:27).

R' Yonah and *Magen Avos* suggest that Abraham's humility is reflected in the way he spoke to the three angels, who he thought were simple nomads: "*Inasmuch as you have passed your ser-*

⇜§ **Portrait.** The Kozhnitzer *Maggid* sees our mishnah as a word portrait of someone with the proper orientation toward his relationship with God. A person with a *good eye* always focuses on the greatness of God, with a *humble spirit* realizes his insignificance in relation to his Maker, and one with a *meek soul* always doubts whether he has done enough for God. Such a person is truly a disciple of Abraham our forefather.

⇜§ **Prerequisites to kindness.** Seemingly the most identifiable trademark of Abraham our forefather was his *chessed,* or kindness, care, and concern for all, yet the mishnah does not list it. *Nesivos Shalom* explains that one must free himself of egocentric tendencies before he can be genuinely kind to others. The disciples of Abraham, who want to develop the trait of caring, seek to be happy with the success of others, to be humble, and to develop an undemanding soul. But people who are obsessed with wealth, honor and the pleasures of this world are so busy with themselves they have no room for others.

---

vant's way" (ibid. v. 5). *Sforno* sees his interpersonal humility mirrored in his deference to the people of Heth (*Genesis* 23:7). Even though they considered him a prince of God (ibid. v. 6), he displayed no arrogance and bowed to them.

Rav sees his lack of lust in the fact that he did not take note of Sarah's great physical beauty until they were forced to go the licentious land of Egypt (see *Genesis* 12:11 and *Rashi* ad loc.). Until then, he was aware only of her spiritual refinement. Another indication is his response to Sarah's complaint that his younger, fertile wife Hagar was disrespectful. Abraham did not let personal considerations stand in the way, and told Sarah that she, as Hagar's mistress, could deal with Hagar as she saw fit.

Clearly, even though Hagar was his wife and was carrying his child, he did not allow considerations of personal pleasure to govern his reaction to Sarah's legitimate complaint. Furthermore, when Abraham was finally forced to send Hagar and their son Ishmael away, the Torah teaches: *The matter greatly distressed Abraham regarding his son* (*Genesis* 21:11). God commanded him to banish Ishmael, because he was a menace to the spiritual health — and perhaps the very life — of Isaac. His only concern was regarding the spiritual future of his son. The loss of his conjugal relationship with Hagar played no role in his emotions (*Rambam, R' Yonah et al.*).

עַיִן רָעָה — *Those who have an evil eye.* One cursed with an insatiable appetite for wealth tends to be jealous, and begrudges others any success (*Rambam, R' Yonah*).

Rashi interprets evil eye as *negative vision*, which is epitomized by the intolerant and jealous way in which he perceived the Jews. *Balaam raised his eyes and saw Israel dwelling according to its tribes* (*Numbers* 24:2). He saw the exemplary order of the Israelite camp, how tribes maintained their separate identities, and arranged their tents so that their entrances did not face one another, so that each family's privacy would be undisturbed. Balaam could not tolerate the humble beauty of the Israelite camp; he sought to inflict damage upon them with his evil and jealous eye (see *Rashi* ad loc. and *Avos* 2:16, s.v. עין הרע).

Thus, people who are jealous, dissatisfied, and crave for things beyond their means are numbered among the disciples of Balaam.

וְרוּחַ גְּבוֹהָה — *an arrogant spirit.* According to *R' Yonah*, Balaam showed his delusionary sense of self-importance when he refused to accompany the first group of Balak's officers. *Balaam arose in the morning and said to the officers of Balak, "Go to your land, for God refuses to let me go with you"* (*Numbers* 22:13). He chose his words carefully. Too arrogant to admit that God had categorically forbidden him

---

◦§ **In the mind.** Sarah's intent was not malicious, but to force Hagar to cease her insulting demeanor. Instead of acknowledging Sarah's authority, however, Hagar fled (*Abarbanel; Sforno*). Rabbi Aryeh Levin noted that it is incongruous to believe that a woman as righteous as Sarah would persecute another human merely to assert her own status. Rather, Sarah treated Hagar as she always had, but Hagar had begun to consider herself Abraham's primary wife, because she had become pregnant, while Sarah was barren. In the light of her newly inflated self-image, Hagar began to look at Sarah's normal, considerate behavior as persecution.

◦§ **Ishmael's character.** Presumably Abraham noticed the same things about Ishmael that Sarah did, but he must have felt that he should not let Ishmael leave the wholesome influence of his home. If Hagar had corrupted the boy in Abraham's home, surely it would be much worse if she were to become the sole influence over him (*R' S. R. Hirsch*).

To signify Ishmael's vulgar nature, the Torah describes him as *the son of Hagar, the Egyptian*. Despite her many years in the home of Abraham and Sarah, Hagar remained an Egyptian princess, and Ishmael gravitated to her influence rather than to Abraham's. Abraham found it repugnant to send them away but he was strong enough to do whatever he was commanded. As the Patriarch of Israel, his primary responsibility was to subordinate his feelings of love to the dictates of the future (*R' Nosson Scherman*).

מַה בֵּין תַּלְמִידָיו שֶׁל אַבְרָהָם אָבִינוּ לְתַלְמִידָיו שֶׁל בִּלְעָם
הָרָשָׁע? תַּלְמִידָיו שֶׁל אַבְרָהָם אָבִינוּ אוֹכְלִין בָּעוֹלָם הַזֶּה,
וְנוֹחֲלִין הָעוֹלָם הַבָּא, שֶׁנֶּאֱמַר: ,,לְהַנְחִיל אֹהֲבַי יֵשׁ,
וְאֹצְרֹתֵיהֶם אֲמַלֵּא". אֲבָל תַּלְמִידָיו שֶׁל בִּלְעָם הָרָשָׁע
יוֹרְשִׁין גֵּיהִנֹּם, וְיוֹרְדִין לִבְאֵר שַׁחַת, שֶׁנֶּאֱמַר: ,,וְאַתָּה

---

to go, he said "with you," implying that it was only with *this* delegation that he could not go — but if Balak were to send a more prestigious delegation, the answer might be different (*Rashi* ad loc.).

וְנֶפֶשׁ רְחָבָה — *and a greedy soul.* Men of insatiable desires will stop at nothing to fulfill them. They possess נֶפֶשׁ רְחָבָה, lit. a wide soul, meaning that they feel a misleading emptiness, which they can never fill. Such people are obsessed with their lusts, and can never satisfy them (*Midrash Shmuel*).

Balaam's excessive lust led to his nearly successful plan to bring God's wrath upon Israel. After Balaam's utter failure to curse Israel, he had one last hope. He knew that sexual morality is a foundation of Jewish holiness and that God does not tolerate immorality — in fact, the only times the Torah describes God's anger with the severe term אַף, *wrath,* is when it is provoked by immorality (*Moreh Nevuchim* 1:36). Therefore Balaam counseled Balak to entice Jewish men to debauchery. So intent were the Moabites and their Midianite allies to undo Israel that even members of the aristocracy sent their daughters to carry out the plan, which the Talmud describes in detail (see *Sanhedrin* 106a). Balaam's own excessive lust motivated him to suggest spiritually entrapment of the Jews in this obscene way. As *Rambam, R' Yonah* and *Meiri* explain, one's advice and suggestions are heavily influenced by his own predispositions and desires. Good people do not suggest an evil course of behavior; it repulses them. In the words of *Meiri,* "The mouth is the messenger of the heart."

תַּלְמִידָיו שֶׁל בִּלְעָם הָרָשָׁע — *are the disciples of the wicked Balaam.* The Torah testifies that all three of these contemptuous traits were an integral part of Balaam's personality. (a) His *evil eye* was shown by his readiness to sell his services to Balak for a hefty price, for when Balak summoned him to curse the

Israelites, Balaam replied, "*If Balak will give me his houseful of silver and gold, I cannot transgress the word of God*" (*Numbers* 22:18). Following the Midrashic interpretation, *Rashi* (ad loc.) notes that by speaking of a houseful of gold and silver he implied that he was ready to comply — but only for a huge sum of money. (See *Meiri* and *Rav*.)

(b) His arrogance showed itself time and time again. [See above, s.v. רוח גבוהה.] *Rambam* quotes his boastful description of himself as *the one who hears the sayings of God, and knows the knowledge of the Supreme One (Numbers* 24:16). (c) For proof of his wanton immorality, see above, s.v. ונפש רחבה; see also *Sanhedrin* 105a.

מַה בֵּין תַּלְמִידָיו שֶׁל אַבְרָהָם אָבִינוּ לְתַלְמִידָיו שֶׁל בִּלְעָם הָרָשָׁע — *How are the disciples of our forefather Abraham different from the disciples of the wicked Balaam.* Since the differences between them have already been described at length, the question seems superfluous. *Rashi* renders it as a rhetorical question. According to *Ikvei HaTzon,* the question refers to the differences in the quality of their respective lives, both in this world and in the World to Come.

תַּלְמִידָיו שֶׁל אַבְרָהָם אָבִינוּ אוֹכְלִין בָּעוֹלָם הַזֶּה, וְנוֹחֲלִין הָעוֹלָם הַבָּא — *The disciples of our forefather Abraham enjoy [the fruits of their good deeds] in this world and inherit the World to Come.* Even the quality of their existence in this world is vastly improved because they have the three trademark traits that confer on them the title "disciples of Abraham" (*Tiferes Yisrael*). They enjoy the dividends of their good deeds in this world, yet retain the principal reward for the World to Come (*Rashi*).

שֶׁנֶּאֱמַר: ,,לְהַנְחִיל אֹהֲבַי יֵשׁ, וְאֹצְרֹתֵיהֶם אֲמַלֵּא" — *As it is said: "To cause those who love Me to inherit an everlasting possession [the World to Come], and I*

the disciples of our forefather Abraham different from the disciples of the wicked Balaam? The disciples of our forefather Abraham enjoy [the fruits of their good deeds] in this world and inherit the World to Come, as it is said: *To cause those who love Me to inherit an everlasting possession [the World to Come], and I will fill their storehouses [in this world]* (Proverbs 8:21). But the disciples of the wicked Balaam inherit *Gehinnom* and descend into the well of destruction, as it is said: *And You,*

---

will fill their storehouses [in this world]" (Proverbs 8:21). God has abundant wealth and goodness to bestow on man (*Rashi*), and He bestows them on those who love Him and follow in the footsteps of Abraham, whom God calls (Isaiah 41:8) אַבְרָהָם אֹהֲבִי, *Abraham who loves Me* (*Rambam, R' Yonah, Rav*).

The Sages teach that God will grant each righteous person 310 worlds in the World to Come (*Uktzin* 3:12). This is based on the word יֵשׁ in this verse, which has the numerical equivalent of 310. Thus the verse has the further implication that the disciples of loving Abraham will be granted reward that is equivalent to 310 worlds as we know it.

אֲבָל תַּלְמִידָיו שֶׁל בִּלְעָם הָרָשָׁע יוֹרְשִׁין גֵּיהִנָּם, וְיוֹרְדִין לִבְאֵר שַׁחַת — *But the disciples of the wicked Balaam inherit Gehinnom and descend into the well of destruction.* Even this world is a purgatory for those who suffer from greed, arrogance and lust. Thus, *Gehinnom* is a metaphor for worldly misfortune (*Meiri, Tosafos Yom Tov*). Furthermore such people will descend into the well of destruction in the next world.

Tiferes Yisrael interprets the phrase conversely,

⤚§ **Deceiving appearances.** The mishnah questions the difference between Abraham's *students* and those of Balaam, instead of the difference between Abraham and Balaam themselves. Certainly the chasm between the mentors themselves is even greater than between their disciples!

The *Maggid* of Mezritch explained: It was easier to see the differences between their respective disciples than between Abraham and Balaam. Disciples are molded by the character and piety of their teachers; it is a familiar truism that students cannot be deceived for long, no matter how hard their teachers try to conceal their essence, so it is inevitable that the students will reflect the essence of their teachers. Thus, one can differentiate between the students of our forefather and those of the prophet of impurity, as long as one learns the guidelines given by our mishnah. But Balaam himself may well have looked as saintly and righteous as Abraham. The unpracticed eye might never realize that Balaam was nothing more than a greedy charlatan; to the untrained eye they looked the same.

Historically, it has often been easier to recognize the relative greatness of people from their students and descendants than from the people themselves. The Chasam Sofer and Rabbi S. R. Hirsch left families and generations of disciples that testify eloquently to their spiritually legacy, whereas the opponents they fought so strenuously left many descendants who converted to other religions, or drifted from the tenets of the Torah.

⤚§ **Added dimension.** The Chasam Sofer adds an insight to the fruits that Abraham's disciples will enjoy in this world. Not only will they be blessed with health and prosperity, but even their temporal blessings will enjoy an added spiritual dimension. The disciples of Abraham eat in this world as a means to serve God. Their Sabbath and Festival meals are holy, and even their ordinary eating is in order to provide energy for spiritual pursuits. Thus, they redefine a physical function as an exercise in spirituality and they inherit reward in the World to Come for having eaten in this world. True love of God permeates all corners of their lives, transforming the mundane into the sublime. The mishnah teaches that even in areas where there seems to be no difference between Abraham's students and Balaam's, there is no comparison between the two.

[כג] **יְהוּדָה** בֶּן תֵּימָא אוֹמֵר: הֱוֵי עַז כַּנָּמֵר, וְקַל כַּנֶּשֶׁר,

---

rendering *Gehinnom* as punishment in the World to Come, and the "well of destruction" as the ominous fear of death, which dampens one's enjoyment of this world. Even people who achieve their desires of wealth and physical pleasure may find their success soured by the fear of death.

שֶׁנֶּאֱמַר: ,,וְאַתָּה אֱלֹהִים תּוֹרִדֵם לִבְאֵר שַׁחַת, אַנְשֵׁי דָמִים וּמִרְמָה לֹא יֶחֱצוּ יְמֵיהֶם, וַאֲנִי אֶבְטַח בָּךְ״ — *as it is said: "And You, O God, shall lower them into the well of destruction, men of bloodshed and deceit shall not live out half their days; but as for me, I will trust in You"* (*Psalms* 55:24). Balaam was a prime example of a man of bloodshed and deceit. He caused the death of 24,000 people, who perished in a plague that resulted of his plan to use immorality to entice Israelite men to idolatry.

The Moabite women invited the Jews to feast and drink with them. When the men became aroused and wanted to cohabit, the women drew their Baal Peor idols from their robes and insisted that the men bow to them [see *Rashi* to *Numbers* 25:2].

The Talmud relates that a Sadducee asked how old Balaam was when he was killed. R' Chanina replied, "Scripture does not give this information, but we can assume that he lived to the age of thirty-three or thirty-four, since King David teaches

that men of bloodshed and deceit will not live out half their days." This is based on the verse that the normal lifespan is seventy years (*Psalms* 90:10).

The Sadducee responded, "You are right. I myself saw the Chronicle of Balaam [a non-Scriptural work], and in it was written, 'Balaam the lame was thirty-three years old when he was killed by Phineas the outlaw' " (*Sanhedrin* 106b).

Maharal comments that men of bloodshed and deceit do not deserve to live at all; at the very least, it is not fitting that they should live the majority of a normal life span. Alternatively, *Maharsha* suggests that it can be assumed that one who has not repented by midlife will not do so during the second half of his life either. There is therefore no purpose in letting him continue to live.

Tiferes Yisrael interprets *half their days* as half of their expectations, i.e., no matter how dazzling their success, they will not achieve even half the pleasures they had imagined. They will even lose this world, the part of one's existence one thinks is his to do as he pleases. They will never achieve even half of their appetites for its pleasures. But as for himself, David concludes, "I will trust in You." No matter how much or how little they have in this world, the disciples of Abraham are always happy, for they know that God provides them with whatever is best for them (*Tiferes Yisrael*).

Mishnah 23

יְהוּדָה בֶּן תֵּימָא אוֹמֵר — *Yehudah ben Tema says.* While this is the only mishnah ascribed to Yehudah ben Tema, the *Baraisos* quote him often (see *Eruvin* 17a). The exact time period in which he lived is unclear.

Avos d'Rabbi Nosson (41) quotes the mishnah and adds: "Love Heaven, fear Heaven, be meticulous and joyful over the *mitzvos*. If you did some small injustice to a friend, view it as a major infraction; if you did him much good, view it as something small and insignificant. If your friend did something small for you, deem it a great favor; if he

did something significant against you, view it as insignificant. Learn to accept pain and forgive those who insult you."

According to *Rashi,* this mishnah was a response to Rabbi Akiva's teaching that one should allow his Sabbath meals to be of weekday quality rather than depend on charity (see *Pesachim* 112a). Yehudah ben Tema teaches that only the absolutely destitute may rely on this permission. Otherwise, one should be "bold as a leopard," making maximum effort to honor the Sabbath and holidays to their fullest.

הֱוֵי עַז כַּנָּמֵר — *Be bold as a leopard.* A leopard is not

O God, shall lower them into the well of destruction, men of bloodshed and deceit shall not live out half their days; but as for me, I will trust in You (Psalms 55:24).

23. **Y**ehudah ben Tema says: Be bold as a leopard, light as an eagle,

---

as strong as many other beasts, but boldly undertakes tasks that seem to be too much for it. Likewise, man should never shirk spiritual opportunities with the claim that such things are only for the truly righteous; he should be bold, fearless, and ambitious as a leopard in assuming spiritual duties beyond his perceived capabilities (*Tiferes Yisrael*), and trust that God will grant him the strength to overcome obstacles.

When man begins to serve God in earnest, he can easily be overwhelmed by the enormity of the task. He hears the Evil Inclination whispering in his ear:

"I can't do it; it's too much." If he seeks to repent, he may remember his old ways: "I have too much spiritual baggage to start over again." The leopard teaches us to have the boldness of spirit and to dream the impossible — and to do it (*Chiddushei HaRim*).

According to *Rav*, this is addressed to students who should not be ashamed to question their teacher. This is a restatement of the principle taught earlier (2:6), *the bashful person cannot learn.*

Sefer HaMussar elaborates: A student ought to be "bold as a leopard" during the course of a lesson and not

---

◦§ **Refuting a challenge.** The Evil Inclination may tap a person on the shoulder in the midst of prayer and say to him, "Aren't you embarrassed to approach God in prayer? Remember all the terrible sins you have committed; don't you think He also remembers?" When this happens, he should not be dismayed, but answer courageously and boldly, "You are right. I *am* unworthy. But God is good, and He will not refuse my prayer" (*Avodas Yisrael*).

When R' Naftali of Ropschitz was a youngster, he tried to begin his service of God by rising early in the day. One icy morning, as he attempted to get out of bed to study and pray, the Evil Inclination accosted him. "It's cold outside, and it is still early; stay in bed for just a few more minutes." The young Naftali answered sharply, "Move out of my way, you scoundrel! You are up already, hard at work to entice me. Why shouldn't I also get up to my work?"

◦§ **A time for boldness; a time for reticence.** *Mesillas Yesharim* (Chapter 5) defines the correct approach:

"If there are among his companions those who subject him to ridicule, he should not take it to heart; on the contrary, he should ridicule and shame them. Let him consider whether, if he had the opportunity to acquire a great deal of money, he would give up the undertaking in order to avoid the ridicule of his companions. How much more averse should he be to forfeiting his soul in order to spare himself ridicule! In this connection, our Sages, of blessed memory, exhorted us (*Avos* 5:23): 'Be bold as a leopard to do the will of your Father in Heaven.' And King David said (*Psalms* 119:46), '*And I will speak of your testimonies before kings, and I will not be ashamed.*' Most of the kings of his time occupied themselves with grandiose schemes and pleasures, and we would tend to expect that David, himself a king, would be ashamed in their presence to speak of Torah and ethical issues instead of discussing great feats and the pleasures of men such as they; but David was not the least perturbed, and his heart was not seduced by these vanities, because he had already attained the truth."

In Chapter 20, *Mesillas Yesharim* continues: "A person must observe all the *mitzvos*, giving attention to all their minute details, without fear or shame, no matter in whose presence he is. This, however, requires discrimination. In relation to the *mitzvah* itself, one must be hard as rock. But there are additional forms of piety that are not required by law, and which, if performed in public, will cause people to laugh at and ridicule him; and thus they will be rendered sinners and liable to punishment because of him. Since such deeds are not absolutely required, it would be better not to do them. As the prophet said (*Micah* 6:8), *And walk modestly with your God.* Many great saints relinquished some of their accustomed ways in public so as not to appear proud.

"In summation, what is essential in respect to *mitzvos* must be performed in the face of all mockery, and what is not essential and provokes laughter and ridicule should not be performed in public."

be ashamed to ask questions. If he has not understood something, he should not pretend that he has; and even if his teacher has taught him something once, twice, or even three times, if he still does not understand, he should ask, "Teach it to me once again," until he does understand. Even if his teacher is annoyed with him, he should not be shamed into silence. If a leopard, a creature of limited intelligence, uses all his daring to seize his prey, how much more should a man, a creature of intelligence, use all his daring to acquire food for his soul and life in the World to Come.

R' Yonah renders הֱוֵי עַז as *be tireless* in your pursuit of Torah and *mitzvos*. The prophet promises (*Isaiah* 40:31): קוֵֹי ה' יַחֲלִיפוּ כֹחַ, *those whose hope is in HASHEM will have renewed strength.* Those who yearn for God will have their energies recharged so that they can continue in their pursuit of God's work.

Alternatively (see also *Rambam*), this is an instruction to be bold in admonishing those who rebel against the word of God. *Tur* (*Orach Chaim* 1) writes: "Yehudah ben Tema begins with [the words] *be bold as a leopard,* since this is a cardinal principle in serving God. Very often one wants to perform a *mitzvah,* but refrains from doing so because of people who scorn and laugh at him. Therefore, he is enjoined to assume an air of obstinacy against such and not refrain from performing the *mitzvah.*"

וְקַל כַּנֶּשֶׁר — *light as an eagle.* According to *Rav* and *Magen Avos,* this is a charge to Torah students to review their studies tirelessly and thus merit the crown of Torah. One may rise above all his contemporaries with the aid of incessant review, just as an eagle rises above all other birds. *Tiferes Yisrael* understands the metaphor as teaching that one should not be dissuaded by difficulties in understanding the Torah. Just as an eagle soars toward the sun, so man should pick himself up again and again to come closer to the warmth and enlightenment of Torah.

Sefer HaMussar views this as an enjoiner against intellectual arrogance in the presence of one's teachers. Just as the eagle soars on high but also swoops down, so must incisive and brilliant scholars not puff themselves up in the presence of

their teachers. Rather, they must listen humbly and minister to the needs of their elders.

According to *Tur* (ibid.), the lesson of the eagle is that man must be swift and agile in ignoring enticement to sin. Just as an eagle glides through the sky and is able to change direction almost effortlessly, so should man teach himself to recoil easily from the beckoning of evil.

רָץ כַּצְּבִי — *swift as a deer.* One should chase after all opportunities to perform *mitzvos.* He should train his legs to run instinctively to perform a *mitzvah* or to help another person. Furthermore, when he is presented with such an opportunity, he should not procrastinate; he should perform the *mitzvah* immediately (*Rav* and *Tur*). The Sages taught: "Just as one does not allow dough to sit around unattended for fear that it will become *chametz,* so one should never delay his performance of a *mitzvah*" (*Mechilta* 67).

The Jews left Egypt in haste (see *Deuteronomy* 16:3), which teaches how one should react to spiritual awakenings. One must seize the moment of inspiration and leave his slavish existence behind, like the Jews, who escaped the impurity of Egypt in the nick of time (see *Tzidkas HaTzaddik* 1).

This is derived from the verse: *You shall safeguard the matzos* (הַמַּצּוֹת) (*Exodus* 12:17). In the plain sense of the verse, the *matzos* must be safeguarded while they are being baked, since even a bit of delay or extra moisture can cause the dough to become leavened. Since the word הַמַּצּוֹת can also be read הַמִּצְוֹת, *the commandments,* the Sages apply this injunction homiletically to all commandments: "If a *mitzvah* comes to your hand, do not allow it to become 'leavened' by delaying its performance" (*Rashi*).

Maskil LeDavid adds: Just as the Jews in Egypt were in such a state of spiritual decline that even a slight delay might have rendered the redemption impossible, so the speedy performance of a single *mitzvah* may be necessary for the salvation of an individual Jew at any given moment.

Like a deer which runs swiftly and does not tire, so one should never weary in his pursuit of *mitzvos* or Torah study. In fact, unlike one who becomes fatigued after a long hard run, the study of Torah will never wear a person out (*R' Yonah*). In *Tiferes Yisrael's* view, the simile is a call to flee swiftly from heretical views, just as a deer flees the hunter.

In a novel interpretation, *Sefer HaMussar* explains this metaphor as a restatement of R' Nehorai's teaching, "Exile yourself to a place of Torah" (4:18). "A man ought to travel from one place to the next, from one country to another, from one city to another [in order to be in a place of Torah]." Following the lead of the deer, which can uproot itself swiftly, Torah students should be ready to forsake the comforts of home in order to search out better teachers and colleagues.

וְגִבּוֹר כָּאֲרִי — *and strong as a lion. Rashi* and *R' Yonah* view this as a reference to Torah study and fulfillment of *mitzvos*. Just as the lion is king of the forest and in full control of all his strength and faculties, so man must commit all his intellectual, emotional, and physical energies to his Godly service. *Tur* adds: One should emulate the lion and approach the service of God with a strong heart and iron will.

Rav, Magen Avos, and *Tiferes Yisrael* interpret the "lion's strength" as the fortitude to defend oneself against the onslaughts of the Evil Inclination. This mirrors Ben Zoma's definition of strength: "Who is strong? He who subdues his personal inclination" [see 4:1] (*HaChassid Yaavetz*).

The idioms "light [or swift] as an eagle" and "brave as a lion" come from King David's eulogy of Saul and Jonathan: *They were swifter than eagles, they were stronger than lions* (*II Samuel* 1:23).

לַעֲשׂוֹת רְצוֹן אָבִיךָ שֶׁבַּשָּׁמָיִם — *to carry out the will of your Father in Heaven.* Many of the traits enumerated above are intrinsically negative. Boldness can smack of arrogance; lightness sometimes becomes synonymous with superficiality; swiftness can be another form of impulsiveness; and strength can be cruelly abused. Therefore Yehudah ben Tema reminds us of the earlier maxim, "Let all your deeds be for the sake of Heaven" (2:17), teaching that we should turn these negatives into positives and channel them into the service of God (*Rambam*).

Meiri summarizes the mishnah by stating that we must serve our Creator with all our might and all our powers. Where strength is needed, let a man be strong as a leopard; where promptness is needed, let him be swift as an eagle; where a stout heart and courage are needed, let him be brave as a lion; and let him be swift as a gazelle to do the will of his Father in Heaven.

◆§ **Looking behind you.** A deer constantly looks over its shoulder to see if a hunter is pursuing it. Likewise, one should never be confident that he is out of reach of iniquity. He should check constantly to be sure the Evil Inclination is not right behind him (*Midrash Shmuel*). *Avos al Banim* suggests that the mishnah teaches one to remember the spiritual needs of his own children even while he is caught up in the race of life. It is not enough that he fulfills God's will himself; he must pay attention to those who are behind him — his children and grandchildren — to be sure that they follow in his footsteps. Hence, he must be like a deer, making his way forward but always looking behind him, to make sure his children are not neglected.

◆§ **Too soon to rest.** *Sefer HaMussar* elaborates: "A man should save his strength so that he will be able to study at night. Let him not say: 'I have studied much and can relax a bit.' On the contrary, he can be sure of one thing — the things he has *not* studied exceed by far the things that he *has* studied. Let him therefore always envy anyone greater than he in wisdom; let him not say, 'I know enough; I am greater than many.' Where bodily comforts are concerned, let his conduct be the reverse; that is, let him take note of those who are more hard pressed than he, and say, 'I am more fortunate than that person.' He should not envy those who enjoy wealth and honor, grumbling, 'Woe is me, I am not like so-and-so! He lives in such comfort!' Torah is to be found only among those who wear themselves out in study. The image of the lion teaches this: With all his might, a man should devote himself to the labors of the Torah only, for this is the soul's source of life."

[כד] **הוּא** הָיָה אוֹמֵר: עַז פָּנִים לְגֵיהִנֹּם, וּבְשֶׁת פָּנִים לְגַן עֵדֶן. יְהִי רָצוֹן מִלְּפָנֶיךָ יהוה אֱלֹהֵינוּ וֵאלֹהֵי אֲבוֹתֵינוּ שֶׁיִּבָּנֶה בֵּית הַמִּקְדָּשׁ בִּמְהֵרָה בְיָמֵינוּ וְתֵן חֶלְקֵנוּ בְּתוֹרָתֶךָ.

Mishnah 24

הוּא הָיָה אוֹמֵר: עַז פָּנִים לְגֵיהִנֹּם — *He* [*Yehudah ben Tema*] *used to say: The brazen goes to Gehinnom.* Yehudah ben Tema here qualifies his earlier statement advocating boldness in the service of God. As a rule, such boldness is a negative trait, since it prevents one from accepting constructive criticism easily and tends to make him chafe against the restraining influence of the Torah (*Meiri*).

Rambam comments that boldness is legitimate when one boldly upbraids people who rebel against the Torah. Even then, however, one must be careful to take such an approach only out of genuine motives; otherwise, it can lead to *Gehinnom.*

Sefer HaMussar summarizes: In the preceding statement, the mishnah taught that one ought to be aggressive in heavenly matters; here we are told that in worldly matters, that affect one's relations with other people, we must beware of all types of brazenness.

According to *Rav* and *Tosafos Yom Tov*, the mishnah refers to someone who obstinately refuses to do God's

⋖§ **Step by step.** Citing the verse *You should reprove your fellow, and do not bear a sin because of him* (*Leviticus* 19:17), *R' Yonah* explains that we bear responsibility for the sins of others if we refrain from rebuking them. Even if one person sins, the entire community may suffer if they were aware of his actions and did not seek to correct him (see *Joshua* 22:20). In order to prevent such communal calamity, it is proper to appoint upstanding members of the community to oversee the moral conduct of their neighbors and to offer reproof, when needed (*Shaarei Teshuvah* 3:72-73).

Rabbi Simcha Zissel of Kelm offers guidelines for appropriate criticism, based on the Talmudic teaching that one must reprove over and over again. It is usually unwise to tell someone bluntly that his actions have been utterly wrong; this will only embarrass and antagonize him. It is wiser to break up the criticism about a particular fault and to approach the other person gradually, a step at a time, in order to draw him closer to your point of view in a friendly, palatable way.

⋖§ **Better to be victim than to victimize.** *Abudraham* notes that in our morning prayers we ask God to rescue us מֵעַזֵּי פָנִים וּמֵעַזּוּת פָּנִים, *from brazen men and from brazenness.* We request that we be saved from others who might act brazenly towards us, and from ourselves acting brazenly towards others.

It is worse to act improperly than to be the victim of others. This is evident from Jacob's reaction to his impending encounter with Esau. *Jacob became very frightened, and it distressed him* (*Genesis* 32:8). He was *frightened* that *he* would be killed, and he was *distressed* that, in defending himself and his family, he might kill others (*Rashi*). Distress is a stronger emotion than fear. The prospect that he might be forced to kill was more disturbing to Jacob than the possibility that he might himself be killed (*Ralbag*).

⋖§ **When and how.** The traits mentioned here and elsewhere in the tractate require the use of good judgment to channel them most effectively; sometimes they must be displayed openly, and at other times kept suppressed.

Ruach Chaim writes, for example, that one should be careful to keep any obstinacy in his personality well hidden in the deep recesses of his heart. It should be allowed to surface only infrequently and only for the service of God.

Alternatively, the term פָּנִים may also be related to פְּנִים, one's *inner self.* Although one may employ brazenness under certain circumstances, he should never become a brazen person. Conversely, shame-facedness is a positive trait since it is a patently Jewish characteristic (see commentary, s.v. וּבְשֶׁת פָּנִים) that *should* be integrated into one's personality. There are instances, however, when one should act out of character in order to further spiritual goals. Hence, "the bashful person cannot learn" (2:6), so that he should shelve his bashfulness for the sake of his learning (*Minchas Shabbos*).

24. He [Yehudah ben Tema] used to say: The brazen goes to *Gehinnom*, but the shamefaced goes to the Garden of Eden. May it be Your will, HASHEM, our God and the God of our forefathers, that the Holy Temple be rebuilt, speedily in our days, and grant us our share in Your Torah.

---

will. The term עַז פָּנִים — literally, one with an arrogant face — is employed since obstinacy and brazenness are emotions worn on the face and not easily hidden.

וּבשֶׁת פָּנִים לְגַן עֵדֶן — *but the shamefaced goes to the Garden of Eden.* People with a sense of shame will not sin habitually; as a natural result, they will be rewarded with *Gan Eden* (*Tiferes Yisrael*). The Talmud teaches: "One who possesses the trait of shamefacedness will not easily come to sin" (*Nedarim* 20a).

This principle is derived from Moses' explanation of the dramatic and awesome character of the Sinaitic revelation: *Do not fear, for God has come in order to elevate you, so that awe of Him shall be on your faces, so that you shall not sin* (*Exodus* 20:17).

Meiri sheds light on the psychological dynamic of shame. One who possesses this trait is drawn toward righteous people and good deeds, since he will be embarrassed if others know of his sins and will be chagrined if his reputation is thus damaged. According to *Rambam*, the ability to feel a sense of shame when contemplating sin is among the greatest gifts that God has bestowed upon the Jewish nation. The Talmud defines three traits as identifying characteristics of the Jewish people: shame, compassion, and kindness (*Yevamos* 97a).

יְהִי רָצוֹן מִלְפָנֶיךָ יהוה אֱלֹהֵינוּ וֵאלֹהֵי אֲבוֹתֵינוּ שֶׁיִבָּנֶה בֵּית הַמִקְדָשׁ בִּמְהֵרָה בְיָמֵינוּ וְתֵן חֶלְקֵנוּ בְּתוֹרָתֶךָ — *May it be Your will, HASHEM, our God and the God of our forefathers, that the Holy Temple be rebuilt, speedily in our days, and grant us our share in Your Torah.* According to *Rambam* and *Rav*, this prayer

is a new request: To our request for the character traits of Abraham, we implore God to bless us also with the rebuilding of the Temple.

R' Akiva Eiger views this prayer as a reaction to the volatile nature of brazenness. While we must employ this dangerous characteristic in the pursuit of Torah knowledge — since students who are ashamed to ask questions will not succeed — we are certainly mindful of its detrimental side effects. We would prefer a situation where we could aspire to Torah knowledge without playing with spiritual fire. Hence, we yearn for the Messianic era, when *God will fill the earth with knowledge of HASHEM as the water fills the seabed* (*Isaiah* 11:9), so that we will no longer need brazenness as a tool for success in Torah study. The mishnah gives expression to this hope with a prayer for the rebuilding of the Temple.

Maharal explains how the Temple and Torah are antidotes to the obstinacy that can lead a person into *Gehinnom*. The Torah and the Temple provide the Jewish people with spiritual sustenance. Just as in the human body, where the heart follows the brain's instructions to pump blood even to the furthest extremities, Torah is the intelligence of the nation and the Temple is its heart. The Torah instruction that emanates from the Temple inspires every facet of the Jewish nation. Since most people are obstinate and one might fear that our people will end up in *Gehinnom*, we pray for a mass awakening to Torah study and fear of God, and for the speedy rebuilding of the Temple so that

---

◆§ **Perform with pride.** *Knesses Yisrael* interprets the mishnah in a homiletic vein, lamenting the distressing contrast between people who exhibit their sordid behavior in full view of the public, without the slightest tinge of embarrassment, while people who are loyal to God and His Torah are ashamed to perform *mitzvos* publicly and with pride. Let the righteous adopt the brazenness of the wicked and perform *mitzvos* with pride and elan.

In the early years of Rabbi Yitzchak Hutner's tenure as *Rosh Yeshivah* of Chaim Berlin, he would agree to perform the marriage of a student only if the young man committed himself to carry his *tallis* and *tefillin* bag openly — not in a paper bag, as was the custom of the time.

[כה] **הוּא** הָיָה אוֹמֵר: בֶּן חָמֵשׁ שָׁנִים לַמִּקְרָא, בֶּן עֶשֶׂר שָׁנִים לַמִּשְׁנָה, בֶּן שְׁלֹשׁ עֶשְׂרֵה

---

our spiritual lifeline will continue to function.

Tiferes Yisrael notes that the inclusion of a prayer in a mishnah is an anomaly. Here it expresses the hope that the great obstinacy that is an unpleasant hallmark of the Messianic era — and which impedes his arrival (see *Sotah* 49b) — will be tempered, and that we merit the swift rebuilding of the Temple as a result of God's mercy. The prayer concludes with a plea that any brazenness we do possess be channeled into Torah study: "Grant us, dear God, that our portion [of obstinacy] be used to advance Torah study and causes."

In a variation on this theme, *B'nayos B'Ramah* suggests that Yehudah ben Tema realized that obstinacy was increasing, in accordance with the description of Messianic times recorded in *Sotah* (ibid.). Therefore, he prayed that the final redemption come to fruition quickly.

Other commentators explain *our share in Your Torah* to refer to each Jew's particular area of Torah, which is his special purpose in life, his singular goal.

On an intellectual level, this means that God awaits specific individuals to elucidate particular ideas or concepts in the Torah, and even to specialize in certain areas of Torah study. Some people have an emotional and intellectual orientation toward halachah, while others are rooted in Aggadah; yet others are drawn toward *pilpul* or study in depth. Even in *mitzvos*, one's personal preference for a particular *mitzvah* is an expression of his share in Torah; so we find, for example, that people may have a particular affinity for study, kindness, *mezuzah*, or *esrog*.

The *Vilna Gaon* (on *Shir HaShirim* 6:4) explains that we add a request for our share in Torah to our request for the reconstruction of the Temple, because as long as the Temple is in ruins and we are in exile, the quality and quantity of our Torah study is drastically diminished. This is the meaning of the verse in *Lamentations* (2:9): מַלְכָּה וְשָׂרֶיהָ בַגּוֹיִם אֵין תּוֹרָה, *Her king and her princes are among the nations; there is no Torah.* With the Temple restored, we will once again be able to study Torah to the fullest extent.

According to the *Vilna Gaon,* the insertion of this prayer here is mistaken. It actually belongs at the end of the chapter, which is where the tractate ends. [Chapter 6 is made up of *Baraisos* which were added on to *Avos* to facilitate a six-week recitation schedule (see 6:1, s.v. שנו חכמים).]

Meiri suggests that R' Yehudah *HaNasi,* the redactor of the Mishnah, ended the tractate here, justifying the insertion of the prayer as a conclusion; the next mishnayos were later additions.

Mishnah 25

הוּא הָיָה אוֹמֵר — *He [Yehudah ben Tema] used to say.* This mishnah continues the theme discussed in the previous mishnayos, that one must exhibit flexibility in the deployment of different character traits, sometimes being bashful while at other times brazen. So too, one must change emphasis at different stages of life. Consistency must always be tempered by the ability to change direction when one achieves a new plateau in his spiritual development (*Doresh LePerakim*).

Mili d'Avos (Warsaw) views this as a qualifier of the prayer that concluded the previous mishnah, that God grant us success in Torah study. While prayer is a necessary component of such achievement, it cannot effective unless it is combined with dedicated study and effort. At every stage of one's

---

⤙§ **Summing up.** Since the goal of *Avos* is to inculcate Torah ethics and morals in us, in order to make us fitting receptacles for the Torah, it is appropriate that we end the tractate with a request for *our* share in the Torah. Each person's particular share is defined by his specific spiritual attributes and inclinations. Now that we have finished *Avos* and have hopefully internalized its lessons, we are ready to receive our specific portion of the Torah.

25. He [Yehudah ben Tema] used to say: A five-year-old begins Scripture; a ten-year-old begins Mishnah; a thirteen-year-

development, vigorous education and character molding is necessary.

According to *Meiri*, the mishnah provides parents with an educational program that meets the needs of children as they advance from level to level. That done, the mishnah goes on to describe the natural changes that occur with age. [See *Tosafos Yom Tov*, who suggests that this mishnah was said by Shmuel *HaKattan*.]

בֶּן חָמֵשׁ שָׁנִים לַמִּקְרָא — *A five-year-old begins Scripture.* According to *Rashi* and *Rav*, in the fourth year of a child's life, i.e., after his third birthday, he should be taught the letters of the Hebrew alphabet and the accompanying vowels, and in his fifth year he should learn to read. From his fifth birthday, the serious, diligent study of Scripture should begin. This schedule inferred homiletically from the verse

in *Leviticus* (19:23-25): *When you shall . . . plant any food tree . . . for three years . . . they shall not be eaten. In the fourth year all its fruit shall be sanctified to laud God. And in the fifth year you may eat its fruit [reading is the fruit of knowledge of the letters] so that it will increase its crop for you (Rashi, Rav).*

Meiri quotes some authorities who hold that the letters should not be taught until the fifth year. According to *Midrash Shmuel*, "Scripture" includes knowledge of the texts, proper spelling, full knowledge of the tenses and rules of Biblical grammar.

Meiri fleshes out the homiletic analogy. The "fruit" is the Torah, and the "tree" is the child. When the child arrives in the land [i.e., he is born] for three years he is allowed to grow and develop physically for the first three years, without any burdens of learning being placed upon him. In the

---

◆§ **Not enough.** A mother asked the Chofetz Chaim for a blessing that her son become a great *talmid chacham* (Torah scholar). The Chofetz Chaim became uncharacteristically agitated. "You are mistaken if you think that my blessing can accomplish this. For success at Torah, blessings are not enough — one must act. Send your son to a good yeshivah and let him labor at Torah study under the tutelage of God-fearing teachers. Let him be surrounded with good friends with whom he can study and grow, and who will be a good influence. Then — maybe then — you will merit a son who is a true scholar. My blessing is certainly not enough."

A similar incident occurred when Rabbi Yaakov Kamenetsky came to a boys' summer camp one evening to deliver an address. Before he spoke, many campers lined up and asked the great sage for blessings that they succeed in learning. Later, he opened his remarks with the following story that he witnessed as a youngster, after the turn of the century:

Rabbi David Friedman of Karlin visited a certain Lithuanian city. Lovingly known as R' David'l, he was recognized as one of the greatest Torah sages of the century, so his visit attracted throngs who came to greet him. Among the crowd was a young man who was being harassed by the Czar's government, and he requested R' David's blessing that he succeed in settling the matter without pain or mishap. The blessing was granted. As the young man turned to leave, R' David'l called after him, "Young man! I am *not* a secretary of the One Above. Do not rely on my blessing — do whatever possible to help your situation."

And so, R' Yaakov concluded, it is with Torah. A blessing may help, but the only way to succeed in Torah is through dedicated study.

◆§ **Proper upbringing.** R' Moshe ibn Machir, author of *Seder HaYom*, offers some advice on child rearing based on this mishnah: One should in no way cause pain or distress to a child below five years old. Such a child lacks the necessary maturity to respond positively to such treatment, and therefore, within reason, should be indulged its desires. One should certainly not hit a child so young.

It is important that the child eat and drink well and sleep enough, so that he does not become ill or weakened. Just as the main support of a building is its foundation, likewise a healthy youth will support a person all his entire life. The Sages relate that at the age of eighty-five, R' Chanina was still able to tie his shoes while standing unsupported on one foot. When questioned about this, he replied, "The warm drinks and oil that my mother provided for me when I was a child have protected me in my old age."

---

fourth year he is "sanctified" by learning to read and in the fifth year he "increases the crop" by beginning to study in earnest.

בֶּן עֶשֶׂר שָׁנִים לַמִּשְׁנָה — *a ten-year-old begins Mishnah.* From five to ten a child should be taught Scripture exclusively. At ten he should begin the study of Mishnah without the elaborate commentary of the Talmud. Simple Mishnah study is not too complex for such a young mind and will not place undue mental or emotional stress on a youngster (*Rashi*). He should not stop studying Scripture, but it should have a secondary place in his schedule. Similarly, one should not abandon the study of Mishnah when he begins Gemara. Since Mishnah is part of the Oral Law, one should try to memorize it. At this young age the mind is still uncluttered, and youngsters can memorize vast amounts of material, albeit on a simple level of understanding (*Midrash Shmuel*).

The Mishnah designates five-year periods for each area of study. This is based on the educational axiom stated in the Talmud (*Chullin* 24a) that if a student has not tasted success within five years of having embarked on the study of a particular area, it is highly unlikely that he ever will (*Rashi, Rav*).

בֶּן שְׁלֹשׁ עֶשְׂרֵה לַמִּצְוֹת — *a thirteen-year-old be-*

comes *obliged to observe the commandments.* A male becomes *bar mitzvah* and is obligated to fulfill the *mitzvos* of the Torah at age thirteen, and a female becomes obligated at twelve. That children are not required to observe the commandments is inferred from *Numbers* 5:6, which imposes responsibility for transgressions on someone who can be considered *a man or a woman*, which indicates that a degree of maturity is required before someone becomes liable. The question remains, therefore, at what age is someone considered a man or woman, as regards the commandments? The definition of אִישׁ, man, is derived from the incident (*Genesis* 34) when Simeon and Levi killed the men of Shechem to avenge the honor of their sister. *And Simeon and Levi, Dinah's brothers, each* **man** *took his sword* (אִישׁ חַרְבּוֹ) (ibid. v. 25). The Midrash notes that Levi was thirteen years old at the time. Thus it is implied in the Midrashic comment that whenever the Torah uses the term אִישׁ, man, it refers to a male at least thirteen years of age (*Rashi to Nazir* 29b, *Tosafos Yom Tov* here).

According to *Teshuvos HaRosh* (Section 16), the ages of twelve and thirteen for girls and boys was conveyed by God to Moses at Sinai.

Alternatively, *Rashi* suggests that thirteen and twelve are the ages at which signs of puberty

---

⊷§ **Hard work.** *Maharal* notes that while the earlier stages in the Mishnah refer to five-year periods — five years for Scripture and five years for Mishnah — the later stages, which involve personal development, are each a ten-year process, because a student has the great advantage of learning from a teacher. Self-improvement, however, is a much more tedious and time-consuming task. Hence, Scripture, Mishnah and Gemara which one learns from a teacher can be absorbed in five years while other steps on the ladder of human growth listed later in the Mishnah take ten years of unassisted hard work.

⊷§ **A significant number.** The author of *Kli Yakar* suggests that thirteen is an appropriate age for a boy to assume the yoke of *mitzvos* since the number thirteen is related to all three of the main foundations of the world's existence — Torah, service, and kind deeds — as taught by Shimon the Righteous, in 1:2 of this tractate. The Torah is interpreted on the basis of the thirteen hermeneutical principles. The service of God is symbolized by the animal offerings brought in the Temple, and, in a sense, man's first blood offering in life is when he enters the covenant with God, by undergoing circumcision. As the Talmud teaches, the word covenant appears thirteen times in the Torah with relation to circumcision. The third pillar of Godly behavior, kind deeds, is rooted in our emulation of God's Thirteen Attributes of Mercy. [The classic *mussar* work *Tomer Devorah*, by the great Kabbalist Rabbi Moshe Cordovero, explains each of these attributes and how man can emulate them in his dealings with others.]

old becomes obliged to observe the commandments; a fifteen-year-old begins to study Gemara; an eighteen-year-old goes to the marriage canopy; a twenty-year-old begins pursuit [of a livelihood]; a thirty-year-old attains full strength; a forty-year-old

---

generally are present.

Meiri cites a Midrash which sees an allusion to this age in the words of the prophet (*Isaiah* 43:21): *I fashioned this people* [עַם זוּ] *for Myself, that it might declare My praise.* The numerical value of the word זוּ is 13, the age at which a male becomes a full-fledged member of God's people.

בֶּן חֲמֵשׁ עֶשְׂרֵה לַגְּמָרָא — *a fifteen-year-old begins to study Gemara.* The term "Gemara" denotes an understanding of the logic and reasons for the laws given without elucidation in the Mishnah. At the time of the Mishnah, the Gemara had not yet been committed to writing; it was still taught by oral transmission, from teacher to student. What we refer to as the "Talmud" is the combination of Mishnah and Gemara. [See *Rashi* to *Succah* 28a, and *Bava Metzia* 33a.]

At the age of fifteen, one is sufficiently developed mentally to delve into the depths of the laws of Torah (*Tiferes Yisrael*). By that age, a boy who has studied Scripture for ten years and Mishnah for five should have become familiar enough with the fundamental concepts of Torah to make the transition to the Torah commentaries, reasonings and inferences. These are contained in the Gemara (from the term לִגְמוֹר, *to finish*), the work that "completes" the Torah. After five years spent in the study of the Mishnah, no subject contained in the Gemara should be foreign to the young scholar; by this time he should be able to follow all its debates with full comprehension and grasp their conclusions (*R' S. R. Hirsch*).

בֶּן שְׁמוֹנֶה עֶשְׂרֵה לַחֻפָּה — *an eighteen-year-old goes to the marriage canopy.* A man should get married

at the *beginning* of his eighteenth year (*R' Akiva Eiger*), but one should not do so before the age of eighteen since the burden of supporting a wife will impede his opportunity for growth in Torah study [see *Kiddushin* 29b] (*Machzor Vitry*).

Rashi and *Rav* see a Biblical allusion to this age in the fact that the word "man" is written nineteen times from the beginning of the Book of *Genesis* until the description of the naming of Eve (see *Tosafos Yom Tov*). One time it is mentioned to teach us Adam's name; the remaining eighteen times, it alludes to the fact that man does not become complete until he marries, which he should do when he is eighteen.

בֶּן עֶשְׂרִים לִרְדּוֹף — *a twenty-year-old begins pursuit [of a livelihood].* Rav, *Tiferes Yisrael,* et al. understand this from the context, for the pursuit of a livelihood naturally follows soon after marriage.

Rashi cites an opinion that it refers to the age when the Heavenly court pursues *man* for his actions, holding him liable for his sins, and subject to Divine punishment. This is derived from the fact that, at the time of the Spies who defamed the Land of Israel, God punished only those over twenty [see *Numbers* 14:29] (*Tosafos Yom Tov*).

According to *Meiri*, this is a continuation of the previous stich. One who was not married by eighteen should actively pursue a mate once he turns twenty. At that point in life, to remain single is detrimental to one's moral fortitude. The Talmud (*Kiddushin* 29b) states that when one approaches twenty, his bones begin to rot [a metaphor for a breakdown of morality and spiritual strength].

R' Moshe Alshakar views this as a call for one to

ᴥ§ **Prophetic words.** In a comment tinged with sadness but hope over the prevailing state of Jewish education in his time, R' Hirsch concludes: "Ah, when shall we see the day when our young people will once again tread the path to spiritual and mental development in accordance with the teaching left us by our wise 'fathers'?!"

History proved that in his generation, it was R' Hirsch who turned the tide and engendered a Torah renaissance that eventually yielded many great Torah scholars.

pursue the path of Torah and *mitzvos.* While one is obligated to fulfill the *mitzvos* from the age of thirteen, it is only after the intense study of Scripture, Mishnah, and Gemara that one is equipped to pursue the Godly path, with maturity and intelligence.

בֶּן שְׁלֹשִׁים לַכֹּחַ — *a thirty-year-old attains full strength.* This fact is derived from the example of the Levites, who were commanded to carry the vessels of the Tabernacle, to erect and disassemble it, and to load and unload the wagons that carried its beams and heavy vessels. Since this work required great strength and stamina, the Levites were allowed to participate only from the age of 30, when one reaches the height of his physical powers [see *Numbers* 4:2-3 and *Rashi* ad loc.] (*Rav, Rashi, Tiferes Yisrael*). *Meiri* adds that one should follow the example of the Levites and take care not to squander his strength on anything but the service of God.

According to *Midrash Shmuel,* כֹּחַ means the power to influence others. Until thirty, one should study in order to increase his own knowledge; at thirty, those who can should begin teaching and guiding others on the path of Torah.

בֶּן אַרְבָּעִים לַבִּינָה — *a forty-year-old attains understanding.* The term בִּינָה indicates the ability to

understand the ramifications of an idea and extrapolate one fact from another. By the age of forty, one's intellectual abilities have matured to the point where he attain this degree of perception (*Tiferes Yisrael*). This type of penetrating understanding gives one the ability to rule on questions of Halachah (*Rashi*).

The special quality of a forty-year period in regard to achieving depth of understanding is derived from Moses' final charge to the Jewish people. Only then, after forty years of miraculous survival and the beginning of a conquest that was clearly accomplished by God, could the people fully appreciate the awesome degree of gratitude and allegiance they owed Him. As the Sages say (*Avodah Zarah* 5b), "a student does not fully understand his teacher until after forty years." Since it was forty years since Moses had led them out of Egypt, he told them that God would now begin to expect more of them as a result of their new level of understanding and gratitude. Thus he said, "*But HASHEM did not give you a heart to know, or eyes to see, or ears to hear, until this day*" (*Deuteronomy* 29:3). Likewise, the passage of forty years in an individual's life gives him a new awareness and depth of understanding (*Rashi, Rav*) [see *Tosafos Yom Tov*].

⟨ **A time to understand.** *Meiri* quotes a Midrash (*Bereishis Rabbah* 30) that Abraham recognized God at the age of forty. The Midrash relates how this happened by way of a parable. A person was once walking through the forest when he noticed a brilliantly lit castle in the distance. As he approached, he thought, "Can it be that the castle has no owner?" Immediately the lord of the manor turned to him and cried out, "I am the owner of the castle." Abraham, too, looked around at the wondrous world in which he lived, and asked himself, "Can it be that the world has no owner?" Immediately God focused His attention on him and cried out, "I am the Owner of the world."

Derech Avos renders בִּינָה as *self-understanding* or *introspection.* Having gone through more than half of his life, one should stop for a moment and reflect, "I have spent most of my life chasing my desires, now it is time to consider what I yet need to do for my soul."

Upon reaching his fortieth birthday, R' Klonymos Kalman of Piaczesna entered the following in his personal diary: "What new commitments should I accept upon myself? To study more? I believe that to the best of my ability, I do not waste any time and am constantly involved in learning. Should I commit myself to keep away from physical desire? Thank God, my Evil Inclination does not dupe me and I am able to avoid becoming enslaved to him. What, then, am I missing? *Simply to be a Jew!* I see myself as a human being, blessed with form, color, body, and everything else that comprises a human being. Only the soul is lacking! Master of the World, allow me to undergo a spiritual conversion, and from now on to *really* be a Jew!"

בֶּן חֲמִשִּׁים לְעֵצָה — *a fifty-year-old can offer counsel.* Fifty was the age at which the Levites were no longer considered fit for heavy work, but they continued to act as guides and counselors to the younger Levites (*Numbers* 8:25). At this age, one can draw on his life experience and intellect to advise others (*Rashi, Rav*). He is better able to weigh conflicting options and opinions impartially before offering his opinion (*Tiferes Yisrael*).

Meiri elaborates: The counsel of a fifty-year-old is invaluable since it combines the two elements necessary for good advice: experience and wisdom. As the ethical philosophers taught, "Time will purify wisdom." One younger than fifty lacks the necessary life experience to offer sage advice, while one who is much older may have begun to experience decline of his intellectual faculties.

בֶּן שִׁשִּׁים לְזִקְנָה — *a sixty-year-old attains seniority* [lit. old age]. This denotes one's appearance at that age (*Rashi, Rav*). Alternatively, it refers to intellectual maturity, since the word זָקֵן is a contraction of the words זֶה קָנָה, *this [person] has acquired [wisdom]* [*Kiddushin* 32b] (*Tiferes Yisrael*).

The age of sixty is a significant milestone, for one who lives past sixty has avoided the Heavenly punishment of a premature death (see *Moed Kattan* 28a). It was for this reason, teaches the Talmud (ibid.), that R' Yosef made a party for his colleagues when he turned sixty. According to *Meiri*, this is the age when man should begin to consider that his end is not far off, and that he should give fuller attention to his duties toward God so that he is prepared for his approaching end.

בֶּן שִׁבְעִים לְשֵׂיבָה — *a seventy-year-old attains a ripe old age.* At seventy, one has reached the fullness of

his years, which is often accompanied by the appearance of white hair. R' Elazar ben Azariah was appointed to the office of *Nasi* when he was only eighteen. Miraculously, his hair turned white, giving him a distinguished appearance that would help him gain the respect of the masses [see *Berachos* 12b] (*Rashi*).

Rav notes that the definition of שֵׂיבָה as 70 is derived from the fact that this was the age at which King David died, of whom it was said: *he died בְּשֵׂיבָה טוֹבָה, in fullness of years* (*I Chronicles* 29:28).

Seder HaYom interprets שֵׂיבָה as related to תְּשׁוּבָה, *repentance.* As man realizes his days are numbered, he feels the urge to repent. Indeed, *Magen Avos* quotes an old philosopher who commented when his hair turned white, "These are the messengers of death."

In a similar context, *Midrash Shmuel* offers a homiletical interpretation of the *Zohar*. The Torah commands מִפְּנֵי שֵׂיבָה תָּקוּם, *before an old person shall you stand* (*Leviticus* 19:32). The *Zohar* comments: Before old age [arrives], stand up [and conquer your Evil Inclination].

בֶּן שְׁמוֹנִים לִגְבוּרָה — *an eighty-year-old shows strength.* At the age of eighty, one's physical powers begin to wane and his soul becomes the dominant force in his life, making it easier for him to study Torah and fulfill the *mitzvos* (*Tiferes Yisrael*). One who lives to eighty does so only due to the strength provided him by God. King David declares: *The days of our lives are seventy years and if due to strength eighty years* (*Psalms* 90:10). Often too weak, or without an appetite, to eat or drink, he does not survive on physical strength alone. God alone strengthens him, and therefore this is an age invested with an abundance of spiritual vigor as well (*Rashi*).

Midrash Shmuel sees this as a reminder that even

⋙ **A new leaf.** The Beis Yisrael of Gur would often visit very old people; even those who were not renowned for their scholarship or piety. When questioned about this, he replied, "They barely have bodies left and their physical lusts are certainly long gone. There is nothing left but a soul."

An eighty-year-old once visited R' Avraham of Kalish and began to complain that he was sick of living. "I'm eighty years old already, and I have had enough. I can't do anything with myself anyway," said the despondent man. The *Rebbe* replied: "Foolish one! It is worthwhile to live a full eighty years just for the opportunity to put on *tefillin* once — even if someone does it out of habit and with little intent!"

[כו] **בֶּן** בַּג בַּג אוֹמֵר: הֲפָךְ בָּה וַהֲפָךְ בָּה, דְּכֹלָּא בָהּ; וּבָהּ תֶּחֱזֵי,

at the advanced age of eighty, one should be ever cautious not to fall into the trap of sin or heresy. Yochanan the Kohen Gadol served in that office for eighty years and later became a victim of heresy. Thus, even at eighty, one needs spiritual fortitude to overcome the panderings of the Evil Inclination.

בֶּן תִּשְׁעִים לָשׂוּחַ — *a ninety-year-old becomes stooped over.* Someone that age generally walks bent over. An alternate reading is לַשּׁוּחַ, *to the pit.* If he is unable to function physically, a ninety-year-old is close to the grave (*Rashi, Rav*).

R' Yonah and HaChassid Yaavetz interpret לָשׂוּחַ as *to pray* based on the Talmudic comment that the term שִׂיחָה refers to prayer (see *Genesis* 24:63 and *Berachos* 26a). Having refined himself and freed himself from the grip of sin, a ninety-year-old should devote himself to Torah study, the perfor-

mance of *mitzvos*, and prayer. According to *Midrash Shmuel*, this also teaches that one who no longer has the strength to sin physically must nonetheless be careful to guard his speech.

בֶּן מֵאָה כְּאִלּוּ מֵת וְעָבַר וּבָטֵל מִן הָעוֹלָם — *a hundred-year-old is as if he were dead, passed away and ceased from the world.* As one approaches the age of one hundred, his mental faculties and physical strength often fail him, sometimes to a very serious degree (*Rashi*). *Tiferes Yisrael* interprets this on a more positive note as a description of one who spiritually and emotionally has disengaged from this world and its false allure. *Midrash Shmuel* elaborates: One who can no longer sin either through deed or word may now focus on repenting his earlier sins without fear of falling into sin again. Nonetheless, one should not delay repentance until such a late stage of life.

Mishnah 26

בֶּן בַּג בַּג אוֹמֵר — *Ben Bag Bag says.* Yochanan ben Bag Bag was one of the early *Tannaim,* a contemporary of Hillel [see *Kiddushin* 10b] (*Tiferes Yisrael*). Like Ben Zoma, he died young and had not received the title rabbi [see 4:1, s.v. בן זומא אמר] (*Tosafos Yom Tov*). *Midrash Shmuel* quotes *Rashbam* that both Ben Bag Bag and Ben Hei Hei (quoted later in the mishnah) were descendants of proselytes whose names were disguised to protect them from informers who would have turned them over to the Romans. Some interpret בַּג בַּג as an acronym of בֶּן גֵּר בֶּן גִּיּוֹרֶת, *the son of male and female proselytes.* *Tosafos Yom Tov* cites a view that the name Hei Hei alludes to the first "proselytes," Abraham and Sarah, to each of whose names God added a ה, *hei.* Thus the name אַבְרָם became אַבְרָהָם and שָׂרַי became שָׂרָה. The name Ben Bag Bag also contains

this allusion because the numerical value of בַּג (2 and 3) equals ה (5). See *Tosafos Chagigah* 9b.

The Talmud cites many questions that Ben Bag Bag asked of R' Yehudah ben Beseira in Netzivin (*Kiddushin* 6b and *Yerushalmi Kesubos* 5:4).

הֲפָךְ בָּה וַהֲפָךְ בָּה — *Delve in it* [the Torah] *and* [continue to] *delve in it.* Study the Torah incessantly, for constant preoccupation with it will uplift you. And through constant review, you will discover new facets of Torah every time you study it (*Rashi, Tosafos Yom Tov*), and review will enable you to clarify subjects that had been murky (*Meiri*). Alternatively, Ben Bag Bag exhorts people to analyze every aspect of the Torah (*Rashi*).

According to *Midrash Shmuel*, Ben Bag Bag responds to the program of study delineated in the

⋖§ **Removing the impediment.** *Yechahein Pe'er* quotes a *Zohar* that "one who has vanquished the snake [a metaphor for the Evil Inclination] is allowed to marry the daughter of the king [a metaphor for the power of prayer]." A ninety-year-old has achieved a spiritual refinement that grants him the power of prayer.

becomes stooped over; a hundred-year-old is as if he were dead, passed away and ceased from the world.

26. Ben Bag Bag says: Delve in it [the Torah] and [continue to] delve in it, for everything is in it; look deeply into it;

---

last mishnah. He insists that one should never suppose that if he studied Scripture, Mishnah, and Gemara for five years each, he has become an accomplished scholar who may now cease studying. Instead, he prescribes lifelong study, for the Torah is endless and even a lifetime is too short to master it.

Ben Bag Bag warns man to never neglect the Torah even after his years of full-time study are over. Though married and bearing the responsibility of earning a living and being a husband and father, one must recognize the primary responsibility to maintain a strong commitment to Torah study. The term הֲפָךְ בָּהּ, *delve in it*, is repeated, to emphasize the crucial importance of every Jew being linked to steady and vibrant Torah study (*Tiferes Yisrael*).

Mili d'Avos adds that even if one has not been successful at his Torah study, he should not despair. Let him continue to delve in the Torah, and

eventually the Torah will share its riches with him, and he will find success.

דְּכֹלָּה בָהּ — *for everything is in it.* The Torah is a self-contained guide to life; all of the world's wisdom is contained in it (*R' Yonah*).

וּבָה תֶּחֱזֵי — *look deeply into it.* The translation follows *Rashi*. One should look deeply and constantly into Torah, for it yields its messages only after one penetrates below the surface.

Rambam and *Sefer HaMussar* render וּבָה תֶּחֱזֵי as *and through it you will view.* Torah refines and sharpens the mind so that one can perceive the truth; one becomes enlightened through the light of Torah and all spiritual darkness is removed from his heart. Thus it grants one the power to view the world around him with a spiritual clarity.

Sfas Emes views this as a continuation of the previous teaching. One who labors continuously and tirelessly in Torah will eventually feel

---

◄§ **Everything is in the Torah.** *Seder HaDoros* reports a harrowing incident that highlights the broad range of information found in the Torah.

Avner, a student of Ramban, drifted from Torah Judaism, and eventually rose to prominence and became a powerful and feared figure in the government. One Yom Kippur he had his former teacher summoned to his palace. In front of Ramban, Avner had a pig beheaded and then cut out a choice slice, which he promptly cooked and ate. Insolently he demanded, "Tell me, how many sins punishable by spiritual excision (*kares*) did I transgress?" Ramban replied, "Four." Avner retorted, "You are wrong — it is five." A hot halachic debate ensued between the two. Finally Ramban gave Avner a sharp stare and the apostate stopped his harangue.

Ramban then asked him why he had abandoned his heritage. Avner replied, "I once heard you expound on the Biblical portion of *Haazinu* and say that all the *mitzvos* of the Torah and future events are alluded to in that portion. I was sure that was impossible, so I began reconsidering the path my life was taking. Before long, I decided to abandon my religion altogether."

The startled sage answered, "I am still sure. Ask about anything you would like and I will show you the allusion in *Haazinu.*" Avner demanded, "Where is my name alluded to in *Haazinu?*" Ramban retired to a corner for a moment and whispered a short prayer for Divine intervention. Suddenly his eyes lit up and he told the Jewish apostate, "The verse אַפְאֵיהֶם אַשְׁבִּיתָה מֵאֱנוֹשׁ זִכְרָם, [*I said*] *I will scatter them, I will cause their memory to cease from man* (*Deuteronomy* 32:26) alludes to you. The third letters of those four words spell your name."

Shocked, Avner broke down and wept. *"Rebbe,* is there any hope for me?" Ramban replied, "You heard the words of *Haazinu.*"

Avner repented. All alone on a boat, he floated out to sea and was never heard from again.

---

its majesty and realize that the Torah contains everything.

The *Baal Shem Tov* taught that the primordial light that God hid away for the righteous (see *Rashi* to *Genesis* 1:4) is found in the Torah. Hence, one who studies Torah enjoys the spiritual illumination of that original, brilliant light.

Tiferes Yisrael comments that this stich refers to the twenty years from the age of forty to sixty. During this period, a person needs wisdom and insight to advise his children on marriage, a means of livelihood, and other such matters. Ben Bag Bag counsels that the Torah should be the source of his inspiration and guidance.

וְסִיב וּבְלֵה בָּה — *grow old and gray over it.* Even in old age, one must toil at Torah study and not imagine that he can retire to more relaxing matters (*Rambam, Rav*).

The Torah is the only thing in life for which it is worth wearing out one's strength. One should not rely on his memory but rather he should grow old and worn from constant review.

Tiferes Yisrael adds: Even in old age, the study of Torah is rejuvenating and grants its students a youthful freshness.

וּמִנָּה לָא תָזוּעַ — *do not stir from it.* Day or night, one should never abandon his study of the Torah (*Rashi*). According to *Midrash Shmuel,* this qualifies the previous mishnah, which prescribed a proscribed amount of time for each area of learning. Nonetheless, Torah study must be a lifelong pursuit. While one can acquire a basic knowledge of Torah in his first twenty years, only through incessant study can one mine the wealth of knowledge and insight of the Torah. *Rav* sees this as a call to refrain from the pursuit of other disciplines at the expense of growth in Torah study.

Alternatively, *Midrash Shmuel* renders the phrase *and from it* [*one may learn*] *not to stir.* A steady connection to God through His Torah inspires a strong sense of confidence and provides the strength of character to fear nothing or no one but God. Even in old age, when one no longer has the physical strength for the grueling regimen that intense Torah study entails, he still must try to the best of his ability (*R' Yonah*).

⋙ **For everything is in it.** Rabbi Elchanan Wasserman offered the following analogy: If someone's friend tells him that his face is dirty and another friend tells him that it is sparkling clean, how can he know the truth? By looking into a mirror. Likewise, when one has doubts in life, whether spiritual or mundane, he should use the Torah as his mirror, allowing him to gain a true and realistic perspective of his own situation. Thus, whenever one is in doubt, the *Tanna* counsels him to look deeply into Torah, for through it he will view all of life with clarity and objectivity.

The Vilna *Gaon* suggested that if someone is in doubt about any major decision, he should study the Torah until he feels sincerely that he is learning purely for the sake of Heaven. Then he should think about his problem. Whatever he decides to do at such a time will be correct.

⋙ **It can give — if you take it.** Rabbi Hirsch of Ziditchov offered a homiletical rendering of the mishnah.

Study Torah constantly, for it humbles man. Then if you realize that you have not accomplished much, and you feel that *you have no good portion,* you should understand that this feeling of humility is הֵימֶנָּה, *from it.*

Rabbi Chaim Soloveitchik of Brisk once upbraided a wealthy Jew who was equally renowned for his scholarship and his stinginess. R' Chaim interpreting our mishnah homiletically, saying, "Even if you study the Talmud page after page, and even if you completed the entire Talmud — even more, even if you worked so hard at Torah study that you became old before your time — nonetheless, it is possible that you have gained no מִדָּה טוֹבָה, *good character trait*, from all of your study."

The wealthy miser took the message to heart and began loosening his purse strings for the benefit of the poor.

grow old and gray over it; do not stir from it, for you can have no better portion than it. Ben Hei Hei says: The reward is in proportion to the exertion.

שֶׁאֵין לְךָ מִדָּה טוֹבָה הֵימֶנָּה — *for you can have no better portion than it.* Man can have no better occupation than the Torah. As the old Yiddish lullaby puts it, תורה איז די אך די בעסטע סחורה, *Torah is in fact the best merchandise.*

Sefer HaMussar explains this statement with the Talmudic teaching that the study of Torah, more than anything else, allows man to enjoy its fruits in this world while storing away the principle for further reward in the World to Come (see *Shabbos* 127a). No investment is as profitable as the time and effort spent by man trying to understand the word of God.

בֶּן הֵא הֵא אוֹמֵר — *Ben Hei Hei says.* See earlier, s.v. בן בג בג.

Mussar Avos offers a novel suggestion about the authorship of this dictum. The Talmud teaches that in order to dissuade potential converts from joining the Jewish people, we warn the candidate of the terrible oppression that Jews suffer in exile. If he replies that he wants to convert in spite of it, he is a viable candidate. Thus Ben Hei Hei said, "The reward is in proportion to the exertion."

לְפוּם צַעֲרָא אַגְרָא — *The reward is in proportion to the exertion.* The reward for observing God's commandments increases in proportion to the effort and difficulty needed for its performance (*Rashi, Rav*).

Midrash Shmuel interprets this stich as a source of solace to people who are not intellectually gifted. God's reward for Torah study is not in proportion to the degree of one's success, but to the amount and quality of effort that one puts into it. If one toiled hard at learning he will be amply rewarded for the exertion, even if he failed to accomplish a great deal.

Rambam comments that the mishnah decries those who feel that the Torah can be acquired casually. It teaches that Torah wisdom is acquired only when a person studies with reverence for his teacher; light reading and superficial study do not produce Torah scholarship. The Sages (*Kesubos* 103b) homiletically interpret the words of King Solomon, אַף חָכְמָתִי עָמְדָה לִי, *still my wisdom stayed with me* (*Ecclesiastes* 2:9), in this vein. The wisdom that I learned with אַף, great effort and under trying conditions, remained with me.

According to *R' Yonah,* this mishnah is addressed to those who continue their spiritual efforts even in old age when their strength wanes and every effort is painful. We are therefore

---

⋖§ **Gold versus flour.** The Chofetz Chaim writes that those who study and support Torah in times when it is unpopular and even scorned receive greater reward than those who do so when spiritual pursuits are honored and respected. He illustrated this idea with a parable:

A city dweller invited his country cousin for a visit. The city dweller took his cousin on a tour and showed him the wealth and plenty of the city's shops. The visitor saw large stores with sacks of flour piled to the ceiling, fabric stores with cotton cloth filling the shelves to capacity. Then he saw shops that sell silk, in which only a few shelves held merchandise. In the silver store, even fewer shelves were full. Finally the city dweller showed him shops that sell gold and diamonds. There, all the merchandise was contained in a few boxes; the rest of the store was empty.

When the country cousin went back to his village, people asked him what he saw. He began praising the large stores with the sacks of flour and rolls of cotton, and spoke disparagingly about the half empty stores. A wise man interjected, "Foolish country bumpkin! Don't you realize that one small box in the gold and diamond shop is worth more than all the merchandise in all the full stores?"

Likewise, concluded the Chofetz Chaim, the few people who study and support Torah in times like these are like the gold and diamonds. Even though they are few, they are more valuable in God's eyes than the thousands of people who waste their lives on purely mundane matters.

❧ ❧ ❧

רַבִּי חֲנַנְיָא בֶּן עֲקַשְׁיָא אוֹמֵר: רָצָה הַקָּדוֹשׁ בָּרוּךְ הוּא לְזַכּוֹת אֶת יִשְׂרָאֵל, לְפִיכָךְ הִרְבָּה לָהֶם תּוֹרָה וּמִצְוֹת, שֶׁנֶּאֱמַר: ,,יהוה חָפֵץ לְמַעַן צִדְקוֹ, יַגְדִּיל תּוֹרָה וְיַאְדִּיר."

---

taught that man receives reward for all the pain.

Magen Avos suggests that Ben Bag Bag and Ben Hei Hei were Babylonians, like Hillel, and thus spoke Aramaic rather than Hebrew. According to

Midrash Shmuel, Rabbi Yehudah *HaNasi* stated this in the vernacular since Torah study and the efforts toward it are so fundamental to human existence that it is imperative that everyone appreciate the

---

❧ **For hard work.** The prayer recited at celebration marking the completion of a Talmudic tractate includes the statement that "We [Jews] toil and receive reward while they [non-Jews] toil and do not receive reward." The Chofetz Chaim explained with a parable:

A craftsman offers a bid based on the cost of materials plus his estimate of how long the job will take. If he could not finish in time or needs more materials, he must absorb the additional cost; he cannot pass it on to the customer. God, however, rewards man not only for the completed *mitzvah* but also for all the toil that went into it.

R' S. R. Hirsch states this truth with his customary eloquence: "It is not the quantitative measure of the moral and spiritual goals you have actually achieved that constitute the true worth of a life's course. It is the measure of earnest striving, of devoted endeavor, of sacrifices made and privation endured, all for the realization of good purposes that determine the truth worth of both a man and his life. Actual success can only come from the hands of God Himself."

An elderly Jerusalemite witnessed an incident that illustrates this concept. He had been a guest of Rabbi Elazar of Poltisk, when a non-Jewish painter who had painted R' Elazar's home came for his pay. The mistress of the house refused to pay him. "The work is unacceptable. Not only did you not make the house look better, you actually made it look worse. How can I pay you?" she said.

The painter agreed. "True, I made nothing better, but how can you send me away with nothing after I put in so many backbreaking hours?" R' Elazar heard his plea and agreed that he should be paid.

That night the guest from Jerusalem heard his host praying, "True, O God, I have not fixed much, and I have even ruined a lot. But Master of the Universe, how can you send me away with nothing after all the backbreaking work I put into Your service?"

Rabbi Chanania ben Akashia says: The Holy One, Blessed is He, wished to confer merit upon Israel; therefore He gave them Torah and *mitzvos* in abundance, as it is said: *HASHEM desired, for the sake of its [Israel's] righteousness, that the Torah be made great and glorious.*

---

beauty of Torah.

Maharal suggests two possible explanations for the use of Aramaic: (a) Ben Bag Bag and Ben Hei Hei were converts who spoke Aramaic. (b) Torah and the free choice that results in reward are two gifts that angels do not enjoy. Since angels do not understand Aramaic, these truths regarding Torah and reward are explained in Aramaic.

⋙ **Reward for effort.** R' Avraham of Slonim wrote a deep Kabbalistic work entitled *Chessed LeAvraham.* When his student and literary scribe Rabbi Yehudah Leib Kostelanitz studied one of the essays contained in the book, he was overwhelmed by its profundity and depth. "Rebbe," he said to R' Avraham, "this must have been written with Divine assistance!" The *Rebbe* interrupted him. "That I can't tell you, but I did study Torah under conditions of privation. The reward I received for this was that God enlightened my eyes to understand His Torah."

פרק ששי ೫

Chapter Six

כָּל יִשְׂרָאֵל יֵשׁ לָהֶם חֵלֶק לָעוֹלָם הַבָּא, שֶׁנֶּאֱמַר:
,,וְעַמֵּךְ כֻּלָּם צַדִּיקִים, לְעוֹלָם יִירְשׁוּ אָרֶץ, נֵצֶר
מַטָּעַי, מַעֲשֵׂה יָדַי לְהִתְפָּאֵר.''

All Israel has a share in the World to Come, as it is said:
*And your people are all righteous; they shall inherit the land
forever; a branch of My plantings, My handiwork, in which to
take pride (Isaiah 60:21).*

שָׁנוּ חֲכָמִים בִּלְשׁוֹן הַמִּשְׁנָה. בָּרוּךְ שֶׁבָּחַר בָּהֶם וּבְמִשְׁנָתָם.

[א] רַבִּי מֵאִיר אוֹמֵר: כָּל הָעוֹסֵק בַּתּוֹרָה לִשְׁמָהּ זוֹכֶה לִדְבָרִים הַרְבֵּה; וְלֹא עוֹד, אֶלָּא

This chapter is not part of the Talmudic Tractate *Avos*, but is a collection of *baraisos*, which were selected because they are related to the major themes of the tractate. This chapter brings to six the number of chapters in the expanded *Avos,* corresponding to the six Sabbaths between Pesach and Shavuos, during which *Avos* is studied, one chapter each Sabbath. The inclusion of the sixth chapter, as well as the custom of reading the tractate on Sabbath afternoons, is of early origin; it is mentioned in the ninth-century *Siddur Rav Amram Gaon* as the custom of the great Babylonian academies.

The first five chapters deal with the proper model of moral and ethical character development, which is a prerequisite to Torah study. This final chapter speaks of the beauty of the Torah itself, and its elevating inspiring effect on those who study it לִשְׁמָהּ, *for its own sake*; consequently this chapter is studied on the Sabbath before Shavuos, the Festival of the Giving of the Torah. Appropriately, the sixth chapter is known as פֶּרֶק קִנְיָן תּוֹרָה, *The Chapter of Acquisition of the Torah.* It is also known as *The Baraisa of R' Meir*, because it begins with a *baraisa* that is attributed to him (*Rashi, Midrash Shmuel, HaChassid Yaavetz*).

In most communities, the Sabbath study of *Avos* is continued throughout the summer, until the Sabbath before Rosh Hashanah.

שָׁנוּ חֲכָמִים — *The Sages taught* [this chapter]. This phrase is the Hebrew equivalent of the familiar Aramaic תָּנוּ רַבָּנָן, which the Talmud generally uses to introduce a *baraisa*. The word *baraisa*, literally *outside*, refers to Tannaitic teachings were not included in the Mishnah, but which were preserved "outside" of it. Alternatively, the Mishnah includes dicta that were taught at the academy of Rabbi Yehudah *HaNasi*, redacter of the Mishnah and leader of the nation, while the teachings known as *baraisos* were formulated "outside" his academy by his disciples, R' Chiya, R' Oshaya, and Bar

Kappara [see *Chullin* 141b and *Yerushalmi, Horayos* 3:5].

בִּלְשׁוֹן הַמִּשְׁנָה — *In the language of the Mishnah.* These teachings were stated in the concise style of the Mishnah. Like the Mishnah, few *baraisos* cite source verses to prove their points, nor do they explicate the meaning of Scriptural verses (*Meiri*), and they were written in Hebrew, following the Mishnaic idiom (*Midrash Shmuel*).

בָּרוּךְ שֶׁבָּחַר בָּהֶם וּבְמִשְׁנָתָם — *Blessed is He Who chose them and their teaching.* God chose the

---

◆§ **In the name of he who said it.** Virtually all of the dicta in *Avos* are quoted in the name of a particular *Tanna*, which implies that it is important to know the identify of the author. The necessity of this is obvious with regard to halachic rulings, because the decision-making process often dictates that a sage is most authoritative in certain subject areas or that the halachah follows him in disputes with specific sages, but not with others. But in matters of morals, ethics, or character development, why is it important to know who made each statement?

Rabbi Meir Shapiro explained that the sages quoted in *Avos* taught more by example than by the spoken word. Moral authority among the Jewish people stems not from eloquent speakers or composers of provocative aphorisms, but from people who actually live by their teachings.

For example, Hillel the Elder was a paragon of humility; even when contentious people conspired to

The Sages taught [this chapter] in the language of the Mishnah. Blessed is He Who chose them and their teaching.

1. Rabbi Meir said: Whoever engages in Torah study for its own sake merits many things; furthermore, [the

---

Sages of Israel as the legitimate expositors of His Torah. The Torah itself enjoins Israel: *According to the teaching that they will teach you, and according to the judgment that they will say to you, shall you do; you shall not deviate from the word that they will tell you, right or left (Deuteronomy 17:11).* The verse requires that even one who is convinced that a decision of the Sages is wrong — even if it seems to be saying that "right is left and left is right" — one must abide by the ruling — and certainly one must abide by the ruling if he understands that it is right (*Rashi* ad loc.).

Thus, God chose the Sages as the legitimate expositors of His will, and this introductory paragraph was written in praise of them as authors of the *baraisos* that comprise this chapter

Mishnah 1

רַבִּי מֵאִיר אוֹמֵר — *Rabbi Meir said.* For a biographical sketch of Rabbi Meir, see 4:12.

כָּל הָעוֹסֵק בַּתּוֹרָה לִשְׁמָהּ — *Whoever engages in Torah study for its own sake.* Ideally, this is how the Torah should be studied, as the Talmud teaches, "Do things for the sake of the deed, study them for their own sake" (*Nedarim* 62a). The exact definition of the term לִשְׁמָהּ, *for its own sake,* and its antonym שֶׁלֹּא לִשְׁמָהּ, *not for its own sake,* is a matter of controversy. A full discussion is beyond the scope of this work, but we will present some of the main views very briefly:

(a) *Shelah* (to *Maseches Shevuos*) defines learning *for its own sake* as study that is a means to the proper practice of the Torah's laws. How good it is if one studies with the feeling that "I wish to study Torah in order that it bring me to practice, to proper character, and to a knowledge of God's Torah."

Rambam (*Hilchos Talmud Torah* 3:3-5) seems to concur with this definition: "Not one of the commandments outweighs the study of Torah; rather, the study of Torah excels all the other commandments, for study leads to practice, therefore study always takes precedence over practice ... Man is first judged on his study, and only afterwards on the rest of his practice. Therefore, the Sages said, 'A man should always engage in Torah whether for its own sake or not for its own sake, for as a result of [study] not for its own sake he will come to [study] for its own sake.' " [See also *Sefer Chassidim* §544 Margolios ed.] Since *Rambam* defines the greatness of study as the vehicle that leads to performance, his later reference to *for its own sake* presumably applies to such study.

(b) In *Hilchos Teshuvah* (10:1-2,4-5), however, *Rambam* seems to apply the concept of *for its own sake* to the practice of all commandments, not just Torah study as a vehicle for fulfillment. There he defines this concept as acting for no ulterior motive except the love of God, saying that one should not practice the commandments and engage in the wisdom of Torah in order to receive God's blessings, nor even in order to merit the life

---

provoke him to anger, he remained calm and friendly, and could not be goaded to anger or to retort sharply, even to people who deserved it (see *Shabbos* 30b-31a). Hillel was the most qualified person, therefore, to teach that one should aspire to be like Aaron, the consummate peacemaker (1:12).

The introductory statement to this chapter alludes to this message. By saying that they taught this chapter *in the language of the Mishnah*, the *baraisa* means to say that they followed the pattern of the Mishnah in attributing statements to those who made them — and the reason for this is because God chose not only their teachings, but He chose *them*, i.e., they earned their role as moral guides of the nation because they personally were people who were of such an exalted stature.

hereafter, nor should one refrain from sin out of fear of punishment and loss of life in the hereafter; for this is the way of the ignorant. However, one who serves out of love is one who is motivated by no extraneous or ulterior cause, but engages in truth for the love of truth, as it is said, *to love HASHEM, your God* (Deuteronomy 6:5): "Whatever you do, you must do only out of love . . . And whoever engages in it not because of fear and not in order to receive reward but only because of love for the Lord of all the earth Who commanded thus — this is engaging in Torah *for its own sake*."

(c) *Likutei Amarim* (*Tanya* chapter 5) defines *for its own sake* as study with the intent to attach one's soul to God through the comprehension of Torah, each person according to his own intellect.

(d) Rabbi Chaim of Volozhin devotes the entire fourth section of *Nefesh HaChaim* to the definition of לִשְׁמָה. Based on *Rosh* to *Nedarim* (62a), he defines it not as "for the sake of knowing how to perform the commandments" (as does the *Shelah*), nor as "for the sake of God" (as does *Rambam* in *Hilchos Teshuvah*), nor even as "a means to cleave to God" (as defined by the *Tanya*). Rather, it means study purely for the sake of the Torah itself, i.e., to know and understand its contents and to apply his knowledge to enhance his understanding and solve new problems (see *Nefesh HaChaim* 4:3).

זוֹכֶה לִדְבָרִים הַרְבֵּה — *merits many things.* I.e., the qualities that are enumerated below (*Rashi, Machzor Vitry*). According to *Midrash Shmuel* and *Tiferes Yisrael*, he merits many things *in addition* to the items enumerated below. The mishnah's list includes instances of spiritual success, which are a natural result of the refining quality of Torah study, but in addition to those, R' Meir promises that there will be many *worldly* benefits, such as long life, health, wealth, and honor. None of these would seem to flow naturally from study, but they are God's additional blessing to those who study the Torah for its own sake.

The blessings that await such a person are too bountiful to be specified. The Talmud (*Berachos* 34b) teaches: "All the prophets prophesied regarding the exalted status of one who marries his daughter to a Torah scholar, does business with Torah scholars [thus helping them earn a living], or allows them to benefit from his property. But regarding the exalted nature of the *talmid chacham* himself, 'no eyes but God's have seen it' " [see *Isaiah* 64:3] (*R' Chaim of Volozhin*).

Chasam Sofer homiletically renders דְּבָרִים הַרְבֵּה as *many words.* While most conversations of average people tend to be fairly insignificant, the words of an authentic Torah scholar are meaningful. The Talmud teaches: "Even the mundane

⋰§ **Chamber leading to chamber.** R' Chaim certainly agrees that Torah study *results* in a connection of one's soul to God. His objection to earlier definitions of לִשְׁמָה is in regard to the *intent* of Torah study. "For when one engages [in the study of] Talmud and Codes and *Tosafos* and in his research and dialectical discourse concerning them, he is attached to the Holy One, for all comes from Sinai . . . The Holy One and Torah are a unity, and he who is attached to His Torah is attached to Him.

". . . The main [purpose of] study is not merely to cleave to God, but to understand, through the Torah, the commandments and laws, and to know all of it, its principles and details, thoroughly; and also, to attain the knowledge of the secrets of the wonders of His works and the contemplation of His glory . . . The more one learns, the more he wants to learn. By means of the light that he has already attained, he can see that there is yet more light, and can hope to attain that too.

"It may be compared to one who enters a room in the royal treasury, which is filled with all kinds of precious objects. There he sees a door leading to an inner chamber, and in it he finds yet another door to yet other inner chambers. The closer one comes to the chamber of the king himself, the more beautiful it is, compared to the chamber before it. Had he not entered the outermost chamber, he would know nothing of other, inner chambers.

"So it is with Torah: By means of the light one attains initially, he sees that there is yet greater light, and so on. Thus one desires to understand and attain more, until he has attained all the mysteries of the world and its fullness" (*Ruach Chaim*).

speech of Torah scholars should be studied" (*Avodah Zarah* 19b). Thus, one who studies Torah for its own sake merits many *words*, since his Torah imbues all of his speech with significance.

וְלֹא עוֹד, אֶלָּא שֶׁכָּל הָעוֹלָם כֻּלּוֹ כְּדַאי הוּא לוֹ — *furthermore, [the creation of] the entire world is worthwhile for his sake alone.* All of Creation is justified for the sake of such a person, since its purpose is realized through him (*Rashi, Midrash Shmuel*).

Tiferes Yisrael clarifies: It befits such a person to make use of all the amenities of this world for his holy mission. In truth, the entire world was created to serve just such a person. *Midrash Shmuel* notes that the *baraisa* speaks of the *entire* world. All of world history, from Creation to the Messianic age, is not in vain even if only one such person ever lives.

Ruach Chaim interprets *the entire world* not as the history of the world, but as its very *existence*, for if there were to be a total absence of Torah study in the world for even a moment, all of Creation would revert to nothingness. Thus, one who studies Torah for its own sake may very likely be the one who sustains the world at any given moment.

נִקְרָא רֵעַ, אָהוּב — *He is called, "Friend, Beloved."* The translation follows *Rashi*, who views *friend* and *beloved* as two separate appellations. That God

considers one who studies Torah for its own sake as His friend is based on *Psalms* 139:17: *To me — how precious are Your dear ones [friends], O God!* Furthermore, the Torah student is considered God's *beloved*, as King Solomon says in the name of God, *I love those who love Me* (*Proverbs* 8:17).

HaChassid Yaavetz renders רֵעַ in the sense of "a junior partner." One who studies Torah with pure motives helps God, so to speak, in sustaining the world, and is therefore His partner, since God provides sustenance for all in the merit of the righteous. King Solomon teaches: צַדִּיק יְסוֹד עוֹלָם, *a righteous man is the foundation of the world* (*Proverbs* 10:25), for he is a conduit through which God showers His beneficence upon all — and because he is God's partner, he is beloved by all who recognize how indispensable he is to their own survival. Such a person was R' Chanina ben Dosa, whose father said that the entire world receives sustenance in his merit (see *Berachos* 17b).

Alternatively, *HaChassid Yaavetz* interprets these two words as a single appellation, i.e., such a person is called a *beloved friend*. In this view, these two words are hardly redundant, because not all friends are truly beloved. Many friendly relationships are nothing more than a functional camaraderie in which each party has a personal vested interest. But once any of the partners no longer stands to gain from the relationship, the friendship

---

◆§ **Positive outlook.** Rabbi Shmuel Alter renders this phrase homiletically: *the entire world* [becomes comprehensible] *to him as being worthwhile.* One who learns Torah for its own sake begins to view everything from a Godly perspective. Just as God's plan includes a function for everything and everyone, so one who studies the Godly wisdom of Torah begins to view all people in a positive light; the entire world becomes *worthwhile,* i.e., meaningful and fulfilling to him. Furthermore, his exposure to the endless depths of the Torah teaches him of his own insignificance, so that he becomes overawed by how little he knows compared to the infinity of God's intelligence. Knowing that there is so much that is beyond human comprehension, he begins to view those around him in a more positive light.

◆§ **Nonstop survival.** It was the practice of the *Netziv* of Volozhin that when Yom Kippur was over and everyone rushed out to break the long fast, he would remain behind and study, until the first students came back after their meal to resume their own studies. He said that since the survival of the universe depends on constant Torah study, there must always be someone in the *bais midrash*, especially at times like the hour after the fast, when famished people are hurrying to refresh themselves. Similarly, there have been yeshivos over the years where the students instituted a system of shifts, so that there would always be people in the study hall, even during the night and at mealtimes.

הַמָּקוֹם, אוֹהֵב אֶת הַבְּרִיּוֹת, מְשַׂמֵּחַ אֶת הַמָּקוֹם, מְשַׂמֵּחַ אֶת הַבְּרִיּוֹת. וּמַלְבַּשְׁתּוֹ עֲנָוָה וְיִרְאָה; וּמַכְשַׁרְתּוֹ לִהְיוֹת צַדִּיק, חָסִיד, יָשָׁר, וְנֶאֱמָן; וּמְרַחַקְתּוֹ מִן הַחֵטְא, וּמְקָרַבְתּוֹ לִידֵי זְכוּת.

of convenience often disintegrates. Of a different ilk is a friendship based on true love. Even when such friends suffer disappointments, the relationship survives the strain. Similarly, one who studies Torah for its own sake will retain his love of God no matter what his lot in life. Hence, such a person deserves to be called רֵעַ אָהוּב, *a beloved friend*. God responds to this love by providing for the world in his merit — even if others do not deserve it.

Rambam (*Deuteronomy* 7:6-8) defines this ability to maintain love in the face of adversity as the reason God chose Israel as His nation. "For in his beloved, a lover seeks one who can bear everything [all the difficulties] that the lover places upon him. Israel, more than all the other nations, befits this role, as the Sages taught (*Beitzah* 25b) . . . Israel is the obstinate one among the nations, for it is able to withstand trials."

אוֹהֵב אֶת הַמָּקוֹם — *He loves the Omnipresent.* The mishnah refers to one who does God's will and studies His Torah out of love [see *Rambam Hilchos Teshuvah* 10:5] (*Tiferes Yisrael*).

According to *Midrash Shmuel*, this is a continuation of the earlier part of the mishnah, which teaches that the merit of Torah study for its own sake sustains the world. The literature of Kabbalah teaches that God created the world because His goodness decreed that He have the opportunity to confer good upon beings other than Himself, and consequently a person who studies Torah in the ideal way affords God with the means of carrying out His wish to bring blessing into the world. In this sense, one who enables God to carry out His desire, so to speak, shows true love for Him.

Chida offers an insight into the profundity of the relationship between a Torah scholar and God. It is an honor for a person when illustrious people love him. It is an even greater honor when those illustrious people are proud to say that person loves them. Similarly, one who studies Torah for its own sake is called God's friend. Then the mishnah goes further and states that God is proud, as it were, to say that such a person *loves the Omnipresent,* so exalted is this person!

אוֹהֵב אֶת הַבְּרִיּוֹת — *he loves* [His] *creatures.* One who studies Torah for its own sake loves all God's creatures without cynicism or malice of any kind, simply because they are God's creatures (*Tiferes Yisrael*). The manifestation of this love, as mentioned above, is that his deeds sustain Creation (*Midrash Shmuel*).

HaChassid Yaavetz views these last two phrases — love of God and love of His creatures — as interrelated. One who loves God *and not himself* is never jealous of others and does not begrudge them anything. Since jealousy and the obsessive

⋖ **A friend in need.** In this light, *HaChassid Yaavetz* interprets the phrase רֵעִים הָאֲהוּבִים, *the beloved friends,* which appears in the blessings recited at wedding celebrations. A loving wife will continue to respect and love her husband even when financial pressures prevent him from providing for her needs and the needs of the household, and a loving husband will reciprocate even if household and emotional pressure interfere with his wife's performance of her tasks. Not so when the marriage is merely a functional relationship. Then, the partners may feel justified in abandoning it if their needs are not being met. Thus we wish a newly married couple that the love between them be deep and enduring, and that they remain *beloved friends* and loyal partners all their lives.

⋖ **The greatest love.** R' Yitzchak Hutner once told a group of students, "The greatest public service a young man can do for *Klal Yisrael* (the Jewish people) is to study Torah." Torah is the lifeblood of the nation and Torah scholars are its heart. The more spiritual blood they pump to the rest of the nation the better the nation's spiritual health. Thus the greatest expression of love for the Jewish nation is deep, passionate, and committed study of Torah.

pursuit of honor are among the greatest causes of hatred among people, one who truly loves God will also love His creatures.

מְשַׂמֵּחַ אֶת הַמָּקוֹם, מְשַׂמֵּחַ אֶת הַבְּרִיּוֹת — *he gladdens the Omnipresent, he gladdens [His] creatures.* By bringing others closer to Torah, either actively or by serving as a role model, one gladdens God. Furthermore, by introducing people to the Torah, he gladdens them and earns their gratitude (*Rashi*).

Unlike the path of sin, which is initially sweet but ultimately bitter, the Torah way is sometimes difficult at the outset, but eventually one comes to appreciate that the words of Torah are *sweeter than honey — than drippings from combs* [*Psalms* 19:11] (*HaChassid Yaavetz*).

Aish Dos sees the two as linked: When a Jew is in pain or emotionally upset, the Divine Presence, so to speak, is also pained (*Sanhedrin* 46a). On the other hand, one who gladdens God's creatures gladdens Him, as well.

וּמַלְבַּשְׁתּוֹ עֲנָוָה וְיִרְאָה — *[The Torah] clothes him in humility and fear [of God].* One who studies Torah for its own sake is humbled by its vastness and depth.

The *Midrash* (*Vayikra Rabbah* 37) portrays the effect of Torah on those who study it: Just as large grapes on the vine hang lower than the smaller grapes, so the more one grows in Torah, the more insignificant he appears in his own eyes.

וּמַכְשַׁרְתּוֹ לִהְיוֹת צַדִּיק, חָסִיד, יָשָׁר, וְנֶאֱמָן — *it makes him fit to be righteous, devout, fair, and faithful.* The study of Torah for its own sake prepares one emotionally to attain elevated spiritual levels. He can aspire to be *righteous* in *mitzvos* between man and God, to be scrupulously *devout* in *mitzvos* between man and his fellow man, and to *fairness* in his own personal deportment and ethical development

(בֵּין אָדָם לְעַצְמוֹ). All of these spiritual attainments will be consistent and enduring [נֶאֱמָן is used in the sense of מֵימָיו נֶאֱמָנִים, *its waters are enduring* (*Isaiah* 33:16)] (*Tiferes Yisrael*).

The Talmud relates the tragic story of Yochanan, who served as Kohen Gadol seventy years, only to become a Sadducee at the end of his life. One who studies Torah for its own sake will be protected against such a downfall (*Midrash Shmuel*). *Emunas Yisrael* relates these four attributes to perfection in different areas of life: *righteous* in faith, *devout* in action (beyond the letter of the law), *fair* in his emotions, *faithful* and honest in his words.

Let no one think that only spiritually great people can achieve Torah study for its own sake. The *baraisa* shatters this misconception, by saying that one who is *not yet* righteous, devout, fair, and faithful can reach these spiritual plateaus by studying Torah for its own sake (*Chiddushei HaRim*).

Midrash Shmuel interprets יָשָׁר as a modifier of חָסִיד; he renders the two words as *scrupulously pious*, in contrast to the sort of person whom the Talmud (*Sotah* 21b) disparages as חָסִיד שׁוֹטֶה, *a foolishly pious person*. Out of an ignorantly false sense of modesty, such a person would ignore a drowning woman for fear of coming into physical contact with her. As another example of such a person, *Yerushalmi* (*Sotah* 3:4) offers the example of one who sees a child floating in the river, and will not jump in to save him until he removes his *tefillin*.

וּמְרַחַקְתּוֹ מִן הַחֵטְא, וּמְקָרַבְתּוֹ לִידֵי זְכוּת — *It moves him away from sin and draws him near to merit.* Torah gives protection not only from physical danger (see 3:5), but also from spiritual harm. The Torah within a person can provide him with the sanity to resist when he is confronted with a temptation to sin. Furthermore, it motivates him to seek opportunities and situations that will enable him to lead a life of merit (*Tiferes Yisrael*).

◆§ **Hard at first.** R' Aharon of Belz is reputed to have said, "Judaism is like a hot *mikveh* (ritual bath). When one steps in, it is hot and uncomfortable, and one bellows that he cannot tolerate the heat. Once in, however, he finds it to be an absolute pleasure, and says, "Ah, what a *mechayah* (pleasurable joy).''

וֹ/א וְנֶהֱנִין מִמֶּנּוּ עֵצָה וְתוּשִׁיָּה, בִּינָה וּגְבוּרָה, שֶׁנֶּאֱמַר: „לִי עֵצָה וְתוּשִׁיָּה, אֲנִי בִינָה, לִי גְבוּרָה". וְנוֹתֶנֶת לוֹ מַלְכוּת, וּמֶמְשָׁלָה, וְחִקּוּר דִּין; וּמְגַלִּין לוֹ רָזֵי תוֹרָה; וְנַעֲשָׂה

Midrash Shmuel interprets this as a promise that the Torah can save someone even from *contemplating* sin. As the Talmud advises, "If the repulsive Evil Inclination engages you, draw him into the study hall [since Torah is the antidote to the Evil Inclination]" (*Kiddushin* 30b). Alternatively, Torah teaches one to repent and distance himself from the sins of his spiritually checkered past.

וְנֶהֱנִין מִמֶּנּוּ עֵצָה וְתוּשִׁיָּה, בִּינָה וּגְבוּרָה — *From him people enjoy counsel and wisdom, understanding and strength.* From a genuine Torah scholar, people gain good *counsel* in mundane matters as well as Torah *wisdom.*

תּוּשִׁיָּה is a reference to Torah wisdom (see *Sanhedrin* 26b).

He gives them *understanding* to delve into the depths of Torah and teaches them its practical details, so that they will have the *strength* to overcome the impediments that stand in the way of living a Torah life (*Midrash Shmuel*).

Emunas Shmuel renders these four qualities as

follows: *counsel* to avoid sinning, *wisdom* on how to fulfill our obligations to God with proper intent and emotion, *understanding* to penetrate the deep meanings of every *mitzvah,* and *strength* to overcome our spiritual foes.

שֶׁנֶּאֱמַר: "לִי עֵצָה וְתוּשִׁיָּה, אֲנִי בִינָה, לִי גְבוּרָה" — *as it is said: "Mine are counsel and wisdom, I am understanding, mine is strength"* (Proverbs 8:14). The "speaker" in this verse is the Torah. It tells its adherents that it provides not only wisdom and counsel to help them, but also the *understanding* and spiritual *strength* to prevail over adversity (*Rashi*).

וְנוֹתֶנֶת לוֹ מַלְכוּת, וּמֶמְשָׁלָה — *[The Torah] gives him kingship and dominion.* To kings and scholars the Torah gives the guidance in law and behavior to exercise moral power.

According to *Tiferes Yisrael, kingship* connotes the air of royalty that the Torah grants its disciples, and *dominion* refers to the power granted him to

---

⧫§ **Reading the blueprint.** Since the Torah is the blueprint of Creation (*Zohar, Terumah*), one who plumbs the depths of Torah can understand the phenomena of the world.

The Chazon Ish, the foremost halachic authority of his time, spent virtually all his life in his small apartment studying Torah, yet his knowledge of medicine and the human anatomy was astounding. Until he died, his advice in health-related matters was sought by patients, their families, and even highly respected doctors. There are many documented instances of his diagnoses and counsel.

A young boy in Israel underwent heart surgery, but did not regain consciousness. The doctor said that if he remained unconscious for another twenty-four hours, all hope would be lost. After hearing the details of the case, the Chazon Ish said that the doctor's ominous prognosis would be true only after seventy-two hours. The boy awoke after twenty-four hours, but before seventy-two hours. Asked to explain how he knew, the Chazon Ish replied, "I knew it from the mishnah in (*Masechta*) *Ohalos.* " No one but the Chazon Ish had seen a connection between that mishnah and medicine.

A renowned Israeli neurosurgeon, Dr. Hardan Ashkenazi, recalled that he was once in doubt as to whether surgery could be performed on a critically ill patient. He received a note from the Chazon Ish in which he described two possible reasons for the uncertainty and requested to be informed which of them it was. "That very day, I related his message to a group of physicians and said, 'See how he summarized the possibilities in a few concise sentences. Any of us would have needed pages to write what he expressed so succinctly.'

"It is many years since the Chazon Ish's death," the doctor once said, "yet when faced with difficulties, I still often think: If only I could discuss this with the Chazon Ish . . ."

From him people enjoy counsel.

From him people enjoy counsel and wisdom, understanding and strength, as it is said: "Mine are counsel and wisdom, I am understanding, mine is strength." [The Torah] gives him kingship and dominion and analytical judgment; the secrets of the Torah are revealed to him; he becomes

influence his surroundings. *Midrash Shmuel* suggests alternatively that *kingship* is the ability to decide halachic issues. The Talmud (*Gittin* 62a) teaches that Torah sages are called kings, based on the verse בִּי מְלָכִים יִמְלֹכוּ, *through me* [the Torah], *kings will reign* (Proverbs 8:15).

וְחִקּוּר דִּין — *and analytical judgment.* A scholar is able to analyze information and arrive at proper and conclusive judgment (*R' Moshe Alshakar*).

וּמְגַלִּין לוֹ רָזֵי תוֹרָה — *the secrets of the Torah are revealed to him.* According to *Machzor Vitry*, this refers to the most esoteric areas of Torah knowledge, such as the mysteries of Creation and the workings of the Heavenly order. R' Meir teaches

> ◆§ **Reading where there are no lines.** A scholar's ability to determine the Torah's opinion on any matter extends even to cases that are not addressed explicitly. Rabbi Yechezkel Abramsky related a fascinating incident that portrayed the ability of Torah scholars to rule on the basis of what is *not* written.
>
> One day a distraught Jew complained to Rabbi Chaim Soloveitchik about an indignity committed against the body of his late father. His father had passed away that morning and a wealthy Jew had died in the early afternoon, but in violation of the halachah, the *chevra kadisha* (burial society) had buried the second deceased person before burying his father. "The *Rav* must do something," cried the man. R' Chaim leafed through some pages of his *Rambam* and told the man, "Go home, I will take care of the problem."
>
> Rav Abramsky, who was present, asked what R' Chaim was looking for, since it was well known that deceased persons must be buried in the order in which they died.
>
> R' Chaim explained, "I was unsure if the basis for this law is due to the proper respect for the deceased or whether it is because of the general rule that 'One may not overlook an opportunity to perform a *mitzvah*' (*Yoma* 33a). If it is because of the honor of the dead, then the man's son has a personal interest and a right to protest the lack of respect shown his father. But if the basis of the law is that the first *mitzvah* must be performed first, then it is *my* responsibility as *rav* to require the *chevra kadisha* to follow the halachah.
>
> "I looked in the *Rambam*'s *Laws of Mourning* and found no reference to this law. I concluded therefore that this injustice is not the mourner's obligation, but mine. Therefore I told him that I would do what is necessary."
>
> ◆§ **Elements of decision making.** Rabbi Elchanan Wasserman wrote: "Five conditions are necessary for giving advice: 1) intelligence; 2) lack of a vested interest in the issue; 3) a general sense of fairness, without which one cannot think clearly; 4) a mindset totally and exclusively shaped by Torah; and 5) Divine assistance in rendering the proper advice."
>
> One who studies Torah for its own sake merits all these aids.
>
> The Chofetz Chaim used to say, "At times when one must make crucial decisions, he would pay a fortune for some sound advice. Were someone to whisper in his ear, 'You can ask God Himself,' he would jump at the opportunity and ask, 'How?' The answer is simple, 'Just look in the Torah.'"
>
> ◆§ *Ibn Ezra* (Numbers 6:7) writes that true kingship is the ability to control one's own desires. Torah grants one freedom to exercise full self-control, hence the Torah *gives him kingship and dominion* (*R' Moshe Almosnino*).
>
> Alexander the Great is reputed to have told his generals, upon their victorious return from the battlefield, to prepare themselves for an even more intense battle. "Who is the foe?" they asked. Replied the great warrior king, "The battle against the evil that lurks in men is the greatest of all wars." It is in this battle that the true student of Torah is granted kingdom and dominion (*Doresh LePerakim*).

כְּמַעְיָן הַמִּתְגַּבֵּר, וּכְנָהָר שֶׁאֵינוֹ פוֹסֵק; וְהֹוֶה צָנוּעַ, וְאֶרֶךְ רוּחַ, וּמוֹחֵל עַל עֶלְבּוֹנוֹ. וּמְגַדַּלְתּוֹ וּמְרוֹמַמְתּוֹ עַל כָּל הַמַּעֲשִׂים.

[ב] **אָמַר** רַבִּי יְהוֹשֻׁעַ בֶּן לֵוִי: בְּכָל יוֹם וָיוֹם בַּת קוֹל

---

that whoever occupies himself with the study of Torah for its own sake merits to have the mysteries of Torah revealed to him.

וְנַעֲשֶׂה כְּמַעְיָן הַמִּתְגַּבֵּר, וּכְנָהָר שֶׁאֵינוֹ פוֹסֵק — *he becomes like a steadily strengthening fountain and like an unceasing river.* Like a stream that gathers strength and never dries up, an authentic Torah scholar espouses ideas that stand the test of time; the clear waters of his Torah constantly increase, and all who seek to quench their thirst draw from the endless well of his Torah (*Emunas Shmuel*).

Tiferes Yisrael shows that the mishnah's two metaphors are complementary. A fountain produces sweet, refreshing water, but in small amounts; a river flows in torrents, but the water is often stale. Someone who studies Torah properly combines the advantages of both: His Torah is both sweet and plentiful. [Additionally, the quality of his ideas will improve, and the quantity of his students will always increase.]

According to *Midrash Shmuel*, however, the analogy of the mishnah portrays the strength of his personality and convictions. Like a spring that constantly grows stronger and can overcome anything that seeks to stop its flow, the true *talmid chacham* does not allow any evil influence to halt his spiritual progress.

וְהֹוֶה צָנוּעַ, וְאֶרֶךְ רוּחַ — *He becomes modest, patient.* A person who attains an elevated spiritual level can easily become arrogant, but R' Meir teaches that when one studies Torah for its own sake, his enhanced qualities are accompanied by modesty. A truly righteous person will perform his good deeds quietly and without fanfare. Furthermore, he will be patient with people (*Tiferes Yisrael*).

According to *Abarbanel*, these attributes are continuations of an earlier stich of the *baraisa*. One to whom the secrets of Torah are revealed must take care to treat these sensitive areas with *modesty,* and not bandy them about in public. Also, when one shares his increasing flow of Torah knowledge with students, R' Meir teaches that he must be *patient* with them, even if they are sometimes immature or cannot absorb the rapid flow of his teachings.

Midrash Shmuel suggest that unlike אֶרֶךְ אַפַּיִם, which indicates delaying punishment in spite of anger, אֶרֶךְ רוּחַ (patience) implies not becoming angry to begin with.

וּמוֹחֵל עַל עֶלְבּוֹנוֹ — *and forgiving of insult to himself.* One who studies Torah for its own sake is among

---

◆§ **Surmounting the distance.** King David says (*Psalms* 25:14), *the secret of God is for those who fear Him.*

While fear is generally a sign of distance, fear of God brings one to an intimate relationship, in which God reveals deep secrets. In the words of R' Tzadok HaKohen, "One who loves the Torah receives its love in return. Like a beloved to a lover, the Torah reveals its intimate thoughts" (*Tzidkas HaTzaddik* 198). *Rashi* describes this process: One who harnesses himself to constant Torah study will merit that the Torah itself will intercede with God on his behalf, begging that God reveal to him the most profound secrets of the Torah (*Sanhedrin* 99b, *Rashi,* s.v. תורה עולמת לו).

◆§ **Public privacy.** One should be modest even in public activities. The *Alter* of Slabodka explained that this is not at all a contradiction in terms. Modesty is an emotional state. Even in the spotlight, one can go about his business quietly, participating without wanting to be noticed and admired. Modesty does not mean that one should not dance enthusiastically at a wedding, but that one should focus on bringing joy to the bride and the groom — not about how many people are looking and how impressed they are with him. Real modesty is being private even in public.

a steadily strengthening fountain and like an unceasing river. He becomes modest, patient, and forgiving of insult to himself. [The Torah] makes him great and exalts him above all things.

2. Rabbi Yehoshua ben Levi said: Every single day, a Heavenly

---

those to whom the Talmud applies the verse *And those who love Him are like the sun coming out in its full intensity* (*Judges* 5:31). This refers to those who are insulted yet do not insult others; who hear themselves degraded yet do not reply in kind (*Shabbos* 88b). He even *forgives* those who insult him, so that they will not be punished for degrading a Torah scholar (*Midrash Shmuel*).

Avos al Banim notes that R' Meir speaks of forgiving *personal* insult. Insults to other Torah scholars or to the Torah itself are another matter. Then, a true Torah scholar must react swiftly and forcefully.

וּמְגַדַּלְתּוֹ וּמְרוֹמַמְתּוֹ עַל כָּל הַמַּעֲשִׂים — *[The Torah] makes him great and exalts him above all things.* The elevated existence of an authentic *talmid chacham* raises him above all the vicissitudes of life. He views everything that God does from a higher

perspective and sees clearly that all God does is for the good.

Avodas Yisrael interprets *all things* as a reference to the mundane functions of daily life. The Torah scholar lives an elevated life not only when he prays and studies, but when he eats, drinks, and conducts commerce. The Torah instills in him an exalted sense of purpose that infuses everything he does. *Ruach Chaim* captures the sentiment: The man who accepts upon himself the yoke of the holy Torah for its own sake is attached to the Torah and to the Holy One, and is sanctified with the holiness of the holy Torah, which is incomparably higher than all the worlds, and which gives vitality and existence to all of them and to all powers. Hence, the man who engages in Torah for its own sake maintains the existence of all the worlds — and even beyond that.

Mishnah 2

אָמַר רַבִּי יְהוֹשֻׁעַ בֶּן לֵוִי — *Rabbi Yehoshua ben Levi said.* One of *Eretz Yisrael's* most prominent first-generation *Amoraim* (i.e., the Sages of the Gemara, who followed the period of the Mishnah), R' Yehoshua ben Levi bridged the eras of the *Tannaim* and *Amoraim,* and is quoted in the Tannaitic literature both here and in the very last mishnah of the Talmud. His main teacher was R' Yehudah ben Pedayah (see *Bereishis Rabbah* 94:5), and he also

studied under Bar Kappara, a student of R' Yehudah *HaNasi* (see *Avodah Zarah* 43a and *Chullin* 56b). Beside his great scholarship, he enjoyed wealth and property, and a household of royal eminence; nonetheless, he was devoted to improving the lot of his brethren and was deeply involved in communal matters. He lived and taught first in Lod and later in Tiberias.

Due to his scholarship, wealth, and family ties

⋖ **The Shechinah suffers.** *Chida* writes that R' Chaim ben Atar (*Ohr HaChaim HaKodesh*) related the following incident: A wealthy, influential man publicly embarrassed a noted Torah scholar. R' Chaim asked the scholar to forgive the culprit. The scholar replied: "I forgave him as soon as he insulted me, because the Holy *Zohar* writes that Jewish sins weigh down the wings of the Divine Presence, as it were. For every moment that I had not forgiven him, the Divine Presence would suffer. Therefore I could not delay."

⋖ **An angel among men.** The Chazon Ish expressed this concept eloquently and poetically: "The human being who is privileged to know the Torah — meaning that the intellect placed in his soul, like a seed in the furrow of a field, unites with his knowledge and they become a single entity — walks among people and seems to any superficial observer like an ordinary person. But in truth, he is an angel dwelling among mortal men, and he lives a life of spiritual ecstasy that is exalted above all blessing and praise" (*Collected Letters* 1:13).

יוֹצֵאת מֵהַר חוֹרֵב, וּמַכְרֶזֶת וְאוֹמֶרֶת: „אוֹי לָהֶם לַבְּרִיּוֹת,
מֵעֶלְבּוֹנָהּ שֶׁל תּוֹרָה!", שֶׁכָּל מִי שֶׁאֵינוֹ עוֹסֵק בַּתּוֹרָה

with the house of the *Nasi* — his son R' Yosef was a son-in-law of R' Yehuda Nesiah, the grandson of R' Yehudah *HaNasi* (see *Kiddushin* 33b) — he often represented the Jewish community before the Roman authorities. *Yerushalmi* (*Berachos* 5:1) relates that when he went with R' Chana bar Chama to Caesaria on a political mission, the Roman governor rose when he entered as a sign of respect, much to the chagrin of the court attendants. When asked to explain, the governor replied, "Their faces look like those of angels." Once, when he returned from a mission to Rome, R' Chanina met him at Acco and noticed that he was limping. "You remind me of your grandfather Jacob who also limped after his confrontation with the angel of Esau" (*Bereishis Rabbah* 78:5). R' Yehoshua ben Levi often complained that his overinvolvement with communal affairs caused him to forget much of what he had learned from R' Yehudah ben Pedayah (*Tanchuma, Va'eira* 5).

He endangered his health in order to teach people with life-threatening communicable diseases, insisting that "the Torah protects those who study it" (*Kesubos* 77b). Believing that Torah had therapeutic powers even in a physical sense, he said, "One who suffers a headache — let him study Torah" (*Eruvin* 54b).

He personally taught his sons and grandchildren. Every Friday his grandson would review the weekly Torah portion with him. One Friday he forgot about his grandson and remembered only after he had entered the bathhouse to bathe for the Sabbath — he rushed home immediately, unbathed. His student R' Chiya bar Abba asked him why he was so meticulous about the matter, and R' Yehoshua replied that when one studies with a grandchild, it is as if one heard the portion directly from Mount Sinai (see *Yerushalmi, Shabbos* 1:2 and *Kiddushin* 30a).

Among his famous maxims were: "Be careful regarding the honor of a scholar who forgot his studies, [this is derived from the fact that] both the Tablets and the broken Tablets were placed in the Ark" (*Berachos* 8b). Regarding public prayer, he taught: "One should arrive early at the synagogue

and be counted among the first ten, since even if a hundred people come afterwards, the first ten receive as much reward as all the rest" (ibid. 47b). He likened support of the Torah to fingernails, which always grow back, no matter how much one cuts them; so too, no matter how much one contributes financially in support of Torah study, God will pay him back (*Shir HaShirim Rabbah*).

A paragon of cleanliness in speech (see *Pesachim* 3b), he viewed slander as severely as transgression of all five books of Moses (*Vayikra Rabbah* 16:6), and was a strong advocate of silence. He said, "If speech is worth one *sela*, then silence is worth two" (*Megillah* 18a).

He stressed humility at home and in the synagogue (*Midrash Shocher Tov* 101:7), and taught that humility is greater than all the offerings brought in the Temple and is the key to the acceptance of one's prayers (*Sanhedrin* 43a).

He fasted on both the ninth and tenth of Av, since the fires raged in the Temple on the tenth (*Yerushalmi, Taanis* 4:6). Once he saw beautiful vineyards and exclaimed, "Land, O Land, hide your fruits! Why do you yield your fruits to the idolaters who occupy our Land, because of our sins?" (*Kesubos* 112a).

R' Yehoshua ben Levi was visited often by Elijah the Prophet, who studied Torah with him (*Sanhedrin* 98b). Once he asked Elijah when the Messiah would arrive. "Ask him yourself," replied the prophet. "He is found in the public square in Rome among the impoverished sick people." R' Yehoshua ben Levi went to Rome and asked the Messiah when he was coming. "Today." When the Messiah did not arrive, R' Yehoshua complained to Elijah, who replied, "He didn't deceive you. הַיּוֹם אִם בְּקֹלוֹ תִשְׁמָעוּ, *Today, if you hearken to His voice* (*Psalms* 95:7) and repent, he will come" (*Sanhedrin* 98a).

So great was his righteousness that the rainbow, which represents God's covenant not to let sins cause total destruction, was not needed while he was alive. He was taken directly from this world to *Gan Eden,* where Elijah called out, "Make way for the son of Levi" (*Kesubos* ibid.).

בְּכָל יוֹם וָיוֹם בַּת קוֹל יוֹצֵאת מֵהַר חוֹרֵב, וּמַכְרֶזֶת וְאוֹמֶרֶת: — *Every single day, a Heavenly voice emanates from Mount Horeb, proclaiming and saying.* *Machzor Vitry* defines בַּת קוֹל [literally: daughter of a voice] not as an angel, but as a voice. According to *R' Saadia Gaon,* it is an echo reverberating from the crags of mountain caves. *Tosafos Yom Tov* (*Yevamos* 16:6) explains it as a diminished form of prophecy, through which God informs those who fear Him what He expects of them. [See *Rashi* to *Sotah* 33a, s.v. שאני בת קול.]

Midrash Shmuel argues that if it is in fact a real voice, why doesn't everybody hear it? Thus he concludes that the term is used figuratively, i.e., when one thinks about transgressions of the Torah, one should imagine as if a voice from Mount Horeb were decrying such disparagement of the Torah. *R' Moshe Alshakar* views this voice as a continuation of the great voice that was heard at Sinai.

Horeb — another name for Mount Sinai — is related to חרב, *destroyed. Ruach Chaim,* based on the Talmud (*Shabbos* 89b), explains that the name Horeb in the context of our mishnah alludes to the destruction that the nations of the world deserve for having rejected the Torah when God offered it to them. Jews should learn the lesson that if they reject their own commitment to the Torah, Mount Sinai can became their own source of destruction, as well.

Midrash Shmuel interprets Horeb as desolate. When Israel fails to occupy itself with Torah, it causes Mount Sinai to become spiritually desolate.

The Heavenly proclamation is described in two ways: *proclaiming,* which implies vehemence; and *saying,* which implies forbearance — for Mount Horeb's call depends on each individual's life situation. One who enjoys the leisure to devote himself to Torah study, yet does not, is much more at fault than one whose responsibilities inhibit him from doing so; to him the Heavenly voice *proclaims,* with a sense of hurt and anger. But to one who is harried and preoccupied, the voice *says,* softly and sympathetically. It pleads, so to speak, that he, too, must make time to imbibe the invigorating waters of Torah (*Chasdei Avos*).

"אוֹי לָהֶם לַבְּרִיוֹת, מֵעֶלְבּוֹנָהּ שֶׁל תּוֹרָה" — *"Woe to them, to the people, because of [their] insult to the Torah."* God occupied Himself with Torah long before the creation of the world, and even the angels protested when God wanted to give the Torah to Moses (*Shabbos* 88b). Thus, in a sense, it was an "insult" to the Torah that it was brought down to this lowly earth and given to man, but it was more than justified by Israel's dedication to its study and commandments. But if Jews turn their backs on the Torah, violating their oath at Sinai, the mountain itself figuratively cries out in pain (*Midrash Shmuel*). The Torah feels insulted and ignored when people do not give it proper attention (*Rashi*).

⋙ **Making words count.** The Baal Shem Tov understands the voice as a figurative reference to thoughts of repentance that God constantly plants in man's heart and mind. A wise person opens his heart to the Heavenly call and returns to God. Spiritually callous people are oblivious to the call and continue their lives as usual. *Divrei Shmuel* of Slonim adds that God sends His message only to those who will listen, as the Sages taught, "Just as one must offer rebuke that will be heeded, so it is a *mitzvah* to refrain from saying things that will not be heeded" (*Yevamos* 65b).

⋙ **Make your choice.** *Ruach Chaim* continues: People often claim that they are prevented from studying the Torah because they must earn a livelihood — but this was the very reason the other nations gave for their refusal to accept the Torah. Each nation asked God what the Torah demanded of it. Some said the prohibition to steal would prevent them from earning a living; others claimed that their livelihood depended on murder (see *Avodah Zarah* 2b). Thus, when we put our livelihoods ahead of the Torah, we disparage God and the Torah, just as they did. When the Jews enthusiastically told Moses, "We will do and we will listen," they accepted the Torah unconditionally — even if it would seem to conflict with their ability to make a living.

נִקְרָא נָזוּף, שֶׁנֶּאֱמַר: „נֶזֶם זָהָב בְּאַף חֲזִיר, אִשָּׁה יָפָה וְסָרַת טָעַם". וְאוֹמֵר: „וְהַלֻּחֹת מַעֲשֵׂה אֱלֹהִים הֵמָּה וְהַמִּכְתָּב מִכְתַּב אֱלֹהִים הוּא חָרוּת עַל הַלֻּחֹת," אַל תִּקְרָא „חָרוּת" אֶלָּא „חֵרוּת," שֶׁאֵין לְךָ בֶּן חוֹרִין אֶלָּא מִי שֶׁעוֹסֵק בְּתַלְמוּד תּוֹרָה.

HaChassid Yaavetz clarifies that man's disrespect cannot in any way diminish the honor of the Torah. Rather it is those who act disrespectfully toward it who are contemptible and disgraced for not living up to the spiritual heritage of their forebears. They may be compared to a servant who was told by the king to count gold coins for two hours and to keep all that he counted. The servant ignored the command and went to sleep, thus indicating that either he did not understand the value of gold or was more enamored by straw than by gold. The servant's foolishness did not diminish the value of the gold; his conduct was a condemnation of himself. Similarly, one who forsakes the Torah indicates only his own ignorance. He insults himself, as indicated by the lament, "Woe is *to them*, to the people."

Mili d'Avos understands the mishnah as referring to the personal harm suffered by one who does not partake of the soul-sustaining power of Torah. Woe is to them who suffer the maladies of the soul yet refuse to avail themselves of the Torah's therapeutic power.

R' S. R. Hirsch summarizes the message of the mishnah with his customary eloquence: As long as there are still people who will not recognize the true worth of the Teaching and the Law thus revealed, and who will not employ it for the spiritual and moral perfection and sanctification of both their inner life and their outer actions, the Revelation on Mount Horeb has not as yet attained its ultimate goal among men. Mount Sinai stands as a silent rebuke, as it were, before mankind. Ceaselessly, it emits a resounding call that says, "It is not the Torah, but only man who will suffer loss and distress because he has despised and insulted the Torah."

שֶׁכָּל מִי שֶׁאֵינוֹ עוֹסֵק בַּתּוֹרָה נִקְרָא נָזוּף — *For whoever does not occupy himself with the Torah is called, "Rebuked."* Based on the earlier mishnah (2:6) that "a boor cannot be fearful of sin, an unlearned per-son cannot be scrupulously pious," *Machzor Vitry* explains that the extent to which one is involved in Torah study affects the quality of his performance of the *mitzvos*. One who does not study cannot fulfill its demands properly, and he is included in the words of the Torah *Accursed is one who will not uphold the words of this Torah, to perform them* (Deuteronomy 27:26). Thus he is *rebuked* by Heaven and unworthy of God's presence (*Tiferes Yisrael*).

Midrash Shmuel renders נָזוּף as *banished*. His disregard for the Torah implies that his soul was not at Mount Sinai; he is figuratively an outcast, outside the spiritual realm of the Jewish people. One who is willing to be considered spiritually excommunicated, rather than commit himself to Torah study and practice, truly insults the Torah, indicating his contempt for it.

Sfas Emes views this stich as portraying the sorry state of one who is deaf to the Heavenly voice. The Torah has so much to teach man; it is the medium through which God speaks, revealing His will, spiritually awakening man. One who refuses to accept this spiritual transmission deserves to be rebuked by Heaven.

שֶׁנֶּאֱמַר: „נֶזֶם זָהָב בְּאַף חֲזִיר, אִשָּׁה יָפָה וְסָרַת טָעַם" — *as it is said: Like a golden ring in a swine's snout is a beautiful woman who turns away from good judgment* (Proverbs 11:22). The precious golden ring becomes degraded and sullied when the pig wallows in dirt. So too, a scholar who scorns Torah study is disgusting, for he shows contempt for something of beauty and value. This proof verse's allusion to "rebuke" is derived by means of the Rabbinic exposition of *notarikon* [abbreviated shorthand], whereby the initial letters of נֶזֶם זָהָב are combined with the last letter of בְּאַף to form נזוף, *rebuke* (*Machzor Vitry; Rashi*).

Torah is more valuable than gold and pearls. For one to abuse it and not allow it to refine his crude and ignoble character is to figuratively "drag it

is called, "Rebuked," as it is said: *Like a golden ring in a swine's snout is a beautiful woman who turns away from good judgment* (Proverbs 11:22). And it says: *The Tablets are God's handiwork and the script was God's script charus (engraved) on the Tablets* (Exodus 32:16). Do not read *charus* (engraved), but *cherus* (freedom), for you can have no freer man than one who is engaged in the study of the Torah.

---

through the mud."

Ruach Chaim and R' S. R. Hirsch explain the verse's comparison of the swine with a golden ring in its snout to a beautiful but crude woman. A beautiful woman with ugly morals is all the more repulsive for her physical attractiveness. Rather than being a source of honor and pride, her physical attributes are obnoxious, because they are an enticement to sin. Physical beauty should be a constant symbol of the spiritual and moral beauty and harmony to which one should aspire. Like a swine degrades the beautiful golden nose ring, so is a woman who employs her charm and beauty in a morally repugnant fashion.

HaChassid Yaavetz comments: Just as a swine's ugliness and stench are not camouflaged by the golden ring in its snout, so a woman's physical beauty cannot conceal her moral blemishes. In the same way, man created in the Godly image should hide his face in shame if he does not nurture that image by studying the Torah. Nothing can disguise the spiritual ugliness of a wasted soul.

וְאוֹמֵר — *And it says.* Having spoken about the baseness of those who neglect the Torah, the *baraisa* now moves on to the personal reward that people derive from from their dedication to it.

״וְהַלֻּחֹת מַעֲשֵׂה אֱלֹהִים הֵמָּה וְהַמִּכְתָּב מִכְתַּב אֱלֹהִים הוּא חָרוּת עַל הַלֻּחֹת,״ אַל תִּקְרָא ,,חָרוּת״ אֶלָּא ,,חֵרוּת,״ שֶׁאֵין לְךָ בֶּן חֹרִין אֶלָּא מִי שֶׁעוֹסֵק בְּתַלְמוּד תּוֹרָה — *"The Tablets are God's handiwork and the*

script was God's script charus (engraved) on the Tablets" (Exodus 32:16). *Do not read "charus" (engraved), but "cherus" (freedom), for you can have no freer man than one who engages in the study of the Torah.* The Torah is not a crushing and constricting yoke; it is a source of freedom that allows man to be loyal to himself and his Godly soul, to be free to live according to the internal harmony of his personality (*Tiferes Yisrael, R' S. R. Hirsch*). Unless man lives as God created him to, he is a slave to his own passions, the mores of society, or the despotism of dominant or fashionable cultures (*Midrash Shmuel*).

Those who think they *must* act, speak, dress, drive, decorate, and vote a certain way to conform to their peers, employers, relatives, and neighbors, can hardly be called free. Better to conform to the life-styles decreed by God as the best and most productive.

Machzor Vitry and *Rashi* explain this freedom in a more practical sense. Due to the respect Jews have for those who are dedicated to Torah study, they will be excused from many of the mundane obligations of the community. *Ruach Chaim* adds: This fits the context of mishnah 3:6: "If someone takes upon himself the yoke of Torah, the yoke of government and the yoke of worldly responsibilities are removed from him."

According to *HaChassid Yaavetz*, R' Yehoshua makes two points with this verse: (a) The Tablets of

---

◦§ **Overruling competing laws.** The mishnah's concept of freedom can be seen in Moses' experience with the First Tablets, which were very heavy stone, but which he was nevertheless able to carry with no difficulty. The Sages relate that after Moses descended the mountain and saw the people worshiping the Golden Calf, the letters of the Ten Commandments miraculously flew from the Tablets — whereupon their weight became too great to bear and Moses dropped them. This implies that the literal word of God, as represented by the letters of the commandments, freed Moses from the limitations of the law of gravity. So too, the Torah provides its adherents with the emotional mettle to overcome life's difficulties and trials.

וְכָל מִי שֶׁעוֹסֵק בְּתַלְמוּד תּוֹרָה הֲרֵי זֶה מִתְעַלֶּה, שֶׁנֶּאֱמַר: ,,וּמִמַּתָּנָה נַחֲלִיאֵל, וּמִנַּחֲלִיאֵל בָּמוֹת.''

[ג] הַלּוֹמֵד מֵחֲבֵרוֹ פֶּרֶק אֶחָד, אוֹ הֲלָכָה אֶחָת, אוֹ פָּסוּק אֶחָד, אוֹ דִבּוּר אֶחָד, אוֹ אֲפִילוּ אוֹת אֶחָת — צָרִיךְ לִנְהָג בּוֹ כָבוֹד. שֶׁכֵּן מָצִינוּ בְּדָוִד מֶלֶךְ יִשְׂרָאֵל, שֶׁלֹּא לָמַד מֵאֲחִיתֹפֶל אֶלָּא שְׁנֵי דְבָרִים בִּלְבָד, וּקְרָאוֹ רַבּוֹ, אַלּוּפוֹ,

the Covenant were made by God Himself, which indicates the Torah's importance in His eyes. Consequently, one who scorns the Torah insults the King Himself. (b) The Torah is the Jew's means of gaining freedom. One who does not use this key to his shackles shows that he is unredeemably chained to his passions and desires; a person who prefers to be imprisoned suffers from a slave mentality.

That the Torah grants freedom is derived through an interpretive method called אַל תִּקְרֵי, *do not read*. This method interprets the word in two ways, the traditional way in which it is vowelized and read, and also by reading its consonants with a different set of vowels. Since the Torah is written without vowels, the letters of the word can be read in more than one way, and the Sages have a tradition that each of the readings may convey its own thought. Nevertheless, of course, the simple meaning of the verse remains unchanged, according to its traditional pronunciation.

וְכָל מִי שֶׁעוֹסֵק בְּתַלְמוּד תּוֹרָה הֲרֵי זֶה מִתְעַלֶּה — *And anyone who engages in the study of Torah becomes elevated*. The Torah affords one the ability to achieve spiritual greatness, to rise above the mundane considerations of this world, and to enjoy a deep and meaningful connection to God (*R' Moshe Almosnino*). Furthermore, the knowledge and refinement of character that result from pure Torah study will help one achieve greatness in this world (*Machzor Vitry*).

Tiferes Yisrael and *Chelek LeOlam Haba* note the usage "*anyone* who engages in Torah study." Even people with limited intellectual ability will rise above their innate limitations as they apply themselves earnestly to Torah. As King David taught, *the testimony of God is trustworthy, making the simple one wise* (Psalms 19:8).

According to *Meiri*, the phrase **anyone** *who* **engages** *in Torah study* includes not only the scholars, but also teachers of Torah, those who spread its word, those who support Torah scholars and institutions, and those who work to advance Torah causes. All will ascend the ladder of spiritual growth through their commitment to the Torah.

שֶׁנֶּאֱמַר: ,,וּמִמַּתָּנָה נַחֲלִיאֵל, וּמִנַּחֲלִיאֵל בָּמוֹת'' — *as it is said: "From Mattanah to Nachaliel and from Nachaliel to Bamos"* (Numbers 21:19). These are the names of places along Israel's way from Egypt to *Eretz Yisrael*. The Sages interpreted these names homiletically in the sense of the literal meaning of the words — מַתָּנָה, *gift* . . . נַחֲלִיאֵל, *Divine heritage* . . . בָּמוֹת, *heights*. Thus they interpret the verse: *From the gift of Torah, man gains a Divine heritage that elevates him and leads him to spiritual heights* (*Rashi*).

The Talmud (*Eruvin* 54a) adds another homiletical interpretation based on the place mentioned just before the ones quoted by this *baraisa*: מִמִּדְבָּר, *from the Wilderness*. This is a call for humility as a prerequisite to advancement in Torah knowledge. "One who makes himself a wilderness, accessible and equal to everyone, will merit the gift of Torah."

Mishnah 3

הַלּוֹמֵד מֵחֲבֵרוֹ פֶּרֶק אֶחָד, אוֹ הֲלָכָה אֶחָת, אוֹ פָּסוּק אֶחָד, אוֹ דִבּוּר אֶחָד — *He who learns from his fellowman a single chapter, a single halachah, a single verse, a*

single Torah statement. Every bit of Torah is of inestimable value: *It is more valuable than pearls; all of your wealth does not equal it* (Proverbs 3:15).

And anyone who engages in the study of the Torah becomes elevated, as it is said: *From Mattanah to Nachaliel and from Nachaliel to Bamos (Numbers 21:19).*

3. He who learns from his fellowman a single chapter, a single halachah, a single verse, a single Torah statement, or even a single letter, must treat him with honor. For thus we find in the case of David, King of Israel, who learned nothing from Achitophel except for two things, yet called him his teacher, his guide,

---

Hence if one gained any Torah knowledge from his fellow, even if the friend did not intend to teach him, the recipient should show him honor (*Midrash Shmuel*).

Even if one gains general knowledge from someone, he must show gratitude (*Rashi*).

אוֹ אֲפִילוּ אוֹת אֶחָת — *or even a single letter.* The nature of the Hebrew language is such that the manner in which we interpret even a single letter can be of decisive importance in our understanding of the whole. In Hebrew, particles, prepositions, and conjunctions are represented by one letter; likewise, tense and mood, number, gender of the object, and so forth, are indicated by changes in individual letters (*R' S. R. Hirsch*).

For example, the letter *vav* can serve as a conjunction connecting two subjects, to show that the laws of one apply to the other, as in *Exodus 21:1:* **And** *these are the ordinances you shall place before them.* The conjunction *and* (from the *vav*) indicates that there is a connection between the chapter of civil and tort law and the previous chapter, which described the Ten Commandments and the Temple

Altar. Just as the Ten Commandments were given at Sinai, so were the "secular" laws, and the Sanhedrin, which rules on pecuniary matters, must be located near the Temple (*Rashi*).

Another example: From slightly varying spellings of the word סֻכּוֹת, which is sometimes spelled without the second *vav*, the Talmud (*Succah* 6b) derives the minimum amount of walls needed for a *succah*. [See *Kesubos* 29b for another example.]

צָרִיךְ לִנְהָג בּוֹ כָּבוֹד — *must treat him with honor.* Honoring such a person shows honor to the Torah, for it shows how much one appreciates the invaluable gift of Torah knowledge (*Midrash Shmuel*).

HaChassid Yaavetz crystallizes the point: Torah knowledge enlightens and refines those who study it. Hence, a teacher — even of a small amount — has shared in molding his friend's essence.

שֶׁכֵּן מָצִינוּ בְּדָוִד מֶלֶךְ יִשְׂרָאֵל, שֶׁלֹּא לָמַד מֵאֲחִיתֹפֶל אֶלָּא שְׁנֵי דְבָרִים בִּלְבָד, וּקְרָאוֹ רַבּוֹ, אַלּוּפוֹ, וּמְיֻדָּעוֹ — *For thus we find in the case of David, King of Israel, who learned nothing from Achitophel except for two things, yet called him his teacher, guide, his intimate (Psalms 55:14).* There are varying opinions as to

---

⋙ **No wall of separation.** The juxtaposition of *Mishpatim* (dealing primarily with civil and tort law) with the Ten Commandments and the laws of the Altar provide a startling insight into Judaism. To God, there is no realm of "religion" in the colloquial sense of the word. Most people think of religion as a matter of ritual and spirituality. Western man differentiates between Church and State. The Torah knows no such distinction. To the contrary, all areas of life are intertwined, and holiness is derived from halachically correct business dealings no less than from piety in matters of ritual. The Sages teach that one who wishes to be a *chassid*, or a devoutly pious person, should be scrupulous in matters of civil and tort law [מִילֵּי דִנְזִיקִין] (*Bava Kamma* 30a), for in Judaism the concept of the "temple" is as much in the courtroom as in the synagogue (*R' Nosson Scherman*).

⋙ **Obligatory honor.** As the king, David was forbidden to honor others at the expense of the honor of the kingdom — unless he was obligated to do so. Therefore, the honor that David conferred on Achitophel proves that David felt obligated to do so and this was not merely a personal stringency.

וּמְיֻדָּעוֹ, שֶׁנֶּאֱמַר: ,,וְאַתָּה אֱנוֹשׁ כְּעֶרְכִּי, אַלּוּפִי וּמְיֻדָּעִי״.

וַהֲלֹא דְבָרִים קַל וָחֹמֶר: וּמַה דָּוִד מֶלֶךְ יִשְׂרָאֵל, שֶׁלֹּא לָמַד

מֵאֲחִיתֹפֶל אֶלָּא שְׁנֵי דְבָרִים בִּלְבָד, קְרָאוֹ רַבּוֹ אַלּוּפוֹ

וּמְיֻדָּעוֹ — הַלּוֹמֵד מֵחֲבֵרוֹ פֶּרֶק אֶחָד, אוֹ הֲלָכָה אֶחָת, אוֹ

פָּסוּק אֶחָד, אוֹ דִבּוּר אֶחָד, אוֹ אֲפִילוּ אוֹת אֶחָת, עַל אַחַת

כַּמָּה וְכַמָּה שֶׁצָּרִיךְ לִנְהָג בּוֹ כָּבוֹד! וְאֵין כָּבוֹד אֶלָּא תוֹרָה,

---

what these two things were. According to *Rashi* and *Machzor Vitry*, Achitophel once found King David studying Torah alone, and criticized this practice, saying, "Did we not learn that scholars who study alone are deserving of the sword and that furthermore they will become fools? (*Berachos* 63b). David asked, "What shall I do?" to which Achitophel replied, " 'Let us take counsel together' (*Psalms* 55:15), i.e., let us study Torah together." Hence he taught King David that one should not study Torah alone, but with a colleague. Another time, David entered the study hall with his head held high. Achitophel said, "Where is your reverence? Did not God command us to fear His Sanctuary?" [See *Leviticus* 19:30.] Again David asked, "What shall I do?" Replied Achitophel, "To the House of God let us walk with emotion" (*Psalms* ibid.). [Others are of the opinion that he taught King David that one should pray together with others.]

Yalkut Shimoni (*Shmuel* 142) cites two different instances where Achitophel taught King David. a) When Uzza allowed the Ark to be carried on a wagon (see *II Samuel* 6:3-6), it was Achitophel who rebuked David, "You should have learned from Moses who calls on the Levites to carry the Ark on their shoulders" (see *Numbers* 7:9). b) When King David excavated to make the subterranean drains under the Altar of the future Temple, the underground waters surged upward and threatened to overflow. David wanted to calm the waters by throwing into them a plate with God's Ineffable Name written on it. He sought the permission of the Sages to do so, and Achitophel was the one who permitted it (see *Succah* 53a).

Radak explains the verse: Although you Achitophel were only my equal and peer, I treated you as my superior, and as one with authority over me. *Targum* renders the verse as "and you Achitophel,

a person who is like my teacher, who taught me wisdom."

שֶׁנֶּאֱמַר: ,,וְאַתָּה אֱנוֹשׁ כְּעֶרְכִּי, אַלּוּפִי וּמְיֻדָּעִי״ — As it is said: *You are a man of my measure, my guide and my intimate"* (*Psalms* 55:14). During Absalom's rebellion that temporarily deposed David, Achitophel was on the side of the revolutionaries. Here David explained why Achitophel differed from the other adversaries. "You are a great man whose stature is equal to my own. I always treated you as an equal, even though I am a king and you are a commoner. You were my closest confidant, the one with whom I shared my most intimate secrets" (*Radak*).

וַהֲלֹא דְבָרִים קַל וָחֹמֶר: וּמַה דָּוִד מֶלֶךְ יִשְׂרָאֵל, שֶׁלֹּא לָמַד מֵאֲחִיתֹפֶל אֶלָּא שְׁנֵי דְבָרִים בִּלְבָד, קְרָאוֹ רַבּוֹ אַלּוּפוֹ וּמְיֻדָּעוֹ — הַלּוֹמֵד מֵחֲבֵרוֹ פֶּרֶק אֶחָד, אוֹ הֲלָכָה אֶחָת, אוֹ פָּסוּק אֶחָד, אוֹ דִבּוּר אֶחָד, אוֹ אֲפִילוּ אוֹת אֶחָת, עַל אַחַת כַּמָּה וְכַמָּה שֶׁצָּרִיךְ לִנְהָג בּוֹ כָּבוֹד — *One can derive from this the following: If David, King of Israel, who learned nothing from Achitophel except for two things, called him his teacher, his guide, his intimate — one who learns from his fellowman a single chapter, a single verse, a single statement, or even a single letter, how much more must he treat him with honor.* By means of a *kal vachomer*, an *a fortiori* derivation, one can deduce the following: If David, who learned nothing from Achitophel except for two things, called him his teacher, his guide, his intimate — surely one must honor his fellow for teaching him only a *single* chapter, a *single* halachah, a *single* verse, a *single* statement, or even a *single* letter!

Many commentaries question this deduction. David's example proves only that one should honor his intimate, as it is said: *You are a man of my measure, my guide and my intimate (Psalms 55:14).* One can derive from this the following: If David, King of Israel, who learned nothing from Achitophel except for two things, called him his teacher, his guide, his intimate — one who learns from his fellowman a single chapter, a single verse, a single statement, or even a single letter, how much more must he treat him with honor! And honor is due only for Torah,

---

one who taught him *two* things. Where is the proof that one must show honor for *one* teaching?

The *Baal Shem Tov* and *Ruach Chaim* resolve this problem based on the esoteric concept that every letter of the Torah is inextricably linked with the entirety of the Torah, as every minute part of God's wisdom is linked with the entire body of sacred knowledge. An example of this concept is found in the "declaration of intent" that many communities recite before performing a commandment: "May it be Your will, HASHEM . . . that the commandment . . . be considered . . . as if I had fulfilled it . . . as well as the six hundred thirteen commandments that are dependent on it." Thus, since every letter of the Torah is linked with the entire infinite body of Divine wisdom, whatever one learns from someone requires him to show gratitude to the teacher.

But if so, why was Achitophel's teaching worthy of gratitude only because he taught *two* things, not one? One letter has significance only if it is learned from a God-fearing person whose teachings are infused with the spirit of the entire Torah. As Achitophel's betrayal of God's anointed showed, he was not God fearing, so his lessons, despite their logic and intellectual appeal, were hollow and profane. As taught in the first *baraisa* of this chapter, Torah confers its lofty, spiritual gifts when it is studied for its own sake. Even when studied with lesser purity, it confers a degree of spiritual majesty, but even then, the student must respect its holiness and have at least a desire to elevate himself to a higher degree of appreciation of its sanctity. Not so Achitophel. His intellect was great, but his spiritual content was negligible.

The *Tanna*'s carefully chosen words allude to this lack of holiness in Achitophel and his teachings. From Achitophel, David learned שְׁנֵי דְבָרִים, *two*

things, rather than genuine Torah teachings; and those two things were בִּלְבָד, literally *only* or *alone.* This implies that these teachings stood alone, totally divorced from the entire body of Torah wisdom. Unlike authentic Torah learning which is fertile and generates new ideas and insights in the vast corpus of Torah knowledge, because every portion of the Torah is like an organ in the entire body of Torah knowledge, Achitophel's Torah was sterile and was *only* two unrelated ideas.

Nevertheless, David showed tremendous gratitude even for Achitophel's limited, fragmented advice. David's example, therefore, is more than adequate proof that a student should venerate the person who links him to the entire Torah, even through the vehicle of only one letter!

וְאֵין כָּבוֹד אֶלָּא תוֹרָה — *And honor is due only for Torah.* I.e., only Torah scholars truly deserve honor (*Rashi*).

According to *R' S. R. Hirsch*, the *baraisa* teaches that only the Torah holds our true human dignity and authentic salvation. Thus Achitophel deserved to be honored even for his meager contribution to David's Torah knowledge.

Maharam Schick renders: *The only lasting honor is that accorded to Torah.* Scientists make new discoveries and are deservedly honored, but often their fame is short lived because their findings are later disproven by others. But Torah knowledge is eternal because even an idea ultimately rejected is considered part of Torah; God cherishes the process, the effort, the contribution to the ultimate discovery of the truth. Like putting on *tefillin* or eating matzah at the *Seder*, the very act of Torah study is the fulfillment of a commandment and adds life and holiness to Creation, whatever the

שֶׁנֶּאֱמַר: ,,כָּבוֹד חֲכָמִים יִנְחָלוּ״; ,,וּתְמִימִים יִנְחֲלוּ טוֹב״

וְאֵין טוֹב אֶלָּא תוֹרָה, שֶׁנֶּאֱמַר: ,,כִּי לֶקַח טוֹב נָתַתִּי לָכֶם,

תּוֹרָתִי אַל תַּעֲזֹבוּ״.

[ד] **כַּךְ** הִיא דַרְכָּה שֶׁל תּוֹרָה: פַּת בַּמֶּלַח תֹּאכֵל, וּמַיִם

בַּמְּשׂוּרָה תִּשְׁתֶּה, וְעַל הָאָרֶץ תִּישָׁן, וְחַיֵּי

צַעַר תִּחְיֶה, וּבַתּוֹרָה אַתָּה עָמֵל; אִם אַתָּה עוֹשֶׂה כֵן,

---

level of the student and the value of his scholarship to others.

One who receives honor for his wealth or beauty is being honored not for what he *is*, but for what he *has*. But the Torah, which bestows honor on the person himself, becomes an integral part of the personality of those who learn it.

שֶׁנֶּאֱמַר: ,,כָּבוֹד חֲכָמִים יִנְחָלוּ״; ,,וּתְמִימִים יִנְחֲלוּ טוֹב״ — *as it is said: "The wise shall inherit honor"* (Proverbs 3:35); *"and the perfect shall inherit good"* (ibid. 28:10). Wise people are those who acquire knowledge; this verse assures that honor will be theirs as well. And students who become so accomplished that they can be called *perfect* will be granted even more goodness. Consequently, they should honor the teachers who made this possible

for them, as David honored Achitophel (*Tiferes Yisrael*).

וְאֵין טוֹב אֶלָּא תוֹרָה, שֶׁנֶּאֱמַר: ,,כִּי לֶקַח טוֹב נָתַתִּי לָכֶם, תּוֹרָתִי אַל תַּעֲזֹבוּ״ — *And only Torah is truly good, as it is said: "I have given you a good teaching, do not forsake My Torah"* (ibid. 4:2). Nothing else in this world is always good. Wealth, for example, is prized by most people, but it causes worry, pain, and strife. Only Torah is unadulterated goodness (*Knesses Yisrael*). This is derived from the verse's description of Torah as a *good teaching*.

The word לֶקַח may also be rendered as *acquisition*. *Ruach Chaim* explains that Torah is something that a person must acquire, but it is so valuable that it is priceless. It is God's gift, but it comes with the caution *not* [to] *forsake My Torah*.

Mishnah 4

כַּךְ הִיא דַרְכָּה שֶׁל תּוֹרָה — *This is the way of the Torah.* According to *Rashi*, the *baraisa* does not advocate asceticism as the vehicle for success at Torah study; a wealthy person need not give up his financial security and live a life of poverty in order to pursue Torah. Rather it is a call to a poor person not to let poverty impede his pursuit of Torah. The serenity of Torah can be experienced even in privation, and one must always be prepared to sacrifice his personal comfort for the sake of Torah study.

In the words of *Rambam* (*Hil. Talmud Torah* 3:7): "Lest one say, 'I will gather money and then return to Torah study; I will buy what I need and be free of preoccupation and then I will study' — know that if such thoughts enter your heart and mind you will never merit the crown of Torah."

Midrash Shmuel and others understand the *baraisa* as addressed to rich and poor alike. The Torah makes its home only among those who understand that one cannot serve two masters, that

---

◆§ **The business trip.** R' Bunam of P'shis'cha compares a Torah scholar's ordeal of poverty to a businessman traveling abroad to find low-cost suppliers. He may pass through places where the food is poor and the accommodations abominable, but he would not even think of canceling his trip. The potential profit more than compensates for the discomfort. Life is a business trip, and the pot of gold is the spiritual profit of Torah, and *mitzvos* can be acquired for great spiritual profit. Only a fool would give it up because of temporary difficulties on the way.

as it is said: *The wise shall inherit honor* (*Proverbs* 3:35); *and the perfect shall inherit good* (*ibid.* 28:10). And only Torah is truly good, as it is said: *I have given you a good teaching, do not forsake My Torah* (ibid 4:2).

4. This is the way of the Torah: Eat bread with salt, drink water in small measure, sleep on the ground, live a life of deprivation — but toil in the Torah! If you do this, *You*

one who becomes dependent on creature comforts will find it difficult to live without them, and that they will usually be purchased at the expense of time that would otherwise have been devoted to Torah study.

As a wise man once said, "Many people have the attitude that they want to learn the entire *Shas* (Talmud) in one night — and they want to sleep, as well." Torah demands a dedication that pampered people are not ready to give it.

Rambam (ibid. 3:6) codifies this approach: "One whose heart has elevated him to want to fulfill the *mitzvah* of Torah study properly and to be crowned with the crown of Torah should not shift his attention to other things. Let him not place the thought in his heart that he will acquire Torah along with wealth and honor. This is the way of the Torah etc."

פַּת בַּמֶּלַח תֹּאכֵל, וּמַיִם בַּמְּשׂוּרָה תִשְׁתֶּה, וְעַל הָאָרֶץ תִּישָׁן — *Eat bread with salt, drink water in small measure, sleep on the ground.* Even if the only way one can free himself to learn is by enduring such privation, he should be ready for it (*Rashi*).

Meiri offers a qualification. While dependence on delicacies does lead to neglect of Torah study, one who can afford to buy good food should eat well, so that he be healthy and strong enough to fulfill his potential.

וְחַיֵּי צַעַר תִּחְיֶה — *Live a life of deprivation.* Most commentator's view this as a general statement which includes the physical deprivations listed above. According to *Tiferes Yisrael*, it is a new aspect of the difficulties one must be willing to bear in order to study Torah. Not only must one be ready to suffer physical want but even to bear emotional strain such as worries, fears and vexation in order to pursue the word of God.

וּבַתּוֹרָה אַתָּה עָמֵל — *but toil in the Torah.* A person's love for Torah should be so deep that he is not even aware of privation or hardship. The Torah gives its

---

◆§ **Wrong-way ride.** A wealthy and successful lawyer visited his childhood friend Rabbi Elchonon Wasserman, and was appalled at the great *rosh yeshivah's* poverty. He exclaimed, "Elchonon, you are much brighter than I am. Had you become a lawyer you would be a wealthy man today!"

R' Elchonon did not react to the comment. The old friends visited together for a few enjoyable hours, and then R' Elchonon accompanied the man to his train. At the station two trains were waiting, one a modern, comfortable one to the east, and another that was old and rickety. The lawyer, who was headed westward, walked toward the old train. R' Elchonon asked him, "Why do you travel in such an uncomfortable train? Go to the luxurious new one!"

The friend stared at him incredulously, and said, "But I'm going in the other direction!"

R' Elchonon ignored the comment. "Nonetheless, isn't it better to travel in a comfortable, plush train?"

The lawyer was exasperated. "Elchonon, you speak nonsense! What good is a comfortable train if it is not taking me where I have to go?"

R' Elchonon quietly replied, "Listen to yourself. You are right. When you want to arrive at a certain destination the comfort level of the vehicle doesn't mean much. The main thing is to get where you have to be. Do you remember you asked me why I did not become a lawyer? Of course that career would be more lucrative, but that is not my goal in life. What good is the comfort if I don't arrive where I want to be?"

„אַשְׁרֶיךָ וְטוֹב לָךְ": „אַשְׁרֶיךָ" – בָּעוֹלָם הַזֶּה, „וְטוֹב לָךְ"
– לָעוֹלָם הַבָּא.

[ה] **אַל** תְּבַקֵּשׁ גְּדֻלָּה לְעַצְמְךָ, וְאַל תַּחְמֹד כָּבוֹד;

---

disciples the serenity to enjoy life with happiness and bliss, oblivious to material privation (*Chida*).

HaChassid Yaavetz comments that this teaches that God does not demand the same level of Torah scholarship from each of us, but He expects us to do our best; the results will be in proportion to the effort. Hence the *baraisa* speaks of *toiling* at Torah. The reward will be in proportion to the effort. Achievement is up to God, but effort is up to man (*HaChassid Yaavetz*).

Mesillas Yesharim qualifies: A person must realize that he is in this world not for rest and relaxation, but for labor and exertion. He should conduct himself like those who work for hire, and in the manner of soldiers in the front lines, who eat in haste, sleep at irregular intervals and are always prepared for battle, כִּי אָדָם לְעָמָל יוּלָד, *for man is born to labor* (*Job* 5:7). If a person accustoms himself to this life-style, he will find Divine service easier, since he will have the proper attitude for it. This is the spirit of what the Sages said: "This is the way of

Torah — eat bread with salt, etc." This discipline embodies the essence of self-denial and removal from comfort and pleasure.

Ruach Chaim notes the change in tense. While the earlier items are in future tense — תֹּאכַל, תִּשְׁתֶּה literally mean *you will eat, you will drink* — the imperative to toil at Torah study, עֲמֹל, is expressed in the present tense. To tend to one's physical needs can sometimes be spiritually counterproductive. Thus one should view them as a necessary evil and delay them for the future, as much as possible. Not so the labor of Torah study, which should be one's constant preoccupation.

אִם אַתָּה עוֹשֶׂה כֵּן, „אַשְׁרֶיךָ וְטוֹב לָךְ": „אַשְׁרֶיךָ" – בָּעוֹלָם הַזֶּה, „וְטוֹב לָךְ" – לָעוֹלָם הַבָּא — *If you do this, "You are praiseworthy and it is well with you"* (*Psalms* 128:2). *"You are praiseworthy"* — in this world; *"and it is well with you"* — in the World to

---

⧉ **The winning ticket.** A Jew who walks God's path should always be ecstatic; poverty and difficulty should seem too insignificant to matter. The Chofetz Chaim offered the analogy of a pauper who won a huge lottery prize. He ran home to share the good news with his wife and children, and they all celebrated together. Passersby looked inside at the poor furnishings and empty cupboard, and wondered how these forlorn people could be happy. What was there to celebrate when there was nothing on the table for supper? But the "demented" family knew better. What did it matter if their pockets were empty today when they were holding a winning ticket that would bring them millions!

True, a life of poverty is difficult, but a Jew with a true perspective knows that he is amassing riches for the World to Come.

⧉ **No words.** Rabbi Eliyahu Lopian elaborates: King David states: וְדֹרְשֵׁי ה׳ לֹא יַחְסְרוּ כָל טוֹב, *Those who seek God will not lack any good* (*Psalms* 34:11). The verse does not say that they will *have* every good; rather, they will not *lack* any good.

Imagine someone who laments that his friend does not possess a single medication. A listener laughs, "How ludicrous! Of course he has no medications — no one in his household is ill!"

Many committed students of Torah live very simply, without the luxuries their neighbors cannot be without. Some may view such a life-style with genuine pity — how wrong they are! *Those who seek God do not lack any good.* Those who are devoted to the Torah experience real satisfaction, not deprivation.

If someone who had never tasted wine would ask me to explain its taste to him, I might say, "Did you ever taste something sweet? Did you ever taste something sour? Well, the taste of wine is a combination of sweet and sour." This may be true, but it is not sufficient; one can know the taste of wine only by actually tasting it.

So is the life of one who toils in Torah. *If you do this . . . you are praiseworthy . . .* The joy of dedicated Torah study cannot be conveyed in words. It must be experienced.

are praiseworthy and it is well with you (Psalms 128:2). You are praiseworthy — in this world; and *it is well with you* — in the World to Come.

5. **D**o not seek greatness for yourself, and do not crave honor;

Come. One who lives frugally in order to toil at Torah will eventually realize how good a life he lives and will enjoy even this world (*Ruach Chaim*).

The *baraisa* states: "If *you* do this." The way of Torah brings one joy and serenity only if it is one's authentic choice of life-style. One who merely imitates others who live an elevated existence will never taste the beauty and serenity of a Torah life (*R' Shlomo Kluger*).

Emunas Shmuel describes the serenity of one who toils in Torah, without pursuing worldly comforts. A person who is constantly preoccupied with wealth and pleasure will never be satisfied. Often he is tempted to meet his "needs" through deceit or worse. Furthermore, a narcissistic lifestyle often leads to physical illness. But one who lives a Torah life is not plagued by this. Satisfied with his basic needs, he is unencumbered by passion and desire, and truly enjoys life.

Mishnah 5

אַל תְּבַקֵּשׁ גְּדֻלָּה לְעַצְמָךְ — *Do not seek greatness for yourself.* In spite of the great reward awaiting him, one who studies Torah and performs *mitzvos* should not seek greatness for himself (*Tiferes Yisrael*).

The Mishnah emphasizes "do not seek greatness for *yourself*," i.e., for personal gratification, but one may demand honor in order to enhance the prestige of Torah and its scholars (*HaChassid Yaavetz*). Likewise, one may seek greatness in order to improve the living conditions and honor of the Jewish people. Mordechai is a prime example of one who sought power and greatness in order to lobby on behalf of his brethren [see *Esther* 10:3] (*Midrash Shmuel*). But one should always bear in mind that he must examine his motives carefully. It is easy to claim that one is concerned only with the honor of the Torah when he really means himself.

Other commentators understand the inference *for yourself* as teaching that one should not pursue greatness for personal ends, but should certainly aspire to spiritual greatness. Alternatively, one should not seek *self-glorification* but should want *others* to attain success and greatness.

וְאַל תַּחְמֹד כָּבוֹד — *and do not crave honor.* By seeking honor for one's scholarly attainments, one does not merit the supreme reward for the study of Torah for its own sake [see 6:1] (*Rashi, Machzor Vitry*). Do not allow yourself to become envious

---

✑ True pleasure. Rabbi Moshe of Kobrin rhapsodized, "World, O world! How beautiful and sweet you are for those who are not mired in the pursuit of your pleasures and enticements! World, O world, how dark and foreboding you are for those who drown in their desires for your mundane thrills. How unfortunate they are. How sad."

A seventeen-year old and his father came to the Chazon Ish. The father claimed that his son had been in the yeshivah long enough, and that it was time for him to deal with the "real world" and earn a living. Bashfully, the son pleaded that his only desire is to study Torah.

Turning to the father, the Chazon Ish cited this *baraisa*, "I understand how 'it is well in the World to Come' for one who lives the diminished life-style of Torah. But how can one be happy in this world if he deprives himself of so many comforts?

"The answer is in the words 'if you do this.' Only someone who lives this way can understand such joy. Your son has tasted the beauty of a Torah life. Believe me, if I could open my chest I would show you what a truly happy heart looks like. Whatever difficulty one suffers for the sake of Torah study is insignificant compared to the Heavenly bliss that comes from toiling in Torah."

יוֹתֵר מִלִּמּוּדֶךָ עֲשֵׂה. וְאַל תִּתְאַוֶּה לְשֻׁלְחָנָם שֶׁל מְלָכִים, שֶׁשֻּׁלְחָנְךָ גָּדוֹל מִשֻּׁלְחָנָם, וְכִתְרְךָ גָּדוֹל מִכִּתְרָם; וְנֶאֱמָן הוּא בַּעַל מְלַאכְתֶּךָ, שֶׁיְשַׁלֶּם לְךָ שְׂכַר פְּעֻלָּתֶךָ.

[ו] **גְּדוֹלָה** תוֹרָה יוֹתֵר מִן הַכְּהֻנָּה וּמִן הַמַּלְכוּת, שֶׁהַמַּלְכוּת נִקְנֵית בִּשְׁלֹשִׁים מַעֲלוֹת,

---

when others are honored while you stand aside unnoticed (R' S. R. Hirsch).

In many versions, the text reads: וְאַל תַּחְמוֹד כָּבוֹד יוֹתֵר מִלִּמּוּדֶךָ, *do not crave more honor than you are accustomed to.* Since honor can have catastrophic spiritual consequences, one should be wary of it. Rather than seeking more accolades, one should keep his honors to a minimum. Alternatively, one should accept honor only for his Torah knowledge and good deeds, for by doing so he honors God and the Torah. Another interpretation: Do not seek any honor other than the opportunity to be privy to the Godly intelligence of the Torah, for there is no greater honor than to be given access to the King's most precious treasure (*Midrash Shmuel*).

יוֹתֵר מִלִּמּוּדֶךָ עֲשֵׂה — *let your performance exceed your learning.* This mirrors an earlier mishnah (3:12), which taught that our good deeds should exceed our wisdom and that everything we learn should be put into practice. Even when one is in doubt as to whether he is obligated in a particular *mitzvah*, he should perform it, lest he transgress

God's will (*Rashi, Machzor Vitry, Midrash Shmuel*).

Ruach Chaim renders: Let your performance [of *mitzvos*] exceed your habit. Always try to upgrade the quality of your performance, investing more time, intelligence, money and emotion than you have in the past.

וְאַל תִּתְאַוֶּה לְשֻׁלְחָנָם שֶׁל מְלָכִים, שֶׁשֻּׁלְחָנְךָ גָּדוֹל מִשֻּׁלְחָנָם — *Do not lust for the table of kings, for your table is greater than theirs.* Do not be tempted by the opulent life-style or the power of royalty. Do not be tempted by the luxuries and pleasures of the good life, because the reward that awaits you in the World to Come is greater than any royal table can provide (*Rashi, Machzor Vitry*).

Even to support people in need, one should not lust for the riches of royalty. Even kings are limited in their ability to help others, but one who lives according to God's will can justify the sustenance of the entire world. Thus the table of the righteous is greater than that of royalty (*Midrash Shmuel*).

Since people of merit eat from God's table, they

✦ The Talmud (*Eruvin* 13b) teaches that one who runs away from honor will be pursued by it. Why, asked R' Mendel of Kotzk, is one who flees from honor punished by having to endure it? He answered that someone who runs from honor reckons with it; he feels that honor is meaningful enough to try and escape from it, that it has some significance. But that should not be the viewpoint of a Jew. Ideally, he should consider honor so insignificant that it need not even be reckoned with. Such a person is punished by having to suffer from honor.

R' Yisrael of Rizhin offered the proper perspective toward honor with a parable. A royal minister traveled throughout the kingdom, and was recognized and honored wherever he went, while the king remained in the capital. Even prestigious officials would bow in the minister's presence. One day the minister went on a trip with the king, but since the king rarely appeared in public, most of the people did not know who he was and ignored him, while they all bowed to the famous minister. How embarrassing it was to him to be honored while his master was ignored!

Likewise, only the King of the Universe deserves honor. How embarrassing it is when we take it for ourselves!

let your performance exceed your learning. Do not lust for the table of kings, for your table is greater than theirs, and your crown is greater than their crown, and your Employer is trustworthy to pay you remuneration for your deeds.

6. Torah is even greater than priesthood or royalty, for royalty is acquired along with thirteen prerogatives,

---

are guests at a table greater than any in the world (*Lechem Shamayim*).

וְכִתְרְךָ גָּדוֹל מִכִּתְרָם — *and your crown is greater than their crown.* The crown of Torah is greater than that of royalty (*Midrash Shmuel*).

Ruach Chaim explains: While the crown of royalty can be removed from one person and granted to another, the crown of Torah is a permanent fixture in the life of one who earns it. [Furthermore, while two kings cannot simultaneously wear the royal crown (see *Chullin* 60b),

everyone can merit the crown of Torah.]

וְנֶאֱמָן הוּא בַּעַל מְלַאכְתֶּךָ, שֶׁיְּשַׁלֶּם לְךָ שְׂכַר פְּעֻלָּתֶךָ — *and your Employer is trustworthy to pay you remuneration for your deeds.* Every person is in the employ of God, and He rewards each person according to the energy and effort he expends at his tasks (*Machzor Vitry*). *Minchas Shabbos* adds that even though ultimately it is God who causes man to succeed at his spiritual tasks, nonetheless God rewards him as his own efforts achieved the success.

Mishnah 6

גְּדוֹלָה תוֹרָה יוֹתֵר מִן הַכְּהֻנָּה וּמִן הַמַּלְכוּת — *Torah is even greater than priesthood or royalty.* There are three crowns: the crown of Torah, the crown of priesthood, and the crown of royalty (4:17), but this *baraisa* teaches that the crown of Torah is greater than the other two. This is not because Torah is acquired by forty-eight qualifications, while royalty and priesthood have fewer prerogatives; the proof is not quantitative, but qualitative. The thirty prerogatives of royalty and the twenty-four gifts of the priesthood are for the purpose of enhancing their dignity and honor; these prerogatives are all materialistic and transitory.

The forty-eight qualifications required for the crown of Torah, however, are moral and spiritual virtues that elevate man above the materialism of society and the temporal values of this world; they assure him eternal honor and dignity. Furthermore, the crowns of priesthood and royalty, as well as their prerogatives, are hereditary, but the crown of Torah is available to all who earn it. It must be earned by developing the forty-eight items listed below as the means to acquire Torah (*Midrash Shmuel*).

שֶׁהַמַּלְכוּת נִקְנֵית בִּשְׁלֹשִׁים מַעֲלוֹת — *for royalty is*

acquired along with thirty prerogatives. A king receives thirty privileges with the office of king. When the Jewish people asked Samuel to appoint a king for them, he warned them that their king would have a significant degree of authority and privilege (see *I Samuel* 8:11-17).

Machzor Vitry enumerates them based on *Sanhedrin* (18a) and *Deuteronomy* (17:15-16). Those listed in the mishnah are: (1) The king may not act as judge; (2) nor is he brought to trial; (3) he is never a witness; (4) nor do witnesses testify for or against him; (5) he does not perform *chalitzah* (the rite in which a woman is released from having to participate in levirate marriage — see *Deuteronomy* 25:7-10); (6) nor is *chalitzah* performed for his wife; (7) he does not take a *yevamah* (a woman in levirate marriage); (8) nor is his wife taken as a *yevamah*; (9) no one may marry his widow; (10) even if a relative died, the king does not leave his palace to accompany the dead; (11) when he is in mourning and people come to pay their condolences, they must sit on the ground while he reclines on a couch; (12) he is permitted to confiscate private property to make a highway for himself; (13) when the nation brings back the spoils or booty captured in war,

ו/ו

וְהַכְּהֻנָּה נִקְנֵית בְּעֶשְׂרִים וְאַרְבָּעָה, וְהַתּוֹרָה נִקְנֵית בְּאַרְבָּעִים וּשְׁמוֹנָה דְבָרִים, וְאֵלּוּ הֵן: בְּתַלְמוּד,

they place it before him and he takes whatever he wishes; (14) he may have no more horses than he requires for his chariot; (15) he may not accumulate silver and gold beyond the needs of his household and escorts; (16) a Torah Scroll is written especially for him and (17) must always be with him in battle, (18) in the city or state, (19) when traveling, (20) and when he is at rest; (21) no one may sit on his throne, (22) ride on his horse, (23) or handle his scepter; (24) no one may see him while he receives a haircut, while he is naked or in the bathhouse. From the Scriptures we know that a king is (25) appointed by the word of a prophet; (26) that a king must be *from among you* and not from outside the land; (27) he must be *your brother,* and not of alien birth; (28) he may not be a convert; (29) a *mamzer,* or (30) a slave.

וְהַכְּהֻנָּה נִקְנֵית בְּעֶשְׂרִים וְאַרְבָּעָה — *and the priesthood with twenty-four [gifts].* The translation follows *Rashi* and *Machzor Vitry,* who interpret the twenty-four as a reference to the gifts that the Torah confers upon the Kohanim. These are enumerated in the Talmud (*Chullin* 133b and *Bava Kamma* 110b). From the Temple service they receive parts of (1) an animal brought as a *chatas* (sin offering); (2) a bird brought as a sin offering; (3) an *asham* (guilt offering); (4) an *asham* brought in cases of doubt (see *Leviticus* 5:17-18); (5) a communal *shelamim* offering; (6) the *log* of oil brought along with the meal offering of a *metzora*; (7) the remainder of the *omer* (after the portion of the Altar's portion [*kometz*] is removed); (8) the two loaves offered on Shavuos; (9) the showbread; (10) the remainder of all *menachos.*

Of those things eaten in Jerusalem they receive (11) *bechor,* the firstborn animal which is offered in the Temple; (12) *bikkurim* — first fruits; (13) the breast and hind leg of the *todah* (thanksgiving offering) and four of the forty breads that are offered with it; parts of the ram offered by a nazirite along with a bread and a wafer from the offering; (14) hides of offerings.

They also received the following ten items: (15) *terumah* (approximately a fiftieth of the crops); (16)

the *terumah* taken by the Levites from the *maaser* they receive; (17) *challah* (from dough); (18) the first shearings of wool; (19) the right foreleg, jaws and maw of an ox, sheep or goat slaughtered for non-sacrificial purposes; (20) the money offered in redemption of a firstborn; (21) the sheep offered in redemption of a first-issue donkey (see *Exodus* 13:13); (22) שְׂדֵה אֲחוּזָה, *an ancestral field,* which was not redeemed by its owner before the Jubilee year (see *Leviticus* 27:20-21); (23) שְׂדֵה חֵרֶם, a field which was consecrated for the benefit of the Kohanim; (24) property stolen from a proselyte who dies before it is returned. If he has no living relatives it is given to the Kohanim.

According to *Chida,* the twenty-four refers to special laws that apply to the priests. They are: (1) They must conduct themselves with holiness (2) and purity; (3) they wear linen clothing for honor and beauty; (4) they trim their hair and beard every thirty days; the Kohen Gadol every seven days; (5) they must not defile themselves for the dead; (6) they should not make their heads bald; (7) they are not to shave off the corners of their beard; (8) they are not to cut their flesh; (9) they are not permitted to marry a harlot; (10) a woman who is profaned (i.e., is born from a marriage prohibited to a Kohen), (11) or who is divorced. Furthermore, they are unfit to serve if they (12) have a blemish, (13) are blind, (14) lame, (15) have a sunken nose, (16) if one arm or leg is longer than the other, (17) have a broken arm, (18) a broken leg, (19) thick eyebrows, (20) cataracts, (21) disarrangement in the eye, (22) scabs, (23) scurvy, (24) crushed testicles.

וְהַתּוֹרָה נִקְנֵית בְּאַרְבָּעִים וּשְׁמוֹנָה דְבָרִים, וְאֵלּוּ הֵן — *but the Torah is acquired by means of forty-eight qualities, which are.* Unlike the prerogatives and gifts that are automatically awarded to kings and Kohanim, the forty-eight qualities enumerated in connection with Torah, however, are moral and spiritual virtues. One who aspires to the crown of the Torah must acquire them through diligent labor upon his own personality before he can gain the crown of the Torah. These forty-eight attributes are not *gifts* which are acquired together with the Torah, but *means* through which it is possible to acquire the crown of the Torah.

R' Aharon Kotler defines the function of these forty-eight qualities. The *baraisa* refers to them as *kinyanim*, the same technical term that is used for the means by which property changes hands, and the new owner acquires possession. This clearly implies that just as a given item can be acquired only through its designated method of acquisition, so it is with the Torah; it can be acquired only through these forty-eight means, and in no other way. This applies to all the qualities listed, even those that seem to have no natural connection to acquiring Torah knowledge.

Among them are purity of soul and correctness in outlook and conduct. To the degree that one lacks these attributes, his attainment of Torah wisdom is lacking, and to that degree he will be unable to arrive at the truth. Aside from the fact that they themselves are fundamentals of spiritual perfec-

tion, the Torah itself is acquired through them — and through Torah, one attains these qualities with yet greater majesty and strength, so that it is a reciprocal process: The qualities bring Torah to their possessor, and the Torah one learns intensifies the qualities with the person, thus increasing his mastery of the Torah.

בְּתַלְמוּד — *Study.* Diligent study is the most basic prerequisite, for the Torah yields itself to those who are dedicated to it. Furthermore, one must be ready to learn from all men (*Midrash Shmuel*).

A key to successful study is the teacher-student relationship, for unlike most secular disciplines one cannot properly absorb the Torah only from books; personal guidance and instruction by a teacher are essential (*HaChassid Yaavetz*). The reason the Oral Law was not to be written was so that students could absorb the spirit and nuances of the Law from the transmitters of its sacred tradition (*Kiryas Sefer*), and even though the oral tradition has been committed to writing, it still remains

---

◄§ **The crown is what you make it.** The first twenty-four qualities on the list are related to the development of the intelligence and methodology by which one can, through toil, come to know the Torah. The other twenty-four are means to sublimate one's character and personality, and refine his essence so that he becomes a fitting receptacle for the holiness of the Torah. As *Maharal* teaches, ''The Godly intelligence cannot reside in a body consumed by its own physicality.'' If man does not become purified and elevated, can he not merit the crown of Torah?

True, one can study Torah just as he can perform other *mitzvos* without all these prerequisites of one who seeks to connect himself to God, but it is through the Torah that a Jew can become Godly. And it is only through these forty-eight qualities that one's love for God and His Torah is awakened. To taste deeply of its wisdom and beauty, one must make all his abilities, senses and talents subservient to the Torah (*Nesivos Shalom*).

Torah is compared to water (*Devarim Rabbah* 7:3). Just as water assumes the shape of the vessel into which it is poured it becomes square in a square vessel and round in a round one — so Torah knowledge can be either a potent force for good, or, God forbid, a destructive, negative force, depending on the vessel one makes of himself. By developing good and refined character, man creates the appropriate vessel for Torah (*R' Mendel of Vitebsk*). One can study civil and tort law in order to know how to be vigilant with other people's property, or he can study it to know how he can defraud others by taking advantage of their gullibility and ignorance.

◄§ **Intentional ambiguity.** Rabbi Yitzchak Hutner suggests that this is why the Mishnah was purposely composed rather unsystematically, even, as the Talmud explains on occasion, with missing words, without which it cannot be properly understood. Such devices made it necessary to have a teacher in order to understand the Mishnah, thus retaining an *oral* tradition. [See *Pachad Yitzchak* (*Chanukah* 1) and *Ohr Gedalyahu* (*Chanukah)*) for explanations of the oral character of the Torah.]

inaccessible unless one has a teacher (R' S. R Hirsch).

בִּשְׁמִיעַת הָאֹזֶן — *attentive listening* [lit. *hearing of the ears*]. One must carefully listen to his teachers and repeat only what he learned from them. If he is inattentive for even a moment, he might miss something important (*Midrash Shmuel*). Proper, accurate and thorough listening is the first demand made on the learner. Intent listening precludes carelessness, inattention or distraction (*R' S. R. Hirsch*).

The *baraisa* emphasizes the ears, because things that enter the ears penetrate deeply into one's consciousness and remain etched on the heart and mind (*Ruach Chaim*).

בַּעֲרִיכַת שְׂפָתַיִם — *articulate speech*. One should not study the Torah through silent reading. The Sages find support for this through a homiletical interpretation of the phrase כִּי חַיִּים הֵם לְמֹצְאֵיהֶם, *for they are life for those that find them* (*Proverbs* 4:22). The Sages taught that the last word of the phrase should be read as לְמוֹצִיאֵיהֶם, *for those who verbally bring forth the words of Torah*.

The Talmud further quotes the admonition of Beruriah, wife of R' Meir, that only if one participates with all his limbs will the Torah be secure and not forgotten.

Rambam (*Hil. Talmud Torah* 3:12) writes: "One who raises his voice while studying will assure the retention of his learning. One who studies quietly will soon forget." Verbalization clarifies thinking and also helps to permanently fix one's learning in his mind.

According to *Tiferes Yisrael*, one should try to always

repeat things in the mode of expression used by his teacher or the book from which he studied. *Midrash Shmuel* interprets this as a call for constant review.

בְּבִינַת הַלֵּב, בְּשִׂכְלוּת הַלֵּב — *intuitive understanding, discernment. Intuitive understanding* is an intuitive understanding of the underlying reasons for the laws. This often requires an instinctive feel for ideas that cannot be put into words (*Tiferes Yisrael*). *Discernment* connotes careful analysis of one's studies in order to understand its implications. *Midrash Shmuel* views this as a continuation of the previous clause, which he interpreted as review. Even though one must review constantly, this does not mean mere rote repetition. One must pay careful attention to the meaning of the material and seek to understand clearly what he studies.

According to *HaChassid Yaavetz*, these two qualities demand that one comprehend whatever he is taught with sufficient clarity to see the connections between ideas and to break down the ideas to their most basic components. In this way one's questions will be pertinent and one's solutions will be clear.

בְּאֵימָה, בְּיִרְאָה — *awe, reverence*. One must study Torah with reverence and awe of the One Who gave us His Torah. The Talmud derives that one should study the Torah with awe and reverence that the Jewish people felt when they received it at Sinai (see *Rashi* to *Berachos* 22a).

Maharal suggests that *awe* is a clear understanding of how removed and elevated God's Torah is from human perception, and *reverence* is a fear engendered by focusing on one's own spiritual

---

◄§ **Value of hearing.** *R' Yonah* writes: "The eye is a very important part of man's body, yet the ear is even more important. While the eye can see the most beautiful visions and light that gladdens the heart, the ear is able to hear glad tidings which penetrate to man's very core and saturate one's essence: It is for this reason that we are taught (*Bava Kamma* 85b) that if one blinds his servant he must pay for the value of the eye, but if one makes his servant deaf he must pay the servant's entire value. The ability to hear enables one to totally restructure his life."

The Midrash (*Shemos Rabbah* 27:9) teaches this by way of a parable: A person fell off a roof and all his limbs were smashed. He needed a separate bandage for every limb. However, a person who sinned with every limb of his body needs only one bandage. God gave him ears to hear words of rebuke and improve. This is the meaning of the words of *Isaiah* (58:50): "Incline your ears and come toward Me, listen and enliven your souls" (*Shaarei Teshuvah* 2:12).

puniness in comparison to the vast wisdom contained in Torah.

Even the High Priest could not enter the Holy of Holies except on Yom Kippur due to the intense Divine Presence found there. Certainly, one must engage in Torah study with awe and reverence, for an even more intense expression of God's Presence is found in Torah (*Ruach Chaim*). In this vein, *Mili d'Avos* quotes the *Zohar* which teaches that Torah studied without love and fear of God is like a bird without wings; it cannot ascend to Heaven.

Midrash Shmuel views it as reverence for teachers and mentors, as well as fear of Heaven.

Machzor Vitry qualifies the two qualities. A student must be in awe of God lest he make errors; and must fear his teacher, so that he not conduct himself frivolously in his presence.

בַּעֲנָוָה — *modesty*. As explained earlier (see 1:1), humility is the key to receiving Torah. Moses was the proper conduit to bring the word of God to His people because of his humility, and Mount Sinai, because it symbolizes humility, was the proper venue to impart His Torah to His people. Furthermore, only one modest enough to learn from all men can succeed at Torah study (*Midrash Shmuel*).

According to *Machzor Vitry*, humility allows one to ask questions when he does not understand; conceit and arrogance are impediments to the acquisition of Torah.

One who overestimates his own intellectual abilities is liable to denigrate the dignity and sanctity of the Torah and its teachers and bearers, thus blocking his own path towards its wisdom. Hence, awe and reverence born of humility will protect him from missteps and errors in

---

⊷ **You must serve me.** Just as water flows from high places to low ones, so the Torah can be transmitted only when the student feels subservient to his teacher (see *Rambam, Hilchos Talmud Torah* 3:9).

The Talmud (*Bava Kamma* 20a) relates that R' Chisda asked Rami bar Chama a very difficult question. Rami replied, "When you will serve me I will answer you," whereupon R' Chisda placed a towel on his arm as a sign of readiness to cater to Rami's needs.

Rabbi Shimon Shkop explained Rami's seemingly strange demand, in the name of his brother-in-law R' Shlomo Zalman Abel of Telshe. Rami bar Chama's answer to the question would be complex and profound, and he wanted to be sure that R' Chisda would regard himself as a student before his teacher and be ready to exert himself to understand. Only when the student-mentor relationship was cemented could Rami teach the matter effectively.

As if at Sinai. The *Aderes* (R' Eliyahu David Rabinowitz-Teumim) related the story of a Jew from Vilna, who traveled to Prussia on business. Before he left Vilna he asked Rabbi Abeli Pasviler, the chief rabbinical judge, for a letter of introduction to the great *gaon* Rabbi Akiva Eiger. In his warm letter, R' Abeli mentioned that the man had seen the Vilna *Gaon*.

As soon as the merchant arrived in Posen, he rushed to R' Akiva Eiger's synagogue, and entered just as the *gaon* was removing his *tefillin*. He handed the letter to R' Akiva Eiger and waited. After reading the letter, R' Akiva Eiger asked, "Did you personally know the Vilna *Gaon*? Can you repeat a Torah thought you heard from him?" When the man replied in the affirmative, R' Akiva Eiger immediately put his *tefillin* back on and with a serious and reverent face listened, all the while murmuring, "The words of the *Gaon* are like Torah from Sinai. One must listen to them as we heard the Ten Commandments from God at Sinai — with awe and reverence."

⊷ **Special preparaton.** Rabbi Eliyahu Botchko, *rosh yeshivah* in Montreux, Switzerland, once befriended a professor who was in Montreux on vacation. During a mid-morning walk, the professor asked the *rosh yeshivah* where he was going. "I am giving a *shiur* (lecture) today and I am on the way to the *mikveh*," he answered, and explained the significance of a *mikveh* to the professor.

"Why do you have to go to the *mikveh* before a lecture?" asked the professor. Replied Rabbi Botchko, "Your teaching of physics has nothing to do with your personal spiritual state. But the Torah is of Divine origin and its teachers must have spiritual purity. I always go to the *mikveh* before presenting a lecture."

practical observance and moral judgment (*R' S. R. Hirsch*).

בְּשִׂמְחָה — *joy.* The Divine Presence does not reside with man unless he is joyous in fulfilling God's will. Since Torah study is the most intimate encounter with the Divine wisdom, it requires joy (*Rashi*). A person in a joyful mood can learn more in an hour than a depressed person can learn in many hours (*Ruach Chaim*). There is no greater means for spiritual progress and elevation than that serenity and joy of the spirit which will cause a man to rejoice in life with all its tasks and burdens (*R' S. R. Hirsch*).

The Sages teach us that man is worthy to attain the nearness of the Divine Spirit neither through apathy nor sadness, nor jest, levity, or aimless talk, but only through the joy of *mitzvos* (*Pesachim* 117a).

Midrash Shmuel notes that joy is a prerequisite to Torah study since if one does not enjoy it he will not have the tenacity of spirit to toil at the task. On the other hand, if one approaches Torah joyfully it will respond in kind.

בְּטָהֲרָה — *purity.* Before beginning to study, one must purify his thoughts, for Torah is holy and pure and can only reside in pure places (*Midrash Shmuel*).

בְּשִׁמּוּשׁ חֲכָמִים — *ministering to the sages.* A student must wait upon scholars and attend to their needs in order to learn their methods of study and reasoning. The Talmud states "Attendance upon the scholars is greater than study with them" (*Berachos*

7b). For this reason it is suggested here that one attend to even their mundane needs so as to always be in close proximity to them.

Rashi adds that one must seek every opportunity to hear the words of the sages, for one has much to learn even from the mundane conversation of scholars (*Avodah Zarah* 19b). According to *Tiferes Yisrael*, one should minister to the sages to observe their practice of halachah in everyday circumstances.

בְּדִקְדּוּק חֲבֵרִים — *closeness with colleagues.* Through study with colleagues, one can analyze the teachings of their mentor (*Rashi*). *Emunas Shmuel* renders *careful choice of friends.* In order to successfully study and internalize Torah, one must surround oneself with friends of good character and intellectual clarity, who are both good hearted and perform good deeds.

Maharal notes that friendship is essential to Torah knowledge, since the gift of Torah is not accessible to individuals; only the nation as a whole can receive God's greatest gift. Friendship is the way to build bridges to others and turn many individuals into a united nation.

The Talmud relates that the spiritually sensitive people of Jerusalem would not accept an invitation to a meal unless they were aware of who else would attend (*Sanhedrin* 23a).

בְּפִלְפּוּל הַתַּלְמִידִים — *sharp discussion with students.* Debate generated by students sharpens the mind and clarifies subject matter. The Sages compared

⤳ **So much, yet . . .** How can one be humble, fearful, and joyous simultaneously? The Baal Shem Tov based his answer on King David's words, *I rejoice over Your words as one who found great treasure* (*Psalms* 119:162). One who found an enormous treasure has mixed emotions. He is ecstatic over his find, but he is disappointed that no matter how much wealth he can stuff into his bags, it will be insignificant compared to everything he must leave behind. Such mixed emotions were the lot of King David. He thrilled at the opportunity to fulfill God's commandments, but his joy was tinged with sadness that he could not accomplish nearly as much as he wanted to.

Likewise, one may be joyous that he can absorb the wisdom of God Himself, yet he is humbled that he can learn so little of the infinitude of Torah (*R' Moshe Adler*).

the effect of students on their teachers to the effect of twigs on large logs. The small branches can kindle a fire on the large log. Similarly, students enlighten their mentors (see *Taanis* 7a).

Isolation is incompatible with Jewish knowledge; it is only by association with living sages, in close communion with associates, and by the clarity of thought and judgment that can be attained by teaching it to disciples that the knowledge of Torah can be nurtured and allowed to flourish. Hence, one must combine a relationship with sages, a closeness with colleagues and sharp discussion with students in order to tap all the resources of Torah knowledge (*R' S. R. Hirsch*).

בְּיִשּׁוּב — *deliberation.* One should never rush to reply to questions; rather, one should carefully analyze a question before replying. This prevents jumping to premature conclusions (*Midrash Shmuel, Machzor Vitry*). *Mili d'Avos* renders *with calmness.* The most advantageous pursuit of Torah demands a calm environment.

Midrash Shmuel cites an alternative text בִּישִׁיבָה, through attendance at an *academy of learning.* Only in an atmosphere of intellectual ferment can one's full potential be brought out.

בְּמִקְרָא, בְּמִשְׁנָה — *[knowledge of] Scripture, Mishnah.* Scripture and Mishnah are prerequisites for success at Torah since they are the foundation of Torah knowledge (*Midrash Shmuel*).

Since Mishnah is the basis of the Oral Law, only one with a broad knowledge of Mishnah can properly engage in Talmudic debate (see *Sanhedrin* 42a).

בְּמִעוּט סְחוֹרָה — *limited business activity.* Torah scholarship is rarely found among those totally engrossed in trade and commerce [see *Eruvin* 55a] (*Rashi*). The *baraisa* does not say that one should be *without* business activity, since one must have the means to provide a livelihood. One should, however, restrict his business activities to what is necessary, even when there is an opportunity for a quick profit; the time could be better spent on spiritual activities (*Midrash Shmuel*). [See *Rambam, Hil. Talmud Torah* 3:10.]

בְּמִעוּט דֶּרֶךְ אֶרֶץ — *limited sexual activity.* Involvement in social, communal, and civic affairs can become an almost full-time preoccupation, allowing little time for growth in Torah (*Rashi, Machzor Vitry*).

Midrash Shmuel defines דֶּרֶךְ אֶרֶץ as *sexual activity.* Even within marriage, it should be practiced in moderation (see *Berachos* 22a).

According to *Lechem Shamayim,* דֶּרֶךְ אֶרֶץ denotes the real sciences. One must have some knowledge of math, geometry, biology, earth science and the like, but one should understand that they are only tools to understand certain areas of Torah, but secondary to the Divine Torah.

בְּמִעוּט תַּעֲנוּג — *limited pleasure.* Even wealthy people should not seek pleasure for its own sake; to do so is spiritually detrimental (*Midrash Shmuel*). Even required physical pleasures, such as Sabbath and festival meals, should be enjoyed in moderation. Rather than being an end in itself, physical pleasure should serve as a means to set the stage for spiritual enjoyment (*B'nayos B'Ramah*). In the words of *Tanna d'Vei Eliyahu,* "Before one prays that Torah enter him, let him pray that the delicacies of the world not enter his intestines" (*Ruach Chaim*).

The *Baal Shem Tov* suggests that the term should more accurately be rendered as *diminishment of pleasure.* One must cultivate such a love for God and His Torah and *mitzvos* that all other worldly pleasures become insignificant and diminished. Let one strengthen the love of God in his heart to such a degree that all other pleasures are insignificant to him.

בְּמִעוּט שֵׁנָה — *limited sleep.* Sleep is necessary in order to maintain a healthy body; in moderation, sleep is very positive (see *Berachos* 62b). One should therefore not deprive his body of its needed respite.

Sleep is symbolic of all legitimate bodily needs,

but in tending to the needs of one's soul and body one dare not devote equal amounts of time to the two. Just as one should sleep for only one third of the day, so the soul deserves twice the time one devotes to his body. Thus one should allot two thirds of his time to spiritual pursuits and only one third to the maintenance of his physical health and needs (*Chasam Sofer*).

Midrash Shmuel suggests rising early and going to sleep late as the key to being able to devote sufficient time to Torah study. The *Zohar* speaks in glowing terms about the special quality of night-time Torah study.

The Talmud (*Eruvin* 65) relates that R' Chisda's daughter once noticed that her father was very tired. When she asked him if he would like to lie down a bit and rest he replied, "The long days spent in the grave are soon upon us. Since then one can no longer learn more Torah or do more *mitzvos*, I will have plenty of time to rest."

בְּמִעוּט שִׂיחָה — *limited conversation.* Superfluous chatter is generally detrimental to the earnestness and spiritual composure essential for productive Torah study (*R' S. R. Hirsch*). Even in the study of Torah, man should try to be succinct and to the point, using the least amount of words possible (*Midrash Shmuel*).

Ruach Chaim cites a teaching of the Sages that every word of mundane and frivolous talk which enters man's ears causes words of Torah to be dislodged. Hence, idle talk, even of others, is detrimental to one's retention of Torah.

בְּמִעוּט שְׂחוֹק — *limited laughter.* Although excessive frivolity leads to immorality (3:17), too somber a mood is not conducive to study or growth in Torah. Thus the Talmud reports that Rabbah would commence his lectures with an amusing statement in order to put his disciples in a relaxed state of mind. Afterwards he would sit in awe and deliver his presentation [see *Pesachim* 117a] (*Midrash Shmuel, Tiferes Yisrael*).

בְּאֶרֶךְ אַפַּיִם — *slowness to anger.* Calm, persevering patience is generally a virtue, but especially so for Torah study, for anger causes errors in judgment and leads one to forget his learning (*Machzor Vitry*).

The Talmud is replete with statements linking failure at Torah study to anger: "If a wise man becomes angry he will lose his wisdom" (*Pesachim* 66b). "Anyone who gets angry will forfeit his learning and will increase his foolishness" (*Nedarim* 22b).

Patience is needed by teachers and students alike. An impatient teacher will never benefit from discussions with his students since they will be afraid to raise questions and incur his wrath. On the other hand, a student who angers easily will not be able to bear the admonishments and discipline imposed by his master, or accept his corrections of their errors (*Midrash Shmuel*).

בְּלֵב טוֹב — *a good heart.* A good heart includes a soft nature and the ability to act joyfully for the benefit of others (*Tiferes Yisrael*). According to *Midrash Shmuel,* this refers to the constant battle for man's heart between good and evil. To become a fitting receptacle for the Torah, man must banish the evil, leaving himself with a purely *good heart*.

Avos d'Rabbi Nosson (16) explains a good heart as the ability not to begrudge others' success at Torah study. A true Torah scholar is as joyful about others' success in Torah as he is about his own. R' S. R. Hirsch elaborates: A person free of envy, jealousy and hate is free in both mind and spirit to be completely immersed in the task of seeking knowledge. This is beneficial in our associations with teachers, students and colleagues. One who enjoys a good heart will rejoice in the spiritual achievements of his companions. He will never allow carping envy to obscure the fact that much of what he knows is the fruit of his colleagues' efforts.

Midrash Shmuel views a *good heart* as complementary to the previous virtue of patience. Often a patient person masks his hurt, he suffers inwardly — and this prevents him from learning at his best. Thus, the *baraisa* teaches that success is predicated on the sort of patience that does not leave emotional scars. *B'nayos B'Ramah* relates these two prerequisites: One must be slow to anger, and when anger does overtake him he should have a *good heart*, to forgive easily.

בֶּאֱמוּנַת חֲכָמִים — *faith in the Sages.* Firm faith in the authenticity of the teachings of the Sages is the bedrock of Torah study, Only when one understands that his teachers are part of the tradition of the Oral Law given to Moses at Sinai can he earnestly apply himself to plumbing its depths. Otherwise, he may fall into the trap of cynicism and become like the ancient Sadducees and Boethusians, who rejected the entire Oral Law (*Machzor Vitry*).

A fool believes everything; a scoffer nothing. Although the wise are skeptical of what they hear and read, they accept the Torah's teachings with unquestioning faith. Thus, one must have the type of faith that the Sages themselves had. According to this interpretation, this phrase of the *baraisa* would be rendered, *the faith of the Sages* (*Tiferes Yisrael* and *Toras Avos*).

According to *Meshivas Nefesh*, one will succeed in understanding the words of the Sages only if he believes that they were infinitely greater than he. Then, even if a particular statement of the Sages seems unclear and incomprehensible, one will realize that his failure is due to his own deficiency, and will exert himself to understand. As the Sages taught, "If the earlier generations were like angels, then we are like humans. If they were like humans, then we are like donkeys." Only if we trust the Sages, can we, as humans, perceive their wisdom.

Rabbeinu Tam wrote that if we understand a complex teaching of the Torah [or the Sages], it is not proof of *their* brilliance. Rather, it means that God has endowed man with so much intelligence that sometimes he can plumb the depths of the Divine wisdom (*Sefer HaYashar*).

בְּקַבָּלַת הַיִּסוּרִין — *acceptance of suffering.* Everyone undergoes some suffering in life. Only one who can keep it from distracting him will succeed at Torah study (*Midrash Shmuel*). If one undergoes suffering, let him not question God's ways or His sense of justice. Rather than rebelling since the Torah did not protect him from suffering, let him remember that no reward in this world is sufficient for one who fulfills God's wishes. His reward will surely come in the World to Come; what happens here is transitory (*Machzor Vitry*).

According to *Ruach Chaim*, the *baraisa* does not mean actual suffering, but the diminished life-style that the Torah demands. When one willingly gives up creature comforts and commits himself to the regimen of the Torah, one's suffering is a *mitzvah* and is duly rewarded (see 6:4). Furthermore, suffering serves to purge one of the detrimental effects of sin.

❧ **Realism with faith.** One need not believe that his teacher has achieved great spiritual heights; nothing is gained by such belief and one may experience great disappointment if he learns as he becomes older that his expectations were unreasonably high. Rather one must accept what his teachers tell him as if he heard it from Moses or even as if he heard it from God Himself, not because they are on such a level, but because they are links in the chain of tradition.

Even if one knows that his spiritual level is greater than his mentor's, he should remain connected to him, since God chose to bring spiritual sustenance to the world through him (*R' Avraham of Slonim*).

❧ **Maybe it was too little?** A man poured out his heart to R' Yisrael of Rizhin. "*Rebbe*, life is unbearable. My suffering has no end." The *Rebbe* sought to comfort him and told him the following story.

A man passed away and came to the Heavenly court to be judged. Angels of mercy brought all his good deeds and placed them on the scale and angels of strict justice brought his sins and the sins outweighed the merits. Just as sentence was to be passed, the angel Gabriel cried out, "What about this man's suffering? Doesn't that count for anything?" The man's many difficult years and his long tear-filled nights were added to the scale of merit but still, the side of evil was just a bit heavier.

The man wept, "Master of the Universe, You created everything, even my suffering. Couldn't you have given me just a little bit more?"

The brokenhearted Jew left the holy Rizhiner with a bit more strength to keep on going with life.

הַמַּכִּיר אֶת מְקוֹמוֹ, וְהַשָּׂמֵחַ בְּחֶלְקוֹ, וְהָעוֹשֶׂה סְיָג לִדְבָרָיו, וְאֵינוֹ מַחֲזִיק טוֹבָה לְעַצְמוֹ, אָהוּב, אוֹהֵב אֶת הַמָּקוֹם, אוֹהֵב אֶת הַבְּרִיּוֹת, אוֹהֵב אֶת הַצְּדָקוֹת, אוֹהֵב אֶת הַמֵּישָׁרִים,

הַמַּכִּיר אֶת מְקוֹמוֹ — *knowing one's place.* One who thinks that this world is his ultimate destination sees no need to invest most of his effort and energy in spiritual matters. Only one who recognizes that he is a stranger in this world and that the World to Come is his true place will succeed at Torah (*Midrash Shmuel*).

Ruach Chaim offers a variation on this idea: Man's body will eventually return to the earth while his soul will hopefully ascend to a better world. One must recognize that his soul is the real person, and that his efforts must be directed toward allowing it to earn its true home.

According to *Tiferes Yisrael*, the *baraisa* refers to self-knowledge. One must have an honest estimate of himself and recognize his own inadequacies in order that he be ready to strive for more Torah knowledge and wisdom. As *Maharal* writes: Only one who senses he is lacking something will seek out the Torah, which brings completion to the incomplete.

וְהַשָּׂמֵחַ בְּחֶלְקוֹ — *being happy with one's lot.* One who broods over his share of this world's pleasures will not concentrate properly on Torah study. Depression and anxiety are detrimental to one's memory, mental agility and power of concentration. Only through happiness can one study Torah with an open mind (*Machzor Vitry*). In a more positive sense, one must be happy that he can be involved in the study of God's word (*Midrash Shmuel*).

According to *Ruach Chaim,* the *lot* is his own ability to learn and comprehend. Rather than being dissatisfied if he cannot live up to his ambitions or the standards of others with greater innate ability, one should do his best and constantly review, until he masters his studies. In the end he will succeed and even excel.

וְהָעוֹשֶׂה סְיָג לִדְבָרָיו — *making a [protective] fence around his personal matters.* The translation follows *Midrash Shmuel*'s first interpretation. One who makes precautions to avoid sin indicates the esteem in which he holds the Torah. The Torah responds by sharing its wisdom with him.

According to *HaChassid Yaavetz*, the phrase should be rendered as *around his words.* A true lover of Torah takes care that his words are exact and leave no room for misinterpretation. [Antigonos was not careful with his words, a flaw which resulted in the formation of the deviant Sadducees and Boethusians. See commentary to 1:3.]

Midrash Shmuel, in a very literal rendering, views this as a call to guard one's tongue and keep his words to a minimum. As Rabbi Yisrael Salanter said, "Not everything one thinks should be said. Not everything one says should be written. Not everything one writes should be printed and not everything printed should be read."

R' S. R. Hirsch offers a novel but insightful interpretation. One who is truly modest will never force his views on others. While he is outspoken and has no compunctions about voicing his convictions forcefully when necessary, he qualifies his words with the reservation that they are true only to the best of his knowledge.

וְאֵינוֹ מַחֲזִיק טוֹבָה לְעַצְמוֹ — *claiming no credit for himself.* This *baraisa* mirrors the earlier mishnah (2:9) which teaches, "If you have studied much Torah, do not take credit for yourself, because that is what you were created to do" (*R' Yosef Nachmias*). *Machzor Vitry* explains: One may never swell with pride over his spiritual accomplishments. Whatever he has learned or done is an obligation; certainly he is far from having discharged his responsibility to God.

R' S. R. Hirsch elaborates: He knows how much of his attainments he owes to favorable circumstances and influences that were not of his own making, but were expressions of God's love. He knows how dependent he has always been upon God's help in everything he has ever done and that therefore he can claim credit only for his good intentions and effort.

Ramban wrote in his famous letter to his son: "For indeed, of what should man be prideful? If he has wealth, it is God Who makes one poor or prosperous. If it is knowing one's place, being happy with one's lot, making a [protective] fence around his personal matters, claiming no credit for himself, being beloved, loving the Omnipresent, loving [His] creatures, loving righteous ways, loving justice,

---

honor, does not honor belong to God? How can one glorify himself with the honor of his Maker? If he takes pride in wisdom let him realize that *God may remove speech from even the most competent and may take away wisdom even from the aged* (see *Job* 12:20).

אָהוב — *being beloved.* A true Torah scholar is a paragon of amicability and noble conduct and thus is beloved by all [see *Yoma* 86a] (*Tiferes Yisrael*). All people will want to share his company and study with him (*Midrash Shmuel*). A true disciple of Torah will so fully inculcate the refinement and nobility of spirit that Torah induces in her best sons that he gains the love of his fellow men without even seeking it (*R' S. R. Hirsch*).

אוהב אֶת הַמָּקוֹם — *loving the Omnipresent.* One who loves the King occupies himself with the King's most valuable treasure. Diligent study of Torah is therefore an expression of a love for God (*Midrash Shmuel*). Through such study, he learns to recognize the Godly path and express his love of God by emulating His ways.

אוהב אֶת הַבְּרִיּוֹת — *loving [His] creatures.* The Torah gives one the perspective to see how all of God's creations are part of His plan for the world, engendering a love for them all. Furthermore, when one teaches Torah to others and brings them closer to God's ways it is the greatest expression of caring and love (*Midrash Shmuel*).

אוהב אֶת הַצְּדָקוֹת — *loving righteous ways.* The Torah personality minimizes the social and moral obligations others may have toward him, but he takes his obligations towards others very seriously. He loves righteousness, is upset by strife among people, and has the strength of character to defend the weak from oppression. Moses exemplified this when he defended Jethro's daughters at the well [*Exodus* 2:16-17] (*Tiferes Yisrael*).

According to *Yalkut Yehudah*, this refers to the practice of righteousness, kindness, and charity even beyond the letter of the law. This heightened sense of justice is highlighted in the Talmud (*Bava Metzia* 83). Rabbah bar bar Chana hired stevedores to carry a barrel of wine for him. Negligently, they dropped it and it broke. Since they were responsible for the damages, Rabbah seized their coats as a security against payment. The stevedores complained to Rav, who summoned Rabba bar bar Chana and demanded that he return the coats. Rabbah bar bar Chana asked Rav, "Is it the law that I must do so?" Rav replied by quoting the verse לְמַעַן תֵּלֵךְ בְּדֶרֶךְ טוֹבִים, *in order that you follow the path of the good* (*Proverbs* 2:20). ["You, Rabbah bar bar Chana, must live with a higher standard and go beyond the strict letter of the law."] Then the stevedores told Rav, "We are poor people. Our meager living depends on getting paid for the work we do. We will starve if we aren't paid." Rav told Rabbah bar bar Chana to pay them. "Is this, too, the law?" asked Rabbah bar bar Chana. Rav answered, "*and the byways of the righteous you shall keep*" (*Proverbs* ibid.).

HaChassid Yaavetz notes that this trait, צְדָקוֹת, and the next two traits, תּוֹכָחוֹת and מֵישָׁרִים, are in the plural. This is meant to imply that one should not only seek these qualities for himself but should desire that they be acquired by others as well.

אוהב אֶת הַמֵּישָׁרִים — *loving justice.* He deals with people in a straightforward fashion and wants others to deal with him in the same fashion. He appre-

---

◄§ **A higher standard.** Rabbi Shlomo Freifeld offered an explanation of Rav's extra-legal ruling. Of course, Rav's ruling cannot be found in *Choshen Mishpat*, the code of damages and restitution, but there is a higher standard, based on God's own conduct. Just as God created the world as an act of unmitigated mercy and kindness, in order to bestow pure goodness on His creatures, so man, in emulation of God's ways, can live on a level from which he emits pure kindness. It was this mode of existence that Rav expected from outstanding Torah scholars.

ciates fairness in talk and action (*HaChassid Yaavetz, Sfas Emes*).

Midrash Shmuel offers two perspectives: (a) An authentic student of Torah loves straight-forwardness and does not flatter others. [Flattery is a distortion that undermines the intellectual honesty needed for success at learning.] Alternatively, the phrase should be rendered *He loves straight thinking*; convoluted logic does not lead to clear conclusions in the halachic process.

אוֹהֵב אֶת הַתּוֹכָחוֹת — *loving reproof.* A mature person welcomes constructive criticism; he puts spiritual growth ahead of his ego. One must always understand that whoever offers rebuke is merely a messenger of God sent to make us focus on our shortcomings. Thus, do not reject the criticism of humans for if you do so, you really detest the rebuke of God (*Mili d'Avos*).

Since moral and ethical perfection is the ultimate goal of a Torah scholar, he will never be angry with someone who points out his errors and faults. Such a person is a friend, not an enemy, and one should thank him with all his heart and regard him as a benefactor (*R' S. R. Hirsch*).

The plural תּוֹכָחוֹת implies that even if one heard the criticism before, he should be willing to hear it again. [Let one never brush off rebuke with the rejoinder, "I know"] (*Chelek Yaakov*).

According to *Midrash Shmuel*, this also includes the willingness to give rebuke to others. People often are afraid to ruffle others' feathers and risk jeopardizing their relationship with them, but people who live by the Torah do not shirk their responsibility for the spiritual welfare of their friends — even if it may hurt them socially. The Talmud speaks glowingly of such a person: "One who rebukes his friend for the sake of Heaven merits to be brought inside the partition of God. Furthermore, he merits to find favor in the eyes of people" (*Tamid* 28a).

וּמִתְרַחֵק מִן הַכָּבוֹד — *keeping far from honor.* He studies Torah not for honor, but in order to express his love of God. In this fashion he is able to learn

◆§ **A rare opportunity.** When the Sfas Emes was a teen-ager, his study partner was Rabbi Yitzchak Feigenbaum (later *Rav* of Warsaw). They would study until 11 a.m. and then attend a private lecture with the Chiddushei HaRim, grandfather of the Sfas Emes. One day the two young men became so engrossed in learning that they lost track of time. At 11:30 they rushed to the home of the Chiddushei HaRim, and as soon as they entered, the grandfather sharply admonished his grandson. "Leibel, what will become of you? If you waste time, you will make nothing of yourself."

The young Sfas Emes remained silent, not offering a word of defense. When they finished the study session and left, Yitzchak Feigenbaum asked his friend, "Why didn't you tell your grandfather the truth; that we became engrossed in learning and lost track of the time? You should have explained."

Leibel answered, "How often does one get a chance to hear rebuke from a Jew like my grandfather? Such an opportunity may not be missed even if a good excuse exists. One must love rebuke!"

His son and successor, the Imrei Emes, shared this love of rebuke. He spoke fondly of the time when he was bested by a *chassid* of his. "Once I was walking up the steps to my apartment after receiving many *chassidim*. An elderly Jew followed me and handed me a petitionary note. I said to him, 'Please believe me, I don't have even a minute now.' The Jew answered, 'I have had time for over twenty years to care of my sick daughter, and the *Rebbe* doesn't have even one minute for her?!' "

◆§ **Hesitant flight.** The famous maxim has it that if one flees from honor, the honor pursues him. Someone once complained to his rabbi that he flees from honor and yet it does not pursue him. "Why is this?"

Answered the rabbi, "The problem is that you keep looking over your shoulder to see if the honor is following."

from *all* persons, even those less knowledgeable than he (*Midrash Shmuel*). Not only does he not seek honor, he even shuns it when offered (*Machzor Vitry*).

A true Torah scholar realizes how far he is from perfection. He understands the spiritual danger inherent in honor and public recognition. He therefore seeks to keep as far as possible from honor and accolades (*Tiferes Yisrael, R' S. R. Hirsch*).

וְלֹא מֵגִיס לִבּוֹ בְּתַלְמוּדוֹ — *not being arrogant with his learning.* Not only does he not seek honor, he even feels no sense of superiority because of his knowledge. He constantly feels that whatever he knows is insignificant to what he should have learned. Such spiritual thirst will propel him to true greatness (*Midrash Shmuel*).

Tiferes Yisrael suggests that to be arrogant about one's knowledge is a glaring ethical flaw. Rather, he interprets this phrase in the sense of *overfamiliarity* (see *Sotah* 1:6). People long married develop a casual familiarity that allows them to speak unabashedly to each other. Not so a groom who is just getting to know his betrothed; he is careful with every word he says. Likewise, the true Torah scholar speaks about Torah and its Sages with utmost discretion.

וְאֵינוֹ שָׂמֵחַ בְּהוֹרָאָה — *not enjoying halachic decision-making.* Ever humble, he feels he is unworthy to decide on halachic issues, and follows the advice of the Sages, who teach that a judge must always view himself as one standing on the edge of *Gehinnom* with a sword poised over his neck

(see *Yevamos* 109b). Afraid to err, he does not want to be included in the words of the mishnah (4:9), "One who is too self-confident in handing down legal decisions is a fool, wicked and arrogant of spirit" (*Midrash Shmuel, Machzor Vitry*).

On the other hand, he realizes that it his responsibility to rule when he is the most qualified to do so. A student of the *Chofetz Chaim* once said that he was afraid to assume a rabbinical position for fear of erring in halachic judgment. Replied the *Chofetz Chaim*, "Who then should be a rabbi — someone who has no fear of erring?"

נוֹשֵׂא בְעֹל עִם חֲבֵרוֹ — *sharing his fellow's yoke.* He helps others any way he can, whether the help entails physical strain, financial expense, or emotional strain. He feels the friend's pain and does whatever he can to help. He is interested in what is good for his friend in this world and the next (*Tiferes Yisrael*). In this way he draws others close to Torah (*HaChassid Yaavetz*). This also entails having the patience and sensitivity to retain relationships with people in spite of their unpleasant personalities (*Midrash Shmuel*).

Alternatively, this is a call to be ready to study with others, even though he prefers to study alone (*Midrash Shmuel*). One should seek to understand his friend's opinion rather than immediately dismissing it as incorrect. This too is a form of bearing the yoke of friendship (*Ruach Chaim*).

◆§ **A personal need.** Rabbi Avraham Grodzinski, famed prewar *mashgiach* of Slabodka, submitted that empathy with the pain of others is easier to achieve than empathy with their joy.

Once, while visiting his family in Warsaw, R' Abraham noted the time — and began to dance! After some time he stopped and explained to his bewildered relatives. "At this moment, a student of mine is going to the *chupah* (wedding canopy). I cannot be at the wedding, but I can join him in his joy even from here."

This ability to so totally throw oneself into his friend's situation is the key to the adage of the Sages, "Anyone who entreats on behalf of a friend for something he himself needs will be answered [by God] first" (*Bava Kamma* 92a). One who cares so much for a friend that he prays to God as if it were his personal problem deserves to be answered (*Ohr Yitzchak*).

וּמַכְרִיעוֹ לְכַף זְכוּת, וּמַעֲמִידוֹ עַל הָאֱמֶת, וּמַעֲמִידוֹ
עַל הַשָּׁלוֹם, וּמִתְיַשֵּׁב לִבּוֹ בְּתַלְמוּדוֹ, שׁוֹאֵל וּמֵשִׁיב,
שׁוֹמֵעַ וּמוֹסִיף, הַלּוֹמֵד עַל מְנָת לְלַמֵּד, וְהַלּוֹמֵד עַל
מְנָת לַעֲשׂוֹת, הַמַּחְכִּים אֶת רַבּוֹ, וְהַמְכַוֵּן אֶת שְׁמוּעָתוֹ,

---

וּמַכְרִיעוֹ לְכַף זְכוּת — *judging him favorably.* He will judge his fellow favorably, even if he does something that seems to be sinful (*Midrash Shmuel*). In his desire to help others, he will accentuate the good in them and attempt to overlook their shortcomings (*HaChassid Yaavetz*). Since Torah is the inheritance of the nation, anything that enhances national unity is a preparatory stage for Torah (*Maharal*).

וּמַעֲמִידוֹ עַל הָאֱמֶת — *setting him on the truthful course.* When a colleague makes a mistake in debate, the true Torah scholar derives no pleasure. Instead, he tactfully corrects his colleague and attempts to focus him on the truth (*Midrash Shmuel*).

Machzor Vitry suggests that this quality calls on one to avoid arbitrarily dismissing a colleague's arguments.

וּמַעֲמִידוֹ עַל הַשָּׁלוֹם — *setting him on the peaceful course.* By being flexible and ready to compromise when possible and legitimate, the Torah scholar promotes peace among people (*Midrash Shmuel*). *Ruach Chaim* and *Mili d'Avos* view the last two stiches as connected. One must seek to rectify his friend's misconceptions without demeaning him. Truth must be served; but only in a peaceful fashion. According to the Talmud (*Berachos* 64a), Torah scholars increase peace in the world.

וּמִתְיַשֵּׁב לִבּוֹ בְּתַלְמוּדוֹ — *thinking deliberately in his study.* Rather than learning quickly and haphazardly, he studies in a composed and steady manner. Alternatively, this means that he reviews the lesson afterwards in order to be sure that everything is clear (*Midrash Shmuel*).

According to *Tiferes Yisrael*, the *baraisa* speaks of the thorough preparation necessary before one presents a Torah lecture or address. A competent and conscientious scholar prepares well, both in terms of content and how it should be presented.

Sfas Emes seeks to differentiate between the ear-lier mentioned בְּיִשּׁוּב, *deliberation*, and this stich. Thus, he renders *his heart becomes composed by Torah study.* One who suffers from problems in life and yet is able to quell this inner tempest by means of deep Torah study demonstrates clearly his powerful connection to the Torah. Rabbi Yitzchak Hutner offered the following analogy: One who has something in his hand may or may not be grasping it. The way to know is by trying to pull it away. Likewise, only when the vicissitudes of life threaten to pull man away from Torah study can we know the depth of his connection to it. King David put it succinctly. *Had Your Torah not been my preoccupation, then I would have perished in my affliction* (*Psalms* 119:92).

The *Chofetz Chaim* homiletically rendered the phrase as *his heart derives the lessons of his learning.* One must not only study but also internalize the messages of Torah, so that it elevates his mundane existence.

For this reason, there are no spaces between the paragraphs of Balaam's prophecy, while there *are* spaces between paragraphs of Moses' prophecy. The purpose of the spaces is to provide time for contemplation and analysis (*Rashi, Leviticus* 1:1), but Balaam, who had no interest in putting his sacred prophecies into practice, had no need for the opportunity to contemplate the lessons God was granting him. Moses, however, needed time to internalize God's teaching.

שׁוֹאֵל וּמֵשִׁיב — *asking and answering.* This process of give and take provides the clarity that engraves knowledge deeply and permanently into the heart and mind. One's questions should be pertinent rather than tangential and inconsequential. When queries are motivated by a genuine desire to learn and know, rather than to engage in intellectual jousting, they will yield added clarity (*Tiferes Yisrael*).

Many texts read שׁוֹאֵל כְּעִנְיָן וּמֵשִׁיב כַּהֲלָכָה, *he asks pertinent questions and answers to the point.* His

yoke, judging him favorably, setting him on the truthful course, setting him on the peaceful course, thinking deliberately in his study, asking and answering, listening and contributing to the discussion, learning in order to teach, learning in order to practice,

---

questions relate to the subject matter presently being taught by his teacher so that the teacher can answer to the point. As the Talmud admonishes, one should never ask a Torah scholar regarding one issue when he is occupied with another area of study.

שׁוֹמֵעַ וּמוֹסִיף — *listening and contributing* [lit. *adding*] *to the discussion.* One must listen to his teachers and understand the ramifications of their words so that he is able to expand upon what he learned. [However, he should seek to support rather than contradict the words of his mentor] (*Rashi*).

Alternatively, he *listens and continues to do so,* never tiring or getting bored of learning (*Midrash Shmuel*).

In *Tiferes Yisrael's* view this is directed to teachers who should listen carefully to their students. If they have not fully understood the lesson, the teacher should be willing to explain as many more times as is necessary.

Machzor Vitry renders *he listens and adds to his knowledge.* He endeavors to enrich his knowledge by listening to others. By working to understand his mentor's words in depth, he can use his newly discovered knowledge as a key to unlock new areas of wisdom.

הַלּוֹמֵד עַל מְנָת לְלַמֵּד — *learning in order to teach.* Learning with the intent of sharing one's knowledge helps to achieve success at learning, in two ways: one practical and one metaphysical. The constant review one experiences when teaching, combined with the necessity to understand the material clearly, in order to convey it to others, helps one master the subject matter. Metaphysically, the desire to teach is a form of praying for others. The Sages promised that the supplicant will be answered by God first (*Midrash Shmuel*).

The Talmud compares a Torah scholar to a flask of scented oil. Covered, its aroma does not spread; uncovered, it lends a fine fragrance to its surroundings. Such is the difference between a scholar who studies, and one who also teaches. Furthermore, a

teacher's capacity expands, so that, in time, he will come to understand areas of Torah knowledge that were once too difficult for him (*Avodah Zarah* 35b; *Rashi* ad loc.).

וְהַלּוֹמֵד עַל מְנָת לַעֲשׂוֹת — *learning in order to practice.* Torah may not be studied in a purely theoretical sense; it must lead to action (see 1:17). One who studies with the intent of learning all the details necessary for proper performance of the *mitzvos* is considered to have already fulfilled the *mitzvos* (see 3:12) and is granted success at his studies (*Tiferes Yisrael*). *Midrash Shmuel* adds: Since he studies all the details carefully, he will retain what he learns.

הַמַּחְכִּים אֶת רַבּוֹ — *making his teacher wiser.* He sharpens his mentor by asking incisive questions and seeking constant clarification of his teachings. Of such a student a teacher may legitimately declare, "Much have I learned from my teachers, more from my colleagues but most of all from my students" (*Taanis* 7a). Reish Lakish was a classic example of this type of student. When he died, someone else became the senior disciple of R' Yochanan, but R' Yochanan grieved over the difference between the two. "Whenever I propounded an idea, the son of Lakish would ask twenty-four questions and raise twenty-four objections. This led to a deeper and fuller understanding of the law. The new study partner only provides twenty-four proofs to my words" [see *Bava Metzia* 84a] (*Midrash Shmuel*).

Tiferes Yisrael and *Midrash Shmuel* offer an alternative rendering: *He deems his teacher wise.* In order to succeed at learning one must respect his teacher's wisdom. Then, even after the student has become an accomplished scholar, he will still try to understand fully the words of his mentor. When one learns from someone whom he regards as a great man, he will always remember his words.

וְהַמְכַוֵּן אֶת שְׁמוּעָתוֹ — *pondering over what he has learned.* The translation follows *Midrash Shmuel*. Torah study cannot be conducted in a superficial manner; to fully understand, one must give careful

וְהָאוֹמֵר דָּבָר בְּשֵׁם אוֹמְרוֹ. הָא לָמַדְתָּ, כָּל הָאוֹמֵר דָּבָר
בְּשֵׁם אוֹמְרוֹ, מֵבִיא גְאֻלָּה לָעוֹלָם, שֶׁנֶּאֱמַר: ,,וַתֹּאמֶר
אֶסְתֵּר לַמֶּלֶךְ בְּשֵׁם מָרְדֳּכָי.''

[ז] גְּדוֹלָה תוֹרָה, שֶׁהִיא נוֹתֶנֶת חַיִּים לְעוֹשֶׂיהָ בָּעוֹלָם

consideration to each idea.

Rashi renders *he notes accurately what he has learned.* When quoting his teacher, he is careful to repeat it exactly as he received it.

Midrash Shmuel further suggests rendering the phrase as *he seeks out the intent of the teaching.* A good student wants to know not only the outcome, but also the underlying rationale for the ideas he learns. In this fashion his knowledge will remain lodged in his heart and mind. Alternatively, one should *focus* on what he learns and connect it to other pertinent ideas.

וְהָאוֹמֵר דָּבָר בְּשֵׁם אוֹמְרוֹ — *and repeating a saying in the name of the one who said it.* Not only should one refuse to pass off as his own whatever he has heard from others, thus falsely taking credit for someone else's statement, but he should also mention *by name* the person from whom he heard it, thus displaying indebtedness to the source (*Tiferes Yisrael*).

Even to anonymously ascribe the thought to "others" is insufficient (*Yalkut Yehudah*).

That it is forbidden to take credit for someone's else's idea is derive from the verse, *Do not steal from the poor man, for he is poor* (Proverbs 22:22). One may not steal from anyone, even one so poor that he owns nothing more than his Torah thoughts (*Midrash Tanchuma, Bamidbar* 27).

The Midrash (*Koheles Rabbah* 2) teaches that one who

habitually does not repeat things in the name of his teacher will forget his learning.

The efficacy of ascribing things to their source in causing success at learning is explained by *Midrash Shmuel*: Since he cannot pass off the ideas of others as his own, he will have to exert great effort in order to formulate his own original ideas. *Ruach Chaim* suggests that many questions and seeming contradictions are resolved by the Talmud by ascertaining the source of the idea. By knowing who said what, many apparent contradictions can be resolved.

Repeating something in the name of the one who said it is a great source of merit for that person — even after his passing. Tradition has it that his lips move in the grave when one of his Torah ideas is repeated.

הָא לָמַדְתָּ, כָּל הָאוֹמֵר דָּבָר בְּשֵׁם אוֹמְרוֹ, מֵבִיא גְאֻלָּה לָעוֹלָם — *For you have learned this: Whoever repeats a thing in the name of the one who said it brings redemption to the world.* In addition to the moral responsibility to attribute ideas to their source, there is an additional benefit to doing so. It is a cause for redemption, both communal and personal (*Midrash Shmuel*).

Maharal explains the dynamic of why attribution is a catalyst for redemption. Exile is a state in which people are displaced, in both a physical and spiritual sense. The physical expression of redemp-

◆§ **Personal liberation.** The Talmud is filled with ideas quoted in the name of their source, yet we still are in exile! The *Chozeh* of Lublin understood from this that people can feel a *personal* sense of spiritual redemption by dealing honestly with the ideas of others. Even in national exile, individual Jews should experience a sense of freedom due to the merit of honest attribution.

◆§ **Impeding redemption?** Rabbi Shmuel Alter suggested humorously that this maxim is the source for the custom of public speakers to end their comments with a prayer for the advent of the Messiah and the redemption of Zion. Since public speakers often appropriate the ideas of others without bothering to give them credit, they fear that they may have delayed the redemption. To compensate for this impediment of salvation, they add a personal prayer for redemption.

making his teacher wiser, pondering over what he has learned, and repeating a saying in the name of the one who said it. For you have learned this: Whoever repeats a thing in the name of the one who said it brings redemption to the world, as it is said: *And Esther said to the king in the name of Mordechai* (*Esther* 2:22).

7. **G**reat is the Torah, for it confers life upon its practitioners,

---

tion is when people are returned to their natural habitat. One who returns ideas to their natural place by citing them in the name of their promulgators mirrors the process of redemption by redeeming the ideas and returning them to their source.

שֶׁנֶּאֱמַר: ,,וַתֹּאמֶר אֶסְתֵּר לַמֶּלֶךְ בְּשֵׁם מָרְדְּכָי'' — *as it is said: "And Esther said to the king in the name of Mordechai"* (*Esther* 2:22). When Bigthan and Teresh, two of King Ahasuerus's chamberlains, plotted to assassinate him, the plot became known to Mordechai who told Queen Esther. She in turn related it to the king in the name of Mordechai, and the act of loyalty to the king was recorded in the royal chronicles. Later when Ahasuerus sought to reward Mordechai, Haman "happened" to be present and was charged with honoring his archenemy Mordechai. That was the beginning of Haman's downfall and the subsequent salvation of the Jews. Thus, repeating something in the name

of the original source was the catalyst for redemption.

Yaaros D'vash questions the premise. Maybe the Purim story was an isolated incident? How does it prove a sweeping generality that attribution is a harbinger of redemption? In truth, it was dangerous for Esther to report it in the name of Mordechai, for if an investigation corroborated Mordechai's claim, both he and his fellow Jews would have been placed in jeopardy. In fact, the Sages report that the investigators tampered with the evidence and removed the poison that Bigthan and Teresh had planned to use, but an angel put it back. Why did Esther not wait for an investigation before revealing her source?

Very clearly, then, Esther knew that attribution brings redemption and that no harm could come from revealing the plot in the name of Mordechai. Esther's lack of fear clearly proves that one who reports something in the name of the one who said it brings redemption to the world.

Mishnah 7

גְּדוֹלָה תוֹרָה, שֶׁהִיא נוֹתֶנֶת חַיִּים לְעוֹשֶׂיהָ — *Great is the Torah, for it confers life upon its practitioners.*

Midrash Shmuel notes that the *baraisa* speaks of those who *practice* Torah, not those who learn it. The primary purpose and focus of learning is doing. As we are taught earlier (1:17), not study but practice is the main thing. If one studies purely for theoretical knowledge, it would be better had he not been created (*Yerushalmi, Shabbos* 1:2). King David writes: *Torah offers a good understand-*

ing to all their practitioners (*Psalms* 111:10). The Talmud notes that this speaks of those who practice, rather than of those who only study. It is the study of the theory, plus its application in practice, that provides man with life both here and in the hereafter.

Luach Erez adds: God grants life not only to those who learn, but also to those who support scholars. [It is for this reason that God does not give scholars their livelihood directly. He allows

---

∽§ **Life-giving Torah.** R' Shlomo of Vilna, author of *Cheshek Shlomo*, became deathly ill when he was seventeen. The doctors warned him that he must immediately stop all his learning, since the mental strain could be catastrophic for his health. He refused to comply: "If I can't learn, I am dead; the Torah gives me life. Even if the doctors are right and learning could be fatal, I prefer dying while learning to dying without learning."

R' Shlomo kept on learning to a ripe old age!

הַזֶּה וּבְעוֹלָם הַבָּא, שֶׁנֶּאֱמַר: „כִּי חַיִּים הֵם לְמֹצְאֵיהֶם, וּלְכָל
בְּשָׂרוֹ מַרְפֵּא.״ וְאוֹמֵר: „רִפְאוּת תְּהִי לְשָׁרֶּךָ, וְשִׁקּוּי
לְעַצְמוֹתֶיךָ.״ וְאוֹמֵר: „עֵץ חַיִּים הִיא לַמַּחֲזִיקִים בָּהּ וְתֹמְכֶיהָ
מְאֻשָּׁר.״ וְאוֹמֵר: „כִּי לִוְיַת חֵן הֵם לְרֹאשֶׁךָ, וַעֲנָקִים
לְגַרְגְּרֹתֶיךָ.״ וְאוֹמֵר: „תִּתֵּן לְרֹאשְׁךָ לִוְיַת חֵן, עֲטֶרֶת תִּפְאֶרֶת

---

others to be linked to life by providing for Torah scholars.] Thus Torah gives life even to its *doers* — those who provide the wherewithal for Torah study.

Tiferes Yisrael explains the novel thought expressed in this *baraisa*. While all other types of wisdom can grant man many good things *in* life, only Torah grants man life. And without life all else is worthless.

Unlike the non-Jewish perception that holiness is rooted in asceticism and that study of Godly ideas can be conducted only in isolation from the mundane details of life, Torah gives man the key to sanctify all facets of human existence (*Darkei Yosher*). According to *Knesses Yisrael,* the Torah gives man satisfaction and a sense of purpose in life.

בְּעוֹלָם הַזֶּה וּבְעוֹלָם הַבָּא — *both in this world and in the World to Come.* One enjoys the fruits of learning Torah and fulfilling its *mitzvos* in this world with the principal reward reserved for the next world (*Rashi;* see *Peah* 1:1). The greatness of Torah is exemplified by the fact that even though this world and the next are diametrically opposite one another, the Torah has the power to grant man life and happiness in both worlds (*Even Shleimah*).

The *baraisa* now cites many verses from *Proverbs* that speak of the life and happiness the Torah

grants those who adhere to its dictates and messages. Each verse is couched in dual terms to indicate that Torah is a source of life in both worlds.

שֶׁנֶּאֱמַר: „כִּי חַיִּים הֵם לְמֹצְאֵיהֶם, וּלְכָל בְּשָׂרוֹ מַרְפֵּא״ — *"For they [the teachings of the Torah] are life to those who find them, and a healing to his entire flesh"* (*Proverbs* 4:22). The fruits of one's Torah observance will provide life in this world, and even in the next world (after death), when man's body is but flesh without a soul, Torah provides life (*Rashi*).

Sfas Emes interprets conversely. True life is in the World to Come. Even in this world where the power of man's soul is restricted by his physicality, the Torah still provides life. According to *Malbim,* the verse teaches that one who acquires Torah knowledge merits physical and spiritual life. While each physical ailment needs a different medicine, Torah is a generic elixir for all ailments.

Maharal (Nesiv HaTorah 1) views the therapeutic power of Torah as rooted in the fact that it is the blueprint of creation. One who is linked to Torah returns to a world without flaw or illness.

וְאוֹמֵר: „רִפְאוּת תְּהִי לְשָׁרֶּךָ, וְשִׁקּוּי לְעַצְמוֹתֶיךָ״ — *And it says: "It shall be healing to your flesh and marrow to your bones"* (*ibid.* 3:8). The Torah's healing power can overcome all the physical and spiri-

---

  The lifeline. *Maharal* explains: Man cannot take life by himself; he must be connected to the Source of all life. Just as the leaves and branches of a tree draw sustenance when they are attached to the roots and wilt when that connection is severed, so too when man studies Torah it provides him with the means to connect to the Living God. Hence, it provides man with life both in this world and the next.

  Nesivos Shalom elaborates: Just as the body needs food for its sustenance, so the soul needs its source of spiritual sustenance — Torah. The wicked are considered dead even during their lifetimes (*Berachos* 18b) because they have severed their lifeline to Torah and hence to God.

  Antidote. *Divrei Shmuel* related that whenever he found himself in a bad mood or under stress, he would study a page of the Talmud. If his problem was exceptionally difficult, he would learn two pages. If the situation was utterly unbearable, he would learn three pages of the Talmud — and he could cope with any pain in the world. Thus, Torah gives life to man for with Torah he lacks nothing.

both in this world and in the World to Come, as it is said: *For they [the teachings of the Torah] are life to those who find them, and a healing to his entire flesh* (Proverbs 4:22). And it says: *It shall be healing to your flesh and marrow to your bones* (ibid. 3:8). And it says: *It is a tree of life to those who grasp it, and its supporters are praiseworthy* (ibid. 3:18). And it says: *They are a tiara of grace for your head and necklaces for your neck* (ibid. 1:9). And it says: *It will give to your head a tiara of grace, a crown of glory it will*

---

tual maladies of this world and sustain one's bones [i.e., essence] even in the grave (*Rashi*). Let one not think that Torah study and the life-style it demands are detrimental to life and health. Even though the Torah proscribes much in the way of food or other physical indulgence, this only enhances one's health, body and soul. One's source of sustenance will be fresh and his bones will enjoy vibrancy. This is true physically, since overindulgence is unhealthy, and spiritually, since God protects those who follow His Torah (*Malbim*).

וְאוֹמֵר: ,,עֵץ חַיִּים הִיא לַמַּחֲזִיקִים בָּהּ וְתֹמְכֶיהָ מְאֻשָּׁר" — *And it says: It is a tree of life to those who grasp it, and its supporters are praiseworthy* (ibid. 3:18). The Talmud enlightens us as to the life-giving power of Torah: "The Torah is a life-giving medicine for those who engage in its study for its own sake" (*Taanis* 7a). Among those who study Torah, there are two types: (a) Those who do not possess sharp minds and who, through perseverance, succeed at Torah because they *grasp it*: for them, the Torah becomes a tree of life because they cling to it, never letting go. (b) Regarding those with brilliant minds who do not need to exert much effort to learn, it says, *And its supporters are praiseworthy*. It requires less effort to lean on something and support it than it does to grasp it (*Midrash Shmuel*).

Ruach Chaim offers the counterpoint of the two halves of the verse with a lovely analogy: Imagine a person caught in a raging storm at sea, where each wave threatens to engulf him and pull him under. The only thing standing between him and death is the branch of a tree that he managed to grasp as he was being swept away by the current. He holds on to that branch for dear life because his life depends on it. Man, in this world, is also in the midst of a raging sea of desire and ambition. The waves of pride and passion threaten to drown him in an ocean of worldly pleasure, and only one thing can save him — Torah, the Tree of Life. As long as he clings to it, grasping it firmly as though his very life depends on it, he may weather the storm. Should he let go, all is lost. Thus, Torah is a tree of life for those who grasp it. Reward will come even to those who feel that in a world where few are involved in the search for God they are doing the Torah a favor by studying it. Thus, even those who mistakenly think that they support and carry the Torah will also find happiness.

According to *Mili d'Avos*, the two parts of the verse are connected. Unlike physical food, which can provide sustenance only to the person who eats it, the Torah provides sustenance not only to those who *grasp* it and study it, but even to those who merely *support* it.

וְאוֹמֵר: ,,כִּי לִוְיַת חֵן הֵם לְרֹאשֶׁךָ, וַעֲנָקִים לְגַרְגְּרֹתֶיךָ" — *And it says: "They are a tiara of grace for your head and necklaces for your neck"* (ibid. 1:9). Both the intellectual content of one's Torah study, symbolized by the head, as well as his ability to verbalize his thoughts, symbolized by the neck, will be pleasing to others and will enjoy a special grace.

It is through the Torah that your head, your mind and your understanding will gain the gift of the Divine approval that causes man's spiritual life to flourish. Then, its blessings will extend even to all of your physical body, culminating in the neck that bears your head. Everything will be so ennobled that the whole man will be worthy of honor (*R' S. R. Hirsch*).

וְאוֹמֵר: ,,תִּתֵּן לְרֹאשְׁךָ לִוְיַת חֵן, עֲטֶרֶת תִּפְאֶרֶת תְּמַגְּנֶךָ" — *And it says: "It will give to your head a tiara of grace, a crown of glory it will deliver to you"*

תְּמַגְּנֶךָ.'' וְאוֹמֵר: ,,כִּי בִי יִרְבּוּ יָמֶיךָ, וְיוֹסִיפוּ לְךָ שְׁנוֹת חַיִּים.''
וְאוֹמֵר: ,,אֹרֶךְ יָמִים בִּימִינָהּ, בִּשְׂמֹאולָהּ עֹשֶׁר וְכָבוֹד.''
וְאוֹמֵר: ,,כִּי אֹרֶךְ יָמִים וּשְׁנוֹת חַיִּים, וְשָׁלוֹם יוֹסִיפוּ לָךְ.''.

[ח] רַבִּי שִׁמְעוֹן בֶּן יְהוּדָה מִשּׁוּם רַבִּי שִׁמְעוֹן בֶּן יוֹחַאי
אוֹמֵר: הַנּוֹי, וְהַכֹּחַ, וְהָעֹשֶׁר, וְהַכָּבוֹד, וְהַחָכְמָה,
וְהַזִּקְנָה, וְהַשֵּׂיבָה, וְהַבָּנִים — נָאֶה לַצַּדִּיקִים וְנָאֶה לָעוֹלָם,

(*ibid.* 4:9). According to *R' Yonah* (*Commentary to Proverbs*), this teaches that the words of one who studies Torah will be heard and accepted. *Malbim* adds: The Torah gives its love and grace to all who love it. Thus those who earnestly seek the enlightenment of Torah will enjoy grace in the eyes of God and man, and will reap extraordinary and eternal signs of honor.

Tiferes Yisrael interprets the verse as promising that in the same way that the Torah provides physical welfare to those who learn it, so it safeguards one's prestige. The true devotee of Torah will merit an unassailable crown of glory.

Midrash Shmuel views the verse as teaching that the loyal Torah personality will receive the gracious gift of life in this world and will enjoy his deserved reward in the World to Come.

— וְאוֹמֵר: ,,כִּי בִי יִרְבּוּ יָמֶיךָ, וְיוֹסִיפוּ לְךָ שְׁנוֹת חַיִּים''
And it says: "Indeed, through me [the Torah] your days shall be increased, and years of life shall be added to you" (*ibid.* 9:11). *Metzudos David* explains: King Solomon promises that due to involvement in Torah study one may merit increased time in this world. With this extra time one can do *mitzvos* and good deeds which will earn him yet additional years of life.

— וְאוֹמֵר: ,,אֹרֶךְ יָמִים בִּימִינָהּ, בִּשְׂמֹאולָהּ עֹשֶׁר וְכָבוֹד''
And it says: "Lengthy days are at its right, and at its left are wealth and honor" (*ibid.* 3:16). The verse now enumerates the various types of success that accompany Torah study. For those who study Torah for its own sake (*its right*), it provides longevity and certainly wealth and honor. Even for those who study for ulterior motives, it provides

wealth and honor (*Rashi* to *Proverbs* ibid.). *Rashi* (to *Shabbos* 88b) defines *its right* as those who study with all their might, earnestly seeking to know the Torah's secrets; much like a person who works with his right, usually stronger, hand.

According to *Malbim*, right and left denote the importance one attaches to things. While most people deem wealth and honor to be their most important goals, and figuratively hold them in their right hand, the authentic lover of Torah knows *that length of days*, i.e., the World to Come, deserves priority, and that honor and wealth are secondary.

וְאוֹמֵר: ,,כִּי אֹרֶךְ יָמִים וּשְׁנוֹת חַיִּים, וְשָׁלוֹם יוֹסִיפוּ לָךְ''
— *And it says: "For lengthy days and years of life, and peace shall they add to you"* (*ibid.* 3:2). The study of Torah and the fulfillment of *mitzvos* will grant man secure and tranquil longevity (*Rashi*). The merit of these endeavors will plead one's case in front of God (*Metzudos David*). The Talmud (*Yoma* 71a) questions the usage "years of life." Are there years of life and years without life? Rather, years of life are times when life turns from bad to good. It is this power to mitigate difficulties that the Torah gives to those who loyally study it.

According to *Midrash Shmuel, lengthy days* refers to life in this temporary world while *years of life* refers to the World to Come. It is there that God will give man true peace.

According to *Rashi,* the verses cited here come to describe yet an additional gift that the Torah bequeaths to its loyal adherents. The first three verses prove that Torah provides man with vibrant life, but we do not know that it also provides wealth. In fact, we have seen many who suffer such poverty

deliver to you (ibid. 4:9). And it says: Indeed, through me [the Torah] your days shall be increased, and years of life shall be added to you (ibid. 9:11). And it says: Lengthy days are at its right, and at its left are wealth and honor (ibid. 3:16). And it says: For lengthy days and years of life, and peace shall they add to you (ibid. 3:2).

8. Rabbi Shimon ben Yehudah says in the name of Rabbi Shimon ben Yochai: Beauty, strength, wealth, honor, wisdom, old age, hoary age, and children — these befit the righteous and befit the

---

that they lose their appetite to live. Therefore, the verse teaches that he will attain wealth and thus find grace among people. The next verse teaches that Torah grants honor as well to its loyal sons.

Let one not think that these gifts are granted even to one that studies for ulterior motives. Therefore, we are taught that only those who study Torah for its own sake merit all these things. Finally, we are taught that peace, the greatest of all blessings, is the lot of those who learn Torah.

Mishnah 8

רַבִּי שִׁמְעוֹן בֶּן יְהוּדָה מִשּׁוּם רַבִּי שִׁמְעוֹן בֶּן יוֹחָאִי אוֹמֵר — *Rabbi Shimon ben Yehudah says in the name of Rabbi Shimon ben Yochai.* A resident of Kfar Akko, he was a fifth-generation *Tanna* and a prized student of R' Shimon ben Yochai whose dicta he frequently conveyed.

הַנּוֹי, וְהַכֹּחַ, וְהָעשֶׁר, וְהַכָּבוֹד, וְהַחָכְמָה, וְהַזִּקְנָה, וְהַשֵּׂיבָה, וְהַבָּנִים – נָאֶה לַצַּדִּיקִים וְנָאֶה לָעוֹלָם — *Beauty, strength, wealth, honor, wisdom, old age, hoary age, and children — these befit the righteous and befit the world.* All of the desirable qualities listed here will enhance and elevate a person if they are channeled toward the service of God. Thus they will be ornaments both for their bearer and his surroundings. When righteous people use such qualities properly, they can transpose the transitory into the eternal.

Ruach Chaim adds: These attributes are like zeros. If one places something before them, they become meaningful and valuable; if not, they remain worthless. (a) Beauty can be a terrible trap. Joseph was almost a victim of his own beauty, but because he overcame its temptation, he became known historically as Joseph the Righteous. He turned his beauty into a catalyst towards greatness (*Midrash Shmuel*). Furthermore, the beauty of one's words makes him a fitting spokesman to teach the word of God.

(b) Strength is good, since Torah study is physically draining and one must recharge his energies. Strength as power, however, can be detrimental. Another positive factor is the power to protect the weak and vulnerable.

(c) Wealth can enable one to be charitable and to study without financial pressures. Furthermore, one can advance causes honestly, since he need not flatter anybody. However, an open account allows one to indulge in forbidden pleasures.

(d) Honor is a powerful force for good and bad. An honorable person can exercise influence on those around him in a very positive fashion. The negative side of honor is the arrogance it can bring, and the abuses of power it can cause.

(e) Wisdom is a two-edged sword; it can lead either to the service of God or to negative behavior.

(f) Old and hoary age is a decidedly positive force in the art of rebuke, since an older person speaks from experience and thus has a deep effect on his listeners. On the other hand, the extra years can become extra time to sin.

(g) Children are the greatest source of merit for a person, if he raises them in the Torah way. When one uses his children to fight his battles, however, he has turned a potential for good into evil.

We are therefore taught to use these characteristics only for good (*Midrash Shmuel*).

שֶׁנֶּאֱמַר: "עֲטֶרֶת תִּפְאֶרֶת שֵׂיבָה, בְּדֶרֶךְ צְדָקָה תִּמָּצֵא."

וְאוֹמֵר: "עֲטֶרֶת זְקֵנִים בְּנֵי בָנִים, וְתִפְאֶרֶת בָּנִים אֲבוֹתָם."

וְאוֹמֵר: "תִּפְאֶרֶת בַּחוּרִים כֹּחָם, וַהֲדַר זְקֵנִים שֵׂיבָה."

וְאוֹמֵר: "וְחָפְרָה הַלְּבָנָה וּבוֹשָׁה הַחַמָּה, כִּי מָלַךְ יהוה צְבָאוֹת בְּהַר צִיּוֹן וּבִירוּשָׁלַיִם, וְנֶגֶד זְקֵנָיו כָּבוֹד." רַבִּי שִׁמְעוֹן בֶּן מְנַסְיָא אוֹמֵר: אֵלּוּ שֶׁבַע מִדּוֹת, שֶׁמָּנוּ חֲכָמִים לַצַּדִּיקִים, כֻּלָּם נִתְקַיְּמוּ בְּרַבִּי וּבְבָנָיו.

[ט] **אָמַר** רַבִּי יוֹסֵי בֶּן קִסְמָא: פַּעַם אַחַת הָיִיתִי מְהַלֵּךְ בַּדֶּרֶךְ, וּפָגַע בִּי אָדָם אֶחָד. וְנָתַן לִי שָׁלוֹם, וְהֶחֱזַרְתִּי לוֹ שָׁלוֹם. אָמַר לִי: "רַבִּי, מֵאֵיזֶה מָקוֹם אָתָּה?"

שֶׁנֶּאֱמַר: "עֲטֶרֶת תִּפְאֶרֶת שֵׂיבָה, בְּדֶרֶךְ צְדָקָה תִּמָּצֵא" — *as it is said: "Ripe old age is a crown of splendor, it can be found in the path of righteousness"* (*Proverbs* 16:31). This verse shows that old age will not cause true Torah personalities to lose their drive for spiritual matters (*Tiferes Yisrael*).

וְאוֹמֵר: "עֲטֶרֶת זְקֵנִים בְּנֵי בָנִים, וְתִפְאֶרֶת בָּנִים אֲבוֹתָם" — *And it says: "The crown of the aged is grandchildren, and the splendor of children is their fathers"* (*ibid.* 17:6). Children, if not educated properly, can serve as a great and shameful indictment of parents. The verse promises that children and grandchildren will only be a source of pride to those who are truly dedicated to the Torah.

וְאוֹמֵר: "תִּפְאֶרֶת בַּחוּרִים כֹּחָם, וַהֲדַר זְקֵנִים שֵׂיבָה" — *And it says: "The splendor of young men is their strength, and the glory of old men is hoary age"* (*ibid.* 20:29). The young should be proud of their strength while the elderly should be proud of the wisdom that comes with years (*Tiferes Yisrael*).

וְאוֹמֵר: "וְחָפְרָה הַלְּבָנָה וּבוֹשָׁה הַחַמָּה, כִּי מָלַךְ ה' צְבָאוֹת בְּהַר צִיּוֹן וּבִירוּשָׁלַיִם, וְנֶגֶד זְקֵנָיו כָּבוֹד" — *And it says: "The moon will grow pale and the sun be shamed, when God, Master of Legions, will have reigned on Mount Zion and in Jerusalem, and honor shall be before His elders"* (*Isaiah* 24:23). The ultimate honor, wealth, and strength will come only when the Messiah arrives (*Mussar Avos*).

רַבִּי שִׁמְעוֹן בֶּן מְנַסְיָא אוֹמֵר: אֵלּוּ שֶׁבַע מִדּוֹת, שֶׁמָּנוּ חֲכָמִים לַצַּדִּיקִים, כֻּלָּם נִתְקַיְּמוּ בְּרַבִּי וּבְבָנָיו — *Rabbi Shimon ben Menasya said: These seven qualities that the Sages attributed to the righteous were all realized in Rabbi and his sons.* Actually, *eight* adornments appear to be enumerated in this *baraisa*. The *Vilna Gaon* omits "wisdom" as it is not referred to in the proof texts, while the parallel dictum in *Yerushalmi Sanhedrin* 11:4 omits "old age." Rabbi is רַבֵּנוּ הַקָּדוֹשׁ, *our sainted teacher*, רַבִּי יְהוּדָה הַנָּשִׂיא, *Rabbi Yehudah the Prince.* He was called by three names for the following reasons: *Rabbi* because he was the master of all Israel and taught them the Torah; *Rabbi Yehudah the Prince* because he was the most honored of Israel and was its prince; *our sainted teacher* because his body was as pure as his soul. The Sages relate that on the day he departed from this world, he stretched his ten fingers towards Heaven and said: "Master of the Universe, let it be known before You that at no time in my life did I take advantage of the pleasures of this world by as much as my little finger." The mention of Rabbi's sons was necessary since he was sick and frail for much of his life (*Mussar Avos*).

world, as it is said: *Ripe old age is a crown of splendor, it can be found in the path of righteousness (Proverbs 16:31). And it says: The crown of the aged is grandchildren, and the splendor of children is their fathers (ibid. 17:6). And it says: The splendor of young men is their strength, and the glory of old men is hoary age (ibid. 20:29). And it says: The moon will grow pale and the sun be shamed, when God, Masters of Legions, will have reigned on Mount Zion and in Jerusalem, and honor shall be before His elders (Isaiah 24:23).* Rabbi Shimon ben Menasya said: These seven qualities that the Sages attributed to the righteous were all realized in Rabbi and his sons.

9. Rabbi Yose ben Kisma said: Once I was walking on the road, when a certain man met me. He greeted me and I returned his greeting. He said to me, "Rabbi, from what place are you?"

Mishnah 9

אָמַר רַבִּי יוֹסֵי בֶּן קִסְמָא — *Rabbi Yose ben Kisma said.* A third-generation *Tanna* and one of the leaders of his generation, he taught Torah in Caesarea, Israel. His literary legacy is small and few details of his life remain with us. During the Bar Kochba revolt, which occurred in R' Yose's later years, he was among the pacifists who felt that Rome was too powerful to revolt against. His warning to R' Chanania ben Tradyon to cease teaching Torah publicly fell on deaf ears (see 3:3, s.v. רבי חנניא). R' Yose predicted many of the terrible tragedies that befell the Jewish people after his death. Many of his pithy maxims are famous: "Two are better than three" [two legs in one's youth are better than two old legs plus a cane in one's old age] (*Shabbos* 152a), or "Woe to the one who goes away and does not return" (i.e., youth).

פַּעַם אַחַת הָיִיתִי מְהַלֵּךְ בַּדֶּרֶךְ — *Once I was walking on the road.* Here R' Yose ben Kisma relates a story to highlight the importance of living in an environment conducive to spiritual growth. Furthermore, it is taught in contrast to the last *baraisa*, which taught the positive value of wealth among other virtues. R' Yose teaches that while wealth is desirable, one should never forfeit Torah in pursuit of wealth (*Tiferes Yisrael*).

According to *Midrash Shmuel*, the word *once* is meant quite literally. Generally, R' Yose spent his time in the study hall and had no occasion to meet strangers. Perhaps he was traveling on a *mitzvah*-related mission. According to *Tiferes Yisrael*, he was on the road in search of a means to support himself.

וּפָגַע בִּי אָדָם אֶחָד — *when a certain man met me.* He does not say: I met a certain man, rather a certain man met me. Until the moment the man greeted him, R' Yose had not noticed him. Had R' Yose noticed him, he would have been first to offer greetings (see 4:20).

וְנָתַן לִי שָׁלוֹם, וְהֶחֱזַרְתִּי לוֹ שָׁלוֹם — *He greeted me and I returned his greeting.* R' Yose tells us this so that there be no misunderstanding on the part of those who heard his tale; the other person was amicable. It was not a personal dislike that caused R' Yose to refuse the man's offer; rather, it was the primacy of Torah (*Tiferes Yisrael*).

אָמַר לִי: ,,רַבִּי, מֵאֵיזֶה מָקוֹם אַתָּה'' — *He said to me, "Rabbi, from what place are you?"* The man addressed him as Rabbi either because he observed him learning Torah and assumed he was a Rabbi, or due to his distinctive rabbinic garb (see *Pesachim*

אָמַרְתִּי לוֹ: ,,מֵעִיר גְּדוֹלָה שֶׁל חֲכָמִים וְשֶׁל סוֹפְרִים
אֲנִי.׳׳ אָמַר לִי: ,,רַבִּי, רְצוֹנְךָ שֶׁתָּדוּר עִמָּנוּ בִּמְקוֹמֵנוּ וַאֲנִי
אֶתֵּן לְךָ אֶלֶף אֲלָפִים דִּינְרֵי זָהָב וַאֲבָנִים טוֹבוֹת
וּמַרְגָּלִיּוֹת?׳׳ אָמַרְתִּי לוֹ: ,,אִם אַתָּה נוֹתֵן לִי כָּל כֶּסֶף
וְזָהָב וַאֲבָנִים טוֹבוֹת וּמַרְגָּלִיּוֹת שֶׁבָּעוֹלָם, אֵינִי דָר אֶלָּא
בִּמְקוֹם תּוֹרָה.׳׳ וְכֵן כָּתוּב בְּסֵפֶר תְּהִלִּים עַל יְדֵי דָוִד
מֶלֶךְ יִשְׂרָאֵל: ,,טוֹב לִי תוֹרַת פִּיךָ מֵאַלְפֵי זָהָב וָכָסֶף.׳׳

111b and *Bava Metzia* 85a). Following *Tiferes Yisrael*, the man's question was an unstated indictment of R' Yose's hometown. "From what type of place are you that its inhabitants allow you to go in search of a livelihood? A scholar of your caliber should be supported by the local residents."

אָמַרְתִּי לוֹ: ,,מֵעִיר גְּדוֹלָה שֶׁל חֲכָמִים וְשֶׁל סוֹפְרִים אֲנִי׳׳ — *I said to him, "I am from a great city of scholars and sages."* According to *Midrash Shmuel*, R' Yose confirmed the man's perception that he was a scholar. *Tiferes Yisrael* understands the answer as a rejoinder to the man's attempted indictment. "Since I come from a great city of scholars, none of whom is very wealthy, they cannot provide for my needs, so I am in search of a livelihood." The term סוֹפְרִים denotes Talmudic knowledge while חֲכָמִים means Scriptural experts.

אָמַר לִי: ,,רַבִּי, רְצוֹנְךָ שֶׁתָּדוּר עִמָּנוּ בִּמְקוֹמֵנוּ וַאֲנִי אֶתֵּן לְךָ אֶלֶף אֲלָפִים דִּינְרֵי זָהָב וַאֲבָנִים טוֹבוֹת וּמַרְגָּלִיּוֹת׳׳ — *He said to me, "Rabbi, would you be willing to live with us in our place? I would give you thousands*

upon thousands of golden dinars, precious stones and pearls." The man invited R' Yose to serve as the rabbi of his town. All the honor he lacked in his great city he would receive in the man's town (*Divrei Shaul*). Furthermore, he would not have to worry about a living — the man himself would provide R' Yose's needs so that R' Yose would not have to debase himself to ask for his salary (*Midrash Shmuel*).

The figure quoted here of course is an exaggeration. He meant to say that he would give R' Yose whatever he needed. The man wanted to enhance the prestige of his town by hiring such a venerable rabbi. Alternatively, he felt that his businesses would be blessed in merit of supporting such an exemplary personality (*Tiferes Yisrael*).

אָמַרְתִּי לוֹ: ,,אִם אַתָּה נוֹתֵן לִי כָּל כֶּסֶף וְזָהָב וַאֲבָנִים טוֹבוֹת וּמַרְגָּלִיּוֹת שֶׁבָּעוֹלָם, אֵינִי דָר אֶלָּא בִּמְקוֹם תּוֹרָה׳׳ — *I replied, "Even if you were to give me all the silver and gold, precious stones and pearls in the world, I would dwell nowhere but in a place of Torah."* This is based on the dictum of R' Nehorai (4:18) that one

---

‏ **No surrogates.** *Arvei Nachal* renders בִּמְקוֹמֵנוּ as *instead of us.* From this key phrase, R' Yose understood that the man came from a city of highly successful businessmen, who were totally preoccupied with their commercial affairs and did not devote time to Torah study or a spiritual agenda. They wanted to hire R' Yose as the token Torah scholar of the town, and have him learn on their behalf. He replied, "Furthermore, when a man departs from this world, neither silver, nor gold, nor precious stones, nor pearls escort him, but only Torah study and good deeds." One must find time and make opportunities for Torah study and good deeds of his own. A surrogate will not do.

‏ **What counts.** Often cities seek a new rabbi based on the prestige of the rabbinic position he last occupied. When R' Yose answered that he comes from a great city of scholars and sages, the man thought he had the right candidate. R' Yose replied, "Since the major qualification in your eyes is the size of my last position rather than my scholarly standing, you are unable to assess Torah scholarship, which is the true qualification of a rabbi. Apparently you do not live in a place of Torah."

I said to him, "I am from a great city of scholars and sages." He said to me, "Rabbi, would you be willing to live with us in our place? I would give you thousands upon thousands of golden dinars, precious stones and pearls." I replied, "Even if you were to give me all the silver and gold, precious stones and pearls in the world, I would dwell nowhere but in a place of Torah." And so it is written in the Book of Psalms by David, King of Israel: *"I prefer the Torah of Your mouth above thousands in gold and silver."*

---

should exile himself to a place of Torah and not rely on self-study. Thus, a scholarly environment is integral to real Torah living (*Tiferes Yisrael*).

The man offered to pay R' Yose when he would move to the town. R' Yose replied that even if the man gave him the money then, he would not be tempted. Just as a fish cannot survive out of water, so Jews cannot survive without Torah. R' Yose

enunciated this basic truth: A Jew needs to live in a place of Torah. Only where authentic Torah study takes place is there the power to generate spiritual growth (*Avos al Banim*).

וְכֵן כָּתוּב בְּסֵפֶר תְּהִלִּים עַל יְדֵי דָוִד מֶלֶךְ יִשְׂרָאֵל: ,,טוֹב לִי תוֹרַת פִּיךָ מֵאַלְפֵי זָהָב וָכָסֶף'' — *And so it is written in the Book of Psalms by David, King of Israel: "I prefer the Torah of Your mouth above thousands in*

⋘§ **Torah is not a luxury.** How did R' Yose ben Kisma know that the man's hometown was not a place of Torah? When he heard the man speak about money so quickly and easily he understood that the man did not come from a place of Torah. In a place where the Torah has primary importance, people do not talk so brazenly about money. Furthermore, we know that the barest necessities of life, such as air or water, do not cost much. Only delicacies and luxuries are very expensive. When R' Yose heard the man speak of paying such an exorbitant sum for a Torah scholar and his Torah, he understood that the man representing that city viewed the Torah as a rare luxury. Such an attitude is symptomatic of such places (*R' Meir Don Plotzki*).

⋘§ **Money cannot buy it.** Why did not R' Yose ben Kisma simply take the fortune the man offered him and open a yeshivah in the man's town, thus turning it into a place of Torah? The Chofetz Chaim explained: "Even though the supporters of Torah are ready to invest and finance a yeshivah, the spiritual tone of a yeshivah must be set by Torah scholars. Not every place has the elements necessary to forge such an environment. It takes sweat, tears, self-sacrifice and a special type of idealism to make a place into an abode for Torah — not only money."

⋘§ **City planner.** On the first Rosh Hashanah after he arrived in the Holy Land, the Chazon Ish prayed at the Yeshivah Beis Yosef in Bnei Brak where his brother-in-law the Steipler *Gaon* was *rosh yeshivah*. Customarily, a prominent person speaks before the sounding of the *shofar*, seeking to inspire the assembled to repentance. The people in the yeshivah asked the Chazon Ish to speak to the assembled. He consented with two conditions: (a) He would only speak in an anteroom; he did not feel it was fitting for him to speak in the study hall/synagogue; (b) he would repeat a mishnah rather than offer a discourse.

All the assembled went out to the anteroom, and the Chazon Ish sat down and began softly to read this *baraisa*. When he reached the phrase, "Even if you were to give me all the silver, gold, precious stones and pearls in the world, I would dwell nowhere but in a place of Torah," his voice rose. Three times he repeated the *baraisa* and then he signaled the people to go to the *shofar*-blowing. At the time, Bnei Brak was a far cry from the Torah metropolis it is today, and all the assembled felt that he had issued his manifesto as to what he planned for the city.

On another occasion he is reputed to have explained why he moved to Bnei Brak rather than Jerusalem. "Jerusalem," he said, "is full of scholars and God-fearing Jews. I want to move to the *yishuv hachadash* (the new settlement of the Land), where the Torah is not yet supreme. Either we will succeed at transforming it into a place of Torah or we will all go together to *Gehinnom*."

וְלֹא עוֹד אֶלָּא שֶׁבִּשְׁעַת פְּטִירָתוֹ שֶׁל אָדָם אֵין מְלַוִּין לוֹ לְאָדָם לֹא כֶסֶף וְלֹא זָהָב וְלֹא אֲבָנִים טוֹבוֹת וּמַרְגָּלִיּוֹת, אֶלָּא תוֹרָה וּמַעֲשִׂים טוֹבִים בִּלְבַד, שֶׁנֶּאֱמַר: "בְּהִתְהַלֶּכְךָ תַּנְחֶה אֹתָךְ, בְּשָׁכְבְּךָ תִּשְׁמֹר עָלֶיךָ, וַהֲקִיצוֹתָ הִיא תְשִׂיחֶךָ." "בְּהִתְהַלֶּכְךָ תַּנְחֶה אֹתָךְ" — בָּעוֹלָם הַזֶּה; "בְּשָׁכְבְּךָ תִּשְׁמֹר עָלֶיךָ" — בַּקֶּבֶר; "וַהֲקִיצוֹתָ הִיא תְשִׂיחֶךָ" — לָעוֹלָם הַבָּא. וְאוֹמֵר: "לִי הַכֶּסֶף וְלִי הַזָּהָב, נְאֻם יהוה צְבָאוֹת."

[יז] **חֲמִשָּׁה** קִנְיָנִים קָנָה הַקָּדוֹשׁ בָּרוּךְ הוּא בָּעוֹלָמוֹ, וְאֵלּוּ הֵן: תּוֹרָה — קִנְיָן אֶחָד, שָׁמַיִם וָאָרֶץ — קִנְיָן

---

gold and silver" (Psalms 119:72). This verse proves that spiritual wealth is far more valuable than mundane riches. R' Yose identifies the author of *Psalms* as King David to emphasize that the statement regarding Torah being so much more valuable than gold and silver was made by King David, who himself enjoyed great wealth. Were a Torah scholar who never tasted luxury to make the statement, it would have much less impact (*Ruach Chaim, K'sav Sofer*).

Midrash Shmuel offers an alternative: Even though kindness and charity are of great merit, a person should realize that they are in no way comparable to the merit of Torah study. We deduce this from what King David said: *I prefer the Torah of Your mouth above thousands in gold and silver.* No one was more charitable than King David, who dedicated everything he had for charity; and yet declared that the merit of Torah was greater than the merit of his charity.

The *Midrash* teaches that Solomon, who had tasted the opulence of this world, was the right person to declare, "Futility of futilities! All is futile!" (*Ecclesiastes* 1:2).

The *Chasam Sofer* adds a different perspective as to why Torah is more valuable than money. The Torah was given to authentic Torah scholars, hence the Torah is theirs. On the other hand, God says regarding gold and silver, *Mine is the silver, Mine is the gold* (*Chaggai* 2:8). Since it is human nature for a person to prefer one thing which is really his own

to nine that he receives from someone else, the Torah that he mastered through his own effort is more valuable to him than gold and silver.

וְלֹא עוֹד אֶלָּא שֶׁבִּשְׁעַת פְּטִירָתוֹ שֶׁל אָדָם אֵין מְלַוִּין לוֹ לְאָדָם לֹא כֶסֶף וְלֹא זָהָב וְלֹא אֲבָנִים טוֹבוֹת וּמַרְגָּלִיּוֹת, אֶלָּא תוֹרָה וּמַעֲשִׂים טוֹבִים בִּלְבַד — *Furthermore, when a man departs from this world, neither silver, nor gold, nor precious stones nor pearls escort him, but only Torah study and good deeds.* Not only should one study Torah and do good deeds because of their intrinsic worth and the sense that nothing in this world is as valuable, but also because of their eternal quality. Man takes nothing with him besides his Torah and good deeds. The *Midrash* (*Koheles Rabbah* 5) teaches that man enters the world with closed fists, symbolic of an ambition to grasp the whole world, but when he leaves his hands are open, as if to say, "I leave it all behind." This is what King Solomon meant when he said, *As he emerged from his mother's womb, naked will he return, as he had come; he can salvage nothing from his labor to take with him* (*Ecclesiastes* 5:14).

It is only his spiritual wealth that can pass over the abyss of death.

שֶׁנֶּאֱמַר: "בְּהִתְהַלֶּכְךָ תַּנְחֶה אֹתָךְ, בְּשָׁכְבְּךָ תִּשְׁמֹר עָלֶיךָ, וַהֲקִיצוֹתָ הִיא תְשִׂיחֶךָ." "בְּהִתְהַלֶּכְךָ תַּנְחֶה אֹתָךְ" — בָּעוֹלָם הַזֶּה — *as it is said: "When you walk, it shall guide you; when you lie down, it shall guard you; and when you awake, it shall speak on your behalf"*

Furthermore, when a man departs from this world, neither silver, nor gold, nor precious stones nor pearls escort him, but only Torah study and good deeds, as it is said: "When you walk, it shall guide you; when you lie down, it shall guard you; and when you awake, it shall speak on your behalf." "When you walk, it shall guide you" — in this world; "when you lie down, it shall guard you" — in the grave; "and when you awake, it shall speak on your behalf" — in the World to Come. And it says: "Mine is the silver, and Mine is the gold, says HASHEM, Master of Legions."

10. Five possessions did the Holy One, Blessed is He, acquire for Himself in His world, and they are: Torah, one possession; heaven and earth, one possession; Abraham,

---

(*Proverbs* 6:22). *"When you walk, it shall guide you"* — *in this world.* King David says: *Your word is a lamp for my feet and a light for my path* (*Psalms* 119:105). The Torah illuminates man's path in life, enabling him to proceed to his destination with vigor and surefootedness. Whenever a doubt arises, one can consult with the Torah and its scholars in order to ascertain the proper course. Hence, Torah is man's guide in this world, saving him from spiritual detours and mistakes (*Ruach Chaim*).

בְּשָׁכְבְּךָ תִּשְׁמֹר עָלֶיךָ״ — בַּקֶּבֶר — *"when you lie down, it shall guard you"* — *in the grave.* When you lie down with your ancestors — namely, after death — the Torah and good deeds you performed in your lifetime will shield you from decay and pain in the grave (*Midrash Shmuel*).

וַהֲקִיצוֹתָ הִיא תְשִׂיחֶךָ״ — לָעוֹלָם הַבָּא — *"and when you awake, it shall speak on your behalf"* — *in the*

World to Come. During the resurrection of the dead, when man will stand up again and be judged, it is the good he accomplished that will plead on his behalf (*Rashi to Proverbs*).

וְאוֹמֵר: ,,לִי הַכֶּסֶף וְלִי הַזָּהָב, נְאֻם ה׳ צְבָאוֹת״ — *And it says: "Mine is the silver, and Mine is the gold, says HASHEM, Master of Legions"* (*Chaggai* 2:8). R' Yose ben Kisma added this quotation to correct the person who sought to entice him with money. The man had said, "I will give you etc." R' Yose therefore told him that it is God Who owns all the money and He gives it to whomever He wants (*Midrash Shmuel*). *Rashi* alludes to the reason for this extra verse: R' Yose expressed the reality that he would lose nothing by not going to the city of wealth. God controls all wealth and can grant it even to people in fiscally poor, spiritually wealthy communities of Torah (*Tiferes Yisrael*).

Mishnah 10

חֲמִשָּׁה קִנְיָנִים קָנָה הַקָּדוֹשׁ בָּרוּךְ הוּא בְּעוֹלָמוֹ, וְאֵלּוּ הֵן — *Five possessions did the Holy One, Blessed is He, acquire for Himself in His world, and they are.* While the whole world is God's, He designated five special things to advance His design for Creation and bring glory to His Name (*Tiferes Yisrael, Bikkurei Yechezkel*).

Sfas Emes renders קִנְיָנִים as modes of acquisition. While God is intrinsically inaccessible, He provides man in general and His people specifi-

cally the means by which to acquire a relationship with Him. These are the five items listed.

תּוֹרָה – קִנְיָן אֶחָד — *Torah, one possession.* Since Torah is the master plan for all of Creation and the guide for man to generate honor for God, it is essential to the world. Furthermore, man achieves closeness to God by studying His wisdom.

שָׁמַיִם וָאָרֶץ – קִנְיָן אֶחָד — *heaven and earth, one possession.* Heaven and earth in all their splendor testify to the existence of one God.

אֶחָד, אַבְרָהָם – קִנְיָן אֶחָד, יִשְׂרָאֵל – קִנְיָן אֶחָד, בֵּית הַמִּקְדָּשׁ – קִנְיָן אֶחָד. תּוֹרָה מִנַּיִן? דִּכְתִיב: "יהוה קָנָנִי רֵאשִׁית דַּרְכּוֹ, קֶדֶם מִפְעָלָיו מֵאָז." שָׁמַיִם וָאָרֶץ מִנַּיִן? דִּכְתִיב: "כֹּה אָמַר יהוה, הַשָּׁמַיִם כִּסְאִי, וְהָאָרֶץ הֲדֹם רַגְלָי, אֵי זֶה בַיִת אֲשֶׁר תִּבְנוּ לִי, וְאֵי זֶה מָקוֹם מְנוּחָתִי"; וְאוֹמֵר: "מָה רַבּוּ מַעֲשֶׂיךָ יהוה, כֻּלָּם בְּחָכְמָה עָשִׂיתָ, מָלְאָה הָאָרֶץ קִנְיָנֶךָ." אַבְרָהָם מִנַּיִן? דִּכְתִיב: "וַיְבָרְכֵהוּ וַיֹּאמַר, בָּרוּךְ אַבְרָם לְאֵל עֶלְיוֹן, קֹנֵה שָׁמַיִם וָאָרֶץ."

See *Rambam* (*Hil. Yesodei HaTorah* 2) for a poetic framing of this concept.

Furthermore, they were created in order that man will have optimal conditions with which to serve God. Heaven and earth provide whatever man needs for his spiritual quest (*Tiferes Yisrael*).

אַבְרָהָם – קִנְיָן אֶחָד — *Abraham, one possession.* The first to light up the world with the doctrine of monotheism, a belief in one God, was Abraham. He walked in God's ways and illuminated the people of the earth with a vibrant awareness that the world is not a conductorless train (*Tiferes Yisrael*).

With Abraham there began a profound change in the spiritual nature of mankind. The plan of Creation was for all human beings to have an equal share in fulfilling the Divine mission and for the Torah to be given to all mankind. But after twenty generations of failure, the privilege of being God's Chosen People was earned by Abraham and his offspring. They would receive the Torah and they would be in the vanguard of perfecting the world and bringing all people to accept the sovereignty of the One God (*Derech God*).

יִשְׂרָאֵל – קִנְיָן אֶחָד — *Israel, one possession.* The Children of Israel are God's messengers in this world, extending the world view of their forefather Abraham to all of mankind (*R' S. R. Hirsch*).

Ramban captures the sentiment in his touching portrayal of Jewish survival: "God created man among the lower creatures in order that he acknowledge his Creator and be thankful to Him, and He placed in man's hand the choice to do evil or

good. But when people sinned willingly and they all denied Him, only this people [Israel] remained devoted to His Name, and so He made known through them by means of signs and wonders that *He is God of gods, and Lord of lords,* (*Deuteronomy* 10:17) and this became known to all nations. Now, if He were to reconsider and [Israel's] memory be lost, the nations will forget His wonders and His deeds and will no longer recount them. And if a person should mention them, they will think that it was [done by] one of the powers of the constellations. Thus, the purpose of the creation of man will be annulled completely, for no one will be left among them who knows his Creator — only those who provoke Him. Therefore, it is appropriate as a consequence of the [Divine] Will that existed at the creation of the world for Him to establish for Himself a people for all time, who are nearer to Him and who know Him more than all the [other] peoples. And the meaning of the verse *For God will judge His people, and for His servants He will reconsider* (*Deuteronomy* 32:36) is that God will remember in mercy that they are His people of old, and He will remember that they are His servants, for they stood by Him in their exile like servants to suffer the troubles and pains."

בֵּית הַמִּקְדָּשׁ – קִנְיָן אֶחָד — *the Holy Temple, one possession.* The Holy Temple was the repository of God's Presence in the world. It was there that man was able to see, without any distortion, the hand of Providence (see 5:7). *Ramban* (*Tetzaveh*) teaches that the Temple was a miniature of what the entire world was before Adam's sin. Thus it is a possession

one possession; Israel, one possession; the Holy Temple, one possession. From where do we know this about the Torah? Since it is written: *God acquired me [the Torah] at the beginning of His way, before His works in time of yore (Proverbs 8:22).* From where do we know this about heaven and earth? Since it is written: *So says God. The heaven is My throne, and the earth is My footstool; what House can you build for Me, and where is the place of My rest? (Isaiah 66:1).* And it says: *How abundant are Your works, God, with wisdom You made them all, the earth is full of Your possessions (Psalms 104:24).* From where do we know this about Abraham? Since it is written: *And He blessed him and said: Blessed is Abram of God the Most High, Who acquired heaven and earth (Genesis 14:19).*

---

of God employed to advance the Divine plan for the world and mankind (*Midrash Shmuel*).

תּוֹרָה מִנַּיִן? דִּכְתִיב: ,,ה' קָנָנִי רֵאשִׁית דַּרְכּוֹ, קֶדֶם מִפְעָלָיו מֵאָז" — *From where do we know this about the Torah? Since it is written: "God acquired me [the Torah] at the beginning of His way, before His works in time of yore"* (*Proverbs* 8:22). Torah long predated Creation and served as its blueprint. Furthermore, it is Torah and its quantification in the universe that is the *raison d'etre* of everything (*Rashi*). Since it was the reason for which Creation was brought into existence, the concept of Torah preceded Creation and was employed by the Creator as its guiding standard (*R' S. R. Hirsch*).

שָׁמַיִם וָאָרֶץ מִנַּיִן? דִּכְתִיב: ,,כֹּה אָמַר ה', הַשָּׁמַיִם כִּסְאִי, וְהָאָרֶץ הֲדֹם רַגְלָי, אֵי זֶה בַיִת אֲשֶׁר תִּבְנוּ לִי, וְאֵי זֶה מָקוֹם מְנוּחָתִי"; וְאוֹמֵר: ,,מָה רַבּוּ מַעֲשֶׂיךָ ה', כֻּלָּם בְּחָכְמָה עָשִׂיתָ, מָלְאָה הָאָרֶץ קִנְיָנֶךָ" — *From where do we know this about heaven and earth? Since it is written: "So says God. The heaven is My throne, and the earth is My footstool; what House can you build for Me, and where is the place of My rest?"* (*Isaiah* 66:1). *And it says: "How abundant are Your works, God, with wisdom You made them all, the earth is full of Your possessions"* (*Psalms* 104:24). By juxtaposing the two verses we may conclude that just as the earth is deemed a possession of God, likewise the heavens (*Midrash Shmuel*). *Sfas Emes* renders קִנְיָנֶךָ as "the earth is full of *ways of acquiring You.*" The heavens and the earth and all they contain are means by which a person can

aspire to a greater relationship with God.

While Creation happened only once, the heavens and the earth continue to relate Creation to the Creator. Now and forever, the heavens are God's throne from which He fashions human destiny, and the earth is His footstool on which He leaves the footprints of progress (*R' S. R. Hirsch*).

אַבְרָהָם מִנַּיִן? דִּכְתִיב: ,,וַיְבָרְכֵהוּ וַיֹּאמַר, בָּרוּךְ אַבְרָם לְאֵל עֶלְיוֹן, קֹנֵה שָׁמַיִם וָאָרֶץ" — *From where do we know this about Abraham? Since it is written: "And he blessed him and said: Blessed is Abram of God the Most High, Who acquired heaven and earth"* (*Genesis* 14:19).

The verse praises Abraham, whose existence justified all of Creation. The Sages homiletically interpret בְּהִבָּרְאָם, *when they were created* (*Genesis* 2:4), as alluding to Abraham, since the letters of this word can be rearranged to spell בְּאַבְרָהָם, meaning that God created the world *for the sake of Abraham* (*Bereishis Rabbah* 12), because he was the epitome of kindness, one of the pillars of the world. This suggests further that Abraham was the one who achieved God's purpose for the universe, because until he came on the scene, humanity consistently failed to live up to its mission. That is why Abraham earned the right to be the progenitor of Israel, the nation that was chosen by God to receive the Torah (*Zohar*).

Rashi views the outreach work of Abraham as the possession referred to since through this he acquired souls for God.

יִשְׂרָאֵל מִנַּיִן? דִּכְתִיב: ,,עַד יַעֲבֹר עַמְּךָ יהוה, עַד יַעֲבֹר עַם זוּ קָנִיתָ"; וְאוֹמֵר: ,,לִקְדוֹשִׁים אֲשֶׁר בָּאָרֶץ הֵמָּה, וְאַדִּירֵי כָּל חֶפְצִי בָם." בֵּית הַמִּקְדָּשׁ מִנַּיִן? דִּכְתִיב: ,,מָכוֹן לְשִׁבְתְּךָ פָּעַלְתָּ יהוה, מִקְדָּשׁ אֲדֹנָי כּוֹנְנוּ יָדֶיךָ"; וְאוֹמֵר: ,,וַיְבִיאֵם אֶל גְּבוּל קָדְשׁוֹ, הַר זֶה קָנְתָה יְמִינוֹ."

[יא] **כָּל** מַה שֶּׁבָּרָא הַקָּדוֹשׁ בָּרוּךְ הוּא בְּעוֹלָמוֹ לֹא בְרָאוֹ אֶלָּא לִכְבוֹדוֹ, שֶׁנֶּאֱמַר: ,,כֹּל הַנִּקְרָא בִשְׁמִי וְלִכְבוֹדִי בְּרָאתִיו, יְצַרְתִּיו אַף עֲשִׂיתִיו"; וְאוֹמֵר: ,,יהוה יִמְלֹךְ לְעוֹלָם וָעֶד."

❦ ❦ ❦

רַבִּי חֲנַנְיָא בֶּן עֲקַשְׁיָא אוֹמֵר: רָצָה הַקָּדוֹשׁ בָּרוּךְ הוּא לְזַכּוֹת אֶת יִשְׂרָאֵל, לְפִיכָךְ הִרְבָּה לָהֶם תּוֹרָה וּמִצְוֹת, שֶׁנֶּאֱמַר: ,,יהוה חָפֵץ לְמַעַן צִדְקוֹ, יַגְדִּיל תּוֹרָה וְיַאְדִּיר."

יִשְׂרָאֵל מִנַּיִן? דִּכְתִיב:,,עַד יַעֲבֹר עַמְּךָ הי, עַד יַעֲבֹר עַם זוּ קָנִיתָ"; וְאוֹמֵר:,,לִקְדוֹשִׁים אֲשֶׁר בָּאָרֶץ הֵמָּה, וְאַדִּירֵי כָּל חֶפְצִי בָם" — *From where do we know this about the people Israel? Since it is written: "Until your people passes through, God, until it passes through — this people You acquired" (Exodus 15:16), and it [also] says: "But for the holy ones who are in the earth and for the mighty all my desires are due to them" (Psalms 16:3). The first verse proves that the people of Israel are a possession of God, the second that they are the focus of Creation. Furthermore, the second verse teaches that even when Jews sin, the merit of their mighty forefathers justifies their continued existence (Midrash Shmuel).*

בֵּית הַמִּקְדָּשׁ מִנַּיִן? דִּכְתִיב:,,מָכוֹן לְשִׁבְתְּךָ פָּעַלְתָּ הי, מִקְדָּשׁ אֲדֹנָי כּוֹנְנוּ יָדֶיךָ"; וְאוֹמֵר:,,וַיְבִיאֵם אֶל גְּבוּל קָדְשׁוֹ, הַר זֶה קָנְתָה יְמִינוֹ" — *From where do we know this about the Holy Temple? Since it is written: "Your dwelling place which You, God, have made; the Sanctuary, my Lord, that Your hands established" (Exodus 15:17). And it says, "And He brought them to His sacred boundary, to this mountain which His right hand acquired" (Psalms 78:54). The verse from Exodus explicitly refers to the Temple as God's dwelling place. The words of the Psalmist teach that even after its destruction the Temple site is still sanctified (Midrash Shmuel).*

Mishnah 11

כָּל מַה שֶּׁבָּרָא הַקָּדוֹשׁ בָּרוּךְ הוּא בְּעוֹלָמוֹ לֹא בְרָאוֹ אֶלָּא לִכְבוֹדוֹ — *All that the Holy One, Blessed is He, created in His world, He created solely for His glory.* In spite of the five special items enumerated in the previous *baraisa*, we are taught that everything has its place in the Godly scenario,

adding to the greater glory of God (*Tiferes Yisrael*).

According to R' S. R. Hirsch, this comes at the heels of the last *baraisa* to teach us the universality of the Godly message.

Not only the Jewish people but, in fact, every molecule of Creation bears the Name of God, and

From where do we know this about the people Israel? Since it is written: *Until Your people passes through, God, until it passes through — this people You acquired (Exodus 15:16)*, and it [also] says: *But for the holy ones who are in the earth and for the mighty all my desires are due to them (Psalms 16:3)*. From where do we know this about the Holy Temple? Since it is written: *Your dwelling place which You, God, have made; the Sanctuary, my Lord, that Your hands established (Exodus 15:17)*. And it says: *And He brought them to His sacred boundary, to this mountain which His right hand acquired.*

11. All that the Holy One, Blessed is He, created in His world, He created solely for His glory, as it is said: *All that is called by My Name, indeed, it is for My glory that I have created it, formed it, and made it (Isaiah 43:7)*. And it says: *God shall reign for all eternity (Exodus 15:18)*.

❦ ❦ ❦

Rabbi Chanania ben Akashia says: The Holy One, Blessed is He, wished to confer merit upon Israel; therefore He gave them Torah and mitzvos in abundance, as it is said: *HASHEM desired, for the sake if its [Israel's] righteousness, that the Torah be made great and glorious.*

---

has no other purpose but to serve the glorification of God, its Creator. It is inevitable that all things should fulfill this destiny, for God has created each one of them especially for this purpose, and fashioned and guided it accordingly.

After six chapters of teaching and exhortation, *Avos* concludes with the stirring and inspirational declaration that everything in Creation is a tool for His glory. Clearly, since God created the universe for His service, no force can prevent man from utilizing it properly. God has shown us the way; it is for us to supply the will and the wisdom (*R' Meir Zlotowitz*).

שֶׁנֶּאֱמַר: ,,כֹּל הַנִּקְרָא בִשְׁמִי וְלִכְבוֹדִי בְּרָאתִיו, יְצַרְתִּיו אַף עֲשִׂיתִיו'' — *as it is said: "All that is called by My Name, indeed, it is for My glory that I have created it, formed it, and made it" (Isaiah 43:7).* There are four levels of Creation: (a) בְּרִיאָה, *creating*; (b) יְצִירָה, *forming*; (c) עֲשִׂיָּה *making*; and (d) אֲצִילוּת, a level

that is unfathomable to humans. On every level of Creation there is a Master Plan of the glory of God, which is supposed to emerge (*Midrash Shmuel*).

וְאוֹמֵר: ,,ה' יִמְלֹךְ לְעוֹלָם וָעֶד'' — *And it says: "God shall reign for all eternity" (Exodus 15:18).* Many explanations are offered for this additional citation. According to *Tiferes Yisrael*, the verse comes to supplement the statement that everything was created and exists to enhance the glory of God. Often we are witness to calamities and the like, which seemingly challenge the idea that everything is for God's greater glory. Even though we presently sense that much of what happens seemingly detracts from God's honor in the future, the kingship of God over earth will be absolute and clear. *Mili d'Avos* understands this verse as an explanation of the earlier clause. Since God rules absolutely, nothing can impede His plans for the world.